S0-BBO-917

PARALLEL COMPUTING FOR BIOINFORMATICS AND COMPUTATIONAL BIOLOGY

PARALLEL COMPUTING FOR BIOINFORMATICS AND COMPUTATIONAL BIOLOGY

MODELS, ENABLING TECHNOLOGIES, AND CASE STUDIES

Edited by

Albert Y. Zomaya
The University of Sydney, Australia

WILEY-
INTERSCIENCE

JOHN WILEY & SONS, INC

Copyright © 2006 by John Wiley & Sons, Inc. All rights reserved.

Published by John Wiley & Sons, Inc., Hoboken, New Jersey.
Published simultaneously in Canada.

No part of this publication may be reproduced, stored in a retrieval system, or transmitted in any form or
by any means, electronic, mechanical, photocopying, recording, scanning, or otherwise, except as
permitted under Section 107 or 108 of the 1976 United States Copyright Act, without either the prior
written permission of the Publisher, or authorization through payment of the appropriate per-copy fee to
the Copyright Clearance Center, Inc., 222 Rosewood Drive, Danvers, MA 01923, (978) 750-8400, fax
(978) 750-4470, or on the web at www.copyright.com. Requests to the Publisher for permission should
be addressed to the Permissions Department, John Wiley & Sons, Inc., 111 River Street, Hoboken, NJ
07030, (201) 748-6011, fax (201) 748-6008, e-mail: permcoordinator@wiley.com.

Limit of Liability/Disclaimer of Warranty: While the publisher and author have used their best efforts in
preparing this book, they make no representations or warranties with respect to the accuracy or
completeness of the contents of this book and specifically disclaim any implied warranties of
merchantability or fitness for a particular purpose. No warranty may be created or extended by sales
representatives or written sales materials. The advice and strategies contained herein may not be suitable
for your situation. The publisher is not engaged in rendering professional services, and you should
consult with a professional where appropriate. Neither the publisher nor author shall be liable for any loss
of profit or any other commercial damages, including but not limited to special, incidental, consequential,
or other damages.

For general information on our other products and services please contact our Customer Care Department
within the United States at (800) 762-2974, outside the United States at (317) 572-3993 or fax (317)
572-4002.

Wiley also publishes its books in a variety of electronic formats. Some content that appears in print may
not be available in electronic format. For more information about Wiley products, visit our web site at
www.Wiley.com.

Library of Congress Cataloging-in-Publication Data is available.

ISBN-13 978-0-471-71848-2
ISBN-10 0-471-71848-3

Printed in the United States of America

10 9 8 7 6 5 4 3 2 1

To our families for their help, support, and patience.
Albert Zomaya

■ CONTENTS

Preface   xv

Contributors   xxv

Acknowledgments   xxix

PART I   ALGORITHMS AND MODELS   1

1   **Parallel and Evolutionary Approaches to Computational Biology**   3
    Nouhad J. Rizk

    1.1   Introduction   4
    1.2   Bioinformatics   13
    1.3   Evolutionary Computation Applied to Computational Biology   20
    1.4   Conclusions   23
    References   25

2   **Parallel Monte Carlo Simulation of HIV Molecular Evolution in**
    Response to Immune Surveillance   29
    Jack da Silva

    2.1   Introduction   30
    2.2   The Problem   30
    2.3   The Model   32
    2.4   Parallelization with MPI   39
    2.5   Parallel Random Number Generation   43
    2.6   Preliminary Simulation Results   46
    2.7   Future Directions   52
    References   55

3   **Differential Evolutionary Algorithms for In Vivo Dynamic Analysis of**
    Glycolysis and Pentose Phosphate Pathway in *Escherichia coli*   59
    Christophe Chassagnole

    3.1   Introduction   59
    3.2   Mathematical Model   61
    3.3   Estimation of the Parameters of the Model   67
    3.4   Kinetic Parameter Estimation by DE   69

3.5   Simulation and Results   70
3.6   Stability Analysis   73
3.7   Control Characteristic   73
3.8   Conclusions   75
References   76

4   Compute-Intensive Simulations for Cellular Models   **79**
K. Burrage

4.1   Introduction   79
4.2   Simulation Methods for Stochastic Chemical Kinetics   81
4.3   Aspects of Biology — Genetic Regulation   92
4.4   Parallel Computing for Biological Systems   96
4.5   Parallel Simulations   100
4.6   Spatial Modeling of Cellular Systems   104
4.7   Modeling Colonies of Cells   109
References   115

5   Parallel Computation in Simulating Diffusion and Deformation in
Human Brain   **121**
Ning Kang

5.1   Introduction   121
5.2   Anisotropic Diffusion Simulation in White Matter Tractography   122
5.3   Brain Deformation Simulation in Image-Guided Neurosurgery   132
5.4   Summary   142
References   143

PART II   SEQUENCE ANALYSIS AND MICROARRAYS   **147**

6   Computational Molecular Biology   **149**
Azzedine Boukerche

6.1   Introduction   149
6.2   Basic Concepts in Molecular Biology   150
6.3   Global and Local Biological Sequence Alignment   152
6.4   Heuristic Approaches for Biological Sequence Comparison   158
6.5   Parallel and Distributed Sequence Comparison   161
6.6   Conclusions   164
References   165

7   Special-Purpose Computing for Biological Sequence Analysis   **167**
Bertil Schmidt

7.1   Introduction   167
7.2   Hybrid Parallel Computer   169

7.3 Dynamic Programming Communication Pattern 172
7.4 Performance Evaluation 179
7.5 Future Work and Open Problems 185
7.6 Tutorial 188
References 190

8 Multiple Sequence Alignment in Parallel on a Cluster of Workstations 193

Amitava Datta

8.1 Introduction 193
8.2 CLUSTAL W 194
8.3 Implementation 201
8.4 Results 207
8.5 Conclusion 209
References 210

9 Searching Sequence Databases Using High-Performance BLASTs 211

Xue Wu

9.1 Introduction 211
9.2 Basic Blast Algorithm 212
9.3 Blast Usage and Performance Factors 214
9.4 High Performance BLASTs 215
9.5 Comparing BLAST Performance 221
9.6 UMD-BLAST 226
9.7 Future Directions 228
9.8 Related Work 229
9.9 Summary 230
References 230

10 Parallel Implementations of Local Sequence Alignment: Hardware and Software 233

Vipin Chaudhary

10.1 Introduction 233
10.2 Sequence Alignment Primer 235
10.3 Smith–Waterman Algorithm 240
10.4 FASTA 244
10.5 BLAST 245
10.6 HMMER — Hidden Markov Models 249
10.7 ClustalW 252
10.8 Specialized Hardware: FPGA 257
10.9 Conclusion 262
References 262

11   Parallel Computing in the Analysis of Gene Expression Relationships   **265**

Robert L. Martino

11.1	Significance of Gene Expression Analysis	265
11.2	Multivariate Gene Expression Relations	267
11.3	Classification Based on Gene Expression	274
11.4	Discussion and Future Directions	280
	References	282

12   Assembling DNA Fragments with a Distributed Genetic Algorithm   **285**

Gabriel Luque

12.1	Introduction	285
12.2	DNA Fragment Assembly Problem	286
12.3	DNA Fragment Assembly Using the Sequential GA	289
12.4	DNA Fragment Assembly Problem Using the Parallel GA	292
12.5	Experimental Results	294
12.6	Conclusions	301
	References	301

13   A Cooperative Genetic Algorithm for Knowledge Discovery in Microarray Experiments   **303**

Mohammed Khabzaoui

13.1	Introduction	303
13.2	Microarray Experiments	304
13.3	Association Rules	306
13.4	Multi-Objective Genetic Algorithm	308
13.5	Cooperative Multi-Objective Genetic Algorithm (PMGA)	313
13.6	Experiments	315
13.7	Conclusion	322
	References	322

PART III PHYLOGENETICS   **325**

14   Parallel and Distributed Computation of Large Phylogenetic Trees   **327**

Alexandros Stamatakis

14.1	Introduction	327
14.2	Maximum Likelihood	330
14.3	State-of-the-Art ML Programs	332
14.4	Algorithmic Solutions in RAxML-III	334
14.5	HPC Solutions in RAxML-III	337
14.6	Future Developments	341
	References	344

15 Phylogenetic Parameter Estimation on COWs   **347**
    Ekkehard Petzold

    15.1 Introduction   347
    15.2 Phylogenetic Tree Reconstruction using Quartet Puzzling   349
    15.3 Hardware, Data, and Scheduling Algorithms   354
    15.4 Parallelizing PEst   356
    15.5 Extending Parallel Coverage in PEst   359
    15.6 Discussion   365
    References   367

**16 High-Performance Phylogeny Reconstruction Under
     Maximum Parsimony**   **369**
    Tiffani L. Williams

    16.1 Introduction   369
    16.2 Maximum Parsimony   374
    16.3 Exact MP: Parallel Branch and Bound   378
    16.4 MP Heuristics: Disk-Covering Methods   381
    16.5 Summary and Open Problems   390
    References   392

PART IV PROTEIN FOLDING   **395**

**17 Protein Folding with the Parallel Replica Exchange Molecular
     Dynamics Method**   **397**
    Ruhong Zhou

    17.1 Introduction   397
    17.2 REMD Method   399
    17.3 Protein Folding with REMD   403
    17.4 Protein Structure Refinement with REMD   420
    17.5 Summary   422
    References   423

18 High-Performance Alignment Methods for Protein Threading   **427**
    R. Andonov

    18.1 Introduction   427
    18.2 Formal Definition   431
    18.3 Mixed Integer Programming Models   434
    18.4 Divide-and-Conquer Technique   444
    18.5 Parallelization   448
    18.6 Future Research Directions   453
    18.7 Conclusion   454
    18.8 Summary   454
    References   455

**19   Parallel Evolutionary Computations in
Discerning Protein Structures**   459
Richard O. Day

   19.1   Introduction   459
   19.2   PSP Problem   460
   19.3   Protein Structure Discerning Methods   461
   19.4   PSP Energy Minimization EAs   471
   19.5   PSP Parallel EA Performance Evaluation   477
   19.6   Results and Discussion   479
   19.7   Conclusions and Suggested Research   483
   References   483

PART V   PLATFORMS AND ENABLING TECHNOLOGIES   **487**

**20   A Brief Overview of Grid Activities for Bioinformatics and
Health Applications**   **489**
Ali Al Mazari

   20.1   Introduction   489
   20.2   Grid Computing   490
   20.3   Bioinformatics and Health Applications   491
   20.4   Grid Computing for Bioinformatics and Health Applications   491
   20.5   Grid Activities in Europe   492
   20.6   Grid Activities in the United Kingdom   494
   20.7   Grid Activities in the USA   497
   20.8   Grid Activities in Asia and Japan   498
   20.9   International Grid Collaborations   499
   20.10 International Grid Collaborations   499
   20.11 Conclusions and Future Trends   500
   References   501

21   Parallel Algorithms for Bioinformatics   **509**
Shahid H. Bokhari

   21.1   Introduction   509
   21.2   Parallel Computer Architecture   511
   21.3   Bioinformatics Algorithms on the Cray MTA System   517
   21.4   Summary   527
   References   528

**22   Cluster and Grid Infrastructure for Computational Chemistry
and Biochemistry**   **531**
Kim K. Baldridge

   22.1   Introduction   531
   22.2   GAMESS Execution on Clusters   532

22.3 Portal Technology 537
22.4 Running GAMESS with Nimrod Grid-Enabling Infrastructure 538
22.5 Computational Chemistry Workflow Environments 542
22.6 Conclusions 546
References 548

23 Distributed Workflows in Bioinformatics **551**
Arun Krishnan
23.1 Introduction 551
23.2 Challenges of Grid Computing 553
23.3 Grid Applications 554
23.4 Grid Programming 555
23.5 Grid Execution Language 557
23.6 GUI-Based Workflow Construction and Execution 565
23.7 Case Studies 570
23.8 Summary 578
References 579

**24 Molecular Structure Determination on a
Computational and Data Grid** **583**
Russ Miller
24.1 Introduction 583
24.2 Molecular Structure Determination 585
24.3 Grid Computing in Buffalo 586
24.4 Center for Computational Research 588
24.5 ACDC-Grid Overview 588
24.6 Grid Research Collaborations 596
24.7 Grid Research Advancements 601
24.8 Grid Research Application Abstractions and Tools 603
24.9 Conclusions 616
References 616

**25 GIPSY: A Problem-Solving Environment for Bioinformatics
Applications** **623**
Rajendra R. Joshi
25.1 Introduction 623
25.2 Architecture 626
25.3 Currently Deployed Applications 634
25.4 Conclusion 647
References 648

**26 TaskSpaces: A Software Framework for Parallel Bioinformatics on
Computational Grids** **651**
Hans De Sterck
26.1 Introduction 651
26.2 The TaskSpaces Framework 655

26.3   Application: Finding Correctly Folded RNA Motifs   661
26.4   Case Study: Operating the Framework on a Computational Grid   663
26.5   Results for the RNA Motif Problem   664
26.6   Future Work   668
26.7   Summary and Conclusion   669
       References   669

**27   The Organic Grid: Self-Organizing Computational Biology on
       Desktop Grids   671**
       Arjav J. Chakravarti

27.1   Introduction   672
27.2   Background and Related Work   674
27.3   Measurements   686
27.4   Conclusions   698
27.5   Future Directions   699
       References   700

28   FPGA Computing in Modern Bioinformatics   705
       H. Simmler

28.1   Parallel Processing Models   706
28.2   Image Processing Task   708
28.3   FPGA Hardware Accelerators   711
28.4   Image Processing Example   716
28.5   Case Study: Protein Structure Prediction   720
28.6   Conclusion   733
       References   734

**29   Virtual Microscopy: Distributed Image Storage, Retrieval,
       Analysis, and Visualization   737**
       T. Pan

29.1   Introduction   737
29.2   Architecture   738
29.3   Image Analysis   747
29.4   Clinical Use   752
29.5   Education   755
29.6   Future Directions   756
29.7   Summary   759
       References   760

Index   765

■■■■■■ PREFACE

Bioinformatics and Computational Biology are fields that requires skills from a variety of fields to enable the gathering, storing, handling, analyzing, interpreting, and spreading of biological information. It requires the use of high-performance computers and innovative software tools to manage enormous quantities of genomic and proteomic data. It also involves the development and application of innovative algorithmic techniques necessary for the analysis, interpretation, and prediction of data to provide insight into the design and validation of experiments for the life sciences.

Most of the above functionalities require the capabilities that are beyond those of a desktop machine and can only be found in a supercomputer. This is especially true now with the rapid increase of the amounts of data generated on a daily basis. Therefore, high-performance computing systems are expected to play an increased role in assisting life scientists in exploring possibilities that were impossible in the past. In return, the variety and richness of problems offered by bioinformatics and computational biology open up new vistas for computer scientists, which could keep them occupied for the next 50 years.

The book is based on a number of standalone chapters that seek to provide an opportunity for researchers to explore the rich and complex subjects of bioinformatics and computational biology and the use of parallel computing techniques and technologies (parallel computing, distributed computing, grid computing, etc.) in solving problems in these dynamic disciplines.

However, as with any new discipline, related applications should be designed and implemented in such a way that enables users to depend on the application availability and results. This book aims to highlight some of the important applications in bioinformatics and computational biology and to identify how parallel computing can be used to better implement these applications.

BOOK OVERVIEW

This is the first book that deals with the topic of parallel computing and its use to drive applications in bioinformatics and computational biology in such a comprehensive manner. The material included in this book was carefully chosen for quality and relevance. This book also provides a mixture of algorithmics, experiments, and simulations, which provide not only qualitative but also quantitative insights into the rich field of bioinformatics and computational biology.

This book is intended to be a repository of case studies that deal with a variety of difficult problems and how parallel computing was used to produce better results in a more efficient manner. It is hoped that this book will generate more interest in developing parallel solutions to wider life sciences applications. This should enable researchers to deal with more complex applications and with larger and richer data sets.

Although the material in this book spans a number of bioinformatics and computational biology applications, the material is written in a way that makes the book self-contained so that the reader does not have to consult with external material. This book offers (in a single volume) a comprehensive coverage of a range of bioinformatics and computational biology applications and how they can be parallelized to improve their performance and lead to faster rates of computations.

This book is intended for researchers, educators, students, and practitioners in the fields of bioinformatics, computational biology, and computer science, who are interested in using high-performance computing to target applications in the life sciences. This book can also be used as a reference for graduate level courses. This book is divided into five parts: algorithms and models, sequence analysis and microarrays, phylogenetics, protein folding, and platforms and enabling techniques. In what follows is a brief précis of the chapters included.

Chapter 1, after an introduction to genes and genomes, describes several efficient parallel algorithms that efficiently solve applications in computational biology. An evolutionary approach to computational biology is presented based first on the search space, which is the set of all possible solutions. The second factor used for the formulation of an optimization problem is the determination of a fitness function that measures how good a particular answer is. Finally, a significant deviation from the standard parallel solution to genetic parallel algorithms approach theory is pointed out by arguing that parallel computational biology is an important sub-discipline that merits significant research attention and that combining different solution paradigms is worth implementing.

Chapter 2 introduces an approach to simulating the molecular evolution of human immunodeficiency virus type 1 (HIV-1) that uses an individual virus-based model of viral infection of a single patient. Numerical methods, including Monte Carlo, are used to realistically simulate viral mutation, recombination, replication, infection, and selection by cell-surface receptor molecules and neutralizing antibodies. The stochastic nature of various events being simulated, such as mutation and recombination, requires that simulations be replicated to account for stochastic variation. In addition, because of the high level of realism, simulations may take a long time to run, and so replicate simulations are preferably run in parallel. The applications of the message-passing interface and the scalable parallel random number generator interface to this problem are described.

To analyze a biological system it is necessary to find out new mathematical models allowing to explain the evolution of the system in a dynamic context or to dread doing of a simple manner the complex situations where the human experience overtakes the mathematical reasoning. Computers have been used since the 1940s to simulate the kinetics of biochemical reactions. Using a pathway structure and a kinetic scheme, the time of reaction and the admissible steady states can be computed. These are discussed in Chapter 3.

A cell is an incredibly complex object as are the dynamical processes that take place within the cell. In spite of this complexity we can hope to understand the dynamics of a cell by building up a set of models and simulation approaches that can lock together in a modular fashion. The focus of Chapter 4 is on how stochasticity manifests itself in cellular processes and how this stochasticity can be modeled, simulated, and visualized. In particular, this chapter addresses the issues of how to simulate stochastic chemical kinetics in both temporal and spatial settings using both sequential parallel computing environments. The models for these simulations are associated with genetic regulation within a single cell but this work also considers colonies of cells.

The purpose of Chapter 5 is to survey some recent developments in the application of parallel and high-performance computation in simulating the diffusion process in the human brain and in modeling the deformation of the human brain. Computational neuroscience is a branch of biomedical science and engineering in which sophisticated high-performance computing techniques can make a huge difference in extracting brain anatomical information non-invasively and in assisting minimal invasive neurosurgical interventions. This chapter demonstrates that there are lots of potential opportunities for computational scientists to work with biomedical scientists to develop high-performance computing tools for biomedical applications.

In Chapter 6, the authors first introduce several basic concepts of molecular biology. This is then followed by a definition of the global and local sequence alignment problems and the exact algorithms used to solve them which are normally based on dynamic programming to solve them. The authors also present several heuristics that can be used to solve the local alignment problem. The chapter concludes with a description of some parallel algorithms that can be used to solve the alignment problems in shorter time.

Chapter 7 presents a hybrid parallel system based on commodity components to gain supercomputer power at low cost. The architecture is built around a coarse-grained PC cluster linked to a high-speed network and fine-grained parallel processor arrays connected to each node. Identifying applications that profit from this kind of computing power is crucial to justify the use of such a system. This chapter presents an approach to high-performance protein database scanning with hybrid computing. To derive an efficient mapping onto this architecture, we have designed instruction systolic array implementations for the Smith–Waterman and Viterbi algorithm. This results in a database scanning implementation with significant run-time savings.

Chapter 8 presents a parallel version of ClustalW for multiple sequence alignment. The algorithm is implemented using the message-passing interface (MPI), a platform for implementing parallel algorithms on a distributed shared memory model. This chapter presents a tutorial introduction to the ClustalW algorithm. First, the authors discuss the dynamic programming algorithm for pairwise sequence alignment. Then this is followed by a discussion of the neighbor-joining method of Seitou and Nei for constructing a phylogenetic tree using the pairwise distances. Finally, the authors present the progressive sequence alignment step based on this phylogenetic tree.

They discuss their strategy for parallelizing the ClustalW algorithm next and provide detailed results for their implementation and analyze the results extensively.

Chapter 9 examines several high-performance versions of BLAST, which is one of the most widely used search tools for screening large sequence databases. Even though BLAST is very efficient in practice, the growing size of sequence databases has created a demand for even more powerful versions of BLAST for use on multiprocessors and clusters. This chapter briefly reviews the basic BLAST algorithm, then describe and analyze several parallel versions of BLAST designed for high performance.

The purpose of pairwise alignment is to extract the sequences that are similar (homologous) to a given input sequence from a database of target sequences. While CPU architectures are struggling to show increased performance, the volume of biological data is greatly accelerating. For example, GenBank, a public database of DNA, RNA, and protein sequence information, is doubling every 6 months. Parallel algorithms for analyzing DNA and protein sequences are becoming increasingly important as sequence data continue to grow. Novel parallel architectures are also being proposed to deal with the growth in computational complexity. Chapter 10 reviews the parallel software and hardware implementations of local sequence alignment techniques. These include various implementations of Smith–Waterman algorithm, FASTA, BLAST, HMMER, and ClustalW.

DNA microarrays provide the technology needed to study gene expression. This technology facilitates large-scale surveys of gene expression in which transcript levels can be determined for thousands of genes simultaneously. These experiments generate an immense quantity of data. Investigators need computational methods to analyze this data to gain an understanding of the phenomena the data represent. Chapter 11 presents two advanced methods for analyzing gene expression data that go beyond standard techniques but require the use of parallel computing. The first method provides for the assessment of the codetermination of gene transcriptional states from large-scale simultaneous gene expression measurements with cDNA microarrays. The parallel implementation exploits the inherent parallelism exhibited in the codetermination methodology that the authors apply. The second method involves classification using cDNA microarrays. The goal is to perform classification based on different expression patterns such as cancer classification. The authors present an efficient parallel implementation of the σ-classifier where the computational work is distributed among available system processors.

As more research centers embark on sequencing new genomes, the problem of DNA fragment assembly for shotgun sequencing is growing in importance and complexity. Accurate and fast assembly is a crucial part of any sequencing project and many algorithms have been developed to tackle it. As the DNA fragment assembly problem is NP-hard, exact solutions are very difficult to obtain. Various heuristics, including genetic algorithms, were designed for solving the fragment assembly problem. Although the sequential genetic algorithm has given good results, it is unable to sequence very large DNA molecules. In Chapter 12, the authors present a distributed genetic algorithm that surmounts that problem. They show how the distributed genetic algorithm can tackle problem instances that are 77K base pairs long accurately.

DNA microarrays allow the simultaneous measurement of the expression level of thousands of genes. This is a great challenge for biologists who see in this new technology the opportunity to discover interactions between genes. The main drawback is that data generated with such experiments is so large that very efficient knowledge discovery methods have to be developed. This is the aim of Chapter 13. The authors propose to study microarray data by using association rules via a combinatorial optimization approach. A cooperative method, based on an evolutionary algorithm, is proposed and several models are tested and compared.

Chapter 14 provides a brief review of phylogenetics and provides an introduction to the maximum likelihood method (one of the most popular techniques used in phylogeney) and describes the abstract computational problems which arise at the computation of the likelihood score for one single-tree topology. This is followed by state-of-the-art description of sequential and parallel maximum likelihood programs. This chapter also explains the maximum likelihood program development cycle and describes algorithmic as well as technical enhancements of RAxMLIII. The chapter concludes by addressing promising technical and algorithmic developments and solutions which could enable the computation of larger and more accurate trees in the near future.

Phylogenetic analysis is a routine task in biological research. Chapter 15 discusses the different factors that influence the performance of parallel implementations. Using the example of parameter estimation in the TREE-PUZZLE program, the authors analyze the performance and speedup of different scheduling algorithms on two different kinds of workstation clusters, which are the most abundant parallel platform in biological research. To that end different parts of the TREE-PUZZLE program with diverse parallel complexity are examined and the impact of their characteristics is discussed. In addition, an extended parallelization for the parameter estimation part of the program is introduced.

Phylogenetic trees are extremely useful in many areas of biology and medicine, and one of the primary tools for understanding evolution. Unfortunately, for a given set of organisms, the number of possible evolutionary trees is exponential. Many phylogenetic algorithms exist, but the most popular approaches attempt to solve difficult optimization problems such as maximum parsimony (NP-hard) or maximum likelihood (conjectured to be NP-hard). Chapter 16 surveys the state-of-the-art in phylogenetic algorithms for reconstructing maximum parsimony trees. Each new algorithmic development attempts to get us closer to reconstructing the "Tree of Life," the holy grail of phylogenetics. Thus, this chapter concludes with a list of research questions that must be addressed to reconstruct extremely large-scale phylogenies such as the "Tree of Life."

A highly parallel replica exchange molecular dynamics (REMD) method and its application in protein folding and protein structure prediction are described in Chapter 17. The REMD method couples molecular dynamics trajectories with a temperature exchange Monte Carlo process for efficient sampling of the conformational space. Two sample protein systems, one α-helix and one β-hairpin, are used to demonstrate the power of the algorithm. Up to 64 replicas of solvated protein systems are simulated in parallel over a wide range of temperatures. Very high efficiency ($>98\%$) can be achieved with this embarrassingly parallel algorithm. The simulation results show that the combined trajectories in temperature and configurational space allow a replica to overcome free energy barriers present at low temperatures. These large-scale simulations also reveal detailed results on folding mechanisms, intermediate-state structures, thermodynamic properties, and the temperature dependencies for both protein systems. Furthermore, the extensive data from REMD simulations are used to assess the various solvation models and force fields, which provide insights to the fix of the problems and further improvement of the models. Finally, the usage of the REMD method in protein structure refinement is also discussed.

Chapter 18 deals with a method known as threading which uses information about already known protein structures stored in databases. The authors present the point of view of a computer scientist with particular interests in combinatorial optimization problems. They focus on the computational aspects of finding the optimal sequence-to-structure alignment referred as protein-threading problem (PTP). A formal definition of the PTP is given, and several mixed integer models are presented in a unified framework, analyzed, and compared. Different divide-and-conquer strategies are also described. They reduce the time needed to solve the master problem by solving auxiliary sub-problems of a moderate size. One section is particularly dedicated to a parallel implementation of such a technique, which happened to be efficient even in a sequential implementation. The results in this chapter demonstrate that a careful combination of modeling, decomposing, and a parallel implementation leads to solving PTP real-life instances of tremendous size in a reasonable amount of time.

In Chapter 19, the authors report results of a parallel modified fast messy GA (fmGA), which is found to be quite "good" at finding semi-optimal protein structure prediction solutions in a reasonable time. They focus on modifications to this EA called the fmGA, extensions to the multiobjective implementation of the fmGA (MOfmGA), constraint satisfaction via Ramachandran plots, identifying secondary protein structures, a farming model for the parallel fmGA (pfmGA), and fitness function approximation techniques. These techniques reflect marked improvement over previous GA applications for protein structure determination. Problem definition, protein model representation, mapping to algorithm domain, tool selection modifications, and conducted experiments are discussed.

Over the last few years Grid Computing has generated considerable interest among researchers, scientific institutions, research centers, universities, governments, funding bodies, and others. Grid technology can be used for many applications in the life sciences that require high computational power, data-intensive processing, storage management, and resource sharing. Chapter 20 reviews the current worldwide activities in Grid Computing as used to drive applications in bioinformatics and the health sciences. The chapter attempts to categorize grid activities by region and by the nature of the application. The review is by no means exhaustive and it is only meant to give the reader an appreciation that current applications that are benefiting from grid deployment and could also provide the thrust for future developments.

Chapter 21 discusses parallel algorithms for bioinformatics in the context of the Cray MTA architecture. This chapter shows how several bioinformatics algorithms can be implemented on this machine and develops an entirely new algorithm for DNA sequencing with very long reads that was developed with the MTA as target architecture. The chapter provides the insights that the authors gained by using the MTA architecture and shows that parallel algorithms may be implemented on this machine with a minimum of rewriting or reorganization. Finetuning of code requires only a basic understanding of the architecture and of the behavior of the tagged memory. The issues of data reorganization, partitioning, scheduling, mapping, and so on, which are central to conventional parallel processors, are nonexistent on this machine. The MTA is thus the ideal machine for a rapidly advancing field like bioinformatics, where algorithm development and coding must charge ahead in tandem.

Many computational chemists requiring significant and relatively flexible resources have turned to parallel clusters to solve increasingly complex problems. Evolving hardware technology and grid resources present new opportunities for chemistry and biology, yet introduce new complexity related to grid, web, and computational difficulties. Chapter 22 describes the author's experience in using the GAMESS quantum chemistry program on clusters, and their utilization of evolving portal, grid, and workflow technologies to solve problems that would not be practical on individual machines.

Chapter 23 sets forth the challenges faced by grid computing and discusses the nature of applications that can be grid-enabled. It introduces a framework that can be used to develop grid-enabled bioinformatics applications and provide examples that show how this can be achieved. The author argues that a software development framework for bioinformatics can only receive acceptance if all the complexity can be hidden away from the scientists. That is why such environments need to have sophisticated graphical user interfaces that enable the easy composition and execution of bioinformatics workflows.

Chapter 24 focuses on the design and implementation of a critical computer program in structural biology onto two computational and data grids. The first is the Buffalo-based ACDC grid, which uses facilities at SUNY–Buffalo and several research institutions in the greater Buffalo area. The second is Grid2003, an international grid established late in 2003 primarily for physics and astronomy applications. The authors present an overview of the ACDC Grid and Grid2003, focusing on the implementation of several new tools that they have developed for the integration of computational and data grids, lightweight job monitoring, predictive scheduling, and opportunities for improved grid utilization through an elegant backfill facility. A new computational framework is developed for the evolutionary determination, an efficient implementation of an algorithm to determine molecular crystal structures using the Shake-and-Bake methodology. Finally, the grid-enabled data mining approach that the authors introduce is able to exploit computational cycles that would otherwise go unused.

Recently, there has been an increase in the number of completely sequenced genomes due to the numerous genome-sequencing projects. The enormous biological sequence data thus generated necessitate the development of efficient tools for mining the information on structural and functional properties of biomolecules. Such a kind of information can prove invaluable for pharmaceutical industries, for in silico drug target identification and new drug discovery. However, the enormity of data and complexity of algorithms make the above tasks computationally demanding, necessitating the use of high-performance computing. Lately, the cost-effective general-purpose clusters of PCs and workstations have been gaining importance in bioinformatics. However, to use these techniques one must still have significant expertise not only in the bioinformatics domain but also in parallel computing. A problem-solving environment (PSE) relieves the scientist of the burdens associated with the needless and often confidential details of the hardware and software systems by providing a user-friendly environment either through web portals or graphical user interfaces. The PSE thus leaves the scientist free to concentrate on the job. This chapter describes the design and development of GIPSY, a PSE for bioinformatics applications.

Chapter 26 describes the TaskSpaces software framework for grid computing. TaskSpaces is characterized by two major design choices: decentralization, provided by an underlying tuple space concept, and platform independence, provided by implementation in Java. This chapter discusses advantages and disadvantages of this approach, and demonstrate seamless performance on an ad hoc grid composed of a wide variety of hardware for a real-life parallel bioinformatics problem. Specifically, the authors performed virtual experiments in RNA folding on computational grids composed of fast supercomputers, to estimate the smallest pool of random RNA molecules that would contain enough catalytic motifs for starting a primitive metabolism. These experiments may establish one of the missing links in the chain of events that led to the origin of life.

Desktop grids have been used to perform some of the largest computations in the world and have the potential to grow by several orders of magnitude. However, current approaches to using desktop resources require either centralized servers or extensive knowledge of the underlying system, limiting their scalability. The authors propose a new design for desktop grids that relies on a self-organizing, fully decentralized approach to the organization of the computation. Their approach, called the Organic Grid, is a radical departure from current approaches and is modeled after the way complex biological systems organize themselves. Similar to current desktop grids, a large computational task is broken down into sufficiently small subtasks. Each subtask is encapsulated into a mobile agent, which is then released on the grid and discovers computational resources using autonomous behavior. In the process of "colonization" of available resources, the judicious design of the agent behavior produces the emergence of crucial properties of the computation that can be tailored to specific classes of applications. The authors demonstrate this concept with a reduced-scale proof-of-concept implementation that executes a data-intensive independent-task application on a set of heterogeneous, geographically distributed machines. They present a detailed exploration of the design space of our system and a performance evaluation of our implementation using metrics appropriate for assessing self-organizing desktop grids.

A new computing approach is introduced in Chapter 28 that makes use of field programmable gate arrays (FPGAs). This new approach uses FPGA processors that are integrated into existing computing nodes. The FPGA processors provide a computing structure that enables to execute the algorithms in a parallel architecture.

The transformation from the sequential algorithm to the parallel architecture is described by the energy calculation part of a protein structure prediction task.

Technological advances in microscopy, digital image acquisition, and automation have allowed digital, virtual slides to be used in pathology and microbiology. Virtual microscopy has the benefits of parallel distribution, on-demand reviews, rapid diagnosis, and long-term warehousing of slides. Sensor technologies combined with high-power magnification generate uncompressed images that can reach 50 GB per image in size. In a clinical or research environment, the number of slides scanned can compound the challenges in storing and managing these images. A distributed storage system coupled with a distributed execution framework is currently the best way to overcome these challenges to perform large-scale analysis and visualization. Chapter 29 demonstrates an implementation that integrates several middleware components in a distributed environment to enable and optimize the storage and analysis of this digital information. These systems support and enable virtual slide reviews, pathology image analysis, and three-dimensional reconstruction and visualization of microscopy data sets in both clinical and research settings.

ALBERT Y. ZOMAYA

CONTRIBUTORS

David Abramson, Monash University, Clayton, Victoria, Australia

Enrique Alba, Universidad de Málaga, Málaga, Spain

Ali Al Mazari, The University of Sydney, Sydney, Australia

Ilkay Altintas, University of California, San Diego, California, USA

Celine Amoreira, University of Zurich, Zurich, Switzerland

R. Andonov, Campus de Beaulieu, Rennes, France

Santosh Atanur, Pune University, Pune, India

David A. Bader, University of New Mexico, Albuquerque, New Mexico, USA

Kim K. Baldridge, University of Zurich, Zurich, Switzerland and University of
   California, San Diego, California, USA

S. Balev, Université du Havre, Le Havre, France

Gerald Baumgartner, The Ohio State University, Columbus, Ohio, USA

Dattatraya Bhat, Pune University, Pune, India

Adam Birnbaum, University of California, San Diego, California, USA

Shahid H. Bokhari, University of Engineering and Technology, Lahore, Pakistan

Azzedine Boukerche, University of Ottawa, Ottawa, Ontario, Canada

K. Burrage, University of Queensland, Queensland, Australia

P. M. Burrage, University of Queensland, Queensland, Australia

Eric S. Carlson, University of Alabama, Auburn, Alabama, USA

U. Catalyurek, The Ohio State University, Columbus, Ohio, USA

Arjav J. Chakravarti, The MathWorks, Natick, Massachusetts, USA

Christophe Chassagnole, Institut National de Sciences Appliquées, Lyon, France

Vipin Chaudhary, Wayne State University, Troy, Michigan, USA

Janaki Chintalapati, Pune University, Pune, India

D. Cowden, The Ohio State University, Columbus, Ohio, USA

Jack da Silva, The University of Adelaide, Adelaide, Australia

Amitava Datta, University of Western Australia, Perth, Australia

Richard O. Day, Air Force Institute of Technology, Wright-Patterson Air Force Base, Dayton, Ohio, USA

Alba Cristina Magalhaes Alves de Melo, Universidade de Brasilia, Brasil

Hans De Sterck, University of Waterloo, Waterloo, Ontario, Canada

Clarisse Dhaenens, Universite des Sciences et Technologies de Lille, Lille, France

Andrei Doncescu, Laboratory of Analysis and Architecture of Systems LAAS CNRS 8001, Toulouse, France

Justin Ebedes, University of Western Australia, Perth, Australia

Colin Enticott, Monash University, Clayton, Victoria, Australia

Slavisa Garic, Monash University, Clayton, Victoria, Australia

Mark L. Green, State University of New York, Buffalo, New York, USA

Jerry P. Greenberg, University of California, San Diego, California, USA

N. Hamilton, University of Queensland, Queensland, Australia

S. Hastings, The Ohio State University, Columbus, Ohio, USA

Sameer Ingle, Pune University, Pune, India

S. Jewel, The Ohio State University, Columbus, Ohio, USA

Calvin A. Johnson, National Institutes of Health, Bethesda, Maryland, USA

Rajendra R. Joshi, Centre for Development of Advanced Computing, Ganeshkhind, Maharashtra, India

Ning Kang, University of Kentucky, Lexington, Kentucky, USA

Mohammed Khabzaoui, Universite des Sciences et Technologies de Lille, Lille, France

Sami Khuri, San Jose State University, San Jose, California, USA

Rob Knight, University of Colorado at Boulder, Boulder, Colorado, USA

Arun Krishnan, Bioinformatics Institute, Matrix, Singapore

T. Kurc, The Ohio State University, Columbus, Ohio, USA

Gary B. Lamont, Air Force Institute of Technology, Wright-Patterson Air Force Base, Dayton, Ohio, USA

S. Langella, The Ohio State University, Columbus, Ohio, USA

Mario Lauria, The Ohio State University, Columbus, Ohio, USA

Feng Liu, Wayne State University, Troy, Michigan, USA

Gabriel Luque, Universidad de Málaga, Málaga, Spain

Rob Markel, National Center for Atmospheric Research, Boulder, Colorado, USA

Robert L. Martino, National Institutes of Health, Laurel, Maryland, USA

Vijay Matta, Wayne State University, Troy, Michigan, USA

Xiandong Meng, Wayne State University, Troy, Michigan, USA

Daniel Merkle, Universität Leipzig, Leipzig, Germany

Martin Middendorf, Universität Leipzig, Leipzig, Germany

Russ Miller, State University of New York, Buffalo, New York, USA

Bernard M.E. Moret, University of New Mexico, Albuquerque, New Mexico, USA

Satish Mummadi, Pune University, Pune, India

Anil Nambiar, Wayne State University, Troy, Michigan, USA

S. Oster, The Ohio State University, Columbus, Ohio, USA

T. Pan, The Ohio State University, Columbus, Ohio, USA

Ekkehard Petzold, MPI fur Evolutionare Anthropologie, Germany

Yohann Potier, University of Zurich, Zurich, Switzerland

Jithesh P.V., Pune University, Pune, India

Nouhad J. Rizk, Notre Dame University, Zouk Mosbeh, Lebanon

Juan Carlos A. Rodríguez, University of Barcelona, Barcelona, Spain

Daniel E. Russ, National Institutes of Health, Bethesda, Maryland, USA

J. Saltz, The Ohio State University, Columbus, Ohio, USA

Jon R. Sauer, Eagle Research & Development, Boulder, Colorado, USA

Bertil Schmidt, Nanyang Technological University, Singapore

Heiko A. Schmidt, Institut fuer Bioinformatik, Duesseldorf, Germany

Heiko Schröder, RMIT University, Melbourne, Australia

Harald Simmler, Bgm.-Horlacherstr., Ludwigshafen, Germany

Uddhavesh Sonavane, Pune University, Pune, India

Alexandros Stamatakis, Institut fur Informatik, Technische Universitat, Munchen, Germany

Wibke Sudholt, University of Zurich, Switzerland and Computational Laboratory, ETH Zurich, Switzerland

El-Ghazali Talbi, LIFL — University of Lille, Villeneuve d'Ascq, France

T. Tian, University of Queensland, Queensland, Australia

Arndt von Haeseler, Bioinformatik, HHU Dusseldorf and von-Neumann Institut fur Computing, NA, Germany

Chau-Wen Tseng, University of Maryland at College Park, Maryland, USA

Tiffani L. Williams, Radcliffe Institute, Cambridge, Massachusetts, USA

Xue Wu, University of Maryland at College Park, Maryland, USA

Ganesh Yadav, Wayne State University, Troy, Michigan, USA

Mi Yan, Texas A&M University, College Station, Texas, USA

N. Yanev, University of Sofia, Bulgaria

Laurence T. Yang, St. Francis Xavier University, Antigonish, Nova Scotia, Canada

Jun Zhang, University of Kentucky, Lexington, Kentucky, USA

Ruhong Zhou, IBM Thomas J. Watson Research Center, Yorktown Heights, New York, USA

Albert Y. Zomaya, Sydney University, Sydney, NSW, Australia

ACKNOWLEDGMENTS

First and foremost I would like to thank and acknowledge the contributors to this volume for their support and patience, and the reviewers for their useful comments and suggestions that helped in improving the earlier outline of the book and presentation of the material. Also, I should extend my deepest thanks to Val Moliere and Emily Simmons from Wiley for their collaboration, guidance, and most importantly, patience in finalizing this book. Finally, I would like to acknowledge the efforts of the team from Wiley's production department for their extensive efforts during the many phases of this project and the timely fashion in which the book was produced by.

PART I

ALGORITHMS AND MODELS

CHAPTER 1

Parallel and Evolutionary Approaches to Computational Biology

NOUHAD J. RIZK

Many of the today's problems, such as those involved in weather prediction, aerodynamics, and genetic mapping, require tremendous computational resources to be solved accurately. These applications are computationally very intensive and require vast amounts of processing power and memory requirements. Therefore, to give accurate results, powerful computers are needed to reduce the run time, for example, finding genes in DNA sequences, predicting the structure and functions of new proteins, clustering proteins into families, aligning similar proteins, and generating phylogenetic trees to examine evolutionary relationships all need complex computations. To develop parallel computing programs for such kinds of computational biology problems, the role of a computer architect is important; his or her role is to design and engineer the various levels of a computer system to maximize performance and programmability within limits of technology and cost. Thus, parallel computing is an effective way to tackle problems in biology; multiple processors being used to solve the same problem. The scaling of memory with processors enables the solution of larger problems than would be otherwise possible, while modeling a solution is as much important as the computation.

In this chapter, after an introduction to genes and genomes, we describe some efficient parallel algorithms that efficiently solve applications in computational biology. An evolutionary approach to computational biology is presented based first on the search space, which is the set of all possible solutions. The second factor used for the formulation of an optimization problem is the determination of a fitness function that measures how good a particular answer is. Finally, a significant deviation from the standard parallel solution to genetic parallel algorithms approach theory is pointed out by arguing that parallel computational biology is an important sub-discipline that merits significant research attention and that combining different solution paradigms is worth implementing.

Parallel Computing for Bioinformatics and Computational Biology, Edited by Albert Y. Zomaya
Copyright © 2006 John Wiley & Sons, Inc.

1.1   INTRODUCTION

Computational biology is the use of computational techniques to model biological systems at various levels of complexity — atomic, metabolic, cellular, and pathologic. The field of computational biology covers many areas: structural biology, biochemistry, physical chemistry, molecular biology, genomics and bioinformatics, control theory, statistics, mathematics, and computer science. Bioinformatics provides a wealth of potential challenges that can be used to advance the state of the art by creating scalable applications that can be used in customer environments. Thus, in computational biology, conducting research related to the realization of parallel/distributed scalable applications requires an understanding of the basics of all related fields. Therefore, this chapter starts with a detailed explanation of certain technical terms that have proved to be essential for researchers in computational biology.

1.1.1   Chromosome

A chromosome is a long string of double-stranded deoxyribonucleic acid (DNA), the molecule that serves as a primary repository of genetic information. Thomas Hunt Morgan found that genes on a chromosome have a remarkable statistical property, that is, genes appear as being linearly arranged along the chromosome and also that chromosomes can recombine and exchange genetic material. A gene is a unit of heredity used to describe a unit of phenotype variation.

1.1.2   Allele

Alleles are alternate forms of the same gene. There may be hundreds of alleles for a particular gene, but usually only one or a few are common. A homologous pair of chromosomes contain two alleles, one in the chromosome derived from the father and the other in the chromosome derived from the mother. If, for example, the chromosome inherited from the mother has a mutant allele at a specific position, this position on a chromosome is called a locus, and the presence of a single mutant allele creates the trait of disease. However, the child will not suffer from the disease caused by this mutation unless both the genes inherited from parents are defective or one of them is on the X chromosome, for example, hemophilus. In brief, an allele is a type of the DNA at a particular locus on a particular chromosome.

1.1.3   Recombination

Recombination or crossing over is defined as the recombination of maternal chromosome pairs with its paternal chromosome and exchanges material in the genesis of a sperm or egg. This formation of new gene combination is the result of the physical event of crossing over. The intensity of linkage of two genes can be measured by the frequency of the recombinants. The probability that a recombination event occurs between two loci is a function of the distance between these loci. In fact, the alleles at two loci that are far apart on a chromosome are more likely to combine than the alleles that are close together on a chromosome. Genes that tend to stay together during recombination are called linked. Sometimes, one gene in a linked pair serves as a *marker* that can be used by geneticists to infer the presence of the other genes causing disease.

1.1.4 Meiosis

Before explaining meiosis, let us explain the relationship between genes and alleles. In Figure 1.1, we notice two gametes inherited from the father AD, which are called the gene 1, and the two gametes inherited from the mother ad, which are called gene 2. Therefore, the formation of haploid germ cells from diploid parent cell is called meiosis. Meiosis is informative for linkage when we identify whether the gamete is recombinant.

1.1.5 Genetic Linkage

Geneticists seek to locate genes for disorder traits (gene disease) among the genome, which is pairs of 23 human chromosomes. The statistical procedure used to trace the transmission of a disordered allele within a family is called linkage analysis. This analysis is based on genes, whose locations on a particular chromosome are already known, and are called markers [1].

Genes will be inherited together if they are close on the same chromosome because recombination is less likely. Recombinant chromosomes will occur less frequently

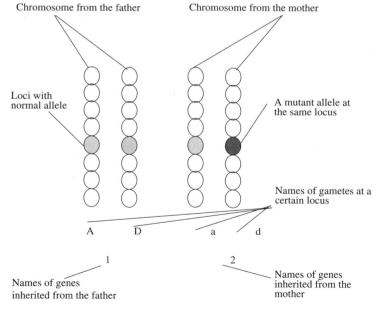

Figure 1.1 Genes and alleles at a specific locus.

TABLE 1.1 Expected Frequency of Children Through the Mother

Mother's Gametes	Recombinant	Probability
Ad	No	1
Ad	No	1
Ad	No	1
Ad	No	1

(less than half of the time) than nonrecombinant chromosomes (more than half of the time). The recombination is measured by the recombination fraction denoted by θ, which is the probability of a recombination between two loci. The lowest possible value for θ is zero, which means that there is no recombination between the marker and the trait locus. In fact, either the marker is the trait or the two loci are so close together that they rarely recombine. The upper limit of θ is 0.5, which means that the loci are not linked. The recombination frequency θ for unlinked loci is 0.5. In brief, $0 \leq \theta \leq 0.5$ [2].

The family is said to be idealized pedigree if no recombination has taken place. If there are recombinations, it is quite easy to calculate θ; it is the summation of the number of recombinants among offspring divided by the total number of offspring. For example, if one recombinant out of nine offspring means that θ is equal to $1/9 = 0.11$.

1.1.6 Expected Frequency of Offspring

The computation of expected frequency of offspring genotypes in linkage is as follows [3]: As an example, consider a father who has haplotype AD/ad and a mother with haplotype ad/ad. All the mother's gametes will be genotyped ad. Thus, the probability that the mother gives the alleles ad is equal to 1 (see Table 1.1).

Father, however, may have one of the four different gametes, AD, Ad, aD, ad. In addition, the probability that the father gives the alleles AD is equal to the probability that the father gives allele A at marker multiplied by the probability of having no recombination between marker and trait. In fact, it is equal to $1/2(1 - \theta)$. Similarly, the probability that the father gives the alleles Ad is equal to the probability that the father gives allele A at marker multiplied by the probability of having recombination between marker and trait. In fact, it is equal to $1/2\theta$. The probability that the father

TABLE 1.2 Expected Frequency of Children Through the Father

Father's Gametes	Recombinant	Probability
AD	No	$1/2(1 - \theta)$
Ad	Yes	$1/2\theta$
AD	Yes	$1/2\theta$
Ad	No	$1/2(1 - \theta)$

TABLE 1.3   Expected Frequency of Children

Father's and Mother's Gametes	Recombinant	Probability
AD/ad	No	$1/2(1-\theta)$
AD/ad	Yes	$1/2\theta$
aD/ad	Yes	$1/2\theta$
ad/ad	No	$1/2(1-\theta)$

gives the alleles aD is equal to the probability that the father gives allele a at marker multiplied by the probability of having no recombination between marker and trait. In fact, it is equal to $1/2\theta$. Finally, the probability that the father gives the alleles ad is equal to the probability that the father gives allele a at marker multiplied by the probability of having recombination between marker and trait. In fact, it is equal to $1/2(1-\theta)$ (see Tables 1.2–1.4). Then, the expected frequency among the offspring is a function of θ.

1.1.7   Multipoint Linkage Analysis

In the previous section, we assumed that we know where is the gene affected but what if we do not know? Therefore, we need to gather a large number of families in which we observe a disorder and we extract some biological specimen from each member of the family to study the linkage, but this time with many markers simultaneously; this procedure is called multipoint linkage [4]. There are two types of statistical techniques used in the linkage analysis, parametric linkage analysis and nonparametric linkage analysis. Parametric linkage analysis uses statistical procedures to estimate θ and sometimes other quantities. The odds for linkage is a quantity that is equal to the ratio of two probabilities; the numerator is the probability of observing the data given that θ is less than 0.5 (i.e., the marker and the trait loci are linked) and the denominator is the probability of observing the data given that θ is equal to 0.5 (i.e., the marker and the trait loci are not linked). The common logarithm (base 10) of the odds (likelihood) of linkage is specific to geneticists for the computation of parametric linkage analysis. It is called the LOD scores. The second method used in linkage analysis is suitable for complex gene disorders, unlike the first one suitable for single gene analysis. It is called the nonparametric approach. The advantages of nonparametric techniques are that it is not necessary to make assumptions about the mode of inheritance for the disorder; their disadvantage is they are less powerful than

TABLE 1.4   Expected Frequency Function of Theta

Offspring	Recombinant	Probability	$\theta=0$	$\theta=0.10$	$\theta=0.2$	$\theta=0.3$	$\theta=0.4$	$\theta=0.5$
AD	No	$1/2(1-\theta)$	0.5	0.45	0.40	0.35	0.30	0.25
Ad	Yes	$1/2\theta$	0.00	0.05	0.10	0.15	0.20	0.25
aD	Yes	$1/2\theta$	0.00	0.05	0.10	0.15	0.20	0.25
ad	No	$1/2(1-\theta)$	0.50	0.45	0.40	0.35	0.30	0.25

the parametric techniques. An example of nonparametric techniques is the affected sib-pair method. The geneticists gather data on a large number of sibships to locate those that have at least two members of a sibship who are affected with the disorder. The affected sib pairs are then genotyped at the marker locus, and the sib pairs are placed into one of the two mutually exclusive categories based on their genotypes at the marker. The first category includes all sib pairs who have the same genotype at the marker, these being called marker-concordant pairs. The second category is for the marker-discordant pairs, those sib pairs who have different genotypes at the marker. If the marker is not linked to the gene for the disorder, then we should expect an equal number in both categories. However, if the marker is linked to the disease locus, then there should be more marker-concordant pairs than marker-discordant pairs.

Sib Pair Analysis   The sib pair analysis is the probability of having 0, 1 or 2 common alleles. This analysis is known as identity by descent (IBD) (Fig. 1.2). Consider a sib pair and suppose we wish to identify the parental origin of the DNA inherited by each sib at a particular locus, say. Label the paternal chromosomes containing the locus of interest by (a, c), and similarly label the maternal chromosomes by (b, d).

The inheritance vector of the sib-pair at the locus l is the vector $x = (x_1, x_2, x_3, x_4)$, where x

x_1 is the label of the paternal chromosome from which sib1 inherited DNA at locus l (a),

x_2 is the label of the maternal chromosome from which sib1 inherited DNA at locus l (b),

x_3 is the label of the paternal chromosome from which sib2 inherited DNA at locus l (c), and

x_4 is the label of the maternal chromosome from which sib1 inherited DNA at locus l (d).

In practice, the inheritance vector of a sibship is determined by finding enough poly-morphism in the parents to be able to identify the chromosomal fragments transmitted

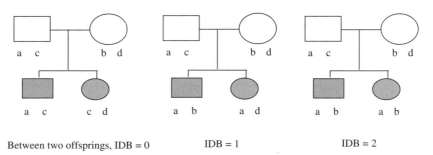

Figure 1.2   Identity by descent (IBD).

to individuals in the sibship. When IBD information is incomplete, partial information extracted from marker data may be summarized by the inheritance distribution, a conditional probability distribution over the possible inheritance vectors at the marker locus [5].

For sib-pairs, there are 16 inheritance vectors; however these are usually grouped into three distinct IBD configurations corresponding to the number of chromosomes sharing DNA IBD at the locus (Table 1.5).

Under Mendel's first law, all 16 inheritance patterns (inheritance vectors) are likely equally, hence the probabilities that two sibs share DNA IBD on 0, 1, and 2 chromosomes are $1/4$, $1/2$, and $1/4$, respectively [6].

1.1.7.1 Joint Genotype Probabilities

The joint genotypes probabilities are conditioned on the number of pairs of genes (one from each individual), which are IBD. The value p_i represents the population frequency of allele i. Genes not IBD are assumed to be statically independent. Genotypes are considered to be unordered pairs of genes. For example, consider two offspring with respectively ab and cd alleles; the probability of having one common identical alleles is equal to zero, and the probability of having two common identical alleles is also equal to zero, but the probability of having zero common identical alleles is equal to the multiplication of probabilities of alleles frequency in such a population multiplied by the number of possible states $S(p_a * p_b * p_c * p_d * S)$ [1, 7].

Example of Computation: Consider $A = (1, \ldots, v)$ a set of different alleles. $P_a = (p_1, \ldots, p_v)$ a set of probabilities of alleles frequency. $G = (x_1, x_2, x_3, x_4)$ an ordered vector of alleles from the set A of two individual X with alleles x_1 and x_2 and the individual Y with alleles x_3 and x_4, and s is a random gene state of G belonging to a set S of IBD states.

If $s = $ abcd implies that there is zero IBD ($m = 0$). If $s = $ abbc implies that there is one IBD (x_2 and x_3 are common). Assumed that x_1 and x_2 are never IBD and also x_3 and x_4 are never IBD. The technical definition of this assumption is that the individuals X and Y are not inbred. This implies that the set of states S contains only IBD states compatible with this assumption and the resulting states are mutually exclusive.

TABLE 1.5   Sib-Pair IBD Configurations

Number IBD	Inheritance Vectors
0	(a, b, c, d), (c, b, a, d), (a, d, c, b), (c, d, a, b)
1 (paternal)	(a, b, a, d), (c, b, c, d), (a, d, a, b), (c, d, c, b)
1 (maternal)	(a, b, c, b), (c, b, a, b), (a, d, c, d), (c, d, a, d)
2	(a, b, a, b), (a, b, a, b), (c, d, c, d), (c, d, c, d)

TABLE 1.6   **Probabilities of Pairwise Genotypes Given Number of IBD**

Genotypes	0 IBD pairs	1 IBD pair	2 IBD pairs
aa–aa	p_a^4	p_a^3	p_a^2
ab–aa	$2p_a^3 p_b$	$p_a^2 p_b$	0
aa–bb	$p_a^2 p_b^2$	0	0
ab–ab	$4p_a^2 p_b^2$	$p_a p_b (p_a + p_b)$	$2p_a p_b$
ab–bc	$4p_a p_b^2 p_c$	$p_a p_b p_c$	0
ab–cc	$2p_a p_b p_c^2$	0	0
ab–cd	$4p_a p_b p_c p_d$	0	0

In the first column of the Table 1.6, there are zero common alleles inherited. The relative probabilities of different states can be calculated by

$$P\{s = (x_1, x_2, x_3, x_4) \in S | m = 0\} = p_{x1} * p_{x2} * p_{y1} * p_{y2} * \text{States' cardinality.}$$

Note that x_i are all independent conditional on $m = 0$. Thus, if all the possible states for this case are only one abcd, this implies that $S = \{abcd\}$ with cardinality equal to 1. Therefore, the probability of having zero IBD between the two pairs ab–cd (row number 7) in this table is equal to $p_a * p_b * p_c * p_d * 1$.

In addition, for the two pairs ab–aa (row number 2), there are ab–aa and ba–aa, implies that $S = \{abcc, bacc\}$ with cardinality equal to 2. The probability is then $p_a * p_b * p_c * p_d * 2$.

1.1.7.2 *Joint Distribution of Genotype*   The distribution of a set of genes is derived by enumerating all possible IBD states, then calculating the probability of each of the states [8]. These probabilities depend only on the pedigree itself, while the actual probability of observing a given genotype is calculated by conditioning on the IBD states, recognizing that non-IBD genes are conditionally independent [3]. In the example described in the previous section, the joint distribution of genotypes g given the states s belongs to $A * A * A * A * S$, where S is the cardinality of the set S:

$$P\{g = (i, j, k, j) \cap s = abcb\} = p\{x_1 = i\} p\{x_2 = j\} p\{x_3 = k\} p\{s = abcb\}.$$
$$P\{g = (i, j, k, j) \cap s = abac\} = 0.$$

As allele configuration (i, j, k, j) is incompatible with state abac. i, j, k represent alleles of unordered genotypes of two ordered individuals. This probability is noted as

$$P\{g \, \text{in} (A * A * A * A) | m = k\}, \quad k = 0, 1, 2.$$

The multi-locus computation of sib-pair genotypes depends on the genotypes of parents. Parents with unknown genotypes are called founders and the offspring with known genotypes are called nonfounders.

Consider an arbitrary family (known as a pedigree) with f founders and n nonfounders. (A sib-pair pedigree is a special case with two founders and two nonfounders). The length of the inheritance vector is now $2n$ (paternal and maternal alleles of each nonfounder), and the number of possible vectors also called possible states is 2^{2n}. Denote by $a_l = (a_{l,1}, \ldots, a_{l,2f})$ the vector of alleles assigned to the founders at locus. The formulation of the computation of the probability of the observed marker genotypes m_l given the inheritance vector v_l at marker locus l is

$$P\{m_l|v_l\} = \sum a_l P\{m_l, a_l|v_l\}.$$

The IBD probabilities at locus l is the summation of $P\{m_l|v_l\}$ over v_l corresponding to IBD = 0, 1 or 2.

1.1.8 Pedigree Probabilities

For a pedigree composed of k persons, each person K has an ordered genotype relative to many locations (called loci): $X_k = (x_k^1, x_k^2, \ldots, x_k^l) = (x_{km}^1, x_{kp}^1, x_{km}^2, x_{kp}^2, \ldots, x_{km}^l, x_{kp}^l)$ where x_{km}^i is the allele inherited from the mother at locus i and x_{kp}^i is the allele inherited from the father at locus i. The problem is to calculate the probability of phenotypes (unknown genotype) of all persons of a family, when knowing the genotype at different positions.

Another way of defining the problem, given the family with many loci in an order and the phenotypes of members of the pedigree, given also the recombination's fractions between consecutive loci θ_i, the problem will be to reconstruct the best genetic map by maximizing the chance of having data presented and to replace the old recombination fractions by the new one calculated by the algorithm. Genetic mapping is placing genes and other genetic markers on chromosomes, ordering them in relation to one another and other landmarks (such as centromeres), and assigning genetic distance to adjacent pairs.

1.1.8.1 Probability Types We distinguish three types of probabilities:

1. *Founder Probabilities*: If the person K is a founder, the probability of the ordered genotype across all loci is equal to the multiplication of all allele frequencies at different loci. $P[X_k] = P[x_k^1] * P[x_k^2] * \cdots * P[x_k^l]$.

   If X_k has as alleles 1 and 3 at locus $l \to P[X_k^l = 1, 3] = P_1^l * P_3^l$. Thus, the allele frequency at locus 1 is the multiplication of population frequency of each allele at the specific locus.

2. *Transmission Probabilities*: This is the probability that a child inherits a particular genotype from his/her parents. $P[X_k = x_k | X_m = x_m, X_p = x_p]$, then all genotypes are ordered $P[X_k | x_m, x_p] = P[X_{km} | x_m] * P[X_{kp} | x_p]$.

3. *Penetrance Probabilities*: This is the probability of phenotypes. When genotypes are given, they are compared with phenotypes; if they are compatible then the penetrance probability is equal to 1, otherwise it is equal to zero.

1.1.8.2 Existing Methods
Performing calculations on multi-locus data means calculating probabilities on pedigrees using different algorithms. The traditional algorithm is to choose new θ values by approximating the derivative of the likelihood function $L(\theta^{old})$. The main disadvantage of this method, called quasi-Newton, is that the new θ may have lower likelihood. The Expectation and Maximization (EM) algorithm overpasses this drawback by offering a powerful general approach to obtain maximum likelihood estimates from incomplete data. The algorithm starts by making an initial guess of θ distribution. Then, it calculates the expected values for complete data such as the number of recombinant and nonrecombinant meioses in each interval. Afterward, it maximizes the likelihood estimate θ^{new}. The algorithm keeps on repeating expectations and maximizations until the likelihood converges to a maximum. The theoretical advantages of EM search are: less computation time per iteration, increased likelihood on each iteration, good initial convergence properties, exact expressions for derivatives of the likelihood, and ease of generalization.

However, the problem is also stated as the construction of multi-locus linkage maps in humans or as a missing data problem. The efficient solutions are to determine the expected number of recombinations that occur in each interval, given the recombination fractions $\theta = (\theta_1, \theta_2, \ldots, \theta_l)$ and the phenotypes for all loci ($l_1, \ldots, l_l$).

A special case reconstruction: in this case we suppose that we can observe the genotypes of each individual in a pedigree, including which alleles are on the paternally and maternally derived chromosomes. In each interval, it is then easy to find out by inspection if there is recombination or nonrecombination. Thus, the computational time is proportional to the square of the number of loci.

Elston-Stewart algorithm: this is the general case of genetic reconstruction, the algorithm is applied recursively up the family tree, with probabilities computed for each possible genotype of each child, conditional on the genotypes of his parents, the phenotype of the child, and the phenotypes for the child's descendents. The computation time scales with the number of alleles on each locus. This becomes impractical if the number of loci is more than 5.

Hidden Markov algorithm: this algorithm can be applied with any number of loci but with pedigrees of limited size. It is based on a nonhomogeneous Markov chain of inheritance vectors $v_1, \ldots, v_l$ at different loci with known transition matrices between any two consecutive loci. An inheritance vector v_i is a vector of 2^* nonfounder binary bits. A coordinate is 0 if the allele is inherited from the father; otherwise, it is 1.

Thus, the molecular biological approach to understanding the flow and expression of genetic information involves studying the structure of macromolecules (DNA, RNA, and protein) and the metabolic steps that mediate the flow of information from the genome to the phenotype of the organism. With the advent of large databases of genetic information for these macromolecules, a completely new approach to studying gene expression and its regulation has developed. This field is known as bioinformatics.

1.2 BIOINFORMATICS

Bioinformatics is a subset of a larger area of computational molecular biology which includes the application of computer and information science to areas such as genomics, mapping, sequencing, and determination of sequence and structure by classical means. The primary goals of bioinformatics are predicting three-dimensional structure from primary sequences, predicting biological or biophysical functions from either sequence or structure, and simulating metabolism and other biological processes based on these functions. Many methods of computer and information science are applied to these goals including machine learning, information theory, statistics, graph theory, algorithms, artificial intelligence, stochastic methods, simulation, logic, and so on. Bioinformatics is the recording, annotation, storage, analysis, and searching/retrieval of gene sequences, protein sequences, and structural information. Thus, the purpose of the human genome project is to map the 24 pairs of human chromosomes (including X and Y chromosomes) and delineate the location of all genes. The parallelization is dealing with gigantic amounts of data, repeated comparisons, and retrievals. But the question remains of what is the relationship between bioinformatics and computational biology.

1.2.1 Computational Biology

Computational biology is the application of computational tools and techniques to (primarily) molecular biology. It is the use of computational techniques to model biological systems at various levels of complexity — atomic, metabolic, cellular, and pathologic. It enables new ways of study in life sciences, allowing analytic and predictive methodologies that support and enhance laboratory work. It is a multidisciplinary area of study that combines biology, computer science, and statistics.

Computational biology is also called bioinformatics, although many practitioners define bioinformatics somewhat more narrowly by restricting the field to molecular biology only.

In computational biology, there are different types of problems such as how to find genes in DNA sequences, to predict the structure and functions of newly discovered proteins, to cluster proteins into families, and to align similar proteins, and to generate phylogenetic trees to examine evolutionary relationships. Therefore, there are different models of genetic change such as the long-term model that deals with the evolutionary changes among species. Another model deals with reconstructing evolutionary trees from sequences, a short-term model that deals with the genetic variations in a population and a final model that deals with finding genes by linkage and association.

1.2.2 What Drives Computational Biology?

Computational biology is one of the most rapidly growing areas of scientific computation. It is driven by two factors, the first of which is the recent explosion in the amount of available biological (particularly molecular biological) data, whereas the second is the commercial incentive to exploit the available biological data for drug development and other discoveries.

We see, therefore, that the biological data explosion is due to the increased interest in the study of molecular biology over the past few decades, to the significant improvements in the reliability and speed of automated techniques available to gather molecular biological data over the past few years [9], and to the mapping of the human genome completed recently by both publicly and privately funded efforts (The International Human Genome Project and Celera Genomics Group). These advances have caused the amount of information available in international DNA databases to increase exponentially over the last few years. Organization, retrieval, and interpretation of this vast amount of data have become a key computational challenge.

1.2.3 Key Areas of Computational Biology

The computational biology field focuses on three key areas of computational molecular biology:

1. *Sequence Analysis*: Analyzing sequences of DNA and proteins to try to determine their structure, function, and control information. Given two sequences of characters (representing DNA or proteins), the key problem of sequence analysis is to align them to achieve the optimal match between them on a character-by-character basis. The optimality of the alignment is determined by a scoring system that gives credit for suitably matched characters and penalizes mismatches. However, gaps may be inserted between characters to try to increase the optimality of the match and therefore may lead to certain complications such as the scoring system penalizing gap insertion [10].

   The advantage of aligning sequences is that, if a sequence with unknown properties aligns with a sequence with known properties, it may be possible to extrapolate the structure and function of the unknown sequence. Besides, two sequences with common ancestry may add or remove some amino acids during evolution. There are different types of sequence analysis: pairwise alignment, heuristic pairwise alignment, and multiple alignments [11–13].

2. *Structure Analysis*: Analyzing biological structures to try to determine their sequence and function, and to control information. The key problem in structure analysis is to find an optimal correspondence between the arrangements of atoms in two molecular structures (say A and B) to align them in three dimension. The optimality of the alignment is determined by using a root-mean-square measure of the distances between corresponding atoms in the two molecules. However, it is not known a priori which atom in molecule B corresponds to a given atom in molecule A (the two molecules may not even have the same number of atoms). Structure is believed to be more closely related to function of proteins than sequence. Structural alignment makes clear the common ancestry of two or more proteins (if such a common ancestry exists). It allows identification of common substructures of interest and it allows classification of proteins based on structural similarities.

3. *Function Prediction*: Understanding how sequences and structures lead to the specific functions. The key problem is to predict the function of protein structures based on sequence and structure information. The function is loosely defined, and can be thought of at many levels atomic or molecular [14, 15]. Currently, relatively little progress has been made in function prediction, particularly for higher-order processes. The current methods of function prediction are:

- *Experimentation*, used to determine the function of proteins and other structures but expensive in terms of time and money.
- *Annotation Transfer*: When sequence or structure analysis yields correspondences between structures, the known properties and function of one is used to extrapolate the properties and function of the other. This method has been extremely successful, but the facts that similar sequence or structure does not always imply similar function and that the annotated information about the "known" protein or its sequence or structure information in the database may be incomplete or incorrect are drawbacks to be considered [16].

1.2.4 On the Parallelization of Bioinformatics Applications

This section surveys the computational strategies followed to parallelize the most commonly used software in the bioinformatics arena. The studied algorithms are computationally expensive and their computational patterns range from the regular, such as database searching applications, to very irregularly structured patterns such as phylogenetic trees. Fine- and coarse-grained parallel strategies are discussed for these very diverse sets of applications. This overview outlines computational issues related to parallelism, physical machine models, parallel programming approaches, and scheduling strategies for a broad range of computer architectures.

Exploring a few general concepts about computer architectures, as well as about the parallel programming approaches that have been used to address bioinformatics applications, seems to be essential.

A parallel computer uses a set of processors that are able to cooperate in solving computational problems. This cooperation is made possible, first, by splitting the computational load of the problem (tasks or data) into parts and, second, by reconnecting the partial computations to create an accurate outcome. The way in which load distribution and reconnection (communications) are managed is heavily influenced by the system that will support the execution of a parallel application program.

Parallel computer systems are broadly classified into two main models based on Flynn's (1972) specifications: single-instruction multiple-data (SIMD) machines and multiple-instruction multiple-data (MIMD) machines.

SIMD machines were powerful in the field of parallel computing, but now facing extinction. A typical SIMD machine consists of many simple processors (hundreds or even thousands), each with a small local memory. The complexity and often the inflexibility of SIMD machines, strongly dependent on the synchronization requirements, have restricted their use mostly to special-purpose applications.

MIMD machines are more amenable to bioinformatics. In MIMD machines, each computational process works at its own rhythm in an asynchronous fashion with complete independence of the other computational processes [17]. Memory architecture has a strong influence on the global architecture of MIMD machines, becoming a key issue for parallel execution, and frequently determines the optimal programming model.

1.2.4.1 *Parallel Programming Models*

In simple terms, parallel software enables a massive computational task to be divided into several separate processes that execute concurrently the solution of a common task through different processors. The method used to divide tasks and rejoin the end result can be used as a point of reference to compare different alternative models for parallel programs. In particular, two key features can be used to compare models: granularity, the relative size of the units of computation that execute in parallel; and communication, the way that separate units of computation exchange data and synchronize their activity.

The finest level of software granularity is intended to run individual statements over different subsets of a whole data structure. This concept is called data-parallel, and is mainly achieved through the use of compiler directives that generate library calls to create lightweight processes called threads, and distribute loop iterations among them. A second level of granularity can be formulated as a block of instructions. At this level, the programmer identifies sections of the program that can safely be executed in parallel and inserts the directives that begin to separate tasks. When the parallel program starts, the run-time support creates a pool of threads that are unblocked by the run-time library as soon as the parallel section is reached. At the end of the parallel section, all extra processes are suspended and the original process continues to execute.

Ideally, if we have n processors, the run time should also be n times faster with respect to the wall-clock time. In real implementations, however, the performance of a parallel program is decreased by synchronization between processes, interaction (information interchanges), and load imbalance (idle processors while others are busy). Coordination between processes represents sources of overhead, in the sense that they require some time added to the pure computational workload.

Much of the effort that goes into parallel programming involves increasing efficiency. The first attempt to reduce parallelization penalties is to minimize the interactions between parallel processes. The simplest way, when it is possible, is to reduce the number of task divisions; in other words, to create coarsely-grained applications.

Once the granularity has been decided, communications are needed to enforce correct behavior and create an accurate outcome. When shared memory is available, interprocess communication is usually performed through shared variables. When several processes are working over the same logical address space, the locks, semaphores, or critical sections (blocks of code that only one process can execute at a time) are required for safe access to shared variables.

When the processors use distributed memory, sending messages over the network must perform all interprocess communication. With this message-passing paradigm, the programmer needs to keep in mind where the data is, what to communicate, and when to communicate to whom. Library subroutines are available to facilitate message-passing constructions: PVM and MPI.

1.2.4.2 *Bioinformatics Applications* In this section, different routinely used algorithms will be presented to describe the strategies followed to parallelize bioinformatics software. The discourse has been organized by the task-level computational pattern observed in such algorithms, from regular to irregular structure [18]. Traditionally, a regular–irregular classification, also named synchronous/asynchronous, has been used in such a way that it was closely related to the characteristic that computations were performed over dense or sparse matrices.

However, when working with nonnumerical applications, as is the case for most of the bioinformatics applications, the rate of free-dependent tasks, the data access pattern, and the task homogeneity, are appropriate indices used to classify applications.

Regular Computational Pattern: Database Searching Database searching (DBsrch) is the most heavily used bioinformatics application. It is also one of the most familiar applications to begin a discussion about parallelization in bioinformatics. It has a very simple form as far as data flow is concerned, and a broad range of strategies have been proposed to apply parallel computing.

The primary influx of information for bioinformatics applications is in the form of raw DNA and protein sequences. Therefore, one of the first steps toward obtaining information from a new biological sequence is to compare it with the set of known sequences contained in the sequence databases. Results often suggest functional, structural, or evolutionary analogies between the sequences.

DBsrch applications allow two different granularity alternatives to be considered: fine- and coarse-grained parallelism. Early approaches focused on data-parallel over SIMD machines starting with the work of Coulson et al. [8]. Deshpande et al. [20] and Jones [21] presented a work on hypercubes and CM-2 computers. Soon after, Sturrock and Collins implemented the exhaustive dynamic programming algorithm of Smith and Waterman in the MasPar family of parallel machines (from the minimum 1024 processors configuration of MP-1 systems up to a 16,384 processors MP-2 system [22, 23].)

The advantage of fine-grained approach is that this strategy only requires local communications. A coarse-grained approach is best for a great number of tasks such as most of today's parallel bioinformatics problems. However, several other applications exist for which there are not enough independent tasks to be solved concurrently. It is still possible to learn from early approaches, and obtain fruitful conclusions that improve new parallel solutions.

Enhanced algorithms may be proposed, taking into consideration the fact that when more tasks than processors are available, the simplest and most effective strategy is coarse-grained parallelization. This is so fundamental that presenting a new algorithm with this feature goes together with its parallel coarse-grained implementation. Some good examples are as follows:

Structural Biology (Electron Microscopy), which determines viral assembly mechanisms and identifies individual proteins. The compute-intensive task in this algorithm is associated with imaging the three-dimensional structure of viruses from electron micrographs (two-dimensional projections). The number of tasks is related to the set of candidate orientations for each particle, such calculations being at different orientations, completely independent of each other.

Protein Structure Prediction: This task involves searching through a large number of possible structures representing different energy states. One of the most computationally intensive tasks calculates the solvent accessible surface area that can be measured on individual atoms if the location of neighboring atoms is known.

Searching Three-Dimensional Structure Databases: As the number of protein structures known in atomic detail increases, the demand for searching by similar structures also grows. A new generation of computer algorithms has been developed for searching by the following methods: extending dynamic programming algorithms [24]; importing strategies from computer vision areas [25] using intramolecular geometrical information, as distances, to describe protein structures [14]; and finding potential alignments based on octomeric C alpha structure fragments, and determining the best path between these fragments using a final dynamic programming step followed by least-squares superposition [26].

Linkage Analysis: Genetic linkage analysis is a statistical technique used for rapid and largely automated construction of genetic maps from gene-linkage data. One key application of linkage analysis aims to map human genes and locate disease genes. The basic computational goal in genetic linkage analysis is to compute the probability that a recombination occurs between two loci L1 and L2. Most frequently used programs estimate this recombination function by using a maximum likelihood approach [7].

All the previous examples fit perfectly to coarse-grained parallel applications, due to the large number of independent tasks and the regular computational pattern they exhibit, together with the low communication/computation rate they present. All these features make them suitable for parallelism with high efficiency rates. However, several other interesting examples have nonregular computational patterns, and they need particular strategies to better exploit parallelism.

In conclusion, it is important to integrate parallelization strategies for individual function evaluation (coarse-grained), with a strategy to parallelize the gradient estimation (fine-grained).

Semi-Regular Computational Patterns   A similar problem arises in the parallelization of hierarchical multiple sequence alignments (MSA) [27–30]. The first step for solving an MSA includes calculating a cross-similarity matrix between each pair of sequences, followed by determining the alignment topology and finally solving the alignment of sequences, or clusters themselves.

Pairwise calculation provides a natural target for parallelization because all elements of the distance matrix are independent (for a set of n sequences $n(n-1)/2$ pairwise comparisons are required [31]). Certainly, parallel strategies for the cross-matrix calculation have been proposed [32, 33], all of them in a coarse-grained approach. In addition, when the MSA is embedded in a more general clustering procedure [34], combining a dynamic planning strategy with the assignment of priorities to the different types of active tasks, using the principles of data locality, has allowed both the exploitation of the inherent parallelism of the complete applications, and the obtaining of performances that are very close to optimal. A full solution probably should combine a coarse-grained solution when computing the cross-similarity matrix with a fine-grained solution for solving the topology.

Irregular Computational Patterns   Applications with irregular computational patterns are the hardest to deal with in the parallel arena. In numeric computation, irregularity is mostly related to sparse computational spaces, which introduce hard problems for data parallel distributions (fine-grained approaches) and data dependencies. The latter reduces the number of independent tasks, which affords little opportunity for developing efficient coarse-grained parallel implementations. A good example of this comes from another routine task in biological sequence analysis; that of building phylogenetic trees [35–38].

The algorithm proceeds by adding sequences into a given tree topology in such a way as to maximize the likelihood topology (suitable for coarse-grained parallelism). Once the new sequence is inserted, a local-optimization step is performed to look for minor rearrangements that could lead to a higher likelihood.

There is no generic procedure to address this type of irregular problem; hence, a good initial approach includes a detailed analysis of the computational behavior of the algorithm such as careful run-time analysis of the algorithm [34, 39].

1.2.4.3 *Successful Applications of Genetic Linkage Analysis*   Many genetics projects were intended to develop which have at least one specific goal, which is to develop a comprehensive human genetic map, which would be used in the identification of the genes associated with genetic diseases and other biological properties and as a backbone for building physical maps. The online resources for gene mapping are very frequent on the Internet as many genome centers develop their own sets of databases to study the inherited diseases and genes and to use a multi-point analysis to locate a disease gene within a framework of markers. Early multi-point linkage analysis based on the Elston–Stewart algorithm [40] was limited to the analysis of few markers.

Lander and Green [6] described the use of hidden Markov models in calculating inheritance distribution, which allowed a more comprehensive multi-point linkage analysis and in the speed of computation subsequently implemented in the Genehunter computer program [5], which is available for download at the homepage of the Whitehead Institute for Biomedical Research [41].

In addition to rapid computation of multi-point LOD scores with dozens of polymorphic markers, the Genehunter program allows calculation of the information content for each region and the construction of multi-marker haplotypes in the pedigrees. The only limitation for the Genehunter algorithm is the size of the pedigree, which is dictated by the power of the computer. Thus, there is a need to parallelize this program. The Whitehead Institute developed a Genehunter with OpenMP support. Minor modifications were made to this program to make it thread-safe and efficient, and to be used with the parallel environment of the OpenMP.

Geneticists are always facing the limitations of the sequential Genehunter version that are memory allocation and CPU time consumption. Kuhn and Peterson from the Whitehead Institute parallelize the same sections of code from Genehunter in both Pthreads and OpenMp. Their result proves that OpenMP is a parallel programming model that facilitates parallelizing debugging and tuning bioinformatics applications, which other implementers use MPI [42, 43]. Rizk provided a new strategy for solving linkage packages analysis based on a parallel program capable of managing these two main handicaps. Conant et al. [42] parallelize the Genehunter by distributing markers among different processors — we call this algorithm the low-level parallel model. However, the high-level model is based on a master–slave paradigm. A more general strategy would be the possibility of selecting either one of these models or a combination of both. In the high-level model, the granularity of a task is one family. Future work includes the implementation of the combined model on different platforms, and using a classification of parameters so that the appropriate model of parallelism can be selected. Moreover, the linkage analysis problem can be a classification problem to predict the optimized complexity based on the selection of the appropriate model. Thus, linkage analysis problem is an application area for evolutionary algorithms.

1.3 EVOLUTIONARY COMPUTATION APPLIED TO COMPUTATIONAL BIOLOGY

Evolutionary computation is, like neural networks, an example *par excellence* for an information-processing paradigm that was originally developed and exhibited by nature and later discovered by man, who subsequently transformed the general principle into computational algorithms to be put to work on computers. Nature makes in an impressive way the use of the principle of genetic heritage and evolution. Application of the simple concept of performance-based reproduction of individuals ("survival of the fittest") led to the rise of well-adapted organisms that can endure in a potentially adverse environment. Mutually beneficial interdependencies, cooperation, and even apparently altruistic behavior can emerge solely by evolution.

Evolutionary computation comprises the four main areas: genetic algorithms (GAs) [44], evolution strategies [45], genetic programming [46], and simulated annealing [47]. GAs and evolution strategies emerged at about the same time in the United States of America and Germany. Both techniques model the natural evolution process to optimize either a fitness function (evolution strategies) or the effort of generating subsequent, well-adapted individuals in successive generations (GAs). Evolution strategies in their original form were basically stochastic hill-climbing algorithms and used for optimization of complex, multi-parameter objective functions that in practice cannot be treated analytically. GAs in their original form were not primarily designed for function optimization but to demonstrate the efficiency of genetic crossover in assembling successful candidates over complicated search spaces. Genetic programming takes the idea of solving an optimization problem by evolution of potential candidates one step further in that not only the parameters of a problem but also the structure of a solution is subject to evolutionary change. Simulated annealing is mathematically similar to evolution strategies. It was originally derived from a physical model of crystallization. Only two individuals compete for the highest rank according to a fitness function and the decision about accepting suboptimal candidates is controlled stochastically.

All methods presented in this chapter are heuristic, that is, they contain a random component. As a consequence (in contrast to deterministic methods) it can never be guaranteed that the algorithm will find an optimal solution or even any solution at all. Evolutionary algorithms are therefore used preferably for applications were deterministic or analytic methods fail, for example, because the underlying mathematical model is not well defined or the search space is too large for systematic, complete search (n.-p. completeness). Another application area for evolutionary algorithms that is rapidly growing is the simulation of living systems starting with single cells and proceeding to organisms, societies, or even whole economic systems [48, 49]. The goal of artificial life is not primarily to model biological life as accurately as possible but to investigate how our life or other, presumably different forms of life could have emerged from nonliving components.

Work with evolutionary algorithms bears the potential for a philosophically and epistemologically interesting recursion. At the beginning, evolution emerged spontaneously in nature. Next, man has discovered the principle of evolution and acquired knowledge on its mathematical properties. He defines GAs for computers. To complete the recursive cycle, computational GAs are applied to the very objects (DNA and proteins) from which they had been derived in the beginning.

1.3.1 Evolutionary Approaches

The explosion of biological sequence data and many of the problems posed by it require tremendous computational resources to solve exactly. Thus, many of the interesting problems arising in the analysis of biological sequence data are in the class of NP-hard. Evolutionary algorithms are one possible tool for addressing such problems. These algorithms use the techniques of survival of the fittest and natural selection to evolve solutions to particular problem instances.

Many sequence analysis problems are optimization problems. The formulation of an optimization problem is based on two factors, namely the search space which is the set of all possible solutions and the fitness function which is the measure used to determine how good a particular answer is.

The evolutionary approaches explore the search space of a problem by working from individuals. Each individual represents an encoding of a potential solution. They modify individuals using artificial operators inspired by natural mechanisms. These individuals compete on the basis of their value under the fitness function. Finally, the selected ones reproduce and live into the next generation [50].

The fitness function embodies the essential aspects of the problem to be solved. It is desirable for individuals with significant shared characteristics to have similar fitness values. The fitness function should point the GA toward the correct value, rather than away from it. In contrast, choosing a representation for a problem is a critical design decision and defines the search space. The representation specifically should help preserve the building blocks of the problem.

The interaction of each of the GA component, affecting the ability of the GA to search the space of available solutions and the design of an efficient GA to solve a particular problem, necessitates some understanding of how the individual components will work together. Their interaction is the primary driver of effective performance of the GA. The complex interactions of the GA components and the generality of the approach are both a strength and a weakness. Therefore, proper understanding of the approach allows one to avoid the weakness and exploit the strength of the GA approach.

1.3.2   Constructing an Algorithm

The work of constructing algorithms that address problems with biological relevance, that is, the work of constructing algorithms in computational biology, consists of two interacting steps. The first step is to pose a biological interesting question and to construct a model of the biological reality that makes it possible to formulate the posed question as a computational problem. The second step is to construct an algorithm that solves the formulated computational problem.

The first step requires knowledge of the biological reality, whereas the second step requires knowledge of algorithmic theory. The quality of the constructed algorithm is traditionally measured by standard algorithmic methodology in terms of the resources, most prominently time and space, it requires for solving the problem. However, as the problem solved by the algorithm originates from a question with biological relevance, its quality should also be judged by the biological relevance of the answers it produces.

The quality of an algorithm that solves a problem with biological relevance is thus a combination of its running time and space assumption and the biological relevance of the answers it produces. These two aspects of the quality of an algorithm depend on the modeling of the biological reality that led to the formulation of the computational problem that is addressed by the algorithm [51].

Constructing a good algorithm that addresses a problem with biological relevance is therefore an interdisciplinary activity that involves interchanging between modeling the biological reality and constructing the algorithm, until a reasonable balance between the running time and space assumption of the algorithm, as well as the biological relevance of the answers it produces, is achieved. The degree of interchanging between modeling and constructing of course depends on how closely related the problem addressed by the algorithm is to a specific biological application, and therefore how relevant it is to judge the algorithm by the biological relevance of the answers it produces.

1.3.3 Application GA

There are several approaches that have been followed in field of evolutionary computation. The general term for such approaches is evolutionary algorithms. The most widely used form of evolutionary algorithm is GA.

Genetic Algorithms are unorthodox search methods. GAs were developed based on the work of John Holland and his colleagues in the 1960s and 1970s at the University of Michigan. In contrast with evolution strategies and evolutionary programming, Holland's original goal was not to design algorithms to solve specific problems, but rather to formally study the phenomenon of adaptation as it occurs in nature and to develop ways in which the mechanisms of natural adaptation might be imported into computer systems. Holland presented the GA as an abstraction of biological evolution and gave a theoretical framework for adaptation under the GAs. Genetic Algorithms have the ability to perform well over a wide range of problems. The following points make them different from other algorithms [52] in GA, variables are represented as strings of binary variables, called chromosomes, GA starts a search from a population of points instead of a single point, which avoids false peaks, GA uses the values of the objective function and GA uses probabilistic transition rules to select improved population points.

The key idea in GAs is the manipulation of chromosomes. Each chromosome represents several variables, encoded as a combination of binary digits (ones and zeroes). Hence by manipulating the chromosome, we will be able to find an optimal or near-optimal solution to the problem. Implementation of GAs requires two main functions, the creation of an initial population and the reproduction of the initial population, which leads to a new one. The reproduction itself is based on three factors: the selection of chromosomes, the crossover, and the mutation. Note that the whole reproduction process is random.

The simplest version of a GA consists of a population and a fitness function. A population of candidate represents solutions to a given problem (e.g., candidate circuit layouts), each encoded according to a chosen representation scheme (e.g., a bit string encoding a spatial ordering of circuit components). The encoded candidate solutions in the population are referred to metaphorically as chromosomes, and units of the encoding (e.g., bits) are referred to as genes. The candidate solutions are typically haploid rather than diploid.

A fitness function assigns a numerical value to each chromosome in the population, measuring its quality as a candidate solution to the problem at hand.

1.4 CONCLUSIONS

Molecular biology and computer science have grown explosively as separate disciplines. However, just as two complementary DNA strands bind together in a double helix to better transmit genetic information, an evolving convergence has created an interrelationship between these two branches of science. In several areas, the presence of one without the other is unthinkable. Not only has traditional sequential Von Neumann-based computing been fertilized through this interchange of programs, sequences, and structures, but the biology field has also challenged high-performance computing with a broad spectrum of demanding applications (for CPU, main memory, storage capacity, and I/O response time). Strategies using parallel computers are driving new solutions that seemed unaffordable only a few years ago.

Parallel computing is an effective way to deal with some of the hardest problems in bioinformatics. The use of parallel computing schemes expands resources to the size of the problem that can be tackled, and there is already a broad gallery of parallel examples from which we can learn and import strategies, allowing the development of new approaches to challenges awaiting solution, without the need to "re-invent the wheel."

Today, it should be natural to think in parallel when writing software, and it should be natural to exploit the implicit parallelism of most applications when more than one processor is available. In most bioinformatics applications, due to a high number of independent tasks, the simplest approaches are often the most effective. These applications scale better in parallel, are the least expensive, and are the most portable among different parallel architectures.

However, several other challenges in bioinformatics remain unsolved as far as parallel computing is concerned. They represent attractive challenges for biologists and computer scientists in the years ahead.

Evolutionary computation is an area of computer science that uses ideas from biological evolution to solve computational problems. Many such problems require searching through a huge space of possibilities for solutions, such as among a vast number of possible hardware circuit layouts for a configuration that produces desired behavior, for a set of equations that will predict the ups and downs of a financial market, or for a collection of rules that will control a robot as it navigates in its environment. Such computational problems often require a system to be adaptive, that is, to continue to perform well in a changing environment.

Thus, the genomic revolution is generating so much data in such rapid succession that it has become difficult for biologists to decipher. In particular, there are many problems in biology that are too large to be solved with standard methods. Researchers in evolutionary computation (EC) have turned their attention to these problems. They understand the power of EC to rapidly search very large and complex spaces and return reasonable solutions. While these researchers are increasingly interested in problems from the biological sciences, EC and its problem-solving capabilities are generally not yet understood or applied in the biology community.

This chapter offers a definitive resource to bridge between the computer science and biology communities. Fogel and Corne [53], well-known representatives of these fields, introduce biology and bioinformatics to computer scientists, and evolutionary computation to biologists and to computer scientists unfamiliar with these techniques.

Biological evolution is an appealing source of inspiration for addressing difficult computational problems. Evolution is, in effect, a method of searching among an enormous number of possibilities, for example, the set of possible gene sequences, for solutions that allow organisms to survive and reproduce in their environments. Evolution can also be seen as a method for adapting to changing environments. In addition, viewed from a high level, the rules of evolution are remarkably simple: species evolve by means of random variation (via mutation, recombination, and other operators), followed by natural selection in which the fittest tend to survive and reproduce, thus propagating their genetic material to future generations.

In conclusion, problems like these require complex solutions that are usually difficult to program by hand. Artificial intelligence practitioners once believed that it would be straightforward to encode the rules that would confer intelligence on a program; expert systems were one result of this early optimism. Nowadays, however, many researchers believe that the rules underlying intelligence are too complex for scientists to encode by hand in a top-down fashion. Instead they believe that the best route to artificial intelligence and other difficult computational problems is through a bottom-up paradigm in which humans write only very simple rules and provide a means for the system to adapt. Complex behaviors such as intelligence will emerge from the parallel application and interaction of these rules. Neural networks are one example of this philosophy; evolutionary computation is another.

REFERENCES

1. J. Olson, J. Witte, and R. Elston, Tutorial in biostatistics genetic mapping of complex traits, *Statist. Med.*, 18, 2961–2981 (1999).

2. S. W. Guo, Computation of multilocus prior probability of autozygosity for complex inbred pedigrees, *Gene. Epidemiol.*, 14, 1–15 (1997).

3. R. L. Martino, C. A. Johnson, E. B. Suh, B. L. Trus, and T. K. Yap, Parallel computing in biomedical research, *Science*, 256, 902–908 (1994).

4. J. R. O' Connell and D. E. Weeks, The VITESSE algorithm for rapid exact multilocus linkage analysis via genotype set — recording and fuzzy inheritance, *Nat. Gene.*, 11, 402–408 (1995).

5. L. Kruglayk, M. J. Daly, M. P. Reeve-Daly, and E. S. Lander, Parametric and nonparametric linkage analysis: a unified multipoint approach, *Am. J. Hum. Genet.*, 58, 1347–1363 (1996).

6. E. S. Lander and P. Green, Construction of multilocus genetic linkage maps in humans, *Proc. Natl. Acad. Sci. USA*, 84, 2363–2367 (1987).

7. J. Ott, *Analysis of Human Genetic Linkage*, The Johns Hopkins University Press, Baltimore (revised edition), 1991.

8. A. B. Smith Cedric and A. Stephens David, Simple Likelihood and Probability Calculations for Linkage Analysis, in I. H. Pawlowitzki, J. H. Edwards, and E. A. Thompson, Eds., *Genetic Mapping of Disease Genes*, Academic Press, London, 1997, pp. 73–96.

9. J. Hodgson, Gene sequencing's industrial revolution, *IEEE Spectrum*, 38, 37–42 (2000).

10. S. B. Needleman and C. D. Wunsch, A general method applicable to the search for similarities in the amino acid sequence of two proteins, *J. Mol. Biol.*, 48, 443–453 (1970).

11. S. F. Altschul, W. Gish, W. Miller, E. W. Myers, and D. J. Lipman, Basic local alignment search tool, *J. Mol. Biol.*, 215, 403–410 (1990).

12. S. F. Altschul, T. L. Madden, A. A. Schaffer, J. Zhang, Z. Zhang, W. Miller, and D. J. Lipman, Gapped BLAST and PSI-BLAST: a new generation of protein DB search programs, *Nucl. Acids Res.*, 25 (17), 3389–3402 (1997).

13. A. Krogh, M. Brown, I. S. Mian, K. Sjölander, and D. Haussler, Hidden Markov models in computational biology: applications to protein modeling, *J. Mol. Biol.*, 235, 1501–1531 (1994).

14. L. Holm and Ch. Sander, Searching protein structure databases has come of age, *Proteins*, 19, 165–173 (1994).

15. D. J. Lipman and W. R. Pearson, Rapid and sensitive protein similarity searches, *Science*, 227, 1435–1441 (1985).

16. P. Bork, T. Dandekar, Y. Diaz-Lazcoz, F. Eisenhaber, M. Huynen, and Y. Yuan, Predicting function: from genes to genomes and back, *J. Mol. Biol.*, 283, 707–725 (1998).

17. Hwang Kai and Xu Zhiwei, *Scalable Parallel Computing: Technology, Architecture, Programming*, McGraw-Hill Series in Computer Engineering, 1998.

18. A. Rodriguez, L. G. de la Fraga, E. L. Zapata, J. M. Carazo, and O. Trelles, Biological Sequence Analysis on Distributed-Shared Memory Multiprocessors, in *Proceedings of the 6th Euromicro Workshop on Parallel and Distributed Processing*, Madrid, Spain, 1998.

19. A. F. W. Coulson, J. F. Collins, and A. Lyall, Protein and nucleic acid sequence database searching: a suitable case for parallel processing, *Comput. J.*, 39, 420–424 (1987).

20. A. S. Deshpande, D. S. Richards, and W. R. Pearson, A platform for biological sequence comparison on parallel computers, *CABIOS*, 7, 237–247 (1991).

21. R. Jones, Sequence pattern matching on a massively parallel computer, *CABIOS*, 8, 377–383 (1992).

22. T. F. Smith and M. S. Waterman, Identification of common molecular subsequences, *J. Mol. Biol.*, 147, 195–197 (1981).

23. S. S. Sturrock and J. Collins, MPsrch version 1.3, *BioComputing Research Unit*, University of Edinburgh, UK, 1993.

24. C. A. Orengo, N. P. Brown, and W. T. Taylor, Fast structure alignment for protein databank searching, *Proteins*, 14, 139–167 (1992).

25. D. Fisher, O. Bachar, R. Nussinov, and H. Wolfson, An efficient automated computer vision based technique for detection of three-dimensional structural motifs in proteins, *J. Biomol. Struct. Dyn*, 9, 769–789 (1992).

26. I. N. Shindyalov and P. E. Bourne, Protein structure alignment by incremental combinatorial extension (CE) of the optimal path, *Protein Eng.*, 11 (9), 739–747 (1998).

27. F. Corpet, Multiple sequence alignments with hierarchical clustering, *Nucl. Acid Res.*, 16, 10881–10890 (1988).

28. O. Gotoh, Optimal alignment between groups of sequences and its application to multiple sequence alignment, *CABIOS*, 9 (2), 361–370 (1993).

29. W. Miller, Building multiple alignments from pairwise alignments, *CABIOS*, 9 (2), 169–176 (1993).

30. J. D. Thompson, D. G. Higgins, and T. J. Gibson, Clustal W: improving the sensitivity of progressive multiple sequence alignment through sequence weighting position-specific gap penalties and weight matrix choice, *Nucl. Acids Res.*, 22, 4673–4680 (1994).

31. O. Trelles, E. L. Zapata, and J. M. Carazo, Mapping Strategies for Sequential Sequence Comparison Algorithms on LAN-Based Message Passing Architectures, in *Lecture Notes in Computer Science, High Performance Computing and Networking*, Springer-Verlag, Berlin, Vol. 796, 1994, pp. 197–202.

32. G. H. Gonnet, M. A. Cohen, and S. A. Benner, Exhaustive matching of the entire protein sequence database, *Science*, 256, 1443–1445 (1992).

33. S. Date, R. Kulkarni, B. Kulkarni, U. Kulkarni-Kale, and A. Kolaskar, Multiple alignment of sequences on parallel computers, *CABIOS*, 9 (4), 397–402 (1993).

34. O. Trelles, M. A. Andrade, A. Valencia, E. L. Zapata, and J. M. Carazo, Computational space reduction and parallelization of a new clustering approach for large groups of sequences, *BioInformatics*, 14 (5), 439–451 (1998).

35. M. Gribskov and J. Devereux, *Sequence Analysis Primer*, UWBC Biotechnical Resource Series, 1991.

36. L. L. Cavalli-Sforza and A. W. F. Edwards, Phylogenetic analysis: models and estimation procedures, *Am. J. Hum. Genet.*, 19, 233–257 (1967).

37. J. Felsenstein, Maximum-likelihood estimation of evolutionary trees from continuous characters, *Soc. Hum. Genet.*, 25, 471–492 (1973).

38. J. Felsenstein, Phylogenies from molecular sequences: inference and reliability, *Annu. Rev. Genet.*, 22, 521–565 (1988).

39. C. Ceron, J. Dopazo, E. L. Zapata, J. M. Carazo, and O. Trelles, Parallel implementation for DNAml program on message-passing architectures, *Parallel Comput. Appl.*, 24 (5–6), 701–716 (1998).

40. R. C. Elston and J. Stewart, A general model for the genetic analysis of pedigree data, *Hum. Heredity*, 21, 523–542 (1971).

41. Whitehead Institute for Biomedical Research. http://www-genome.wi.mit.edu.

42. G. C. Conant, S. J. Plimpton, W. Old, A. Wagner, P. R. Fain, and G. Heffelfinger, Parallel genehunter: implementation of a linkage analysis package for distributed-memory architectures, *J. Parallel Distrib. Comput.*, 63, 674–682 (2003).

43. N. Rizk, Parallelization of IBD computation for determining genetic disease maps, *Concurrency Comput. Pract. Exp.*, 16, 933–943 (2004).

44. J. Holland, Genetic algorithms and the optimal allocations of trials, *SIAM J. Comput.*, 2 (2), 88–105 (1973).

45. I. Rechenberg, Bioinik, evolution und optimierung, *Naturwissenschaftiche Rundschau*, 26, 465–472 (1973).

46. J. Koza, *Genetic Programming*, MIT Press, 1993.

47. S. Kirkpatrick, C. D. Gelatt, and M. P. Vecchi, Optimization by simulated annealing, *Science*, 220 (4598), 671–680 (1983).

48. S. M. Le Grand and K. M. Merz, The application of the genetic algorithm to the minimization of potential energy functions, *J. Global Optimization*, 3, 49–66 (1993).

49. S. Y. Lu and K. S. Fu, A sentence-to-sentence clustering procedure for pattern analysis, *IEEE Trans. Sys., Man Cybernetics*, 8, 381–389 (1978).

50. D. E. Goldberg, *Genetic Algorithms in Search, Optimization and Machine Learning*, Addison-Wesley, 1989.

51. H.-P. Schwefel, *Numerical Optimization of Computer Models*, John Wiley, Chichester, (originally published in 1977), 1981.

52. S. Schulze-Kremer and A. Levin, Search for Protein Conformations with a Parallel Genetic Algorithm: Evaluation of a Vector Fitness Function, Final Report and Technical Documentation of Protein Folding Application (Work package 1), European ESPRIT project # 6857 PAPAGENA, 1994.

53. G. Fogel and D. Corne, *Evolutionary Computation in Bioinformatics*, Morgan Kaufmann, 2002.

54. A. Whittemore and J. Halpern, Probability of gene identity by descent: computation and applications, *Biometrics*, 50(1), 109–117 (1994). Department of Health Research and Policy, Stanford University School of Medicine, California, 94305.

CHAPTER 2

Parallel Monte Carlo Simulation of HIV Molecular Evolution in Response to Immune Surveillance

JACK DA SILVA

This chapter introduces an approach to simulating the molecular evolution of human immunodeficiency virus type 1 (HIV-1) that uses an individual virus-based model of viral infection of a single patient. Numerical methods, including Monte Carlo, are used to realistically simulate viral mutation, recombination, replication, infection, and selection by cell-surface receptor molecules and neutralizing antibodies. The stochastic nature of various events being simulated, such as mutation and recombination, requires that simulations be replicated to account for stochastic variation. In addition, because of the high level of realism, simulations may take a long time to run, and so replicate simulations are preferably run in parallel. The applications of the message-passing interface and the scalable parallel random number generator interface to this problem are described.

For an HIV-1 virus particle (virion) to infect a cell, exterior envelope glycoprotein (gp120) molecules on its surface must interact with the receptor protein CD4 and one of the two chemokine coreceptor proteins, either CCR5 or CXCR4, on the cell surface. The V3 loop of gp120 plays important roles in the interactions with coreceptors and as a target of neutralizing antibodies. The fitness of a virion, based on its V3 loop sequence, is modeled with respect to V3's interaction with coreceptors (functional component) and V3's resistance to neutralization (neutralization component). Simulations explore the interactions between these fitness components. Preliminary results indicate that viral recombination hastens adaptation and that there is a clear trade-off between the functional and neutralization components of fitness. Open problems are discussed. These include the refinement of parameter values, the expansion of the model, and the computing limitations that will be encountered with model expansion.

· *Parallel Computing for Bioinformatics and Computational Biology,* Edited by Albert Y. Zomaya
Copyright © 2006 John Wiley & Sons, Inc.

2.1   INTRODUCTION

This chapter introduces an approach to simulating the molecular evolution of human immunodeficiency virus type 1 (HIV-1) that uses an individual virus-based model of viral infection of a single patient. Numerical methods, including Monte Carlo, are used to realistically simulate viral mutation, recombination, replication, infection, and selection by cell surface receptor molecules and neutralizing antibodies. Simulation with a high level of realism is possible for HIV-1 because the values of important model parameters, such as the number of infected cells, the number of virus particles (virions), mutation and recombination rates, and the effects of some amino acid replacements in viral proteins on viral fitness, are well established empirically. This high level of realism provides the opportunity to investigate the complexities of adaptation within the bounds of realistic parameter values and to predict the course of evolution of HIV-1 in response to important selective forces.

The stochastic nature of various events being simulated, such as mutation and recombination, requires that simulations be replicated to account for stochastic variation. Because of the high level of realism, simulations may take a long time to run, and so replicate simulations are preferably run in parallel. The straightforward way in which the message-passing interface (MPI) can be used to run parallel replicate simulations and consolidate their results is described. Monte Carlo simulation depends on a good random number generator, and in a parallel environment a good generator must be able to spawn independent streams of random numbers in each process [1]. A good generator for this purpose is the scalable parallel random number generator (SPRNG), and its use is described.

2.2   THE PROBLEM

In order for an HIV-1 virion to infect a cell, exterior envelope glycoprotein (gp120) molecules on its surface must interact with the receptor protein CD4 and one of the two chemokine coreceptor proteins, either CCR5 or CXCR4, on the cell surface [2]. $CD4^+$ T-lymphocytes, among other cells, express these receptors and are typically targeted by HIV-1. Antibodies that bind to gp120 may interfere with either of these interactions and, thereby, block the virion's entry. Therefore, gp120 is under two potentially opposing selective pressures. It is being selected, first, to interact optimally with cell surface receptors and second, to escape binding by circulating neutralizing antibodies.

2.2.1   The V3 Loop

A key region of gp120 in these interactions is the third variable loop, V3. This 35-amino acid (typically) region is an important determinant of which chemokine coreceptor is utilized by a virion [3] and is an important target of neutralizing antibodies [4]. Its importance in infection and neutralization has resulted in a great deal of knowledge accumulating on the structure, function, antigenicity, and amino acid replacement dynamics of V3. This early version of the model, therefore, focuses on the evolution of V3 in response to selection by chemokine coreceptors and antibodies.

Amino acid replacements at sites throughout V3 affect the utilization of CCR5 as a coreceptor or cause a switch in coreceptor use between CCR5 and CXCR4 [5–7]. Amino acid replacements in the central region of V3 have also been implicated in escape from neutralization [8–10]. These sites correspond to linear antibody epitopes, that is, consecutive V3 amino acid sites that define a region bound by antibodies. The overlap between sites affecting coreceptor utilization and those affecting neutralization resistance means that amino acid replacements selected by antibodies may affect coreceptor usage and vice versa. This antagonistic pleiotropy may constrain adaptation to either antibodies or coreceptors, thereby limiting the extent or rate of adaptation by V3.

2.2.2 HIV Replication Cycle

To understand the factors affecting the evolution of V3, or any other protein region, we must consider the replication cycle of HIV-1 [2]. Virions carry two copies of their genome in the form of single-stranded RNA sequences, and can, therefore, be considered diploid. Successful infection requires that, after entering a cell, the RNA genome is reverse transcribed to double-stranded DNA and then integrated into the cell's genome. This integrated viral DNA is known as a provirus. During reverse transcription, the RNA copy of the genome that is used as a template is, for reasons that are not entirely understood, frequently switched. This switching results in recombination between the RNA copies during the reverse transcription to the DNA copy. Reverse transcription is also very error-prone, giving rise to the characteristically high mutation rate of retroviruses such as HIV-1. After some period of stable integration, the proviral DNA is transcribed into RNA copies and these are translated into viral proteins. Pairs of RNA sequences may then be packed into immature virus particles by the newly translated viral proteins and then budded from the cell to form free virions.

2.2.3 Cell Superinfection and Recombination

Interestingly from the standpoint of the effect on virion production and the outcome of recombination, more than one virion may infect a single cell [11]. The significance of this is that superinfected cells may produce virions with two different copies of their RNA genome (heterozygous virions) and whose protein structures are translated from one, both, or neither genome copy. This weakened link between a virion's genotype and its phenotype, or reduced heritability of its structure, should interfere with viral adaptation because selection of viral protein regions, such as V3, will not necessarily correspond to selection at the genetic level. Another outcome is that when a heterozygous virion infects a cell, recombination between its different RNA genome copies will produce a recombinant provirus. Such effective recombination is expected to hasten adaptation under strong directional selection, as is likely to occur with antibody surveillance.

2.3 THE MODEL

2.3.1 The Cell Data Structure

Each HIV-1-infected cell in a patient is represented in the model as a defined data structure containing the V3-coding DNA sequence of each provirus infecting the cell as well as fitness-related information about each provirus (Fig. 2.1). The population of these cells is represented as a vector of such structures. As a cell may contain more than one provirus, the simplest way to represent superinfection is to have as a component of the structure a vector of proviruses whose dimension is the maximum number of proviruses allowed in a cell. Obviously, this number should be large enough to contain the maximum number of proviruses expected per cell, given the simulation conditions, but not so large as to occupy an excessive amount of computer memory. In the simulations described here, the mean number of proviruses per cell is 3 (see Section 2.3.5) and the maximum number of proviruses allowed per cell is set at 10. Although such a representation occupies unused memory, it increases the ease of replicating proviruses, as described below. Additional information stored for each provirus in the structure includes the translated V3 amino acid sequence, the coreceptor usage phenotype of the V3 sequence, fitness components and total fitness based on the V3 sequence, and the amino acid sequence, coreceptor usage phenotype, and fitness of the provirus with the highest fitness in the cell.

```
TYPE Cell
    CHARACTER(aaSeqLen*3) DNA    (maxNumProvCell)
    CHARACTER(aaSeqLen)   aa     (maxNumProvCell)
    CHARACTER(4)          Trop   (maxNumProvCell)
    REAL(8)               Wfunc  (maxNumProvCell)
    REAL(8)               Wneut  (maxNumProvCell)
    REAL(8)               W      (maxNumProvCell)
    REAL(8)               Wmax
    REAL(8)               Wmax_rel
    REAL(8)               Wmax_Wfunc
    REAL(8)               Wmax_Wneut
    CHARACTER(aaSeqLen)   Wmax_aa
    CHARACTER(4)          Wmax_trop
    INTEGER               nProv
    LOGICAL               Productive
    LOGICAL               Burst
END TYPE
```

Figure 2.1   Fortran 90 type definition for a cell structure (Cell). Proviral V3 DNA (DNA), its translated amino acid sequence (aa), the V3 coreceptor usage phenotype (Trop), and the functional component of fitness (Wfunc), neutralization component of fitness (Wneut), and total fitness (W) of V3 are each vectors of size equal to the maximum number of proviruses allowed per cell (maxNumProvCell). The fitness (Wmax), relative fitness (Wmax_rel), fitness components (Wmax_Wfunc, Wmax_Wneut), amino acid sequence (Wmax_aa), and coreceptor usage phenotype (Wmax_trop) of the provirus with the highest fitness in the cell are recorded. The number of proviruses in the cell (nProv), and indicators of whether the cell is productive (Productive) and has burst (Burst) are also stored. The V3 amino acid sequence length is aaSeqLen.

2.3.2 Simulation Flow

The flow of the simulation follows the HIV-1 replication cycle (Fig. 2.2). Infected cells produce virions, which infect a new generation of cells, until a constant number of proviruses are produced. An infected cell is chosen at random and a number of virions (burst size) are assembled from the cell. A virion consists of a pair of randomly chosen proviruses infecting the cell (transcribed RNA sequences in reality). The virion then enters a random cell in the next generation (all cells in the current generation will die) with a probability equal to its relative fitness (fitness is discussed below). This step constitutes selection in the model. The reverse-transcribed DNA copy of the virion's genome is then integrated into the host genome with a constant probability (infectivity). During the reverse transcription step, the two RNA copies of the virion genome recombine and the resulting single-copy provirus is mutated. As virions infect cells at random, the ratio of the number of proviruses to cells can be adjusted to produce the desired cell superinfection rate.

2.3.3 Genetic Variation

The ultimate source of genetic variation is mutation, and this variation may be recombined by crossovers between the two copies of a virion's RNA genome. Mutation is

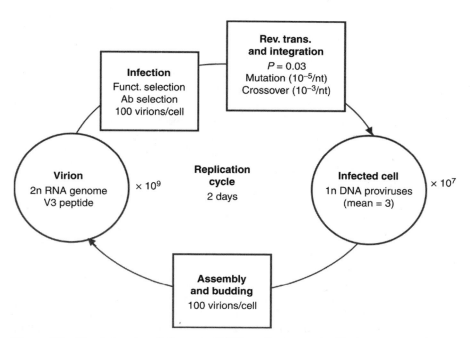

Figure 2.2 Simulation flow follows the HIV-1 replication cycle. Circles represent the two states of viral genomes and rectangles represent processes acting on the genetic information. Some of the major parameter values are shown.

applied at a specified rate by testing each nucleotide of proviral DNA for mutation. If a nucleotide is to be mutated, it then changes to one of the three other nucleotides with equal probability or with a specified bias. Recombination is applied at a specified rate by testing each nucleotide of a randomly chosen member of a pair of RNA genome copies for a recombination event. If a nucleotide is the site of a recombination event, then the portions of the RNA sequences to the left of the nucleotide are swapped between the RNA genome copies.

2.3.4   Fitness

The fitness of a virion is partitioned into two components. One component is based on the optimality of the interaction of V3 with a chemokine coreceptor and is the probability that a virion enters a cell (W_{func}, the functional component). The other component is based on the resistance of V3 to neutralization by antibodies and is the probability that a virion escapes neutralization (W_{neut}, the neutralization component). Total fitness is the product of the probabilities of these two independent events:

$$W = W_{func} W_{neut}.$$

Relative fitness refers to the fitness of a virion relative to the highest fitness in the population:

$$W_{rel} = \frac{W}{W_{max}}.$$

As the protein structures of a virion may be translated from either, both, or neither of the two proviruses from which the two copies of its RNA genome were transcribed (assuming there were more than two proviruses present in the cell), in reality a virion may carry several different V3 loops (as regions of gp120 molecules) on its surface. Assuming that the probability of a virion escaping neutralization and infecting a cell is limited by the V3 loop with the highest fitness, the V3 amino acid sequence assigned to a virion in the model, and therefore the fitness of the virion, is that of the provirus with the highest fitness in the cell.

2.3.4.1   V3 Functional Component of Fitness

Coreceptor Usage Phenotype   The component of fitness based on the interaction between V3 and a coreceptor is referred to as the functional component, W_{func}, because it reflects the presumed function of V3. W_{func} depends on the coreceptor usage phenotype of V3. Coreceptor usage may be predicted from V3's amino acid sequence because V3 sequences from virions using different coreceptors vary in the amino acids present at some sites and in the frequencies of amino acids observed at other sites (Fig. 2.3). The site-specific amino acid frequencies of V3 from virions that use CCR5 (R5 phenotype), CXCR4 (X4 phenotype), and virions that use both coreceptors (X4R5 phenotype) were calculated from aligned V3 sequences from patients infected

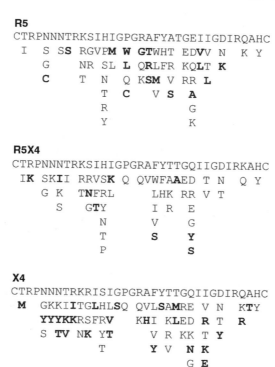

Figure 2.3 Site-specific V3 amino acid composition of chemokine coreceptor usage phenotypes in order of decreasing frequency at each site. Residues in bold font are unique to a phenotype at the specific site. Frequencies were calculated from 181 sequences from 36 patients for R5, 43 sequences from 12 patients for R5X4, and 83 sequences from 10 patients for X4.

with subtype B virus. These sequences were obtained from the Los Alamos National Laboratory's HIV Sequence Database (http://www.hiv.lanl.gov/). To avoid sampling bias, site-specific amino acid counts from each patient were weighted by the inverse of the number of sequences sampled from the patient. Therefore, for a given phenotype, the frequency of amino acid i at site j was calculated as

$$ p_{ij} = \frac{\sum_{k=1}^{N}\left(f_{ijk}\frac{1}{n_k}\right)}{N}, $$

where f_{ijk} is the count of amino acid i at site j in a sequence from patient k, n_k the number of sequences sampled from patient k, and N the number of patients. These site-specific frequencies from patient data are then used to calculate the probability of a given V3 sequence belonging to each phenotype. Thus, the probability of a sequence belonging to phenotype ρ is simply the product of the observed site-specific frequencies from phenotype ρ for the amino acids found at each of the L sites of the sequence

$$P_\rho = \prod_{j=1}^{L} p_{ij}.$$

The phenotype that gives the highest P is assigned to the V3 sequence. P may also be thought of as a measure of how similar the sequence of interest is to the phenotype consensus sequence, the sequence with the most common amino acid at each site, which is assumed to represent the optimal sequence for the phenotype. P is standardized to equal 1 for each consensus sequence.

Fitness Due to Independent Sites   The contribution of amino acid i at site j to W_{func} is proportional to p_{ij}. The maximal effect of this amino acid on W_{func} relative to the most common amino acid at the site, which has p_{ij} set to 1, is $s_{\max} = 1 - p_{ij}$. We do not know the actual effect of the amino acid on fitness, its selection coefficient, s, but assume it lies between zero and $s_{\max}$. Therefore, $s_{\max}$ is adjusted by multiplying by a value ranging from zero, for no selection, to 1, for the maximal strength of selection, to obtain s. For the simple case of amino acids at each site affecting fitness independently, this factor, the relative strength of selection, y, is applied to all amino acids at all sites (Fig. 2.4). For the case of synergistic epistasis, in which the effect

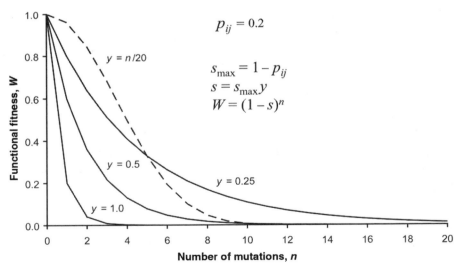

Figure 2.4   The functional component of fitness in relation to the number of mutations. Here, mutations are defined as amino acid changes from the most common residue at a site. In this example, the observed frequency of amino acid i at site j, p_{ij}, is equal for all mutations. $s_{\max}$ is the maximum selection coefficient and s the adjusted selection coefficient. Solid lines show the relationship when mutations act independently on fitness, and the dashed line shows the relationship when there is synergistic epistasis.

on fitness of an amino acid different from that of the consensus sequence increases with the total number of such differences, y increases with the number of differences (Fig. 2.4). The functional component of fitness is then calculated as

$$W_{\text{func}} = \prod_{j=1}^{L} \left(1 - s_{ij}\right).$$

Fitness Due to Covarying Sites   Finally, W_{func} is adjusted to take into account the covariation of amino acids at pairs of sites. These are sites at which pairs of amino acids are found in the same sequence more often than expected from their individual frequencies, presumably because they complement each other in their effects on V3 structure or function [12]. If only one of a pair of covarying amino acids is present in a sequence, then fitness is reduced by the ratio of the expected frequency of the pair (the product of their individual observed frequencies) to the observed frequency of the pair.

2.3.4.2 V3 Neutralization Component of Fitness

The neutralization component of fitness is a measure of the resistance of a V3 sequence to neutralization by antibodies. The degree to which a V3 sequence is neutralized depends on the circulating neutralizing antibodies and the number of viral generations for which they have been stimulated (their maturity). The time dependence reflects the affinity maturation of an antibody, during which its affinity to antigen slowly increases (as a result of an increased rate of division and hypermutation of B-cells that are stimulated by the antigen). Monoclonal neutralizing antibodies elicited during HIV-1 subtype B infection of humans are listed in the Los Alamos National Laboratory's HIV Immunology Database (http://www.hiv.lanl.gov/). In the model, each antibody is elicited when the segment of the V3 sequence to which it binds, its epitope, is present in a V3 sequence in the viral population; the potency of a particular antibody's response is determined by the number of viral generations in which the antibody's epitope is present in the viral population. Potency is assumed to reflect the expansion of high-affinity variants of an antibody, and is modeled as the logistic growth of the antibody's population

$$N_t = \frac{K}{1 + (K/N_0 - 1)\, e^{-rt}},$$

where N_t is the antibody population size after t viral generations of stimulation, K the carrying capacity (asymptotic population size), N_0 the population size at $t = 0$, and r the intrinsic rate of increase (the maximal growth rate when the population is small). K is set to 1 so that N_t will vary from N_0 (set to a small value such as 10^{-4}) at $t = 0$ to approaching 1 at some higher value of t. The fitness of a V3 sequence due to a single antibody for which it contains an epitope is then simply $w_\alpha = 1 - N_t$ (Fig. 2.5). As the probability of V3 being bound by a particular antibody, and the virion being neutralized is independent of the probability of being bound by any other antibody, the fitness of a V3 sequence due to all the antibodies for which it contains epitopes,

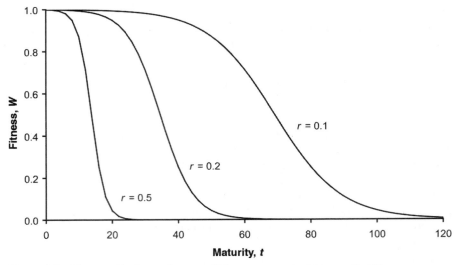

Figure 2.5   The contribution to the neutralizing component of fitness of a V3 sequence containing an epitope recognized by an antibody of a given maturity. Fitness is $1 - N_t$, where N_t is the potency of the antibody at maturity t, as determined by the logistic growth equation. r is the intrinsic rate of increase in antibody potency. In this example, the values of the other logistic parameters are: $K = 1$, $N_0 = 0.001$.

its neutralization fitness component, is the product of the fitness effects of each antibody:

$$W_{\text{neut}} = \prod_{\alpha=1}^{A} w_\alpha,$$

where A is the number of antibodies for which the sequence contains epitopes.

2.3.5   Parameter Values

Values for the most important parameters in the model have been determined empirically. The number of productively infected cells is approximately 10^7 [13]. However, several recent studies suggest that the effective number of infected cells is much lower, about 10^3 to 10^4 [14–17]. The effective population size is the theoretical size that would produce the same amount of genetic drift observed for the real population, given a constant population size, no selection, and other idealized conditions. This discrepancy suggests that selection, population subdivision, or other factors result in a low effective population size. The number of proviruses per infected cell (splenocytes) has recently been observed to be between 3 and 4, with 78 to 80 percent of infected cells harboring more than one provirus [11]. The number of virions budded by an infected cell, the burst size, is variously estimated as being about 10^2 to 10^3, with the lower number likely more accurate for conditions in vivo [18]. The mutation rate is approximately 10^{-5} per nucleotide per replication cycle [19], and the recombination rate is two orders of magnitude higher, approximately 10^{-3} per nucleotide per replication cycle for virus infecting T-cells [20]. The length of the HIV-1 replication cycle is estimated at between 1 and 3 days [21].

2.4 PARALLELIZATION WITH MPI

The simulation model described earlier will benefit from parallelization by simply having replicate simulations run simultaneously. Replicates have identical starting conditions, but because of the stochastic nature of mutation, recombination, selection, and other events, the states of replicate simulations diverge. This problem is referred to as embarrassingly, or naturally, parallel because of the ease with which a parallel programming model is implemented. More formally, this is an example of a single program multiple data (SPMD) parallel programming model [1]. MPI is particularly well suited to this programming model and was used to run replicate simulations in parallel. MPI provides a set of calls (an interface) to a library of subroutines (Fortran) or functions (C) that control communication between processors. Descriptions of the MPI-1 and MPI-2 standards can be found at http://www-unix.mcs.anl.gov/mpi/. A good primer on MPI is the book *Using MPI* [22].

2.4.1 Initialization and Termination of MPI

The basic parallelization strategy applied here is to run each replicate simulation on a separate processor and afterward gather results from each process, summarize these, and write a single output file to disk. Figure 2.6 gives the Fortran 90 pseudocode in the main program for this approach. These instructions are executed on each processor. Near the beginning of the code is a C preprocessor directive that begins with # include. This directive identifies the MPI header file for Fortran, *mpif.h*, which contains definitions of variables and constants used by MPI. For example, the default communicator, MPI_COMM_WORLD, which defines the communication context and set of all processes used, is defined in this header file. This directive must be used in every program and subprogram that makes MPI calls. Invoking preprocessing usually requires setting a compiler switch or identifying files for automatic preprocessing with the suffix ".F" or ".F90," as opposed to ".f" or ".f90" for files that do not require preprocessing.

Then, after some variable declarations, MPI is initialized with a call to the MPI subroutine MPI_INIT. This must be the first MPI call. The variable istat is used to store the error status of the MPI call. Following this statement, two calls are made, one to MPI_COMM_SIZE to query the number of processors being used (npes) and the other to MPI_COMM_RANK to identify the processor number on which execution is taking place (mype). The next statement identifies the replicate number being run on the processor. Processors are counted from zero, so the replicate number is mype +1. This information is used when summarizing the results from replicate simulations.

```
PROGRAM Main
  USE types_module

#include "mpif.h"          ! C preprocessor directive

  INTEGER, PARAMETER :: numGens = 100
  INTEGER, PARAMETER :: numCells = 100000
  TYPE( Cell ), DIMENSION( numCells ) :: CellPop
  REAL(8), DIMENSION ( 0:numGens ) :: repdata
  INTEGER istat, npes, mype
  INTEGER rep, gen

  ! Initialize MPI & query communicator
  CALL MPI_INIT( istat )
  CALL MPI_COMM_SIZE( MPI_COMM_WORLD, npes, istat)
  CALL MPI_COMM_RANK( MPI_COMM_WORLD, mype, istat)

  rep = mype + 1            ! Identify replicate

  ! Loop through viral generations
  DO gen = 0, numGens
    IF( gen == 0 ) then
      CALL inoculate( CellPop )
    ELSE
      CALL replicate( CellPop )
    END IF
      CALL fitness( CellPop, repdata )
  END DO

  ! Gather results from processes
  CALL summarize            ! Internal subroutine

  ! Terminate MPI
  CALL MPI_FINALIZE( istat )

  CONTAINS                  ! Internal subroutines

    SUBROUTINE summarize
      .
      .
      .
    END SUBROUTINE summarize

END PROGRAM Main
```

Figure 2.6   Fortran 90 pseudocode with actual MPI calls for the main program.

Next, a DO loop simulates the viral life cycle, for the desired number of generations, by calls to subroutines. Upon completion of the loop, a call is made to a subroutine (summarize) that gathers the results of the simulations from all processors, summarizes these, and writes the summary statistics to a file. This subroutine uses MPI calls and is described below.

Finally, the MPI environment is terminated by a call to MPI_FINALIZE, and no MPI calls may be made after execution of this statement. Every process must make this call.

2.4.2 Consolidation of Replicate Simulation Results

The subroutine `summarize` consolidates the results from all processes (replicate simulations). Each replicate simulation stores a result from each generation simulated, say the population mean fitness, in a vector of results for each generation of that replicate (`repdata`). This subroutine passes these vectors from each process to the root process (usually process 0) where they are assigned to a two-dimensional array (replicates × generations) that stores all the data (`alldata`). The root process then passes this array to a subroutine that computes means and other statistics across replicates for each generation and writes these to a file. Two methods of accomplishing this are described.

2.4.2.1 Using `MPI_RECV` and `MPI_SSEND`
With the first method (Fig. 2.7), the first step is to check whether the process is the root (`mype == 0`). If so, the process' results vector is assigned to the array. Then a DO loop is used to receive the

```
SUBROUTINE summarize

    REAL(8), DIMENSION( 0:numGens ) :: pedata
    REAL(8), DIMENSION( numReps, 0:numGens ) :: alldata
    INTEGER pe, totgens, datatag, request
    INTEGER irecvstat( MPI_STATUS_SIZE )

    totgens = numGens + 1          ! Include generation 0
    datatag = 101                  ! Arbitrary tag

    ! If root process, assign root's data...
    IF( mype == 0 ) THEN

      alldata( :, : ) = 0.0
      alldata( 1, : ) = repdata( : )

      ! ...and receive data from remaining processes
      DO pe = 1, npes - 1
        CALL MPI_RECV( pedata, totgens, MPI_REAL8, pe, &
             datatag, MPI_COMM_WORLD, irecvstat, istat )
        alldata( pe + 1, : ) = pedata( : )
      END DO

      CALL stats( alldata )

    ! If not root process, send data to root
    ELSE

      CALL MPI_SSEND( repdata, totgens, MPI_REAL8, 0, &
           datatag, MPI_COMM_WORLD, request, istat )

    END IF

END SUBROUTINE summarize
```

Figure 2.7 Fortran 90 pseudocode with actual MPI calls for a version of subroutine `summarize` that uses MPI_RECV and MPI_SSEND. This is an internal subroutine of the main program.

results vectors from all remaining processes in turn and assign these to the array. This is accomplished through a pair of "send and receive" MPI calls. These can be used in any order; following their order of presentation in the code, the root process prepares to receive data from another process through a call to MPI_RECV. MPI_RECV requires the following arguments (using names from this example, except for MPI predefined names): the variable in which to receive the data (pedata), the number of elements of data being passed (totgens), the data type of the data (MPI_REAL8), the rank of the process sending the data (pe), a tag that may be used to identify the communication (datatag), the communicator (MPI_COMM_WORLD), a vector containing the status of the message (irecvstat), and the error status of the message (istat). The data type is specified using a predefined MPI type (MPI_REAL8) and the extent of the status vector is predefined by MPI_STATUS_SIZE.

If the process is not the root, then it sends its results vector to the root by a call to MPI_SSEND. This is a synchronized send, meaning that it does not complete until its message has started to be received, which is a safe way to send data. MPI_SSEND requires the following arguments: the variable containing the data being sent (repdata), the number of data elements being sent (totgens), the data type (MPI_REAL8), the destination process (0), a tag (datatag), the communicator (MPI_COMM_WORLD), a request identification (request), and the error status (istat).

2.4.2.2 Using MPI_GATHERV

An alternative method is, for each process, to make a single call to MPI_GATHERV, but this requires more preparation (Fig. 2.8). MPI_GATHERV automatically sends data to the destination process from all other processes and the destination process automatically receives these data. MPI_GATHERV requires the following arguments: the data being sent from each process (repdata), the number of elements of sent data from each process (totgens), the data type of the sent data (MPI_REAL8), the vector in which all received data are stored (recvbuf), a vector containing the number of elements received from each process (recvcounts), a vector containing the displacement in number of elements in the receiving vector after which the data from each send is stored (displs), the data type of the receiving vector (MPI_REAL8), the destination process (0), the communicator (MPI_COMM_WORLD), and the error status (istat).

The receiving vector, recvbuf, must be large enough to contain the data from the results vectors from all processes, that is, it must have an extent of npes $\times$ numGens. Also, data are placed in recvbuf in rank order, that is, the data sent from process i are placed in the ith portion of recvbuf. The ith portion of recvbuf begins at an offset of displs[i] elements. These offsets were calculated by summing the number of elements sent from all processes of rank lower than i.

Then, finally, the root process assigns the data in recvbuf to the two-dimensional array alldata by reshaping, and alldata is passed to a subroutine that computes summary statistics for each generation and write these to a file.

```
SUBROUTINE summarize

  INTEGER, DIMENSION( 0 : npes - 1 )        :: recvcounts
  INTEGER, DIMENSION( 0 : npes - 1 )        :: displs
  REAL(8), DIMENSION( numReps, 0:numGens ) :: alldata
  REAL(8), DIMENSION(:), ALLOCATABLE        :: recvbuf
  INTEGER pe, totgens

  totgens = numGens + 1                 ! Include generation 0

  ! Receiving vector holds all replicates & generations
  ALLOCATE( recvbuf( npes * totgens ) )

  recvcounts(:) = totgens
  displs(:)     = 0

  ! Displacements are sums of previous counts
  DO pe = 1, npes - 1
    displs( pe ) =  SUM( recvcounts( 0 : pe - 1 ) )
  END DO

  CALL MPI_GATHERV( repdata, totgens, MPI_REAL8, &
       recvbuf, recvcounts, displs, MPI_REAL8, 0, &
       MPI_COMM_WORLD, istat )

  IF( mype == 0 ) THEN
    alldata(:,:) = 0.0
    alldata(:,:) = RESHAPE( recvbuf, (/npes, totgens/), &
                   ORDER= (/2,1/) )
    CALL stats( alldata )
  END IF

END SUBROUTINE summarize
```

Figure 2.8 Fortran 90 pseudocode with actual MPI calls for a version of the subroutine `summarize` that uses `MPI_GATHERV`. This is an internal subroutine of the main program.

2.5 PARALLEL RANDOM NUMBER GENERATION

A good random number generator produces a stream of random numbers with a period of sufficient length that the stream will not be repeated during a simulation. A good parallel random number generator in addition produces streams on separate processes that are independent of each other [1]. The SPRNG library provides several random number generators that meet these criteria for different-sized simulation problems. SPRNG is free and can be downloaded from http://sprng.cs.fsu.edu/. Here, I describe the use of the default interface.

2.5.1 Setting Up and Shutting Down SPRNG

SPRNG is initialized and terminated in the main program unit. Figure 2.9 shows the use of SPRNG functions, in addition to the MPI calls described earlier, in the main program. Two C directives are added: the first defines `USE_MPI`, which allows SPRNG to make MPI calls, and the second includes the SPRNG header file *sprng_f.h*.

```fortran
PROGRAM Main
  USE types_module

  IMPLICIT NONE

! C directives
#define USE_MPI 1        ! Allows SPRNG to make MPI calls
#include "mpif.h"        ! MPI header file
#include "sprng_f.h"     ! SPRNG header file

  INTEGER, PARAMETER :: numGens = 100
  INTEGER, PARAMETER :: numCells = 100000
  INTEGER, PARAMETER :: numProvs = 3*numCells
  TYPE(Cell), DIMENSION(numCells) :: CellPop
  REAL(8), DIMENSION (0:numGens) :: repdata
  INTEGER istat, npes, mype
  INTEGER rep, gen
  INTEGER junk, seed, gtype, streamnum, nstreams
  SPRNG_POINTER stream

  ! Initialize MPI & query communicator
  CALL MPI_INIT( istat )
  CALL MPI_COMM_SIZE( MPI_COMM_WORLD, npes, istat)
  CALL MPI_COMM_RANK( MPI_COMM_WORLD, mype, istat)

  ! Generate seed, select generator & initialize SPRNG
  seed      = make_sprng_seed()
  streamnum = mype
  nstreams  = npes
  gtype     = SPRNG_LFG
  stream    = init_sprng( gtype, streamnum, nstreams, &
              seed, SPRNG_DEFAULT )

  ! Processor 0 prints SPRNG seed & generator info
  IF( mype == 0 ) junk = print_sprng( stream )

  ! Identify replicate
  rep = mype + 1

  ! Loop through viral generations
  DO gen = 0, numGens
    IF( gen == 0 ) then
      CALL inoculate(CellPop)
    ELSE
      CALL replicate(CellPop, numCells, numProvs, stream)
    END IF
      CALL fitness(CellPop, repdata)
  END DO

  ! Gather results from processes
  CALL summarize          ! Internal subroutine

  ! Free memory used by SPRNG
  junk = free_sprng( stream )

  ! Terminate MPI
  CALL MPI_FINALIZE( istat )

  CONTAINS                 ! Internal subroutines

    SUBROUTINE summarize
      .
      .
      .
    END SUBROUTINE summarize

END PROGRAM Main
```

Figure 2.9 Fortran 90 pseudocode with actual MPI calls and SPRNG functions in the main program.

USE_MPI must be defined before including *sprng_f.h*. Then a SPRNG pointer of type SPRNG_POINTER (stream) is declared; this points to the location in memory where the state of a stream is stored.

The first SPRNG function used, make_sprng_seed, produces a new seed for the generator using the system time and date, and broadcasts the seed to all processes. This function must be called in all processes. Using the same seed to initialize each stream ensures that independent streams are produced. Streams are distinguished by their stream number (streamnum), and the number of streams required (nstreams) must also be specified. As streams are counted from zero and in these simulations a single stream is used per process, the stream number is equal to the process rank (mype) and the number of streams is equal to the number of processes (npes).

Next, the identity of the specific generator to be used is stored in gtype. In this example, the generator is the modified lagged Fibonacci generator (SPRNG_LFG), which, with default parameter values, has a period of approximately 2^{1310} random numbers and produces 2^{39648} independent streams.

The last step in setting up SPRNG is to initialize each stream's state by assigning a value to the SPRNG pointer stream with the function init_sprng. init_sprng requires the following arguments: the generator type (gtype), the stream number for the process (streamnum), the number of streams required (nstreams), the seed (seed), and the parameter values for the generator, which in this case are the default values (SPRNG_DEFAULT).

Following initialization, it is a good idea to have the root process print to standard output the value of the seed and the identity of the generator. This is done with function print_sprng, which takes stream as its argument.

At this point, SPRNG may be used to generate random numbers. In this example, the subroutine replicate (in the viral generation loop) uses SPRNG to generate random numbers and is passed stream as an argument to identify the stream of numbers being generated in the processes. The contents of replicate are described below.

Finally, after all random numbers have been generated, the memory used to store the state of the random number stream for each process is freed with the function free_sprng.

2.5.2 Using SPRNG in a Subprogram

The use of SPRNG to generate random numbers in a subprogram is shown with the subroutine replicate in Fig. 2.10. As mentioned earlier, replicate requires the SPRNG pointer stream as an argument to generate random numbers from the correct stream. Each subprogram that uses SPRNG functions must include the SPRNG header file, *sprng_f.h*. A double-precision, uniform random number in the range 0 to 1 may then be generated with the function sprng, which takes stream as an argument.

```
SUBROUTINE replicate(CellPop, numCells, numProvs, stream)
  USE types_module

  IMPLICIT NONE

#include "sprng_f.h"

  TYPE(Cell), DIMENSION(*), INTENT(INOUT) :: CellPop
  INTEGER, INTENT(IN) :: numCells, numProvs
  SPRNG_POINTER stream

  REAL(8) r
  INTEGER cellnum, numNewProv

  numNewProv = 0
  DO WHILE ( numNewProv < numProv )
    r = sprng( stream )
    cellnum = INT( r * numCells + 1 )
    .
    .
    .
  END DO
  .
  .
  .

END SUBROUTINE replicate
```

Figure 2.10 Fortran 90 pseudocode with actual MPI calls and SPRNG functions in the subprogram `replicate`.

2.6 PRELIMINARY SIMULATION RESULTS

2.6.1 The Parallel Computing Environment

Simulations were carried out on an IBM eServer 1350 Linux cluster administered by the South Australian Partnership for Advanced Computing (SAPAC). The cluster comprised 129 IBM xSeries 335 servers as nodes connected via a high-speed Myrinet 2000 network. Each node contained dual 2.4 GHz Intel Xeon processors (a multiprocessor-capable Pentium 4 architecture) and 2 GB of random access memory (RAM). MPICH, a portable implementation of MPI, was used for message passing. The simulations described here generally took 1 to 4 h to complete, depending on parameter values. As simulations were run in replicate 20 times, in serial such runs would take 20 to 80 h to complete.

2.6.2 Model Parameters

Simulations were run with the parameter values in Table 2.1, unless otherwise noted. The number of productively infected CD4$^+$ T-cells simulated, 10^5, is lower than the total number of such cells estimated per patient, 10^7, for two reasons. First, because of the distributed nature of RAM in a computer cluster, each replicate simulation could access only the RAM available on a single node. Therefore, a single replicate

TABLE 2.1 Values of Main Model Parameters

Parameter	Value
No. of productively infected cells	10^5
No. of proviruses	3×10^5
No. of mutations/nucleotide/cycle	10^{-5}
No. of crossovers/nucleotide/cycle	10^{-3}
Burst size	100
Probability of integration	0.03
Relative strength of coreceptor selection	0.5
Antibody potency at generation 0	0.0001
Antibody potency intrinsic rate of increase	0.1

running on a node could access a maximum of 2 GB, which is insufficient to simulate all productively infected cells (10^7 cells would require 30 GB with the current implementation of the model). Second, recent estimates of the effective population size of infected cells (10^3 to 10^4) suggest that it is much smaller than the census population size, because of population subdivision among other factors. Therefore, 10^5 cells may be a reasonable estimate of the census number of infected cells in a subpopulation within which recombination among viral genomes may take place.

The number of proviruses was set to three times the number of infected cells to achieve a cell superinfection rate of about 3. Given a burst size of 100 virions per cell, the probability of viral DNA integrating into the host cell's genome was set to 0.03 to be consistent with the superinfection rate.

The relative strength of selection by chemokine coreceptors (y) was set to 0.5. The parameters for the logistic growth of the potency of an antibody response were as follows: the potency at time zero (N_0) was set to 0.0001 and the intrinsic growth rate (r) was set to 0.1.

2.6.3 Adaptation to CCR5

The first simulation investigated adaptation to CCR5 by a viral population with a V3 loop that was suboptimal in its interaction with this coreceptor.

2.6.3.1 *The Functional Component of Fitness* Without antibody selection, only the functional fitness component is of interest. Population mean fitness was averaged over 20 replicate simulations and the change in this value over time is shown in Fig. 2.11. Fitness increased over time and appears to have done so in two phases, corresponding to the spread of two beneficial mutations (see below).

2.6.3.2 *Sequence Evolution* Figure 2.12 shows 20 randomly selected amino acid sequences from the 50th generation of one replicate simulation compared with the inoculum and optimal R5 sequences. The optimal sequence differs from the inoculum sequence at three sites and the simulated sequences show changes that match the

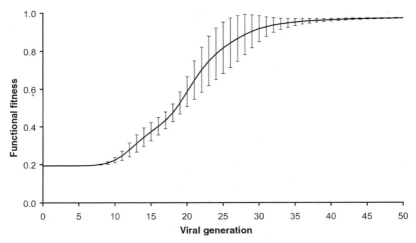

Figure 2.11 The change in functional fitness over time, starting with a V3 sequence with a suboptimal R5 phenotype. The curve is drawn from points representing means across 20 replicate simulations; bars are standard errors across replicates. Parameter values are given in the text.

```
CTRPNNNTRKGIHIGPGRTFYTTGEIIGDIRQAHC  Inoculum
..........S.......A.................  Simulated:
..........S.......A.................  50th generation
..................A.................
.........S.......A.................
.........S.......A.................
.........S.......A.................
.........S.......A.................
.........S.......A.................
.........S.......A.................
.........S.......A.................
.........S.......A.................
.........S.......A.................
.........S.......A.................
.........S.......A.................
.........S.......A.................
.........S.......A.................
.........S.......A.................
.........S.......A.................
.........S.......A.................
.........S.......A.................
..........S.......A..A.............  R5 optimal
```

Figure 2.12 Sequences at the end of one replicate of simulation of the adaptation of V3 to CCR5. Periods indicate identity with the inoculum sequence.

optimal sequence at two of these sites. At the third site, the threonine in the inoculum sequence and the alanine in the optimal sequence have nearly identical observed frequencies in the R5 phenotype, and therefore a threonine → alanine change would have a negligible effect on fitness.

2.6.4 Effects of Superinfection and Recombination on Adaptation

To investigate the effects of cell superinfection and recombination on the rate of adaptation to CCR5, simulations with reduced superinfection and with no recombination were carried out.

2.6.4.1 Superinfection As superinfection is expected to give rise to hybrid virions and thus reduce the heritability of a virion's phenotype, reducing the rate of superinfection is expected to hasten the rate of adaptation. Superinfection was reduced by increasing the number of cells available for infection from 10^5 to 6×10^5 and maintaining the number of proviruses at 3×10^5. The recombination rate was maintained at 10^{-3}. Lowering the rate of superinfection seems to have actually slowed the second phase of adaptation, that is, the spread of the second beneficial mutation (Fig. 2.13).

2.6.4.2 Recombination As recombination is expected to hasten adaptation under strong directional selection, reducing the recombination rate is predicted to reduce the rate of adaptation. Eliminating recombination did indeed result in a marked

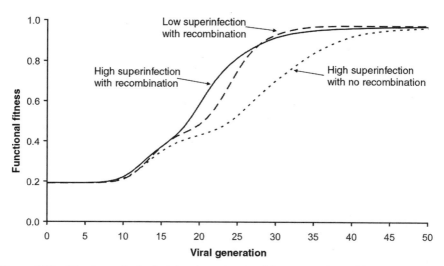

Figure 2.13 The change in the functional component of fitness over time with varying degrees of cell superinfection and viral recombination. Curves are drawn from means of 20 replicate simulations. Error bars have been omitted for clarity.

reduction in the rate of adaptation, mainly by slowing the second phase (Fig. 2.13). Therefore, under the simulation conditions described here, cell superinfection had a minor effect on the rate of adaptation, but recombination appears to hasten adaptation substantially.

2.6.5 Adaptation to Antibody Surveillance

2.6.5.1 *Functional and Neutralization Components of Fitness*   To investigate the relationship between the functional and neutralization components of fitness, selection by antibodies was added to the simulation. In this simulation, the production of antibodies with increased affinity for their epitope is stimulated when the epitopes are detected in the viral population.

As in the previous simulations, adaptation to CCR5 is observed as an increase in the functional component of fitness, but in this case, this component does not remain near one indefinitely (Fig. 2.14). Rather, the functional component begins to decline after 75 generations. This is due to the emergence of a neutralization escape mutant as seen in the increase in the neutralization component after an initial decrease. The neutralization component begins at 1, because antibody production has not been stimulated at generation 0, and decreases as the potency of antibodies increases. The increase in the neutralization component at generation 75 indicates that a viral variant with a previously unrecognized epitope is spreading in the population. However, this variant is suboptimal in its interaction with CCR5, resulting in a concomitant decline in the functional component of fitness.

Then, the neutralization component decreases shortly after it began to increase due to a new antibody response, and this coincides with stabilization of the functional

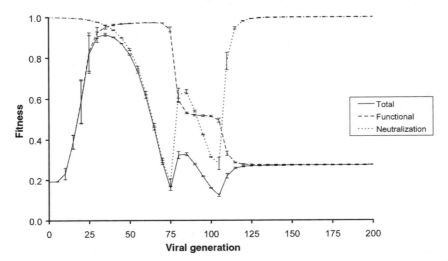

Figure 2.14   The changes in total fitness, and the functional and neutralization components of fitness over time. Curves are based on means of 20 replicate simulations and bars are standard deviations across replicates.

component. Finally, another neutralization escape mutant emerges and the neutralization component increases again, this time reaching its maximal value and remaining there, while the functional component declines again.

Therefore, in this simulation, the viral population escapes antibody control altogether by generation 125. However, the cost of escaping neutralization is a reduction in V3 function, resulting in low total fitness. These results show a clear trade-off between the functional and neutralization components of fitness.

2.6.5.2 *Sequence Evolution*

Figure 2.15 shows 20 randomly selected amino acid sequences from the 500th generation of one replicate of this simulation. As in the simulation without antibody selection, amino acids changed at two sites to match the optimal R5 sequence. However, in this simulation, amino acid changes occurred at two additional sites. These additional changes do not match amino acids in the optimal R5 sequence; rather they disrupt any epitope recognized by antibodies used in the simulation and, therefore, represent neutralization escape mutations.

2.6.5.3 *Antibody Maturation*

Table 2.2 shows the states of antibodies in the 500th generation of the same replicate simulation described earlier. The production of most antibodies was stimulated in generation 0, the inoculation generation, and continued to the 500th generation. A V3 sequence carrying an epitope recognized by

```
CTRPNNNTRKGIHIGPGRTFYTTGEIIGDIRQAHC  Inoculum
..........S......GA.HA............  Simulated:
..........S......GA.H.............  500th
..........S......GA.H.............  generation
..........S......GA.H.............
..........S......GA.H.............
..........S......GA.H.............
..........S......GA.HA............
..........S......GA.HA............
..........S......GA.HA............
..........S......GA.H.............
..........S......GA.HA............
..........S......GA.HA............
..........S......GA.HA............
..........S......GA.H.............
..........S......GA.H.............
..........S......GA.H.............
..........S......GA.HA............
..........S......KA.H.............
..........S......GA.H.............
..........S......GA.H.............
..........S......A..A............  R5 optimal
```

Figure 2.15 Sequences at the end of one replicate of simulation of the adaptation of V3 to CCR5 and antibody surveillance. Periods indicate identity with the inoculum sequence.

TABLE 2.2   Antibody Maturity After 500 Viral Generations

Antibody	V3 Epitope[a]	Stimulation[b] First	Stimulation[b] Last	Maturity[c]	Fitness
412-D	RKRIHIGPGRAFYTT	12	94	0	1.0
DO142-10	KRIHIGPGRAFYTT	12	94	0	1.0
391/95-D	KRIHIGPGRAFY	12	94	0	1.0
41148D	KRIHIGP	0	500	496	0.0
311-11-D	KRIHIGP	0	500	496	0.0
257-D	KRIHI	0	500	496	0.0
908-D	KSITKG	—	—	0	1.0
782-D	KSITKG	—	—	0	1.0
838-D	KSITK	—	—	0	1.0
MN215	RIHIGPGRAFYTTKN	—	—	0	1.0
19b	I....G..FY.T	0	500	500	0.0
419-D	IHIGPGR	0	500	500	0.0
504-D	IHIGPGR	0	500	500	0.0
453-D	IHIGPGR	0	500	500	0.0
4117C	I.IGPGR	0	500	500	0.0
418-D	HIGPGRA	0	500	500	0.0
386-D	HIGPGR	0	500	500	0.0
268-D	HIGPGR	0	500	500	0.0
537-D	IGPGR	0	500	500	0.0
447-52D	GP.R	0	500	500	0.0
N70-1.9b	PGRAFY	0	324	0	1.0
694/98-D	GRAF	0	500	500	0.0

[a] Periods indicate any amino acid.
[b] Viral generation; dash indicates no stimulation.
[c] Number of viral generations of net stimulation.

one of these antibodies has a neutralization fitness component of zero and, therefore, its genome is not replicated. The presence of V3 variants with these epitopes in the 500th generation, as indicated by the stimulation of the corresponding antibodies, indicates that these epitopes are being re-created by mutation and likely occur at very low frequency. Four other antibodies, three of which have similar epitopes, never had their production stimulated. These antibody's epitopes are found only in V3 sequences with the X4R5 or X4 phenotype.

2.7   FUTURE DIRECTIONS

This simulation approach provides the opportunity to investigate the process of adaptation at the molecular level with realistically constrained parameters. If there is a high degree of confidence in the parameter values and relatively complete knowledge of the interacting components, then this approach may also be used to predict the evolution of HIV-1 in response to specific scenarios of immune surveillance. Unanswered questions that may be addressed with this approach include: (1) What is the form of the neutralizing antibody response to V3? (2) Does adaptation to chemokine coreceptors impede adaptation to antibody surveillance? (3) Does adaptation to antibody surveillance change the coreceptor usage phenotype? (4) Does V3 always evolve to escape neutralization regardless of the cost to function? (5) Are cell superinfection and recombination important determinants of the rate of adaptation? For this approach to be successful, values for several parameters or parameter sets must be refined.

2.7.1 Refining Parameter Values

2.7.1.1 Intrahost HIV-1 Population Size
The question of what is the population size of HIV-1 infecting a patient, either in terms of infected cells or proviruses, is an important one. This is related to the question of whether there is substantial population structure or compartmentalization within a host. A large population with little structure is conducive to adaptive evolution because such a population will produce a large number of competing mutations, the raw material for selection.

2.7.1.2 Functional Selection Coefficients
The functional selection coefficients of amino acids at specific sites of V3 are unknown. In this version of the model, we assume that the relative sizes of these coefficients are related to the observed frequencies of the amino acids at specific sites in each phenotype. This assumption, however, does not address the magnitudes of these coefficients. The magnitudes of selection coefficients will have to be measured empirically, and until such measures become available, a scaling factor can be applied to coefficients to produce reasonable rates of adaptation to coreceptors, perhaps based on data on adaptation to a new coreceptor in culture.

2.7.1.3 The Form of the Neutralizing Antibody Response
The dynamics of the neutralizing antibody response to HIV-1 are poorly understood. It seems reasonable to assume that the maturation of antibody affinity is described by a curve resembling logistic growth. The two unknown parameters of the logistic equation, the population size (potency) at time zero and the intrinsic growth rate (for the purposes of this model, the carrying capacity is 1 by definition), could in principle be measured in vivo. For now, these parameters may be adjusted to give an antibody response whose tempo matches that observed in patients [23, 24]. Other questions about the form of the neutralizing antibody response also remain: Is there an epitope frequency threshold above which antibody production is stimulated? How frequently must this stimulation occur? How narrow is the antibody response? And, probably the most vexing question: What is the form of humoral memory of HIV-1 epitopes? Answers to these questions obviously require empirical investigation, but again parameter values

could be adjusted to conform to reasonable expectations based on current knowledge and to produce a response tempo matching that observed in patients.

A related and equally important question is: What are the V3 epitopes recognized by neutralizing antibodies? The linear epitopes of monoclonal antibodies used in the current simulations may not represent the epitopes of the most effectively neutralizing antibodies in vivo, which may actually recognize conformational epitopes [4]. Such conformational epitopes have not been described. One possible interim solution is to assume that covarying sites in V3 are responsible for V3 conformation and, therefore, dictate the possible conformational epitopes for neutralizing antibodies.

2.7.1.4 Cell Superinfection and Viral Recombination

As shown in this chapter, cell superinfection and viral recombination have potentially strong impacts on the rate of adaptation by HIV-1. Although the only study to attempt to quantify the rate of superinfection reports a high rate in splenocytes, it is uncertain whether this rate applies to other cell populations and whether proviruses in a multiply infected cell are nearly identical clones. Nevertheless, the rate of recombination is well established empirically and the rate of superinfection may simply be varied to explore its potential effect.

2.7.2 Importance of Selection

Although selection by antibodies and cytotoxic T-lymphocytes (CTLs) has been demonstrated beyond any reasonable doubt [23–25], estimates of a low intra-patient effective population size for HIV-1 have lead to the question of how deterministic is the evolution of HIV-1 [14, 17, 26]. In other words, does knowing the nature of a selective force allow us to predict the evolution of HIV-1, or is its evolution largely the result of a long series of random events whose endpoints can only be assigned probabilities? The refinement of parameter values discussed earlier should allow the simulation approach described here to answer this fundamental question.

2.7.3 Model Expansion

The interactions between HIV-1 and the immune system and target cells involve many other components than just the V3 loop. It will be useful to expand the model to include these other components in order to more realistically capture the dynamics of HIV-1 evolution. The V1/V2 loops affect sensitivity to neutralizing antibodies and affect coreceptor usage [27]. Glycosylation of V1/V2, V3, and other surface regions of gp120 also affects coreceptor usage and neutralization [24, 27, 28]. The CD4-binding region of gp120 [29, 30] and the ectodomain of the interior envelope glycoprotein, gp41 [31], are also targets of neutralizing antibodies. In addition, selection by the cell-mediated branch of the immune system is clearly important; CTLs recognize class I MHC-bound epitopes processed from HIV-1 proteins, but for reasons that are not entirely understood, may have an impact upon only some of these [32].

2.7.4 Computing Limitations

The expansion of the current model will be challenging. Already, with just the V3 loop, it is difficult to simulate the total population of infected cells in a single patient because of the modest amounts of RAM per node on distributed-memory computer systems. A simple solution is to divide the vector of cell data structures among several processors and perform calculations on the subvectors in parallel (data parallelization). This could even be done as a way of simulating population structure. Including other components in the model will require innovative ways of minimizing memory usage and the use of large shared-memory systems. Coupled with the need to run replicate simulations in parallel to achieve reasonable run times, the increase in total memory requirements will be daunting. One solution may be to store the proviral components on different processors, perform calculations on these in parallel, and consolidate the results in each viral generation. For example, a single replicate simulation would be executed on four processors, one for each of the V3 loops, the V1/V2 loops, the CD4-binding region of gp120, and the ectodomain of gp41.

REFERENCES

1. I. Foster, *Designing and Building Parallel Programs: Concepts and Tools for Parallel Software Engineering*, Addison-Wesley, Reading, MA, 1995.

2. J. M. Coffin, "Molecular biology of HIV," in K. A. Crandall, Ed., *The Evolution of HIV*, The John Hopkins University Press, Baltimore, 1999, 504 p.

3. J. P. Moore, A. Trkola, et al., "Co-receptors for HIV-1 entry," *Curr. Opin. Immunol.*, 9 (4), 551–562 (1997).

4. M. K. Gorny, C. Williams, et al., "Human monoclonal antibodies specific for conformation-sensitive epitopes of V3 neutralize human immunodeficiency virus type 1 primary isolates from various clades," *J. Virol.*, 76 (18), 9035–9045 (2002).

5. J. J. De Jong, A. De Ronde, et al., "Minimal requirements for the human immunodeficiency virus type 1 V3 domain to support the syncytium-inducing phenotype: analysis by single amino acid substitution," *J. Virol.*, 66 (11), 6777–6780 (1992).

6. R. F. Speck, K. Wehrly, et al., "Selective employment of chemokine receptors as human immunodeficiency virus type 1 coreceptors determined by individual amino acids within the envelope V3 loop," *J. Virol.*, 71 (9), 7136–7139 (1997).

7. C. S. Hung, N. Vander Heyden, et al., "Analysis of the critical domain in the V3 loop of human immunodeficiency virus type 1 gp120 involved in CCR5 utilization," *J. Virol.*, 73 (10), 8216–8226 (1999).

8. J. A. McKeating, J. Gow, et al., "Characterization of HIV-1 neutralization escape mutants," *AIDS*, 3 (12), 777–784 (1989).

9. A. McKnight, R. A. Weiss, et al., "Change in tropism upon immune escape by human immunodeficiency virus," *J. Virol.*, 69 (5), 3167–3170 (1995).

10. K. Yoshida, M. Nakamura, et al., "Mutations of the HIV type 1 V3 loop under selection pressure with neutralizing monoclonal antibody NM-01," *AIDS Res. Hum. Retroviruses*, 13 (15), 1283–1290 (1997).

11. A. Jung, R. Maier, et al., "Multiply infected spleen cells in HIV patients," *Nature*, 418 (6894), 144 (2002).

12. B. T. Korber, R. M. Farber, et al., "Covariation of mutations in the V3 loop of human immunodeficiency virus type 1 envelope protein: an information theoretic analysis," *Proc. Nat. Acad. Sci. USA*, 90 (15), 7176–7180 (1993).

13. T. W. Chun, L. Carruth, et al., "Quantification of latent tissue reservoirs and total body viral load in HIV-1 infection," *Nature*, 387 (6629), 183–188 (1997).

14. A. J. Leigh Brown, "Analysis of HIV-1 env gene sequences reveals evidence for a low effective number in the viral population," *Proc. Nat. Acad. Sci. USA*, 94 (5), 1862–1865 (1997).

15. T. K. Seo, J. L. Thorne, et al., "Estimation of effective population size of HIV-1 within a host: a pseudomaximum-likelihood approach," *Genetics*, 160 (4), 1283–1293 (2002).

16. G. Achaz, S. Palmer, et al., "A robust measure of HIV-1 population turnover within chronically infected individuals," *Mol. Biol. Evol.*, 21 (10), 1902–1912 (2004).

17. D. Shriner, R. Shankarappa, et al., "Influence of random genetic drift on human immunodeficiency virus type 1 env evolution during chronic infection," *Genetics*, 166 (3), 1155–1164 (2004).

18. A. T. Haase, "Population biology of HIV-1 infection: viral and CD4+ T cell demographics and dynamics in lymphatic tissues," *Annu. Rev. Immunol.*, 17, 625–656 (1999).

19. L. M. Mansky, and H. M. Temin, "Lower in vivo mutation rate of human immunodeficiency virus type 1 than that predicted from the fidelity of purified reverse transcriptase," *J. Virol.*, 69 (8), 5087–5094 (1995).

20. D. N. Levy, G. M. Aldrovandi, et al., "Dynamics of HIV-1 recombination in its natural target cells," *Proc. Nat. Acad. Sci. USA*, 101 (12), 4204–4209 (2004).

21. M. Markowitz, M. Louie, et al., "A novel antiviral intervention results in more accurate assessment of human immunodeficiency virus type 1 replication dynamics and T-cell decay in vivo," *J. Virol.*, 77 (8), 5037–5038 (2003).

22. W. Gropp, E. Lusk, et al., *Using MPI: Portable Parallel Programming With the Message-Passing Interface*, MIT Press, Cambridge, MA, 1999.

23. D. D. Richman, T. Wrin, et al., "Rapid evolution of the neutralizing antibody response to HIV type 1 infection," *Proc. Nat. Acad. Sci. USA*, 100 (7), 4144–4149 (2003).

24. X. Wei, J. M. Decker, et al., "Antibody neutralization and escape by HIV-1," *Nature*, 422 (6929), 307–312 (2003).

25. D. T. Evans, D. H. O'Connor, et al., "Virus-specific cytotoxic T-lymphocyte responses select for amino-acid variation in simian immunodeficiency virus Env and Nef," *Nat. Med.*, 5 (11), 1270–1276 (1999).

26. S. D. Frost, M. J. Dumaurier, et al., "Genetic drift and within-host metapopulation dynamics of HIV-1 infection," *Proc. Natl. Acad. Sci. USA*, 98 (12), 6975–6980 (2001).

27. A. Ly and L. Stamatatos "V2 loop glycosylation of the human immunodeficiency virus type 1 SF162 envelope facilitates interaction of this protein with CD4 and CCR5 receptors and protects the virus from neutralization by anti-V3 loop and anti-CD4 binding site antibodies," *J. Virol.*, 74 (15), 6769–6776 (2000).

28. C. A. Pikora, "Glycosylation of the ENV spike of primate immunodeficiency viruses and antibody neutralization," *Curr. HIV Res.*, 2 (3), 243–254 (2004).

29. P. D. Kwong, M. L. Doyle, et al., "HIV-1 evades antibody-mediated neutralization through conformational masking of receptor-binding sites," *Nature*, 420 (6916), 678–682 (2002).

30. T. Beaumont, E. Quakkelaar, et al., "Increased sensitivity to CD4 binding site-directed neutralization following in vitro propagation on primary lymphocytes of a neutralization-resistant human immunodeficiency virus IIIB strain isolated from an accidentally infected laboratory worker," *J. Virol.*, 78 (11), 5651–5657 (2004).

31. G. Ofek, M. Tang, et al., "Structure and mechanistic analysis of the anti-human immunodeficiency virus type 1 antibody 2F5 in complex with its gp41 epitope," *J. Virol.*, 78 (19), 10724–10737 (2004).

32. T. M. Allen, D. H. O'Connor, et al., "Tat-specific cytotoxic T lymphocytes select for SIV escape variants during resolution of primary viraemia," *Nature*, 407 (6802), 386–390 (2000).

Differential Evolutionary Algorithms for In Vivo Dynamic Analysis of Glycolysis and Pentose Phosphate Pathway in *Escherichia coli*

CHRISTOPHE CHASSAGNOLE, JUAN-CARLOS A. RODRIGUEZ, ANDREI DONCESCU, and LAURENCE T. YANG

3.1   INTRODUCTION

Most of the kinetic models in biology are described by coupled differential equations, and simulators implement the appropriate methods to solve these systems. The biochemical reaction is very often involved a series of steps instead of a single one. Therefore, one of the biochemical research problems has been to capture or describe the series of steps called pathways.

Although the cells have different morphologies and structures, and their roles in different organisms are varied, their basic functionality is the same.

One of the main activities of the cell is to ensure its own surviving. Altogether, this activity can be summarized in two points as

1. The cell needs to find the necessary energy for its activity. This energy is mainly obtained by degradation of mineral or organic molecules, named catabolism.
2. The cell needs to produce simple molecules for its survival, named anabolism.

These two activities are grouped under the name of metabolism; it is the result of a great number of mechanisms and reactions. All these biochemical reactions, unfolding in the cell, are catalyzed by special molecules, constituted of proteins, called enzymes.

All reactions that allow to go from one molecule to another are a metabolic pathway, the most known is the glycolysis. Each compound that participates in the different metabolic pathways is regrouped under the term of metabolite. Taking into account

Parallel Computing for Bioinformatics and Computational Biology, Edited by Albert Y. Zomaya
Copyright © 2006 John Wiley & Sons, Inc.

the entirety of the different metabolic pathways, one considers that they form a real system, given that several of these ways can have the metabolites in common.

Our goal is to analyze, to understand, and to model these systems of reactions and the mechanisms that govern them, to better understand the behavior of cells. What made the wealth and the complexity of a cell is its number of genes, on the one hand, and the degree of interactions between the different interactions, on the other hand (protein/protein, protein/ADN, protein/metabolite). It is therefore necessary to make an analysis taking into account the totality of interactions. In addition, the complexity of this system comes from the strong concentration of intercellular macromolecules.

This basic complexity of the biological systems has slowed the impact of the metabolic engineering into industrial applications. If the databases concerning the *Escherichia coli* (*E. coli*) increase each year with results about the discovery of new proteins and behavior of new genes, the mathematical modeling of the prokaryote cells is always an open question which excites the scientific community.

When applying metabolic engineering concepts to improve the production of metabolites such as amino acids, vitamins, organic acids, and so on, there is a crucial necessity to understand the central metabolism in its flux distribution, regulation phenomena, and control properties, as these pathways are responsible for the production of precursors for the biosynthetic pathways. For this purpose, a kinetic model including glycolysis and the pentose phosphate pathway has been developed for *E. coli* [1]. To determine the parameters of this model, the experimental observations of intracellular metabolites to a pulse of glucose were measured in continuous culture employing automatic stopped flow and manual fast sampling techniques in the time span of seconds and milliseconds after the stimulus with glucose.

The extracellular glucose, the intracellular metabolites (glucose-6-phosphate, fructose-6-phosphate, fructose-1, 6-bisphosphate, glyceraldehyde-3-phosphate, phosphoenolpyruvate, pyruvate, 6-phosphate-gluconate, and glucose-1-phosphate), and the cometabolites (atp, adp, amp, nad, nadh, nadp, and nadph) were measured using enzymatic methods or high-performance liquid chromatography (HPLC).

This dynamic model for the central metabolism of *E. coli* includes a quantitative description of the phosphotransferase system (PTS) system. The industrial production of certain metabolites such as amino acids, vitamins, organic acids, and so on is performed by microorganisms. To improve these microbial processes, the more rational concepts of metabolic engineering, rather than the classical genetic techniques, have been developed [2, 3]. For this purpose, there is a crucial necessity to understand the central metabolism in its flux distribution, regulation phenomena, and control properties, as these pathways are responsible for the production of precursors in biosynthetic pathways. This has been demonstrated experimentally in *E. coli* in the case of tryptophan by the groups of Liao and Berry [4–10] or in the case of ethanol by Emmerling et al. [11]. To understand the central metabolism, a kinetic model including the PTS, the glycolysis, and the pentose phosphate pathway has been implemented for *E. coli*. Several models of glycolysis have been published for *Saccharomyces* (for a review cf. [12]), trypanosome [13], or human erythrocytes (see [14] for a review). Torres [15] used an erythrocyte model developed by Schuster et al. [16].

The dynamic model with a Michaelis–Menten formalism has been made because it is a better representation for a nonlinear allosteric regulation system. The major criticism with this formalism as discussed by Ni and Savageau [17] is the use of in vitro kinetic data, for an in vivo representation. To avoid this problem, the approach suggested by Rizzi et al. [12] for an in vivo diagnosis of the kinetic parameters of the model has been used.

The response of intracellular metabolites to a pulse of glucose was measured in continuous culture employing automatic stopped flow and manual fast sampling technics in the time span of seconds and milliseconds after the stimulus with glucose [18–21]. The metabolic control analysis [22, 23] has been used to determine the controlling step of the central metabolism on the glucose uptake.

3.2 MATHEMATICAL MODEL

3.2.1 Metabolite Flux Balancing

Metabolite flux balancing is one of the first approaches to determine the intracellular fluxes based on the measures of the extracellular fluxes. In fact it is necessary to measure the consummation of the substrate, the new products obtained similar biomass and gas exchanges. However, this technique is not sufficient in determining all the intracellular fluxes of central metabolism without making some assumptions about the enzymatic activity and energetic yields which limit the validity of the results. This approach is not sufficient to determine the metabolite tendencies.

3.2.2 Model Structure

Figure 3.1 shows the dynamic model of the Embden–Meyerhof–Parnas pathway and pentose phosphate pathway of E. coli that consists of mass balance equations for extracellular glucose and for the intracellular metabolites.

These mass balances have the general structure

$$\frac{dC_i}{dt} = \sum_i v_{ij} r_j - \mu C_i \tag{3.1}$$

where C_i denotes the concentration of metabolite i, μ the growth rate, and v_{ij} the stoichiometric coefficient for this metabolite in reaction j, which occurs at the rate r_j. Because masses were balanced, the equation for extracellular glucose needs to include a conversion factor for the difference between the intracellular volume and the culture volume. It thus becomes

$$\frac{dC_{\text{glc}}^{\text{extracellular}}}{dt} = D(C_{\text{glc}}^{\text{feed}} - C_{\text{glc}}^{\text{extracellular}}) + f_{\text{pulse}} - \frac{Xr_{\text{PTS}}}{\rho_x} \tag{3.2}$$

Here, $C_{\text{glc}}^{\text{feed}}$ is the glucose concentration in the feed, X the biomass concentration, and ρ_x the specific weight of biomass in the culture volume. The term f_{pulse} represents the sudden change of the glucose concentration due to a glucose pulse.

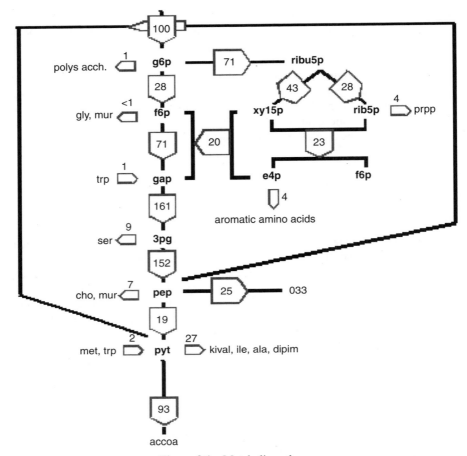

Figure 3.1   Metabolic pathway.

Dynamic reaction rates consist of mechanism-based kinetic rate expressions and maximum reaction rates, the latter of which are assumed to be constant. As the maximum reaction rates represent the amount and catalytic activity of enzymes, this assumption implies that effects of genetic regulation of the enzymes included are negligible. This assumption appears reasonable, considering dynamic experiments were simulated in the range of less than 1 min.

3.2.3   Estimation of Maximum Reaction Rates

The in vitro enzymatic activities determination is not really representative of the in vivo maximal rates. To avoid this problem, these values were estimated with the approach suggested by Rizzi et al. [12], which is based on a calculation of the flux distribution under steady-state conditions. The rate of the enzyme i at steady state is

$$\tilde{r}_i = r_i^{\max} f_i(\tilde{C}_i, \tilde{P}_i) \tag{3.3}$$

where $\tilde{P}_i$ is the parameter vector and $\tilde{C}_i$ the steady-state concentration vector of the metabolites involved in the reaction. From the above equation, the maximal rate could be calculated as

$$r_i^{\max} = \frac{\tilde{r}_i}{f_i(\tilde{C}_i, \tilde{P}_i)} \tag{3.4}$$

In this flux analysis, the reactions of the Embden–Meyerhof–Parnas pathway, pentose phosphate pathway, tricarboxylic acid cycle, oxidative phosphorylation, membrane transport processes, and the formation of monomers and their successive polymerization were included. The flux model also contains phosphoenol pyruvate carboxylase activity, an overall atp hydrolysis reaction, and reactions for the regeneration of C1-transfer cometabolites. The stoichiometry of these reactions was primarily taken from the Internet database EcoCyc [24] or from Neidhardt et al. [25]. Linear pathways were combined into overall reactions. The p/o ratio was taken to be variable by specifying a respiratory efficiency η. As atp was not balanced in the present model, it had no influence on the fluxes there and thus no assumption on the p/o ratio had to be made.

Macromolecular composition of biomass was estimated according to Domach et al. [26], Neidhardt et al. [25], and Pramanik and Keasling [27].

The set of equations was solved analytically based on measurements in the steady state of a continuous culture at a growth rate of $\mu = 0.1\ h^{-1}$. The rates of glucose uptake and acetate excretion were calculated from measurements of the extracellular glucose and acetate concentrations. The glucose uptake rate was 9.2 mmol $L^{-1}h^{-1}$ and the extracellular acetate was not detected. For determination of oxygen uptake rate and carbon dioxide excretion rate, the composition of the exhaust gas was measured. A value of 24.3 and 24.8 mmol $L^{-1}h^{-1}$, respectively, was obtained. As no extracellular acetate could be detected, the degree of freedom of the linear equation system reduced to (3.2), which means that the measurement of two independent fluxes is sufficient to determine the system. The third flux, the carbon dioxide excretion rate, was used for a χ^2-test, serving the statistical verification of the consistency of the measured data set.

Other pathways like the pathway or the glyoxylate shunt as well as polymer and monomer degradation reactions were neglected, because their fluxes could not be distinguished by the approach specified. To get more information on these pathways, for example, gas chromatography–mass spectrometry (GC–MS) or nuclear magnetic resonance (NMR) analyses could be applied.

3.2.4 Kinetic Rate Expressions

This section summarizes the kinetic types and the regulations used for the description of the different enzymatic reactions. These equations taken from the literature or some empirical formulae have been used when no equation is available. Some complementary information about some of the assumptions made are given below.

3.2.4.1 Glucose Transport System

Prior the glucose pulse, the chemostat culture is glucose-limited. Under these conditions, two different systems for glucose transport across the cytoplasmic membrane are active in *E. coli*: the Mgl transport system with a very high affinity for glucose (Km 0.2 μM) and the PTS with a medium affinity. There are two different PTSs, PTS G with a higher affinity and PTS M with a lower affinity. Both affinities are in the range of 10 μM to 1 mM. It has been shown that the contribution of the PTS G for the glucose transport is greater even for saturating glucose concentrations (for a complete review, cf. [28]). In our model, the glucose uptake has been described only in terms of the PTS kinetics. We used the PTS rate equation described by Liao et al. [6] with some modifications: a g6p inhibition term was added to this equation according to Kaback [29] and Clark et al. [30]. In the equation of Liao et al., the PTS rate (Eq. (3.1)) is assumed to be a function of the pep/pyruvate ratio. Assuming a high pep/pyruvate ratio, it is possible to derive a simple equation from this expression, where KPTS,a2 represents the Km value of glucose. Since the PTS G system seems to be responsible for most of the uptake, the KPTS,a2 parameter was fixed to its glucose Km value of 10 μM, according to Notley-McRobb et al. [31].

3.2.4.2 Glycolysis

Two glucose-6-phospho isomerase (PGI) isoenzymes are present in *E. coli*, but in this model only one equation is used to describe the PGI activity as the kinetic properties of both forms are identical [32]. Two forms of phosphofructokinase (PFK) are present in *E.. coli* of which PFK-1 is the predominant form accounting for 90 percent of the total activity. Thus, only this form was considered in this model. The atp inhibition present in yeast was replaced by pep inhibition as described for *E. coli* by Kotlarz et al. [33]. The pyruvate kinase activity is catalyzed by two isoenzymes in *E. coli*: PKI, which is activated by fdp and inhibited by atp, and the amp-activated PKII. These two enzymes seem to be of equal importance. As the steady-state activity of these enzymes cannot be distinguished by flux analysis, only one rate equation was used, including a combination of the different effectors. This rate equation was based on the formula described by Johannes et al. [34] with an additional term for amp activation.

3.2.4.3 Biosynthetic and Anaplerotic Reactions

The flux toward polysaccharide synthesis was assessed based on the activity of G1PAT, the enzyme catalyzing the initial reaction of this pathway. The biochemical pathways leading to the synthesis of nucleotides and glycerol are represented in the model by the first reaction of these pathways, ribose phosphate pyrophosphokinase, and glycerol-3-phosphate-dehydrogenase, respectively. The anabolic fluxes from pep to mureine and chorismate were lumped together in one empirical reaction (Eq. 3.1). A similar equation (Eq. 3.2) represents the different anabolic fluxes from pyruvate to isoleucine, alanine, alpha-ketoisovalarate, and diaminopimelate synthesis.

3.2.4.4 Pentose Phosphate Pathway The model of this part of the metabolism is based on the model developed for *Saccharomyces cerevisiae* by Vaseghi et al. [35]. The non-oxidative part of the pentose phosphate pathway (ppp) comprises the reactions of ribulose phosphate epimerase (Ru5P), ribose phosphate isomerase (R5PI), transketolase, which catalyzes two reactions, TKa and TKb, and transaldolase (TA). Like in the model of Vaseghi et al., these five reactions were described simply by first-order kinetics, assuming that they are fast near-equilibrium reactions. The glucose-6-phosphate dehydrogenase (G6PDH) and 6-phosphogluconate dehydrogenase (PGDH) rate equations were modified to account for regulatory differences of these two enzymes in *E. coli*. As compared with *S. cerevisiae*, G6PDH is only inhibited by nadph and not by atp [36], while for PGDH the inhibition by nadph and atp is similar [37]. 6-Phosphoglucono-delta-lactone was not balanced in our model for the same reasons as assumed by Vaseghi et al. [35].

All rate equations cited earlier are summarized as follow:

$$\frac{dC_{glc}^{extracellular}}{dt} = D(C_{glc}^{feed} - C_{glc}^{extracellular}) + f_{pulse} - \frac{Xr_{PTS}}{\rho_x} \tag{3.5}$$

$$\frac{dC_{g6p}}{dt} = r_{PTS} - r_{PGI} - r_{G6PDH} - r_{PGM} - \mu C_{g6P} \tag{3.6}$$

$$\frac{dC_{f6p}}{dt} = r_{PGI} - r_{PFK} + r_{TKb} + r_{TA} - 2r_{MurSynth} - \mu C_{g6P} \tag{3.7}$$

$$\frac{dC_{fdp}}{dt} = r_{PFK} - r_{ALDO} - r_{G6PDH} - \mu C_{fdp} \tag{3.8}$$

$$\frac{dC_{gap}}{dt} = r_{PTS} - r_{PGI} - r_{G6PDH} - r_{PGM} - \mu C_{gap} \tag{3.9}$$

$$\frac{dC_{dhap}}{dt} = r_{ALDO} - r_{TIS} - r_{G3PDH} - \mu C_{dhap} \tag{3.10}$$

$$\frac{dC_{pgp}}{dt} = r_{GAPDH} - r_{PGK} - \mu C_{pgp} \tag{3.11}$$

$$\frac{dC_{3pg}}{dt} = r_{PGK} - r_{PGluMu} - r_{SerSynth} - \mu C_{3pg} \tag{3.12}$$

$$\frac{dC_{2pg}}{dt} = r_{PGluMu} - r_{ENO} - r_{PGM} - \mu C_{2pg} \tag{3.13}$$

$$\frac{dC_{pep}}{dt} = r_{ENO} - r_{PK} - r_{PTS} - r_{PEPCxylase} - r_{DAHPS} - r_{Synth1}^{a} - \mu C_{pep} \tag{3.14}$$

$$\frac{dC_{pyr}}{dt} = r_{PK} + r_{PTS} - r_{PDH} - r_{Synth2}^{b} + r_{MetSynth} + r_{TrpSynth} + \mu C_{pyp} \tag{3.15}$$

$$\frac{dC_{6pg}}{dt} = r_{G6PDH} - r_{PGDH} - \mu C_{6pg} \tag{3.16}$$

$$\frac{dC_{ribu5p}}{dt} = r_{PGDH} - r_{Ru5P} - r_{R5PI} - \mu C_{ribu5p} \tag{3.17}$$

$$\frac{dC_{xyl5p}}{dt} = r_{Ru5P} - r_{5PI} - \mu C_{xyl5p} \tag{3.18}$$

$$\frac{dC_{sed7p}}{dt} = r_{TKa} - r_{TA} - \mu C_{sed7p} \tag{3.19}$$

$$\frac{dC_{rib5p}}{dt} = r_{R5PI} - r_{TKa} - r_{RPPK} - \mu C_{rib5p} \tag{3.20}$$

$$\frac{dC_{e4p}}{dt} = r_{TA} - r_{TKb} - r_{DAHPS} - \mu C_{e4p} \tag{3.21}$$

$$\frac{dC_{g1p}}{dt} = r_{PGM} - r_{G1PAT} - \mu C_{g1p} \tag{3.22}$$

3.2.5 Estimation of Non-Measured Steady-State Concentrations

Statistical optimization process utilizes linear estimation techniques (least-square estimation) to produce models that describe the research space. Today, owing to the development of high computing, we are able to implement new algorithms which use nonlinear optimization techniques. Computational optimization methods such as genetic algorithm, neural networks, and particle swarm optimization have shown some promise in developing optimization strategies.

Steady-state concentrations for all intermediate metabolites were needed for V_m calculation. Some of these had to be estimated because no experimental results were available. Owing to our measured values of fdp and gap, it was impossible to estimate the steady-state concentration of dhap from a near-equilibrium assumption for triosephosphate isomerase (TIS). Likewise a near-equilibrium assumption for aldolase and TIS is impossible either. Therefore, the same mass action ratio as experimentally measured by Schaefer et al. [18] was employed ([gap]/[dhap] = 3 mM/2.3 mM). Thus a concentration of 0.167 mM was calculated for dhap based on a measured value of 0.218 mM for gap. For the estimation of pgp, 3pg, and 2pg concentrations, a near-equilibrium assumption for the enzymes PGK, PGluMu, and ENO was reasonable. The concentrations of the three metabolites were calculated using the measured pep concentration and the Keq values of the different enzymes as taken from Ni and Savageau [17] for PGK, and from Bakker et al. [13] for PGluMu and ENO, respectively. The resulting ratio of the intracellular concentration of pep and 3pg was found to be close to the values measured by Schaefer et al. [18] and Bhattacharya et al. [38] for *E. coli*. A similar ratio was also found by Bakker et al. [13] in the case of trypanosome and by Mulquinay [14] for human erythrocyte. Thus, there is substantial experimental evidence that the assumption of near-equilibrium conditions is valid. Concordant with Vaseghi et al. [35], near-equilibrium conditions were assumed for the five reactions of the non-oxidative part of the ppp (Ru5P, R5PI, TK1, TK2, and TAL). The metabolite concentrations of ribu5p, rib5p, xyl5p, sed7p, and e4p were estimated from measured steady-state concentrations of f6p and gap.

Table 3.1 summarizes all the estimated and measured steady-state concentrations.

3.3 ESTIMATION OF THE PARAMETERS OF THE MODEL BY DIFFERENTIAL EVOLUTIONARY ALGORITHM

The kinetic parameters of these equations were fit to the measurements by minimizing the sum of relative squared errors using differential evolutionary algorithm. Differential evolution (DE) is one of evolutionary algorithms (EAs), which are a class of stochastic search and optimization methods including genetic algorithms (GAs), evolutionary programming, evolution strategies, genetic programming, and all methods based on genetic and evolution. The DE algorithm was introduced by Rainer Storn and Kenneth Price. DE is a higher implementation of GAs. Owing to its fast convergence and robustness properties, it seems to be a promising method for optimizing real-valued multi-modal objective functions. Compared with traditional search and optimization methods, the EAs are more robust and straightforward to use in complex problems: they are capable of working with minimum assumptions about the objective functions. Only the value is required to guide the research process of parameters.

The generation of the vectors containing the parameters of the model is attained by an independent procedure:

$$X_{i,G} = X_{1,i} \cdots X_{D,i} \tag{3.23}$$

TABLE 3.1 Concentrations for Steady States

Metabolite	Concentration (mM)
Glucose extracellular	0.0556
xg6p	3.480
f6p	0.600
fdp	0.272
gap	0.218
dhap	0.167 (estimation)
pgp	0.008 (estimation)
3pg	2.130 (estimation)
2pg	0.399 (estimation)
pep	2.670
pyr	2.670
6pg	0.808
ribu5p	0.111 (estimation)
xyl5p	0.138 (estimation)
sed7p	0.276 (estimation)
rib5p	0.398 (estimation)
e4p	0.098 (estimation)
g1p	0.653
amp	0.955
adp	0.595
atp	4.270
nadp	0.195
nadph	0.062
nad	1.470
nadh	0.100

with $i = 1, \ldots, NP$, D the number of parameters, NP the cardinal of $G =$ number of individuals, G the current population, i one individual of the population, and $X_{j,i}$ the parameter j of the individual i.

The initial population is chosen randomly, inside the intervals given by an expert biologist. Trial parameter vectors are evaluated by the objective function. For simple GAs, the new vectors are the result of the difference between two population vectors, and the result is added to a new one. The objective function determines if the new vector is more efficient than a candidate population member and replace it if this simple relation is true. In the case of the DE, the generation of the new vectors is realized by the difference between the "old vectors," given equal weightage to all.

We have tested and compared different schemes:

- *DE/rand/1*

  For each vector $X_{i,G}$ a perturbed vector $V_{i,G+1}$ is generated according to

$$V_{i,G+1} = X_{R1,G} + F * (X_{R2,G} - X_{R3,G})$$

where $R1, R2, R3 \in [1, NP]$ are the individuals of population, chosen randomly, $F \in [0, 1]$ controls the amplification $(X_{R2,G} - X_{R3,G})$, and $X_{R1,G}$ the perturbed vector. There is no relation between $V_{i,G+1}$ and $X_{i,G}$. The objective function must evaluate the quality of this new trial parameter for the old member. If $V_{i,G+1}$ yields a lower objective function value, $V_{i,G+1}$ is set to $X_{i,G+1}$ for the future generation or there is no effect.

- $DE/best/1$

  It is like $DE/rand/1$ and generating $V_{i,G+1}$ integrating the more performance vector:

$$V_{i,G+1} = X_{best,G} + F * (X_{R1,G} - X_{R2,G})$$

where $X_{best,G}$ is the best vector of population G, and $R1, R2 \in [1, NP]$ the individuals of population, chosen randomly. At $DE/rand/1$, the objective function compared the quality of $V_{i,G+1}$ and $X_{i,G}$; only the smaller is saved.

- Hybrid differential evolution algorithms

  As DE algorithms, a perturbed vector is generated but the weight F is a stochastic parameter.

To increase the potential diversity of the perturbed vector, a crossover operation is introduced. $X_{i,G+1} = (X_{1i,G+1}, X_{2i,G+1}, \ldots, X_{Di,G+1})$ becomes

$$V_{ji,G+1} \begin{cases} j = (n)_D, (n+1)_D, (n+L-1)_D \\ X_{ij,G} \quad \text{otherwise} \end{cases}$$

where $n \in [1, D]$ is the starting index, chosen randomly, $(n)_D = n \bmod D$, and $L \in [1, D]$ the number of parameters which are going to be exchanged.

3.4 KINETIC PARAMETER ESTIMATION BY DE

In this study, the parameters have been estimated by EA. We describe the principal steps of the estimation:

- Generation of a population randomly with NP individuals: one individual refers to D parameters that have to be evaluated.
- Simulation of NP models: one individual identifies one model because of it specifies.
- Evaluation of each model generated using the objective function which calculates the time-weighted least-squares error for each experiment. For example, the error is given by

$$\text{Error} = \frac{1}{N} \sum \left\{ \frac{[x_e(t_j) - x(t_j)]^2}{x_{e\,max}^2} + \frac{[s_e(t_j) - s(t_j)]^2}{s_{e\,max}^2} + \frac{[p_e(t_j) - p(t_j)]^2}{p_{e\,max}^2} \right\}$$

where the sum is calculated reporting to $j = 1$ to N_S where N_S is the number of the sampling data. $x_e(t_j), s_e(t_j), p_e(t_j)$ are the measured data at $t = t_j, x(t_j), s(t_j), p(t_j)$ are the concentrations calculated using the model, and $x_{e\,max}, s_{e\,max}, p_{e\,max}$ are the maximum measured concentrations.

- Search the lower value of the objective function: the best individual is marked as "bestind" and the lower value is "bestval".
- Generation/selection of the population $G + 1$ by
  1. Create new individual with DE algorithm
  2. For each individual: simulation of a model with NR
  3. Evaluation of the new individual with the objective function
  4. Comparison between old and new values of objective function for the individual

     If the new value is lower, the trial individual is stored

     If the new value is lower than the best value for the population G, it becomes the new reference
  5. Go to step (1) and stop where there are NP individuals
- Repeat the generation until a criterion like a number of iteration or a minimum for the best value is founded.

3.5   SIMULATION AND RESULTS

Initially, the whole model is divided into submodels. Afterward a global optimization is carried out with the complete set of equations. For the intermediate estimations, analytical functions were used to describe the dynamic behaviors of some balanced metabolites, but in the final optimization only the metabolites not balanced were represented by such functions.

Figure 3.2 shows a comparison between experimental data and model simulations. For some parameters, small differences between the optimized values and initial values were observed that might result from discrepancy between in vitro and in vivo kinetics.

The patterns of simulations are similar to that of the experimental data. If millisecond experiments were available, they would combined well with the data from the manual sampling technic. An exception is the pyruvate curve where the rapid decrease of the first peak is not observed. The discrepancy between simulation and experimental points can be explained by various factors, for example, experimental measurement errors, as some metabolites like pep and pyruvate are especially difficult to measure. Another reason could be a lack in the model structure for the mass balance equations or the rate expressions. Most of the stoichiometry is well known, but some effectors are involved in a great number of reactions. As a first approach, a mass balance equation for these metabolites was avoided by keeping the analytical functions. The use of analytical functions for certain metabolites may impose strong

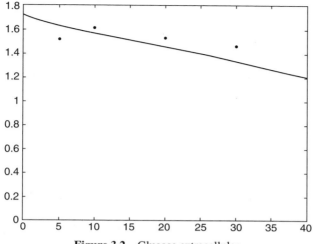

Figure 3.2 Glucose extracellular.

boundary conditions to our system that could also cause deviations. Other critical points are the assumptions in the kinetic expressions. The metabolic regulations and allosteric properties used in these equations have been determined by in vitro studies. Some of these effects might be different under in vivo conditions.

Figures 3.3–3.5 show the same simulations, only for the millisecond experiments, carried out with stopped flow technic. Only four metabolites (g6p, f6p, pep, and pyr) have been measured in this short period of time. Despite the very short period,

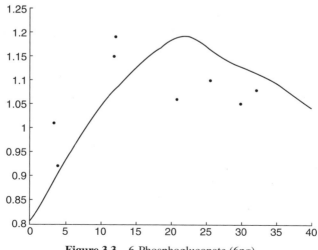

Figure 3.3 6-Phosphogluconate (6pg).

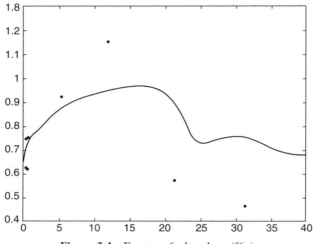

Figure 3.4 Fructose-6-phosphate (f6p).

we could observe noticeable variations in the concentrations. This emphasizes the importance of these measurements. Like for the longer time scale, the model obtains a reasonable fitting for all metabolites, except pyruvate.

All these equations had been implemented on Simulink/Matlab allowing us to introduce new equations as subsystems and to validate the results of the estimation (the Simulink model could be downloaded from www.laas.fr).

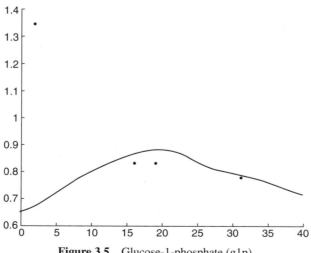

Figure 3.5 Glucose-1-phosphate (g1p).

3.6 STABILITY ANALYSIS

The stability of the system is an important property of the model, as it is unlikely that a cell remains in an unstable steady state. Moreover, a stable model of a steady state is an essential prerequisite for control analysis, as control analysis quantifies the system's infinite reaction on infinite deviations. In Figure 3.4, the concentrations did not yet return to the values before the pulse, so the stability of the model could be doubted. Evidence of the dynamic reaction system's stability can be obtained by an investigation of the eigenvalues of the Jacobian matrix. Also, these eigenvalues contain information on how fast a deviation from the given steady state will disappear. The time constants are defined as the reciprocal values of the real parts of the eigenvalues. They represent the time at which a perturbation needs to decline to e^{-1} of its starting value. In addition, potential non-zero imaginary parts of the eigenvalues point out the system's ability to oscillate.

All real parts of the eigenvalues are found to be negative, indicating a stable dynamic system behavior. The small simulated time and the presence of the analytical functions may impede a return to the steady state.

The range of time constants in the dynamic system is from $t_1 = 0.29$ ms to $t_2 = 120$ s. This large range of time constants reflects the high inflexibility of the system. The highest time constant yet is still four orders of magnitude smaller than the time constant for the dilution by growth, which is 10 h. This finding indicates that growth has a negligible influence on the system's capability to return to steady state after a perturbation.

Among the eigenvalues of the dynamic system, there are two pairs of complex conjugate eigenvalues. Oscillations are due to two natural frequencies, which can be calculated from the imaginary part Im of the complex eigenvalues λ by $\mathrm{Im}(\lambda)/2\pi$. For the given system, the natural frequencies are $f_1 = 0.022$ s^{-1}, in agreement with a period of 46 s, and $f_2 = 0.014$ s^{-1} (period of 71 s). The calculated periods not only fit the data presented here, but are also in the same order of magnitude as the oscillations noticed by Schaefer et al. [18].

3.7 CONTROL CHARACTERISTIC

From the dynamic model, flux control coefficients (FCCs) of the reactions in the system on the glucose uptake by the PTS were determined. The results are given in Figure 3.6.

PTS is having the highest control on glucose uptake, but only with an FCC of 0.4. Almost as high are the values of the FCCs of R5PI, PFK, G6PDH, PDH, and the absolute value of the FCC of Ru5P. Thus, both the glucose-degrading pathways depicted in this model are remarkably involved in the control of glucose uptake. In the Embden–Meyerhof–Parnas pathway, PFK is the enzyme with the highest control. In the ppp, G6PDH exerts a significant control on glucose uptake, but also R5PI and Ru5P, whereas the absolute values of the FCCs of R5PI and Ru5P are virtually the same. FCC of Ru5P is negative that suggests that the important role of R5PI and Ru5P

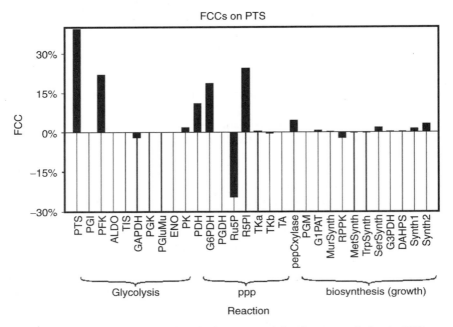

Figure 3.6   FCCs of the reactions in the system on the glucose uptake by the PTS.

is to ensure a balanced production of Xyl5P and Rib5P to achieve a high flux through TKa, TKb, and TA. This suggestion would also explain the negative FCC of RPPK. Also, the removal of pyr by PDH has a high control on glucose uptake. The main role of this reaction in the control is to remove carbon from the reaction system. It also lowers the pep/pyr ratio, which plays an important role in the PTS kinetics, but for the whole system this effect is negligible as shown below by the response coefficients of pep and pyr. Although with a small absolute value, the negative FCC of GAPDH is a surprise, as this reaction is crucial for the degradation of glucose. It can be explained in a equivalent way as the high flux control by R5PI and Ru5P. A lowered expression level of GAPDH seems to enhance the fluxes in the non-oxidative part of the ppp.

The elasticity of PDH for pyruvate is 3.6. The elasticities of R5PI and Ru5P for Ribu5P are 1. The elasticities of the other three reactions with the highest absolute values of FCCs are given in Figure 3.7.

The PTS rate is determined by both substrates and products, but the high g6p elasticity stands out. The f6p concentration exerts the main influence on the PFK rate, followed by a noticeable inhibition by pep. In this model, the role of atp in the PFK rate expression is almost negligible. The elasticities of G6PDH indicate that there is a noticeable influence of the anabolic reduction charge, which is defined as $C_{nadph}/(C_{nadph} + C_{nadp})$ on the G6PDH rate. The roles of pep and pyr in glucose uptake are ambiguous, although both metabolites are directly involved in the PTS. Although pep is a substrate of PTS, it has a non-negligible inhibitory effect on PFK. Pyruvate, which is a product of PTS, is also a substrate of PDH. Both PFK and PDH exert a significant control on glucose uptake.

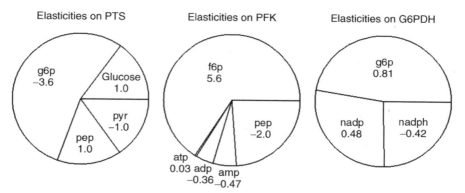

Figure 3.7   Elasticities of different substrates and effectors on the PTS, PFK, and G6PDH.

Mathematical equations and one-dimensional equations (ODEs) have been used to capture the structure of the model. However, a pure mathematical formulation of the model is difficult due to parametric uncertainty and incomplete knowledge and mechanism.

3.8   CONCLUSIONS

A dynamic model of glycolysis and the ppp in *E. coli* has been constructed. This model is able to give a reasonable description of the experimental data obtained by adding a glucose pulse to a continuous culture. The capability of the model to describe the observed oscillations has been proven. For some metabolites analytical functions were used, which should be avoided in the future model development for two reasons: First, the analytical functions are valid only under the specific experimental conditions. Predictive simulations with these functions will always retain erroneous assumption. Second, the analytical functions impose strong boundary conditions to the model which might impede good fitting. With all metabolites balanced, the model could be extended to biosynthetic pathways to optimize the production of metabolites of industrial interest. The identification of metabolic systems such as metabolic pathways enzyme actions and gene regulations is a complex task due to the complexity of the system and limited knowledge about the model.

GLOSSARY

AlaSynth: alanine synthesis
ALDO: aldolase
ChoSynth: chorismate synthesis
DHAPS: DHAP synthases
DipimSynth: diaminopimelate synthesis
ENO: enolase

G1PAT: glucose-1-phosphate adenyltransferase
G3PDH: glycerol-3-phosphate dehydrogenase
G6PDH: glucose-6-phosphate dehydrogenase
GAPDH: glyceraldehyde-3-phosphate dehydrogenase
IleSynth: isoleucine synthesis
KivalSynth: alpha-ketoisovalerate synthesis
MetSynth: methionine synthesis
MurSynth: mureine synthesis
PFK: phosphofructokinase
PGDH: 6-phosphogluconate dehydrogenase
PGI: glucose-6-phosphoisomerase
PGK: phosphoglycerate kinase
PGluMu: phosphoglycerate mutase
PDH: pyruvate dehydrogenase
PEPCxylase: PEP carboxylase
PGM: phosphoglucomutase
PK: pyruvate kinase
ppp: pentose phosphate pathway
PTS: phosphotransferase system
R5PI: ribose-phosphate isomerase
RPPK: ribose-phosphate pyrophosphokinase
Ru5P: ribulose-phosphate epimerase
Synth1: synthesis 1
Synth2: synthesis 2
TA: transaldolase
TIS: triosephosphate isomerase
TKa: transketolase

REFERENCES

1. C. Chassagnole, N. Noisommit-Rizzi, J. W. Schmid, K. Mauch, and M. Reuss, Dynamic modeling of the central carbon metabolism of *Escherichia coli*, *Biotechnol. Bioeng.*, 79, 53–73 (2002).

2. J. E. Bailey, Lessons from metabolic engineering for functional genomics and drug discovery, *Nat. Biotechnol.*, 17, 616–661 (1999).

3. J. Nielsen, Metabolic engineering: techniques for analysis of targets for genetic manipulations, *Biotechnol. Bioeng.*, 58, 125–132 (1998).

4. R. Patnaik and J. C. Liao, Engineering of *Escherichia coli* central metabolism for aromatic metabolite production with near theoretical yield, *Appl. Environ. Microbiol.*, 60 (11), 3903–3908 (1994).

5. R. Patnaik, R. G. Spitzer, and J. C. Liao, Pathway engineering for production of aromatics in *Escherichia coli*: confirmation of stoichiometric analysis by independent modulation of aroG, tktA, and pps activities, *Biotechnol. Bioeng.*, 46, 361–370 (1995).

6. J. C. Liao, S. Hou, and Y. Chao, Pathway analysis, engineering and physiological considerations for redirecting central metabolism, *Biotechnol. Bioeng.*, 52, 129–140 (1996).

7. J. Lu and J. C. Liao, Metabolic engineering and control analysis for production of aromatics: role of transaldolase, *Biotechnol. Bioeng.*, 53, 132–138 (1997).

8. G. Gosset, J. Yong-Xiao, and A. Berry, A direct comparison of approaches for increasing carbon flow to aromatic biosynthesis in *Escherichia coli*, *J. Ind. Microbiol.*, 17 (1), 47–52 (1996).

9. N. Flores, J. Xiao, A. Berry, F. Bolivar, and F. Valle, Pathway engineering for the production of aromatic compounds in *Escherichia coli*, *Nat. Biotechnol.*, 14 (5), 620–623 (1996).

10. A. Berry, Improving production of aromatic compounds in *Escherichia coli* by metabolic engineering, *Trends Biotechnol*, 14 (7), 250–256 (1996).

11. M. Emmerling, J. E. Bailey, and U. Sauer, Glucose catabolism of *Escherichia coli* strains with increased activity and altered regulation of key glycolytic enzymes, *Metab. Eng.*, 1 (2), 117–127 (1999).

12. M. Rizzi, M. Baltes, U. Theobald, and M. Reuss, In vivo analysis of metabolic dynamics in *Saccharomyces cerevisiae*. II. Mathematical model, *Biotechnol. Bioeng.*, 55, 592–608 (1997).

13. B. M. Bakker, P. A. M. Michels, F. R. Oppperdoes, and H. V. Westterhoff, Glycolysis in bloodstream from trypanosoma brucei can be understood in terms of the kinetics of the glycolytic enzymes, *J. Biol. Chem.*, 272, 3207–3215 (1997).

14. P. J. Mulquiney and P. W. Kuchel, Model of 2,3-bisphosphoglycerate metabolism in the human erythrocyte based on detailed enzyme kinetic equations: equations and parameter refinement, *Biochem. J.*, 342, 581–596 (1999).

15. J. C. Torres, V. Guixe, and J. Babul, A mutant phosphofructokinase produces a futile cycle during gluconeogenesis in *Escherichia coli*, *Biochem. J.*, 327, 675–684 (1997).

16. R. Schuster and H. G. Holzhütter, Use of mathematical models for predicting the metabolic effect of large-scale enzyme activity alterations: application to enzyme deficiencies of red blood cells, *Eur. J. Biochem.*, 229, 403–418 (1995).

17. T.-C. Ni and M. A. Savageau, Model assessment and refinement using strategies from biochemical systems theory: application to metabolism in human red blood cells, *J. Theor. Biol.*, 179, 329–368 (1996).

18. U. Schaefer, W. Boos, R. Takors, and D. Weuster-Botz, Automated sampling device for monitoring intracellular metabolite dynamics, *Anal. Biochem.*, 270, 88–96 (1999).

19. U. Theobald, W. Mainlinger, M. Reuss, and M. Rizzi, In vivo analysis of glucose-induced fast changes in yeast adenine nucleotide pool applying a rapid sampling technique, *Anal. Biochem.*, 214, 31–37 (1993).

20. U. Theobald, W. Mainlinger, M. Baltes, M. Rizzi, and M. Reuss, In vivo analysis of metabolic dynamics in *Saccharomyces cerevisiae*. I. Experimental observations, *Biotechnol. Bioeng.*, 55, 305–316 (1997).

21. D. Weuster-Botz, Sampling tube device for monitoring intracellular metabolite dynamics, *Anal. Biochem.*, 246, 225–233 (1997).

22. H. Kacser and J. A. Burns, The control of flux, *Symp. Soc. Exp. Biol.*, 27, 65–104 (1973). Reprinted in *Biochem. Soc. Trans.*, 23, 341–366 (1995).

23. R. Heinrich and T. A. Rapoport, A linear steady-state treatment of enzymatic chains: general properties, control and effector strength, *Eur. J. Biochem.*, 42, 89–95 (1974).

24. P. Karp, M. Riley, S. Paley, A. Pellegrini-Toole, and M. Krummenacker, EcoCyc: electronic encyclopedia of *E. coli* genes and metabolism, *Nucl. Acids Res.*, 27 (1), 55 (1999).

25. F. C. Neidhardt, R. Curtiss, III, J. L. Ingraham, E. C. C. Lin, K. B. Low, B. Magasanik, W. S. Reznikoff, M. Riley, M. Schaechter, and H. E. Umbarger, *Escherichia coli and Salmonella*: *Cellular and Molecular Biology*, ASM Press, Washington, DC, 1996.

26. M. M. Domach, S. K. Leung, R. E. Cahn, G. G. Cocks, and M. L. Shuler, Computer model for glucose-limited growth of a single cell of *Escherichia coli* B/r-A, *Biotechnol. Bioeng.*, 26, 203–216 (1984).

27. J. Pramanik and J. D. Keasling, Effect of *Escherichia coli* biomass composition on central metabolic fluxes predicted by a stoichiometric model, *Biotechnol. Bioeng.*, 60, 230–238 (1998).

28. T. Ferenci, Adaptation to life at micromolar nutrient levels: the regulation of *Escherichia coli* glucose transport by endoinduction and cAMP, *FEMS Microbiol. Rev.*, 18, 301–317 (1996).

29. H. R. Kaback, Regulation of sugar transport in isolated bacterial membrane preparations from *Escherichia coli*, *Proc. Nat. Acad. Sci.*, 63, 724–731 (1969).

30. C. Clark and W. H. Holms, Control of the sequential utilisation of glucose and fructose by *Escherichia coli*, *J. Gen. Microbiol.*, 95, 191–201 (1976).

31. L. Notley-McRobb, A. Death, and T. Ferenci, The relationship between external glucose concentration and cAMP levels inside *Escherichia coli*: implications for models of phosphotransferase-mediated regulation of adenylate cyclase, *Microbiology*, 143, 1909–1918 (1997).

32. R. Schreyer and A. Bock, Phosphoglucose isomerase from *Escherichia coli* K10: purification, properties and formation under aerobic and anaerobic condition, *Arch. Microbiol.*, 127, 289–298 (1980).

33. D. Kotlarz, H. Garreau, and H. Buc, Regulation of the amount and of the activity of phosphofructokinase and pyruvate kinase in *Escherichia coli*, *Biochim. Biophys. Acta*, 381, 257–268 (1975).

34. K.-J. Johannes and B. Hess, Allosteric kinetics of pyruvate kinase of *Saccharomyces cerevisiae*, *J. Mol. Biol.*, 76, 181–205 (1973).

35. S. Vaseghi, A. Baumeister, M. Rizzi, and M. Reuss, In vivo dynamics of the pentose phosphate pathway in *Saccharomyces cerevisiae*, *Metab. Eng.*, 1, 128–140 (1999).

36. B. D. Sanwal, Regulatory mechanisms involving nicotinamide adenine nucleotides as allosteric effectors. III. Control of glucose 6-phosphate dehydrogenase, *J. Biol. Chem.*, 245, 1626–1631 (1970).

37. A. Orozco de Silva, The 6-phosphogluconate dehydrogenase reaction in *Escherichia coli*, *J. Biol. Chem.*, 254, 10237–10242 (1979).

38. M. Bhattacharya, L. Fuhrman, A. Ingram, K. W. Nickerson, and T. Conway, Single-run separation and detection of multiple metabolic intermediates by anion-exchange high-performance liquid chromatography and application to cell pool extracts prepared from *Escherichia coli*, *Anal. Biochem.*, 232, 98–106 (1995).

CHAPTER 4

Compute-Intensive Simulations for Cellular Models

K. BURRAGE, P. M. BURRAGE, N. HAMILTON, and T. TIAN

4.1 INTRODUCTION

A cell is an incredibly complex object as are the dynamical processes that take place within the cell. Yet computational cell biology, a relatively new discipline, attempts to understand these complexities by a mixture of sophisticated applied mathematics, innovative algorithm development, and implementation informed by experimental observations. Figure 4.1 shows the ultrastructure of just a small part of a mammalian insulin-secreting cell. It was produced by Brad Marsh (while at the University of Colorado) using electron microscope tomography and the volumetric rendering of a series of two-dimensional images to create a three-dimensional image.

The focus of this chapter is to understand the dynamics of a cell by building up a set of models and simulation approaches that can lock together in a modular fashion, irrespective of the complexity. The main idea is how stochasticity manifests itself in cellular processes and how it can be modeled and simulated.

The outline of this chapter is as follows. Section 4.2 discusses various approaches for simulating the time evolution of a well-stirred chemically reacting system by considering the inherent randomness associated with the timing and occurrence of a reaction based on Gillespie's stochastic simulation algorithm (SSA). We show how the state of a chemically reacting system can be described by the time evolution of a discrete Markov process that is characterized by the propensity functions and stoichiometric vectors associated with the reactions. As the SSA can be computationally very expensive, because at any time point the next time step must be sufficiently small to guarantee that only one reaction occurs in that time interval, we consider ways of improving on the efficiency of SSA. The idea is to take a larger time step and allow for more reactions to take place in that step under the proviso that the propensity functions do not change too much in that step. This leads us to discuss simulation methods that sample from Poisson or Binomial distributions. We also discuss the three

Parallel Computing for Bioinformatics and Computational Biology, Edited by Albert Y. Zomaya
Copyright © 2006 John Wiley & Sons, Inc.

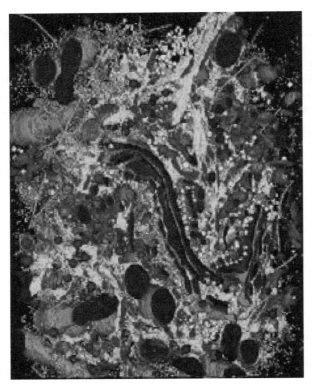

Figure 4.1   Three-dimensional image of a mammalian insulin-secreting cell, produced by Dr. Brad Marsh (University of Queensland).

modeling regimes: systems with small numbers of molecules, systems where in any small time interval all the reactions can fire many times but none of the propensity functions changes appreciably, and systems with large numbers of molecules. These three regimes are sometimes called the discrete regime (described by discrete Markov processes), the chemical Langevin regime (CLE, described by stochastic differential equations driven by Wiener processes), and the standard chemical kinetic rate equations regime (described by ordinary differential equations). Thus at the end of this section we describe multi-scaled simulation approaches that allow us to move back and forth between these regimes as appropriate.

Section 4.3 gives a brief overview of some of the modeling and simulation issues associated with genetic regulation. Because of its simplicity we focus on bacteriophage λ, which is a virus that infects the bacterium *Escherichia coli*. This phage can be in two states: lysis or lysogen, and in this section we review some of the modeling and simulation approaches applied to this system in terms of some of the issues raised in Section 4.2. In particular, we show that there are still issues in developing mathematical models that agree with experimental results for biologically reasonable values of the model parameters.

Sections 4.4 and 4.5 give a brief overview of some of the issues associated with the use of parallel and grid computing for simulating biological systems. The main focus is on simulation parallelism, as algorithms such as the SSA require hundreds if not thousands of independent simulations to calculate meaningful statistics about the behavior of these systems. As a particular example we perform a parallel simulation of the expression and activity of LacZ and LacY proteins in *E. coli*. Because we only track the genetic regulation of one cell through many cell cycles the only effective form of parallelism is simulation parallelism. However, we do discuss what would happen if we tracked the genetic regulatory effects of proliferating cells through a number of cell cycles and how parallelism could be exploited in this setting.

In Section 4.6, we turn our attention to the modeling of cellular processes both in time and space. We show how the diffusion equation arises as a parabolic partial differential equation and relate this to evolution of the probability density function of a stochastic process described by a particle acting under Brownian motion. We then show how to add chemical reactions in this formulation and this leads to the concept of Turing models, that are coupled sets of partial differential equations describing the diffusion and chemical interaction of chemical species in some domain. We then mention that if a method of lines approach is used to approximate the spatial derivatives by finite difference operators then this leads to large, block-structured systems of ordinary differential equations (ODEs) that can be solved by domain decomposition techniques in parallel.

Finally in Section 4.7 we attempt to bring all the issues raised in this chapter into one framework when we discuss the modeling and simulation associated with colonies of cells. In this setting we either have a fixed large number of cells that adhere to one another and possibly respond to chemical signaling as in epithelial models for wound healing, or we attempt to model the proliferation of cells by considering genetic regulation and the cell cycle for each individual cell, chemical signaling between the cells and cell adhesion through force models.

4.2 SIMULATION METHODS FOR STOCHASTIC CHEMICAL KINETICS

The basis of our discussion in this section is the stochastic simulation approach to biochemical reactions that was developed by Gillespie [1] through the SSA. This is an essentially exact procedure for numerically simulating the time evolution of a well-stirred chemically reacting system by taking proper account of the randomness inherent in such a system. It is based on the same microphysical assumption that underlies the chemical master equation [2] and gives a more realistic representation of a system's evolution than the deterministic reaction rate equation (RRE). In particular, the RRE is entirely inappropriate if the molecular population of some critical reactant species is so small that microscopic fluctuations can produce macroscopic effects. This is especially true for the genetic/enzymatic reactions in living cells. In recent years, the SSA has been successfully applied for simulating genetic/enzymatic reactions in which the molecular population of some critical reactant species is relatively small.

Despite continued refinements to the numerical methods used in the SSA, it remains a computationally demanding approach limiting its applicability, especially for large reaction networks required for modeling most realistic gene networks. The cost of this detailed SSA is the large amount of computing time. Recently, considerable attention has been paid to reducing the computational time of simulation algorithms for stochastic chemical kinetics. This section consists of a brief review of the up-to-date progress of these approaches.

4.2.1   Stochastic Simulation Algorithm

We first give a brief description of the SSA for chemical reaction systems. We will, for the meantime, assume that we have a well-stirred mixture at constant temperature in a fixed volume Ω. This mixture consists of $N \geq 1$ molecular species $\{S_1, \ldots, S_N\}$ that chemically interact through $M \geq 1$ reaction channels $\{R_1, \ldots, R_M\}$. The restriction that Ω is fixed can be relaxed but we will not do that here.

The dynamical state of this system is $X(t) \equiv (X_1(t), \ldots, X_N(t))^\top$, where $X_i(t)$ is the number of S_i molecules in the system at time t. The initial state is given by $X(t_0) = X_0$. For each j, $j = 1, \ldots, M$, we will define the propensity function $a_j(X)$ such that $a_j(X(t)) \, dt$ is the probability that given $X(t) = X$, one reaction R_j will occur inside Ω in the next infinitesimal time interval $[t, t + dt)$.

When that reaction occurs, $X(t)$ changes its state. The amount by which X_i changes is given by v_{ji}, that represents the change in the number of S_i molecules produced by one R_j reaction. The $N \times M$ matrix v with elements v_{ji} is called the stoichiometric matrix. In particular, if just the jth reaction occurs in the time interval $[t, t + \tau)$, the jth vector v_j of the stoichiometric matrix is used to update the state of the system by

$$X(t + \tau) = X(t) + v_j.$$

We see that the propensity functions and state-change vectors completely characterize the chemical reaction system.

Example 4.1. As a particular example, consider a simple chemical reaction system with three molecular species and four reaction channels, namely

$$
\begin{aligned}
R_1 : && S_1 &\xrightarrow{k_1} 0, \\
R_2 : && S_1 + S_1 &\xrightarrow{k_2} S_2, \\
R_3 : && S_2 &\xrightarrow{k_3} S_1 + S_1, \\
R_4 : && S_2 &\xrightarrow{k_4} S_3.
\end{aligned}
$$

This system contains a reversible dimerization of the monomer S_1 into an unstable S_2, that can convert to a stable form S_3 by reaction R_4. In this case the propensity functions are given by

$$a_1 = k_1 S_1,$$

$$a_2 = \frac{k_2 S_1 (S_1 - 1)}{2},$$

$$a_3 = k_3 S_2,$$

$$a_4 = k_4 S_2,$$

and the stoichiometric matrix is given by

$$\begin{bmatrix} -1 & -2 & 2 & 0 \\ 0 & 1 & -1 & -1 \\ 0 & 0 & 0 & 1 \end{bmatrix}. \tag{4.1}$$

In the discrete and stochastic case, $X_i(t)$ represents the number of S_i molecules at time t and thus $X(t)$ takes on integer values in a nonnegative integer lattice of dimension N. In fact $X(t)$ is a discrete (jump) Markov process. As such it has a time evolution equation associated with it that describes the probability $P(x, t|x_0, t_0)$ that $X(t) = x$ given $X(t_0) = x_0$. This equation is called the chemical master equation (CME) and it can be written as

$$\frac{\partial P(x; t)}{\partial t} = \sum_{j=1}^{M} \left(a_j(x - v_j) P(x - v_j; t) - a_j(x) P(x; t) \right). \tag{4.2}$$

In general this discrete parabolic partial differential equation is too difficult to solve (either analytically or numerically) and other techniques are needed to simulate the $X(t)$.

A method for simulating such systems is the so-called SSA of Gillespie [1], that is an exact and direct representation of the evolution of $X(t)$. There are several forms of this algorithm. The direct method works in the following manner.

Method 4.1 (The direct method). With two independent samples r_1 and r_2 of the uniformly distributed random variable $\mathbf{U}(0, 1)$, the length of the time interval $[t, t + \tau)$ is determined by

$$\tau = \frac{1}{a_0(X)} \ln \left(\frac{1}{r_1} \right),$$

where $a_0(X(t))$ is the sum of all the propensity functions

$$a_0(X) = \sum_{k=1}^{M} a_k(X).$$

The determination of the specific reaction occurring in $[t, t + \tau)$ is given by the index j satisfying

$$\sum_{k=1}^{j-1} a_k(X) < r_2 a_0(X) \leq \sum_{k=1}^{j} a_k(X).$$

The update of the system is then given by

$$X(t + \tau) = X(t) + \nu_j.$$

Example 4.2. For the system in Example 4.1, with $X(t) = (2400, 290, 50)^\top$ and reaction rates $\mathbf{k} = (0.1, 0.005, 0.1, 0.5)^\top$, values of the propensity functions are

$$(a_1, a_2, a_3, a_4) = (240, 14394, 29, 145),$$

and $a_0 = 14808$. Then

$$\frac{(a_1, a_2, a_3, a_4)}{a_0} = (0.01620, 0.97204, 0.00195, 0.00979).$$

If the generated samples are $r_1 = 0.21$ and $r_2 = 0.478$, the stepsize is determined by

$$\tau = \frac{1}{14808} \ln\left(\frac{1}{0.21}\right) = 1.054 \times 10^{-4},$$

and the second reaction will occur in $[t, t + 1.054 \times 10^{-4})$. Finally the system is updated by $t \leftarrow t + \tau$ and

$$\begin{bmatrix} X_1 \\ X_2 \\ X_3 \end{bmatrix} = \begin{bmatrix} 2400 \\ 290 \\ 50 \end{bmatrix} + \begin{bmatrix} -2 \\ 1 \\ 0 \end{bmatrix} = \begin{bmatrix} 2398 \\ 291 \\ 50 \end{bmatrix},$$

where $(-2, 1, 0)^\top$ is the second column of the stoichiometric matrix (4.1).

The point about the SSA is that the time step τ is taken small enough to guarantee that only one reaction occurs in that time interval. Clearly the SSA can be very computationally inefficient especially when there are large numbers of molecules or the propensity functions are large.

Gillespie [3] proposed two new methods, namely the τ-leap method and the midpoint τ-leap method to improve the efficiency of the SSA while maintaining acceptable losses in accuracy. The key idea here is to take a larger time step and allow for more reactions to take place in that step, but under the proviso that the propensity functions do not change too much in that interval. Thus in the time interval $[t, t + \tau)$ and with the present state $X(t)$ at time t, the number of times that the reaction channel R_j will fire is a Poisson random variable

$$K_j(\tau; X, t) = \mathcal{P}(a_j(X), \tau), \quad j = 1, \dots, M. \tag{4.3}$$

Here the notation $\mathcal{P}(\lambda, t)$ denotes a stochastic Poisson process with mean λt and variance λt, whose probability function is given by

$$P\{\mathcal{P}(\lambda, t) = k\} = \frac{(\lambda t)^k}{k!} e^{-\lambda t}, \quad k = 0, 1, \ldots . \tag{4.4}$$

These considerations lead to the τ-leap method.

Method 4.2 (The τ-leap method). Choose a value for τ that satisfies the Leap Condition: that is, a temporal leap by τ will result in a state change λ such that for every reaction channel R_j, $|a_j(X + \lambda) - a_j(X)|$ is "effectively infinitesimal." Generate for each $j = 1, \ldots, M$ a sample value k_j of the Poisson random variable $\mathcal{P}(a_j(X), \tau)$, and compute $\lambda = \sum_{j=1}^{M} k_j v_j$. Finally, perform the updates by replacing t by $t + \tau$ and X by $X + \lambda$.

As the τ-leap method uses the initial state X to approximate the states in the time interval $[t, t + \tau)$, its efficiency can be improved by computing a better approximation to the states in the given time interval — for example, by an estimation at the midpoint $t + \tau/2$. This leads to the midpoint τ-leap method.

Method 4.3 (The midpoint τ-leap method). For the selected leaping time τ (which satisfies the Leap Condition), compute the expected state change $\bar{\lambda} = (\tau/2) \sum_{j=1}^{M} a_j(X) v_j$ during the time period $[t, t + \tau/2)$. Then use the estimated state $X' \equiv X + [\bar{\lambda}]$ to generate for each $j = 1, \ldots, M$ a sample value k_j of the Poisson random variable $\mathcal{P}(a_j(X'), \tau)$. Compute the actual state change, $\lambda = \sum_{j=1}^{M} k_j v_j$, and perform the updates by replacing t by $t + \tau$ and X by $X + \lambda$. Here $[\,]$ denotes the integer part.

It is clear that robust leap control strategies should be developed before these leap methods can be considered for practical applications [3]. More recently, Tian and Burrage [4] have considered sampling from a binomial distribution rather than a Poisson distribution in (4.4) to improve computing efficiency. In the proposed binomial leap methods, the number of times that the reaction channel R_j will fire is a binomial random variable $\mathcal{B}(N_j, b_j(\mathbf{x})\tau)$ under the condition $0 \leq b_j(\mathbf{x})\tau \leq 1$. Here the notation $\mathcal{B}(N, p)$ denotes a binomial process with mean Np and variance $Np(1 - p)$. The probability function of $\mathcal{B}(N, p)$ is defined by

$$P(\mathcal{B}(N, p) = k) = \frac{N!}{k!(N - k)!} (p)^k (1 - p)^{N-k}, \quad k = 0, 1, \ldots, N. \tag{4.5}$$

For three types of elementary reactions, functions N_j and $b_j(\mathbf{x})$ are defined below.

1. First-order reaction:

$$S_1 \xrightarrow{c_1} S_3, \qquad N_j = X_1, \qquad b_j(\mathbf{x}) = c_1.$$

2. Second-order reaction:

$$S_1 + S_2 \xrightarrow{c_2} S_4, \qquad N_j = \min\{X_1, X_2\}, \qquad b_j(\mathbf{x}) = c_2 \max\{X_1, X_2\}.$$

3. Homodimer formation ($X_1 \geq 2$):

$$S_1 + S_1 \xrightarrow{c_3} S_5, \qquad N_j = \left[\frac{1}{2}X_1\right], \qquad b_j(\mathbf{x}) = \frac{1}{2N_j} c_3 X_1 (X_1 - 1),$$

where $[x]$ is the integer part of x.

In addition a sampling technique has been proposed for the simultaneous occurrence of different reaction channels if a reactant species undergoes two or more reaction channels. Suppose that the propensity functions of the reaction channels R_j and R_k can be written as

$$a_j(\mathbf{x}) = N_j b_j(\mathbf{x}), \qquad a_k(\mathbf{x}) = N_k b_k(\mathbf{x}),$$

where N_j and N_k are functions of the population X_i of species S_i. The reaction numbers of channels R_j and R_k can be generated by the following sampling technique.

(1) Generate a sample value K_{jk} for the total reaction number of R_j and R_k from the binomial random variable

$$\mathcal{B}\left(N_i, \frac{N_j b_j(\mathbf{x}) + N_k b_k(\mathbf{x})}{N_i} \tau\right)$$

under the condition $0 \leq ((N_j b_j(\mathbf{x}) + N_k b_k(\mathbf{x}))/N_i)\tau \leq 1$, with $N_i = \min\{N_j, N_k\} \neq 0$.

(2) Generate a sample value K_j for the reaction number of R_j from

$$\mathcal{B}\left(K_{jk}, \frac{N_j b_j(\mathbf{x})}{N_j b_j(\mathbf{x}) + N_k b_k(\mathbf{x})}\right).$$

(3) The reaction number of channel R_k is $K_k = K_{jk} - K_j$.

Then the binomial τ-leap method is given below.

Method 4.4 (Binomial τ-leap method). For a given criterion ϵ, choose a stepsize τ satisfying the Leap Condition and stepsize conditions for each reaction channel. Then generate a sample value K_j from the binomial random variable $\mathcal{B}(N_j, b_j(\mathbf{x})\tau)$ for $j = 1, \ldots, M$. If there are reactant species undergoing two or more reaction channels, apply the simultaneous reaction stepsize condition and sampling technique for these reaction channels. Finally update the system by

$$\mathbf{x}(t + \tau) = \mathbf{x}(t) + \sum_{j=1}^{M} v_j K_j. \tag{4.6}$$

In addition to the above binomial τ-leap method, the binomial midpoint τ-leap method has also been proposed. Numerical results for three test systems [4] indicate that the binomial leap methods can be used to simulate a wide range of chemical reaction systems with very good accuracy and significant improvement of efficiency over existing approaches.

4.2.2 Methods for Continuous Models

Now if a chemical reaction system possesses a macroscopically infinitesimal time scale so that during any dt all the reaction channels can fire many times, yet none of the propensity functions change appreciably, then the jump Markov process can be approximated by a continuous Markov process. This Markov process is described by the CLE, which is a stochastic ordinary differential equation (SDE); see [5]. It takes the Itô form

$$\mathrm{d}X = \sum_{j=1}^{M} v_j a_j(X)\,\mathrm{d}t + \sum_{j=1}^{M} v_j\sqrt{a_j(X)}\,\mathrm{d}W_j(t), \qquad (4.7)$$

where $W_j(t)$ are independent Wiener processes whose increment $\Delta W_j(t) \equiv W_j(t + \Delta t) - W_j(t)$ is a Gaussian random variable with mean 0 and variance Δt, written as $N(0, \Delta t) = \sqrt{\Delta t}N(0, 1)$. The CLE represents chemical kinetics in the so-called intermediate regime, that is those processes that are stochastic and continuous.

The CLE is an example of the more general class of Itô SDEs given by

$$\mathrm{d}y(t) = g_0(y(t))\,\mathrm{d}t + \sum_{j=1}^{d} g_j(y(t))\,\mathrm{d}W_j(t), \qquad y(t_0) = y_0, \quad y \in \mathbb{R}^m. \qquad (4.8)$$

Thus general classes of methods that can be used to solve (4.8) can also be used to simulate solutions of (4.7) (see e.g., [6]).

Now the simplest numerical method for solving (4.8) is the Euler–Maruyama method. It takes the form

$$y_{n+1} = y_n + hg_0(y_n) + \sum_{j=1}^{d} \Delta W_j^{(n)} g_j(y_n), \qquad t_{n+1} = t_n + h.$$

Here $\{y_n\}$ are approximations to the solution of (4.8) $\{y(t_n)\}$ on the mesh $\{t_n\}$. At each step, $d + 1$ function evaluations of the $g_j(y_n)$ are needed along with the simulation of d normal random variables $G_1, \ldots, G_d$. The Wiener increments are then computed as

$$\Delta W_j^{(n)} = \sqrt{h}G_j, \quad j = 1, \ldots, d.$$

The Euler–Maruyama method converges with strong order 0.5 and weak order 1 to the Itô form of the SDE. If it is applied to (4.7) it takes the form

$$X_{n+1} = X_n + \tau \sum_{j=1}^{M} v_j a_j(X_n) + \sum_{j=1}^{M} \Delta W_j^{(n)} v_j\sqrt{a_j(X_n)}. \qquad (4.9)$$

Now an SDE of the form (4.8) is said to be stiff if it has widely varying Lyapunov exponents (these are the stochastic counterparts of eigenvalues). In this case there are three possible simulation approaches: explicit, semi-implicit (implicit only in the deterministic component), and fully-implicit methods. In the first case, explicit methods can be suitable for stiff problems only if the stepsize is not too small or if the additional computation associated with implicit methods is prohibitive. Perhaps the simplest method in the second class is the semi-implicit Euler method which takes the form

$$y_{n+1} = y_n + hg_0(y_{n+1}) + \sum_{j=1}^{d} \Delta W_j^{(n)} g_j(y_n).$$

This method works well if (4.8) is stiff only in the deterministic component but less well if there is also stiffness in the stochastic components. The method requires the solution of a nonlinear system of equations, usually by some variant of the Newton–Raphson method, at each step. Note that the fully-implicit Euler method cannot guarantee convergence at any particular time step (see e.g., [7]).

To solve SDEs with stiffness in the stochastic components, Milstein et al. [8] introduced the balanced Euler method to overcome this limitation. In addition, Alcock and Burrage [9] have considered improvements over the balanced Euler method in terms of better order and stability properties while Tian and Burrage [10] have constructed high order implicit Taylor methods for stiff SDEs. Both the semi-implicit Euler method and the balanced Euler method have strong order 0.5 and weak order 1.

In the case that the deterministic component dominates the noise terms then this leads to the standard chemical kinetic approach that is described by the reaction rate equations

$$X'(t) = \sum_{j=1}^{M} v_j a_j(X(t)). \tag{4.10}$$

Equation (4.10) represents the third regime for modeling chemical reaction systems and there are standard techniques for computing numerical approximations to this ODE system (Butcher [86]).

4.2.3   Poisson Runge–Kutta Methods

Just as there is a natural relationship between the modeling of the discrete, continuous stochastic, and deterministic regimes so there is a relationship between the simulation techniques.

A Poisson random variable $\mathcal{P}(a_j(X), \tau)$ with a large mean $a_j(X)\tau$ can be approximated by a Gaussian random variable $N(a_j(X)\tau, a_j(X)\tau)$, because

$$\mathcal{P}(a_j(X), \tau) \approx N(a_j(X)\tau, a_j(X)\tau) = a_j(X)\tau + \sqrt{a_j(X)\tau}N(0, 1),$$

where $N(\mu, \sigma^2)$ is a Gaussian random variable with mean μ and variance σ^2. This can be viewed as

$$\mathcal{P}(a_j(X), \tau) \approx a_j(X)\tau + \sqrt{a_j(X)}\Delta W(t).$$

Hence the Euler–Maruyama method (4.9) can be written as

$$X_{n+1} = X_n + \sum_{j=1}^{M} v_j \mathcal{P}(a_j(X_n), \tau).$$

This method is nothing but the τ-leap method of Gillespie. Thus the τ-leap method is the Euler–Maruyama method applied in the discrete setting when there are small numbers of molecules.

This has led Burrage and Tian [11] to consider a general class of explicit Poisson–Runge–Kutta (PRK) methods in which s intermediate approximations are simulated within a given step. This class of method takes the form

$$Y_i = X_n + \sum_{k=1}^{M} v_k P_k \left(\sum_{j=1}^{s} W_{ij} a_k(Y_j), \tau \right), \quad i = 1, \ldots, s,$$

$$X_{n+1} = X_n + \sum_{k=1}^{M} v_k P_k \left(\sum_{j=1}^{s} \beta_j a_k(Y_j), \tau \right).$$

In general it is sufficient to consider simulation methods in which s is 1 or 2, and this gives rise to a general class of two-stage methods of the form

$$X = X_n + \sum_{k=1}^{M} v_k P_k(\theta a_k(X_n), \tau)$$

$$X_{n+1} = X_n + \sum_{k=1}^{M} v_k P_k((1 - \beta)a_k(X_n) + \beta a_k(X), \tau).$$

Burrage and Tian [11] consider two new stochastic simulation methods with $\beta = 1/(2\theta)$: the Heun PRK method ($\theta = 1$) and the R2 PRK method ($\theta = 2/3$). The latter is so-called because it is directly related to the R2 method for solving Stratonovich SDEs (see, [12]).

An important issue here is that of stiffness. In the case of stochastic simulations, Rathinam et al. [13] consider how stiffness manifests itself at both the continuous deterministic and discrete stochastic levels. In this case explicit methods become impractical. The authors construct two implicit versions of the explicit τ-leap method known as the rounded and unrounded implicit τ-leap method that have better stability properties than the explicit τ-leap method and are suitable for solving stiff chemical systems. The rounded method has the form

$$X = X_n + \tau \sum_{j=1}^{M} v_j \left(a_j(X) - a_j(X_n)\right) + \sum_{j=1}^{M} v_j P_j \left(a_j(X_n), \tau\right),$$

$$X_{n+1} = X_n + \sum_{j=1}^{M} v_j \left[\tau \left(a_j(X) - a_j(X_n)\right)\right] + \sum_{j=1}^{M} v_j P_j \left(a_j(X_n), \tau\right),$$

where again [   ] denotes the nearest nonnegative integer.

What we see from the above discussion is an attempt to construct families of simulation methods that can move between the discrete, continuous stochastic, and deterministic chemical kinetics regimes in a natural manner. This is very important when dealing with mixed chemical systems as such systems can be viewed as consisting of three different regimes and can be solved by coupling together three different simulation approaches applied to each of these regimes. For example, for mixed systems Burrage et al. [14] use the SSA when there are only a very few molecules; the explicit PRK approach (as typified by the τ-leap method) is used for components of the system with moderate numbers of molecules and a simple SDE method for solving the CLE (4.7) is used when there are very large numbers of molecules.

4.2.4 Multi-Scaled Approaches

Recently two new approaches by Rao and Arkin [15] and Haseltine and Rawlings [16] have been considered in an attempt to speedup the performance of the SSA. Both these ideas are based on partitioning of the system. In the case of Rao and Arkin, they consider a time scale separation in which a subset of the system is asymptotically at steady state. This is called the quasi-steady-state assumption (QSSA) and eliminates the fast dynamics that is responsible for the poor performance of the SSA. If the QSSA is applied in deterministic kinetics, the ODEs describing the intermediate species are set to 0. In the stochastic setting the system $x = (y, z)$ is split into primary (y) and ephemeral (z) subsystems. Then the CME (4.2) can be written as

$$\frac{\partial P(y, z; t)}{\partial t} = \sum_{j=1}^{M} \left(a_j(y - v_j^y, z - v_j^z)P(y - v_j^y, z - v_j^z; t) - a_j(y, z)P(y, z; t)\right).$$

Let $P(y, z; t)$ be the probability density function of the entire system so that

$$P(y, z; t) = P(z|y; t) \, P(y; t).$$

Then Rao and Arkin assume that z conditional on y is Markovian, so that for fixed y the conditional probability distribution $P(z|y; t)$ approximately satisfies a master equation. If, in addition,

$$\frac{dP(z|y; t)}{dt} \approx 0$$

so that

$$P(z|y; t) \approx P(z|y),$$

then a chemical master equation for describing the evolution of the probability density function can be obtained solely in terms of the primary species y, namely

$$\frac{\partial P(y; t)}{\partial t} = \sum_{j=1}^{M} \left[b_j(y - v_j^y) P(y - v_j^y; t) - b_j(y) P(y, t) \right],$$

where $b_j(y) = \sum_z a_j(y, z) P(z|y)$ is the conditional expectation of the function a_j.

The SSA can then be applied to this subsystem in a transparent manner. As a particular case Rao and Arkin [15] show how a simple enzymatic reaction involving an enzyme (E), substrate (S), and enzyme–substrate (ES) complex in which the substrate concentration is much larger than the enzyme concentration leads, via QSSA arguments, to applying the SSA with a propensity function of the form $a(s) = \alpha s/(\beta + s)$, which is of course the Michaelis–Menten approximation.

Example 4.3. The Michaelis–Menten reaction is one of the most important chemical reactions. It takes the form

$$E + S \rightleftharpoons ES$$

$$ES \longrightarrow P + E.$$

Finally, Rao and Arkin [15] consider, as a specific example, the behavior of the P_R promoter in conjunction with the Cro protein in λ bacteriophage. The P_R promoter is an important regulatory component for determining the lysis or lysogenic pathways in the lambda infection of *E. coli* (see, e.g., [17–19]).

Using the ideas of Rao and Arkin [15], Haseltine and Rawlings [16] attempt to speedup the performance of the SSA by partitioning a chemical reaction system into slow and fast reaction subsets. The slow subsystem corresponds to extents with small propensity functions and few numbers of reactions, whereas the latter corresponds to large propensity functions and large numbers of reactions. This partitioning is achieved by exploiting the structure of the CME and deriving master equations that describe the evolution of the probability density function for both the slow and fast subsystems. The slow system is treated by the SSA, whereas the fast one is treated either deterministically or by applying the explicit Euler–Maruyama method to the CLE. Thus at each time point t_n the CLE is repeatedly solved until $t_{n+1} = t_n + \tau$ is reached and then the SSA is applied to the slow subsystem with a stepsize of τ.

In the Haseltine and Rawlings approach, it is not clear what the specific details for partitioning into slow and fast reactions are but they recommend maintaining at least two orders of magnitude difference between the partitioned reaction probabilities. However, it is important for the partitioning to be adaptive and to change throughout the interval of integration. Burrage et al. [14] extended this approach to classifying reactions into slow, intermediate, and fast regimes. These regimes are characterized by the presence of one or more slow, intermediate, and fast reacting species. The classification is in terms of the size of the propensity functions but also in terms of the number of molecules in the system. Thus at every time step they classify the system as slow, intermediate, or fast, then form three vectors corresponding to the slow, intermediate, and moderate regimes, and place in those vectors the corresponding reaction number. If there are no reactions in the intermediate vector for a given time step, then there are no intermediate reactions for that step and the simulation regime changes accordingly.

In some cases it is possible to scale systems such that each term in the governing equations is composed of an expression of order of magnitude unity, multiplied by a dimensionless parameter, and this can lead to semiautonomous simplification procedures. However, the approach adopted by Burrage et al. [14] is based on trying to get a completely general, adaptive, partitioning approach for simulating chemical reaction systems.

4.3   ASPECTS OF BIOLOGY — GENETIC REGULATION

Genetic networks are defined as sets of genes whose state of activity is connected by sequence-specific regulatory interactions. The regulation of gene expression is achieved through genetic regulatory systems structured by networks of interactions between DNA, RNA, proteins, and small molecules. To understand the functioning of organisms on the molecular level, we need to know which genes are expressed, when and where in the organism, and to what extent. A major focus of modern research in molecular biology is in identifying the architecture of these genetic networks. As most genetic regulatory networks of interest involve many components connected through interlocking positive and negative feedback loops, an intuitive understanding of their dynamics is hard to obtain (Endy [87]).

This study of genetic regulatory systems has received a major impetus from the recent development of experimental techniques such as cDNA microarray and oligonucleotide chips, that permit the spatiotemporal expression levels of genes to be rapidly measured in a massively parallel way. Although still in their infancy, these techniques have become significant experimental tools by opening up a window on the dynamics of gene expression. For these massive gene expression data sets, Bayesian networks, Boolean network models, and differential equation models are key mathematical tools for the reverse engineering of genetic regulatory networks. Here we just refer to a very good review by de Jong [20].

Recently, there have been many efforts toward modeling gene regulatory networks using different classes of mathematical models [20, 21]. These mathematical models can be classified into fine-grained or coarse-grained approaches. Fine-grained approaches are based on detailed biochemical knowledge and complex networks of biochemical reactions and can be modeled by a mix of ODEs, SDEs, and discrete systems simulated by SSAs. Significant progress has been made in studying, for instance, bistability and genetic switching [22] and oscillating cellular processes

[23]. However, instead of going down to the exact biochemical reactions, coarse-grained approaches analyze large gene networks at some intermediate levels by using macroscopic variables in a global fashion.

In the last few years there has been extensive research in investigating noise in genetic regulatory networks. The origin of noise has been studied through a methodology that directly couples theory and experiments [24–26, 88], and there is considerable experimental evidence that indicates the presence of significant stochasticity in transcriptional regulation in eukaryotes and prokaryotes [27, 28, 90]. We should note that in general, the amount of protein produced by a particular gene varies from cell to cell.

Random fluctuation (noise) in biological systems can be classified into external noise, due to the random variation of external control parameters, and internal noise, due to chance events in biochemical reactions [22]. Some care must be taken with how we represent this noise; oscillation and bistability may not exist if noise is just added to a deterministic model [29–31]. For example, Barkai and Leibler [29] needed to propose strict constraints on oscillation mechanisms when the discrete nature of reaction events is taken into account. As living systems are optimized to function in the presence of stochastic fluctuations [28], mathematical models that attempt to explain these systems should also be robust. Stochastic models can not only allow realistic simulations of biological systems, but also be used as a criterion for measuring the robustness of mathematical models against stochastic noise.

To illustrate some of these issues we will focus on the fine-grained approach by reviewing a well-studied system for bacteriophage-λ. λ phage is a virus that infects the bacterium *E. coli*. It is called a temperate phage because it can be in the form of either lysis or lysogen. In the lysogenic form, the virus will replicate passively whenever the host bacterium replicates. Under the right conditions, a lysogen can be induced from the lysogenic pathway to the lysis pathway. λ phage has been studied extensively because it is one of the simplest developmental switches, and has often been used as a testing ground for modeling methodology.

Figure 4.2 gives the right operator region (O_R) control system of λ phage. Transcription of CI from the P_{RM} promotor is enhanced when the λ repressor binds to O_R2 (positive feedback) but is blocked by the binding to O_R3 by either a λ repressor (self-negative feedback) or cro (negative feedback). However, binding of either protein to O_R1 or O_R2 halts transcription of cro. Thus the lysogenic state is reflected by high concentrations of CI while in the lysis state high levels of cro will be observed.

The dynamics of this system was first studied by a rate-equation approach. This system contains 40 possible binding configurations with λ-repressor protein, cro, and RNA polymerase. The rate-equation of this system is given by [17]

$$\frac{dx}{dt} = S_x P_x(x, y) - d_x x, \qquad \frac{dy}{dt} = S_y P_y(x, y) - d_y y, \qquad (4.11)$$

where x and y are concentrations of repressor and cro, S_x and S_y are the synthesis rates of repressor and cro, and d_x and d_y are the degradation rates for repressor and

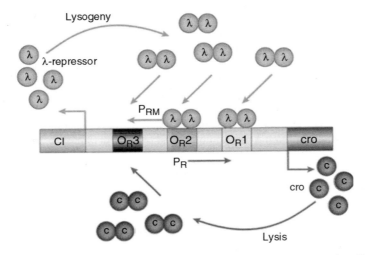

Figure 4.2   The right operator region (O_R) of λ phage. The three operator sites $O_R 1, O_R 2$, $O_R 3$ bind two proteins: λ repressor (λ) and cro (c). Reproduced with permission from *Nature Reviews Genetics* [21], copyright 2001, Macmillan Magazines Ltd.

cro, respectively. Functions $P_x(x, y)$ and $P_y(x, y)$ are given by

$$\frac{\sum_{j\in\Sigma(x)} k_j x^{j1} y^{j2}[\text{RNAP}]^{j3}}{\sum_{j=1}^{40} k_j x^{j1} y^{j2}[\text{RNAP}]^{j3}}, \qquad \frac{\sum_{j\in\Sigma(y)} k_j x^{j1} y^{j2}[\text{RNAP}]^{j3}}{\sum_{j=1}^{40} k_j x^{j1} y^{j2}[\text{RNAP}]^{j3}},$$

where $\Sigma(x)$ is a subset of the binding configurations of all 40 binding configurations in which gene CI can be expressed. Similarly $\Sigma(y)$ is defined for gene cro. Although this model gives a good description of the regulatory control of the right operator region, it cannot realise genetic switching with experimental data.

Hasty et al. [22] first derived SDE models for studying external noise in this biological system via the induction process (genetic switching from lysogen to lysis) due to DNA damage caused by ultraviolet light. By introducing noise to the synthesis rate S_x and additive noise to the system, Hasty studied the influence of noise on the bistability properties by means of a simplified system. However, it is still an open problem to realize bistability by using a more detailed model with experimentally estimated data. The key issue being the representation of those reactions that occur in low frequencies at a given system state.

However, Arkin et al. [18] developed a stochastic kinetic model of the λ lysis–lysogeny genetic regulatory circuit to study the dynamical behavior of the circuit, including effects of random patterns of gene expression. Rather than considering switching behavior, this study addressed the initial occurrence between the two available developmental pathways (lysis and lysogeny) made shortly after a bacterium is first infected with the phage. This is a system containing 75 equations in 57 chemical species. In the stochastic simulation, the protein concentrations (including several proteins other than CI and cro) vary with a strong random component and the fluctuations are large enough to send some cells down the lysogenic pathway (with high concentration of CI but low concentration of cro), whereas other cells proceed down the lytic pathway (with high concentration of cro but low concentration of CI). The predictions of the model agree quite well with experimental results.

This is pioneering work on the role of fluctuations in gene regulation. Apparently the lysogenic or lytic path in individual cells results from the inevitable fluctuations in the temporal pattern of protein concentration growth. The central conclusion is that fluctuations cannot always be viewed as simply small perturbations as they can, in fact, induce different developmental pathways.

By using a model with full binding configurations and experimental data, Tian and Burrage realized bistability by introducing threshold values into a mathematical model [19]. This approach represents an attempt to describe the regulatory mechanisms in a genetic regulatory network under the influence of intrinsic noise in the framework of continuous models. The threshold values are used for indicating the effect of positive and negative feedback regulatory mechanisms. For example, the synthesis rate S_x is now a function of the concentration of CI, given by

$$\overline{S}_x = \begin{cases} S_x, & x \geq x_1^*, \\[2mm] \dfrac{S_x x}{x_1^*}, & x < x_1^*. \end{cases}$$

This functional reaction rate is used to represent different developmental stages due to different concentrations of proteins in the system. Using these mathematical representations, Tian and Burrage constructed a quantitative model for describing the evolutional pathways of λ phage that agrees well with experimental results.

In addition, a stochastic model has been introduced for describing switching in induction from the lysogenic pathway to the lysis pathway. A stochastic degradation rate has been used to represent intrinsic noise so that the first equation in (4.11) is (see [19])

$$dx = S_x P_x(x, y) \, dt - k_x x \, dt - \sqrt{k_x x} \, dW(t). \tag{4.12}$$

Figure 4.3 gives two simulations of this model with $k_x = 1.0$ at 40–70 min. A successful switching is given in the left figure while the right figure is a simulation of unsuccessful switching. Numerical simulations have also been used to predict the proportionally induced λ phage through a large number of simulations and this percentage is consistent with the experimental data.

The power of the stochastic kinetics approach lies in its completeness and attention to detail. This might lead, for example, to more rapid hypothesis testing, by indicating which experiments would be expected to distinguish most sharply among the competing hypotheses. The drawback of the simulations is the large computational load compared with other methods. But that is the motivation for us to discuss parallel computation in the following sections.

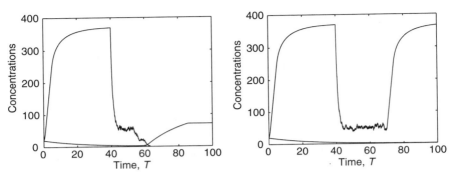

Figure 4.3   Simulations of the stochastic model (4.12) in [19].

4.4   PARALLEL COMPUTING FOR BIOLOGICAL SYSTEMS

With the levels of computational intensity required for the simulation of even simple gene complexes, it is clear that parallelism is necessary and desirable to make progress with numerical simulation in the field of computational biology. The inclusion of stochastic effects greatly enhances the realism of the model but also significantly increases the computational complexity, and again we need to consider parallel computing. There are a number of different techniques that could be implemented. These include "parallelism across the simulations" and "parallelism across the method"; the latter approach involves domain decomposition, either at a functional level or at a data level (see, e.g., [32]). An overview of these approaches is presented in this section, followed by a detailed discussion of the particular implementation approach adopted in this chapter.

4.4.1   Parallelism Across the Simulations

To understand the nature of a biological system, multiple simulations (approximately 1000 or more) can be run and various statistics (most commonly, the mean and variance, and sometimes higher-order moments) are generated at various time points. It is a straightforward parallelization technique to run a different simulation on separate processors (e.g., on a multi-processor supercomputer), as these simulations are independent of each other. This can be programmed using, for example, OpenMP, that is an application programmer's interface for shared memory parallelism. OpenMP uses a single master thread, with a team of slaves (processors) executing code in parallel. When running multiple simulations, communication between the processors is only required at the end of the simulations to generate the statistics; such an implementation is referred to as coarse-grain parallelism (in contrast to fine-grain parallelism where only small amounts of computation can be carried out between processor synchronization).

OpenMP requires compiler directives to be issued to control the parallel implementation; as such it allows for incremental parallelization from the programmer. It is possible for different numbers of processors to be used in different sections of the program. Load-balancing is an extremely important aspect of parallelizing code, although for parallelizing across the simulations this is usually easy to achieve.

The compiler directives for OpenMP take the form

```
!$OMP                          in Fortran
#pragma omp directive          in C or C++.
```

Parallel regions are placed within the statements

```
!$OMP PARALLEL

    ⋮

!$OMP END PARALLEL
```

and there are various optional clauses that can be included here to specify the nature of variables being used in such a block; variables can be `private`, in which case they only have a value within the parallel region, or the variable could be `shared`.

Directives for sharing the work in a loop (within a parallel region) are implemented via `!$OMP DO`, followed by the sequential specification of the loop. The iterations within the loop are allocated to the processors depending on the schedule specified; for example, the iterations could be divided evenly among the processors, or the iterations may only be allocated when processors are available for work. Such control allows the programmer to manage the issues of load-balancing more effectively.

If a shared-memory machine is not available, then we use the message passing interface (MPI) approach. MPI is the standard message-passing library, and its functions can be called from Fortran, C or C++. MPI Header Files must be included in the program, and then calls are made explicitly to the various MPI functions, for example

```
CALL MPI_INIT(istat)           in Fortran
MPI_Init(& arg c,& arg v);     in C or C++
```

There are functions to determine the number of processors available, the processor number, as well as `send` and `receive` functions. Data can be broadcast to all the processors, and there are also global reduction functions that will calculate the sum, product, maximum, or minimum of all the data on the processors. Synchronization between the processors is also possible.

One important issue in simulation parallelism is guaranteeing the independence of the generated random numbers in each process as this directly influences the statistical results of the stochastic simulations. In the `MPI/PVM` environment we generate different random seeds for different processes and each process receives a seed from the MASTER process at the beginning of the simulation. Then each process can use the generator RANDOM_NUMBER in Fortran90 to generate uniformly distributed random numbers. To generate Gaussian random numbers, the Box–Muller method, given by

$$G_1 = \sqrt{-2\ln(U_1)}\cos(2\pi U_2), \qquad G_2 = \sqrt{-2\ln(U_1)}\sin(2\pi U_2)$$

can be used. Here U_1 and U_2 are two independent $U(0,1)$ uniformly distributed random numbers and G_1 and G_2 are two independent $N(0,1)$ standard Gaussian samples.

An alternative to running the code on a multi-processor supercomputer is to use grid computing. See, for example, Burrage et al. [33] and McCollum et al. [34] for the implementation details of using grid computing for chemical kinetic simulation methods. The approach in [33] utilizes a mix of PCs and a number of workstations on a network, using MPI for the message-passing. For the user–computer interface and for the presentation of results we use MathML, which is a markup language for mathematics that can be incorporated into a web browser [35]. This interface allows interactive and dynamic elements as part of the implementation.

The MathML interface allows easy input of the parameters required for the simulations, and this information is passed to the C-code via a CGI script written in Perl that processes the input and invokes a shell script using a system call. The shell script creates an application schema, which defines which executables will run on which computers, and also starts MPI. It sets up the network on the same machine (master) that the web server is running on, based on the MPI configuration file. The master merely submits tasks to the slaves. When there are no more tasks to submit, the master informs the slaves to shut down. The slaves, however, wait for the master to send them a task, execute it, return the results to the master, and wait for another task. When all the tasks are complete, the master gathers all the relevant information, computes the necessary statistics, and generates plots. Figures 4.4 and 4.5 show the MathML interface and results being displayed back in the browser.

We note that currently there are a number of software environments that couple the visualization and simulation of cellular processes. These include ECELL [36], MCELL [37], and Virtual Cell [38].

4.4.2 Parallelism Across the Method

Although parallelism across the simulations is an effective technique when many simulations are required ([85]), there are other instances when only a single simulation (but for a colony of cells) may be required. This implementation may be simulating genetic regulation within each cell along with chemical signaling between cells. The implementation then requires the code to be analyzed for sections that can be run independently/concurrently. This technique is called domain decomposition at a functional level, with different processors performing different functions. It can be difficult to program successfully as it may require considerable synchronization and

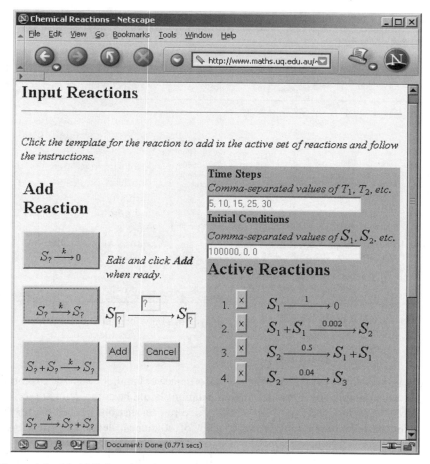

Figure 4.4 MathML Interface for performing stochastic chemistry in a Grid environment.

data movement (in this case through the chemical signaling), and is also difficult to "scale" as the number of processors increases.

An easier alternative is to perform domain decomposition at the data level. This is often called data parallelizm and involves different processors performing the same function but on different sets of data. The data need to be spread among the processors in a manner that minimizes the data transfer costs. Load-balancing must also be taken into account; it is inefficient to have some processors idle while others are busy. Data decomposition can be either explicit (where the programmer directs how the data are placed on the processors) or implicit (which is where a compiler directive may distribute some array data among the processors). In particular, the data may be distributed cyclically by rows or columns, or subblocks of data could be distributed. In some cases, data may be replicated locally to minimize communication costs.

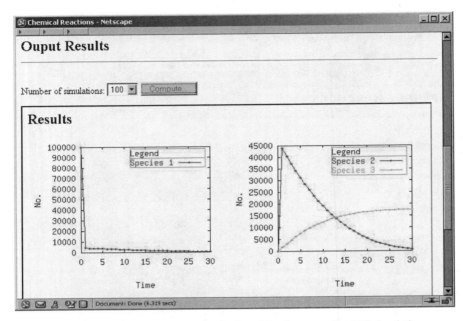

Figure 4.5   MathML output results displayed in a browser after 100 simulations.

4.4.3   Parallel Performance

There are various ways of measuring the performance of parallel code. To be rigorous, the speedup obtained by a parallel implementation should be compared with the best available sequential code (not the parallel code run on just one processor) for that problem. Also of importance is the concept of efficiency, defined as the ratio of speedup to number of processors (the best result is an efficiency value close to 1), and the computation to communication ratio. In practice, the performance of a parallel implementation is limited by

- Number of processors available;
- Load-balancing;
- Parallel overheads (e.g., synchronization time); and
- Communication costs.

It is important to note that more processors do not always equate to less computational time.

4.5   PARALLEL SIMULATIONS

To illustrate some of the issues discussed in Section 4.4, we will simulate the expression and activity of LacZ and LacY proteins in *E. coli*. A detailed description of the biological significance of the model is given in Kierzek [39] but we give the full list of reactions here in Table 4.1. There are 22 reactions and 23 molecular species in this model. The initial state is PLac $= 1$, RNAP and ribosome are generated from random pools at each step, and all other elements 0.

In a single generation it is assumed that the cell doubles its volume from 1 to 2. This is achieved by allowing the volume grow as $V(t) = 1 + t/T$, where T is the cell generation time. Thus at each simulation time step, the rates of all the second-order reactions are divided by the current volume. When the system reaches the cell generation time, all the reactants that model the DNA elements are doubled (implemented by a separate set of reactions from that being modeled). Then the numbers of all the molecules present in the system are divided by 2, the volume of the cell is reset and the behavior of a new cell is simulated for the next generation time.

We first propose a general formula for representing propensity functions for different types of biochemical reactions. Here we are interested in biological systems modeled by three types of elementary reactions, namely the first-order reaction, the second-order reaction, and the homodimer formation. These reactions can be written

TABLE 4.1 A Full List of Reactions and Rates for the Expression and Activity of LacZ and LacY Proteins in *E. coli*

	Reaction	Rate Constant
1	PLac + RNAP → PLacRNAP	0.17
2	PLacRNAP → PLac + RNAP	10
3	PLacRNAP → TrLacZ1	1
4	TrLacZ1 → RbsLacZ + PLac + TrLacZ2	1
5	TrLacZ2 → TrLacY1	0.015
6	TrLacY1→ RbsLacY + TrLacY2	1
7	TrLacY2 → RNAP	0.36
8	Ribosome + RbsLacZ → RbsRibosomeLacZ	0.17
9	Ribosome + RbsLacY → RbsRibosomeLacY	0.17
10	RbsRibosomeLacZ → Ribosome + RbsLacZ	0.45
11	RbsRibosomeLacY → Ribosome + RbsLacY	0.45
12	RbsRibosomeLacZ → TrRbsLacZ + RbsLacZ	0.4
13	RbsRibosomeLacY → TrRbsLacY + RbsLacY	0.4
14	TrRbsLacZ → LacZ	0.015
15	TrRbsLacY → LacY	0.036
16	LacZ → dgrLacZ	6.42×10^{-5}
17	LacY → dgrLacY	6.42×10^{-5}
18	RbsLacZ → dgrRbsLacZ	0.3
19	RbsLacY → dgrRbsLacY	0.3
20	LacZ + lactose → LacZlactose	9.52×10^{-5}
21	LacZlactose → product + LacZ	431
22	LacY → lactose + LacY	14

in a general form

$$X_i + X_j \xrightarrow{c} X_k \qquad (4.13)$$

with propensity function $a(X) = cX_iX_j$. Third- and higher-order reactions are not studied here as they can be reasonably estimated by the combination of second-order reactions [39]. For the three types of elementary reactions, the molecular species, reaction rates, and propensity functions are defined in the following way:

(1) The first-order reaction

$$X_i \xrightarrow{c_1} X_k, \quad a(X) = c_1 X_i X_{M+1},$$

where X_{M+1} denotes a pseudo-molecular species whose molecular number is always 1;

(2) The second-order reaction

$$X_i + X_j \xrightarrow{c_2} X_k, \quad a(X) = c_2 X_i X_j.$$

(3) The homodimer formation

$$X_i + X_i \xrightarrow{c_3} X_k, \quad a(X) = \frac{c_3}{2} X_i (X_i - 1).$$

Using the general form (4.13), the propensity functions can be written as

$$a_j(X) = k_{j1} X_{j1} X_{j2} - k_{j2} X_{j1}, \quad j = 1, \dots, M$$

that can be defined by a rate vector $k = (k_1, \dots, k_M)^\top$ and a $(M \times 2)$ index matrix with elements j_1 and j_2 in the ith row. Then the calculation of propensity functions can be implemented in parallel if the number of reactions is large.

In the OpenMP environment we use the command

```
!\$OMP PARALLEL DO PRIVATE(i), shared(a,b)
     DO I = 1, M
     ⋮
     END DO
!\$OMP END PARALLEL DO
```

to perform the following parallel computations:

(1) Calculate the propensity functions for 22 reactions at each step of SSA;
(2) Simulate samples from random pools for RNAP and ribosome;
(3) Generate uniformly distributed random numbers.

As we record the numbers of proteins after every 10,000 steps in SSA, the samples for the random pools and for the uniformly distributed random variable are generated in advance for every 10,000 reactions.

As the number of reactions in this system is just 22, it is hard to see any speedup in the OpenMP environment for a single simulation of just one cell. The computing time with two processes is just a few minutes less than the sequential computing time which is one hour, thirty-six minutes and thirty-four seconds. If four processes are used, the computing time is longer than the sequential computing time due to communication and latency overloads.

However, if we simulate the chemistry of all proliferating cells through N cell cycles then parallel computing can be very effective even with just one simulation. If T is the time to simulate one cell then the sequential time, T_S, to simulate all proliferating cells through N cycles is $T_S = T\left(2^{N+1} - 1\right)$. However, given 2^p processors, then assuming negligible latency and communication times the time T_p is given by

$$T_p = T\left(\sum_{j=1}^{p} (1) + 2 + 4 + \cdots + 2^{N-p}\right) = T\left(2^{N+1-p} + p - 2\right).$$

Thus the speedup $S = T_S/T_p$ is approximately

$$S = 2^p - (p-2)2^{2p-(N+1)}$$

so that for $N \geq 2p - 1$, $S \in (2^p - (p-2), 2^p)$.

Numerical results are obtained from parallel computing carried out on an SGI Origin 3000 scalable shared memory parallel computer at the University of Queensland. The command in Fortran 90 DATE_AND_TIME is used to measure the program's elapsed time. The timings were calculated from five runs, discarding the slowest and fastest and then averaging the remaining times. From the simulation results given in Figure 4.6, we can see the efficiency is very close to 1, based on 120 simulations with 6, 8, 10, or 15 processes in use.

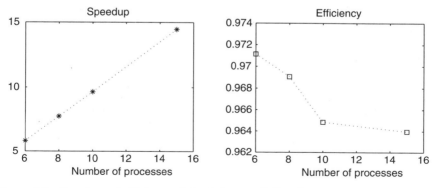

Figure 4.6 Speedup and efficiency of simulation parallelism for *E. coli* reactions described in Table 4.1.

4.6   SPATIAL MODELING OF CELLULAR SYSTEMS

4.6.1   Turing Models

There are many situations arising in molecular cell biology that require an understanding of dynamic processes both in time and space. Models described by ODEs
or SDEs usually assume that the region in which chemical reactions take place is
homogeneous and "well-stirred." In many practical situations this is not true. Ions
pass through membrane channels, chemical signals diffuse to a nucleus, C_a^{2+} waves
propagate through eggs after fertilization, and so on. These situations require a
modeling framework based on diffusion coupled with chemistry and so in this section
we introduce the concept of Turing models which are coupled sets of partial differential equations. Turing [40] originally introduced these models to describe pattern
formation in organisms through chemical signaling.

To develop these issues further we need to understand the process of diffusion.
Consider some chemical species C whose concentration in some region Ω is a function
of the spatial coordinates x and time t given by $c(t, x)$. If C is free to move within Ω
then the behavior of C can be described through two laws: the conservation law and
Fick's law of diffusion.

The conservation law for any subdomain R of Ω can be written as

$$\text{rate of change of } C \text{ in } R = \text{ rate at which } C \text{ flows in}$$

$$- \text{ rate at which } C \text{ flows out}$$

$$+ \text{ rate of production of } C$$

$$- \text{ rate of destruction of } C.$$

The first two terms on the right-hand side can be considered as the change in flux
$J(t, x)$ whereas the second two terms represent the chemistry and can be characterized
by a function $f(t, x, c(t, x))$. Thus the conservation law gives

$$\frac{\partial c}{\partial t} + \nabla J = f, \tag{4.14}$$

where ∇ is the divergence operator.

Fick's law states that the rate of movement of C from regions of high concentration
to those of low concentration is proportional to the concentration gradient. Thus

$$J(t, x) = -D\nabla c(t, x). \tag{4.15}$$

Equations (4.14) and (4.15) lead to the reaction-diffusion equation (see, e.g., [41])

$$\frac{\partial c}{\partial t} - \nabla (D\nabla c) = f. \tag{4.16}$$

D is often a constant (the diffusion constant), in which case (4.16) becomes

$$\frac{\partial c}{\partial t} - D\nabla^2 c = f, \tag{4.17}$$

where ∇^2 is the Laplacian operator, which in three dimensions is given by

$$\nabla^2 c = \frac{\partial^2 c}{\partial x^2} + \frac{\partial^2 c}{\partial y^2} + \frac{\partial^2 c}{\partial z^2}.$$

If C is diffusing in a solvent with a velocity v, then (4.15) is replaced by

$$J(t, x) = vc(t, x) - D\nabla c(t, x),$$

and this leads to the advection-diffusion equation

$$\frac{\partial c}{\partial t} + v\nabla c - \nabla (D\nabla c) = f. \tag{4.18}$$

The case of two chemical species u and v, say, chemically interacting with each other in some domain, is the basis of the so-called Turing model given by

$$\frac{\partial u}{\partial t} = D_u \nabla^2 u + f(u, v), \qquad \frac{\partial v}{\partial t} = D_v \nabla^2 v + g(u, v). \tag{4.19}$$

In two spatial dimensions, this model was used by Turing to describe pattern formation on the skins of certain types of animals ([40]). We observe that if there is no diffusion then (4.19) reduces to a coupled set of ODEs.

Turing models have been developed for two important classes of kinetics, namely activator–inhibitor and substrate depletion. Using a Michaelis–Menten approximation (see e.g., [42]) and dimensionless variables the f and g take the forms:

Activator (u)–Inhibitor (v)

$$f(u, v) = k_1 \frac{u^2}{v} - k_2 u, \qquad g(u, v) = k_3 u^2 - k_4 v.$$

Activator–Substrate

$$f(u, v) = k_1 u^2 v - k_2 u, \qquad g(u, v) = k_3 - k_4 u^2 v.$$

In the case of one chemical species, the equation

$$\frac{\partial u}{\partial t} = D\nabla^2 u + f(u) \tag{4.20}$$

has been used to model, for example, the propagation of C_a^{2+} waves through eggs after they have been fertilized [43]. Such a model is of course a gross simplification assuming that a cell is homogeneous, whereas in reality it is an incredibly complex structure consisting of a wide variety of ultrastructure. Nevertheless simplifying assumptions based on the size of the diffusion constants and the chemical kinetics (such as QSSA leading to the Michaelis–Menten formulation or fast and slow time scale approximations) can often reduce the model to the form of (4.20) again.

4.6.2 Brownian Motion

The spatial formalism described in the previous section works well for systems with large numbers of molecules (concentrations) but is not appropriate for systems that have small numbers of molecules. We have already discussed the continuous time Markov process modeling regime for describing small molecular interactions and various simulation techniques for analyzing such chemical systems. In addition, we have shown how this approach should be modified if there are moderate numbers of molecules and the noise terms are still relevant, thus leading to the CLE, that describes the temporal evolution of the system. Now we address the issue of how to model molecular motion. The fundamental principle is that of Brownian motion. Brownian motion is caused by changes in the velocity of a large molecule subject to random thermal motion of smaller molecules in a fluid. It is named after the botanist Robert Brown who first observed the phenomenon in 1827.

If a molecule is moving in a potential field characterized by $\phi(x)$ then the Langevin equation for the position of the molecule moving through a fluid, as a function of time $x(t)$, is given by the additive noise SDE

$$dx = \frac{-1}{\xi} \nabla \phi(x)\, dt + \sqrt{2D}\, dW. \tag{4.21}$$

Here (see [44]) ξ represents the hydrodynamic drag coefficient of a molecule. For a spherical molecule with radius 10^{-8} m,

$$\xi \approx 10^{-10}\, \text{N s/m},$$

and the diffusion coefficient D is approximately given by

$$D \approx 10^{-11} \text{m}^2/\text{s}.$$

Note that in (4.21) there is no inertia term. This is because typical velocities of molecules are at the molecular scale and so the Reynolds number is approximately 10^{-8} ([44]). Note also that if we use units of nanometers (10^{-9} m) rather than metres then

$$\xi \approx 10^{-19}\, \text{N s/nm}, \qquad D \approx 10^7 (\text{nm})^2/\text{s}.$$

Einstein in 1905 related ξ and D by the formula

$$D = \frac{1}{\xi} k_B T \tag{4.22}$$

where k_B is Boltzmann's constant and T the absolute temperature. At room temperature

$$k_B T \approx 4.10^{-12}\, \text{N nm}.$$

Thus we can rewrite (4.21) as

$$dx = \frac{-D}{k_B T} \nabla \phi(x)\, dt + \sqrt{2D}\, dW. \tag{4.23}$$

There are two approaches to solving (4.23). First we could perform a simulation of a number of trajectories, noting that each trajectory will be different depending on the Brownian path (the set of Wiener increments) that is evaluated. Or an alternative approach is to work with the probability of finding a single particle at the point (t, x). If this probability is denoted by $p(t, x)$, then we can apply Fokker–Planck theory that describes $p(t, x)$ as the solution of a deterministic partial differential equation.

The Fokker–Planck equation (see, e.g., [6]) for (4.23) takes the form

$$\frac{\partial p}{\partial t} = D \left(\nabla^2 p + \frac{1}{k_B T} \nabla (p \nabla \phi) \right).$$

This is sometimes called the Smoluchowski equation and in one spatial dimension takes the form

$$\frac{\partial p}{\partial t} = D \left(\frac{\partial^2 p}{\partial x^2} + \frac{1}{k_B T} \frac{\partial}{\partial x} \left(p \frac{\partial \phi}{\partial x} \right) \right). \tag{4.24}$$

The first term on the right-hand side can be considered as the diffusion term and the second term is the drift.

In general, equations such as (4.24) need to be solved numerically, but the steady-state solution can be found analytically. Thus if $p_S(x) = \lim_{t \to \infty} p(t, x)$ then

$$\frac{dp_S(x)}{dx} = -\frac{1}{k_B T} p_S(x) \frac{\partial \phi}{\partial x}.$$

Hence

$$p_S(x) = C\, e^{-\phi(x)/k_B T}. \tag{4.25}$$

This is sometimes called the Boltzmann distribution.

The approach as typified by Eq. (4.24) can now be generalized to chemical species that are chemically interacting. In this case we can mix (4.24) with the time-dependent continuous time Markov process that can describe the evolution of probabilities through a matrix of transition rates. We interpret therefore the rate constants as some sort of average of the statistical behavior of a large number of reactions [45].

Consider the simple chemical interaction between two species in time and space. Assume the reactions are given by

$$A \xrightarrow{k_1} B$$

$$B \xrightarrow{k_2} A$$

Let $p_1(t,x)$ and $p_2(t,x)$ be the probability distribution of A and B, respectively, and assume that each chemical state is characterized by a separate potential $\phi_1(t,x)$ and $\phi_2(t,x)$. Then in one spatial dimension the coupled Smoluchowski equations are in vector form

$$\frac{\partial p}{\partial t} = D\left(\frac{\partial^2 p}{\partial x^2} + \frac{1}{k_B T}\frac{\partial}{\partial x}\left(p\frac{\partial \phi}{\partial x}\right)\right) + Lp. \tag{4.26}$$

Here $p = (p_1, p_2)^\top$,

$$\frac{\partial \phi}{\partial x} = \left(\frac{\partial \phi_1}{\partial x}, \frac{\partial \phi_2}{\partial x}\right)^\top,$$

and L is the transition probability matrix given by

$$L = \begin{pmatrix} -k_1 & k_2 \\ k_1 & -k_2 \end{pmatrix}.$$

Of course for more complicated reactions the chemistry term will, in general, be nonlinear. Clearly in three spatial dimensions and for even a moderate number of chemical species, equations of the form (4.26) need substantial computing time. For example, in a cuboid with N voxels in each of the three spatial dimensions, a method of lines approach to (4.26) leads to a system of time-dependent ODEs of dimension $2N^3$ and for m chemical species, a system of dimension mN^3. Such a system of equations has a block structure and so domain decomposition and parallel techniques can be used effectively (see, e.g., [32]).

4.6.3 Other Spatial Issues

Despite the computational complexity of the problem formulation in Section 4.6.2, even this formulation may not be realistic. A cell is not a homogeneous structure, but comprises a wide range of dynamically changing ultrastructure, that is, it is heterogeneous. Not only does heterogeneity affect the development of simple conceptual models, but also it can affect the nature of the chemical reactions. Kopelman [46] showed that some simple chemical reactions in crowded spatial environments exhibit fractal-like kinetics for the "rate constants." This can lead to spatial self-organization of the reactants. Berry [47], Schnell and Turner [48] and Turner et al. [49] have modeled and confirmed these effects using Monte-Carlo lattice simulations for the Michaelis–Menten reactions. The necessity for a Monte-Carlo approach is because SSA does not readily adapt to spatial considerations. It relies on the assumption that even for small numbers of molecules the system is well-mixed. This is not the case in highly ordered or compartmentalized media.

One of the first approaches to address these issues was the StochSim algorithm of Firth and Bray [50]. In StochSim, molecules are treated as individual software objects. At each time step a molecule is selected at random followed by either another molecule or a pseudomolecule (if a unimolecular reaction) can take place. Whether a reaction occurs is determined by sampling from a probability distribution. If the reaction takes place the state of the system is updated. In its original form, however, Brownian motion is not explicitly modeled and it is difficult to incorporate ultrastructure into StochSim.

Berry [47] has refined this approach. Thus a domain is populated with internal structures with certain properties (absorbing, repelling, etc.) and the space is discretized into voxels and seeded by a certain initial distribution. A molecule is then selected at random. A look-up table decides if a molecule should move and if it can move one voxel to an empty neighboring voxel. If it cannot move due to the existence of another molecule in that voxel then the appropriate chemical reaction takes place.

This detailed approach is clearly compute-intensive but can give us significant insights into the nature of spatial organization and anomalous diffusion. A significant challenge in computational cell biology is to develop algorithms that are much faster than these Monte-Carlo simulations but that generate similar spatial effects.

4.7 MODELING COLONIES OF CELLS

The mathematical modeling of processes within a cell has a long history going back to Hodgkin and Huxley's classic papers on the squid axon [51]. However, because of the computational complexity involved, attention has only recently turned to modeling the behavior of colonies of cells. The central aims of such modeling are to understand how cells organize themselves into complex structures, and how processes such as embryo development, cancer, and wound healing occur.

There have been a variety of approaches to modeling these processes. Perhaps the most common has been to use coupled partial differential equations to describe cell density and chemical gradients over space and time. Typically cell density is described changing over time according to cell generation, death, and diffusion, where the cell generation is dependent on both the density of cells and the concentration of a growth factor [52, 53]. Growth factors change over time by diffusing, decaying, and being produced by cells. In some cases stochastic effects are considered [54], as well as hybrids of PDEs and cellular automata [55].

Another approach has been to describe cells as polygons or polyhedra. For instance, using Voronoi domains the center of each cell is used to generate a polygon or polyhedra associated with the cell [56–58], and the set of polyhedra cover the space that the cells are contained within. Typically, the dynamics of the cell structure in the polyhedra approach are modeled by considering forces acting variously through the center, vertices, or edges of the polyhedra (see [59] for a detailed bibliography). In many of the models cell division, migration, and chemical signaling are also considered.

Recently, a more direct approach to modeling cell colonies has been taken where each cell is modeled as a sphere or oval in space, and physical forces between them are considered in the evolution of the geometry of the colony [60–63]. In the next section the fundamentals of the physical model will be given. In Section 4.7.2 some ways to extend the model to include factors such as cell signaling will be outlined. In Section 4.7.3 we examine how parallelization can be applied to modeling colonies.

Finally we conclude with some applications and discussion of the ultimate aims of modeling colonies of cells.

4.7.1   Modelling the Forces Between Cells

In [60] colonies of cells are modeled by considering each cell to be a circle in two dimensions (see also [61, 62, 64]). In its most basic form each cell is characterized by its position, radius, and a list of neighbors with which it is bonded. Each cell can then exert a force on the neighbors to which it is bonded.

For a collection of n cells, the forces acting on the ith cell are modeled using Newton's second law as follows:

$$m_i \frac{d^2 u_i}{dt^2} + c_i \frac{du_i}{dt} = \sum_{j=1}^{n} F_{ij}, \tag{4.27}$$

where u_i is the physical displacement of the ith cell, m_i its mass, c_i a damping constant, and F_{ij} the force between the ith and jth cells. Note that F_{ij} is only nonzero for cells that are bonded.

The ith cell has a radius r_i, which can change as the cell grows, and the mass is proportional to the area of the cell. The damping constant is also proportional to the mass.

The force F_{ij} between the ith and jth cells is assumed to be related to the separation as

$$F_{ij} = r_{ij}(r_{ij} - (r_i + r_j)),$$

where r_{ij} is the separation of the centers of cells i and j. Hence, when the surfaces of a pair of cells are just touching there is no force between them, while overlapping cells experience a repulsive force, and separated cells an attractive force. Note that the pairs of bonded cells that are most distant experience the greatest attractive force. However, as the forces only apply to bonded pairs this is not unreasonable. Another approach to intercellular forces is taken in [64] where the force peaks when the cells are in close contact, and tails off quickly with greater distance.

The next step is to consider the components of the forces along the x and y axes. Using elementary geometry, the components of Eq. (4.27) along the axes are readily obtained, giving a total of $2n$ differential equations. To solve these the standard Euler approximations

$$\frac{du_{i,x}}{dt} = \frac{u_{i,x}(t) - u_{i,x}(t - \delta t)}{\delta t},$$

$$\frac{d^2 u_{i,x}}{dt^2} = \frac{u_{i,x}(t + \delta t) - 2u_{i,x}(t) + u_{i,x}(t - \delta t)}{(\delta t)^2}$$

may be used, where δt is a small time interval and $u_{i,x}$ the component of u_i along the x-axis, and similarly for the y-components. This gives a system of $2n$ linear equations in $2n$ unknowns.

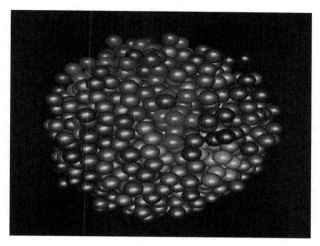

Figure 4.7 A colony of 2048 cells with three cell types. The shade of a cell represents its age, darker being older.

The matrix is sparse because each cell has relatively few neighbors, but it is not blocked as cell contacts do not naturally fall into cliques. The system of equations is readily solved using standard techniques such as Gaussian elimination or conjugate gradients.

This approach is readily extended to three dimensions. In [65], colonies of dividing cells in three dimensions were modeled using the above approach, and colonies of up to 2^{16} cells could be run on a desktop machine (see Fig. 4.7). Tests on dividing colonies of cells found that the conjugate gradients method converged within a few iterations. Iterating over time then shows the system evolving with cells jostling for position as they overlap. Hatherley [66] has also used this model with the inclusion of several cell types in an attempt to understand the positioning of cell types in a neurosphere.

4.7.2 Extending the Physical Model

There are a variety of ways that the modeling of physical forces may be extended to give a more realistic model of the development of a colony of cells. These include modeling different cell types; modeling the cell cycle of growth, division, and death; chemical signaling between cells; bonding between cells; bonding to the substrate; ion concentrations on the substrate; and motility of cells. Understanding and modeling each of these processes is a substantial challenge often involving incomplete information and guesswork, and any number of approaches may be taken.

Cell division in multicellular organisms is controlled by a complex array of signals, growth factors, and regulatory networks. The cell cycle in eukaryotes is in four phases [67]. The quiescent phase stage in animal cells may last for years, then in response to external growth factors and signals, the cell enters the G1 phase. In this phase, if sufficient stimulation occurs, the cell reaches a point where it is no longer dependent on external signals to drive the cell cycle forward. Next, in the S phase, DNA in the nucleus and related molecules and structures are replicated. In the G2 phase the cell checks that DNA synthesis and repair are finished, and that the cell has grown to a critical size. Finally, in the M phase, division into two daughter cells occurs. Transitions between phases are governed by a variety of mechanisms and checkpoints. For instance, S to G2 is governed by the protein complex cdk-cyclin A [67].

Each phase of cell division is an intricate process requiring interactions of multiple molecules, subprocesses, and checkpoints, not all of which are well understood, and which have been mathematically modeled to varying degrees. For instance, the maturation promotion factor (MPF) is required to initiate and drive the cell cycle. MPF is a heterodimer comprising the proteins cdc2 and cyclin. The cyclin combines with cdc2 to form an inactive MPF complex. The complex is then autocatalytically activated, and then stimulates the cell to start mitosis. Later the MPF complex dissociates, and the cyclin subunit degrades [68]. During the cell cycle, MPF is low during the G1 phase, intermediate during S2 and G, and high in the M phase.

In [68], MPF production is modeled using a set of six coupled ODEs, that shows a wide variety of behaviors such as steady states and limit cycle oscillations. More recently, stochastic effects on MPF production have been modeled [31, 69]. However, as in Smallwood et al. [60] simple rule based systems such as "if enough nutrients then begin division" are sometimes used to reduce the computational complexity.

Another important consideration is the nature of the cleavage plane for a cell division. The distribution of cell types can be radically different in a colony that has random cleavage planes to one that has some order [66]. Cell shape can affect the axis of division as mitotic spindles tend to align to the long axis of the cell, and the cleavage plane is perpendicular to the long axis of the spindles. In some cases it is known that neighboring cells mediate the direction of division [70], and wounds can also affect the axis of division [71].

As cell shape influences the cell division cleavage plane, cell deformation due to forces applied by neighbors has been extensively modeled. In [64], cells are modeled as deformable ellipsoids with the forces acting between the cells in a way similar to that outlined in the previous section. Tensegrity ideas have also been used to model deformation [72], as well as rod and spring models of the cell cytoskeleton [73]. More complex models that attempt to describe how forces act on the major surface and interior structures of a cell have also been constructed [74].

Cell to cell and cell to substrate adhesions are also important factors in colonies of cells. In Smallwood et al. [60], the approach used is to maintain a list of cell pairs that have "bonded" and only consider forces to act between bonded cells. Hence distant bonded cells have a strong attractive force. A similar approach, with the modification being that all cells interact, but the force function drops off sharply with distance is taken by Palsson [64]. Zhu [75] takes a stochastic approach to how strongly a pair of cells bond based on experimental data on ligand densities and applied forces.

Here we have only considered a few of the influences that affect cell colony growth and some of the ways in which they may be modeled. Many other important influences occur that can have a dramatic effect on colony growth such as substrate ion concentrations and movement of animal cells through size and shape deformations. In modeling a colony of cells, the challenge is to integrate the many types of models: ordinary and partial differential, stochastic differential, probabilistic and discrete into a single model to understand the growth and structure of colonies of cell. The limiting factors are available computational time and how well the processes are understood.

4.7.3 Parallelization and Visualization

There are many opportunities to apply parallelization to solving models of colonies of cells, depending on the model and the architecture of the parallel environment. In earlier sections, we saw how parallelism across simulation could be used to understand stochastic processes such as gene regulatory networks that underly the control of growth, division, and differentiation of colonies of cells. Here we consider some other ways in which parallelism might be exploited in the modeling of colonies.

The modeling of physical forces in a colony of n cells in three dimension requires a system of $3n$ linear equations to be solved. As the eventual aim is to model of the order 10^6 cells, the problem becomes computationally very intensive. However, parallel algorithms for solving systems of linear equations have been much studied and methods such as conjugate gradients or Gaussian elimination are readily parallelizable on shared memory multi-processor machines [76].

In some cases a colony with cells might be considered as a collection of semi-autonomous agents representing the cells, with signaling occurring between them. For instance, juxtacrine signaling is a method of cellular communication whereby signaling molecules anchored to a cell membrane bind to and activate receptors on the surface of neighboring cells [77]. In this way the signaling molecules are passed between cells. A system can then be envisaged whereby the cell cycle is modeled in each cell, perhaps by SDEs, with the cells communicating via juxtacrine signaling. The bulk of the computation would then be within each cell with a small amount of communication between adjacent cells. One way to model this in a multi-processor environment would be to have a group of cells assigned to a node on the multi-processor. On that node the calculations for each cell's cycles would be performed. Information on exchange of molecules involved in juxtacrine signaling could then sent between cells using MPI.

The question then becomes how to assign groups of cells to nodes of the computer in as efficient a manner as possible. If the communication between cells is relatively small or there are more nodes than cells then it probably does not matter as to which node a cell is assigned, except to balance the load between nodes. However, as communication between processes on the same node is typically orders of magnitude faster than communication between nodes, the problem becomes much more interesting if there are many more cells than nodes, and considerable communication between cells.

To analyze how best to assign cells to nodes, a graph can be constructed whose vertices are the cells of the colony, and with two vertices having an edge between them if the corresponding cells are in contact. Suppose there are N nodes and C cells. Then, to load-balance, each node should be assigned $[C/N]$ or $[C/N] + 1$ processes, where $[C/N]$ is the integer part of C/N. The problem is then to find a partition of the graph, such that each element of the partition has size $[C/N]$ or $[C/N] + 1$ and the number of edges between vertices in different elements of the partition is minimized. The elements of a partition of the graph are then assigned to a single node on the multi-processor system. By assigning in this way, the number of messages sent between nodes is minimized.

This is a standard problem called the *minimal cut partition problem*, and has been well studied [78]. In fact, as well as a minimal cut partition we would like a further property of the partition: that there are not "too many" edges coming out of one element of the partition, for then one node would have much more network communication than the others. The *subdomain degree* of an element of the partition is defined to be the number of edges that join vertices of the partition element to vertices in other partition elements. So we would also like to minimize the maximum subdomain degree. Again, this is a well-studied problem and several algorithms have been developed. Of course, in all the above it has been assumed that the colony is static. If the colony is allowed to grow, divide, and move then the problem of node assignment becomes *really* interesting. For an excellent overview on graph partition problems and algorithms, see [78].

Another interesting problem is how to visualize large colonies of cells. Typically OpenGL, or something similar, is used to draw and animate the scene. The programmer creates a list of positions and radii of spheres representing each cell, and these are then rendered using OpenGL libraries. However, calculating the surface lighting on perhaps 10^5 or 10^6 spheres is a nontrivial task to do in real time. In fact the majority of the calculations are not needed because only a very small fraction of the cells are on the surface, and so visible. What is needed is a way of deciding which cells are visible, or at least on a surface, before sending them to be rendered. One approach might be via Scene Graphs [79]. A scene graph is a hierarchical graph that describes the objects in a scene. In its simplest form the relationship between the objects would be containment. In a colony of cells, one object might be a surface layer of the epithelium, and the objects within it would be the cells of that layer. A scene graph renderer can then use the graph of the scene to cull unnecessary objects before they are rendered.

4.7.4 Applications

The central aim of modeling colonies of cells is to understand the mechanisms controlling how cells organize themselves into complex structures. Broadly the models fall into two overlapping classes. The first is more structural. For instance, it has been shown how the differential adhesion of distinct cell types can lead to cell sorting and to structure formation in a colony [54, 64]. It has also been shown how stresses across the colony structure can produce global alignment of the cleavage planes of cell division and so drive the shaping of the colony [71]. The second class of models, while still structural, have more emphasis on the chemical signaling both within cells and the inter-cellular environment, and the effects these have on the form of the colony. For instance, in [61, 62] the effects of calcium ion concentration on the cell cycle and colony structure are modeled, and in [80] the outcomes of the cancer therapy drug paclitaxel on cell population growth are considered. In other work, models of how a whole colony of cells can migrate under the influence of waves of chemo-attractant have been developed [81].

By modeling and then comparing with experiment it is possible to make and test conjectures about the major influences on growth and organization, as well as improve the models. In [61], a model was built of healing in scratch wounds in the epithelium and the effect of calcium ion concentrations. It was found that coverage of the wound in low calcium ion concentrations was achieved principally by cell migration rather than cell division "filling up" the gap, a conclusion that may have important consequences in the treatment of wounds. However, there were significant differences found between in vitro and in silico experiments and this led the authors to conclude that the model could be improved by more detailed modeling of molecular pathways and regulation (see also [62]). More generally, because of the availability of experimental results (and rabbits!), a relatively large literature exists on the modeling of corneal would healing [53]. As the models become increasingly complex it will be possible to make ever more precise predictions and the theory will begin to drive experiment (and maybe even save a few rabbits).

The majority of the papers published in the area have thus far attempted to answer fairly specific questions on structure and signaling. On a much more ambitious scale there is the *Physiome Project* [82], an initiative of the International Union of Physiological Sciences. It broadly aims to have "quantitative description of physiological dynamics and functional behavior of the intact organism" [83]. It will provide a hierarchy of integrated models on a range of scales from molecular, protein, cells, tissues, up to organs and body. Associated with this project is the *Epitheliome Project*, that aims to provide a computational model of cellular interaction of up to 10^6 cells with a focus on skin as the best characterized epithelial tissue [64].

The Physiome Project is a "grand challenge" that is to be a focus for the IUPS over the next decade. If it is to be successful it will need to combine on a wide range of scales, stochastic, differential, discrete, and spatial models of the types we have discussed in this chapter, along the way exploiting parallel and distributed computer architectures and visualization methods to the limits of current techniques and technology.

REFERENCES

1. D. T. Gillespie, Exact stochastic simulation of coupled chemical reactions, *J. Phys. Chem.*, 81, 2340–2361 (1977).

2. D. T. Gillespie, *Markov Processes: An Introduction for Physical Scientists*, Academic Press (1992).

3. D. T. Gillespie, Approximate accelerated stochastic simulation of chemical reaction systems, *J. Chem. Phys.*, 115, 1716–1733 (2001).

4. T. Tian and K. Burrage, Binomial leap methods for simulating chemical kinetics, *J. Chem. Phys.*, 121, 10356–10364 (2004).

5. D. T. Gillespie, A rigorous derivation of the chemical master equation, *Physica A*, 188, 404–425 (1992).

6. P. E. Kloeden and E. Platen, *Numerical Solution of Stochastic Differential Equations*, Springer-Verlag, Berlin, 1992.

7. K. Burrage and T. Tian, The composite Euler method for solving stiff stochastic differential equations, *J. Comp. Appl. Math.*, 131, 407–426 (2001).

8. G. Milstein, E. Platen, and H. Schurz, Balanced implicit methods for stiff stochastic systems, *SIAM J. Numer. Anal.*, 35, 1010–1019 (1998).

9. J. Alcock and K. Burrage, A note on the balanced method, *BIT*, in press.

10. T. Tian and K. Burrage, Implicit Taylor methods for stiff stochastic differential equations, *Appl. Numer. Math.*, 38, 167–185 (2001).

11. K. Burrage and T. Tian, "Poisson Runge–Kutta Methods for Chemical Reaction Systems," in Advances in Scientific Computing and Applications, Y. Lu et al. Eds, Science Press, Beijing/New York, 82–96 (2004).

12. P. M. Burrage, *Runge–Kutta Methods for Stochastic Differential Equations*, Ph.D. thesis, University of Queensland, Brisbane, Australia, 1999.

13. M. Rathinam, L. R. Petzold, Y. Cao, and D. T. Gillespie, Stiffness in stochastic chemically reacting systems: the implicit tau-leap method, *J. Chem. Phys.*, 119, 12784–12794, 2003.

14. K. Burrage, T. Tian, and P. M. Burrage, A multi-scaled approach for simulating chemical reaction systems, *Prog. Biophys. Mol. Bio.*, 85, 217–234 (2004).

15. C. Rao and A. Arkin, Stochastic chemical kinetics and the quasi-steady-state assumption: application to the Gillespie algorithm, *J. Chem. Phys.*, 118, 4999–5010 (2003).

16. E. L. Haseltine and J. B. Rawlings, Approximate simulation of coupled fast and slow reactions for stochastic chemical kinetics, *J. Chem. Phys.*, 117, 6959–6969 (2002).

17. M. A. Shea and G. K. Ackers, The O_R control system of bacteriophage lambda: a physical–chemical model for gene regulation, *J. Mol. Biol.*, 181, 211–230 (1985).

18. A. Arkin, J. Ross, and H. H. McAdams, Stochastic kinetic analysis of developmental pathway bifurcation in phage lambda-infected *Escherichia coli* cells, *Genetics*, 149, 1633–1648 (1998).

19. T. Tian and K. Burrage, Bistability and switching in the lysis/lysogeny genetic regulatory network of bacteriophage λ, *J. Theor. Biol.*, 227, 229–237 (2004).

20. H. de Jong, Modeling and simulation of genetic regulatory systems: a literature review, *J. Comput. Biol.*, 9, 67–103 (2002).

21. J. Hasty, D. McMillen, F. Isaacs, and J. J. Collins, Computational studies of gene regulatory networks: in numero molecular biology, *Nat. Rev. Genet.*, 1 (4), 268–279 (2001).

22. J. Hasty, J. Pradines, M. Dolnik, and J. J. Collins, Noise-based switches and amplifiers for gene expression, *Proc. Natl. Acad. Sci.*, 97, 2075–2080 (2000).

23. M. B. Elowitz and S. Leibler, A synthetic oscillatory network of transcriptional regulators, *Nature*, 403, 335–338 (2000).

24. M. B. Elowitz, A. J. Levine, E. D. Siggia, and P. S. Swain, Stochastic gene expression in a single cell, *Science*, 297, 1183–1186 (2002).

25. E. M. Ozbudak, M. Thattai, I. Kurster, A. D. Grossman, and A. van Oudenaarden, Regulation of noise in the expression of a single cell, *Nat. Genet.*, 31, 69–73 (2002).

26. W. J. Blake, M. Kaern, C. R. Cantor, and J. J. Collins, Noise in eukaryotic gene expression, *Nature*, 422, 633–637 (2003).

27. T. B. Kepler and T. C. Elston, Stochasticity in transcriptional regulation: origins, consequences, and mathematical representations, *Biophys. J.*, 81, 3116–3136 (2001).

28. M. Thattai, and A. van Oudenaarden, Intrinsic noise in gene regulatory networks, *Proc. Natl. Acad. Sci.*, 98, 8614–8619 (2001).

29. N. Barkai and S. Leibler, Biological rhythms: circadian clocks limited by noise, *Nature*, 403, 267–268 (2000).

30. D. Gonze, J. Halloy, and A. Goldbeter, Robustness of circadian rhythms with respect to molecular noise, *Proc. Natl. Acad. Sci.*, 99, 673–678 (2002).

31. R. Steuer, Effects of stochasticity in models of the cell cycle: from quantized cycle times to noise-induced oscillations, *J. Theor. Bio.*, 228, 293–301 (2004).

32. K. Burrage, *Parallel and Sequential Methods for Ordinary Differential Equations*, Oxford University Press, Oxford, 1995.

33. K. Burrage, P. Burrage, S. Jeffrey, T. Pickett, R. Sidje, and T. Tian, "A Grid Implementation of Chemical Kinetic Simulation Methods in Genetic Regulation," in *Proceedings of APAC03 Conference on Advanced Computing, Grid Applications and eResearch*, 2003.

34. J. M. McCollum, C. D. Cox, M. L. Simpson, and G. D. Peterson, "Accelerating gene regulatory network modeling using grid-based simulation," University of Tennessee, 2002.

35. D. Carlisle, et al., Eds., *Mathematical Markup Language (MathML) 2.0, W3C Recommendation*, 2001. http://www.w3.org/TR/MathML2/.

36. http://www.e-cell.org.

37. http://www.mcell.enl.salk.edu.

38. http://www.nream.ucbc.edu.

39. A. M. Kierzek, STOCKS: stochastic kinetic simulations of biochemical systems with Gillespie algorithm, *Bioinformatics*, 18, 470–481 (2002).

40. A. M. Turing, The chemical basis of morphogenesis, *Phil. Trans. Roy. Soc. Lond. B*, 237, 37–72 (1952).

41. C. P. Fall, E. S. Morland, J. M. Wagner, and J. T. Tyson, *Computational Cell Biology*, Springer-Verlag, 2002.

42. Y. Bar-Yam, *Dynamics of Complex Systems*, Addison-Wesley, 1997.

43. G. D. Smith, J. E. Pearson, and J. E. Keizer, "Modelling Intracellular Calcium Waves and Sparks," in Fall, Marland, Wagner, and Tyson, Eds., *Computational Cell Biology*, 2002.

44. A. Moligner, T. C. Elston, H. Wang, and G. Oster, "Molecular Motors: Examples," in Fall, Marland, Wagner and Tyson, Eds., *Computational Cell Biology*, 2002, Springer, New York.

45. P. Hanggi, P. Talkner, and M. Borkovec, Reaction-rate theory: 50 years after Kramers, *Rev. Mod. Phys.*, 62, 254–341 (1990).

46. R. Kopelman, Rate-processes on fractals — theory, simulations and experiments, *J. Stat. Phys.*, 42, 185–200 (1986).

47. H. Berry, Monte Carlo simulations of enzyme reactions in two dimensions: fractal kinetics and spatial segregation, *Biophys. J.*, 83, 1891–1901 (2002).

48. S. Schnell and T. E. Turner, Reaction kinetics in intracellular environments with macromolecular crowding: simulations and rate laws, *Prog. Biophys. Mol. Biol.*, 85, 235–260 (2004).

49. T. E. Turner, S. Schnell, and K. Burrage, Stochastic approaches for modelling in vivo reactions, *J. Comput. Biol. Chem.*, 28, 3, 165–178 (2004).

50. C. J. Firth and D. Bray, "Stochastic Simulation of Cell Signaling Pathways," in J. M. Bower and H. Bolouri, Eds., *Computational Modeling of Genetic and Biochemical Networks*, MIT Press, Cambridge, MA, 2000, pp. 263–286.

51. A. L. Hodgkin and A. F. Huxley, A quantitative description of membrane current and its application to conduction and excitation in nerve, *J. Physiol.*, 117, 500–544 (1952).

52. P. D. Dale, J. A. Skerratt, and P. K. Maini, The speed of corneal epithelial wound healing, *Appl. Math. Lett.*, 7, 11–14 (1994).

53. E. A. Gaffney, P. K. Maini, J. A. Sherratt, and S. Tuft, The mathematical modeling of cell kinetics in corneal epithelial wound healing, *J. Theor. Biol.*, 197, 15–40 (1999).

54. A. Mochizuki, Y. Iwasa, and Y. Takeda, A stochastic model for cell sorting and measuring cell-cell adhesion, *J. Theor. Biol.*, 179, 129–143 (1996).

55. N. J. Savill and P. Hogeweg, Modelling morphogenesis: from single cells to crawling slugs, *J. Theor. Biol.*, 184, 229–235 (1997).

56. C. Indermitte, Th. M. Liebling, M. Troyanov, and H. Clémençon, Computer simulations of mitosis and interdependencies between mitosis orientation, cell shape and epithelia reshaping, *J. Theor. Biol.*, 197, 15–40 (1999).

57. D. Morel, R. Macelpoil, and G. Brugal, A proliferation control network model: the simulation of two-dimensional epithelial homeostasis, *Acta Biotheor.*, 49, 219–234 (2001).

58. T. Rudge, "A computational system for modelling cellular morphogenesis in plants," *preprint*, University of Queensland.

59. H. Honda, M. Tanemura, and T. Nagai, A three-dimensional vertex dynamics cell model of space-filling polyhedra simulating cell behavior in a cell aggregate, *J. Theor. Biol.*, 226, 439–453 (2004).

60. R. H. Smallwood, M. Holcombe, D. Walker, D. R. Hose, S. Wood, S. MacNeil, and J. Southgate, "Modelling emergent order: from individual cells to tissue," *preprint*, Sheffield University, UK, 2004.

61. D. C. Walker, G. Hill, R. H. Smallwood, and J. Southgate, Agent-based computational modeling of wounded epithelial cell monolayers. *IEEE Trans. Nanobioscience*, 3, 153–163 (2004).

62. D. C. Walker, J. Southgate, G. Hill, M. Holcombe, D. R. Hose, S. M. Wood, S. MacNeil, and R. H. Smallwood, The Epitheliome: modeling the social behaviour of cells," *Biosystems*, 76, 89–100 (2004).

63. R. H. Smallwood, W. M. L. Holcombe, and D. C. Walker, "Development and validation of computational models of cellular interaction," *preprint*, Sheffield University, UK, 2004.

64. E. Palsson, A three-dimensional model of cell movement in multicellular systems, *Future Gen. Comput. Syst.*, 17, 835–852 (2001).

65. D. Woolford, *Modelling globular cell colony growth*, ACMC Project Report, University of Queensland, 2004.

66. K. Hatherley, *Computational Model of the Proliferation Patterns of Neural Stem Cells*, Honours Thesis, Department of Mathematics, University of Queensland, 2004.

67. A. Tözeren and S.W. Byers, *New Biology for Engineers and Computer Scientists*, Pearson, 2004.

68. J. J. Tyson, Modeling the cell division cycle: cdc2 and cyclin interactions, *Proc. Natl. Acad. Sci.*, 88, 7328–7332 (1991).

69. A. Sveiczer, J. J. Tyson, and B. Novak, A stochastic, molecular model of the fission yeast cell cycle: role of the nucleocytoplasmic ratio in cycle time regulation, *Biophys. Chem.*, 92, 1–15 (2001).

70. R. Goldstein, When cells tell their neighbors which direction to divide, *Dev. Dyn.*, 218, 23–29 (2000).

71. G. W. Brodland and J. H. Veldhuis, Computer simulations of mitosis and interdependencies between mitosis orientation, cell shape and epithelia reshaping, *J. Biomech.*, 35, 637–681 (2002).

72. D. Stamenovic, J. J. Fredberg, N. Wang, J. P. Butler, and D. E. Ingber, A microstructural approach to cytoskeletal mechanics based on tensegrity, *J. Theor. Biol.*, 181, 125–136 (1996).

73. Y. Shafrir and G. Forgacs, Mechanotransduction through the cytoskeleton, *Am. J. Physiol. Cell Physiol.*, 282, C479–C486 (2002).

74. J. G. McGarry and P. J. Prendergast, A three-dimensional finite element model of an adherent eukaryotic cell, *Eur. Cell. Matter.*, 7, 27–34 (2004).

75. C. Zhu, Kinetics and mechanics of cell adhesion, *J. Biomech.*, 33, 23–33 (2000).

76. J. M. Ortega, *Introduction to Parallel and Vector Solution of Linear Systems*, Plenum Press, 1988.

77. M. R. Owen and J. A. Sherratt, Mathematical modelling of juxtacrine cell signalling, *Math. Biosci.*, 153, 125–150 (1998).

78. K. Schloegel, G. Karypis, and V. Kumar, "Graph Partitioning for High Performance Scientific Simulations," in J. Dongarra, et al., Eds., *CRPC Parallel Computing Handbook*, Morgan Kaufmann, 2000.

79. A. E. Walsh, Understanding scene graphs, *Dr. Dobbs J.*, 27 (7), 17–26 (2002).

80. B. Basse, B. C. Baguley, E. S. Marshall, G. C. Wake, and D. J. N. Wall, Modelling cell population growth with applications to cancer therapy in human tumour cell lines, *Prog. Biophys. Mol. Biol.*, 85, 353–368 (2004).

81. B. Vasiev and C. J. Weijer, Modelling of Dictyostelium discoideum slug migration, *J. Theor. Biol.*, 223, 347–359 (2003).

82. P. J. Hunter and T. K. Borg, Integration from proteins to organs: the Physiome Project, *Nat. Rev., Mol. Cell. Biol.*, 4, 237–243 (2003).

83. J. B. Bassingthwaighte, Strategies for the Physiome Project, *Ann. Biomed. Eng.*, 28, 1043–1058 (2000).

84. K. Burrage, P. M. Burrage, and T. Tian, "Numerical Methods for Solving Stochastic Differential Equations on Parallel Computers," in *Proceedings of the Fifth International Conference on High-Performance, Computing in the Asia-Pacific Region*, 2001.

85. J. C. Butcher, *The Numerical Analysis of Ordinary Differential Equations*, Wiley, UK, 1987.

86. D. Endy and R. Brent, Modelling cellular behaviour, *Nature*, 409, 391–395 (2001).

87. N. Federoff and W. Fontana, Small numbers of big molecules, *Science*, 297, 1129–1131 (2002).

88. D. A. Hume, Probability in transcriptional regulation and its implications for leukocyte differentiation and inducible gene expression, *Blood*, 96, 2323–2328 (2000).

Parallel Computation in Simulating Diffusion and Deformation in Human Brain

NING KANG, JUN ZHANG, and ERIC S. CARLSON

The purpose of this chapter is to survey some recent developments in the application of parallel and high-performance computation in simulating the diffusion process in the human brain and in modeling the deformation of the human brain. Computational neuroscience is a branch of biomedical science and engineering in which sophisticated high-performance computing techniques can make a huge difference in extracting brain anatomical information non-invasively and in assisting minimal invasive neurosurgical interventions. This chapter will demonstrate that there are lots of potential opportunities for computational scientists to work with biomedical scientists to develop high-performance computing tools for biomedical applications.

5.1 INTRODUCTION

We present a survey on two types of computer simulations conducted in the human brain involving parallel computation. The first one is to simulate the anisotropic diffusion process in the human brain, using the measured diffusion tensor magnetic resonance imaging (DT-MRI) data. DT-MRI technique is the only non-invasive in vivo approach available so far to investigate the three-dimensional architecture of brain white matter with the potential to generate fiber tract trajectories in the white matter. The simulation of the diffusion over the brain could play a critical role in the development of improved approaches for the reconstruction of nerve fiber tracts in the human brain. The second type is the simulation of brain deformation during image-guided neurosurgery. The challenge that a neurosurgeon has to face is

Parallel Computing for Bioinformatics and Computational Biology, Edited by Albert Y. Zomaya
Copyright © 2006 John Wiley & Sons, Inc.

the removal from the brain of as much diseased tissue as possible and meanwhile the removal of normal tissue must be minimized and the disruption of important anatomical structures must be avoided. Therefore, it is crucial to capture the brain deformation during the neurosurgical interventions on patients by aligning preoperatively acquired image data with intraoperative images. To be practical, the brain deformation simulation has to meet real-time constraints as well as achieve robustness and high accuracy.

5.2 ANISOTROPIC DIFFUSION SIMULATION IN WHITE MATTER TRACTOGRAPHY

5.2.1 Background

The solution of the general unsteady-state anisotropic diffusion equation could be important in the development of improved approaches for the analysis of DT-MRI. DT-MRI is an extension of conventional MRI with the added capability of measuring the random motion of water molecules in all three dimensions, usually referred to as diffusion or "Brownian motion." As water diffusion is influenced by the microstructure, architecture, and physical properties of tissues, DT-MRI can render the information about how water diffuses in biological tissues containing a large number of fibers, like muscles or brain white matter, into intricate three-dimensional representations of the tissues architecture. Thus, it can be exploited to visualize and extract information about the brain white matter and nerve fibers by reconstructing the fiber pathways, which has raised promises for achieving a better comprehension of the fiber tract anatomy of the human brain. In combination with functional MRI, it might potentially bring tremendous improvements in deeply understanding the crucial issue of anatomical connectivity and functional coupling between different regions of the brain [1–3]. Therefore, the neuroanatomical knowledge on connectivity interpreted from the DT-MRI information has been playing an indispensable role in neurosurgery planning [4] and in tackling a lot of brain diseases and disorders, such as Alzheimer's disease [5, 6], attention-deficit hyperactivity disorder, and schizophrenia [7, 8].

It is known that water diffusion is anisotropic in brain white matter. The significant anisotropy presented in white matter reveals microscopic properties of the anatomy of the nerve fibers, because water tends to diffuse predominantly along the long axis of the fibers, because the longitudinally oriented structures, the dense packing of axons, and the inherent axonal membranes, which are widely assumed to be the main barrier, hinder water diffusion perpendicular to the fibers [9]. DT-MRI is sensitive to this structural anisotropy and is able to characterize it by noninvasively quantifying and assessing the self-diffusion of water in vivo. The information concerning the local orientation of fibers, extracted from the water anisotropic diffusion in white matter, forms the basis of utilizing DT-MRI to track fiber pathways and build connectivity mapping in vivo. The water diffusion behavior elucidated by the diffusion tensor imaging reflects the directional organization of the underlying white matter microstructure. DT-MRI characterizes the behavior on a voxel-by-voxel basis, and for each voxel, the diffusion tensor yields the diffusion coefficient corresponding to any direction in space [10]. The direction of the greatest diffusion can be determined by evaluating the diffusion tensor in each voxel, which is believed to point along the dominant axis of the white matter fiber bundles traversing the voxel. Thus, the panoramic view of the fastest diffusion direction can be generated to provide a visualization of the white matter pathways and their orientations.

A number of fiber tracking algorithms have been developed since the appearance of DT-MRI. In Refs. [11, 12] a variety of these algorithms are described and reviewed. As the measured quantity in DT-MRI is water diffusion, an intuitive way to gain insights from the diffusion tensor data is to carry out a virtual simulation of water diffusion, which is anisotropic and governed by the diffusion equation, over the brain. The white matter fiber bundles are assumed to proceed along the direction where the diffusion is the greatest. The idea of studying brain connectivity by simulating the anisotropic diffusion has been explored in Refs. [13–15]. Batchelor et al. [13] specify a starting point for tractography where a seed is diffused. A virtual concentration peak of water is spread in Ref. [14]. In Ref. [15], successive virtual anisotropic diffusion simulations are performed over the whole brain, which are utilized to construct three-dimensional diffusion fronts and then the fiber pathways. This technique of solving a diffusion equation makes use of the full information contained in the diffusion tensor, and it is not dependent upon a point-to-point eigenvalue/eigenvector computation along a trajectory, thus in that sense may enhance the robustness and reliability of fiber reconstruction algorithms. It is also intuitively related to the underlying physical–chemical process in the central nervous system [16, 17]. The diffusion process and related transport mechanism in the brain are discussed in detail in Ref. [18].

Simply, anisotropic systems are those that exhibit a preferential flow direction, in which the flow field does not follow the concentration gradient directly, for the material properties also affect diffusion. Therefore, the diffusion tensor, D, is introduced to fully describe the molecular mobility along each direction and the correlation between these directions. We have

$$D = \begin{pmatrix} D_{xx} & D_{xy} & D_{xz} \\ D_{yx} & D_{yy} & D_{yz} \\ D_{zx} & D_{zy} & D_{zz} \end{pmatrix},$$

where the subscripts xx, xy, xz, and so on, denote the values of the individual coefficients in the matrix that can be seen as the influence from directions in the input (being the concentration) on the various directions in the output (being the flux). For the brain system and other typical systems, the tensor is symmetric. Figure 5.1 shows an axial slice of a diffusion tensor volume from the human brain.

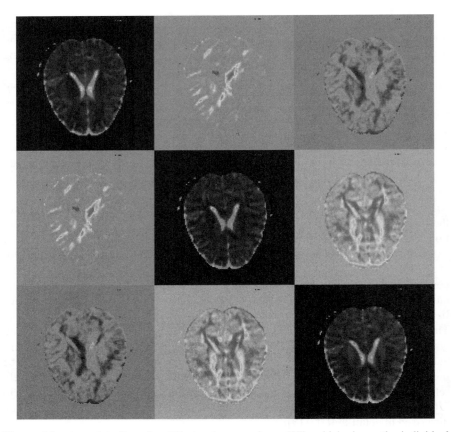

Figure 5.1   An axial slice of a diffusion tensor volume [27], which shows the individual diffusion tensor components, corresponding to the diffusion tensor matrix D.

Essentially, the fiber tracking schemes based on diffusion simulation mentioned earlier are seeking to solve an unsteady-state diffusion equation in an anisotropic medium based on the measured diffusion tensor D. The anisotropic diffusion process, due to the conservation of mass, is governed by

$$\frac{\partial C}{\partial t} = \nabla \cdot (D\nabla C),$$ (5.1)

where t is the independent time variable. This equation shows that over the time, the rate of change in concentration is proportional to the divergence of the flux.

In a Cartesian coordinate system, Eq. (5.1) is expressed as

$$
\begin{aligned}
\frac{\partial C}{\partial t} = \ & \frac{\partial}{\partial x}\left(D_{xx}\frac{\partial C}{\partial x} + D_{xy}\frac{\partial C}{\partial y} + D_{xz}\frac{\partial C}{\partial z}\right) \\
& + \frac{\partial}{\partial y}\left(D_{yx}\frac{\partial C}{\partial x} + D_{yy}\frac{\partial C}{\partial y} + D_{yz}\frac{\partial C}{\partial z}\right) \\
& + \frac{\partial}{\partial z}\left(D_{zx}\frac{\partial C}{\partial x} + D_{zy}\frac{\partial C}{\partial y} + D_{zz}\frac{\partial C}{\partial z}\right).
\end{aligned}
\tag{5.2}
$$

This equation could be very difficult to solve under the circumstance of the human brain for several reasons. First, because the brain structure is heterogeneous where anisotropy requires full tensor representation, the second-order cross derivatives must be calculated. Second, the diffusion tensor changes drastically between adjacent small regions in the brain tissues. Thus, fine gridding must be used to avoid a crude approximation to the true geometry of interesting structures, and this leads to large systems of equations. The third challenge is that time plays a crucial role in the real environment, such as clinical diagnosis, surgical planning, and neurosurgery [4]. Actually the solution must meet the real-time constraints and must achieve good reliability and robustness as well.

5.2.2 Simulating the Diffusion Process

As mentioned earlier, the anisotropic diffusion process is simulated in Refs. [13–15], where each employs different tensor data set and uses different approach to solve the governing diffusion equation. The diffusion tensor data are extracted and estimated from the collected echo-planar images with different diffusion weighting, at least six independent gradient directions, and one unweighted image by solving the Stejskal–Tanner equation for anisotropic diffusion, as the symmetric tensor matrix has at least six independent components [19].

In Ref. [13], the diffusion tensor data set used is obtained from the acquired 25 slices with voxel size being 2 mm $\times$ 2 mm $\times$ 2 mm, and the diffusion equation is discretized in space with Galerkin finite element method and in time with finite difference method. The semi-implicit system is then solved by using a Crank–Nicholson scheme. Initially, the concentration distribution in the brain, which is the seed, is described as

$$
C(x,0) = \begin{cases} 1 & \text{in starting region,} \\ 0 & \text{elsewhere,} \end{cases}
\tag{5.3}
$$

and the simplified anisotropic diffusion equation being solved is

$$
\nabla \cdot D\nabla C(x,t) = -\frac{\partial C(x,t)}{\partial t},
\tag{5.4}
$$

where $C(x, t)$ is the concentration function. The Neumann boundary condition is enforced in the computation, that is, $D\nabla C \cdot n = 0$ on the boundary, in which n is the direction normal to the surface of the boundary.

Both two- and three-dimensional diffusion tensor data sets are applied to solve the anisotropic diffusion equation in Ref. [14], with the resolution of the tensor data being $128 \times 128 \times 43$ corresponding to a uniform voxel size of $1.8\,\text{mm}^3$. The equation is solved using a finite element method from the software package "FEMLAB" (www.femlab.com). The solved euqation is also simplified as

$$\frac{\partial C}{\partial t} = \sum_{i,j=1}^{3} D_{ij} \frac{\partial^2 C}{\partial x_i \partial x_j} \tag{5.5}$$

with an initial water concentration peak specified by a Gaussian function with a standard deviation of 2. The time cost for the finite element computations in a two-dimensional grid with 128×128 voxels is reported in the order of minutes on a PC with a 700 MHz Pentium III CPU and 512 MB memory. The three-dimensional simulation runs for about 4 min before completion, using a mesh with 19,651 voxels generated by a Delaunay algorithm.

In Ref. [15], successive virtual anisotropic diffusion simulations are performed over the whole brain, where the resolution of the tensor data set is $128 \times 128 \times 48$ with each voxel size being $2.5\,\text{mm} \times 2.5\,\text{mm} \times 2.5\,\text{mm}$ defined on the Cartesian mesh. The anisotropic diffusion equation (5.2) on the Cartesian grid is discretized using a finite difference approximation. The central difference in space and backward differentiation formula in time are applied to approximate the spatial and time derivative terms in Eq. (5.2), respectively. On the boundaries of the heterogeneous system, it is assumed to be insulated, that is, $D\nabla C \cdot n = 0$, which corresponds to the Neumann condition as well. This condition means that the normal part of the gradient of the concentration on the boundary is zero. Nothing diffuses outside the brain image boundary. The initial condition uses Eq. (5.3), where the start region is a single voxel and it changes with the growth of the fiber pathways.

In Ref. [20], a steady-state concentration distribution is created in the diffusion tensor field by solving

$$\nabla \cdot (D\nabla C) = 0. \tag{5.6}$$

As for the boundary and initial conditions, they simulate a sink at one point of interest and a source at another, to estimate the steady-state flow between the regions. Batchelor et al. [21] further extend the diffusion equation to a diffusion–convection equation by adding a convection term

$$\frac{\partial C}{\partial t} = \nabla \cdot (D\nabla C) + fv \cdot \nabla C, \tag{5.7}$$

where v is a vector field and f a coefficient to control the convection term which could be chosen to rely on anisotropies. Equation (5.7) is discretized by a finite element method with Crank–Nicholson scheme.

The anisotropic diffusion equation is also solved in the environment of the human brain with measured DT-MRI data in Ref. [22], where the resolution of the tensor data set is $128 \times 128 \times 16$ with each voxel size being 2.5 mm $\times$ 2.5 mm $\times$ 7.5 mm defined on the Cartesian mesh. A different yet efficient gridding scheme, the face-centered cubic (FCC) grids, is employed to do the discretization [23]. In the case of three dimension (3D), Figure 5.2 displays the three-dimensional FCC mesh and the grid has a 13-point cuboctahedral stencil, as shown in Figure 5.3. The node at the center of Figure 5.3 is symmetrically surrounded by 12 equidistant nodes. The external 12 nodes are the 12 vertices of a cuboctahedron. Thus, the actual number of computational nodes in the FCC grid is half the size of that in the Cartesian grid, by the way of generating the FCC grid as described in Ref. [22]. A three-dimensional Gaussian function with an equal standard deviation of $\sigma = 0.2$ is selected to be the initial distribution profile of the water concentration in the brain

$$C\big|_{t=0} = \frac{1}{\sigma^3 \sqrt{8\pi^3}}\, e^{-[(x-\mu_x)^2+(y-\mu_y)^2+(z-\mu_z)^2]/2\sigma^2}, \tag{5.8}$$

where μ_x, μ_y, and μ_z are the mean in the x, y, and z directions, respectively.

The discretization of Eq. (5.2) and its boundary conditions on the FCC grid or the Cartesian grid generates a large-scale system of semi-explicit differential-algebraic equations (DAEs) with the form

$$F(t, y, y') = 0, \tag{5.9}$$

where y and y' are N-dimensional vectors corresponding to the discretized values of C and C'. In Refs. [15, 22] a high-performance DAE solver is given, the IDA solver

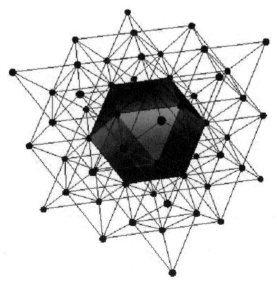

Figure 5.2 The 3D FCC grid (the center unit is a cuboctahedron) [22].

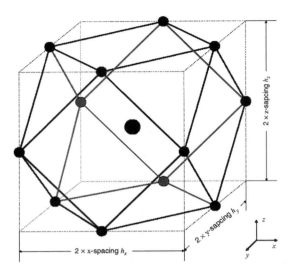

Figure 5.3   The 13-point cuboctahedral stencil in a 3D FCC grid [22].

in the SUNDIALS suite, one of the software packages contained in the ACTS Toolkit (www.acts.nersc.gov). IDA stands for implicit differential-algebraic solver, which is a general-purpose solver for the initial value problem for systems of DAEs. SUNDIALS stands for Suite of Nonlinear and Differential/Algebraic equation Solvers. Detailed explanations of the DAEs theories and its numerical solution methods on initial-value problems are given in Ref. [24]. More detailed information about the SUNDIALS suite and the IDA solver can be found in Ref. [25] and at the web site of SUNDIALS (http://acts.nersc.gov/sundials/).

For the solution of the linear system

$$Ax = b, \qquad (5.10)$$

resulted from Eq. (5.9), the IDA includes both direct and iterative methods. Owing to the large-scale nature of the 3D simulation problem, direct solution methods based on Gaussian elimination are not suitable for their prohibitive central processing unit (CPU) and memory costs. Another thing about solving the time-dependent system is that it is often possible to use a preconditioner over more time steps when using iterative methods than it would be possible to keep an iteration matrix in the direct method, because the iterative methods do the rest of the work in solving the system. Therefore, Kang et al. [15, 22] choose the preconditioned iterative methods based on the Krylov subspaces.

As the preconditioning of the linear iteration is essential and beneficial for both robustness and efficiency, Kang et al. [22] apply a number of different preconditioning techniques, based on incomplete lower-upper (LU) factorizations of the coefficient matrix, to the GMRES [26] method embedded in the IDA solver. The basic idea of preconditioning is as follows. Let P be a matrix which approximates the coefficient matrix A in some way. Preconditioning is an iterative method for solving the linear system, Eq. (5.10), which means applying this method instead to the equivalent system $P^{-1}Ax = P^{-1}b$. The preconditioned system is expected to become easier to solve than the original problem, that is, the matrix $P^{-1}A$ is better conditioned than A or $P^{-1}A$ and has a more favorable eigenvalue distribution than A. For an efficient preconditioning, P should be in some sense close to A and its construction should be inexpensive.

Numerical experiments are performed in Ref. [22] to investigate the efficiency and effectiveness of several standard ILU preconditioners in solving the linear systems arising at each Newton iteration, which are conducted on a Sun Blade 100 workstation with a single 500 MHz UltraSPARC-IIe processor and 128 MB memory. The overall time cost runs in several hundred seconds, including the preconditioner setup time and iteration time. The ILU preconditioners based on the static pattern scheme, ILU(k), are found to be inefficient for solving the current problem. The best choice among all the preconditioners that are investigated is the dynamic-pattern-scheme-based ILUT, with optimum choices of its two thresholding parameters p and τ. The composite preconditioner in which ILU(0) uses the ILUT data pattern shows better performance than ILU(0), but no better than ILUT. The numerical tests in Ref. [22] illustrate that, regardless of the thresholding strategies applied in the ILU preconditioning, the choice of the corresponding parameters has direct and distinct influences on the accuracy and the construction cost of the preconditioner, the convergence rate of the iterative solution, and the total computational efforts. Generally, the more the entries kept in the factorization, the higher the quality of the ILU preconditioner will be, which makes the iterative solution more robust but with the price of more construction time, and higher per iteration cost.

Figure 5.4 shows the simulated concentration distribution profiles of the anisotropic diffusion in the human brain from Ref. [22]. The simulated result on the 3D Cartesian

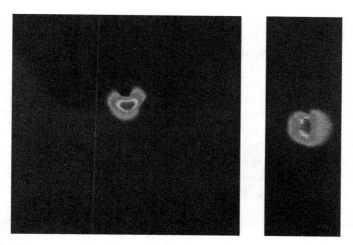

Figure 5.4   The concentration distribution profiles of the anisotropic diffusion in the human brain [22]. Left: the profile on the cutting plane of $z = 8$. Right: the profile on the cutting plane of $y = 75$.

grid is derived from interpolation when the solution on the FCC grid is mapped back to the Cartesian grid.

5.2.3   A Parallel Implementation

All the above-mentioned implementations of solving the anisotropic diffusion equation in a human brain with the measured DT-MRI data are done in a serial computing environment. To perform diffusion simulations over the whole brain with sufficient accuracy and acceptable computational time and memory cost, a parallel implementation of the solution is presented in Ref. [27]. The tensor data set used in the simulation is the same as that used in Ref. [22], where the resolution of the data set is $128 \times 128 \times 16$ with each voxel size being $2.5\,\text{mm} \times 2.5\,\text{mm} \times 7.5\,\text{mm}$ defined on the Cartesian mesh. The 3D diffusion equation (5.2) is discretized on the Cartesian grid using finite difference approximation. The central difference in space and backward differentiation formula in time are applied to approximate the spatial and time derivative terms in Eq. (5.2), respectively. Kang et al. [27] apply the same boundary and initial condition as those used in Ref. [22]. The resulting coefficient matrix after the discretization process is distributed to different processors with the scheme of row-wise block striping, that is, the matrix is divided into groups of complete rows and each group is assigned to one processor. Then the parallel version of the IDA solver in the ACTS Toolkit is exploited as the primary integration tool. For the large-scale sparse linear system arising from each integration step, the Krylov subspace method, preconditioned GMRES, is used and a number of highly efficient and robust parallel preconditioners are also applied to achieve speedy solutions with good accuracy.

The parallel version of IDA uses a revised version of the vector module NVECTOR in its package to achieve parallelism and the (message-passing interface) (MPI) library for all interprocessor communication. The NVECTOR module is the key to make possible the shift from the serial computing environment to the parallel computing environment. It contains a set of mathematical operations on N vectors (N-dimensional vectors), including vector linear combinations, scaling, vector norms, scalar products, and so forth. By separating these operations from the rest of the code, all operations in IDA with significant potential for parallel computation are isolated, which allows parallel computation to be neatly implemented with these codes. The fact that the parallel form of IDA is intended for a SPMD (single program multiple data) programming model with distributed memory, all N vectors are identically distributed across processors such that each processor is solving a contiguous subset of the DAE system. For any given vector operation, each processor performs the operation on its contiguous elements of the input vectors, followed by a global reduction operation when needed. In this way, vector calculations can be done simultaneously with each processor working on its own segment of the vector.

The incomplete LU preconditioners studied in Ref. [22] are not suitable for implementations on parallel computers. In the parallel computing environment, it is desirable that both the preconditioner construction phase and the preconditioned solution phase possess a high degree of parallelism. In Ref. [27], two classes of preconditioners suitable for parallel implementation are investigated. The first parallel preconditioning technique is a class of sparse approximate inverse (SAI) preconditioners. The SAI preconditioner, as its name implies, is an approximation to A^{-1}, the inverse of a matrix A. Both its construction and application in the iterative solution, which require nothing but matrix by vector products, allow a high degree of parallelism and can be implemented in parallel without much difficulty. The SAI preconditioning technique discussed in Ref. [27] is based on the idea of the least-squares (Frobenius norm) minimization [28], using a priori sparsity patterns [29], where people seek to approximate the inverse of a matrix A (usually sparse) by a sparse matrix P, such that $AP \approx I$ in some sense, where I is the identity matrix. Another class of preconditioners that are involved in Ref. [27] is the block-diagonal preconditioning, which is also suitable for the parallel architecture. Actually, close attention is paid to the banded-block-diagonal (BBD) preconditioners. This class of preconditioners is based on the block Jacobi method where a preconditioner can be derived by a partitioning of the variables. The basic idea is to isolate the preconditioning so that it is local to each processor. In fact, on parallel computers it is natural to let the partitioning coincide with the division of the variables over the processors.

In Ref. [27] a number of numerical results are presented to compare the performance of SAI and BBD preconditioners on the simulation of the anisotropic diffusion in the human brain. The numerical tests are conducted on a 32-processor (HP PA-RISC 8700 processors running at 750 MHz) subcomplex of an HP superdome supercomputer at the University of Kentucky. Each processor has 2 GB local memory. The running time reported in all cases is less than 100 s. The experimental results show that the SAI preconditioners based on a priori sparsity pattern provide a more robust and efficient parallel preconditioning technique than the BBD preconditioners for the brain diffusion simulation problem. It is the SAI preconditioner whose convergence performance is not affected by the number of processors employed, although both the SAI and BBD preconditioners demonstrate a good speedup, which is close to linear. The SAI preconditioners take more CPU time to construct, but need less memory space to store, than the BBD preconditioners. The numerical tests also illustrate that the best performance of the preconditioners can be obtained by choosing optimum values for their corresponding parameters, τ_1 and τ_2 in SAI, and w_1 and w_2 in BBD, which have direct and distinct influences on the quality and the construction expense of the preconditioners, the convergence rate of the iterative solutions, and the total computational efforts. The comparison of scalability between the SAI and BBD preconditioners is given in Figure 5.5, where there exists superlinear speedups for the BBD preconditioner. This can be attributed to the caching effects. When the problem is dispatched onto multiple processors, the subproblems are obviously a fraction of the original problem size. With a smaller problem size, it is most likely to get a higher cache hit rate, and the result, even after considering the communication time, is still better than the time on a single processor with more cache misses.

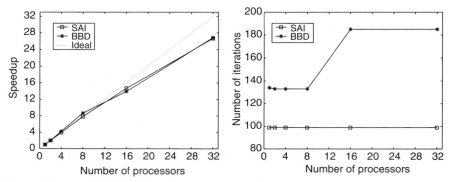

Figure 5.5   The diagram for scalability comparison of the SAI and BBD preconditioners [27]. Parameters are selected as: for SAI, $\tau_1 = 0.05$, $\tau_2 = 0.001$; for BBD, $w_1 = 8$, $w_2 = 5$. Left: speedup obtained versus. the number of processors used. Right: the number of iterations versus. the number of processors used.

5.3   BRAIN DEFORMATION SIMULATION IN IMAGE-GUIDED NEUROSURGERY

5.3.1   Background

During the past decade, the development of image-guided surgery techniques has been playing a crucial role in minimizing invasive neurosurgery. The neurosurgeon is allowed to acquire new images during surgery by exploiting these newly developed and advanced techniques, which are performed in operating rooms equipped with imaging devices for special purposes. These images, as acquired by intraoperative ultrasound or intraoperative magnetic resonance imaging, can provide improved contrast between normal and diseased tissues, and enable people to gain better understanding of the brain by exposing deeper structure of the brain through the surface, because the major difficulty a neurosurgeon has to confront is the removal from the brain of as much tumor tissue as possible, while minimizing the removal of healthy tissue and preventing the disruption of important anatomical structures like white matter fiber tracts [4].

Image-guided neurosurgery heavily relies upon the visualization of the underlying brain tissue structure. Recent reviews by Jolesz [30] and Warfield et al. [4] point out the importance and great potential impact of the image-guidance on more invasive surgical procedures. Efforts have been largely focused on the issues concerned with image acquisition, visualization, and registration of intraoperative and preoperative data, to supply the surgeon with a better visualization environment to derive quantitative assessment of intraoperative imaging data and qualitative judgments. Intraoperative image guidance is based on functional integration of the previously acquired and processed three-dimensional image-based visual information and the corresponding anatomy of the patient within the same frame of reference, which requires matching of the two frames of reference [30]. The actual coordinates used by the models of surgical planning and simulation must be mapped or registered onto the physical space of the patient. These two ingredients are connected together by combining image-to-patient registration and by tracking instruments within the surgical field. They are the crucial components of frameless stereotactic targeting methods, which capitalize on the interactive control of image planes and explore the full information contained in the perceived three-dimensional space. Reliable and completely automated registration techniques are desired to integrate the image-based information with the patient's anatomy. However, as noticed in Ref. [4, 30], the existing methods for rigid registration and visualization impose limitations on image-guided treatment process in deep brain structures with large resections. The restrictions motivate the development of improved approaches for visualization and better algorithms for registration, which can capture the non-rigid deformation of the brain during operation.

During the process of neurosurgery, the shape of the brain gets deformed in response to mechanical and physiological changes related to the surgery. Many different approaches have been proposed to characterize these changes and to construct integrated visualizations of preoperative data in the architecture of the deformed brain, which can be roughly divided into three types. Techniques classified in the first category rely on some form of physics-oriented deformation models, which assume that the image space deformation is subject to the theory of physical laws, like elasticity in continuum mechanics. The second type of techniques is purely image-based approaches based on some image-related constraint criteria [31–33]. The third category uses physical deformation models to constrain the deformation field derived from image data using elastic [34, 35] or viscous fluid deformation models [36–39]. The third category is different from the techniques in the first category in that it does not take into consideration the actual material characteristics of the brain, where the matching is trying to minimize an energy measure that includes a weighted sum of an image similarity term and a relaxation term representing the potential energy of a physical body. This survey will only focus on the techniques in the first category, which take into account the physical properties and material characteristics of the underlying depicted objects, and thus are believed to be able to drastically improve the robustness and accuracy of deformable models [4, 40].

A very good review can be found in Ref. [4] for physics-based models in support of the image-guided neurosurgery, which ranges from less physically plausible, but very fast models, to extremely accurate biomechanical models demanding hours of computational time to get the solution and are developed and implemented under serial computing environments. We first briefly go through a couple of the typical physics-based models for capturing the brain deformations. Then in the following sections, the elasticity theory-based biomechanical models and simulations are surveyed in more detail, with the focus on the ones which have been implemented in parallel under different parallel environments.

5.3.2 Physics-Based Brain Deformation Models

In Ref. [41], a biomechanical model for brain deformation simulation based on linear elasticity theory is proposed to deal with the deformations rising during surgical interventions, by using a finite element discretization method. Two-dimensional implementation of the model is carried out with two different materials being distinguished, namely brain tissue and skull bone. Instead of applying forces in the model, a set of manually determined correspondences is used to drive the deformation of the preoperative image. The finite element mesh is constructed by using four-node quadrilateral finite elements, in accordance with the underlying pixel grid of 2D images. The registration experiments are performed for the case of synthetic images and for real brain image data, with a preoperative MR image of the human brain and a corresponding postoperative image simulating an intraoperative image. The tests from both the cases yield physically plausible deformation results. The time cost to process an image with a size of 256×256 pixels is around 45 min on a Sun Ultra 2/1300 machine with a 300 MHz CPU.

An algorithm attempting to track the intraoperative tissue deformation is presented in Ref. [42], which is based on a simple 2D three-component model consisting of rigid, deformable, and fluid regions. The deformable region is allowed to have a number of energy characteristics, such as stiffness and tension energies, and a fold avoidance strategy is used in this algorithm. The clinical data are utilized to carry out the tests. Their multigrid implementation on 2D images with a size of 128×128 pixels takes about 120 to 180 min to obtain the solution when the test is run on a Sun Sparc 20 machine.

The Kelvin solid model, a simplified homogeneous brain tissue material model, is exploited by the model proposed in Ref. [43] for the interconnection of mass nodes to capture real-time brain shift under gravity, with boundary conditions to simulate the interaction of the brain with the skull. The surface displacement is calculated by tracking the brain surface points in this approach. In the discretized deformation model, there are 2088 nodes, 11,733 connections, and 1521 brick elements, and the time required to simulate the system typically runs in 10 min on an SGI Octane R10000 machine with one 250 MHz processor.

Ferrant et al. [44] present an integrated approach that uses surface-based correspondences to derive a biomechanical model of the brain instead of using estimates of forces, which allows the analysis of the characteristics of the deformed tissues, like stress measures. More specifically, the biomechanical model is driven by imposing displacements to critical boundary surfaces. The displacements at the boundary surfaces are calculated using an active surface-matching algorithm, which determines the correspondences between landmark surfaces in the pre- and intraoperative images. The finite element method is used for discretization which results in approximately tetrahedra in the finite element mesh. Under such 100,000 size mesh, the running time of the entire deformation algorithm is around 30 min on a Sun Ultra 10 workstation with one 440 MHz processor, whereas with four CPUs, the computation time is about 10 min.

A three-dimensional physical model adapted from consolidation theory in soil mechanics is developed in Refs. [45–48], which treats the brain as a solid tissue filled with interstitial fluid where the tissue displacement is characterized by an instantaneous deformation at the contact area followed by subsequent additional deformation due to interstitial fluid draining in the direction of strain-induced pressure gradients. Miga et al. [47] augment the technique to incorporate the simulation of brain tissue retraction and resection. This computational model, combined with the intraopera-tively acquired data, which is usually incomplete and sparse, is exploited to update high-resolution preoperative images and then to estimate the brain deformation in vivo through a series of controlled repeat-experiments during surgery. The finite element method is applied to discretize the model, and the intraoperative computation with the real human brain image data takes about 5–18 min to get the numerical solutions in a 3D tetrahedra mesh with 19,000 nodes.

5.3.3 Biomechanical Models with Parallel Implementation

5.3.3.1 Elastic Deformation of Volumetric Solid A real-time model for surgery simulation to calculate the elastic deformation of a volumetric solid is devel-oped and described in Ref. [49]. The mesh-based 3D finite element scheme with linear elastic deformation is exploited to model the general elastic volumetric deformation. The strain energy of a linear elastic solid Ω is defined as

$$E(u) = \frac{1}{2} \int \int \int_{\Omega} \epsilon^{\mathrm{T}} \sigma \, dx, \tag{5.11}$$

where u is the displacement of particle $x \in \Omega$, ϵ the strain vector, and σ the stress vector, which is related to the strain vector through Hook's law by $\sigma = D \cdot \epsilon$, where D is a symmetric 6×6 material stiffness matrix. Then the domain Ω of the volu-metric solid is discretized into a number of finite elements in the form of four-node tetrahedrons with linear interpolation of the displacement field between the nodes. The solution to the deformation problem can be found when the potential energy of the system takes its minimum value, which happens when $\delta E(u) = 0$, that is , the first variation of the functional E vanishes. This results in a large sparse linear system

$$Ku = f, \tag{5.12}$$

where K is the stiffness matrix and f the force vector. The linear system (5.12) models the behavior of the solid object and includes both the surface nodes and the internal nodes of the model. As this work only concerns speed instead of precision and memory cost, in the actual simulation, condensation is used to convert the volumetric model into a model with only surface nodes, which is achieved by removing the internal nodes from the linear equation system (5.12). In addition, numerical experiments are performed with explicit inversion, conjugate gradient method with and without preconditioner, Gauss elimination, and several factorization techniques such as QR and Cholesky. Mass and damping are added to the model to have a physically correct model of the solid, which leads to a Lagrangian dynamic system. An alternative simulation method, selective matrix vector multiplication method, is also developed, which is considerably faster for sparse force vectors, based on the idea that uses the original static linear system (5.12) instead of the Lagrangian dynamic system and exploits the sparse structure of the force vector.

The simulation system is implemented on a Silicon Graphics ONYX with four MIPS R4400 processors using SGI Performer graphics library. The actual deformation simulation system runs on a single processor, although the entire system is a parallel one, and the parallel feature is only used to separate rendering from simulation. A model of the lower leg is used as an example to perform the real-time simulation of solid volumetric deformable models. Performance of the dynamic simulation methods is determined only by the size of the linear system, whereas it is more difficult to predict the performance of the methods using the selective matrix vector multiplication scheme [49]. Using the dynamic simulation scheme, the rate of 20 frames/s is achieved with up to 250 nodes in the system equation. The model presented in [49] is applicable for real-time surgical simulation where video frame rates are required.

Bro-Nielsen [50] also employs the finite element model of linear elasticity to simulate the elastic deformation of a volumetric solid object in real-time. Condensation is used to remove the internal nodes from the linear matrix system (5.12), which has the same size as would result from a finite element surface model. The condensed problem shows exactly the same behavior for the surface nodes as the original solid volumetric system. The selective matrix vector multiplication approach is applied to solve the linear system (5.12), which is based on the fact that only a few positions of the force vector f are non-zero. As Eq. (5.12) is solved by using the inverted stiffness matrix K as $u = K^{-1}f$, the scheme will reduce the complexity to $O(n/N)$ times the time of a normal matrix vector multiplication if n of the N positions in f is non-zero. The solution of the linear system (5.12) is implemented in parallel using domain decomposition, where the domain of the solid Ω is decomposed into a number of non-overlapping sub-domains Ω_i with a common boundary Γ. The nodes of the global stiffness matrix K are ordered in such a way that the nodes on the boundary Γ are ordered first, followed by sections of nodes corresponding to the subdomains Ω_i. Then the condensation technique is used to separate the computation of the individual subdomains, each of which can be handled by one processor with the result reduced to a root processor. The simulation system is implemented on the same platform with the same physical organ data set, the lower leg as used in Ref. [49], but no result or performance data is reported under the parallel environment.

5.3.3.2 *Elastic Deformation Model Integrated with Optical Flow*   In Ref. [40], an integrated hybrid approach is proposed to implicitly compute the forces applied to the 3D deformation model by constraining the deformation field to satisfy both the elasticity model and the model based on optical flow methods, where the objects are modeled as elastic bodies. The optical flow methods for recovering image deformation are largely based on local image structure [51, 52], which simulates the deformation field between images to satisfy some prechosen smoothness constraints by minimizing local similarity criteria. The satisfaction with both models is achieved in Ref. [40] by embedding an image similarity constraint on the deformation field into the minimization scheme, which results in the constitutive equations of the deformation model. The main difference between the hybrid technique and the purely image-based optical flow method is that the former technique takes into account the actual physical properties of the deformed objects to be deformed and

allows the thorough investigation of the characteristics of the deformed objects by providing information about the physically realistic deformation field, while the latter does not. Another difference is that the hybrid technique computes a global solution to the deformation field instead of a collection of local solutions as the optical flow method does. The integrated model could be very useful for the inspection of stresses induced by the deformation of certain objects on their surroundings, which might be used to predict deformations due to the growth of tumors and brain shift during neurosurgery. The hybrid model [40] is discussed in detail, subsequently.

The fundamental step behind the integrated approach is to formulate the elastic matching of two images as an energy minimization procedure, where the energy consists of two terms. One term is used to simulate the physical behavior of the object to be deformed, while the other one drives the model in order to make both images match. The deformation field minimizes the sum of the squared differences between the images to be matched and at the same time is constrained by the biomechanical properties of the different objects represented by the image.

Under the assumption of a linear elastic continuum with no initial stresses or strains, the potential energy of an elastic body subject to externally applied forces can be described as

$$E = \int_{\Omega} \sigma^{\mathrm{T}} \epsilon \, d\Omega + \int_{\Omega} Fu \, d\Omega, \tag{5.13}$$

where F is the force vector applied to the elastic body, u the displacement vector, and Ω the elastic body. The strain vector, ϵ, is defined as

$$\epsilon = \left(\frac{\partial u}{\partial x}, \frac{\partial u}{\partial y}, \frac{\partial u}{\partial z}, \frac{\partial u}{\partial x} + \frac{\partial u}{\partial y}, \frac{\partial u}{\partial y} + \frac{\partial u}{\partial z}, \frac{\partial u}{\partial x} + \frac{\partial u}{\partial z} \right)^{\mathrm{T}} = Lu. \tag{5.14}$$

The constitutive equation of the material regulates the relationship between the stress vector σ and the strain vector ϵ, and in the case of linear elasticity without initial stresses or strains, it is expressed as

$$\sigma = (\sigma_x, \sigma_y, \sigma_z, \tau_{xy}, \tau_{yz}, \tau_{xz})^{\mathrm{T}} = D\epsilon, \tag{5.15}$$

where D is the elasticity matrix characterizing the properties of the material.

The deformation field governed by the elastic model is first initialized to be the optical flow field, as the external forces F can be calculated as a typical optical flow field between the images to be matched (I_1 and I_2). The initial estimate can then be iteratively refined until an equilibrium is reached by a semi-implicit method. In Ref. [40], the deformation field is computed to simultaneously satisfy both the elasticity constraint and a local image similarity constraint between the images I_1 and I_2, to avoid the separate computation of the forces F, the elastic deformation, and the matching criterion. Thus Eq. (5.13) can be expressed as

$$E = \int_{\Omega} \sigma^{\mathrm{T}} \epsilon \, d\Omega + \int_{\Omega} (I_1(x + u(x)) - I_2(x))^2 \, d\Omega, \tag{5.16}$$

where $I_1(x + u(x))$ is approximated by the first-order Taylor expansion as in Ref. [40] the deformation field is assumed to be small relative to the variation of I_1 smooth.

Finite-element-based scheme is exploited in Ref. [40] to solve Eq. (5.16) and compute the deformation field, which corresponds to the global minimum of the total energy. Within their finite element discretization framework, the physical domain is discretized by using tetrahedral elements that are simpler than other elements according to the shape function and data structure, with linear interpolation of the displacement field. The displacements are a function of the displacement at the element's nodal points weighted by the element's shape function. The elastic body can then be approximated as an assemblage of discrete tetrahedral elements interconnected at nodal points on the element boundaries. The mesh structure is constructed in the way such that for images containing multiple objects, a fully connected and consistent tetrahedral mesh is generated for each cell, with a given label corresponding to the object the cell belongs to. Likewise various biomechanical properties are assigned to the different cells or objects composing the mesh without difficulty.

After the implementation of finite element algorithm, the linear system is solved in parallel by using the portable, extensible toolkit for scientific computation (PETSc) library, which provides a collection of numerical software tools for solving large-scale sparse nonlinear systems of equations in parallel and relies on the MPI for interprocessor communication (http://acts.nersc.gov/petsc/main.html). The timing of the matching algorithm, which uses a tetrahedra mesh with the size of approximately a 100,000, is reported to be around a couple of minutes when the simulation is carried out on a parallel machine with 20 Ultra Sparc II 250 MHz CPUs. Synthetic image data and real medical data are used in the experiments to test the proposed integrated model, where the objects are considered to be homogeneous elastic bodies. The tested medical applications include the muscle exercise imaging and ventricular deformation in multiple sclerosis obtained from 3D brain MRI images. In these examples, the hybrid model is well suited for the small biomechanical deformations which deform the shape of objects over time.

5.3.3.3 *Linear Elastic Model*   Warfield et al. [4] present an algorithm to create enhanced visualization of tumor and critical brain structure during neurosurgery by combining both preoperatively generated surface models of the corticospinal tract from an anatomical atlas with intraoperative MRI and the biomechanical model inferring the 3D volumetric deformation of the brain and ventricles of the patient. The algorithm tracks the surface changes of key structures in intraoperatively acquired brain images by aligning preoperatively acquired image data with intraoperative images of the patient's brain, as its shape changes during the neurosurgical procedure. A volumetric deformation field is derived from the shape changes to capture the non-rigid deformations of the shape of the brain in response to mechanical and physiological changes associated with the surgery. An enhanced and integrated visualization is then constructed by exploiting the solution to the deformation field simulated by the biomechanical model and the projection of a preoperatively built model of the brain into the configuration of the deformed brain.

In Ref. [4], the biomechanical simulation of the volumetric brain deformation is conducted by modeling the brain as an elastic object with homogeneous linear elasticity. When there is no initial stresses or strains, the deformation energy of this elastic body submitted to externally applied forces is modeled as

$$E = \frac{1}{2} \int_{\Omega} \sigma^{T} \epsilon \, d\Omega + \int_{\Omega} F^{T} u \, d\Omega, \tag{5.17}$$

where F is the vector denoting the forces applied to the elastic body, u the unknown displacement vector field, Ω the elastic body, ϵ the strain vector, and σ the stress vector. ϵ and σ are related to each other by the constitutive equations of the material, Eq. (5.15). Strain is linked to displacement by the assumption $\epsilon = L^{T} u$, where L is a linear operator.

The finite element method is used to generate a volumetric unstructured tetrahedral mesh in the image domain, on which the biomechanical simulation of deformation is performed. The volumetric deformation of the brain is obtained by solving the displacement field that minimizes the deformation energy described in Eq. (5.17). This yields a linear equation system, which is solved for the displacements due to the forces applied to the elastic body

$$Ku = -F, \tag{5.18}$$

where K is the stiffness matrix. Equation (5.18) is solved in a way such that the derived deformation field over the entire mesh matches the prescribed displacements at the boundary surfaces by fixing the displacements at the boundary surface nodes to match those generated by the active surface model. The entries of the rows in K corresponding to the nodes at which a displacement is to be imposed are set to zero and the diagonal elements of these rows are set to 1. The force vector F is set to be the displacement vector, to be imposed at the boundary nodes.

To achieve the timing constraint set by the real-time situation of neurosurgery as well as robustness and high accuracy in the matching of brain image data, the linear equation system (5.18) is implemented and solved in parallel with the PETSc package using the generalized minimal residual (GMRES) solver with a block Jacobi preconditioning scheme. The rows of the global stiffness matrix K are divided equally among the different processors such that each processor has an equal number of rows to compute and it assembles the local K^{e} matrix for each element in its subdomain. After the global matrix K is assembled in parallel, it is adjusted to reflect the enforced boundary conditions determined by the surface matching. The total number of mesh nodes is 43,584, which specifies 214,035 tetrahedral elements and represents a system of 130,752 unknown displacements to be identified. The brain deformation simulation during neurosurgery is carried out on a Sun Microsystems StarFire 6800 symmetric multi-processor machine with 12 UltraSPARC-III processors running at 750 MHz and 12 GB of RAM.

A set of parallel scaling experiments are performed to demonstrate the scaling characteristics of the implementation with the timings for solving the biomechanical model under serial and parallel environment reported as well as good simulation results of volumetric brain deformation. In the case of serial computing environment, that is, on a single processor, it takes 17 s to assemble the system of equations, 37 s to get the solution of the linear system of equations, and 57 s for the overall solution time, which includes the time for initialization. Under the parallel environment, 12 processors are used and the parallel assembly of system of equations costs 3 s, solving the linear system costs 9 s, and the overall solution time requires 15 s. In Ref. [4], a context is provided to compare the timings for the biomechanical simulation with the other intraoperative image analysis and acquisition tasks that are intraoperatively indispensable. The results show that the most computationally demanding task, the deformation simulation, becomes the fastest component and, the complete execution time for the intraoperative image analysis is less than 10 min. Their experiments demonstrate the capability of the algorithm to meet the real-time constraints of neurosurgery, and even a relatively complicated biomechanical simulation of brain deformation could be simulated sufficiently fast at a rate that is practical for routine use during neurosurgery.

5.3.3.4 Volumetric Biomechanical Model with A Priori Knowledge A patient-specific biomechanical model based on block matching to register MRI images of the same patient with a parallel implementation is illustrated in [53], which combines a viscoelastic mechanical regularization with a correlation-based iconic energy term. It relies on a dynamic law of motion of a tetrahedral mesh, which leads to iteratively solving a linear system of equations.

In the registration algorithm of [53], a priori anatomical and mechanical knowledge is integrated through a volumetric biomechanical model of the brain. In the deformable model framework, a balance between mechanical and iconic influences is considered during the full registration process through an energy minimization. The internal energy which manipulates the displacement field is based upon linear elasticity in continuum mechanics. The volumetric external energy based on 3D block matching is used in their biomechanical model. With such an energy, full motion of the organ can be registered, more complicated deformation can be estimated inside the model, and the quality of the registration does not count on the surface segmentation accuracy. The external energy exploited is relied on the assumption that the intensity around a given vertex of the mesh should be similar in the two images with the difference only from noise and anatomical changes. A surrounding block of voxels from the reference image is attached to each vertex and the most similar block around the current position is searched in the target image. The center of the block is chosen to be the matching voxel, which maximizes the prescribed similarity criterion. The external force calculated for each voxel is then proportional to the distance to the matching voxel, and its orientation is from the vertex current position to the position of the matching voxel.

The inertia effect is also taken into consideration in the brain deformation model by using a dynamic approach, which is efficient and stable to find a balance between external and internal energies. The dynamic equation of motion is described as

$$M\frac{\mathrm{d}^2 U}{\mathrm{d}t^2} + C\frac{\mathrm{d}U}{\mathrm{d}t} + KU = F, \tag{5.19}$$

where M is the mass density matrix, C the damping matrix, K the stiffness matrix, U the displacement from the rest position ($P(t) = P(0) + U(t)$ with $P(t)$ the position at time t), and F the external force vector computed from the image matching.

The finite element method is used to discretize the physical domain, with linear tetrahedral elements in space and the semi-implicit Houbolt scheme in time. The discretization results in a linear system to solve in $U(t + \Delta t)$ at each iteration. The stiffness matrix K is chosen to be constant with the assumption of linear elasticity. The numerical integration of the discretized time-dependent system involves two steps, the initialization step and the procedure of solving the linear system. The initialization procedure includes matrix assembly, the effective stiffness matrix calculation, $\bar{K} = K + a_0 M + a_1 C$ with a_0 and a_1 being constants, and the preconditioner matrix construction for $\bar{K}$ which is performed only once for the overall process. Then at each time step, a linear system of equations, $\bar{K}U(t + \Delta t) = \bar{F}(t + \Delta t)$, is iteratively solved with the computed effective external forces $\bar{F}(t + \Delta t)$, and then the node positions are updated. The parallelization of the registration process uses a distributed memory model, where each processor computes the biomechanical and image forces in a subdomain of the global mesh. The tetrahedral mesh is partitioned using the METIS software (www-users.cs.umn.edu/~karypis/metis) and each vertex of the mesh is assigned to a processor in such a way to minimize the communication cost. Each processor computes the external forces for the vertices corresponding to the associated submesh.

The PETSc library is applied to solve the linear system of equations in parallel. The stiffness matrix is computed, preconditioned, and distributed at the beginning of the process. Several different iterative solvers, conjugate gradient (CG), GMRES, and BIConjugate Gradient STABilized (BICGSTAB), with the ILUT and Incomplete Cholesky (IC) preconditioners are tested and compared for a mesh of 2000 nodes on a PC equipped with an Intel Pentium IV 2 GHz processor. It is found that BICGSTAB with ILUT has the least number of iterations and the shortest total solution time, whereas CG with IC has the largest number of iterations and the longest total solution time and GMRES with ILUT sits between the number of iterations and the total solution time.

The performance of the algorithm is evaluated on synthesized images and on real brain images. The experiments are conducted on a cluster of PCs consisting of 14 Intel Pentium IV 2 GHz processors interconnected by a gigabit-ethernet switch.

In the case of synthesized image data, the underlying tetrahedral mesh of the brain contains around 2000 vertices with block-matching searching range being 5 mm and searching step being 2 mm. The relationship between the number of processors and the speedup of one time step shows that the speedup decreases fast, due to the relatively coarse mesh used in the test. The influence of the damping factor on the convergence of the algorithm is also investigated. It demonstrates that the dynamic effects of the damping factor is critical in the registration computation process, where a small value of it leads to an instability whereas a large value results in a large computation time. The optimum damping factor for this case is found to be 0.015, by which the error tolerance is reached in less than 3 min on 14 processors. The analysis of the robustness of the algorithm to noise is also presented, which shows that it performs well with a high degree of noise (white Gaussian noise on intensity) on images with a similar measure of the correlation coefficient.

In the case of tests on real brain images, there are 30,000 vertices in the tetrahedral mesh with block-matching searching range and searching step being 5 and 2 mm, respectively. Each image is computed in less than a minute. The results show that the volumetric biomechanical registration is well suited to recover a physical deformation and a good capability of deforming internal structure illustrated in the difference image. The efficiency of the volumetric external energy is also demonstrated by the ability to recover the surface displacement with only internal constraints. However, there are no tests reported on timing, damping factor, and robustness comparisons with the real brain image data.

5.4 SUMMARY

Parallel computation in simulating diffusion and deformation of the human brain is a new field of exploration. The driving force in the use of parallel computing in these biomedical applications is the need to increase real-time speed. The response time is of vital importance in image-guided neurosurgery, and more accurate simulations usually demand more computing time.

It can be said that parallel computation in biomedical applications is still in its early development stage, with the gradual realization of the importance of reducing computing time in simulations in the application community. With more sophisticated and complicated simulations to be designed in the future, and the need for fast and high definition imaging techniques, parallel computation will undoubtedly find its way in large-scale biomedical applications. There are ample opportunities for computational scientists to work with biomedical scientists to develop high-performance computing tools and platforms for biomedical applications.

ACKNOWLEDGMENTS

Ning Kang thanks the U.S. Department of Energy Office of Science for its support under grant DE-FG02-02ER45964. Jun Zhang was partly supported by the U.S. National Science Foundation under grants CCR-9988165, CCR-0092532 and CCR-0202934, partly supported by the U.S. Department of Energy Office of Science under grant DE-FG02- 02ER45961 and partly supported by the university of Kentucky Research Committee. Carlson was supported by the U.S. Department of Energy office of science under grant DE-FG02-02 ER45961.

REFERENCES

1. D. Le Bihan, J. F. Mangin, C. Poupon, C. A. Clark, S. Pappata, N. Molko, and H. Chabriat, "Diffusion Tensor Imaging: Concepts and Application," *J. Mag. Res. Imaging*, 13, 534–546 (2001).

2. T. E. Conturo, N. F. Lori, T. S. Cull, E. Akbudak, A. Z. Snyder, J. S. Shimony, R. C. McKinstry, H. Burton, and M. E. Raichle, Tracking Neuronal Fiber Pathways in the Living Human Brain, *Proc. Natl. Acad. Sci. U.S.A.*, 96, 10422–10427 (1999).

3. M. Guye, G. J. M. Parker, M. Symms, P. Boulby, C. A. M. Wheeler-Kingshott, A. Salek-Haddadi, G. J. Barker, and J. S. Duncana, "Combined Functional MRI and Tractography to Demonstrate the Connectivity of the Human Primary Motor Cortex in vivo," *NeuroImage*, 19, 1349–1360 (2003).

4. S. K. Warfield, F. Talos, A. Tei, A. Bharatha, A. Nabavi, M. Ferrant, P. M. Black, F. A. Jolesz, and R. Kikinis, "Real-Time Registration of Volumetric Brain MRI by Biomechanical Simulation of Deformation during Image Guided Neurosurgery," *Comput. Visual. Sci.*, 5, 3–11 (2002).

5. S. E. Rose, F. Chen, J. B. Chalk, F. O. Zelaya, W. E. Strugnell, M. Benson, J. Semple, and D. Doddrell, "Loss of Connectivity in Alzheimer's Disease: An Evaluation of White Matter Tract Integrity with Colour Coded MR Diffusion Tensor Imaging," *J. Neurol. Neurosurg. Psychiat.*, 69, 528–530 (2000).

6. B. Stieltjes, M. Schluter, H. K. Hahn, T. Wilhelm, and M. Essig, "Diffusion Tensor Imaging: Theory, Sequence Optimization and Application in Alzheimer's Disease," *Radiologe*, 43 (7), 562–565, July (2003).

7. B. A. Ardekani, J. Nierenberg, M. J. Hoptman, D. C. Javitt, and K. O. Lim, MRI study of white matter diffusion anisotropy in schizophrenia, *Neuroreport*, 14 (16), 2025–2029 (2003).

8. J. Foong, M. Maier, C. A. Clark, G. J. Barker, D. H. Miller, and M. A. Ron, Neuropathological abnormalities of the corpus callosum in schizophrenia: a diffusion tensor imaging study, *J. Neurol. Neurosurg. Psychiat.*, 68 (2), 242–244 (2000).

9. C. Beaulieu, "The Basis of Anisotropic Water Diffusion in the Nervous System — a Technical Review," *NMR Biomed.*, 15, 435–455 (2002).

10. P. J. Basser, J. Mattiello, and D. Le Bihan, Estimation of the effective self-diffusion tensor from the NMR spin echo," *J. Mag. Res.*, Ser. B, 103, 247–254 (1994).

11. A. B. M. Björnemo, "White Matter Fiber Tracking Using Diffusion Tensor MRI," Master's Thesis, Linkoping University, Sweden, 2002.

12. S. Mori and P. C. M. van Zijl, "Fiber Tracking: Principles and Strategies — a Technical Review," *NMR Biomed.*, 15, 468–480 (2002).

13. P. G. Batchelor, D. L. G. Hill, F. Calamante, and D. Atkinson, Study of Connectivity in the Brain Using the Full Diffusion Tensor from MRI, *Information Processing in Medical Imaging*, in Proceedings of the 17th International Conference, IPMI'01, UC Davies, USA (Published by Springer, *Lecture Notes in Computer Science 2082*, June 2001, pp. 121–133).

14. D. Gembris, H. Schumacher, and D. Suter, "Solving the Diffusion Equation for Fiber Tracking in the Living Human Brain," in *Proceedings of the International Society for Magnetic Resonance Medicine (ISMRM)*, Vol. 9, Glasgow, Scotland, April, 2001, pp. 1529.

15. N. Kang, J. Zhang, E. S. Carlson, and D. Gembris, *White Matter Fiber Tractography via Anisotropic Diffusion Simulation in the Human Brain*, IEEE Trans. Med. Imaging (in press).

16. C. Nicholson and E. Syková, "Extracellular Space Structure Revealed by Diffusion Analysis," *Trends Neurosci.*, 21 (5), 207–215 (1998).

17. I. Vorisek and E. Sykova, "Evolution of Anisotropic Diffusion in the Developing Rat Corpus Callosum," *J. Neurophysiol.*, 78, 912–919 (1997).

18. C. Nicholson, "Diffusion and Related Transport Mechanism in Brain Tissue," *Rep. Prog. Phys.*, 64, 815–884 (2001).

19. P. J. Basser, Inferring microstructural features and the physiological state of tissues from diffusion-weighted images, *NMR Biomed.*, 8, 333–344 (1995).

20. L. O'Donnell, S. Haker, C. F. Westin, "New Approaches to Estimation of White Matter Connectivity in Diffusion Tensor MRI: Elliptic PDEs and Geodesics in a Tensor-Warped Space," in *Proceedings of the MICCAI*, Tokyo, Japan, September, 2002.

21. P. G. Batchelor, D. L. G. Hill, D. Atkinson, F. Calamante, and A. Connelly, Fibre-Tracking by Solving the Diffusion-Convection Equation, *Proc. Intl. Soc. Mag. Res. Med.*, (2002).

22. N. Kang, J. Zhang, and E. S. Carlson, "Performance of ILU Preconditioning Techniques in Simulating Anisotropic Diffusion in the Human Brain," *Future Gener. Comput. Sys.*, 20 (4), 687–698 (2004).

23. J. Xu, "Multidimensional Finite Differencing (MDFD) with Hypersphere-Close-Pack Grids for Numerical Solution of PDE Defined on Irregular Domains," Ph.D. Thesis, University of Alabama, Tuscaloosa, AL, 2001.

24. K. E. Brenan, S. L. Campbell, and L. R. Petzold, *Numerical Solution of Initial-Value Problems in Differential-Algebraic Equations*, SIAM, Philadelphia, PA, 1996.

25. A. C. Hindmarsh and A. G. Taylor, *User Documentation for IDA, a Differential-Algebraic Equation Solver for Sequential and Parallel Computers*, LLNL Report UCRL-MA-136910, Center for Applied Scientific Computing, LLNL, Livermore, CA, 1999.

26. Y. Saad and M. H. Schultz, "GMRES: A Generalized Minimal Residual Algorithm for Solving Nonsymmetric Linear Systems," *SIAM J. Sci. Stat. Comput.*, 7, 856–869 (1986).

27. N. Kang, J. Zhang, and E. S. Carlson, "Parallel Simulation of Anisotropic Diffusion with Human Brain DT-MRI Data," *Comput. Struct.*, 82, 2389–2399 (2004).

28. M. J. Grote and T. Huckle, "Parallel Preconditioning with Sparse Approximate Inverses," *SIAM J. Sci. Comput.*, 18, 838–853 (1997).

29. E. Chow, A priori sparsity patterns for parallel sparse approximate inverse preconditioners, *SIAM J. Sci. Comput.*, 21, 1804–1822 (2000).

30. F. Jolesz, "Image-Guided Procedures and the Operating Room of the Future," *Radiology*, 204, 601–612 (1997).

31. N. Hata, A. Nabavi, W. M. Wells, S. K. Warfield, R. Kikinis, P. M. Black, and F. A. Jolesz, "Three-Dimensional Optical Flow Method for Measurement of Volumetric Brain Deformation from Intraoperative MR Images," *J. Comput. Assisted Tomography*, 24, 531–538, July (2000).

32. D. Hill, C. Maurer, R. Maciunas, J. Barwise, J. Fitzpatrick, and M. Wang, "Measurement of intraoperative brain surface deformation under a Craniotomy," *Neurosurgery*, 43, 514–526 (1998).

33. S. Tang and T. Jiang, "Nonrigid Registration of Medical Image by Linear Singular Blending Techniques," *Pattern Recog. Lett.*, 25 (4), 399–405 (2004).

34. R. Bajcsy and S. Kovacic, Multi-resolution elastic matching, *Comput. Vision Graph. Image Process.*, 46, 1–21 (1989).

35. C. Davatzikos, "Spatial Transformation and Registration of Brain Images Using Elastically Deformable Models," *Comput. Vision Image Understanding*, 66 (2), 207–222 (1997).

36. M. Bro-Nielsen and C. Gramkow, "Fast Fluid Registration of Medical Images," in *Proceeding of the Visualization in Biomedical Computing (VBC'96)*, 1996, pp. 267–276.

37. G. E. Christensen, S. C. Joshi, and M. I. Miller, "Volumetric transformation of brain anatomy," *IEEE Trans. med. Imaging*, 16 (6), 864–877 (1997).

38. G. E. Christensen, M. I. Miller, M. Vannier, and U. Grenander, Individualizing neuroanatomical atlases using a massively parallel computer," *IEEE Comput.*, 29 (1), 32–38 (1996).

39. G. E. Christensen, R. D. Rabbit, and M. I. Miller, "Deformable templates using large deformation kinematics," *IEEE Trans. Image Process.*, 5 (10), 1435–1447 (1996).

40. M. Ferrant, S. K. Warfield, C. R. G. Guttmann, R. V. Mulkern, F. A. Jolesz, and R. Kikinis, "3D Image Matching Using a Finite Element Based Elastic Deformation Model," *in* C. Taylor and A. Colchester, Eds., *Proceedings of the MICCAI 99: Second International Conference on Medical Image Computing and Computer-Assisted Intervention; September 19–22 1999, Cambridge, England*, Springer-Verlag, Heidelberg, Germany, 1999, pp. 202–209.

41. A. Hagemann, K. Rohr, H. S. Stiel, U. Spetzger, and J. M. Gilsbach, "Biomechanical Modeling of the Human Head for Physically Based, Non-Rigid Image Registration," *IEEE Trans. Med. Imaging*, 18 (10), 875–884 (1999).

42. P. J. Edwards, D. L. G. Hill, J. A. Little, and D. J. Hawkes, "Deformation for Image Guided Interventions Using a Three Component Tissue Model," in *proceedings of the IPMI'97*, 1997, pp. 218–231.

43. O. Skrinjar and J. S. Duncan, "Real Time 3D Brain Shift Compensation," in *Proceedings of the IPMI'99*, Visegrad, Hungary, 1999, pp. 42–55.

44. M. Ferrant, S. K. Warfield, A. Nabavi, B. Macq, and R. Kikinis, "Registration of 3D Intra-operative MR Images of the Brain Using a Finite Element Biomechanical Model," in A. M. DiGioia and S. Delp, Eds., *Proceedings of the MICCAI 2000: Third Internation conference on Medical Robotics, Imaging, and Computer Assisted Surgery*, Springer-Verlag, 2000, pp. 19–28.

45. M. I. Miga, K. D. Paulsen, P. J. Hoopes, F. E. Kennedy, Jr., A. Hartov, and D. W. Roberts, "In vivo Quantification of a Homogeneous Brain Deformation Model for Updating Preoperative Images During Surgery," *IEEE Trans. Biomed. Eng.*, 47 (2), 266–273 (2000).

46. M. I. Miga, K. D. Paulsen, F. E. Kennedy, P. J. Hoopes, A. Hartov, and D. W. Roberts, "In vivo Analysis of Heterogeneous Brain Deformation Computations for Model-Updated Image Guidance," *Comput. Meth. Biomech. Biomed. Eng.*, 3 (2), 129–146 (2000).

47. M. I. Miga, D. W. Roberts, F. E. Kennedy, L. A. Platenik, A. Hartov, K. E. Lunn, and K. D. Paulsen, "Modeling of Retraction and Resection for Intraoperative Updating of Images," *Neurosurgery*, 49, 75–85 (2001).

48. K. D. Paulsen, M. I. Miga, F. E. Kennedy, P. J. Hoopes, A. Hartov, and D. W. Roberts, "A Computational Model for Tracking Subsurface Tissue Deformation During Stereotactic Neurosurgery," *IEEE Trans. Biomed. Eng.*, 46 (2), 213–225 (1999).

49. M. Bro-Nielsen and S. Cotin, "Real-Time Volumetric Deformable Models for Surgery Simulation Using Finite Elements and Condensation," in J. Rossignac and F. Sillion (Guest Editors) *Proceedings of the Eurographics'96*, Blackwell Publishers, 15 (3), 57–66 (1996).

50. M. Bro-Nielsen, "Surgery Simulation Using Fast Finite Elements," *Visualization in Biomedical Computing*, Springer-Verlag, Heidelberg, Germany, 1996, pp. 529–534.

51. S. Bauchemin and J. L. Barron, The Computation of Optical Flow, *ACM Comput. Surv.*, 27 (3) (1995).

52. J. Dengler and M. Schmidt, The Dynamic Pyramid — a Model for Motion Analysis with Controlled Continuity, *Int. J. Pattern Recogn. Artif. Intell.*, 2, 275–288 (1988).

53. M. Sermesant, O. Clatz, Z. Li, S. Lantéri, H. Delingette, and N. Ayache, "A Parallel Implementation of Non-Rigid Registration Using a Volumetric Biomechanical Model," J. C. Gee et al. Eds. in *proceeding of the WBIR 2003 LNCS 2717*, 2003, pp. 398–407.

PART II

SEQUENCE ANALYSIS AND MICROARRAYS

CHAPTER 6

Computational Molecular Biology

AZZEDINE BOUKERCHE and ALBA CRISTINA MAGALHÃES ALVES DE MELO

6.1 INTRODUCTION

Proteins are the fundamental building blocks of all living organisms. They are made up of chains of aminoacids, which are obtained in the DNA (deoxyribonucleic acid) translation process. Protein sequences are usually determined from the DNA sequences which encode them. The process of discovering the properties of a newly sequenced DNA is very difficult for several reasons. First, the proteins are encoded in pieces of DNA and most genomes contain some pieces of DNA which do not encode proteins. Thus, biologists are faced with the problem of determining where a protein sequence starts and stops. After determining a protein sequence, one must infer its function. Usually, this is done by comparing the newly sequenced DNA against DNA sequences for which the functionality has already been established. Many efforts have been made to collect the determined sequences and place them in publicly accessible databases. The problem is that these databases are huge and, by now, they have presented an exponential growth rate. Therefore, biological sequence comparison is one of the most important and basic problems in computational biology, given the number and diversity of the sequences and the frequency on which it is needed to be solved daily all over the world [27]. Sequence comparison, also called sequence alignment, is in fact a problem of finding an approximate pattern matching between two biological sequences, possibly introducing spaces (gaps) into them.

The most important types of sequence alignment problems are global and local. To solve a global alignment problem is to find the best match between the entire sequences. Local alignment algorithms must find the best match (or matches) between parts of the sequences. Needleman and Wunsh (NW) [21] proposed an algorithm based on dynamic programming to solve the global alignment problem. This is an exact algorithm that finds the best global alignment(s) between two genomic sequences of size n in quadratic time complexity and space complexity $O(n^2)$. Smith and Waterman (SW) [28] proposed an algorithm which is a variation of the algorithm proposed by NW, which finds the best local alignment(s) between two genomic sequences. Its time

Parallel Computing for Bioinformatics and Computational Biology, Edited by Albert Y. Zomaya
Copyright © 2006 John Wiley & Sons, Inc.

and space complexities are also $O(n^2)$. In genome projects, the size of the sequences to be compared is constantly increasing, thus an $O(n^2)$ solution is still expensive. For this reason, heuristics were proposed to reduce time complexity to $O(n)$. BLAST [8] and FASTA [22] are examples of widely used heuristics to compute local alignments. Some heuristics [9, 30] were also proposed to reduce space complexity.

In this chapter, we first introduce some basic concepts in molecular biology that are related to the DNA sequence comparison problem (Section 6.2). In Section 6.3, the global and local sequence alignment problems are defined and the exact algorithms based on dynamic programming to solve the global and local sequence alignment problems are discussed in detail. Section 6.4 presents some heuristics, which are widely used to solve the local alignment problem. Finally, Section 6.5 discusses some parallel and distributed algorithms proposed to achieve biological sequence alignment in a shorter time.

6.2 BASIC CONCEPTS IN MOLECULAR BIOLOGY

The DNA is a biochemical macromolecule comprised of nucleotide chains, which contain genetic information [27]. DNA is responsible for propagate the characteristics of one organism from one generation to another. It is comprised by sequences of four nitrogenous bases or nucleotides: adenine (A), thymine (T), guanine (G), and cytosine (C). In the DNA chain, adenine always pairs with thymine. Similarly, guanine always pairs with cytosine. This can be explained as adenine and thymine are linked together through two hydrogen bonds, whereas guanine and cytosine establish three hydrogen bonds. The pairs A–T and G–C are called base pairs (bp). Multiplier prefixes are usually used, such as kb and Mb, indicating thousands and millions of nucleotides, respectively. The DNA molecule has the shape of a double helix and the nucleotides are connected to each other forming a strand with two termini: 5' and 3'. The full DNA sequence of an organism is known as a genome. Figure 6.1 represents a fragment of a DNA sequence.

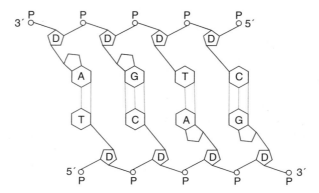

Figure 6.1   Fragment of a DNA sequence containing 4 bp.

Proteins are made up of chains of aminoacids, which are obtained in the DNA translation process. The information needed to obtain aminoacids is organized in codons, which are triplet series of nucleotides. The proteins alphabet contains 20 symbols, which are presented in Table 6.1.

The goal of a genome–sequencing project is to determine the exact order in which the nucleotides appear in a particular genome. Sometimes, it cannot be decided exactly which nucleotide occupies a given position. This is called ambiguity and, in this case, the standard IUPAC (International Union of Pure and Applied Chemistry) one-letter codes are used.

Once the genome sequence was obtained, it has to be analyzed. This analysis can be made at the nucleotide level or at the protein level, and it is usually achieved by comparing the newly sequenced DNA against DNA sequences for which the characteristics are already known. The goal of sequence comparison is to determine the similarities between two genetic sequences. For the similarity regions, the biologists can infer that both sequences are homologous, that is, they diverged during evolution from a common origin. Homologous sequences may or may not present the same functionality [27].

Many genomic databases are available all over the world. By now, the most widely used are GenBank from the NCBI (National Center for Biotechnology Information), SwissProt from the Swiss Institute of Bioinformatics, and PIR from the Protein Information Resource. These three databases can be found in www.ncbi.nlm.nih.govgenbank, ca.expasy.org, and pir.georgetown.eduhome.shtml, respectively.

TABLE 6.1   Proteins Alphabet

Name	Symbol (Three Letters)	Symbol (One Letter)
Alanine	Ala	A
Cystine	Cys	C
Aspartic acid	Asp	D
Glutamic acid	Glu	E
Phenylalanine	Phe	F
Glycine	Gli	G
Histidine	His	H
Isoleucine	Ile	I
Lysine	Lys	K
Leucine	Leu	L
Methionine	Met	M
Asparagine	Asn	N
Proline	Pro	P
Glutamine	Gln	Q
Arginine	Arg	R
Serine	Ser	S
Threonine	Thr	T
Valine	Val	V
Tryptophan	Trp	W
Tyrosine	Tyr	Y

6.3 GLOBAL AND LOCAL BIOLOGICAL SEQUENCE ALIGNMENT

DNA sequences and protein sequences are treated as long sequences depicted, respectively, by {A, T, G, C} and {A, C, D, E, F, G, H, I, K, L, M, N, P, Q, R, S, T, V, W, Y}. To compare two biological sequences, we need to determine whether a given pattern (sequence 1) appears in a given text (sequence 2). Exact searching is not usually done in this case, because it is unlikely that biological patterns match the text exactly.

Therefore, the problem of comparing two biological sequences is in fact a problem of approximate pattern matching, where the goal is to find a given pattern in a given text, allowing a limited number of errors in the matches [20]. In this context, a key concept is the error model, which defines how different two strings are. Depending on the type of errors being considered, the time needed to obtain solutions can range from linear to exponential.

For any string, $s \in \Sigma^*$, we denote its length as $|s|$. We also denote s_i, the ith character of s, for an integer $i \in \{1 \cdots |s|\}$. We also denote $s_{i,\ldots,j} = s_i s_{i+1} \cdots s_j$.

Using these previously defined notations, the problem of approximate pattern matching can be defined as follows [20]:

- Let Σ be a finite alphabet of size $|\Sigma| = \sigma$.
- Let $T \in \Sigma^*$ be a *text* of length $n = |T|$.
- Let $P \in \Sigma^*$ be a *pattern* of length $m = |P|$.
- Let $k \in \Re$ be the maximum error allowed.
- Let $d: \Sigma^* \times \Sigma^* \to \Re$ be a *distance function*.
- Given T, P, k, and $d(\cdot)$ return the set of all the text positions j such that there exists i with $d(P, T_{i,\ldots,j}) \le k$.

The distance $d(x, y)$ between strings x and y is the minimal cost of a sequence of operations of the form $\delta(z, w) = t$, where z and w are different substrings, which transform x into y [20].

In biological sequence comparison applications, the set of possible operations δ is [27]:

- Insertion ($\delta(\epsilon, a)$): insertion of the letter a.
- Deletion ($\delta(a, \epsilon)$): deletion of the letter a.
- Substitution ($\delta(a, b)$): substitution of the letter a by letter b.

Two basic notions widely used in biological sequence comparison algorithms are similarity and alignment. The similarity is a measure how similar two sequences are. In general, the more the sequences are similar, the less the errors are present. The alignment is obtained by placing one sequence above the other, making clear the correspondence between similar characters or substrings from the sequences [27]. In an alignment, spaces are inserted in arbitrary locations along the sequences so that they end up with the same size.

G	A	-	C	G	G	A	T	T	A	G
G	A	T	C	G	G	A	A	T	A	G
+1	+1	−2	+1	+1	+1	+1	−1	+1	+1	+1

$$\Sigma = 6$$

Figure 6.2 Alignment between $s = $ GACGGATTAG and $t = $ GATCGGAATAG.

There are three basic cases to be considered: matches, mismatches, and gaps. A match occurs when $s_i = t_j$ and, for this case, a positive value is associated. If $s_i \neq t_j$, a mismatch occurs and a negative value is associated with it. If s_i or t_j is aligned with a space, a gap occurs and also a negative value is assigned.

Given an alignment between two sequences s and t, a score can be associated with it as follows. For instance, for each column, we associate $+1$ if a match occurs, -1 for a mismatch, and -2 for a gap. The score is the sum of the values computed for each column. The maximal score is the similarity between the two sequences, denoted by $\text{sim}(s, t)$. In general, there are many alignments with maximal score. Figure 6.2 shows the alignment of sequences s and t, with the score for each column. In this case, there are nine columns with identical characters, one column with distinct character and one column with a space, giving a total score six.

The most important types of alignments are global and local. If the whole sequences are considered to obtain an alignment, then we are dealing with global alignment. However, if only parts of the sequences are used to compose the alignment, then we are dealing with local alignment.

6.3.1 Global Sequence Alignment

NW [21] proposed an algorithm based on dynamic programming to solve the global alignment problem. It is divided into two parts, explained in the following sections: the calculation of the *similarity array* and the retrieval of the local alignments.

6.3.1.1 *Part 1: Calculation of the Similarity Array* As input, the algorithm receives two sequences s, with $|s| = m$, and t, with $|t| = n$. There are $m + 1$ possible prefixes for s and $n + 1$ prefixes for t, including the empty string. An array $A_{m+1,n+1}$ is built, in which the $A[i,j]$ entry contains the value of the similarity between two prefixes of s and t, $\text{sim}(s[1 \cdots i], t[1 \cdots j])$. Figure 6.3 shows the similarity array between $s = $ ATAGCT and $t = $ GATATGCA. To obtain global alignments, the first row and column are initialized with the gap penalty associated with the introduction of gaps at the beginning of one of the sequences (s or t). The other entries are computed using Eq. (6.1).

$$\text{sim}(s[1 \cdots i], t[1 \cdots j])$$

$$= \max \begin{cases} \text{sim}(s[1 \cdots i], t[1 \cdots j - 1]) - 2, \\ \text{sim}(s[1 \cdots i - 1], t[1 \cdots j - 1]) + (\text{ if } s[i] = t[j] \text{ then } 1 \text{ else } -1), \\ \text{sim}(s[1 \cdots i - 1], t[1 \cdots j]) - 2 \end{cases}$$

$$(6.1)$$

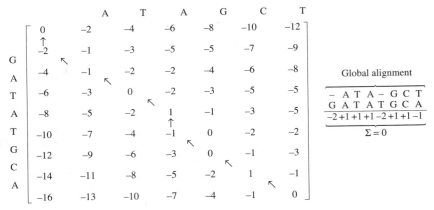

Figure 6.3   Similarity array to compute the similarity between the sequences ATAGCT and GATATGCA, using global alignment.

The values $A[i,j]$, for $i,j > 0$, are defined as $\text{sim}(s[1 \cdots i], t[1 \cdots j])$.

We have to compute the array A row by row, left to right on each row, or column by column, top to bottom on each column. Finally, arrows are drawn to indicate where the maximum value comes from, according to Eq. (6.1).

The time and space complexity of this part of the algorithm is $O(mn)$, where m and n are the lengths of the two sequences, and, if both sequences have approximately the same length, n, we get $O(n^2)$ [21].

6.3.1.2 *Part 2: Retrieval of the Local Alignments* An optimal global alignment between two sequences can be obtained as follows. We begin at value $A[s + 1, t + 1]$ and follow the arrow going out from this entry until we reach $A[0, 0]$.

A west arrow leaving entry $A[i,j]$ corresponds to a column with a space in s matching $t[j]$, a north arrow corresponds to $s[i]$ matching a space in t, and a northwest arrow means $s[i]$ matching $t[j]$. After computing A, an optimal global alignment is constructed from right to left following these arrows. Many optimal global alignments may exist for two sequences. This second part of the algorithm has time and space complexity $O(n)$.

6.3.2 Local Sequence Alignment

For long sequences, it is unusual to obtain a global alignment. Instead, the local alignment algorithm is executed to detect regions that are similar inside both sequences. For instance, for two 400 kb DNA sequences, we can obtain around 2000 similarity regions with an average size of 300×300 bytes. Global alignment algorithms are executed only for similarity regions. Figure 6.4 illustrates this.

To obtain local alignments, the algorithm proposed by Smith and Waterman (SW) [28] is used. In this algorithm, some minor changes are made to the algorithm described in Section 6.3.1. First, negative values are not allowed and, thus, entries are

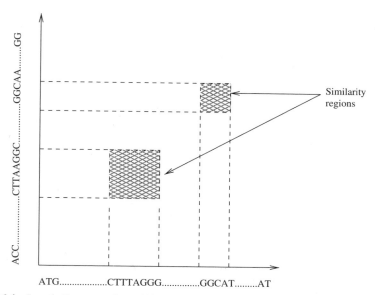

Figure 6.4   Local alignment of two 400 kb sequences, which produced two similarity regions.

still computed using Eq. (6.1) but including zero in the set to be maximized. Secondly, the first row and column of A are filled with zeros, as shown in the Figure 6.5. In this way, gaps introduced in the beginning of the sequences are not penalized and the differences between both sequences are computed in a less aggressive way, because zero is the minimal value.

To retrieve the local alignments, we begin in a maximal value at array A and follow the arrow going out from this entry until we reach another entry with no arrow going out or until we reach an entry with value 0, as shown in Figure 6.5.

6.3.3 Variations on the Basic Algorithms

The algorithms described in Sections 6.3.1 and 6.3.2 are exact algorithms that can be used to obtain the optimal global and local sequence alignments. However, with the increasing size of the biological sequences and the number of comparisons to be made, quadratic time and space complexity is prohibitive.

For this reason, some variations are proposed on the basic algorithms that aim to reduce computation time and/or memory space. An exact algorithm with the same generality that runs on less asymptotic time than the NW and SW algorithms is not known. Nevertheless, there are faster algorithms for particular cases.

Hirschberg [13] proposed an exact algorithm that calculates a local alignment between two sequences s and t in quadratic time but in linear space. The approach used splits sequence s in the middle, generating subsequences $s1$ and $s2$, and calculates the corresponding place to cut sequence t, generating subsequences $t1$ and $t2$, in such a way that the alignment problem can be solved in a divide and conquer recursive

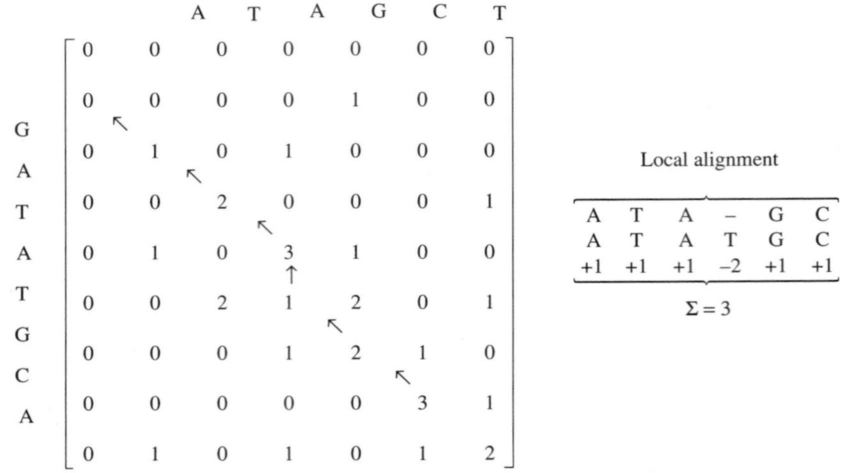

Figure 6.5 Array to compute the similarity between the (sub)sequences ATAGC and ATATGC, using the SW algorithm.

manner. This recursion roughly doubles the execution time when compared with the original algorithm. Nevertheless, for long biological sequences, which would otherwise generate very huge similarity arrays, this approach can be appropriate.

The method proposed by Fickett [9] considers only very similar sequences. In this case, the array A generated by the dynamic programming method is square and its main diagonal starts at $A[0, 0]$ and ends at $A[n, n]$, where n is the size of the sequences. To follow the main diagonal is to align both sequences without gaps. As long as gaps are introduced, the alignment leaves the main diagonal. If the sequences are very similar, the alignment between them is near the main diagonal. Thus, to compute the best global alignment(s), it is sufficient to fill only a small band (k-band) near the main diagonal. If k is the distance between the array element being computed and the element that composes the main diagonal on the same row, the algorithm has time complexity $O(kn)$.

Other algorithms that achieve improvements over the basic algorithms for particular situations are the ones proposed by Ukkonen [30], Myers [19], and Chang and Lawler [5].

6.3.4 Scoring Matrices

The methods described in Sections 6.3.1 and 6.3.2 typically deal only with nucleotides and do not take into account biological information to generate alignments. However, some information must indeed be taken into account to provide results which are consistent with the real world.

This is the case for penalties associated with mismatches. So far, we associated a unique value for a mismatch (-1 in the example) regardless of the parts involved. This works well with nucleotides but not with proteins. For instance, some mismatches are more likely to occur than others and can indicate evolutionary aspects [27]. For this reason, the alignment methods for proteins use score matrices which associate distinct values with distinct mismatches and reflect the likelihood of a certain change.

The most widely used scoring matrices are percent accepted mutations (PAM) and blocks substitution matrix (BLOSUM) and they are briefly explained as follows.

PAM matrices are result of an extensive work done by Dayhoff et al. [7] that analyzes the frequencies in which an amino acid a is replaced by an amino acid b during evolution. In the PAM matrices, each score is represented in such a way that positive scores indicate that the substitution occurs more often than expected by chance. A PAM matrix entry (i, j) is generated using the expected frequency of i and j and the number of times i and j are aligned in global alignments of homologous sequences. The resulting matrix is multiplied n times by itself to generate a PAMn matrix. PAM80, PAM120, and PAM250 are examples of PAM matrices. The most appropriate PAM matrix to use depends on the sequences being compared.

BLOSUM are scoring matrices, which were proposed by Henikoff and Henikoff [12]. These matrices are generated considering evolutionary rates of a region of a protein (block) rather than the entire protein. If two sequences are identical for more than a certain threshold of positions, they are clustered. BLOSUMn matrices have a clustering level of n. For instance, BLOSUM62 has sequence blocks clustered with 62% identity level. As in the PAM case, selecting the best BLOSUM matrix depends on the sequences being compared. Figure 6.6 shows the BLOSUM62 substitution matrix.

	A	R	N	D	C	Q	E	G	H	I	L	K	M	F	P	S	T	W	Y
A	4	-1	-2	-2	0	-1	-1	0	-2	-1	-1	-1	-1	-2	-1	1	0	-3	-2
R	-1	5	0	-2	-3	1	0	-2	0	-3	-2	2	-1	-3	-2	-1	-1	-3	-2
N	-2	0	6	1	-3	0	0	0	1	-3	-3	0	-2	-3	-2	1	0	-4	-2
D	-2	-2	1	6	-3	0	2	-1	-1	-3	-4	-1	-3	-3	-1	0	-1	-4	-3
C	0	-3	-3	-3	9	-3	-4	-3	-3	-1	-1	-3	-1	-2	-3	-1	-1	-2	-2
Q	-1	1	0	0	-3	5	2	-2	0	-3	-2	1	0	-3	-1	0	-1	-2	-1
E	-1	0	0	2	-4	2	5	-2	0	-3	-3	1	-2	-3	-1	0	-1	-3	-2
G	0	-2	0	-1	-3	-2	-2	6	-2	-4	-4	-2	-3	-3	-2	0	-2	-2	-3
H	-2	0	1	-1	-3	0	0	-2	8	-3	-3	-1	-2	-1	-2	-1	-2	-2	2
I	-1	-3	-3	-3	-1	-3	-3	-4	-3	4	2	-3	1	0	-3	-2	-1	-3	-1
L	-1	-2	-3	-4	-1	-2	-3	-4	-3	2	4	-2	2	0	-3	-2	-1	-2	-1
K	-1	2	0	-1	-3	1	1	-2	-1	-3	-2	5	-1	-3	-1	0	-1	-3	-2
M	-1	-1	-2	-3	-1	0	-2	-3	-2	1	2	-1	5	0	-2	-1	-1	-1	-1
F	-2	-3	-3	-3	-2	-3	-3	-3	-1	0	0	-3	0	6	-4	-2	-2	1	3
P	-1	-2	-2	-1	-3	-1	-1	-2	-2	-3	-3	-1	-2	-4	7	-1	-1	-4	-3
S	1	-1	1	0	-1	0	0	0	-1	-2	-2	0	-1	-2	-1	4	1	-3	-2
T	0	-1	0	-1	-1	-1	-1	-2	-2	-1	-1	-1	-1	-2	-1	1	5	-2	-2
W	-3	-3	-4	-4	-2	-2	-3	-2	-2	-3	-2	-3	-1	1	-4	-3	-2	11	2
Y	-2	-2	-2	-3	-2	-1	-2	-3	2	-1	-1	-2	-1	3	-3	-2	-2	2	7
V	0	-3	-3	-3	-1	-2	-2	-3	-3	3	1	-2	1	-1	-2	-2	0	-3	-1

Figure 6.6   Substitution matrix BLOSUM62.

6.4 HEURISTIC APPROACHES FOR BIOLOGICAL SEQUENCE COMPARISON

Usually, one given biological sequence is compared against hundreds or even thousands of sequences that compose genetic data banks. One of the most important gene repositories is the one that is part of a collaboration that involves *GenBank* at the NCBI, the *EMBL* at the European Molecular Biology Laboratory and *DDBJ* at the DNA Data Bank of Japan. These organizations exchange data daily and a new release is generated every two months. By now, there are millions of entries composed of billions of nucleotides.

In this scenario, the use of exact methods as the ones presented in Sections 6.3.1 and 6.3.2 is prohibitive. For this reason, faster heuristic methods are proposed which do not guarantee to produce the optimal alignment.

Usually, these methods are evaluated using the concepts of sensitivity and sensibility. Sensitivity is the ability to recognize more distantly related sequences, that is, it consists of finding *all* real alignments (true positives). Searches with a high sensitivity are more likely to discard false positive matches. Selectivity is the ability to narrow the search in order to retrieve *only* the true positives. Typically, there is a tradeoff between sensitivity and sensibility.

FASTA [22] and BLAST (Basic Local Alignment Search Tool) [1] are the most widely used heuristics for sequence comparison and will be detailed in Sections 6.4.1 and 6.4.2, respectively.

6.4.1 FASTA

In 1985, Lipman and Pearson [18] proposed FastP (fast protein), an algorithm that searches amino acids data banks for shared identities between two sequences, taking into account biological restrictions. In 1988, Pearson and Lipman [22] created Fasta (Fast-All), which is an improved version of FastP.

The Fasta algorithm has four steps: identification of similarity regions, re-scoring the best regions, selection of the more similar sequences, and alignment of the more similar sequences.

The goal of the first step is to locate the similarity regions between a query sequence and the sequences contained in a database. Therefore, it is run for every sequence in the database. Assume s and t are sequences with length m and n, respectively. First, all exact matches of length k (k-tuples) are identified. The k-tuples are also called *hot spots*. The offset of a k-tuple is then calculated as follows. If a shared k-tuple starts at positions $s[i]$ and $t[j]$, the offset is $i - j$. An offset vector and a search table are built indicating the number of matches found for each offset [18]. This method is known as diagonal, because an offset can be seen as a diagonal at the dynamic programming similarity matrix. Subsequently, the algorithm tries to merge two or more k-tuples which are in the same diagonal and not too far from each other. The criterion used to do this merging is heuristic [18]. The merged k-tuples form a *region*, which is a local alignment without gaps. A score is calculated for each region, which is a function of the matches and mismatches. The 10 regions that have the highest score are selected and the first step ends.

At the second step, new scores are associated with the best 10 regions using a substitution matrix. The best score obtained this way is called the *initial score*, which is the first similarity measure between s and t.

The initial score is used in the third step to rank the sequences in the database. Fasta also attempts to merge the best 10 regions in such a way that gaps are restrictively treated, that is, gaps are considered only in the junction of two regions [22]. The best region combination is calculated using a dynamic programming algorithm and the score for this combination is called *initn*. The score initn is calculated for every sequence in the database and only sequences which have this score above a given threshold are considered in the fourth step.

In the fourth step, the k-band variant of the SW algorithm (Section 6.3.3) is executed for each pair of sequences to generate the alignments.

6.4.2 BLAST

BLAST was proposed by Altschul et al. [1] in 1990. It is based on an heuristic algorithm which was designed to run fast, while still maintaining high sensibility.

The first BLAST version searched for local alignments without considering gaps. Its motivation was to improve the performance of the Fasta algorithm by obtaining less k-tuples with higher quality. This was achieved by integrating the use of PAM matrices in the first step of the algorithm. In 1996 and 1997, improved gapped versions of the original BLAST, NCBI-BLAST2, and WU-BLAST2, were proposed by Altschul et al. [8] and States and Gish [29], respectively.

The BLAST algorithm is divided into three well-defined phases: seeding, extension, and evaluation.

6.4.2.1 *Seeding* As in Fasta, BLAST also compares in the first phase a query sequence against all sequences in a database. BLAST uses the concept of words, which is very similar to the k-tuples concept (Section 6.4.1). A word is defined to be a finite set of letters with length w that appear in a given sequence. For instance, the sequence TCACGA contains four words with length three: TCA, CAC, ACG, and CGA. The BLAST algorithm assumes that significant alignments have words in common.

In this first phase, the location of all shared w-letter words between sequences s and t is determined by doing exact pattern matching. These locations are known as *identical words*. Only regions with identical words can be used as seeds for the alignment.

For the cases where significant alignments do not contain words in common, the concept of neighborhood is used. The neighbor of a word includes the word itself and every other word whose score is at least equal to T when compared through a substitution matrix. For instance, if we consider $T = 11$ and a substitution matrix PAM200, RGD, and KGD are neighbors, then the score between them is 14 [17].

An appropriate choice of w, T, and the substitution matrix is an effective way to control the performance and the sensibility of BLAST.

In BLASTN (BLAST nucleotide) from NCBI-BLAST, the minimum length of a word is seven and the T parameter is not used. In BLASTP (BLAST protein) and other BLAST programs that deal with proteins, usually w is equal to 2 or 3 and a two-hit algorithm [17] is used to detect identical words, where only words within a distance are examined. Typically, this distance is 40 amino acids.

In WU-BLAST, any value of w can be specified. If w is adjusted to a value which is greater than four and the T parameter is not specified, the concept of neighborhood is not used.

There are some combinations of amino acids that occur frequently in biological sequences but have low biological interest. To mask these combinations, both NCBI-BLAST and WU-BLAST allow the replacement by N or X, which have negative scores.

6.4.2.2 Extension The seeds obtained in the previous phase must be extended to generate an alignment. This is done by inspecting the characters near the seed in both directions and concatenating them to the seed until a *drop-off score X* is reached. The drop-off score defines how much the score can be reduced, considering the last maximal value. Having the seed A, the X parameter equal to three, and a punctuation of $+1$ for matches and -1 for mismatches, the following result is obtained:

```
ATGC GATA CTAGA
ATTC GATC GATGA
1212 3454 32123 <-- score
0010 0001 23432 <-- drop off score
```

In this case, the extension of the first A gives us the alignment:

```
ATGC GATA CT
ATTC GATC GA
```

6.4.2.3 Evaluation The alignments generated in the extension phase must be evaluated to remove the nonsignificant ones. The significant alignments, called high score segment pairs (HSPs) are the ones whose scores are higher or equal to a threshold S. In addition, consistent HSP groups are generated, which include non-overlapped HSPs that are near the same diagonal. The consistent HSP groups are compared against a final threshold, known as the E parameter [15], and only the alignments that are above this threshold are considered.

6.4.2.4 BLAST Variations Owing to the success in obtaining significant alignments fastly, many BLAST variations and wrappers were proposed. PSI-BLAST [8], PHI-BLAST [32], Mega-BLAST [33], BLASTZ [26], and MPBLAST [16] are a non-exhaustive list of these variations.

6.5 PARALLEL AND DISTRIBUTED SEQUENCE COMPARISON

6.5.1 Parallel SW

In the SW algorithm (Section 6.3.2), most of the time is spent calculating the similarity matrix between two sequences and this is the part which is parallelized. The access pattern presented by the matrix calculation is nonuniform and has been extensively studied in the parallel programming literature [24]. The parallelization strategy that is traditionally used in this kind of problem is known as the "wavefront method" as the calculations that can be done in parallel evolve as waves on diagonals.

Figure 6.7 illustrates the wavefront method. At the beginning of the computation, only one node can compute value $A[1, 1]$. Then, values $A[2, 1]$ and $A[1, 2]$ can be computed in parallel, and then $A[3, 1]$, $A[2, 2]$, and $A[1, 3]$ can be computed independently, and so on. The maximum parallelism is attained at the main matrix diagonal and then decreases again.

In the following paragraphs, most of the strategies discussed use the wavefront method. In addition, assume sequences s and t with lengths m and n, respectively.

Galper and Brutlag [10] proposed a parallel SW algorithm that uses the wavefront method in a row basis or in a diagonal basis. Each processor communicates with two neighbors and computations evolve as waves on the similarity matrix diagonals. Synchronous and asynchronous modes are provided. In addition, a mode called *windowed asynchronous diagonal* is provided for space saving on the similarity matrix calculation. The size of the window depends on the cost functions for insertion, deletion, and substitution (Section 6.3) and is the maximum cost of converting the query sequence s on sequence t. This algorithm was implemented in C with parallel macroextensions. Experimental results were collected in a 12-processor Encore Multimax shared memory machine. For sequences with lengths $m = 118$ and $n = 14,908$, a speedup of 10.29 was achieved for 12 processors.

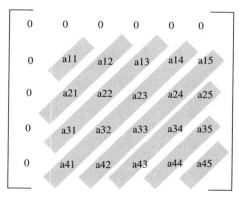

Figure 6.7 The wavefront method used to exploit the parallelism presented by the SW algorithm.

Boukerche et al. [3, 4] proposed a parallel heuristic SW variant that reduces the size of the similarity matrix to $2m$ and thus only the row being calculated and the previous one are kept in memory. To do that, an additional data structure is used to keep the potential alignments, which are the ones whose score is above a given threshold. Work is assigned to the p processors in a row basis and the wavefront method is used. Each processor acts on a set of columns inside the row and communicates with two neighbors through a lazy synchronization protocol. This approach was implemented in C using the JIAJIA distributed shared memory system [14]. The results were collected in a eight-processor cluster, and real DNA sequences were used. The sequences tested were of approximately the same length and the lengths analyzed were 15, 50, 80, 150, and 400 kB. A speedup of 4.58 was achieved in the 400 kB sequence comparison with eight processors. A variant of this approach which uses blocking factors is proposed in Ref. [2]. This variant was implemented in JIAJIA and message passing interface (MPI), and a speedup of 7.28 was achieved in the comparison of 50 kB sequences with eight processors.

Zhang et al. [31] proposed PSW-DC, a parallel heuristic SW variant that uses the divide and conquer method to reduce the size of the similarity matrix to $(mn)/p$, where p is the number of processors. In this approach, the similarity matrix is spread over the parallel system. The query sequence s is divided in such a way that each processor i receives only a subsequence s'_{pi} whose length is m/p and the whole sequence t, with length n. The SW algorithm is executed for these data, with no communication between the processors, producing p optimal local alignments Alig_i between the subsequences s'_{pi} and t. In this case, the wavefront method is not used. A heuristic method called *combine and extend* is proposed to generate the local alignments between s and t from the p similarity matrices between t and s'_i. The PSW-DC algorithm was implemented in C using MPI. The results were collected in a 16-processor cluster and indicated that as long as processors are added, the sensitivity is reduced. The test sequences were artificially produced and had the following lengths: 1, 2, 4, 8, and 16 kB.

Rajko and Aluru [25] proposed an algorithm that solves the global sequence alignment problem in $O(mn/p)$ time and requires $O(mn/p)$ space. The sequence alignment algorithm is extended to treat the affine gap penalty function. Thus, the extended alignment problem is (A, B, start_type, and end_type), where A and B are sequences and start_type and end_type are in $-3, -2, -1, 1, 2, 3$, where types 1, 2, and 3 correspond to a_i matched to b_j, a_i matched to a gap, and b_j matched to a gap, respectively. Besides that, in the case of negative values, the original scores of the alignments can be modified to enforce a particular type of match. The scores for the extended alignment problem are calculated by adding the score obtained from the standard alignment problem with the modified score.

Using these ideas, the key idea of this algorithm is to find add an additional phase to find a partial balanced partition between subsequences of A and B. The partial balanced partition allows the subdivision of the original problem in independent subproblems, which can be solved in parallel [25]. To compute the partial balanced partition in parallel, three dynamic tables are used to find the cells where a recursive decomposition of the problem can be performed. A partial balanced partition starts at the intersection of an optimal path with a diagonal. If the intersection is in a_i, b_j, then the problem can be decomposed in two independent subproblems: the alignment of $a_1, a_2, \ldots, a_i$ with $b_1, b_2, \ldots, b_j$ and the alignment of $a_{i+1}, a_{i+2}, \ldots, a_m$ with $b_{j+1}, b_{j+2}, \ldots, b_n$. This decomposition can be done recursively. k regions are composed by k tuples (i_x, j_x, t_x), where i_x and j_x are the upper left coordinates of the corner of region x and t_x is the start_type of the same region. An optimal alignment C between sequences A and B is proved to be the concatenation of optimal alignments to the subproblems corresponding to each region [25]. Note that this algorithm finds only one optimal global alignment. The authors state that this algorithm can be easily modified to solve the local alignment problem.

The proposed algorithm was implemented in C++ and MPI and executed on an IBM xSeries cluster with 60 machines. Only the complete match (where both sequences are equal) and complete mismatch (where both sequences are entirely different) cases were analyzed. Sequence sizes of 40, 80, 160, and 320 kB were considered. The results obtained show good speedups for both the complete match and the complete mismatch cases for 60 processors when the sequence size is big enough (320 kB). The authors also show a test for 1.1 MB sequences in 60 processors. The complete match took around 2.58 h, where 2.55 h were spent in the first phase (computation of the partial balanced partition).

6.5.2 Distributed BLAST

As the time complexity of BLAST is linear $O(n)$, most strategies focus on query distribution. In this way, the many query sequences are distributed among the processors, but computation of one sequence comparison against the data bank remains sequential.

MpiBLAST [6] is a strategy that focus on data distribution for NCBI-BLAST and was proposed for clusters of workstations. The algorithm has two phases. First, the data bank is segmented by tools provided by NCBI-BLAST and put in a shared storage medium. Next, the queries are distributed among the cluster nodes. If the node does not have a data bank fragment, a local copy is made. A method that associates data fragments to cluster nodes is proposed, to minimize the number of copies. MpiBLAST was tested on Green Destiny, a 240-node Beowulf cluster. With 128 nodes, it achieved a superlinear speedup of around 170 due to data fragmentation in smaller pieces as long as processors are added. MpiBLAST can be found in mpiblast/.lanl/.gov.

BLAST++ parallel [23] uses query packing [11] to group multiple sequences to reduce the number of database accesses. A master/slave approach is used, which divides the queries of BLAST++ in n sets, each one composed by k queries, where n is the number of workers. Each worker executes BLAST++ independently for the k queries and, finally, the results are collected and combined by the master. This approach was implemented in C using MPI and the results were collected in a 14-node cluster. The size of the query sequence used was 64 bp and a real protein databank was used. A speedup of around 13 was achieved for 1024 queries.

6.6 CONCLUSIONS

Computational molecular biology is rapidly becoming a very important research area. Owing to the amount and complexity of the organisms that are being constantly sequenced all over the world, it is becoming unthinkable to analyze these new genomes without the aid of computers.

One of the most fundamental problem in computational molecular biology is biological sequence comparison, which aims to determine the similarity between two DNA (or protein) sequences. This comparison is very important because biologists often infer the properties of newly sequenced genomes by comparing them against genomes which are already determined.

Formally speaking, this is a problem of approximate pattern matching where the goal is to determine which sequences are similar to a query sequence. Algorithms such as the ones proposed by NW [21] and SW [28] are exact algorithms which use dynamic programming techniques to solve the sequence comparison problem. However, the time and space complexities of these algorithms is $O(n^2)$, where n is the size of the sequences. Therefore, they are often considered impracticable when huge sequences are compared against huge databases.

Hirschberg [13] proposed an exact algorithm that can be adapted to solve the sequence alignment problem, which requires $O(n)$ space, at the expense of doubling the execution time. Other exact methods were proposed but, as far as we know, there is still no exact algorithm that runs on less asymptotic time than NW.

For this reason, heuristic methods such as FASTA and BLAST were proposed. Although those methods are much faster than the exact algorithms, their sensibility is often reduced and a great effort must be done to find appropriate parameter tuning.

An obvious way to accelerate these algorithms is by running them in multiple processors or multiple nodes. Many techniques were proposed to parallelize the SW algorithm, and good results were indeed obtained. As the time complexity of BLAST is $O(n)$, the common approach is to distribute the database's sequences among the nodes to reduce the execution time of the whole process. In this sense, many algorithms were proposed and good reductions on execution time were achieved. However, in real genome projects, SW is rarely used as its execution time, even in multiple processors, is still very high. Thus, biologists often use heuristic methods such as BLAST, sacrificing sensitiveness for the sake of performance.

To conclude, biological sequence comparison is a very challenging problem. This is mainly due to the fact that we must find approximate pattern matching between a query sequence and a very huge database. There is a clear need for new algorithms that could obtain results with high sensitivity in a reasonable time. In addition, new ways to accelerate the known algorithms must be found. In this direction, parallel and distributed processing seems to be a very good approach. Biological sequence comparison is, thus, still an open problem and very intensive research activity is done in this area.

ACKNOWLEDGMENTS

We are greatful to many colleagues for many helpful and stimulating discussions on these topics. In particular, we would like to thank Maria Emilia M. T. Walter, Mauricio Ayala-Rincon, Ricardo P. Jacobi, Marcelo S. Silva, Rodolfo B. Batista, and Marcelo N. P. Santana. Dr. A. Boukerche work was partially supported by NSERC, Canada Research Chair (CRC) Program, Canadian Foundation for Innovation, and Ontario Innovation Funds.

REFERENCES

1. S. F. Altschul, W. Gish, W. Miller, E. W. Myers, and D. J. Lipman, Basic local alignment search tool, *J. Mol. Biol.*, 215 (3), 410–413 (1990).

2. R. B. Batista, D. N. Silva, A. C. M. A. Melo, and L. Weigang, Using a DSM Application to Locally Align DNA Sequences, in *Proceeding of the IEEE/ACM International Symposium on Cluster Computing and the Grid*, IEEE Computer Society, 2004.

3. A. Boukerche and A. C. M. A. Melo, Parallel DNA Sequence Alignment Algorithm, in *Proceeding of the International Parallel and Distributed Processing Symposium (IPDPS2005)*, IEEE Computer Society, 2005.

4. A. Boukerche, A. C. M. A. Melo, M. E. M. T. Walter, R. C. F. Melo, M. N. P. Santana, and R. B. Batista, Performance Evaluation of a Local DNA Sequence Alignment Algorithm on a Cluster of Workstations, in *Proceeding of the International Parallel and Distributed Processing Symposium (IPDPS2004)*, IEEE Society, 2004.

5. W. I. Chang and E. W. Lawler, Approximate String Matching in Sublinear Expected Time, in *IEEE Thirty-first Annual Symposium on Foundations of Computer Science*, 1990, pp. 116–124.

6. A. darling, L. Carey, and W. Feng, The Design, Implementation and Evaluation of mpiblast, in *Proceeding of the fourth International Conference on Linux Clusters*, 2003.

7. M. Dayhoff, R. M. Schwartz, and B. C. Ortcutt, A model of evolutionary changes in proteins, *Atlas Protein Sequence Struct.*, 5, 345–352 (1978).

8. S. F. Altschul et al., Gapped blast and psi-blast: a new generation of protein database search programs, *Nucleic Acids Res.*, 25 (17), 3389–3402, 1997.

9. J. Fickett, Fast optimal alignments, *Nucleic Acids Res.*, 12 (1), 175–179 (1984).

10. A. R. Galper and D. R. Brutlag, Parallel Similarity Search and Alignment with the Dynamic Programming Method, in *Technical Report KSL 90-74*, Stanford University, 1990, pp. 1–14.

11. B. C. Ooi, H. Wang, T. Ong, and K. Tan, Blast++: a Tool for Blasting Queries in Batches, in *Proceeding of the Asia-Pacific Bioinformatics Conference (APBC2003)*, 2003.

12. S. Henikoff, and J. G. Henikoff, Amino Acid Substitution Matrices from Protein Blocks, in *Proceedings of the National Academy of Science*, Vol. 89, 1992, pp. 10915–10919.

13. D. S. Hirschberg, A linear space algorithm for computing maximal common subsequences, *Commun. ACM*, 18 (6), 341–343 (1975).

14. S. Hu, W. Shi, and Z. Tang, Jiajia: an svm System Based on a New Cache Coherence Protocol, in *High Performance Computing and Networking (HPCN)*, Springer-Verlag, 1999, pp. 463–472.

15. S. Karlin and S. F. Altschul, Methods for Assessing the Statistical Significance of Molecular Sequence Features by Using General Scores, in *Proceedings of the National Academy of Sciences*, Vol. 87, 1990, pp. 2264–2268.

16. I. Korf and W. Gish, Mpblast: improved blast performance with multiplexed queries, *Bioinformatics*, 16 (11), 1052–1053 (2000).

17. I. Korf, M. Yandell, and J. Bedell. *BLAST — An Essential Guide to the Basic Local Alignment Search Tool*, OReilly Associates, 2003.

18. D. Lipman and W. Pearson, Rapid and sensitive protein similarity searches, *Science*, 227, 1435–1441 (1985).

19. E. W. Myers, An o(nd) difference algorithm and its variations, *Algorithmica*, 1 (2), 251–266 (1986).

20. G. Navarro, A guided tour to approximate string matching, *ACM Comput. Surv.*, 33 (1), 31–88 (2001).

21. S. B. Needleman and C. D. Wunsh, A general method applicable to the search of similarities of amino acid sequences of two proteins, *J. Mol. Biol.*, 48 (2), 443–453 (1970).

22. W. R. Pearson and D. L. Lipman, Improved Tools for Biological Sequence Comparison, in *Proceedings of the National Academy of Science USA*, NAS, 1988, pp. 2444–2448.

23. D. Peng, W. Yan, and Z. Lei, Parallelization of Blast++, Technical Report, Singapore-MIT Alliance, 2004.

24. G. Pfister, *In Search of Clusters — The Coming Battle for Lowly Parallel Computing*, Prentice-Hall, 1995.

25. S. Rajko and S. Aluru, Space and time parallel sequence alignments, *IEEE Trans. Parallel Distributed Syst.*, 15 (12), 1070–1081 (2004).

26. S. Schwartz, W. J. Kent, A. Smit, Z. Zhang, R. Baertsch, R. C. Hardison, D. Haussler, and W. Miller, Human-mouse alignments using blastz, *Genome Res.*, 13, 103–107 (2003).

27. J. C. Setubal and J. Meidanis, *Introduction to Computational Molecular Biology*, Brooks/Cole Publishing Company, 1997.

28. T. F. Smith and M. S. Waterman, Identification of common molecular sub-sequences, *J. Mol. Biol.*, 147 (1), 195–197 (1981).

29. D. J. States and W. Gish, Combined use of sequence similarity and codon bias for coding region identification, *J. Comput. Biol.*, 1, 39–50 (1994).

30. E. Ukkonen, Algorithms for approximate string matching, *Information Control*, 64 (1), 100–118 (1985).

31. F. Zhang, X. Qiao, and Z. Liu, A Parallel Smith Waterman Algorithm Based on Divide and Conquer, in *Fifth International Conference on Algorithm and Architectures for Parallel Processing (ICA3PP02)*, IEEE Society, 2002, pp. 162–169.

32. Z. Zhang, A. A. Schaffer, W. Miller, T. L. Madden, and D. J. Lipman, Protein sequence similarity searches using patterns as seeds, *Nucleic Acids Res.*, 26 (17), 3986–3990 (1998).

33. Z. Zhang, S. Schwartz, L. Wagner, and W. Miller, A greedy algorithm for aligning DNA sequences, *J. Comput. Biol.*, 7 (1–2), 203–214 (2000).

Special-Purpose Computing for Biological Sequence Analysis

BERTIL SCHMIDT and HEIKO SCHRÖDER

We present a hybrid parallel system based on commodity components to gain super-computer power at low cost. The architecture is built around a coarse-grained PC cluster linked to a high-speed network and fine-grained parallel processor arrays connected to each node. Identifying applications that profit from this kind of computing power is crucial to justify the use of such a system. In this chapter, we present an approach to high-performance protein database scanning with hybrid computing. To derive an efficient mapping onto this architecture, we have designed instruction systolic array implementations for the Smith–Waterman and Viterbi algorithm. This results in a database scanning implementation with significant runtime savings.

7.1 INTRODUCTION

SIMD architectures looked very promising around 1990, as they delivered highest performance at the price of being special purpose engines rather than general purpose. Then, with the end of the cold war, the western military stopped the support for such systems. In 1998, the last SIMD supercomputer vanished from the list of the top 500 most powerful supercomputers (see http://www.top500.org/lists/2004/06/overtime.php?c=1). What was it that made the SIMD concept compelling in first place and what caused the end of this concept? Advantages of the SIMD concept over the MIMD concept include the following aspects:

- Massively parallel SIMD computers typically consist of at least 2^{10} processing elements, but only one control unit. This single control unit broadcasts a single

Parallel Computing for Bioinformatics and Computational Biology, Edited by Albert Y. Zomaya
Copyright © 2006 John Wiley & Sons, Inc.

stream of instructions to all processing elements that execute these instructions in lockstep.

- Communication between processors does not need any hand shaking — due to the perfect synchronization, the receiving processor is always ready to receive when data is sent to it.
- Typically, the processing elements are tailored towards a special type of applications and thus the processing elements can be smaller (which means more of them can be placed on a single chip) and can be clocked faster.

In contrast, arguments in favour of MIMD machines include the following:

- MIMD machines are typically comprised of off-the-shelf processors, which are cheap and due to the strong competition in this market have matured; reaching the limits of what is possible using state-of-the-art technology.
- MIMD machines are programmed with standard programming languages, whereas SIMD machines typically use languages, that have similarity to assembly languages, and in addition, require the programmer to develop a deep understanding of parallel processing (in which most IT specialists are not trained).
- Owing to the use of standard components, MIMD machines can be designed faster than SIMD machines. SIMD machines of the past needed ASIC design — a process that has increasingly become prohibitively expensive, justified only if vast quantities can be produced.
- As standard processors are used, MIMD machines come closer to being general-purpose machines than SIMD machines.

There are probably many more advantages and disadvantages for both concept. Fact is that the SIMD concept has been defeated on the market. Thus, it requires strong arguments in its defense to convince anybody to invest again into the SIMD concept. In many countries, the research community and the pharmaceutical industry are investing heavily in the area of "life science." The Blue Gene supercomputer project will produce the world fastest supercomputer in 2005, tailored toward biomolecular simulation, at a price of about 100M US$. This certainly makes for a large application. FPGA technology is advancing fast — already now we can place on a single FPGA chip as much compute power as we were able to place on an PCI card 10 years ago. FPGAs have several advantages over ASIC design:

- An FPGA can be programmed in few days, whereas an ASIC design requires typically at least 1 year.
- FPGAs are low risk as design mistakes can easily be corrected.
- An FPGA can be tailored for a single algorithm and its design can be changed any time to run a different algorithm.
- FPGA designs are much more cost effective, as long as only few machines are produced.

- FPGA designs can easily be used for the implementation of SIMD architectures and even for systolic architectures.
- FPGA designs are particularly good for architectures that do not require large and fast random access memory.

Thus, we expect that FPGAs will continue their current dramatic increase in use and will enter several niche markets to cater for special-purpose applications where supercomputer power is required as well as for smaller systems such as embedded systems. As soon as the market allows selling large numbers of systems, SoC is the most cost-effective solution.

The particular applications we are looking at are the area of biological sequence analysis. This area is particularly promising for the use of special-purpose architectures as the required data type is short integers and the performed arithmetic operations are mainly additions, max/min comparisons, and table lookups. Thus, the processing elements can be made very small and many processing elements can be fitted on a single FPGA.

The communication structure required by the algorithms we intend to use is strictly local, that is, we are basing our algorithms on dynamic programming. Such algorithms can be implemented in a systolic manner, requiring a constant data stream but no substantial on-chip memory. Thus, long distance communication can be avoided allowing for high clock frequencies.

In this chapter, we make a case for SIMD architectures for the area of biological sequence analysis. In Section 7.2, we introduce a concept of special-purpose SIMD computing, the instruction systolic array (ISA), and its incorporation into an MIMD computing which we call "hybrid parallel computer." In Section 7.3, we introduce two algorithmic approaches and their solution via dynamic programming. Section 7.4 evaluates the performance under varying technologies.

7.2 HYBRID PARALLEL COMPUTER

Hybrid computing describes combination of fine-grained and coarse-grained parallelism within an architecture, that is, within the processors of a computer cluster (MIMD) tightly coupled processor arrays (SIMD) are embedded to accelerate compute intensive regular tasks. The driving force and motivation behind hybrid computing is the price-to-performance ratio. Using PC-cluster as in the Beowulf approach is currently the most efficient way to gain supercomputer power for a reasonable price. Installing, in addition, massively parallel processor add-on boards within each PC can further improve the cost-to-performance ratio significantly. Of course, not all computing problems are suitable for mapping onto a hybrid architecture. The problem mix to be handled requires a high percentage of tasks that are suitable for SIMD computing to justify the use of hybrid computing. Hence, suitable applications for hybrid computing are high performance visualization and image/video processing and also typical supercomputer applications that deal with simulations of large and regular physical structures. In this chapter, we will demonstrate that bioinformatics is another application area that can benefit from the hybrid computing concept.

We have built a hybrid MIMD–SIMD architecture from general available components (Fig. 7.1). The MIMD part of the system is a cluster of 16 PCs (PentiumII, 450 MHz) running Linux. The machines are connected via a gigabit-per-second LAN (using Myrinet M2F-PCI32 as network interface cards and Myrinet M2L-SW16 as a switch). For application development, we use the MPI library MPICH v. 1.1.2. For the SIMD part, we plugged a Systola 1024 PCI board [21] into each PC. Systola 1024 contains an ISA of size 32×32. ISAs have been developed to combine the speed and simplicity of systolic arrays with flexible programmability [20]. Originally, the main application field of ISAs was supposed to be scientific computing. However, in the mid-90s, the suitability of the ISA architecture for other applications was recognized, for example, [10, 27–31].

7.2.1   Principle of the ISA

The ISA [20] is a mesh-connected processor grid, where the processors are controlled by three streams of control information: instructions, row selectors, and column selectors (Fig. 7.2). The instructions are input in the upper left corner of the processor array and from there they move step by step in horizontal and vertical direction through the array. This guarantees that within each diagonal of the array, the same instruction is active during each clock cycle. In clock cycle, $k + 1$ processor $(i + 1, j)$ and $(i, j + 1)$ execute the instruction that has been executed by processor (i, j) in clock cycle k.

The selectors also move systolically through the array: the row selectors horizontally from left to right and column selectors vertically from top to bottom. Selectors mask the execution of the instructions within the processors, that is, an instruction is

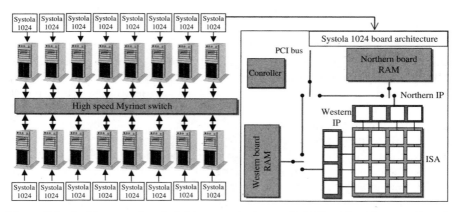

Figure 7.1   Architecture of our hybrid system: A cluster of 16 PCs with 16 Systola 1024 PCI boards (left). The data paths in Systola 1024 are depicted (right).

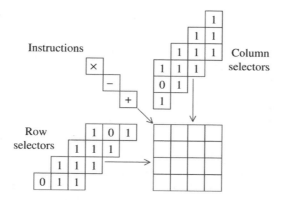

Figure 7.2 Control flow in an ISA.

executed if and and only if both selector bits, currently in that processor, are equal to one. Otherwise, a no-operation is executed.

Every processor has read-and-write access to its own memory. Besides that, it has a designated *communication register* (*C-register*), which can also be read by the four neighbor processors. Within each clock phase, reading access is always performed before writing access. Thus, two adjacent processors can exchange data within a single clock cycle in which both processors overwrite the contents of their own C-register with the contents of the C-register of its neighbor. This convention avoids read-and-write conflicts and also creates the possibility to perform *aggregate functions* within one instruction (or a constant number of instructions).

Aggregate functions on a processor array are associative and commutative functions to which every processor provides an argument value. As they are commutative and associative, aggregate functions can be evaluated in many different ways (orders). The ISA supports top-down column operations and left-right row operations, due to the systolic flow of the instructions. Thus, an aggregate function can be implemented on the ISA by executing it first in all columns, placing the corresponding results within the last processor within each column, and secondly, applying the aggregate function to these results in the last row, executing it within the last row (left-to-right). Simple examples of aggregate functions are the sum of all and the maximum of all. Other important operations that can be executed particularly well on the ISA are *row broadcast* (left-to-right), *column broadcast* (top-down), and *ringshift operations*. These are explained subsequently.

Row broadcast. Each processor reads the value from its left neighbor. As the execution of this operation is pipelined along the row, the same value is propagated from one C-register to the next, until it finally arrives at the rightmost processor. Note that the row broadcast requires only a single instruction (Fig. 7.3, left).

Row ringshift. The contents of the C-registers can be ringshifted along the processor rows by two instructions (Fig. 7.3, right). Every two horizontally adjacent processors exchange data (using one read left and one read right operations). Because

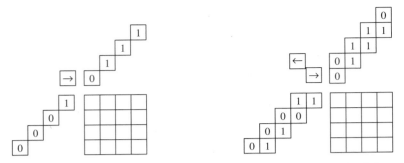

Figure 7.3   (Left) Broadcast along the first row of a 4 × 4 ISA. The arrow "→" denotes the instruction C:=C[WEST] (read the contents of the C-register of the western neighbor and write it into the own C-register). (Right) Ringshift of a data item in the first row of a 4 × 4 ISA. The arrow "→" denotes again the instruction C:=C[WEST] and "←" denotes C:=C[EAST].

of the instruction flow from west to east, this implements a ringshift. Of course, a column ringshift can be executed in the same way.

7.2.2   Architecture of Systola 1024

Systola 1024 is a low cost add-on board for standard PCs [21]. The ISA on the board is integrated on a 4 × 4 array of processor chips. Each chip contains 64 processors, arranged as an 8 × 8 square. This provides 1024 processors on the board. To exploit the computation capabilities of this unit, a cascaded memory concept is implemented on Systola 1024, which forms a fast input and output environment for the parallel processing unit. For the fast data exchange with the ISA, there are rows of intelligent memory units at the northern and western borders of the array called *interface processors* (IPs). Each IP is connected to its adjacent array processor for data transfer in each direction. The IPs have access to an on-board memory by means of special fast data channels, those at the northern interface chips with the northern board RAM and those at the western chips with the western board RAM. The northern and the western board RAM can communicate bidirectionally with the PC memory over the PCI bus. The data transfer between every two memory units within this hierarchy is controlled by an on-board controller chip (Fig. 7.1, right).

At a clock frequency of $f = 50$ MHz and using a word format of $m = 16$ bits, each (bitserial) processor can execute $f/m = 50/16 \times 10^6 = 3.125 \times 10^6$ word operations per second. Thus, one board with its 1024 processors performs up to 3.2 GIPS. This adds up to a theoretical peak performance of 51.2 GIPS for 16 boards inside the cluster.

7.3   DYNAMIC PROGRAMMING COMMUNICATION PATTERN

Scanning sequence databases is a common and often repeated task in molecular biology. The need for speeding up this treatment comes from the recent developments in genome-sequencing projects, which are generating an enormous amount of data. This results in an exponential growth of the biosequence banks: every year their size scaled by a factor 1.5 to 2 (see http://www.ncbi.nlm.nih.gov/Genbank/genbankstats.html). The scan operation consists in finding similarities between a particular query sequence and all the sequences of a bank. This operation allows biologists to point out sequences sharing common sub-sequences. From a biological point of view, it leads to identify similar functionality.

Comparison algorithms whose complexities are quadratic with respect to the length of the sequences detect similarities between the query sequence and a subject sequence. One frequently used approach to speed up this time-consuming operation is to introduce heuristics in the search algorithms [1]. The main drawback of this solution is that the more time efficient the heuristics, the worse is the quality of the results [25]. Another approach to get high-quality results in a short time is to use parallel processing. There are two basic methods of mapping the scanning of protein sequence databases to a parallel processor: one is based on the systolization of the sequence comparison algorithm and the other is based on the distribution of the computation of pairwise comparisons. Systolic arrays have been proven as a good candidate structure for the first approach [7, 16, 26], whereas supercomputers and networks of workstations are suitable architectures for the latter [5, 13, 14, 24, 25].

The alignment algorithms investigated in this chapter are the Smith–Waterman (SW) algorithm and the Viterbi algorithm. Both algorithms are based on the dynamic programming concept. We will first explain both algorithms and then show how they can be mapped onto the hybrid parallel architecture using the same communication pattern.

7.3.1 Smith–Waterman Algorithm

Surprising relationships have been discovered between protein sequences that have little overall similarity but in which similar sub-sequences can be found. In this sense, the identification of similar sub-sequences is probably the most useful and practical method for comparing two sequences. The SW algorithm [33] finds the most similar sub-sequences of two sequences (the local alignment) by dynamic programming.

The algorithm compares two sequences by computing a distance that represents the minimal cost of transforming one segment into another. Two elementary operations are used: match/mutation and insertion/deletion (also called a gap operation). Through series of such elementary operations, any segments can be transformed into any other segment. The smallest number of operations required to change one segment into another can be taken into as the measure of the distance between the segments.

Consider two strings S1 and S2 of length 11 and 12. To identify common subsequences, the SW algorithm computes the three similarity values $M(i, j)$, $I(i, j)$, and $D(i, j)$ of two sequences ending at position i and j of the two sequences S1 and S2. Their computation for all $1 \leq i \leq 11$ and $1 \leq j \leq 12$ is given by the following recurrence relations:

$$M(i, j) = \max\{0, D(i, j), I(i, j), M(i - 1, j - 1) + \text{sbt}(\text{S}1_i, \text{S}2_j)\}$$

$$I(i, j) = \max\{M(i - 1, j) - \alpha, I(i - 1, j) - \beta\}$$

$$D(i, j) = \max\{M(i, j - 1) - \alpha, D(i, j - 1) - \beta\}$$

where sbt is a character substitution cost table. Initialization of these values are given by $M(i, j) = I(i, j) = D(i, j) = 0$ when $i, j = 0$. Multiple gap costs are taken into account as follows: α is the cost of the first gap and β is the cost of the following gaps. At every matrix element, three values are computed corresponding to the best score so far if the characters defining the matrix elements are matched $[M(i, j)]$, inserted $[I(i, j)]$, or deleted $[D(i, j)]$. The inclusion of the constant zero in the match equation implements local scoring. The two segments of S1 and S2 producing the highest score value can then be determined by a traceback procedure. Figure 7.4 illustrates an example.

7.3.2 Viterbi Algorithm

Biologists have characterized a growing resource of protein families that share common function and evolutionary ancestry. Hidden Markov models (HMMs) have been identified as a suitable mathematical tool to statistically describe such families. Consequently, databases of HMMs for protein families have been created [3]. HMMs have become a powerful tool for high sensitivity database scanning, because they can provide a position-specific description of protein families. HMMs can identify that a

	Ø	A	T	C	T	G	G	T	C	C
Ø	$_00^0$	$_00^0$	$_00^0$	$_00^0$	$_00^0$	$_00^0$	$_00^0$	$_00^0$	$_00^0$	$_00^0$
G	$_00^0$	$_{-1}0^{-1}$	$_{-2}0^{-1}$	$_{-2}0^{-1}$	$_{-2}0^{-1}$	$_{-2}2^{-1}$	$_02^{-1}$	$_00^{-1}$	$_{-1}0^{-1}$	$_{-2}0^{-1}$
T	$_00^0$	$_{-1}0^{-2}$	$_{-2}2^{-2}$	$_00^{-2}$	$_{-1}2^{-2}$	$_00^0$	$_{-1}1^0$	$_{-1}4^{-2}$	$_20^{-2}$	$_10^{-2}$
C	$_00^0$	$_{-1}0^{-2}$	$_{-2}0^0$	$_{-2}4^{-2}$	$_20^0$	$_11^{-1}$	$_00^{-1}$	$_{-1}0^2$	$_{-2}6^{-2}$	$_44^{-2}$
T	$_00^0$	$_{-1}0^{-2}$	$_{-2}2^0$	$_00^2$	$_{-1}6^{-2}$	$_41^{-1}$	$_30^{-2}$	$_22^1$	$_11^4$	$_05^2$
T	$_00^0$	$_{-1}0^{-2}$	$_{-2}2^0$	$_01^1$	$_{-1}4^4$	$_25^{-1}$	$_33^{-2}$	$_25^0$	$_31^3$	$_23^3$
C	$_00^0$	$_{-1}0^{-2}$	$_{-1}0^0$	$_{-2}4^0$	$_20^3$	$_13^3$	$_14^1$	$_22^3$	$_17^2$	$_55^2$
A	$_00^0$	$_{-1}2^{-2}$	$_00^{-1}$	$_{-1}0^2$	$_{-2}3^2$	$_12^2$	$_02^2$	$_03^2$	$_12^5$	$_06^3$

Figure 7.4 Example of the SW algorithm to compute the local alignment between two DNA sequences ATCTGGTCC and GTCTTCA. The three values M, I, and D at each position are shown as follows: $_DM^I$. The matrix is computed with gap costs $\alpha = 2$ and $\beta = 1$, and a substitution table of $+2$ if the characters are identical and -1 otherwise. From the highest score ($+7$ in the example), a traceback procedure (in italics) delivers the following optimal local alignment:

```
T  C  T  G  G  T  C
|  |  |        |  |
T  C  T  -  -  T  C
```

new protein sequence belongs to the modeled family, even with low sequence identity [11, 12]. A protein sequence can be aligned to an HMM to determine the probability if it belongs to the modeled family. This alignment can be computed by another by dynamic programming based alignment algorithm: the Viterbi algorithm.

The structure of an HMM to model a protein sequence family is called a profile HMM (Fig. 7.5). It consists of a linear sequence of nodes. Each node has a match (M), insert (I), and delete state (D). Between the nodes are transitions with associated probabilities. Each match state and insert state also contains a position-specific table with probabilities for emitting a particular amino acid. Both transition and emission probabilities can be generated from a multiple sequence alignment of a protein family [11].

An HMM can be compared (aligned) with a given sequence to determine the probability that the sequence belongs to the modeled family. The most probable path through the HMM that generates a sequence equal to the given sequence determines the similarity score. The well-known Viterbi algorithm computes this score by dynamic programming. The computation is given by the following recurrence relations.

$$M(i,j) = e(M_j, s_i) + \max\{M(i-1, j-1) + t(M_{j-1}, M_j), I(i-1, j-1)$$
$$+ t(I_{j-1}, M_j), D(i-1, j-1) + t(D_{j-1}, M_j)\}$$

$$I(i,j) = e(I_j, s_i) + \max\{M(i-1, j) + t(M_j, I_j), I(i-1, j) + t(I_j, I_j), D(i-1, j)$$
$$+ t(D_j, I_j)\}$$

$$D(i,j) = \max\{M(i, j-1) + t(M_{j-1}, D_j), I(i, j-1) + t(I_{j-1}, D_j), D(i,j-1)$$
$$+ t(D_{j-1}, D_j)\}$$

where tr (state1, state2) is the transition cost from state1 to state2 and $e(M_j, s_i)$ is the emission cost of amino acid s_i at state M_j. $M(i,j)$ denotes the score of the best path matching sub-sequence $s_1, \ldots, s_i$ to the submodel up to state j, ending with s_i being emitted by state M_j. Similarly $I(i,j)$ is the score of the best path ending in s_i being emitted by I_j, and, $D(i,j)$ for the best path ending in state D_j. Initialization

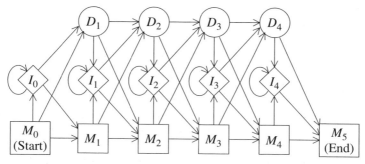

Figure 7.5 The transition structure of a profile HMM of length 4. Squares represent match states, circles represent delete states, and diamonds represent insertions.

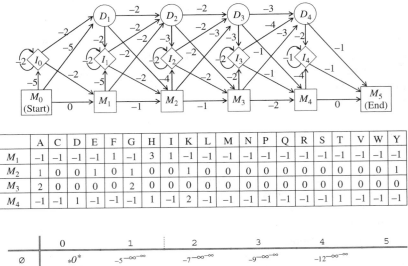

	A	C	D	E	F	G	H	I	K	L	M	N	P	Q	R	S	T	V	W	Y
M_1	-1	-1	-1	-1	1	-1	3	1	-1	-1	-1	-1	-1	-1	-1	-1	-1	-1	-1	-1
M_2	1	0	0	1	0	1	0	0	1	0	0	0	0	0	0	0	0	0	0	1
M_3	2	0	0	0	0	2	0	0	0	0	0	0	0	0	0	0	0	0	0	0
M_4	-1	-1	1	-1	-1	-1	1	-1	2	-1	-1	-1	-1	-1	-1	-1	1	-1	-1	-1

	0	1	2	3	4	5
∅	$*0*$	$_{-\infty}{-5}^{-\infty}$	$_{-\infty}{-7}^{-\infty}$	$_{-\infty}{-9}^{-\infty}$	$_{-\infty}{-12}^{-\infty}$	
H	$_{-\infty}{-\infty}^{-5}$	$_{-7}3^{-7}$	$_{1}7^{-9}$	$_{-1}9^{-12}$	$_{-4}9^{-14}$	
E	$_{-\infty}{-\infty}^{-7}$	$_{-9}8^{-2}$	$_{-4}3^{-2}$	$_{0}1^{-4}$	$_{-3}3^{-6}$	
I	$_{-\infty}{-\infty}^{-9}$	$_{-11}6^{-4}$	$_{-6}4^{-1}$	$_{-3}2^{-3}$	$_{-1}2^{-5}$	
K	$_{-\infty}{-\infty}^{-11}$	$_{-13}10^{-6}$	$_{-8}5^{-3}$	$_{-5}3^{0}$	$_{-4}2^{-3}$	
Q	$_{-\infty}{-\infty}^{-13}$	$_{-15}12^{-8}$	$_{-10}8^{-5}$	$_{-7}5^{-2}$	$_{-6}2^{-2}$	
						-2

Figure 7.6 Given is a profile HMM of length 4 with structure and transition scores shown at the top. The emission scores of the M-states are shown in the table in the middle. Emission scores of the I-states are all set to zero, that is, $e(I_j, s_i) = 0$ for all i, j. The Viterbi dynamic programming matrix for computing the global alignment score of the protein sequence HEIKQ and the given HMM is shown in the lower table. The three values M, I, and D at each position are displayed as $_D M^I$. A traceback procedure starting at $M(6, 5)$ and ending at $M(0, 0)$ (in italics) delivers the optimal path through the given HMM emitting the sequence HEIKQ.

and termination are given by $M(0,0) = 0$ and $M(n + 1, m + 1)$ for a sequence of length n and an HMM of length m. An example is illustrated in Figure 7.6. By adding jump-in/out costs, null model transitions and null model emission costs the equation can be easily extended to implement Viterbi local scoring (equivalent to 0 in the SW equations, [11]).

7.3.3 Dynamic Programming Computation on a Linear Systolic Array

The three values of I, D, and M of any cell in the SW or Viterbi dynamic programming matrices can only be computed if the values of all cells to the left and above have been computed. However, the calculations of the values of diagonally arranged cells parallel to the minor diagonal are independent and can be done simultaneously. On a linear array of processing elements (PEs), this parallelization is achieved by mapping the SW/Viterbi calculation as follows: one PE is assigned to each character/node of

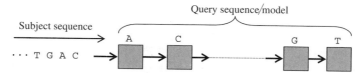

Figure 7.7 Systolic sequence comparison on a linear processor array: the query sequence/model is loaded into the processor array (one character/node per PE) and a subject sequence flows from left to right through the array. During each step, one elementary matrix computation is performed in each PE.

the query sequence/model. The subject sequence is then shifted through the linear chain of PEs (Fig. 7.7). If l1 is the length of the subject sequence and l2 is the length of the query string/model, the comparison is performed in l1 + l2 − 1 steps on l1 PEs, instead of l1 × l2 steps required on a sequential processor.

7.3.4 Mapping onto the Hybrid Architecture

To extend the linear array algorithm to a mesh architecture, we take advantage of the ISA's capabilities to perform row broadcast and row ringshift in a very efficient way. As the length of the sequences/models may vary (several thousands in some cases, however, commonly the length is only in hundreds), the computation must also be partitioned on the $N \times N$ ISA. For sake of clarity, we first assume the processor array size N^2 to be equal to the query sequence length M, that is, $M = N^2$.

Figure 7.8 shows the data flow in the ISA for aligning the sequences $A = a_0 a_1 \cdots a_{M-1}$ and $B = b_0 b_1 \cdots b_{K-1}$ with the SW algorithm, where A is the query sequence and B is a subject sequence of the database. As a preprocessing step, symbol $a_i, i = 0, \ldots, M - 1$, is loaded into PE (m, n) with $m = N - i \operatorname{div} N - 1$ and $n = N - i \bmod N - 1$ and B is loaded into the lower western IP. After that, the row

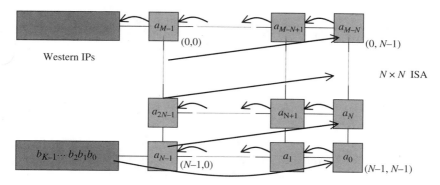

Figure 7.8 Data flow for aligning two sequences A and B on an $M = N \times N$ ISA: A is loaded into the ISA one character per PE and B is completely shifted through the array in $M + K - 1$ steps. Each character b_j is input from the lower western IP and results are written into the upper western IP.

of the substitution table corresponding to the respective character is loaded into each PE as well as the constants α and β. B is then completely shifted through the array in $M + K - 1$ steps as displayed in Figure 7.8.

In iteration step k, $1 \leq k \leq M + K - 1$, the values $M(i,j)$, $D(i,j)$, and $I(i,j)$ for all i,j with $1 \leq i \leq M$, $1 \leq j \leq K$, and $k = i + j - 1$ are computed in parallel in the PEs (m,n) with $m = N - i \operatorname{div} N - 1$ and $n = N - i \operatorname{mod} N - 1$. For this calculation, PE (m,n) receives the values $M(i - 1, j)$, $I(i - 1, j)$, and b_j from its eastern neighbor $(m, n + 1)$ if $n < N - 1$ or from PE $(m + 1, 0)$ if $n = N - 1$ and $m < N - 1$, whereas the values $M(i - 1, j - 1)$, $M(i, j - 1)$, $D(i, j - 1)$, a_i, α, β, and $\operatorname{sbt}(a_i, b_j)$ are stored locally. The lower right PE $(N - 1, N - 1)$ receives b_j in steps j with $0 \leq j \leq K - 1$ from the lower western IP and zeros otherwise.

Because of the efficient row ringshift and row broadcast, these routing operations can be accomplished in constant time on the ISA. Thus, it takes $M + K - 1$ steps to compute the alignment cost of the two sequences with the SW algorithm. However, notice that after the last character of B enters the array, the first character of a new subject sequence can be input for the next iteration step. Thus, all subject sequences of the database can be pipelined with only one step delay between two different sequences. Assuming k sequences of length K and $K = O(M)$, we compute K sequence alignments in time $O(KM)$ using $O(M)$ processors. As the best sequential algorithm takes $O(KM^2)$ steps, our parallel implementation achieves maximal efficiency. The same technique can be applied for mapping the Viterbi algorithm onto the ISA.

Because of the limited PE memory, only the highest score of matrix M is computed on Systola 1024 for each pairwise comparison. Ranking the compared sequences and reconstructing the alignments are carried out by the front-end PC. Because this last operation is only performed for very few subject sequences, its computation time is negligible. In our ISA algorithm, the maximum computation of the matrix M can be easily incorporated with only a constant time penalty: After each iteration step, all PEs compute a new value max by taking the maximum of the newly computed H-value and the old value of max from its neighboring PE. After the last character of a subject sequence has been processed in PE $(0,0)$, the maximum of matrix M is stored in PE $(0,0)$, which is written into the adjacent western IP.

So far, we have assumed a processor array equal in size of the query sequence length $(M = N^2)$. In practice, this rarely happens. Assuming a query sequence length of $M = kN$ with k a multiple of N or N a multiple of k, the algorithm is modified as follows:

1. $k \leq N$: In this case, we can just replicate the algorithm for a $k \times N$ ISA on an $N \times N$ ISA, that is, each $k \times N$ subarray computes the alignment of the same query sequence with different subject sequences.

2. $k > N$: A possible solution is to assign k/N characters of the sequences to each PE instead of one. However, in this case, the memory size has to be sufficient to store k/N rows of the substitution table (20 values per row, as there are 20 different amino acids), that is, on Systola 1024, it is only possible to assign maximally two characters per PE for the SW algorithm (only one character

per PE for the Viterbi algorithm). Thus, for $k/N > 2$, it is required to split the sequence comparison into $k/(2N)$ passes.

The first $2N^2$ characters of the query sequence are loaded into the ISA. The entire database then crosses the array; the M-value and I-value computed in PE (0,0) in each iteration step are written into the adjacent western IP and then stored in the western board RAM. In the next pass, the following $2N^2$ characters of the query sequence are loaded. The data stored previously is loaded into the lower western IP together with the corresponding subject sequences and from there sent again into the ISA. The process is iterated until the end of the query sequence is reached. Note that no additional instructions are necessary for the I/O of the intermediate results with the processor array, because it is integrated in the dataflow. The additionally required data transfer between IPs and board RAM can be performed concurrently with the computation.

For distribution of the computation among the PCs, we have chosen a static split load balancing strategy: A similar sized subset of the database is assigned to each PC in a preprocessing step. The subsets remain stationary regardless of the query sequence. Thus, the distribution has only to be performed once for each database and does not influence the overall computing time. The input query sequence is broadcast to each PC and multiple independent subset scans are performed on each Systola 1024 board. Finally, the highest scores are accumulated in one PC. This strategy provides the best performance for our homogenous and dedicated architecture, where each processing unit has the same processing power. However, a dynamic split load balancing strategy as used in Ref. [22] is more suitable for heterogeneous environments such as computational grids.

7.4 PERFORMANCE EVALUATION

A performance measure commonly used in computational biology is millions of dynamic cell updates per second (MCUPS). A CUPS represents the time for a complete computation of one entry of the matrices M, D, and I including all comparisons,

TABLE 7.1   IC to Update Two cells of the SW Algorithm and One Cell of the Viterbi Algorithm in One PE of Systola 1024 with the Corresponding Operations

Operation in Each PE per Iteration Step	IC (SW)	IC (Viterbi)
Get data from left neighbor	20	20
Compute $I(i,j)$	8	29
Compute $D(i,j)$	8	10
Compute $M(i,j)$	20	29
Compute temporary max-score	4	N.A.
Sum	68	88

additions and maxima computations. To measure the MCUPS performance on Systola 1024, we have given the instruction count (IC) to update two cells per PE for the SW algorithm and to update one cell per PE for the Viterbi algorithm in Table 7.1.

Because two new SW cells are computed for two characters within 68 instructions in each PE, the whole 32×32 processor array can perform 2048 cell updates in the same time. This leads to a performance of $(2048/68) \times (50/16) \times 10^6 \text{ CUPS} = 94 \text{ MCUPS}$ for the SW algorithm. The corresponding performance for the Viterbi algorithm is $(1024/88) \times (50/16) \times 10^6 \text{ CUPS} = 36 \text{ MCUPS}$.

Because MCUPS does not consider data transfer time and query length, it is often a weak measure that does not reflect the behavior of the complete system. Therefore, we will use execution times of database scans for different query lengths in our evaluation. The involved data transfer in each iteration step of the SW algorithm is input of a new character b_j into the lower western IP of each $k \times N$ subarray for query lengths ≤ 2048 and input of a new b_j and a previously computed cell of M and I and output of an M-cell and I-cell from the upper western IP for query lengths greater than 2048. Thus, the data transfer time is totally dominated by above computing time of 68 instructions per iteration step.

Table 7.2 reports times for scanning the TrEMBL protein databank for query sequences of various lengths with the SW algorithm. The first two rows of the table give the execution times for Systola 1024 and the cluster with 16 boards compared to a sequential C-program on a Pentium III 1 GHz. As the times show, the parallel implementations scale almost linearly with the sequence length. Because of the used static split strategy, the cluster times also scale almost linearly with the number of PCs. Table 7.3 reports times for scanning the SwissProt databank for HMMs of various lengths with the Viterbi algorithm.

A single Systola 1024 board is around four times faster than a Pentium III 1 GHz for the SW algorithm and around 3.5 times faster than a single Pentium III 1 GHz for the Viterbi algorithm. The reason for these relatively poor speedups is that Systola has been built in 1994 [21]. However, a board redesign based on technology used for processors such as the Pentium III would make this factor significantly higher.

For the comparison of different parallel machines, we have taken data from Dahle et al. [8] for a database with the SW algorithm for different query length.

TABLE 7.2   Scan Times (in seconds) of the TrEMBL Protein Databank (release 14, Which Contains 351,834 Sequences and 100,069,442 Amino Acids) for Various Length of the Query Sequence on Systola 1024 and the PC Cluster with 16 Systola 1024

Query sequence length	256	512	1024	2048	4096
Systola 1024	294	577	1137	2241	4611
Speedup	4	4	4	4	4
PC cluster of 16 Systolas	20	38	73	142	290
Speedup	53	56	58	60	59

Note: The speedup compared to the Pentium III 1 GHz is also reported.

TABLE 7.3   Scan Times (in seconds) of SwissProt (release
40, 113997 Protein Sequences) for Various HMM Lengths
with the Viterbi algorithm on Systola 1024 and a PC
Cluster with 16 Systolas

HMM length	112	222	490
Systola 1024	152	288	546
Speedup	3	3.5	4
PC cluster of 16 Systolas	12	22	40
Speedup	37	45	56

Note: The speedup compared to a Pentium III 1 GHz is also reported.

Systola 1024 is around two times faster than the much larger 1K-PE MasPar and the cluster of 16 Systolas is around two times faster than a 16K-PE MasPar. The one-board Kestrel is four to five times faster than a Systola board. Kestrel's design [8] is also a programmable fine-grained parallel architecture implemented as a PC add-on board. It reaches the higher performance, because it has been built with $0.5\,\mu$m CMOS technology, in comparison with $1.0\,\mu$m for Systola 1024. Extrapolating to this technology both approaches should perform equally. However, the difference between both architectures is that Kestrel is purely a linear array, whereas Systola is a mesh. This makes the Systola 1024 a more flexible design, suitable for a wider range of applications; see, for example, [27–32].

7.4.1   Performance Evaluation of a Reconfigurable Platform

To evaluate our approach on a device based on state-of-the-art technology, we have implemented the SW algorithm on a modern reconfigurable architecture. Figure 7.9 shows our PE design for computing one cell of the SW dynamic programming matrix. A linear systolic array of this PE can be built to compute the SW algorithm as shown in Figure 7.7.

As the query sequence is usually larger than the processor array, we have to do a partitioning on a fixed-size linear processor array. For sake of clarity, we first assume a query sequence of length M and a processor array of size N, where M is a multiple of N, that is, $M = kN$ where $k \geq 1$ is an integer. A possible solution is to split the computation into k passes. Unfortunately, this solution requires a large amount of off-chip memory. The memory requirement can be reduced by factor p by splitting the database into p equal-sized pieces and computing the alignment scores of all subject sequences within each piece.

However, this approach also increases the loading time of substitution table columns by factor p. To eliminate this loading time, we have slightly extended our PE design. Each PE now stores k columns of the substitution table instead of only one. Although this increases the area of each PE, it allows for alignment of each database sequence with the complete query sequence without additional delays. It also reduces the required off-chip memory for storing intermediate results to four times the longest

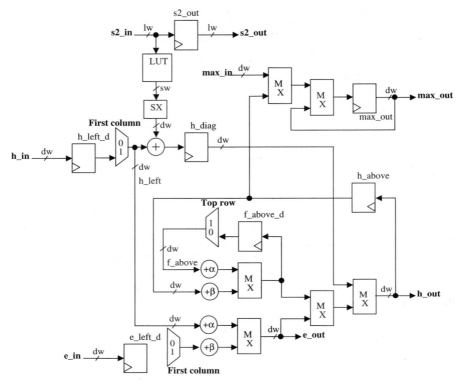

Figure 7.9 PE design for computing on SW cell. Data width (dw) is scaled to the required precision (usually dw = 16 is sufficient). The LUT depth is scaled to hold the required number of substitution table rows. Substitution width (sw) is scaled to accommodate the dynamic range required by the substitution table. Look-up address width (lw) is scaled in relation to the LUT depth. Each PE has local memory to store $M(i, j-1)$, $M(i-1, j)$, and $M(i-1, j-1)$. The PE holds a column of the substitution table in its LUT. The look-up of sbt($S1_i$, $S2_j$) and addition to $M(i-1, j-1)$ is done in one cycle. The score is calculated in the next cycle and passed to the next PE in the array. The PE keeps track of the maximum score computed so far and passes it to the next PE in the array. The PE has additional storage for $D(i, j-1)$ and $I(i-1, j)$ and additional score computation circuitry. Additions are performed using saturation arithmetic.

database sequence size. Figure 7.10 illustrates our solution. Different configurations are designed for different values of k. This allows us to load a particular configuration that is suited for a range of query sequence lengths.

We have described the PE design in Verilog and targeted it to the Xilinx Virtex II architecture. The size of a PE is 6×8 configurable logic blocks (Figure 7.11). Using a Virtex II XC2V6000, we are able to accommodate 168 PEs using $k = 3$. This allows for query sequence lengths up to 504, which is sufficient in most cases

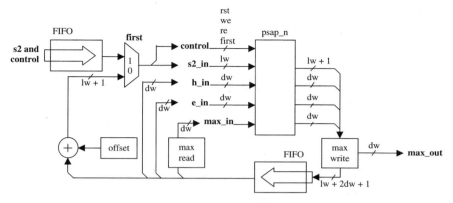

Figure 7.10 System implementation: The linear array of PEs is encapsulated in psap_n. The database sequences are passed in from the host one by one through an FIFO to the s2 interface. The database sequences have been preconverted to LUT addresses. For query lengths longer than the PE array, the intermediate results are stored in the FIFO of width $2 \times dw + lw + 1$. The FIFO depth is sized to hold the longest sequence in the database. The database sequence is also stored in the FIFO. On each consecutive pass, an LUT offset is added to address the next column of the substitution table stored within the PEs. The maximum score on each pass is compared with those from all other passes and the absolute maximum is returned to the host.

(74% of sequences in Swiss-Prot are ≤ 500 [4]). For longer queries, we have a design with $k = 12$, which can accommodate 126 PEs. The clock frequencies are both 45 MHz. The corresponding CUPS performances are shown in Table 7.4. Table 7.5 reports the performance for scanning the Swiss-Prot protein databank (release 42.5, which contains 138,922 sequences comprising 51,131,444 amino acids [4]) for query sequences of various lengths using our design on an RC2000 FPGA Mezzanine PCI-board with a Virtex II XC2V6000 from Celoxica [6].

For the same application, an optimized C-program on a Pentium IV 1.6 GHz has a performance of ~40 MCUPS. Hence, our FPGA implementation achieves a speedup of ~125. The Virtex II XC2V6000 is around ten times faster than the much larger 16K-PE MasPar. Kestrel is 12 times slower [8] and Systola 1024 is around 50 times slower than our solution. All these boards reach a lower performance, because they have been built with older CMOS technology (Kestrel: 0.5 μm, Systola 1024: 1.0 μm) than the Virtex II XC2V6000 (0.15 μm). Extrapolating to this technology both SIMD and reconfigurable FPGA platforms have approximately equal performance. However, the difference between both approaches is that FPGAs allow easy upgrading, for example, targeting our design to a Virtex II XC2V8000 would improve the performance by around 30%.

Our implementation is slower than the FPGA implementations described in Refs. [15, 18, 35]. However, all these designs only implement edit distance. This greatly simplifies the PE design and, therefore, achieves a higher PE density as well

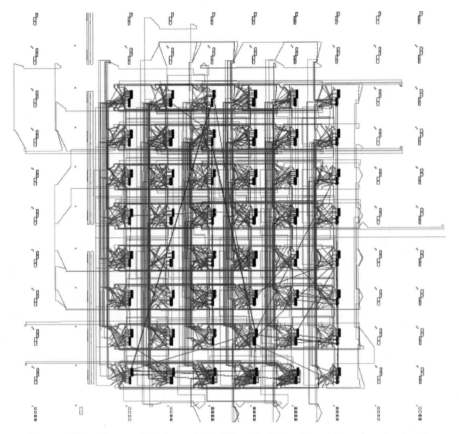

Figure 7.11   Layout plans for a single PE on the Virtex II architecture using $k = 3$.

as a higher clock frequency. Although of theoretical interest, edit distance is not used in practice because it does not allow for different gap penalties and substitution tables. The FPGA implementation presented in Ref. [34] on a Virtex XCV2000E is around three times slower than our solution. Unfortunately, the design only implements global alignment.

TABLE 7.4   Achieved Number of PEs and Clock Frequencies of our Different Designs on a Virtex II XC2V6000

Design	Number of PEs	Clock Frequency	Max Query Length	Peak Performance
$k = 3$	168	45 MHz	504	7.6 GCUPS
$k = 12$	126	45 MHz	1512	5.7 GCUPS

Note: The maximal query sequence lengths and performance (in Giga CUPS) for each design is also reported.

TABLE 7.5   Performance Evaluation for Various Query Sequence Length Ranges of our Implementation on a Virtex II XC2V6000 FPGA

Query length range	1–168	169–336	337–504	505–630	631–756
Mean performance	3.2 GCUPS	5.1 GCUPS	5.8 GCUPS	4.8 GCUPS	5.0 GCUPS

Note: Mean performance indicates the performance for the mean value of the corresponding query length range.

7.5 FUTURE WORK AND OPEN PROBLEMS

We are currently working on improving and complementing our already successful protein structure prediction algorithm [9, 32]. The first area of improvement is in its speed and the second is in relation to what (and how much) information should be extracted from the context to achieve optimal predictions. The third problem is in relation to whether we can produce indications in which cases our predictions are good and in which cases the prediction quality is not high. The fourth problem is in relation to visualization tools that help experts use this approach. The fifth area is about making use of the fact that protein structures are mainly determined by their dihedral angles and developing a method for finding similar structures to a given structure (instead of finding similar sequences to a given sequence). The sixth problem is about developing special-purpose architectures particularly in relation to algorithms such as those developed in relation to problems 1, 2, 4, and 5. The seventh problem deals with a variation of the ISA concept, which does allow using different processors in the same architecture.

7.5.1   Fast Algorithms and Data Structures for Finding Short Patterns

In Refs. [9, 32], we have presented an algorithm for protein structure prediction that requires for every predicted dihedral angle to retrieve all sequences that match the context of this angle. Thus, fast retrieval of such sequences is most essential. The problem is for a given database of known protein structures to develop a data structure together with a search algorithm such that the memory requirement is not too large and the search time is as small as possible. One obvious approach to this problem is setting up a keyword tree for the complete set of sub-sequences. This would create a structure that is in size proportional to the database and has optimal access time as long as we are looking for perfect matches for a given pattern. In the course of refining our approach, we do not insist on exact matches though. Instead we are looking for sub-sequences in the database that are similar to a given pattern, but not necessarily identical. For such cases, there might be better solutions — in particular, we are looking at sorting all sub-sequences of a given length and develop a system of pointers that supports fast traversal of the sorted list.

7.5.2   Finding the Optimal Context

In our approach, we rely on finding several matches or several sub-sequences that are similar to a given pattern (combined with a certain tolerance that defines the maximal deviation from the given pattern). There is a trade-off between the length of the pattern and the tolerance expected number of matches of this pattern in the database. The longer the pattern, the less likely it is to find a match in the database. The larger the tolerance, the easier it is to find a match. Both dependencies are exponential, that is, if the sequence is a sequence over an alphabet with k letters and the pattern length is n, then there are k^l different patterns of length l, and if the database contains M patterns, the expected number of sub-sequences that match the given pattern is $E = M/k^l$. To do any statistical analysis on the matches found, we need E to be of sufficient size. To increase E for a fixed l, we can reduce the size of the alphabet, that is, instead of requesting a match with the given amino acids (there are 20 different amino acids) we might only request the corresponding amino acid is in the same class of amino acids (there we might place every amino acid into only 2 classes, such as hydrophilic and hydrophobic). The following two cases demonstrate the potential advantage of such an approach.

Case 1: We look for all amino acid sub-sequences in the PDB database that match a given sequence of five amino acids. Given the fact that the PDB database currently contains about 10^7 amino acids and the fact that there are 3.2×10^6 different amino acid sequences of length 5, we can expect to find about three matches.

Case 2: We look for all amino acid sub-sequences in the PDB database that match a given pattern that has a given amino acid in its central position and specifies to its left an right a pattern of hydrophobicity of length 3 (i.e., we specify in which position we expect to have a hydrophobic amino acid and in which position we expect to have a hydrophilic amino acid). There are 1280 such patterns of length 7 and thus we can expect to find about 10^4 such patterns in the PDB database — a much better basis for statistical analysis than in Case 1.

7.5.3   Develop Interactive Visualization Tools that Allow Fast Correction of Incorrect or Improbable Predictions

There are several open source visualization tools available, which allow visualization and rotation of proteins in a wide variety of modes. For our application, we would like to develop interactive visualization tools that present the histogram of an angle as soon as the curser is pointing at it. Then, it should be possible to point at the histogram and change the corresponding dihedral angles (arrows in Figure 7.12). The visualization tool should also have the option of highlighting amino acids of particular interest and positions that might be involved in hydrogen bonds.

7.5.4   Extracting Structure Similarity Based on Dihedral Angles

Having the structures almost totally represented by sequences of dihedral angles, opens the option of looking for similar structures, that is, similar sequences of dihedral

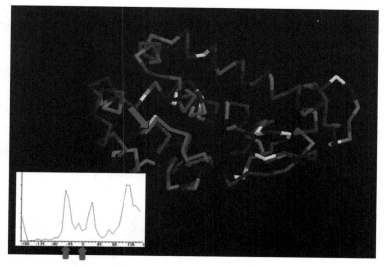

Figure 7.12   An interactive visualisation tool.

angles. To this end, we envisage to develop an algorithm that works similar to the SW algorithm, but instead of comparing sequences of symbols (amino acids) we would compare sequences of real numbers. It needs to be worked out what kind of formula should be used for the determination of penalties and what angles difference is regarded a match. Being able to search for similar structures might contribute toward giving additional insight into understanding the functions of proteins.

7.5.5   Development of Special-Purpose Architectures in Relation to Protein Structure Predictions

All structural prediction algorithms as well as interactive visualization tools are compute intensive and, at the same time, do not make good use of standard CPUs. Thus, it is desirable to develop special-purpose architectures. It is very likely that algorithms will be improved over time and new algorithms will be designed. Therefore, it is essential that the corresponding architectures are flexible. We envisage making use of the concept of the ISA and embedding it on FPGAs. This way we can not only change the programs but can even change the ALUs and the set of instructions, and thus we will be able to optimally adjust the architecture to the application.

7.5.6   ISA Architectures with Nonidentical Processors

In many situations, it might be desirable to have different processors working collaboratively. This is a new concept in the area of SIMD computing. In particular, some processors might compare amino acids, whereas others compare only classes of amino acids. Although comparing amino acids requires at least 5 bit data and corresponding ALUs, comparing classes would in cases where we have only two classes (e.g. hydrophobic and hydrophilic) only require 1 bit. Thus, we can save significant number of gates and increase the number of processors implemented on the FPGAs.

7.6 TUTORIAL

1. In solving this problem, you are free to define your own instructions for the ISA.

   a. Design an ISA program for the 4×4 ISA, which performs a vertical rotate operation on all rows, that is, data of the first row is moved to the last row and data from all other rows is moved one row up.

   b. Design an ISA program for the 4×4 ISA, which performs a broadcast operation within every row, that is, data form the leftmost processor is sent to all processors within its row.

   c. Design an ISA program for the 4×4 ISA, which produces the transitive closure of a directed graph.

   d. Analyze the time complexity and the period of the above programs.

2. Find the optimal global and local alignment of the two sequences GACGGGT and ACT using the following scoring system: substitution matrix $sbt(x, y) = +3$ if $x = y$ and -1 if $x \neq y$, gap opening penalty $h = -3$, and gap extension penalty $g = -1$.

3. Several optimal alignments may exist for a pair of sequences. For instance, the sequences ATAT and TATA have the following two optimal global alignments when using the substitution matrix $sbt(x, y) = +1$ if $x = y$ and -1 if $x \neq y$ and the linear gap penalty $g = -2$

$$\begin{array}{ccccc} - & A & T & A & T \\ T & A & T & A & - \end{array} \quad \text{and} \quad \begin{array}{ccccc} A & T & A & T & - \\ - & T & A & T & A \end{array}$$

Each optimal alignment corresponds to a distinct traceback path in the dynamic programming matrix.

   a. Develop the pseudocode of an algorithm using the dynamic programming concept, which computes the number of optimal global alignments of two sequences according to a linear gap penalty and a substitution matrix as parameters.

   b. Explain how your algorithm works.

   c. What is the time and space complexity of your algorithm? Justify your answer.

4. Given is the following alignment algorithm in pseudocode [17]. It uses the gap penalty g and substitution matrix sbt( ) as parameters.

   Algorithm Wrap

   Input: sequences $T = t_1, \ldots, t_m, P = p_1, \ldots, p_n$.

Output: score
for $i = 0$ to m do $H[i, 0] = 0$;
for $j = 0$ to n do $H[0, j] = 0$;
for $i = 1$ to m do begin
for $j = 1$ to n do
$\quad H[i,j] = \max\{0, H[i, j-1] - g, H[i-1, j-1] - \text{sbt}(t_i, p_j),$
$\quad\quad H[i-1,j] - g\}$;
$H[i, 0] = H[i, k]$;
for $j = 1$ to n do
$\quad H[i, j] = \max\{0, H[i, j-1] - g, H[i-1, j-1] - \text{sbt}(t_i, p_j),$
$\quad\quad H[i-1, j] - g\}$;
end;
score = maximal value of matrix H;

a. Compute score for the input sequences $T = $ KFGFGFGM and $P = $ FG using $\text{sbt}(t_i, p_j) = +2$ if $t_i = p_j$ and -1 if $t_i \neq p_j$ and $g = 1$.

b. Which alignment problem is the algorithm solving in general? State a possible bioinformatics application where this algorithm could be used.

c. Parallelize this algorithm on a PC cluster using MPI and parallel prefix computations. The concept of prefix computations is described in Ref. [2].

d. Parallelize the algorithm on an ISA using C:=max{C,CW} as one of the instruction. This instruction computes the maximum of the C-register of the western neighbor and the own C-register and writes it into the own C-register.

5. Given the HMM shown in Figure 7.6.

a. Compute the optimal global alignment of the protein sequence ERTIG to this model using the Viterbi algorithm.

b. Design a PE of a linear systolic array, which computes one cell of the Viterbi dynamic programming matrix in one clock cycle.

c. Compare the size of your PE design to the PE design for the SW algorithm shown in Figure 7.9.

d. Lookup the structure of a profile HMM for local alignment, for example in Ref. [11]. Extend your PE design in part b to implement the Viterbi algorithm for local alignment.

6. Nussinov has introduced another dynamic programming algorithm in 1978 for RNA folding [26]. Given an RNA sequence A of length L with symbols $x_1, \ldots, x_L$. Let $\delta(i,j) = 1$ if x_i and x_j are a complementary base pair (the nucleotides G–C and A–U are said to be complementary) and $\delta(i,j) = 0$ otherwise. We then calculate a two-dimensional dynamic programming matrix $M(i,j)$ as follows:

$$M(i, i-1) = 0 \quad \text{for } i = 2 \text{ to } L$$
$$M(i, i) = 0 \quad \text{for } i = 1 \text{ to } L$$

$$M(i,j) = \max \begin{cases} M(i+1,j) \\ M(i,j-1) \\ M(i+1,j-1) + \delta(i,j) \\ \max_{i<k<j}[M(i,k) + M(k+1,j)] \end{cases} \quad \begin{array}{l} \text{for } i = 1 \text{ to } L \text{ and} \\ j = i+1 \text{ to } L. \end{array}$$

The value of $M(1,L)$ then represents the number of base pairs in the maximally base-paired structure of A.

a. Compute $M(1,L)$ for the input sequence CCCUUUAGG.

b. What is the main difference of Nussinov's algorithm when compared with the SW and Viterbi algorithm?

c. Develop a strategy how Nussinov's algorithm can be efficiently computed on an ISA. You are free to define your own instruction set.

REFERENCES

1. S. F. Altschul, W. Gish, W. Miller, E. W. Myers, and D. J. Lipman, Basic local alignment search tool, *J. Mol. Biol.*, 215, 403–410 (1990).

2. S. Aluru, N. Futamura, and K. Mehrotra, Parallel biological sequence comparisons using prefix computations, *J. Parallel Distributed Comput.*, 63, 264–272 (2003).

3. A. Bateman, et al., The PFAM protein families database, *Nucleic Acid Res.*, 32, 138–141, (2004).

4. B. Boeckmann, A. Bairoch, R. Apweiler, M.-C. Blatter, A. Estreicher, E. Gasteiger, M. J. Martin, K. Michoud, C. O'Donovan, I. Phan, S. Pilbout, and M. Schneider, The SWISS-PROT protein knowledgebase and its supplement TrEMBL in 2003, *Nucleic Acids Res.*, 31, 365–370 (2003).

5. M. Borah, R. S. Bajwa, S. Hannenhalli, and M. J. Irwin, A SIMD Solution to the Sequence Comparison Problem on the MGAP, in *Proceedings of ASAP'94*, IEEE CS, 1994 144–160.

6. Celoxica Corporation, www.celoxica.com, 2004.

7. E. Chow, T. Hunkapiller, J. Peterson, and M. S. Waterman, Biological information signal processor, *Proc. ASAP'91*, IEEE CS, 144–160 (1991).

8. D. Dahle, L. Grate, E. Rice, and R. Hughey, The UCSC Kestrel general Purpose Parallel Processor, in *Proceedings of International Conference in Parallel and Distributed Processing Techniques and Appilcations*, 1243–1249 (1999).

9. S. Dayalan, S. Bevinakoppa, and H. Schröder, A Dihedral Angle Database of Short Sub-Sequences for Protein Structure Prediction, in *Proceedings of the Second Asia Pacific Bioinformatics Conference*, Dunedin, New Zealand, 2004.

10. A. Dittrich and H. Schmeck, Givens's rotation on an instruction systolic array, *Proc. Parcella'88*, LNCS 342, Springer, 340–346 (1988).

11. R. Durbin, S. Eddy, A. Krogh, and G. Mitchison, *Biolgcial Sequence Analysis, Probabilistic Models of Proteins and Nucleic Acids*, Cambridge University Press, 1998.

12. S. R. Eddy, Profile hidden markov models, *Bioinformatics*, 14, 755–763 (1998).

13. E. Glemet and J. J. Codani, LASSAP, a large scale sequence comparison package, *CABIOS*, 13 (2), 145–150 (1997).

14. M. Gokhale, et al., Processing in memory: the Terasys massively parallel PIM array, *Computer*, 28(4), 23–31 (1995).

15. S. A. Guccione and E. Keller, Gene matching using JBits, *Proceedings of 12th International Workshop on Field-Programmable Logic and Applications* (FPL'02), Springer, LNCS 2438, 1168–1171 (2002).

16. P. Guerdoux-Jamet, and D. Lavenier, SAMBA: hardware accelerator for biological sequence comparison, *CABIOS*, 12 (6), 609–615 (1997).

17. D. Gusfield, *Algorithms on Strings, Trees and Sequences: Computer Science and Computational Biology*, Cambridge University Press, 1997.

18. D. T. Hoang, Searching Genetic Databases on Splash 2, in *Proceedings of IEEE Workshop on FPGAs for Custom Computing Machines*, IEEE CS, 185–191 (1993).

19. R. Hughey, Parallel Hardware for sequence comparison and alignment, *CABIOS* 12 (6), 473–479 (1996).

20. H.-W. Lang, The instruction systolic array, a parallel architecture for VLSI, *Integration, VLSI J.*, 4, 65–74 (1986).

21. H.-W. Lang, R. Maaß, and M. Schimmler, The Instruction Systolic Array — Implementation of a Low-Cost Parallel Architecture as Add-On Board For Personal Computers, in *Proceedings of HPCN'94*, LNCS 797, Springer, 487–488 (1994).

22. D. Lavenier and J.-L. Pacherie, Parallel Processing for Scanning Genomic Data-Bases, in *Proceedings of PARCO'97*, Elsevier, 81–88, 1998.

23. D. P. Lopresti, P-NAC: A systolic array for comparing nucleic acid sequences, *Computer*, 20 (7), 98–99 (1987).

24. R. Nussinov, G. Pieczenik, J. R. Griggs, and D. J. Kleitman, Algorithms for loop matchings, *SIAM J. App. Math.*, 35, 68–82 (1978).

25. W. R. Pearson, Comparison of methods for searching protein sequence databases, *Protein Sci.*, 4 (6), 1145–1160 (1995).

26. R. K. Singh, et al., BIOSCAN: a network sharable computational resource for searching biosequence databases, *CABIOS*, 12 (3), 191–196 (1996).

27. M. Schimmler and H.-W. Lang, The Instruction Systolic Array in Image Processing Applications, in *Proceedings of Europto 96*, SPIE 2784, 136–144 (1996).

28. B. Schmidt and M. Schimmler, A Parallel Accelerator Architecture for Multimedia Video Compression, in *Proceedings of EuroPar'99*, LNCS 1685, Springer, 950–959, 1999.

29. B. Schmidt, M. Schimmler, and H. Schröder, High-speed Cryptography, in *Embedded Cryptographic Hardware: Methodologies and Architectures*, Nova Science Publishers, 2004.

30. B. Schmidt, M. Schimmler, and H. Schröder, Tomographic image reconstruction on the instruction systolic array, *Comput. Inform.*, 20, 27–42 (2001).

31. B. Schmidt, Design of a Parallel Accelerator for Volume Rendering, in *Proceedings of Euro-Par'2000*, LNCS 1900, Springer, 1095–1104, 2000.

32. H. Schröder, B. Schmidt, and J. Zhu, A new approach to protein structure prediction, in *Proceedings International Conference on Bioinformatics*, Bangkok, Thailand, 2002.

33. T. F. Smith and M. S. Waterman, Identification of common molecular sub-sequences, *J. Mol. Biol.*, 147, 195–197 (1981).

34. Y. Yamaguchi, T. Maruyama, and A. Konagaya, High Speed Homology Search with FPGAs, in *Proceedings of Pacific Symposium on Biocomputing'02*, 271–282 (2002).

35. C. W. Yu, K. H. Kwong, K. H. Lee, and P. H. W. Leong, A Smith-Waterman Systolic Cell, in *Proceedings of 13th International Workshop on Field Programmable Logic and Applications (FPL'03)*, Springer, LNCS 2778, 375–384 (2003).

Multiple Sequence Alignment in Parallel on a Cluster of Workstations

AMITAVA DATTA and JUSTIN EBEDES

In this chapter, we present a parallel version of CLUSTAL W for multiple sequence alignment. Our algorithm is implemented using the Message Passing Interface (MPI), a platform for implementing parallel algorithms on a distributed shared memory model. We first present a tutorial introduction to the CLUSTAL W algorithm. First we discuss the dynamic programming algorithm for pairwise sequence alignment. Then we discuss the neighbor-joining method of Seitou and Nei for constructing a phylogenetic tree using the pairwise distances. Finally, we discuss the progressive sequence alignment step based on this phylogenetic tree. We discuss our strategy for parallelizing the CLUSTAL W algorithm next. We give detailed results for our implementation and analyze the results extensively. Our program is available from the web server: http://mason.csse.uwa.edu.au

8.1 INTRODUCTION

Multiple sequence alignment is the problem of aligning DNA or amino acid sequences in an optimal way to match as many characters as possible from each sequence. Given a scoring scheme for evaluating matching characters and for penalizing gaps in the sequences, the problem concerns placing gaps in each sequence in such a way to maximize the alignment score.

The main purpose of sequence alignment is to infer homology between sequences, but there are also many other applications. These include finding diagnostic patterns to characterize protein families, to detect similarity between new sequences and well-known families of sequences, and to aid in evolutionary analysis [5, 10, 15].

Multiple sequence alignment is, however, an NP-hard problem, so approximation algorithms are generally required for most multiple alignment tasks [8]. One such

Parallel Computing for Bioinformatics and Computational Biology, Edited by Albert Y. Zomaya
Copyright © 2006 John Wiley & Sons, Inc.

approximation algorithm is used by the popular program CLUSTAL W [15] and consists of three stages. The first of these stages uses the sequences to construct a *distance matrix*, which tabulates the similarity between every pair of sequences. The second stage involves the construction of a phylogenetic or *guide tree*, using the information in the distance matrix. This tree is used as input to the final stage, where the sequences are progressively aligned in an order specified by the guide tree to produce the final sequence alignment.

Given that sequences can be many hundreds or even thousands of *residues* or *base pairs* long and that molecular biologists may require the alignment of thousands of sequences, even these approximation algorithms require long periods of time to compute a near-optimal alignment. Thus, a natural step forward to reduce the running time required is to parallelize one of these algorithms. This chapter examines the algorithm used by CLUSTAL W and explains how its steps can be parallelized. The performance of the parallel implementation is then examined.

We have developed a parallel version of CLUSTAL W, named MASON (multiple alignment of sequences over a network), using the methods described in this chapter. The source code of MASON is available on request from the first author. MASON was written using the C programming language and MPICH [9], an implementation of the message passing interface (MPI).

The use of network of workstations as parallel computing environments is becoming increasingly popular. This is due to the fact that today's desktop machines are extremely powerful as well as affordable. In contrast, dedicated parallel computers are often very expensive and most research groups have only limited access to such machines. Hence, we have used an ordinary cluster of PCs as a parallel computer. However, our implementation can be run on a dedicated parallel machine using other MPI implementations with little changes in the code.

The rest of the chapter is organized as follows. We discuss the algorithm used in CLUSTAL W in Section 8.2. We discuss our parallel implementation in Section 8.3. Our results are discussed in Section 8.4 and finally, we conclude with some comments in Section 8.5.

8.2 CLUSTAL W

This section outlines the three stages of the algorithm used by CLUSTAL W. The first stage, calculating the distance matrix, uses the sequences themselves as input. The distance matrix is then used to construct the guide tree, which in turn is used in the final progressive alignment stage.

8.2.1 Calculating the Distance Matrix

The first stage of the CLUSTAL W algorithm requires the calculation of a distance matrix, which simply tabulates the results from pairwise aligning each sequence with every other sequence. For N sequences, $N(N-1)/2$ pairwise alignments must be calculated.

A pairwise alignment is performed using the dynamic programming algorithm of Needleman and Wunsch [11], as modified by Gotoh [3] to obtain $O(m^2)$ performance, where m is the length of the sequences being aligned. For aligning two sequences S and T, the process involves filling in a matrix that represents all possible alignments of the two sequences. If S_i is the ith amino acid of protein S and T_j is the jth amino acid of protein T, then the cell $A(i,j)$ represents a particular alignment of the two sequences, where S_i is aligned with T_j. The matrix is also used to penalize gaps in the alignment, to encourage fewer and shorter gaps. In general, there are many different ways of assigning scores for *gap*, *match*, and *mismatch*; see, for example, the article by Thompson et al. [15] for a detailed discussion of score assignments in CLUSTAL W. In the example given subsequently, we assume that a gap is assigned a score of -2 and a match (or mismatch) is assigned a score of $+1$ (or -1). The aim is to find an alignment that has a maximum score. Each step in the dynamic programming algorithm can be summarized as follows:

- Each entry $A(i,j)$ can be filled in three ways [$A(i-1,j-1)$, $A(i-1,j)$, and $A(i,j-1)$ are the three elements immediately preceding $A(i,j)$ in the matrix]
    1. The last *nucleotide* of $S(i)$ is aligned with $T(j)$. There are two possibilities, either they match ($+1$) or they mismatch (-1). The cost is $A(i-1,j-1) \pm 1$
    2. $S(i)$ is aligned with a gap in T. The cost is $A(i-1,j) - 2$
    3. $T(j)$ is aligned with a gap in S. The cost is $A(i,j-1) - 2$
- In each case, the rest of prefix of S should be optimally aligned with the rest of prefix of T.

We can write these three possibilities in a more mathematical form as follows:

$$A(i,j) = \max \begin{cases} A(i-1,j) - 2, & \text{align } S(i) \text{ with a gap} \\ A(i,j-1) - 2, & \text{align } T(j) \text{ with a gap} \\ A(i-1,j-1) \pm 1 & \text{align } S(i) \text{ with } T(j) \end{cases}$$

Hence, we need the three entries $A(i-1,j)$, $A(i,j-1)$, and $A(i-1,j-1)$ for filing the entry $A(i,j)$. Note that all these three entries have been already computed when we are trying to compute $A(i,j)$.

The time to fill the entire matrix is $O(m \times n)$ when the two sequences are of length m and n, respectively. The cost of the optimal alignment is the cost in the $A(m,n)$th entry of the dynamic programming matrix. At every step, we can keep back pointers to indicate where the optimal cost came from. Hence, we can determine the optimal alignment by following these back pointers when the dynamic programming is completed.

The value of the $A(m,n)$th entry in this matrix is the *distance* or *score* for the optimal alignment of the two sequences; the higher the score, the closer the relationship between the two sequences. This is because a higher score can be achieved only if a large number of residues or bases in the two strings match. Recall that only matches are given a positive score and both mismatches and gaps are given negative scores. This distance between S and T is then inserted into the corresponding entry that stores the distance of the sequences S and T in the distance matrix. Further details of the dynamic programming method can be found in the book by Gusfield [5].

8.2.2   Constructing the Guide Tree

Once it has been calculated, the distance matrix is used in the next phase of the algorithm to produce a phylogenetic or "guide" tree, which will determine the order of alignments in the final phase of the algorithm [15]. The idea here is to use the information contained in the distance matrix to construct a tree that shows the evolutionary relationship between proteins or DNA sequences.

A number of algorithms are available to construct guide trees, with varying levels of accuracy and performance. The neighbor-joining method of Saitou and Nei [13] is the algorithm used by CLUSTAL W, undoubtedly due to its tremendous speed advantage over other, more accurate methods. In tests run by Kuhner and Felsenstein [6], the neighbor-joining method was more than 40 times quicker than the next fastest method on one set of data and was over 70 times quicker on the other data set used by the authors. Furthermore, the neighbor-joining method produced acceptable results in the majority of test cases. The neighbor-joining method, later simplified by Studier and Kelper [14] and shown to be of $O(n^3)$ complexity for n sequences, gradually constructs the guide tree by combining sequences or groups of sequences called operational taxonomic units (OTUs), which are either protein or DNA sequences.

The main task in the neighbor-joining method is to compute the branch lengths of the guide tree from the pairwise distances of the sequences computed in the previous section. We discuss subsequently this process in detail. Our discussion is based on the paper by Saitou and Nei [13]. We refer to Figure 8.1 for our discussion. There are N sequences in our example and we start with a *star*-like tree (Fig. 8.1a). After the first iteration of the neighbor-joining method, we arrive at a tree shown in Figure 8.1b. The two branches $X1$ and $X2$ are shown with double lines to indicate that these two branch lengths have been computed already. Hence, sequences 1 and 2 are connected to node X after the first iteration. All the remaining sequences are connected to node Y in a star-like structure. This process is repeated until all the edges in the tree are

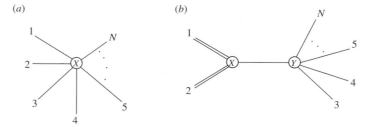

Figure 8.1   Illustration for the computation of sum of branch lengths by the algorithm by Saitou and Nei [13].

assigned weights. We discuss subsequently the first iteration in constructing the guide tree in detail assuming that we have N OTUs.

We denote by D_{ij} the distance between OTUs i and j. Note that all these pairwise distances have been computed through the dynamic programming algorithm in Section 8.2.1. We denote by L_{ab} the branch length between nodes a and b. The purpose of the neighbor-joining method is to compute all the branch lengths from the pairwise distances.

Our first task is to compute the sum of branch lengths of the tree in Figure 8.1a. We represent this by S_0.

$$S_0 = \sum_{i=1}^{N} L_{iX} = \frac{1}{N-1} \sum_{i<j} D_{ij} \tag{8.1}$$

We can derive Eq. (8.1) in the following way. We can write the distances from OTU 1 to all other OTUs as:

$$\sum_{j=2}^{N} D_{1j} = (L_{1X} + L_{2X}) + (L_{1X} + L_{3X}) + \cdots + (L_{1X} + L_{NX}) \tag{8.2}$$

$$\sum_{j=2}^{N} D_{1j} = (N-1)L_{1X} + \sum_{k=2}^{N} L_{kX} \tag{8.3}$$

Equation (8.2) follows from the fact that a distance like D_{12} is essentially the sum $L_{1X} + L_{2X}$ following the tree branches. The sum $\sum_{i<j} D_{ij}$ is the sum of all the pairwise distances such that $i < j$, in other words, each distance is counted only once. Similarly, we can write

$$\sum_{j=3}^{N} D_{2j} = (N-2)L_{2X} + \sum_{k=3}^{N} L_{kX}$$

The equations for $\sum_{j=4}^{N} D_{3j}$ and so on can be written in a similar way. The following equation results from adding the left-hand and right-hand sides of the earlier equations and doing some simplifications.

$$\sum_{i<j} D_{ij} = (N-1) \sum_{i=1}^{N} L_{ix} \tag{8.4}$$

Hence, Eq. (8.1) follows from Eq. (8.4).

Our next task is to identify a pair of OTUs so that the tree has the smallest sum of branch lengths. The OTUs 1 and 2 indicate this pair in Figure 8.1. Note that there are $N(N-1)/2$ ways of choosing this pair and we assume that OTUs 1 and 2 as neighbors give the smallest sum of branch lengths. Once the pair is chosen, we consider it as a single OTU and the next pair of OTUs that gives the smallest sum of branch lengths is again chosen. This process is continued until all the $N - 3$ interior branch lengths are determined. Note that a consequence of choosing OTUs 1 and 2 as the first pair is the determination of the branch lengths L_{1X} and L_{2X}. This is indicated by the double lines for these two branches in Figure 8.1b. We discuss subsequently the procedure of choosing a pair of OTUs that gives us the smallest sum of branch lengths for the entire tree.

We discuss how to compute the sum of branch lengths when OTUs 1 and 2 are considered as the first pair. In practice, the following steps are repeated for every possible pair and then the pair that gives the smallest sum of branch lengths is chosen. Figure 8.1 gives the shape of the guide tree when OTUs 1 and 2 constitute the pair. We denote by S_{12} the sum of the branch lengths of the tree when OTUs 1 and 2 are chosen as the pair. This sum can be expressed as (Fig. 8.1b):

$$S_{12} = L_{XY} + (L_{1X} + L_{2X}) + \sum_{i=3}^{N} L_{Yi} \tag{8.5}$$

Our first task is to determine the branch length L_{XY}.

$$\sum_{k=3}^{N} D_{1k} = D_{13} + D_{14} + \cdots + D_{1N}$$

$$= (L_{1X} + L_{XY} + L_{Y3}) + (L_{1X} + L_{XY} + L_{Y4}) + \cdots + (N - 2) \text{ terms}$$

$$= (N - 2)(L_{1X} + L_{XY}) + \sum_{p=3}^{N} L_{Yp}$$

Similarly, $\sum_{k=3}^{N} D_{2k}$ can be written as:

$$\sum_{k=3}^{N} D_{2k} = (N - 2)(L_{2X} + L_{XY}) + \sum_{p=3}^{N} L_{Yp}$$

$$\sum_{k=3}^{N} (D_{1k} + D_{2k}) = (N - 2)(L_{1X} + L_{2X}) + 2(N - 2)L_{XY} + 2 \sum_{p=3}^{N} L_{Yp}$$

Hence,

$$L_{XY} = \frac{1}{2(N - 2)} \left[\sum_{i=3}^{N} (D_{1k} + D_{2k}) - (N - 2)(L_{1X} + L_{2X}) - 2 \sum_{p=3}^{N} L_{Yp} \right] \tag{8.6}$$

Note that $L_{1X} + L_{2X} = D_{12}$. In addition, from Eq. (8.1), $\sum_{p=3}^{N} L_{Yp} = 1/(N-3)$ $\sum_{3 \le i \le j} D_{ij}$. Hence, we can rewrite Eq. (8.5) as

$$S_{12} = L_{XY} + (L_{1X} + L_{2X}) + \sum_{i=3}^{N} L_{Yi}$$

$$= \frac{1}{2(N-2)} \sum_{k=3}^{N} (D_{1k} + D_{2k}) - \frac{1}{2}(L_{1X} + L_{2X})$$

$$- \frac{1}{N-2} \sum_{i=3}^{N} L_{iY} + (L_{1X} + L_{2X}) + \frac{1}{N-3} \sum_{i<j} D_{ij}$$

Substituting $L_{1X} + L_{2X} = D_{12}$ and $\sum_{p=3}^{N} L_{Yp} = 1/(N-3) \sum_{3 \le i \le j} D_{ij}$, we get the following equation after some simplifications:

$$S_{12} = \frac{1}{2(N-2)} \sum_{k=3}^{N} (D_{1k} + D_{2k}) + \frac{1}{2}D_{12} + \frac{1}{N-2} \sum_{3 \le i < j} D_{ij} \qquad (8.7)$$

Note that Eq. (8.7) expresses the sum of branch lengths in terms of the pairwise distances computed through dynamic programming in Section 8.2.1. In general, we do not know which pairs of OTUs should be combined, that is, which pair is closest to each other. Therefore, we compute the sum of branch lengths S_{ij} for all the $N(N-1)/2$ pairs of OTUs and the pair that gives the smallest value is chosen as a pair of neighbors. If OTUs 1 and 2 are chosen as neighbors, they are combined to form an OTU $(1-2)$. The distance between this combined OTU and another OTU j is given by

$$D_{(1-2)j} = \frac{D_{1j} + D_{2j}}{2}, \quad 3 \le j \le N$$

This process reduces the number of OTUs by one and it is repeated for finding the next pair of neighbors. The algorithm stops when the number of OTUs becomes three.

The branch lengths of a tree can be estimated by a method by Fitch and Margoliash [4]; see also Nei [12] and Mount [10]. Suppose OTUs 1 and 2 are the first pair to be selected as neighbors as shown in Figure 8.1b. L_{1X} and L_{2X} can be estimated by the method by Fitch and Margoliash [4] as follows:

$$L_{1X} = \frac{D_{12} + D_{1Z} - D_{2Z}}{2}$$

$$L_{2X} = \frac{D_{12} + D_{2Z} - D_{1Z}}{2}$$

where $D_{1Z} = 1/(N-2) \sum_{i=3}^{N} D_{1i}$ and $D_{2Z} = 1/(N-2) \sum_{i=3}^{N} D_{2i}$. Z represents all the OTUs except 1 and 2. D_{1Z} and D_{2Z} are the distances between 1 and Z and 2 and Z, respectively.

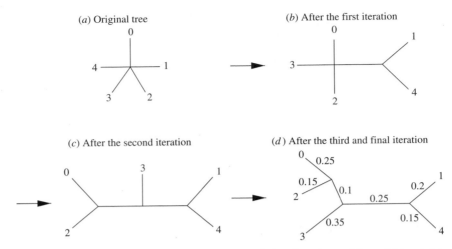

Figure 8.2 The formation of the guide tree through four iterations of the neighbor-joining algorithm.

After these iterations are complete, a root must be placed along the correct branch of the tree. This is done using a "mid-point" method by Thompson et al. [16], which places the root such that the means of the branch lengths on either side of the root are equal. An example of formation of the guide tree is shown in Figure 8.2. This concludes our discussion of the construction of the guide tree through the neighbor-joining method.

8.2.3   Performing the Progressive Alignment

The basic procedure to produce a multiple sequence alignment, outlined by Thompson et al. [15], and Feng and Doolittle [2], is to use a series of pairwise alignments on larger and larger groups of sequences. The order in which these pairwise alignments are performed is dictated by the guide tree. Once two sequences are aligned, the gaps that are introduced in creating the alignment remain fixed. Thus, the ordering of the pairwise alignments has a considerable effect on the resulting multiple sequence alignment.

The pairwise alignments are performed proceeding from the leaves of the guide tree to the root. Figure 8.3 shows a sample guide tree where the nine leaves represent sequences numbered 0–8. The alignments that must be computed initially are those that are represented by the internal nodes closest to the leaves of the tree. In this example, sequence 0 must be aligned with 1, 2 must be aligned with 3, 4 must be aligned with 5, and 7 must be aligned with 8.

Then, the internal nodes that are next closest to the leaves of the guide tree are computed. In this case, the result of the alignment of sequences 2 and 3 (labeled 2-3) must be aligned with the result of the alignment between sequences 4 and 5

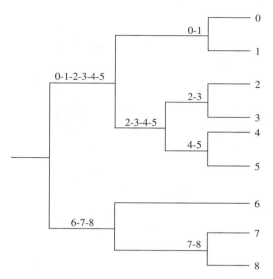

Figure 8.3 A sample guide tree. This tree contains nine leaves, numbered 0–8, that represent nine sequences. The tree's eight internal nodes each represent an alignment that must be calculated; nodes with the same depth can be computed in parallel.

(labeled 4-5). Next, the 0-1 alignment must be aligned with the 2-3-4-5 alignment and sequence 6 must be aligned with the 7-8 alignment. Finally, the two alignments 0-1-2-3-4-5 and 6-7-8 must be aligned together to produce the required alignment of all the sequences.

There are thus eight alignments that must be calculated, each corresponding to one internal node in the tree. In general, to align N sequences, $N - 1$ alignments must be calculated.

8.3 IMPLEMENTATION

This section examines ways in which the different stages of the CLUSTAL W algorithm can be parallelized. Figure 8.4 shows the overall work done by the CLUSTAL W algorithm when it is run sequentially as well as in parallel. With 1 processor (sequential execution), almost 96% of the time is spent in computing the $N(N - 1)/2$ alignments in the first stage. Approximately 2% time is spent for the construction of the guide tree and another 2% for the final progressive alignment stage. Hence, we decided to concentrate our effort in parallelizing the first stage of the algorithm. However, as can be seen from Figure 8.4, the proportion of work done in the second and third stages increases with increasing number of processors. Hence, a parallelization of the second and third stages of the algorithm is also needed in speeding up the CLUSTAL W algorithm.

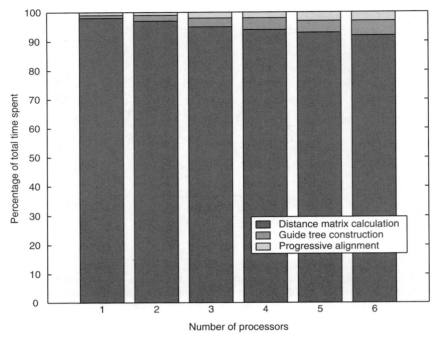

Figure 8.4 Percentage of time spent in each stage of the alignment algorithm with a varying number of processors.

We discuss later the parallelization of the third stage. However, we have not parallelized the second stage (construction of guide tree) in our current implementation. The main reason is that this stage requires fine grain parallelization, which is usually difficult to implement in a message passing environment. The main parallelization in the second stage is the computation in each iteration of the construction of the guide tree. As we have to consider all possible pairs of OTUs for computing the sum of branch lengths, it is possible to compute all these sums of branch lengths in parallel. However, the communication overhead in this parallelization is more than the computational efficiency.

8.3.1 Calculating the Distance Matrix

For n sequences, there are $n(n-1)/2$ unique pairs of sequences that must be aligned. Thus, for P processors, $n(n-1)/2P$ sequence alignments must be calculated per processor. There are, however, an enormous number of ways in which these alignments can be divided among the processors. Three ways in which this can be done were investigated, as shown in Figure 8.5.

The most obvious and direct way to construct the distance matrix is to broadcast all n sequences to each processor to compute exactly $n(n-1)/2P$ pairwise alignments. The alignments are simply allocated row by row throughout the distance matrix, with

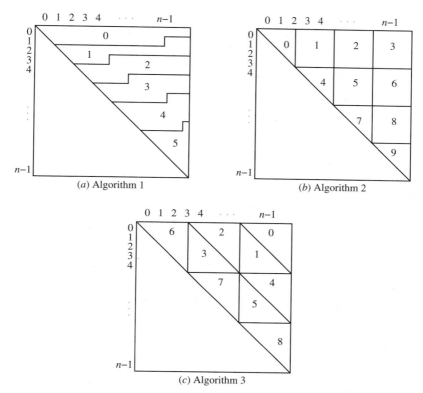

Figure 8.5 Three methods of dividing up the calculation of the distance matrix among processors. The aim is to minimize the amount of message passing, while still balancing the workload fairly among processors.

each processor computing an identical number of alignments. This method is shown in Figure 8.5a for six processors. While the balance between processors is ideal, the amount of message passing is clearly far more than required, as all processors receive all n sequences, whether they are required or not.

The second method investigated for 10 processors is shown in Figure 8.5b. The majority of the processors are allocated a square section of the distance matrix, except for processors that are allocated a triangular section along the diagonal of the matrix. Using this method, P must now be a square number. If P is the ith triangular number, then each processor is sent a maximum of a fraction of $2/i$ of the sequences. Although less message passing is required, the workload is far less balanced than in Algorithm 1.

Finally, a third method, as shown in Figure 8.5c, was investigated. Here, the aim was to minimize the number of messages being passed, while still maintaining an even distribution of alignments between processors.

We decided to use Algorithm 1 for aligning protein sequences as the communication is still not too high for aligning up to several hundred protein sequences each of several hundred residues long. However, Algorithms 2 and 3 are more appropriate for aligning DNA sequences that are very long.

8.3.2   Performing the Progressive Alignment

As previously explained, $N - 1$ alignments are required to be calculated to align N sequences. However, not all of these alignments need to be computed sequentially. In general, nodes with the same depth may be computed in parallel.

In the example shown in Figure 8.3, the alignments at the bottom of the tree (0-1, 2-3, 4-5, and 7-8) can be done in parallel, as they require no other alignments to have been computed before being calculated. Then, the 0-1-2-3-4-5 alignment can be produced at the same time as the 6-7-8 alignment, because the alignments they require have already been produced. Thus, there is considerable scope for exploiting parallelism in this stage.

In the example in Figure 8.3, the fourth level of the tree contains four nodes, so the program may make use of four processors when computing these alignments. Note, however, that if more than four processors were available, they would be unused in this example. Although this significantly limits the speedup obtainable in small examples such as the one described here, this is not usually a concern in practice, because inputs generally contain many hundreds of sequences. The number of nodes at the leaf level of the guide tree is thus usually many times more than the number of processors available.

In addition, affecting the speedup obtainable is the fact that later alignments close to the root of the tree take many times longer to compute than earlier alignments close to the leaves of the tree. The time required to compute a single alignment is proportional to the number of sequences in each set of sequences being aligned. As the more computationally intensive alignments appear close to the root at levels of the tree containing few nodes, the potential speedup is greatly reduced.

By making a number of realistic assumptions, we can analyze the performance of the parallel algorithm to obtain an equation that can be used to predict speedup for a given input. First, assume that the guide tree is perfectly balanced; experimental results show that this is a realistic assumption for a large number of sequences. Secondly, assume that after a pairwise alignment, the sequences being aligned grow in length by a constant factor c, which is dependent on the gap penalties used to perform the alignment. In our implementation, we use a master–slave relationship between the processors. A master processor is responsible for initiating the computation and distributing the tasks to the slave processor.

Each level of depth of the guide tree can be put into one of two categories: either the number of nodes at a particular depth is greater than the number of processors, P, or it is less than it. If the number of nodes is less than P, then the master processor is only required to calculate one of the alignments at that depth; otherwise, it is necessary for the master processor to perform more than one alignment.

Consider, first, the situation where the number of nodes at a particular depth is greater than P. The number of nodes at the final level of the tree is $n/2$, at the level before it, there are $n/4$ nodes, and so on. If each processor calculates an equal number of alignments at a particular depth, then the total number of alignments required to be calculated by the master processor is

$$\frac{n/2}{P} + \frac{n/4}{P} + \frac{n/8}{P} + \cdots + \frac{n/2^{a+1}}{P}$$

However, not each of these of alignments requires the same amount of time. The first term in the earlier expression represents those alignments where only one sequence is aligned with another sequence. However, the next term, assuming a perfectly balanced guide tree, is the number of alignments involving two sequences being aligned with two sequences, thus requiring twice as much time to perform the alignment. In the third term, four sequences are aligned with four sequences, thus requiring four times as much time to perform the alignment.

To predict the amount of time required, then, we need to weight each of the earlier terms to reflect the amount of time required to calculate the alignment. We also need to take into account our assumption that the length of the sequences grow by a constant factor c (due to introduction of gaps) after each alignment.

Thus, an expression approximating the length of time required for these alignments is

$$\frac{n/2}{P} + \frac{2c(n/4)}{P} + \frac{4c^2(n/8)}{P} + \cdots + \frac{2^a c^a (n/2^{a+1})}{P}$$

$$= \frac{n}{2P} + \frac{nc}{2P} + \frac{nc^2}{2P} + \cdots + \frac{nc^a}{2P}$$

This expression represents a geometric series of $a + 1$ terms with a common ratio of c. Thus, the sum of the series is given by

$$\frac{(n/2P)(c^{a+1} - a)}{c - 1} \tag{8.8}$$

Given that a is defined at the point where

$$\frac{n/2^{a+1}}{P} = 1 \quad \text{or} \quad \frac{n}{P} = 2^{a+1}$$

Thus

$$a + 1 = \log\left(\frac{n}{P}\right) \tag{8.9}$$

Note that all logarithms in this Chapter have base 2. Thus, combining Eq. (8.8) with Eq. (8.9), the sum of the geometric series can be rewritten as:

$$\frac{n(c^{\log(n/P)} - 1)}{2P(c - 1)} \tag{8.10}$$

Now, consider the levels of the tree that have a number of nodes less than P. In each of these levels, the master processor is required to perform one alignment only. There are $\log P$ levels where this occurs. If we assume that n is a power of 2, then the time required to calculate these alignments is proportional to:

$$2^{a+1}c^{a+1} + 2^{a+2}c^{a+2} + \cdots + \frac{n}{2}c^{\log(n)} - 1$$

This is again a geometric series, consisting of $\log P$ terms with a common ratio of $2c$. The sum of the series is thus

$$\frac{(2c)^{a+1}((2c)^{\log(P)} - 1)}{2c - 1} = \frac{(2c)^{\log(n/P)}((2c)^{\log(P)} - 1)}{2c - 1} \tag{8.11}$$

The total time required to perform all alignments is proportional to the sum of Eqs. (8.10) and (8.11).

$$\frac{n(c^{\log(n/P)} - 1)}{2P(c - 1)} + \frac{(2c)^{\log(n/P)}((2c)^{\log(P)} - 1)}{2c - 1} \tag{8.12}$$

Figure 8.6 shows a comparison of the actual speedup achieved by our algorithm with the predicted speedup computed in Eq. (8.12). In most cases, the predicted speedup was close to the actual speedup achieved by our implementation.

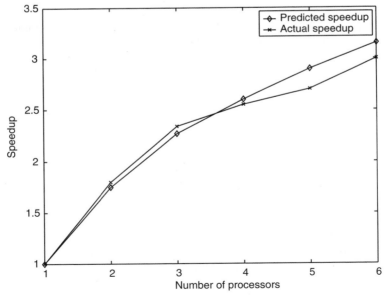

Figure 8.6 Predicted vs. actual speedup of the progressive alignment (third) stage of our implementation for 400 sequences each of 400 residues long.

8.4 RESULTS

This section analyzes the performance of each of the three stages of the algorithm separately. The performance tests were run in Linux, using a 100 MB Ethernet network of up to six Pentium 4 1.8 GHz machines, each with 1 GB of RAM.

8.4.1 Distance Matrix

The three proposed methods to calculate the distance matrix were implemented and compared. As Algorithm 2 requires a triangular number of processors and Algorithm 3 requires a square number of processors, each was only compared directly to Algorithm 1, which can be run on any number of processors.

Algorithm 2 is far inferior to Algorithm 1. This can simply be explained by the poor distribution of the alignments between processors. More surprising, however, is that Algorithm 1 slightly outperforms Algorithm 3, despite it requiring far more message passing over the network.

The algorithms were tested on randomly generated inputs containing between 50 and 500 sequences, with each sequence being between 50 and 500 characters in length. Of the 100 test cases, Algorithm 2 was outperformed by Algorithm 1 in every test. Furthermore, Algorithm 1 has a slight edge in performance over Algorithm 3, outperforming it in 70 of the test cases. Algorithm 3 will outperform Algorithm 1 when the sequences are very long. For example, DNA sequences are usually longer by several orders of magnitude when compared with protein sequences. In case of very long sequences, the distribution of all sequences to all processors over a network (as is required by Algorithm 1) is very expensive.

8.4.2 Guide Tree

Owing to its largely iterative nature, the construction of the guide tree was not parallelized. However, Figure 8.4, which illustrates the percentage of time spent in each stage of the algorithm for a typical input, shows that this is not necessarily a great concern. As shown in the figure, the time spent in constructing the guide tree represents a rather small amount of the total processing time required, so the fact that this stage was not parallelized does not affect overall speedup significantly. In fact, when running the algorithm on one processor, constructing the guide tree generally requires by far the least amount of time of the three stages, especially when the sequences are particularly long or few in number.

8.4.3 Progressive Alignment

One feature of Eq. (8.12) is that it implies that after the input exceeds a certain number of sequences, the obtainable speedup reaches a maximum level. Of interest, of course, is how close the predictions of speedup are to the speedup actually obtained experimentally. Figure 8.6 shows the running time for one particular input, consisting of 400 sequences each of 400 residues long. Other inputs exhibit an almost identically shaped graphs, as long as the input is of a reasonable size.

Many other experiments confirm that the predictions are generally very close to the actual speedup on a wide variety of inputs, just as in Figure 8.6. The only requirement for the predicted values to be close to the actual results is that the input be of a considerable size. As long as the input contains 300 or more sequences, of length 300 or more characters each, the results are comparable to that shown in Figure 8.6.

8.4.4 Overall Result

Our tests were run on a small cluster of six Pentium IV machines (1.8 GHz, 1 GB of RAM, 100 MB Ethernet network). We used both synthetic data sets and real data sets for protein sequences. We show some results in Figure 8.7. Three widely varying inputs are shown, which are reasonably close to best-case (small number of very large sequences), average-case (average number of sequences of average length), and worst-case (large number of short sequences) scenarios. As is clear from the graph, even in the cases with "bad" input, there is still a significant level of speedup, which in this case was 4.96 with six processors. When using inputs closer to the average and best cases, even greater speedup is possible, which in the two cases were 5.56 and 5.81 with six processors. We found that an overall speedup of about 5.5 with six processors, for an efficiency of approximately 90%, is obtainable for most inputs. Our speedup for the first stage was almost linear and efficiency was close to 100%.

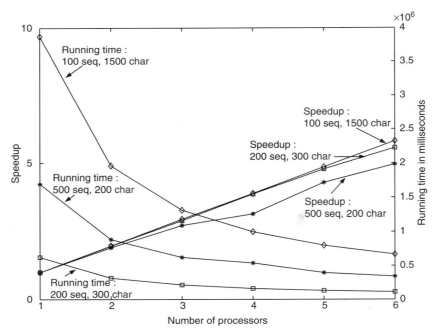

Figure 8.7   The results for different data sets executed on a six processor cluster.

There was no speedup for the second stage as we did not parallelize the construction of the guide tree. The average speedup for the third stage was about three with six processors, that is, about 50% efficiency.

Our method and the speedup we achieved are quite similar to those reported by Li [7]. Our program and his program work well for small clusters. However, from our experience, the speedup decreases as we employ more processors. The main reason is the poor load balancing in the third stage of the algorithm. During the progressive alignment at the higher levels of the guide tree, some processors are loaded with large alignment tasks. In contrast, more and more processors become idle as the alignments progress at the higher levels of the guide tree. The extreme example is when there is only one large alignment to be done at the last level. The speedup of our implementation decreases when the number of sequences in the input is large. Again, this inefficiency comes due to the poor load balancing in the third stage. With a large number of input sequences, the alignments at the higher levels of the guide tree involve very large sequences as more and more gaps are introduced at the lower levels. Hence, these sequential alignments at the higher levels dominate the speedup. The proportion of the work in the third stage compared with the total work done by the algorithm increases with increasing number of processors. This is due to the fact that the first stage can be completed faster if we employ more processors.

8.5 CONCLUSION

To improve the speedup in the third stage of our implementation, we need to devise a method to split up a single alignment task among multiple processors. This will require a new algorithm for parallel dynamic programming, which keeps the communication costs low. This is an important future direction for improving the parallel CLUSTAL W algorithm. Another important problem is the establishment of correspondence between biologically meaningful alignments through structural superposition. Most multiple alignment algorithms including CLUSTAL W work on mathematical alignments based on general scoring schemes.

A previous version of our work has been published in Ref. [1]. Our program can be used for multiple sequence alignment through the web server: http://mason.csse.uwa.edu.au

The server can take inputs as sequence ids or files in FASTA format. The ids are then validated from the EMBL sequence database, the alignment is performed on a small cluster and the result is sent back by email. The code for this program is also available on request from the first author.

ACKNOWLEDGMENTS

The first author's research is partially supported by Western Australian Interactive Virtual Environments Centre (IVEC) and Australian Partnership in Advanced

Computing (APAC). The authors would like to thank S. Soundaralakshmi for reading an earlier draft of this chapter and suggesting many improvements. The authors would like to thank Justus Ong, Joel Huang, Serence Chow, Victor Loh, David Ow, Derrick Wong, and Gene Lim for developing the web server available at: http://mason.csse.uwa.edu.au.

REFERENCES

1. J. Ebedes and A. Datta, Multiple sequence alignment in parallel on a workstation cluster, *Bioinformatics*, 20, 1193–1195 (2004).

2. D. F. Feng and R. F. Doolittle, Progressive sequence alignment as a prerequisite to correct phylogenetic trees, *J. Mol. Evol.*, 25, 351–360 (1987).

3. O. Gotoh, An improved algorithm for matching biological sequences, *J. Mol. Biol.*, 162, 705–708 (1982).

4. W. M. Fitch and E. Margoliash, Construction of phylogenetic trees, *Science*, 155, 279–284 (1967).

5. D. Gusfield, *Algorithms on Strings, Trees, and Sequences*, Cambridge University Press, 1997.

6. M. K. Kuhner and J. Felsenstein, A simulation comparison of phylogeny algorithms under equal and unequal evolutionary rates, *Mol. Biol. Evol.*, 11, 459–468 (1994).

7. K.-B. Li, ClustalW-MPI: ClustalW analysis using distributed and parallel computing, *Bioinformatics*, 19 (12), 1585–1586 (2003).

8. W. S. Martins, J. B. Del Cuvillo, F. J. Useche, K. B. Theobald, and G. R. Gao, A multi-threaded parallel implementation of a dynamic programming algorithm for sequence comparison, *Pac. Symp. Biocomput.*, 311–322 (2001).

9. http://www-unix.mcs.anl.gov/mpi/mpich/

10. D. W. Mount, *Bioinformatics: Sequences and Genome Analysis*, Cold Spring Harbor Laboratory Press, New York, 2001.

11. S. B. Needleman and C. D. Wunsch, A general method applicable to the search for similarities in the amino acid sequences of two proteins, *J. Mol. Biol.*, 48, 443–453 (1970).

12. M. Nei, *Molecular Evolutionary Genetics*, Columbia University Press, New York, 1987.

13. N. Saitou and M. Nei, The neighbor-joining method: a new method for reconstructing phylogenetic trees, *Mole. Biol. Evol.*, 4 (4), 406–425 (1987).

14. J. A. Studier and K. J. Keppler, A note on the neighbor-joining algorithm of Saitou and Nei, *Mol. Biol. Evol.*, 5 (6), 729–731 (1988).

15. J. D. Thompson, D. G. Higgins, and T. J. Gibson, CLUSTAL W: improving the sensitivity of progressive multiple sequence alignment through sequence weighting, position-specific gap penalties and weight matrix choice, *Nucleic Acids Res.*, 22 (22), 4673–4680 (1994).

16. J. D. Thompson, D. G. Higgins, and T. J. Gibson, Improved sensitivity of profile searches through the use of sequence weights and gap excision, *Comp. Appl. Biosci.*, 10 (1), 19–29 (1994).

CHAPTER 9

Searching Sequence Databases Using High-Performance BLASTs

XUE WU and CHAU-WEN TSENG

9.1 INTRODUCTION

Recent advances in molecular biology techniques have allowed scientists to quickly gather huge amounts of DNA sequence data. For instance, a single high-throughput automated DNA sequencer (e.g., ABI Prism 3730xl) can output up to two million nucleotides (bases) of sequence per day. In addition, much of this data have been collected and annotated in large sequence databases publicly available at institutions such as NCBI GenBank. The reason researchers find sequence information so useful is that close sequence matches (in terms of nucleotides or amino acids) frequently provide clues to biological function (by identifying sequences of similar genes or proteins with known behavior or structure) without requiring long and expensive laboratory experiments.

The ability to exploit sequence information is one of the fundamental reasons behind current advances in the field of computational biology and bioinformatics. Efficiently extracting information from large sequence databases is thus a very common and important task for computational biologists. One of the most popular and widely used tools used in the bioinformatics community for performing such searches is basic local alignment search tool (BLAST) [1, 2], a program designed to quickly perform pairwise sequence alignments. Its search strategy is based on using scoring matrices to compare short subsequences (words) in the query sequence against the entire target DNA or protein sequence database to find statistically significant matches, then extending these matches to find the most similar sequences or sub-sequences.

Even though BLAST uses a very efficient algorithm, the growing size of sequence databases and number of searches needed are quickly expanding beyond the computational capabilities of individual computers. The ever-increasing need for higher performance has created a demand for even more powerful versions of BLAST for use on multiprocessors and PC clusters and has led to the development of enhanced

Parallel Computing for Bioinformatics and Computational Biology, Edited by Albert Y. Zomaya
Copyright © 2006 John Wiley & Sons, Inc.

versions of BLAST, which attempt to exploit parallelism to improve performance. This chapter examines and compares these high-performance versions of BLAST.

We begin by briefly reviewing the basic BLAST algorithm, then discussing how sequence searches are typically conducted in bioinformatics and some important parameters affecting performance. We examine different methods of exploiting parallelism for BLAST, then we examine in detail how several versions of BLAST attempt to achieve high performance. We experimentally evaluate the performance of each version of BLAST under an important set of parameters and we show that although each version of BLAST has its own strengths, none is able to consistently achieve the best performance when sequence search parameters such as sequence database size, query batch size, and query sequence length are varied. On the basis of our evaluation, we design UMD-BLAST, a wrapper capable of selecting between different versions of BLAST and BLAST parameters, and show how it can improve performance. We discuss some future directions and finish with a comparison to related work.

9.2   BASIC BLAST ALGORITHM

BLAST [1, 2] is a program that efficiently calculates local *pairwise alignments* between sequences, based on a sophisticated statistical model [3, 4]. BLAST is based on the premise of sequence similarity, that is, similarity between two DNA or protein can suggest similar structure or function based on a common ancestor. BLAST searches thus attempt to find sequences in the database that are "similar" to the query sequence, where similarity is calculated using methods that increase the likelihood of common structure or function.

BLAST searches are comprised of a series of pairwise sequence comparisons of a single query sequence to all the sequences in a sequence database. Each comparison finds a number of possible alignments between all or part of the query sequence to some part of a sequence in the database, where an alignment is a one-to-one mapping between elements of the query and matching sequences, possibly with gaps, insertions/deletions, or substitutions. A *scoring matrix* based on experimental analysis of known similarity in DNA and protein sequences is usually used to estimate the statistical probability of the match/mismatch at each position in the sequence. Penalties are also assigned to introducing and extending gaps in the alignment. Probabilities are combined to produce a single score for the entire alignment. The scores of different possible alignments are compared and the most likely alignment and score (or several top candidates) are returned as the result of the BLAST search.

The BLAST program is actually a set of programs used to search DNA and protein sequences against database DNA and protein sequences, possibly with on-the-fly frame shifts and codon translations. Although optimal (with respect to a particular scoring matrix and gap penalties), pairwise alignment algorithms such as Smith–Waterman require dynamic programming and can take $O(n^2)$ time [5] and the BLAST algorithm takes only $O(n)$ time (with respect to the size of the query and sequence database) and seems to be quite precise in practice [1, 2]. BLAST manages to achieve high efficiency by filtering its searches based on finding exact matches between short fragments (called words) of the query sequence and database.

The overall BLAST algorithm has several steps: build words, find seeds, extend, and evaluate. We describe each step in more detail in this section. The overall basic BLAST algorithm is shown in Figure 9.1. To better explain the algorithm, we will use DNA query sequence "ACTGA" and database sequence "GACTGC" as an example.

Build List First, BLAST breaks the query into fragments ("words") and compiles a word list. For protein sequences, the words in the list must include all the words with length W and score at least T when compared with the query word using a given substitution matrix. For DNA sequences, the word list simply includes all the words with length W in the query sequence. Therefore, for "ACTGA," if the value of W is 3, the word list is: ACT, CTG, and TGA.

Find Seeds BLAST then scans through every database sequence to find all the occurrences of the words in the list. These words are used as "seeds" for the extension step. For the initial implementation of BLAST algorithm, the scanning step uses a finite state machine algorithm to speed up the process. In our example, the seeds generated by seed scanning step are ACT and CTG.

Extend In the next step, the matching words (seeds) are extended into ungapped local alignments between the query sequence and the sequence from the database. Extensions are made in both directions and continued until the score of the alignment drops below a threshold X. The resulting pairwise alignments are called high-scoring pairs (HSPs). Some versions of the BLAST algorithm require two hits, in which case seed extension is performed only when sequences sharing two nonoverlapped seeds

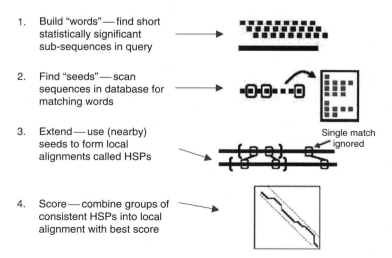

1. Build "words" — find short statistically significant sub-sequences in query

2. Find "seeds" — scan sequences in database for matching words

3. Extend — use (nearby) seeds to form local alignments called HSPs

Single match ignored

4. Score — combine groups of consistent HSPs into local alignment with best score

Figure 9.1 Basic BLAST algorithm.

are within a given distance. In our example, the seed extension result is the query sequence "ACTG."

Score   Finally, the top-scoring HSPs are combined into *consistent* local alignments. HSPs are consistent if they can be combined without overlapping and while maintaining the same order in both the query and database sequences. Statistical scores are generated for both top-scoring and local alignments to assess the significance of the results and to select the most likely alignment.

BLAST uses the W and T parameters to adjust the sensitivity and speed of sequence searches. Increasing the length of a word (W) may result in a shorter word list and thus speed up the BLAST searching process. However, BLAST may then miss some alignments with shorter lengths. Similarly, increasing the value of parameter T will result in fewer words in the initial word list, but may also cause BLAST to miss some alignments, reducing the sensitivity of the final results.

9.3   BLAST USAGE AND PERFORMANCE FACTORS

9.3.1   Typical BLAST Usage

If computational biologists searched only for matches for individual sequences, performance would be less of an issue. Instead, in practice, biologists frequently perform a large number (batch) of sequence comparisons at once. Some reasons why BLAST searches tend to occur in batches include:

Data Collection   Biologists gather and analyze a large amount of sequence data simultaneously. For instance, researchers may collect and sequence a large number of expressed DNA sequences known as expressed sequence tags (ESTs) in a single tissue sample, then compare all ESTs collected against known sequence databases to estimate their biological function [6, 7]. Each sequence collected would become a single BLAST query.

Self Comparisons   Biologists may also wish to compare data with itself to discover similarities and differences. After collecting a number of sequences, they may compare each sequence collected against each other to discover highly expressed sequences or fragments that may be combined into longer sequences. Such comparisons require on the order of $O(n^2)$ pairwise BLAST searches for a collection of n sequences [8].

Database Comparisons   Finally, biologists may also perform comparisons using existing sequence databases, either comparing databases against one another or against itself. For instance, researchers may compare all human gene sequences against mouse gene sequences for comparative genomics, compare some genes for all known organisms to perform phylogenetic analysis, or even compare the genomes of different species [9, 10].

9.3.2 Factors Affecting BLAST Performance

Because batched BLAST searches tend to cause most computationally intensive work-loads, we will focus on factors affecting the performance of batched BLAST searches. For typical batched BLAST queries, there are a number of factors that affect performance. From our experiments, we find some important factors: database size, query batch size, and search sequence length.

Database Size　There are a variety of sequence databases for a number of organisms, and the database size can vary greatly. Nucleotide (DNA) sequence databases consisting of the nucleotides (A, C, T, G) are typically the largest, because the DNA sequencing techniques are the most developed. DNA databases range from thousands to billions of bases and may consist of known genes, genomic DNA, or large collections EST sequences. Protein (amino acid) sequence databases tend to be smaller, both because protein sequences are shorter and because there are many fewer proteins that have been identified and sequenced.

Query Batch Size　We have already seen that biologists frequently compare a large set of sequences against a sequence database simultaneously by sending batched searches. Depending on the application, query batch sizes may range from hundreds to potentially millions of sequences simultaneously.

Search Sequence Length　Finally, the length of the search sequence may also vary, depending on the bioinformatic application. Sequence lengths may range from 50–100 (micro-cDNAs or ESTs), through 300–500 (proteins), to more than 10,000 (contigs, genes).

9.4　HIGH PERFORMANCE BLASTS

Because of the importance of BLAST to biologists, many researchers have attempted to exploit parallelism to improve BLAST performance. These high-performance BLASTs usually take one or more of the following approaches for improving BLAST performance: vector instructions, multithreading, replicated databases, distributed databases, and optimized batch queries. In this section, we describe and comment on each approach.

9.4.1　Vector Instructions

One approach for improving BLAST performance for individual searches is to exploit low-level vector parallelism to speedup calculating scores for candidate alignments. Recall that once BLAST finds hits between statistically significant words and sequences in the database, it must find a local pairwise alignment and calculate a score for the alignment, before returning the best score found. Local alignments calculations can be parallelized in a fine-grain manner using vector parallelism.

Such parallelism can be exploited using fine-grain vector instructions found in common microprocessors, such as Altivec (for the PowerPC) and MMX/SSE (for the Pentium).

A version of BLAST called AGBLAST developed by researchers at Apple and Genentech exploited the Altivec instructions in the PowerPC family of CPUs to improve BLAST performance. Experimental results showed performance improvements up to a factor of five for BLAST queries with long sequences, which required more time for calculating local alignments. Improvements were more limited for short sequences such as ESTs.

9.4.2 Multithreading

A second approach for improving BLAST performance for individual searches is to exploit thread-level parallelism in comparing queries to different parts of a sequence database. As a BLAST search is usually performed against sequence databases consisting of multiple sequences, searches can easily be performed in parallel using multiple threads. A threaded BLAST search simply slices the given databases into equal sized chunks according to the number of available processors. Each database chunk is then distributed to a predefined processor using memory mapping. Each processor is responsible for a thread scanning, a different database fragment. The sorted results are stored in a global structure, which is shared by all the processors and then combined to produce the final BLAST search result. Figure 9.2 shows the algorithm used by multithreaded BLAST searches.

The current release of both NCBI BLAST [11] and WU BLAST [12] can be run in multithreaded mode on shared-memory multiprocessor (SMP) machines. As BLAST search needs to scan each database sequence at least once for each query sequence, threaded BLAST searches are both memory and I/O intensive and are

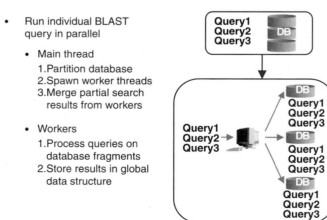

Figure 9.2 Multithreaded BLAST algorithm.

most effective on large SMPs. Database partitioning, thread creation and management, memory contention, and collecting search results can result in large overheads, which prevent BLAST from achieving good scalability. However, according to experimental studies [13], multithreaded BLAST appears to achieve good performance in practice.

9.4.3 Replicated Databases

Replicating sequence databases on distributed memory systems (replicated BLAST) is one of the most popular methods for providing high performance BLAST searches. The implementations usually adopt a master/worker paradigm to maintain load balance. When the database size is relatively small, a full copy of the sequence database may be stored in memory on each node. Batched queries can be split up evenly and assigned to each node. The computing nodes then perform local BLAST searches and send the results back to the master node. Although this method will not reduce the search time for individual queries, the total search time can be reduced when there are a large number of number batched queries. Figure 9.3 shows the algorithm used by BLAST searches using replicated sequence databases.

One obvious advantage of replicated BLAST is that the only parallelization overhead is distributing the queries and collecting the final results. It is thus fairly easy to achieve near-linear speedups for large numbers of BLAST queries, as long as the database is not too large. The disadvantages of replicated BLAST are that it needs sufficient memory and disk space to store the database on each node and requires a large number of queries (at least equal to the number of computing nodes) to exploit

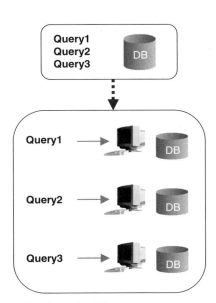

1. Replicate database on
   cluster of PCs

2. Run multiple BLASTs in
   parallel

   - Master
     1. Assign query sequences
        to workers
     2. Collect search results
        from workers

   - Workers
     1. BLAST assigned queries
        on database
     2. Send results back to
        master

Figure 9.3 Replicated BLAST algorithm.

parallelism. Replicating sequence databases for BLAST search has been proposed and examined by several researchers [14, 15]. Versions of BLAST that employ replicated databases include BeoBLAST [16] and Hi-per BLAST [17].

9.4.4   Distributed Databases

As sequence databases increase in size, they may no longer fit in the memory of individual computers. This may reduce performance for batched BLAST queries as each query will need to reload the sequence database into memory to scan for seeds. One approach to improving performance is to exploit the large amount of aggregate memory available in parallel computers through distributed sequence databases.

In a distributed database, the sequence database can be split up, with each processor maintaining a portion of the sequence database small enough to fit in memory. Multiple BLAST queries may then be processed without retrieving the database from slower disk storage requiring disk I/O. Implementation is more complex as sequence databases need to be partitioned and physically distributed between processors. Greater overheads are incurred as only partial results are calculated for each query on a single processor. These partial results must be combined between processors for each query. Nonetheless, overall performance can be improved due to reduced disk accesses. Using distributed databases is proposed by Braun [14] and has been implemented in mpiBLAST [18].

mpiBLAST   mpiBLAST [18] is a version of BLAST, which exploits distributed databases to improve performance. Figure 9.4 shows the algorithm used by mpi-BLAST using distributed sequence databases. mpiBLAST's task partition strategy for improving the performance of BLAST is similar to that of threaded BLAST. It is designed to work on a computer cluster using MPI library. The major difference is mpiBLAST also tries to use the distributed memory of the whole cluster to reduce disk I/O. The program adopts a master/worker paradigm for task distribution and maintaining load balance. The master is only responsible for broadcasting query sequences, assigning database fragments to worker nodes, and merging search results from worker nodes. The workers process the queries and send back the results. BLAST query processing is accomplished using NCBI BLAST's core functions.

The details of the algorithm are as follows. Initially, the master node sends a message to each worker node to ask for a list of database fragments in its local directory. The master node then assigns jobs to worker nodes according to the database fragments at each node. If a node is idle and has a local copy of a database fragment, the master node will send a message to that node, directing it to search the fragment. The worker node then performs a local BLAST search for the database fragment assigned by the master.

If the worker node has already searched all database fragments stored locally, the master will instruct it to copy one of the remaining unsearched database fragments from the master before continuing. Once the search is finished, a worker will send its

1. Partition database on
   cluster of PCs

2. Run individual BLAST
   query in parallel

   • Master
     1. Broadcast query
        sequences to workers
     2. Merge partial search
        results from workers

   • Workers
     1. Process queries on
        database fragments
     2. Send results back to
        master

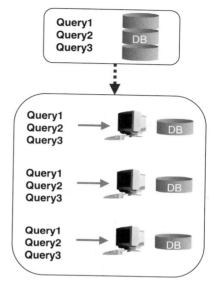

Figure 9.4   mpiBLAST algorithm.

results and also an idle message to the master node, then wait for a new job assignment. As partial search results arrive from workers, the master merges them into the master result list. Once all fragments have been searched, the master node will notify all worker nodes to terminate, then output the merged results.

Although mpiBLAST attempts to minimize the number of database fragments copied during execution, nontrivial communication overhead is incurred due to query sequence broadcasts, database fragment distribution, and collection of partial search results. In addition, the master node may become a bottleneck because it is the center for task distributing and merging results. According to Amdahl's law, the master node can become the system bottleneck if there are too many database fragments or query sequences, because the master node executes sequentially.

9.4.5 Batch Query Optimizations

Finally, researchers have also learned to improve the performance of BLAST by exploiting redundancies between multiple queries found in batch BLAST queries. By combining multiple BLAST queries, results and data structures may be reused and the number of scans through sequence databases may be reduced. Reducing the number of scans through sequence databases is particularly important for large databases that do not fit in memory, as slow disk accesses can be considerably reduced.

Although these batch query improvements do not exploit multiple processors directly, they can greatly improve performance and can be executed in parallel as with replicated BLAST. These optimizations also may impact the strategies used by parallel versions of BLAST. Versions of BLAST that perform batch query optimizations include BLAST++ [19] and HT-BLAST [20, 21].

The current version of NCBI BLAST also tried to optimize batch queries when searching DNA sequence database. It does so by concatenating the batched queries (interspaced with stop codons) into a single virtual query, then searching the database with the virtual query. However, performance is reduced because significant work is required to translate results back to the original batched queries.

BLAST++   BLAST++ improves the performance of BLAST by adapting the algorithm to exploit sharing of results on common sub-sequences of batched queries. The structure of the BLAST++ algorithm is similar to BLAST. The major difference is in how BLAST++ compiles its word list. First, BLAST++ creates a virtual query consisting of all queries. When building the word list, BLAST++ maintains a list of (query ID, list of offsets) pairs for each word to record all the occurrences of the word in the entire set of batched BLAST queries. The remaining steps of BLAST++ are the same as those of BLAST. However, as a common word is searched only once for all the batched queries, as compared to once for each query, the computation time is greatly reduced.

In addition, the sequence database is only scanned once for all batched queries combined by BLAST++, potentially increasing performance when the database is too large to fit in memory. Unfortunately, a side effect of maintaining all the additional information for the combined query is increased memory usage for BLAST++ compared with BLAST. As a result, BLAST++ will run out of memory for longer query sequences and larger databases faster than standard BLAST searches. Figure 9.5 shows the algorithm used by BLAST++ searches for batched BLAST queries. Like BLAST, batched BLAST++ queries may be executed in parallel with replicated sequence databases on PC clusters, although larger batch sizes are needed.

1. Combine words from multiple queries

2. Perform a single scan for multiple queries

   ▪ Create virtual query from all queries in batch

   ▪ Share words used by multiple queries

   ▪ Reuse information (word-hits) from queries

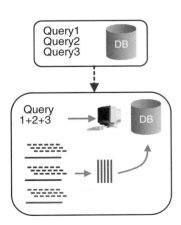

Figure 9.5   BLAST++ algorithm.

9.5 COMPARING BLAST PERFORMANCE

As described in the previous section, different high-performance BLAST algorithms have different strengths and weaknesses. It is interesting to study the characteristics of different algorithms through experiments. In this section, the performance of several representative algorithms is compared.

9.5.1 Experiment Environment

To evaluate and compare the performance of threaded BLAST, mpiBLAST, and BLAST++, we downloaded and installed the most current versions of NCBI BLAST, mpiBLAST, and BLAST++ software packages as of December 2003. All three programs were compiled and installed on a Sun SunFire 6800 SMP with 24 processors and 12G memory and a Linux PC cluster with 10 worker nodes (each with dual AMD Athlon 1.6 GHz processors and 1 GB of memory) and a file server node (with Pentium III 750 MHz processor and 256 MB memory). When the performance of BLAST and BLAST++ are evaluated on the PC cluster, we used replicated sequence databases to run BLAST and BLAST++ in parallel on multiple nodes.

We created several test sequence databases by using subsets of the GenBank *nt* (nonredundant nucleotide) database, with sizes varying from 250 million to 20 billion nucleotides. All queries used by the experiments are randomly generated nucleotide sequences with specified lengths. Most experiments involve batches of 10 queries at a time, where all query sequences are of the same length. When batch query sizes are varied, the length of the query sequences is 64. Experiments are performed on the PC cluster unless otherwise noted.

9.5.2 Performance vs. Database Size

We begin by investigating the impact of sequence database size on performance. Nucleotide databases can generally compress and store four nucleotides as a single byte, so a sequence database with 4 billion bases would generate a 1 GB of storage. Figure 9.6 presents the performance of replicated BLAST, replicated BLAST++, and mpiBLAST for a range of database sizes for nine processors on our PC cluster. Note that the Y-axis represents execution time with a *logarithmic scale* and the X-axis represents sequence database size in billions of nucleotides.

As expected, we find execution times tend to increase for larger databases as more sequences must be examined for each query. The results show that before the database size reaches the memory limit, both replicated BLAST and replicated BLAST++ perform better than mpiBLAST because of lower parallelization overhead. BLAST++ achieves better performance than BLAST by optimizing batched queries. However, once database sizes exceed 4 billion bases, databases no longer fit in the memory of a single node (because our PC nodes have 1 GB memory). The performance of replicated BLAST and replicated BLAST++ then degrades sharply, as portions of the database are evicted from the file cache (in memory) and need to be slowly reloaded

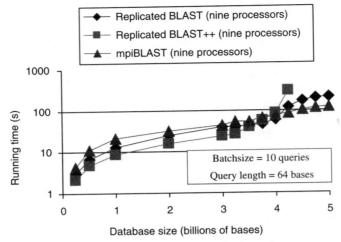

Figure 9.6   Impact of sequence database size.

from disk. BLAST++ performance degrades earlier than BLAST at smaller database sizes, as it requires additional memory for its search algorithm.

In comparison, the performance of mpiBLAST does not experience major performance degradations when database size exceeds the memory size on individual PC nodes. Instead, performance continues to degrade almost linearly as database size increases. Steep performance dropoffs are avoided as each node only performs searches on a portion of the partitioned database. Performance for mpiBLAST will only drop sharply when each database partition becomes too large for the memory of individual nodes. These experimental results thus demonstrate that mpiBLAST works best for large sequence databases that do not fit in the memory of a single node.

9.5.3   Performance vs. Batch Size

We investigate the performance of different versions of BLAST with respect to the number of queries in a batched query. Figure 9.7 presents the performance of replicated BLAST, replicated BLAST++, and mpiBLAST as the batch size varies between 32 and 256. The results are obtained on PC cluster using eight processors. In the figure, note that the Y-axis represents execution times with a log scale and the X-axis represents query batch size. The database size is 0.25 billion bases and query sequence length is 64 bases.

Results show that as expected, execution time increases for all three BLAST algorithms as the batch size increases, because more sequences need to be searched. When compared with BLAST and mpiBLAST, BLAST++ is able to significantly reduce execution times for batched BLAST queries, even for fairly small batches. In fact, it does such a good job of exploiting redundancy that execution times only increase slightly as batch size grows. However, BLAST++ does require more memory, so there is a limit to the batch query size, which can be supported before BLAST++

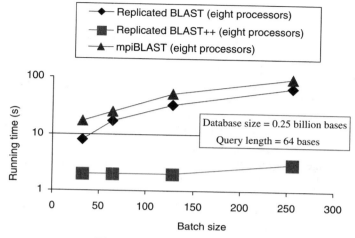

Figure 9.7   Impact of batch size.

performance degrades instead of improving, although that limit is not reached in Figure 9.7.

9.5.4   Performance vs. Query Length

Now, we examine the impact of query length on the performance of BLAST, BLAST++, and mpiBLAST. Results are shown in Figure 9.8 for execution times obtained with nine processors on PC cluster, using a 8 billion base database and a batch size is 10. We varied the length of query sequences from 256 to 4096 bases.

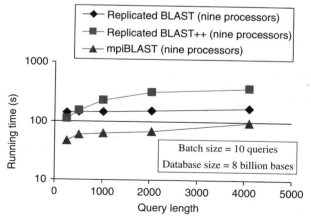

Figure 9.8   Impact of query length.

In the figure, the Y-axis represents execution times with a log scale and the X-axis shows the length of query sequences.

We find that mpiBLAST achieves the best performance because the large sequence database cannot fit in the memory of a single node. Replicated BLAST++ achieves the next lowest execution times for short queries, but performance quickly degrades for longer query sequences. This is because BLAST++ requires much more memory than BLAST or mpiBLAST as query length increases, due to its algorithm and internal data structures needed to combine words from multiple queries. BLAST++ performance becomes significantly worse than BLAST once memory is exhausted. As a result, for larger databases, BLAST++ becomes increasingly sensitive to memory overhead incurred by longer query sequences. As a result, we find that using BLAST is more efficient than BLAST++ for very long query sequences.

9.5.5 Parallel Performance

Finally, we evaluate the scalability of parallel implementations of BLAST. We used a batch of 10 queries of 1024 bases for two database sizes, a database with 8 billion bases and a larger database with 20 billion bases. Figure 9.9 presents the parallel performance of both threaded BLAST and mpiBLAST on both a Sun SunFire 6800 SMP and a Linux PC cluster. The Y-axis displays parallel speedup, and the X-axis represents the number of processors. Speedups are calculated relative to execution time of the sequential version of BLAST running on a single node. A line is provided showing linear speedups.

First, we consider the speedups for mpiBLAST on the PC cluster for both small and large database sizes. We see that mpiBLAST can achieve large, even superlinear

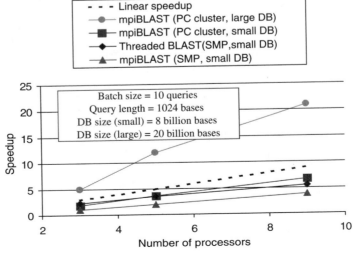

Figure 9.9   Parallel performance on SMP and PC cluster.

speedups on a cluster for large sequence databases by taking advantage of the aggregate memory in a cluster. Improvements are greater for the larger database. This is because when databases are very large, sequential BLAST performance is very poor due to the need for disk I/O to fetch data that does not fit in memory. In these cases, mpiBLAST obtains major performance improvements by partitioning the database and using the memory from multiple nodes.

Next, we consider the speedups for both threaded BLAST and mpiBLAST on a SMP. We can evaluate mpiBLAST on a SMP, because there are shared-memory implementations of the MPI interface. We see that although near-linear speedups are possible for very small numbers of processors, for larger numbers of processors, speedups are poor for both threaded BLAST and mpiBLAST on an SMP. Because they parallelize individual BLAST queries in a fine-grain manner, both versions of BLAST incur lots of parallelism overhead and have difficulty in achieving scalable parallel performance. The performance of mpiBLAST is even worse than for threaded BLAST, as it encounters additional overhead to set up, partition databases, and communicate messages. In comparison, we can obtain near-linear speedups using replicated BLAST and replicated BLAST++ for batched queries because they eliminate parallel overhead by executing entire queries in parallel.

9.5.6 Observations

Our experiments have shown that there are many factors affecting the performance of BLAST searches. Among these factors, sequence database size seems to be the most important in determining the total search time. This is mainly because databases can take up a lot of memory and because BLAST is an exhaustive search algorithm, which examines every sequence in the database for every query. Researchers are investigating new data indexing and organization methods [22, 23] for bioinformatics databases. These methods have potential for improving BLAST performance further.

Query batch size is another important factor which affects BLAST search times. As BLAST will repeatedly scan the entire database for each sequence in the batch query, properly dealing with batched queries will improve search throughput. BLAST++ exploits redundancy and the data locality of the BLAST algorithm by changing how words are compiled. Our experimental results demonstrate BLAST++ can dramatically improve the throughput of BLAST search. The performance of sequential versions of BLAST++ can compete with threaded BLAST with eight threads and mpiBLAST with nine threads. Query length is the least important factor affecting BLAST performance, but the fact that BLAST is more efficient than BLAST++ for very long query sequences may still be important for some applications.

Another class of factors affecting BLAST performance is related to BLAST parallelization strategies. We see that different high performance BLASTs have their own strengths and weaknesses. In general, partitioning a batch of BLAST queries seems to be more efficient than partitioning the sequence database or attempting to parallelize individual BLAST queries. However, on computation clusters with large aggregate memories, combining these distributed memories across the system can achieve better speedups.

9.6   UMD-BLAST

From our experimental results, it is clear that although each version of BLAST can achieve high-performance under the right set of circumstances, no single version achieves the best performance under all conditions. This motivated us to develop UMD-BLAST, a wrapper program that can be used as a single intelligent interface to several high-performances BLASTs. UMD-BLAST is designed to select and invoke the most efficient version of BLAST for the selected database size, batch size, and query length. The current version is implemented for replicated BLAST, replicated BLAST++, and mpiBLAST on PC clusters.

Algorithm   The basic algorithm for UMD-BLAST is as follows:

```
For each batched sequence search query
    If database is too large to fit in memory on a single
      node, use mpiBLAST
    Else
        If (batch size >B) and (query length <L) use
            replicated BLAST++
        Else use replicated threaded-BLAST
        Combine outputs for batch from replicated BLASTs
(where B and L are parameters determined by the
  available memory on each node)
```

The goal is to use replicated BLAST++ if there is sufficient memory, else use replicated threaded-BLAST on each multiprocessor node and switch to mpiBLAST for very large sequence databases that do not fit in the memory of a single node.

9.6.1   UMD-BLAST Performance

To demonstrate the feasibility of an intelligent BLAST wrapper, we implemented UMD-BLAST as a small C program. The current prototype only selects parameters for nucleotide BLAST searches (blastn). Nonetheless, we feel that it can be very useful for bioinformatics researchers who are setting up their own BLAST servers on PC clusters. We present some preliminary performance improvements here for DNA sequence searches.

Figures 9.10 and 9.11 present the performance of UMD-BLAST with varied database and batch sizes. Instead of execution times, performance is measured as throughput, the number of bases processed per processor per second. For the experiments, batch size varies from 28 to 256 and sequence database size range from small

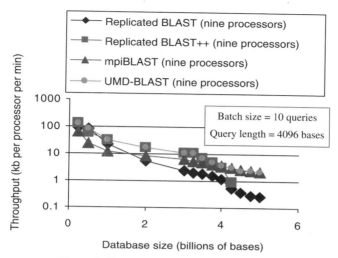

Figure 9.10   UMD-BLAST vs. database size.

databases for which most searches can finish in seconds to large databases that cannot fit into memory on a single node.

As results show, UMD-BLAST can intelligently choose the best performing BLAST version and produce good speedups against individual versions of BLAST. When compared with individual high-performance BLASTs, UMD-BLAST achieved average improvements ranging from a factor of 10 to a hundred. For some cases, where BLAST++ was running out of memory, UMD-BLAST can finish searches in

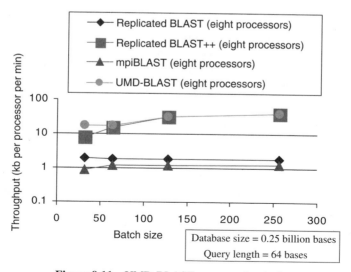

Figure 9.11   UMD-BLAST vs. query batch size.

a relative short time. Even for small database where BLAST searches can be finished quickly, UMD-BLAST can still achieve reasonable improvements.

9.7 FUTURE DIRECTIONS

As we have seen, there are a number of methods for improving the performance of BLAST searches by exploiting parallelism at a number of levels. We believe that BLAST performance can continue to be improved in the future through a number of approaches.

Integration of Existing Approaches   Researchers will develop versions of BLAST that combine the approaches described in this chapter in a single, well-tuned program. The UMD-BLAST wrapper is a first step in this direction.

Precomputing and Caching Intermediate Results   As storage space becomes ever less expensive, intermediate results may be precomputed and saved for sequence databases, reducing the apparent time required for future BLAST searches. Results saved may range from low level results such as the location of word hits to complete pairwise BLAST sequences comparisons for speeding up all-to-all BLAST comparisons.

Preprocessing Sequence Databases   Another approach is to analyze and preprocess sequence databases to make them more efficient for BLAST searches. Unlike caching intermediate results, such preprocessing can take advantage of knowledge of properties of the BLAST algorithm. For instance, the BLAST scoring algorithm may be analyzed to index and partition sequence databases to reduce the portion of the database that must be scanned [22, 23].

Exploiting Grid Resources   For truly large BLAST searches, researchers may attempt to take advantage of CPU cycles in large *grid* systems. Grid computing attempts to provide a common interface for a variety of computing resources, ranging from dedicated computing clusters at supercomputing centers to spare CPU cycles harvested from pools of idle PCs [24]. Researchers are beginning to look into the interfaces and infrastructure required for supporting BLAST in a grid environment. Prototype grid-based versions of BLAST [25, 26] attempt to provide transparent user interfaces for performing BLAST searches on a grid. Such systems will increase in importance as grid computing becomes more popular.

Alternative Pairwise Sequence Alignment Methods   Finally, researchers are continuing to work on developing algorithms that can yield results as precise (or better) than BLAST with better performance. Examples include BLAT [27], PatternHunter [28], and MEGABLAST [29]. Although these methods can be quite powerful and precise, BLAST is so firmly entrenched that convincing biologists to use new sequence search tools will require much evidence of positive results.

9.8 RELATED WORK

As BLAST is an exhaustive searching tool, both database size and number of queries are factors that slow the query processing. A lot of research has been conducted on how to fragment/replicate sequence databases or batch queries to improve the performance of BLAST searches. Julich [30] performed some of the earliest work in this area, porting BLAST to a variety of parallel computers (the shared memory machine Cray Y-MP 8/864, the distributed memory architectures Intel iPSC/860 and nCUBE, and workstation clusters) and discussing the pros and cons of different techniques. More recent work [14, 15], further examine database fragmentation/replication and query distribution issues, giving an overview of different performance enhancement strategies.

Currently, there are many software packages that uses one or more techniques to improve BLAST performance. The standard, most popular BLAST programs are NCBI BLAST [11] and WU BLAST [12]. These versions of BLAST both support parallel processing on a variety of SMP architectures using multiple threads to process queries concurrently.

mpiBLAST [18] is the most recent version of parallel BLAST for distributed memory architecture. It partitions the sequence database into equal sized pieces and distributes the databases to the computing nodes for performing BLAST searches. mpiBLAST can achieve superlinear speedup for large sequence databases by exploiting large aggregate memories.

Another approach is to replicate databases on each computing node. BeoBLAST [16] and Hi-Per BLAST [17] are two softwares that adopt this approach. BeoBLAST implements replicated BLAST/PSI-BLAST on Beowulf linux cluster with perl. It distributes BLAST queries across a cluster through communication between the core of BeoBLAST, perl scripts, and the perl daemon on each computing node. Hi-Per BLAST is another implementation of Replicated BLAST based on NCBI BLAST. The system is comprised of one "control node" and a number of "computing nodes." The control node is responsible for distributing jobs and the actual BLAST search is done by computing nodes. Nblast [8] is a version of replicated blast customized to conduct all-to-all BLAST comparisons. Unlike mpiBLAST, these methods will all experience performance degradation for larger sequence databases that do not fit in the memory on a single node.

One reason that BLAST is computationally intensive is because to process a batch of queries, the default strategy of most BLAST implementations is to run BLAST on each of the queries one at a time. This is clearly inefficient as it does not consider the data locality or the possibility of amortizing search costs. A more efficient algorithm can exploit the common subsequences exist among query sequences and share the computation.

BLAST++ [19] is one BLAST-like batch-processing algorithm that is discussed comprehensively in this chapter. MEGABLAST [29] is another batch processing program embedded in NCBI BLAST. It employs a greedy algorithm to align DNA sequences that differ only by sequencing errors or by equivalent errors. A similar commercial product for improving the efficiency of BLAST is SGI HT-BLAST [20].

It speeds up BLAST query processing by replicating the databases for each processor and dynamically scheduling the batched queries for multiple processors. Benchmark results provided by SGI show that HT-BLAST achieves better scalability than NCBI-BLAST.

Several researchers have also investigated parallelization of other more precise but expensive sequence alignment (search) algorithms [5] than BLAST, in hopes of making them more practical for larger sequence databases [31–33]. Their methods typically require more fine-grain parallelization algorithms and can exploit parallel hardware support [34].

Some research work has been done to investigate the performance of different parallel BLAST strategies. Chi et al. [13] evaluated the performance of BLAST on three different SMP architectures — SGI Challenge, Sun Sparc Center 2000, and Cray CS6400. The results showed that the throughput performance was linearly scalable with little degradation. A more recent paper by Costa and Lifschitz [35] investigated the database distribution issues related to parallel BLAST on clusters of workstations. Performance of parallel BLASTs with different database partition strategies were discussed without experimental comparison. Other researchers [21] tried to provide benchmarks for different versions of BLAST.

9.9 SUMMARY

In this chapter, we examined several high-performance versions of BLAST, the most widely used search tool for screening large sequence databases. The BLAST algorithm is based on comparing words in the query sequence against the entire target DNA or protein sequence database to find statistically significant matches. Even though BLAST is very efficient in practice, the growing size of sequence databases has created a demand for even more powerful versions of BLAST for use on multiprocessors and clusters.

This chapter briefly reviewed the basic BLAST algorithm, then described and analyzed several parallel versions of BLAST designed for high performance. We found that mpiBLAST is good for keeping large sequence databases in memory, whereas BLAST++ can amortize search costs for batched searches. We developed UMD-BLAST, a wrapper for high-performance BLASTs, which can automatically select the appropriate version and configuration of BLAST based on the target database size, query batch size, and query sequence length.

REFERENCES

1. S. Altschul, W. Gish, E. Miller, E. Myers, and D. Lipman, A basic local alignment search tool, *J. Mol. Biol.*, 215, 403–410 (1990).

2. I. Korf, M. Yandell, and J. Bedell, *BLAST*, O'Reilly (2003).

3. S. Karlin and S. Altschul, Applications and statistics for multiple high-scoring segments in molecular sequences, *Proc. Natl. Acad. Sci. USA*, 90 (12), 5873–5877 (1993).

4. S. Altschul and W. Gish, Local alignment statistics, *Methods Enzymol.*, 266, 460–480 (1996).

5. T. F. Smith and M. S. Waterman, Identification of common molecular subsequences, *J. Mol. Biol.*, 147, 195–197 (1981).

6. F. Liang, I. Holt, G. Pertea, S. Karamycheva, S. Salzberg, and J. Quackenbush, An optimized protocol for analysis of est sequences, *Nucleic Acids Res.*, 28, 3657–3665 (2000).

7. J. Parkinson, D. Guiliano, and M. Blaxter, Making sense of EST sequences by CLOBBing them, *BMC Bioinformatics*, 3 (31), October (2002).

8. M. Dumontier and C. Hogue, Nblast: a cluster variant of blast for nxn comparisons, *BMC Bioinformatics*, 3 (1), 13 (2002).

9. A. Delcher, S. Kasif, R. Fleischmann, J. Peterson, O. White, and S. Salzberg, Alignment of whole genomes, *Nuclear Acids Res.*, 27 (11), 2369–2376 (1999).

10. S. Schwartz, Z. Zhang, K. Fraser, A. Smit, C. Riemer, J. Bouck, R. Gibson, R. Hardisson, and W. Miller, Pipmaker — a web server for aligning two genomic dna sequences, *Genome Res.*, 10, 577–586 (2000).

11. National Center for Biotechnology Information, NCBI BLAST, http://www.ncbi.nih.gov/BLAST/.

12. Washington University School of Medicine, WU blast, http://blast.wustl.edu/blast/README.html.

13. E.-H. Chi, E. Shoop, J. Carlis, E. Retzel, and J. Riedl, Efficiency of shared-memory multiprocessors for a genetic sequence similarity search algorithm, *Technical Report TR97-05*, University of Minnesota, Minneapolis, CS Department, January, 1997.

14. R. Braun et al., Three complementary approaches to parallelization of local BLAST service on workstation clusters, *Fifth International Conference on Parallel Computing Technologies (PaCT)*, Vol. 1662, Lecture Notes in Computer Science (LNCS), 1999.

15. R. Costa and S. Lifschitz, Database allocation strategies for parallel BLAST evaluation on clusters, *Distributed Parallel Databases*, 13, 99–127 (2003).

16. J. Grant, R. Dunbrack, F. Manion, and M. Ochs, BeoBLAST: distributed BLAST and PSI-BLAST on a Beowulf cluster, *Bioinformatics*, 18 (5), 765–766 (2002).

17. A. Naruse and N. Nishinomiya, Hi-per BLAST: high Performance BLAST on PC cluster system, *Genome Informatics*, 13, 254–255 (2002).

18. A. Darling, L. Carey, and W.-C. Feng, The design, implementation, and evaluation of mpiBLAST, ClusterWorld Conference & Expo and the 4th International Conference on Linux Clusters: The HPC Revolution, San Jose, CA, June (2003).

19. H. Wang, T. Ong, B. Ooi, and K. Tan, BLAST++: a Tool for BLASTing queries in batches, *Proceedings of the First Asia-Pacific Bioinformatics Conference*, Adelaide, Australia, February, 2003.

20. N. Camp, H. Cofer, and R. Gomperts, High-throughput blast, http://www.sgi.com/industries/sciences/chembio/resources/papers/HTBlast/HT_Whitepaper.html.

21. SGI, SGI bioinformatics performance report, Fall (2001), http://www.sgi.com/solutions/sciences/chembio/resources.

22. R. Mao, W. Xu, N. Singh, and D. Miranker, An assessment of a metric space database index to support sequence homology, *Third IEEE Symposium on BioInformatics and BioEngineering (BIBE'03)*, March, 2003.

23. T. Ong, K. Tan, and H. Wang, Indexing genomic databases for fast homology searching, *Proceedings of the 13th International Conference on Database and Expert Systems Applications (DEXA'02)*, Aix-en-Provence, France, September, 2002.

24. I. Foster, C. Kesselman, and S. Tuecke, The anatomy of the Grid: enabling scalable virtual organizations, *Lecture Notes in Computer Science*, 2150, 2001.

25. F. Konishi, Y. Shiroto, R. Umetsu, and A. Konagaya, Scalable BLAST service in OBIGrid environment, *Genome Informatics*, 14, 535–536 (2003).

26. V. Breton, R. Medina, and J. Montagnat, Datagrid, prototype of a biomedical grid, *Methods Inf. Med.*, 2 (42), 143–147 (2003).

27. W. Kent, Blat — the blast-like alignment tool, *Genome Res.*, 12 (4), 656–664 (2002).

28. B. Ma, J. Tromp, and M. Li, PatternHunter: faster and more sensitive homology search, *Bioinformatics*, 18 (3), 440–445 (2002).

29. Z. Zhang, S. Schwartz, L. Wagner, and W. Miller, A greedy algorithm for aligning DNA sequences, *J. Comput. Biol.*, 7, 203–214 (2000).

30. A. Julich, Implementations of BLAST for parallel computers, *Comput. Appl. Biosci.*, 11 (1), 3–6 (1995).

31. W. Martins, J. del Cuvillo, F. Useche, K. Tehobald, and G. Gao, A multithreaded parallel implementation of a dynamic programming algorithm for sequence comparison, *Pacic Symposium on Biocomputing*, January, 2001.

32. T. Rognes, Paralign: a parallel sequence alignment algorithm for rapid and sensitive database searches, *Nucleic Acids Res.*, 29 (7), 1647–1652 (2001).

33. D. Lavenier and J. Pacherie, Parallel processing for scanning genomic data-bases, *Parallel Computing 97 (PARCO'97)*, Bonn, Germany, pp. 81–88, September 1997.

34. T. Rognes and E. Seeberg, Six-fold speed-up of Smith-Waterman sequence database searches using parallel processing on common microprocessors, *Bioinformatics*, 16, 699–706 (2000).

35. R. Costa and S. Lifschitz, Database allocation strategies for parallel blast evaluation on clusters, *Distributed Parallel Databases*, 13, 99–127 (2003).

CHAPTER 10

Parallel Implementations of Local Sequence Alignment: Hardware and Software

VIPIN CHAUDHARY, FENG LIU, VIJAY MATTA, and LAURENCE T. YANG

10.1 INTRODUCTION

With the progress in computer science and raw computational power available today, human quest to learn and understand the complex relationships between the subsets of biology, for example, biological response, biodiversity, genetics, medicine, and so on has got a new promise. Computational biology represents the combination of computer science and biology and spans many disciplines such as bioinformatics (genomics and postgenomics), clinical informatics, medical imaging, bioengineering, and so on. It finds application in many areas of life science, for example, the development of human therapeutics, diagnostics, pyrognostics, and forensics, up through the simulation of large entities such as populations and ecosystems.

Genomics is the determination of the entire DNA sequence of an organism. The goal of modern human genomics is preventive, predictive, and individualized medicine. In agriculture, the goal is the production of foods with improved production characteristics and increasingly beneficial consumer traits. Postgenomics refers to the biological processes that follow from DNA sequence (e.g., transciptomics, proteomics, metabolomics, etc.).

Modern biopharm companies currently have about 2–10 TB of genomics data, large phrama have 10–40 TB, and genomic data providers have over 100 TB. The genomics effort is to collect and process terabytes of such heterogeneous and geographically disperse data into *information* (translating the spots into the sequence of nucleotide bases A, C, G, and T consisting sequences of DNA or the 3D structure of a protein with the relative location of all of its atoms), then *knowledge* (the location of genes in the sequence, the proteins that come from the genes, the function of the genes and proteins, how they interact, their relationship to each other, etc.), and then take *action*

Parallel Computing for Bioinformatics and Computational Biology, Edited by Albert Y. Zomaya
Copyright © 2006 John Wiley & Sons, Inc.

(the simple decision to run another experiment or the decision to risk $2 billion to develop the drug candidate). Eventually, they ship the information to the regulatory agencies. Only after approval does the company become a manufacturer of a tangible product (drug, therapy, diagnostic, etc.).

Although CPU architectures are struggling to show increased performance, the volume of biological data is greatly accelerating. For example, GenBank, a public database of DNA, RNA, and protein sequence information, is doubling about every 6 months. In keeping up with Moore's law, the density of the transistors on a chip has doubled for four decades, but may slow, according to Semiconductor Industry Association, as certain physical limits are reached. In addition, DRAM speeds have not kept up with the CPU speeds, thus hitting the *"memory wall."* Most science and engineering problems tend to plateau beyond eight CPUs. However, genomics algorithms can achieve much better parallelization (sometimes called "embarrassingly parallel") because they can be deconstructed into a large number of independent searches with little message passing, or coordination, between jobs/threads, if the data is appropriately passed to the appropriate processors. The final results are then assembled when the independent jobs are completed.

10.1.1 Types of Sequence Alignment

Sequence alignment refers to the procedure of comparing two or more sequences by searching for a series of characters (nucleotides for DNA sequences or amino acids for protein sequences) that appear in the same order in the input sequences. Although residues are mostly used to refer to amino acids, for brevity purposes, residues will be used to imply both nucleotides and amino acids in the remainder of this discussion. A distinction will be made when necessary. The sequence alignment problem is often referred to as the longest common substring problem. Regions in the new sequence and the known sequence that are similar can help decipher biological functions or evolutionary information about the new sequence. The alignment of two or more sequences is anchored around the longest common substring and the remaining, nonmatching residues can represent gaps, insertion, or deletion. When aligning multiple sequences, the goal is to discover signatures or motifs that are common to all the sequences. A motif or a signature is a sequence of residues that is common to the aligned sequences and can help identify a family of nucleic acid sequences or protein sequences.

The alignment of two sequences (pairwise alignment), or multiple sequences (multiple alignment) and the alignment of short or long sequences such as an entire genome may require different types of algorithms. The algorithms used in all of these four cases can be dynamic programming based or heuristic based or a combination of both. Dynamic programming is a general optimization technique, which relies on the fact that the solution to a problem consists of the combined solutions of the sub-problems. Furthermore, several of the sub-problems may be the same. Thus, they are solved only once. Dynamic programming based algorithms generate optimal solutions. However, they are computationally intensive, which makes them impractical for a large number of sequence alignments. A more practical solution is one that uses a heuristic to generate a near-optimal solution. Heuristics are approximation algorithms. In the case of sequence alignment, these heuristics often use a combination of a restricted form of dynamic programming (e.g., dynamic programming is only used for a small subset of the residues in a sequence rather than on the entire sequence) and other approximations to reduce the search space of possible solutions.

10.1.1.1 *Pairwise Alignment*

Pairwise alignment is the alignment of two sequences. In general, the purpose of this alignment is to extract the sequences that are similar (homologous) to a given input sequence from a database of target sequences. That is, the input sequence is aligned with each target sequence in the database and the top ranking sequences represent the sequences with the highest level of similarity to the input sequence. The input sequence is also called the query sequence. Each alignment between the input sequence and a target sequence is one pairwise alignment. A score is associated with each pairwise alignment to indicate the level of similarity between the query sequence and the corresponding target sequence. This score is determined based on a scoring matrix and specific penalties for insertions, deletions, and gaps. The scoring matrix represents the weight associated with a match for all different types of nucleotides or amino acids.

10.1.1.2 *Multiple Sequence Alignment*

In multiple sequence alignment, the objective is to find a common alignment for multiple sequences. Several approaches for multiple sequence alignment have been proposed. Initial implementations were based on an extension of the Smith–Waterman algorithm to multiple sequences. This implementation, which is based on dynamic programming, generates an optimal solution, but is computationally very intensive. More recent approaches incrementally build multiple sequence alignment using heuristics.

10.2 SEQUENCE ALIGNMENT PRIMER

10.2.1 Parallel Programming Models

Parallel algorithms for analyzing DNA and protein sequences are becoming increasingly important as sequence data continues to grow. In simple terms, parallel software enables a massive computational task to be divided into several separate processes, which execute concurrently through different processors to solve a common task [1].

In particular, two key features can be used to compare models: granularity and communication. Granularity is the relative size of the units of computation that execute in parallel, for example, fineness or coarseness of task division; communication is the way that separate units of computation exchange data and synchronize their activity.

10.2.1.1 *Coarse and Fine-Grain Parallelism*

The finest level of software granularity is intended to run individual statements over different subsets of a whole data structure. This concept is called data parallel and is mainly achieved through the use of compiler directives, which generate library calls to create lightweight processes called threads and distribute loop iterations among themselves. A second level of granularity can be formulated as a "block of instructions." At this level, the programmer identifies sections of the program that can be safely executed in parallel and inserts the directives that begin to separate tasks. When the parallel program starts, the run-time support creates a pool of threads, which are unblocked by the run-time library as soon as the parallel section is reached. At the end of the parallel section, all extra processes are suspended and the original process continues to execute.

Ideally, if we have n processors, the run time should also be n times faster with respect to the wall-clock time. In reality, however, the speedup of a parallel program is decreased by synchronization between processes, interactions, and load imbalances. In other words, the overhead to coordinate multiple processes require some time added to the pure computational workload.

Much of the effort that goes into parallel programming involves increasing efficiency. The first attempt to reduce parallelization penalties is to minimize the communication cost between parallel processes. The simplest way, when possible, is to reduce the number of task divisions; in other words, to create coarsely grained applications. Once the granularity has been decided, communications are needed to enforce correct behavior and create an accurate outcome.

10.2.1.2 *Inter-Process Communication*

When shared memory is available, inter-process communication is usually performed through shared variables. When several processes are working over the same logical address space, locks, semaphores, or critical sections are required for safe access to shared variables.

When the processors use distributed memory, all inter-process communication must be performed by sending messages over the network. The message-passing paradigms, for example, MPI, parallel virtual machine (PVM), and so on, are used to specify the communication between a set of processes forming a concurrent program. The message-passing paradigm is attractive because of its wide portability and scalability. It is easily compatible with both distributed-memory multi-computers and shared-memory multiprocessors, clusters, and combinations of these elements. Writing parallel code for a distributed memory machines is a difficult task, especially for applications with irregular data access patterns. To facilitate this programming task, software distributed shared memory provides the illusion of shared memory on top of the underlying message-passing system [2].

Task scheduling strategies suggest that obtaining an efficient parallel implementation is fundamental to achieving a good distribution for both data and computations. In general, any parallel strategy represents a trade-off between reducing communication time and improving the computational load balance.

A simple task scheduling strategy is based on a master–slave approach. The master–slave paradigm consists of two entities: a master and multiple workers. For coarse-grain parallelism, the database is divided into blocks of sequences. These blocks can be assigned to the slaves following the work pool approach with dynamic load balancing. When one slave finishes generating all the pairwise alignments for the target sequences in its block, another block is assigned to it. This process is continued until all the sequences in the database are processed. The number of blocks is usually orders of magnitude higher than the number of processors, and blocks are assigned to processors dynamically. This dynamic load balancing approach is more efficient than a static load balancing approach because the execution time associated with the pairwise alignment is not known a priori and can vary from a pair of sequences to the next. The factors that have an impact on the execution time required by a pairwise alignment include the length of the two sequences and how similar they are. The results generated from the individual slaves have to be combined and sorted according to the score calculated for each pairwise alignment. To perform this task, the slaves can send their results to the master, which take care of generating this final result. Usually, the communication takes place only between the master and the workers at the beginning and at the end of the processing of each task.

10.2.2 Parallel Computer Architectures

The algorithms for database searching can be implemented to run efficiently on various types of hardware with the ability to perform several operations simultaneously. There is a wide range of different hardware available on which the algorithms can be implemented. Hughey [3] has reviewed various types of hardware that can be used and their performance. The hardware can be divided into a group of general purpose computers, which can be used for many different kinds of computations, and a group of hardware specifically designed for performing sequence alignments and database searches.

10.2.2.1 General-Purpose Parallel Computers   General-purpose computers with parallel processing capabilities usually contain a number of connected processors, ranging from dual-CPU workstations to supercomputers. The well-known dynamic programming or heuristic algorithms must be rewritten to run on such computers. The algorithms can be parallelized at different scales, from a simple coarse-grained parallelization where, for example, the database sequences are divided on two or more processors, each comparing the sub-database sequence against the query sequence, to a complicated fine-grained parallelization where the comparison of the query sequence against one database sequence is parallelized. The speed gained varies according to the type of algorithm and computer architecture.

A cluster of workstations (either single- or multi-CPU) connected by an Ethernet network is loosely connected processors, is very interesting for sequence database searches, because of the independence between the different sequences in the database.

Microparallelism can be classified into SIMD (single instruction, multiple data) and MIMD (multiple instruction, multiple data) types according to whether the processing units perform the same or different operations on their data. It is an interesting form of SIMD, where a 128 bit wide integer register of a CPU is divided into 16 smaller 8 bit units and where the same arithmetic or logical operation can be performed simultaneously and independently on the data in each of the individual units. This technique can be performed on ordinary CPUs using normal instructions combined with a technique involving masking of the high order bits in each unit. However, it has become much easier recently with the introduction of MMX/SSE from Intel, MMX/3DNow from AMD, and VIS from SUN, which allows fine-grain parallelism to be exploited for a single pairwise alignment.

10.2.2.2 *Special-Purpose Parallel Hardware* A number of different designs for special-purpose hardware for performing sequence alignments and database searching have been proposed and implemented. Their advantage over general-purpose computers is that they can be tailored specifically to perform sequence comparisons at a high speed, whereas the disadvantage is high cost.

Special-purpose hardware is usually built using either FPGA (field-programmable gate arrays) or custom VLSI (very large scale integration) technology. The advantage of FPGA is that they are reprogrammable and can be built to work in a given function, and hence can be changed to remove bugs or to work with different algorithms, whereas VLSI is customarily designed to a very specific purpose and cannot be changed. The advantage of VLSI is a lower cost per unit (at least in large volumes) and a higher processing speed. However, the design and initial costs for VLSI systems are higher than for FPGA.

10.2.3 Local Sequence Alignment Software

10.2.3.1 *Sequence Alignment Parallelization* Sequence alignment is the most widely used bioinformatic application. It is also one of the most familiar applications to begin a discussion about parallelization in bioinformatics. Sequence alignment has a very simple form as far as data flow is concerned, and a broad range of strategies have been proposed to apply parallel computing.

Searching on DNA or protein databases using sequence comparison algorithm has become one of the most powerful technique to help determine the biological function of a gene or the protein it encodes. The primary influx of information for database searching is in the form of raw DNA and protein sequences. Therefore, one of the first steps towards obtaining information from a new biological sequence is to compare it with the set of known sequences contained in the sequence databases, using algorithms such as BLAST [4], Needleman–Wunsch [5], and Smith–Waterman [6]. Results often suggest functional, structural, or evolutionary analogies between the sequences.

Two main sets of algorithms are used for pairwise comparison: exhaustive algorithms and heuristic-based algorithms. The exhaustive algorithms are based on dynamic programming methodologies such as Needleman–Wunsch [5] and Smith–Waterman [6] algorithm. The heuristic approaches are widely used, such as the FASTA [7] and BLAST [4] families. Most of the currently used pairwise alignment algorithms are heuristic based.

The first widely used program for database similarity searching was FASTA [7]. FASTA stands for FAST-All, reflecting the fact that it can be used for a fast protein comparison or a fast nucleotide comparison. This program achieves a high level of sensitivity for similarity searching at high speed. The high speed of this program is achieved by using the observed pattern of word hits to identify potential matches before attempting the very time consuming optimized search. The trade-off between speed and sensitivity is controlled by the k-tuple parameter, which specifies the size of the word. Increasing the k-tuple decreases the number of background hits. The FASTA program does not investigate every word hit encountered, but instead looks initially for segments containing several nearby hits. Using a heuristic method, these segments are assigned scores and the score of the best segment found appears in the output. For those alignments finally reported, a full Smith–Waterman alignment search is performed.

BLAST [4] is another heuristic-based algorithm for sequence homology search. As in FASTA, it finds database sequences that have k consecutive matches to the query sequence. The value of k is 3 for protein sequence and 11 for DNA sequence. Several variations [4, 8] of the original BLAST algorithm were developed to accommodate different types of sequence alignments. For example, MEGABLAST uses the XDrop alignment algorithm [8]. It is particularly tuned for the alignment of two DNA sequences that are highly similar. This algorithm is computationally efficient because it considers long runs of identical adjacent nucleotides. If the two sequences differ by 3%, the expected length of the run is 30 nucleotides. The algorithm is also computationally efficient because it completely avoids the use of dynamic programming even in a limited context. It uses a greedy algorithm instead. A greedy algorithm is one type of a heuristic that is developed with the assumption that a global optimal can be obtained by making a sequence of local optimal decisions, whereas dynamic programming is a global optimization algorithm. XDrop was used to align entire genomes and it was found [8] to be 10 times faster than BLAST for long and highly similar sequences.

PSI-BLAST [4] executes several iterations of the BLAST algorithm. However, the scoring matrix, which is used to score the pairwise alignment, is not fixed in PSI-BLAST. The scoring matrix includes the weights corresponding to a match for all types of nucleotides or amino acids. After every iteration, the top ranking target sequences in the pairwise alignment are used to update the scoring matrix. In addition, PSI-BLAST uses a position-specific scoring matrix where two matching residues are assigned a score based not only on the importance of the match but also on the position of the residue in the sequence. PSI-BLAST is more sensitive than BLAST in detecting weak sequence similarities.

Regardless of the algorithm used, in the case of pairwise alignment, an input sequence is aligned against a list of target sequences from a database resulting in multiple pairwise alignments. In each pairwise alignment, one of the two sequences is the input sequence and the other one is sequence from the database. This process can be parallelized in two ways: (1) multiple pairwise alignments can be executed in parallel (coarse-grain parallelism) and (2) a parallel version of the alignment algorithm can be used to speedup each individual pairwise alignment (fine-grain parallelism).

Given a set of input sequences, ClustalW [9] implements multiple alignments using a tree-based method. Pairwise alignments are first constructed for each pair of sequences from the input set. These alignments are used to construct a similarity matrix. Each entry in the matrix represents the similarity distance between any two sequences from the input set. The similarity matrix is used to construct a tree that will guide the multiple sequence alignment. Closely related sequence pairs are aligned first resulting in partial alignments. These partial alignments are then either combined with other neighboring partial alignments or sequences in the guiding tree. The computational complexity of ClustalW is reduced from being exponential when dynamic programming based multiple alignment is used to a second-order polynomial.

For n sequences, the number of comparisons to be made are $n(n-1)/2$, which is very large as the number of sequences increases. This pairwise comparison can be done in parallel. There are different approaches such as ClustalW-MPI, SGI's HT ClustalW, and MULTICLUSTAL. These approaches increase the speed of aligning multiple sequences. ClustalW-MPI and HTClustalW will be discussed in detail in the following sections.

The demand for computational power in the bioinformatic field will continue to grow as the complexity and the volume of data increases. This computational power can only be delivered by large-scale parallel computers that either have distributed memory architecture or shared memory architecture. Distributed computing has been already used successfully in sequence alignment. In general, most of these applications have been implemented using the work pool approach with coarse grain parallelism. This type of implementation is ideal for clusters built with off-the-shelve personal computers. Sequence alignment is expected to continue to draw increasing attention and it will drive several high performance computing efforts.

10.3 SMITH–WATERMAN ALGORITHM

When looking for similarities between subsequences of two sequences, as is usually the goal in the methods used to find homologies by database searches, a local alignment method is more appropriate than a global. The simple dynamic programming algorithm described by Smith and Waterman [6] is the basis for this type of alignments. The Smith–Waterman algorithm is perhaps the most widely used local similarity algorithm for biological sequence database searching.

In Smith–Waterman database searches, the dynamic programming method is used to compare every database sequence against the query sequence and assign a score to each result. The dynamic programming method checks every possible alignment between two given sequences. This algorithm can be used both to compute the optimal alignment score and to create the actual alignment. It uses memory space proportional to the product of the lengths of the two sequences, mn, and computing time proportional to $mn(m+n)$. The recursion relations used in the original Smith–Waterman algorithm are the following:

$$H_{i,j} = \max\{H_{i-1,j-1}, S[ai, bj], E_{i,j}, F_{i,j}\}$$

where

$$E_{i,j} = \max_{0<k<i}\{H_{i-k,j} - g(k)\}, \quad F_{i,j} = \max_{0<l<j}\{H_{i,j-l} - g(l)\}$$

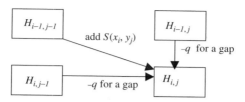

Figure 10.1 Dynamic programming illustration.

Here, $H_{i,j}$ is the score of the optimal alignment ending at position (i, j) in the matrix, whereas $E_{i,j}$ and $F_{i,j}$ are the scores of optimal alignments that ends at the same position but with a gap in sequence A or B, respectively. S is the match/mismatch value of ai and bj or amino acid substitution score matrix, whereas $g(k)$ is the gap penalty function. The computations should be started with $E_{i,j} = F_{i,j} = H_{i,j} = 0$ for all $i = 0$ or $j = 0$ and proceeded with i going from 1 to m and j going from 1 to n (Fig. 10.1).

The order of computation is strict, because the value of H in any cell in the alignment matrix cannot be computed before all cells to the left or above it have been computed. The overall optimal alignment score is equal to the maximum value of $H_{i,j}$.

Gotoh [10] reduced the time needed by the algorithm to be proportional to mn when affined gap penalties of the form $g(k) = q + rk; (q \geq 0, r \geq 0)$ are used, where q is the gap opening penalty and r is the gap extension penalty. When only the actual optimal local alignment score is required, the space requirements were reduced to be proportional to the smallest of m and n. The new recursion relations for $E_{i,j}$ and $F_{i,j}$ are as follows:

$$E_{i,j} = \max_{0<k<i}\{H_{i-1,j} - q + E_{i-1,j} - r\}$$

$$F_{i,j} = \max_{0<l<j}\{H_{i,j-l} - q + E_{i,j-1} - r\}$$

All the searching process can be divided into two phases [11]. In the fist phase, all the elements of two sequences have to be compared and form a scoring matrix. Following the recurrence equation in Figure 10.1, the matrix is filled from top left to bottom right with each entry $H_{i,j}$ requiring the entries $H_{i-1,j}$, $H_{i,j-1}$, and $H_{i-1,j-1}$ with gap penalty $q = r$ at each step. Once scores in all cells are calculated, the second phase of the algorithm identifies the best local alignments. As they might be biologically relevant, alignments with score value above a given threshold are reported. Thus, for each element of the matrix, a backtracking procedure is applied to find out the best local alignment.

Figure 10.2 shows the data dependencies in Smith–Waterman algorithm. As mentioned in the previous section, there are three possible alignments to choose from when calculating one element: alignment of the symbol in the row considered with gap — horizontal arrow; alignment between the symbols in the row and column considered with match/mismatch — diagonal arrow; alignment of the symbol in the column considered with a gap — vertical arrow. This means that rows or columns

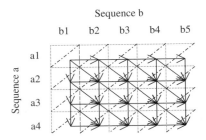

Figure 10.2 Data dependency in Smith–Waterman alignment matrix.

can not be computed in parallel. The only elements on each successive anti-diagonal (labeled dashed line in Fig. 10.2) are processed in parallel. These data dependencies present a serious challenge for sufficient parallel execution on a general-purpose parallel processor.

10.3.1 Parallel Computation Approach for Smith–Waterman Algorithm

Database searching applications allow two different granularity alternatives to be considered: fine-grained and coarse-grained parallelism. Early approaches focused on data parallel over SIMD machines.

10.3.1.1 *Fine-Grain Parallelism* Typical dynamic programming-based algorithms, such as Smith–Waterman algorithm, compute an $H_{m,n}$ matrix (m and m being the sequence lengths) depending on the three entries $H_{i-1,j}$, $H_{i,j-1}$, and $H_{i-1,j-1}$. Fine grain means that processors will work together in computing the H matrix, cell by cell. Some researchers organized the parallel machine as an array of processors to compute in diagonal-sweep fashion the matrix H (Fig. 10.3). An advantage is that this strategy only requires local communications in each step. PE_i sends $H_{i,j}$ to PE_{i+1} to allow it to compute $H_{i+1,j}$ in the next step, whereas PE_i computes $H_{i,j+1}$. Query

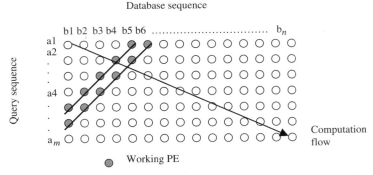

Figure 10.3 Diagonal-sweep fine-grained workload distribution for multiprocessors machines to avoid data dependencies in Smith–Waterman algorithm.

sequence length determines the maximum number of processors able to be assigned and processors remain idle at begin/end steps.

Rognes [12] implemented the Smith–Waterman algorithm using Intel's MMX/SSE technology. Six-fold speed-up relative to the fastest known Smith–Waterman implementation on the same hardware was achievied by optimized eight-way parallel processing approach.

10.3.1.2 *Coarse-Grain Parallelism*

There are several proposed strategies for achieving coarse-grained parallelism in sequence-alignment applications. Most of them can be explained on the basis of the flow chart shown in Figure 10.4. First of all, the program sets the initial stage of the algorithm. Next, it manages the algorithm extension, which works until the number of database sequences is exhausted, then fetches the next database sequence to be compared against the query sequence. The result value is saved to rank the best results as in the following step. Finally, statistical significance can incorporate a optimization process and the last step is to output results.

As should be noted, the algorithm has a very simple form as far as data flow is concerned. The database sequence corresponds to the data set to be searched, which

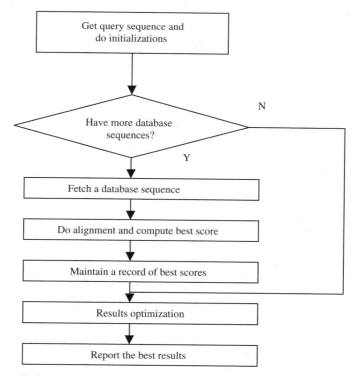

Figure 10.4 Sequential flow chart for a sequence database searching application.

is a set of sequences of different lengths. In essence, in a typical coarse-grained parallel implementation, one of the processors acts as a "master", dispatching blocks of sequences to the "slaves" which, in turn, perform the algorithm calculations. When the slaves report results for one block, the master sends a new block. This strategy is possible because results from the comparison between query and database sequences are independent of the previous results deriving from the comparison of the query with other sequences.

However, the time required in the processing of any given sequence depends not only on the length of the sequence but also on its composition. Therefore, the use of a dynamic load balancing strategy is necessary. The simplest way is to modify the way in which the master processor distributes the load on demand from the slaves. Obviously, sending one-sequence messages introduces additional expensive time overhead due to the high number of messages interchanged. Thus, rather than distributing messages sequence-by-sequence, better results are achieved by dispatching blocks of sequences.

10.4 FASTA

FASTA [7] finds homologous sequences using a four-step process. First, sequences that have sub-sequences of at least k adjacent residues, which match sub-sequences in the query sequence, are identified. The recommended value of k for a protein sequence alignment is 2 and for a DNA sequence alignment is between 4 and 6. The second step combines groups of these matching sub-sequences into longer matching regions called initial regions. Each initial region consists of one or more matching sub-sequence separated by mismatching regions of residues. Gaps are not allowed within the mismatching regions. That is, the number of residues between two consecutive matching sub-sequences within the same initial region has to be the same in the query sequence and the target sequence. These initial regions are scored and the best 10 initial regions are selected. During the third step, dynamic programming is used to combine nearby initial regions and new scores are assigned to the combined regions. This is an example of how dynamic programming is used in a limited context (i.e., only for nearby initial regions) within heuristics. In this third step, mismatching regions between the initial regions may contain gaps. The scores generated in the third step are used to rank the database sequences. During the fourth step, the Smith–Waterman [6] algorithm is applied to the top ranking sequences from the previous step. Specifically, this algorithm is used to align the query sequence and the database sequences within the selected initial regions and their neighboring residues. The fourth step in FASTA is another example of the use of dynamic programming in a limited context within a heuristic based alignment algorithm. The Smith–Waterman [6] algorithm is only used for top ranking sequences and only within selected regions of these sequences. Limiting the use of dynamic programming increases the computational efficiency of the alignment algorithm. However, it also means that the generated solution is only a sub-optimal solution rather than an optimal one.

FASTA provides different executables for different types of sequence alignment.

- FASTA: Nucleotide sequence/nucleotide sequence database.
- SSEARCH: Protein sequence/protein sequence database.
- TFASTA: Protein sequence/six-frame translations of a nucleotide sequence database (treats each frame separately).
- FASTX: Six-frame translations of a nucleotide sequence/protein sequence database.
- TFASTX: Protein sequence/six-frame translations of a nucleotide sequence database (treats the forward or reverse three frames as one sequence).

10.4.1 Parallel Implementation of FASTA

To study the performance of parallel FASTA, a large quantity of research work has been done. The parallel efficiency of FASTA programs on Sun servers [13] can be quite high, especially for large searches. The experiment results show a 54-fold speedup of FASTA search when it runs on 62 CPUs of the Sun Enterprise 10000 (64 CPUs of 400 MHz with 8 MB L2 cache). Parallel scaling for smaller queries is typically much lower.

The performance of the FASTA programs was studied on PARAM 10000 [14], a parallel cluster of workstations. The FASTA program executes very quickly when a small query or database is chosen, but becomes compute intensive when searching a query of longer length against huge databases. The parallel FASTA ported with Sun-MPI libraries was used to run on Fast Ethernet across 2–64 processors and a speedup of 44-fold was observed on 64 processors. Although searching a longer query sequence against a huge database using parallel FASTA, better speedup was observed than with smaller query lengths. Thus, parallel FASTA can be more effectively used when long genome sequences of human chromosomes, that is, those having more than 10 MB, need to be searched against large genome sequence databases.

10.5 BLAST

BLAST [15] or basic local alignment search tool is a heuristic-based search algorithm to match sequences. This heuristic search method seeks words of length W that score at least T when aligned with the query and scored with a substitution matrix. Words in the database that score T or greater are extended in both directions in an attempt to find a locally optimal un-gapped alignment or high scoring pair (HSP) with a score of at least S or an E value lower than the specified threshold. HSPs that meet these criteria will be reported by BLAST, provided they do not exceed the cutoff value specified for number of descriptions and/or alignments to report.

In the first step, BLAST uses words of length w instead of k-tuples. These words also include conservative substitutions. The words used in BLAST contain all w-tuples that receive a score T, above a certain level, when compared using the amino acid substitution matrix. By default, BLAST uses $w = 3$ and $T = 11$. A given triplet in the query sequence will then match the triplets in the database sequence that has a score of 11 or more when the three pairs of amino acids are compared.

In the second step, BLAST extends the initial words into so-called HSPs using the amino acid substitution matrix. This extension is performed in both directions along the diagonal from the initial word and is stopped when the potential score falls a level X below the currently found maximum score of the HSP.

It was found that 90% of the time was spent in extending the word and most of this extension would not lead to a HSP. It was also found that most of the HSPs found would have multiple hits. Therefore, rather than extending the word on a single hit, one would only extend a word if there were multiple hits. To keep the probability of finding a similarity constant, one reduces the threshold T. This is known as the two-hit alignment method. In addition, the first version of BLAST does not consider gapped alignments at all, but computes a statistical measure of significance based on the highest scoring HSPs using sum-statistics [16].

Altschul et al. [4] describe version 2 of NCBI BLAST, which includes a few improvements and increases both the speed and the sensitivity of the program. In the first step, BLAST 2 uses the two-hit alignment method to improve performance. This double-hit method not only reduces the number of hits substantially but also reduces sensitivity relative to the first version of BLAST. The extension of HSPs in the second step is performed in the same manner as with the previous version, although with far fewer HSPs, and hence much faster. Using midpoints on the HSPs as seeds, BLAST 2 performs an accurate gapped alignment constrained not to contain any low-scoring regions. This gapped alignment leads to much increased sensitivity over the original BLAST program. The alignments take a lot of time and are hence only performed for the HSPs scoring 40 or above, which represents only about 2% of the database sequences. NCBI BLAST 2 uses the new statistics for gapped alignments described by Altschul [17] to compute an E-value expressing the expected number of random matches in the database having a given score.

To utilize these heuritics for sequence alignments, NCBI provides different executables for different types of sequence alignment. Blastp is used for matching protein query sequence against protein database. Blastn is used for matching neucleotide query sequence against neucleotide database. Blastx is used for matching nucleotide query sequence translated in all reading frames against a protein sequence database. Tblastn is used for matching protein query sequence against a nucleotide sequence database dynamically translated in all reading frames. Tblastx is used for matching the six-frame translations of a nucleotide query sequence against the six-frame translations of a nucleotide sequence database. Although they are different programs, they all use the same tow-hit heuristic for the comparison of query against the database.

10.5.1 TurboBLAST

TurboBLAST [18] is an accelerated, parallel deployment of NCBI BLAST, which delivers high performance, not by changing the BLAST algorithm but by coordinating the use of multiple copies of the unmodified serial NCBI BLAST application on networked clusters of heterogeneous PCs, workstations, or Macintosh computers. As a result, TurboBLAST supports all of the standard variants of the BLAST algorithm supported in NCBI BLAST (blastn, blastp, blastx, tblastn, and tblastx). It provides results that are effectively identical to those obtained with the NCBI application.

An individual BLAST job specifies a number of input query sequences to be searched against one or more sequence databases. To achieve parallel speedup, TurboBLAST implements a distributed Java "harness" that splits BLAST jobs into multiple small pieces, processes the pieces in parallel, and integrates the results into a unified output. The harness coordinates the following activities on multiple machines

- Creation of BLAST tasks, each of which requires the comparison of a small group of query sequences (typically 10–20 sequences) against a modest-sized partition of one of the databases sized, so that the entire task can be completed within the available physical memory without paging.
- Application of the standard NCBI blastall program to complete each task
- Integration of the task results into a unified output.

This approach has the advantage that it is guaranteed to generate the same pairwise sequence comparisons as the serial version of BLAST, because it uses exactly the same executable to perform the search computations. High performance is achieved in two ways. First, the size of each individual BLAST task is set adaptively so that blastall processing will be efficient on the processor that computes the task. Secondly, a large enough set of tasks is created so that all the processors have useful work to do and so that nearly perfect load balance can be achieved.

Initial benchmarks of TurboBLAST on a network of 11 commodity PCs running Linux reduced the serial time of 5 days, 19 h, and 13 min BLAST run to just a parallel time of 12 h, 54 min. It was able to achieve a speedup of nearly 10.8.

10.5.2 mpiBLAST

mpiBLAST [19, 42] is an open-source parallelization of BLAST, which achieves superlinear speedup by segmenting a BLAST database and then having each node in a computational cluster search a unique portion of the database. Database segmentation permits each node to search a smaller portion of the database (one that fits entirely in memory), eliminating disk I/O and vastly improving BLAST performance. Because database segmentation does not create heavy communication demands, BLAST users can take advantage of low-cost and efficient Linux cluster architectures such as the bladed Beowulf.

mpiBLAST is a pair of programs that replace *formatdb* and *blastall* with versions that execute BLAST jobs in parallel on a cluster of computers with MPI installed. There are two primary advantages to using mpiBLAST versus traditional BLAST. First, mpiBLAST splits the database across each node in the cluster. Because each node's segment of the database is smaller, it can usually reside in the buffer-cache, yielding a significant speedup due to the elimination of disk I/O. In addition, the data

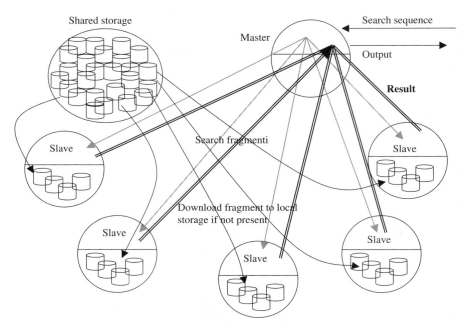

Figure 10.5   Master–slave worker model of mpiBLAST.

decomposition is done offline. The fragments reside in a shared storage as shown in Figure 10.5. Secondly, it allows BLAST users to take advantage of efficient, low-cost Beowulf clusters because the inter-processor communication demands are low.

The mpiBLAST algorithm consists of three steps:

1. Segmenting and distributing the database, for example, see Figure 10.5
2. Running mpiBLAST queries on each node
3. Merging the results from each node into a single output file

The first step consists of a front-end node formatting the database via a wrapper around the standard NCBI *formatdb* called *mpiformatdb*. The *mpiformatdb* wrapper generates the appropriate command-line arguments to enable NCBI *formatdb* to format and divide the database into many small fragments of roughly equal size. When completed, the formatted database fragments are placed on shared storage. Next, each database fragment is distributed to a distinct worker node and queried by directly executing the BLAST algorithm as implemented in the NCBI development library. Finally, when each worker node completes searching on its fragment, it reports the results back to the front-end node who merges the results from each worker node and sorts them according to their score. Once all the results have been received, they are written to a user-specified output file using the BLAST output functions of the NCBI development library. This approach to generating merged results allows mpiBLAST to directly produce results in any format supported by NCBI's BLAST, including XML, HTML, tab-delimited text, and ASN.1.

The extra overhead incurred by the coordination and message passing may not pay off for small databases and small-to-medium length queries, but for databases that are very big to fit in the physical memory of a single node, it clearly offers an advantage.

10.5.3 Green Destiny

Green destiny is a 240-processor supercomputer that operates at a peak rate of 240 gigflops [20]. It fits in 6 ft^2 and consumes 3.2 kW of power. mpiBLAST is benchmarked on the Green Destiny cluster by the Los Alamos National Laboratory. Each node of this cluster consists of a 667 MHz Transmeta Crusoe TM5600 processor with 640 MB RAM and a 20 GB hard disk. Nodes are interconnected with switched 100Base-Tx Ethernet. Each node runs Linux 2.4 operating system. It is able to achieve a speedup of over 160 for 128 processors. The database used is the GenBank nt of size 5.1 GB to run a query of predicted genes from bacterial genome of size 300 kB. The cluster with one worker runs for about 22.4 h, whereas with 128 workers, the query takes just 8 min. However, the scalability of this system is largely constrained by the time to merge results, which typically increase with the number of fragments.

10.6 HMMER — HIDDEN MARKOV MODELS

HMMER [21] is a statistical model, which is suited for many tasks in molecular biology, such as database searching and multiple sequence alignment of protein families and protein domains, although they have been mostly developed for speech recognition since 1970s. Similar to the ones used in speech recognition, a HMM is used to model protein families such as globins and kinases. The most popular use of the HMM in molecular biology is as a probabilistic profile of a protein family, which is called profile HMM. From a family of proteins or DNA, a profile HMM can be made for searching a database for other members of the family.

The Internet sources for profile HMM and HMM-like software package are listed in the following table.

Software Tool	Web Site
HMMER	http://hmmer.wustl.edu
SAM	http://www.cse.ucsc.edu/research/compbio/sam.html
Pfam	http://pfam.wustl.edu
PFTOOLS	http://www.isrec.isb-sib.ch/ftp-server/pftools/
BLOCKS	http://blocks.fhcrc.org/
META-MEME	http://metameme.sdsc.edu
PSI-BLAST	http://www.ncbi.nlm.nih.gov/BLAST/

HMMER offers a more systematic approach to estimating model parameters. The HMMER is a dynamic kind of statistical profile. Like an ordinary profile, it is built by analyzing the distribution of amino acids in a training set of related proteins. However, an HMMER has a more complex topology than a profile. It can be visualized as a finite state machine, familiar to students of computer science. Finite state machines typically move through a series of states and produce some kind of output either when the machine has reached a particular state or when it is moving from state to state. The HMMER generates a protein sequence by emitting amino acids as it progresses through a series of states. Each state has a table of amino acid emission probabilities similar to those described in a profile model. There are also transition probabilities for moving from state to state.

Figure 10.6 shows one topology for a hidden Markov model. Although other topologies are used, the one shown is very popular in protein sequence analysis. Note that there are three kinds of states represented by three different shapes. The squares are called match states, and the amino acids emitted from them form the conserved primary structure of a protein. These amino acids are the same as those in the common ancestor or, if not, are the result of substitutions. The diamond shapes are insert states and emit amino acids which result from insertions. The circles are special, silent states known as delete states and model deletions.

Transitions from state to state progress from left to right through the model, with the exception of the self-loops on the diamond insertion states. The self-loops allow deletions of any length to fit the model, regardless of the length of other sequences in the family. Any sequence can be represented by a path through the model. The probability of any sequence, given the model, is computed by multiplying the emission and transition probabilities along the path.

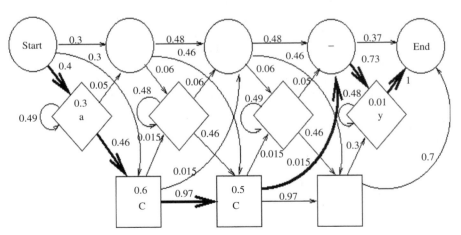

Figure 10.6   A possible hidden Markov model for the protein ACCY. The protein is represented as a sequence of probabilities. The numbers in the boxes show the probability that an amino acid occurs in a particular state, and the numbers next to the directed arcs show probabilities which connect the states. The probability of ACCY is shown as a highlighted path through the model.

10.6.1 Scoring a Sequence with the HMMER

In Figure 10.6, a path through the model represented by ACCY is highlighted. In the interest of saving space, the full tables of emission probabilities are not shown. Only the probability of the emitted amino acid is given. For example, the probability of A being emitted in position 1 is 0.3, and the probability of C being emitted in position 2 is 0.6. The probability of ACCY along this path is

$$0.4 * 0.3 * 0.46 * 0.6 * 0.97 * 0.5 * 0.015 * 0.73 * 0.01 * 1 = 1.76 \times 10^{-6}$$

As in the profile case described earlier, the calculation is simplified by transforming probabilities to logs so that addition can replace multiplication. The resulting number is the raw score of a sequence, given the HMMER. One common application of HMMER is classifying sequences in a database. The method is to build the HMMER with a training set of known members of the class, and then to compute the score of all sequences in the database. The resulting scores are ranked and a suitable threshold is selected to separate class members from the other sequences in the database.

10.6.2 Parallel Implementation of HMM

HMMER 2.2g provides a parallel *hmmpfam* program based on PVM, which is a widely used tool for searching one or more sequences against the HMM database and is provided by Dr. Eddy's Lab at the Washington University. In this implementation, the computation for one sequence is executed concurrently, the master node dynamically assigns one profile to a specific slave node for comparison. Upon finishing its job, the slave node reports the results to the master, which will respond by assigning a new profile. When all the comparison regarding this sequence is completed, the master node sorts and ranks all the results it collects and outputs the top hits. Then the computation on the next sequence begins.

Using state-of-the-art multi-threading computing concept, some researchers [22] implement a new parallel version of *hmmpfam* on EARTH (efficient architecture for running threads). EARTH is an event-driven fine-grain multi-threaded programming execution model, which supports fine-grain, nonpreemptive fibers, developed by CAPSL (Computer Architecture and Parallel System Laboratory) at the University of Delaware. In its current implementations, the EARTH multi-threaded execution model is built with off-the-shelf microprocessors in a distributed memory environment. The EARTH runtime system (version 2.5) performs fiber scheduling, inter-node communication, inter-fiber synchronization, global memory management, dynamic load balancing, and SMP node support. The EARTH architecture executes applications coded in Threaded-C, a multi-threaded extension of C.

For parallelizing *hmmpfam*, two different schemes are developed: one predetermines job distribution on all computing nodes by a round-robin algorithm; the other takes advantage of the dynamic load balancing support of EARTH runtime system, which simplifies the programmer's coding work by making the job distribution completely transparent. It shows a detailed analysis of the hmmpfam program and different parallel schemes, and some basic concepts regarding multi-threaded parallelization of HMM-pfam on EARTH RTS 2.5. When searching 250 sequences against a 585-family Hmmer database on 18 dual-CPU computing nodes, the PVM version gets absolute speedup of 18.50, whereas EARTH version gets 30.91, achieving a 40.1% improvement on execution time. On a cluster of 128 dual-CPU nodes, the execution time of a representative testbench is reduced from 15.9 h to 4.3 min.

10.7 ClustalW

ClustalW is a tool used in computational biology to perform "multiple sequence alignment." In practice, it means reading in a number of sequences representing sequences of biological data, calculating pairwise rankings of "alignedness" between them, forming a hypothetical tree of relationships between the sequences, and then performing adjustments to the sequences to make them all "align" with one another by introducing some gaps, and so on. The following discussion involves basic steps involved in performing multiple sequence alignment. We then discuss how this is computationally intensive and discuss some parallel implementations using different approaches.

The basic alignment method was first devised by Thompson et al. [23]. The basic multiple alignment algorithm consists of three main stages: (1) all pairs of sequences are aligned separately to calculate a distance matrix giving the divergence of each pair of sequences; (2) a guide tree is calculated from the distance matrix; and (3) the sequences are progressively aligned according to the branching order (from tips to root) in the guide tree.

In the original Clustal programs, the pairwise distances were calculated using a fast approximate method [24]. This allows very large numbers of sequences to be aligned, even on a microcomputer. The scores are calculated as the number of k-tuple matches (runs of identical residues, typically 1 or 2 long for proteins or 2–4 long for nucleotide sequences) in the best alignment between two sequences minus a fixed penalty for every gap. One can use either fast approximate method or the slower but more accurate scores from full dynamic programming alignments using two gap penalties (for opening or extending gaps) and a full amino acid weight matrix. These fast approximate methods virtually yield the same results as the exact methods as long as the sequences are not very dissimilar.

The guided tree which is used in the final multiple alignment process are calculated from the distance matrix of step 1 using the neighbor-joining method [25]. This produces unrooted trees with branch lengths proportional to estimated divergence along each branch. The root is placed by a "midpoint" method [26] at a position where the means of the branch lengths on either side of the root are equal. These trees are also used to derive a weight for each sequence. The weights are dependent upon the distance from the root of the tree but sequences which have a common branch with other sequences share the weight derived from the shared branch. In contrast, in the normal progressive alignment algorithm, all sequences would be equally weighted.

Progressive alignment is the final stage in the ClustalW. This stage uses the series of pairwise alignments to align larger and larger groups of sequences, following the branching order in the guide tree. You proceed from the tips of the rooted tree towards the root. At each stage of the tree, a full dynamic programming [26, 27] algorithm is used with a residue weight matrix and penalties for opening and extending gaps. It is appropriate to use dynamic programming here because the number of comparisons will be less compared to initial stage; thus, leading to more accurate alignments. Each step consists of aligning two existing alignments or sequences. Gaps that are present in older alignments remain fixed. In the basic algorithm, new gaps that are introduced at each stage get full gap opening and extension penalties, even if they are introduced inside old gap positions. The average of all the pairwise weight matrix scores from the amino acids in the two sets of sequences is used to calculate the score between a position from one sequence or alignment and one from another.

If either set of sequences contains one or more gaps in one of the positions being considered, each gap versus a residue is scored as zero. The default amino acid weight matrices we use are rescored to have only positive values. Therefore, this treatment of gaps treats the score of a residue versus a gap as having the worst possible score. When sequences are weighted, each weight matrix value is multiplied by the weights from the two sequences.

If the total number of sequences is N, then the pairwise comparison step requires $N * (N - 1)/2$ number of comparisons. N can be a very large number. As at each step either fast approximation or full dynamic programming techniques are used, this step will be more computationally intensive and throws a significant challenge for the researchers at improving the speed at this stage. As the pairwise comparison state takes up most of the time and as it is easy to implement on multiprocessors, several parallel computing methods have been introduced. The next two sections will discuss about the two very useful parallel programming approaches.

10.7.1 ClustalW-MPI

ClustalW-MPI is a distributed and parallel implementation of ClustalW [28]. All three stages are parallelized to reduce the execution time. It uses a message-passing library called MPI and runs on distributed clusters as well as on traditional parallel computers. The first step in ClustalW is to calculate a distance matrix for $N * (N - 1)/2$ pairs of sequences. This is an easy target for coarse-grained parallelization as all elements of the distance matrix are independent. The second step of ClustalW determines the guided tree (topology) of the progressive alignments. Finally, the last step obtains the multiple alignments progressively. For the last two steps, there is no simple coarse-grained parallel solution because of the data dependency between each stage in the guided tree.

The parallelization of the distance-matrix calculation is simply allocating the time-independent pairwise alignments to parallel processors. The scheduling strategy used in ClustalW-MPI is called fixed-size chunking [29] where chunk of tasks are to be allocated to available processors. Allocating large chunk of sequences to available processors minimizes the communication overhead but may incur high processor idle time, whereas small batches reduce the idle time but may lead to high overhead.

Once we have the distance matrix, a guide tree needs to be produced to serve as the topology of the final progressive alignment. The algorithm for generating the guide tree is the neighbor-joining method [25]. Slight modifications were made so that the neighbor-joining tree can be done in $O(n^2)$ time, while still retain the same results as the original ClustalW. For the 500-sequence test data, the tree generation takes about 0.04% of the overall CPU time. In most cases, the CPU time spent on this stage is less than 1% even for data containing 1000 sequences. ClustalW-MPI implementation parallelizes the searching of sequences having the highest divergence from all other sequences. A mixed fine- and coarse-grained approach is used for the final progressive alignment stage. It is coarse grained in that all external nodes in the guide tree are to be aligned in parallel. The efficiency obviously depends on the topology of the tree. For well-balanced guide tree, the ideal speedup can be estimated as $N/\log N$, where N is the number of nodes in the tree. Finally, the calculations of the forward and backward passes of the dynamic programming are also parallelized.

Experiments were conducted on test data comprising of 500 protein sequences with an average length of about 1100 amino acids. They were obtained from the BLASTP results with the query sequence (GI: 21431742), a cystic fibrosis transmembrane conductance regulator. Experiments were performed on a cluster that is made of eight dual-processor PCs (Pentium III, 800 MHz) and interconnected with the standard Fast Ethernet. The calculations of pairwise distances scale up as expected, up to 15.8 using 16 processors. For the essentially not parallelizable progressive alignment, this implementation shows that the speedup of 4.3 can be achieved using 16 processors.

From the earlier discussion, it is evident that with the features of ClustalW-MPI, it is possible to speedup lengthy multiple alignments with relatively inexpensive PC clusters.

10.7.2 Parallel ClustalW, HT ClustalW, and MULTICLUSTAL

Another parallel programming approach for ClustalW is undertaken by the SGI. This parallel version shows speedups of up to 10 when running ClustalW on 16 CPUs and significantly reduces the time required for data analysis. The development of a high throughput version of ClustalW called HT ClustalW and the different methods of scheduling multiple MA jobs are discussed subsequently. Finally, the improvements of recently introduced MULTICLUSTAL algorithm and its efficient use for parallel ClustalW are discussed.

The basic ClustalW algorithm was parallelized by SGI using OpenMP [30] directives. Time profile analysis of the original ClustalW, using different numbers of G-protein coupled receptor (GPCR) proteins as inputs leads to the following discussion. Stages of the ClustalW algorithm: pairwise calculation (PW), guide tree calculation (GT), and progressive alignment (PA). Most of the time is spent in PW stage, although the relative fraction is lower (50%) for larger number of sequences when compared with 90% for smaller alignments. Therefore, the focus of parallelization needs to be PW stage first. For larger number of sequences (>1000 and length of nucleotides 390), the time taken by the GT stage is also significant. For sequences greater than 1000, it is necessary to parallelize both PW and GT stages to get significant speedup.

10.7.2.1 *PW Stage Optimization*

As mentioned earlier, during the first stage $N * (N - 1)/2$, pairwise comparisons have to be made to calculate the distance matrix. Because each comparison is independent of another, this part of the algorithm can be easily parallelized with the OpenMP "for" construct:

```
/* SGI pseudocode: Parallelism for pairwise
distance matrix calculation */

#pragma omp parallel private(i,j) {
#pragma omp for schedule(dynamic)
for(i=start;i<numseqs;i++)} {
    for(j=i+1;j<numseqs;j++)
        calc_pw_matrix_element();
    }
} /* End of pragma parallel */
```

Because inner "*j*-loop" varies, the OpenMP "dynamic" schedule is used to avoid load unbalance among different threads. In principle, the "static" interleave schedule can be used here as well, but because each pairwise comparison takes varying amounts of time, the "dynamic" type works better. This implementation is only efficient on a shared memory system such as the SGI Origin 3000 series. However, even if this stage is parallelized, the scaling would still be limited to a low number of processors if no further optimization is done. For example, without parallelization second and third stages (GT and PA), the alignment of 1000 GPCR protein sequences, where PW stage accounts for 50% of total time, would be only 1.8 times faster when running on eight CPUs according to Amdahl's Law [27]. Therefore, to achieve better scaling for larger, more compute-intensive alignments and efficient parallelization techniques are needed for the GT and PA stages.

10.7.2.2 *GT Stage Optimization*

In the second stage (GT calculation), the most time-consuming part is determining the smallest matrix element corresponding to the next tree branch. This can be done in parallel by calculating and saving the minimum element of each row concurrently and then using the saved minimum row elements to find the minimum element of the entire matrix.

Experimental results have shown that the relative scaling of the parallel-optimized ClustalW for 100 and 600 GPCR sequences with the average length of 390 amino acids (in terms of fraction of parallel code P [27]) is better for larger inputs as most of the time spent is in the first and second stages. For the larger inputs, the time consumed by first and second stages is almost equal. Parallelization of these stages is more coarse grained, and as a result, the OpenMP overhead becomes minimal when compared with the finer grained parallelization of the third stage. The speedup of more than 10 times is obtained for the MA of 600 GPCR proteins using 16 CPUs when compared with the one which was run on a single processor. Total time to solution is reduced from 1 h, 7 min (single processor) to just over 6.5 min (on 16 CPUs of the SGI Origin 3000 series), and hence significantly increasing research productivity.

10.7.2.3 *HT ClustalW Optimization*   The need to calculate large numbers of multiple alignments of various sizes has become increasingly important in high-throughput (HT) research environments. To address this need, SGI has developed HT Clustal, basically, a wrapper program that launches multiple ClustalW jobs on multiple processors, where each ClustalW job is usually executed independently on a single processor. To reproduce this high throughput environment, the following mix of heterogeneous MAs is constructed.

HT Clustal is used to calculate 100 different MAs for GPCR proteins (average length 390 amino acids). Each input file contains between 10 and 100 sequences taken randomly from a pool of 1000 GPCR sequences. The number of sequences conforms to a Gaussian distribution with the average of 60 sequences and standard deviation of 20.

To optimize the throughput performance, the input sequences are presorted based on a relative file size. The purpose of the presorting is to minimize load unbalance and hence improve the scaling of HT Clustal. Experimental studies have shown that the improvement from presorting becomes significant when the average number of jobs per CPU is on the order of five. When the average number of jobs per CPU is greater than five, it shows that the statistical averaging reduces the load unbalance and there is only minor improvement with presorting.

With presorting, it is possible to achieve almost linear speedups. For the earlier example, the speedups of 31 times were achieved on 32 CPUs. For the larger test cases, speedup of 116 times was found on a 128-CPU SGI Origin 3000 series server, and hence reducing total time to solution from over 18.5 h to just less than 9.5 min. Because individual ClustalW jobs are processed on a single processor, HT Clustal can be used efficiently on both single system image SGI Origin 3000 series servers and distributed Linux clusters.

10.7.2.4 *MULTICLUSTAL Optimization*   The MULTICLUSTAL algorithm was introduced as an optimization of the ClustalW MA [31]. The MULTICLUSTAL alignment gives a domain structure, which is more consistent with the 3D structures of proteins involved in this alignment.

The algorithm searches for the best combination of ClustalW input parameters to produce more meaningful multiple sequence alignments (i.e., smaller number of gaps with more clustering). It does so by performing ClustalW calculations for various scoring matrices and gap penalties in the PW/GT and PA stages.

SGI has optimized the original MULTICLUSTAL algorithm by reusing the tree calculated in the PW/GT steps. Therefore, the guide tree is calculated only once for a given combination of PW parameters and is then used for all possible combinations of PA parameters. The performance (relative to that of original MULTICLUSTAL on one CPU) gives speedups range from 1.5 to 3.0 when compared with the original algorithm running on the same number of processors. Similar time to solution can be obtained using the SGI modified MULTICLUSTAL on smaller number of CPUs when compared with the original MULTICLUSTAL, thereby freeing additional computer resources without a performance degradation.

10.8 SPECIALIZED HARDWARE: FPGA

Over the past several years, key computational biology algorithms such as the Smith–Waterman have been implemented on FPGAs and have enabled many computational analysis that were previously impractical. Many problems in computational biology are inherently parallel and benefit from concurrent computing models. There are several commercial systems currently available, which all take different approaches. In academic area, many researchers proposed their implementations to address this problem. For a comparison, clusters of machines and custom VLSI systems are also included.

The first system listed in Table 10.1 is from Celera Genomics, Inc. Celera uses an 800 node Compaq Alpha cluster for their database searches. This arrangement is able to perform approximately 250 billion comparisons per second. The major advantage of such a multiprocessor system is its flexibility. The drawback, however, is the large cost associated with purchasing and maintaining such a large server farm.

The second system in the table is made by Paracel, Inc. Paracel takes a custom ASIC approach to do the sequence alignment. Their system uses 144 identical custom ASIC devices, each containing approximately 192 processing elements. This produces 276 billion comparisons per second, which is comparable to Celera's sever farm approach, but using significantly less hardware.

TimeLogic, Inc. also offers a commercial system but uses FPGAs and describes their system as using "reconfigurable computing" technology. They currently have six processing elements per FPGA device and support 160 devices in a system. This

TABLE 10.1 Performance for Different Implementation

Implementation	Type	Processors per Devices	Devices	Comparisons per Seconds (bytes)
Celera	Alpha Cluster	1	800	250
Paracel	ASIC	192	144	276
Timelogic	FPGA	6	160	50
StarBridge	FPGA	Unpublished	1	Unpublished
Splash 2	FPGA	14	272	43
JBits (XCV1000)	FPGA	4,000	1	757
JBits (XC2V6000)	FPGA	11,000	1	3,225
Researcher from Japan (XCV2000E)	FPGA	144	1	4

system performs approximately 50 billion matches per second. This is significantly lower in performance than the Celera or Paracel systems, but the use of FPGAs results in a more flexible system, which does not incur the overheads of producing a custom ASIC.

StarBridge Systems [32] has developed a reconfigurable computing system using FPGAs, which can deliver 10–100 times or greater improvement in computational efficiency (compared with traditional RISC processor based machines) as per their white paper. Their system employs a dual processor motherboard and a single hyper-computer board with nine Xilinx XC2V6000-BG1152 Virtex-II FPGAs and two XC2V4000-BG1152 Virtex-II FPGAs, yielding approximately 62 million gates per board. Details about processing elements are unpublished and the market price for this tailored system is relatively high.

Splash 2 [33] is a legacy system loaded with 272 FPGAs, each supplying 14 processing elements, producing a match rate of 43 billion matches per second. These are respectable numbers for 10 year old technology in a rapidly changing field.

The JBits [34] implementations using a Xilinx XCV1000 Virtex device implements 4000 processing elements in a single device running at 188 MHz in the fully optimized version. This results in over 750 billion matches per second. In addition, if the newer Virtex II family is used, a single XC2V6000 device can be used to implement approximately 11,000 processing elements. At a clock speed of over 280 MHz, this gives a matching rate of over 3.2 trillion elements per second.

Finally, the research group from Japan [35] also proposed their implementation using FPGAs. They use one PCI board with Xilinx XCV2000E FPGAs and implement 144 processing elements. The time for comparing a query sequence of 2048 elements with a database sequence of 64 million elements by Smith–Waterman algorithm is about 34 s, which is about 330 times faster than a desktop computer with a 1 GHz Pentium III.

10.8.1   Implementation Details

The data dependencies from the Smith–Waterman algorithm indicate that calculations may proceed in parallel across the diagonals of the array. That is, if the nxm comparisons performed in the algorithm is viewed as a 2D array, then the algorithm can be seen as proceeding from the upper left corner of the array, where S0 is compared to T0, downward and to the right until the final value of d is computed using the comparison of Sn and Tm. There are two major implement approaches: multi-threaded computation and systolic array.

10.8.1.1   Multi-Threaded Computation   The parallelism elements on each diagonal line are processed simultaneously. Therefore, the order of the computation can be reduced to $m + n - 1$ from mn if m elements can be processed in parallel. If the size of the hardware is not large enough to compare m elements at once, the first p elements (suppose that the hardware process p elements in parallel) of the query sequence are compared with the database sequence at once and the scores of all pth elements are stored in temporal memory. Then, the next p elements of the query sequence are compared with the database sequence using the scores stored in the temporal memory.

Suppose that the length of the query sequence (m) is longer than the number of processing units on the FPGA (p). Then, in the naive approach

1. The first p elements of the query sequence are compared and the intermediate results (all pth scores on lower edge of upper half) are stored.
2. Then, the next p elements of the query sequence are compared using the intermediate results.

In this case, it takes $2x2x(p + n - 1)$ cycles to compare the two sequences and processing units become idle for one clock cycle in every two clock cycles as described earlier.

We can reduce the computation time by the multi-threaded computation method. In the multi-threaded computation:

1. P elements on the diagonal line in upper half are processed, and the score of pth element is stored on temporal registers
2. Then, the next p elements on the diagonal line in lower half are processed without waiting for one clock cycle using the intermediate result. By interleaving the processing of elements in upper half and lower half, we can eliminate the idle cycles of the processing elements. The clock cycles become $2x(p + n - 1) + 2xp$, which is almost equal to $2xn$ because n is much longer than p in most cases.

When the length of the query sequence (m) is longer than twice the number of the processing units ($2p$), the multi-threaded computation is repeated according to the length of the query sequence.

The advantage of this approach is that it can use the off-the-shelf boards from FPGA manufacturers. It is easy to obtain the boards with latest FPGAs (namely, larger FPGAs) and the performance of the approach is almost proportional to the size of FPGAs. The disadvantage is that off-the-shelf FPGA boards do not have enough hardware resources for homology search. Especially memory size and memory bandwidth are not sufficient. Because of this limitation, query sequences can not be compared with long database sequences simultaneously. Therefore, query sequences are always compared with subsequences of the database sequences (automatically divided during the search) and only results against the fragments in the subsequences can be shown. Research group from Japan takes this approach.

10.8.1.2 *Systolic Sequence Comparison*

A property of the dynamic programming for computing edit distances is that each entry in the distance matrix depends on adjacent entries. This locality can be exploited to produce systolic algorithms in which communications is limited to adjacent processors. There are two mappings, both exploiting the locality of reference by computing the entries along each anti-diagonal in parallel [36–39].

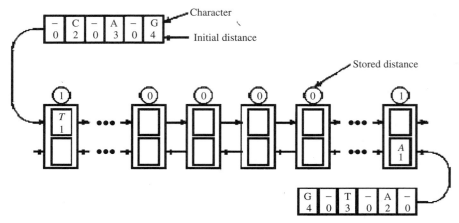

Figure 10.7   Systolic array for sequence comparison.

The first one is "bidirectional array" as shown in Figure 10.7. The source and target sequences are shifted simultaneously from the left and right, respectively. Interleaved with the characters are the data values from the first row and column of the dynamic programming matrix. When two nonnull characters enter a processor from opposite directions, a comparison is performed. On the next clock tick, the characters shift out and the values following them shift in. This processor now determines a new state based on the result of the comparison, the two values just shifted in, and its previous state value, using the same rule as in the dynamic programming algorithm. When the string are shifted out, they carry with them the last two row and column of the dynamic programming matrix, and hence the answer. Comparing sequences of lengths m and n requires at least $2 \max(m + 1, n + 1)$ processors. The number of steps required to compute the edit distance is proportional to the length of the array. With the bidirectional array, the source sequence must be cycled through the array once for each target sequence in the database. The source and target sequences are both limited in length to half of the array's length.

With respect to the shortcomings of the bidirectional array, "unidirectional array" process data in one direction. The source sequence is loaded once and stored in the array starting from the leftmost PE. The target sequences are streamed through the array one after another, separated by a control character. With the source sequence loaded and the target sequences streaming through, the array can achieve near 100% PE utilization. The length of the array determines the maximum length of the source sequence. The target sequence, however, can be of any length. Altogether, these properties make the unidirectional array more suitable and efficient than the bidirectional array for database searches. A unidirectional array of length n can compare a source sequence of length at most n and to a target sequence of length m in $O(n + m)$ steps.

Both bidirectional systolic array and unidirectional array have been implemented on the Splash 2 system using Xilinx FPGAs. The JBits implementation follows the same approach but use more advanced features of FPGAs.

10.8.1.3 *Runtime Reconfiguration*

The JBits implementation explore the use of the run-time reconfiguration using Xilinx JBit toolkit. The JBits toolkit is a set of Java tools and APIs that permit direct impementation and reconfiguration of circuits for the Xilinx Virtex family of FPGAs. JBits was particularly useful in the implementation of this algorithm because there were several opportunities to take advantage of run-time circuit customization. In addition, the systolic approach to the computation permitted a single parameterizable core representing the processing element to be designed, then replicated as many times as necessary to implement the fully parallel array.

The logic implementation of the algorithm is shown in Figure 10.8. Each gray box represents a LUT/flip-flop pair. This circuit demonstrates four different opportunities for run-time circuit customization. Three of these are the folding of the constants for the insertion, deletion, and substitution penalties into the LUTs. Rather than explicitly feeding a constant into an adder circuit, the constant can be embedded in the circuit, resulting in (in effect) a customized constant adder circuit. Note that these constants can be set at run time and may be parameters to the circuit.

The fourth run-time optimization is the folding of the match elements into the circuit. In genomic databases, a four character alphabet is used to represent the four bases in the DNA molecule. These characters are typically denoted A, T, G, and C. In this circuit, each character can be encoded with two bits. The circuit used to match S_i and T_j does not require that both strings be stored as data elements. In this implementation, the S string is folded into the circuit as a run-time customization. Note that unlike the previous optimizations, the string values are not fixed constants and will vary from one run to another. This means that the entire string S is used as a run-time parameter to produce the customized circuit.

This design uses a feature of the algorithm first noted by Lipton and Lopresti [39]. For the commonly used constants, 1 for insert/delete and 2 for substitution, b and c can only differ from a by $+1$ or -1, and d can only differ from a by either 0 or 2. Because of this modulo 4 encoding can be used, only 2 bits to represent each value is required. The final output edit distance is calculated by using an up-down counter at the end of the systolic array. For each step, the counter decrements if the previous

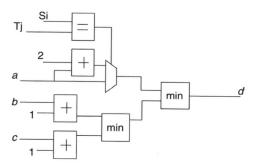

Figure 10.8   The combinational logic of the Smith–Watermann circuit.

output value is 1 less than the current one and it increments otherwise. The up-down counter is initialized to the match string length, which makes 0 the minimum value for a perfect match.

10.9   CONCLUSION

Relying on Moore's law alone for performance demands of computational biology applications may prove detrimental. An amalgamation of better architectures, clever algorithms, computation system with higher raw CPU performance, with less power consumption, and higher bandwidth will be required to meet demands of computational biology. We do not expect the general purpose computers to provide the cost performance for most of these problems. We expect architectural changes to support computational biology.

REFERENCES

1. O. Trelles, On the parallelization of bioinformatic applications, *Briefings Bioinformatics*, 2 (May), pp. 6–7 (2001).

2. S. Roy and V. Chaudhary, Design issues for a high-performance distributed shared memory on symmetrical multiprocessor clusters, cluster Comput. *J Networks Software Tools Appl.*, 2 (3), 177–186 (1999).

3. R. Hughey, Parallel hardware for sequence comparison and alignment, *Comput. Appl. Biosci.*, 12, 473–479 (1996).

4. S. F. Altschul, T. L. Madden, A. A. Schaffer, J. Zhang, Z. Zhang, W. Miller, and D. J. Lipman, Gapped BLAST and PSI-BLAST: a new generation of protein database search programs, *Nucleic Acids Res.*, 25 (17), 3389–3402 (1997).

5. S. Needleman and C. Wunsch, A general method applicable to the search for similarities in the amino acid sequence of two sequences, *J. Mol. Biol.*, 48 (3), 443–453 (1970).

6. T. F. Smith and M. S. Waterman, Identification of common molecular subsequences, *J. Mol. Biol.*, 147, 195–197 (1981).

7. W. R. Pearson, Rapid and sensitive sequence comparison with FASTP and FASTA, *Methods Enzymol.*, 183, 63–98 (1990).

8. Z. Zhang, S. Schwartz, L. Wagner, and W. Miller, A greedy algorithm for aligning DNA sequences, *J Comput Biol.*, 7 (1–2), 203–214 (2000).

9. J. Cheetham, F. Dehne, S. Pitre, A. Rau-Chaplin, and P. J. Taillon, Parallel CLUSTAL W for PC Clusters, *International Conference on Computational Sciences and Its Applications*, 2003.

10. O. Gotoh, An improved algorithm for matching biological sequences, *J. Mol. Biol.*, 162, 705–708 (1982).

11. X. Meng and V. Chaudhary, Bio-Sequence Analysis with Cradle's 3SoC^{TM} Software Scalable System on Chip, *SAC '04*, March 14–17, (2004).

12. T. Rognes and E. SeeBerg, Six-fold speedup of Smith–Waterman sequence database searches using parallel processing on common microprocessors, *Bioinformatics*, 16 (8), 699–706 (2000).

13. Ilya Sharapov, Computational Applications for Life Sciences on Sun Platforms: Performance Overview, Whitepaper, 2001.

14. C. Janaki and Rajendra R. Joshi, Accelerating comparative genomics using parallel computing, *Silico Biology*, 3 (4), 429–440 (2003).

15. S. F. Altschul, W. Gish, W. Miller, E. W. Myers, and D. J. Lipman, Basic local alignment search tool, *J. Mol. Biol.*, 215, 403–410 (1990).

16. S. Karlin and S.F. Altschul, Method for Assessing the Statistical Significance of Molecular Sequence Features by Using General Scoring Schemes, *Proceedings of the National Academy of Science*, USA 87, 2264–2268, 1990.

17. S. F. Altschul and W. Gish, Local alignment statistics, *Methods Enzymol.*, 266, 460–480 (1996).

18. R. D. Bjornson, A.H. Sherman, S. B. Weston, et al., TurboBLAST: A Parallel Implementation of BLAST Built on the TurboHub, *International Parallel and Distributed Processing Symposium: IPDPS Workshops*, 2002, (CD proceedings).

19. ftp://ftp.ncbi.nih.gov/toolbox/ncbi_tools/, NCBI Toolbox download site.

20. M. Warren, E. Weigle, and W. Feng, High-Density Computing: A 240-Node Beowulf in One Cubic Meter, *Proceedings of SC2002*, November, 2002.

21. S. R. Eddy, Profile hidden Markov models, *Bioinformatics*, 14 (9), 755–763 (1998).

22. Weirong Zhu, Yanwei Niu, Jizhu Lu, and Guang R. Gao, Implementing Parallel Hmm-pfam on the EARTH Multithreaded Architecture, *Proceedings of the Computational Systems Bioinformatics*, 2003.

23. J. D. Thompson, D. G. Higgins, and T. J. Gibson, CLUSTAL W: improving the sensitivity of progressive multiple sequence alignment through sequence weighting, positions-specific gap penalties and weight matrix choice, *Nucleic Acids Res.*, 22, 4673–4680 (1994).

24. D. Bashford, C. Chothia, and A. M. Lesk, Determinants of protein fold: unique features of globin amino acid sequences., *J. Mol. Biol.*, 196, 199–216 (1987).

25. N. Saitou and M. Nei, The neighbor-joining method: a new method for reconstructing phylogenetic trees, *Mol. Biol. Evol.*, 4, 406–425 (1987).

26. J. D. Thompson, Higgins and Gibson, Improved sensitivity of profile searches through the use of sequence weights and gap excision, *CABIOS*, 10, 19–29 (1994).

27. G. Amdahl, Validity of the Single-Processor Approach to Achieving Large-Scale Computing capabilities, *Proceeding of AFIPS Conference*, 1967.

28. K.-B. Li, ClustalW-MPI: ClustalW analysis using distributed and parallel computing *Bioinformatics*, 19 (12), 1585–1586 (2003).

29. T. Hagerup, Allocating independent tasks to parallel processors: an experimental study., *J. Parallel Distrib. Comput.*, 47, 185–197 (1997).

30. www.openmp.org.

31. J. Yuan, A. Amend, J. Borkowski, R. DeMarco, W. Bauiley, Y. Liy, G. Xie, and R. Blevins, MULTICLUSTAL: a systematic method for surveying Clustal W alignment parameters, *Bioinformatics*, 15 (10), 862 (1999).

32. Starbridge Systems, www.starbridgesystems.com

33. D. T. Hoang, Searching genetic databases on Splash 2, *IEEE Workshop on FPGAs for Custom Computing Machines*, IEEE Computer Society Press, 1993, pp. 185–191.

34. S. A. Guccione and Eric Keller, Gene matching using JBits, *Field-Programmable Logic and Applications*, Springer-Verlag, Berlin, 2002.

35. Y. Yamaguchi, T. Maruyama, and A. Konagaya, High Speed Homology Search with FPGAs, *Pacific Symposium on Biocomputing*, 7, 271–282 (2002).

36. D. T. Hoang, FPGA implementation of systolic sequence alignment, *International Workshop on Field Programmable Logic and Applications, Vienna, Austria*, August 31–September 2, 1992.

37. D. Lavenier, SAMBA: systolic accelerators for molecular biological applications, *IRISA Report*, March 1996.

38. D. Lavenier, Speeding up genome computations with a systolic accelerator, *SIAM News*, 31 (8), 6–7 (1998).

39. R. J. Lipton and D. Lopresti, *A systolic array for rapid string comparison*, Chapel Hill Conference on VLSI, Computer Science Press, 1985, pp. 363–376.

40. Aaron E. Darling, L. Carey, and W.-C. Feng, The design, implementation, and evaluation of mpiBLAST, *ClusterWorld Conference and Expo in Conjunction with the Fourth International Conference on Linux Clusters: The HPC Revolution 2003*, June 2003.

CHAPTER 11

Parallel Computing in the Analysis of Gene Expression Relationships

ROBERT L. MARTINO, DANIEL E. RUSS, and CALVIN A. JOHNSON

DNA microarrays provide the technology needed to study gene expression. This technology facilitates large-scale surveys of gene expression in which transcript levels can be determined for thousands of genes simultaneously. These experiments generate an immense quantity of data. Investigators need computational methods to analyze this data to gain an understanding of the phenomena the data represents.

This chapter presents two advanced methods for analyzing gene expression data that go beyond standard techniques but require the use of parallel computing. The first method provides for the assessment of the codetermination of gene transcriptional states from large-scale simultaneous gene expression measurements with cDNA microarrays. The parallel implementation exploits the inherent parallelism exhibited in the codetermination methodology that we apply. The second method involves classification using cDNA microarrays. The goal is to perform classification based on different expression patterns such as cancer classification. We present an efficient parallel implementation of the σ-classifier where the computational work is distributed among available system processors.

11.1 SIGNIFICANCE OF GENE EXPRESSION ANALYSIS

DNA microarrays provide the technology needed to study gene expression [1–5]. This technology facilitates large-scale surveys of gene expression in which transcript levels can be determined for thousands of genes simultaneously. DNA microarray data result from a complex biochemical–optical system incorporating robotic spotting and computer image formation and analysis. Many laboratories are now obtaining reproducible results from this RNA-based assay. The final result of a microarray

Parallel Computing for Bioinformatics and Computational Biology, Edited by Albert Y. Zomaya
Copyright © 2006 John Wiley & Sons, Inc.

experiment is a set of numbers associated with the expression levels of various genes or DNA fragments. A single DNA microarray can provide thousands of such numbers. Studies may involve many such experiments to obtain an understanding of some biological phenomena. Expression levels are compared between species, between healthy and diseased individuals, or at different time points for the same individual or population of individuals. These experiments generate an immense quantity of data. Investigators need computational methods to analyze these data to gain an understanding of the phenomena the data represent.

Widely available techniques for analyzing microarray data include principal component analysis (PCA) and cluster analysis [6, 7]. In gene expression experiments, each gene and each experiment can represent one dimension, which can result in a significant number of dimensions. PCA reduces the number of dimensions by determining those dimensions that account for a large variance in the data and by ignoring the dimensions in which the data do not vary much. Cluster analysis is the most frequently used multivariate technique to analyze expression data. Clustering is appropriate when there is no a priori knowledge about the data. Cluster analysis allows for the study of the similarity between different samples or experiments. Clustering programs use predefined algorithms to group significantly changed genes, according to their strength of expression or pattern of expression across different experiments.

This chapter presents two advanced methods for analyzing gene expression data that go beyond the standard PCA and clustering techniques but require the use of parallel computing. The first method is used for the assessment of the codetermination of gene transcriptional states from large-scale simultaneous gene expression measurements with cDNA microarrays. The implementation of this method is based on the coefficient of determination (CoD), which has been proposed for the analysis of gene interaction via multivariate expression arrays and the construction of genetic regulatory network models. Parallel computing is essential in the application of the CoD to a large set of genes owing to the large number of expression-based functions that must be statistically designed and compared. The parallel implementation exploits the inherent parallelism exhibited in the codetermination methodology.

The second method involves classification using cDNA microarrays. The goal is to perform classification based on different expression patterns such as cancer classification. Classification can be between different kinds of cancer, different stages of tumor development, or many other such differences. A novel method for classification based on gene expression, the σ-classifier, is successfully applied to cancer classification via cDNA microarrays. However, the time to perform the calculations required to implement this method on a single processor system is prohibitive if the number of genes exceeds several thousand. We present an efficient parallel implementation of the σ-classifier, where the computational work is distributed among available system processors. Classification analyses that would have taken over 2 months of computer time on a single processor system can now be completed in 2 days using 32 processors.

11.2 CODETERMINATION ANALYSIS OF MULTIVARIATE GENE EXPRESSION RELATIONS

An important goal of functional genomics is to develop methods for determining ways in which individual actions of genes are integrated in the cell. One way of gaining insight into a gene's role in cellular activity is to study its expression pattern in a variety of circumstances and contexts, as it responds to its environment and to the action of other genes. As mentioned in Section 11.1, microarray technology provides large-scale surveys of gene expression in which transcript levels can be determined for thousands of genes simultaneously. As transcription control is accomplished by a method involving the interpretation of a variety of inputs, analytical tools are required for expression profile data, which can detect the types of multivariate influences on decision-making produced by complex genetic networks.

Kim et al. proposed using the method of CoD for finding associations between genes [8–10]. The method assesses the codetermination of gene transcriptional states on the basis of statistical evaluation of reliably informative subsets of data derived from large-scale gene-expression measurements with cDNA microarrays. The CoD measures the degree to which the transcriptional levels of a small gene set can be used to predict the transcriptional state of a target gene in excess of the predictive capability of the mean level of the target. In addition to purely transcriptional features, the method allows incorporation of other conditions as predictive elements, thereby broadening the information that can be evaluated in modeling biological regulation. The CoD has also been used for choosing gene predictor sets and for determining their selection probabilities in the design of probabilistic Boolean networks [11], which form a special class of Markovian regulatory networks that generalize the classical Boolean genetic networks [12, 13].

Data from cDNA microarrays are preprocessed before CoD calculation occurs. An algorithm calibrates the data internally to each microarray and determines statistically whether the data justify the conclusion that an expression is up- or downregulated [14]. The complexity of expression data from a microarray is reduced by quantizing changes in expression level into ternary values: -1 (downregulated), $+1$ (upregulated), or 0 (invariant). The number of genes from the microarray is reduced from several thousand to several hundred by requiring at least c changes in the quantized gene expression data over the samples. For the data set used in this chapter, $c = 4$.

Application of the statistical framework to a large set of genes requires a prohibitive amount of computer time on a classical single-CPU computing machine. To meet the computational requirement, we have developed a parallel implementation of the codetermination method.

11.2.1 Codetermination Algorithm

The genomic regulation patterns seen in microarray data can be viewed as a biological system with a k-input expression level vector $X = \{X_1, X_2, \ldots, X_k\}$. The target Y is the output expression value of the system. A nonlinear predictor L is constructed to estimate Y, and it can be either a perceptron or a ternary logic filter. The results from the optimal predictor Y_{pred} are the closest approximation to Y. The logic of L represents an operational model of our understanding of the biological system.

Theoretically, the optimal predictor has minimum error across the population. It is unknown and must be statistically estimated; that is, it must be designed from a sample by some training (estimation) method. How well a designed predictor estimates the optimal predictor depends on the training procedure and the sample size n. The error ε_n of a designed predictor must exceed the error ε_{opt} of the optimal predictor. For a large number of microarrays, ε_n approximates ε_{opt}, but for the small numbers typically used in practice, ε_n may substantially exceed ε_{opt} [15].

The data problem can be made less severe if, instead of estimating the best predictor, we estimate the best predictor from a constrained set of predictors. The theoretical error of a best-constrained predictor exceeds that of the best predictor; however, the best-constrained predictor can be designed more precisely from the data. Hence, the error of a designed estimate of an optimal constrained predictor is often less than the error of a designed estimate of the optimal unconstrained predictor. This work focuses mainly on the full-logic (unconstrained) predictor.

The CoD of the optimal predictor θ_{opt} is the relative decrease in error owing to the presence of the observed variables:

$$\theta_{opt} = \frac{\varepsilon_b - \varepsilon_{opt}}{\varepsilon_b} \tag{11.1}$$

where ε_b is the error for the best predictor in the absence of observations. Since the error, ε_{opt}, of the optimal predictor cannot exceed ε_b, $0 \leq \theta_{opt} \leq 1$. If optimization is relative to mean-square error (MSE), which is the expectation $E[|Y_{pred} - Y|^2]$, then the best predictor based on the predictor variables $X_1, X_2, \ldots, X_k$ is the conditional expectation of Y given $X_1, X_2, \ldots, X_k$. The best predictor of Y in the absence of observations is its mean, μ_Y, and the corresponding error is the variance of Y. Predicting Y by its mean might yield small or large MSE because the variance of Y is small or large, respectively. Thus, there is normalization by ε_b in Eq. (11.1) to measure the effect of the observations. In our setting, the conditional expectation needs to be quantized to ternary values and ε_b is the error from predicting Y by applying the ternary threshold of the mean of Y. The CoD measures normalized predictive capability in a probabilistic, not causal, sense. A high CoD may indicate causality of the predictors on the target or vice versa. It may also indicate diffuse control along network pathways or coregulation of both predictors and target by another mechanism. That is why the CoD is being called the *codetermination* in biological applications.

For designed predictors, ε_b is replaced by $\varepsilon_{b,n}$ the error resulting from using the ternary threshold of the sample mean of Y to predict Y, and ε_{opt} is replaced by ε_n to give the estimate θ_n of the CoD:

$$\theta_n = \frac{\varepsilon_{b,n} - \varepsilon_n}{\varepsilon_{b,n}} \tag{11.2}$$

We use cross-validation to estimate θ_n. The data are split into training and test data, a predictor is designed from the training data, and estimates of $\varepsilon_{b,n}$ and ε_n are obtained.

An estimate of θ_n is found by putting the error estimates into Eq. (11.2). The procedure is repeated a number of times and a final estimate, $\hat{\theta}_n$, is obtained by averaging $\hat{\theta}_n$ for a conservative estimate of θ_{opt}. We could also use resubstitution to estimate the CoD (by training with the full data set and computing the error on the same training). This would have two effects: it would decrease computation time and would yield an optimistic (high-biased) estimate of the CoD.

There are $_mC_k = m!/k!(m-k)!$ predictor combinations for k predictor genes out of m total genes. For t target genes where $1 \le t \le m$, there are $tm!/k!(m-k)!$ coefficients to be calculated. As incremental relations between smaller and larger predictor sets are important, it is necessary to calculate the CoD for k predictor gene combinations, for each k of 1, 2, 3, ..., to some stopping point. A large storage space is required for all or part of the CoD results.

11.2.2 Prediction System Design

This section discusses design issues for the codetermination algorithm. As mentioned earlier, the focus of this work is the design of a logic-filter-based prediction system. A ternary logic filter is a nonlinear predictor that has a k-gene input and an output. The input is ternary data for the k genes, and the output is the predicted value of the quantized target expression. Rather than using the ternary-quantized conditional expectation for the predictor, the conditional mode is used. This requires less computation, the differences between it and the conditional expectation are small, and it avoids predicting values that have not occurred in the samples, a desirable property for coarse quantization. The ternary logic filter is defined by a logic table constructed via the conditional probability of the output Y given input data $\mathbf{X}$ as follows:

$$Y = \Psi(\mathbf{X}) = \begin{cases} -1 & \text{if } P(Y = -1|\mathbf{X}) \text{ is highest,} \\ 0 & \text{if } P(Y = 0|\mathbf{X}) \text{ is highest,} \\ 1 & \text{if } P(Y = 1|\mathbf{X}) \text{ is highest.} \end{cases} \quad (11.3)$$

Filter design becomes the computation of the conditional probability for each input–output pair, $(\mathbf{x}, y)$. For any observation vector $\mathbf{x}$, $\Psi(\mathbf{x})$ is the value of Y seen most often with $\mathbf{x}$ in the sample data. The size of table defining the predictor grows exponentially with the number of predictor variables, and the number of conditional probabilities to estimate increases accordingly. For two input variables and ternary data, there are $3^2 = 9$ conditional probabilities to estimate; for three variables, there are $3^3 = 27$. For gene expression ratio data, the number of input vectors available for filter design is very limited; in fact, we often do not observe all vectors. When applying the filter to test data, there may be inputs not observed during design. The quantized expected value of Y, $T(E[Y])$, is used as the output from the filter for all input vectors that are not observed in the training.

We can increase the information content of the input by providing additional inputs to the filter. This additional information increases the ability to predict the target gene expression value and decreases ε_n. In the worst case, when the additional gene carries no information, ε_n remains constant. This is not observed in the designed filters. Statistical fluctuations caused by the estimation error resulting from a small number of samples allow logic filters designed with more inputs to have a larger ε_n and smaller CoD value than the same filter without one of the inputs. After CoD values are calculated for gene combinations with more than one input value, the results are compared with the CoD values from all gene combination with one less input. If the new CoD value is less than the CoD value calculated with the smaller number of inputs, then the CoD value is assigned to the CoD value from the smaller input set. This assures that the estimated CoD increases as information content increases.

11.2.3 Parallel Implementation of Codetermination Algorithm

The parallel implementation of the codetermination algorithm discussed earlier consists of three main modules, which perform the following three functions: (1) generate all k-predictor gene combinations for a target T, (2) calculate the CoD, and (3) adjust the CoD. A diagram of this implementation is shown in Figure 11.1. For any target T, all one-gene predictor combinations are determined. The predictor combinations are

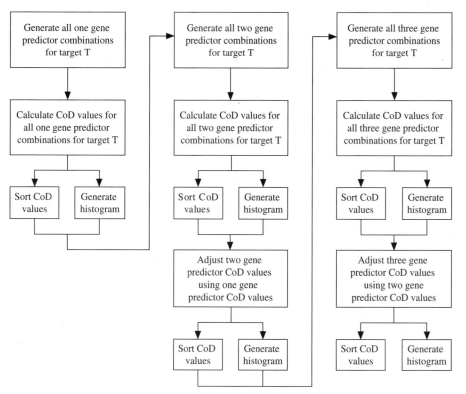

Figure 11.1 Diagram of parallel implementation of the codetermination algorithm.

then passed into the CoD calculator, which constructs the logic filters and calculates a CoD value for each combination. The values are sorted and CoD histograms are created. For the one-gene predictor, there is no CoD adjustment. After analyzing the CoD values all one-gene predictor combinations, all two-gene predictor combinations are then determined and the CoD values for each predictor combination are calculated. Results are sorted and histograms are created. At this point, CoD values calculated from two-gene combinations and from one-gene combinations exist.

The CoD values from the two-gene combinations are adjusted using the CoD values from the one-gene combinations. The adjusted results are sorted and adjusted histograms are created. The CoD values from the two-gene combinations are again compared with the CoD values from the one-gene combinations. This time, instead of adjusting the CoD values, instances where the CoD values from two-gene combinations are less than the CoD values from the one-gene combinations are deleted from the results. These results are considered redundant because all the information is carried by the one-gene predictor and the addition of the second gene is unnecessary. The results that are not redundant are sorted and histograms are created. This procedure continues for the three-gene combinations as it did for the two-gene combinations: all combinations are determined, CoD values are calculated, the results are adjusted, and a redundancy check is performed. The results from all stages are sorted and histograms are created. The procedure could continue for a larger combination of genes but, in practice, the number of combinations greater than three makes the calculations impractical.

For any target T, all one-gene predictor combinations are determined. The number of combinations is $_{m-1}C_k = (m-1)!/(m-k-1)!k!$, where m is the number of genes in the microarray data and k is the number of genes in the predictor. The value of $m-1$ arises from the fact that the target is not allowed to be a predictor. As the predictor combinations exclude the target gene, the list of the predictors needs to be recreated for every target.

For each predictor gene combination, a CoD value is calculated. The number of gene combinations becomes very large quickly, so the CoD calculation is performed in parallel as shown schematically in Figure 11.2. The combinations are partitioned evenly across p processors. Each processor then randomly partitions the sample from the microarray data into a training and test set. The training set develops the logic filter, and the test set is used to get a CoD value. The training and testing is repeated many times ($N = 128$ times for our studies) to estimate the CoD. The average of the CoD values is reported. After each processor has completed its share of the work, the CoD values are written to a file on a shared disk.

We tested the parallel implementation with data obtained from a study of 31 melanoma samples [16]. For that study, total messenger RNA was first isolated directly from melanoma biopsies. Fluorescent cDNA, produced from the acquired messenger RNA, was then prepared and hybridized to a microarray containing probes for 8150 cDNA (representing 6971 unique genes). Preprocessing the microarray data produced a data set of 587 genes from the melanoma samples.

We measured the performance of calculating the CoD values in parallel by performing this task for all three-gene predictor combinations for one target of this data using

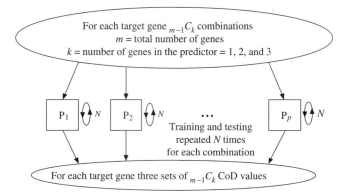

Figure 11.2 Diagram showing the parallel calculation of the CoD values. For each target gene, the predictor gene combinations are partitioned by the number of processors and a partition is allocated to each processor. The CoD is calculated N times for each predictor gene combination.

31 of the 587 genes. The measured efficiencies for 1, 2, 4, 8, 16, and 32 processors are shown in Table 11.1. The speedup that can be achieved by having p processors work concurrently on a computational problem is at most p times faster than that of a single processor. Although attempts are made to achieve this ideal speedup, the ability to attain it, in practice, is determined by the efficiency of the developed parallel algorithm or method to exploit the natural concurrency in the computing problem [17]. The actual speedup is equal to the time required to solve the problem on one processor divided by the time required for the parallel algorithm to solve the problem with p processors. The efficiency of an algorithm is the speedup per processor multiplied by 100, $((T_{\text{single}}/T_{\text{parallel}})/p) * 100$, with the ideal efficiency being 100%. Most of the inefficiencies for the CoD calculation task is due to the amount of disk input/output being performed. In the serial case, the results are written directly to the global disk; in the parallel case, writing to the global disk causes disk contention problems, which increase with the number of processors. This issue was partially alleviated by writing

TABLE 11.1 Parallel Performance for the Calculation of the CoD for all Three-Gene Predictor Combinations (33, 366, and 840) for a Single Gene Target Using 31 of the 587 Genes of a Melanoma Data Set

Number of Processors	Runtime (h)	Efficiency (%)
1	55.94	100
2	33.90	83
4	17.00	82
8	8.55	82
16	4.30	81
32	2.29	76

to a local disk, and then copying from local to the global disk. Some of the overhead involved in the recopying data is hidden by small load imbalances.

As mentioned earlier, CoD values are compared to the CoD values obtained from predictor combinations with fewer inputs. As an example, assuming that the calculated CoD value using genes G_1, G_2, and G_3 is smaller than the calculated CoD value using genes G_1 and G_3, then the adjusted CoD value for combination $(G_1, G_2,$ and $G_3)$ would be set to the CoD value of combination $(G_1$ and $G_3)$.

The algorithm used to adjust the CoD data is also performed in parallel and is shown schematically in Figure 11.3. The CoD values are partitioned equally across p processors. Each processor stores its partition as an array in memory. A lookup table is created for the CoD values in the array with the first combination that starts with $0, 1, 2, \ldots, m - k$. Given any combination of predictors, the CoD value is compared to the CoD values for all combination subsets with one less gene. The lookup table facilitates accessing the array in memory. The array indices for the subset are not known and the array must be searched for subsets. There are bounds that can be set to limit the search space, but no closed expression for the indices has been determined.

We measured the performance of adjusting the CoD values in parallel by performing the adjustment task on the results of the three-gene predictor CoD calculations discussed earlier. The results of the three-gene predictor CoD calculations were adjusted using the two-gene CoD results for the same target. The measured efficiencies for 1, 2, 4, 8, 16, and 32 processors are shown in Table 11.2. As seen in this table, the efficiencies deteriorated significantly as more processors were added, making it less desirable to increase the number of processors used to perform this task. We would like to mention that the efficiencies obtained for the parallel adjustment of the results of the two-gene predictor CoD calculations were better than the three-gene

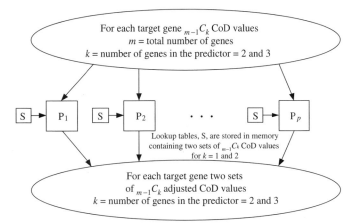

Figure 11.3 Diagram showing the parallel adjustment of the CoD values. These values are partitioned by the number of processors and a partition is allocated to each processor. The CoD values of the two- and three-gene predictors are compared to the CoD values of one- and two-gene predictors, respectively.

TABLE 11.2   Parallel Performance for the Adjustment of the CoD, Which was Calculated for all Three-Gene Predictor Combinations (33, 366, and 840) Using the CoD Results Calculated for all Two-Gene Predictor Combinations (171 and 405). These Results are for a Single Gene Target Using 31 of the 587 Genes of a Melanoma Data Set

Number of Processors	Runtime (h)	Efficiency (%)
1	0.51	100
2	0.36	70
4	0.20	65
8	0.12	50
16	0.08	39
32	0.06	25

efficiencies presented here. We used the same single gene target to obtain both the two-gene and three-gene parallel performance measurements.

Finally, we performed a complete CoD analysis on the 587 gene melanoma data set, which required 2 months of computer time using four sets of 32 processors, a total of 128 processors. This same analysis would have required approximately 4 years using four single processor systems with the same performance rating as the processors that formed the parallel system. The complete analysis generated hundreds of millions of CoD values, which provided the fundamental information needed to identify genes involved in causing the melanoma. This CoD information helped in identifying 10 genes of interest for further study.

11.3   CLASSIFICATION BASED ON GENE EXPRESSION

Classification of disease states using cDNA microarrays, which provide expression measurements for thousands of genes simultaneously, has become a key application of expression data and has had many successes including the following cancer examples: rhabdomyosarcoma [18], colon cancer [19], lymphoma [20], breast cancer [21], and melanoma [16]. Classification based on gene expression data can separate samples into different classes using a variety of methods such as neighborhood analysis with p-value with random permutation [22], TNoM score [23], and neural network [24].

A novel method, the σ-classifier, was recently proposed and successfully applied to a few data sets [25]. The σ-classifier uses an exhaustive search of combinatorial space to find the best feature vectors. As the number of features increases, however, this task becomes computationally prohibitive. Sub-optimal search algorithms were also introduced as alternatives to a full search. These algorithms reduce the feature space by removing less informative features, but a full search is still required in cases where the sub-optimal solution fails to find good feature sets.

In this section, we present a parallel version of the σ-classifier that significantly reduces the time to complete a classification analysis by efficiently distributing the computational work to many processors.

11.3.1 Design of σ-Classifiers and Feature Selection

When designing classifiers, we often do not know which features are required. Therefore, the selection of good features is important in addition to the design of specific classifiers. A classifier design method should provide a reasonable estimation of error for each classifier relative to other classifiers, to help find the desired features. If the number of samples available for analysis is very limited, then error estimation for the classifiers becomes difficult. To alleviate these problems, the σ-classifier is designed from a probability distribution resulting from spreading the mass of the sample points via a circular distribution to make classification more difficult, while maintaining sample geometry. The algorithm is parameterized by the variance of the circular distribution. By considering increasing variances, the algorithm finds feature sets whose classification accuracy remains strong relative to greater spreading of the sample. The error then gives a measure of the strength of the feature set as a function of the variance. The σ-classifier designs classifiers and estimates errors analytically to minimize the computational load. This property is crucial because of the immense size of the feature space that will be searched.

An exhaustive search of combinatorial space results in the best feature sets for a σ-classifier. This approach has been successfully applied to a few sets of microarray data of reasonable size containing a few thousand genes. Even though the σ-classifier algorithm is designed for this type of search, as the number of features increases, the computational load increases significantly, often becoming computationally prohibitive. If n be the total number of features and k be the number of features in a classifier, then there are $M = \binom{n}{k}$ classifiers to design and σ-errors to estimate. Even with reasonably sized data, n being larger than a few thousand, M may be so large that it is not feasible to perform an analysis on a single CPU. Therefore, parallel processing becomes inevitable.

11.3.2 Parallel Implementation of the σ-Classifier

When designing a parallel implementation, evenly distributing the computational work among the processors reduces the time that some processors are idle, while other processors are doing their work. The most efficient way to distribute the work would be to take the total number of classifiers and divide them equally among the processors. However, the number of classifiers quickly exceeds the largest signed 32-bit integer. Therefore, with three features per classifier, only 2345 features would be possible. Using unsigned 32-bit integers does not solve the problem, as only 2954 features would be possible. Although using 64-bit integers is an option, we preferred a simple, sub-optimal method for distributing the work, one that does not depend on such system constraints and remained surprisingly efficient for our study.

A full exploitive combinatorial generator makes the sequence of feature vectors, $\{x_1, x_2, \ldots, x_{k-1}, x_k\}$, $\{x_1, x_2, \ldots, x_{k-1}, x_{k+1}\}, \ldots, \{x_1, x_2, \ldots, x_{k-1}, x_n\}$, $\{x_1, x_2, \ldots, x_k, x_{k+1}\}, \ldots, \{x_1, x_{n-k+1}, \ldots, x_{n-1}, x_n\}, \ldots, \{x_2, x_3, \ldots, x_k, x_{k+1}\},$ $\ldots, \{x_3, x_4, \ldots, x_{k+1}, x_{k+2}\}, \ldots, \{x_{n-k+1}, x_{n-k+2}, \ldots, x_{n-1}, x_n\}$. These vectors can be grouped as $t_1, t_2, \ldots,$ and t_{n-k+1}, where t_i is the group with all feature vectors starting with feature x_i. For each group, t_i is also called a task, the *size of task* t_i

$$q(i) = \binom{n-i}{k-1}$$

where $i = 1, \ldots, n - k + 1$. The whole search space, $\binom{n}{k}$, now is broken into $n - k + 1$ tasks, each having $q(i)$ feature vectors. An individual task size is substantially smaller than the size of the total search space. The ratio between two tasks, $q(i)$ and $q(j)$, is

$$\frac{q(i)}{q(j)} = \frac{\binom{n-i}{k-1}}{\binom{n-j}{k-1}} = \frac{(n-i)\cdots(n-(j-1))}{(n-(k-1)-i)\cdots(n-(k-1)-(j-1))} \tag{11.4}$$

$$= \prod_{m=i}^{j-1} \frac{n-m}{n-(k-1)-m}$$

where $1 \leq i < j \leq n$. If this ratio is equal to 1, the work would be perfectly balanced. However, as j gets larger, $q(j)$ gets smaller, resulting in a larger ratio. This difference gives rise to a workload imbalance when tasks are distributed.

We studied three ways of distributing tasks to the processors as shown in Figure 11.4. Allocation schema A initially assigns to processor P_i all feature vectors that start with feature i. When the processor is completed, it then begins working on $i + p, i + 2p, \ldots$, where p is the number of processors, until it runs out of work to do. The total size of all the tasks assigned to each processor corresponds to the total computational load of processor $P_i, c(i)$. In the schema A, processor 1 will consistently have more work to do than all other processors, hence a significant workload imbalance will ensue. Allocation schema B is a first-order correction. Initially, processor 1 is assigned more work; however, during the second round of assignments, processor p is assigned more work. This is repeated many times, yielding a workload imbalance smaller than obtained with schema A. Allocation schema C includes a second-order correction that assigns more work to processor p in the third round because the correction in schema B does not fully account for workload imbalance that was created in schema A.

On the basis of allocation schemata described earlier, the total computational workloads on processor $i, c_A(i)$ using schema A and $c_B(i)$ using schema B, respectively, are represented by the following equations.

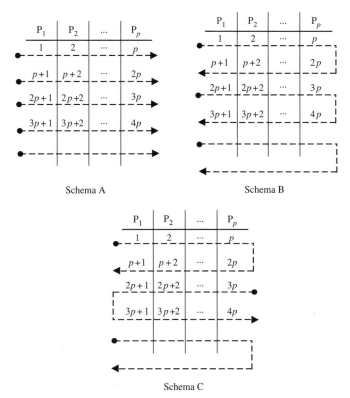

Figure 11.4 Three approaches to distributing tasks to the processors for the σ-classifier. Allocation schema A uses a cyclic distribution starting with the first feature in the set. This results in a large computational load imbalance as the amount of work decreases when the numbered feature in a classifier increases. Schema B reverses the direction of every other row in an attempt to rebalance the load. A higher order correction is shown as schema C, where every other direction of allotment is reversed.

For schema A,

$$c_{\mathrm{A}}(i) = \sum_{j=0}^{K_1} \binom{n - (i + jp)}{k - 1},$$ (11.5)

where

$$K_1 = \begin{cases} K & n - [i + Kp] \geq k - 1 \\ K - 1 & \text{otherwise} \end{cases}$$

$$K = \left\lfloor \frac{n}{p} \right\rfloor,$$

where $\lfloor x \rfloor$ is the greatest integer less than or equal to x.

For schema B,

$$c_{\mathrm{B}}(i) = \sum_{j=0}^{K_1} \binom{n - (i + j\,(2p))}{k - 1} + \sum_{j=0}^{K_2} \binom{n - (j\,(2p) + 2p - i + 1)}{k - 1}, \qquad (11.6)$$

where

$$K_1 = \begin{cases} K & n - (i + 2Kp) \geq k - 1, \\ K - 1 & \text{otherwise,} \end{cases}$$

$$K_2 = \begin{cases} K & (n - (2Kp + 2p - i + 1)) \geq k - 1, \\ K - 1 & \text{otherwise,} \end{cases}$$

$$K = \left\lfloor \frac{n}{2p} \right\rfloor.$$

In Eq. (11.6), the first summation is for forward distribution and the second for backward distribution in each round. The workload imbalance is defined as the difference between the amount of work on the processor with maximum workload and on the processor with the minimum workload. The workload imbalance was calculated as a function of the total number of features for 2, 4, 8, 16, 32, and 64 processors using schemata A and B. The results of this calculation are shown in Figure 11.5. In the figure, the plain lines represent the work imbalance calculated using schema A. The lines with dots represent the work imbalance calculated using schema B. There is a several orders of magnitude difference in the work imbalance between the schemata. Using schema B, the imbalance increases with the number of processors. This simply occurs because the correction that is introduced by reversing the direction of work assignment is much smaller when there are many processors than when there are only a few. As the differences between schemata B and C are small compared with the differences between A and B, only schemata A and B are shown. For simplicity, we selected schema B for implementation.

We implemented a parallel version of the σ-classifier using schema B and tested this implementation with a lymphoma data set [26] consisting of 30 samples with 2303 genes. The measured run times and efficiencies for 1, 2, 4, 8, 16, and 32 processors are shown in Table 11.3 with $k = 3$ and $n = 2303$. The schema B partitioning worked well as the implementation scaled to 32 processors with a high efficiency. The efficiency exceeds 100% due to slight differences between the parallel and serial versions of the software. The serial version was designed to allow the user a selection of several options. The parallel version was optimized to run full searches only; therefore, several conditional statements were removed from the main loop of the parallel version leading to a significant performance improvement. The parallel version does not run on a single processor. The adjusted efficiency shown in the table is the efficiency calculated assuming a serial time of double the two-processor time. When compared with the two-processor timing, the efficiency remains at over 95% even for 32 processors.

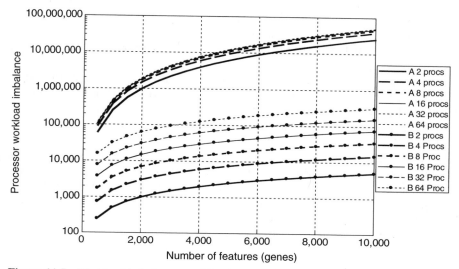

Figure 11.5 Workload imbalance resulting from calculations using the parallel σ-classifier on 2, 4, 8, 16, 32, and 64 processors as a function of the total number of features. The workload imbalance is the difference between the maximum and minimum number of classifiers handled by individual processors. The lines without dots show the workload imbalance using schema A. The lines with dots are the workload imbalance using schema B. Changing the work distribution from schemata A to B improves the efficiency by decreasing the workload imbalance several orders of magnitude.

After testing, we used the parallel version to classify a much larger published data set consisting of 31 samples with 8067 genes [16]. The analysis attempted to distinguish the melanoma primary cluster from noncluster. Even though the number of unique genes in the arrays is smaller (6971), we used all of them as a test for the new parallel software with a large data set. With 64 processors, the analysis required

TABLE 11.3 Performance of the Parallel σ-Classifier Using Schema B and a Lymphoma Data Set Consisting of 30 Samples with 2303 Genes ($k = 3$ and $n = 2303$)

Number of Processors	Runtime (h)	Adjusted Efficiency[a] (%)
1	14.60	
2	6.93	100
4	3.50	99
8	1.78	97
16	0.90	96
32	0.45	95

[a]The single processor version is slightly different than the parallel version. The adjusted efficiency assumes a single processor time of half the two processor time.

864.17 min or 14.5 h to complete. The same analysis required 1713 and 3406 min with 32 and 16 processors, respectively. Using these results, we determined that it would require more than 38 days to complete this analysis using the serial version on a single processor.

The parallel version of the σ-classifier has been extensively used for the following cancer classification problems: (1) a lymphoma study with 2303 unique genes for further understanding the sub-type of diffuse large B-cell lymphomas (DLBCLs) at the molecular level and to find genes that are differentially expressed in de novo CD5+ DLBCL, CD5− DLBCL, and mantle cell lymphoma (MCL), (2) a multiple sclerosis study with 4222 unique genes for distinguishing patients with multiple sclerosis from healthy controls by gene expression profiling of peripheral mononuclear cells by cDNA microarrays, and (3) a melanoma study with 5450 unique genes to study the response of the tumor patients to high-dose IL-2 treatment. All these problems, with the number of genes involved, would take a significantly longer time to analyze whether the serial version of the program was used.

11.4 DISCUSSION AND FUTURE DIRECTIONS

Gene expression is regulated at many levels of the molecular chain starting from the DNA level to the mRNA level and to the protein level. Challenging problems remain in developing methods to analyze microarray data so that we can model and understand regulatory as well as other complex biological processes from the molecular view to the systems perspective. When attempting to obtain a better understanding of gene regulation, parallel computing provides a means to greatly reduce the time it takes to process microarray data and allows for the consideration of new approaches to analyzing it.

The parallel method described earlier in this chapter for assessing the codetermination of gene transcriptional states from large-scale simultaneous gene expression measurements with cDNA microarrays provides a good example. Although the CoD analysis mainly focuses on finding individual connections among genes, using this information in the context of a biological problem remains a difficult challenge and an open problem. Studies of the ability to predict a gene's state based on the states of other genes, such as CoD analysis, suggest that it may be possible to abstract sufficient information to build models of the system that retain some characteristics of the real system.

A case study by Kim et al. [27] investigated whether the network of interactions that regulate gene expression can be modeled by existing mathematical techniques. As an attempt to determine whether certain biological behavior could be captured in a Markov chain model, a small network based on microarray data observations of a human cancer, melanoma, was built and simulated by a Markov chain. The Markov chain is a widespread statistical methodology to enable estimation of complex models via simulation, in particular, in the context of a biological system. This required developing criteria to select a small set of genes from which to build a Markov chain and developing a method to construct transition rules from microarray data. As it would be unrealistic to study all genes in one regulatory network because of the limit on computational resources and the perception that biological systems seems to be comprised small, function-centered regulatory sub-networks, a small set of genes was chosen based on the predictive relationships obtained from CoD analysis using the parallel method described earlier and available biological knowledge. The focus of the study was the steady-state behavior of the Markov chain constructed from the multivariate relationships and the transition rules, both estimated from the data. This modeling would not have been possible without availability of the parallel CoD analysis.

When developing parallel methods for gene expression analysis, researchers are presented with the opportunity provided by the availability of new parallel computer architectures. At the level of the individual processor, taking advantage of parallelism among instructions is critical to achieving high performance. Modern superscalar processors provide this instruction-level parallelism by pipelining the instruction execution cycle in addition to issuing multiple instructions per clock cycle. However, providing parallelism at the system level with multiple superscalar processors is necessary to reduce the time needed to complete the required calculations. The calculations are divided into parts that are independently executed on different processors. As mentioned earlier, the speedup that can be achieved by having p processors work concurrently on the calculations is at most p times faster than a single processor. Although attempts are made to achieve this ideal speedup, the ability to attain it, in practice, is determined by the efficiency of the developed parallel method to exploit the natural concurrency for the computing problem.

Modern vector architectures can offer advantages over superscalar processors for a range of compute-intense applications. Vector processors provide high-level operations that work on vectors — linear arrays of numbers. With computer architects developing vector microprocessors for multimedia applications, it will be possible to implement multiple processor systems where each processor contains a number of vector processors in addition to a superscalar processor core. For example, Kozyrakis and Patterson [28] are developing the CODE (Clustered Organization for Decoupled Execution) architecture, a vector processor that contains a number of functional units with a unique clustered vector register file.

A block diagram of the CODE processor is shown in Figure 11.6. In addition to the scalar core, the processor has N clusters. A cluster contains an integer, floating point,

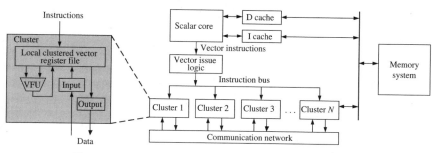

Figure 11.6   Block diagram of the CODE vector processor.

or load-store vector functional unit (VFU) and a number of vector registers. A cluster also includes an instruction queue as well as one input and one output interface, which allow vector register transfers from and to other clusters. Architectures such as the CORE vector processor have the potential to reduce the time required to perform the CoD calculations described earlier. For example, when developing the logic filter during the CoD calculations, this computational task can be further divided by distributing the training and testing calculations among the clusters within a processor in addition to partitioning the gene combinations across the multiple processors.

REFERENCES

1. P. Baldi and G.W. Hatfield, *DNA Microarrays and Gene Expression*, Cambridge University Press, Cambridge, 2002.
2. J. L. DeRisi, V. R. Iyer, and P. O. Brown, Exploring the metabolic and genetic control of gene expression on a genomic scale, *Science*, 278, 680–686 (1997).
3. D. J. Duggan, M. L. Bittner, Y. Chen, P. S. Meltzer, and J. M. Trent, Expression profiling using cDNA microarrays, *Nature Gene.*, 21, 10–14 (1999).
4. S. Knudsen, *Guide to Analysis of DNA Microarray Data*, John Wiley and Sons, Hoboken, New Jersey, 2004.
5. M. Schena, D. Shalon, R. W. Davis, and P. O. Brown, Quantitative monitoring of gene expression patterns with a complementary DNA microarray, *Science*, 270, 467–470 (1995).
6. S. Draghici, *Data Analysis Tools for DNA Microarrays*, Chapman and Hall/CRC, Boca Raton, 2003.
7. R. M. Simon, E. L. Korn, L. M. McShane, M. D. Radmacher, G. W. Wright, and Y. Zhao, *Design and Analysis of DNA Microarray Investigations*, Springer, New York, 2003.
8. S. Kim, E. R. Dougherty, M. L. Bittner, Y. Chen, K. Sivakumar, P. Meltzer, and J. M. Trent, A general nonlinear framework for the analysis of gene interaction via multivariate expression arrays, *J. Biomed. Optics*, 5, 411–424 (2000).
9. S. Kim, E. R. Dougherty, Y. Chen, K. Sivakumar, P. Meltzer, J. M. Trent, and M. Bittner, Multivariate measurement of gene expression relationships, *Genomics*, 67, 201–209 (2000).
10. E. R. Dougherty, S. Kim, and Y. Chen, Coefficient of determination in nonlinear signal processing, *Signal Process.*, 80, 2219–2235 (2000).
11. I. Shmulevich, E. R. Dougherty, S. Kim, and W. Zhang, Probabilistic boolean networks: a rule-based uncertainty model for gene regulatory networks, *Bioinformatics*, 18, 261–274 (2002).
12. S. A. Kauffman, Metabolic stability and epigenesis in randomly constructed genetic networks, *Theoret. Biol.*, 22, 437–467 (1969).
13. S. A. Kauffman, *The Origins of Order: Self-organization and Selection in Evolution*, Oxford University Press, New York, 1993.
14. Y. Chen, E. R. Dougherty, and M.L Bittner, Ratio-based decisions and the quantitative analysis of cDNA microarray images, *J. Biomed. Optics*, 2, 364–374 (1997).
15. E. R. Dougherty, Small sample issues for microarray-based classification, *Comp. Funct. Genomics*, 2, 28–34 (2001).

16. M. L. Bittner, P. Meltzer, Y. Chen, Y. Jiang, E. Seftor, M. Hendrix, M. Radmacher, R. Simon, Z. Yakhini, A. Ben-Dor, N. Sampas, E. R. Dougherty, E. Wang, F. Marincola, C. Gooden, J. Lueders, A. Glatfelter, P. Pollock, J. Carpten, E. Gillanders, D. Leja, K. Dietrich, C. Beaudry, M. Berens, D. Alberts, V. Sondak, N. Hayward, and J. Trent. Molecular classification of cutaneous malignant melanoma by gene expression profiling, *Nature*, 406, 536–540 (2000).

17. R. L. Martino, C. A. Johnson, E. B. Suh, B. L. Trus, and T. K. Yap, Parallel computing in biomedical research, *Science*, 265, 902–908 (1994).

18. J. Khan, et al., Gene expression profiling of alveolar rhabdomyosarcoma with cDNA microarrays, *Cancer Res.*, 58 (22), 5009–5013 (1998).

19. U. Alon, N. Barkai, D. A. Notterman, K. Gish, S. Ybarra, D. Mack, and A. J. Levine, Broad patterns of gene expression revealed by clustering analysis of tumor and normal colon tissues probed by oligonucleotide arrays, *Proc. Natl. Acad. Sci. USA*, 96 (12), 6745–6750 (1999).

20. A. Alizadeh, M. Eisen, R. E. Davis, C. Ma, H. Sabet, T. Tran, J. I. Powell, L. Yang, G. E. Marti, D. T. Moore, J. R. Hudson, Jr., W. C. Chan, T. Greiner, D. Weisenburger, J. O. Armitage, I. Lossos, R. Levy, D. Botstein, P. O. Brown, and L. M. Staudt, The lymphochip: a specialized cDNA microarray for the genomic-scale analysis of gene expression in normal and malignant lymphocytes, *Cold Spring Harb. Symp. Quant. Biol.*, 64, 71–78 (1999).

21. C. M. Perou, et al., Molecular portraits of human breast tumours, *Nature*, 406, 747–752 (2000).

22. T. R. Golub, D. K. Slonim, P. Tamayo, C. Huard, M. Gaasenbeek, J. P. Mesirov, H. Coller, M. L. Loh, J. R. Downing, M. A. Caligiuri, C. D. Bloomfield, and E. S. Lander, Molecular classification of cancer: class discovery and class prediction by gene expression monitoring, *Science*, 286, 531–537 (1999).

23. A. Ben-Dor, et al., Tissue classification with gene expression profiles, *J. Comput. Biol.*, 7 (3–4), 559–583 (2000).

24. J. Khan, J. S. Wei, M. Ringnér, L. H. Saal, M. Ladanyi, F. Westermann, F. Berthold, M. Schwab, C. R. Antonescu, C. Peterson, and P. S. Meltzer, Classification and diagnostic prediction of cancers using gene expression profiling and artificial neural networks. *Nature Med.*, 7 (6), 673–679 (2001).

25. S. Kim, E. R. Dougherty, J. Barrera, Y. Chen, M. L. Bittner, J. M. Trent, Strong feature sets from small samples, *J. Comput. Biol.*, 9 (1), 127–146 (2002).

26. T. Kobayashi, M. Yamaguchi, S. Kim, J. Morikawa, S. Ueno, E. Suh, E. R. Dougherty, I. Shmulevich, H. Shiku, and W. Zhang, Gene expression profiling identifies strong feature genes that classify de novo CD5+ and CD5 diffuse large B-cell lymphoma and mantle cell lymphoma, *Cancer Res.*, 63, 60–66 (2003).

27. S. Kim, H. Li, E. R. Dougherty, N. Chao, Y. Chen, M. L. Bittner, and E. B. Suh, Can Markov chain models mimic biological regulation? *J. Biol. Syst.*, 10 (4), 447–458 (2002).

28. C. Kozyrakis and D. Patterson, Overcoming the Limitations of Conventional Vector Processors, in *Proceedings of the 30th International Symposium on Computer Architecture*, ACM Press, 2003, pp. 283–293.

CHAPTER 12

Assembling DNA Fragments with a Distributed Genetic Algorithm

GABRIEL LUQUE, ENRIQUE ALBA, and SAMI KHURI

As more research centers embark on sequencing new genomes, the problem of DNA fragment assembly for shotgun sequencing is growing in importance and complexity. Accurate and fast assembly is a crucial part of any sequencing project and many algorithms have been developed to tackle it. As the DNA fragment assembly problem is NP-hard, exact solutions are very difficult to obtain. Various heuristics, including genetic algorithms (GAs), were designed for solving the fragment assembly problem. Although the sequential GA has given good results, it is unable to sequence very large DNA molecules. In this work, we present a distributed genetic algorithm (dGA) that surmounts the problem. We show how the dGA can tackle problem instances that are 77 kb long accurately.

12.1 INTRODUCTION

DNA fragment assembly is a technique that attempts to reconstruct the original DNA sequence from a large number of fragments, each having several hundred base-pairs. The DNA fragment assembly is needed because current technology, such as gel electrophoresis, cannot directly and accurately sequence DNA molecules longer than 1000 bases. However, most genomes are much longer. For example, a human DNA is about 3.2 billion nucleotides in length and cannot be read simultaneously.

The following technique was developed to deal with this limitation. First, the DNA molecule is amplified, that is, many copies of the molecule are created. The molecules are then cut at random sites to obtain fragments that are short enough to be sequenced directly. The overlapping fragments are then assembled back into the original DNA molecule. This strategy is called *shotgun sequencing*. Originally, the assembly of

Parallel Computing for Bioinformatics and Computational Biology, Edited by Albert Y. Zomaya
Copyright © 2006 John Wiley & Sons, Inc.

short fragments was done by hand, which is inefficient and error prone. Hence, a lot of effort has been put into finding techniques to automate the shotgun sequence assembly. Over the past decade, a number of fragment assembly packages have been developed and used to sequence different organisms. The most popular packages are PHRAP [1], TIGR assembler [2], STROLL [3], CAP3 [4], Celera assembler [5], and EULER [6]. These packages deal with the previously described challenges to different extend, but none of them solves all. Each package automates fragment assembly using a variety of algorithms. The most popular techniques are greedy based. This work reports on the design and implementation of a parallel distributed genetic algorithm (dGA) to tackle the DNA fragment assembly problem.

The remainder of this chapter is organized as follows. In Section 12.2, we present background information about the DNA fragment assembly problem. In Section 12.3, the details of the sequential genetic algorithm (GA) are presented. We discuss the GA operators, fitness functions [7], and how to design and implement a GA for the DNA fragment assembly problem. In Section 12.4, we present the parallel dGA. We analyze the results of our experiments in Section 12.5. We end this chapter by giving our final thoughts and conclusions in Section 12.6.

12.2 DNA FRAGMENT ASSEMBLY PROBLEM

We start this section by giving a vivid analogy to the fragment assembly problem: "Imagine several copies of a book cut by scissors into thousands of pieces, say 10 millions. Each copy is cut in an individual way such that a piece from one copy may overlap a piece from another copy. Assume one million pieces lost and remaining nine million are splashed with ink, try to recover the original text." [6]. We can think of the DNA target sequence as being the original text and the DNA fragments as being the pieces cut out from the book. To further understand the problem, we need to know the following basic terminologies:

- *Fragment*: A short sequence of DNA with length up to 1000 bp.
- *Shotgun Data*: A set of fragments.
- *Prefix*: A substring comprising the first n characters of fragment f.
- *Suffix*: A substring comprising the last n characters of fragment f.
- *Overlap*: Common sequence between the suffix of one fragment and the prefix of another fragment.
- *Layout*: An alignment of collection of fragments based on the overlap order.
- *Contig*: A layout consisting of contiguous overlapping fragments.
- *Consensus*: A sequence derived from the layout by taking the majority vote for each column of the layout.

To measure the quality of a consensus, we can look at the distribution of the coverage. Coverage at a base position is defined as the number of fragments at that position. It is a measure of the redundancy of the fragment data. It denotes the number of fragments, on average, in which a given nucleotide in the target DNA is expected to appear. It is computed as the number of bases read from fragments over the length of the target DNA [8].

$$Coverage = \frac{\sum_{i=1}^{n} \text{length of the fragment } i}{\text{target sequence length}} \tag{12.1}$$

where n is the number of fragments. TIGR uses the coverage metric to ensure the correctness of the assembly result. The coverage usually ranges from 6 to 10 [9]. The higher the coverage, the fewer the gaps are expected and the better the result.

12.2.1 DNA Sequencing Process

To determine the function of specific genes, scientists have learned to read the sequence of nucleotides consisting a DNA sequence in a process called DNA sequencing. The fragment assembly starts with breaking the given DNA sequence into small fragments. To do that, multiple exact copies of the original DNA sequence are made. Each copy is then cut into short fragments at random positions. These are the first three steps depicted in Figure 12.1 and they take place in the laboratory. After the fragment set was obtained, traditional assemble approach is followed in this order: overlap, layout, and consensus. To ensure that enough fragments overlap, the reading of fragments continues until the coverage is satisfied. These are the last three steps depicted in Figure 12.1. In what follows, we give a brief description of each of the three phases, namely, overlap, layout, and consensus.

12.2.1.1 *Overlap Phase* Finding the Overlapping Fragments. This phase consists in finding the best or longest match between the suffix of one sequence and the prefix of another. In this step, we compare all possible pairs of fragments to determine their similarity. Usually, the dynamic programming algorithm is used in this step to find semiglobal alignment. The intuition behind finding the pairwise overlap is that fragments with a significant overlap score are very likely next to each other in the target sequence.

12.2.1.2 *Layout Phase* Finding the order of fragments based on the computed similarity score. This is the most difficult step because it is hard to determine the true overlap due to the following factors:

1. *Unknown Orientation.* After the original sequence is cut into many fragments, the orientation is lost. The sequence can be read in either 5′–3′ or 3′–5′. One does not know which strand should be selected. If one fragment does not have any overlap with another, it is still possible that its reverse complement might have such an overlap.

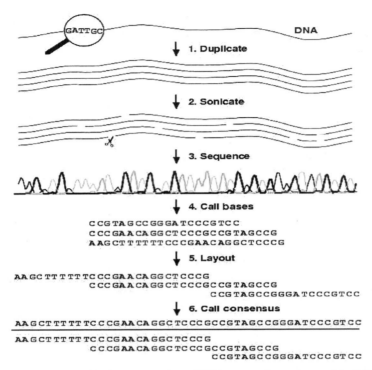

Figure 12.1   Graphical representation of DNA sequencing and assembly [10].

2. *Base Call Errors.* There are three types of base call errors: substitution, insertion, and deletion. They occur due to experimental errors in the electrophoresis procedure. Errors affect the detection of fragment overlaps. Hence, the consensus determination requires multiple alignments in high coverage regions.

3. *Incomplete Coverage.* It happens when the algorithm is not able to assemble a given set of fragments into a single contig.

4. *Repeated Regions.* Repeats are sequences that appear two or more times in the target DNA. Repeated regions have caused problems in many genome-sequencing projects, and none of the current assembly programs can handle them perfectly.

5. *Chimeras and Contamination.* Chimeras arise when two fragments that are not adjacent or overlapping on the target molecule join together into one fragment. Contamination occurs due to the incomplete purification of the fragment from the vector DNA.

After the order was determined, the progressive alignment algorithm is applied to combine all the pairwise alignments obtained in the overlap phase.

12.2.1.3 *Consensus Phase* Deriving the DNA Sequence From the Layout.

The most common technique used in this phase is to apply the majority rule in building the consensus.

Example We next give an example of the fragment assembly process. Given a set of fragments {F1 = GTCAG, F2 = TCGGA, F3 = ATGTC, F4 = CGGATG}, assume the four fragments are read from 5′ to 3′ direction. First, we need to determine the overlap of each pair of the fragments using the semiglobal alignment algorithm. Next, we determine the order of the fragments based on the overlap scores, which are calculated in the overlap phase. Suppose we have the following order: F2 → F4 → F3 → F1. Then, the layout and the consensus for this example can be constructed as follows:

```
F2  →      TCGGA
F4  →        CGGATG
F3  →          ATGTC
F1  →            GTCAG
_____

Consensus  →  TCGGATGTCAG
```

In this example, the resulting order allows to build a sequence having just one contig. As finding the exact order takes a huge amount of time, a heuristic such as GA can be applied in this step [7, 11, 12]. In the following section, we illustrate how the GA is implemented for the DNA fragment assembly problem.

12.3 DNA FRAGMENT ASSEMBLY USING THE SEQUENTIAL GA

The GA was invented in the mid-1970s by Holland [13]. It is based on Darwin's evolution theory. GA uses the concept of survival of the fittest and natural selection to evolve a population of individuals over many generations using different operators: selection, crossover, and mutation. As the generations are passed along, the average fitness of the population is likely to improve. GA can be used for optimization problems with multiple parameters and multiple objectives. It is commonly used to tackle NP-hard problems such as the DNA fragment assembly and the traveling salesman problem. NP-hard problems require tremendous computational resources to solve exactly. GAs help to find good solutions in a reasonable amount of time. Next, we present the sequential GA for the fragment assembly problem. More details about the inner workings of the algorithm can be found in Ref. [14].

1. Randomly generate the initial population of fragment orderings.
2. Evaluate the population by computing fitness.
3. While (NOT termination condition)

(a) Select fragment orderings for the next generation through ranking selection.
(b) Alter population by
    i. Applying the crossover operator.
    ii. Applying the mutation operator.
    iii. Re-evaluate the population.

12.3.1 Implementation Details

Let us give some details about the most important issues of our implementation.

12.3.1.1 *Population Representation*

We use the permutation representation with integer number encoding. A permutation of integers represents a sequence of fragment numbers, where successive fragments overlap. The population in this representation requires a list of fragments assigned with a unique integer ID. For example, eight fragments will need eight identifiers: 0, 1, 2, 3, 4, 5, 6, and 7. The permutation representation requires special operators to make sure that we always get legal (feasible) solutions. To maintain a legal solution, the two conditions that must be satisfied are (a) all fragments must be presented in the ordering and (b) no duplicate fragments are allowed in the ordering. For example, one possible ordering for four fragments is 3 0 2 1. It means that fragment 3 is at the first position, fragment 0 is at the second position, and so on.

12.3.1.2 *Population Size*

We use a fixed size population to initialize random permutations.

12.3.1.3 *Program Termination*

The program can be terminated in one of two ways. We can specify the maximum number of generations to stop the algorithm or we can also stop the algorithm when the solution is no longer improving.

12.3.1.4 *Fitness Function*

A fitness function is used to evaluate how good a particular solution is. It is applied to each individual in the population and it should guide the genetic algorithm toward the optimal solution. In the DNA fragment assembly problem, the fitness function measures the multiple sequences alignment quality and finds the best scoring alignment. Parsons et al. [7] mentioned two different fitness functions.

Fitness function F1 sums the overlap score for adjacent fragments in a given solution. When this fitness function is used, the objective is to maximize such a score. It means that the best individual will have the highest score.

$$F1(l) = \sum_{i=0}^{n-2} w(f[i]f[i+1]) \tag{12.2}$$

Fitness function F2 sums not only the overlap score for adjacent fragments but also the overlap score for all other possible pairs.

$$F2(l) = \sum_{i=0}^{n-1}\sum_{j=0}^{n-1} |i - j| \times w(f[i]f[j]) \tag{12.3}$$

This fitness function penalizes solutions in which strong overlaps occur between nonadjacent fragments in the layouts. When this fitness function is used, the objective is to minimize the overlap score. It means that the best individual will have the lowest score.

The overlap score in both F1 and F2 is computed using the semiglobal alignment algorithm.

12.3.1.5 Recombination Operator
Two or more parents are recombined to produce one or more offspring. The purpose of this operator is to allow partial solutions to evolve in different individuals and then combine them to produce a better solution. It is implemented by running through the population, and for each individual, deciding whether it should be selected for crossover using a parameter called *crossover rate* (P_c). A crossover rate of 1.0 indicates that all the selected individuals are used in the crossover. Thus, there are no survivors. However, empirical studies have shown that better results are achieved by a crossover rate between 0.65 and 0.85, which implies that the probability of an individual moving unchanged to the next generation ranges from 0.15 to 0.35.

For our experimental runs, we use the order-based crossover (OX) and the edge-recombination crossover (ER). These operators were specifically designed for tackling problems with permutation representations.

The order-based crossover operator first copies the fragment ID between two random positions in Parent 1 into the offspring's corresponding positions. We then copy the rest of the fragments from Parent 2 into the offspring in the relative order presented in Parent 2. If the fragment ID is already present in the offspring, then we skip that fragment. The method preserves the feasibility of every string in the population.

Edge recombination preserves the adjacencies that are common to both parents. This operator is appropriate because a good fragment ordering consists of fragments that are related to each other by a similarity metric and should therefore be adjacent to one another. Parsons [7] uses edge-recombination operator as follows:

1. Calculate the adjacencies.
2. Select the first position from one of the parents, call it s.
3. Select s' in the following order until no fragments remain:
   (a) s' adjacent to s is selected if it is shared by both parents.
   (b) s' that has more remaining adjacencies is selected.
   (c) s' is randomly selected if it has an equal number of remaining adjacencies.

12.3.1.6   Mutation Operator   This operator is used for the modification of single individuals. The reason we need a mutation operator is for the purpose of maintaining diversity in the population. Mutation is implemented by running through the whole population, and for each individual, deciding whether to select it for mutation, based on a parameter called *mutation rate* (P_m). For our experimental runs, we use the swap mutation operator. This operator randomly selects two positions from a permutation and then swaps the two fragment positions. As this operator does not introduce any duplicate number in the permutation, the solution it produces is always feasible. Swap mutation operator is suitable for permutation problems such as ordering fragments.

12.3.1.7   Selection Operator   The purpose of the selection is to weed out the bad solutions. It requires a population as a parameter, processes the population using the fitness function, and returns a new population. The level of the selection pressure is very important. If the pressure is too low, convergence becomes very slow. If the pressure is too high, convergence will be premature to a local optimum.

In this work, we use ranking selection mechanism [15] in which the GA first sorts the individuals based on the fitness and then selects the individuals with the best fitness score until the specified population size is reached. Note that the population size will grow whenever a new offspring is produced by crossover or mutation. The use of ranking selection is preferred over other selections such as fitness proportional selection [16].

12.4   DNA FRAGMENT ASSEMBLY PROBLEM USING THE PARALLEL GA

This section introduces the parallel model that we use in the experiments discussed in the next section. The first part of this section describes the parallel model of GA, whereas the second part presents the software used to implement that model.

12.4.1   Parallel GA

A parallel GA (PGA) is an algorithm having multiple component GAs, regardless of their population structure. A component GA is usually a traditional GA with a single population. Its algorithm is augmented with an additional phase of *communication* code so as to be able to convey its result and receive results from the other components [17].

Different parallel algorithms differ in the characteristics of their elementary heuristics and in the communication details. In this work, we have chosen a kind of decentralized distributed search because of its popularity and because it can be easily implemented in clusters of machines. In this parallel implementation, separate subpopulations evolve independently in a ring with sparse exchanges of a given number of individuals with a certain given frequency (Figure 12.2). The selection of the emigrants is through binary tournament [16] in the GAs, and the arriving immigrants replace the worst ones in the population only if the new ones is better than the current worst individuals.

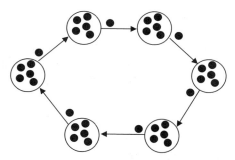

Figure 12.2 Graphical representation of the parallel dGA.

Before moving on to Section 12.5, in which we analyze the effects of several configurations of migration rates and frequencies, we introduce MALLBA which we used in this work and where all our programs can be found.

12.4.2 MALLBA Project

The MALLBA research project [18] is aimed at developing a library of algorithms for optimization that can deal with parallelism in a user-friendly and, at the same time, efficient manner. Its three target environments are sequential, LAN, and WAN computer platforms. All the algorithms described in the next section are implemented as *software skeletons* (similar to the concept of software pattern) with a common internal and public interface. This permits fast prototyping and transparent access to parallel platforms.

MALLBA skeletons distinguish between the concrete problem to be solved and the solver technique. Skeletons are generic templates to be instantiated by the user with the features of the problem. All the knowledge related to the solver method (e.g., parallel considerations) and its interactions with the problem are implemented by the skeleton and offered to the user. Skeletons are implemented by a set of *required* and *provided* C++ classes, which represent an abstraction of the entities participating in the solver method:

- *Provided Classes*: They implement internal aspects of the skeleton in a problem-independent way. The most important provided classes are `Solver` (the algorithm) and `SetUpParams` (setup parameters).
- *Required Classes*: They specify information related to the problem. Each skeleton includes the `Problem` and `Solution` required classes, which encapsulate the problem-dependent entities needed by the solver method. Depending on the skeleton, other classes may be required.

Therefore, the user of a MALLBA skeleton only needs to implement the particular features related to the problem. This speeds considerably the creation of new algorithms with minimum effort, especially if they are built up as combinations of existing skeletons (*hybrids*).

The infrastructure used in the MALLBA project is made of communication networks and clusters of computers located at the Spanish universities of Málaga, La Laguna, and UPC in Barcelona. These nodes are interconnected by a chain of Fast Ethernet and ATM circuits. The MALLBA library is publicly available at http://neo.lcc.uma.es/mallba/easy-mallba/index.html.

Using this library, we were able to perform a quick coding of algorithmic prototypes to cope with the inherent difficulties of the DNA fragment assembly problem.

12.5 EXPERIMENTAL RESULTS

A target sequence with accession number BX842596 (GI 38524243) was used in this work. It was obtained from the NCBI website (http://www.ncbi.nlm.nih.gov). It is the sequence of a *Neurospora crassa* (common bread mold) BAC, and is 77,292 bp long. To test and analyze the performance of our algorithm, we generated two problem instances with GenFrag [19]. The first problem instance, 842596_4, contains 442 fragments with average fragment length of 708 bp and coverage 4. The second problem instance, 842596_7, contains 733 fragments with average fragment length of 703 bp and coverage 7.

We evaluated each assembly result in terms of the number of contigs assembled and the percentage similarity of assembled regions with the target sequence. As we obtain fragments from a known target sequence, we can compare our assembled consensus sequence with the target.

We use a sequential GA and several dGAs (having 2, 4, and 8 islands) to solve this problem. As the results of the GA vary depending on the different parameter settings, we begin this section by discussing how the parameters affect the results and the performance of the GA. We then elaborate on how these parameters are used for solving the DNA fragment assembly problem.

12.5.1 Analysis of the Algorithm

We studied the effects of the fitness function, crossover operator, population size, operator rates, and migration configuration for the dGA. In our analysis, we perform different runs of the GA in the following manner: change one GA parameter of the basic configuration, while keeping the other parameters to the same value. The basic setting uses F1 (Eq. 12.2) as fitness function and the order-based crossover as recombination operator. The whole population is compried of 512 individuals. In dGA, each island has a population of $512/n$, where n is the number of islands. Migration occurs in a unidirectional ring manner, sending one single randomly chosen individual to the neighbor subpopulation. The target population incorporates this individual only if it is better than its current worst solution. The migration step is performed every 20 iterations in every island in an asynchronous way. All runs were performed on a Pentium 4 at 2.8 GHz linked by a Fast Ethernet communication network. Our parameter values are summarized in Table 12.1. We performed 30 independent runs of each experiment.

TABLE 12.1   Basic Configuration

Independent runs	30
Popsize	512
Fitness function	F1
Crossover	OX (0.7)
Mutation	Swap (0.2)
Cutoff	30
Migration frequency	20
Migration rate	1
Instance	38524243_4.dat

12.5.1.1 *Function Analysis*

We begin our study with the choice of the fitness function because it is one of the most important steps in applying a GA to a problem. Especially, in this problem, choosing an appropriate fitness function is an open research line, because it is difficult to capture the dynamics of the problem into a mathematical function. The results of our runs are summarized in Table 12.2. The table shows the fitness of the best solution obtained (b), the average fitness found (f), average number of evaluations (e), and average time in seconds (t). Recall that F1 is a maximization function, whereas F2 is a minimization one. Our conclusion is that although F2 takes longer than F1, both functions need the same number of evaluations to find the best solution (differences are not statistically significant in sequential and distributed ($n = 2$) versions). This comes as no surprise, because F2 has a quadratic complexity, whereas the complexity of F1 is linear. In fact, this amounts to an apparent advantage of F1, as it provides a lower complexity when compared with F2 while needing a similar effort to arrive to similar or larger degrees of accuracy. In addition, when distributed ($n = 4$ or 8) F1 does allow for a reduction in the effort, whereas F2 seems not to profit from a larger number of machines.

The number of contigs is used as the criterion to judge the quality of the results. As it can be seen in Table 12.3, F1 performs better than F2 as it produces fewer contigs.

12.5.1.2 *Crossover Operator Analysis*

In this section, we analyze the effectiveness of two recombination operators: the order-based crossover and the edge recombination. Table 12.4 summarizes the results obtained using these operators. A

TABLE 12.2   Results with F1 and F2 Fitness Functions

	F1				F2			
	b	f	e	t	b	f	e	t
Sequential	26,358	24,023	808,311	56	55,345,800	58,253,990	817,989	2.2E+03
$n = 2$	98,133	86,490	711,168	25	58,897,100	61,312,523	818,892	1.1E+03
$n = 4$	75,824	66,854	730,777	14	66,187,200	68,696,853	818,602	5.4E+02
$n = 8$	66,021	56,776	537,627	6.3	77,817,700	79,273,330	817,638	2.7E+02

TABLE 12.3 Best Contigs with F1 and F2 Fitness Functions

	F1 Contig	F2 Contig
Sequential	6	8
$n = 2$	6	7
$n = 4$	6	6
$n = 8$	6	7

close look at the columns devoted to running times reveals that the ER is slower than the OX operator. This is due to the fact that ER preserves the adjacency present in the two parents, whereas OX does not. Despite the theoretical advantage of ER over OX, we noticed that the GA performs equally with the order-based crossover operator as with the edge recombination, because it computes higher fitness scores for two out of two cases for the two operators (recall that F1 is a maximization function). OX operator is much faster at an equivalent accuracy.

12.5.1.3 Population Size Analysis   In this section, we study the influence of the population in our algorithms. Table 12.5 shows the average fitness score and the average time for several population sizes. As can be seen in the table, small population sizes lead to fast convergence to low average fitness values. The best average fitness in our experiments is obtained with a population of 512 individuals. For population sizes larger than 512, the execution time is increased, whereas the average fitness does not improved. This observation leads us to believe that a population size of 512 might be optimal.

12.5.1.4 Operator Rate Analysis   We now proceed to analyze the effects of the operator rates in the GA behavior. Table 12.6 summarizes the results using different combinations of crossover rates (P_c) and mutation rates (P_m). Our findings show that the fitness values tend to increase as the crossover and mutation rate increase. In fact, the best fitness values are reached when we use the highest rates ($P_c = 1.0$ and $P_m = 0.3$). The mutation operator is very important in this problem, because when the algorithm does not apply mutation ($P_m = 0.0$), the population converges very quickly and the algorithm yields very bad solutions.

TABLE 12.4 Crossover Operator Analysis

	OX				ER			
	b	f	e	t	b	f	e	t
Sequential	26,358	24,023	808,311	56	26,276	23,011	801,435	2.01E3
$n = 2$	98,133	86,490	711,168	25	99,043	84,238	789,585	1.1E3
$n = 4$	75,824	66,854	730,777	14	73,542	65,893	724,058	5.3E2
$n = 8$	66,021	56,776	537,627	6.3	62,492	53,628	557,128	1.9E2

TABLE 12.5 Population Size Analysis

| | Sequential | | LAN | | | | | |
| | $n = 1$ | | $n = 2$ | | $n = 4$ | | $n = 8$ | |
Popsize	f	t	f	t	f	t	f	t
128	8,773	1.7	53,876	11	16,634	3	23,118	3.5
256	7,424	0.01	76,447	29	44,846	7	21,305	1.9
512	24,023	56	86,490	25	66,854	14	56,776	6.3
1024	21,012	60	76,263	30	60,530	13	47,026	7.1
2048	23,732	67	54,298	32	49,049	14	32,494	3.3

12.5.1.5 *Migration Policy Analysis* We conclude this analysis by examining the effects of the migration policy. More precisely, we study the influence of the migration rate (rate) and the migration frequency (freq). The migration rate indicates the number of individuals that are migrated, whereas the migration frequency represents the number of iterations between two consecutive migrations. These two values are crucial for the coupling between the islands in the dGA. Table 12.7 summarizes the results using different combinations of these parameters. Upon examining the average fitness column (f), we observe that a lower value of migration rate (rate = 1) is better than a higher value. A high coupling among islands (a low value of migration frequency) is not beneficial for this problem. The optimum value of migration frequency is 20, because if we still increase this value (resulting in a looser coupling among islands), the average fitness decreases.

12.5.2 Analysis of the Problem

In this section, we report the results aimed at solving the problem as accurately and efficiently as possible.

From the previous analysis, we conclude that the best settings for our problem instances of the fragment assembly problem is a population size of 512 individuals, with F1 as fitness function, OR as crossover operator (with probability 1.0), and with a swap mutation operator (with probability 0.3). The migration in dGAs occurs in a unidirectional ring manner, sending one single randomly chosen individual to the neighbor sub-population. The target population incorporates this individual only if it is better than its presently worst solution. The migration step is performed every 20 iterations in every island in an asynchronous way. A summary of the conditions for our experimentation is found in Table 12.8.

Table 12.9 shows all the results and performance with all data instances and algorithms described in this chapter. We discuss some of the results found in the table. First, for both instances, it is clear that the distributed version outperforms the serial version. The distributed algorithm yields better fitness values and is faster than the sequential GA. Let us now go in deeper details on these claims.

TABLE 12.6 Operator Rate Analysis ($P_c - P_m$)

| | Sequential | | | LAN | | | | | | | | |
| | n = 1 | | | n = 2 | | | n = 4 | | | n = 8 | | |
$P_c - P_m$	b	f	t	b	f	t	b	f	t	b	f	t
0.3–0.0	8,842	7,817	0	12,539	9,148	0.2	11,500	8,775	0.1	10,284	7,932	0.01
0.3–0.1	15,624	12,223	33	91,989	61,549	16	51,109	43,822	8	34,645	29,582	3.6
0.3–0.2	22,583	17,567	33	90,691	70,342	15	70,608	59,581	8.1	50,336	41,728	3.6
0.3–0.3	27,466	20,476	33	96,341	77,048	15	78,339	66,137	7.8	59,242	51,174	3.6
0.5–0.0	8,908	7,620	0	12,981	12,981	0.5	13,629	10,236	0.2	12,788	8,522	0.03
0.5–0.1	18,103	12,600	45	83,121	61,355	20	54,930	47,894	11	40,523	31,871	4.9
0.5–0.2	22,706	19,038	44	95,352	77,583	20	73,333	62,963	11	53,326	45,378	5
0.5–0.3	28,489	23,180	45	101,172	84,300	22	80,102	70,013	11	59,946	53,567	5
0.7–0.0	9,157	7,459	0	28,221	12,540	0.6	14,702	11,099	0.2	16,089	8,935	0.05
0.7–0.1	17,140	14,065	56	86,284	67,225	27	59,714	50,899	14	39,862	33,719	6.3
0.7–0.2	26,358	24,023	56	98,133	86,490	25	75,824	66,854	14	66,021	56,776	6.3
0.7–0.3	28,359	25,026	56	104,641	84,065	28	84,732	71,897	14	63,482	53,212	6.1
1.0–0.0	8,692	7,505	0	21,664	14,561	1.1	26,294	12,888	0.4	16,732	9,897	0.11
1.0–0.1	19,485	16,242	74	90,815	71,252	35	67,067	55,713	19	42,650	33,783	7.9
1.0–0.2	27,564	22,881	74	103,231	81,300	35	81,417	71,963	20	56,871	50,154	8.4
1.0–0.3	33,071	27,500	74	107,148	88,653	36	88,389	74,048	18	66,588	58,556	8.5

TABLE 12.7 Migration Policy Analysis (freq–rate)

| | LAN | | | | | |
| | $n = 2$ | | $n = 4$ | | $n = 8$ | |
freq–rate	b	f	b	f	b	f
5–1	99,904	76,447	75,317	62,908	52,127	35,281
5–10	61,910	37,738	68,703	55,071	56,987	52,128
5–20	92,927	72,445	72,029	66,368	59,473	54,312
20–1	98,133	86,490	75,824	66,854	66,021	56,776
20–10	82,619	45,375	70,497	57,898	53,941	48,968
20–20	89,211	74,236	72,170	65,916	59,324	53,352
50–1	95,670	70,728	77,024	65,257	64,612	55,786
50–10	92,678	41,465	66,046	51,321	59,013	51,842
50–20	95,374	76,627	72,540	62,371	59,923	52,650

For the first problem instance, the parallel GAs sampled less points in the search space than the serial one, whereas for the second instance, the panmictic algorithm is mostly similar in the required effort with respect to the parallel ones.

Increasing of the number of islands (and CPUs) results in a reduction in search time, but it does not lead to a better fitness value. For the second problem instance, the average fitness was improved by a larger number of islands. However, for the first problem instance, we observed a reduction in the fitness value as we increased the number of CPUs. This counterintuitive result clearly states that each instance has a different number of optimum number of islands from the accuracy point of view.

The best tradeoff is for two islands ($n = 2$) for the two instances, as this value yields a high fitness at an affordable cost and time.

Table 12.10 gives the speed-up results. As it can be seen in the table, we always obtain an almost linear speedup for the first problem instance. For the second instance, we also have a good speedup with a low number of islands (two and four islands); eight islands make the efficiency decrease to a moderate speedup (6.42).

TABLE 12.8 Parameters When Heading and Optimum Solution of the Problem

Independent runs	30
Popsize	512
Fitness function	F1
Crossover	OR (1.0)
Mutation	Swap (0.3)
Cutoff	30
Migration frequency	20
Migration rate	1

TABLE 12.9   Results of Both Problem Instances

	38524243_4				38524243_7			
	b	f	e	t	b	f	e	t
Sequential	33,071	27,500	810,274	74	78,624	67,223	502,167	120
n = 2	107,148	88,653	733,909	36	156,969	116,605	611,694	85
n = 4	88,389	74,048	726,830	18	158,021	120,234	577,873	48
n = 8	66,588	58,556	539,296	8.5	159,654	119,735	581,979	27

TABLE 12.10   Speedup

	38524243_4			38524243_7		
	n CPUs	1 CPU	Speedup	n CPUs	1 CPU	Speedup
n = 2	36.21	72.07	1.99	85.37	160.15	1.87
n = 4	18.32	72.13	3.93	47.78	168.20	3.52
n = 8	8.52	64.41	7.56	26.81	172.13	6.42

Finally, Table 12.11 shows the global number of contigs computed in every case. This value is used as a high-level criterion to judge the whole quality of the results because, as we said earlier, it is difficult to capture the dynamics of the problem into a mathematical function. These values are computed by applying a final step of refinement with a greedy heuristic regularly used in this application [14]. We have found that in some (extreme) cases, it is possible that a solution with a better fitness than other one generates a larger number of contigs (worse solution). This is the reason for still needing research to get a more accurate mapping from fitness to contig number. The values of this table confirm again that all the parallel versions outperform the serial versions, thus advising the utilization of parallel GAs for this application in the future.

TABLE 12.11   Final Best Contigs

	38524243_4	38524243_7
Sequential	5	4
n = 2	3	2
n = 4	4	1
n = 8	4	2

12.6 CONCLUSIONS

The DNA fragment assembly is a very complex problem in computational biology. Since the problem is NP-hard, the optimal solution is impossible to find for real cases, except for very small problem instances. Hence, computational techniques of affordable complexity such as heuristics are needed for this problem.

The sequential GA we used here solves the DNA fragment assembly problem by applying a set of genetic operators and parameter settings, but does take a large amount of time for problem instances that are over 15 kb. Our distributed version has taken care of this shortcoming. Our test data are over 77 kb long. We are encouraged by the results obtained by our parallel algorithms not only because of their low waiting times but also because of their high accuracy in computing solutions of even just one contig. This is noticeable because it is far from triviality to compute optimal solutions for real-world instances of this problem.

We plan to analyze other kinds of distributed algorithms created as extensions of the canonical GA skeleton used in this chapter. To curb the problem of premature convergence, for example, we propose a restart technique in the islands. Another interesting point of research would be to incorporate different algorithms in the islands, such as greedy or simulated annealing, and to study the effects that could have on the observed performance.

ACKNOWLEDGMENTS

The first two authors are partially supported by the Ministry of Science and Technology and FEDER under contract TIC2002-04498-C05-02 (the TRACER project).

REFERENCES

1. P. Green, Phrap (http://www.mbt.washington.edu/phrap.docs/phrap.html.)
2. G. G. Sutton, O. White, M. D. Adams, and A. R. Kerlavage, TIGR assembler: a new tool for assembling large shotgun sequencing projects, *Genome Sci. Technol.*, 2, 9–19 (1995).
3. T. Chen and S. S. Skiena, Trie-Based Data Structures for Sequence Assembly, in *The Eighth Symposium on Combinatorial Pattern Matching*, 1998, pp. 206–223.
4. X. Huang and A. Madan, CAP3: a DNA sequence assembly program, *Genome Res.*, 9, 868–877 (1999).
5. E. W. Myers, Towards simplifying and accurately formulating fragment assembly, *J. Comput. Biol.*, 2 (2), 275–290 (2000).
6. P. A. Pevzner, *Computational Molecular Biology: An Algorithmic Approach*, The MIT Press, London, England, 2000.
7. R. Parsons, S. Forrest, and C. Burks, Genetic algorithms, operators, and DNA fragment assembly, *Machine Learn.*, 21, 11–33 (1995).
8. J. Setubal and J. Meidanis, Fragment assembly of DNA, *Introduction to Computational Molecular Biology*, chap. 4, University of Campinas, Brazil, 1997, pp. 105–139.

9. S. Kim, A Structured Pattern Matching Approach to Shotgun Sequence Assembly. PhD Thesis, Computer Science Department, The University of Iowa, Iowa City, 1997.

10. C. F. Allex, Computational Methods for Fast and Accurate DNA Fragment Assembly, UW Technical Report CS-TR-99-1406, Department of Computer Sciences, University of Wisconsin-Madison, 1999.

11. C. Notredame and D. G. Higgins, SAGA: sequence alignment by genetic algorithm, *Nucleic Acids Res.*, 24, 1515–1524 (1996).

12. R. Parsons and M. E. Johnson, A case study in experimental design applied to genetic algorithms with applications to DNA sequence assembly, *Am. J. Math. Manage. Sci.*, 17, 369–396 (1995).

13. J. H. Holland, *Adaptation in Natural and Artificial Systems*, The University of Michigan Press, Ann Arbor, Michigan, 1975.

14. L. Li and S. Khuri, A comparison of DNA fragment assembly algorithms, in *International Conference on Mathematics and Engineering Techniques in Medicine and Biological Sciences*, 2004, pp. 329–335.

15. D. Whitely, The GENITOR algorithm and selection pressure: Why Rank-Based Allocation of Reproductive Trials is Best, in J. D. Schaffer, Ed., *Proceedings of the Third International Conference on Genetic Algorithms*, Morgan Kaufmann, 1989, pp. 116–121.

16. D. E. Goldberg and K. Deb, A Comparative Analysis of Selection Schemes Used in Genetic Algorithms, in G. J. E. Rawlins, Ed., *Foundations of Genetic Algorithms*, Morgan Kaufmann, 1991, pp. 69–93.

17. E. Alba and M. Tomassini, Parallelism and evolutionary algorithms, *IEEE Trans. Evol. Comput.*, 6 (5), 443–462 (2002).

18. E. Alba and MALLBA Group, MALLBA: A Library of Skeletons for Combinatorial Optimisation, in R. Feldmann and B. Monien, Eds., *Proceedings of the Euro-Par*, Volume 2400 of *Lecture Notes in Computer Science*, Paderborn (GE), Springer-Verlag, 2002, pp. 927–932.

19. M. L. Engle and C. Burks, Artificially generated data sets for testing DNA fragment assembly algorithms, *Genomics*, 16 (1993).

CHAPTER 13

A Cooperative Genetic Algorithm for Knowledge Discovery in Microarray Experiments

MOHAMMED KHABZAOUI, CLARISSE DHAENENS, and EL-GHAZALI TALBI

DNA microarrays allow to measure the expression levels of thousands of genes simultaneously. This is a great challenge for biologists who see in this new technology the opportunity to discover interactions between genes. The main drawback is that data generated with such experiments are so huge that very efficient knowledge discovery methods have to be developed. This is the aim of this work. We propose to study microarray data on the basis of association rules and to adopt a combinatorial optimization approach. Therefore, a cooperative method based on an evolutionary algorithm is proposed and several models are tested and compared.

13.1 INTRODUCTION

DNA microarray experiments have a great interest for biologists, because of their ability to measure the expression and interactions of thousands of genes simultaneously [1]. Although microarrays have been applied in many biological studies [2–7], the analysis of the large volumes of data generated (large matrices of expression levels of genes under different experimental conditions) is not trivial and requires advanced knowledge discovery methods. There exist several kinds of representations to express knowledge that can be extracted from microarray data. Many data mining techniques have been proposed to analyze microarray data.

Here, we propose to deal with such data through association rules. This is a general model that allows to find associations between subsets of genes. Moreover, associations obtained are interesting to understand the relations between genes on the basis of the notions of antecedent and prediction.

Parallel Computing for Bioinformatics and Computational Biology, Edited by Albert Y. Zomaya
Copyright © 2006 John Wiley & Sons, Inc.

In this work, the association rule problem is modeled as a multi-objective combinatorial optimization problem. On the basis of an genetic algorithm (GA) we propose to solve it using a cooperative evolutionary algorithm. Therefore, specific mechanisms (mutation and crossover operators, elitism, etc.) have been designed and a parallel model is proposed and tested.

In this chapter, we first present the microarray technology. Then, we present a multi-objective model for the association rule problem, which is followed by an evolutionary algorithm to extract association rules in a multi-objective way. This is followed by a cooperative scheme, which is tested in the last section. Experiments show that the cooperation allows to introduce more diversity and to find better solutions.

13.2 MICROARRAY EXPERIMENTS

13.2.1 Microarray Technology

Microarray technology is now widely used in many areas of biomedical research. It provides access to expression levels of thousands of genes simultaneously to identify co-expressed genes, relationships between genes, patterns of gene activity, changes in gene activity under specific medical treatment, and so on. This technology consists in hybridizing previously "colored" (where different colors — red/green — may be used for the sample under study and the control) extracts of DNA with probes that match a single gene. The more a gene is active, the more it will be hybridized with the probe and the more the corresponding probe will be colored. Then, arrays are scanned and images are produced and analyzed to obtain an intensity value for each probe (Fig. 13.1). In this manner, the gene expression level may be calculated on the basis of the hybridization level.

13.2.2 Data Preprocessing

Before a possible analysis of microarray data, some preparative tasks are required. The most common way to deal with these data is to compute the differential gene expression. The differential gene expression is calculated by dividing the intensity of the gene in the sample under study by its intensity level in the control. This intensity ratio has a highly asymmetric distribution. To avoid this problem, a $\log_2$-transformation is usually used to make a normal-like distribution.

There are many sources of variations of measures in microarray experiments (variations in cells or individuals, mRNA extraction, isolation, hybridization condition, optical measurement, scanner noise, etc.). Normalization can remove such variations. Many techniques for normalization aim to make the data more normally distributed (log-transformation, per chip and per gene). This is an important issue to be able to analyze data [1].

Moreover, there may have numerous missing values in microarray data due to the empty spots or when the background intensity is higher than the spot intensity. Two

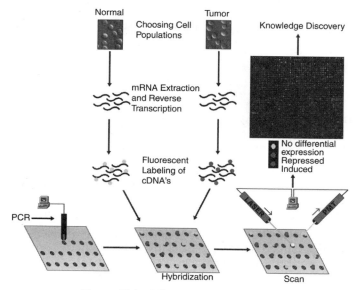

Figure 13.1 Microarray technology.

ways are commonly used for the treatment of missing values: they may be replaced by estimated values (e.g., median) or corresponding experiments are deleted. However, these two approaches have drawbacks: replacing missing values with estimating values may introduce errors and deleting corresponding experiments should be avoided in this context of microarray data, where the number of experiments is often very small in regard to the number of genes under study. Therefore, we choose to adopt another approach, which will be explained in Section 13.3.3.

Finally, as we are interested in finding genes that show significant changes between two groups of patients (most of the time samples under study and control people), we propose to remove genes that show no difference in their expression levels between these two groups over all the experiments.

13.2.3 Dealing with Microarray Data

Once data preprocessing has been done, the knowledge discovery task may start. Several knowledge discovery approaches have been used to deal with microarray data. For example, cluster analysis and classification techniques have been proposed to identify genes expression profiles. Eisen et al. [8] grouped the genes sharing similar types of behavior over experiments into clusters. Kurra et al. [9] described a classification method to discriminate two types of leukemia using heuristic feature selection and a certain variant of perceptron-based classification method that separates these two classes of leukemia. Friedman et al. [10] used Bayesian networks to analyze gene expression data and to discover and describe interactions between genes. To have a general overview, the reader may refer to the survey of Aas [11].

In this chapter, we propose to deal with microarray data through association rules discovery, which is a very general model. This model has already shown its capability to extract knowledge of such data.

13.3 ASSOCIATION RULES

13.3.1 Initial Problem

Association rules were first formulated in Ref. [12] and were called the market-basket problem. The initial problem was the following: given a set of items and a large collection of sales records, which consist in a transaction date and the items bought in the transaction, the task is to find relationships between the items contained in the different transactions.

Since this first application, many other problems have been studied with association rules, which may be defined in a more general way.

Let us consider a database comprised transactions (rows) described according to several — may be a lot — attributes (columns). The value of the attributes may be a presence/absence marker (binary data), a description belonging to a small number of possibilities (nominal data), or a real value (numerical data).

Then, an association rule is an expression of the form: IF C THEN P. This kind of rules contains two parts: the IF part is called the rule condition (C) and the THEN part is called the rule prediction (P), where both parts, the C and P parts, contain a conjunction of terms indicating specific values for specific attributes.

The most famous and the most commonly used algorithm to solve association rules is Apriori [12]. The aim of this algorithm is to enumerate in a very efficient way all the rules that respect a minimal given *support* (frequent rules) and a minimal level of *confidence* (truth of the rule). The support is the percentage of rules containing both the C and P parts of the rules and the confidence is the proportion of the rules containing C and P (see subsequently for a more formal description). A lot of improvements of the initial Apriori algorithm have been proposed, and in particular, there exist parallel versions of it. Now, we can say that Apriori-like methods are able to deal with problems with a large number of transactions and quite a large number of attributes.

Therefore, why do we not use such an algorithm? According to biologists, frequent rules are not necessarily interesting. Conversely, rare rules for which the confidence is very high may be relevant, but those rules are impossible to find by the Apriori algorithm. Moreover, the efficiency of the Apriori algorithm is based on the monotony property of the support, which cannot be replaced by any other usual quality criteria that could be used to look for rare patterns.

Hence, to overpass this problem, we choose to adopt another approach. One important characteristic of association rules, when the number of attributes (here genes) is important, is the huge number of possible rules. Therefore, we choose to adopt a combinatorial optimization approach using an evolutionary algorithm for the resolution.

13.3.2 A Multi-objective Optimization Problem

To solve association rule discovery problem as a combinatorial optimization problem, the optimization criterion has to be defined. A lot of measures exist for estimating the quality of association rules. For an overview, readers can refer to Freitas [13], Tan et al. [14] or Hilderman and Hamilton [15].

In a previous work [16, 17], we made a statistical study of different criteria found in the literature. This study lead us to determine five groups of criteria, where each group comprised correlated criteria. We choose to take one criterion of each group and obtain five complementary criteria, which allow to evaluate rules in a complete way. Chosen criteria are Support, Jmeasure, Interest, Surprise, and Confidence. Those criteria are presented with their formula in Table 13.1. Formulas are given for a set of N instances, where $|C|$ (respectively, $|P|$) represents the number of instances satisfying the C (respectively, the P) part of the rule and $|C$ and $P|$ is the number of instances satisfying simultaneously the C and P parts of the rule.

Support (S): It is the classical measure of association rule. It enables to measure rule frequency in the database. It is the percentage of transactions containing, both the C part and the P part, in the database.

Confidence (Cf): The confidence measures the validity of a rule. It is the conditional probability of P given C.

Interest (I): The interest measures the dependency, while privileging rare patterns in the region of weak support.

Surprise (R): It is used to measure the affirmation. It enables to search surprising rules.

Jmeasure (Jm): Smyth and Goodman [18] have proposed the Jmeasure, which estimates the degree of interest of a rule and combines support and confidence. It is used in optimization [19, 20].

TABLE 13.1 Quality Criteria for Association Rules

Measure	Formula
S	$\dfrac{|C \text{ and } P|}{N}$
Cf	$\dfrac{|C \text{ and } P|}{|C|}$
I	$\dfrac{N * |C \text{ and } P|}{|C| * |P|}$
R	$\dfrac{|C \text{ and } P| - |C \text{ and } \overline{P}|}{|\overline{P}|}$
J	$\dfrac{|P|}{N} * \left[\dfrac{|C \text{ and } P|}{|P|} \log\left(\dfrac{N * |C \text{ and } P|}{|C| * |P|} \right) \right.$ $\left. + \left(1 - \dfrac{|C \text{ and } P|}{|P|} \right) \log\left(\dfrac{1 - |C \text{ and } P|/|P|}{1 - (|C|/N)} \right) \right]$

13.3.3 Microarray Data and Association Rules

There are two ways to present DNA microarray data in a "market-basket" fashion [21]:

- *Gene Table*: Genes constitute the rows, whereas treatments to which the genes were exposed are the columns. The values are in normalized red/green color ratios, representing the abundance of transcript for each spot on the microarray. Clustering and classification may be applied to this table (clusters of genes).
- *Treatment Table*: Experiments or treatments constitute the rows in the data-table, whereas genes form the columns. Values are the gene expression levels. In this case, association rules can be applied to the analysis of gene expressions to identify a set of regulated genes (associations between genes).

In our study, we consider that data in the treatment table form and differential gene expressions are discretized into three values: under_expressed, over_expressed and no_change. Our objective is to look for rules combining genes where a term can be in the form <gene = value>. Value belongs to the discretized gene expression level. An example of a rule could be: IF($gene_{12}$ = over_expressed) AND ($gene_{504}$ = under_expressed) THEN ($gene_{8734}$ = over_expressed).

Concerning the missing values, we adopt a specific strategy: we propose that all genes that have missing values are kept without modification. This allows not to replace missing values by computed, but may be wrong, values and this avoid to remove some of the experiments from the whole set of data. But how to deal with such missing values? When a missing value does not concern any attribute of the rule under study, it has no consequence, and when it concerns an attribute of a rule, the corresponding experiment is excluded from the computation of the quality of this specific rule.

13.4 MULTI-OBJECTIVE GENETIC ALGORITHM

To deal with the multi-objective association rule problem, we develop a specific GA [22], as GAs have been widely used to solve multi-objective optimization problems and have been applied with success to mono-objective rule mining problems [23]. We adopt a "A posteriori" approach while looking for all the solutions of best compromise between criteria. We expose the main features of the proposed GA scheme for association rules problem (encoding, mutation, and crossover operators) and its multi-objective aspects (archive of Pareto solutions, ranking, and management of the population).

13.4.1 General Scheme

GAs are inspired from Darwin's theory of evolution. By simulating nature evolution and emulating biological selection and reproduction techniques, a GA can solve complex problems in a strong search domain.

The algorithm starts with a set of randomly generated solutions (population). The population size remains constant throughout the GA. At each iteration, solutions are selected, according to their fitness quality to form new solutions (offspring). Offspring are generated through a reproduction process (crossover and mutation).

As in a multi-objective optimization, we are looking for all the solutions of best compromise, best solutions encountered over generations are filed into a secondary population called the "Pareto archive." In the production process, solutions can be selected also from "Pareto archive," this mechanism is called "elitism." A part of the offspring solutions replace their parents according to the replacement strategy.

Figure 13.2 presents the multi-objective GA scheme.

13.4.2 Operators for Association Rules

Crossover and mutation operators are two basic operators of GAs.

Crossover: The crossover mixes the features of two rules by the combination of their attributes. The proposed crossover operator has two versions:

- *Crossover by Value Exchange.* If two rules X and Y have one or several common attribute(s) in their C parts, one common attribute is randomly selected. The value of the selected attribute in X is exchanged with its counterpart in Y (Fig. 13.3).
- *Crossover by Insertion.* Conversely, if X and Y have no common attribute, one term is randomly selected in the C part of X and inserted in Y with a probability inversely proportional to the length of Y. The similar operation is performed to insert one term of Y in X (Fig. 13.4).

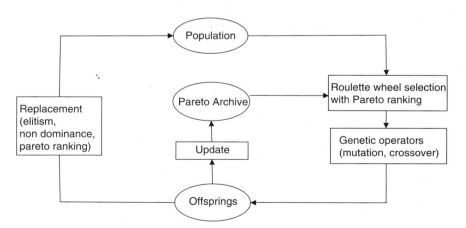

Figure 13.2 A multi-objective GA.

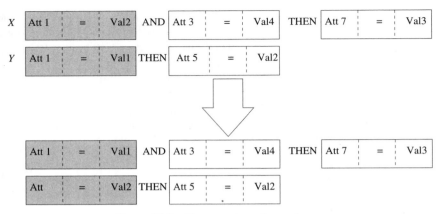

Figure 13.3 Crossover by value exchange.

Mutation: Four mutation operators were implemented.

- The *value mutation* replaces an attribute value by a randomly chosen one (Fig. 13.5).
- The *attribute mutation* replaces a term by another. The value of the new attribute is randomly chosen in its domain (Fig. 13.6).
- The *insertion operator* adds a term (randomly chosen attribute with a randomly chosen value) in the rule.
- The *delete operator* removes a term of the rule (if the number of terms is greater or equal to 3).

Adaptive Mutation Rate Setting the probabilities of appliance of these four mutation operators may be difficult. Moreover, the more interesting operator at a given time of the search is not always the same. To overcome this problem, we implement an adaptive strategy for calculating the rate of application of each mutation operator.

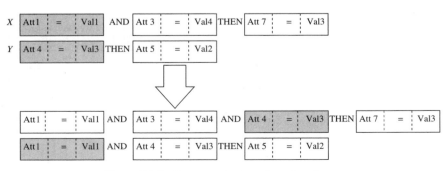

Figure 13.4 Crossover by insertion of attributes.

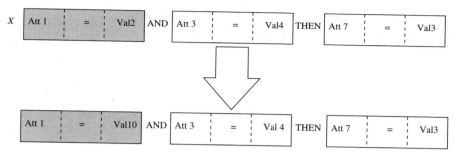

Figure 13.5 Value mutation.

Many authors have worked on setting automatically the probabilities of applying operator. Hong et al. [24] proposed to compute the new rate of mutation by calculating the progress of the jth application of mutation M_i, for an individual ind mutated into an individual mut as follows:

$$\text{progress}_j(M_i) = \text{Max}(\text{fitness}(\text{ind}, \text{fitness}(\text{mut})) - \text{fitness}(\text{ind})) \qquad (13.1)$$

Then, for each mutation operator M_i, assume $\text{Nb\_mut}(M_i)$ applications of the mutation are done during a given generation ($j = 1, \ldots, \text{Nb\_mut}(M_i)$). Then, we can compute the profit of a mutation M_k:

$$\text{Profit}(M_k) = \frac{\sum_j \text{progress}_j(M_k)/\text{Nb\_mut}(M_k)}{\sum_i \left(\sum_j \text{progress}_j(M_i)/\text{Nb\_mut}(M_i) \right)} \qquad (13.2)$$

We set a minimum rate δ and a global mutation rate p_{mutation} for N mutation operators. The new mutation ratio for each M_i is calculated using the following formula [24]:

$$p(M_i) = \text{Profit}(M_i) \times (p_{\text{mutation}} - N \times \delta) + \delta \qquad (13.3)$$

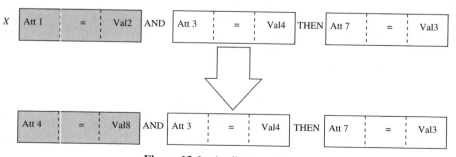

Figure 13.6 Attribute mutation.

The sum of all the mutation rates is equal to the global rate of mutation $p_{mutation}$. The initial rate of application of each mutation operator is set to $p_{mutation}/N$.

13.4.3 Multi-objective Aspects

13.4.3.1 Specificities of Multi-objective Optimization

Dealing with a multi-objective problem requires adaptation of optimization methods. The main difference with mono-objective optimization problems is that in multi-objective problems, there is not a single solution for which all criteria are optimal but a set of solutions for which there are no other solutions better for all the criteria. These solutions are called Pareto-optimal. The notion of Pareto-optimality is defined in terms of dominance. Let us consider a multi-objective minimization problem with k criteria. A solution $x = (x_1, x_2, \ldots, x_k)$ is said to be dominated another solution $y = (y_1, y_2, \ldots, y_k)$ iff $\forall i,\ x_i \leq y_i$ and $\exists i\ /\ x_i < y_i$. A solution x is a member of the Pareto-set or said to be nondominated, if there is no other solution w such that w dominates x.

We propose to use a GA to find all the Pareto-optimal solutions (solutions of best compromise), which are all interesting potential rules. They are located on a boundary, known as the Pareto-front. We would like the solutions to cover the Pareto-front as well as possible to obtain a good representation of this front. This "A priori" approach offers multiple solutions to the decision maker, which can select the solution that is best suited according to nonformal additional criteria, without requiring additional searches.

13.4.3.2 Multi-objective Operators

To deal with multi-objective optimization problems, different mechanisms have to be used. For example, the notion of dominance has to be defined (to be able to compare solutions between them) and population management has to be carefully studied.

Selection Operator: We use the classical roulette selection based on the ranking notion. The probability of selection of a solution is proportional to its rank. We use the Pareto ranking [25]. The rank of a solution corresponds to the number of solutions, in the current population, by which it is dominated (Fig. 13.7) for a bicriteria minimization problem.

Replacement Operator: We use the elitist nondominated sorting replacement. The worst ranked solutions are replaced by dominating solutions (if there is any) generated by mutation and crossover operators (offspring). The size of the population remains unchanged.

Archive: Nondominated association rules are archived into a secondary population called the "Pareto archive" to keep track of them. It consists in archiving all the Pareto association rules encountered over generations. This archive has to be updated each time a solution is added.

Elitism: The Pareto solutions (best solutions) are not only stored permanently but also take part in the selection and may participate to the reproduction.

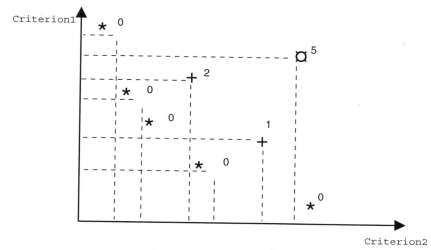

Figure 13.7   Pareto ranking.

13.5 COOPERATIVE MULTI-OBJECTIVE GENETIC ALGORITHM (PMGA)

13.5.1 Choice of the Model

Parallel GAs may be classified into three main models: Master-Slave (global), fine gained (cellular), and coarse gained (island).

The global model uses parallelism to speed up the sequential GA. This model uses a global shared population and the fitness evaluation is done on different processors.

The cellular model seeks to exploit the fine-gained, massively parallel architectures. The population is separated into a large number of very small subpopulations (one solution), which are maintained by different processors.

In the island model, the population is divided into a few large independent subpopulations (islands). Each processor evolve their population using a serial GA. For each island, some solutions occasionally migrate to another island.

We choose the island model because this model seems to be adapted for the problem under study, where the search space is very large and require a good diversity. Moreover, this model is easily implemented on a clustered computer. Let us note that converting a serial GA into this model requires to add migration operators.

13.5.2 Island Model

The island model implemented has been designed according to the ring topology (Fig. 13.8). The model typically runs a serial multi-objective GAs on each processor (island) with independent populations and Pareto archives (Fig. 13.9). Each GA starts with its proper parameters (population, parameters of GAs). Periodically, each island

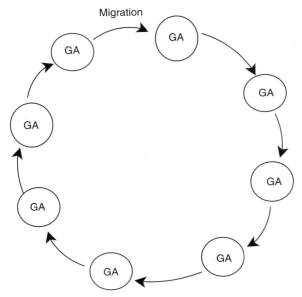

Figure 13.8   Ring topology.

sends some solutions from its Pareto archive (randomly selected) to the neighboring island (this neighbor is always the same and is defined by the topology).

An island model requires to identify the migration policy. The main questions are:

- How and when do migrations occur?
- How to select emigrating solutions?
- How many solutions have to be sent?
- Which solutions are to be replaced by the received solutions?
- What is the neighborhood structure?

Our model can be summarized in the following steps:

Each Island has to:

- Create its population
- Evolve its population for a global number of generations and update its archive every generation
- Send some solutions of its "Pareto archive" to the neighboring island (according to the migration policy)
- Receive migrating solutions and replace the worst solutions by those immigrants (according to the ranking)

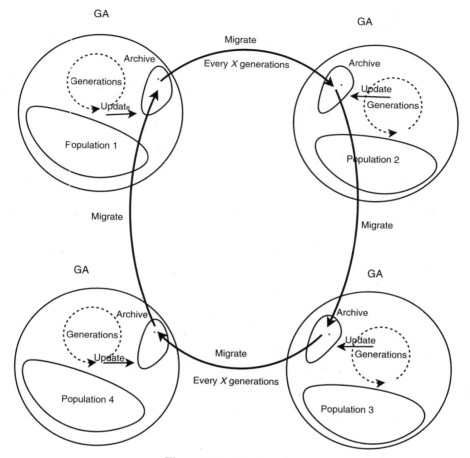

Figure 13.9   Island model.

At the end, a specific island waits for all the others to have finish their execution and collects all the final Pareto archives to create the global Pareto archive.

To develop those GAs (sequential and parallel versions), we used the PARADISEO (parallel and distributed evolving objects) platform (http://eodev.sourceforge.net), which allows to easily develop parallel and distributed evolutionary algorithms.

13.6 EXPERIMENTS

The aim here is to validate the interest of developing cooperative algorithms in making cooperate parallel GAs. First, we expose the indicators used to compare several models as they are specific to multi-objective optimization. Then, we describe the general experimental design. Finally, we present results in two phases: we first try to find the best migration policy (when and how many solutions must be exchanged) and then we compare the cooperative model with noncooperative ones to assess the contribution of cooperation.

To evaluate the algorithm, we tested it on several microarray databases and expose here results for the public microarray database "MIPS Yeast Genome Database" containing 2467 genes for 79 chips.

13.6.1 Indicators for Multi-objective Experiments

In multi-objective optimization, solutions quality can be assessed in different ways. Some approaches compare the obtained front with the optimal Pareto front [26]. Others approaches evaluate a front with a reference point [27]. Some performance measures do not use any reference point or front to evaluate an algorithm [28, 29], especially when the optimal Pareto front is not known at all.

Here, we have to compare different versions of the proposed model, without knowing the true Pareto front. We propose to use two complementary types of performance indicators that allow to compare two by two Pareto fronts obtained by different algorithms: the contribution and the entropy [30]. The contribution indicator quantifies the domination between two sets of nondominated solutions. The entropy indicator gives an idea about the diversity of the solutions found.

These indicators have been integrated to GUIMOO (graphical user interface for multi-objective optimization — http://www.lifl.fr/OPAC/guimoo), which offers tools to analyze results of multi-objective methods.

13.6.1.1 Contribution The contribution of a set of solutions PO_1 relative to a set of solutions PO_2 is the ratio of nondominated solutions produced by PO_1.

Let C be the set of solutions in $PO_1 \cap PO_2$.

Let W_1 (respectively, W_2) be the set of solutions in PO_1 (respectively, PO_2), which dominate some solutions of PO_2 (respectively, PO_1).

Let L_1 (respectively, L_2) be the set of solutions in PO_1 (respectively, PO_2), which are dominated by some solutions of PO_2 (respectively, PO_1).

Let N_1 (respectively, N_2) be the other solutions of PO_1 (respectively, PO_2): $N_i = PO_i / (C \cup W_i \cup L_i)$.

Let PO^* be the set of Pareto solutions of $PO_1 \cup PO_2$. Therefore, $\|PO^*\| = \|C\| + \|W_1\| + \|N_1\| + \|W_2\| + \|N_2\|$.

The contribution of the algorithm PO_1 relative to PO_2 is stated as:

$$C\left(\frac{PO_1}{PO_2}\right) = \frac{\|C\|/2 + \|W_1\| + \|N_1\|}{\|PO^*\|}$$

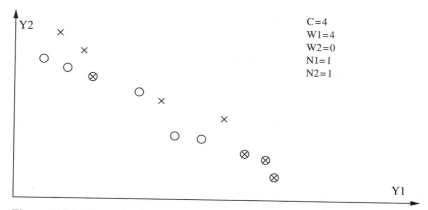

Figure 13.10 Example of contribution ($C = 4$, $W_1 = 4$, $W_2 = 0$, $N_1 = 1$, $N_2 = 1$).

For example, for the two sets of solutions PO_1 and PO_2 of Figure 13.10, where solutions of PO_1 (respectively, PO_2) are represented by circles (respectively, crosses), the contributions are $C(PO_1, PO_2) = 0.7$ and $C(PO_2, PO_1) = 0.3$.

Let us remark that $C(PO_1/PO_2) + C(PO_2/PO_1) = 1$ and hence a contribution greater than 0.5 indicates an improvement of the Pareto front.

13.6.1.2 *Entropy* The entropy allows to appreciate the diversity of the Pareto front obtained. It is based on the definition of *niche* of a solution s, which represents all the solutions that are closed to the solution s (a size of the niche has to be defined).

Let PO_1 and PO_2 be two sets of solutions.

Let PO^* be the set of optimal Pareto solutions of $PO_1 \cup PO_2$.

Let N_i be the cardinality of solutions of $PO_1 \cup PO^*$, which are in the niche of the ith solution of $PO_1 \cup PO^*$.

Let n_i be the cardinality of solutions of PO_1, which are in the niche of the ith solution of $PO_1 \cup PO^*$.

Let C be the cardinality of the solutions of $PO_1 \cup PO^*$.

Let $\gamma = \sum_{i=1}^{C} 1/N_i$ be the sum of the coefficients affected to each solution. The more concentrated is a region of the solution space, the lower will be the coefficients of its solutions.

Then, the following formula is applied to evaluate the entropy E of PO_1, relative to the space occupied by PO^*:

$$E(PO_1, PO_2) = \frac{-1}{\log(\gamma)} \sum_{i=1}^{C} \left(\frac{1}{N_i} \frac{n_i}{C} \log \frac{n_i}{C} \right)$$

An entropy value belongs to the interval $[0, 1]$, and the more the entropy is close to 1, the better diversified is the front.

13.6.2 Experimental Design

Several versions of the algorithms will be compared. We indicate the values of the parameters used subsequently, when the corresponding parameter is not under study.

The default values of the parameters used:

- Population size: 300
- Selection in population: 2/3 (200)
- Global mutation rate: 0.5
- Crossover rate: 0.8
- Selection in Pareto archive (elitism): 0.5
- Minimal number of generations: 300

The stopping criterion used is the nonamelioration during 10 generations, once the minimal number of generations has been overpassed.

Regarding the technical aspects, the used clustered machine comprised six workstations with Intel Pentium 4 3 GHz and 512 MB main memory.

13.6.3 Selecting Best Parameters

To select the best migration policy, we must answer to the questions of when and how many solutions should have to be sent by island. Therefore, these two parameters have been specifically studied.

13.6.3.1 Answer to the Question "How Many"
The number of solutions sent by an island will be a proportion of the Pareto archive of this island. The tested proportions are 2, 7, 10, 20, and 50%.

Ten executions with each values have been executed. Results are reported in Table 13.2. Each configuration is compared with all the others. Information about the average of the contribution is given.

Figure 13.11 allows to compare each configuration two by two. We recall that a contribution greater than 0.5 indicates an improvement of the Pareto front. We can

TABLE 13.2 Comparison of Several "How Many" Scenarios: Contribution

	Average Contribution				
	2%	7%	10%	20%	50%
2%	—	0.47	0.47	0.51	0.51
7%	0.53	—	0.48	0.54	0.54
10%	0.53	0.52	—	0.54	0.56
20%	0.49	0.46	0.46	—	0.50
50%	0.49	0.46	0.44	0.50	—

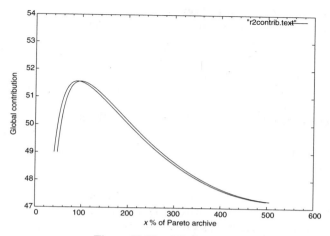

Figure 13.11   "How many."

easily see here that the configuration 10% has all its contributions greater than 0.5. It seems to be the best configuration tested.

This may be confirmed by Figure 13.12, which represents for a given configuration, the global average contribution regarding all the other configurations. We can see that the 10% configuration has the best value. Another important remark is that the figure shows that very few or too much exchanges will not lead to a good cooperation and will not produce a very efficient front. Hence, it seems important to choose a medium value for the number of solutions sent by islands. For the rest of the experiments, we will use the value of 10% of the local Pareto archive.

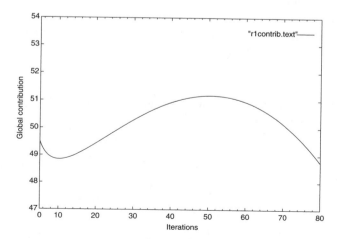

Figure 13.12   "When."

13.6.3.2 Answer to the Question "When" The other very important question is "when" do islands have to exchange their Pareto solutions. To determine the best configuration, several tests have been realized with different occurences. The different versions tested are every 5 iterations, every 10 iterations, every 25 iterations, every 50 iterations, and every 80 iterations.

This parameter has a great importance as it allows to let islands evolving independantly or to cooperate very often. Once again, 10 executions of each configurations have been tested and results report different statistics about comparisons between the configurations.

Table 13.3 indicates the two by two contributions. We can see again that a parameter (here 50 generations) seems to overpass all the other, as its contribution is always greater than 0.5.

This may also be visualized in Figure 13.12, where the global average contribution is represented. Again, we can see that exchanging information very often or very rarely does not help the cooperation. It seems to be important to let each island evolving alone, while receiving regularly good individuals from its neighbor.

13.6.4 Parallel vs Nonparallel

To assess the contribution of the cooperation, three different configurations have been tested (Fig. 13.13):

- *Conf 1.* A single GA, with a population size of 3000 individuals (all the other parameters are the default parameters). The Pareto archive of the GA is the final archive.
- *Conf 2.* Ten independent GAs with a population size of 300 individuals each (all the other parameters are the default parameters). The 10 GAs contribute to the final Pareto archive.
- *Conf 3.* Ten cooperative GAs with a population size of 300 individuals each. The migration policy is to send 10% individuals every 50 iterations. The 10 GAs contribute to the final Pareto archive.

TABLE 13.3   Comparison of Several "When" Scenarios: Contribution

	Average Contribution				
	5%	10%	25%	50%	80%
5%	—	0.50	0.48	0.46	0.54
10%	0.50	—	0.47	0.44	0.50
25%	0.52	0.53	—	0.46	0.49
50%	0.54	0.56	0.54	—	0.52
80%	0.46	0.50	0.51	0.48	—

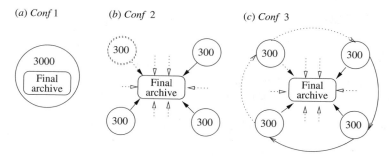

Figure 13.13 The three configurations tested.

These configurations have been chosen to give to each configuration the same global population size.

Table 13.4 indicates the two by two contributions of the different configurations tested. With this table, it is clear that Conf 3 is the best configuration. In fact, we can remark that Conf 3 > Conf 2 > Conf 1. This first shows that the cooperation allows to improve the quality of the Pareto front obtained. Moreover, these results show that as the Conf 2 is better than the Conf 1, this problem requires a lot of diversity search, which may be difficult to achieve with a single GA.

The need of diversity may be confirmed by Table 13.5, which indicates the two by two entropies of the different configurations. Again, this table shows that the Pareto fronts obtained with Conf 3 are the most diversified fronts.

Hence, the cooperation allows to obtain efficient and diversified pareto fronts, which was the initial objective of the study.

TABLE 13.4   Comparison of the Different Configurations: Contribution

	Average Contribution		
	Conf 1	Conf 2	Conf 3
Conf 1	—	0.39	0.28
Conf 2	0.61	—	0.40
Conf 3	0.72	0.60	—

TABLE 13.5   Comparison of the Different Configurations: Entropy

	Average Entropy		
	Conf 1	Conf 2	Conf 3
Conf 1	—	0.56	0.50
Conf 2	0.69	—	0.53
Conf 3	0.71	0.70	—

13.7 CONCLUSION

This chapter propose to deal with a very challenging problem: Knowledge discovery in microarray experiments data. The analysis of this problem lead us to choose the rule mining model to extract interesting knowledge. However, this interesting knowledge discovery task is a difficult problem and we adopt an optimization approach to get solutions.

As we have explained in this chapter, the search space of this rule mining problem is very large and only heuristics are able to cope with it. Moreover, while defining the optimization criterion, the necessity of defining a multi-objective model appeared, which still make the problem more complex.

Hence, we develop an evolutionary approach and propose a cooperative model, based on parallel GAs, which evolve independently and exchange information.

This parallel model has been tested to determine the best parameter configuration. This model has also been compared with noncooperative approaches and results show the contribution of the cooperation.

REFERENCES

1. D. P. Berrar, W. Dubitzky, and M. Granzow, *A Practical Approach to Microarray Data Analysis*, Kluwer Academic Publishers, 2003.

2. P. O. Brown and D. Botstein. Exploring the new world of the genome with DNA microarrays, *Nat. Genet. Suppl.*, 21, 33–37 (1999).

3. D. J. Duggan, M. Bittner, Y. Chen, P. Meltzer, and J. M. Trent, Expression profiling using cDNA microarrays, *Nat. Genet. Suppl.*, 21, 10–14 (1999).

4. P. T. Spellman, G. Sherlock, and M. Q. Zhang, Comprehensive identification of cell cycle-regulated genes of the yeast saccharomyces cerevisiae by microarray hybridization, *Mol. Biol. Cell*, 9, 3273–3297 (1998).

5. M. A. Behr, M. A. Wilson, and W. P. Gill, Comparative genomics of beg vaccines by whole-genome DNA microarray, *Science*, 284, 1520–1523 (1999).

6. M. J. Marton, J. L. DeRisi, and H. A. Bennett, Drug target validation and identification of secondary drug target effects using DNA microarrays, *Nat. Genet.*, 4, 1293–1301 (1998).

7. J. G. Hacia, L. C. Brody, M. S. Chee, S. P. Fodor, and F. S. Collins, Detection of heterozygous mutations in brcal using high density oligonucleotide arrays and two-colour fluorescence analysis, *Nat. Med.*, 14, 441–447 (1996).

8. M. B. Eisen, P. T. Spellman, P. O. Brown, and D. Botstein, Cluster analysis and display of genome-wide expression patterns, *Proc. Natl. Acad. Sci.*, 95 (25), 14863–14868 (1998).

9. G. Kurra, W. Niu, and R. Bhatnagar, Mining Microarray Expression Data for Classifier Gene-Cores, in *Proceedings of BIOKDD 01*, 2001.

10. N. Friedman, M. Linial, I. Nachman, and D. Peér, Using Bayesian Networks to Analyze Expression Data, in *Proceedings of the Fourth Annual International Conferenceon on Computational Molecular Biology (RECOMB-2000)*, 2000.

11. K. Aas, Microarray data mining: a survey, Technical report SAMBA/02/01, Norsk Regnesentral/Norwegian Computing Center, January, 2001.

12. R. Agrawal and R. Srikant, Fast Algorithms for Mining Association Rules, in *Proceedings of the 20th International Conference on Very Large Databases*, Santiago, Chile, September, 1994.

13. A. Freitas, On rule interestingness measures, *Knowledge-Based Syst. J.*, 1999.

14. P.-N. Tan, V. Kumar, and J. Srivastava, Selecting the Right Interestingness Measure for Association Patterns, in *Proceedings of the Eight ACM SIGKDD Conference*, Edmonton, Canada, 2002.

15. R. Hilderman and H. Hamilton, Knowledge discovery and interestingness measures: a survey, technical report cs 99-04, Technical report, Department of Computer Science, University of Regina, October, 1999.

16. M. Khabzaoui, C. Dhaenens, A. N'Guessan, and E.-G. Talbi, Etude exploratoire des critères de qualité des règies d'association en datamining, in *Journées Françaises de Statistique*, 2003, pp. 583–587.

17. M. Khabzaoui, C. Dhaenens, and E.-G. Talbi, A Multicriteria Genetic Algorithm to Analyze DNA Microarray Data, in *Congress on Evolutionary Computation (CEC)*, Vol II, Portland, USA, IEEE Service center, June, 2004, pp. 1874–1881.

18. P. Smyth and R. M. Goodman, Rule Induction Using Information Theory, in G. Piatetsky-Shapiro and J. Frawley, *Knowledge Discovery in Databases*, AAAI/MIT Press, 1991, pp. 159–176.

19. K. Wang, S. H. W. Tay, and B. Liu, Interestingness-Based Interval Merger for Numeric Association Rules, in R. Agrawal, P. E. Stolorz, and G. Piatetsky-Shapiro, Eds., in *Proceedings of Fourth International Conference Knowledge Discovery and Data Mining, KDD*, AAAI Press, New York, USA, 1998, pp. 121–128.

20. D. L. A. Araujo, H. S. Lopes, and A. A. Freitas, A Parallel Genetic Algorithm for Rule Discovery in Large Databases, in *Proceedings of 1999 IEEE Systems, Man and Cybernetics Conference*, Vol. III, Tokyo, Japan, October, 1999, pp. 940–945.

21. P. Kotala, P. Zhou, S. Mudivarthy, W. Perrizo, and E. Deckard, Gene Expression Profiling of DNA Microarray Data Using Peano Count Trees, in *Online Proceedings of the First Virtual Conference on Genomics and Bioinformatics, URL: http://midas-10.cs.ndsu.nodak.edu/bio/*, October, 2001.

22. D. E. Goldberg, *Genetic Algorithms — in Search, Optimization and Machine Learning*, Addison-Wesley Publishing Company, 1989.

23. L. Jourdan, C. Dhaenens, and E. G. Talbi, Rules Extraction in Linkage Disequilibrium Mapping with an Adaptive Genetic Algorithm, in *Proceedings of the European Conference on Computational Biology (ECCB '03)*, 2003, pp. 29–31.

24. T. P. Hong, H. Wang, and W. Chen, Simultaneously applying multiple mutation operators in genetic algorithms, *J. Heuristics*, 6, 439–455 (2000).

25. C. M. Fonseca and P. J. Fleming, An overview of evolutionary algorithms in multiobjective optimization, *Evol. Comput.*, 3 (1), 1–16 (1995).

26. D. A. van Veldhuizen and G. B. Lamont, On Measuring Multiobjective Evolutionary Algorithm Performance, in *In 2000 Congress on Evolutionary Computation*, Piscataway, New Jersey, Vol. 1, July, 2000, pp. 204–211.

27. A. Jaszkiewicz, On the performance of multiple objective genetic local search on the 0/1 knapsack problem, a comparative experiment, Technical report RA-002/2000, Institute of Computing Science, Poznan University of Technology, Poznan, Poland, July, 2000.

28. J. D. Knowles, D. W. Corne, and M. J. Oates, On the Assessment of Multiobjective Approaches to the Adaptive Distributed Database Management Problem, in *Proceedings*

of the Sixth International Conference on Parallel Problem Solving from Nature (PPSN VI), September, 2000, pp. 869–878.

29. E. Zitzler and L. Thiele, Multiobjective evolutionary algorithms: a comparative case study and the strength pareto approach, *IEEE Trans. Evol. Comput.*, 3(4): 257–271 (Nov), (1999).

30. M. Basseur, F. Seynhaeve, and E.-G. Talbi, Design of multi-objective evolutionary algorithms: application to the flow-shop scheduling problem, in *Congress on Evolutionary Computation CEC'02*, Honolulu, USA, 2002, pp. 1151–1156.

PART III

PHYLOGENETICS

CHAPTER 14

Parallel and Distributed Computation of Large Phylogenetic Trees

ALEXANDROS STAMATAKIS

The computation of ever larger as well as more accurate phylogenetic trees with the ultimate goal to compute the "tree of life" represents one of the grand challenges in high performance computing (HPC) bioinformatics. Statistical methods of phylogenetic analysis such as Maximum Likelihood and Bayesian inference have proved to be the most accurate models for evolutionary tree reconstruction. Unfortunately, the size of trees which can be computed in reasonable time is limited by the severe computational cost induced by these methods. There exist two orthogonal research directions to overcome this challenging computational burden: First, the development of novel, faster, and more accurate heuristic algorithms. Second, the application of high performance computing techniques, the deployment of supercomputers, and Grid-computing to provide the required computational power, mainly in terms of CPU hours. This Chapter initially provides an introduction to the computational aspects of the Maximum Likelihood model and reviews some popular state-of-the art phylogeny programs. It then outlines the algorithmic and technical development cycle of an HPC phylogeny program by example of RAxML-III. Finally, future research directions in the field are addressed.

14.1 INTRODUCTION

Phylogenetic (evolutionary) trees are used to represent the evolutionary history of a set of n organisms, which are often also called taxa within this context. A multiple alignment of a, in a biological context, suitable small region of their DNA or protein sequences can be used as input for the computation of such phylogenetic trees. Note that a high-quality multiple alignment of the organisms is a necessary prerequisite to conduct a phylogenetic analysis: The quality of the evolutionary tree can only be as good as the quality of the multiple alignment.

Parallel Computing for Bioinformatics and Computational Biology, Edited by Albert Y. Zomaya
Copyright © 2006 John Wiley & Sons, Inc.

In a computational context, phylogenetic trees are usually strictly bifurcating (binary) unrooted trees. The organisms of the alignment are located at the tips (leaves) of such a tree, whereas the inner nodes represent extinct common ancestors. The branches of the tree represent the time that was required for the mutation of one species into another, new, one. An example for the evolutionary tree of the monkeys and the *Homo sapiens* is provided in Figure 14.1.

The inference of phylogenies with computational methods has many important applications in medical and biological researches such as drug discovery and conservation biology. A paper by Bader et al. [1] addresses potential industrial applications of evolutionary tree inference and contains numerous useful references to important biological results obtained by phylogenetic analyses.

Owing to the rapid growth of available sequence data over the last years and the constant improvement of multiple alignment methods it has now become feasible to compute very large trees, which comprise more than 1000 organisms. The computation of the tree-of-life containing representatives of all living beings on Earth is considered to be one of the grand challenges in bioinformatics.

The main focus of this chapter is on algorithmic as well as technical problems and solutions for the computation of large trees (containing ≥ 1000 sequences) based on statistic models of sequence evolution.

The most fundamental algorithmic problem computational phylogeny faces consists in the immense amount of potential alternative tree topologies. This number

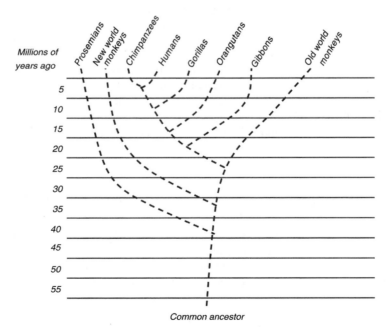

Figure 14.1   Phylogenetic tree representing the evolutionary relationship between monkeys and *Homo sapiens*.

grows exponentially with the number of sequences n, for example, for $n = 50$ organisms, there already exist 2.84×10^{76} alternative topologies; a number almost as large as the number of atoms in the Universe ($\approx 10^{80}$). Thus, given some, biologically meaningful, optimality criterion for evaluating all alternative configurations (topologies) to search for the best tree, one can quickly assume that the problem might be NP-hard. In fact, this has been already demonstrated for the general version of the *perfect phylogeny* problem [2] and *maximum parsimony* (MP) [3]. The *maximum likelihood* (ML) criterion [4] is also believed to be NP-hard, although this could not be demonstrated so far because of the significantly superior mathematical complexity of the model which is not discrete.

Another important aspect for the design of heuristic tree searches consists in the very high degree of accuracy (difference to the score of the optimal or best-known solution), which is required to obtain reasonable biological results. Although an accuracy of 90% is considered to be a "good" value for heuristics designed to solve other NP-hard optimization problems, for example, the traveling salesman problem, recent results suggest that phylogenetic analyses require an accuracy $\geq 99.99\%$, particularly for large trees [5]. This observation yields the whole field more difficult and challenging.

When comparing the various optimality criteria which have been devised for phylogenetic trees, one can observe a *trade-off* between speed and quality. This means that a phylogenetic analysis conducted with an elaborate model such as ML requires significantly more time but yields trees with superior accuracy than, for example, *neighbor joining* (NJ) [6] or MP [7, 8]. However, because of the higher accuracy, it is desirable to infer large and complex trees with ML.

Within this context, it is important to emphasize that the design of ML programs is primarily an *algorithmic discipline*, because of the gigantesque number of alternative tree topologies and the high computational cost of the likelihood function (Section 14.2). Thus, progress in the field has been attained mainly by algorithmic improvements rather than by brute force allocation of all available computational resources. As an example, consider the performance of parallel fastDNAml [9] (state-of-the-art parallel ML program in 2001) and RAxML-III [10] (randomized accelerated ML, one of the fastest sequential ML programs in 2004) on a 1000-organisms alignment: For this large alignment, parallel fastDNAml consumed approximately 9000 accumulated CPU hours on a Linux PC cluster in contrast to less than 20 hours required by RAxML-III on a single processor. In addition, the likelihood of the tree computed by RAxML-III was significantly better than the likelihood score obtained by parallel fastDNAml.

Therefore, a reasonable approach to design ML phylogeny programs for high-performance computing consists in adapting an iterative development cycle as outlined in Figure 14.2. Consequently, this chapter covers one typical iteration of this development process by example of algorithmic and technical improvements implemented in RAxML-III.

The remainder of this chapter is organized as follows. Section 14.2 provides a brief introduction to the ML method and describes the abstract computational problems,

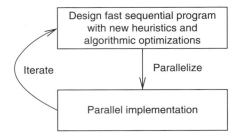

Figure 14.2   High performance ML phylogeny program development cycle.

which arise at the computation of the likelihood score for one single tree topology. Section 14.3 gives an overview over the most popular state-of-the-art sequential and parallel ML programs. Sections 14.4 and 14.5 illustrate the aforementioned stages of the ML program development cycle and describe algorithmic and technical enhancements of RAxML-III. Finally, Section 14.6 addresses promising technical and algorithmic developments and solutions, which could enable the computation of larger and more accurate trees in the near future.

14.2   MAXIMUM LIKELIHOOD

This section does not intend to provide a detailed introduction to ML for phylogenetic trees. The goal is to give the reader a notion of the complexity and amount of arithmetic operations required to compute the ML score for one *single* tree topology, that is, to answer the question: Where do all the floating point operations (FLOPs) come from?

The seminal paper by Felsenstein [4] actually introduces the application of ML to phylogenetic trees and the comprehensive and readable chapter by Swofford et al. [11] provide detailed descriptions of the mathematical background.

To calculate the likelihood of a tree topology with given branch lengths, one requires a probabilistic model of nucleotide substitution $P_{ij}(t)$, which allows for computing the probability P that a nucleotide i mutates to another nucleotide j within time t (branch length). The model for DNA data must therefore provide substitution probabilities for all possible 16 transitions:

A|C|G|T -> A|C|G|T

To significantly reduce the mathematical complexity of the overall method, the model of nucleotide substitution must be time reversible [4], that is, the evolutionary process has to be identic if followed forward or backward in time. Essentially, this means that the maximum number of possible transition types in the general time reversible model of nucleotide substitution (GTR [12, 13]) is reduced to 10 due to required symmetries. The less general time-reversible models of nucleotide substitution such as the Jukes–Cantor (JC69 [14]) or Hasegawa–Kishino–Yano (HKY85 [15]) model can be derived from GTR by further restriction of possible transition types. It is

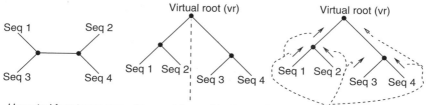

Figure 14.3   Computation of the likelihood vectors of four-taxon tree.

important to note that there also exists a trade-off between speed and quality among substitution models. The simple JC69 model which offers only one single transition type requires significantly less FLOPs to compute $P_{ij}(t)$ than GTR, which is the most complex and accurate one.

Given the model of nucleotide substitution and a tree topology with branch lengths where the data (the individual sequences of the multiple alignment) is located at the tips, one can proceed with the computation of the likelihood score for that tree. To compute the likelihood, a *virtual root* (vr) has to be placed into an *arbitrary* branch of the tree to calculate/update the individual entries of each *likelihood vector* with length n (alignment length) in the tree bottom-up, that is, starting at the tips and moving towards vr. It is important to note that if the model of nucleotide substitution is time reversible, the likelihood of the tree is identic irrespective of where vr is placed. After having updated all likelihood vectors, the vectors to the right and left of vr can be used to compute the overall likelihood of the tree. The process of rooting and updating the likelihood vectors for a four-taxon tree is outlined in Figure 14.3.

To understand how the individual likelihood vectors are updated, consider a subtree rooted at node p with immediate descendants r and q and likelihood vectors l_p, l_q, and l_r respectively. When the likelihood vectors l_q and l_r have been computed, the entries of l_p can be calculated, in an extremely simplified manner, as outlined by the pseudocode subsequently and in Figure 14.4:

```
for (i = 0; i < n; i++)
    l_p[i] = f(g(l_q[i], b_pq), g(l_r[i], b_pr));
```

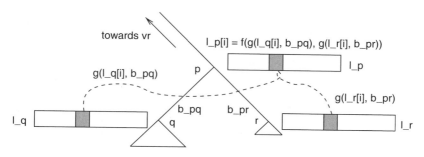

Figure 14.4   Updating the likelihood vector of node p at position i.

where `f()` is a simple function, that is, requires just a few FLOPs, to combine the values of `g(l_q[i], b_pq)` and `g(l_r[i], b_pr)`. The `g()` function, however, is more complex and computationally intensive as it contains the evaluation of $P_{ij}(t)$. The parameter t corresponds to the branch lengths `b_pq` and `b_pr` respectively. Note that the `for-loop` can easily be parallelized on a fine-grained level as entries `l_p[i]` and `l_p[i + 1]` can be computed independently (Section 14.6).

Up to this point, it has been described how to compute the likelihood of a tree given some arbitrary branch lengths. However, to obtain the ML value for a given tree topology, the length of all branches in the tree has to be optimized. As the likelihood of the tree is not altered by distinct rootings of the tree, the virtual root can be subsequently placed into all branches of the tree. Each branch can then be individually optimized to improve the likelihood value of the entire tree. In general, depending on the implementation, this process is continued until no further branch length alteration yields an improved likelihood score. Branch length optimization can be regarded as maximization of a one-parameter function lh(t), where lh is the phylogenetic likelihood function and t the branch length.

Some of the most commonly used optimization methods are, for example, the Newton–Raphson method in fastDNAml [16] or Brent's rule in PHYML [7]. Note that branch length optimization is not as trivial as it appears because multiple local optima for distinct branch length configurations might exist [17].

Typically, the two basic operations, computation of the likelihood value and optimization of the branch lengths, require $\approx$90% of the complete execution time of every ML program. Thus, an acceleration of these functions on a technical level by optimization of the C code and the memory access behavior or on an algorithmic level by reuse of previously computed values is very important.

A technically extremely efficient implementation of the likelihood function has been coded in fastDNAml. The subtree equality vector method [18] represents an algorithmic optimization of the likelihood function which exploits alignment pattern equalities to avoid a substantial amount of re-computations of `f()` and `g()`.

However, the perhaps most important question still remains to be answered: How to efficiently search for a near-optimal tree topology in the vast search space? The following Sections 14.3 and 14.4 address this problem.

14.3   STATE-OF-THE-ART ML PROGRAMS

Heuristic search algorithms for ML analyses can be roughly divided into two categories: *progressive algorithms* and *global algorithms*.

Progressive algorithms build the tree by progressively inserting the organisms into the tree and eventually applying some intermediate optimizations. A well-known representative is the stepwise addition algorithm [4] by Joe Felsenstein, which is also used with some modifications in fastDNAml.

Global algorithms usually start with a comprehensive tree already containing all organisms, which can either be a random tree or a tree obtained by a simpler method such as NJ or MP. The tree is then optimized by application of a standard or random pattern of topological alterations to find a topology with a better likelihood score. The most common tree alteration techniques are subtree rearrangements (Section 14.4), nearest-neighbor interchange (NNI) and tree bisection reconnection (TBR). The NNI and TBR operations are well outlined in Ref. [11]. Except RAxML-III which uses MP starting trees, all other global optimization algorithms either use random or NJ starting trees.

In addition, the various programs for ML phylogenetic inference can be further classified by the strategy deployed to find improved trees:

Hill-Climbing: Many implementations such as PAUP* [19], PHYML [7], RAxML-III, and fastDNAml [16] deploy strict hill-climbing approaches, that is, searches which do not carry out any backward steps, that is, accept trees with inferior likelihood values. Those algorithms are usually very fast but hill-climbing searches face a potentially high risk of getting trapped in local maxima. At present, PHYML and RAxML-III represent the fastest and partially most accurate programs available. For fastDNAml, there also exist a parallel MPI-based [9] and a shared-memory parallelization [20]. Finally, some efforts are undertaken lately to implement a distributed version of fastDNAml [21] and to design a general distributed JAVA-based framework for phylogeny computations called DPRml [22]. Despite the popularity of parallel fastDNAml, one should be aware of the fact that the original sequential fastDNAml algorithm dates back to the year 1994 and is extremely slow in respect to recent algorithmic developments.

Genetic Algorithms: To avoid local optima to some extent, genetic search algorithms have recently been proposed [23, 24], which maintain a collection (population) of trees that is altered and recombined at each step of the algorithm. Genetic algorithms tend, however, to be slower than hill-climbing algorithms. The program MetaPIGA [25] appears to be the most efficient implementation of a genetic search algorithm currently available [7]. Brauer et al. [26] have describe, a parallel MPI-based implementation of their genetic algorithm.

Stochastic Optimization: The simulated annealing technique represents another alternative search method, which explicitly allows for backward steps. There already exists a simulated annealing algorithm for ML phylogenetic tree search [27], which has not become very popular, however. Generally speaking, simulated annealing is the slowest of the three approaches.

One of the main advantages of simulated annealing and genetic algorithms is that they create a collection (population) of almost equally good trees. This set of trees can be used to approximate the posterior probabilities for all individual clades of the phylogenetic tree.

Some recent reviews and articles [7, 8, 10] contain detailed comparative studies on the performance of ML programs.

Finally, Bayesian phylogenetic inference which is closely related to ML has recently received much attention. Owing to space limitations, the problems and advantages of this method cannot be discussed in this chapter. A review by Holder and Lewis [28] provides an overview over differences between ML and Bayesian inference. Furthermore, a paper by Huelsenbeck et al. [29] discusses potential advantages and pitfalls of this approach.

14.4   ALGORITHMIC SOLUTIONS IN RAxML-III

The heuristics of RAxML-III belong to the aforementioned class of global algorithms, which optimize the likelihood of a starting tree already comprising all sequences. In contrast to other programs, RAxML-III starts by building an initial parsimony tree with dnapars from Felsenstein's PHYLIP package [30] for two reasons.

First, parsimony is related to ML under simple evolutionary models [31], such that one can expect to obtain a starting tree with a relatively good likelihood value when compared with random or NJ starting trees. For example, a 500-taxon MP starting tree already showed a better likelihood than the final tree of PHYML [32].

Secondly, dnapars uses stepwise addition [4] for tree building and is relatively fast. The stepwise addition algorithm enables the construction of distinct starting trees by using a randomized input sequence order. Thus, RAxML-III can be executed several times with different starting trees and thereby compute a set of distinct final trees. This set of final trees can be used to build a consensus tree and augment confidence into the final result because RAxML-III explores the search space from different starting points. To speed up computations, some optimization steps have been removed from dnapars.

The tree optimization process represents the second and most important part of the heuristics. RAxML-III performs standard subtree rearrangements by subsequently removing all possible subtrees from the current best tree t_{best} and re-inserting them into neighboring branches up to a specified distance of nodes. RAxML-III inherited this optimization strategy from fastDNAml. One rearrangement step in fastDNAml consists of moving all subtrees within the current best tree by the minimum up to the maximum distance of nodes specified (lower/upper rearrangement setting). This process is outlined for a single subtree (ST5) and a distance of 1 in Figure 14.5 and for a distance of 2 in Figure 14.6 (not all possible moves are shown). In fastDNAml, the likelihood of each thereby generated topology is evaluated by exhaustive branch length optimizations. If one of those alternative topologies improves the likelihood, t_{best} is updated accordingly and once again all possible subtrees are rearranged within t_{best}. This process of rearrangement steps is repeated until no better topology is found.

The implementation of the rearrangement process in RAxML-III differs in two major points: In fastDNAml, after each insertion of a subtree into an alternative branch, the branch lengths of the entire tree are optimized. As depicted in Figure 14.5

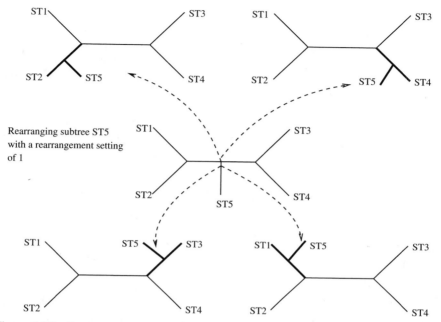

Figure 14.5 Rearrangements traversing one node for subtree ST5, branches which are optimized by RAxML-III are indicated by bold lines.

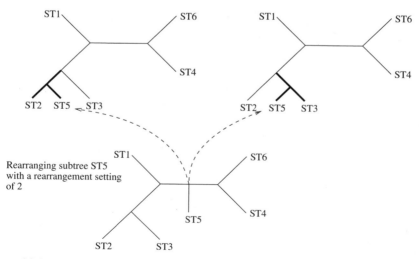

Figure 14.6 Example rearrangements traversing two nodes for subtree ST5, branches which are optimized by RAxML-III are indicated by bold lines.

with bold lines, RAxML-III only optimizes the three local branches adjacent to the insertion point either analytically (fast) or by the Newton–Raphson method (slower) before computing its likelihood value. As the likelihood of the tree strongly depends on the topology per se, this fast prescoring can be used to establish a small list of potential alternative trees, which are very likely to improve the score of t_{best}. RAxML-III uses a list of size 20 to store the best 20 trees obtained during one rearrangement step. This list size proves to be a practical value in terms of speed and thoroughness of the search [10]. After completion of one rearrangement step, the algorithm performs global branch length optimizations only on those 20 best topologies. Owing to the capability to analyze significantly more alternative and diverse topologies in less time, a higher upper rearrangements setting can be used, for example, 5 or 10 which results in significantly improved final trees.

Another important change concerning particularly the initial optimization phase, that is, the first three to four rearrangement steps, consists in the subsequent application of topological improvements during one rearrangement step. During the insertion of one specific subtree into an alternative branch, a topology with a better likelihood is encountered; this tree is kept immediately and all subsequent subtree rearrangements of the current step are performed on the improved topology. This mechanism allows for rapid initial optimization of random starting trees [32].

The exact implementation of the RAxML-III algorithm is indicated in the C-like pseudocode subsequently. The algorithm is passed the user/parsimony starting `tree` `t`, the initial rearrangement setting `rStart` (default: 5), and the maximum rearrangement setting `rMax` (default: 21). Initially, the rearrangement stepwidth ranges from `rL = 1 to rU = rStart`. Fast analytical local branch length optimization `a` is turned off when functions `rearr($\cdots$)`, which actually performs the rearrangements, and `optimizeList20()` fail to yield an improved tree for the first time. As long as the tree does not improve the lower and upper rearrangement parameters `rL`, `rU` are incremented by `rStart`. The program terminates when the upper rearrangement setting is greater or equal to the maximum rearrangement setting, that is, `rU >= rMax`.

Comparative performance studies of the sequential RAxML-III algorithm can be found in Ref. [10]. The following section describes how this algorithm can be parallelized.

```
RAxML-III(tree t, int rStart, int rMax)
{
  int rL, rU;
  boolean a = TRUE;
  boolean impr = TRUE;
  while(TRUE)
    {
      if(impr)
        {
          rL = 1;
          rU = rStart;
```

```
        rearr(t, rL, rU, a);
      }
    else
      {
       if(!a)
         {
          a = FALSE;
          rL = 1;
          rU = rStart;
         }
       else
         {
          rL += rStart;
          rU += rStart;
         }
       if(rU < rMax)
         rearr(t, rL, rU, a);
       else
         goto end;
      }
    impr = optimizeList20();
   }
 end:
}
```

14.5   HPC SOLUTIONS IN RAxML-III

This section describes the second step of the development cycle: the parallel and distributed implementations of RAxML-III.

14.5.1   Parallel RAxML-III

The parallel implementation is based on a simple master–worker architecture and consists of two phases.

In phase I, the master distributes the alignment file to all worker processes if no common file system is available, otherwise it is read directly from the file. Thereafter, each worker independently computes a randomized parsimony starting tree and sends it to the master process. Alternatively, it is also possible to start the program directly in phase II by specifying a starting tree file name in the command line.

In phase II, the master initiates the optimization process for the best parsimony or specified starting tree. Owing to the high speed of a single topology evaluation of a specific subtree rearrangement by function `rearrangeSubtree()` and the high communication cost, it is not feasible to distribute work by single topologies as, for example, in parallel fastDNAml. Another important argument for a parallelization based upon whole subtrees is that only in this way likelihood vectors at nodes can be reused efficiently within a slightly altered tree. Therefore, work is distributed by sending the subtree ID (of the subtree to be rearranged) along with the current best topology t_best to each worker.

The sequential and parallel implementation of RAxML on the master-side is outlined in the pseudocode of function rearr(), which actually executes subtree rearrangements. Each worker simply executes function rearrangeSubtree().

```
void rearr(tree t_best, int rL, int rU, boolean a)
{
 boolean impr;
 worker w;
 for(i = 2; i < #species * 2 - 1; i++){
    if(sequential){
       impr = rearrangeSubtree(t_best, i, rL, rU, a);
       if(impr) applySubsequent(t_best, i);
    }
    if(parallel){
       if(w = workerAvailable)
          sendJob(w, t_best, i);
       else putInWorkQueue(i);
    }
 }
 if(parallel){
    while(notAllTreesReceived){
       w = receiveTree(w_tree);
       if(likelihood(w_tree) > likelihood(t_best))
          t_best = w_tree;
       if(notAllTreesSent)
          sendJob(w, t_best, nextInWorkQueue());
    }
 }
}
```

In the sequential case, rearrangements are applied to each individual subtree i. If the tree improves through this subtree rearrangement, t_best is updated accordingly, that is, subsequent topological improvements are applied. In the parallel case, subtree IDs are stored in a work queue. Obviously, the subsequent application of topological improvements during one rearrangement step [1 invocation of rearr()] is closely coupled. Therefore, the algorithm is slightly modified to break up this dependency according to the following observation: Subsequent improved topologies occur only during the first three to four rearrangement steps (initial optimization phase).

After the initial optimization phase, likelihood improvements are achieved only by function `optimizeList20()` (Section 14.4). This phase requires the largest amount of computation time, especially with huge alignments ($\approx$80% of execution time).

Thus, only one single subtree ID $i = 2, \ldots,$ `#species * 2 - 1` is sent along with the current best tree `t_best` to each worker for rearrangements during the initial optimization phase. Each worker returns the best tree `w_tree` obtained by rearranging subtree i within `t_best` to the master. If `w_tree` has a better likelihood than `t_best` at the master, `t_best = w_tree` is set and the updated best tree is distributed to each worker along with the following work request. The program assumes that the initial optimization phase IIa is terminated if no subsequently improved topology has been encountered during the last three rearrangement steps.

In the final optimization phase IIb, communication costs are reduced and granularity is increased by generating only 5 * #workers jobs (subtree ID spans). Finally, irrespective of the current optimization phase, the best 20 topologies (or #workers topologies if #workers > 20) computed by each worker during one rearrangement step are stored in a local worker tree list. When all `#species * 2 - 3` subtree rearrangements of `rearr()` have been completed, each worker sends its tree list to the master. The master process merges the lists and redistributes the 20 (#workers) best tree topologies to the workers for branch length optimization. When all topologies have been globally optimized, the master starts the next iteration of function `RAxML-III()` (Section 14.4).

The program flow of the parallel algorithm is outlined in Figure 14.7. Owing to the required changes to the algorithm, the parallel program is nondeterministic, as final output depends on the number of workers as well as on the arrival sequence of results for runs with equal numbers of workers, during the initial optimization phase IIa. This is due to the altered implementation of the subsequent application of topological improvements during the initial rearrangement steps, which leads to a traversal of search space on different paths. However, this solution represents a feasible and efficient approach both in terms of attained speedup values and final tree likelihood values. A recently published paper [33] on parallel RAxML-III reports on parallel program performance and describes the, to the best of the author's knowledge, largest ML inference to date for a multiple alignment of 10,000 sequences.

14.5.2 Distributed RAxML-III

The motivation to build a distributed seti@home-like [34] code is driven by the computation time requirements for trees containing more than 1000 organisms and by the desire to provide inexpensive solutions for this problem, which do not require supercomputers.

The main design principle of the distributed code is to reduce communication costs as far as possible and accept potentially worse speedup values than achieved with the parallel implementation. The algorithm of the http-based implementation is similar to the parallel program.

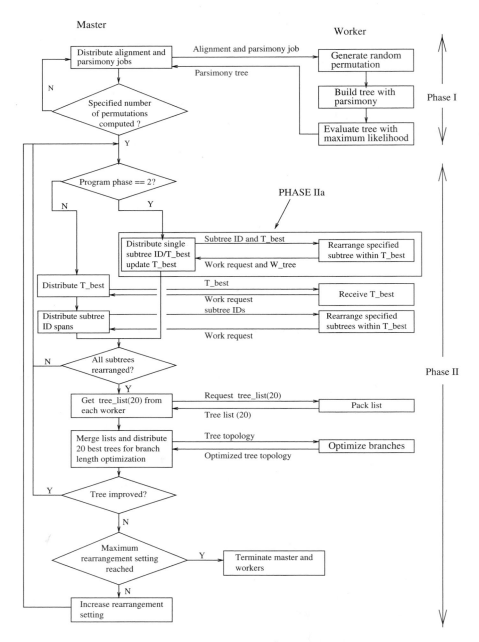

Figure 14.7 Parallel program flow of RAxML-III.

Initially, a compressed (zipped) alignment file is transferred to all workers, which start with the computation of a local parsimony starting tree. The parsimony tree is then returned to the master as in the parallel program.

However, the parallel and distributed algorithms differ in two important aspects which have a positive impact on communication costs.

First, RAxML@home does not implement phase IIa but only phase IIb of the parallel algorithm, to avoid frequent communication and frequent exchange of tree topologies between master and workers.

Secondly, the lists containing the 20 best trees, irrespective of the number of workers, are optimized locally at the workers after completion of subtree rearrangements. The branch lengths of the trees in the list are optimized less exhaustively than in the sequential and parallel program. After this initial optimization, only the best local tree is thoroughly optimized and returned to the master.

This induces some computational overhead and a slower improvement rate of the likelihood during the initial optimization phase (phase IIa of the parallel program) but remains within acceptable limits.

A more detailed technical description of distributed RAxML-III can be found in Ref. [35].

14.6 FUTURE DEVELOPMENTS

Future developments cover a wide range of issues such as appropriate visualization tools for huge trees, further refinement of evolutionary models, as well as new algorithms and computer systems for the inference of huge trees. Despite the fact that visualization and modeling are very important issues, they cannot be discussed here as they are outside the scope of this chapter. Sanderson and Driskell [36] provide a more comprehensive review of the challenges for large phylogeny reconstruction.

Consequently, this final section covers only future algorithmic and technical developments of high performance phylogenetic inference.

14.6.1 Algorithmic Developments

The main goal of future algorithmic improvements is to compute better trees, that is, with higher accuracy, in less time than the currently fastest and most accurate programs. Given the at least quadratic complexity of search algorithms, one very evident idea, at least for a computer scientist, to further accelerate tree building algorithms consists in devising a divide-and-conquer approach.

In the concrete case, this means that the alignment has to be (intelligently) split up into overlapping subalignments. Thereafter, a subtree is inferred for each subalignment by application of some fast base method, for example, PHYML or RAxML-III. Finally, the subtrees are merged into a single comprehensive tree (also called supertree) by appropriate supertree methods. As the subtrees overlap, that is, share some common organisms, they provide information to the supertree method at which points they should be reconnected. Mostly, supertree methods will return a multifurcating (unresolved) tree, which must be transformed (resolved) to a strictly bifurcating tree. Although this method appears to be very simple and efficient, it faces some serious limitations.

First, apart from the family of DCMs (disk covering methods) [37–39] and an experimental (unpublished) tree-based alignment division method in RAxML-III, there exist practically no methods to intelligently divide alignments into subalignments.

Secondly, the optimal resolution of multifurcations represents a hard optimization problem [40] and requires numerous likelihood evaluations and optimizations in the supertree. However, those global tree evaluations and optimizations should be avoided by the divide-and-conquer approach due to the high computational cost.

To solve this problem, researchers have recently devised "iterative guide-tree approaches," which work in a similar way as the "classic" supertree approach. The idea of those approaches is to quickly calculate a comprehensive starting tree (initial guide-tree), for example, by using the NJ or MP and then iteratively improve the guide tree by optimization and reconstruction/reconnection of appropriately chosen sub-trees. The two most promising approaches are PhyNav (phylogenetic navigator) [41] and Rec-I-DCM3 (recursive iterative DCM3) [39].

Rec-I-DCM3 has so far only been tested for MP but shows very promising results in terms of speed and accuracy when compared with the fastest and most accurate MP methods available. An integration of fast ML base methods into Rec-I-DCM3 could yield substantial benefits.

PhyNav computes ML trees but the implementation of the likelihood function and the basic tree optimization method is comparatively inefficient. In a series of experiments with large real-world alignment data, PhyNav was significantly out-competed by RAxML-III in terms of execution time and final likelihood values. Therefore, the integration of this promising algorithmic concept into, for example, RAxML-III or PHYML could reveal the real potential of this method.

The computation of confidence values for large trees represents a quite distinct problem. Even if algorithms are developed, which allow for rapid and accurate computation of large phylogenetic trees, it will still be hard to conduct even 100 bootstrap analyses for a 10,000-taxon tree in the near future. Thus, methods are required, which are able to compute a large set of equally good trees with high score accuracy. The simulated annealing technique might serve as a solution because it explores a larger number of equally good trees and avoids local maxima. The key advantage is that only one single analysis of an alignment may be required to obtain reliable results in contrast to several independent analyses with standard hill-climbing techniques. Some initial (unpublished) experiments with RAxML-SA (RAxML simulated annealing) yielded encouraging results. In a series of experiments with real data alignments comprising 101 up to 1000 taxa RAxML-SA was not significantly slower than a single RAxML-III run. Note that for each alignment of this analysis, 10 distinct RAxML-III runs with randomized parsimony starting trees have been executed. In addition, RAxML-SA returned best-known trees, that is, with the best-known likelihood value, for the three large alignments of 500, 500, and 1000 taxa, respectively.

TABLE 14.1   Memory Consumption of RAxML-III, MrBayes, and PHYML for Large Data Sets

Program	1000 taxa	10,000 taxa
RAxML-III	200 MB	750 MB
PHYML	900 MB	8.8 GB
MrBayes	1.2 GB	Not available

14.6.2 Technical Developments

As mentioned in Section 14.1, currently, most of the research carried out in phylogenetics is very algorithmic and theoretical for good reasons. However, as phylogenetics come of age and computation of 5000 organism ML trees has become feasible, it is also important to consider technical aspects such as cache efficiency, memory consumption, and further technical optimizations of the codes.

An often underestimated problem concerning the computation of large trees is memory consumption. The general tendency in phylogenetics is that alignment sizes will grow in both dimensions, that is, number of organisms and number of base pairs. Yet already for alignments of 1000 and 10,000 taxa, PHYML and MrBayes [42] (the program for Bayesian phylogenetic analysis) showed a relatively high memory consumption when compared with RAxML-III as outlined in Table 14.1. (Data for MrBayes with the 10,000-taxon alignment is not available as the code could not be ported to a 64 bit architecture.)

Another relatively easy way to improve performance of ML programs and partially resolve memory problems at the same time consists in shared memory parallelizations. As already mentioned in Section 14.2, the compute-intensive for-loops which can typically be found in every ML program consume up to 90% of overall execution time. Owing to the absence of dependencies, they can easily and efficiently be parallelized using the shared memory paradigm. A parallelization of RAxML-III with OpenMP [43] (called RAxML-OpenMP) showed, however, that the speedup is extremely hardware dependent. Table 14.2 lists the speedup values measured for simulated 100-taxon alignments with lengths of 1000, 5000, 10,000, and 20,000 bp for a Quad-Opteron and Quad-Itanium2 processor.

The bad parallel performance on the Itanium2 processor is most probably due to the memory access architecture of the processor, which represents a significant

TABLE 14.2   Speedup of RAxML-OpenMP on Opteron and Itanium2 Architectures

Number of Base Pairs	Quad-Opteron	Quad-Itanium2
1,000	2.11	0.88
5,000	3.58	1.38
10,000	4.30	1.51
20,000	4.22	1.42

bottleneck. The partially super-linear speedups attained on the Opteron processor are due to the "classic" reason: improved cache efficiency for large data sets.

An important advantage of this implementation consists in the minimal effort required for parallelization: a student who had never ever heard before about phylogenetics required just one week to parallelize the program after being shown the critical `for`-loops in the RAxML-III source code. As already mentioned, other programs such as PHYML can easily be parallelized with OpenMP as well. Apart from solving memory problems, this approach can also be used for parallel implementations on hybrid supercomputers. Finally, one could also try to use peripheral vector processors such as GPUs (graphics processing units) to exploit the fine-grained parallelism of ML programs, as there already exist implementations of scientific codes on GPUs [44].

Another easy way, in terms of required effort, to technically accelerate ML programs consists in using highly optimized math-libraries such as the Intel Math Kernel Library (MKL) [45]. Typically, ML programs perform many calls to the `exp()` and `log()` functions. MKL can be used to accelerate those functions by minor changes to the source code. For example, an MKL implementation of RAxML-III yielded a speedup of ≈30% over the nonoptimized program after just half a day of work.

Finally, in a combination of algorithmic and technical approaches, the aforementioned guide-tree approach could be ideally suited for a coarse-grained distributed or grid-enabled implementation. Such a system could potentially be used to infer reliable trees comprising 20,000 or 30,000 organisms in the near future. However, given the large number of unresolved theoretical and technical challenges, of which only a few have been covered in the present chapter, one can conclude that it is still a long way to go for the tree-of-life.

REFERENCES

1. D. A. Bader, B. M. E. Moret, and L. Vawter, Industrial Applications of High-Performance Computing for Phylogeny Reconstruction, in *Proceedings of SPIE ITCom: Commercial Applications for High-Performance Computing*, Vol. 4528, 2001, pp. 159–168.

2. H. L. Bodlaender, M. R. Fellows, M. T. Hallett, T. Wareham, and T. Warnow, The hardness of perfect phylogeny, feasible register assignment and other problems on thin colored graphs, *Theor. Comp. Sci.*, 244, 167–188 (2000).

3. W. E. Day, D. S. Johnson, and D. Sankoff, The computational complexity of inferring rooted phylogenies by parsimony, *Math. Bios.*, 81, 33–42 (1986).

4. J. Felsenstein, Evolutionary trees from DNA sequences: a maximum likelihood approach, *J. Mol. Evol.*, 17, 368–376 (1981).

5. T. L. Williams, B. M. Berger-Wolf, U. Roshan, and T. Warnow, The relationship between maximum parsimony scores and phylogenetic tree topologies, *Technical Report*, TR-CS-2004-04, Department of Computer Science, The University of New Mexico, 2004.

6. O. Gascuel, BIONJ: an improved version of the NJ algorithm based on a simple model of sequence data, *Mol. Biol. Evol.*, 14, 685–695 (1997).

7. S. Guindon and O. Gascuel, A simple, fast, and accurate algorithm to estimate large phylogenies by maximum likelihood, *Syst. Biol.*, 52 (5), 696–704 (2003).

8. T. L. Williams and B. M. E. Moret, An Investigation of Phylogenetic Likelihood Methods, in *Proceedings of 3rd IEEE Symposium on Bioinformatics and Bioengineering (BIBE'03)*, 2003, pp. 79–86.

9. C. Stewart, D. Hart, D. Berry, G. Olsen, E. Wernert, and W. Fischer, Parallel Implementation and Performance of fastDNAml — A Program for Maximum Likelihood Phylogenetic Inference, *Proceedings of 14th Supercomputing Conference (SC2001)*, 2001.

10. A. Stamatakis, T. Ludwig, and H. Meier, RAxML-III: a fast program for maximum likelihood-based inference of large phylogenetic trees, *Bioinformatics*, 21(4), 456–463, 2005.

11. D. L. Swofford, G. J. Olsen, P. J. Wadell, and D. M. Hillis, Phylogenetic Inference, in D. M. Hillis, C. Moritz, and B. K. Mabel, Eds., *Molecular Systematics*, Chapter 11, Sinauer Associates, Sunderland, MA, 1996.

12. C. Lanave, G. Preparata, C. Saccone, and G. Serio, A new method for calculating evolutionary substitution rates, *J. Mol. Evol.*, 20, 86–93 (1984).

13. F. Rodriguez, J. L. Oliver, A. Marin, and J. R. Medina, The general stochastic model of nucleotide substitution, *J. Theor. Biol.*, 142, 485–501 (1990).

14. T. Jukes and C. Cantor, Evolution of Protein Molecules, in H. Munro, Ed., *Mammalian Protein Metabolism*, Academic Press, New York, 1969, Vol. 3, pp. 21–132.

15. M. Hasegawa, H. Kishino, and T. Yano, Dating of the human-ape splitting by a molecular clock of mitochondrial DNA, *J. Mol. Evol.*, 22, 160–174 (1985).

16. G. Olsen, H. Matsuda, R. Hagstrom, and R. Overbeek, FastDNAml: a tool for construction of phylogenetic trees of DNA sequences using maximum likelihood, *Comput. Appl. Biosci.*, 10, 41–48 (1994).

17. B. Chor, M. Hendy, B. Holland, and D. Penny, Multiple maxima of likelihood in phylogenetic trees: an analytic approach, *Mol. Biol. Evol.*, 17, 1529–1541 (2000).

18. A. Stamatakis, T. Ludwig, H. Meier, and M. J. Wolf, Accelerating Parallel Maximum Likelihood-Based Phylogenetic Tree Calculations Using Subtree Equality Vectors, in *Proceedings of 15th Supercomputing Conference (SC2002)*, 2002.

19. D. L. Swofford, *PAUP*: Phylogenetic Analysis Using Parsimony* (*and Other Methods), Sinauer, Sunderland, Massachusetts, 1999.

20. veryfastDNAml distribution: BIOWEB.PASTEUR.FR/SEQANAL/SOFT-PASTEUR.HTML.

21. D. Hart, D. Grover, M. Liggett, R. Repasky, C. Shields, S. Simms, A. Sweeny, and P. Wang, Distributed Parallel Computing Using Windows Desktop Systems, in *Proceedings of HPDC-12, Challenges for Large Applications in Distributed Environments (CLADE2003)*, 2003.

22. DPRml: Distributed Phylogeny Reconstruction by Maximum Likelihood: WWW.CS.MAY.IE/~TKEANE/DISTRIBUTED/DPRML.HTML.

23. P. Lewis, A genetic algorithm for maximum likelihood phylogeny inference using nucleotide sequence data, *Mol. Biol. Evol.*, 15, 277–283 (1998).

24. A. Skourikhine, Phylogenetic Tree Reconstruction Using Self-Adaptive Genetic Algorithm, in *Proceedings of IEEE International Symposium on Bio-Informatics and Biomedical Engineering (BIBE'00)*, 2000.

25. A. Lemmon and M. Milinkovitch, The metapopulation genetic algorithm: an efficient solution for the problem of large phylogeny estimation, *Proc. Natl. Acad. Sci. USA*, 99, 10516–10521 (2002).

26. M. J. Brauer, M. T. Holder, L. A. Dries, D. J. Zwickl, P. O. Lewis, and D. M. Hillis, Genetic algorithms and parallel processing in maximum-likelihood phylogeny inference, *Mol. Biol. Evol.*, 19, 1717–1726 (2002).

27. L. Salter and D. Pearl, Stochastic search strategy for estimation of maximum likelihood phylogenetic trees, *Syst. Biol.*, 50, 7–17 (2001).

28. M. T. Holder, P. O. Lewis, Phylogeny estimation: traditional and Bayesian approaches, *Nat. Rev. Genet.*, 4, 275–284 (2003).

29. J. P. Huelsenbeck, B. Larget, R. E. Miller, and F. Ronquist, Potential applications and pitfalls of Bayesian inference of phylogeny, *Syst. Biol.*, 51 (5), 673–688 (2002).

30. PHYLIP package: EVOLUTION.GENETICS.WASHINGTON.EDU.

31. C. Tuffley and M. Steel, Links between maximum likelihood and maximum parsimony under a simple model of site substitution, *Bull. Math. Biol.*, 59 (3), 581–607 (1997).

32. A. Stamatakis, T. Ludwig, and H. Meier, New Fast and Accurate Heuristics for Inference of Large Phylogenetic Trees, in *Proceedings of 18th International Parallel and Distributed Processing Symposium (IPDPS2004)*, 2004, p. 193.

33. A. Stamatakis, T. Ludwig, and H. Meier, Parallel Inference of a 10,000-taxon Phylogeny with Maximum Likelihood, in *Proceedings of Euro-Par 2004*, Vol. 3149 of Lecture Notes in Computer Science, Springer Verlag, 2004, pp. 997–1004.

34. Seti@home project site: SETIATHOME.SSL.BERKELEY.EDU.

35. A. Stamatakis, M. Ott, T. Ludwig, and H. Meier, DRAxML@home: a distributed program for computation of large phylogenetic trees, *Future Generation Comp. Sys.*, 21(5), 725–730, 2005.

36. M. J. Sanderson and A. C. Driskell, The challenge of constructing large phylogenetic trees, *Trends Plant Sci.*, 8 (8), 374–378 (2003).

37. D. Huson, S. Nettles, and T. Warnow, Disk-covering, a fast converging method for phylogenetic tree reconstruction, *Comp. Biol.*, 6 (3), 369–386 (1999).

38. D. Huson, L. Vawter, and T. Warnow, Solving Large Scale Phylogenetic Problems Using DCM2, in *Proceedings of ISMB99*, 1999, pp. 118–129.

39. U. Roshan, B. M. E. Moret, T. L. Williams, and T. Warnow, Rec-I-DCM3: A Fast Algorithmic Technique for Reconstructing Large Phylogenetic Trees, in *Proceedings of 3rd IEEE Computational Systems Bioinformatics Conference (CSB2004)*, 2004.

40. M. L. Bonet, M. Steel, T. Warnow, and S. Yooseph, Better methods for solving parsimony and compatibility, *J. Comp. Biol.*, 5, 391–408 (1998).

41. L. S. Vinh, H. A. Schmidt, and A. Haeseler, PhyNav: a novel approach to reconstruct large phylogenies, *Proceedings of GfKl Conference*, 2004.

42. J. P. Huelsenbeck and F. Ronquist, MRBAYES: Bayesian inference of phylogenetic trees, *Bioinformatics*, 17 (8), 754–755 (2001).

43. OpenMP: WWW.OPENMP.ORG/DRUPAL.

44. J. Krüger and R. Westermann, Linear algebra operators for GPU implementation of numerical algorithms, *Proceedings of SIGGRAPH2003*, 2003, pp. 908–916.

45. Intel Math Kernel Library: WWW.INTEL.COM/SOFTWARE/PRODUCTS/MKL.

CHAPTER 15

Phylogenetic Parameter Estimation on COWs

EKKEHARD PETZOLD, DANIEL MERKLE, MARTIN MIDDENDORF,
ARNDT VON HAESELER, and HEIKO A. SCHMIDT

Phylogenetic analysis is a routine task in biological research. The growing amounts of biological sequence data makes the computational part a bottleneck of the analysis of these data. Parallel computing is applied to reduce the computational burden. In this chapter we discuss different factors that influences the performance of parallel implementations. Using the example of parameter estimation in the TREE-PUZZLE program, we analyze the performance and speedup of different scheduling algorithms on two different kinds of workstation clusters, which are the most abundant parallel platform in biological research. To that end different parts of the TREE-PUZZLE program with diverse parallel complexity are examined and the impact of their characteristics are discussed. In addition, an extended parallelization for the parameter estimation program is introduced.

15.1 INTRODUCTION

Phylogenetic analysis aims to reconstruct the relationship between species, organisms, etc. With the advent of molecular biology, DNA and protein sequences are routinely used to reconstruct the relationships based on gene trees. Thus, the reconstruction of evolutionary or phylogenetic trees is a fundamental task in everyday biological and biomedical researches.

Genome sequencing projects and efficient sequencing techniques lead to the doubling of the amount of data in the public sequence databases every 9 months. Therefore, when analyzing this tremendous data set, the computational part of tree reconstruction causes a bottleneck.

Several facts contribute to this problem. On one hand the large number of possible binary unrooted tree topologies $B(n) = (2n - 5)!/(2^{n-3}(n - 3)!)$ [1] with n labeled leaves (typically n sequences) prevents exhaustive searches of the tree space to find a tree that fits the data best with respect to some objective function. In addition, a number

Parallel Computing for Bioinformatics and Computational Biology, Edited by Albert Y. Zomaya
Copyright © 2006 John Wiley & Sons, Inc.

of phylogeny reconstruction problems are known to be NP-hard [2–4a]. Therefore, it is unlikely that they can be solved in polynomial time. Thus, phylogenetic reconstruction relies on the use of heuristics for even moderately sized data [5–7].

Currently, the computationally most intensive tree reconstruction methods are based on the likelihood principle [8], which tends to give more accurate results when compared with other heuristics. However, those likelihood methods get more and more with common with increasing processor speeds.

Unfortunately, the gain of speed is foiled by the increasing amount of data. Accordingly, also parallel computing has been applied since the 1990s to limit the runtime of phylogenetic analyses [9, 10]. The parallelization of tree reconstruction was intuitive because it requires the computation of large numbers of independent tasks. This is typical for many analyses in molecular biology, for example, comparing a number of sequences against all sequences in a biological sequence database.

Before we start with the description of the parallelization, we introduce some basic notation from computer science and molecular evolution.

15.1.1 Parallel Platforms

Three types of parallel computing platforms are popular

1. Massively parallel processors (MPPs) consisting of a large number of processing elements (PEs) communicating via a fast interconnection facility
2. Symmetric multiprocessors (SMPs) where a number of processors share a common memory
3. Clusters of workstations (COWs) typically consisting off-the-shelf workstations coupled with a local area network (LAN) like Ethernet.

In biological sciences, COWs are the most abundant parallel platforms [10]. Typically, such COWs either originate as a network of desktop workstations or have been bought as a dedicated cluster, which typically has been or will be later extended with additional up-to-date machines. Both developments produce heterogeneous workstation clusters — a setting to be considered in the development of parallel software suitable for genetic sequence analysis.

15.1.2 Parallel Performance

To effectively use parallel platforms, it is crucial to keep all processors equally busy while keeping the communication overhead low. According to *Amdahl's law* [11] the parallel performance is limited by the sequential fraction S of the program, because only the runtime of the parallelized fraction P, also called the *coverage*, can be reduced by parallel computing with p processors. Thus, it is favorable to parallelize large portions of a program. The parallel performance of a parallel program is commonly measured by its *speedup*

$$\text{speedup}(p) = \frac{\text{runtime with one processor}}{\text{runtime with } p \text{ processors}} \tag{15.1}$$

where the runtime with one processor is typically measured with the corresponding sequential program missing the overhead of a parallel version. The success of a parallel implementation often depends on the granularity, that is, the amount of independent problems that are executed by the processors until communication is necessary, as well as the way the workload is distributed among the available processors.

In the following, the parameter estimation part of the TREE-PUZZLE program [12] serves as an example to demonstrate the impact of task granularity and the scheduling algorithm on the parallel performance. TREE-PUZZLE implements a maximum likelihood (ML) based method, quartet puzzling [13], to reconstruct evolutionary trees from (biological) sequences. To infer ML based trees, it is necessary to estimate the model parameters by ML method. In sequential programs, this is a time-consuming task and several heuristics are employed [7, 14, 15]. The parallelization of the sequential ML based optimization technique is nontrivial, when developing parallel phylogenetic analysis software.

In the following, we will examine the parallel version of TREE-PUZZLE [12] that uses MPI (Message Passing Interface [16, 17]) for parallel execution on a heterogeneous and a homogeneous COW.

15.2 PHYLOGENETIC TREE RECONSTRUCTION USING QUARTET PUZZLING AND ITS PARALLELIZATION

15.2.1 Modeling Molecular Evolution

Here, we give a short introduction to the probabilistic framework that is used in phylogenetic analysis. In the following, we confine ourselves to DNA sequence evolution. However, we note that everything transforms easily to model protein sequence evolution. As input serves a DNA sequence alignment (cf. Table 15.1) of n sequences $S_1, \ldots, S_n$ with length L (measured in nucleotides or base pairs, bp). All characters within one column trace back to one common ancestor nucleotide.

The ML reconstruction of a tree with n sequences requires a model of evolution describing how substitutions from one character to another occur at a given position in a sequence alignment A (cf. Table 15.1). Typically, this is modeled by time-homogeneous reversible-time Markov process [18, 19]. This stochastic process

TABLE 15.1 Alignment Example for Eight DNA Sequences $S_1, \ldots, S_8$[1]

S_1	...TGTCTCAAGG	ACTAAGCCAT	GCAAGTGTAA	GTATA**A**GT**AT**...
S_2	...TGTCT**A**TAGG	ACTAAGCCAT	GCAAGTG**C**AA	GTAT**G**GAGTGA...
S_3	...TGTCTCAAA**G**	A**T**TAAGCCAT	GCA**T**GT**C**TAA	GTATAAAC**A**T...
S_4	...TGTCTCAAGG	ACTAAGCCAT	GCAAGTGTAA	GTAT**G**GAGTGA...
S_5	...TG**TTT**AAGG	ACTAAGCCAT	GCAAGTG**C**AA	GTAT**G**GAGTGA...
S_6	...TGTCTCAAA**G**	ACTAAGCCAT	GCA**T**GT**C**TAA	GTATAAAC**A**T...
S_7	...TGTCTCAAA**G**	A**T**TAAGCCAT	GCA**T**GT**C**TAA	GTATAAAC**G**T...
S_8	...TGTCTCAAA**G**	ACTAAGCCAT	GCAAGT**C**TAA	GTATA**A**GT**GT**...

[1]Columns in boldface contain substitutions

describes the evolutionary history for a single nucleotide position. To specify the evolutionary process, one typically defines an instantaneous rate R_{ij} of substituting nucleotide i by j. All possible substitutions are given by an instantaneous rate matrix $\mathbf{Q}$. Additionally, it is usually assumed that the composition of the nucleotides $\pi = (\pi_A, \pi_C, \pi_G, \pi_T)$ remains stationary over time. Because we assume time-reversibility, the elements of $\mathbf{Q}$ can be written as

$$Q_{ij} = \begin{cases} R_{ij}\pi_j & \text{if } i \neq j \\ -\sum_k R_{ik}\pi_k & \text{if } i = j \end{cases} \tag{15.2}$$

where the 4×4 matrix $\mathbf{R} = (R_{ij})$ is symmetrical and the elements on the main diagonal are 0. $\mathbf{R}$ comprises the nucleotide-specific substitution rates. Equation (15.2) describes the general time-reversible model (GTR) [18, 20], which has six independent rate parameters and three independent frequency parameters (the nucleotide composition). The GTR model can be reduced to a number of simpler models such as the HKY model [21] or Jukes–Cantor model [22], which have less parameters. Given $\mathbf{Q}$, a probability matrix $\mathbf{P}(t) = (P_{ij}(t))$ can be computed [23]. The off-diagonal elements of $\mathbf{P}(t)$ determine the probabilities to observe a substitution from nucleotide i to j in time t. The probability of one sequence S_1 to evolve to sequence S_2 during a given period of time t is the product of the probabilities $P_{s_1(l),s_2(l)}(t)$ to observe the nucleotide pair $[s_1(l), s_2(l)]$ at each alignment column l. For two sequences, one can estimate $\mathbf{P}(t)$ by counting the observed nucleotide pairs in the alignment. This estimate of $\mathbf{P}(t)$ can then be used to compute the ML estimate $\hat{t}$, which for simplicity we will call evolutionary distance D between two sequences (see Ref. [24] for details).

This approach can be extended [8] to compute the probability of the data to be produced by a given tree T and an evolutionary model M. M includes the necessary parameters such as the character frequencies π and the independent rate parameters of $\mathbf{R}$. The probability $\Pr(A_l|T, M)$ of an alignment column A_l is the product of all pairwise probabilities along each branch, summed over all possible (typically unknown) character states at the internal nodes of the tree T [7, 8]. To efficiently compute this probability of the alignment given the tree, Felsenstein [8] suggested a recursive algorithm that avoids multiple redundant computations along the tree. The probability of the entire alignment A of length L is the product of all column probabilities

$$\Pr(A|T, M) = \prod_{l=1}^{L} \Pr(A_l|T, M) \tag{15.3}$$

The probability $\Pr(A|T, M)$ is also called the likelihood $\mathcal{L}(T|A, M)$ of the tree T with branch lengths, interpreted as evolutionary distances between the corresponding nodes of the branch (edge), given the data A. To avoid multiplications of small numbers, one computes the log-likelihood

$$\log \mathcal{L}(T|A, M) = \log \Pr(A|T, M) = \sum_{l=1}^{L} \log \Pr(A_l|T, M) \tag{15.4}$$

of the tree.

Biological sequences usually do not evolve with the same rate at all positions of an alignment. Thus, it is often necessary to introduce a column specific rate parameter r_l, which is typically assumed to be distributed according to a discrete Γ-distribution with expectation 1 and variance $1/\alpha$ [25, 26]. If the so-called shape parameter α of the Γ-distribution is high, there is almost no rate heterogeneity observed among the columns, whereas a low α implies that a high amount of columns evolve at low rates while a small number of sites are evolving fast.

Assuming Γ-distributed rate heterogeneity, the likelihood of a tree T is computed by

$$\mathcal{L}(T|A, M, \alpha) = \prod_{l=1}^{L} \left(\sum_{h=1}^{c} \Pr(r_h)\Pr(A_l|T, M, r_h) \right) \tag{15.5}$$

or taking the log-likelihood

$$\log \mathcal{L}(T|A, M, \alpha) = \sum_{l=1}^{L} \log \left(\sum_{h=1}^{c} \Pr(r_h)\Pr(A_l|T, M, r_h) \right) \tag{15.6}$$

where c is the number of discrete rate categories and each rate r_h is equally likely $[\Pr(r_h) = 1/c]$.

The likelihood is used as a measure for the goodness-of-fit of a tree. Moreover, it can be used to compare different tree topologies and parameter estimates. The parameters of the evolutionary model M, namely, the nucleotide distribution π, the rate matrix **R**, and the shape parameter α, have to be inferred from the given alignment A.

15.2.2 Quartet Puzzling Algorithm

TREE-PUZZLE uses the ML principle to reconstruct evolutionary trees from biological sequence alignments (Table 15.1), applying the quartet puzzling algorithm [13, 27]. The reconstruction is partitioned in four main steps of different computational complexity

1. *Initialization and Estimation of Evolutionary Parameters (PEst).* The input data are given in the form of an alignment of biological sequences (DNA or protein sequences, cf. Table 15.1). For the underlying model of sequence evolution, the most appropriate model parameters (e.g., rate matrix, rate heterogeneity shape parameter α) are estimated from the input data. The estimation procedure will be detailed subsequently.

2. *Maximum Likelihood Step (MLStep).* On the basis of evolutionary model and the estimated parameters, we compute for all $\binom{n}{4}$ quartets (subsets of size 4 from the n input sequences) the ML value (Eq. (15.6) and cf. [8]) of each of the three possible tree topologies (Fig. 15.1) to determine the collection of highly supported quartet topologies [13, 27]. The ML values are computed applying the ML principle as outlined in Section 15.2.1.

3. *Puzzling Step (PStep)*. From the quartet topologies with high ML values, so-called *intermediate trees* containing all given sequences are constructed in a stepwise procedure by inserting sequence by sequence [13]. To that end, we use the neighborhood relations induced from the highly supported quartet topologies. We order all sequences in a random order, say {A, B, C, D, E, F, ...}. We start with the supported topology of the first quartet {A, B, C, D}. For the starting quartet in Figure 15.2*a*, the sequences A and B are neighbors as are C and D. This neighborhood relation is denoted by AB|CD, depicting the bipartition of the sequences induced by the splitting inner edge (see also Fig. 15.1). To insert the next sequence E, we examine the neighborhood relations in all quartets {u, v, w, E} with u, v, w being part of the already reconstructed subtree. In Figure 15.2*a*, and *b*, the considered quartet topology is AE|BC. To maintain the neighborhood relations, E should not be inserted on the path between sequences B and C. Accordingly, every branch on this path gets a penalty of one. This is repeated for all quartets {u, v, w, E}, counting how many quartets contradict the insertion of E into each branch (Fig. 15.2*b–e*). Sequence E is inserted at the branch with lowest penalty (Fig. 15.2*e* and *f*). Then, the next sequences are inserted accordingly (cf. Fig. 15.2*g–i*) until all *n* sequences are contained in the tree. As ties are broken randomly, this step is repeated many (thousand) times, producing many intermediate trees.

4. *Consensus Step (CStep)*. From all intermediate trees, a majority-rule consensus tree [28] is constructed. This consensus tree contains all branches (bipartitions), which were observed in more than 50% of all intermediate trees.

The four steps leave ample space for parallelization on various levels. The parallel implementations of the MLStep and PStep, which together use well over 90% of the total serial computing time, have shown to be almost optimal [29]. Owing to the large number of independent tasks and the use of an efficient dynamic scheduling algorithm, the speedup of the parallelized steps was almost linear up to 64 processors [12, 29]. Parts of the CStep are also executed in parallel, as the preprocessing of the intermediate trees for consensus construction moved to the end of the PStep and is done concurrently by the worker processes.

In the following we explain the PEst part of the serial TREE-PUZZLE program in more detail. In the subsequent paragraphs, we will describe our current parallel implementation of this part. PEst consists of the following steps:

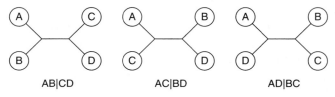

Figure 15.1 The three possible topologies for a sequence quartet (A, B, C, D) and their corresponding neighborhood relations are shown.

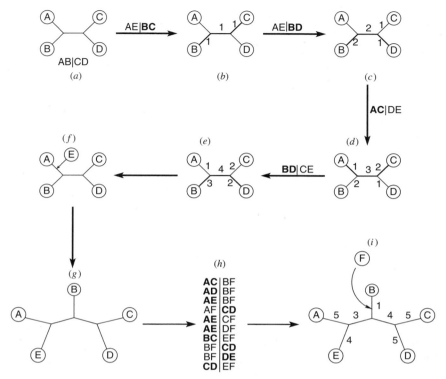

Figure 15.2   Puzzling step constructing a tree of six sequences: From a starting quartet AB|CD (*a*), sequence F is inserted (*f*) according to the lowest penalty accumulated from the neighborhood relations (*b–e*) in the relevant quartets (AE|BC, AE|BD, and AC|DE, and BD|CE) resulting in a five-tree (*g*). To the five-tree sequence, *F* is again added (*i*) to the branch with lowest penalty computed from the relevant quartets (*h*). Neighborhood relations and associated penalty paths are denoted in bold. Penalties are given at the branches.

(i) Let θ denote the parameters of the evolutionary model M. Initialize $\theta \equiv \theta_0$.

(ii) Compute all pairwise ML distances between sequences (this produces the ML distance matrix **D**, cf. Section 15.2.1) using θ_0. (ML Dist)

(iii) Construct a neighbor-joining tree T from **D** [30].

(iv) Compute branch lengths of the neighbor-joining tree T by a least-square fit method to distance matrix **D** [31]. (LS Len)

(v) Re-estimate θ_0 as the ML estimate over all admissible θ using tree T and least-square branch lengths.

(vi) Repeat steps (ii)–(v) until the likelihood of T does not be improved any more.

Figure 15.3 displays the flowchart of the most recent version of parallel TREE-PUZZLE, where the three steps PEst, PStep, and MLStep are parallelized. A master process computes the sequential parts of the program and distributes the parallel parts to several worker processes, which send the results back to the master. The main parts of steps PStep and MLStep are done by the worker processes.

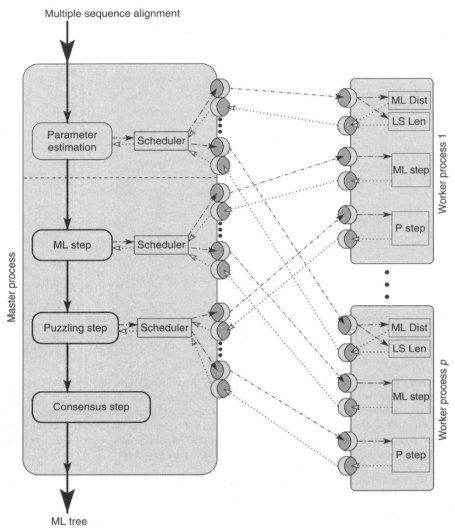

Figure 15.3   Parallelized work-flow of the current TREE-PUZZLE program. The master process performs the sequential code and distributes the parallel parts to the workers; parallel parts are steps PStep, MLStep, and substeps (ii) and (iv) of PEst.

15.3   HARDWARE, DATA, AND SCHEDULING ALGORITHMS

15.3.1   Parallel Hardware

Two types of parallel workstation clusters are used to evaluate the performance of the parallelized parameter estimation of TREE-PUZZLE. One cluster is a homogeneous COW (homoCOW) consisting of eight SMP nodes each with four Intel Pentium III

Xeon 550 MHz processors, 512 kb on-chip cache, and 2 Gb RAM. The nodes are coupled with a fast Myrinet network.

The other cluster is a heterogeneous COW (heteroCOW) comprising 12 different SUN Ultra workstations with between one and three CPUs, a total of 15 processors. The machines have CPU clock rates ranging from 143 to 440 MHz and with memory capacities between 128 and 1024 Mb per processor (see Table 15.2 for more detail). A total number of 15 processors is available. The communication between the nodes is handled by 100 Mbit Fast Ethernet.

15.3.2 Data Sets

To study the effects of problem size, granularity, and scheduling on the parallel performance, data sets with different alignment lengths (192, 384, 768, and 1536 bp) and numbers of sequences (16, 32, 64, and 128 sequences) were generated using the Seq-Gen program [32].

The implementation was also applied on two biological data sets: data derived from the set of small-subunit ribosomal RNA sequences from Rhodophyta in the European rRNA Database [33] and another data set of Cadherin protein sequences (HBG003908) was collected from the Hovergen database [34].

15.3.3 Scheduling Algorithms

To distribute the tasks, a scheduling strategy is required, which facilitates an even load balancing while simultaneously keeping the communication overhead low. The latter is especially important for COWs where a large number of concurrent communication operations cannot be executed very fast.

Scheduling algorithms distribute a set of N tasks to the p processors executing the parallel processes. The two naïve scheduling algorithms are distributing the N independent tasks to the p processes, either in equally sized packages of $B = N/p$ tasks or in an one-by-one scheme ($B = 1$). Whenever a processor finished a batch of tasks, it receives a new batch until all tasks are done. The former algorithm, *static chunking* (SC) [35], although having a low communication overhead, usually performs

TABLE 15.2 Specifications of the Heterogeneous COW

No. of Machines	CPU Speed (MHz)	No. of CPUs	System Clock (MHz)	Memory (Mb)	Cache (Mb)	Type
2	143	1	71	160	0.5	Sun Ultra 1 SBus
2	167	1	84	288–448	0.5	Sun Ultra 1 SBus
1	200	2	100	2048	2×1.0	Sun Ultra 2 UPA/SBus
3	270	1	90	128	0.2	Sun Ultra 5/10
2	360	1	90	320	0.2	Sun Ultra 5/10
1	400	3	100	4096	4×4.0	Sun Enterprise 450
1	440	1	111	384	2.0	Sun Ultra 5/10

badly if the speed of the processors or the computing times for the tasks differ. The latter algorithm, *self-scheduling* (SS) [35] can guarantee an equal workload on the processors but has in turn a very high communication overhead.

In the first parallel version of TREE-PUZZLE, the parts MLStep and PStep were parallelized [12]. For this implementation, we tested different scheduling algorithms [29, 35], which do not require estimates of a task's runtime. Among the considered schedulers, *guided self-scheduling* (GSS) [36] turned out to show the best performance. GSS assigns task packages of $B_{GSS} = N/p$ tasks, starting with a pth of the full task set and decreasing B_{GSS} exponentially with every batch of tasks to a minimum of (single) tasks. After a batch of B_{GSS} tasks has been assigned to a process, the number N of tasks to be scheduled is decreased by B_{GSS}. To gain an even better performance, the GSS algorithm has been generalized by decreasing the starting size of the first package and introducing an *atomic batch size A*, which determines the minimum size of a batch as well as the step size. This *smooth guided self-scheduling* (SGSS) [29] assigns batches of size

$$
B_{SGSS} = \begin{cases} N & \text{if } N \leq A \\ \left\lceil \dfrac{N}{2p} \right\rceil + A - \left(\left\lceil \dfrac{N}{2p} \right\rceil \bmod A \right) & \text{otherwise} \end{cases} \tag{15.7}
$$

The first line schedules all remaining tasks if less than the atomic batch size A, whereas the second line ensures that each batch size B is divisible by A (for details, see [29]). Again, after scheduling a batch of tasks, N is decreased by B_{SGSS}.

15.4 PARALLELIZING PEST

Although parallelizing the parts MLStep and PStep of the TREE-PUZZLE program was straightforward, the PEst part is more difficult to parallelize and needs different scheduling strategies.

15.4.1 Parallelizing PEst-(ii): ML Distance Estimation

The pairwise distance estimation [step (ii)] comprises $(n^2 - n)/2$ independent estimations for n input sequences. Owing to the ML optimization of the distances (cf. Section 15.2.1), the runtime of each estimation is long relative to the time required for a single communication event.

The large number of tasks combined with their long runtime makes this step prominent for an elaborate scheduling approach. We implemented a master–worker scheme where one master process assigns and coordinates the tasks to the $p - 1$ worker processes. As scheduling strategies, GSS and SGSS have been applied. The results are given in the next section.

15.4.2 Parallel Performance of PEst-(ii) on a Heterogeneous COW

In this section, we analyze the performance of the SGSS scheduling algorithm to keep the CPUs of a heterogeneous COW equally busy [29] and compare it to the efficiency of GSS [36]. To evaluate the efficiency of GSS and SGSS, we measured the computation times for the pairwise distance computation step (ii) of PEst for the Cadherin data set on the heterogeneous COW.

To simulate the best and worst case scenario with respect to the runtime, we applied two different processor permutations for the assignment of the tasks. In the best case, the first (largest) batches are assigned to the processors in the order of decreasing speed (fastest to slowest CPU). Thus, the fastest processor gets the largest chunk. The second permutation is just the opposite, assigning the chunks from the slowest first to the fastest last, that is, ascending speeds. The latter assignment sequence is supposed to perform worse than the first because the slowest processor gets the largest chunk of tasks. This can be regarded as the worst case scenario that can happen to these scheduling algorithms.

The Gantt charts of a typical pairwise distance estimation [step (ii)] with SGSS and GSS are shown in Figures 15.4 and 15.5, respectively, using identical time scales. Both scheduling algorithms perform well for the best case (Figs. 15.4*b* and 15.5*b*). This means that the load is almost evenly distributed among the worker processes without much idle time at the end of the parallel region. In the worst case, however (Figs. 15.4*a* and 15.5*a*), the GSS scheduler performs badly on the heterogeneous COW. Although

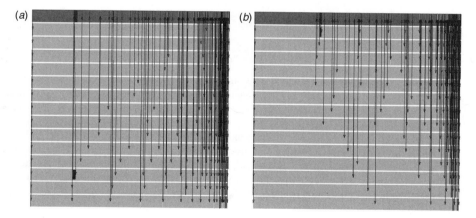

Figure 15.4 Gantt charts of a single execution of the pairwise distance computation step for Cadherin protein data using SGSS on a heterogeneous COW. Assignment order under (*a*) worst case scenario: The slowest processor receives the largest available batch; (*b*) best case: starting with the fastest CPU. Each row corresponds to one processor sorted by speed according to the earlier assignments. The first row represents the master process distributing tasks to the processors from top to bottom sending new task batches whenever a processor has finished its last batch. Light gray areas depict work and dark gray areas depict idle time and communication or, in case of the master process (first line), coordinating and scheduling the tasks. Vertical arrows represent communication events.

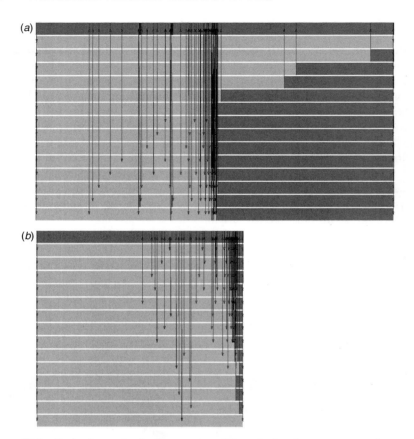

Figure 15.5   Gantt charts of a single execution of the pairwise distance computation step for Cadherin protein data using GSS on a heterogeneous COW. Assignment order under (*a*) worst case scenario: The slowest processor receives the largest available batch; (*b*) best case: starting with the fastest CPU. Each row corresponds to one processor sorted by speed according to the above assignments. The first row represents the master process distributing tasks to the processors from top to bottom sending new task batches whenever a processor has finished its last batch. Light gray areas depict work and dark gray areas depict idle time and communication or, in case of the master process (first line), coordinating and scheduling the tasks. Vertical arrows represent communication events.

there is no significant difference among the runtimes of the GSS in the best case and SGSS under both scenarios (about 9 s), GSS shows a significant increase of about 60% of its runtime to about 15 s for the worst case scenario (compared with the other cases) and keeping more than 50% of the workers waiting for the tasks to be finished. Although the impact might not be as harsh on average, one can clearly see that there will be a severe increase of running time whenever one of the slower machines gets one of the larger task packages. This effect has been eliminated efficiently by the SGSS algorithm.

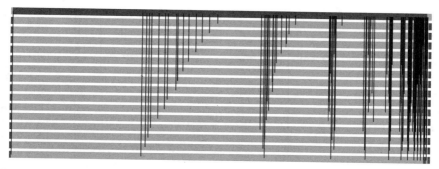

Figure 15.6   Gantt chart of pairwise distance computation for Cadherin protein data on a homogeneous COW with SGSS: Each row corresponds to one processor, the first as a master process handling the distribution of tasks to the other (worker) processes. Light gray areas depict work and dark gray areas depict idle time and communication or, in case of the master process (first line), coordinating and scheduling the tasks. Vertical lines represent communication events.

For comparison, we also show a Gantt chart from a typical run with Cadherin data on the homogeneous cluster (Fig. 15.6). Note that for this cluster, both assignment sequences are the same because all processors have the same speed. It can be seen that the first chunks have slightly different runtime because of the different size of the chunks. Although the performance results were shown, only for the Cadherin data set, similar results are gained for other protein, DNA, and simulated data sets.

15.4.3   PEst-(iii) and (iv): Neighbor-Joining and Least-Square Branch Lengths

The construction of the neighbor-joining tree [30] in step (iii) is very fast and, hence, no parallelization is needed (cf. [29]). The optimization of the branch lengths [step (iv)] in tree T using the least-square method, in contrast, incorporates $N = (2n - 3)$ $(n - 1)$ calculations for n sequences. However, each of the calculations is very short when compared with communication. Hence, the communication overhead was kept minimal by assigning an even share of N/p calculations to each processor (static chunking, cf. Section 15.3.3).

15.5   EXTENDING PARALLEL COVERAGE IN PEST

As we have pointed out earlier, it is favorable according to Amdahl's law to increase the parallel coverage within a program if possible.

To identify potential time-consuming blocks in PEst of TREE-PUZZLE, we evaluate its runtime relative to the overall runtime of the program. The aim is to determine

TABLE 15.3 Runtime of PEst in a TREE-PUZZLE Analysis on homoCOW

Data Set		Sequential Run			Parallel (32 Processors)		
Seqs[a]	Length (bp)	PEst (s)	Total (s)	Ratio	PEst[b] (s)	Total (s)	Ratio
16	192	26.1	44.6	0.59	0.4	0.5	0.86
16	384	14.6	51.7	0.28	0.0	0.0	0.69
16	768	28.3	115.9	0.25	1.6	2.4	0.68
32	192	33.8	777.7	0.04	10.9	22.8	0.48
32	384	57.1	1,083.3	0.05	17.1	31.6	0.54
32	768	102.7	1,994.6	0.05	33.3	58.5	0.57
64	192	180.2	28,199.0	<0.01	103.4	862.0	0.12
64	384	276.8	32,522.0	<0.01	211.4	1,006.5	0.21
64	768	465.3	48,206.0	<0.01	326.8	1,485.6	0.22

[a]Number of sequences.
[b]With parallelized steps (ii) and (iv).

how much increase in performance can be gained by an improved parallelization. The time measurements were performed on the homogeneous cluster for simulated DNA data with different numbers of the sequences and different sequence lengths (see Table 15.3 for details) using TREE-PUZZLE with the SGSS scheduler as described earlier. As the main parts of the quartet puzzling analysis have been shown to be efficiently parallelized [29], we were particularly interested in the runtime of the parameter estimation step. Table 15.3 shows the relative runtimes that are consumed for PEst in sequential as well as parallel runs with 32 processors.

The table shows that the relative amount of time spent for PEst strongly depends on the number of sequences in the test set. For a small number of sequences, 16 sequences, the relative amount of time is more than 25%, whereas for 64 sequences, it is less than 1%. The absolute amount of time consumed in a sequential run has been substantially reduced by the parallelization described in the previous section. This holds especially for small data sets. The relative amount of time needed for PEst in a parallel run on 32 processors has dramatically increased to more than 67% for 16 sequences and still between 12 and 22% for 64 sequences. This clearly indicates that an improved parallelization of PEst is advantageous for further improvement of the overall parallel performance of the program.

15.5.1 Parallelizing PEst: Tree Likelihood Computation

The runtimes of all steps of PEst were more closely examined to identify the time-consuming parts. The Gantt chart in Figure 15.7 shows that step (v), which evaluates the likelihood of the tree based on θ_0, should be targeted to extend the parallelization of PEst additionally to the already parallelized steps (ii) and (iv).

Although the overall running time of step (v) covers a long duration likelihood, computations are repeated for 10 to over 100 sequential estimates of θ to

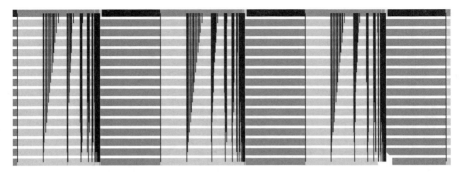

Figure 15.7 Gantt chart covering 7.16 s of optimization cycles, that is, PEst steps (ii)–(v), with the nonparallelized step (v). The dark parts identify the duration consumed by executing PEst step (v). In the master (first line), the dark gray areas depict step (ii) and black areas depict step (v). Steps (iii) and (iv) are located in the light gray area between steps (ii) and (v). Vertical arrows represent communication events.

find an ML estimate. Hence, the runtime of each iteration is very short relative to communication.

The following parallelization strategy has been chosen to parallelize step (v). The tree likelihood for the parameter θ is the product over all partial likelihoods over the sites of the sequence alignment. The likelihoods for each alignment position are computed recursively in a tree traversal. As the number of columns in the alignment is typically much higher than the number of $2n - 3$ edges in the tree, the computation of the likelihoods for equal subsets of the alignment columns to the p processors was adopted as a strategy to improve the performance. It is possible to split the alignment such that each processor gets its corresponding section of all sequences in the alignment (Fig. 15.8). After a processor has computed the likelihoods for all sites in its section of the alignment, it computes the likelihood product of that section and returns the result to the master processor. The master computes the overall likelihood product of the entire alignment given the tree and the parameters from the collected section likelihoods.

Owing to the time constraints highlighted earlier, again a hard-wired SC approach was used to avoid communication overhead.

15.5.2 Results for PEst-(v) on a Homogeneous COW

To exemplify the performance of the parallel step (v), we analyze its speedup for simulated data. As representative speedup measurements are hardly possible on heterogeneous platforms, we used the homogeneous COW described in Section 15.3.1. Figure 15.9a presents the speedup of step (v) for 64 sequences of varying lengths. The parallelization shows promising results. Although a speedup of 9.7 is observed for short sequences (length 192 bp), long sequences show even super-linear speedup (e.g., a speedup of 17.9 for 16 processors with sequences of length 1536 bp).

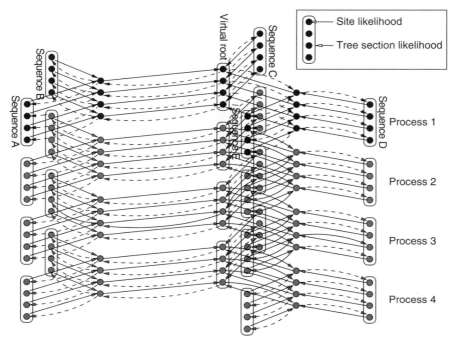

Figure 15.8   Visualization of the parallel likelihood computation [step (v)] for five sequences (A–D) with alignment length $N = 16$ columns using $p = 4$ processes (1–4). The sequences are depicted vertically, columns horizontally. The dots denote (partial) likelihoods that have to be computed recursively for each position along the structure of tree T starting at the root. The 16 positions are assigned in sections of $B = N/p = 4$ columns to the processors. The section likelihoods at the root are then collected to compute the overall likelihood.

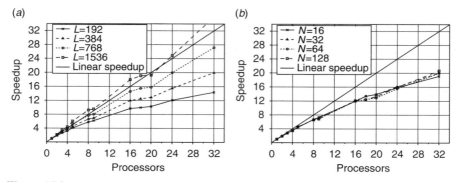

Figure 15.9   Speedup for step (v) of PEst for simulated data with (a) $N = 64$ sequences of different length and (b) sequences of length $L = 384$ bp and different numbers of sequences on the homogeneous COW.

This super-linear speedup is due to cache effects. The tree structure with the short sequence sections can be cached completely during the parallelized likelihood computation, whereas the tree with the complete data set does not fit into the local cache of the homogeneous COW causing a caching overhead in the sequential run.

For sequences of length 384 bp, Figure 15.9b indicates that the speedup is almost independent of the number of sequences in the data sets. The speedup values are satisfactory for all numbers of sequences examined. For instance, for 32 processors, the speedup for 16 up to 128 sequences is between 19.1 and 20.2.

15.5.3   Performance of the Full-Parallel PEst on HomoCOW

Now, we examine the the performance of the parallel version of PEst as presented here. The Gantt chart in Figure 15.10 demonstrates the runtime improvement with the parallelized step (v). Within the time scale of 7.16 s about five estimation cycles could be executed compared with three cycles as shown in Figure 15.7.

The influence of the parallelization on the speedup of the whole PEst step is shown in Figure 15.11. The figure relates the speedup of PEst with (Fig. 15.11a and b) and without (Fig. 15.11c and d) the parallelized step (v) for simulated data with $N = 64$ sequences with varying lengths (Fig. 15.11a and c) and varying numbers sequences of length $L = 384$ bp (Fig. 15.11b and d).

The speedup obtained without the parallelized step (v) shows early saturation (Fig. 15.11a and b). An effect that is more pronounced for longer sequences (Fig. 15.11a). For instance, the speedup is 6.7 with 16 processors for sequences of length 192 bp, but only 2.9 for longer sequences of length 1536 bp. This is due to the nonparallelized step (v), its time consumption grows almost linearly with the length of sequences.

The speedup substantially improves with step (v) parallelized (Fig. 15.11c). The saturation is reached later (i.e., when more processors are used). In addition the level of saturation is higher, thus the speedup is better. Furthermore, the speedup gained for

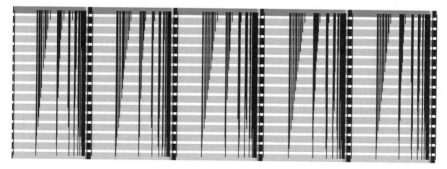

Figure 15.10   Gantt chart covering 7.16 s of optimization cycles, that is, PEst steps (ii)–(v), after parallelizing step (v) as introduced in Section 15.5. The dark parts identify the duration consumed by executing PEst step (v) on the different processors. Vertical arrows represent communication events.

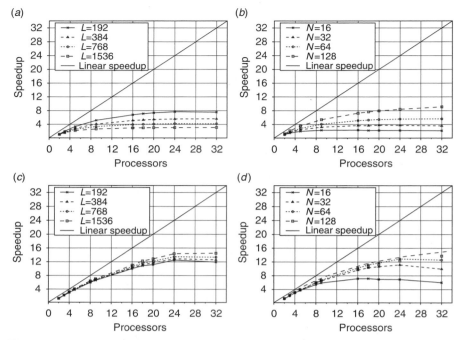

Figure 15.11 Speedup for PEst without (top) and with (bottom) parallelization of step (v) on simulated data with $N = 64$ sequences of different lengths (left) and sequences of length $L = 384$ bp for different numbers of sequences (right) on the homogeneous cluster.

different sequence lengths is almost identical. Best speedup is reached for the longest sequence this time. Although there is a good speedup up to 16 processors (speedup of > 10 for all lengths), it reached saturation (between 11.9 and 13.7) with 24 processors.

For a fixed length and sets of different numbers of sequences, the results show (Fig. 15.11d) that the speedup for sets with less sequences is worse (earlier saturation) than for larger instances. For large sets with 128 sequences, saturation has not been reached with 32 processors. On the whole, the parallelization of step (v) has significantly increased the speedup for all data set sizes. Using 16 processors, speedup values for data sets with 16 and 128 sequences have increased from 2.3 (and 7.3) to 7.1 (and 9.9). For 32 processors, the speedup has reached saturation for data sets with less than 128 sequences.

Biological example. The speedup values for PEst with the improved parallel PEst version of TREE-PUZZLE for the rRNA and protein data are shown in Figure 15.12.

First, we discuss the rRNA example. The speedup saturates early (12–24 processors) for most data sets, only for more than 64 sequences saturation has not been reached with 24 processors. For 16 processors, the speedup is at least 8.6. The speedup becomes worse with 16 and more processors for a small number of sequences and is only 3.9 for 32 processors.

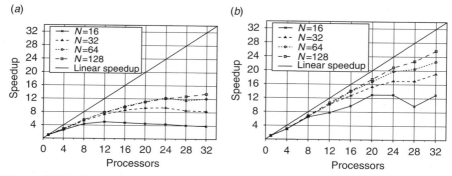

Figure 15.12 Speedup of the parameter estimation for (*a*) Rhodophyta rRNA data and (*b*) Cadherin protein data measured on the homogeneous COW.

For the protein data, the obtained speedup is better than for the DNA data. For sets with 32 and more sequences, it is at least 12.8 for 16 processors. Even for the small number of 16 sequences, it is 9.8 for 16 processors. The effect of increasing speedup for larger problem sizes on identical numbers of processors is called Amdahl effect [37, 38]. It is caused by a lower complexity of the communication overhead compared with the time complexity of the problem size.

15.6 DISCUSSION

The parallel performance of an implementation is limited mainly by the coverage, that is the parallel proportion of the problem, and *granularity*, that is, the amount of work performed until communication is necessary.

The two targets of parallelizing the parameter estimation prior to phylogenetic analysis as delineated earlier exhibit nicely the effects of coverage as well as granularity. The improved parallelization introduced in Section 15.5 aims at the increase of the coverage, after runtime measurements have identified step (v) as consuming most of the runtime (nonparalelized on one processor). After parallelization of step (ii), the relative duration of step (v) became dramatically apparent (cf. Fig. 15.7), now being the limiting time factor to the parameter estimation.

Increasing the coverage alone does not guarantee a good parallel performance. Within the different parallel regions their granularity plays an important role, determined by the size of the independent tasks as well as the scheduling technique assigning batches of tasks (grains) to the processors. Finding efficient ways to parallelize the parameter estimation was much more difficult than in the MLStep and the PStep of the subsequent tree reconstruction analysis, where we have to execute a large number of independent tasks with long durations relative to the communication overhead [39].

Two characteristics of the targeted sequential part determine the achievable granularity of the parallelization, namely, the number of independent tasks and the runtime relative to the communication overhead.

The pairwise distance estimation [step (ii)] comprises $(n^2 - n)/2$ independent tasks for n input sequences. Owing to the maximum likelihood optimization of the distances, the runtime of each estimation is long relative to communication. In contrast, the likelihood computation [step (v)] based on the parameters along the tree consists of the calculation of a large number (alignment length) of independent (column) likelihoods. The calculation time per task, however, is very short.

These facts allow the application of more elaborate scheduling algorithms like SGSS for step (ii), because the communication overhead is small when compared with the computation time. In step (v), the application of such a dynamic load balancing tool is not possible. Experiments, prior to parallelization, had shown that the communication overhead would have substantially increased the parallel runtime. This is the case even more, if Ethernet is used to communicate among the processes within the COW.

Owing to the relatively short parallel regions within the sequential parameter estimation strategy and its inherent high interdependence, the performance of its parallel implementation is not expected to be optimal. Nevertheless, we have to consider that parameter estimation is a minor part of the tree reconstruction procedure, which has been shown to scale well even for large numbers of processors [12, 29]. This makes the results even more valuable, as it reduces substantially the role of the parameter estimation as a bottleneck to the whole analysis.

Considering the positive results in speedup improvement and runtime reduction presented in Figures 15.12 and 15.10, which have been achieved by the additional parallelization of the likelihood computation, makes the effort worthwhile. Moreover, these improvements are very promising, as they have been obtained on COWs, where the parallel performance is hampered by the high communication overhead determined by the high latencies on their relatively slow interconnections. Application on SMP and MPP platforms produces even better results.

Future improvements of the parallel parameter estimation could be achieved approaching the computation using exact likelihood estimation. Unfortunately, the necessary optimization of the tree branch lengths by means of the ML principle is done in a sequential manner. However, this would surely increase the quality of the parallel parameter estimation.

ACKNOWLEDGMENTS

The authors wish to thank the iBIOS group at DKFZ, Heidelberg, for access to the heterogeneous COW. The Zampano Cluster of the ZAM/NIC at FZ Jülich, Germany, has been used to study the homogeneous COW. E.P. was supported by the *Gaststudentenprogramm 2002* of NIC/ZAM. Support by the *Deutsche Forschungsgemeinschaft* is gratefully acknowledged. The TREE-PUZZLE program is available free of charge at http://www.tree-puzzle.de.

REFERENCES

1. J. Felsenstein, The number of evolutionary trees, *Syst. Zool.*, 27, 27–33 (1978).

2. H. Bodlaender, M. Fellows, and T. Warnow, Two Strikes Against Perfect Phylogeny, in *Proceedings of the 19th International Colloquium on Automata, Language, and Programming (ICALP 1992)*, Vol. 623 of *Lecture Notes in Computer Science*, Springer, New York, 1992, pp. 273–283.

3. W. H. E. Day and D. Sankoff, Computational complexity of inferring phylogenies by compatibility, *Syst. Zool.*, 35, 224–229 (1986).

4. L. R. Foulds and R. L. Graham, The Steiner problem in phylogeny is NP-complete, *Adv. Appl. Math.*, 3, 43–49 (1982).

4a. B. Chor and T. Tuller, Maximum Likelihood of Evolutionary Trees is Hard, Proceedings of the 9th Annual International conference on Research in Computational Molecular Biology (RECOMB 2005), Vol. 3500 of Lecture Notes in Computer Science, Springer, Berlin, 2005, pp. 296–310.

5. A. D. Baxevanis, D. B. Davison, R. D. M. Page, G. Stormo, and L. Stein, Eds., *Current Protocols in Bioinformatics*, Wiley and Sons, New York, USA, 2002.

6. J. Felsenstein, *Infering Phylogenies*, Sinauer Associates, Sunderland, Massachusetts, 2004.

7. D. L. Swofford, G. J. Olsen, P. J. Waddell, and D. M. Hillis, Phylogeny Reconstruction, in D. M. Hillis, C. Moritz, and B. K. Mable, Eds., *Molecular Systematics*, Sinauer Associates, Sunderland, Massachusetts, 2nd ed., 1996, pp. 407–514.

8. J. Felsenstein, Evolutionary trees from DNA sequences: A maximum likelihood approach, *J. Mol. Evol.*, 17, 368–376 (1981).

9. G. J. Olsen, H. Matsuda, R. Hagstrom, and R. Overbeek, fastDNAml: A tool for construction of phylogenetic trees of DNA sequences using maximum likelihood, *Comput. Appl. Biosci.*, 10, 41–48 (1994).

10. O. Trelles, On the parallelisation of bioinformatics applications, *Brief. Bioinform.*, 2, 181–194 (2001).

11. G. M. Amdahl, Validity of the Single Processor Approach to Achieving Large Scale Computing Capabilities, in *American Federation of Information Processing Societies Conference Proceedings: Spring Joint Computing Conference (AFIPS 1967)*, Vol. 30, Afips Press, Reston, Va, 1967, pp. 483–485.

12. H. A. Schmidt, K. Strimmer, M. Vingron, and A. von Haeseler, TREE-PUZZLE: Maximum likelihood phylogenetic analysis using quartets and parallel computing, *Bioinformatics*, 18, 502–504 (2002).

13. K. Strimmer and A. von Haeseler, Quartet puzzling: A quartet maximum–likelihood method for reconstructing tree topologies, *Mol. Biol. Evol.*, 13, 964–969 (1996).

14. J. Sullivan, K. E. Holsinger, and C. Simon, The effect of topology on estimates of among-site rate variation. *J. Mol. Evol.*, 42, 308–312 (1996).

15. Z. Yang, Maximum-likelihood models for combined analyses of multiple sequence data, *J. Mol. Evol.*, 42, 587–596 (1996).

16. W. Gropp, S. Huss-Lederman, A. Lumsdaine, E. Lusk, B. Nitzberg, W. Saphir, and M. Snir, *MPI: The Complete Reference. The MPI Extensions*, 2nd ed., Vol. 2, The MIT Press, Cambridge, Massachusetts, 1998.

17. M. Snir, S. W. Otto, S. Huss-Lederman, D. W. Walker, and J. Dongarra, *MPI: The Complete Reference — The MPI Core*, Vol. 1, 2nd ed., The MIT Press, Cambridge, Massachusetts, 1998.

18. S. Tavaré, Some probabilistic and statistical problems on the analysis of DNA sequences, *Lec. Math. Life Sci.*, 17, 57–86 (1986).

19. A. Zharkikh, Estimation of evolutionary distances between nucleotide sequences, *J. Mol. Evol.*, 39, 315–329 (1994).

20. Z. Yang, Estimating the pattern of nucleotide substitution, *J. Mol. Evol.*, 39, 105–111 (1994).

21. M. Hasegawa, H. Kishino, and T.-A. Yano, Dating of the human–ape splitting by a molecular clock of mitochondrial DNA, *J. Mol. Evol.*, 22, 160–174 (1985).

22. T. H. Jukes and C. R. Cantor, Evolution of protein molecules, in *Mammalian Protein Metabolism*, H. N. Munro, Ed., Vol. 3, Academic Press, New York, 1969, pp. 21–123.

23. X. Gu and W.-H. Li, A general additive distance with time-reversibility and rate variation among nucleotide sites, *Proc. Natl. Acad. Sci. USA*, 93, 4671–4676 (1996).

24. E. Baake and A. von Haeseler, Distance measures in terms of substitution processes. *Theor. Popul. Biol.*, 55, 166–175 (1999).

25. T. Uzzel and K. W. Corbin, Fitting discrete probability distributions to evolutionary event, *Science*, 172, 1089–1096 (1971).

26. J. Wakeley, Substitution rate variation among sites in hypervariable region 1 of human mitochondrial DNA, *J. Mol. Evol.*, 37, 613–623 (1993).

27. K. Strimmer, N. Goldman, and A. von Haeseler Bayesian probabilities and quartet puzzling, *Mol. Biol. Evol.*, 14, 210–213 (1997).

28. T. Margush and F. R. McMorris, Consensus n-trees, *Bull. Math. Biol.*, 43, 239–244 (1981).

29. H. A. Schmidt, E. Petzold, M. Vingron, and A. von Haeseler, Molecular phylogenetics: Parallelized parameter estimation and quartet puzzling, *J. Parallel Distrib. Comput.*, 63, 719–727 (2003).

30. N. Saitou and M. Nei, The neighbor–joining method: A new method for reconstructing phylogenetic trees, *Mol. Biol. Evol.*, 4, 406–425 (1987).

31. J. Adachi and M. Hasegawa, *MOLPHY Version 2.3 — Programs for Molecular Phylogenetics Based on Maximum Likelihood*, Vol. 28 of *Computer Science Monographs*, Institute of Statistical Mathematics, Minato-ku, Tokyo, 1996.

32. A. Rambaut and N. C. Grassly, Seq-Gen: An application for the Monte Carlo simulation of DNA sequence evolution along phylogenetic trees, *Comput. Appl. Biosci.*, 13, 235–238 (1997).

33. J. Wuyts, G. Perrière, and Y. van de Peer, The European ribosomal RNA database, *Nucl. Acids Res.*, 32, D101–D103 (2004).

34. L. Duret, D. Mouchiroud, and M. Gouy, HOVERGEN, a database of homologous vertebrate genes, *Nucl. Acids Res.*, 22, 2360–2365 (1994).

35. T. Hagerup, Allocating independent tasks to parallel processors: An experimental study, *J. Parall. Distrib. Comput.*, 47, 185–197 (1997).

36. C. D. Polychronopoulos and D. J. Kuck, Guided self-scheduling: A practical scheduling scheme for parallel supercomputers, *IEEE Trans. Comput.*, 36, 1425–1439 (1987).

37. S. E. Goodman and S. T. Hedetniemi, *Introduction to the Design and Analysis of Algorithms*, McGraw-Hill, New York, 1977.

38. M. J. Quinn, *Parallel Programming in C with MPI and OpenMP*, McGraw-Hill, New York, 2004.

39. H. A. Schmidt, *Phylogenetic Trees from Large Datasets*, Ph.D. thesis, Universität Düsseldorf, 2003.

■■■■■ **CHAPTER 16**

High-Performance Phylogeny Reconstruction Under Maximum Parsimony

TIFFANI L. WILLIAMS, DAVID A. BADER, BERNARD M. E. MORET, and MI YAN

16.1 INTRODUCTION

The similarity of the molecular matter of the organisms on Earth suggests that they all share a common ancestor. Thus any set of species is related, and this relationship is called a phylogeny. The links (or evolutionary relationships) between a set of organisms (or taxa) form a phylogenetic tree, where modern organisms are placed at the leaves and ancestral organisms occupy internal nodes, with the edges of the tree denoting evolutionary relationships. Phylogenies are the organizing principle for most biological knowledge. They are a crucial tool in identifying emerging diseases, predicting disease outbreaks, and protecting ecosystems from invasive species [1, 2]. The greatest impact of phylogenetics will be reconstructing the Tree of Life, the evolutionary history of all known organisms. The precise number of organisms that exist is not known; estimates range from 10 to 100 million species. Today only about 1.7 million species are known.

Reconstructing the evolutionary history of a set of taxa is a very difficult problem, given the enormous implications of phylogenetic analysis. For n organisms, there are $(2n - 5)(2n - 3) \cdots (5)(3)$ distinct binary trees — each a possible hypothesis for the "true" evolutionary history. For example, there are over 13 billion possible trees for 13 taxa. As the size of the tree space increases exponentially with the number of taxa, it is impossible to consider all the possible trees within a reasonable time frame. Most phylogenetic methods use exhaustive searches on small datasets and heuristic strategies for larger datasets. Another difficulty is accessing the accuracy of the reconstructed tree. Short of traveling back into time, there is no way of determining whether the proposed evolutionary history is 100% correct.

Parallel Computing for Bioinformatics and Computational Biology, Edited by Albert Y. Zomaya
Copyright © 2006 John Wiley & Sons, Inc.

16.1.1 Phylogenetic Data

Early evolutionary trees were built by examining the similarities and differences of form and structure of the organisms of interest. Such an approach relies on identifying morphological characters (i.e., presence of wings) and classifying organisms based on the presence or absence of these features. Species are represented by binary sequences corresponding to the morphological data. Each bit corresponds to a character. If a species has a given feature, the corresponding bit is set to 1; otherwise, it is zero. Yet, relying solely on morphological characters can be a major source of phylogenetic error.

With the advent of molecular data, scientists hope to avoid the problems with morphological criteria of relatedness. Today, most trees are built exclusively from molecular sequences. In sequence data, characters are individual positions (or sites) in the string, in which characters can assume one of the four states for nucleotides (A, C, G, T) or one of the 20 states for amino acids. Sequence evolution is studied under a simplifying assumption that each site evolves independently. Data evolve through point mutations (i.e., changes in the state of a character), plus insertions (including duplications) and deletions.

Figure 16.1 shows a simple evolutionary history, from the ancestral sequence at the root (AAGACTT) to modern sequences at the leaves, with evolutionary events occurring on each edge. This history is incomplete, as it does not detail the events that have taken place along each edge of the tree. Thus, one might conclude that, to reach the leftmost leaf, labeled AGGCAT, from its parent, labeled AGGGCAT, one should infer the deletion of one nucleotide (one of the three Gs in the parent). Yet, a more complex scenario may in fact have unfolded. If one were to compare the leftmost leaf with the rightmost one, labeled AGCGCTT, one could account for the difference with two changes: starting with AGGCAT, insert a C between the two Gs to obtain AGCGCAT, then mutate the penultimate A into a T. Yet, the tree itself indicates that the change occurred in a far more complex manner: the path between these two leaves

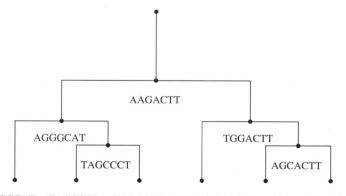

Figure 16.1   Evolving sequences down a fixed tree.

in the tree goes through the series of sequences

AGGCAT $\leftrightarrow$ AGGGCAT $\leftrightarrow$ AAGACTT $\leftrightarrow$ TGGACTT $\leftrightarrow$ AGCACTT $\rightarrow$ AGCGCTT

and each arrow in this series indicates at least one evolutionary event.

Obtaining sequence data is relatively easy given that large amounts of sequence data are easily attainable from databases such as GenBank, along with search tools (such as BLAST). However, "raw" sequence data must first be refined into a format suitable for use in a phylogenetic analysis. The refinement process is comprised the following four steps.

1. Identifying *homologous* genes (i.e., genes that have evolved from a common ancestral gene — and most likely fulfill the same function in each organism) across the organisms of interest.

2. Retrieving followed by aligning the sequences of these genes across the entire set of organism, to identify gaps (corresponding to insertions or deletions) and matches or mutations.

3. Deciding whether to use all available data at once for a *combined* analysis or to use each gene separately and *reconcile* the resulting trees.

4. Applying a phylogenetic method to the aligned sequence data (see Section 16.1.2).

Many packages requiring sequence data are available to reconstruct phylogenetic trees such as PAUP* [3], Phylip [4], MrBayes [5], and TNT [6]. These are available either free of cost or for a modest fee, are in widespread use, and have provided biologists with satisfactory results on many datasets.

Phylogenetic inference based on gene order data provides an alternative to sequence data [7, 8]. Gene order data are based on the structural arrangement of genes in an organism's entire genome. Hence, the gene tree/species tree problem (i.e., the evolution of any given gene need not be identical to that of the organism) is avoided by using gene order data. Gene order data are sparsely available compared to sequence data. So, most tree reconstruction efforts have focused on the reconstruction of phylogenetic trees based on sequence data.

16.1.2 Phylogenetic Methods

There are a plethora of methods — each accounting for some aspect of the evolutionary process — that can be used to infer a phylogenetic tree. The methods can be divided into two broad categories: *distance methods* transform the sequence data into a numerical representation of the data whereas *criteria-based methods* rely on optimality criteria to score the tree based on the individual contribution of the characters in the sequence data.

16.1.2.1 *Distance Methods* Nucleotide sequence similarities can be converted to sequence distances to infer a phylogenetic tree. For n sequences, pairwise distances

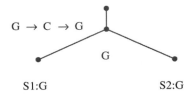

$$G \rightarrow C \rightarrow G$$

G

S1:G   S2:G

Figure 16.2   Silent mutation. The C mutation is unobserved in S1. There are no mutations from the root node to S2. The Hamming distance between sequences S1 and S2 is 0, which is an underestimation of the pattern of evolution (G $\rightarrow$ C $\rightarrow$ G $\rightarrow$ G) from S1 to S2.

are calculated to produce an $n \times n$ distance matrix. One could compute the Hamming distance between two sequences as an estimate of their evolutionary distance. However, the Hamming distance is an underestimate of the true genetic distance between a pair of sequences. If mutations occur randomly, there will be a certain number of positions with *silent mutations* — changes that are subsequently reversed in the course of evolution, leaving no trace in modern organisms (Fig. 16.2). Therefore, in distance-based methods, one estimates the number of substitutions that have actually occurred by applying a specific *evolutionary model*, which makes assumptions about the nature of evolutionary changes. For example, the Jukes–Cantor model simply assumes that when a base changes, it is equally-likely to change to each of the three alternatives [9]. Other models, such as Kimura's two-parameter model [10], provide additional parameters to compute the probability of change from a given state to another given state.

Distance-based methods build the search for the "true" tree into the algorithm, thus returning a unique final topology for a distance matrix associated with a given set of sequences. Neighbor-joining (NJ), the most popular distance-based algorithm [11], begins with each organism in its own subtree. The algorithm joins the pair with the minimum distance, making a subtree whose root replaces the two chosen taxa in the matrix. Distances are recalculated based on this new node, and the joining continues until three nodes remain. These nodes are joined to form an unrooted binary tree. Appealing features of NJ are its simplicity and speed; it runs in $O(n^3)$ time. Other distance methods include refinements of NJ are BioNJ [12] and Weighbor [13].

16.1.2.2   *Criteria-Based Methods*

Criteria-based methods explicitly rank the tree topologies by defining an objective function to score the trees. Tree scores allow any two or more trees to be ranked according to the chosen optimality criterion. Unlike distance-based approaches, there are many possible solutions for a given set of sequences in this approach. Hence, there is an explicit search for the "optimal" tree. Maximum parsimony (MP) and maximum likelihood (ML) are two of the major optimization problems in phylogeny reconstruction, but both are quite difficult to solve (MP is NP-hard [14], and ML harder in practice). We briefly discuss each in turn below. MP is discussed more thoroughly in Section 16.2.

Maximum Parsimony   An intuitive approach for ranking phylogenetic trees is counting the total number of mutations required to explain all the observed character sequences. MP attempts to minimize this score following the philosophy of Occam's razor — the simplest explanation of the data is preferred. Under MP, a total cost is assigned to each tree, and the optimal tree (i.e., the most parsimonious tree) is defined as the one with the smallest total cost. In this approach, a unit cost is given for each nucleotide substitution. A central step in the procedure is allocating sequences to the internal nodes in the tree. For any set of sequence allocations, the total cost of the tree is the sum of the costs of the various edges, where the cost of joining two internal nodes, or an internal node and a leaf, is the number of substitutions needed to move from the sequence at one to the sequence at the other (i.e., the Hamming distance). The most popular software packages that implement MP heuristics are PAUP* [3], Phylip [4], and TNT [6].

Likelihood Methods Likelihood methods require the specification of an evolutionary model. For a given phylogenetic arrangement, the question is: what is the likelihood that evolution under the specified parameters will produce the observed nucleotide sequences? For a given evolutionary hypothesis, the likelihood of the observed change is computed for each position, and then the product of the likelihoods is expressed as a distance or branch length between the sequences. The parameters are then varied, and the combination with the highest likelihood is accepted. This procedure is then repeated for another arrangement, the two topologies compared, and the one with the highest likelihood selected. The selective process is continued until an arrangement is found with the combined ML of both an evolutionary hypothesis and a topology. Finding the best tree under ML is the most computationally demanding of the methods discussed here.

Like MP, ML is an optimization problem. ML seeks the tree and associated model parameter values that maximize the probability of producing the given set of sequences. ML thus depends explicitly on an assumed model of evolution. For example, the ML problem under the Jukes–Cantor model needs to estimate one parameter (the substitution probability) for each edge of the tree, while under the General Markov model 12 parameters must be estimated on each edge. Scoring a fixed tree cannot be done in polynomial time for ML [15], whereas it is easily accomplished in linear time for MP [16]. Various software packages provide heuristics for ML, include PAUP* [3], Phylip [4], fastDNAml [17], and PHYML [18].

Bayesian methods deserve a special mention among likelihood-based approaches; they compute the posterior probability that the observed data would have been produced by various trees (in contrast to a true ML method, which computes the probability that a fixed tree would produce various kinds of data at its leaves). Their implementation with Markov chain Monte-Carlo (MCMC) algorithms often run significantly faster than pure ML methods. Moreover, the moves through state space can be designed to enhance convergence rates and speedup execution. Mr-Bayes [5] is the most popular software package for reconstructing trees based on Bayesian analysis.

16.1.3 Large-Scale Phylogenies

The remainder of this paper considers high-performance approaches to inferring trees under MP. Our reasons for focusing on MP are twofold. First, MP remains the major approach by which phylogenies are reconstructed. A survey of 882 phylogenetic analyses published in 76 journals revealed that 60% of the phylogenies were constructed using MP heuristics [19]. Second, ML methods are too slow to infer trees for large data sets (>1000 sequences). Although distance methods can handle large data sets, studies show that they produce trees with very high topological error [20–22].

16.2 MAXIMUM PARSIMONY

MP is an optimization problem for inferring phylogenetic trees, where each taxon in the input is represented by a string over some alphabet. The input consists of a set S of n strings over a fixed alphabet Σ, where $\Sigma = \{A, C, G, T\}$ represents the set of four nucleotides. Σ could also represent the set of 20 amino acids. The elements of Σ are also called states (or characters). We assume that the sequence data have been properly prepared; particularly, the sequences are already aligned so that all sequences are of length k. Positions within the sequences are sometimes called sites.

Formally, given two sequences a and b of length k, the *Hamming distance* between them is defined as $H(a,b) = |\{i : a_i \neq b_i\}|$. Let T be a tree whose nodes are labeled by sequences of length k over Σ, and let $H(e)$ denote the Hamming distance of the sequences at each endpoint of e. Then the *parsimony length* of the tree T is $\sum_{e \in E(T)} H(e)$. The MP problem seeks the tree T with the minimum length; this is the same as seeking the tree with the smallest number of point mutations for the data. MP is an NP-hard problem [14], but the problem of assigning sequences to internal nodes of a fixed leaf-labeled tree is polynomial [16].

16.2.1 Scoring a Fixed Tree

Fitch's algorithm can be applied to calculate the parsimony score of a fixed tree [23]. First, we define the possible states for each internal node that minimizes the score. Let $S_v \subseteq \Sigma$ denote the set of state assignments for node v. We assume that T is binary and the children of v are x and y. If v is a leaf, then S_v is simply the state of v. If v is an internal node, then its state is based on the state of its two children x and y (i.e., S_x and S_y). If $S_x \cap S_y \neq \varnothing$, then $S_v = S_x \cap S_y$. Otherwise, $S_v = S_x \cup S_y$.

Using a postorder traversal, the above equalities allow us to compute S_v for every node v in T, from the bottom-up (Fig. 16.3). Moreover, the optimal cost (or MP score) of T can be calculated from the bottom-up at the same time. Every time $S_x \cap S_y = \varnothing$, we increment the parsimony score of the tree by 1. The sum of these values over all the sites is the parsimony score of the tree.

After states have been assigned to all internal nodes, we can obtain a labeling of them using a preorder traversal. Once again, we can compute the positions (sites) independently. The root r arbitrarily assign its state to be any element of S_r. Next we visit the remaining nodes in turn, each time assigning a state to the node v from its set S_v. When we visit a node v, we will have already set the state of its parent, p. If the selected state for p is an element of S_v, then we use the same state. Otherwise we pick a state arbitrarily from S_v.

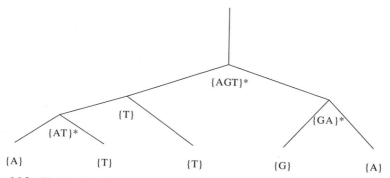

Figure 16.3 Fitch's algorithm applied to single site. Sets denoted by an asterisk increase the parsimony score by 1. Thus, the parsimony score of this tree is 3.

Fitch's algorithm requires $O(nk)$ time to compute the labeling of every node in T and the optimal length (i.e., MP score) of T, where $n = |S|$ and k is the sequence length.

16.2.2 Parsimony-Informative Sites

When computing the parsimony score, one only needs to consider *informative* sites. Parsimony-informative sites include only those sites where at least two distinct characters are observed two or more times. Consider the sequences for four taxa in Table 16.1. The four sequences can be related to one another in three different ways (Fig. 16.4). Let us now consider one site after the other in terms of the minimum changes it involves.

Site 1 has not changed and can therefore be ignored. Site 2 must have suffered at least one change, no matter how we arrange the tree. (This site could, of course, have undergone more than one change, but this assumption is not maximally parsimonious and so is not taken into consideration.) For site 2, all three trees are equally likely and so the site is regarded, like site 1, as being uninformative and not considered any further. Site 3 is informative because it enables us to choose the most parsimonious

TABLE 16.1   DNA Sequences Used in Figure 16.4

	Sites			
	1	2	3	4
S1	G	T	A	G
S2	G	T	A	C
S3	G	T	G	G
S4	G	C	G	C

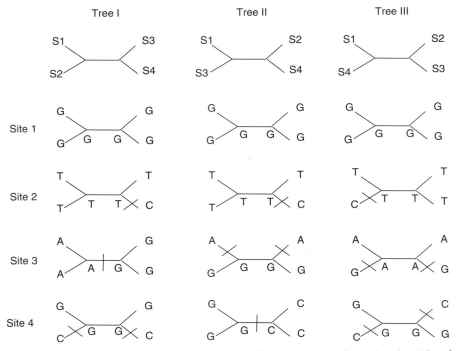

Figure 16.4   Finding the most parsimonious tree. Using only the informative sites (sites 3 and 4), the optimal MP score is 3 as shown by trees I and II. The DNA sequences represented by S1, S2, S3, and S4 are GTAG, GTAC, GTGG, and GCGC, respectively. These sequences are shown in Table 16.1.

tree. Tree I requires one change, whereas trees II and III each require two changes. Finally, site 4 is also informative and identifies tree II as the most parsimonious tree for this site. Thus, trees I and II are the optimal MP trees.

So for four taxa, only three site patterns are informative: *aabb*, *abab*, *abba*, where *a* and *b* are two different states from Σ. Informative and noninformative sites affect only parsimony. All sites, including the constant site, affect the calculation of distance and likelihood methods.

16.2.3   Exact MP Search

One approach to solving MP is to evaluate all possible trees to guarantee that the most parsimonious tree is found. Thus, an algorithm is needed to generate all possible trees. One procedure for generating all possible trees is as follows. Consider the unrooted tree T for three taxa. To create all trees with four taxa, we add the fourth taxon to each edge in T. Thus, the algorithm adds the ith taxon in a stepwise fashion to all possible trees containing the first $i - 1$ taxa until all n taxa have been joined.

The above algorithm makes it clear that the number of possible trees grows by a factor of 2 with each additional taxon. This relationship is expressed as $B(n) = \prod_{i=3}^{n}(2i - 5)$, where $B(n)$ is the number of unrooted binary trees for n taxa. As stated earlier, for 13 taxa there are over 13 billion trees to score. Clearly, the exhaustive search method can only be used for a relatively small number of taxa. An alternative exact procedure, the branch-and-bound (B&B) method [24], operates implicitly by evaluating all possible trees, but cutting off paths of the search tree when it is determined that they cannot possibly lead to optimal trees. We describe a high-performance B&B algorithm in Section 16.3.

16.2.4   MP Heuristics

When data sets become too large to use the exact searching methods, one must resort to the use of heuristics. The fundamental technique is to take an initial estimate of the tree and rearrange branches in it, to reach neighboring trees. If a rearrangement yields a better scoring tree, it becomes the new "best" tree and it is then submitted to a new round of rearrangements. The process continues until no better tree can be found in a full round.

Nearest-neighbor interchange (NNI) is one type of tree rearrangement operation (Fig. 16.5). The NNI operation effectively swaps two adjacent branches on the tree. In particular, an interior edge is removed from the tree, and the two branches connected to it at each end (i.e., a total of five branches are erased). Four subtrees remain that are disconnected from one another. These subtrees can be hooked together into a tree in three possible ways. One of the three trees is the original one, so that each NNI examines two alternative trees. In an unrooted bifurcating tree with n taxa, there will be $n - 3$ interior edges. At each edge, we can examine two neighboring trees. Thus, $2(n - 3)$ neighbors can be examined for a given tree. Other rearrangement operations include subtree pruning and regrafting (SPR), which breaks part of a tree and attaches it elsewhere in the tree, and tree-bisection reconnection (TBR), which breaks a phylogenetic tree into two parts and then reconnects them at a random edge.

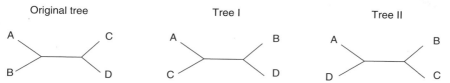

Figure 16.5   Nearest-neighbor interchange. An interior edge is dissolved and the four subtrees (A, B, C, D) connected to it are isolated. The subtrees can be reconnected in two different ways as represented by trees I and II.

16.3 EXACT MP: PARALLEL BRANCH AND BOUND

Although it takes polynomial time to compute the tree cost by Fitch's method [16], it is still very time-consuming to compute the exact MP by exhaustive search due to the enormous size of search space. Hence we use B&B to prune the search space in phylogeny reconstruction [25, 26]. The underlying idea of the B&B algorithm is successive decomposition of the original problem into smaller disjoint subproblems and pruning subproblems whose lower bound is greater than the upper bound until all optimal solutions are found.

16.3.1 Basic Issues in B&B Approach

Our B&B approach has five aspects that affect the performance of the algorithms: branching scheme, search strategy, lower bounding function, initial global upper bound, and the data structure. We will discuss these five aspects in the following sections.

16.3.1.1 Branching Scheme The branch scheme decides how to decompose a subproblem in the search space. Here, each subproblem is associated with a partial tree and the aim is to find the exact MP score among those trees built from the partial tree. Our branching scheme employs the same mechanism to generate all possible unrooted binary trees for a given set of taxa. Consider the unrooted tree for three taxa. The remaining $n - 3$ taxa are added to the tree in stepwise fashion as described in Section 16.2.3. Each new position for taxon i of the partial tree is considered a subproblem. Thus, a subproblem associated with the original partial tree is decomposed into a set of disjoint subproblems, each associated with a new partial tree.

16.3.1.2 Search Strategy The search strategy decides which of the currently open subproblems to be selected for decomposition. The two strategies most commonly used are *depth-first search* (DFS) and *best-first search* (BeFS). DFS is a space-saving strategy and BeFS is targeted more toward a better global upper bound. In the case when the initial global upper bound obtained by heuristic approaches is exactly optimal or very close to exact optimal value, there is no significant difference in the number of examined subproblems between DFS and BeFS search. Therefore DFS has more advantage for reasons of space efficiency. As our experiment shows that heuristics can provide a very good solution, we employ DFS as our primary B&B search strategy and adopt BeFS as a secondary strategy to break ties.

16.3.1.3 Lower Bounding Function of the Subproblems Hendy and Penny [24] use the cost of the associated partial tree as the lower bound of a subproblem. Purdom et al. [27] used the sum of the single-column discrepancy and the cost of the associated tree as the lower bound. For each column (character), the single-column discrepancy is the number of states that do not occur among the taxa in the associated tree but only occur among the remaining taxa. We employ Purdom's lower bounding function as it is much tighter than the one described by Hendy and Penny.

16.3.1.4   Initial Global Upper Bound   We do not compute the upper bound for each subproblem. Instead, before the B&B search, a global upper bound is obtained by a fast heuristic algorithm. We investigate the performance of both the NJ and greedy algorithms. From experiments, we found that the tree obtained from NJ is usually much worse than the one obtained from the greedy algorithm. The greedy algorithm constructs a tree in a stepwise fashion; at each step, the new taxon is added into the best position that results in a partial tree with the minimum score. As adding taxa in different orders yields different trees, we use the greedy algorithm with two different addition orders and use the best score as the initial global upper bound.

16.3.1.5   Data Structure   Each subproblem in the search space of the B&B phylogeny reconstruction is associated with a partial tree and the lower bound. The lower bound serves as the priority, and priority queues are used to save the open problems. As we use DFS search, it is natural to use a priority queue for each depth. Several types of heaps can be found in literature. For simplicity, a traditional D-heap [28] is chosen to represent a priority queue. A D-heap is organized as an array, using the rule that the first location is the root of the tree, and the locations $2i$ and $2i + 1$ are the children of location i.

16.3.2   Preprocessing Before B&B Search

We adopt a series of preprocessing to conduct the B&B search efficiently.

16.3.2.1   Binary Encoding of Original States   The basic operation of Fitch's method is to compute the intersection or union of state sets. As most modern computers can perform efficient bitwise logical operations, we decide to use the binary encoding of state sets to implement intersection and union by bitwise AND and bitwise OR. We assign a one-to-one map between the bits of code and the character states. Given a species, if a state is present, then the corresponding bit is set to 1 otherwise it is set to zero.

16.3.2.2   Decide the Addition Order of the Species   Our experiments show that the overall execution time of B&B phylogeny reconstruction can change drastically depending on the order in which the taxa are added. This can be explained in theory. The lower bounding function we adopt heavily depends on the cost of the associated partial tree. This can also explain why the addition order decided by max–mini rule performs best in most cases. Starting with the initial core tree of three taxa, at each step, for each of the remaining taxa, we find the best inserting position which results the minimum score. Then, we choose the taxon with maximum minimum-score to be added at its best position and go on to next step until all taxa are added. This procedure is called the max–mini approach.

16.3.2.3   Reorder Sites   Fitch made a basic classification of sequence sites (the columns of the sequence matrix) [23]. At a given site, the state that appears more than once is said to be a *nonsingleton state*. A site with at most one nonsingleton states is said to be a *parsimony-uninformative site* because the state changes at such kind of a site can always be explained by the same number of substitutions in all topologies. At the lower levels of B&B phylogeny reconstruction, only a few sites are parsimony-informative. However, with the addition of taxa, many sites turn from parsimony-uninformative to parsimony-informative. Hence, we may compute at which level a site turns into parsimony-informative, then reorder sites so that at each level all the parsimony-informative sites are kept in a contiguous segment of memory. By reordering sites, not only the computation on parsimony-uninformative sites is saved, but also the ratio of cache misses is greatly reduced.

16.3.3   A Fast Algorithm to Compute Tree Length

In a B&B search, an enormous number of trees must be evaluated. Given an original tree, how can we compute the scores of each new tree generated by adding a taxon in the original one? As described in Section 16.2.1, Fitch's method involves one bottom-up pass and one top-down pass of the tree. Each pass computes a set of states for each internal node by different rules, the states obtained in the first pass are *preliminary states* and the states obtained in the second pass are *final states*. Goloboff [29] proposed a method to preprocess the original tree in two passes, which takes constant time to compute the score for each new tree. Gladstein [30] described an incremental algorithm based on preliminary state sets obtained from Fitch's first pass. In practice, Goloboff's method works better than that of Gladstein's. We developed an approach that requires preprocessing the original tree in one pass and for each new tree it takes constant time to compute the score.

Our approach is similar to Fitch's algorithm. Our first pass is identical to Fitch's first pass. However, our second pass uses the rules of Fitch's first pass — not Fitch's second pass rules. We obtain a set of states for each edge, which are the preliminary states of the root. Therefore, when inserting a new taxon in the original tree at an edge, we only compare the states of the new taxon and the states of that edge. We obtain the same result as our bottom-up pass does on the new tree. If the result of the new tree is kept in memory, when we decompose this new tree later, only the top-down pass is required. Thus, in B&B search, our method saves one pass compared with Goloboff's method. Besides the B&B search, our method can also be applied to heuristic-search-based SPR and TBR rearrangement operations.

16.3.4   Parallel Implementation on Symmetric Multiprocessors (SMPs)

To utilize the computation power of parallel computers, we implement the B&B phylogeny reconstruction on Cache-Coherent Uniform Memory Access (CC-UMA) SMPs. In the parallel implementation, each processor selects different active nodes, then processes the computation on it. We use the SPMD (Single Program, Multiple Data) asynchronous model in which each processor works at its own pace and does not have to wait at predetermined points for predetermined data to become available. As the B&B search space tends to be highly irregular, any static distribution of search space is bound to result in significant load imbalance, and the dynamic distribution methods usually involve very complex protocols to exchange subspace between processors to obtain load balance. Compared with the distributed data structure, a single shared data structure is easily maintained on SMPs because there is no load balance problem. We modify the serial data structure by adding a lock for each heap to get the shared data structure. Each heap is protected by a lock and the entire heap is locked whenever it is being modified. Due to the small size of heaps in B&B phylogeny reconstruction, the D-heap is used for simplicity and efficiency.

To minimize the concurrent access contention, a relaxed DFS search strategy is adopted. A heap is accessed if all the heaps at higher levels are empty or locked by other processors. When a processor detects that all the heaps are unlocked and empty, this processor can terminate its own execution of the algorithm.

16.3.5 Experimental Results

We use the benchmark collection at http://www.lirmm.fr/ranwez/PHYLO/ benchmarks24.html. Each data set consists of 24 sequences and the length of each DNA sequence is 500. These tests allow comparison on trees whose internal branch lengths are not all equal, and over a wide variety of tree shapes and evolutionary rates.

We compared the running time between our serial code and PAUP* using the subcommand *bandb addseq=maxmini* on a Sun UltraSparcII workstation. Among the 20 datasets randomly chosen from the benchmark, for 10 datasets our code is 1.2 to 7 times faster than PAUP*, for 5 datasets our code runs as fast as PAUP*, and for 5 datasets our code is 1.2 to 2 times slower than PAUP*. The experiments on our parallel code was carried out on Sun E4500, a uniform-memory-access (UMA) shared-memory parallel machine with 14 UltraSparcII 400MHz processors. We conducted the experiment on 200 datasets randomly chosen from the benchmark, on average we achieve speedups of 1.92, 2.78, and 4.34, on two, four, and eight processors, respectively. The above experimental results show that our strategies on the B&B phylogeny reconstruction are efficient.

16.4 MP HEURISTICS: DISK-COVERING METHODS

Disk-covering methods (DCMs) [22, 31–34] are a family of divide-and-conquer methods designed to "boost" the performance of existing phylogenetic reconstruction methods. All DCMs require four steps.

1. Decompose the data set into subproblems;
2. Apply a "base" phylogenetic method to each subproblem;
3. Merge the subproblems;
4. Refine the resulting tree.

Variants of DCMs come from different decomposition techniques for the initial step; the last three phases are unaffected. The first DCM [31], also called DCM1, was designed for use with distance-based methods and has provable theoretical guarantees about the sequence length required to reconstruct the true tree with high probability under Markov models of evolution [34]. The second DCM [32], also called DCM2, was designed to speedup heuristic searches for MP trees; we showed that when DCM2 was used with PAUP*-TBR search, it produced better trees faster on simulated data sets.

16.4.1 DCM3

We designed the third DCM, or DCM3, from the lessons learned with our first two DCMs. DCM1 can be viewed, in rough terms, as attempting to produce overlapping clusters of taxa to minimize the intracluster diameter; it produces good subproblems (small enough in size), but the structure induced by the decomposition is often poor. DCM2 computes a fixed structure (a graph separator) to overcome that drawback, but the resulting subproblems tend to be too large. Moreover, both DCM1 and DCM2 operate solely from the the matrix of estimated pairwise distances, so that they can produce only one (up to tiebreaking) decomposition. In contrast, DCM3 uses a dynamically updated *guide tree* (in practice, the current estimate of the phylogeny) to direct the decomposition, so that DCM3 will produce different decompositions for different guide trees. This feature enables us to focus the search on the best parts of the search space and is at the heart of the iterative use of the decomposition: roughly speaking, the iteration in *Rec-I-DCM3* consists of successive refinements of the guide tree. By using the guide tree, DCM3 also produces smaller subproblems than DCM2: the guide tree provides the decomposition structure, but does so in a manner responsive to the phylogenetic estimation process. Finally, we designed DCM3 to be much faster than either DCM1 or DCM2 in producing the decompositions (mostly by not insisting on their optimality), as previous experiments had shown that dataset decomposition used most of the running time with DCM2.

16.4.1.1 *Short Subtree Graph*

An essential component of our DCM3 decomposition algorithm is computing the short subtree graph. Consider a tree T on our set S of taxa and an edge weighting w of T, $w: E(T) \rightarrow \Re^+$. (A possible edge weighting is given by the Hamming distances under the MP labeling of the nodes of T.) We construct the *short subtree graph*, which is the union of cliques formed on "short subtrees" around each edge. Let e be an internal edge (not touching a leaf) in T; then removing e and its two endpoints from T breaks T into four subtrees. A *short quartet* around e comprises of four leaves, one from each of these four subtrees, where each leaf is selected to be the closest (according to the edge weights) in its tree to e. This short quartet need not be unique: several leaves in the same subtree may lie at the same shortest distance from e. Thus we define the *short subtree* around e to be the set $X(e)$ of all leaves that are part of a short quartet around e. Figure 16.6 provides an example of computing a short subtree around an edge e. We will use the *clique* on $X(e)$: the graph with $X(e)$ as its vertices and with every pairwise edge present, weighted according to w; denote this clique by $K(e)$. The *short subtree graph* is then the union, over all internal edges e of the guide tree, of $K(e)$.

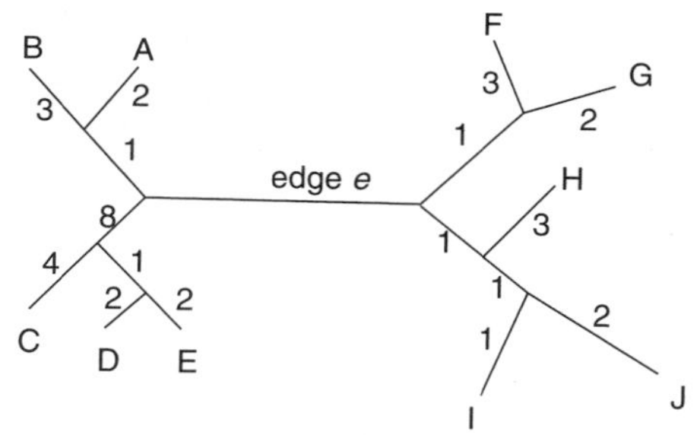

Figure 16.6 Short subtree around edge e. The leaves that form the short subtree around e are A, D, E, G, and I.

16.4.1.2 DCM3 Decomposition
Our decomposition algorithm requires finding a *centroid edge* in the guide tree T — that is, an edge that, when removed, produces the most balanced bipartition of the leaves. Our approach is based on the notion of a *centroid edge* in T — that is, an edge that, when removed, produces the most balanced bipartition of the leaves. Let X be the leaves of the short subtree around a centroid edge e. In our experience, X is always a separator of the short subtree graph, so we can define the subproblems as $A_i = X \cup C_i$, where $G - X$ has m distinct connected components, $C_1, C_2, \ldots, C_m$. (Should X fail to be a separator in the short subtree graph, we would then resort to computing all maximal clique separators in G.) As we cannot afford to compute the short subtree graph, we cannot directly verify that X is a separator. However, we can proceed without knowing the short subtree graph [33]. By using this result, we can compute a decomposition that is not exactly that induced by the centroid edge, but that retains good characteristics (i.e., small number of small subproblems).

Finding a centroid edge e through a simple tree traversal requires linear time. Computing $X(e)$ and then the subproblems $A \cup X(e)$, $B \cup X(e)$, $C \cup X(e)$, and $D \cup X(e)$ also require linear time. Thus, a DCM3 decomposition can be computed in $O(n)$ time, where A, B, C, and D are the sets of leaves in the four subtrees obtained by deleting e from T.

16.4.1.3 Comparison of DCM Decompositions
We designed DCM3 in part to avoid producing large subsets, as DCM2 is prone to do. Yet, of course, the subproblems produced from a very large data set remain too large for immediate solution by a base method. Hence we used the approach successfully pioneered by Tang and Moret [35] with DCM-GRAPPA and used DCM3 recursively, producing smaller and smaller subproblems until every subproblem was small enough to be solved directly. Figure 16.7 shows that DCM3 produces subproblems much smaller than those produced by DCM2. (Recursive-DCM3 in this series of tests was set up to recurse until each subproblem was of size at most one-eighth of the original size.) The characteristics of the datasets are given in Section 16.4.2.1.

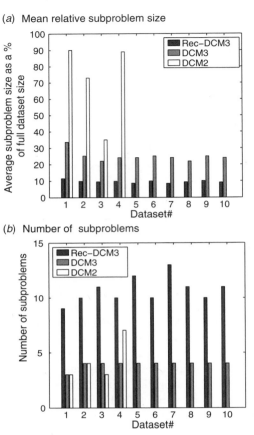

Figure 16.7   Comparison of DCM2, DCM3, and Recursive-DCM3 decompositions. DCM2 decompositions on datasets 5 to 10 could not be computed due to memory limitations.

16.4.1.4 Subtree Construction and Assembly   Once the data set is decomposed into overlapping subsets $A_1, A_2, \ldots, A_m$ (for us, $m \leq 4$ is typical), subtrees are constructed for each subset, A_i, using the chosen "base method," and then combined using the Strict Consensus Merger [31, 32] to produce a tree on the combined data set. The proof that the resulting tree is accurate (i.e., agrees, with high probability and in the limit, with the unknown underlying "true tree") is similar to the argument shown in Ref. [31].

Our *Rec-I-DCM3* algorithm takes as input the set $S = \{s_1, \ldots, s_n\}$ of n aligned biomolecular sequences, the chosen base method, and a starting tree T. In our experiments, we have used TNT (with default settings) as our base method, as it is the hardest to improve (in comparison, the PAUP* implementation of the parsimony ratchet [36] is easier to improve). Our algorithm produces smaller subproblems by recursively applying the centroid-edge decomposition until each subproblem is of size at most k. The subtrees are then computed, merged, and resolved (from the bottom-up, using random resolution) to obtain a binary tree on the full data set. These steps are repeated for a specified number of iterations.

16.4.2 Experimental Design

The experimental evaluation of algorithms for phylogenetic reconstruction is a difficult endeavor (see Refs. [37, 38] for details). Because credible simulations of evolution remain lacking at the scale of 10,000 or more taxa, we chose to use biological data sets in our study. This choice ensures biological relevance of our results, but it prevents us from evaluating the accuracy of reconstructed trees, as the "true" tree is not available. However, other work from our group [39] tells us that we need to achieve excellent approximation of the parsimony score (tree length) to have any chance at reconstructing the true topology. Thus, we focused our testing on the quality of approximation in terms of the parsimony score.

16.4.2.1 Biological Data Sets
We present our results on 10 large biological datasets — because of their large size, all but one are RNA data, ranging from a smallest set of 1322 sequences to a largest of 13,921 sequences, all with sequence lengths between 800 and 1600. Seven of these 10 sets have over 4500 sequences and thus are not, in practice, accurately analyzable with existing MP heuristics.

1. A set of 1322 aligned large subunit ribosomal RNA of all organisms (1078 sites) [40].
2. A set of 2000 aligned eukaryotes ribosomal RNA sequences (1326 sites) obtained from the Gutell Lab at the Institute for Cellular and Molecular Biology, the University of Texas at Austin.
3. A set of 2594 *rbcL* DNA sequences (1428 sites) [41].
4. A set of 4583 aligned 16s ribosomal actinobacteria RNA sequences (1263 sites) [42].
5. A set of 6590 aligned small subunit ribosomal eukaryotes RNA sequences (1661 sites) [40].
6. A set of 7180 aligned ribosomal RNA sequences (1122 sites) from three phylogenetic domains obtained from the Gutell Lab at the Institute for Cellular and Molecular Biology, the University of Texas at Austin.
7. A set of 7233 aligned 16s ribosomal firmicutes (bacteria) RNA sequences (1352 sites) [42].
8. A set of 8506 aligned ribosomal RNA sequences (851 sites) from three phylogenetic domains, plus organelles (mitochondria and chloroplast), obtained from the Gutell Lab at the Institute for Cellular and Molecular Biology, the University of Texas at Austin.
9. A set of 11,361 aligned small subunit ribosomal bacteria RNA sequences (1360 sites) [40].
10. A set of 13,921 aligned 16s ribosomal proteobacteria RNA sequences (1359 sites) [42].

16.4.2.2 Parameters and Measurements   We chose to test performance during the first 24 hours of computation on each dataset for each method, taking
hourly "snapshots" along the way to evaluate the progress of each method. We
asked the following two questions: (i) how much of an improvement is gained
by using *Rec-I-DCM3* versus TNT, if any? and (ii) how long does the best TNT
trial (out of five runs) take to attain the average MP score obtained at 24 hours by
Rec-I-DCM3?

To answer these questions, we ran TNT and *Rec-I-DCM3(TNT)*, which uses TNT
as its base method, on our 10 biological data sets, using five independent runs, all on
the same platform, with computed variances for all measurements.

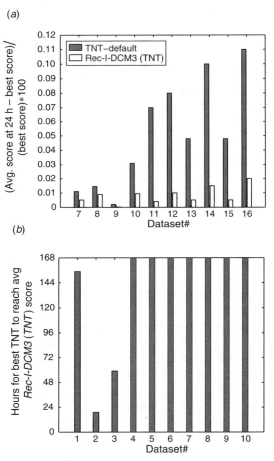

Figure 16.8   (*a*) Average deviation above optimal after 24 hours by TNT and
Rec-I-DCM3(TNT). (*b*) Time taken by the single best TNT trial, extended to run for up to
a week, to match the average *Rec-I-DCM3(TNT)* score at 24 hours — bars that reach the top
indicate that TNT could not reach a match after a week of computation.

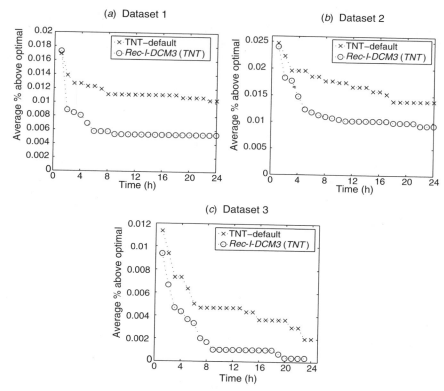

Figure 16.9 Average MP scores of TNT and *Rec-I-DCM3(TNT)* on datasets 1, 2, and 3, given as the percentage above the optimal score. *Note*: The vertical range varies across the datasets.

16.4.2.3 *Implementation and Platform*

Our DCM implementations are a combination of LEDA, C++, and Perl scripts. The TNT Linux executable was obtained from Goloboff, one of the authors of TNT. We ran our experiments on three sets of processors, all running Linux: the Phylofarm cluster of 9 dual 500 MHz Pentium III processors; a part of the 132-processor SCOUT cluster, consisting of 16 dual 733 MHz Pentium III processors; and the Phylocluster of 24 dual 1.5 GHz AMD Athlon processors, all at the University of Texas at Austin. For each data set, all the methods were executed on the same cluster; larger data sets were run on the faster machines.

16.4.3 Results

We defined the "optimal" MP score on each hour data set to be the best score found over all five runs among all methods in the 24-hour period we allowed; on our data sets, this optimal score was always obtained by *Rec-I-DCM3(TNT)*. On each data set and for each method, we computed the average MP score at hourly intervals and reported this value as a percentage of deviation from optimality. In our experiments, on

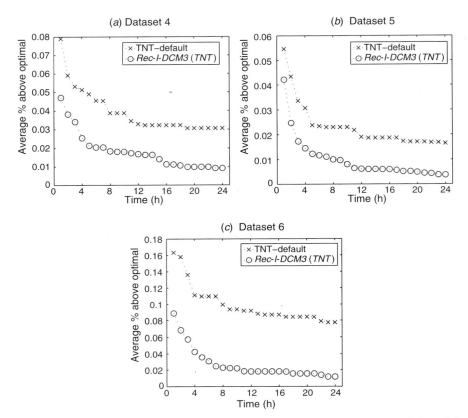

Figure 16.10 Average MP scores of TNT and *Rec-I-DCM3(TNT)* on datasets 4, 5, and 6, given as the percentage above the optimal score. *Note*: The vertical range varies across the datasets.

every dataset and at every point in time (within these 24 hours), the best performance was obtained by *Rec-I-DCM3(TNT)*. As only error rates <0.01% are tolerable, *Rec-I-DCM3*'s performance is very impressive; all trees are at least 99.99% correct. TNT failed to reach this level of accuracy consistently, especially on data sets with more than 4500 sequences.

Figure 16.8a shows the performance of *Rec-I-DCM3(TNT)* and of TNT at 24 hours. As the size of the data set increases, the relative error in MP scores increases, but at a much faster rate for TNT than for *Rec-I-DCM3(TNT)*, so that the accuracy gap between the two increases quite rapidly. Figure 16.8b indicates how long it took TNT, in the best of five runs, to match the average scores obtained by *Rec-I-DCM3(TNT)* after 24 hours — we stopped the clock after 1 week of computation if the TNT run had not achieved a match by then, something that happened on the seven largest data sets. (The standard deviations of the MP scores at 24 hours for all the methods on all the data sets were very low, at most 0.035%.)

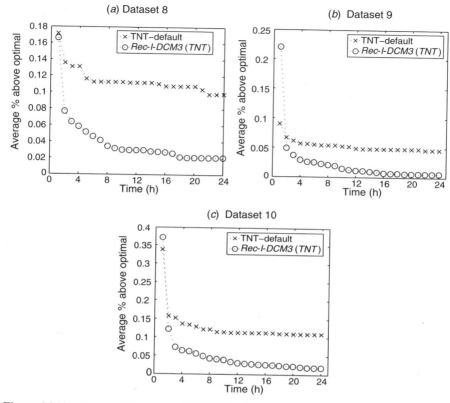

Figure 16.11 Average MP scores of TNT and *Rec-I-DCM3(TNT)* on datasets 8, 9, and 10, given as the percentage above the optimal score. *Note*: The vertical range varies across the datasets.

Figure 16.9 compares the time-dependent behaviors of TNT and *Rec-I-DCM3(TNT)* on our three smallest datasets (1, 2, and 3), while Figures 16.10 and 16.11 show the same for three medium datasets (4, 5, and 6) and three largest datasets (8, 9, and 10), respectively. (It should be noted that the 24 hour time limit was perhaps overly limiting for the largest dataset: a quick look at the curves appears to indicate that even *Rec-I-DCM3(TNT)* has not yet reached a plateau at that point.) The improvement achieved by boosting TNT with *Rec-I-DCM3* is significant on all datasets and at all time intervals. In particular, the boosted version of TNT shows much stronger decreases in MP scores in the first several hours than the unboosted version.

Figure 16.12 shows how the error rate (deviation above the optimal MP score) of *Rec-I-DCM3(TNT)* decreases with computation time on each of the 10 datasets. While the initial trees computed for the large datasets tend to exhibit large error (as large as 0.35%), the error drops very rapidly — even more rapidly for the large datasets than

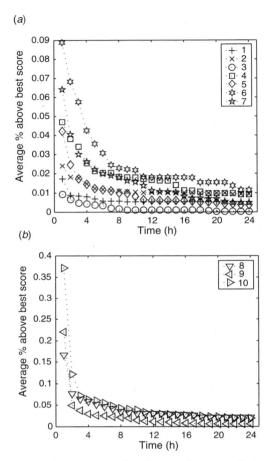

Figure 16.12   Decrease in error rates with time on all datasets for *Rec-I-DCM3(TNT)*

for the smaller ones. Thus, not only do the error rates of *Rec-I-DCM3(TNT)* fall more rapidly than those of TNT alone, but also they have a positive second derivative: the larger they are, the faster they fall.

16.5 SUMMARY AND OPEN PROBLEMS

MP is the most popular optimization criterion for analyzing large datasets. Because of the importance of MP analyses in phylogeny reconstruction, systematists and algorithm researchers have studied existing methods (specifically implementations of heuristics in different software packages) to see which performed the best. We have provided an overview of two high-performance phylogenetic algorithms, which dramatically outperform traditional techniques. Hence, larger analyses can be performed within a reasonable time period. Each performance gain brings us closer to reconstructing the "Tree of Life." Yet, much work still remains to be done. Below, we provide a biased sample of open problems that appear to be the most promising or important avenues for further exploration.

- *Tree Accuracy*. Bootstrapping is one technique for estimating the support of the inferred tree [43]. The bootstrap proceeds by resampling the original data matrix with replacement of the sites. The process is repeated many times (1000 times or more) and phylogenies are reconstructed for each bootstrap replicate. The bootstrap support for any internal edge is the number of times it was recovered during the bootstrapping procedure. However, it is not clear how to access the accuracy of large-scale phylogenies on real data sets as a single analysis may require weeks or months to complete.

- *Evolutionary Models for DNA Sequences*. Of course, no simulation can be accurate enough to replace real data. However, simulated data sets enable evaluations of solution quality (because the model, and thus the "true" answer, is known) and can be generated in arbitrarily large numbers to ensure statistical significance. Often the performance ranking of phylogenetic methods on simulated data is different from that on real data. Hence, realistic models for generating simulated data are needed.

- *Stopping Criteria*. Currently, phylogenetic analyses are stopped when one is tired of waiting for a result. Depending on the user's current needs, an analysis can be short (i.e., 24 hours) or it could run for several months. However, there is little work on determining when a search should terminate.

- *Multiple Sequence Alignment*. Although alignment was mentioned briefly in Section 16.1.1, it is probably the most crucial phase of inferring an accurate tree. More work is needed to understand the effect sequence alignment has on inferring the "true" evolutionary tree.

ACKNOWLEDGMENTS

This work was supported by the National Science Foundation under grants ACI-00-81404 (Bader), ACI-00-93039 (Bader), ANI 02-03584 (Moret), DEB 01-20709 (Moret), DEB 99-10123 (Bader), EF 03-31654 (Bader and Moret), IIS 01-13095 (Moret), IIS 01-21377 (Moret), by an Alfred P. Sloan Foundation Postdoctoral Fellowship in Computational Molecular Biology DE-FG03-02ER63426 (Williams), and by the Radcliffe Institute for Advanced Study (Williams). We thank Pablo Goloboff for providing us with a Linux executable for TNT.

REFERENCES

1. D. Bader, B. M. Moret, and L. Vawter, Industrial Applications of High-Performance Computing for Phylogeny Reconstruction, in H. Siegel, Ed., *Proceedings of the SPIE Commercial Applications for High-performance Computing*, Vol. 4528, Denver, CO. SPIE, 2001, pp. 159–168.

2. J. Cracraft, The seven great questions of systematic biology: an essential foundation for conservation and the sustainable use of biodiversity, *Ann. Missouri Bot. Gard.*, 89, 127–144 (2002).

3. D. L. Swofford, PAUP*: Phylogenetic Analysis Using Parsimony (and other Methods). Sinauer Associates, Sunderland, Massachusetts, Version 4.0.

4. J. Felsenstein, Phylogenetic inference package (PHYLIP), version 3.2, *Cladistics*, 5, 164–166 (1989).

5. J. P. Huelsenbeck and F. Ronquist, "MR-BAYES: Bayesian inference of phylogenetic trees," *Bioinformatics*, 17 (8), 754–755 (2001).

6. P. Goloboff, Analyzing large data sets in reasonable times: solutions for composite optima, *Cladistics*, 15, 415–428 (1999).

7. B. Moret, J. Tang, and T. Warnow, Reconstructing Phylogenies from Gene-Content and Gene-Order Data, in O. Gascuel, Ed., *Mathematics of Evolution and Phylogeny*, Oxford University Press, 2005, pp. 321–352.

8. B. M. E. Moret and T. Warnow, "Advances in Phylogeny Reconstruction from Gene Order and Content Data," in Molecular Evolution: Producing the Biochemical Data, Part B, E. A. Zimmer and E. H. Roalson, eds., Vol. 395 of Methods in Enzymology, Elsevier (2005), 673–700.

9. T. Jukes, Evolution of Protein Molecules, in M. Munro, Ed., *Mammalian Protein Metabolism*, Vol. III, Academic Press, New York, 1969, pp. 21–132.

10. M. Kimura, A simple model for estimating evolutionary rates of base substitutions through comparative studies of nucleotide sequences, *J. Mol. Evol.*, 16, 111–120 (1980).

11. N. Saitou and M. Nei, The neighbor-joining method: A new method for reconstructing phylogenetic trees, *Mol. Biol. Evol.*, 4, 406–425 (1987).

12. O. Gascuel, BIONJ: an improved version of the NJ algorithm based on a simple model of sequence data, *Mol. Biol. Evol.*, 14, 685–695 (1997).

13. W. Bruno, N. Socci, and A. Halpern, Weighted neighbor joining: a likelihood-based approach to distance-based phylogeny reconstruction, *Mol. Biol. Evol.*, 17 (1), 189–197 (2000).

14. L. R. Foulds and R. L. Graham, The Steiner problem in phylogeny is NP-complete, *Adv. App. Math.*, 3, 43–49 (1982).

15. M. Steel, The maximum likelihood point for a phylogenetic tree is not unique, *Systematic Biol.*, 43 (4), 560–564 (1994).

16. W. M. Fitch, Toward defining the course of evolution: minimal change for a specific tree topology, *Syst. Zool.*, 20, 406–416 (1971).

17. G. Olsen, H. Matsuda, R. Hagstrom, and R. Overbeek, fastdnaml: a tool for construction of phylogenetic trees of DNA sequences using maximum likelihood, *Comput. Appl. Biosci.*, 10, 41–48 (1994).

18. S. Guindon and O. Gascuel, A simple, fast, and accurate algorithm to estimate large phylogenies by maximum likelihood, *Syst. Biol.*, 52 (5), 696–704 (2003).

19. M. Sanderson, B. Baldwin, G. Bharathan, C. Campbell, D. Ferguson, J. Porter, C. V. Dohlen, M. Wojciechowski, and M. Donoghue, The growth of phylogenetic information and the need for a phylogenetic database, *Systematic Biology*, 42, 562–568 (1993).

20. B. Moret, U. Roshan, and T. Warnow, Sequence Length Requirements for Phylogenetic Methods, in *Proceedings of the second International Workshop Algorithms in Bioinformatics* (WABI'02), Vol. 2452, *Lecture Notes in Computer Science*, Springer-Verlag, 2002, pp. 343–356.

21. L. Nakhleh, B. Moret, U. Roshan, K. S. John, J. Sun, and T. Warnow, The Accuracy of Fast Phylogenetic Methods for Large Data Sets, in *Proceedings of the seventh Pacific Symposium Biocomputing* (PSB'2002), World Scientific Publication, 2002, pp. 211–222.

22. L. Nakhleh, U. Roshan, K. St. John, J. Sun, and T. Warnow, Designing Fast Converging Phylogenetic Methods, in *Proceedings of the Ninth International Conference on Intelligent Systems for Molecular Biology* (ISMB'01), Vol. 17, Bioinformatics, Oxford Univeristy Press, 2001, pp. S190–S198.

23. W. Fitch, On the problem of discovering the most parsimonious tree, *Am. Nat.* 111 (978), 223–257 (1977).

24. M. Hendy and D. Penny, Branch and bound algorithms to determine minimal evolutionary trees, *Math. Biosci.*, 59, 277–290 (1982).

25. D. A. Bader, W. E. Hart, and C. A. Phillips, Parallel Algorithm Design for Branch and Bound, in H. Greenberg, Ed., *Tutorials on Methodologies and Applications in Operation Research*, Chapter 5, Academic Press, 2004, pp. 1–44.

26. M. Yan and D. A. Bader, High-Performance Algorithms for Phylogeny Reconstruction with Maximum Parsimony, in S. Aluru, Ed., *Handbook on Computational Molecular Biology*, Chapman & Hall/CRC Computer and Information Science Series, 2005, in press.

27. P. J. Purdom, P. Bradford, K. Tamura, and S. Kumar, Single column discrepancy and dynamic max–mini optimization for quickly finding the most parsimonious evolutionary trees, *Bioinfomatics*, 2 (16), 140–151 (2000).

28. D. Knuth, *The Art of Computer Programming: Sorting and Searching*, Vol. 3, Addison-Wesley, Reading, MA, 1973.

29. P. A. Goloboff, Character optimization and calculation of tree lengths, *Cladistics*, 9, 433–436 (1993).

30. D. S. Gladstein, Efficient incremental character optimization, *Cladistics*, 13, 21–26 (1997).

31. D. Huson, S. Nettles, and T. Warnow, Disk-covering, a fast-converging method for phylogenetic tree reconstruction, *J. Comput. Biol.*, 6, 369–386 (1999).

32. D. Huson, L. Vawter, and T. Warnow, Solving Large-scale Phylogenetic Problems using DCM2, in *Proceedings of the 7th International Conference on Intelligent Systems for Molecular Biology* (ISMB'99), AAAI Press, 1999, pp. 118–129.

33. U. Roshan, B. M. E. Moret, T. L. Williams, and T. Warnow, Rec-I-DCM3: A Fast Algorithmic Technique for Reconstructing Large Phylogenetic Trees, in *Proceedings of the IEEE Computer Society Bioinformatics Conference* (CSB 2004), IEEE Press. 2004, pp. 98–109.

34. T. Warnow, B. Moret, and K. St. John, Absolute Convergence: True Trees from Short Sequences, in *Proceedings of the 12th Ann. ACM-SIAM Symp. Discrete Algorithms* (SODA'01), SIAM Press, 2001, pp. 186–195.

35. J. Tang and B. Moret, Scaling Up Accurate Phylogenetic Reconstruction from Gene-Order Data, in *Proceedings of the 11th International Conference on Intelligent Systems for Molecular Biology* (ISMB'03), Vol. 19 (Suppl. 1), *Bioinformatics*, 2003, pp. i305–i312.

36. O. Bininda-Emonds, Ratchet Implementation in PAUP*4.0b10. http://www.tierzucht.tum.de:8080/WWW/Homepages/Bininda-Emonds.

37. B. Moret, Towards a Discipline of Experimental Algorithmics, in M. Goldwasser, D. Johnson, and C. McGeoch, Eds., *Data Structures, Near Neighbor Searches, and Methodology: Fifth and Sixth DIMACS Implementation Challenges*, Vol. 59, *DIMACS Monographs*, American Mathematical Society, 2002.

38. B. Moret and T. Warnow, Reconstructing Optimal Phylogenetic Trees: A Challenge in Experimental Algorithmics, in R. Fleischer, B. Moret, and E. Schmidt, Eds., *Experimental Algorithmics*, Vol. 2547, *Lecture Notes in Computer Science*, Springer-Verlag, 2002, pp. 163–180.

39. T. Williams, B. M. Berger-Wolf, U. Roshan, and T. Warnow, The Relationship Between Maximum Parsimony Scores and Phylogenetic Tree Topologies, Technical Report TR-CS-2004-04, Department of Computer Science, The University of New Mexico, 2004.

40. J. Wuyts, Y. V. de Peer, T. Winkelmans, and R. D. Wachter, The European database on small subunit ribosomal RNA, *Nucl. Acids Res.*, 30, 183–185 (2002).

41. M. Kallerjo, J. S. Farris, M. W. Chase, B. Bremer, and M. F. Fay, Simultaneous parsimony jackknife analysis of 2538 *rbcL* DNA sequences reveals support for major clades of green plants, land plants, seed plants, and flowering plants, *Plant. Syst. Evol.*, 213, 259–287 (1998).

42. B. Maidak, J. Cole, T. Lilburn, C. T. Parker, Jr., P. R. Saxman, J. Stredwick, G. Garrity, B. Li, G. Olsen, S. P. Pamanik, T. Schmidt, and J. Tiedje, The RDP (ribosomal database project) continues, *Nucl. Acids Res.*, 28, 173–174 (2000).

43. J. Felsenstein, *Inferring Phylogenies*, Sinauer Associates, 2003.

PART IV

PROTEIN FOLDING

CHAPTER 17

Protein Folding with the Parallel Replica Exchange Molecular Dynamics Method

RUHONG ZHOU

A highly parallel replica exchange molecular dynamics (REMD) method and its application in protein folding and protein structure prediction are described in this chapter. The REMD method couples molecular dynamics trajectories with a temperature exchange Monte Carlo process for efficient sampling of the conformational space. Two example protein systems, one α-helix and one β-hairpin, are used to demonstrate the power of the algorithm. Up to 64 replicas of solvated protein systems are simulated in parallel over a wide range of temperatures. Very high efficiency ($>98\%$) can be achieved with this embarrassingly parallel algorithm. The simulation results show that the combined trajectories in temperature and configurational space allow a replica to overcome free energy barriers present at low temperatures. These large-scale simulations also reveal detailed results on folding mechanisms, intermediate state structures, thermodynamic properties, and the temperature dependences for both protein systems. Furthermore, the extensive data from REMD simulations are used to assess the various solvation models and force fields, which provides insights into the fix of the problems and further improvement of the models. Finally, the usage of the REMD method in protein structure refinement is also discussed.

17.1 INTRODUCTION

How to efficiently sample the conformational space of complex biological systems, such as protein folding, remains a great challenge in molecular biology [1–6]. The free energy landscape of protein folding is believed to be at least partially rugged. At room

Parallel Computing for Bioinformatics and Computational Biology, Edited by Albert Y. Zomaya
Copyright © 2006 John Wiley & Sons, Inc.

temperature, protein systems get trapped in many local minima. This trapping limits the capacity to effectively sample the conformational space. Many methods have been proposed to enhance the conformation space sampling. These methods include multi-canonical sampling, simulated tempering, parallel tempering, catalytic tempering, and expanded ensembles. For a good review, the readers are directed to the paper by Berne and Straub [7]. Despite the enormous efforts from many groups, it is still difficult to perform realistic all-atom folding simulations for normal size proteins, which often take microseconds to milliseconds to fold. The only microsecond simulation with an all-atom model and explicit solvent was done by Duan and Kollman [8] on a 36-residue α-helical villin headpiece protein. Thus, more efficient simulation methods, particularly algorithms for parallel computing [9, 10], and more powerful supercomputers such as IBM's BlueGene machine (http://www.research.ibm.com/bluegene) or super PC-clusters such as folding@home (http://folding.stanford.edu), are in great demand to tackle this problem.

Proteins are mainly comprised of two major secondary structural features: α-helices and β-sheets. It is observed that 40–70% of secondary structure in proteins falls into these two categories. It is believed that understanding the folding of these elements will be a foundation for investigating larger and more complex structures. As a result, these secondary structures have been studied extensively using both theoretical and experimental approaches. The α-helices are very fundamental structural units and are believed to be the early structural elements in the protein evolution history. They are highly ordered and are stabilized by local interactions — the backbone hydrogen bonds between the ith and the $(i + 4)$th residues. The β-sheets, in contrast, are more complex, as the long-range interactions play an important role in their formation. The interest in β-sheet structures is enhanced by the fact that they can form amyloid fibrils involved in fatal diseases such as Alzheimer's disease [1]. The β-hairpins, two anti-parallel β-strands, are the simplest of β-sheet structures.

The simplicity of these α-helix and β-hairpin structures makes them amenable to thorough studies. It should be pointed out that although these peptides still have many of the complexities associated with the folding free energy landscape despite of their structural simplicity, they are ideal systems to understand the role of competing interactions in determining protein structures. Experimental approaches to studying these structures include NMR, infrared, circular dichroism, T-jump experiments, and so on [1]. These experimental techniques have been more than complemented by computational methods, of which molecular dynamics (MD) simulations are much favored [3–5]. The MD simulations, which make use of classical Newton equation to generate trajectories, are playing an ever-expanding role in biochemistry and biophysics because of substantial increases in computational power and concomitant improvements in force fields.

Generally speaking, there are two types of parallel computing in protein folding studies, one is the force decomposition and/or volume decomposition based "true" parallel MD useful for kinetics studies [8] and the other is loosely coupled parallel replica based approach mainly for thermodynamics studies [11, 12]. Here, we will focus on the later approach for its high efficiency and easy implementation. The best known algorithm in this category is arguably the replica exchange method (REM), also known as parallel tempering [11–17]. In the REM method, replicas are run in parallel at a sequence of temperatures ranging from the desired temperature to a high temperature at which the replica can easily surmount the energy barriers. From time to time, the configurations of neighboring replicas are exchanged and this exchange is accepted by a Metropolis acceptance criterion that guarantees the detailed balance. Thus, REM is essentially a Monte Carlo (MC) method. Because the high temperature replica can traverse high energy barriers, there is a mechanism for the low temperature replicas to overcome the quasi-ergodicity they would otherwise encounter in a single temperature replica. The replicas can be generated by MC, hybrid Monte Carlo (HMC), or MD with velocity rescaling. Okamoto and co-workers [13] have developed a temperature rescaling scheme for coupling MD with REM — the replica exchange molecular dynamics (REMD) method. These large-scale simulations cannot only study the protein folding mechanism but also provide extensive data for force field and solvation model assessment and further improvement.

Two example small protein systems, one α-helix [Ace-A5(AAARA)3A-Nme] and one β-hairpin (Ace-GEWTYDDATKTFTVTE-Nme), are used to illustrate the power of the parallel algorithm in this chapter. Larger protein systems have also been studied with the REMD method, and interested readers can refer to previous publications for details [16, 18–22]. Here, we select these two structurally simpler systems, largely because there are a lot of data available for comparison of solvation models and force fields with the same peptide — one of the major benefits of the large-scale simulations. We will also briefly discuss the application of REMD in protein structure refinement. This chapter is not aimed to be a complete review of the subject, but instead to pick a few specific examples, some from our own, to illustrate the parallel REMD method and its application in protein folding and protein structure prediction.

17.2 REMD METHOD

A brief discussion of the REM method based on molecular dynamics (REMD) is described subsequently. We have also implemented a combination of HMC with REM, which is more efficient for smaller systems. The implementations are basically very similar; therefore, for simplicity, we will only describe the MD based implementation following Okamoto's velocity rescaling approach [13, 23].

Suppose there is a protein system (or any other molecular systems) of N atoms with masses m_k ($k = 1, 2, \ldots, N$), and coordinates and momenta $q \equiv \{q_1, q_2, \ldots, q_N\}$ and $p \equiv \{p_1, p_2, \ldots, p_N\}$, the Hamiltonian $H(p, q)$ of the system can be expressed as,

$$H(p, q) = \sum_{k=1}^{N} \frac{p_k^2}{2m_k} + V(q) \qquad (17.1)$$

where $V(q)$ is the potential energy of the N atom system. In the canonical ensemble at temperature T, each state $x \equiv (p, q)$ with the Hamiltonian $H(p, q)$ is weighted by the Boltzmann factor

$$\rho(x;T) = \frac{1}{Z} \exp^{[-\beta H(p,q)]} \tag{17.2}$$

where $\beta = 1/k_B T$ (k_B is the Boltzmann constant) and Z is the partition function $Z = \int \exp^{[-\beta H(p,q)]} \, dp \, dq$. The generalized ensemble for REM consists of M non-interacting replicas of the original system at M different temperatures T_m ($m = 1, 2, \ldots, M$). The replicas are arranged such that there is always exactly one replica at each temperature. Then, there is an one-to-one correspondence between replicas and temperatures; the label i ($i = 1, 2, \ldots, M$) for replicas is a permutation of the label m ($m = 1, 2, \ldots, M$) for temperatures and vice versa,

$$i = i(m) \equiv f(m)$$
$$m = m(i) \equiv f^{-1}(i) \tag{17.3}$$

where $f(m)$ is a permutation function of m and $f^{-1}(i)$ is its inverse.

The meta state X of this generalized ensemble will be a collection of all the M sets of coordinates $q^{[i]}$ and momenta $p^{[i]}$ of the N atoms in replica i at temperature T_m: $x_m^{[i]} \equiv (p^{[i]}, q^{[i]})_m$

$$X = \left(x_1^{[i(1)]}, \ldots, x_M^{[i(M)]} \right) = \left(x_{m(1)}^{[1]}, \ldots, x_{m(M)}^{[M]} \right) \tag{17.4}$$

where the superscript and the subscript in $x_m^{[i]}$ label the replica and the temperature indices, respectively, which have an one-to-one correspondence. Because the replicas are noninteracting, the weight factor for the state X in this generalized ensemble is given by the product of Boltzmann factors for each replica or each T

$$\rho_{REM}(X) = \exp\left\{ -\sum_{i=1}^{M} \beta_{m(i)} H\left(p^{[i]}, q^{[i]} \right) \right\} = \exp\left\{ -\sum_{m=1}^{M} \beta_m H\left(p^{[i(m)]}, q^{[i(m)]} \right) \right\}, \tag{17.5}$$

where $i(m)$ and $m(i)$ are the permutation functions defined in Eq. (17.3). Now, suppose a pair of replicas is exchanged. For generality, we assume the pair being swapped is (i, j), which are at temperatures (T_m, T_n), respectively,

$$X = (\ldots, x_m^{[i]}, \ldots, x_n^{[j]}, \ldots) \longrightarrow X' = (\ldots, x_m^{[j]'}, \ldots, x_n^{[i]'}, \ldots) \tag{17.6}$$

The indices i, j and m, n are related by the permutation function. Upon the exchange, the permutation function will be updated, let us rename it f'

$$i = f(m) \longrightarrow j = f'(m)$$
$$j = f(n) \longrightarrow i = f'(n) \tag{17.7}$$

The earlier exchange of replicas can be rewritten in more detail as

$$x_m^{[i]} = (p^{[i]}, q^{[i]})_m \longrightarrow x_m^{[j]'} = (p^{[j]'}, q^{[j]})_m$$
$$x_n^{[j]} = (p^{[j]}, q^{[j]})_n \longrightarrow x_n^{[i]'} = (p^{[i]'}, q^{[i]})_n \tag{17.8}$$

where the new momenta $p^{[i]'}$ and $p^{[j]'}$ will be defined subsequently. It is easy to see that this process of exchanging a pair of replicas (i, j) is equivalent to exchanging the two corresponding temperatures T_m and T_n

$$x_m^{[i]} = (p^{[i]}, q^{[i]})_m \longrightarrow x_n^{[i]'} = (p^{[i]'}, q^{[i]})_n$$
$$x_n^{[j]} = (p^{[j]}, q^{[j]})_n \longrightarrow x_m^{[j]'} = (p^{[j]'}, q^{[j]})_m \tag{17.9}$$

This mathematical equivalence is very useful in practice, as it can be used to reduce the communication costs in REM, that is, rather than exchanging the two full sets of coordinates and momenta, one can just swap the two temperatures for the two replicas and then update the permutation function. In the original implementations of the REM [11, 12], MC algorithms were used, thus only the coordinates q and the potential energy $V(q)$ need to be taken into account. For this exchange process to generate the equilibrium canonical distribution functions, it is necessary and sufficient to impose the detailed balance condition on the transition probability $T(X \to X')$ from meta state X to X'

$$\rho_{REM}(X)T(X \to X') = \rho_{REM}(X')T(X' \to X) \tag{17.10}$$

From Eqs. (17.1), (17.5) and (17.10), one can easily derive that

$$\frac{T(X \to X')}{T(X' \to X)} = \exp(-\Delta) \tag{17.11}$$

where

$$\Delta = (\beta_m - \beta_n)\left(H(x^{[j]}) - H(x^{[i]})\right) \tag{17.12}$$

For MD simulations, both the potential energy and kinetic energy are present in the Hamiltonian, thus Okamoto and Sugita et al. [13] introduced a momenta rescaling scheme to simplify the detailed balance condition

$$p_n^{[i]'} = \sqrt{\frac{T_n}{T_m}} p_m^{[i]}$$

$$p_m^{[j]'} = \sqrt{\frac{T_m}{T_n}} p_n^{[j]}. \tag{17.13}$$

With the earlier velocity rescaling scheme, the detailed balance equation can be reduced to

$$\Delta = (\beta_m - \beta_n)\left(V(q^{[j]}) - V(q^{[i]})\right) \tag{17.14}$$

Note that because of the velocity rescaling in Eq. (17.13), the kinetic energy terms are canceled out in the earlier detailed balance condition and that the same criterion, Eq. (17.14), which was originally derived for MC algorithm, is recovered. It should also be noted that this detailed balance criterion is exactly the same as in Jump Walking methods [24, 25]. The earlier detailed balance condition can be easily satisfied, for instance, by the usual Metropolis criterion

$$T(X \to X') \equiv T\left(x_m^{[i]} | x_n^{[j]}\right) = \begin{cases} 1 & \text{for } \Delta \le 0 \\ \exp(-\Delta), & \text{for } \Delta > 0 \end{cases} \tag{17.15}$$

Thus, the replica exchange method can be summarized as the following two-step algorithm

(1) Each replica i $(i = 1, 2, \ldots, M)$, which is in a canonical ensemble of the fixed temperature T_m $(m = 1, 2, \ldots, M)$, is simulated *simultaneously* and *independently* for a certain MC or MD steps.

(2) Pick some pairs of replicas, for example, $x_m^{[i]}$ and $x_n^{[j]}$, and exchange the replicas with the probability $T(x_m^{[i]} | x_n^{[j]})$ as defined in Eq. (17.15), and then go back to step (1).

In most of the work described in the following sections, the MD algorithm is used in step (1) with velocity rescaling (thus a REMD method) and all the replicas are run in parallel; in step (2), only the replicas in neighboring temperatures are attempted for exchanges because the acceptance ratio of the exchange decreases exponentially with the difference of the two β's. Note that whenever a replica exchange is accepted in step (2), the permutation functions in Eq. (17.3) must be updated.

The major advantage of REM over other generalized-ensemble methods such as multi-canonical algorithm and simulated tempering lies in the fact that the weight factor is a priori known [Eq. (17.5)], whereas in the latter algorithms, the determination of the weight factors can be nontrivial for complex systems and very time consuming. In REM method, a random walk in the "temperature" space is realized for each replica, which in turn induces a random walk in potential energy space. This alleviates the problem of being trapped in states of energy local minimum.

Another way to use MD in REM but without the earlier velocity scaling is through HMC, which utilizes MD as well in the underlying sampling. Either with velocity rescaling or with HMC, REM is essentially a MC method as mentioned earlier. In general, HMC is more efficient for smaller systems, such as protein in a continuum solvent [26], whereas the velocity rescaling approach is more appropriate for the explicit solvent simulations. Either way, the good thing about REMD is that the new advances in MD algorithms can be easily incorporated into replica exchange scheme. As shown subsequently, the REMD method is a powerful tool for protein conformational space sampling.

17.3 PROTEIN FOLDING WITH REMD

17.3.1 Two Example Protein Systems

The α-helix system is a 21-residue peptide with a large propensity of forming α-helical structure in water at room temperature. It contains three Arg residues in its Ace-A_5(AAARA)$_3$A-Nme sequence (called Fs peptide, where Fs stands for folded short and Ace and Nme are capping groups) and has been widely described in the experimental literature [27–30]. The Fs peptide is then solvated in a cubic box with a side of 43.7 Å containing 2660 TIP3P water molecules [14]. The initial configurations are selected from a 1 ns simulation at 700 K of 42 identical solvated systems, starting from an α-helical configuration and random velocities. The helical content of the starting configurations ranges from 15 to 73%. The solvated systems are subjected to 500 steps of steepest descent energy minimization and a 100-ps MD simulation at constant pressure and temperature (1 atm, 300 K). A modified AMBER94 force field is used with a cutoff of 8.0 Å for nonbonded interactions. Nonbonded pair lists were updated every 10 integration steps. The integration step in all simulations is 0.002 ps. The system is coupled to an external heat bath with relaxation time of 0.1 ps. All bonds involving hydrogen atoms are constrained using SHAKE with a tolerance of 0.0005 Å. The Fs peptide is simulated in the temperature range of 275–551 K with up to 42 replicas. The temperatures of the replicas are chosen to maintain an exchange rate among replicas of 8–20%. Exchanges are attempted every 125 integration steps (0.25 ps).

The β-hairpin system, in contrast, is taken from the C-terminus (residues 41–56) of protein G (PDB entry 2gb1). It has 16 residues with a residue sequence of Ace-GEWTYDDATKTFTVTE-Nme. The folding time for this hairpin is about 6 μs. With the explicit solvent, the solvated system has 1361 water molecules [single point charge (SPC) water, with density 1.0 g/cm^3] and also three counter ions (3Na$^+$) for neutralizing the molecular system, which results in a total of 4342 atoms in each replica. A total of 64 replicas are simulated for the explicit solvent systems with temperatures spanning from 270 to 695 K. For the implicit solvent simulations, only the protein atoms are present and 18 replicas are used with the same temperature range (less replicas needed for smaller system size). The OPLSAA force field [31], as well as AMBER94, AMBER96, and AMBER99 force fields, is used. In explicit solvent simulations, the periodic boundary conditions are used, and the long-range electrostatic interactions are calculated by the P3ME method, with a mesh size of $36 \times 36 \times 36$ (grid spacing about 1.0 Å). A time step of 4.0 fs (outer timestep) is used for all temperatures using the RESPA [32–34] algorithm. A standard equilibration protocol is used for each replica. It starts with a conjugate gradient minimization for each system. Then a two-stage equilibration, each consisting of a 100 ps MD, is followed. The final configurations of the earlier equilibration are then used as the starting points for the replica simulations and data are collected after 100 ps REMD simulations. Each replica is run for 3.0 ns for data collection, with replica exchanges attempted every 0.4–2 ps [15, 26, 35, 36].

17.3.2   Optimal Temperature Sequences in REMD

The optimal temperature distributions in the replica exchange method can be obtained by running a few trial replicas with short MD simulations. The temperature gap can thus be determined by monitoring the acceptance ratio desired between neighboring temperatures. The rest of the temperature list can usually be interpolated, as the optimal temperature distribution should be roughly exponential assuming the heat capacity is relatively a constant [15]. Using the β-hairpin as an example, the optimal temperature sequence is found to be 270, 274, 278, . . . , 685, and 695 K, with an acceptance ratio of about 30–40%. The temperature gaps between these replicas range from 4 to 10 K. Both temperature swap and configuration swap (coordinates and velocities) have been implemented in REMD with MPI, and very high efficiency (up to 98%) has been achieved with this embarrassingly parallel algorithm. Figure 17.1 shows the speedup for the example β-hairpin with 1, 2, 4, . . . , 64, 128 processors or replicas (each replica is run on one processor). The speedup is measured by the aggregate MD steps (number of replicas multiplied by the MD steps in one replica) finished by

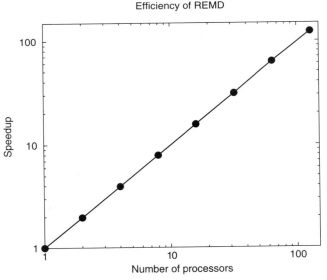

Figure 17.1   The speedup of REMD versus the number of processors used. The speedup is measured by the aggregate MD steps (number of replicas multiplied by the MD steps in one replica) finished by REMD within 1 h of wall-clock time divided by that finished by a single processor and single replica run. The simulations were done on the solvated β-hairpin system with replica exchanges attempted every 250 MD steps.

(a)

(b)

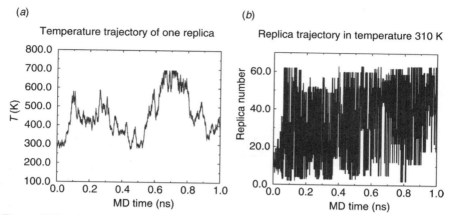

Figure 17.2 The replica exchange trajectory from the β-hairpin simulation: (a) the temperature trajectory for one replica (started at 310 K) and (b) the replica trajectory in temperature 310 K. Both show that the replica exchange method is "surfing" the temperature space effectively.

REMD within 1 h of wall clock time divided by that finished by a single processor and single replica run. Even with the configuration swap, the communication time is minimal when compared with the computing time of each MD step. Furthermore, the swaps happen every hundreds of MD steps. The minimal loss in the efficiency is mainly because of the fluctuations of the CPU time in each processor.

Figure 17.2a shows the "temperature trajectory" for one replica started at 310 K for the β-hairpin. It is clear that this replica walks freely in the temperature space. A similar graph, Figure 17.2b, monitors the "replica trajectory" at one particular temperature 310 K. It shows that various replicas visit this temperature randomly. These two plots basically show the time trajectory of the permutation function and its inverse in Eq. (17.3) as we discussed in Section 17.2. The results indicate that our temperature series is reasonably optimized for this system with sufficiently high acceptance ratios for replica exchanges.

17.3.3   Folding of an α-Helix

In spite of the large number of experimental studies conducted in α-helical peptides, there is still much debate concerning the propensity of Ala residues to stabilize α-helices. Garcia and co-workers have applied the REMD method to the 21-residue Fs peptide folding. Figure 17.3 shows a comparison of the helix content profiles as a function of temperature for the Fs and A21 peptides (a pure Ala 21-residue peptide also simulated for comparison) with a slightly modified AMBER94 force field [14]. A residue is classified whether as helical or not based on the backbone (ϕ, ψ) angles. For the details of the helix residue definition, the readers can refer to the original paper [14]. The simulation gives the folding transition temperature $T_{1/2}$ of 345 K and 90% helical content at 275 K for the Fs peptide. The results seem to agree well with experimental

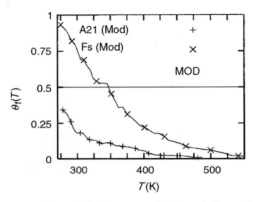

Figure 17.3 Comparison of the helical content of A21 and Fs peptides as a function of temperature obtained from a modified AMBER94 force field. The transition temperatures are 345 K for Fs and <275 K for A21.

data for Fs [27–30]. As for comparison, only 34% helical content is obtained for A21 at 275 K. The thermodynamic properties, such as enthalpy (ΔH) and entropy (ΔS) can be determined from these temperature-dependent data. This is another benefit of the REMD method, as it not only helps the lower temperature replica to cross the free energy barrier but also obtains the equilibrium properties at each temperature. Assuming a linear temperature dependence on the specific heat, and taking the unfolded state as reference, one gets $\Delta H(273\,\text{K}) = -4.6\,\text{kJ/mol}$, $\Delta S(273\,\text{K}) = -15\,\text{J/(K mol)}$ and $\Delta C_p(273\,\text{K}) = -60\,\text{J/(mol K)}$ [14].

Simulations reveal higher stability of the Fs peptide over A21. For example, at 350 K, Fs peptide is 5.8 kJ/mol more stable than the A21 peptide [14]. This difference in stability has to come from the Arg side chains. To test the hypothesis that chain desolvation might be responsible for this stabilization [6] and to provide a molecular description of the shielding, the authors studied the coordination of water to the peptide backbone. Figure 17.4 shows the water coordination number for the peptide backbone carbonyl oxygen. Carbonyl oxygen atoms involved in backbone hydrogen bonding, on average, have one coordinated water molecule. End carbonyl oxygen atoms not participating in hydrogen bonds have two coordinated water molecules. Shielded carbonyl oxygen atoms have zero coordinated water molecules. At low temperature, the peptide is in the α-helical conformation and has an average coordination number about 1. At high temperature, the peptide is in the coil conformation and shows a coordination >1.5 on average. For the Fs peptide, they also observed that at low temperature, the coordination number adopts a number of 0.5 at three positions along the sequence. The atoms with low coordination correspond to carbonyl oxygen four residues before Arg side chains, which are shielded from water by the Arg side chain. There are two configurations, shown in Figure 17.5, which yield coordination numbers of 1 and 0. On average, they are approximately equally populated, yielding an average coordination number of 0.5.

Nc = 0

Arg c=0 bridged water molecule

Nc = 1

Figure 17.4 Illustration of the shielding of the backbone carbonyl oxygen atoms by the Arg side chain of Fs. The Arg side chains stabilize this configuration by a favorable guanidinim group interaction with a carbonyl oxygen four amino acids upstream of the Arg in sequence and by the bridging of water molecules that coordinate to carbonyl oxygen five amino acids upstream of the Arg in sequence. Two equally populated configurations show the carbonyl oxygen to be exposed (Nc = 1) and shielded by the side chain (Nc = 0). The average coordination number for these carbonyl oxygen is ~0.5 for residues 5, 10, and 15.

This analysis indicates that the additional stabilization observed for the Fs peptide relative to the A21 peptide is produced by the partial shielding of the backbone hydrogen bonds from water, provided by the Arg side chains. The enhanced stability of shielded hydrogen bonds can be explained in terms of the competition for backbone hydrogen bonds between water molecules and backbone donors and acceptors. Thermal fluctuations can cause local opening and closing of backbone $CO \cdots NH$ hydrogen bonds. When the local environment is shielded from access to water, the hydrogen bond-breaking event is energetically unfavorable [37]. The destabilization of the opened $CO \cdots NH$ hydrogen bonds by side chain shielding results in the stabilization of the shielded hydrogen bond conformation, which contributes to the overall stability of helical conformations. The Arg side chain partially shields the carbonyl oxygen of the fourth amino acid upstream from the Arg.

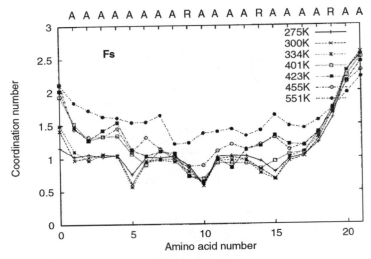

Figure 17.5 Water coordination to the backbone carbonyl oxygen atoms along the peptide sequence. The coordination number is about 1, except when the carbonyl group is four amino acids before an Arg side chain. The Arg side chain shields the carbonyl oxygen atom from exposure to water.

17.3.4 Folding of a β-Hairpin

The second example, the C-terminus β-hairpin of protein G, has recently received much attention from both experimental and theoretical fronts [38–47]. Its fast folding speed (folds in 6 μs) and reasonable stability in aqueous solution make it a system of choice for studying the β-hairpin folding in isolation. Again, we use the highly parallel REMD to study the free energy landscape and folding mechanism of this β-hairpin.

The free energy landscape is often calculated by the histogramming analysis [44, 48]

$$P(X) = \frac{1}{Z} \exp(-\beta W(X)) \qquad (17.16)$$

and

$$W(X_2) - W(X_1) = -kT \log \left(\frac{P(X_2)}{P(X_1)} \right), \qquad (17.17)$$

where $P(X)$ is the normalized probability obtained from a histogram analysis as a function of X. X is any set of reaction coordinates (RCs) or any parameters describing the conformational space. $W(X_2) - W(X_1)$ is thus the relative free energy or so-called potential of mean force (PMF). Here, we will use the number of β-strand hydrogen bonds (N_{HB}^{β}) and the radius of gyration of the hydrophobic core (R_g^{core}) as the RC for the free energy contour map (many other RCs have also been used [15]). N_{HB}^{β} is defined as the number of native β-strand backbone hydrogen bonds excluding the two at the turn of the hairpin (five out of total seven such hydrogen bonds). R_g^{core} is the radius of gyration of the side chain atoms on the four hydrophobic residues, Trp43, Tyr45, Phe52, and Val54.

Figure 17.6 shows the free energy contour map (in units of kT) and representative structures at each local free energy basin. The free energy landscape reveals a few interesting features: (1) The overall free energy contour map shows an "L" shape, indicating that the folding mechanism is likely driven by the hydrophobic core collapse. If it were driven by a "hydrogen bond zipping" mechanism as proposed by experiment [38, 39], the shape would have been a more "diagonal" one in the 2D graph. (2) There are four states at biological temperature: the native folded state (F), the unfolded state (U) and two intermediates, a "molten globule" state, which is similar to Pande and co-workers' [41, 42] state H and a partially folded state (P). (3) The intermediate state H shows a compact hydrophobic core but with no β-strand

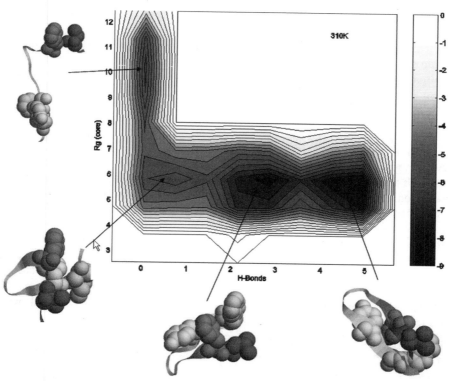

Figure 17.6 Folding free energy contour map of the β-hairpin versus the two reaction coordinates, the number of β-sheet hydrogen bonds N_{HB}^{β} and the radius gyration of the hydrophobic core residues R_g^{core}. The representative structures are shown for each energy state. The hydrophobic core residues, Trp43, Tyr45, Phe52, and Val54, are shown in space-fill mode, whereas all other residues are shown as ribbons. The free energy is in units of kT, and contours are spaced at intervals of 0.5 kT (same for all contour maps in this chapter).

hydrogen bonds. These results, in general, are consistent with what has been found by others [38, 41, 43, 44, 49]. However, there are also some significant differences. One important difference is in the folding mechanism. Eaton and co-workers [38, 39] proposed a "hydrogen bond zipping" mechanism in which folding initiates at the turn and propagates toward the tails, so that the hydrophobic clusters, from which most of the stabilization derives, form relatively late during the reaction. Our analysis shows no evidence of this hydrogen bond zipping model. Pande and Rokhsar [41] and Garcia and Sanbonmatsu [44] found similar results using the CHARMM and AMBER force fields, namely, the β-hairpin system first folds into a compact H state before it folds into the native structure. It is also found that both H and P states have a well-formed hydrophobic core, but the P state (two to three hydrogen bonds) has a significantly higher population than the state H (zero to one hydrogen bonds). The heavy population in the partially folded state P and a low free energy barrier from the H state to the P state (≈ 0.8 kT) implies that the final β-strand hydrogen bonds could be formed nearly simultaneously with the hydrophobic core. Thus, it seems that after an initial core collapse of the peptide, it quickly adopts a partially folded state with two to three hydrogen bonds before folding into the native state.

The simulation also reveals the folding transition temperature, α helical content, hydrogen bond distributions at various temperatures, temperature dependence of the hairpin population, and pair NOE distances, and so on. The detailed results can be found in previous publications [15, 26].

17.3.5 Assessment of Solvation Models and Force Fields

As mentioned earlier, one very useful aspect of these large-scale simulations, such as those from the parallel REMD, is to provide extensive data for assessment of the solvation models and protein force fields. Because explicit solvent simulations require enormous CPU time, many recent studies have been carried out with implicit solvent models [50–53]. However, it is still an open question as to how well these implicit solvent models can predict the thermodynamics as well as the kinetics of protein folding. It is of great interest to see whether implicit solvent models can reproduce the results from explicit solvent simulations or experiment. It is also of interest to see how various protein force fields behave in protein folding simulations with explicit or implicit solvent. In this chapter, we will focus on the implicit solvent models with some exposure to the protein force fields as well.

17.3.5.1 Comparison of Solvation Models Using the Same OPLSAA Force Field   Three solvation models are compared here: explicit solvent model, SPC model [54], and two implicit (or continuum) solvent models, generalized Born (GB) model [51] and Poisson-Boltzmann (PB) model [50]. We first use the same protein force field, the OPLSAA force field [31], for simulations with three different solvation models to avoid any inconsistencies from the protein force fields, and at the same time, we use large-scale simulations such as REMD to eliminate any sampling convergence issues.

The GB model is an empirical method that estimates the electrostatic response from the polarization of the dielectric medium. The surface GB implementation [52] (SGB) was used in this study. Various implementations of the GB model have slight differences in handling the single energy integrations and parametrizations but, in principle, they are the same physical model to approximate the more rigorous PB model discussed subsequently. Both the GB and PB models treat the solute (protein) as some fixed charge distribution contained in a region of low dielectric constant (typically $\epsilon = 1$–4) that is surrounded by a high dielectric continuum solvent ($\epsilon = 80$). The nonpolar cavity term [26, 35, 36] in both GB and PB continuum solvent models is measured by the usual solvent accessible surface areas with a surface tension of $5.0\,\mathrm{cal/mol\,\AA^{-2}}$.

Let us first examine the GB model. Figure 17.7a shows the free energy contour map of the explicit solvent simulation and Figure 17.7b shows that of the SGB simulation. Several important features arise for the SGB model: (1) The native state ($N_{\mathrm{HB}} = 5.0$ and $R_{\mathrm{g}}^{\mathrm{core}} = 5.8\,\text{Å}$) is no longer the lowest free energy state in the SGB continuum solvent model. (2) The most heavily populated state or the lowest free energy state has no meaningful β-strand hydrogen bonds ($N_{\mathrm{HB}} \approx 0$), and also it has a slightly higher radius of gyration for the hydrophobic core ($R_{\mathrm{g}}^{\mathrm{core}} \approx 7.0\,\text{Å}$). It has

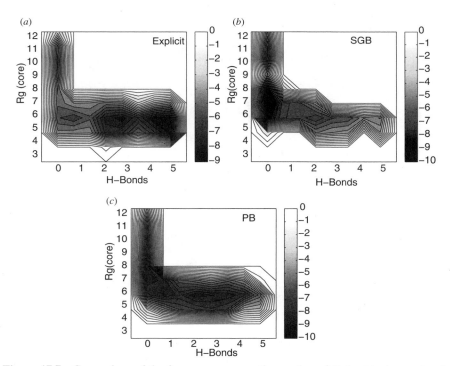

Figure 17.7 Comparison of the free energy versus the number of β-sheet hydrogen bonds N_{HB}^{β} and the hydrophobic core radius gyration $R_{\mathrm{g}}^{\mathrm{core}}$ at 310 K: (a) from the explicit solvent model, (b) from the implicit solvent GB model, and (c) from the implicit solvent PB model.

about 2.92 kcal/mol (4.75 kT) lower free energy than the native state (as this state is similar to the intermediate state H from explicit solvent model [15, 41, 44], we also name it the H state for simplicity in the following). (3) The overall shape of the free energy contour map, however, is still an "L" shape, which is the same as the contour map for the explicit solvent simulation. This indicates that the folding process is probably still driven by hydrophobic core collapse [15].

To understand why the SGB continuum solvent model favors nonnative structures, we analyze the heavily populated state H in detail. Figure 17.8*b* shows one of the representative structures from clustering in state H, and for comparison, we also show one of the representative structures from the explicit solvent model, which is basically the native structure (Fig. 17.8*a*). Two interesting observations emerge from the comparison of these two structures: (1) The hydrophobic residue PHE52

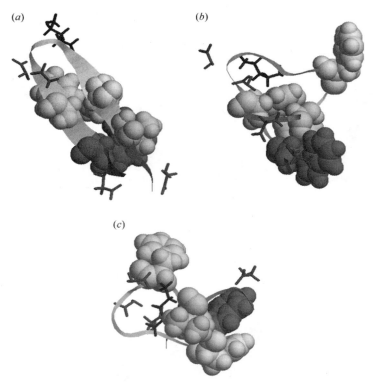

Figure 17.8   Comparison of the lowest free energy structures: (*a*) from the explicit solvent model, (*b*) from the implicit solvent GB model, and (*c*) from the implicit solvent PB model. The hydrophobic residues (TRP43, TYR45, PHE52, and VAL54) are represented by spacefill and charged residues (GLU42, ASP46, ASP47, LYS50, and GLU56) are represented by sticks with positively charged residues colored dark gray and negatively charged residues colored light gray, and the rest are represented by ribbons.

is expelled from the hydrophobic core in the SGB model, whereas it is well packed with other three hydrophobic residues (TRP43, TYR45, and VAL54) in the explicit solvent model. (2) In the SGB model, the charged residues are clustered to form salt bridges between opposite charges. For example, ASP46 and ASP47 form two salt bridges with LYS50 near the β-hairpin turn and the C-terminal end residue GLU56 also swings toward LYS50 to get closer to the positive charge. The net effect of this salt bridge formation brings the oppositely charged residues, two near the β-hairpin turn (ASP46 and ASP47) and one from the C-terminal end (GLU56) into closer contact with residue LYS50, thereby expelling the hydrophobic residue PHE52 from the hydrophobic core. This suggests that the balance between electrostatic interactions and the hydrophobic interactions is no longer preserved in SGB. The electrostatic interactions between the charged residues overwhelm the hydrophobic interactions between the four hydrophobic core residues. In the following section, we will also examine other implementations of the GB model in the AMBER package parameterized with AMBER force fields to see whether the problem arises from the specific implementation or the associated parameterization, however, similar erroneous results were found [36]. Thus, it appears that the problem is common to GB models.

Then, a natural questions arise, "What about the implicit solvent model based on the more rigorous PB solver, such as Delphi [50]?" Would it reproduce experimental results as well as the explicit solvent simulations? In principle, the PB model does not provide a complete electrostatic description either, unless one knows the dielectric constant at any position in the protein. Assuming a uniform dielectric constant for the protein solute, the Poisson–Boltzmann equation can be expressed as

$$\nabla \cdot (\epsilon \nabla \phi) = -\frac{4\pi\rho}{kT} + 4\pi C \sinh(\phi e) \qquad (17.18)$$

where ϵ is the dielectric constant, ϕ the electrostatic potential, and ρ the solute charge density. $C = 2eI/k_B T$, where I is the ionic concentration of the salt dissolved in the solvent.

Figure 17.7c shows the free energy contour map of the β-hairpin from the PB model. Interestingly, the free energy contour map from the PB model is still significantly different from that of the explicit solvent, even though it shows improvement over that of the GB model [26]. A few noticeable differences include: (1) The folded state in the PB model ($N_{HB} \approx 2-3$ and $R_g^{core} \approx 5.8$ Å) has a smaller number of the native β-strand hydrogen bonds and it is not the lowest free energy state. (2) The so-called H state has the lowest free energy. Its free energy is lower by approximately 0.4 kcal/mol (0.7 kT) than that of the folded state. Its radius of gyration for the hydrophobic core is slightly larger than that of the explicit solvent, $R_g^{core} \approx 7.2$ Å versus $R_g^{core} \approx 5.8$ Å. In the previous simulation with the GB model, however, the H state is found to be 2.92 kcal/mol lower than the native state. Thus, the PB model does seem to perform better than the GB model do, even though the improvement is still not sufficient to predict the correct lowest free energy structure.

Again, we examined the representative structures from the lowest free energy state in the PB model (Fig. 17.8c, from the H state). Interestingly, the hydrophobic residue TYR45 is expelled from the hydrophobic core in the PB model. In addition, similar to the GB model, the charged residues from the PB model are clustered to form salt bridges between opposite charges. For example, ASP46 and ASP47 form two salt bridges with LYS50 near the β-hairpin turn, and the N-terminal end residue GLU42 also swings toward LYS50 to get closer to the positive charge. These structural features are surprisingly similar to those of the GB model, except that in the GB model, the hydrophobic residue PHE52 was expelled to make a closer contact between the residues GLU56 and LYS50 [26]. These results suggest that the balance between the electrostatic interactions and the hydrophobic interactions is shifted toward favoring the electrostatic interactions. The strong electrostatic interactions between the charged residues (salt bridges) overwhelm the local hydrophobic interactions.

To fix the problem, it may suffice to devise a more accurate nonpolar cavity term, such as the one recently proposed by Levy and co-workers [55], combined with a stronger dielectric screening (a much larger dielectric constant) of the Coulomb interaction between charged residues as was suggested previously in another context as well [56, 57]. In our opinion, the assignment of a uniform dielectric constant inside proteins is an unjustified assumption, particularly for proteins with heavy charged residues, such as the β-hairpin. Even if one can fix the problem in this β-hairpin system or any other systems by fitting more adjustable parameters, such as atomic radii and/or residue or atom based dielectric constants, it might still be an open question on how portable these parameters are. However, given the large computational savings of implicit solvent models for protein folding simulations, it is important to develop better continuum solvent models.

17.3.5.2 *Comparison of the GB Model in Various Force Fields*   From the earlier discussion, we found that the free energy landscape of the β-hairpin in the SGB implicit solvent model is quite different from that in the explicit SPC solvent model using the same OPLSAA force field. As the GB type model is probably the most widely used implicit solvent model in protein folding simulations due to its fast speed (when compared with the more rigorous PB models [50]), we would like to ask the same question for other variations of the GB model, particularly the implementations based on other force fields. Thus, this section will shift the focus to GBSA (GB with Solvent Accessible Surface Area) models as implemented in the AMBER package in the context of various AMBER force fields, AMBER param94 [58] (named as AMBER94/GBSA), param96 [59] (AMBER96/GBSA), and param99 [60] (AMBER99/GBSA). The results from OPLSAA/SPC and OPLSAA/SGB will also be used for comparison, so a total of five combined force field/solvation models will be compared.

Free Energy Landscape   We first compare the free energy landscapes from the five combined force field/solvation models. Figure 17.9 shows the comparison of the five free energy contour maps. As shown previously [15], the explicit solvent model OPLSAA/SPC in general agrees quite well with experiment near room temperature, thus we use it as a benchmark for comparisons with other models. As some of the

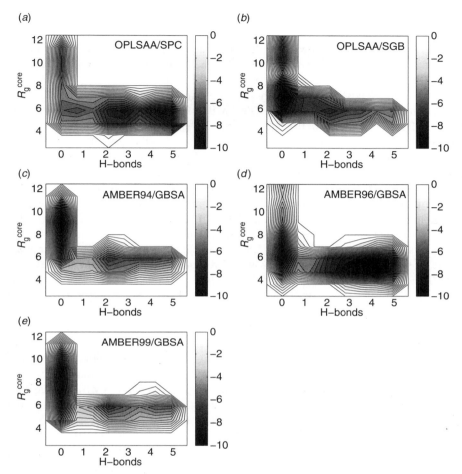

Figure 17.9 Comparison of the free energy contour maps versus the number of β-strand hydrogen-bonds N_{HB}^{β} and the hydrophobic core radius gyration R_g^{core}: (*a*) OPLSAA/SPC, (*b*) OPLSAA/SGB, (*c*) AMBER94/GBSA, (*d*) AMBER96/GBSA, and (*e*) AMBER99/GBSA.

results of OPLSAA/SPC and OPLSAA/SGB models have been described earlier [15, 26], we will mainly focus on the AMBER9x/GBSA results (Fig. 17.9*c-e*).

Interestingly, AMBER94/GBSA and AMBER99/GBSA show very similar free energy contour maps, even though AMBER99 [60] has all parameters refit from AMBER94 [58] (in contrast, AMBER96 [59] has only some backbone torsion parameters refit from AMBER94). The AMBER94 force field by Cornell et al. [58] is probably still the most widely used version of the AMBER force field. It is clear from Figure 17.9*c* and *e* that the native state is again not the lowest free energy state in either AMBER94/GBSA or AMBER99/GBSA, and the lowest free energy state, H state, has a much higher R_g^{core}, about 9.0 Å in AMBER94 and 8.1 Å in AMBER99/GBSA.

The H state also has about 2.95 and 2.60 kcal/mol (4.80 and 4.22 kT) lower free energy than the corresponding native state in AMBER94/GBSA and AMBER99/GBSA, respectively. As will be shown later, the larger core radius gyration is due to the fact that the β-hairpin has been turned into an α-helix in both AMBER94/GBSA and AMBER99/GBSA.

In contrast, AMBER96/GBSA shows a very similar free energy contour map compared to the OPLSAA/SPC model. The AMBER96 force field is a derivative of the AMBER94 force field with the only changes in the torsional parameters. This is the only continuum solvent model examined here that mimics the explicit solvent simulation, even though the β-hairpin populations at low temperatures are not as good as the explicit solvent model, for example, at 282 K, the β-hairpin population is estimated to be 57% in AMBER96/GBSA when compared with 74% in OPLSAA/SPC and about 80% in experiment. Nevertheless, similar features can be seen from the free energy contour maps of AMBER96/GBSA and OPLSAA/SPC, both show the native folded state F having the lowest free energy; both show the intermediate H state [15, 41, 44] having a core radius gyration about 5.8 Å; and both show an "L" shape contour map. The reason why AMBER96/GBSA works reasonable well, but not AMBER94 or AMBER99, might be mainly due to the backbone torsional parameters used in various AMBER force fields. Both AMBER94 and AMBER99 seem to have backbone ϕ and ψ torsional parameters very favorable for α-helix conformations.

Lowest Free Energy Structure   Figure 17.10c shows the lowest free energy structure of AMBER94/GBSA. The most astonishing observation is that the β-hairpin has been turned into an α-helix. Obviously, the AMBER94 force field biases the structure to form an α-helix. It has been previously reported that the AMBER force field has a tendency to overestimate the α-helix due to some backbone torsion parameters [44, 61], for example, Garcia and Sanbonmatsu found that there is about 15–20% α-helix from clustering for this same β-hairpin at 282 K using AMBER94 and an explicit solvent model TIP3P. However, what seems not previously known is that the continuum solvent model GBSA dramatically enhances this α-helix tendency. Following a similar approach as Garcia and Sanbonmatsu [44], first, the α-helix population is estimated to be 77% by clustering H state with $(N_{HB}^{\beta}, R_g^{core}) = (0.0 \pm 1.0,$

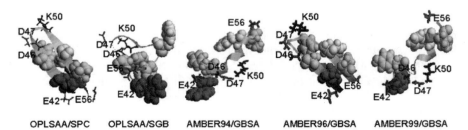

OPLSAA/SPC   OPLSAA/SGB   AMBER94/GBSA   AMBER96/GBSA   AMBER99/GBSA

Figure 17.10   Comparison of the most popular structures at the lowest free energy state for various models, (*a*) OPLSAA/SPC, (*b*) OPLSAA/SGB, (*c*) AMBER94/GBSA, (*d*) AMBER96/GBSA, and (*e*) AMBER99/GBSA.

9.0 ± 1.0). Secondly, the hydrophobic core is completely broken. The four hydrophobic residues, TRP43, TYR45, PHE52, and VAL54, are separated from each other to fit in an α-helix. Another interesting observation is that even though the salt bridge effect is not as strong as in the OPLSAA/SGB case, the charged sidechains still show a tendency to get closer to have stronger electrostatic interactions, for example, residues LYS50 and ASP47 exhibit a clear salt bridge. This is found in all the three AMBER9x/GBSA models as shown in Figure 17.10c–e.

The structure from AMBER99/GBSA shown in Figure 17.10e is very similar to that from AMBER94/GBSA discussed earlier, except that the α-helix turns are not as elegant as those in AMBER94/GBSA. Similarly, the α-helix population is estimated to be 61% with the H state population clustering using $(N_{HB}^{\beta}, R_g^{core}) = (0.0 \pm 1.0, 8.1 \pm 1.0)$. Finally, Figure 17.10d shows the most populated structure in AMBER96/GBSA, which is similar to the native β-hairpin structure except that there is a salt bridge between charged residues ASP47 and LYS50. Nevertheless, this is the only native-like structure found in the lowest free energy state in all four continuum solvent models with both OPLSAA and AMBER force fields.

α-Helix Content Whether there exist significant intermediate α-helical structures during the folding process of this β-hairpin is under heavy debate recently. As mentioned earlier, Garcia and Sanbonmatsu [44] found that significant helical content exists (15–20%) at low temperatures using the AMBER94 force field with TIP3P explicit water and also that these conformations are only slightly unfavorable energetically with respect to hairpin formation at biological temperatures. Pande and co-workers also found significant helical intermediates at 300 K using OPLS united atom force field with GBSA continuum solvent model [42]. These authors speculated that significant helical content was not found in experiment due to the limited time resolution [42, 44]. However, we argue that the significant α-helix content might be mainly due to the artifacts of the protein force fields.

Figure 17.11 shows the "trajectories" of the number of α-helix residues (colored red) and β-sheet residues (colored black) during the simulations. It is clear that both OPLSAA/SPC and OPLSAA/SGB simulations show very little α-helical content. The number of helical residues, including both α-helix and 3_{10}-helix, are less than or equal to 3. In addition, only 1–2% of the conformations show any helical content. Furthermore, almost all of the helices we found are 3_{10}-helices near the original β-turn (residues 47–49). All the other temperatures examined from 270 to 695 K show similar results. This minimal helix content is in contrast to recent results of Garcia and Sanbonmatsu [44] and Pande and co-workers [42], but seems to agree better with experiment [38–40, 63].

In contrast, both AMBER94/GBSA and AMBER99/GBSA turned the β-hairpin into an α-helix, as clearly shown in Figure 17.11c and e. After some initial equilibration period, most of conformations show significant α-helical content. If we count the peptide as an α-helix if four or more residues are in the helical format, the helix population is about 85% in AMBER94/GBSA and 59% in AMBER99/GBSA, generally consistent with the earlier estimates with the H state populations. Meanwhile, only very few residues were found to be in the β-sheet format in both

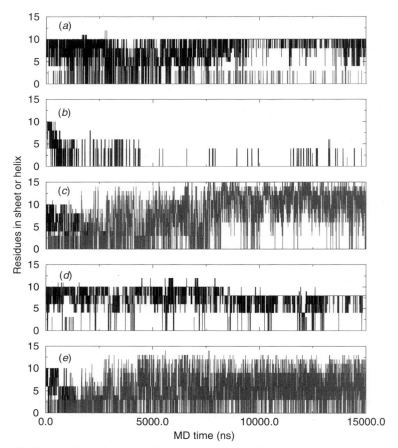

Figure 17.11 Number of residues in α-helix (gray) and beta sheet (black) format at various temperatures as determined by the program STRIDE [62], (*a*) OPLSAA/SPC, (*b*) OPLSAA/SGB, (*c*) AMBER94/GBSA, (*d*) AMBER96/GBSA, and (*e*) AMBER99/GBSA. Both AMBER94/GBSA and AMBER99/GBSA show enormous α-helical content.

AMBER94/GBSA and AMBER99/GBSA. These findings differ significantly from the results of OPLSAA/SPC and OPLSAA/SGB simulations. As speculated earlier [26], this suggests that the helical content is mainly determined by the protein force field, and less by the solvation model. This might make sense because helix formation is mainly driven by local hydrogen bonds and largely determined by torsional potentials, whereas β-sheets involve global interactions and both hydrophobic interactions and hydrogen bonds contribute. Thus, β-sheet formation might be more influenced by solvation models, although the formation of helices is largely determined by protein force fields. Thus, we think the large helical content in AMBER94 and AMBER99 force fields is largely due to the artifacts of AMBER force fields as found by others as well [44, 61, 64].

Interestingly, AMBER96/GBSA seems to have this problem fixed. Similar to OPLSAA/SPC, the number of helical residues, including both the α-helix and the 3_{10}-helix, is typically less than or equal to 3, and only less than 1% of the conformations exhibit helical content at 310 K. Thus, AMBER96/GBSA gives quite reasonable results on the α-helical content as compared to explicit solvent simulation and experiment, and the problem of overestimation of the α-helix seems to have been fixed in AMBER96.

Temperature Dependence Even though the explicit solvent OPLSAA/SPC model gives very reasonable results at low temperatures, the temperature dependence is not quite correct. The β-hairpin populations at higher temperatures are way too high, and the folding transition temperature is also way too high. This is found to be true with CHARMM and AMBER force fields as well with explicit solvent models [15]. This should not be very surprising given that most of the modern force fields are parameterized at room temperature. Nevertheless, we include the temperature dependence data here for all five models to provide information for force field developers to improve the models.

The β-hairpin populations at various temperatures are calculated with the average fraction of native contacts and the results are compared with the experimental populations from the TRP fluorescence yield measurements [38]. Klimov and Thirumalai [49] have used the average fraction of native contacts to estimate the β-hairpin population, and here we follow the same approach. Figure 17.12 shows the

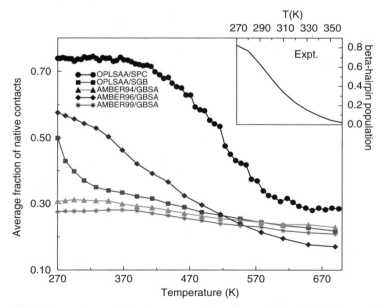

Figure 17.12 Comparison of the temperature dependence of the β-hairpin population for various models. The β-hairpin population is estimated with the average fraction of native contacts. The experimental results [38] are also shown in the inset for comparison.

comparison of the β-hairpin populations at various temperatures for the five different models. The experimental populations are shown in the inset for comparison. The fluorescence yield experiment shows a β-hairpin population of about 80% at a low temperature of 282 K, whereas the calculation shows a 74% population for OPLSAA/SPC, 43% for OPLSAA/SGB, 31% for AMBER94/GBSA, 57% for AMBER96/GBSA, and 28% for AMBER99/GBSA. As expected, the β-hairpin population is seriously underestimated in all the implicit solvent models except AMBER96/GBSA where it shows a decent 57% at 282 K. Although the explicit solvent model simulation predicts populations in reasonable agreement with experiment near the biological temperatures, it overestimates populations at higher temperatures [15]. The folding transition temperature is estimated to be about 470 K for OPLSAA/SPC and 430 K for AMBER96/GBSA. Both are too high when compared with experiment. The transition temperatures for OPLSAA/SGB, AMBER94/GBSA, and AMBER99/GBSA are not very meaningful, as there are no meaningful decays in the β-hairpin population with temperature. As stated earlier, we listed these results here not for head-to-head comparisons with experiments as we should not expect them to be perfect at higher temperatures, but rather for force field developers to use these data to improve the parameters to include some kind of temperature dependence in the future.

In general, the assessment of force fields and solvation models involves huge amount of work, and the examples described here is just an initial try. Other people have also tried to address the same issue, such as Okamoto and co-workers' recent work on comparing various force fields on the folding of polypeptides with REMD [64]. The authors found that α-helix is favored for AMBER94 and AMBER99 and that β-hairpin is favored for GROMOS96, whereas CHARMM22, AMBER96, and OPLS-AA have intermediate tendency. Finally, it should be pointed out that some of these results are obtained with specific peptides or proteins, they should probably not be taken too conclusively. Nevertheless, these large-scale parallel simulations with REMD do provide informative data for further improvement of the force fields and solvation models, which are critical in protein folding simulations.

17.4 PROTEIN STRUCTURE REFINEMENT WITH REMD

Protein structure prediction has been of great interest recently, as witnessed by the past six worldwide competitions in critical assessment of protein structure prediction (CASP). Even with enormous efforts from various groups, protein structure prediction remains a challenging and unsolved problem. A derived and arguably equally challenging problem is how to refine the model structures from homology modeling or fold recognition methods. Even for homology models, the typical RMSDs from the native structures are about 3 Å (fold recognition targets usually have even larger RMSDs). However, structures with higher resolution (1.5–2.0 Å RMSD) are often needed for many important function studies, such as ligand–protein binding affinity prediction in drug design. Thus, how to effectively refine the protein structures is critical. In this section, we illustrate the usage of REMD in a structure refinement protocol.

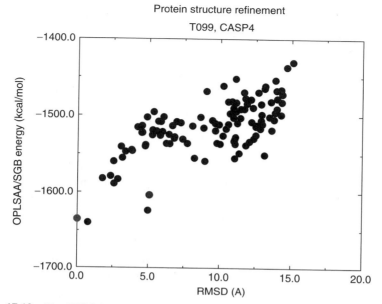

Figure 17.13 The OPLSAA/SGB energy versus the RMSD from the native structure for configurations from the REM sampling for CASP target T099.

Figure 17.13 shows the OPLSAA/SGB energy versus the backbone RMSD from the native structure for configurations from the REMD sampling of CASP target T099 (56 residues). The blue point indicates the starting model structure from homology modeling, which has an initial backbone RMSD of 5.1 Å. The red point indicates the native structure of T099, which obviously has a RMSD of zero. These data are obtained from a 18-replica REMD simulation with the a temperature range from 295 to 590 K [26, 36]. The SGB continuum solvation model is used for its fast speed, even though we learn from above that it might have salt bridge overestimation problem in some proteins. However, due to the enormous CPU request, running protein folding or refinement simulations with explicit solvent for large proteins are currently still out of reach, particularly within the CASP time frame, many targets have only two weeks time window. In these simulations, a dielectric constant of 2.0 is used for the protein and 80.0 used for water in SGB, similar to earlier folding simulations. The sampled configurations are first clustered and then minimized. Figure 17.13 shows the results for the final minimized structures. It is clear that there exists a rough correlation between the energy and RMSD — lower energy structures tend to have a smaller RMSD, which is ideal for protein structure prediction. However, for many other cases, we have examined, there appear to be less or none such correlations indicating that the OPLSAA force field and/or the SGB solvation model still have some problems and further improvements are needed.

In this particular case, we have found a very good improvement in terms of the structure refinement. The best candidate (lowest OPLSAA/SGB energy structure) has

Figure 17.14 Comparison of the native (*a*), initial model (*b*), and refined (*c*) structures of the target T099. The residues 8–18 in the loop region is dark gray, which show large improvements after the refinement, together with the N- and C-terminuses.

a RMSD of 0.8 Å from the native one, which is about 4.3 Å improvement. Figure 17.14 shows the native model and refined structures. The initial model structure has problems in the N- and C-terminuses, as well as the loop region from residues 8–18 (colored red in Fig. 17.14). The refined structure seems to have all these problems fixed through REMD.

We have also applied the same approach to three different classes of model structures for a systematic study of the refinement protocol. It is based on the backbone RMSD from the native structures: (1) RMSD < 3 Å, (2) 3 Å < RMSD < 8 Å, and (3) RMSD > 8 Å. The detailed results are not listed here due to the page limitations, but can be found elsewhere [65]. Overall, we do observe successes in some proteins, particularly those with larger initial RMSDs. We also found that with only a few exceptions the native structures are indeed the lowest total energy structures in all the models examined. However, the improvement is limited for those high homologous models with very small RMSDs. As mentioned earlier, this is probably the most important category for high resolution structures needed for, for example, drug discovery, thus more work is still needed. It is interesting to note that the majority of the conformations sampled are further away from the native structure, indicating that the total sampling space is enormous and the refinement time (local readjustment time) can be very long, may be comparable to the folding time. For further improvement, some biased sampling might be needed as well to somehow constrain the sampling around the "native-like fragments" based on the confidence level from secondary structure predictions, and so on.

17.5 SUMMARY

In this chapter, we have described a highly parallel REMD method and its application in protein folding and protein structure prediction. The REMD method couples MD trajectories with a temperature exchange Monte Carlo process for efficient sampling of the protein conformational space. We have used two example protein systems, one

α-helix and one β-hairpin, to demonstrate the power of the REMD algorithm, with up to 64 replicas of solvated protein systems simulated in parallel over a wide range of temperatures. Very high efficiency (>98%) can be achieved with this embarrassingly parallel algorithm. The simulation results show that the combined trajectories in temperature and configurational space allow a replica to overcome free energy barriers present at low temperatures. These large-scale simulations also reveal detailed results on folding mechanisms, intermediate state structures, thermodynamic properties, and the temperature dependences for both α-helix and β-hairpin systems. For the α-helix, it is found that the Arg residues contribute significantly to the stability of the peptide when compared with the pure Ala counterpart due to the shielding of the backbone hydrogen bonds from water by the Arg side chains. In contrast, the β-hairpin is found to undergo a "hydrophobic core collapse" folding mechanism rather than a "hydrogen bond zipping" mechanism. We have compared the explicit solvent model versus the implicit solvent models, including both the GB and PB models. We have also compared various protein force fields and their combination with solvation models in terms of the folding free energy landscape, lowest free energy structure, α-helical content, and temperature dependence. These large-scale simulations provide extensive data and insights for the possible fix of the problems and further improvement of solvation models and protein force fields. Finally, we also demonstrate the usage of REMD method in protein structure refinement, which remains a serious challenge in protein structure prediction. The future work will include applications to the folding of larger and more complex protein systems such as membrane proteins and multi-domain proteins and also to other related fields such as the protein–protein interactions. More work also needs to be done for generating necessary data for further improving of the solvation models and protein force fields.

ACKNOWLEDGMENTS

I would like to thank Angel Garcia for sending graphs for the α-helix simulations and Bruce Berne, Jed Pitera, William Swope, Vijay Pande and Yuko Okmotto for many helpful discussions and comments.

REFERENCES

1. A. R. Fersht, *Structure and Mechanism in Protein Science*. W. H. Freeman and Company, New York, 1999.
2. C. L. Brooks, J. N. Onuchic, and D. J. Wales, *Science*, 293, 612–613 (2001).
3. C. M. Dobson, A. Sali, and M. Karplus, *Angrew. Chem. Int. Edit. Engl.*, 37, 868–893 (1998).
4. C. L. Brooks, M. Gruebele, J. N. Onuchic, and P. G. Wolynes, *Proc. Natl. Acad. Sci. USA*, 95, 11037 (1998).
5. R. Zhou, X. Huang, C. J. Margulius, and B. J. Berne, *Science*, 305, 1605–1609 (2004).

6. J.A. Vila, D.R. Ripoll, and H. A. Scheraga, *Proc. Natl. Acad. Sci. USA*, 97, 13075–13079 (2000).

7. B. J. Berne and J. E. Straub, *Curr. Opin. Struct. Biol.*, 7, 181 (1997).

8. Y. Duan and P. A. Kollman, *Science*, 282, 740 (1998).

9. J. Dongarra, I. Foster, G. Fox, K. Kennedy, A. White, L. Torczon, and W. Gropp, Eds. *The Sourcebook of Parallel Computing*, Morgan Kaufmann Publisher, 2002.

10. R. Buyya, *High Performance Parallel Computing: Architectures and Systems*, Prentice Hall Printer, 1999.

11. K. Hukushima and K. Nemoto, *J. Phys. Soc. Jap.*, 65, 1604–1608 (1996).

12. E. Marinari, G. Parisi, and J. J. Ruiz-Lorenzo, *World Scientific*, Singapore, 1998, p. 59.

13. Y. Sugita and Y. Okamoto, *Chem. Phys. Lett.*, 329, 261–270 (2000).

14. A. E. Garcia and K. Y. Sanbonmatsu, *Proc. Natl. Acad. Sci. USA*, 99, 2782–2787 (2002).

15. R. Zhou, B. J. Berne, and R. Germain, *Proc. Natl. Acad. Sci. USA*, 98, 14931–14936 (2001).

16. Y. M. Rhee and V. S. Pande, *Biophys. J.*, 84, 775–786 (2003).

17. Y. Z. Ohkubo and C. L. Brooks, *Proc. Natl. Acad. Sci. USA*, 100, 13916–13921 (2003).

18. R. Zhou, *Proc. Natl. Acad. Sci. USA*, 100, 13280–13285 (2003).

19. H. Nymeyer and A. E. Garcia, *Biophys. J.*, 84, 381A (2003).

20. A. E. Garcia and J. N. Onuchic, *Proc. Natl. Acad. Sci. USA*, 100, 13898–13903 (2003).

21. W. Im, M. Feig, and C. L. Brooks, *Biophys. J.*, 85, 2900–2918 (2003).

22. H. Kokubo and Y. Okamoto, *Chem. Phys. Lett.*, 392, 168–175 (2004).

23. R. Zhou, *J. Mol. Graph Model.*, 22, 451–463 (2004).

24. D. L. Freeman, D. D. Frantz, and J. D. Doll, *J. Chem. Phys.*, 97, 5713 (1992).

25. R. Zhou and B. J. Berne, *J. Chem. Phys.*, 107, 9185–9196 (1997).

26. R. Zhou and B. J. Berne, *Proc. Natl. Acad. Sci. USA*, 99, 12777–12782 (2002).

27. S. Williams, T. P. Causgrove, R. Gilmanshin, K. S. Fang, R. H. Callender, W. H. Woodruff, and R. B. Dyer, *Biochemistry*, 35, 691–697 (1996).

28. D. J. Lockhart and P. S. Kim, *Science*, 260, 198–202 (1993).

29. P. A. Thompson, W. A. Eaton, and J. Hofrichter, *Biochemistry*, 36, 9200–9210 (1997).

30. I. K. Lednev, A. S. Karnoup, M. C. Sparrow, and S. A. Asher, *J. Am. Chem. Soc.*, 123, 2388–2392 (2001).

31. W. L. Jorgensen, D. Maxwell, and J. Tirado-Rives, *J. Am. Chem. Soc.*, 118, 11225–11236 (1996).

32. M. Tuckerman, B. J. Berne, and G. J. Martyna, *J. Chem. Phys.*, 97, 1990–2001 (1992).

33. R. Zhou and B. J. Berne, *J. Chem. Phys.*, 103, 9444 (1995).

34. R. Zhou, E. Harder, H. Xu, and B. J. Berne, *J. Chem. Phys.*, 115, 2348–2358 (2001).

35. R. Zhou, G. Krilov, and B. J. Berne, *J. Phys. Chem. B*, 108, 7528–7530 (2004).

36. R. Zhou, *Proteins*, 53, 148–161 (2003).

37. M. Sundaralingam and Y. Sekharudu, *Science*, 244, 1333–1337 (1989).

38. V. Munoz, P. A. Thompson, J. Hofrichter, and W. A. Eaton, *Nature*, 390, 196–199 (1997).

39. V. Munoz, E. R. Henry, J. Hofrichter, and W. A. Eaton, *Proc. Natl. Acad. Sci. USA*, 95, 5872–5879 (1998).

40. F. J. Blanco, G. Rivas, and L. Serrano, *Nature Struct. Biol.*, 1, 584–590 (1994).

41. V. S. Pande and D. S. Rokhsar, *Proc. Natl. Acad. Sci. USA*, 96, 9062–9067 (1999).

42. B. Zagrovic, E. J. Sorin, and V. S. Pande, *J. Mol. Biol.*, 313, 151 (2001).

43. A. R. Dinner, T. Lazaridis, and M. Karplus, *Proc. Natl. Acad. Sci. USA*, 96, 9068–9073 (1999).

44. A. E. Garcia and K. Y. Sanbonmatsu, *Proteins*, 42, 345–354 (2001).

45. D. Roccatano, A. Amadei, A. D. Nola, and H. J. Berendsen, *Protein Sci.*, 10, 2130–2143 (1999).

46. A. Kolinski, B. Ilkowski, and J. Skolnick, *Biophys. J.*, 77, 2942–2952 (1999).

47. B. Ma and R. Nussinov, *J. Mol. Bio.*, 296, 1091 (2000).

48. A. M. Ferrenberg and R. H. Swendsen, *Phys. Rev. Lett.*, 63, 1195–1198 (1989).

49. D. K. Klimov and D. Thirumalai, *Proc. Natl. Acad. Sci. USA*, 97, 2544–2549 (2000).

50. B. Honig and A. Nicholls, *Science*, 268, 1144–1149 (1995).

51. W. C. Still, A. Tempczyk, R. C. Hawley, and T. Hendrickson, *J. Am. Chem. Soc.*, 112, 6127–6129 (1990).

52. A. Ghosh, C. S. Rapp, and R. A. Friesner, *J. Phys. Chem. B*, 102, 10983–10990 (1998).

53. T. Lazaridis and M. Karplus, *Proteins*, 35, 133–152 (1999).

54. H. J. C. Berendsen, J. P. M. Postma, W. F. van Gunsteren, and J. Hermans, in B. Pullman, Ed., *Intermolecular Forces*, Reidel, Dordrecht, 1981, pp. 331–342.

55. E. Gallicchio, L. Y. Zhang, and R. M. Levy, *J. Comp. Chem.*, 23, 517–529 (2002).

56. A. Burykin, C. N. Schutz, J. Villa, and A. Warshel, *Proteins*, 47, 265–280 (2002).

57. E. Garcia-Moreno, J. Dwyer, A. Gittis, E. Lattman, D. Spenser, and W. Stites, *Biophys. Chem.*, 64, 211–224 (1997).

58. W. Cornell, P. Cieplak, C. I. Bayly, I. R. Gould, K. M. Merz, D. M. Ferguson, D. C. Spellmeyer, T. Fox, J. W. Caldwell, and P. A. Kollman, *J. Am. Chem. Soc.*, 117, 5179–5197 (1995).

59. P. A. Kollman, R. Dixon, W. Cornell, T. Fox, C. Chipot, and A. Pohorille, *Computer Simulation of Biomolecular Syatems*, in A. Wilkinson, P. Weiner and W. F. van Gunsteren, Eds. 3, 83–96 (1997).

60. J. Wang, P. Cieplak, and P. A. Kollman, *J. Comput. Chem.*, 21, 1049 (2000).

61. M. Beachy, D. Chasman, R. Murphy, T. Halgren, and R. Friesner, *J. Am. Chem. Soc.*, 119, 5908–5920 (1997).

62. D. Frishman and P. Argos, *Proteins*, 23, 566–579 (1995).

63. F. J. Blanco and L. Serrano, *Eur. J. Biochem.*, 230, 634–649 (1995).

64. T. Yoda, Y. Sugita, and Y. Okamoto, *Chem. Phys. Lett.*, 386, 460–467 (2004).

65. R. Zhou, G. Dent, A. Royyuru, and P. Atham, *RECOMB2004 — Currents in Computational Molecular Biology*, A. Gramada and P. E. Bourne, Eds. 2004, pp. 441–442.

CHAPTER 18

High-Performance Alignment Methods for Protein Threading

R. ANDONOV, S. BALEV, and N. YANEV

Recombinant DNA techniques have provided tools for the rapid determination of DNA sequences and, by inference, the amino acid sequences of proteins from structural genes. The number of such sequences is now increasing almost exponentially, but by themselves these sequences tell little more about the biology of the system than a New York City telephone directory tells about the function and marvels of that city.

— C. Branden and J. Tooze, [1]

18.1 INTRODUCTION

Genome sequencing projects generate an ever-increasing number of protein sequences. For example, the Human Genome Project has identified over 30,000 genes, which may encode about 100,000 proteins. One of the first tasks when annotating a new genome is to assign functions to the proteins produced by the genes. To fully understand the biological functions of proteins, the knowledge of their structure is essential.

Unlike other biological macromolecules (e.g., DNA), proteins have complex, irregular structures. They are built up by amino acids that are linked by peptide bonds to form a polypeptide chain. The amino acid sequence of a protein's polypeptide chain is called its primary or one-dimensional (1D) structure. Different elements of the sequence form local regular secondary (2D) structures, such as α-helices or β-strands. The tertiary (3D) structure is formed by packing such structural elements into one or several compact globular units called domains. The final protein may contain several polypeptide chains arranged in a quaternary structure. By formation of such tertiary and quaternary structures, amino acids far apart in the sequence are brought close together to form functional regions (active sites). The interested reader can find more on protein structure in Ref. [1].

Parallel Computing for Bioinformatics and Computational Biology, Edited by Albert Y. Zomaya
Copyright © 2006 John Wiley & Sons, Inc.

Protein structures can be solved by experimental (in vitro) methods, such as x-ray crystallography or nuclear magnetic resonance (NMR) spectroscopy. Despite the recent advances in these techniques, they are still expensive and slow, and cannot cope with the explosion of sequences becoming available. That is why molecular biology resorts to computational (in silico) methods of structure determining.

The protein-folding problem can be simply stated in the following way. Given a protein 1D sequence, which is a string over the 20-letter amino acid alphabet, determine the coordinates of each amino acid in the protein's 3D folded shape. Surprisingly, in many cases the input information is completely sufficient to produce the desired output.

Although simply stated, the protein-folding problem is quite difficult. The natural folding mechanism is complicated and poorly understood. Most likely, it is a global result of many local, weak interactions. The protein-folding problem is widely recognized as one of the most important challenges in computational biology today [1–6]. Sometimes it is referred to as the "holly grail of molecular biology." The progress of molecular biology depends on the existence of reliable and fast computational structure prediction methods.

The computational methods for structure prediction fall roughly into two categories. The direct methods [7] use the principles of quantum mechanics. They seek a folded conformation minimizing the free energy. The main obstacles to these methods are the large number of interacting atoms, as well as many technical complications related to cumulative approximation errors, modeling surrounding water, and so on.

An important alternative to the direct techniques is the methods using information about proteins of already known structure, stored in databases. These methods are based on the concept of homology, which plays a central role in biology. Two proteins are homologous if they are related by descent from a common ancestor. Homologous proteins have similar 3D structures and often, similar functions.

The easiest way to detect homology between two proteins is to compare their amino acid sequences. If the sequences are "sufficiently" similar then the two proteins are homologous. A number of sequence comparison methods (e.g., BLAST [8], FASTA [9], PSI-BLAST [10]) are available and can be used to detect homology. But if two amino acid sequences are not sufficiently similar, can we conclude that the corresponding proteins are not homologous? In the case of remote homologs, the amino acid sequences have had a plenty of time to diverge. They are no longer similar and lie beyond the sequence comparison recognition threshold, in the so-called twilight zone. Nevertheless, their 3D structures are still similar. In such a case, one of the most promising approaches to the protein-folding problem is protein threading. This method relies on three basic facts.

1. The 3D structures of homologous proteins are much better conserved than their 1D amino acid sequences. Indeed, many cases of proteins with similar folds are known, though having less than 15% sequence identity.
2. There is a limited, relatively small number of protein structural families (between 1000 and 10,000 according to different estimations [11, 12]). Each

structural family defines an equivalence class and the problem reduces to classifying the query sequence into one of these classes. According to the statistics of Protein Data Bank (PDB) [13], 90% of the new proteins submitted in the last 3 years belong to already known structural families.[1]

3. Different types of amino acids have different preferences for occupying a given structural environment (e.g., being in α-helix or β-sheet, being buried in the protein interior or exposed on the surface). In addition, there are different preferences for, or more generally, for spatial proximity, as a function of those environments. These preferences have been estimated statistically and used to produce score functions distinguishing between native and non-native folds.

The process of aligning a sequence to a structure, thereby guiding the spatial placement of sequence amino acids, is known as threading. The term "threading" is used to specialize the more general term "alignment" of a query sequence and a structure template.

The fold recognition methods based on threading are complex and time-consuming computational techniques consisting of the following main components:

1. A database of potential core folds or structural templates;
2. An objective function (score function) which evaluates any alignment of a sequence to a structure template;
3. A method of finding the best (with respect to the score function) possible alignment of a sequence and a structure template;
4. A method to select the most appropriate among the best alignments of a query sequence and each template from the database.

Components (1), (2), and (4) use mainly statistical methods incorporating the biological and physical knowledge on the problem. These methods are beyond the scope of this chapter. Component (3) is the most time-consuming part of the threading methods. It is the most challenging and the most interesting one from computer scientist's point of view. The problem of finding the optimal sequence-to-structure alignment is referred to as protein threading problem (PTP) throughout this chapter. PTP is solved many times in the threading process. The query sequence is threaded to all (or at least to a part of) templates in the database. Component (4) of some methods uses a score normalization procedure which involves threading a large set of queries against each template [14]. The designers of score functions make experiments involving millions of threadings to tune their parameters. That is why, really efficient threading algorithms are needed.

As we will see in the next sections, PTP is a hard combinatorial optimization problem. Till recently, it was the main obstacle to the development of efficient and reliable fold recognition methods. In the general case, when variable-length alignment gaps are allowed and pairwise amino acid interactions are considered in the score function, PTP is NP-hard [15]. Moreover, it is MAX-SNP-hard [16], which means

---

[1] http://www.rcsb.org/pdb/holdings.html.

that there is no arbitrary close polynomial approximation algorithm, unless $P = NP$. These complexity results have guided the research of threading methods to three different directions.

The first approach consists of simplifying the problem by ignoring the pairwise amino acid interactions. In this case the optimal alignment can be found by polynomial dynamic programming algorithms [17, 18]. The methods based on this approach ignore potentially rich source of structural information and, consequently, cannot recognize distant structural homologies.

The second direction is to use approximate algorithms which are relatively fast and capable of finding a good but not necessarily the optimal alignment. These methods include several algorithms based on dynamic programming [19–21], statistical sampling [22], and genetic algorithms [23–25]. As these methods do not guarantee optimality, their use risks to worsen the fold recognition sensitivity and quality.

The third way to attack PTP is to develop dedicated exact methods which are exponential in the worst case, but efficient on most of the real-life instances. This chapter traces the later direction of research and presents recently developed high-performance exact algorithms for solving PTP, which use advanced mathematical programming techniques, as well as parallel and distributed computing methods. Subsequently, we summarize what we feel to be the most important steps in this direction.

Lathrop and Smith [26] designed the first practical branch-and-bound (B&B) algorithm for PTP. This algorithm became the kernel of several structure prediction software packages [14, 27]. Lathrop and Smith's work has shown that the problem is easier in practice than in theory and that it is possible to solve real-life (biological) instances in a reasonable amount of time. However, practical applications of this B&B algorithm remained limited to moderate-size instances. These results have drawn the attention of many researchers to the problem, the authors included.

The second main step involves using mathematical programming techniques to solve PTP. Two teams have been working independently in this direction and their results were published almost simultaneously. Andonov et al. [28–30] proposed different mixed integer programming (MIP) models for PTP. The content of this chapter is based essentially on the results from [30]. Xu et al. [31, 32] also reported successful use of an MIP model in their protein threading package RAPTOR. The main drawback of mathematical programming approaches is that the corresponding models are often very large (over 10^6 variables). Even the most advanced MIP solvers cannot solve instances of such size in reasonable time and, in some cases, even to stock them in computer memory. Different divide-and-conquer methods and parallel algorithms are used to overcome this drawback.

Xu et al. [33, 34] were the first to use divide-and-conquer in their package PROSPECT-I. Their algorithm performs well on simple template interaction topologies, but is inefficient for protein templates with dense pairwise amino acid interactions. The ideas from PROSPECT-I were used in the latest version of RAPTOR [35]. Andonov et al. [29, 30] proposed a different divide-and-conquer strategy. While the splits in Ref. [33] occur along the interactions between template blocks, the splits in Refs. [29, 30] are along the possible positions of a given template block. In addition, in the latter works, the solutions of already solved subproblems are used as "cuts" for the following subproblems. Andonov et al. [29, 30] also proposed an efficient parallel algorithm which solves simultaneously the subproblems generated by their divide-and-conquer technique.

The rest of this chapter is organized as follows. In Section 18.2 we give a formal definition of PTP and introduce some existing terminology. Section 18.3 introduces a network formulation of PTP. On the basis of this formulation, we present the existing MIP models for PTP in a unified framework and compare them. We show that choosing an appropriate MIP model can lead to considerable decrease in solution time for PTP. We demonstrate that PTP is easier in practice than in theory because the linear programming (LP) relaxation of the MIP models provides the optimal solution for most real-life instances of PTP. Section 18.4 presents and analyzes two divide-and-conquer strategies for solving the MIP models. We show that these strategies are a way to overcome the main drawback of the MIP models, their huge size, and lead to significant reduction of the solution time. These strategies are used in Section 18.5 to design an efficient parallel algorithm for PTP. The performance of this algorithm is experimentally evaluated and the question of choosing a good granularity (number of subproblems) for a given number of processors is discussed. In Section 18.6 we discuss some open questions and future research directions and in Section 18.7 we conclude.

18.2 FORMAL DEFINITION

In this section we give a more formal definition of PTP and simultaneously introduce some existing terminology. Our definition is very close to the one given in [4, 16]. It follows a few basic assumptions widely adopted by the protein threading community [1, 4, 6, 30, 32, 33]. Consequently, the algorithms presented in the subsequent sections can be easily plugged in most of the existing fold recognition methods based on threading.

Query Sequence　A query sequence is a string of length N over the 20-letter amino acid alphabet. This is the amino acid sequence of a protein of unknown structure which must be aligned to structure templates from the database.

Structure Template　All current threading methods replace the 3D coordinates of the known structure by an abstract template description in terms of core blocks or segments, neighbor relationships, distances, environments, and so on. This avoids the computational cost of atomic-level mechanics in favor of more abstract, discrete alignment between sequence and structure.

We consider that a structure template is an ordered set of m segments or blocks. Segment i has a fixed length of l_i amino acids. Adjacent segments are connected by variable-length regions, called loops (Fig. 18.1a). Segments usually correspond to the most conserved parts of secondary structure elements (α-helices and β-strands). They trace the backbone of the conserved fold. Loops are not considered as part of

(a)

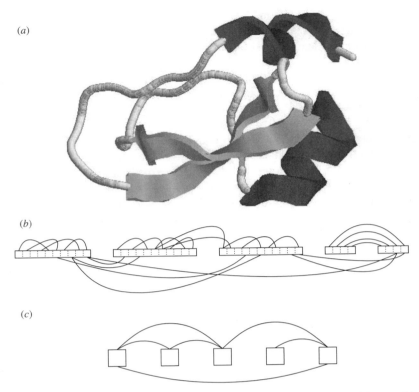

(b)

(c)

Figure 18.1   (a) 3D structure backbone showing α-helices, β-strands, and loops. (b) The corresponding contact map graph. (c) The corresponding generalized contact map graph.

the conserved fold and consequently, the pairwise interactions between amino acids belonging to loops are ignored. It is generally believed that the contribution of such interactions is relatively insignificant. The pairwise interactions between amino acids belonging to segments are represented by the so-called contact map graph (Fig. 18.1b). It is common to assume that two amino acids interact if the distance between their C_β atoms is within p Å and they are at least q positions apart along the template sequence (e.g., $p = 7$ and $q = 4$ in [32]). However, arbitrary contact map graphs can be considered. We say that there is an interaction between two segments, i and j, if there is at least one pairwise interaction between amino acid belonging to i and amino acid belonging to j. Let $L \subseteq \{(i, j) \mid 1 \leq i < j \leq m\}$ be the set of segment interactions. The graph with vertices $\{1, \dots, m\}$ and edges L is called generalized contact map graph (see Fig. 18.1c).

Threading   An alignment or threading of a query sequence and a structure template is covering of contiguous query areas by the template segments. A threading is called feasible if the segments preserve their original order and do not overlap (Fig 18.2a). A threading is completely determined by the starting positions of all segments. For the

(a)

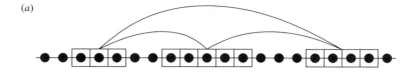

(b)

Abs. position	1	2	3	4	5	6	7	8	9	10	11	12	13	14	15	16	17	18	19	20
Rel. position block 1	1	2	3	4	5	6	7	8	9											
Rel. position block 2				1	2	3	4	5	6	7	8	9								
Rel. position block 3							1	2	3	4	5	6	7	8	9					

Figure 18.2 (*a*) Example of alignment of query sequence of length 20 and template containing three segments of lengths 3, 5, and 4. (*b*) Correspondence between absolute and relative block positions.

sake of simplicity we will use relative positions. If segment i starts at the kth query character, its relative position is $r_i = k - \sum_{j=1}^{i-1} l_j$. In this way the possible (relative) positions of each segment are between 1 and $n = N + 1 - \sum_{i=1}^{m} l_i$ (Fig. 18.2*b*). The set of feasible threadings is

$$\mathcal{T} = \{(r_1, \ldots, r_m) \mid 1 \leq r_1 \leq \cdots \leq r_m \leq n\}.$$

It is easy to see that the number of possible threadings (the search space size of PTP) is

$$|\mathcal{T}| = \binom{m + n - 1}{m},$$

which is a huge number even for small instances (e.g., if $m = 20$ and $n = 100$ then $|\mathcal{T}| \approx 2.5 \times 10^{22}$).

Most of the threading methods impose an additional feasibility condition, upper and lower bounds on the lengths of the uncovered query areas (loops). This condition can be easily incorporated by a slight modification in the definition of relative segment position.

In the previous definition, alignment gaps are not allowed within segments. They are confined only to loops. The biological justification is that segments are conserved so that the chance of insertion or deletion within them is very small.

Score Function   The score function is used to evaluate the degree of compatibility between the sequence amino acids and their positions in the template in a given threading. This evaluation is based on statistically estimated amino acid preferences for occupying different environments. The choice of an adequate score function is essential for the quality of the threading method. The form of the score function varies from method to method. Here we give a general definition, compatible to most of the threading methods. We only assume that the score function is additive and can be computed considering interactions between at most two amino acids at a time. These assumptions allow to represent the score function by two groups of coefficients:

- $c_{ik}, i = 1, \ldots, m, k = 1, \ldots, n$, the score for placing segment i on position k;
- $c_{ikjl}, (i, j) \in L, 1 \le k \le l \le n$, the score induced by the pairwise interaction between segments i and j when segment i is on position k and segment j is on position l.

The coefficients c_{ik} are some function (usually sum) of the preferences of each query amino acid placed in segment i for occupying its assigned position, as well as the scores of pairwise interactions between amino acids belonging to segment i. The coefficients c_{ikjl} include the scores of interactions between pairs of amino acids belonging to segments i and j. Loops may also have sequence-specific scores, included in the coefficients $c_{i,k,i+1,l}$.

Alternatively, we can represent the score function only by the second set of coefficients. To do this, it is sufficient to add c_{ik} to all coefficients $c_{i,k,i+1,l}, l = k, \ldots, n$. In the subsequent sections we will use one of these representations, depending on which one is more convenient.

Protein Threading Problem   Using the earlier definitions, PTP is simply to find the feasible threading of minimum score, or formally,

$$\min \left\{ \sum_{i=1}^{m} c_{ir_i} + \sum_{(i,j) \in L} c_{ir_i jr_j} \mid (r_1, \ldots, r_m) \in \mathcal{T} \right\}.$$

18.3   MIXED INTEGER PROGRAMMING MODELS

In this section we restate PTP as a network optimization problem. On the basis of this reformulation, we present different mixed integer programming models for PTP in a unified framework. At the end of the section we compare the efficiency of these models by experimental results. Subsequently, we make a brief introduction to MIP and LP, necessary to understand the rest of this section. The reader familiar with these topics can skip directly to Section 18.3.1. For a more detailed and consistent introduction, the reader is referred to any good integer programming textbook (e.g., [36]).

MIP deals with problems of optimizing (maximizing or minimizing) a linear function of many variables subject to linear equality and inequality constraints and integrality restrictions on some or all of the variables. Because of the robustness of the general MIP model, a remarkably rich variety of optimization problems can be represented by mixed integer programs. The general form of MIP is

$$z_{\text{MIP}} = \min \left\{ cx + dy \mid Ax + By \le b, \ x \in Z_+^n, \ y \in R_+^p \right\},$$

where Z_+^n is the set of non-negative integral n-dimensional vectors, R_+^p is the set of non-negative real p-dimensional vectors, $x = (x_1, \ldots, x_n)$ and $y = (y_1, \ldots, y_p)$ are variables, c is an n-vector, d is a p-vector, A is an $m \times n$ matrix, B is an $m \times p$ matrix, and b is an m-vector. The function $z = cx + dy$ is called objective function and the set $\{(x, y) \mid Ax + By \leq b, \ x \in Z_+^n, \ y \in R_+^p\}$ is called feasible region. In many models, the integer variables are constrained to equal 0 or 1. Thus we obtain 0–1 MIP, where $x \in Z_+^n$ is replaced by $x \in B^n$, where B^n is the set of n-dimensional binary vectors.

Although the general MIP problem is NP-hard, it can be solved efficiently in many particular cases. Even in the general case, there exist different efficient solution techniques. Most of them use the LP relaxation of MIP

$$z_{\mathrm{LP}} = \min \left\{ cx + dy \mid Ax + By \leq b, \ x \in R_+^n, \ y \in R_+^p \right\},$$

where the integrality constraints are relaxed. LP is much easier than MIP. It can be solved in polynomial time. The most commonly used method to solve LP is the simplex method which, although exponential in the worst case, performs well in practice.

The most important relations between MIP and LP are: (1) $z_{\mathrm{LP}} \leq z_{\mathrm{MIP}}$, that is, the optimal objective value of LP is a lower bound on the optimal objective value of MIP and (2) if (x^*, y^*) is an optimal solution of LP and $x^* \in Z_+^n$ then (x^*, y^*) is an optimal solution of MIP. The B&B algorithms for MIP are based on these relations. They partition MIP into subproblems by fixing some of the x-variables to integer values until either, (1) the optimal solution of the LP relaxation of a subproblem becomes feasible for MIP or (2) the optimal objective value of the LP relaxation of a subproblem becomes greater than the objective value of the best-known solution of MIP.

Most optimization problems can be formulated as MIP in several different ways. Choosing a "good" model is of crucial importance to solving the model. The pruning conditions (1) and (2) will work earlier for a model with "tighter" LP relaxation.

18.3.1 Network Flow Formulation

To find the most appropriate MIP model for PTP, we start by restating it as a network optimization problem. Let $A = \{(i, j) \in L \mid j - i = 1\}$ be the set of interactions between adjacent segments and let $R = L \setminus A$ be the set of remote links. We introduce a digraph $G(V, E)$ with vertex set $V = \{(i, k) \mid i = 1, \ldots, m, \ k = 1, \ldots, n\}$ and arc set $E = E_L \cup E_x$, where

$$E_L = \{((i, k), (j, l)) \mid (i, j) \in L, \ 1 \leq k \leq l \leq n\},$$

$$E_x = \{((i, k), (i + 1, l)) \mid i = 1, \ldots, m - 1, \ 1 \leq k \leq l \leq n\}.$$

A vertex $(i, k) \in V$ corresponds to segment i placed on its kth relative position. The set E_L corresponds to the set of links L between the segments. The arcs from $E_x \setminus E_L$ are added to ensure the order of the segments. Depending on the situation, a set of arcs E_z is defined as either $E_L \setminus E_x$, corresponding in this case to the links from R, or as E_L. The default value is the first definition, but in either case, $E = E_x \cup E_z$. The arcs from E_x are referred to as x-arcs, and the arcs from E_z as z-arcs.

By adding two extra vertices, S and T, and arcs $(S, (1, k))$, $k = 1, \ldots, n$ and $((m, l), T)$, $l = 1, \ldots, n$ (considered as x-arcs), it is easy to see the one-to-one correspondence between the set of the feasible threadings and the set of the S–T paths in (V, E_x). A threading $(r_1, \ldots, r_m)$ corresponds to the S–T path $S - (1, r_1) - \cdots - (m, r_m) - T$, and vice versa. Figure 18.3 illustrates this correspondence.

To each arc $e = ((i, k), (j, l)) \in E$ we associate a cost denoted by c_{ikjl}, or simply c_e. The costs of the arcs are related to the score coefficients introduced in the previous section. The cost of each x-arc is sum of three components: (1) the head of the arc (segment-to-position score), (2) the score of the loop between the adjacent segments (if any), and (3) the score of the interaction between the adjacent segments (if any). If the leading/trailing gaps are scored then their scores are associated to the outgoing/incoming arcs from/to the vertex S/T. The costs of z-arcs correspond to the pairwise segment interaction scores. In some of the models, the cost for placing the segment i on position k will be associated to the vertex (i, k) and denoted by c_{ik}.

An S–T path is said to activate the z-arcs that have both ends on this path. Each S–T path activates exactly $|R|$ z-arcs, one for each pair of segments in R. The subgraph induced by the x-arcs of an S–T path and the activated z-arcs is called an augmented path. Thus, solving PTP is equivalent to finding the shortest augmented path in G (as usual, the length of an augmented path is defined as the sum of the costs of its arcs). Figure 18.4 provides an example of augmented path.

Let us introduce the variables $x_e, e \in E_x$, $z_e, e \in E_z$, and $y_v, v \in V$. These variables will sometimes be denoted by $x_{i,k,i+1,l}$, z_{ikjl}, and y_{ik}. By interpreting x_e as a flow on the arc e, the problem of finding an S–T path in G becomes a problem of sending unit flow from S to T. In other words, there is one-to-one correspondence between the S–T paths and the vertices of the network-flow polytope X, defined by the constraints

$$\sum_{e \in \Gamma(S)} x_e = 1, \tag{18.1}$$

$$\sum_{e \in \Gamma^{-1}(T)} x_e = 1, \tag{18.2}$$

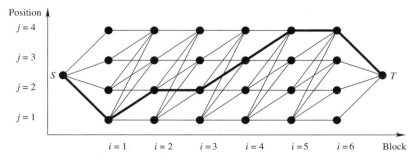

Figure 18.3 Example of the graph (V, E_x). The path in thick lines corresponds to the threading $(1, 2, 2, 3, 4, 4)$.

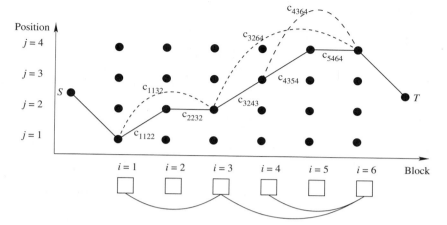

Figure 18.4 Example of augmented path. The generalized contact map graph is given in the bottom. The x-arcs of the S–T path are in solid lines. The activated z-arcs are in dashed lines. The length of the augmented path is equal to the score of the threading $(1, 2, 2, 3, 4, 4)$.

$$\sum_{e \in \Gamma(v)} x_e - \sum_{e \in \Gamma^{-1}(v)} x_e = 0, \quad v \in V, \tag{18.3}$$

$$x_e \geq 0, \quad e \in E_x, \tag{18.4}$$

where $\Gamma(v)$ (respectively $\Gamma^{-1}(v)$) denotes the set of the x-arcs with tail (respectively head) v. Constraint (18.1) (respectively (18.2)) corresponds to unit flow from S (respectively to T), and constraints (18.3) refer to flow conservation for each vertex. The well-known properties of the network polytope X make it possible to replace the integrality requirements $x_e \in \{0, 1\}$ by $x_e \geq 0$.

The set of feasible threadings can also be expressed in the space of y-variables as a set Y, defined by the constraints

$$\sum_{k=1}^{n} y_{ik} = 1, \quad i = 1, \ldots, m, \tag{18.5}$$

$$\sum_{l=1}^{k} y_{il} - \sum_{l=1}^{k} y_{i+1,l} \geq 0, \quad i = 1, \ldots, m-1, \ k = 1, \ldots, n-1, \tag{18.6}$$

$$y_{ik} \in \{0, 1\}, \quad i = 1, \ldots, m, \ k = 1, \ldots, n. \tag{18.7}$$

The binary variable y_{ik} is 1 if and only if segment i is placed on position k. Constraints (18.5) assign each segment to exactly one position and (18.6) ensure the order of segments (if segment i is placed after the kth position, then $i + 1$ must also be placed after the kth position).

Starting from the S–T path defining sets X or Y, an augmented path defining set Z can be constructed by introducing the z-variables and adding appropriate connecting constraints. In this way, different MIP models for PTP can be obtained. Although equivalent, these models will either be easier or more difficult to solve using a given MIP solver, depending on their formulation. The strategy for deriving such models is: while keeping the vertices of the convex hull of the Z projection on X (or Y) invariant, either improve the LP bounds by tightening the linear relaxation $\overline{Z}$ of Z, or restate the model (maybe by chance) in a way that makes its LP relaxation easier for the chosen solver.

In the rest of this section we derive five MIP models for PTP. $F(\mathbf{M})$ and $\overline{F}(\mathbf{M})$ denote the feasible sets of a model $\mathbf{M}$ and its LP relaxation. $v(\mathbf{M})$ and $\overline{v}(\mathbf{M})$ refer, respectively, to the optimal objective values of a model and to its LP relaxation. The models from Sections 18.3.2 to 18.3.4 are first proposed in [28, 29], the model in Section 18.3.5 is from [30], and the one in Section 18.3.6 is introduced in [32]. Before describing the models, two easily verifiable observations that will be useful to remember when reading the model descriptions are given subsequently.

Observation 18.1 Note that adding a constant to all arc costs does not change the set of optimal solutions. The same holds even if different constants d_{ij} are added to the costs c_{ikjl}, $1 \leq k \leq l \leq n$. This allows the objective function to be rotated to minimize the number of iterations of the simplex algorithm.

Observation 18.2 Let C be the set of segments participating in remote interactions, that is, $C = \{i \mid (i, j) \in R$ or $(j, i) \in R$ for some $j\}$. It is easy to see that the number of S–T paths (which is also the number of feasible threadings) is $N_x = \binom{m+n-1}{m}$, and the number of the different z-components of all augmented paths is $N_z = \binom{|C|+n-1}{|C|}$.

For the example shown in Figure 18.4, $C = \{1, 3, 4, 6\}$. The number of S–T paths (the number of possible fixations of the x-variables) is $N_x = \binom{6+4-1}{6} = 84$, and the number of possible fixations of the z-variables is $N_z = \binom{4+4-1}{4} = 35$. For fixed values of the z variables (in our case $z_{1132} = z_{3264} = z_{4364} = 1$, and all others equal to zero), the problem becomes simply a matter of finding the shortest S–T path passing through $(1, 1)$, $(3, 2)$, $(4, 3)$, and $(6, 4)$.

18.3.2 A Nonlinear Model using Vertices

The most straightforward presentation of PTP as a mathematical programming problem is:

$$\min \left\{ \sum_{i=1}^{m} \sum_{k=1}^{n} c_{ik} y_{ik} + \sum_{(i,j)\in L} \sum_{k=1}^{n} \sum_{l=k}^{n} c_{ikjl} y_{ik} y_{jl} \mid y \in Y \right\}.$$

Despite the simplicity of this nonlinear 0–1 programming model, there are currently no algorithms or software able to solve efficiently such nonconvex quadratic problems with thousands of binary variables. It is possible to linearize the model by introducing the z-variables. The products $y_{ik} y_{jl} = \min\{y_{ik}, y_{jl}\}$ can be replaced by z_{ikjl} in the objective function if the following tightest connecting constraints are added to the model [37]:

$$z_{ikjl} \leq y_{ik}, \quad z_{ikjl} \leq y_{jl}, \quad y_{ik} + y_{jl} - z_{ikjl} \leq 1, \quad 0 \leq z_{ijkl} \leq 1,$$
$$(i,j) \in L, \quad 1 \leq k \leq l \leq n.$$

Note that the integrality of z is implied by the integrality of y. Although linear, the obtained model cannot be efficiently solved, mainly because of the weakness of its LP-bounds [28].

18.3.3 A Model using *x*-arcs and *z*-arcs

The following model, later referred to as **MXZ**, is a restatement of the previous one in terms of network flow:

$$\text{Minimize} \quad \sum_{e \in E_x} c_e x_e + \sum_{e \in E_z} c_e z_e, \tag{18.8}$$

$$\text{subject to} \quad z_{ikjl} \leq \sum_{e \in \Gamma(i,k)} x_e, \quad ((i,k),(j,l)) \in E_z, \tag{18.9}$$

$$z_{ikjl} \leq \sum_{e \in \Gamma^{-1}(j,l)} x_e, \quad ((i,k),(j,l)) \in E_z, \tag{18.10}$$

$$\sum_{1 \leq k \leq l \leq n} z_{ikjl} = 1, \quad (i,j) \in R, \tag{18.11}$$

$$x \in X, \tag{18.12}$$

$$z_e \in \{0,1\}, \quad e \in E_z. \tag{18.13}$$

The z-arcs are activated by a nonzero outflow from their tail vertex (constraints (18.9)) and a nonzero inflow into their head vertex (constraints (18.10)). The special ordered set (SOS) constraints (18.11) follow from the rest of the constraints, but even though they are redundant, they are included in the model primarily to control the branching strategy of the MIP solver.

For **MXZ** we can choose either x or z as the integer variables, as the integrality of x follows from the integrality of z, and vice versa. However, the better choice is z because, as mentioned in Observation 18.2, the space of z-variables is smaller than the space of x-variables.

18.3.4 A Model using Vertices, *x*-arcs, and *z*-arcs

To improve the LP-bounds and the branching strategy by imposing branching on SOS constraints (despite the expense of adding extra constraints), we modify the model

MXZ by introducing the y-variables, associated to the vertices of the graph G. Thus we obtain the following model, denoted here by **MXYZ**:

$$\text{Minimize} \quad \sum_{e \in E_x} c_e x_e + \sum_{e \in E_z} c_e z_e, \tag{18.14}$$

$$\text{subject to} \quad y_{ik} = \sum_{l=k}^{n} z_{ikjl}, \quad (i,j) \in R, \quad k = 1, \ldots, n, \tag{18.15}$$

$$y_{jl} = \sum_{k=1}^{l} z_{ikjl}, \quad (i,j) \in R, \quad l = 1, \ldots, n, \tag{18.16}$$

$$y_{ik} = \sum_{e \in \Gamma(i,k)} x_e, \quad i \in C, \quad k = 1, \ldots, n, \tag{18.17}$$

$$\sum_{k=1}^{n} y_{ik} = 1, \quad i \in C, \tag{18.18}$$

$$y_{ik} \in \{0, 1\}, \quad i \in C, \quad k = 1, \ldots, n, \tag{18.19}$$

$$x \in X, \tag{18.20}$$

$$z_e \geq 0, \quad e \in E_z. \tag{18.21}$$

The y-variables control the activation of z-arcs (constraints (18.15) and (18.16)), as well as the flow on x-arcs (constraints (18.17)). Constraints (18.18) and (18.19) correspond to (18.5) and (18.7) from the previous definition of the set Y. This model has no constraints corresponding to (18.6) in the set Y, because the order of the segments is imposed in X. From a computational point of view, even at the expense of adding new variables and constraints, **MXYZ** is preferable mainly for the following two reasons: (1) $\overline{F}(\textbf{MXYZ}) \subset \overline{F}(\textbf{MXZ})$ (see Proposition 18.1), which means that $\overline{v}(\textbf{MXYZ})$ is a better bound on the optimal objective value than $\overline{v}(\textbf{MXZ})$ and (2) given that the y-variables are defined only for the segments in C, the size of the search space for this model is the same as in **MXZ** (see Observation 18.2), while the number of binary variables is $|C|n$, which is much less than $|R|n(n+1)/2$, the corresponding number in **MXZ**.

Proposition 18.1 $\overline{F}(\textbf{MXYZ}) \subset \overline{F}(\textbf{MXZ})$.

Proof It is easy to verify that constraints (18.15) and (18.17) imply (18.9); (18.16) and (18.17) imply (18.10); (18.15) and (18.18) imply (18.11). Therefore, $\overline{F}(\textbf{MXYZ}) \subseteq \overline{F}(\textbf{MXZ})$. To prove that the inclusion is strict, consider the values of x and z shown in Figure 18.5. It is easy to see that these values satisfy (18.9)–(18.12). In contrast from (18.17) it follows that $y_{33} = 0.25$, while according to (18.16), $y_{33} = 0.5$. ∎

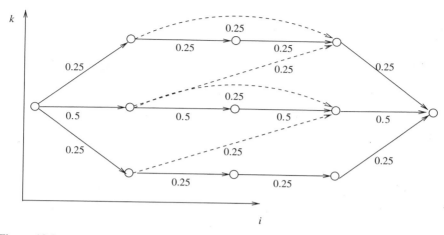

Figure 18.5   An instance of a network flow graph with $m = 3$, $n = 3$, and $L = \{(1,3)\}$. The x-arcs are represented by solid lines and the z-arcs by dashed lines. Only the arcs with nonzero flow are given. The number associated to each arc is the value of the corresponding variable.

18.3.5   A Model using Vertices and z-arcs

The only combination left involves excluding the x-variables and testing the impact on the LP solver's efficiency of the possible reduction in the number of variables versus some increase in the number of constraints. Toward this end, the arcs in $E_x \setminus E_L$ are excluded from G and the arcs from $E_x \cap E_L$ are considered to be z-arcs. More precisely, in this model, $E_z = E_L$. The model **MYZ** obtained in this way is:

$$\text{Minimize} \quad \sum_{i=1}^{m}\sum_{k=1}^{n} c_{ik} y_{ik} + \sum_{e \in E_z} c_e z_e, \tag{18.22}$$

$$\text{subject to} \quad y_{ik} = \sum_{l=k}^{n} z_{ikjl}, \quad (i,j) \in L, \ \ k = 1,\ldots,n, \tag{18.23}$$

$$y_{jl} = \sum_{k=1}^{l} z_{ikjl}, \quad (i,j) \in L, \ \ l = 1,\ldots,n, \tag{18.24}$$

$$y \in Y, \tag{18.25}$$

$$z_e \geq 0, \quad e \in E_z. \tag{18.26}$$

In this model, as in the previous one, the z-arcs are activated by the y-variables (constraints (18.23) and (18.24)). The gain with respect to **MXYZ** is about a 10% reduction in the number of variables, due to exclusion of non-duplicated x variables. Almost the same increase in the number of constraints due to (18.23) and (18.24) for $(i,j) \in A$ is observed for real-life instances. However, these modifications have a significant impact on the performance of the LP solver as we will see later.

18.3.6   The RAPTOR Model

Although derived differently, this model is very similar to the previous two. Let us make the following modifications in the model **MXYZ**: replace $i \in C$ by $i = 1, \ldots, m$ in constraints (18.17)–(18.19); replace the flow-tracing constraints (18.20) by the constraints

$$y_{jl} = \sum_{e \in \Gamma^{-1}(j,l)} x_e, \quad j = 1, \ldots, m, \ l = 1, \ldots, n$$

connecting the y-variables and the tails of the x-arcs. In this way we obtain the **RAPTOR** model. It can also be derived from **MYZ** by replacing E_z with E, L with $L \cup \{(i, i+1) \mid i = 1, \ldots, m-1\}$, and removing constraints (18.6) (contained in (18.25)). Although seemingly minor, these modifications have a significant effect on the performance of the LP solver.

18.3.7   The LS Algorithm and the Self-Threading Case

Lathrop and Smith's B&B algorithm [26] uses lower bounds, which can be easily explained in terms of our network model. Consider a vertex $(i, k) \in V$, where $i \in C$. Let $P = S - (1, r_1) - \cdots - (i, k) - \cdots - (m, r_m) - T$ be an S–T path in G. Let

$$b(i, k, P) = \sum_{(i,j) \in R} c_{ikjr_j} + \sum_{(j,i) \in R} c_{jr_jik}$$

be the sum of the costs of the z-arcs with head or tail (i, k), activated by P. Let $b^*(i, k) = \min_P b(i, k, P)$, where the minimum is over all S–T paths passing through (i, k). If the costs of the x-arcs in $\Gamma(i, k)$ are updated by adding $1/2b^*(i, k)$, then the cost of the shortest S–T path in G is a lower bound on the optimal objective value ($b^*(i, k)$ is multiplied by $1/2$ because each arc is counted twice, once for its head and once for its tail). The $O(m^2 n^2)$ complexity of this procedure could be derived from the complexity of the shortest-path problem and the complexity of the algorithm for computing b^*. Lathrop and Smith provide a list of impressive computational results for a rich set of the so-called self-threading instances (the protein sequence is aligned to its own structure template). Andonov et al. [28–30] tested the MIP models on a large set of self-threading instances, and the results were always the same: the LP relaxation attains its minimum at a feasible (hence optimal) 0–1 vertex. The relaxation used in the **LS** algorithm is based on minimizing a function $\underline{f}(x)$, which is inferior to the objective function $f(x)$, over the set of feasible threadings. For such a relaxation, an optimal solution x^* to the relaxed problem is optimal for the original problem if $f(x^*) = \underline{f}(x^*)$. For the **LS** model, this is a kind of self-threading subclass defining property, and in most of the cases the optimal solution is found at the root of the B&B tree. This is the reason for the efficiency of the **LS** algorithm on instances in this subclass.

18.3.8 Experimental Comparison of the MIP Models

Extensive computational experiments in [28, 29] showed that **MXYZ** significantly outperforms the **LS** algorithm and the **MXZ** model. Here we present results from [30] which compare the models **MXYZ**, **MYZ**, and **RAPTOR**. The models were solved using CPLEX 7.1 on a Pentium 2.40 GHz Linux PC with 4 GB of RAM. The models are compared on real-life instances generated by Fold Recognition Oriented Search Tool (FROST) software [27].

The most important observation is that for almost all (about 95%) the instances, the LP relaxation of all three models is integer-valued, thus providing optimal threading. This is true even for polytopes with more than 10^{46} vertices. Table 18.1 shows the number of simplex iterations and the time for each model on a sample from these instances. More precisely, of the 3600 instances solved by the **MYZ** model, the LP solution is noninteger in only 182 cases (about 5%). In all these cases, the solution contains mainly zeros and ones, and several 0.5 values. The largest number of nodes in the B&B tree for the 182 noninteger instances is 11; only 17 instances have a tree with six or more nodes (these instances are shown in Table 18.2). In most instances, only two nodes are sufficient for attaining optimality. The behavior of the other two models is similar. The number of nodes is slightly different from one model to another, and from CPLEX 7.1 to 8.0, but always stays in the same range of values. Table 18.2 shows that most of the solution time is usually spent in solving the LP relaxation. In addition, the gap between the LP score and the MIP score is so small that the LP relaxation could very well predict the closest template when comparing a query to multiple templates. There are, in fact, many similarities with the classic uncapacitated plant-location problem, in which most of the instances are easy to solve [38, 39]. The good behavior of the LP relaxation is definitely lost when using randomly generated

TABLE 18.1 A Set of Instances where the LP Solution is Integer

Query Length	Space Size	MXYZ		RAPTOR		MYZ	
		Iter.	Time	Iter.	Time	Iter.	Time
491	2.9E21	13624	25	13864	26	7907	13
491	2.5E25	22878	83	25747	118	10566	29
522	1.8E26	20627	111	15723	94	7920	22
491	1.1E27	41234	276	47082	347	16094	58
455	1.5E29	30828	390	36150	596	25046	241
522	1.8E29	18949	161	18598	169	12307	77
491	1.1E30	28968	365	40616	604	13870	68
491	1.4E30	58602	1303	66816	2083	29221	401
491	3.2E30	34074	572	41646	659	22516	186
522	5.3E31	26778	334	33395	468	13752	64
294	4.1E38	43694	619	52312	749	36539	314
583	1.3E39	124321	6084	147828	8019	57912	1120
757	9.9E45	121048	4761	166067	7902	92834	3117

Note: Times are in seconds. For all instances, the **MYZ** model provides the best time.

TABLE 18.2 A Set of Instances with a Noninteger LP Solution

Query Length	Space Size	LP Score	MIP Score	MXYZ		RAPTOR		MYZ	
				LP Time	MIP Time	LP Time	MIP Time	LP Time	MIP Time
300	3.8E20	57.5	60.8	230	468	338	832	207	320
344	5.2E23	152.1	156.2	125	260	196	368	79	319
364	1.1E23	185.5	188.0	466	562	576	1642	262	635
416	4.1E26	314.8	318.8	219	523	357	552	91	168
394	1.9E28	214.2	217.1	425	599	692	1167	117	273
394	2.1E28	201.4	202.9	458	599	834	1140	208	421
427	1.6E29	256.3	261.6	1308	1692	2025	3109	304	653
508	1.3E30	316.2	317.5	195	281	339	447	72	126
491	1.8E30	97.4	98.1	245	262	427	545	70	87
511	1.9E31	415.7	420.1	1908	3893	3129	4053	1012	1773
508	3.9E32	180.3	181.9	841	1008	1389	1666	293	422
508	1.7E33	370.2	370.2	1292	1356	1706	2117	908	1182
491	1.2E33	90.2	90.8	542	927	737	827	202	218
522	6.6E34	−12.4	−11.8	1678	1723	1928	2119	258	293
583	1.3E36	−297.5	−296.6	1900	2533	4372	4648	773	910
508	1.23E38	347.8	354.5	4711	9349	6346	17903	1657	3949
508	1.66E40	201.1	210.4	8031	13449	10588	27055	2504	9631

Note: Times are in seconds. The LP relaxation value is the same for all models, and the gap between this value and the optimal solution is relatively small. **MYZ** is significantly faster than the other models.

score coefficients, but we believe that the behavior will stay good for each reasonable additive scoring scheme. In complexity-theory parlance, these observations can be summarized as: the subset of real-life instances of PTP is polynomially solvable.

These results show that all practical instances of PTP could be solved in affordable time using only a general-purpose LP solver and one of the MIP models described earlier. The problems with noninteger LP solutions could be driven to feasibility by using a simple ad hoc procedure instead of an MIP solver. As for the minimality of the polytope-describing constraints of the proposed MIP models, we must note that any attempt of aggregation (e.g., (18.15), (18.16), and (18.18) in **MXYZ**) spoils the integrality of the LP solution.

All numerical experiments show that the constraints (18.6) influence CPLEX solution times very favorably. Consequently, the **MYZ** model significantly outperforms **MXYZ** and **RAPTOR** for all large instances (see the corresponding columns in Tables 18.1 and 18.2).

18.4 DIVIDE-AND-CONQUER TECHNIQUE

The main drawback of the MIP models presented in the previous section is their huge number of variables and constraints. Although their LP relaxations yield optimal solutions for most real-life instances, solving these relaxations is still computationally expensive, and sometimes even impossible due to memory requirements. A possible approach to increase efficiency is to split the problem into subproblems and to solve them separately. In this section, we present such divide-and-conquer technique for the **MYZ** model.

Let $1 \leq L_1 \leq \cdots \leq L_m \leq n$, $1 \leq U_1 \leq \cdots \leq U_m \leq n$, $L_i \leq U_i$, $i = 1, \ldots, m$ be lower and upper bounds of the segment positions. These bounds can be imposed by setting to zero (removing) the variables y_{ik}, $i = 1, \ldots, m$, $k \notin \overline{L_i, U_i}$ and z_{ikjl}, $(i,j) \in R$, $k \notin \overline{L_i, U_i}$, $l \notin \overline{L_j, U_j}$ in the **MYZ** model. The resulting model is called **MYZ**(L, U) and its optimal objective value is denoted $v(L, U)$. Now if $\{(L^s, U^s) \mid s \in S\}$ is a set of bounds partitioning the space of feasible threadings, then $v(\textbf{MYZ}) = \min\{v(L^s, U^s) \mid s \in S\}$. In other words, the solution to the original problem is the best of the subproblem solutions.

Splitting the problem into subproblems is useful for two reasons. First, each subproblem has a smaller number of variables and is thus easier to solve than the original problem. Second, and more important, information from the previously solved subproblems can be used when solving the next subproblem. Suppose that the first s subproblems have already been solved, and let v^* be the best of their objective values. Then v^* can be used as a cutoff value when solving subproblem $s + 1$. If the LP relaxation of this subproblem is solved using a dual simplex method, the optimization can be stopped prematurely if the objective function exceeds v^*. The same cut can be applied not only at the root, but also in any node of the B&B tree.

There are many ways to split the space of feasible threadings. Andonov et al. [30] have tested two natural, easy-to-implement, and efficient possibilities. Let us fix a segment i and partition the interval $\overline{1, n}$ of its possible positions into q subintervals $\overline{L_i^s, U_i^s}$, $s = 1, \ldots, q$ of lengths approximately n/q each. In this way, a partition of the feasible threadings space (L^s, U^s), $s = 1, \ldots, q$, is obtained, where

$$L_i^s = 1 + (s - 1)\left\lfloor \frac{n}{q} \right\rfloor + \min(s - 1, n \bmod q), \quad U_i^s = s\left\lfloor \frac{n}{q} \right\rfloor + \min(s, n \bmod q),$$

$$L_j^s = 1, \qquad U_j^s = U_i^s, \quad j = 1, \ldots i - 1,$$

$$L_j^s = L_i^s, \quad U_j^s = n, \quad j = i + 1, \ldots m.$$

Intuitively, the feasible space of subproblem s is composed of the S–T paths in the network that pass through the vertices (i, k), $k \in \overline{L_i^s, U_i^s}$ (Fig. 18.6a).

Earlier, we defined a splitting for a fixed segment i and a fixed number of subproblems q. A natural question is how to choose good values for these parameters. For a fixed q, a good strategy is to choose the segment i in such a way that the most difficult of the resulting subproblems become easier to solve. Formally, if the number of variables is considered as an approximate measure of subproblem's difficulty, a good choice would be

$$i = \operatorname*{argmin}_{1 \leq j \leq m} \left\{ \max_{1 \leq s \leq q} v_{js} \right\},$$

where v_{js} is the number of variables of subproblem s, split on the jth segment. The choice of the number of subproblems q is not obvious and will be discussed later.

The order in which the subproblems are solved is very important to the efficiency of this approach. A better record v^* allows earlier cuts in the subproblems that follow. Statistically, the chance of finding the global optimum in a subproblem is proportional to the size of its search space. It is not difficult to see that the number of S–T paths passing through a vertex (i, k) is $\binom{i+k-2}{i-1}\binom{m+n-i-k}{m-i}$. From this, it is easy to compute the search space size of each subproblem and to sort the subproblems in decreasing order according to their size.

This splitting technique can be generalized for two (or more) segments. Consider two segments i and j (Fig. 18.6b). As before, the possible positions for each segment are partitioned into q subintervals, yielding $q(q + 1)/2$ subproblems. Segments i and j can be chosen to minimize the maximal number of variables in the resulting subproblems, and the subproblems can be solved in decreasing order on their search space size. In the following paragraphs, SPLIT1 and SPLIT2 denote partitioning based on one and two segments. Finding the best splitting segment(s) in SPLIT1 requires considering each of the m segments, while in SPLIT2 $m(m - 1)/2$ pairs of segments must be enumerated. In both cases, the time needed to choose the splitting segments is negligible with respect to the time needed to solve the resulting subproblems.

Andonov et al. [30] have tested these splitting techniques on a large set of threading instances. Table 18.3 presents the running times for SPLIT1 and SPLIT2 on a representative subset of these instances. The experiment shows that:

- Splitting reduces the running time by a factor of more than 2 for bigger instances when an appropriate number of subproblems are chosen.
- Running time decreases up to certain number of subproblems, and then begins to increase again. The best number of subproblems is relatively small (no more than 15 for all solved instances). This phenomenon is due not only to the increased

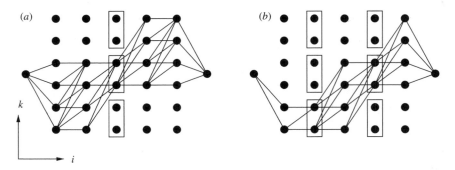

Figure 18.6 Instance with five segments and six free positions. (*a*) The problem is split on segment 3 into three subproblems. The feasible set of the second subproblem is defined by $L^2 = (1, 1, 3, 3, 3)$ and $U^2 = (4, 4, 4, 6, 6)$. (*b*) The problem is split on segments 2 and 4 into six subproblems. The feasible set of the second subproblem is defined by $L^2 = (1, 1, 1, 3, 3)$ and $U^2 = (2, 2, 4, 4, 6)$.

TABLE 18.3 **Running Times for SPLIT1 and SPLIT2 with Different Number of Subproblems**

Number of Subproblems

Space	Split	1	3	6	10	15	21	28	36
2.80E+19	1	13	**9**	11	13	19	24	31	32
	2	13	**10**	10	13	14	17	20	25
2.94E+21	1	33	**16**	17	22	27	35	45	55
	2	33	**21**	22	21	26	28	37	38
2.47E+25	1	80	**39**	40	57	76	102	123	154
	2	80	**40**	40	40	47	57	68	79
1.75E+26	1	99	**72**	101	142	191	257	335	421
	2	99	**77**	101	111	141	179	212	247
1.10E+27	1	308	95	**92**	115	153	189	251	292
	2	308	102	**92**	102	108	122	148	171
1.53E+29	1	1115	**329**	392	491	645	788	993	1163
	2	1115	392	604	**369**	441	635	662	744
1.78E+29	1	364	**144**	192	291	390	528	677	818
	2	364	**163**	175	195	243	312	381	478
1.09E+30	1	292	**134**	181	216	303	388	501	612
	2	292	167	**158**	225	276	273	342	419
1.44E+30	1	1117	482	**463**	512	676	840	1094	1314
	2	1117	511	**457**	464	534	660	768	800
3.20E+30	1	802	**314**	405	515	719	903	1216	1484
	2	802	322	366	**318**	396	525	665	763
5.34E+31	1	524	**277**	352	531	728	908	1020	1308
	2	524	**329**	409	405	475	496	561	701
# instances where SPLIT1 is better		11	3	1	0	0	0	0	
# instances where SPLIT2 is better		0	5	9	11	11	11	11	
Average speedup SPLIT1		2.3	2.0	1.5	1.1	0.9	0.7	0.6	
Average speedup SPLIT2		2.0	1.9	1.9	1.6	1.3	1.1	1.0	

Note: The running times are in seconds. The best running time in each row is in bold.

overhead for the initialization of the subproblems, but also to the smaller chance of finding the globally optimal solution in one of the first subproblems (see also Table 18.4).

- It is difficult to determine the optimal number of subproblems before solving them. This number is different for each instance and depends on the structure of the subproblems.
- SPLIT2 is more robust, in that its running time increases more slowly with the number of subproblems. Although SPLIT1 is clearly the winner for three subproblems, in the case of ten or more subproblems, SPLIT2 is the better choice. This observation is illustrated by rows "# instances where SPLIT1 (SPLIT2) is better" in Table 18.3. Use of SPLIT2 is preferable, because even when the number

TABLE 18.4   Subproblem where the Optimal Solution is Found

Number of Subproblems								
Space	Split	3	6	10	15	21	28	36
2.80E+19	1	1	2	3	2	2	5	5
	2	1	1	2	1	4	2	9
2.94E+21	1	1	1	1	2	1	2	1
	2	1	4	1	8	4	19	12
2.47E+25	1	1	1	1	2	2	3	3
	2	1	1	1	1	3	1	2
1.75E+26	1	1	2	2	3	5	6	7
	2	1	3	1	3	3	6	6
1.10E+27	1	1	1	1	2	2	5	4
	2	1	2	1	1	2	4	2
1.53E+29	1	1	2	3	4	5	7	9
	2	1	2	1	3	2	7	3
1.78E+29	1	1	1	2	3	4	6	5
	2	1	2	1	2	2	4	3
1.09E+30	1	1	2	1	2	3	4	5
	2	1	3	5	6	2	5	9
1.44E+30	1	1	1	1	1	1	1	1
	2	1	1	1	1	2	3	1
3.20E+30	1	1	2	2	4	6	7	11
	2	3	2	8	3	5	5	12
5.34E+31	1	3	4	6	8	12	15	18
	2	3	6	7	10	16	8	13

of subproblems is chosen randomly, there is a smaller chance of making a serious "mistake."

Table 18.4 presents the subproblem in which the global optimum was found. It shows that solving the subproblems in decreasing order on their search-space size yields good results. In many cases, the optimal solution is found when solving the first subproblem, and the rest of the subproblems are quickly abandoned using the obtained cutoff value. Even when the first subproblem does not contain the global optimum, it provides a good record that allows many of the following subproblems to be cut.

18.5   PARALLELIZATION

In the previous sections we have shown that an appropriate MIP model combined with divide-and-conquer strategy can significantly decrease the time for solving PTP. The application of these techniques allows to increase the size of practically solvable instances from 10^{18}–10^{20} to 10^{35}–10^{38}. However, given that PTP is NP-hard, it is not surprising that solving instances of bigger size is still slow. A natural way to accelerate the algorithms for solving PTP is to use parallel computing. There are two possible approaches to parallelization.

The high-level parallelization considers each PTP as a single task. Recall that the query sequence must be aligned to each template (or a filtered subset of templates) from the database. These alignments are independent tasks and can be executed in parallel. Pley et al. [40] propose such parallelization. As the tasks are irregular, dynamic load balance is used.

In this section we present a lower-level parallelization proposed by Andonov et al. [29, 30]. This approach uses the divide-and-conquer strategy from the previous section. The subproblems are considered as tasks to be executed on p processors. The best objective value known by a given processor is called local record, and the global record is the best among the local records. The efficiency of the parallel algorithm depends essentially on propagating the global record quickly among the processors to use it as a cut.

18.5.1 Parallel Algorithm

The parallel algorithm proposed by Andonov et al. [30] is based on centralized dynamic load balancing: tasks are dispatched from a centralized location (pool) in a dynamic way. The work pool is managed by a "master" who gives work on demand to idle "slaves." The master is also responsible for communicating new records to the slaves. Each slave solves the subproblem assigned to it, using the model **MYZ**. Note that dynamic load balancing is the only reasonable task allocation method when dealing with irregular tasks for which the amount of work is not known prior to execution.

To propagate the global record quickly, the CPLEX callback functions are used. These are user functions called at each simplex iteration (LP callback) and at each node of the B&B tree (MIP callback). The slaves use the MIP callback to communicate the local record to the master (if this record is improved at the current node). The LP callback is used to probe for new records coming from outside and to stop the optimization if the LP objective value becomes greater than the record. In the experiments, the local record was hardly ever updated — about once for every 1000 simplex iterations. Furthermore, the only information exchanged between the master and a slave when a new task is transmitted is the number of this task. This information is sufficient for the slave to instantiate the CPLEX problem object directly in its own memory. This, together with the reduced number of record exchanges, makes this parallel implementation very efficient.

18.5.2 Computational Experiments

The numerical results presented in this section were obtained by using the CPLEX 7.1 callable library and the MPI communication library on a cluster of 16, 2 × Pentium III

1 GHz 512 MB Linux PCs connected by a Myrinet network. As in Section 18.3.8, the PTP instances are generated by FROST [27]. As discussed in Section 18.4, it is extremely difficult to predict the number of subproblems that will minimize running time. The problem becomes even more complicated when there are multiple processors. For these reasons, the algorithm was run on a large set of various instances and its behavior was observed, with both varying the problem granularity and the number of processors. Based on the resulting statistics, Andonov et al. [30] derive empirically a range of values for the observed parameters for which the program has close-to-optimal behavior.

Tables 18.5 and 18.6 summarize the execution times of the parallel code on a set of representative instances, using SPLIT1 and SPLIT2, respectively. The pth row gives the running times using p processors, $p = 1, \ldots, 12$. Columns 2–9 correspond to the different granularities (the number of subproblems is shown in the header). ∞ denotes cases in which the problem was not solved due to insufficient memory. This happened only for the original (nonsplit) problem. The "avg" column contains the arithmetic mean of the values in bold from the corresponding row, whereas the "stddev" column gives the standard deviation of the same values. The column "s_up" contains the speedup, computed using the values from the column "avg" (avg_1/avg_p), and the last column shows the corresponding efficiency (s_up_p/p).

The last two columns characterize the average performance of the algorithm when the pair (processors and subproblems) belongs to the bold area in the corresponding row of the table. The bold area itself was determined by statistical analysis. For each row, the bold area consists of consecutive cells that optimize the average values of the last two columns over the set of instances considered in the experiment. Thus, when a pair (processors and granularity) is located in the bold area, the behavior of the algorithm is expected to be close to the data from the last two columns. The performed analysis makes an automatic choice of granularity possible, and transparent to the user.

The data presented in Tables 18.5 and 18.6 show that the SPLIT2 strategy is significantly better than SPLIT1. For SPLIT2, the mean running time decreases much faster than for SPLIT1, which naturally yields more attractive values in the last two columns. SPLIT2 is also more robust, as demonstrated by the standard deviations, which decreases faster with an increasing number of processors. In both cases, parallelism gives robustness to the algorithms: increasing the number of processors lessens the impact of granularity on execution time.

Table 18.7 contains the running time for the biggest instance that was solved. The SPLIT2 strategy was used in this example. Up to 26 processors were used to observe the algorithm's efficiency. Although efficiency decreases below 0.8 when more than 12 processors are used, it remains above 0.5 even with 26 processors. The parallel algorithm is reasonably efficient up to about 10 processors. But this is not a serious drawback, because the query sequence is usually aligned to multiple templates. If there are more processors available, they can be used efficiently by separating them into groups and assigning a different query-to-template threading to each group.

TABLE 18.5   Running Times for SPLIT1

p	1	3	6	10	15	21	28	36	avg	stddev	s_up	eff
				$m=33, n=172, \|R\|=84, \|\mathcal{T}\|=1.23\text{E}38$								
1	17673	**8647**	**2517**	**2431**	2656	2309	2756	2809	4531	2910	1.0	1.0
2		2972	**1915**	**1341**	**1736**				1664	239	2.7	1.4
4			839	**864**	**1051**	1145			1020	116	4.4	1.1
6			810	**503**	**778**	857			712	151	6.4	1.1
8				482	**632**	**708**	716		685	37	6.6	0.8
10				481	**525**	**644**	564		577	49	7.8	0.8
12					523	**595**	**507**	567	556	36	8.1	0.7
				$m=31, n=212, \|R\|=81, \|\mathcal{T}\|=1.29\text{E}39$								
1	3036	**2450**	**1126**	**1520**	868	1137	1381	1257	1698	555	1.0	1.0
2		824	**421**	**796**	**1141**				786	294	2.2	1.1
4			277	**351**	**500**	469			440	64	3.9	1.0
6			276	**279**	**338**	346			321	29	5.3	0.9
8				279	**310**	**232**	325		289	40	5.9	0.7
10				278	**309**	**203**	285		265	45	6.4	0.6
12					311	**189**	**188**	237	204	22	8.3	0.7
				$m=27, n=225, \|R\|=71, \|\mathcal{T}\|=1.33\text{E}36$								
1	∞	712	**497**	**664**	472	557	613	704	624	92	1.0	1.0
2		654	**376**	**438**	485				433	44	1.4	0.7
4			296	**311**	**319**	346			325	15	1.9	0.5
6			294	**312**	**253**	261			275	26	2.3	0.4
8				312	**254**	**260**	279		264	10	2.4	0.3
10				310	**252**	**260**	280		264	11	2.4	0.2
12					252	**260**	**278**	230	256	19	2.4	0.2
				$m=30, n=219, \|R\|=90, \|\mathcal{T}\|=4.13\text{E}38$								
1	∞	680	**699**	**441**	523	693	1719	796	606	117	1.0	1.0
2		1245	**321**	**522**	**980**				607	275	1.0	0.5
4			135	**165**	**276**	340			260	72	2.3	0.6
6			92	**124**	**154**	242			173	50	3.5	0.6
8				114	**111**	**233**	233		192	57	3.2	0.4
10				78	**109**	**127**	203		146	40	4.1	0.4
12					109	**106**	**138**	200	148	39	4.1	0.3
				$m=32, n=123, \|R\|=86, \|\mathcal{T}\|=1.19\text{E}33$								
1	443	**208**	**245**	**139**	179	240	287	290	197	43	1.0	1.0
2		150	**120**	**139**	148				135	11	1.5	0.7
4			82	**88**	**84**	95			89	4	2.2	0.6
6			82	**67**	**63**	69			66	2	3.0	0.5
8				63	**59**	**55**	67		60	5	3.3	0.4
10				63	**59**	**52**	56		55	2	3.5	0.4
12					59	**45**	**52**	56	51	4	3.9	0.3

TABLE 18.6 Running Times for SPLIT2

p	1	3	6	10	15	21	28	36	avg	stddev	s_up	eff
$m = 33, n = 172, \|R\| = 84, \|\mathcal{T}\| = 1.23E38$												
1	17673	8647	2517	2431	2656	2309	2756	2809	4531	2910	1.0	1.0
2		3878	1173	1400	1419	1105	1562	1467	1330	111	3.4	1.7
4			703	714	677	576	700	719	655	58	6.9	1.7
6			657	606	500	397	510	515	501	85	9.0	1.5
8				614	421	374	401	431	398	19	11.4	1.4
10				374	324	313	349	394	328	15	13.8	1.4
12					243	246	336	351	311	46	14.6	1.2
$m = 31, n = 212, \|R\| = 81, \|\mathcal{T}\| = 1.29E39$												
1	3036	2450	1126	1520	868	1137	1381	1257	1698	555	1.0	1.0
2		983	693	771	466	592	663	656	643	129	2.6	1.3
4			342	504	298	336	354	329	379	89	4.5	1.1
6			343	309	230	277	185	222	272	32	6.2	1.0
8				259	228	232	150	179	203	37	8.4	1.0
10				258	185	189	136	154	170	24	10.0	1.0
12					185	190	130	152	157	24	10.8	0.9
$m = 27, n = 225, \|R\| = 71, \|\mathcal{T}\| = 1.33E36$												
1	∞	712	497	664	472	557	613	704	624	92	1.0	1.0
2		904	383	393	316	343	373		364	34	1.7	0.9
4			232	159	173	140	158	182	157	13	4.0	1.0
6			185	123	113	106	116	146	114	7	5.5	0.9
8				119	109	120	90	95	106	12	5.9	0.7
10				119	109	109	89	85	102	9	6.1	0.6
12					146	112	68	70	83	20	7.5	0.6
$m = 30, n = 219, \|R\| = 90, \|\mathcal{T}\| = 4.13E38$												
1	∞	680	699	441	523	693	1719	796	606	117	1.0	1.0
2		591	187	261	318	289	522	417	255	53	2.4	1.2
4			160	146	153	166	192	216	155	8	3.9	1.0
6			104	115	126	115	125	159	118	5	5.1	0.9
8				81	107	89	99	123	98	7	6.2	0.8
10				59	107	93	89	105	96	7	6.3	0.6
12					94	67	78	83	76	6	8.0	0.7
$m = 32, n = 123, \|R\| = 86, \|\mathcal{T}\| = 1.19E33$												
1	443	208	245	139	179	240	287	290	197	43	1.0	1.0
2		127	103	80	102	115	145	159	95	10	2.1	1.0
4			71	51	63	62	75	83	58	5	3.4	0.8
6			54	39	46	48	56	57	44	3	4.5	0.7
8				38	40	39	46	45	41	3	4.7	0.6
10				33	36	35	39	38	36	1	5.4	0.5
12					37	29	34	36	33	2	6.0	0.5

TABLE 18.7 **Running Times for Instance with $m = 41$, $n = 194$, $|R| = 112$, $|T| = 9.89E45$**

p	1	3	6	10	15	21	28	36	45	55	66	avg	stddev	s_up	eff
1	∞	**4412**	**4726**	**3385**	2903	3638	3595	3931	3958			4174	572	1.0	1.0
2		3039	**1841**	**1755**	**1441**	1838	1870	2017	1980			1679	171	2.5	1.2
4			990	**1239**	858	**1010**	943	1019	1010			1035	156	4.0	1.0
6			955	**998**	**614**	**710**	673	680	692			774	163	5.4	0.9
8				686	**543**	**599**	**536**	519	535			559	28	7.5	0.9
10				681	**416**	**478**	**476**	425	440			456	28	9.1	0.9
12					415	**449**	**440**	**367**	387			418	36	10.0	0.8
16						464	**387**	**356**	**333**	352		358	22	11.6	0.7
18						383	**351**	**372**	**326**	313	359	349	18	11.9	0.7
24							343	**308**	**294**	**282**	307	294	10	14.2	0.6
26							373	**320**	**334**	**299**	296	317	14	13.1	0.5

18.6 FUTURE RESEARCH DIRECTIONS

In this section we discuss several possible extensions, improvements, and open questions related to the algorithms presented in this chapter.

Properties of the PTP Polytope   It is well known that the network flow polytope defined by constraints (18.1)–(18.4) has only integral vertices. Unfortunately, it is not the case for the polytopes of the LP relaxations of the MIP models for PTP. It can be shown that even a single pairwise interaction between nonadjacent segments introduces nonintegral vertices. However, as we have seen in Section 18.3.8, the optimum of the LP relaxations is attained in integral vertices for 95% of the real-life instances. Surprisingly, even small perturbations of the score coefficients move the optimum to nonintegral vertex. This phenomenon is still unexplained. It would be interesting to study the structure of the PTP polytope and the relations between the properties of the score coefficients and the integrality of the LP solution. A study in this direction can also help to formulate tighter LP models.

Solving the MIP Models by Special-Purpose Methods   The advantage of MIP models presented in this chapter is that their LP relaxations give the optimal solution for most of the real-life instances. Their drawback is their huge size (both number of variables and number of constraints) which makes even solving the LP relaxation slow. The MIP models have very sparse and structured constraint matrix. Instead of solving them by general-purpose B&B algorithms using LP relaxation, one can try to design more efficient special-purpose algorithms. The first encouraging results in this direction are reported by Balev [41]. He proposes an MIP model similar to the ones discussed in Section 18.3 and solves it by B&B algorithm using Lagrangian relaxation. This algorithm is much faster than the general-purpose methods. Another, still not investigated possibility is to take advantage of the network flow constraints and to design a decomposition network-simplex-like algorithm for solving the LP relaxations of the MIP models.

Variable Segment Lengths   The definition of PTP given in Section 18.2 assumes that the length of each segment is fixed. This assumption is common for many threading methods but is somehow restrictive, because two proteins belonging to the same structural family may have a couple of amino acids attached to or detached from the endpoints of the corresponding secondary structure element. Taking into account this particularity could improve the quality of the threading method. It should not be very difficult to design MIP models with variable segment lengths, but this question is still open.

Semi-Global Threading   The 3D structure of more complex proteins is formed by several compact structural units, called domains. While each database template describes a single domain, the query sequence can be a multi-domain protein. In this case the template must be aligned only to a (unknown) part of the query. We call this kind of alignment semi-global threading. The MIP models described in this chapter are flexible enough and can be easily adapted to semi-global threading. This could be done by introducing extra constraints restricting either the length of each loop, or the sum of all loop lengths. The main difficulty will be to avoid the increase of the size and the complexity of the obtained models.

18.7   CONCLUSION

The protein threading problem is a challenging combinatorial optimization problem with very important practical applications and impressive computational complexity. Mathematical programming techniques, still not very popular in computational biology, can be a valuable tool for attacking problems that arise in this domain. The MIP models confirm that real-life instances are much easier to solve than artificial ones. The complexity of PTP is such that only an appropriate combination of different techniques can yield an efficient solution. By combining a careful choice of MIP formulation, a divide-and-conquer technique, and a parallel implementation, one can solve real-life instances of tremendous size in a reasonable amount of time.

The algorithms described in this chapter are already integrated in FROST [27] fold recognition software tool. They are general and flexible enough and can be readily plugged in (or easily adapted to) other threading-based fold recognition tools to improve their performance.

18.8   SUMMARY

This chapter is dedicated to one challenging problem in the computational molecular biology — the so-called protein-folding problem. The goal is to predict the 3D structure of a protein based on a given sequence of amino acids. As the 3D structure is tightly related to its function, this problem concerns the main task in computational molecular biology — to assign functions to proteins.

More precisely the chapter deals with a method known as threading which uses information about already known protein structures stored in databases. The authors present the point of view of a computer scientist with particular interests in combinatorial optimization problems. They focus on the computational aspects of finding the optimal sequence-to-structure alignment referred as PTP. A formal definition of the PTP is given, and several mixed integer models are presented in a unified framework, analyzed, and compared. Different divide-and-conquer strategies are also described. They allow to reduce the time needed to solve the master problem by solving auxiliary subproblems of a moderate size. One section is dedicated to a parallel implementation of such a technique, which happened to be efficient even in a sequential implementation. The results in this chapter demonstrate that a careful combination of modeling, decomposing, and a parallel implementation leads to solving PTP real-life instances of tremendous size in a reasonable amount of time.

ACKNOWLEDGMENTS

This work has been partially supported by the French–Bulgarian project RILA'2004 "Programme d'actions integrées (PAI)." The authors are grateful to Jean-François Gibrat and Antoine Marin for many helpful discussions and for providing them with the code of Lathrop and Smith algorithm, as well as all data concerning the protein structure prediction problem. Many thanks to Philippe Veber for his careful reading of the manuscript of this chapter.

REFERENCES

1. C. Branden and J. Tooze, *Introduction to Protein Structure*, Garland Publishing, 1999.
2. H. J. Greenberg, W. E. Hart, and G. Lancia, Opportunities for combinatorial optimization in computational biology, *INFORMS J. Comput.*, 16 (3) (2004).
3. T. Head-Gordon and J. C. Wooley, Computational challenges in structural and functional genomics, *IBM Syste. J.*, 40, 265–296 (2001).
4. R. H. Lathrop, R. G. Rogers, Jr., J. Bienkowska, B. K .M. Bryant, L. J. Buturovic, C. Gaitatzes, R. Nambudripad, J. V. White, and T. F. Smith, Analysis and Algorithms for Protein Sequence-Structure Alignment, in S. L. Salzberg, D. B. Searls, and S. Kasif, Eds., *Computational Methods in Molecular Biology*, Chap. 12, Elsevier Science, 1998, pp. 227–283.
5. T. Lengauer, Computational Biology at the Beginning of the Post-Genomic Era, in R. Wilhelm, Ed., *Informatics: 10 Years Back–10 Years Ahead*, Vol. 2000 of *Lecture Notes in Computer Science*, Springer-Verlag, 2001, pp. 341–355.
6. J. C. Setubal and J. Meidanis, *Introduction to Computational Molecular Biology*, PWS Publishing Company, 1997.

7. C. L. Brooks, M. Karplus, and B. M. Pettitt, *Proteins: A Theoretical Perspective of Dynamics, Structure, and Thermodynamics*, John Wiley and Sons, 1990.

8. S. F. Altschul, W. Gish, W. Miller, E. W. Myers, and D. J. Lipman, Basic local alignment search tool, *J. Mol. Biol.*, 215, 403–410 (1990).

9. W. R. Pearson and D. J. Lipman, Improved tools for biological sequence comparison, *Proc. Natl. Acad. Sci. USA*, 85, 2444–2448 (1988).

10. S. F. Altschul, T. L. Madden, A. A. Schäffer, J. Zhang, Z. Zhang, W. Miller, and D. J. Lipman, Gapped BLAST and PSI-BLAST: a new generation of protein database search programs, *Nucl. Acids Res.*, 25, 3389–3402 (1997).

11. C. Chothia, Proteins: one thousand families for the molecular biologist, *Nature*, 357, 543–544 (1992).

12. C. A Orengo, T. D. Jones, and J. M. Thornton, Protein superfamilies and domain superfolds, *Nature*, 372, 631–634 (1994).

13. H. M. Berman, J. Westbrook, Z. Feng, G. Gilliland, T. N. Bhat, H. Weissig, I. N. Shindyalov, and P. E. Bourne, The protein data bank, *Nucl. Acids Res.*, 28, 235–242 (2000).

14. A. Marin, J. Pothier, K. Zimmermann, and J.-F. Gibrat, Protein Threading Statistics: an Attempt to Assess the Significance of a Fold Assignment to a Sequence, in I. Tsigelny, Ed., *Protein Structure Prediction: Bioinformatic Approach*, International University Line, 2002.

15. R. H. Lathrop, The protein threading problem with sequence amino acid interaction preferences is NP-complete, *Prot. Eng.*, 7(9), 1059–1068 (1994).

16. T. Akutsu and S. Miyano, On the approximation of protein threading, *Theor. Comput. Sci.*, 210, 261–275 (1999).

17. R. B. Russel and G. J. Barton, Structural features can be unconserved in proteins with similar folds. An analysis of side-chain to side-chain contacts secondary structure and accessibility, *J. Mol. Biol.*, 244, 332–350 (1994).

18. D. Sankoff and J. B. Kruskal, Eds., *Time Wraps, String Edits and Macromolecules*, Addison-Wesley, Reading, 1983.

19. A. Godzik, A. Kolinski, and J. Skolnik, Topology fingerprint approach to the inverse protein folding problem, *J. Mol. Biol.*, 227, 227–238 (1992).

20. C. A. Orengo and W. R. Taylor, A rapid method for protein structure alignment, *J. Theor. Biol.*, 147, 517–551 (1990).

21. W. R. Taylor and C. A. Orengo, Protein-structure alignment, *J. Mol. Biol.*, 208, 1–22 (1989).

22. C. E. Lawrence, S. F. Altschul, J. S. Boguski, A. F. Neuwald, and J. C. Wootton, Detecting subtle sequence signals: a gibbs sampling strategy for multiple alignment, *Science*, 262, 208–214 (1993).

23. N. Krasnogor, W. E. Hart, J. Smith, and D. A. Pelta, Protein Structure Prediction with Evolutionary Algorithms, in *Proceedings of the Genetic and Evolutionary Computation Conference*, Vol. 2, Morgan Kaufmann, 1999, pp. 1596–1601.

24. A. A. Rabow and H. A. Scheraga, Improved genetic algorithm for the protein folding problem by use of a cartesian combination operator, *Prot. Sci.*, 5, 1800–1815 (1996).

25. J. D. Szustakowski and Z. Weng, Protein structure alignment using a genetic algorithm, *Proteins*, 38 (4), 428–440 (2000).

26. R. H. Lathrop and T. F. Smith, Global optimum protein threading with gapped alignment and empirical pair potentials, *J. Mol. Biol.*, 255, 641–665 (1996).

27. A. Marin, J. Pothier, K. Zimmermann, and J.-F. Gibrat, FROST: a filter-based fold recognition method, *Proteins*, 49 (4), 493–509 (2002).

28. N. Yanev and R. Andonov, The Protein Threading Problem is in P? Research Report 4577, Institut National de Recherche en Informatique et en Automatique, 2002.

29. N. Yanev and R. Andonov, Solving the Protein Threading Problem in Parallel, in *HiCOMB 2003 — Second IEEE International Workshop on High Performance Computational Biology*, 2003.

30. R. Andonov, S. Balev, and N. Yanev, Protein threading: from mathematical models to parallel implementations, *INFORMS J. Comput.*, 16 (4), 393–405 (2004).

31. J. Xu, M. Li, G. Lin, D. Kim, and Y. Xu, Protein Structure Prediction by Linear Programming, in *Proceedings of The Seventh Pacific Symposium on Biocomputing (PSB)*, 2003, pp. 264–275.

32. J. Xu, M. Li, G. Lin, D. Kim, and Y. Xu, RAPTOR: optimal protein threading by linear programming, *J. Bioinformat. Comput. Biol.*, 1 (1), 95–118 (2003).

33. Y. Xu, D. Xu, and E. C. Uberbacher, An efficient computational method for globally optimal threading, *J. Comput. Biol.*, 5 (3), 597–614 (1998).

34. Y. Xu and D. Xu, Protein threading using PROSPECT: design and evaluation, *Proteins: Struct. Funct. Genet.*, 40, 343–354 (2000).

35. J. Xu, Speedup LP Approach to Protein Threading via Graph Reduction, in *Proceedings of WABI 2003: Third Workshop on Algorithms in Bioinformatics*, Vol. 2812 of *Lecture Notes in Computer Science*, Springer-Verlag, 2003. pp. 374–388.

36. G. L. Nemhauser and L. A. Wolsey, *Integer and Combinatorial Optimization*, Wiley, 1988.

37. F. Plastria, Formulating logical implications in combinatorial optimization, *Eur. J. Oper. Res.*, 140, 338–353 (2002).

38. G. Cornuéjols, G. L. Nemhauser, and L. A. Wolsey, The Uncapacitated Facility Location Problem, in P. Mirchandani and R. Francis, Eds., *Discrete Location Theory*, John Wiley and Sons, 1990, pp. 119–171.

39. N. Yanev, Solution of a simple plant-location problem, *USSR Comput. Math. Math. Phys.*, 21, 626–634 (1981).

40. J. Pley, R. Andonov, J.-F. Gibrat, A. Marin, and V. Poirriez, Parallèlisation d'une méthode de reconnaissance de repliements de protéines (FROST), in *Proceedings des Journées Ouvertes Biologie Informatique Mathématiques*, 2002, pp. 287–288.

41. S. Balev, Solving the Protein Threading Problem by Lagrangian Relaxation, in *Proceedings of WABI 2004: Fourth Workshop on Algorithms in Bioinformatics*, LNCS/LNBI, Springer-Verlag, pp. 182–193, 2004.

CHAPTER 19

Parallel Evolutionary Computations in Discerning Protein Structures

RICHARD O. DAY and GARY B. LAMONT

Interest in discerning protein structures through prediction (PSP) is widespread and has been previously addressed using a variety of techniques including X-ray crystallography, molecular dynamics, nuclear magnetic resonance spectroscopy, Monte Carlo analysis, lattice simulation, and evolutionary algorithms (EAs) in energy minimization. We have employed EAs such as the simple genetic algorithm (GA), messy GA (mGA), and the linkage learning GA (LLGA), with associated public domain software. Here, we report results of a parallel modified fast messy GA (fmGA), which is found to be quite "good" at finding semi-optimal PSP solutions in a reasonable time. We focus on modifications to this EA called the fmGA, extensions to the multiobjective implementation of the fmGA (MOfmGA), constraint satisfaction via Ramachandran plots, identifying secondary protein structures, a farming model for the parallel fmGA (pfmGA), and fitness function approximation techniques. These techniques reflect marked improvement over previous GA applications for protein structure determination. Problem definition, protein model representation, mapping to algorithm domain, tool selection modifications, and conducted experiments are discussed.

19.1 INTRODUCTION

Protein structure prediction is a grand challenge problem [1, 2]. Solving this problem involves finding a methodology that can consistently and correctly determine the configuration of a folded protein without regard to the folding process. The problem is simply stated; however, solving this problem is intractable [3] due to the combinatorics. Thus, a variety of algorithmic approaches have been proposed [4, 5], ranging from GAs, simulated annealing (SA), to hybrids between deterministic and

Parallel Computing for Bioinformatics and Computational Biology, Edited by Albert Y. Zomaya
Copyright © 2006 John Wiley & Sons, Inc.

stochastic methodologies using nonlinear optimization techniques and maximum likelihood approaches [6, 7]. In this discussion, we focus on modifications to an evolutionary algorithm (EA) called the fast messy genetic algorithm (fmGA), extensions to the multiobjective implementation of the fmGA (MOfmGA), constraint satisfaction via Ramachandran plots, and a farming model for the parallel fmGA (pfmGA). These techniques reflect marked improvement over previous GA applications for protein structure determination.

All GAs discussed in this chapter utilize the same protein energy model as a fitness function: the Chemistry at HARvard Molecular Mechanics (CHARMm) model. A protein structure is determined by minimizing this energy fitness function. The protein structure is modeled with folded dihedral angles related to the relative position of protein atoms. Of course, a choice between real and binary values of the EA chromosome is required. In our previous research, both of these encodings yielded similar results. Thus, a binary encoding is chosen for ease of implementation, with the protein dihedral angles discretetized into 1024 (1 MB or 2^{10}) sections for every $360°$. Note that a coordinate transformation needs to be employed for evaluating the real-valued fitness function CHARMm based upon these angles.

Regarding parallel computation for EAs, parallel paradigms can be utilized to decompose a problem (EA task and data) which in turn decrease execution time [8]. These paradigms can also allow for searching more of the solution space, potentially finding "better" solutions in the same amount of time as a serial implementation. The four major parallel computational paradigms are considered. They are the "master–slave," "island," and "diffusion" paradigms, the fourth includes the "hierarchical" or "hybrid" paradigms, which may sometimes be seen as a combination(s) of the three major forms. Island paradigms are sometimes defined as coarse-grained paradigms, with diffusion paradigms referred to as cellular or fine-grained paradigms. Note that each paradigm may be implemented in either a synchronized or nonsynchronized fashion; each has its own particular considerations. For purposes of this discussion, synchronized implementations are defined as utilizing "same-generation" populations where some sort of inter-processor communication synchronizes all processes at the end of each generation. Nonsynchronized implementations can greatly reduce processor idle time (assuming varying processor speeds/memory/hardware limitations and data decomposition), but this implies communications occur at random times and possibly without guaranteed delivery of messages to their destinations.

The protein-structure prediction (PSP) problem is addressed first with various folded protein discerning methods presented. The CHARMm model is viewed before discussion of EA energy minimization techniques. The parallel fmGA and associated efforts as discussed in detail are shown to be effective and efficient via various experiments in finding PSP configurations.

19.2 PSP PROBLEM

As indicated, the protein energy evaluation model employed is based on the CHARMm ver. 22 software with our own improvements integrated [9, 10]. In evaluating a

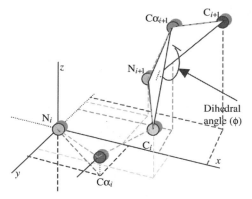

Figure 19.1 This figure illustrates the ϕ angle in a small section of backbone atoms within a protein. This angle representation is the same at each C-N-C$_\alpha$-C instance in any protein; however, each angle is indexed according to how many ϕ angles appear in that particular protein. This method ensures that each dihedral angle is uniquely specified.

protein's potential energy, the program requires the protein be specified by dihedral angles. A dihedral angle is the angle formed by four atoms connected in a chain-like manner. The dihedral angle itself is developed when the two planes (formed by the first three and last three atoms in the chain) make an angle. Figure 19.1 illustrates a dihedral angle. This particular dihedral angle is called ϕ angle within any protein.

The entire process for specifying a protein (polypeptide) is more involved than just identifying dihedral angles of a protein. Assumptions and domain information are also included in the specification process to make the size of the search space more reasonable [11]. After each individual protein is specified with dihedral angles, each atom becomes locatable in a three dimensional space allowing for a potential energy program, like CHARMm, to calculate energy between each atom. The calculation requires the binary angular values to be transferred to real-valued atom positions and distances for the CHARMm variables. It takes approximately 6.8 ms to calculate the potential energy for a single conformation on an Intel PIII 800 MHz machine. It would take considerable computational time to find the absolute lowest energy conformation for general proteins (by calculating the energy for each conformation after discretizing all angles to 1024 bit degrees [11]). The order-of complexity is $O(n^6)$, where n is the number of atoms. The polypeptides analyzed in this study are Met-enkephalin (MET) and polyalanine$_{14}$ (POLY). Note that the fully specified MET/POLY has 24/56 adjustable dihedral angles with 75/141 atoms each.

19.3 PROTEIN STRUCTURE DISCERNING METHODS

Approaches to finding the structure of a fully folded protein are numerous. They range from software to hardware driven, theoretical to empirical, and fine to coarse grained. The more generic methods are X-ray crystallography [12, 13], molecular dynamics, nuclear magnetic resonance spectroscopy [14], Monte Carlo analysis [15], atomistic

TABLE 19.1   Classification of Methodologies Used in Solving the PSP Problem

	Experimental Methods	Simulation	Energy Minimization
X-ray crystallography	2–4 months after crystal		
NMR spectroscopy	2–3 years		
Molecular dynamics		1 ps of the folding process can be simulated	
Monte Carlo analysis		Highly computational	
Lattice simulations		Highly computational	
Off-lattice simulation		Highly computational	
Evolutionary algorithm			Stochastic search

and nonatomistic lattice simulation, off-lattice simulation, and energy minimization. Various methodologies are classified in Table 19.1.

Fundamentally, there are two main reasons for having many alternate techniques. The first reason would be a feasibility issue. Some protein conformations are easily found using empirical methods, such as X-ray crystallography, because they crystallize easily, yet others are easily found in solution using nuclear magnetic resonance spectroscopy [12]. Still others cannot be crystallized at all. The second reason would be a compromise between dihedral angle resolution and time to calculate a solution. It is known that the time involved to find structures using empirical measurement techniques can sometimes be cost prohibitive. Additionally, each approach has resolution limitations. The trade-off between resolution and time is apparent in Table 19.1. Furthermore, having alternate search methods permits their use in complementing one another.

Corporations like International Business Machines (IBM) have recognized the need for extensive computational resources to run experiments and is currently building a petaflop computer specifically designed for simulating the protein folding process [16, 17].

In examination of IBM's petaflop computer chances of solving the PSP problem, we turn to what is known about the computational requirements for a simulation. It is known that the time steps required to accurately account for thermal oscillations of the protein are on the order of 1 fs (10^{-15} s) [18, 19]. Therefore, if a single calculation between two atoms must be computed within a femtosecond, the number of calculations required for a single pair combinatorially rises as the number of atoms is increased. For example, if it takes 4000 floating point operation per second (flops) to calculate one quantum mechanical function between two atoms, the number of flops required would grow exponentially $4000^{\text{number of atoms}}$ per femtosecond for a real-time simulation. IBM's petaflop computer is scheduled to be finished in 2006; however, this computer though built for massive simulations may not meet the simulation requirement for protein folding. To date, these protein folding methods were used in finding 2% of the total number of proteins found in the Protein Data Bank [20].

19.3.1 Atomistic and Nonatomistic Lattice Simulation

19.3.1.1 Energy Minimization Models The energy landscape search algorithms are based on the concept that a protein's final resting conformation is found at the conformation that yields the lowest overall energy of the protein. Force field energy equations, such as assisted model building with energy refinement [21] (AMBER), empirical conformational energy program for peptides [22] (ECEPP), and CHARMm, are typically used in calculating the energy for a specific conformation. The disadvantages to using these methods are two fold: (1) the problem of enumerating every possible conformation a protein could possibly retain and (2) a highly computational fitness or energy evaluation function that needs to be evaluated at each of the possible conformations. Given the fact that the number of conformations a protein could retain is uncountably infinite, it is impossible to enumerate every possible combination of conformations. Moreover, even if a protein is decomposed into dihedral angles, which have a limited set of values, the number of possible conformations based upon $(Dihedral\_angle\_partitions)^{Number\_of\_dihedral\_angles}$ still makes for extremely difficult problems. Furthermore, it has been measured that one fitness evaluation takes 15 ms on today's high end computers; it can be concluded that the fitness evaluations of each conformation alone, for even small proteins, is going to cost much computational time (approximately 2.5×10^{114} ms). This is precisely why alternative algorithms have evolved to solve specific problems. Following is a discussion of GA's employed at the Air Force Institute of Technology (AFIT) for solving the PSP problem [23–26]. The PSP problem has been attacked with many different forms of GAs including: simple GA (sGA), mGA, parallel GA (pGA), fmGA, pfmGA, GAs with local searches (Lamarckian, Baldwinian, and Niching), and other smart operator techniques. The following GAs utilize the same CHARMm energy model as a fitness function. This fitness function was ported from Fortran to C as the choice fitness function [27] in 1991. We have been applying various serial and parallel GA approaches for over a decade starting with a sGA and a mGA [28]. All GAs discussed have originated from the sGA. Understanding the sGA is paramount to understanding such extensions.

19.3.2 CHARMm Protein Energy Model

Search algorithms rely solely upon the ability to be able to recognize good solutions. For the PSP problem, this recognition comes in the form of an energy function or fitness function. Solutions found to be dominated by one may be found to be weaker by others using a different fitness function. That is why it is extremely important to have the most suitable fitness function for the problem. This suitability is particularly difficult to achieve for the PSP problem. Many factors are involved in choosing a suitable energy function. Potential energy [29], quantum mechanical energy, chemistry of the protein [30–34], empirical force fields energy, energy surface with the largest statistical weight [31], and entropy [25] are just a few of the fitness function ingredients that may be used.

Essentially, the selected CHARMm energy function sums the internal terms or bonded atom energy and external terms or nonbonded atom energy of a particular protein in a specific conformation.

$$E_{\text{total}} = \sum_{(i,j)(\text{connect})} E(\text{bonded}) + \sum_{(i,j,k,...,n)(!\text{connect})} E(\text{nonbonded}) \quad (19.1)$$

Bonded energy is the sum of bond stretching, bond rotation, bond bending, improper torsion, and hydrogen bonding energy reduction between each connected or bonded atom.

$$E_{\text{stretching}} = \sum_{(i,i+1)} K_b(b - b_0)^2 \quad (19.2)$$

where K_b is the force constant determining the strength of the bond, b is the actual bond length, and b_0 is the ideal bond length [Eq. (19.2)]. The bending energy is similar to that of the stretching energy, where K_θ is the force constant, θ is the actual measured angle, and θ_0 is the ideal angle. This is primarily a penalty function [Eq. (19.3)].

$$E_{\text{bending}} = \sum_{\text{angles}(i,j,k)} K_\theta(\theta - \theta_0)^2 \quad (19.3)$$

The third term in the bonded energy calculation representing a reduction in the van der Waals term for the interaction between the hydrogen atom and the acceptor atom [35] [Eq. (19.4)].

$$E_{\text{hydrogen}} = \sum_i \left(\frac{A'}{r_{\text{AD}}^i} - \frac{B'}{r_{\text{AD}}^i} \right) \cos^m(\theta_{A-H-D}) * \cos^n(\theta_{AA-A-H}) \quad (19.4)$$

The fourth term in the bonded energy calculation representing the torsion angle potential function, which models the presence of steric barriers between atoms separated by three covalent bonds (1,4 pairs) is shown in Eq. (19.5).

$$E_{\text{torsion}} = \sum_{(i,j,k)\in D} K_\theta(1 - \cos(n\phi)) \quad (19.5)$$

$$E_{\text{Improper-torsion}} = \sum_\omega K_\omega(\omega - \omega_0)^2 \quad (19.6)$$

Equations (19.2)–(19.6) make up the energy for bonded atoms:

$$E_{\text{bonded}} = E_{\text{torsion}} + E_{\text{bending}} + E_{\text{hydrogen}} + E_{\text{stretching}} + E_{\text{Improper-torsion}} \quad (19.7)$$

The final terms for the calculation of energy are the nonbonded related terms, electrostatics, water–water interaction and van der Waals. These terms may be combined into the following sum:

$$E_{\text{lennard-jones}} = \sum_{(i,j)\in \mathcal{N}} \left[\left(\frac{A_{ij}}{r_{ij}} \right)^{12} - \left(\frac{B_{ij}}{r_{ij}} \right)^6 \right] \quad (19.8)$$

Constants A and B are interaction energy using atom-type properties. D is the effective dielectric function for the medium and r is the distance between two atoms having charges q_i and q_k.

$$E_{\text{electrostatics}} = \sum_{(i,j)\in\mathcal{N}} \left[\frac{q_i q_j}{D r_{ij}}\right] \tag{19.9}$$

$$E_{\text{water-water1}} = \sum_i K_i (r_i - r_{i0})^2 \tag{19.10}$$

$$E_{\text{water-water2}} = \sum_i K_i (\theta_i - \theta_{i0})^2 \tag{19.11}$$

Contributions of water–water constraints of distance and dihedral angles are shown in Eqs. (19.10) and (19.11), respectively. Furthermore, the entire contribution of nonbonded energy is given by Eq. (19.12).

$$E_{\text{nonbonded}} = E_{\text{lennard-jones}} + E_{\text{electrostatics}} + E_{\text{water-water1}} + E_{\text{water-water2}} \tag{19.12}$$

The CHARMm energy function is computationally expensive. For example, the search landscape with this model for the polypeptide [Met]-Enkephalin has been experimentally generated using parallel random search [36] over an immense number of dihedral angles. In this case, the PSP landscape structure is an extremely dense set of points at relatively high-energy levels over a wide energy band vs. the range of possible dihedral angles. Few points are close to the minimized energy levels. These points are reflected at the bottom of narrow phenotype energy "wells" with cascading sides. These optimal points are difficult to find even with integrated local search techniques.

Within Table 19.2, a comparison of CHARMm, AFIT CHARMm, AMBER, ECEPP, and optimized potentials for liquid simulations (OPLS) is illustrated. Notice that CHARMm covers each one of the possible energy equations; however, AFIT's CHARMm has reduced this function due to the insignificance of these other forces. AFIT's version of CHARMm was used in our investigations because it has been found to be a valid model [37].

In addition to these energy models, many other models have been used in other studies. The random energy model (REM) was applied to the PSP problem by Bryngelson and Wolynes [7]. This energy model was originally used in spin glass theory [39]. Other such fitness function models have been applied to the PSP problem using enthalpy [25], conformational entropy, hydrophobic/hydrophilic [26], and distance matrix models employing Frobenius norm of differences, Hoeffding inequality keeping corrected distances for fitness function terms [26], and ring closure on local conformations [32]. Moreover, all these models have the same theme in trying to define the properties a protein has when folded. Currently, there is no single model that has prevailed and thus the search for the perfect energy model continues.

TABLE 19.2   Comparison of Common Energy Functions Used in Solving the PSP Problem

Acronym	Name	Equation Number								
		19.2	19.3	19.5	19.6	19.8	19.9	19.4	19.10	19.11
CHARMm	Chemistry at Harvard using molecular mechanics	✓	✓	✓	✓	✓	✓	✓	✓	✓
CHARMm at AFIT [22, 29, 38]		✓	✓	✓	✓	✓	✓			
Amber	Assisted model building with energy refinement	✓	✓	✓		✓	✓	✓		
ECEPP/3	Empirical conformational energy program for peptides				✓		✓	✓	✓	
OPLS	Optimized potentials for liquid simulation				✓		✓	✓		

19.3.3 Approximation of Energy Fitness

Our interest is to reduce via parallel computing the computation time spent evaluating a protein's potential energy with CHARMm given a particular conformation. To reduce the time needed to find some "good" solutions, an approximating fitness function is employed to determine appropriate search landscape points. For example, one could approximate the CHARMm formulation by deleting terms that provide a functional envelope. In addition, a lower-order functional, such as an artificial neural net (ANN), could be used to approximate the deleted terms or the entire function.

In validating the concept that an ANN can approximate the CHARMm model, it is important to find the best ANN structure and determine a good method for collecting data to train that design. In addition, it is required that a certain accuracy be maintained between the CHARMm model and ANN. Furthermore, maintenance of accuracy is not done for the purpose of the ANN replacing the CHARMm model, but to ensure that the ANN can identify solutions which are to be exploited later using a *local search* via the exact CHARMm software. The training set was comprised of over 43K records from fmGA produced data and over 4000K from a random generated data set.

Preliminary tests, using the leave one out algorithm, were run on this data set resulting in nonacceptable mean-squared errors (MSE) (>50). It was then determined that the training records should be localized to a certain dihedral angle area. Further, it was determined records closest to the root-mean squared difference from the average dihedral angle values should be ranked and the top 1K records should be selected. In addition, the top 200 records were used for parameter determination. The justification for selecting only 200 records for parameter determination is mainly to reduce the run time during experimentation. The training data is normalized to zero mean unit variance.

19.3.3.1 ANN Experimentation
Two neural networks are studied to replace our energy model to gain efficiency at the cost of, at most, one percent effectiveness. The first neural network is a radial basis function neural network (RBFNN) and the second is a multilayered perceptron neural network (MLPNN). Both networks have 24 inputs to 1 output. In the case of the MLPNN, many experiments were run to select the best parameters for optimized results. Previous research [40] enabled us to get an estimate for the number of neurons needed for 99% effectiveness.

$$N_{min} \cong \frac{W}{\epsilon} = \frac{24 \times \text{Neurons} + \text{Neurons} + 1}{0.01} \tag{19.13}$$

Equation (19.13) is the relationship between the total number of weights (W), the number of data records (N_{min}), and the fraction of correctly classified fitness values $(1 - \epsilon)$ [40]. This equation is mainly for discrete output values or categorized outputs; therefore, it can be only applied loosely to this problem. We use 3, 4, 10, and 100 neurons in each network for this experiment. Using Eq. (19.13), we can then calculate the theoretical fraction of correctly classified fitness values to be 90, 88, 74, and 0%, respectively.

19.3.3.2 Parameter Determination
The Matlab 6.5 neural network toolbox is used to build both the RBFNN and the MLPNN used in this aspect of the research.

The training parameter is selected first. Matlab 6.5's neural network toolbox has many different settings for this parameter. The training parameter settings tested for selection are listed in Table 19.3. Matlab ANNs can be trained for function approximation (nonlinear regression), pattern association, or pattern classification. The result of testing resulted in **traingdx** as being selected as the training method for these data records.

The transfer parameter is to be selected next. Matlab 6.5's neural network toolbox has many different settings for this parameter. The tested transfer parameters are listed in Table 19.4.

The transfer parameter is used to simulate the network when the *sim* command is called. To put simply, the behavior of this parameter, mathematically, is placed in the position of the neuron in the network. The results of the experiment showed tansig, k, and logsig, d, were both good choices for this data set; however, tansig was the overall better choice having a lower mean-squared error and variance.

TABLE 19.3   Lists of All Tested Training Parameters

No.	Training Parameter	Description
a	trainrp	Resilient backpropagation
b	trainbr	Bayesian regularization
c	trainlm	Levenberg-Marquardt
d	traingd	Gradient descent (GD)
e	traingdm	GD with momentum
f	**traingdx**	Adaptive learning rate
g	traincgf	Fletcher-Reeves conjugate gradient
h	traincgp	Polak-ribiere conjugate gradient
i	traincgb	Powell-beale conjugate gradient
j	trainscg	Scaled conjugate gradient
k	trainscg	BFGS quasi-Newton method
l	trainoss	One step secant method

Note: The best training parameter is indicated by bold face type.

19.3.3.3   *ANN Results*   A successful analysis of any added feature for solving a problem must include both a comparison between effectiveness (indicating the new algorithm now has either better precision or accuracy) and efficiency (indicating the new algorithm now completes sooner than it did before). Mechanisms that excel under both criteria are a positive change and should be adopted. The following discussion evaluates how the neural network fairs in both the effectiveness and efficiency categories when replacing the CHARMm energy fitness function in the fmGA.

The first completed experiment was on the RBFNN. It found the best effectiveness results overall with a mean-squared error of 0.54; see Table 19.5 for the summary of results. Notice also that the RBFNN had the lowest variance.

TABLE 19.4   Lists of All Tested Transfer Parameters

No.	Transfer Parameter	Description
a	compet	Competitive xfer fnc
b	hardlim	Hard-limit (HL) xfer fnc
c	hardlims	Symmetric HL xfer fnc
d	logsig	Log-sigmoid xfer fnc
e	poslin	Pos linear xfer fnc
f	purelin	HL xfer fnc
g	radbas	Radial basis xfer fnc
h	satlin	Saturating linear xfer fnc
i	satlins	Symmetric saturating linear xfer fnc
j	softmax	Soft max xfer fnc
k	**tansig**	Hyperbolic tangent sigmoid xfer fnc
l	tribas	Triangular basis xfer fnc

Note: The best training parameter is indicated by bold face type.

TABLE 19.5   Summary of Effectiveness Results

Neurons	Training fnc	Transform fnc	MSE	Mean (μ)	Var (σ)
25	**RBFNN**	**RBFNN**	**0.54**	**0.0171**	**0.000001**
3	traingdx	tansig	2.10	0.0461	0.0228
3	trainrp	tansig	10.16	0.0699	0.0984
4	trainrp	tansig	10.27	0.0559	0.1024
10	trainrp	tansig	5.01	0.0074	0.0251
100	trainrp	tansig	1.84	0.0102	0.0033
100	traingdx	tansig	1.52	0.0396	0.0007

It is also prudent to test the validity of Eq. (19.13) [40]. MLPNN having 3, 4, 10, and 100 neurons each as tested. Each MLPNN is trained using 1K *gold plated* data records, 500 epochs, hyperbolic tangent sigmoid transfer function, and a resilient training parameter. Results show that the neural network having 100 neurons outperforms the three neuron case; contradicting Eq. (19.13).

The final MLPNN experiment tested an aggregate configuration of validated parameter settings found in previous experiments. Although it was able to perform better than previous tests, it failed to outperform RBFNN. One final test was conducted to compare MLPNN using 100 neurons with RBFNN; even in this configuration, MLPNN was unable to outperform RBFNN.

19.3.4 Farming the Energy Model Calculation

Owing to the complexities associated with the energy fitness function calculation, the addition of a farming model is also proposed instead of the ANN approximation. Farming out the fitness calculations to a set of slave processors allows for a decrease in the overall processing time as long as the computation time is greater than the communications time required. As the slave processors calculate fitness values, the masters can do the same or conduct other computations. In addition to speedup gained for the peptide selected in this investigation, the addition of these slave processors allows for the fmGA to handle larger proteins.

The following pfmGA parameters are kept constant (set at standard values) throughout all of the testing: protein, POLY; string length, 560 bits; cut probability, 0.02; splice probability, 1.00; primordial generations, 200; juxtapositional generations, 100; total generations, 300. An input schedule is also used to specify during which generations building block filtering occurs.

A goal of this testing is to determine the speedup associated with increasing the number of farming processors per algorithm node in the pfmGA. Figure 19.2 illustrates a plot of one algorithm node with a number of different farming nodes. Each BB test point represents the average value for a specific BB size (in increasing order) executed by the pfmGA. As the BB size increases, the average execution time also increases. Additionally, Figure 19.2 shows that as the number of farming processors

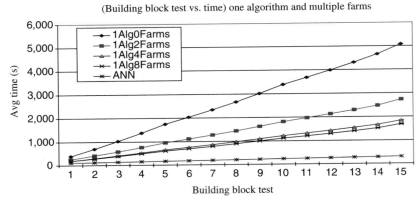

(Building block test vs. time) one algorithm and multiple farms

Figure 19.2   This figure illustrates the achievable 16.7 speedup, which may be realized when implementing a 1K neuron ANN within the fmGA search process. This speedup is not direct and final because there is still runtime required for the local search, which must be accomplished on good solutions found by the ANN.

increases, the average execution time decreases for any given BB test. In this test, there exists a significant improvement in modifying the number of farming nodes from 0 to 2 and from 2 to 4. An increase in the farming nodes from 4 to 8 provides a small improvement. The best speedup obtained was with 8 farming nodes where the serial time was 5080 s, whereas the parallel time was 1684 s yielding a speedup of three times. This validates our model and we can draw a conclusion that this model increases the efficiency.

Efficiency measurements were taken from run times of the original fmGA using the CHARMm code versus a mach-up neural network code in place of the CHARMm function. Table 19.6 summarizes the results. The ANNs are shown to provide an increase in efficiency over the CHARMm code. Figure 19.3a graphically illustrates this speedup. Notice that the 25 neuron RBFNN is not listed. It can be approximated to take 0.021 ms, which is easily more efficient than the CHARMm code. Additionally, Figure 19.3b is provided to illustrate the increase in calculation time spent as the number of neurons is added to the neural network. Furthermore, the ANN also can yield a preprocessing speedup of 16.7 over the farming model parallel implementation. This speedup is illustrated in Figure 19.2, where the ANN is shown to be more efficient than every farming implementation tested.

TABLE 19.6   Average Time for Evaluations on PIII 800 MHz (Efficiency Results)

Application	msec
CHARMm MET(POLY)	6.211(41.04)
One nonlinear layer having (3,4,10,100,1K) neurons	(0.007,0.008,0.012,0.068,0.640)

(*a*) CHARMm vs. ANN runtime increase

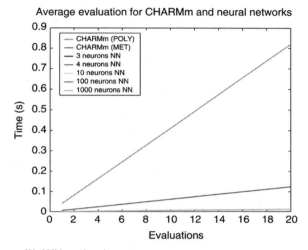

(*b*) ANN runtime increase

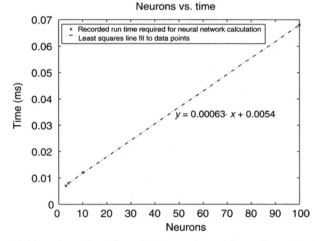

Figure 19.3 (*a*) Run time after 20 evaluations using each configuration in Table 19.6. (*b*) Least-squares line fit to the data points showing the increase in time as the number of neurons are added.

19.4 PSP ENERGY MINIMIZATION EAs

19.4.1 Fast Messy GA

Following our previous sGA and mGA work, the fmGA (Fig. 19.4) was to be named our GA of choice [41–44], having lower complexity (Table 19.7).

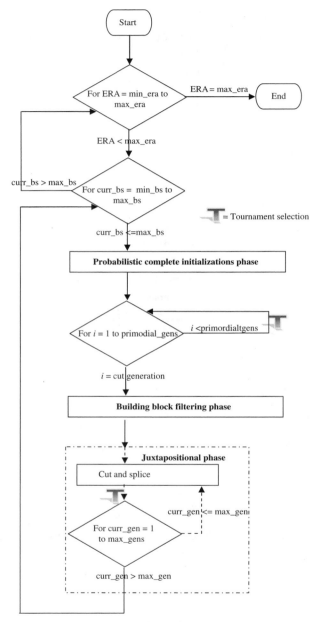

Figure 19.4   Flow of fmGA.

TABLE 19.7 Complexity Estimates for Serial GAs

Phase	sGA[a]	ssGA[b]	mGA	fmGA
Initialization	$O(l^n)$	$O(l^n)$	$O(l^k)$	$O(l)$
Recombination	$O(g*n*q)$	$O(g)$		
Primordial	$O(0)$		$O(0)$	$O(l^2)^c$
Juxtapositional			$O(l \log l)$	$O(l \log l)$
Overall mGA	$O(l^n)$	$O(l^n)$	$O(l^k)$	$O(l^2)$

[a] l is the length of chromosome, n the size of population, q group size for tournament selection, and g the number of generations.
[b] l is the length of chromosome, n the size of population, and g the number of generations of reproduction.
[c] Building block filtering.

The mGA's advantage over the sGA is in its ability to explicitly create tightly linked building blocks for defeating deception by insuring that there is a good solution in the population of building blocks created in the initialization phase. However, it is extremely expensive to build every combination of a particular building block size to put into a population. The fmGA is designed to reduce this complexity by replacing the initialization phase and primordial phase with a probabilistic complete initialization (PCI) and primordial phase, consisting of selection and building block filtering (BBF). PCI and BBF are an alternate means to providing the juxtaposition phase with highly fit building blocks [45].

The PCI phase creates an initial pop-pool size of n as described by Eq. (19.14), which is probabilistically equivalent to the pop-pool size at the end of the primordial phase of mGAs.

The population size is the multiplication of three terms from the equations of the gene-wise probability, the allele-wise combinatoric, and the building block evaluation noise equation [45]. Furthermore, it can be shown that the probability gene-wise equation is the probability of selecting a gene combination of size k in a string of length l' having the total number of genes, l, as given as Eq. (19.15). If, n_g, is assigned to the *inverse* of Eq. (19.15), it is suggested that each subpopulation of size n_g have one needed string, on average, gene combination of size k. Equation (19.16) defines n_g. If we expect to have one of our needed gene combinations for one particular building block of size k, then we can further claim that we require the needed gene combination for each and every possible combination of k building block size, which makes for 2^k allelic combinations or allele-wise combinatoric population size multiplier. A second multiplier is then defined in Eq. (19.17) (the building block evaluation noise equation). This equation makes for a population size calculation where the selection error between two competing building blocks is no more than α different. Finally, we have a simple, more manageable, population sizing calculation [45] in Eq. (19.18).

$$2^k \frac{\binom{l}{l'}}{\binom{l-k}{l'-k}} 2c(\alpha)\beta^2(m-1) \qquad (19.14)$$

$$p(l', k, l) = \frac{\binom{l-k}{l'-k}}{\binom{l}{l'}} \qquad (19.15)$$

$$n_g = \frac{1}{\binom{l-k}{l'-k} \Big/ \binom{l}{l'}} \qquad (19.16)$$

$$n_a = 2c(\alpha)\beta^2(m-1) \qquad (19.17)$$

$$n = n_a n_g \qquad (19.18)$$

Once the population size is determined, the initial population is created and the algorithm begins. The length of the strings, l', is set to $l - k$. The primordial phase performs several tournament selection generations to build up copies of highly fit strings followed by BBF to reduce the string length toward the building block size k. An example of the population sizing calculation can be found [11]. To conclude, instead of having a huge initialization cost as we do with the mGA, the fmGA has allowed a more optimal initial population mechanism, which is statistically equivalent to that of the mGA.

19.4.2 Parallel Fast Messy GA

The pfmGA is an extension of the fmGA [45] and is a binary, population based, stochastic approach that exploits building blocks (BBs) within the population to find solutions to optimization problems. Our pfmGA may be executed in a single program single data (SPSD) or a single program multiple data (SPMD) mode. The parallelization of this algorithm is based on the message passing interface (MPI) constructs. The pfmGA consists of three phases of operation: the initialization, building block filtering, and juxtapositional phases, all using synchronous MPI based communications. The pfmGA operates independently on each of the processors with communications occurring during the initialization and juxtapositional phases (independent mode).

In the initialization phase, a population of individuals is randomly generated on each processor. Subsequently, the population members are evaluated. A competitive template (CT) is also generated on each processor a priori. The CT is a locally optimized and used for calculating the fitness value of partial strings in the later phases of the algorithm.

The BBF phase follows and extracts BBs from the population for the generation of solutions. This process occurs through a random deletion of bits from each of the population members alternated with tournament selection. A BBF schedule is provided a priori to specify the generations for the deletion to occur, the number of bits to be deleted from each population member and the generations to complete tournament selection. This phase completes once the length of the population members' chromosomes have been reduced to a predetermined BB size. To evaluate these BBs ("under-specified" strings), a CT is utilized to fill in the missing allele values. These population members are referred to as "under-specified", as each locus position does not have an associated allele value. The BBF process is alternated with tournament selection to keep only the strings with the best building blocks found or those with the best fitness value around for later processing.

The Juxtapositional phase follows and uses the building blocks found through the BBF phase and recombination operators to create population members that become fully specified (all loci values have corresponding allele values) by the end of the phase. Again the CT is used anytime a population member is missing a locus and in the case of "over-specification," where a specific locus is assigned an allelic value multiple times, the first value encountered is the one recorded. At the end of the juxtapositional phase, the best population member found across all of the processors becomes the new CT on each processor. At this point, the BB size is incremented and each of the three phases is executed again. After all of the specified BB sizes are executed, the best solution found is recorded and presented to the user.

19.4.3 Multiobjective fmGA (MOfmGA)

A modified multiobjective fmGA (MOfmGA) executes using the same basic algorithm structure as the fmGA. The differences include the use of a multiple CT design where each objective function is assigned a CT. This CT evolves to "optimize" that particular objective function. Each population member is overlayed onto this competitive template before evaluation of the objective function. As the juxtapositional phase completes, population members (after overlaying onto a competitive template if necessary) are written to a file for processing and extraction of pareto front points. Finally, after storing the overall best chromosome into the next CT, a protein data bank (PDB) file is generated.

19.4.4 Ramachandran Experiment

The Ramachandran experiment is conducted to take advantage of problem domain information in restricting the search space (not size) for the algorithm. In the preliminary results, the MOfmGA was executed three times for each of the methods to provide statistical results. All results presented here are averaged over three runs. The following MOfmGA parameters are kept constant:

(1) Cut probability = 0.02
(2) Splice probability = 1.00
(3) Primordial generations = 200
(4) Juxtapositional generations = 200
(5) Total generations = 400

An input schedule was used to specify sizes of the building blocks the algorithm uses and during which generations BBF occurs. Tests were conducted using only POLY, with 560 bit length strings and BB sizes 20–24. Furthermore, the n_a variable is set at 100 and, for efficiency of getting results, only a single objective and a single randomly generated competitive template is employed. Figure 19.5 illustrates the

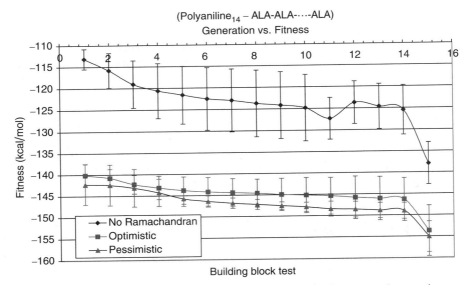

Figure 19.5   Building block test vs. fitness/time plots of results for an experiment using no, pesimistic, and optimistic Ramachandran [11] plots on the protein POLY.

results of the Ramachandran experiment. Clearly, we note that both Ramachandran constraints achieve better results. The mapping cost of using Ramachandran plots is three times that of a non-Ramachandran implementation. This is presented in Figure 19.6. Notice that the mapping for both the optimistic and pessimistic implementation takes exactly the same cost in time; therefore, to use these constraints,

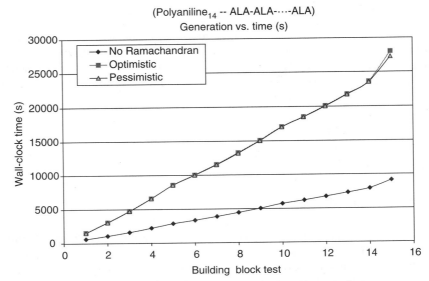

Figure 19.6   Efficiency results of the Ramachandran experiment.

TABLE 19.8 ASPEN and Polywell System Configurations

Variable	Cluster 1 (ASPEN)	Cluster 2 (Polywells)
Operating system	Redhat Linux 7.3	Redhat Linux 7.1
Processors	Dual PIII 1 GHz	AMD 1.4 MHz
Cache(L1 I, D/L2)	(16, 16/256)KB	(64, 64/256) KB
Backplane	Fast Ethernet	Fast Ethernet
RAM	1 GB	768 MB
Switching	Crossbar Switch	Crossbar switch
Disk I/O	RAID 5	RAID 5
Memory type	Distributed	Distributed
Node specifics	48 node, 2 CPUS/node	16 node, 1 CPU/node

the pessimistic values are to be utilized because it is statistically more effective and costs the same in time.

19.5 PSP PARALLEL EA PERFORMANCE EVALUATION

The fmGA is programmed to run in serial and parallel on the following computer systems: pile of PCs (PPCs), cluster of workstations (COWs), and networks of workstations (NOWs). The clusters of computers used in this investigation are listed in Table 19.8. The system configurations for the PPCs are shown in Table 19.9. Specifications for the NOWs are listed in Table 19.10. The algorithm's generic performance metric is two fold: *goodness* of the structure (effectiveness) and the time to converge (efficiency).

Next, the study of both effectiveness and efficiency is discussed for the fmGA when used to determine a protein structure. Specific studies include competitive template generation, a building block size experiment, a Ramachandran constraint experiment, and a multiobjective experiment. Efficiency is tested using a Farming Model. Finally, the "goodness" of solutions are evaluated using RMS differences. In this preliminary study, we chose Polyalanine$_{14}$ (POLY) as a test peptide.

TABLE 19.9 Pile of PCs System Configurations

Number of Nodes	Processor/Operating System
8	1.7 GHz P-IV/Linux 7.1
2	1.2 GHz P-III/Linux 7.1
5	1.0 GHz P-III/Linux 6.2
2	933 MHz P-III/Linux 6.2
8	600 MHz P-III/Linux 6.2
4	450 MHz P-III/Linux 6.2
3	400 MHz P-III/Linux 6.1

TABLE 19.10 Specifications for the NOWs

Network of Workstation Specifications
17 node single processor nodes
16 compute Nodes/1 server node
AMD processor architecture (1.4 MHz)
Work space 3.2 GB per compute node
768 MB memory per compute node
64 L1 and 256 L1 cache per processor on compute nodes

19.5.1 Competitive Template Generation

The fmGA explicitly manipulates BBs in search of the global optimum and uses the idea of speciation through successive phases of the algorithm. The fmGA uses a competitive template, which is a fully specified population member, to evaluate these partially defined strings or building blocks. By focusing on modifying the process that the fmGA uses to create and update the competitive template during the execution of the algorithm, the algorithm's effectiveness is increased.

19.5.2 Building Block Experiment

The BB analysis is performed in an attempt to identify the BB sizes that result in finding better solutions. A BB is a partial string representing bits from one, some, or all of the dihedral angles that each chromosome represents. The BBs are not restricted to be contiguous bits from the chromosomes but instead can be noncontiguous bits from the chromosome.

The BB analysis conducted covers a variety of BB sizes and compares the results to determine which size produces the best statistical results. One expects a BB size of 35 bits to yield the best due to the alpha helical [7] structure of POLY, known to have 3.5 residues per turn [46].

19.5.3 Constraints Based on Ramachandran Maps

Search algorithms having constraints on search space by a feasibility function statistically, over time, must find better solutions. This premise also applies to this experiment; by constraining the search space to have only feasible solutions, it is expected that better solutions are found.

19.5.4 Multiobjective Experiment

In the single objective implementation of the fmGA, the CHARMm energy function was utilized and consists of a summation of several terms. In the multiobjective approach, the objectives are drawn from each of the terms within the CHARMm energy function, defined in terms of bonded and nonbonded interactions.

19.5.5 Farming Model Experiment

Alternate efficiency models, such as the island model, have been previously applied in parallelizing GAs. Owing to our energy fitness function calculation, the addition of a farming model is proposed as discussed.

The component under test for efficiency is the fitness function calculation. The farming out of a computationally expensive fitness evaluation should realize speedup in efficiency without affecting the effectiveness. Wall clock time is measured by system-clock time to complete (seconds).

19.6 RESULTS AND DISCUSSION

19.6.1 Multiple Competitive Templates

The multiple CT experiment is our first design modification to the fmGA. This modification requires the fmGA to have the ability to compute a panmetic competitive template[1] in addition to having multiple competitive templates present during computational search. Statistical techniques used are the Kruskal–Wallis [47] (KW) and Student's t-test for paired observations (PO) [48] and unpaired observations.

Generation of the alpha helix produces good results; however, the multiple and panmetic competitive template methods also performed well. Both the beta sheet and randomly generated competitive template generation approaches performed badly. This is illustrated in Figure 19.7a. There is a clear difference between the random, beta-sheet, and all alpha-helix related templates (alpha-helix, multiple, and panmetic competitive template). Similar results are reported with the PO test. Accordingly, the PO test concluded that the order from best to worst is panmetic, multiple, alpha helix, beta sheet, and randomly generated competitive template method. Finally, the KW test also confirmed that the alpha-helix related, beta-sheet, and randomly generated competitive template methods are different. It concluded conceptually that it was 84% confident that these are different (χ^2 distribution with 2 degrees of freedom (DF) and 3.65 quantile) and computationally it is 100% confident that these are different (χ^2 distribution with 2 DF and 9.24 quantile). A further KW test was conducted on the three alpha-helix related competitive template methods. Conceptually, we conclude that there was no difference between the three (94% confident using DF = 2 and 0.12 quantile of the χ^2 distribution). Moreover, computationally the KW test shows with 45% confidence that these are the same. The KW is more strict regarding differences; therefore, we conclude that the three competitive template methods are the same statistically. Finally, as expected, although having multiple competitive templates increases algorithm effectiveness, runtime is also increased (Fig. 19.7b illustrates the run time increase).

---

[1] A panmetic competitive template is derived from the existing multiple competitive templates.

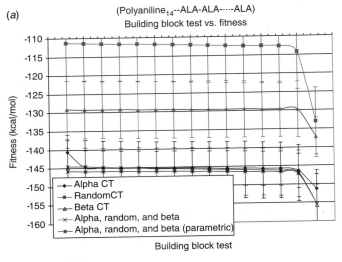

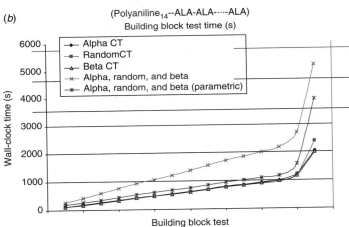

Figure 19.7 (*a*) Building block test vs. fitness plot of results for an experiment using multiple methods of competitive template generation on the protein POLY. (*b*) Building block test vs. time to run experiment using multiple methods of competitive template generation on the protein POLY.

19.6.2 Farming Model Experiment

The pfmGA utilizes an island model paradigm to conduct parallel communications between processors. At each stage of the communications, all of the processors communicate their best found population member to processor 0. Processor 0 then determines which is the "best" and communicates that population member back to all of the processors who then update their CT. After the update, all of the processors continue to execute the algorithm independently with independent population members until the next update communication is necessary.

Owing to the complexities associated with the energy fitness function calculation, the addition of a farming model in combination with the island model is proposed. With the addition of farms, the program becomes multiple program multiple data (MPMD). In the single data model, the GAs execute in parallel and generate populations separately from one another, with interactions only when a migration of a good population member occurs with some probability. Whereas in shared memory machine, a Global population model may be more appropriate as communication cost may not be as much of a concern. In such a shared memory MPMD setup, data does not need to be transferred among processors and data pipelining can be utilized more readily. The systems used in these experiments are not currently shared memory systems but the communication cost is later shown to be insignificant when compared with the cost of the energy fitness function evaluations.

The following pfmGA parameters are kept constant (set at standard values) throughout all of the testing:

(1) String length = 560 bits
(2) Cut probability = 0.02
(3) Splice probability = 1.00
(4) Primordial generations = 200
(5) Juxtapositional generations = 100
(6) Total generations = 300

An input schedule is also used to specify during which generations BBF occurs.

A goal of this testing is to determine the speedup associated with increasing the number of farming processors per algorithm node in the pfmGA. Figure 19.8a illustrates a plot of one algorithm node with a number of different farming nodes. Each BB test point represents the average value for a specific BB size (in increasing order) executed by the pfmGA. As the BB size increases, the average execution time also increases. Additionally, Figure 19.8a and b shows that as the number of farming processors increases, the average execution time decreases for any given BB test. In this test, there exists a significant improvement in modifying the number of farming nodes from 0 to 2 and from 2 to 4. An increase in the farming nodes from 4 to 8 provides a small improvement. The best speedup obtained was with eight farming nodes where the serial time was 5080 s, whereas the parallel time was 1684 s yielding a speedup of three times. This validates our model and we can draw a conclusion that this model increases the efficiency of the fmGA.

Figure 19.8b presents the results for two algorithm nodes tested with a number of different farming nodes. In this testing, the overall population size across all of the algorithm nodes is equivalent to the population size used in the test of a single algorithm node. The serial time was 4140 s and the parallel time with four compute nodes per farm took 887 s yielding a speedup of 4.7.

(a)

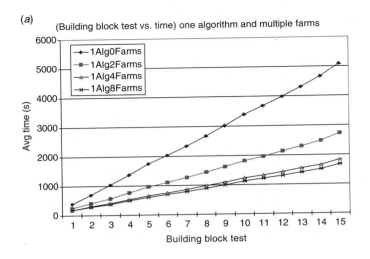

(b)

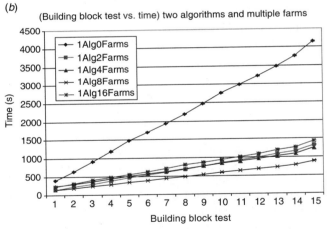

Figure 19.8   (*a*) One algorithm node experiment and (*b*) two algorithm node experiment.

19.6.3   Building Block Size Analysis

The BB analysis is performed in an attempt to identify the building block sizes that result in finding better solutions for POLY. A BB is a partial string representing bits from one, some, or all of the dihedral angles that each chromosome represents [49]. The BBs are not restricted to be contiguous bits from the chromosomes but instead can be noncontiguous bits from the chromosome. This analysis covers a variety of BB sizes and compares the results to determine which size produces the best statistical results. The BB ranges chosen for testing included: 16–18, 18–20, 20–22, . . . , and 38–40.

The results of the BB size experiment show that BB sizes of 30–32 yielded the best results for POLY. Although, this BB size is specific for POLY, it should apply to other proteins having an alpha-helical structure. Additionally, BB size 30–32 yielded the best overall fitness value found during all of the BB testing of -140 kcal, which is in the neighborhood of the accepted CHARMm fitness for this protein.

19.7 CONCLUSIONS AND SUGGESTED RESEARCH

This investigation summarizes our progress with using MOfmGA, modified to scale its efficiency to 4.7 times a serial run time. Algorithm development required a major rewrite to prepare for the implementation of the multiobjective approach. The new algorithm has the capabilities to be single and multiple objective and run with single and multiple competitive templates all configurable. The algorithm now provides for optimistic and pessimistic Ramachandran (per residue) constraints and calculation of RMS dihedral and Cartesian coordinate differences from accepted structures. Computational results support our hypothesis that the MO version provides more acceptable results. Overall preliminary results for a poly(alanine) model are encouraging. Future studies will involve beta structures and the villin headpiece [50, 51] as well as participation in critical assessment of techniques for protein structure prediction (CASP) [52]. In addition, interfacing with the hierarchical bayesian optimization algorithm (hBOA) as extended to the MOP domain may provide for more accurate solutions.

ACKNOWLEDGMENTS

The authors wish to thank AFIT Ph.D. students Larry Merkle, Jesse Zydallis, and others who contributed to this ongoing research. In addition, we are indebted to Dr. Ruth Pachter of the Air Force Research Laboratory who has provided the computational biology knowledge throughout the project. Note that the views expressed herein are those of the authors and do not reflect the official policy or position of the United States Air Force, Department of Defense, or the U.S. Government.

REFERENCES

1. Mathematical Committee on Physical and Engineering Sciences, *Grand Challenges 1993: High Performance Computing and Communications*, Office of Science and Technology Policy, 1982.

2. N. Krasnogor, D. Pelta, P. Mocciola, Pablo E. Martinez Lopex, and E. de la Canal, Enhanced evolutionary search of folding using parsed proteins, *Oper. Res. Symp.*, (1997).

3. Mehul M. L. Khimasia, Np complete problems. http://www.tcm.phy.cam.ac.uk/~mmlk2/report13/node31.html, 1996.

4. K. Lipkowitz and D. Boyd, *Reviews in Computational Chemistry*, Vol. 10, VCH Publishers, Inc., 333 7th Avenue, New York, New York, 1997.

5. S. Schulze-Kremer, Genetic algorithms and protein folding, *Methods Mol. Bilo.*, 143, 175–222 (2000).

6. J. G. Ecker, M. Kupferschmid, C. E. Lawrence, A. A. Reilly, and A. C. H. Scott, An application of nonlinear optimization in molecular biology, *Eur. J. Oper. Res.*, 138 (2), 452–458 (2002).

7. Joseph D. Bryngelson, Eric M. Billings, Ole G. Mouritsen, J. Hertz, Morgens H. Jensen, K. Sneppen, and H. Flyvbjerg, *Physics of Biological Systems: From Interatomic Interactions to Protein Structure*, Vol. 480, From Molecules to Species, Springer-Verlag, New York, 1997, pp. 80–116.

8. E. Cant'u-Paz, *Efficient and Accurate Parallel Genetic Algorithms*, Kluwer, New York, 2000.

9. Donald J. Brinkman and George H. Gates, Implimentation of a CHARMM energy function, /usr/genetic/Toolkit/CHARMm, September, 1994.

10. B. Brooks, R. Bruccoleri, B. Olafson, D. States, S. Swaminathan, and M. Karplus, CHARMM a program for macromolecular energy minimization, and dynamics calculations. *J. Comput. Chem.*, 4 (2), 187–217 (1983).

11. Richard O. Day, A multiobjective approach applied to the protein structure prediction problem, Ms Thesis, Air Force Institute of Technology, March, 2002. Sponsor: AFRL/Material Directorate.

12. L. Stryer, *Biochemistry*, Vol. 1 of 2nd Printing, 4th edn, W.H. Freeman and Company, New York, 1995.

13. F. V. Hartemann, H. A. Baldis, A. K. Kerman, A. Le Foll, N. C. Luhmann Jr., and B. Rupp, Three-dimensional theory of emittance in compton scattering and x-ray protein crystallography, *Am. Phys. Soc., Phys. Rev. E*, 64 (016501) (2001).

14. Thomas L. James, Fundamentals of NMR, Technical report, Department of Pharmaceutical Chemistry, University of CA, San Francisco, CA 94143, 1998.

15. P. Grassberger, W. Nadler, and G. T. Barkema, *Monte Carlo Approach to Biopolymers and Protein Folding*, World Scientic Publishing Company, Incorporated, Forschungszentrum Jlich, Germany, John von Neumann-Institut fr Computing, November 1998.

16. Shannon K. Duntz, Richard C. Murphy, Michael T. Niemier, J. Izaguirre, and Peter M. Kogge, Petaflop Computing for Protein Folding, Project Report, International Business Machines Corporation, 2001.

17. Lawrence Livermore Laboratories, Blue gene project update, Los alamos sandia and lawrence livermore laboratories: Project report, International Business Machines Corporation, January, 2002.

18. T. Lengauer, Algorithmic research problems in molecular bioinformatics, *Arbeitspapiere der GMD 748*, May, 1993.

19. George H. Gates, Predicting Protein Structure using Parallel Genetic Algorithms, Ms Thesis, Air Force Institute of Technology, Wright Patterson AFB, OH, December 1994. Sponsor: AFOSR WL/Material Directorate.

20. P. Fagan, D. Kegler, H. Cheng, J. Westbrook, Z. Feng, P. Bourne, G. Gilliland, D. Hancock, T. N. Bhat, B. Kroeger, D. Padilla, V. Colflesh, H. Weissig, N. Thanki, G. Patel, B. Schneider, H. M. Berman, N. Deshpande, W. Bluhm, K. Burkhardt, L. Iype, W. Fleri, C. Zardecki, and T. Battistuz, Protein data bank annual report 2001, Research collaboratory for structural bioinformatics, National Institute of CA, San Diego, San Diego Super

Computer Center at the University of CA, San Diego, June 2000–2001, Rutgers, The State University of New Jersey.

21. Peter A. Kollman, Department of pharmaceutical chemistry, University of california San Francisco, Energy Function.

22. Daniel R. Ripoll. Electrostatically driven monte carlo (edmc) protein folding, Baker Laboratory of Chemistry.

23. S. Schulze-Kremer, Genetic algorithms and protein folding, Westfalische Strasse 56, D-10711 Berlin, FRG, June, 1996.

24. Mehul M. Khimasia, and Peter V. Coveney, Protein structure prediction asa hard optimization problem: The genetic algorithm approach, June, 1997, Theory of Condensed Matter, Cavendish Laboratory.

25. A. Neumaier, Molecular modeling of proteins and mathematical prediction of protein structure, *SIAM Review*, 39 (3), 407–460 (1997).

26. A. Piccolboni and G. Mauri, Application of evolutionary algorithms to protein folding prediction, *Artificial. Evol.*, 123–136 (1997).

27. Robert L. Gaulk, The application of hybridized genetic algorithms to the protein folding problem, Ms Thesis, Air Force Institute of Technology, Wright-Patterson Air Force Base, Ohio, December 1995.

28. Laurence D. Merkle, Generalization and parallelization of messy genetic algorithms and communication in parallel genetic algorithms. Thesis, Air Force Institute of Technology, December, 1992, Sponsor: WL/Materials Directorate.

29. Harvard University, Charmm energy functions, http://www.ch.embnet.org/MD_tutorial/pages/MD.Part2.html, 2001.

30. Jeffery G. Saven, Designing protein energy landscapes, *Ame. Chem. Soc.*, 101, 3113–3130 (2001).

31. N. Go and Harold A. Scheraga, Calculation of the conformation of pentapeptide cyclo-(glycylglycylglycylprolylprolyl). i. A complete energy map, *Macromolecules*, 3, 188–194 (1969).

32. N. Go and Harold A. Scheraga, Ring closure and local conformational deformation of chain molecules, *Macromolecules*, 3, 178–187 (1969).

33. L. Baltzer, H. Nilsson, and J. Nilsson. De novo design of proteins — what are the rules? *Am. Chem. Soc.*, 101, 3153–3163 (2001).

34. J. Venkatraman, Sasalu C. Shankaramma, and P. Balaram, Design fo folded peptides, *Am. Chem. Soc.*, 101, 3131–3152 (2001).

35. B. Brooks, R. Bruccoleri, B. Olafson, D. States, S. Swaminathan, and M. Karplus, *CHARMm A Program for Macromolecular Energy, Minimization, and Dynamics Calculations*, Vol. 4.2, John Eiley and Sons, Inc., 1983, pp. 187–217.

36. Steven R. Michaud, Protein structure prediction using refined parallel fast messy genetic algorithms, Ms Thesis, Air Force Institute of Technology, March, 2001, Sponsor: AFRL/Material Directorate.

37. Gary B. Lamont and Laurence D. Merkle, Introduction to bioinformatics for computer scientists, Chapter in W. Corne's book, August, 2002.

38. Karl R. Deerman, Protein structure prediction using parallel linkage investigating genetic algorithms, Ms Thesis, Air Force Institute of Technology, Wright Patterson AFB, OH, March, 1999, Sponsor: AFRL/Material Directorate.

39. B. Derrida, Random energy model: limit of a family of disordered models, *Phys. Rev. Lett*, 45 (2), 79–82 (1980).

40. Christopher M. Bishop, *Neural Networks for Pattern Recognition*, Chapter 9, Oxford, Great Clarendon St., Oxford New York, 2002, pp. 377–380.

41. Richard O. Day, Jesse B. Zydallis, Gary B. Lamont, and R. Pachter, Genetic algorithm approach to protein structure prediction with secondary structures, *EUROGEN*, p. 6, September, 2000.

42. Richard O. Day, Jesse B. Zydallis, and Gary B. Lamont, Solving the protein structure prediction problem through a multiobjective genetic algorithm, *ICCN*, p. 4, December, 22, 2001.

43. Richard O. Day, Jesse B. Zydallis, and Gary B. Lamont, Competitive template analysis of the fast messy genetic algorithm when applied to the protein structure prediction problem, *ICCN*, p. 4, December, 22, 2001.

44. Richard O. Day, Jesse B. Zydallis, Gary B. Lamont, and R. Pachter, Analysis of fine granularity in parallelization and building block sizes of the parallel fast messy Ga used on the protein structure prediction problem, *World Congress on Computational Intelligence*, p. 6, December, 2001, Special Biological area.

45. David E. Goldberg, K. Deb, H. Kargupta, and G. Harik, Rapid, accurate optimization of difficult problems using fast messy genetic algorithms, July, 56–64 (1993).

46. C. Branden and J. Tooze, Introduction to protein structure, 1991.

47. Murray R. Spiegel and Larry J. Stephens, *Theory and Problems of Statistics*, Vol. 1, 3rd. ed., McGraw-Hill, 1999.

48. R. Jain, *The Art of Computer Systems Performance Analysis,* Wiley, 1991.

49. Steven R. Michaud, Jesse B. Zydallis, G. Lamont, and R. Pachter, Scaling a Genetic Algorithm to Medium-Sized Peptides by Detecting Secondary Structures with an Analysis of Building Blocks, in *Proceedings of the First International Conference on Computational Nanoscience*, M. Laudon and B. Romanowicz, Eds., Hilton Head, SC, March, 2001, pp. 29–32.

50. B. Zagrovic, Chirstopher D. Snow, Michael R. Shirts, and Vijay S. Pande, Simulation of folding of a small alpha-helical protein in atomistic detail using worldwide-distributed computing, *J. Mol. Biol.*, 323 (5), 927–937 (2002) (CODEN: JMOBAK ISSN: 0022-2836).

51. A. Fernandez, M. Yi Shen, A. Colubri, Tobin R. Sosnick, Stephen R. Berry, and Karl F. Freed, Large-scale context in protein folding: villin headpiece, *Biochemistry*, 42 (3), 664–671, 2003 (CODEN: BICHAW ISSN: 0006-2960).

52. www.predictioncenter.unl.gov, 1998–2003.

PART V

PLATFORMS AND ENABLING TECHNOLOGIES

A Brief Overview of Grid Activities for Bioinformatics and Health Applications

ALI AL MAZARI and ALBERT Y. ZOMAYA

20.1 INTRODUCTION

Bioinformatics and health applications such as genomic computations, protein structures prediction, biologic systems simulations, nucleotide and amino acid sequences, molecular engineering, drug science and pharmacology, biomedical imaging, to name a few, accumulate massive quantities of valuable data over very short periods of time.

Bioinformatics researchers and health scientists require powerful supercomputing infrastructures and need tools as well as techniques developed in other disciplines, such as computer science, mathematics, biology, statistics, physics, and medicine, to drive their disciplines.

In addition, speeding up the results of bioinformatics and health applications or producing early outcomes may save lives, time, and cost. In reality, the rate of production of scientific data is much greater than the rate of the development of supercomputing tools, which are required for handling such massive quantities of data. Therefore, grid computing infrastructure can be used to accelerate the necessary complex computations and enable scientific collaborations. This should lead to the smooth execution of critical tasks necessary for data distribution sharing and transfer, security, access management, analysis, and processing.

Recently, grid computing as a new and continuously evolving promising technology has succeeded in penetrating different industries, such as engineering, aerospace, finance, entertainment, and so on. Furthermore, several research groups and agencies such as the National Cancer Institute (NCI) and the National Foundation for Cancer Research (NFCR) in the USA, Biotechnology and Biological Sciences Research Council (BBSRC) and the Research Council in UK, the European Commission

Parallel Computing for Bioinformatics and Computational Biology, Edited by Albert Y. Zomaya
Copyright © 2006 John Wiley & Sons, Inc.

and Uniform Interface to Computing Resources (UNICORE) in Europe, and the Australian Research Council (ARC) have adopted grid technology to address research challenges, namely, those in bioinformatics and health sciences.

In addition, the European Union and several countries such as Australia, USA, UK, Japan, China, and others have also deployed grid technology to develop applications that require supercomputing capabilities. This chapter provides a brief overview of some of the international grid activities targeting bioinformatics and health sciences.

The chapter is organized as follows: Sections 20.2 and 20.3 give an overview of grid computing and the bioinformatics and health applications. In Section 20.4, the suitability of the grid technology for scientific applications will be examined. In Section 20.5, the grid projects in Europe will be reviewed. In Section 20.6, the international grids will be reviewed. In Sections 20.7, 20.8 and 20.9, the grid projects in UK, USA and France, and Asia and Japan will be reviewed, respectively. Section 20.10, recommends and concludes the future trends and research directions in grid computing for the health and bioinformatics industries as well as explains some research challenges and difficulties that may face the researchers and scientists.

20.2   GRID COMPUTING

Grid computing [1–5] was introduced in the late 1990s to establish large-scale distributed computing infrastructures for problems in advanced sciences and engineering known as "Grid Problems" [2]. These problems have certain requirements of flexible, secure, coordinated resource sharing among dynamic collections of individuals, institutions, and research organizations. In 1998, Foster and Kesselman have explained the early definition of computational grids [6] in their landmark book as an infrastructure of hardware and software that provides consistent, dependable, pervasive, and inexpensive access to high-end computational capabilities [7]. However, this definition was modified later to define grid technology as a system that coordinates resources that are not subject to centralized control, delivers non-trivial qualities of service and uses standard, open, general-purpose protocols and interfaces [8]. Therefore, grid-based infrastructures are decentralized, standardized, and have multi-purpose functionality.

Other studies define grid vision as one that creates simple yet large and powerful self-managing virtual computers from large collections of connected heterogeneous and/or homogeneous systems sharing various combinations of resources [5]. Such infrastructure will help and serve in solving complex problems that need computational power, data analysis, and scientific collaboration. Recently, this vision was reiterated to state that the grid will make it possible for scientific collaborators to share resources and for geographically distributed groups to work together in ways that were previously impossible [3].

20.3 BIOINFORMATICS AND HEALTH APPLICATIONS

Applications in the *life sciences* overlap a number of disciplines such as medicine, biology, pharmacology, neuroscience, physics, chemistry, medicines, and many others. These are also correlated and linked to *information technology* due to the massive computational and storage requirements of most applications in the life sciences [9–12]. Therefore, the creation of a strong and direct relationship between information technology and life sciences is a mandatory and a sensible requirement. According to observations, life scientists and computer technologists have started already, for more than a decade now, developing applications that cross the boundaries of both fields [9, 13]. The growth of this relationship has developed the new *bioinformatics* discipline that combines applications from both fields [5, 9, 11].

Bioinformatics as a discipline, according to the National Institutes of Health (NIH) definition, deals with the research, development, or application of computational tools and approaches for expanding the use of biological, medical, behavioral, or health data, including those to acquire, store, organize, archive, analyze, or visualize such data. One also view bioinformatics as a bridge between the life sciences and mathematical and computer sciences [9, 13–15]. Applications in bioinformatics also include the design and development of algorithmic and computational platforms to solve problems in biomedicine [15]. These applications employ services and tools from computer science in solving extremely complex biomedical research problems. The complexity of biomedical research problems stems from a number of factors, such as, understanding the mechanisms of how cells behave and communicate, the use of genetic data to detect diseases, speed up the rate of discovery of new medicines, production of proteins, to name a few [5, 9, 11, 12].

Such applications require sophisticated computing infrastructure and number crunching capabilities to handle large volumes of processing, perform various functionalities, and access large numbers of distributed and heterogeneous databases. This makes grid computing one of the prime candidates for delivering such capabilities [3].

20.4 GRID COMPUTING FOR BIOINFORMATICS AND HEALTH APPLICATIONS

Many applications in health and bioinformatics produce massive amount of data over very short periods of time, and this requires considerable computational and storage capabilities [5, 16]. To some extent, supercomputing technology have been used to face such needs. However, it is a known fact that data are doubling every 18 months, whereas computer processing power takes over 5 years to meet the challenge of handling such data quantities [3].

Moreover, scientific applications require months or years of data processing to produce results. For example, the drug discovery cycle might take 10 to 15 years of research, data processing, and lab experiments to bring a new drug into market [17–20]. In addition, some drug design problems may involve the job of screening 180,000 compounds that may need up to 540,000 h or over 60 years of execution time on a single desktop computer [18]. These factors re-enforce the need for grid technology because of the role that it can play in facilitating research in the life sciences [3]. The range of problems in the life sciences arena will also lead to the development of a wide range of grid-enabled technologies to play a variety of roles, for example, computational grids [5, 6] can provide number crunching capabilities, and data grid [5, 21] delivers a secure infrastructure for all data managements needs.

In this chapter, an overview of some of the grid activities are presented. These projects will be classified by the country and target application area of the grid project. It is important to note that the list of projects overviewed is by no means exhaustive as there are new grid projects launched on regular basis. However, this review will help in understanding the significance of grid computing technology in driving research in the life sciences, and also shows the level of commitment from many countries and funding bodies in backing this research.

20.5 GRID ACTIVITIES IN EUROPE

Many grid projects in Europe aim to create a consistent and complementary grid services throughout the continent addressing different bioinformatics and health research needs [10, 22–24]. In particular, these grid projects target three distinct areas: grid-enabled scientific infrastructure for biomedical applications, scientific and medical databases for medical images, genes, proteins, and molecular sciences, and medical simulations and visualizations [16, 24–26].

20.5.1 Grid-Enabled Scientific Infrastructure for Biomedical Applications

The majority of the European grid projects are funded by the European Commission (EC). The largest and most ambition of these projects is the European Grid (EuroGrid), which began in November 2000 to establish a European grid infrastructure based on the UNiform Interface to COmputing REsources (UNICORE) system to support scientific and industrial applications like the Biotechnology Grid (BioGrid) for biomolecular research [10, 27, 28]. Other projects include the HEAlthGrid VENture (HEAVEN), which aims to develop a European network that uses grid services for a variety of applications, such as medical informatics, bioinformatics, clinical informatic, or other healthcare applications [29], and the Enabling Grid for E-science in Europe (EGEE) to create a seamless European grid infrastructure that supports biomedical applications covering most of the European community [30].

In addition to these grids, the European Data Grid (EDG) is another EC-funded project that started in January 2001 to build a testbed for next-generation computing infrastructure that will provide the European scientific community with shared data and computing resources [31–34]. EDG will develop the technological infrastructure that supports research activities for computational and data-intensive applications such as medical imaging and processing, biological analysis, and other scientific applications [32, 35].

20.5.2 Scientific and Medical Databases for Medical Images

The other focus of the European grid projects is the development of medical databases for processing medical images and/or analyzing clinical data [10, 25]. The main grid project in this area is the HealthGrid that will support and assist health professionals by providing rapid and intelligent data access to large heterogeneous biomedical databases for molecular, cell, tissue, and population data [16, 26, 36]. Also, the Mammograms Grid (MammoGrid) will develop a European database for mammograms (stored as images) that will be used in healthcare investigations such as in the case of breast cancer through the MammoGrid Acquisition Station (MAS) [36, 37], and the Grid Platform for Computer Assisted Library for MAmmography (GPCALMA) to build a large distributed database of digitized mammography images for assisting in breast cancer diagnosis [36, 38].

Other European grid projects that focus on medical databases and images are the Medical Grid (MEDGRID) to tackle the processing of huge databases of medical images in hospitals [39, 40], the GridSystems to create an individualized healthcare environment that enables analyzing and processing 3D medical images to aid clinical analysis [41, 42], and the Grid-Enabled Medical Simulation Services (GEMSS) testbed for advanced image-processing services [43]. The GEMSS testbed also aids medical services applications in the area of neurosurgery, prosthesis design, advance image reconstruction, and others [44].

20.5.3 Genes, Proteins, and Molecular Sciences

Another focus for European grid efforts is to target genomics and proteomics data and the molecular sciences [16, 26, 36]. The main projects include the Biotechnology Information and Knowledge Grid (BIOGRID) that adopts the EuroGrid infrastructure to support molecular biology and quantum chemistry for the integration of large proteomics and genomics databases that can be used for pharmaceutical research [1], and the Grid Basic Local Alignment Search Tool (Grid-BLAST), which is the first application deployed on the EDG testbed to create the Visual DataGridBlast project that supports comparative genomics facilitating comparative analysis to compare sequences of nucleic or amino acids produced by researchers with those stored in available public databases [45].

Further, the BioInformatics and Genomics GRID for European Research (BIGGER) is also intended to be a platform enabling researchers to access and use biological information and software such as DNA sequence databases, protein sequences and family data, macromolecular structures, metabolic information, and other resources [46]. These facilities and services open new opportunities and initiate the next phase of the biological research. Finally, the Open Computing GRID Molecular Science and engineering (OpenMolGRID) project employs the EuroGrid to integrate heterogeneous and distributed databases for computational molecular engineering and molecular modeling [47–49]. This provides a solid foundation for designing next-generation molecular engineering tools to target large-scale problems.

20.5.4   Medical Simulations and Visualizations

Another area of opportunity for grid services is in medical simulations and visualization applications [10]. The CrossGrid, which began in September 2002, aims to create a European high-performance computing (HPC) platform for bioinformatics and health applications [50, 51]. Another project is GEMSS, which provides medical practitioners and researchers with advanced simulation services within medical applications such as maxillo facial surgery simulation, radio surgery simulation, drug delivery simulation, and cardiovascular system simulation [52, 121].

Other grids that may provide services for medical simulation and visualization are the GridSET, which is developed within the framework of the European WebSET project to provide a complete training system for medical students based on a 3D virtual reality simulator [53], and the GridSystems project which includes projects InnerGrid, OuterGrid, and GridApps targeting pharmaceutical and bioinformatics applications [41, 54].

In France, scientists and technologists have focused on exploiting grid capabilities and services for life sciences research and this can be seen in three main projects. The first is the Realization and Use of a Grid for Bio-computing (RUGBI) which is based on the Data Grid infrastructure to enable flexible and rapid use of genomic and proteomic sequences analysis algorithms, implementing a portal for secondary structures of proteins prediction, and offering services to analyze large-scale protein structures [55, 56, 127]. The second grid project is the GenoGrid that provides an experimental environment for genomic applications that aims to the detection of repeat sequences inside genomes and the implementation of a protein threading algorithms [57]. The third project is the Grid Protein Pattern Scanning (GriPPS), which is funded by the French Programme Action Concerte Incitative (ProgrammACI) in 2002, to develop bioinformatics algorithms that can be used by the biological applications such as genomes sequencing and proteins scanning [58].

20.6   GRID ACTIVITIES IN THE UNITED KINGDOM

Due to massive investment of funding and interest in grid research in the United Kingdom it was decided to dedicate a whole section to the different projects separate from those funded by the European Community.

20.6.1   Grid-Enabled Scientific Infrastructure for Biomedical Applications

There are two main projects in UK that provide the required scientific infrastructure to assist in developing grid-enabled bioinformatics and health applications. The first project which is part of the UK e-Science grid testbed will enable the development of healthcare applications by enabling the implementation of biomedical database architectures [59]. The project supports applications from other disciplines focusing on medical imaging, a dynamic brain atlas, and automated chemical data capture [60]. The second project is the UK myGrid that exploits the grid technology and provides middleware development for bioinformatics applications [61, 62]. The myGrid project also extends the grid framework to develop a virtual laboratory that enables scientists for e-collaboration [10, 63, 64].

20.6.2   Medical Imaging and Databases

The study and analyses of medical images and their conversion into valuable and useable data are some of the major objectives of several grid projects in the UK [24, 26]. A group of these projects includes the Medical Image and Signal Research (MIAS) Grid to enable the MIAS Interdisciplinary Research Consortium (IRC) to transform the huge amount of the medical images and signals into clinical information [65], the Digital Mammography National Database (eDiamond) Grid which provides physicians and hospitals fast access to a vast database of digital mammograms for breast cancer diagnosis [37, 66, 67], and the Information eXtraction from Medical Images (IXI) Grid that facilitates the access, manipulation, and analysis of medical images [68, 69].

Other grid projects that have the same focus include the iX-Grid which is a collaboration between the Manchester Visualization Centre (MVC) and iXimaging plc. to develop a framework that will enable transparent access to medical images data and integrate X-ray image acquisition and processing [70, 125]. Also, there is the 3D Optical Projection Tomography (OPT) Microscopy Grid that speeds up bio-imaging by 20:1 to provide scientists with faster access to data, reduce data-processing time, and provide online processing with data visualization at the scientist's laboratory [119, 120, 123]. In addition, the Op3D-Grid is another project that targets medical imaging and is a collaboration between the MVC, Manchester Royal Infirmary (MRI), and Silicon Graphics (SGI) to deliver innovation in imaging and 3D reconstruction [71]. The goal of this project is to assist in hepato-pancreatic surgery by delivering interactive 3D high-quality images directly into the operating theater [72].

20.6.3   Clinical Informatics and Medical Records

Studying clinical information, patients records, behaviors, reactions, and the need for producing healthcare information, clinical records, and medical databases are some of the concerns of the other grid projects in the UK [6, 24, 26]. For example, the Grid Based Medical Devices for Everyday Health is to improve access to medical information records remotely and enable online analysis and delivery of healthcare information to mobile healthcare professionals for the purpose of monitoring patients and processing their data [73]. The Telemedicine Grid was designed to enable remote delivery of care and provide access to appropriate clinical information and medical images across computer networks [74]. The BioMedical Research Informatics Delivery by Grid Enabled Services (BRIDGES) is a UK e-Science Programme Core project intended to develop and explore database integration over six geographically distributed research sites to maintain the availability of patients' records and support bioinformatics analysis, infrastructure, and visualization tools [126].

Finally, the Clinical E-Science Framework (CLEF) Grid is another project that targets clinical informatics for the purpose of establishing the nucleus of a public domain Clinical e-Science/Grid Community for the UK by focusing on generic methods for capturing, processing, and distributing information about cancer patients and their care [76]. The CLEF project achieves this goal by developing historical repositories on cancer patients that can be correlated with genetic, genomic, and/or image data, to produce a robust framework that can be used in many areas of clinical medicines and drug research [77, 78].

20.6.4 Biomedical Experimentations, Simulations, and Visualizations

Dealing with the complexity associated with biomedical experiments, simulations, and visualizations are issues for many biomedical researchers [16, 24, 26]. Some of the projects that target such needs include the RealityGrid for the modeling and simulation of complex condensed matter at the molecular and meso-scale levels to assist in the discovery of new materials [10, 79, 122]. The COmputing Systems of Microbial Interactions and Communications (COSMIC) Grid was designed for the development of a simulator to support individual-based modeling of evolving bacterial systems for genomic and proteomic studies [80, 81]. Finally, the BioMolecular Simulations Grid (BioSimGrid) is to provide a generic database for comparative simulation analysis of biomolecules for biological and pharmaceutical purposes [82, 83]. Thus, the BioSimGrid facilitates the use of computer simulations of biomolecules and enables a more efficient storage and exchange mechanism for simulation data [75, 84, 85].

20.6.5 Genes, Proteins, and Molecular Sciences

Other grid projects focus on studying genes, molecules, and proteins structures and features. Of these projects is the Chemical Semantic Grid to exploit and develop modern methods of information management that help in discovering new molecular information and thus facilitate computing molecular properties [86]. Also, the ProteomeGrid, which is funded by the BBSRC to build a fully automated distributed pipeline for structure-based proteome annotation [87]. Moreover, the GeneGrid project aims to construct a grid-based virtual bioinformatics laboratory to develop specialist tissue-specific data sets that are relevant to a particular disease like cancer or other infectious diseases [88]. Finally, the e-Family Information Grid project is intended to provide a better view of the information associated with protein sequences and structures for bioinformatics researchers [89].

20.7 GRID ACTIVITIES IN THE USA

Grid projects in the USA mainly focus on genomic and proteomic science, brain activities, and drug discovery for infectious diseases. Of course, the list of projects is not exhaustive, and it is meant to give an indication of the level of research activities.

20.7.1 Genomic and Proteomic Sciences

The most visible project in the USA is the North Carolina Bioinformatics Grid Computing (NC BioGrid or NCBGC) [124]. The project was established in December 2000 by a collaboration between IBM Life Sciences Division, Microelectronics Center of North Carolina (MCNC), the North Carolina Supercomputing Center, North Carolina Research and Education Network, University of North Carolina, and Duke University [90]. The purpose of NC BioGrid is to assist in meeting challenges and taking advantages of the genomic revolution by providing computing, data storage, and networking infrastructure that combines genomic, proteomic, and other scientific data [5]. In addition, NC BioGrid will help in accelerating drug discovery that could lead to new medicines for combating diseases and producing new nutritional crops. The project will give approximately a $10 billion economic boots to the economy of NC by 2010 with the creation of 24,000 additional jobs [91, 92].

20.7.2 Brain Activities and Neuroscience

The Biomedical Informatics Research Network (BIRN) Grid aims to develop a testbed for sharing and mining data or digital magnetic resources images (MRI) in neuroscience including studies of the brain of humans and animals [93]. The BIRN Grid is funded by the National Center for Research Resources (NCRR) at the NIH to study brain disorders by fostering distributed scientific collaboration between biomedical scientists [94].

20.7.3 Drug Discovery

Moreover, the TeraGrid is the major grid project in the USA funded by the US National Science Foundation (NSF). The TeraGrid will support many sciences and applications including those related to drug discovery [95, 96].

20.8   GRID ACTIVITIES IN ASIA AND JAPAN

Consistent with other activities around the world most of the grid projects in Asia and Japan have focused on creating genomic, proteomic and biological databases, and brain activities analysis.

20.8.1   Genomic, Proteomic, and Biological Databases

The Asia Pacific Bioinformatics Grid (APBioGrid) was launched by the Asia Pacific Bioinformatics Network (APBioNet) in late 2001 to build networked computational resources and databases of genomics, proteomic, and other biological data to be easily accessible by scientists in the Pacific region [97]. The National University of Singapore Bioinformatics Grid (NUS BioGrid) was formed in 2002 to empower applications in life sciences and bioinformatics such as genomic analysis and molecular biology [98].

Moreover, scientists and researchers in Japan initiated several grid projects, that include the Open Bioinformatics Grid (OBIGrid) organized by the Japan Committee on Very Large Scale Biocomputing (VLSB) and the Initiative for Parallel Bioinformatics Processing (IPAB) in 2002 to support work on genomics [99]. A year later the BioInformatics Grid Yet Another Gene Network Simulator (OBIYangs) was introduced to provide biological researchers with the use of a simulation system to understand the dynamics and regulation mechanism of biological behavior and to help scientists test hypotheses that could pave the way for better experiments [56].

The Bioinformatics Grid (BioGrid) project is sponsored by the Cybermedia Center of Osaka University to meet information technology needs and research activities in medicine and biology, mainly creating biodatabases [16, 100, 128]. This includes several projects: re-developing Data Online Analysis Technology (DOAT) to enable the sharing of scientific measurement devices, the Computing Grid Technology (CGT) to facilitate bio-simulation at the petascale level, and the Data Grid Technology (DGT) for linking huge biodatabases [36].

Finally, Singapore's Bio-Medical Grid (BMG) project was announced in 2004 to link universities, hospitals, and biomedical research institutions in Singapore, Japan, and other western countries for the purpose of aggregating and sharing distributed computing resources and data storages for genomic, proteomic, and microarray data [101].

20.8.2   Brain Activity and Neuroscience

In addition to the BioGrid project in Japan, the Cybermedia Center of Osaka University has also sponsored the Medical Engineering Grid (MEGRID) which is a collaboration between the Nanyang Technological University in Singapore and Advanced Industrial Science and Technology (AIST) for establishing an infrastructure that allows doctors and researchers in magnetoencephalography (MEG) science to analyze brain activities and functions efficiently for clinical use and neuroscience research [22, 102, 103].

20.9 GRID ACTIVITIES IN AUSTRALIA

A partnership between United Devices, IBM, Sydney University Biological Informatics and Technology Center (SUBIT), and Monash University will utilize grid technology to aid life sciences researchers. The initial work will focus on computationally intensive phylogenetic applications. The project aims at distributing the computational load across a grid at Sydney University using cycle harvesting techniques [104]. The second phase of the project will link several institutions together.

Another project is the Virtual Laboratory to enable molecular modeling for drug design on a grid. This enable the screening of millions of compounds in chemical databases (CDB) against a protein target to identify those with potential use for drug design [17, 18].

20.10 INTERNATIONAL GRID COLLABORATIONS

There are a limited number of grid projects in bioinformatics and the health industry that are international in nature with a high level of publicity and visibility. These projects depend on the use of worldwide dispersed resources that are provided by individual volunteers and research institutions.

20.10.1 Drug Discovery

The main aim of such projects is to reduce the production cycle of new drugs and lead to cures, that could save many lives [17–19, 105]. One of the earlier projects in this area is the FightAIDS@Home (FAAH) Grid which was developed by the company Entropia in September 2000 then transferred to the Oslen Laboratory at the Sripps Research Institute (TSRI) in May 2003 to speedup and assist fundamental research to discover a new cure of AIDS based on the Entropia's distributed computing network [106].

Other international grids for the same purpose also include the Grid Meta Processor (MP) Solutions developed by United Devices and others for drug discovery requests. One such project is the Grid MP Enterprise for creating dynamic computing infrastructures, and is used as a tool to accelerate virtual high-throughput screening (GHTS), applications in drug discovery by the pharmaceutical firm GlaxoSmith-Kline (GSK), which is one of the top five pharmaceutical firms in the world [20, 107]. Another Grid MP Solution is the Grid MP Data Center project launched in 2004, which is a collaboration between Intel, Microsoft, the Department of Chemistry at Oxford University to improve the scope and speed of drug discovery, virtual screening, and clinical developments [108, 109].

Other international grid projects in the area of drug discovery include the UD Patriot Grid projects, which are a family of grids to identify new drugs for diseases that are known to have potential for bioterrorism. The purpose is to create defensive capabilities to accelerate the drug discovery process by using the VHTS techniques

[107, 110]. The first grid in this family is for the Anthrax Research Project that was sponsored by the US Department of Defense (DoD), UD, Intel, and Accelerys in January 2002 to accelerate the process of identifying molecular candidates for treatment of advanced stages of anthrax infection [110, 111]. The second member of this family is the Smallpox Research Grid Project that is sponsored by UD, US DoD, IBM, Accelerys, and Evotec OAI in 2003 to provide researchers at Oxford and Essex Universities in the UK and other smallpox researchers with the computing power needed to identify new antiviral drugs by linking and deploying millions of worldwide computers [112, 113].

The third grid is the Cancer Research Project that runs on the Grid MP Global by UD and is a collaboration with Intel and the NFCR to discover new cancer cures [107].

Other international grid projects in the area of drug discovery are the Cancer Biomedical Informatics Grid (caBIG), which is created by the NCI and other American cancer centers in July 2003, to form a worldwide web of cancer research that helps in understanding of cancer disease and accelerates early detection and treatment [105]. In addition, the Sudden Acute Respiratory Syndrome (SARS) Grid is an international grid sponsored by many research centers and institutions based on the Access Grid technology to include a database of patients to track the infected people a user interface part that provides a platform for enabling radiologists and doctors to review daily X-rays of SARS patients without risk of infection [114].

Finally, the Distributed Computing Grid (DCGrid), which was used by Entropia and the Cambridge Crystallographic Data Centre (CCDC), to establish the grid computing partnership in October 2002 for accelerating virtual screening and drug design [115].

20.10.2   Biomedical Imaging and Brain Activities or Neuroscience

Although, most of the high visibility grid projects focus on drug discovery, there is a very limited number of projects with different focus. The Biomedical Imaging Grid (BIG) is a web-based grid portal for the management of biomedical images [97, 116]. The other project is the NeuroGrid which aims to provide a framework for applications in neurosciences for the analysis of brain activity data gathered from the MEG instrument to help doctors in identifying symptoms of diseases [22, 117, 118].

20.11   CONCLUSIONS AND FUTURE TRENDS

Bio- and health informatics span a wide range of applications. However, most of these applications require massive computing capability and sophisticated storage management resources. Grid computing can facilitate the development of high-performance scientific applications that require collection, management, analysis, processing, and transfer of data among heterogeneous resources. Grid computing also enables collaboration and data exchange among dispersed geographical locations to create a high level of participation between researchers and scientists. This means that grid technology can lead to great time and cost savings for many application domains including those in the life sciences.

Despite many bioinformatics and health grid projects that are sprouting everywhere, there is a clear need for more concerted efforts and developments. Undoubtedly, these technological investments in grid technology will reshape the future of the life sciences and will open new vistas for research and development.

REFERENCES

1. P. Bata, V. Alessandrini, D. Girou, J. MacLaren, J. Brooke, J. Pytlinski, M. Nazaruk, D. Erwin, D. Mallmann, and J. F. Myklebust, "BioGRID — A European grid for molecular biology," in *Proceedings of the 11th IEEE International Symposium on High Performance Distributed Computing (HPDC-11)*, Edinburgh, Scotland, 2002.

2. I. Foster, C. Kesselman, and S. Tuecke, The anatomy of the grid: enabling scalable virtual organizations, *Int. J. Supercomput. Appl.*, 15, 200–222 (2001).

3. I. Foster, The Grid: a new infrastructure for 21st century science, *Phys. Today*, 55, 42–47 (2002).

4. I. Foster, C. Kesselman, M. N. Jeffrey, and S. Tuecke, "The Physiology of the Grid: An Open Grid Services Architecture for Distributed Systems Integration," Argonne National Laboratory, June 22, 2002.

5. L. Ferreira, V. Berstis, J. Armstrong, M. Kendzierski, A. Neukoetter, M. Takagi, R. Bing-Wo, A. Amir, R. Murakawa, O. Hernandez, J. Magowan, and N. Bieberstein, "Introduction to Grid Computing with Globus," IBM Red Book, 2003.

6. I. Foster and C. Kesselman, "Computational Grids," in *The Grid: Blueprint for a Future Computing Infrastructure*, I. Foster and C. Kesselman, Eds., Morgan Kaufmann Publishers, USA 1999.

7. I. Foster and C. Kesselman, *The Grid: Blueprint for a New Computing Infrastructure*, Morgan Kaufmann, USA, 1999.

8. I. Foster, "What is the Grid? A Three Point Checklist," *Grid Today*, 6, 2002.

9. B. Bergeron, *Bioinformatics Computing: the Complete, Practical Guide to Bioinformatics for Life Scientists*. Persons Hall PTR, New Jersey, USA, 2003.

10. S. Farantos, S. Stamatiadis, N. Nellari, and D. Maric, "A Joint Scientific and Technological Activity and Study on Grid Enabling Technologies," in *the Proceedings of the European Network for Advanced Computing Technology for Science (ENACTS)*, 2002.

11. IBM, "IBM Grid Offering for Information Accessibility: Life Sciences," IBM, 2003.

12. B. Jacob, L. Ferreira, N. Bieberstein, C. Gilzean, J. Y. Girard, R. Strachowski, and S. Yu. *Enabling Applications for Grid Computing with Globus.*, IBM Red Book, 2003.

13. C. Ouzounis and A. Valencia, 'Early Bioinformatics: the Birth of a Discipline — a personal view, *Bioinformatics*, 19, 2176–2190 (2003).

14. S. F. Martin, I. Iakovidis, S. Norager, V. Maojo, P. D. Groen, J. V. D. Lei, T. Jones, K. Abraham-Fuchs, R. Apweiler, A. Babic, R. Baud, V. Breton, P. Cinquin, P. Doupi, M. Dugas, R. Eils, R. Engelbrecht, P. Ghazal, P. Jehenson, C. Kulikowski, K. Lampe, G. D. Moor, S. Orphanoudakis, N. Rossing, B. Sarachan, A. Sousa, G. Spekowius,

G. Thireos, G. Zahlmann, J. Zvarova, I. Hermosilla, and F. J. Vicente, Synergy between medical informatics and bioinformatics: facilitating genomic medicine for future health care, *J. Biomed. Inform.*, 37, 30–42 (2004).

15. M. Cannataro, C. Comito, F. L. Schiavo, and P. Veltri, Proteus, a grid based problem solving environment for bioinformatics: architecture and experiments, *IEEE Comput. Intell. Bull.*, 3, 7–18 (2004).

16. I. S. T., "Prospective Study on GRID Technology," Information Society Technology, Portugal 1.1, 2003.

17. R. Buyya, K. Branson, J. Giddy, and D. Absramson, "The Virtual Laboratory: A Toolset for Utilising the World-Wide Grid to Design Drugs," in *Proceedings of the Second IEEE International Symposium on Cluster Computing and the Grid (CCGrid 2002)*, Berlin, Germany, 2002.

18. R. Buyya, K. Branson, J. Giddy, and D. Absramson, The virtual laboratory: A toolset to enable distributed molecular modelling for drug design on the world-wide grid, *J. Concurr. Comput. Prac. Exp.*, 15, 1–25 (2003).

19. A. E. Lunney, Computing in drug discovery: The Design Phase, *Comput. Sci. Eng.*, 3, 105–108 (2001).

20. UD, "GlaxoSmithKline: Implementing Breakthrough Technology for Clinical Development Modeling and Simulation," United Devices (UD), Texas, USA, 2004.

21. A. Chervenak, I. Foster, C. Kesselman, C. Salisbury, and S. Tuecke, The data grid: towards an architecture for the distributed management and analysis of large scientific datasets, *J. Network Comput. Appl.*, 33, 187-200 (2002).

22. R. Buyya, S. Date, Y. Mizuno-Matsumoto, S. Venugopal, and D. Abramson, Neuroscience instrumentation and distributed analysis of brain activity data: a case for eScience on global grids, *J. Concurr. Comput. Prac. Exp.*, 2004.

23. GRIDSTART, GRIDSTART project: turning the GRID into reality, *GRIDSTART Tech. Bull.*, 1, 2002.

24. HealthGrid, "Abstracts of Presentations," in *Proceedings of The First European Health Grid Conference (HealthGrid'03)*, Lyon, France, 2003.

25. P. Graham, M. Heikkurinen, J. Nabrzyski, A. Oleksiak, M. Parsons, H. Stockinger, K. Stockinger, M. Stroinski, and J. Weglar, "EU Funded Grid Development in Europe," in *Proceedings of the Second European Across Grids Conference*, Springer-Verlag, Nicosia, Cyprus, 2004.

26. HealthGrid, "Abstract Booklet: Presentations, Posters and Demonstrations," in *Proceedings of the Second HealthGrid Conference (HEALTHGRID'04)*, Clermont-Ferrand, France, 2004.

27. H. Hoppe, P. G. D. Mallmann, and F. Jülich, "EUROGRID — European testbed for GRID applications," *GRIDSTART Tech. Bull.*, 1, 2002.

28. I. S. T., "EuroGrid: European Testbed for GRID Applications," Information Society Technology (IST), 2002.

29. V. Breton, A. Solomonides, and R. McClatchey, "A Perspective on the Healthgrid Initiative," in *Proceedings of the fourth IEEE/ACM International Symposium on Cluster Computing and the Grid (CCGrid 2004)*, Chicago, USA, 2004.

30. EGEE, "EGEE Project Executive Summary," Enabling Grids for e-Science in Europe (EGEE), 2003.

31. EDG, "Evaluation of Testbed Operation: Overview of Testbed-1 Deployment and Features," European Data Grid Project (EDG), 2002.

32. I. S. T., "Annex 1 — Description of Work — Research and Technological Development for an International Data Grid (DATAGRID) Project," Information Society Technology (IST), 2003.

33. I. S. T., "DataGrid Project: EDG Users," Information Society Technology (IST), UK 2003.

34. R. Wilson, "The European DataGrid Project," Institute de Fisica d'Altes Energies and Colorado State University, Barcelona, Spain and Fort Collins, Colorado, USA, 2001.

35. G. Cancio, S. M. Fisher, T. Folkes, F. Giacomini, W. Hoschek, D. Kelsey, and B. L. Tierney, "The DataGrid Architecture," CERN, RAL, and INFN, 2001.

36. D. Berry, C. Germain-Renaud, D. Hill, S. Pieper, and J. Saltz, "IMAGE 03: Images, Medical Analysis and Grid Environments," UK National e-Science Centre, UK, 2004.

37. A. Solomonides, R. McClatchey, M. Odeh, M. Brady, M. Mulet-Parada, D. Schottlander, and S. R. Amendolia, "MammoGrid and eDiamond: Grids Applications in Mammogram Analysis," in *Proceedings of the IADIS International Conference: e-Society*, Lisbon, Portugal, 2003.

38. U. Bottigli, P. Cerello, P. Delogu, M. Fantacci, F. Fauci, B. Golosio, A. Lauria, E. Torres, R. Magro, G. Masala, P. Oliva, R. Palmiero, G. Raso, A. Retico, S. Stumbo, and S. Tangaro, "GPCALMA, a Mammographic CAD in a GRID Connection," in *Proceedings of the 17th International Congress and Exhibition on Computer Assisted Radiology and Surgery*, London, UK, 2003.

39. L. Seitz, J. Pierson, and L. Brunie, "Semantic Access Control for Medical Applications in Grid Environments," in *Proceedings of Europar'03*, Klagenfurt, Austria, 2003.

40. T. Tweed and S. Miguet, "Medical Image Database on the Grid: Strategies for Data Distribution," in *Proceedings of the First European Health Grid Conference (HealthGrid'03)*, Lyon, France, 2003.

41. GridSystem, "InnerGrid Nitya: A Computing Platform for Pharmaceutical and Chemical Companies," GridSystem Project, Baleares, Spain, 2003.

42. GridSystem, "InnerGrid Nitya: The Solution for Research in Health Sciences," GridSystem Project, Baleares, Spain, 2003.

43. S. Benkner, G. Berti, G. Engelbrecht, J. Fingberg, G. Kohring, S. Middleton, and R. Schmidt, "GEMSS: Grid-infrastructure for Medical Service Provision," in *Proceedings of the Second HealthGrid Conference (HEALTHGRID'04)*, Clermont-Ferrand, France, 2004.

44. I. S. T., "Grid-enabled Medical Simulation Services (GEMSS): First Annual Project Progress Report," Information Society Technology, UK Deliverable D6.2a, 2003.

45. V. Breton, R. Medina, and J. Montagnat, "DataGrid, Prototype of a Biomedical Grid," in *Proceedings of the Conference on the Synergy between Bioinformatics*, Medical Informatics and Neuroinformatics, Brussels, 2003.

46. G. Cameron, "BioInformatics and Genomics Grid for European Research (BIGGER)," in *Proceedings of the First European Health Grid Conference (HealthGrid'03)*, Lyon, France, 2003.

47. F. Darvas, A. Papp, I. Bágyi, G. Ambrus, and L. Ürge, "OpenMolGRID: a GRID Based System for Solving Large-Scale Drug Design Problems," in *Proceedings of the Second IST Concertation Meeting and AxGrids2004*, Nicosia, Cyprus, 2004.

48. I. S. T., "OpenMolGRID: Ecotox — Acquire Data, Specification," Information Society Technology (IST), Negri Document Identifier: OpenMolGRID-1-D1.1c-0103-2-1-AquireDataSpec, 2004.

49. D. McCourt, W. Jing, and W. Dubitzky, "The OpenMolGRID Data Warehouse, MOLDW," in *Proceedings of the Second Across Grids conference*, Nikosia, Cyprus, 2004.

50. I. S. T., "Annex 1 — Description of Work — Development of Grid Environment for Interactive Applications Project," Information Society Technology (IST), 2002.

51. P. Nowakowski, "CROSSGRID — Project at a Glance," *GRIDSTART Tech. Bull.*, Vol. 1, 2002.

52. I. S .T., "GEMSS: Grid-enabled Medical Simulation Services," Information Society Technology (IST), UK, 2001.

53. GridSET, "GridSET Reduces Training Time for Medical Procedures: Closing the Gap between Theory and Practice," GridSET Exchange, 2004.

54. GridSystem, "Using Grid to Shorten Drug Discovery and Commercialization Time Cycles," GridSystem Project, Baleares, Spain, 2003.

55. C. Blanchet, V. Breton, G. Deleáge, N. Demesy, F. Hernandez, N. Jacq, S. Langlois, A. Lecluse, Y. Legré, D. Linglin, J. F. Musso, R. Nougarede, H. Prévoteau, S. Reynaud, and J. P. Roebuck, "RUGBI: Design and deployment of a Grid for BioInformatics," in *Proceedings of the Second HealthGrid Conference (HEALTHGRID'04)*, Clermont–Ferrand, France, 2004.

56. S. Kimura, T. Naka, T. Kawasaki, F. Konishi, M. Hatakeyama, and A. Konagaya, "OBIYagns: A Biochemical Simulator in Grid Environment," in *Proceedings of the 14th International Conference on Genome Informatics (GIW 2003)*, Pacifico Yokohama, Japan, 2003.

57. D. Lavenier, L. Hugues, M. Hurfin, R. Andonov, L. Mouchard, and F. Guinand, "The GenoGRID Project," in *Proceedings of the First European Health Grid Conference (HealthGrid'03)*, Lyon, France, 2003.

58. A. Vernois, P. Vicat-Blanc, F. Desprez, F. Hernandez, and C. Blanchet, "GriPPS Project: Protein Pattern Scanning in a Grid Context," in *Proceedings of the First European Health Grid Conference (HealthGrid'03)*, Lyon, France, 2003.

59. T. Hey and A. Trefethen, The UK e-Science Core Programme and the Grid, *Future Gener. Comput. Sys.*, 18, 1017–1031 (2002).

60. A. Hardisty and J. Giddy, "The UK e-Science Grid: Beyond a Prototype — Project to Establish a Production Quality e-Science Grid," The UK e-Science Grid, Welsh e-Science Centre (WeSC), UK, 2003.

61. C. Goble, C. Wroe, R. Stevens, and myGrid-Consortium, "The myGrid Project: Services, Architecture, and Demonstrator," in *Proceedings of the Second UK e-Science All Hands Meeting (AHM03)*, Nottingham, UK, 2003.

62. R. Stevens, A. Robinson, and C. Goble, "myGrid: personalised bioinformatics on the information grid," *Bioinformatics*, 19, 302–305 (2003).

63. myGrid, "myGRID Project: An e-biologist's Workbench," E-Science North West (ESNW), 2003.

64. R. Stevens, R. McEntire, C. Goble, M. Greenwood, J. Zhao, A. Wipat, and P. Li, "myGrid and the Drug Discov. Process," *Drug Discov. Today: BIOSILICO*, Vol. 2, 2004, pp. 140–148.

65. NeSC, "The UK e-Science Core Programme: Annual Report," National e-Science Centre (NeSC), UK, 2002.

66. S. Lloyd, "eDiaMoND — State of the Art Technology for Breast Screening: 8302 Data Sheet Visuals," UK National e-Science Centre, UK, 2004.

67. M. Brady, D. Gavaghan, M. Simpson, M. Mulet-Parada, and R. Highnam, "eDiamond: a Grid-enabled Federated Database of Annotated Mammograms," in F. Berman, G. Fox, and T. Hey, Eds., Grid Computing — Making the Global Infrastructure a Reality, John Wiley & Sons, Ltd., 2003.

68. R. A. Heckemann, T. Hartkens, K. Leung, D. L. G. Hill, J. V. Hajnal, and D. Rueckert, "Information Extraction from Medical Images: Developing an e-Science Application Based on the Globus Toolkit," in *Proceedings of the Second UK e-Science Conference All Hands Meeting (AHM03)*, Nottingham, UK, 2003.

69. D. Hill, "IXI Provides a Clean Extraction: 8302 Data Sheet Visuals," UK National e-Science Centre, UK, 2004.

70. M. Riding, "iX-Grid Final Report," E-Science North West (ESNW), 2003.

71. J. Leng and N. John, "Scientific Application of OpenGL Vizserver within High Performance Computing," UK High End Computing (UKHEC), 2002.

72. J. Leng, "Op3D — Grid Final Report," E-Science North West (ESNW), 2004.

73. J. Crowe, B. Hayes-Gill, M. Sumner, C. Barratt, B. Palethorpe, C. Greenhalgh, O. Storz, A. Friday, J. Humble, C. Setchell, C. Randell, and H. Muller, "Modular Sensor Architecture for Unobtrusive Routine Clinical Diagnosis," in *Proceedings of the 24th International Conference on Distributed Computing Systems (ICDCSW'04)*, Hachioji, Tokyo, Japan, 2004.

74. M. Graves and K. Caldwell, "Telemedicine on the Grid," Cambridge eScience Center (CeSC) and The West Anglia Cancer Network (WACN), UK, 2003.

75. M. H. Ng, S. Johnston, S. Murdock, B. Wu, K. Tai, H. Fangohr, S. Cox, J. Essex, M. Sansom, and P. Jeffrey, "Efficient Data Storage and Analysis for Generic Biomolecular Simulation Data," in *Proceedings of the Third UK e-Science Conference All Hands Meeting (AHM04)*, Nottingham, UK, 2004.

76. D. Kalra, P. Singleton, D. Ingram, J. Milan, J. MacKay, D. Detmer, and A. Rector, "Security and Confidentiality Approach for the Clinical E-Science Framework (CLEF)," in *Proceedings of the Second UK e-Science Conference All Hands Meeting (AHM03)*, Nottingham, UK, 2003.

77. N. C. R. I., "Strategic Framework for the Development of Cancer Research Informatics in the UK," National Cancer Research Institute (NCRI), UK, 2003.

78. A. Rector, J. Rogers, A. Taweel, D. Ingram, D. Kalra, J. Milan, P. Singleton, R. Gaizauskas, M. Hepple, D. Scott, and R. Power, "CLEF — Joining up Healthcare with Clinical and

Post-Genomic Research," in *Proceedings of the UK e-Science Conference All Hands Meeting (AHM03)*, Nottingham, UK, 2003.

79. J. Brooke, M. Foster, S. Pickles, K. Taylor, and T. Hewitt, "Mini-Grids: Effective Test-beds for Grid Applications," in *Proceedings of The First IEEE/ACM International Workshop on Grid Computing (GRID 2000)*, Bangalore, India, 2000.

80. R. Gregory and R. Paton, "Cosmic-Grid Project, Progress Report 1," Biocomputing and Computational Biology Group, Liverpool, UK, 2004.

81. R. Gregory, R. C. Paton, J. R. Saunders, and Q. H. Wu, "Cosmic-Grid: Grid for the Modeling and Simulation of Bacterial Evolution," E-Science North West (ESNW), 2003.

82. Y. Arinaminpathy, O. Beckstein, P. Biggin, P. Bond, C. Domene, A. Pang, and M. Sansom, "Large Scale Biomolecular Simulations: Current Status and Future Prospects," in *Proceedings of the Second UK e-Science Conference All Hands Meeting (AHM03)*, Nottingham, UK, 2003.

83. B. Wu, K. Tai, S. Murdock, H. M. Ng, S. Johnston, H. Fangohr, P. Jeffreys, S. Cox, J. Essex, and M. Sansom, "Biosimgrid: A Distributed Database for Biomolecular Simulations," in *Proceedings of the Second UK e-Science Conference All Hands Meeting (AHM03)*, Nottingham, UK, 2003.

84. M. Sansom, "Stimulating Simulated Biology," UK National e-Science Centre BioSim-Grid Project, UK, 2004.

85. B. Wu, M. Dovey, M. H. Ng, K. Tai, S. Murdock, P. Jeffreys, S. Cox, J. Essex, and M. Sansom, "A Web/Grid Portal Implementation of BioSimGrid: A Biomolecular Simulation Database," in *Proceedings of the International Conference on Information Technology: Coding and Computing (ITCC)*, Vol. II, Las Vegas, USA, 2004.

86. R. P. Murray, R. Glen, H. Rzepa, J. Stewart, J. Townsend, E. Willighagen, and Y. Zhang, "A Semantic GRID for Molecular Science," in *Proceedings of the Second UK e-Science Conference All Hands Meeting (AHM03)*, Nottingham, UK, 2003.

87. L. McGuffin, S. Street, S. A. Sorensen, and D. Jones, The genomic threading database, *Bioinformatics*, 20, 131–132 (2004).

88. P. Donachy, T. J. Harmer, R. H. Perrott, J. Johnston, A. McBride, and M. Townsley, "GeneGrid: Grid Based Virtual Bioinformatics Laboratory," in *Proceedings of the Second UK e-Science Conference All Hands Meeting (AHM03)*, Nottingham, UK, 2003.

89. A. Bateman, "Keep it in the e-Family: 8302 Data Sheet Visuals," UK National e-Science Centre, UK, 2004.

90. MCNC, "MCNC's North Carolina Grid Computing Initiative," MCNC Grid Computing & Network Services, North Carolina, USA, 2004.

91. MCNC, "MCNC and IBM to collaborate on First-of-a-kind Computer Grid for Life Sciences: New Grid to Accelerate Drug Discovery and Agricultural Research," MCNC Grid Computing & Network Services and IBM, North Carolina, USA, 2001.

92. MCNC, "Grid Computing To Have $10 Billion Impact on N.C. Economy Through 2010," MCNC Grid Computing & Network Services, e-NC and UNC, North Carolina, USA, 2003.

93. M. Ellisman, Brain imaging research data will be shared in new research network, *NPACI & SDSC On-Line Quart. Sci. Mag.*, 5 (2001).

94. M. Maisel, Biomedical Informatics Research Network to Improve Understanding of Brain Disorders, *NPACI SDSC On-Line Quart. Sci. Maga.*, Vol. 17, 2001.

95. C. Catlett, "The TeraGrid: A Primer," TeraGrid Project, USA, 2002.

96. R. Wilhelmson and D. Reed, "A Report on Plans for a TeraGrid," in *Proceedings of the 18th International Conference on IIPS (18IIPS)*, Orlando, FL, USA, 2002.

97. T. T. Wee and O. G. Sin, "Asia Pacific BioGRID Initiative," in *Proceedings of the Second ApGrid Core Meeting Phuket*, Taipei, Taiwan, 2002.

98. P. T. Cheok, "Development in Grid Activities Development in Grid Activities in Singapore," in *Proceedings of the Third Pacific Rim Applications and Grid Middleware Assembly (PRAGMA) Workshop*, Fukuoka, Japan, 2003.

99. F. Konishi, T. Yamamoto, A. Fukuzaki, X. Defago, K. Satou, and A. Konagaya, "OBIGrid: A New Computing Platform for Bioinformatics," in *Proceedings of the 13th International Conference on Genome Informatics (GIW 2002)*, Tokyo, Japan, 2002.

100. S. Date, "BioGrid project in Japan: For Accelerating Science and Industry," Department of Bioinformatics Engineering, Osaka University, Japan, 2003.

101. K. Sakharkar, "BioMedGrid (BMG): Singapore Effort to Build Grid Computing Infrastructure for the BioMedical R& D community," Bioinformatics Institute (BII): a member of Agency for Science, Technology And Research (A∗STAR) Biomedical Sciences Institutes, Matrix, Singapore, 2003.

102. S. Date, "An Application of Grid Technology to Medical Data Analysis," Department of Information Systems Engineering, Osaka University, Japan, 2004.

103. K. Ichikawa, S. Date, Y. M. Mastumoto, and S. Shimojo, "A Grid-enabled System for Analysis of Brain Function," in *Proceedings of the Third IEEE/ACM International Symposium on Cluster Computing and the Grid (CCGrid 2003)*, Tokyo, Japan, 2003.

104. D. Braue, Grid Speed Analysis of Genomic Heritage, *Aust. Life Sci.*, 9, 10 (2004).

105. N. C. I., "caBIG: Cancer Biomedical Informatics Grid," National Cancer Institute, USA, 2004.

106. ENTROPIA, "The Scripps Research Institute and Entropia Fight AIDS at Home: PC Grid Project Successfully Completes First Phase," Entropia, Inc, 2003.

107. UD, "GRID MP Solutions: A Comprehensive Suite for Creating a Dynamic IT Infrastructure," United Devices (UD), Texas, USA, 2004.

108. UD, "Life Sciences Solutions: Discovery, Clinical, Sales & Marketing," United Devices (UD), Texas, USA, 2004.

109. UD, "The University of Oxford: Intel and United Devices Team Up to Speed Cancer Research," United Devices (UD), Texas, USA, 2004.

110. UD, "Supporting Biodefense by Speeding Development of Countermeasures," United Devices (UD), Texas, USA, 2003.

111. UD, "U.S. Department of Defense: Unprecedented Pre-Clinical Research Acceleration to Find an Anthrax Treatment," United Devices (UD), Texas, USA, 2004.

112. IBM, "IBM Life Sciences Solutions: Smallpox Research Grid Project," IBM, 2003.

113. UD, "Accelerating the Discovery of a Smallpox Cure," United Devices (UD), Texas, USA, 2003.

114. PRAGMA, "Collaboration Overview," Pacific RIM Applications and Grid Middleware Assembly (PRAGMA), 2003.

115. ENTROPIA, "ENTROPIA and Cambridge Crystallographic Data Centre Launch: Grid Computing Partnership to Accelerate Virtual Screening," Entropia, Inc. and Cambridge Crystallographic Data Centre (CCDC), 2002.

116. G. Aloisio, "BIG-Biomedical Imaging Grid Project," The International Summer School on Grid Computing, Vico Equense, Naples, Italy, 2003.

117. R. Buyya, S. Date, Y. Mizuno-Matsumoto, S. Venugopal, and D. Abramson, "Composition and On Demand Deployment of Distributed Brain Activity Analysis Application on Global Grids," in *Proceedings of the International Conference on High Performance Computing (HiPC 2003)*, Hyderabad, India, 2003.

118. R. Buyya, S. Date, Y. Mizuno-Matsumoto, S. Venugopal, and D. Abramson, "Economic and On Demand Brain Activity Analysis on Global Grids," University of Melbourne, Melbourne, Australia, 2003.

119. R. Baxter, H. N. Chue, M. Parsons, R. Baldock, B. Hill, and J. Sharpe, "3D OPT Microscopy Grid — Bringing the Grid to the Biomedical Workbench," in *Proceedings of the SUN High Performance Computing (HPC) Consortium*, Baltimore, Maryland, 2003.

120. R. Baxter, N. C. Hong, R. Baldock, B. Hill, and J. Sharpe, "Bringing the Grid to the Biomedical Workbench," in *Proceedings of the 11th IEEE International Symposium on High Performance Distributed Computing (HPDC-11)*, Edinburgh, Scotland, 2002.

121. S. Benkner, G. Engelbrecht, W. Backfrieder, G. Berti, J. Fingberg, G. Kohring, J. G. Schmidt, S.E. Middleton, D. Jones, and J. Fenner, "Numerical Simulation for eHealth: Grid-enabled Medical Simulation Services," in *Proceedings of Parallel Computing 2003 (PARCO2003)*, Dresden, Germany, 2003.

122. J. M. Brooke, P. V. Coveney, J. Harting, S. Jha, M. S. Pickles, R. L. Pinning, and R. A. Porter, "Computational Steering in RealityGrid," in *Proceedings of the Second UK e-Science Conference All Hands Meeting (AHM03)*, Nottingham, UK, 2003.

123. GO, "3D OPT Microscopy Grid: Bringing the Grid to the Biomedical workbench," Grid Outreach Organization (GO): UK National e-Science Centre for 3D OPT Microscopy Grid, UK, 2002.

124. IBM, "IBM Life Sciences Solutions: North Carolina Bioinformatics Grid links Genomic, Proteomic and Related Data to Accelerate the Pace of Genomic Research," IBM, 2003.

125. N. W. John, "iX-Grid: Integrating Emerging Grid Components with State-of-the-Art Medical Visualization and Image Processing Software," E-Science North West (ESNW), UK, 2003.

126. NeSC, "IBM's Blue Dwarf Arrives," *NeSC Newslett.*, Vol. 5, 2003.

127. RUGBI, "Genomics and Medical Innovations," Realization and Use of a Grid for Biocomputing (RUGBI), project 2002.

128. S. Shimojo, "BioGrid Project: Construction of a Super Computer Network," Osaka University, Japan, 2003.

■■■■■ **CHAPTER 21**

Parallel Algorithms for Bioinformatics

SHAHID H. BOKHARI and JON R. SAUER

21.1 INTRODUCTION

The end of the 20th century saw a great surge in the applications of computing to biology. As we move into the 21st century, bioinformatics is well established as one of the leading areas of scientific endeavor.

Bioinformatics is concerned with the computational study, analysis, and design of the essential materials that life is composed of. As such, it is a subject whose importance is appreciated by all. Developments in this field could result in cures for many of the diseases that affect humans, assuage the impacts of aging, provide the means to protect the fragile biosphere that we inhabit, and lead the way toward the establishment of an environment in which all species coexist harmoniously.

The application of computation to biology became possible only after biology itself had evolved to the point where the structure and behavior of organisms could be quantified. Certainly, the discovery of DNA structure and its coding mechanism followed by the understanding of the roles of DNA and RNA in the production of proteins were landmark events in this regard. The study of *what* the various coding mechanisms for different constituents of living matter are, and *how* these codes determine the characteristics of organisms, is a complex field. Currently, we have barely been able to find the sequences for a few individuals each of a small number of species. The goal of unambiguously recording the code for every individual belonging to even a small population, with a restricted budget and within a reasonable amount of time is at least 10 years from realization. Yet, this goal must be attained if we are to embark on a comprehensive study of how the code of life influences the structure and behavior of living things.

21.1.1 The Computational Challenge of Bioinformatics

The human genome is approximately 3×10^9 bases spread over 23 pairs of chromosomes. Merely storing, in a form that permits easy retrieval, the genomes of the

Parallel Computing for Bioinformatics and Computational Biology, Edited by Albert Y. Zomaya
Copyright © 2006 John Wiley & Sons, Inc.

inhabitants of a small city would sorely tax the capabilities of our largest computer systems. Beyond mere storage, the computational burden of assembling and analyzing genomes would be enormous. Moving further afield, the problem of correlating this set of genomes against a set of observable properties (the genotype–phenotype mapping problem) would have, in its general form, computational requirements that could not be satisfied by current technology even if the raw data were available.

The previous paragraph establishes the need for massive amounts of computational power for solving worthwhile bioinformatic problems. Such power is only achievable through parallelism, providing the motivation for this volume and, in particular, this chapter.

We have four main objectives:

1. To describe the general characteristics of some important classes of bioinformatic computation and to show how these characteristics influence the development of algorithms, especially parallel algorithms.
2. To demonstrate that the architecture and programming models used in traditional parallel computers constrain programmer productivity and hardware utilization and thus yield a poor return on investment.
3. To introduce the revolutionary Cray Multithreaded Architecture (MTA), which has been called the "world's most interesting computer," [1]. The philosophy behind this architecture is sketched and the way in which it provides an easy to program platform for high-performance computing described through examples.
4. To establish the relevance of the MTA to bioinformatic computing by reporting on our experiences with a set of representative problems.

21.1.2 Representative Bioinformatic Algorithms

Over the past 5 years, we have implemented on the MTA, algorithms for

(1) Exact string matching;
(2) Approximate string matching;
(3) Molecular dynamics; and
(4) DNA sequencing.

String matching problems (1) and (2) are classical topics from bioinformatics. We show that algorithms for these problems can easily be implemented on the MTA to yield excellent performance. The codes for these algorithms are not significantly different from serial codes and are easy to comprehend. Finetuning of these codes requires some attention to the structure of the problem and to the MTA architecture but can, however, be done with very little disruption to the code.

In the case of molecular dynamics (3) we report our experience in porting an existing C code of about 14,000 lines involving heavy use of fast fourier transforms and other numerical techniques. This port took 3 months and required careful optimization for high utilization.

The DNA sequencing algorithm (4) was developed from the scratch for an ultrafast silicon-based nanosequencer. This is a graph-theoretic algorithm that also incorporates a concurrently accessed hashed data structure.

Taken together, these four algorithms span several key areas of bioinformatic computing. Successful implementation of these algorithms on the MTA demonstrates the relevance of its architecture to the field of bioinformatic computing.

21.2 PARALLEL COMPUTER ARCHITECTURE

21.2.1 The State of Parallel Computing

Although parallel computing has been an area of vigorous research and development for nearly half a century, truly general-purpose parallel computing remains an elusive goal. In the majority of cases, very careful programming and a good knowledge of the target computer's architecture are needed to achieve even modest performance. This discourages practitioners, for example, bioinformaticians, from exploring parallel computing and limits the field to experts, researchers, and academicians. An inordinate amount of effort is required to parallelize an algorithm and the achieved performance is often poor compared with the theoretical peak. Applications that are successfully parallelized are often "embarrassingly parallel," that is, can trivially be split up into independent subproblems that can be executed without communicating with each other. Most of the worthwhile problems in scientific computing do not fall in this category.

There are a number of reasons for this state of affairs. The architecture of most large-scale parallel computers that are commercially available today is a hybrid. Small clusters (4–16) of CPUs (usually commodity processors) physically share memory, and the clusters themselves are distributed over a high-performance network. Obtaining high utilization from such machines depends on how well the structure of the computation matches (or can be transformed to match) the structure of the machine. The process of transformation may involve partitioning, mapping and reordering of data, as well as reformulation of the computation. These transformational requirements lead to major combinatorial problems that are often more difficult than the actual problem being solved. The programmer is required to have extensive knowledge of the interconnect network, cache hierarchy, arithmetic unit, and other architectural features.

A traditional parallel processor requires large hardware and software investments to obtain adequate utilization. Figure 21.1 depicts the substantial investment in hardware and software that is required in such a machine to obtain a small amount of useful computation. The hardware that carries out the actual computations for the target program has to be augmented with additional hardware and software to enhance performance. The augmentation would include, for example, memory caches, high-speed interconnect, synchronization mechanisms, instruction pipelines, and pipelined arithmetic units. Considerable investment may be needed in the areas of compilers, operating systems, and analysis tools. Parallel programming platforms such as PVM

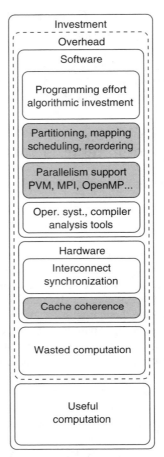

Figure 21.1 A traditional parallel processor. Large investments in hardware and software yield a small fraction of useful computation. The block labeled "wasted computation" represents the time processors are idle, waiting for memory accesses or communications.

(www.csm.ornl.gov/pvm), MPI (www.mcs.anl.gov/mpi), and OpenMP (www.openmp.org) constitute part of the software overhead. The programmer needs to invest considerable effort in developing his program, including rethinking algorithms and, of course, the difficult issues of partitioning, mapping, and scheduling. Despite this effort, the utilization achieved by such processors is often low; indeed, there are large classes of problems for which these machines are considered unsuitable.

21.2.2 The Cray MTA

The Cray MTA is a revolutionary parallel computer that has been under development for over a decade. At the present time several versions of this machine are installed in research institutes around the world. The original MTA was installed at San Diego Supercomputing Center (www.sdsc.edu) but was decommissioned in 2001. The current model, the MTA-2, is installed at the Electronic Navigation Research Institute in Japan (www.enri.go.jp) and the Naval Research Laboratory in Washington (www.cmf.nrl.navy.mil). The latter machine has 40 processors and 160 GB memory.

The MTA breaks away from the traditional styles of implementing parallel processors in several respects. The machine is based on a custom designed processor that has zero-overhead switching between threads. The memory has tag bits that permit fine-grained synchronization at the word level. The entire memory is uniformly accessible from all processors. A sophisticated compiler and run-time environment takes over from the programmer the task of spawning, synchronizing, and allocating work to threads. The end result is that the user sees a familiar Fortran, C, or C++ programming environment into which the implementation details of parallelism intrude very occasionally, if at all. The MTA thus permits the programmer to be highly productive without having to be concerned with details of the parallel architecture. The MTA philosophy is shown in Figure 21.2 and can be compared with the traditional parallel processor of Figure 21.1.

A useful collection of technical papers on the MTA is available at www.cray.com/products/programs/mta_2/. Two well-known papers are [2, 3]. A conceptual view of a multiprocessor MTA is given in Figure 21.3. Subsequently, we present a brief overview of the key features of the MTA that is based in part on Refs. [4, 5].

21.2.2.1 *Zero-Overhead Thread Switching*

At the heart of the MTA is special-purpose hardware to hold the state of threads. There are 128 of these *streams* per processor; each can hold the state[1] of one thread. The processor is designed to execute one instruction from a different stream on each clock tick. A stream holding a thread that is blocked, for example, waiting for a word from memory, will cause no overhead as the processor will ignore it in favor of some other ready stream.

21.2.2.2 *Pipelined Processors*

Each processor in the MTA has a 21-stage pipeline. Thus 21 of the 128 streams must hold ready threads at all times to keep the processor fully utilized, as one instruction is executed from a different stream at each clock tick. This target is easy to achieve because most large computational problems have far more than 21-way parallelism.

21.2.2.3 *Flat-Shared Memory*

The MTA has 64-bit words, the addresses of which are deliberately scrambled by hardware to scatter them across memory banks [3]. Delays in accessing memory locations, because of long memory cycles or network congestion, are overcome by having multiple accesses outstanding at any one time. The stream hardware makes this possible with little overhead so that threads whose memory accesses cannot be satisfied at a particular instant are ignored in favor

---

[1] State includes registers, condition codes, program counter, and so on.

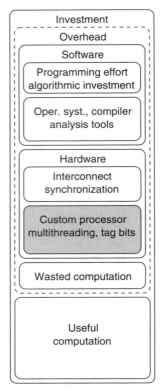

Figure 21.2   The Cray MTA philosophy. Investment in a custom processor, tagged memory, and a sophisticated compiler reduces the programmer's burden and achieves a higher fraction of useful computation. Shaded blocks indicate the differences between the two approaches.

of those whose operands are available. As a result of this revolutionary feature, the memory has no locality, and no issues of partitioning data or mapping memory arise on this machine. The only performance issue that has ordinarily to be considered by the programmer with regard to memory is that of "hotspotting", that is, the concentration of accesses to a single memory location by multiple threads. As we shall show later in this chapter, very simple techniques can be used to minimize the impact of hotspotting.

21.2.2.4   Extremely Fine-Grained Synchronization   Each word of memory has an associated *full/empty* tag bit. A memory location may be written or read using ordinary loads and stores, as in conventional machines. These operations may also be under the control of the full/empty bit. The "read-when-full, then set-empty" (y=readfe(x)) operation automatically reads data from location x only after that location's full/empty bit is set *full*. The full/empty bit is automatically set to *empty*

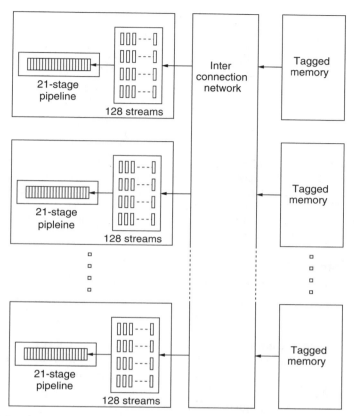

Figure 21.3 A conceptual view of a multiprocessor MTA. Each processor has a 21-stage pipeline, each stage of which can execute an instruction from a different thread. The states of threads are stored in special hardware called "streams" that allow *zero-overhead* switching between different threads. A thread that is blocked (e.g., waiting for a word from memory or for a synchronization event) causes no overhead as the processor switches over to another ready thread. To obtain high utilization, the pipeline must be kept as full as possible. This is made easy by the comparatively large number of streams. The entire memory is uniformly accessible from all processors and, other than hotspotting (discussed in Section 21.2.2.3), *no* locality issues arise on this machine.

during the read operation. If the full/empty bit is not set when a readfe() is executed, the corresponding thread suspends (with very low overhead, its state being saved in the stream hardware) and is later retried. It resumes when the read operation has completed. The writeef() writeef ("wait-until-empty then write-and-set-full") operation is the complement of readfe(). The readfe(), writeef(), and similar operations that manipulate the full/empty tag bits are called *intrinsics* and compile into *individual* machine instructions. Thus they allow very fine-grained synchronization.

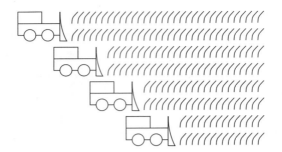

Figure 21.4 A traditional parallel processor behaves like a team of harvesters sweeping through a large field. This team will perform well if the field is uniform and rectangular. Considerable efficiency is lost if the field has variations in density or irregular shape. A significant proportion of the resources of such a processor (and a sizable amount of the time of the programmer) is consumed by the issues of data partitioning, reordering, mapping, interprocessor communications, and so on.

21.2.2.5 An Analogy The custom-designed processors of the MTA give it great flexibility in attacking parallel problems. This flexibility relieves the programmer of most of the burdens of explicit parallel programming, as described by the analogies of Figures 21.4 and 21.5.

21.2.2.6 A Programming Example A simple example demonstrates the power of the MTA hardware–software combination. In the following code fragment we compare two arrays to find the number of locations in which they differ and save the contents of the locations that differ in a third array. The listing given below is an edited version of the output of the MTA CANAL (Compiler ANAlysis) tool. The "P" annotation indicates that the compiler was able to detect the parallelism in this code. The "$" indicates that the compiler employed full/empty bits to safely perform the incrementing of the variable count. The compiler also added code (that is not visible to the programmer) to efficiently compute the cumulative sum (this process is called "reduction"). Although the MTA uses multithreading, the programmer does not have to be concerned with the details of spawning, scheduling, synchronizing, and stopping thread. These details are handled by the compiler, the runtime system, and the hardware.

```
|        for(i=0; i<n; i++){
|P          if(string1[i] != string2[i]){
|P              place[i] = string2[i];
|P:$            count++;
|** reduction moved out of 1 loop
|            }
|            else{
|P              place[i] = 0;
|            }
|        }
|
```

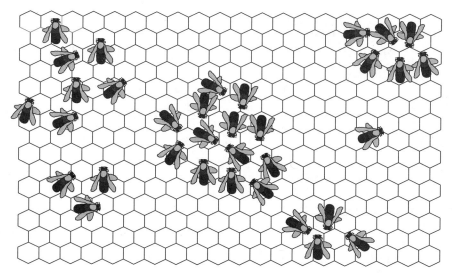

Figure 21.5 The MTA may be viewed as a swarm of bees attending to the duties of a beehive. The bees move to wherever there is work to be done and, when a task is completed, quickly move on to the next task. The "streams" of the MTA divide the computational power of the machine into such small, agile workers. These relieve the programmer of the onerous burdens of explicit parallel programming.

The above code fragment is from a program that uses static arrays. If dynamic arrays (allocated, e.g., with malloc) had been used in the main program and the code above had been in a function with array addresses passed to it, the compiler would have had no way of knowing if these would overlap at run time (and thereby make parallel execution impossible). We could use the following pragma in the function to reassure the compiler that there would be no overlap.

```
#pragma mta noalias *string1, *string2, *place
```

This is a signal to the MTA compiler that would be ignored by other compilers. The code shown above is thus completely portable between the MTA and conventional machines.

21.3 BIOINFORMATICS ALGORITHMS ON THE CRAY MTA SYSTEM

21.3.1 Approximate String Matching

The problem of finding an approximate match between two DNA sequences is very central to bioinformatic computing. The objective in this case is to compare two strings that are not identical to determine the degree of similarity. The motivations and overall relevance of this problem are covered in detail in the texts by Gusfield

[6, Chapter 11] and Pevzner [7, Chapter 6]. In the following, we will concentrate on parallelization issues related to this problem in the context of the Cray MTA.

When dynamic programming is used to find the approximate matching of a pattern P against text T, the essential step is to update a matrix according to the following recurrence:

$$D(i,j) = \min\,(D(i-1,j)+1,\ D(i,j-1)+1,$$

$$D(i-1,j-1) + \text{if } (P(i) \neq T(i)) \text{ then } 1 \text{ else } 0)$$

The updating of matrix D may be done in row, column, or antidiagonal (wavefront) order as shown in Figure 21.6. Wavefront order is usually the most efficient. The following code fragment shows the conventional way of expressing this update in row-order.

```
for (i=1; i<=n; i++) {
   int j;
   for(j=1; j<=n ; j++){
PS:w    D[i][j]=MIN(MIN(D[i-1][j]+1,D[i][j-1]+1),
                       D[i-1][j-1]+(P[i]!=T[j]));
   }
}
```

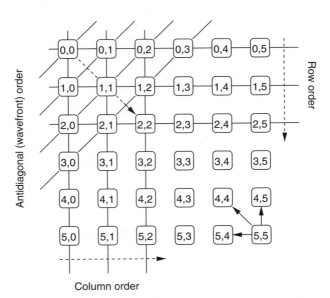

Figure 21.6 The matrix used for dynamic programming may be updated in row, column, or antidiagonal (wavefront) order (dashed arrows). Each entry in the matrix depends on three neighbors, as exemplified for cell [5,5].

Although we have expressed the update using a conventional rectangular loop, the compiler is able to detect that wavefronting is possible. This is indicated by the "w" in the CANAL annotation above. It parallelizes the outer loop and inserts synchronization operations in the inner loop so that wavefronting is effected.

A detailed study of the various tradeoffs in dynamic programming for approximate string matching appears in [5], which describes how explicit use of the full/empty tag bits can lead to excellent scaling. The following is a carefully optimized row-order loop adapted from that paper. The operation readff(x) causes a thread to wait until the tag bit of x is set, read the value of x, and then leave the tag bit set. The matrix D is initialized to have all tag bits clear, except for the zeroth row and column.

```
#pragma mta assert parallel
for (i=1; i<=n; i++) {
    int j, tempP;
    tempP = P[i];
    for(j=1; j <= n ; j++){
        int vert, horiz, diag, min1, min2;
        vert  = readff(&D[i-1][j])+1;
        diag  = readff(&D[i-1][j-1])+
                    (tempP!=T[j]);
        min1  = MIN(diag, vert);
        horiz = readff(&D[i][j-1])+1;
        min2  = MIN(min1,horiz);
        writeef(&D[i][j], min2);
    }
}
```

The declaration of variables only inside the scope in which they are used, in addition to being good programming practice, makes the compiler's task easier as these variables can be made local to a thread without having to investigate if they are used elsewhere. Similarly, the use of the scratch variable tempP eliminates the hotspotting caused by repeated access to P[i] by multiple threads.

Simple code transformations of the type shown above are usually enough to achieve very good performance on the MTA. To keep the code portable for purposes of program development, debugging and testing, we use header files that define the MTA-specific intrinsics readff(), writeef(), and so on, as identity operations for non-MTA platforms.

21.3.2 Molecular Dynamics

Our interest in molecular dynamics arises because of our involvement in the design of a silicon-based nanosequencer [8] that is expected to directly sense the bases of a single-stranded DNA string that passes through it. Molecular dynamic analysis is needed to study the behavior of DNA molecules in such a nanosequencer. The code used for this analysis, SIMU-MD [9] has heavy requirements for floating point computations.

At the same time its data are "unstructured", that is, they cannot be conveniently stored in matrix data structures that permit easy parallel or vector processing. This code is thus an ideal candidate for porting to the MTA because of that machine's insensitivity to data locality and memory access patterns. This code is about 14,000 lines of C and took 3 months to port to the MTA. The final result was a highly optimized MTA code that obtained very good hardware utilization [4].

When carrying out molecular dynamics computations, various types of interatomic forces need to be analyzed. For "short-range" forces it is sufficient to consider the influence of an atom on other atoms only within a cutoff radius r_c. This is because short-range interatomic forces decay very rapidly with distance. The forces on a set of atoms occupying a cuboid of space are analyzed by dividing up the cuboid into cells and storing the locations of atoms as a linked list associated with each cell. This is illustrated in Figure 21.7 (for simplicity, this figure shows a two-dimensional domain). For an atom i located in cell $c[i]$ we need to evaluate the interaction between i and all other atoms in $c[i]$ as well as all atoms in the *cell neighborhood* $n[c[i]]$. The cell neighborhood is determined by the cutoff radius r_c. To examine all atoms in a neighborhood cell we need to traverse the corresponding linked list, considering only those atoms that lie within distance r_c of atom i. The end result is that an elaborate series of indirections is required to evaluate the forces on a single atom. This is an excellent example of the type of "unstructured" problem the MTA excels at, as its

$n[c[i]]$

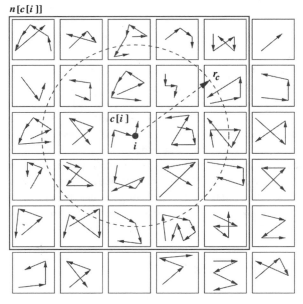

Figure 21.7   Cell list data structure for SIMU-MD. To evaluate the forces at atom i, we examine all atoms in the linked list of the cell $c[i]$ to which i belongs. We also need to examine all cells in $n[c[i]]$, the cell, neighborhood of $c[i]$ (solid square). We traverse the linked list in each cell of $n[c[i]]$ and only consider the atoms within cutoff radius r_c (dashed circle).

flat and uniformly accessible memory does not require the atom data structure to be partitioned or mapped in any way. Furthermore, because of the MTA's insensitivity to access patterns, there is no difficulty in concurrently updating several hundred atoms in arbitrary order, provided simple rules of exclusive access are followed.

As an example of careful performance tuning for SIMU-MD, consider the CANAL output for the function pme_R. This implements the "particle mesh Ewald reciprocal", technique, complete details of which are irrelevant to the present discussion.

```
|//Original Code                         |//Transformed code
|void pme_R(double *PECR,                |void pme_R(double *PECR,
|           double **VCR){               |           double **VCR){
|double uC, vC ...                       |double //shadow variables:
|                                        |   pecr=0.0,
|   ...                                  |   vcr00=0.0,vcr01=0.0,vcr02=0.0,
|   *PECR=0.0;                           |   vcr11=0.0,vcr12=0.0,vcr22=0.0;
|   for(i=0; i < 3; ++i)                 |
|     for(j=i; j < 3; ++j)               |   #pragma mta assert parallel
|       VCR[i][j]=0.0;                   |   for (mz=1; mz<=..; ++mz){
|   ...                                  |   #pragma mta assert parallel
|   for(mz=0; mz<=..; ++mz){             |     for (my=..; my<=..; ++my){
|     for(my=..; my<=..; ++my){          |       for (mx=..; mx<=..; ++mx){
|       for(mx=..; mx<=..; ++mx){        |       //local variables:
|                                        |       double uC, vC ...
|         uC = ...                       |pp-    uC = ..
|         vC = ...                       |pp-    vC = ..
|SSS      *PECR += uC;                   |pp-:$ pecr += uC;
|SSS      VCR[0][0] += uC*(vC*..);       |** reduction moved out of 3 loops
|SSS      VCR[1][1] += uC*(vC*..);       |pp-:$    vcr00 += uC*(vC*..);
|           ...                          |** reduction moved out of 3 loops
|SSS      VCR[1][2] += uC*(vC*..);       |pp-:$    vcr11 += uC*(vC*..);
|                                        |** reduction moved out of 3 loops
|     }                                  |        ...
|   }                                    |pp-:$ vcr12 += uC*(vC*..);
| }                                      |** reduction moved out of 3 loops
|}                                       |       }
                                         |     }
                                         |   }
                                         |   *PECR = pecr;
                                         |   VCR[0][0] = vcr00;
                                         |   VCR[1][1] = vcr11;
                                         |   ...
                                         |   VCR[1][2] = vcr12;
                                         |}
```

As seen from the original code on the left, none of the three triply nested loops is parallelized automatically by the compiler because the addresses of the arrays PECR and VCR are passed as pointers. The compiler cannot establish if the arrays overlap and thus cannot guarantee that parallelization of these loops would be provably safe. The annotation "SSS" indicates that these loops are executed serially.

A number of interesting transformations are performed to obtain the code on the right. The rules followed in carrying out these transformations are as follows.

Assure Compiler that Loop is Parallelizable   This is done via the `#pragma mta assert parallel` compiler directives after manual inspection reveals that there are no dependencies or overlaps.

Do not Overparallelize   The parallel assertion is applied only to the outer two loops as these are enough to saturate the machine, given that $mx = my \approx 100$ in this specific case. Parallelizing the innermost loop would have bogged down the machine as it tried to schedule 10^6 indexes instead of 10^4. The compiler signals via the annotation "pp" that it has parallelized the outer two loops. The lower-case "p" denotes parallelization carried out in response to an assertion, in contrast to the uppercase "P" (encountered in some of the earlier examples), which signals an automatic parallelization. In the annotation "pp-" the final "-" indicates that the innermost loop was not parallelized. The compiler automatically uses the full/empty mechanism to synchronize the updating of `pcr`, `vcr00`, and so on, as indicated by the annotation "$".

Declare Variables within the Appropriate Scope   The declarations of `uC`, `vC`, and so on are moved to the innermost loop, as these scratch variables are not used elsewhere. The compiler creates private copies of these for each thread to improve performance.

Use Local Shadow Variables   The variable `PECR` is shadowed by the local variable `pecr`. Similarly, the small upper triangular matrix `VCR` is shadowed by scalar local variables `vcr00`, and so on. After accumulating values in these local scalars, they are copied back at the end of the function. These shadow scalar variables permit the compiler to allocate private copies of reduction variables (used behind the scenes to speedup accumulation of sums) for each thread. This reduces the need for synchronization, as each thread executes serially, and leads to significant performance improvements. It is only when the inner loops terminate, and the private loop variables have to be accumulated into the final sum, that there is a need for synchronization. This process reduces quite substantially the overhead of synchronization.

21.3.3   DNA Sequencing with Very Long Reads

Recent developments in nanopore technology promise exciting improvements in the speed and cost of DNA sequencing. Ultrafast nanosequencers may soon be able to provide direct "reads" of single-stranded DNA of length 10^5 bases or more. With reads of this length, the process of assembling DNA takes on an entirely new form, and the automated reconstruction of the entire DNA of an organism becomes feasible. Our recent research on this topic [10] describes how the Cray MTA can be used to implement a parallel algorithm for sequencing with very long reads.

The basic idea underlying nanosequencers is to pass a single-stranded DNA (ssDNA) string through a pore that is a few atoms wide in diameter. There are various

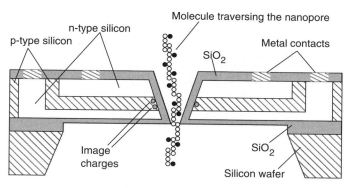

Figure 21.8 A cross-section of the silicon-based nanosequencer [8]. Field effect transistors are fabricated integrally with the nanopore. A single-stranded DNA molecule translocating the nanopore induces image charges in the the silicon that are amplified and transmitted to a computer. Differences in the dipole moments of the bases (A, C, T, or G) allow discrimination between these bases [4].

proposals for discriminating between the bases (i.e., C, T, A, or G). In the silicon-based nanosequencer proposed by Sauer and Van Zeghbroeck [8], bases are detected by sensing the charge on the atoms that pass through, using field-effect transistors embedded in the walls of the pore (Fig. 21.8).

A number of factors complicate the process of reassembling the target DNA from the reads provided by a nanosequencer.

1. It is unlikely that the entire DNA of an organism could pass through (or translocate) a nanopore without breaking. It is expected that reads will be of 10^5 bases in length.
2. The direction of translocation of a specific piece of ssDNA cannot be known.
3. The complementarity of a piece cannot be known.
4. There may be errors of biological or electrical origin in the sensed information.

It is possible to reconstruct the entire DNA of an organism, even under the conditions enumerated earlier. In [10] we demonstrate how a variant of the Eulerian path technique can reconstruct the entire 816394-base sequence of *Mycoplasma pneumoniae* from erroneous randomly sized reads, provided multiple DNA strands are input to the sequencer.

The basic approach is to break all reads into k-mers and then create a histogram of mer frequencies. A threshold frequency f_t is then chosen to reject infrequently occurring erroneous mers and create a deBruijn graph from the remaining. If the resulting graph can be decomposed into exactly four disjoint paths, the reconstruction is a success. If not, the process is repeated with a different k and f_t. A 3D histogram of mer frequencies for a range of f and k is shown in Figure 21.9.

Of immediate interest to us is the process of creating a mer frequency histogram at a fixed value of k, which would correspond to a slice through the surface of Figure 21.9.

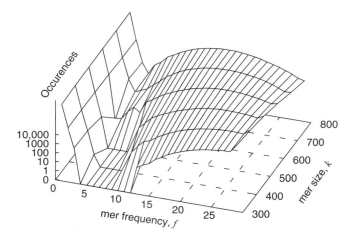

Figure 21.9   A 3D histogram of k-mer frequencies for 80 strands of DNA (160 ssDNA) of *M. pneumoniae*. Each strand is randomly broken up at 20 locations; the probability of errors (indels or mutations) at any base position is 0.0005. As k varies from 300 to 800 in steps of 100, the generated deBruijn graph can unambiguously reconstruct the sequence only at $k = 500$, $f = 5, \ldots, 9$. When k is large, the errors in the bases overlap with too many k-mers, destroying resolution. When k is small, erroneous and nonerroneous k-mers map onto each other. We can always improve the resolution by increasing the number of DNA strands, at the cost of greater time and space usage.

The following code fragment shows how this would be implemented using hashing[2] on the MTA. It is assumed that all reads have been loaded into memory and stored in a long array of bases. As each mer is generated, we check to see if it is in the hash table. If it is not, its position is inserted in the table. If it is already present, the number of occurrences are incremented and so on. The code fragment demonstrates how the full/empty bits of the MTA (described in Section 21.2.2.4) are used to ensure automatic access to a data structure shared across hundreds of threads.

```
insertHashTable(int *Table, int* Occur, int pos){
    // Table holds staring addresses of strings
    // Occur = no. of occurences of corresp. string
    // 'pos' = starting location of string in bases array
    // 'place' is the first hash table probe
    while (true){

        this = readfe(&Table[place]);// Table[place] locked
```

---

[2]We use open addressing with double hashing, as described by Cormen et al. [11, Chapter 11].

```
    if (this == -1){ // empty location -- enter 'pos'
        Occur[place] = 1;
        writeef(&Table[place], pos);  return;
    }

    if (this == pos){
        // 'pos' already there, no need to do anything
        // but must write value back to release lock
        writeef(&Table[place], this);  return;
    }

    if (compareStrings(this, pos) == true){
        // strings pointed to by 'this' & 'pos' match
        // a new occurrence has been found
        Occur[place]++;
        writeef(&Table[place], this);  return;
    }

    writeef(&Table[place], this);
    // failed: release location & compute next place
    ...
    }
}
```

Once the hash table has been constructed, we can compute the total mers and the number whose occurrences are above a threshold as follows.

```
#pragma mta assert parallel
for(i=0; i<n; i++){
    if(Table[i] != -1){
        int_fetch_add(&numEdges,1);
        if (Occur[i] > threshold){
            int_fetch_add(&above,1);
        }
    }
}
```

The well-known int_fetch_add primitive is used to ensure atomic updating of variables shared across multiple threads. The pragma is required to make the compiler parallelize this loop.

21.3.4   Exact String Matching

The naive algorithm for exact string matching is perhaps the simplest algorithm encountered in bioinformatics. However, we have chosen to discuss it at the end of this section because, despite its simplicity, it brings out a deep aspect of parallel processing. Regardless of the power and elegance of a parallel architecture, there are some problems that are simply not amenable to simple solutions. This material is based on Ref. [5].

The main loop of the naive algorithm to match a pattern of length m against a text of length n is easily parallelized on the MTA.

```
#pragma mta assert parallel
   for (i=0; i < n-m+1; i++) {
      int j;
      for(j=0; j < m ; j++){
         if (P[j]!=T[i+j])
            break;
      }
      if (j >= m){
         found++;
         F[int_fetch_add(&Ptr,1)]=i;
      }
   }
```

This implementation gives excellent performance when m is much smaller than n. Its performance deteriorates catastrophically when m becomes large. This is because, although many threads are launched in parallel to search different parts of the text, only one thread can execute the matching for the successful substring. When m is large, the unsuccessful threads quickly die out leaving only one thread to complete the job of checking for this substring. This is clear from Figure 21.10, which shows the performance on the MTA-2 when comparing substrings of length m against the entire DNA sequence of *H. influenzae* with $n = 1.8 \times 10^6$ bases. The naive algorithm shows excellent times up to $m = 10^4$ and a catastrophic increase after that.

We have developed a two-phase algorithm for exact matching that does not suffer from the drawback described earlier. In the first phase this algorithm identifies multiple candidate starting positions. In the second phase the pattern P is equipartitioned into blocks that are tested in parallel. If each block matches the corresponding block of text, the algorithm signals success. As should be expected, the two-phase algorithm has a small constant overhead for small patterns but performs significantly better than the naive algorithm beyond $m = 10^4$.

This final example illustrates that, in certain cases, the structure of the problem requires a more careful solution than might originally be contemplated. This is very similar to the cutting-stock problem in operations research, which deals with the minimization of waste when cutting out various required strips of material from a large roll. Careful choices of layout can reduce the waste considerably and this is standard practice in, for example, the paper industry. However, if the requirement includes one

Time (s)

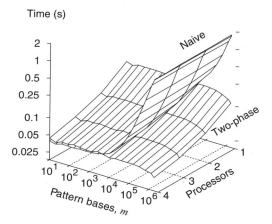

Figure 21.10   MTA-2 runtimes for the naive and two-phase algorithms for exact matching. The text is the DNA sequence of *H. influenzae*, which has 1.8 million bases. The pattern to be tested for is taken from the end of *H. influenzae*.

very long and narrow strip, no amount of optimization will produce a solution without enormous waste unless the decision is made to cut this strip into manageable lengths. This is analogous to what is being done in the two-phase algorithm described earlier.

21.4 SUMMARY

We have discussed parallel algorithms for bioinformatics in the context of the Cray MTA. After presenting our viewpoint on the nature of bioinformatic algorithms, we proceeded to describe the architecture of the MTA, with emphasis on its hardware support for multithreading and its tagged, uniformly accessible memory. We then went on to describe the implementation of several bioinformatic algorithms on this machine. These include the well-known algorithms for exact and approximate string matching and the port of an existing molecular dynamics code. We also described an entirely new algorithm for DNA sequencing with very long reads, which was developed with the MTA as a target architecture.

Our experience with this unusual parallel architecture reveals that it is well suited to the types of problems encountered in bioinformatics. Parallel algorithms may be implemented to this machine with a minimum of rewriting or reorganization. Finetuning of code requires only a basic understanding of the architecture and of the behavior of the tagged memory. The issues of data reorganization, partitioning, scheduling, mapping, and so on, which are central to conventional parallel processors, are nonexistent on this machine.

The MTA is thus the ideal machine for a rapidly advancing field like bioinformatics, where algorithm development and coding must charge ahead in tandem. This machine permits the quick evaluation of new algorithmic ideas with small investments of time and effort. Indeed, that is how most of the algorithms described in this chapter were developed. We feel that the MTA, its successor machines, and related architectures will provide a path toward the goal of a truly general-purpose parallel architecture that combines high performance with increased programmer productivity.

There are numerous opportunities for further research and development in bioinformatics on the MTA. Within the context of approximate string matching, we would like to explore how to efficiently implement an algorithm with less than quadratic space requirements. For molecular dynamics with SIMU-MD, it would be of great interest to explore performance scaling on larger configurations of the MTA. Finally, for the DNA sequencing algorithm, the next objectives are extensions to multichromosomal organisms with longer genomes. The ultimate objective in this case is a simulation of the sequencing of the entire human genome.

ACKNOWLEDGMENTS

We are grateful to Bracy Elton, Simon Kahan, John Feo, and our other colleagues at Cray for many useful discussions over the past 7 years that have contributed significantly to our work on the Cray MTA system. We acknowledge the unceasing efforts of Dick Russell in maintaining our access to the MTA. We are indebted to Jeff Schloss for his encouragement of our sequencing and alignment work. We thank Albert Zomaya for his patience in tolerating many delays in the delivery of this chapter. We affectionately recall the many long and helpful discussions with the late Harry Jordan, who was the primary motivating force behind our involvement with the MTA. This work was supported by the National Institutes of Health, Grant Number HG03588-01. Access to the MTA was provided by Cray Inc., Cray (Japan) Inc., and the Electronic Navigation Research Institute (ENRI), Japan.

REFERENCES

1. A. Orlowski, World's most interesting computer in jeopardy, *The Register*, 12 March 2002. www.theregister.co.uk/2002/03/12/worlds_most_interesting_computer.

2. G. Alverson, R. Alverson, D. Callahan, B. Koblenz, A. Porterfield, and B. Smith, Exploiting heterogeneous parallelism on a multithreaded multiprocessor, in *Proceedings of the Sixth International Conference on Supercomputing*, ACM Press, 1992, pp. 188–197.

3. R. Alverson, D. Callahan, D. Cummings, B. Koblenz, A. Porterfield, and B. Smith, The Tera computer system, in *Proceedings of the Fourth International Conference on Supercomputing*, ACM Press, 1990, pp. 1–6.

4. S. H. Bokhari, M. A. Glaser, H. F. Jordan, Y. Lansac, J. R. Sauer, and B. V. Zeghbroeck, Parallelizing a DNA simulation code for the Cray MTA-2, in *Proceedings of the IEEE Computer Society Bioinformatics Conference*, 2002, pp. 291–302.

5. S. H. Bokhari and J. R. Sauer, Sequence alignment on the Cray MTA-2, *Concurr. Comput. Prac. Exp.*, 16, 823–839 (2004).

6. D. Gusfield, *Algorithms on Strings, Trees, and Sequences*, Cambridge University Press, 1997.

7. P. A. Pevzner, *Computational Molecular Biology — An Algorithmic Approach*, The MIT Press, 2000.

8. J. R. Sauer and B. Van Zeghbroeck, Ultra-fast nucleic acid sequencing device and a method for making and using the same, 2002, US Patent No. 6,413,792.

9. M. Glaser, Atomistic Simulation and Modeling of Smectic Liquid Crystals, in P. Pasini and C. Zannoni, Eds., *Advances in the Computer Simulations of Liquid Crystals*, Kluwer Academic Publishers, Dordrecht, 1999, pp. 263–331.

10. S. H. Bokhari and J. R. Sauer, A parallel path decomposition algorithm for DNA sequencing with nanopores, *Bioinformatics*, 21(7), 889–896 (2005).

11. T. H. Cormen, C. E. Leiserson, R. R. Rivest, and C. Stein, *Introduction to Algorithms*, 2nd ed., MIT Press, 2001.

CHAPTER 22

Cluster and Grid Infrastructure for Computational Chemistry and Biochemistry

KIM K. BALDRIDGE, WIBKE SUDHOLT, JERRY P. GREENBERG,
CELINE AMOREIRA, YOHANN POTIER, ILKAY ALTINTAS,
ADAM BIRNBAUM, DAVID ABRAMSON, COLIN ENTICOTT,
and SLAVISA GARIC

Many computational chemists requiring significant and relatively flexible resources have turned to parallel clusters to solve increasingly complex problems. Evolving hardware technology and grid resources present new opportunities for chemistry and biology, yet introduce new complexity related to grid, web, and computational difficulties. Here, we describe our experience in using the GAMESS quantum chemistry program on clusters and our utilization of evolving portal, grid, and workflow technologies to solve problems that cannot be solved on individual machines.

22.1 INTRODUCTION

Computational chemists tend to require multiple types of facilities based on the rather large diversity of chemical problems studied, and the interoperability of resources sought, to carry out increasingly complex computational science experiments. The complexity of the associated computational chemistry software forces chemists to focus on advanced high-performance computing methodologies to exploit rapidly changing architectures. In particular, many groups have long recognized the importance of parallel computers in increasing the range of chemical systems that can be treated by quantum mechanical techniques. In the computational chemistry community, for example, a code called *GAMESS* (general atomic and molecular electronic structure system) [1, 2] has been the focus of many years of community code development. GAMESS has evolved over the years into a highly reputable code

Parallel Computing for Bioinformatics and Computational Biology, Edited by Albert Y. Zomaya
Copyright © 2006 John Wiley & Sons, Inc.

for accurate representations of molecular structure and properties through quantum mechanical techniques. In addition, much effort has gone into providing optimal performance on cutting-edge, high-end architectures, and more recently, it has been central to the development of robust and user-friendly working environments.

On the basis of our experiences from a hard science background and a significant information technology (IT) depth, we believe that the effective use of such infrastructures is limited by (1) rapid pace of technological change in IT infrastructure, which requires users to constantly learn new terminology and tools, (2) lack of flexibility from system components that inhibit exploratory analysis by the end users, (3) IT-oriented abstractions that are difficult for domain scientists to work with, and (4) communication optimization between the computer science, physical science, and life science communities.

Computational infrastructure technology has been rapidly evolving over the past few years: Hardware resources have been moving away from traditional high-end supercomputers and turning toward commodity clusters, remote grid computing, and even desktop grid systems. In addition, new large-scale data-management systems and services-based software infrastructures are significantly enabling the management of software on such architectures. User portals, applications, and environments in which end users directly interact have been effective at shielding the end user from the changing technologies by providing a domain-specific layer, which provides stable interfaces for users, while adapting to new technologies under covers.

What we describe in this contribution are our experiences as we have evolved the GAMESS computational chemistry community of users through new opportunities offered by the cluster and grid revolution, including (1) standard running of computations on simple cluster computers, including the evolution in node quality, (2) the use of portal technology for ease of execution on cluster architectures, (3) the employment of efficient grid-execution systems for large-scale computing, and (4) exploitation of middleware technology for running complex computational experiments.

22.2   GAMESS EXECUTION ON CLUSTERS

In the GAMESS code, parallelism is programmed through the distributed data interface (DDI) [3] layer. Beneath the DDI layer are calls to sockets, MPI [4], or shared memory. On Linux clusters, GAMESS typically uses sockets for communication between the processors. A separate program starts two GAMESS processes on each host, which then establish socket communication between themselves. The "compute processes" do almost all the work. The "data server" processes control shared memory distributed over all the hosts and store and retrieve data when requested by the compute processes. At present, only a limited number of higher order quantum chemistry computational methods use the distributed memory facilities. All GAMESS processes run on the compute nodes. The "master" node (node 0) handles all user input and output tasks, in addition to contributing to the computational tasks that all other compute server processes perform.

The conventional means of running GAMESS on clusters has been to log on to a cluster front end directly and to run shell scripts provided for GAMESS installation and execution. Typically, the shell scripts are tailored to the particular platform being used, with variations in such system-dependent considerations as parallel APIs (e.g., sockets, MPI) and queuing systems (PBS [5] and SGE [6]). This poses somewhat of a burden on users who want to solve their computational chemistry problems of interest and are not necessarily concerned with system architecture. Subsequently, we will describe our efforts to provide a layer of abstraction for users from the computational resource.

Another difficulty facing users and cluster managers is the system environment, which may vary widely between clusters. For a cluster with N hosts, there are N copies of the operating system to manage. Furthermore, each host must be updated with items such as new software, security patches, and account information. If the system is not maintained with a consistent set of software on each host, it may become unstable and endanger long running calculations. The ROCKS cluster-management system [7] provides a means to deploy a cluster in a short period of time and to maintain consistency between all the nodes. ROCKS provides not only a solution for maintaining and updating Linux clusters but also provides a common interface for the user regardless of cluster hardware. In terms of a GAMESS installation, deployment to a ROCKS cluster involves minimal, if any, reconfiguration.

GAMESS performance is quite good on cluster architectures, providing scaling close to linearity for large molecular systems. Quantum codes, in general, have many different task types, which are invoked depending on the specifics of the requested computation. These tasks range from being highly serial to fairly parallel, as well as requiring anywhere from moderate to extreme memory and disk resources. Thus, various parts of the code will have different levels of performance characteristics. An example would be the comparison of the matrix multiplication type steps to the calculation/processing of the atomic orbital integrals. As such, the move to parallel cluster architectures has been very beneficial to the performance of GAMESS, and through careful algorithmic enhancements such as those discussed earlier, we have been able to see significant scaling improvements.

Figure 22.1a shows the performance of GAMESS across a wide variety of platforms, from tightly coupled supercomputers such as SDSC-Blue Horizon to the large shared-memory SDSC-SUNHPC platform, to the TERA-InCore platform, and to clusters of computers (Meteor = Pentium III based and Compaq = Alpha based). In fact, the Alpha cluster is one of the better platforms in terms of overall performance, as it retains high efficiencies (>95%) with increasing nodes. We should also note that the TERA performance is artificially high because of the incompleteness of the computation that is enabled in GAMESS for that platform. In fact, the clusters are, in general, quite competitive to the large supercomputer infrastructures, with essentially linear performance even on a small test case involving the luciferin molecule with the chemical formula $C_{11}N_2S_2O_3H_8$ and no molecular symmetry. The total memory required for processing of atomic orbital integrals in this case is 3.8 GB. In general, one should expect a faster reduction in performance for distributed platforms when

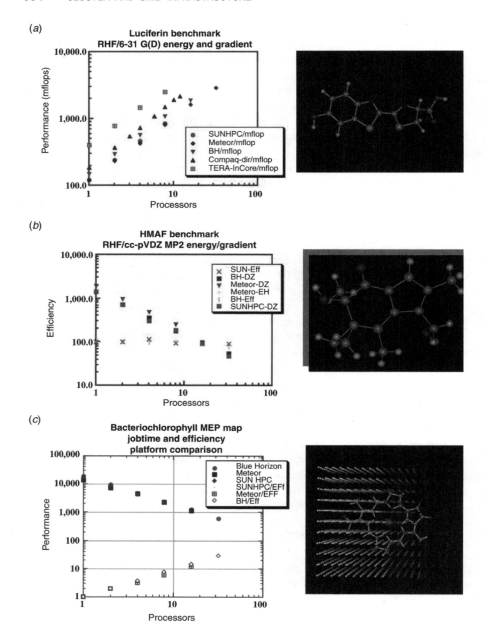

Figure 22.1 (*a*) Performance vs. number of processors for an RHF energy and gradient calculation on luciferin. (*b*) Efficiency vs. number of processors for an MP2 energy and gradient calculation on hydroxy-methyl fulvene. (*c*) Performance vs. number of processors for an electrostatic map calculation on bacteriochlorophyll. (*d*) CPU time per optimization step for an MP2 optimization of hydrocarbon molecules of varying lengths for two processors. (*e*) CPU time vs. number of processors for the optimization of a particular hydrocarbon (butane).

(d)

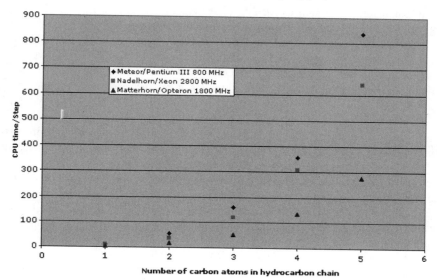

Hydrocarbon benchmark MP2/DZV (2d,p) optimization

(e)

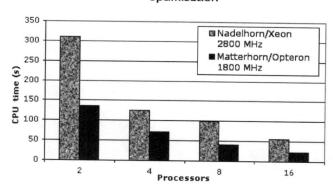

Butane benchmark MP2/DZV (2d,p) optimization

Figure 22.1 *Continued.*

tasks run out (e.g., computations involving small molecular systems on large numbers of nodes).

A particularly good example of scalability occurs with a rather CPU and memory intensive capability of GAMESS, involving the dynamic correlation method — second-order Møller–Plesset (MP2) theory. In this case, our scalable distributed-data algorithms target the increasingly large aggregate memories available with cluster architectures. The design of the distributed-data algorithms is enhanced considerably by the availability of one-sided forms of communication that facilitate remote data access in a shared-memory style of environment. This has shown to be particularly important in methods such as MP2. A distributed-data second-order MP2 energy algorithm is now available, which typically maintains an efficiency of over 90% with increased problem size. Figure 22.1b illustrates the performance for a relatively modest calculation involving an important cancer drug target, hydroxy-methyl fulvene (17 heavy atoms). Here, we show MFLOPS (solid) and efficiencies (cross-lines) again on three different architecture types. This computation retains more than 90% efficiency with increasing node application on the Pentium III cluster (triangles) on which it was run.

We have also investigated the computational performance of molecular property computations, which typically involve the calculation and handling of potentially very large N^3 grid points. The time to calculate 3D surfaces can be a significant, or even the major, portion of the calculation when computed on a single node. When the calculations are parallelized, the 3D serial grid calculations become much more significant relative to the parallel calculations. All these effects are multiplied, when several levels of grid properties have to be computed at once (e.g., 10 or more grids per molecular system). For example, on a R12000 processor, the time to compute one $60 \times 60 \times 60$ grid exceeds 1 h (and this is a very small grid size).

To improve efficiency on clusters, we have divided the grid into groups of processors and accumulated the results via the DDI layer. Figure 22.1c illustrates the overall performance in terms of CPU and efficiency measures for the computation involving the moderately large bacteriochlorophyll molecule electrostatic field.

Finally, we have the opportunity to make a few comparisons due to enhancements in processor speed as we have now cluster systems with Pentium III processors, Xeon processors, and Opteron processors. Here, we have performed several benchmark computations on hydrocarbons with increasing number of carbons (for comparative purposes, we consider all-staggered forms of the hydrocarbons here). Figure 22.1d shows the CPU time (in seconds) per optimization step as a function of hydrocarbon length across these three platform types. The processor speeds for the three platforms are shown. The Opteron cluster shows the best performance. It is important to keep in mind that there are other considerations to the overall speed of the calculations other than just the clock speed on the particular processor. Figure 22.1e shows the performance of a geometry optimization calculation for a single hydrocarbon across a sequence of node combinations. This illustrates the difference in performance particularly for the Xeon vs. the Opteron cluster type. For this small molecular system, the efficiency is optimal up to 16 nodes, at which point the workload is no longer an issue.

Although it is certainly the case that GAMESS performance is enhanced by the continued increase in processor speed, processors on the slower side can also compete in total performance by executing multi-tasking, which has been enabled by the compiler. In addition to the importance of speed to main memory, the capacity of the main memory, the speed of access to the disk drives, and the latency and bandwidth on the network controllers all contribute to the overall performance observed for GAMESS jobs.

22.3 PORTAL TECHNOLOGY

Our first attempt at providing a means to shield users from the intricacies of parallel computational systems involved several schemes for submitting GAMESS jobs to remote resources and retrieving the results through the *QMView* visualization software [8]. We also developed tools such as a cluster submission/monitoring program, which allows users to choose nodes and submit jobs via an X11 interface. These were primarily for "proof of concept" and demonstration purposes; they were never established as production "services." All of those methods were originally designed before the advent of the world wide web and are now essentially obsolete, superseded by new grid technologies.

Subsequently, the SDSC portals group created the GridPort Toolkit [9], which provided portal developers with a Perl API for establishing secure web portals capable of submitting, controlling, and gathering the output of jobs to remote high-performance computing resources. The GridPort API also includes file transfer capabilities that a portal developer can use to transfer files such as input and output data using GridFTP or the storage resource broker (SRB). To access a GridPort Portal like the *GAMESS Portal* [10], a user logs on to a website, selects input files, and chooses a remote platform to run their jobs on. The portal provides information on job status and stores the output on the SDSC SRB system [11]. GridPort uses the Globus Toolkit [12] to handle authentication, security, and job submission and control. Figure 22.2 gives a flowchart of jobs and data through a portal.

In our initial implementations of the GAMESS Portal, the "storage device" used to archive the simulation results was an NFS-exported file system. In the updated system, all data files are "collections" within the SRB. Access to data stored on the SRB is provided by web portals, which allow a user to download and upload files by SRB client tools on UNIX systems using the "srbBrowser" program on Windows systems, or via the SRB website. We are also building infrastructure for computational chemistry database technologies to be included in the environment.

Although GridPort has proven to be a useful tool and is widely utilized, it lacks a basis on which to build complex and dynamically reconfigurable workflows. Although complexity is hidden from the end user, it is not hidden from the application scientist or portal developer: Many CGI scripts and HTML documents have to be created or copied and modified from existing portals. More complications come in when new computational platforms are added, since all runtime details on the new platform must be added, including the queuing mechanism and location of the executable and directory structures. What is lacking is an overall architecture that provides the user and the application programmer with an interface that shields them from the complexity of the HPC resources available and allows them to concentrate on solving their scientific problem, while allowing scientific programmers to integrate their software into the system in a simple and effective manner. The next generation of portal technology provides a further layer of abstraction for the applications programmer and exploits the latest grid technologies.

The web and grid technologies briefly described earlier can be used to run GAMESS jobs without making changes in the GAMESS program itself nor in the

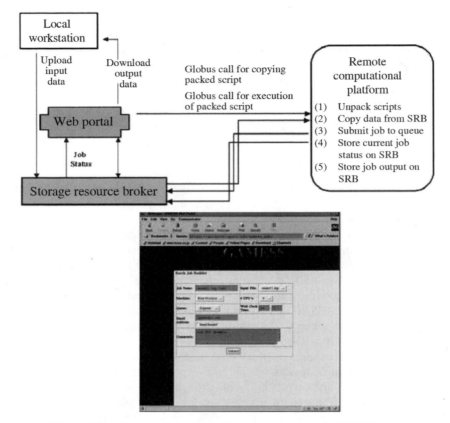

Figure 22.2   Flowchart illustrating the operation of the GAMESS Portal.

mechanism of deployment. Work is currently in progress to enable GAMESS to output structured data in the form of extensible markup language (XML) documents and JAVA objects based on the GAMESS schema [13–15]. This will facilitate data transfer between programs in a workflow and also provide a basis for a database structure (Section 22.5).

22.4   RUNNING GAMESS WITH NIMROD GRID-ENABLING INFRASTRUCTURE

Over the last few years, combinations of computers, called "grids," have been developed, which couple geographically distributed resources such as supercomputers, workstations, clusters, and scientific instruments [16, 17]. Newly constituted grid organizations such as the U.S.-based *TeraGrid* [18] and the Swiss-based *SwissBioGrid* [19] have begun to provide the infrastructure to support global and interdisciplinary collaboration in science and engineering in ways that were not previously possible. They enable a new discipline called "*e-Science*." In addition, because of involvement in various projects, computational researchers may even build their own "private" grids when they combine access to several computers at different institutions worldwide.

Unlike traditional high-performance computing systems, grids provide more than just computing power, they provide a new "Cyberinfrastructure." Computational grids address issues of long-distance networking, distributed storage, wide-area scheduling, and resource discovery in ways that allow many resources (e.g., computers and scientific instruments) to be assembled, on demand, to solve large, complex problems. Grid applications potentially allow real-time processing of data streams from scientific instruments such as synchrotrons and telescopes in ways that are much more flexible and powerful than those currently available. Through the pooling of resources, grids provide significant and flexibly adjustable computational power, which can be exploited by quantum chemistry and other compute-intense calculations.

Common challenges in establishing a grid infrastructure present the diversity of hardware and software, restrictions in the network connections, different site policies, and communication difficulties between the various institutions and disciplines involved. In addition, scientific program codes are often complex and were developed over many years by many people, with specific applications and efficiency in mind. As exemplified in Section 22.2 for the quantum chemical package GAMESS [1, 2], selected codes have been adapted to run in parallel on various compute cluster and supercomputer systems. Despite this portability, the adaptation to loosely connected and heterogeneous grid environments is challenging. Although clusters, with similar hardware and fast, reliable network backbone between the nodes, make parallel computations very efficient, geographically distributed grids suffer from high network latency, uncontrollable downtimes, and diverse hardware. This makes it currently less desirable to run a single job in parallel on different grid machines. Therefore, we concentrate less on the specifics of the optimization of the application codes for parallel usage on grids at the moment, and instead, we focus here on connecting the compute clusters to distribute many independent jobs onto a personal "grid queuing system." As we have seen, even this much-needed capability is still a challenging mission.

An obvious way of using such widely distributed grid resources is when a single "experiment" requires processing multiple different input scenarios, as this is a typical embarrassingly parallel task. We have initially undertaken to provide such a capability with two separate strategies, each having their advantages and implications for computational chemistry applications: One mechanism involves calling GAMESS within the Nimrod Toolkit [20] for distributed parametric modeling, which we will discuss in this section. The other mechanism involves calling GAMESS within a desktop grid environment, which will not be covered here (for more details, see Ref. [21]).

The experimental or computational scanning of a parameter space and the search for optimal solutions to construct or test hypotheses or algorithms is a common and fundamental task in scientific research. Although the generation of such jobs sounds relatively easy, the computational requirements and the amount of bookkeeping steeply rise with the number of generated jobs. Furthermore, it is almost impossible for application scientists to adjust the load of their calculations on various resources in an adequate and efficient manner manually. However, as all jobs are basically similar to each other — they only differ in the values of certain parameters — and they are not directly coupled to each other, this is a perfect task to be solved by grid computing.

We used the Nimrod family of tools for distributed parametric modeling [22–24] to construct, launch, control, and gather a quantum chemical parameter scan with GAMESS. Developed at the Distributed Systems Technology Centre at Monash University, Australia, *Nimrod/G* [22, 23] manages the execution of studies with varying parameters across distributed computers. This software responsibility for the overall management of an experiment as well as the low-level issues of distributing files to remote systems, performing the remote computations, and gathering the results. When users describe an experiment to Nimrod/G, a declarative "plan file" is developed, which describes the parameters, their default values, and the commands needed to perform the work. Apart from this high-level description, users are freed from much of the complexity of the grid. As a result, Nimrod/G has been very popular among application scientists.

Nimrod/O [24] is a variant of Nimrod/G, which performs a guided search of the design space rather than exploring all combinations. Nimrod/O allows users to phrase questions such as: "What set of design parameters will minimize (or maximize) the output of my model?" If the model computes metrics such as cost and lifetime, it is then possible to perform automatic optimal design. A commercial version of Nimrod, called *EnFuzion*, has also been produced. A web portal, called the *Nimrod Portal*, provides access to Nimrod via conventional browser technology. Of the different modes of user interfaces offered by the Nimrod software, we utilized the portal interface in this work.

Nimrod is built on a variety of middleware layers, most importantly Globus [12], through which it can, for example, interact with remote cluster queuing systems. Considering constraints such as time or cost, Nimrod dynamically detects suitable resources from a user-provided list of grid-enabled computers, modifies and ships the corresponding input files to those resources, submits the individual jobs via "agents" scheduled to run on the machines, and collects the results, while handling events such as node and network failures. Nimrod's core is a relational database, which stores the experimental details.

In our case, we prepared, executed, controlled, and gathered GAMESS calculations with the help of the Nimrod Toolkit. As an application, we used the GAMESS/Nimrod setup to parameterize a so-called "group difference potential" (GDP) [25, 26]. This is a quantum chemical pseudopotential designed to be used in future research, to cap atoms at carbon–carbon single bonds cut in hybrid quantum mechanics–molecular mechanics (QM/MM) calculations or to allow free energy difference determinations between fluorine and methyl groups. The former method enables accurate yet fast modeling of chemical reactions in realistic, yet large and complex molecular systems such as solutions, biomolecules, and materials, by subdividing the system into an active QM and a surrounding MM parts. The latter allows estimation of the effects of functional group substitutions in derivatives of the original compounds, for example, in drug or catalyst development.

Our potential function consists of four adjustable parameters, and the parameterization is carried out using quantum chemical calculations involving the GAMESS package, in this case, for the small prototype molecule ethane. The integrity of each parameter combination is measured by a weighted least-square difference cost function, which compares various properties of the original molecule with the pseudomolecule. First, we scanned subsequent regions of the parameter space in their entirety, applying different types and densities of point spacing, using the Nimrod/G sweeping tool to identify the most interesting region for our purposes. Secondly, we performed cost function minimizations on this subspace with the Nimrod/O parameter optimization tool.

The parameter sweeps resulted in experiment sizes of up to about $60,000 \times 4$ single GAMESS calculations. Performing this number of tasks manually on a single machine is practically impossible, but with the Nimrod technologies lasted only a few days when distributed automatically on a grid of computers. The actual experiments were mainly performed during the Fourth Pacific Rim Applications and Grid Middleware Assembly (PRAGMA) workshop and the Supercomputing (SC) 2003 conference. For these events, we were able, with the help of the PRAGMA collaboration [27], to accumulate the necessary number of resources to form a huge grid testbed, spanning a range of hardware architectures, software setups, organizations, and countries. Many of these machines were compute clusters running Linux, often under ROCKS configuration management. Analysis of the resource usage shows the efficient, dynamic, and flexible distribution of jobs over the grid testbed to minimize the overall execution time for each experiment. Considering the enormous success of such experiments, there was one considerable obstacle, involving misconfigured Globus installations on a few of the machines, which again shows the difficulties in dealing with the grid middleware directly.

At the end of the cost function minimizations, we obtained an optimal parameter set for our ethane GDP. Currently, this result is tested under different environmental conditions, for larger molecules, and with other quantum chemical methods. Up to now, the outcomes are encouraging and the pseudopotential seems to be stable under a variety of circumstances. More details of the GAMESS/Nimrod experiments can be found in Refs. [25, 26]; further publications are in preparation.

The success of this project encouraged us to apply Nimrod also in other fields of our research. Of particular interest in our current efforts is the behavior of ligands in proteins, but similar principles can also be used, for example, to study the driving forces involved in protein–protein interactions. Both topics are of invaluable importance for the understanding of biological processes and the design of pharmaceutical agents.

In recent years, we developed techniques that simplify the modeling of the protein environmental influence on a ligand via a combination of quantum chemical and continuum electrostatics approaches. Our current work targets the automation of a molecular docking procedure, which is typically known to be computationally challenging both from the perspective of computational resources and computational accuracy. Such calculations are difficult because of the fact that one would like to investigate all possible configurations in the ligand–protein interaction space to find their best relative position. However, the correct representation of electrostatic and non-electrostatic energies as well as entropic contributions in the overall scoring cost function is not fully established. We target both the configurational as well as the energetic surface analysis, since the optimal protein–ligand interaction is not determined solely by one or the other but by a complex interplay between energetic stabilization and configuration selection. The initial parameterization will be done on systems for which the real positions of ligand and protein are known from experimental results in the Protein Data Bank (PDB) [28].

Tools such as Nimrod greatly facilitate carrying out procedures such as described, as they can manage the rather large set of individual calculations that one would like to do to obtain the most accurate and thorough results. Furthermore, apart from existing parameter sweeping and objective parameter optimization facilities in Nimrod/G and Nimrod/O, recently an interactive subjective optimization algorithm was implemented into the Nimrod Toolkit (*Nimrod/OI*). An objective cost function can thus be applied to monitor the energetics associated with the protein–ligand interaction in any particular molecular configuration of the ligand docked into the protein, and a subjective cost function to monitor the steric and overall configuration details in terms of special parameters. The subjective optimization procedure needs direct user intervention and decisions, and therefore, requires the use of a visualization tool, for which we plan to invoke our QMView [8] molecular computation and analysis tool.

As such, our particular docking protocol requires executing two major computational chemistry or biophysics packages: The GAMESS software, which was discussed earlier, has just to be the invoked once for each ligand structure, to obtain its hydrogen positions and atomic charge distribution. Then, the adaptive Poisson–Boltzmann solver (APBS) [29, 30], a code for biomolecular dielectric continuum solvation calculations, computes the electrostatic energies of protein, ligand, and protein–ligand complex in solution for each of their relevant positions, from which the corresponding binding energies can be determined. However, particularly due to the complexity of protein structures, a variety of auxiliary tools is also required, to prepare, manipulate, and analyze the docking calculations such as those to access the protein data, to set up the GAMESS and APBS input files, to bring the quantum chemical results into the right format, to assign the molecular force field, to estimate non-electrostatic contributions, and to visualize the results. A principal methodology to automate this overall procedure will be introduced in the next chapter.

22.5 COMPUTATIONAL CHEMISTRY WORKFLOW ENVIRONMENTS

Although Nimrod plan files allow the user to construct basic pipelines, there is a considerable interest in the ability to combine more than one computational code, to build flexible, complex, and reusable workflows for high-throughput studies on significant numbers of molecules or with a variety of methods. Recently, we have begun to develop a "computational chemistry prototyping environment," which would enable researchers to design computational experiments which span multiple computational and analytical models, and in the process, to store, access, transfer, and query information. This requires the integration of a variety of computational tools, including the chemistry software, preparation, visualization, and analysis toolkits, as well as database programs. The overall infrastructure is being referred to as the "Resurgence" RESearch sURGe ENabled by CyberinfrastructurE project.

We are realizing this with the help of the *Kepler* collaborative system for scientific workflows [31–33], which is based on dataflow process networks. Exploiting Kepler addresses various levels of complexity, detail, and control desired by different factions of the rather diverse computational chemistry community. A major focus here is not to provide predefined workflows for pure application, but a set of highly modular and extensible elementary and composite workflow pieces, which by individual combination allow researchers to explore new paradigms for their science. Such explorations particularly include new ideas in complex molecular modeling, such as exist in the biological or material sciences. For example, we would like to refer here to our efforts in protein–ligand docking, described in detail in Section 22.4.

Underlying Kepler is the Java-based *Ptolemy II* system [34] for heterogeneous, concurrent modeling and design. It also provides the foundation for the graphical user interface (GUI) called *Vergil*, which facilitates the setup and execution of complex workflow scenarios with a convenient workflow editor and libraries of component workflow tools. Dragging and dropping a number of predefined so-called "actors" into the workspace construct a functional model, which comprises a complete chemistry computational process. These are then connected together between their input and output "ports," defining the routes for the transfer of data or the triggering of other actors. Certain "parameters" of the actors can also be modified after double clicking. Examples of fundamental Kepler actors for computing are command-line execution, Globus jobs, GridFTP, proxy certificate management, and web service consumers. Several actors may be combined to build more complex "composite" actors, which allows defining hierarchies. Finally, a so-called "director" for each workflow part is used to steer execution of the merged actors and to manage scheduling, dispatching threads, running of code, and similar tasks. The created workflow is saved in a Ptolemy II-specific XML dialect called modeling markup language (MoML). For the GUI and an example computational chemistry workflow, see Figure 22.3.

Overall, the software under development can be described as consisting of three different layers: (1) the "control layer" on the top guarantees communication between different molecular modeling applications and databases, (2) the "translation layer" in the middle is responsible for constructing the inputs and analyzing the outputs of each program involved, and (3) the "execution layer" on the bottom provides the connection to the computational resources, the transfer of files between machines, and the running of individual jobs.

Following the previous success, the dynamic grid distribution facilities on the execution layer are realized by Nimrod/G, as described in Section 22.4. Combined with the static grid-execution facilities of Globus, we believe that this will give scientists a tool that has the ability to catapult computational chemistry research to new heights. In such a complex workflow, it is possible to invoke a Nimrod run as just one component of a series of calculations. From the corresponding list of input files and a template, a plan file is automatically constructed. The template is specific for

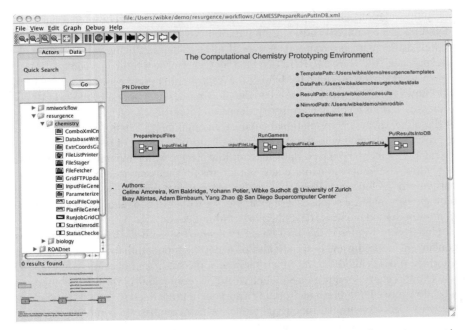

Figure 22.3   Example workflow of the computational chemistry prototyping environment in the Kepler GUI, developed within the Resurgence project.

each computational code or installation. Currently, this setup works for the GAMESS quantum chemical program package [1, 2]. The corresponding experiment is then added to the Nimrod database. The same applies to the grid resources, which the user selects prior to running the workflow. Finally, the computational experiment is started and monitored until execution stops. At the end, the list of generated output files is given back. Although Nimrod is currently accessed via its command-line API, such a service could also be implemented by adding a web service interface for Nimrod. In both ways, Kepler will be able to invoke parameter scans and searches, and the results can be processed and passed to later computations.

The translation and control layers are more difficult to realize. Here, the diversity of the computational chemistry software represents a considerable issue. Although the codes mostly read or write text or binary input and output files, these generally have proprietary file formats, which are incompatible to each other. In addition, not all corresponding sources are open or they are hard to adapt due to their grown complexity. Thus, researchers usually apply a variety of transformation procedures in between two programs to connect these. Either these are self-written scripts, freely available molecular file format conversion tools such as OpenBabel [35], or the two codes involved are directly called from one another.

To solve this very general problem, two aspects are of importance: First, the input and output files should be in an easier format to process, which allows both automatic and human reading and writing. For this, XML [36] seems to be a perfect choice. Secondly, a common data format may also be desirable. An attempt into this direction is the chemical markup language (CML) [37, 38] or its recently started computational chemistry derivate CMLComp. Unfortunately, experience shows that it is very difficult to define one overall data format for a complex field such as molecular modeling, and we ultimately even want to connect codes across disciplines. In addition, ontologies should be part of the research and not part of the file format. Therefore, we believe it is best for now to provide the user with code-specific XML, so that he or she does not need to think about the file formats any more, but only about the correct mapping of data. This means that the individual calculation programs need to be internally or externally (e.g., by XSLT) wrapped to be able to communicate with each other (Fig. 22.4). We have already performed a corresponding integration for the GAMESS quantum chemistry package inside the code (Section 22.3) and within the Resurgence project.

When one considers high-throughput calculations, another important issue is the interfacing to databases. On one hand, only databases provide access to the large numbers of molecular geometries needed as input for the computational chemistry calculations. Thus, we plan to interface our workflow system to experimental structure databases such as the RCSB PDB [28] and the CCDC Cambridge Structural Database [39]. On the other hand, the outcomes need to be stored in databases as well, as only these allow managing the huge amounts of newly computed data. In addition, the detailed and systematic storage permits to perform data mining on the results to find relationships between properties that were not known before and could also not easily be deduced from small numbers of calculations.

Therefore, we are currently building a relational databank to store the XML output of GAMESS jobs, named "QM-DB." When it is based, for example, on the professional IBM DB2 database system [40], the storage of data could work by XML-relational mapping defined in a document access definition file and processing of the results via a corresponding stored procedure. Our overall view is that — to guarantee the integrity and accessibility of the data — there should be only one open worldwide GAMESS data repository, similar in spirit to the PDB. In addition, analogous layouts could be introduced for other molecular modeling codes. Federation may then combine all these databases. This strategy is parallel to our ideas on XML and CML.

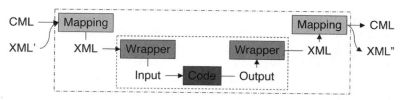

Figure 22.4 Wrapping of a computational chemistry code to read and write XML and mapping of the XML information for connection with other codes.

We are currently implementing some of these features into the Resurgence add-on module [41] for the Kepler workflow collaboration. A semi-automatic installation procedure might ease the setup of the large number of different necessary software tools (Ptolemy II, Kepler, Resurgence, Python, PostgreSQL, and Nimrod/G). Nevertheless, even though MoML-defined workflows can be executed independently from the GUI, the overall system is inherently coupled to a central machine where Kepler and Nimrod need to be installed. In the age of grid computing, however, ultimately a more flexible and dynamically reconfigurable design is desirable. Thus, the next generation of workflow architecture, constructed under the impetus of the newly interdisciplinary chemical and biological outlook, will be more generally layered (e.g., an interface layer, a middleware layer, and a resource layer), shielding users even more from the complexity of the underlying grid system. The associated tool, INFORMNET [42], developed in parallel to our Kepler efforts by Stephen Mock et al. at the San Diego Supercomputer Center, provides convenient mechanisms of abstraction of functionality, interface, hardware, and software, tested in an application-rich environment.

22.6 CONCLUSIONS

Calculations that predict the structures, energetics, and other properties of experimentally known or unknown molecules are a fundamental resource in modern chemical and biological research. Understanding molecular systems at a variety of levels of detail and accuracy requires a variety of different types of computational capabilities to be accessible. The goal is nevertheless the solution of problems of general chemical and biological interest, especially for the experimental side — how molecular and electronic forces determine the details of structures and the dynamics and energetics of chemical reactions.

In the past 5 years, the quantum chemistry program package GAMESS [1, 2] has served as a strategic application for prototyping advances in cluster and grid architecture and connectivity. First of all, sophisticated parallelization approaches and interfaces allow running GAMESS jobs very efficiently on clusters and supercomputers. Together with the steady advances in hardware, this enables researchers to study increasingly larger systems of chemical and biological interest in more detail and with greater accuracy. A GAMESS GridPort web portal at SDSC permits job submissions on a variety of platforms, most predominately clusters, using the technologies of the SRB and Globus middleware tools to assemble, carry out, and monitor jobs and store the results. This shields the complexity of the grid middleware from the end user (although not from the application developer) and eases the calculations by client-independent Internet access and flexible server selection.

The execution of GAMESS or other experiments via the Nimrod Toolkit permits the easy setup and distribution of parameters sweeps and optimizations on computational grids. Also here, the scientist does not have to deal directly with the middleware software and, in addition, does not need to worry about the allocation of jobs to machines, which is done automatically and in a high-throughput manner, opening new possibilities for research. Desktop grids provide an alternative approach based on different platforms and with different targets for application, but similar advantages. Finally, the complex combination of diverse computational chemistry — and later biology — tasks and the grid distribution of the resource-intensive calculations can be realized by the scientific workflow systems currently under development. Here, the goal is to flexibly integrate a variety of computational tools including molecular calculation software such as GAMESS, visualization and analysis toolkits, and database programs, thereby providing reusable building blocks.

This advanced set of cluster, portal, grid, and workflow infrastructure is now enabling considerable progress toward the integration of chemical and biochemical calculations across all scales from molecules to cells to organisms, with the quantum chemical GAMESS application providing the basis for a more generalized chemistry and biology framework. Examples for this are the GridPort and Nimrod integrations of APBS and further scientific software. The objective is to put experimental data and computational modeling within reach of users in a variety of disciplines through intuitive, configurable, and easy-to-use graphical and web interfaces, but also to still support all possibilities for experts in each field.

Our ultimate goal is to create a software environment that is able to run applications from any scientific domain with little configuration effort by users or developers, and perhaps more relevant to the scientific community, to offer a working environment that enables creative new computational chemistry possibilities for research, from high-throughput analyses to difficult and complex individual computational research problems. We will continue to use our prior experience with GAMESS, QMView, web portals, as well as new workflow and grid middleware technologies as our guide in the design. Careful choice of protocols is crucial to ensure the reusability of developed infrastructure across an entire spectrum of computational science applications. The main parts of our software are planned to be available free of charge under an open source license.

ACKNOWLEDGMENTS

K.K.B. and J.P.G. acknowledge NSF-ANI-0223043, NSF-PRAGMA, and NIH-NBCR-RR08605 for support. W.S. thanks for support by J. Andrew McCammon and by a fellowship within the Postdoc Program of the German Academic Exchange Service (DAAD) during her time at the University of California, San Diego (UCSD). We are grateful to Laura Brovold, UCSD, for some of the benchmark studies, to Chris Kondric, UCSD, for his protein–ligand docking work, while funded by the PRAGMA-Prime program, and to Yang Zhao, University of California, Berkeley, for her help in the computational chemistry workflow project, under project funding NSF-DBI-0078296. Nimrod/G has been funded partly by the Cooperative Centre for Enterprise Distributed Systems Technology (DSTC) through the Australian Federal Government's CRC Programme (Department of Education, Science, and Training). Nimrod/O has been funded by the Australian Research Council. The UZ-ROCKclimber group, the SDSC-ROCKS cluster group, the PRAGMA collaboration,

NBCR, the W.M. Keck Foundation, and UCSD all provided computing resources for the work discussed here.

REFERENCES

1. M. Schmidt, K. K. Baldridge, J. A. Boatz, S. Elbert, M. Gordon, J. H. Jenson, S. Koeski, N. Matsunaga, K. A. Nguyen, S. J. Su, T. L. Windus, M. Dupuis, and J. A. Montgomery, The general atomic and molecular electronic structure system, *J. Comp. Chem.*, 14, 1347 (1993).

2. *The General Atomic and Molecular Electronic Structure System (GAMESS)*, Ames Laboratory, Iowa State University, Ames, Iowa, 2004. Available at http://www.msg.ameslab.gov/ GAMESS/GAMESS.html.

3. G. D. Fletcher, M. W. Schmidt, B. M. Bode, and M. S. Gordon, The distributed data interface in GAMESS, *Comp. Phys. Commun.*, 128, 190 (2000).

4. *MPICH — A Portable Implementation of MPI,* Argonne National Laboratory, Argonne, Illinois, 2004. Available at http://www-unix.mcs.anl.gov/mpi/mpich/.

5. *OpenPBS*, Altair Engineering, Inc., Troy, Michigan, 2004. Available at http:// www.openpbs.org/.

6. *Sun Grid Engine*, Sun Microsystems, Inc., Santa Clara, California, 2004. Available at http://gridengine.sunsource.net/.

7. P. M. Papadopoulos, C. A. Papadopoulos, M. J. Katz, W. J. Link, and G. Bruno, Configuring Large High-Performance Clusters at Lightspeed: A Case Study, *International Journal of High Performance Computing Applications*, 18, 317 (2004).

8. K. K. Baldridge and J. P. Greenberg, QMView: a computational 3D visualization tool at the interface between molecules and man, *J. Mol. Graphics*, 13, 63 (1995).

9. M. Thomas, S. Mock, M. Dahan, K. Mueller, D. Sutton, and J. R. Boisseau, The Gridport Toolkit: A System for Building Grid Portals, *10th IEEE International Symposium on High Performance Computing*, San Francisco, CA, 2001.

10. K. K. Baldridge and J. P. Greenberg, *GAMESS Web Portal*, 2004. Available at http://gridport.npaci.edu/gamess/.

11. A. K. Rajasekar and M. Wan, SRB and SRBRack — Components of a Virtual Data Grid Architecture, *Advanced Simulation Technologies Conference (ASTC02)*, San Diego, California, 2002.

12. I. Foster and C. Kesselman, Globus: a metacomputing infrastructure toolkit. *Int. J. Supercomput. Appl.*, 11, 115 (1997).

13. J. P. Greenberg, GAMESS/QMVIEW, *Computational Representation of Bio-Molecules (CRBM) Workshop*, University of California, San Diego, 2003.

14. K. Baldridge and J. Greenberg, Representation of Computational Quantum Chemistry Data in a Structured Format and Incorporation into a Scientific Workflow, *Toward a Common Data and Command Representation for Quantum Chemistry*, Edinburgh, UK, 2004. Available at http://www.nesc.ac.uk/talks/394/data_rep_apr4.pdf.

15. J. Greenberg, S. Mock, M. J. Katz, G. Bruno, F. D. Sacerdoti, P. Papadopoulos, and K. Baldridge, Incorporation of Middleware and Grid Technologies to Enhance Usability in

Computational Chemistry Applications, *Computational Science — ICCS 2004: Proceedings of 4th International Conference, Part I,* Krakow, Poland, Springer-Verlag, Heidelberg, 2004.

16. I. Foster and C. Kesselman, Eds., *The Grid 2: Blueprint for a New Computing Infrastructure,* 2nd ed., Morgan Kaufmann, San Francisco, 2003.

17. F. Berman, G. Fox, and A. J. G. Hey, Eds., *Grid Computing: Making the Global Infrastructure a Reality,* Wiley, 2003.

18. *TeraGrid,* 2004. Availale at http://www.teragrid.org/.

19. *Swiss Bio Grid,* 2004. Available at http://www.swissbiogrid.org/.

20. *Nimrod: Tools for Distributed Parametric Modelling,* Monash University, Clayton, Australia, 2004. Available at http://www.csse.monash.edu.au/~davida/nimrod/.

21. K. K. Baldridge, J. P. Greenberg, W. Sudholt, S. Mock, K. Bhatia, A. Birnbaum, C. Amoreira, Y. Potier, and M. Taufer, The Computational Chemistry Prototyping Environment, *Proceedings of the IEEE,* 93, 510 (2005).

22. D. Abramson, R. Sosic, J. Giddy, and B. Hall, Nimrod: A Tool for Performing Parametised Simulations Using Distributed Workstations, *The 4th IEEE Symposium on High Performance Distributed Computing,* Virginia, 1995.

23. D. Abramson, J. Giddy, and L. Kotler, High Performance Parametric Modeling with Nimrod/G: Killer Application for the Global Grid? *International Parallel and Distributed Processing Symposium (IPDPS),* Cancun, Mexico, 2000.

24. D. Abramson, A. Lewis, and T. Peachy, Nimrod/O: A Tool for Automatic Design Optimization, *The 4th International Conference on Algorithms and Architectures for Parallel Processing (ICA3PP 2000),* Hong Kong, 2000.

25. W. Sudholt, K. K. Baldridge, D. Abramson, C. Enticott, and S. Garic, Parameter scan of an effective group difference pseudopotential using grid computing, *New Generation Comput.,* 22, 137 (2004).

26. W. Sudholt, K. K. Baldridge, D. Abramson, C. Enticott, and S. Garic, Applying Grid Computing to the Parameter Sweep of a Group Difference Pseudopotential, *Computational Science — ICCS 2004: Proceeding of 4th International Conference, Part I,* Krakow, Poland, Springer-Verlag, Heidelberg, 2004.

27. *Pacific Rim Applications and Grid Middleware Assembly (PRAGMA),* 2004. Available at http://www.pragma-grid.net/.

28. *The RCSB Protein Data Bank,* 2004. Available at http://www.rcsb.org/pdb/.

29. N. A. Baker, D. Sept, S. Joseph, M. J. Holst, and J. A. McCammon, Electrostatics of nanosystems: application to microtubules and the ribosome, *Proc. Natl. Acad. Sci.,* 98, 10037 (2001).

30. *APBS: Adaptive Poisson-Boltzmann Solver,* Washington University of St. Louis, St. Louis, Missouri, 2004. Available at http://agave.wustl.edu/apbs/.

31. I. Altintas, C. Berkley, E. Jaeger, M. Jones, B. Ludäscher, and S. Mock, Kepler: Towards a Grid-Enabled System for Scientific Workflows, *Workflow in Grid Systems Workshop in GGF10 — The Tenth Global Grid Forum,* Berlin, Germany, 2004.

32. I. Altintas, C. Berkley, E. Jaeger, M. Jones, B. Ludäscher, and S. Mock, Kepler: an Extensible System for Design and Execution of Scientific Workflows, *16th International Conference on Scientific and Statistical Database Management (SSDBM),* Santorini Island, Greece, 2004.

33. *Kepler: A System for Scientific Workflows*, 2004. Available at http://kepler.ecoinformatics. org/ and http://www.kepler-project.org/.

34. *Ptolemy II: Heterogenous Modeling and Design*, University of California, Berkeley, California, 2004. Availale at http://ptolemy.eecs.berkeley.edu/ptolemyII/.

35. *Open Babel: A Package to Decypher Computational Chemistry*, 2004. Available at http://openbabel.sourceforge.net/.

36. *Extensible Markup Language (XML)*, W3C, 2004. Available at http://www.w3.org/XML/.

37. P. Murray-Rust, H. S. Rzepa, and M. Wright, Development of chemical markup language (CML) as a system for handling complex chemical content, *New J. Chem.*, 25, 618 (2001).

38. *Chemical Markup Language (CML)*, 2004. Available at http://www.xml-cml.org/ and http://cml.sourceforge.net/.

39. *Cambridge Structural Database (CSD)*, Cambridge Crystallographic Data Centre (CCDC): Cambridge, UK, 2004. Available at http://www.ccdc.cam.ac.uk/products/csd/.

40. *DB2 Product Family*, IBM, 2004. Available at http://www-306.ibm.com/software/data/db2/.

41. *Resurgence Project Home Page*, University of Zurich, Zurich, Switzerland, 2004. Available at http://www.Baldridge.unizh.ch/resurgence.

42. *INFORMNET: INformation Flow and Operation Resource Management on the NET*, San Diego Supercomputer Center, San Diego, California, 2004. Available at http://chemport.sdsc.edu/informnet/.

CHAPTER 23

Distributed Workflows in Bioinformatics

ARUN KRISHNAN

23.1 INTRODUCTION

The development of improved DNA (deoxyribonucleic acid) sequencing technologies in the 1980s and 1990s heralded the start of a new era in biology. Biology and, in fact, biomedical science have slowly transformed into a multidisciplinary arena where there is a confluence of such diverse fields of research as genetics, molecular biology, computer sciences, mathematics, biostatistics, and bioinformatics. A vast amount of data is also being generated from DNA microarrays, mass spectrometry, DNA sequencing, and structure analysis. To be useful, the data acquired with these technologies need to be processed and interpreted. This requires new and innovative computational paradigms, techniques, and algorithms that can effectively process the large volume of data. In addition, it requires large parallel computing resources.

The field of high performance computing has undergone even more rapid and drastic changes over the past few years. Improvements in the performance of processors and networks have made it feasible to treat collections of workstations, servers, clusters, and supercomputers as integrated computing resources or *Grids*. However, heterogeneity, while allowing for scalability on one hand, makes application development and deployment for such an environment extremely difficult on the other. For grids to be widely useful, application design must be flexible enough to exploit widely differing and geographically distributed resources, matching application requirements and characteristics with grid resources.

Grid computing, as a distributed computing framework, offers a powerful, high performance computing environment, particularly for coarse-grained, data-parallel applications. The vision of geographically distributed, heterogeneous high-performance systems [22] is quickly becoming a reality, especially with grid middleware technologies, such as Globus, rapidly maturing and reaching stability. Many large-scale

Parallel Computing for Bioinformatics and Computational Biology, Edited by Albert Y. Zomaya
Copyright © 2006 John Wiley & Sons, Inc.

Grid projects, such as Grid Physics Network (GriPhyN) [12], the EU Datagrid [2], and NASA's Information Power Grid (IPG) [38], have sprung up, resulting in greater interdisciplinary osmosis. This has lead to the metamorphosis of fields such as computational biology, from an insular, compute-intensive realm to that of a collaborative, high-throughput, and data-driven science [13].

Despite the technological innovations accompanying the grid computing paradigm, the issue of how best to utilize a functional grid still poses a significant problem. More specifically, the problem deals with developing grid-aware applications. Current networking technologies impose an unavoidable limitation on grid computing in the form of high inter-grid node communication. As a result, the most viable applications are those that can benefit from coarse-grained parallelism.

The field of biosciences is one which lends itself easily to be adapted to a distributed, grid computing environment with its rich array of embarrassingly parallel applications. The large resource needs of bioinformatics allied to the large number of data-parallel applications in this field and the availability of a powerful, high performance, distributed, computing environment lead naturally to opportunities for developing grid-enabled bioinformatics applications.

Bioinformatics analysis typically consists of a number of applications being run one after the other resulting in pipelines or more complex workflows. For example, let us consider the simplest workflow, namely, a regular pipeline as shown in Figure 23.1. In a typical analysis of a protein sequence, homologous proteins are found using *BLASTP* [8]. Next, the most similar protein sequences from the various organisms are selected and then aligned using *ClustalW* [58]. The alignment results are finally provided as input to a phylogenetic tree generator such as *PHYLIP* [21], which renders a graphical representation of the evolutionary relationship between the proteins. These applications are, or could be, geographically dispersed and may require specialized resources such as large protein sequence databases. Thus, a Grid computing environment is ideally suited for such workflow applications.

The rest of this chapter is organized as follows. Section 23.2 sets forth the challenges faced in grid computing. Section 23.3 discusses the characteristics of applications that can typically be grid enabled. Section 23.4 details the different grid programming approaches. Section 23.5 introduces the grid execution language (GEL). Section 23.6 introduces graphical workflow construction and also describes the architecture of the graphical user interface (GUI)-based, grid-enabled worflow execution and enactment engine, *Wildfire*. Section 23.7 provides examples of three different

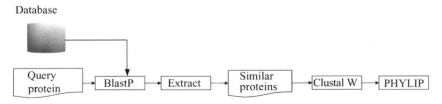

Figure 23.1   A typical pipeline used repeatedly by bioinformaticians.

bioinformatics workflows and how they can be run on a distributed environment using *Wildfire*. Section 23.8 summarizes the chapter.

23.2 CHALLENGES OF GRID COMPUTING

Grid computing is still in a stage of infancy with regard to the technologies for constructing a working grid as well as for creating applications that can take advantage of the geographically distributed resources making up a grid. A number of challenges need to be overcome by application programmers for creating grid-enabled applications in general. Some of the main challenges in grid application development are highlighted subsequently.

- *High-Latency Communications*. Grids, being loosely connected and made up of geographically distributed resources by definition, tend to have poor internode communications performance, especially in terms of latency. However, the prevailing parallel-programming formalisms, such as MPI, PVM and OpenMP, support mostly fine-grained parallelism and are suited to tightly integrated parallel computers such as clusters and, to a greater extent, shared-memory computers. Thus, there are inherent limitations placed on application developers as a result of the intrinsic nature of grids.

- *Heterogeneity: A Janus-Faced Entity*. One of the distinguishing characteristics of a computational Grid is its heterogeneity. One view of heterogeneity is that it is a necessary evil to allow for the integration of existing computational hardware/software and future extensibility of the resulting set up. A contrary view is that heterogeneity with its nonuniformity gives rise to immense challenges for grid system deylopers, administrators, and application programmers. However, we believe that heterogeneity should be embraced, as it allows the execution of subtasks on different nodes, depending on suitability. As grids are supposed to be comprised of widely differing resources, tasks can be scheduled on to particular nodes based on a "best-fit" with its requirements. For example, consider the following areas of resource heterogeneity and how these can be taken advantage of by applications.

  1. *Hardware Architecture*: Subtasks might require different hardware configurations, operating systems, and CPU architectures.

  2. *Data*: Replication of large databases (e.g., genomic databases) might not be feasible across all Grid nodes, in which case, subtasks should run on Grid nodes which are "close" to the data on which they are dependent.

  3. *Software*: Certain tasks might require specialized software that have expensive licenses tied to them. In such cases, it would be prohibitively expensive to purchase licences for all compute resources and hence moving such a task to the node on which the software resides might be a better option.

- *Legacy Applications.* Legacy applications, that is, applications that have been used (and work well) for a significant period of time, are present in various computing fields. In particular, bioinformaticians typically use large collections (e.g., EMBOSS [51] and Accelrys [32]) of software tools and utilities, which are used on a daily basis. Mainly, because such applications work well in their current environment, the users (and thus programmers) are often hesitant to port or re-implement their programs to make them Grid enabled or web-services enabled. Furthermore, given the sheer volume of existing applications, porting is a tremendous effort in itself.

- *Middleware Dependency.* Owing to the nascent stage of current grid technology, a lot of competing middleware are being developed by different groups (despite the widespread acceptance of Globus [23] as a de facto standard). As developers race to create grid-enabled applications, they often find that the resulting code becomes middleware specific. Not only does this present problems when moving to other middleware implementations, for example, Unicore [7], but also it slows down the development process as the underlying middleware must be set-up, configured, and tested to develop the code. For example, short of providing each team member with their own test bed, it would be extremely hard to test development code in isolation.

23.3 GRID APPLICATIONS

Grid application development remains limited to a small class of applications due to a number of issues, some of which were discussed earlier, such as high latency, heterogeneity, legacy applications, and middleware dependency. Another challenge for grid application developers lies in the absence of generic schedulers for grid environments. As a result, application developers need to incorporate aspects of scheduling into the applications. Although application level schedulers [14] and problem solving environments are being developed, these are not ubiquitous enough for generic application development. Keeping in mind the challenges mentioned earlier, it seems reasonable to classify grid applications that can be developed using currently available technology into the following main classes [34], namely,

1. *Single Program Multiple Data*: This category also includes the class of parameter sweep applications. The primary characteristic of this category of applications is the very minimal inter-node communication. These applications typically tend to be embarrassingly parallel in nature.

2. *Hierarchical Parallelism*: Applications belonging to this category are those that have a mix of fine-grained and coarse-grained parallelism. These applications can typically be re-engineered so that fine-grained parallelism at the intra-cluster level and coarse-grained parallelism at the inter-node level coexist.

3. *Data-Driven Applications*: Applications belonging to this class are not computationally intensive. They deal with enabling the access of data from remote locations.

4. *Work Flow*: These applications are typically made up of a number of distinct stages that can be run independent of one another. In the sense, these applications can also be said to be embarrassingly parallel as the individual components making up a pipeline are mostly independent.

In a sense, workflows are a superset of the other three classes of applications. Any application belonging to the other three classes can be expressed as a workflow. Hence, given the constraints on latencies and bandwidths and the current state of grid technology, workflows seem to be the best way to adapt applications to the grid.

23.4 GRID PROGRAMMING

Grid programming, at the most basic level, consists of working with APIs provided by middleware packages such as Globus to develop programs from scratch or to port from existing codes. In general, such API calls are often relatively low level in relation to the application domain. However, such low-level APIs make it relatively difficult to grid-enable applications. Ideally, a higher-level option for grid applications development, which makes transparent a lot of the complexity of core middleware API calls, should be available.

Initial attempts tended to focus on porting existing parallel programming formalisms to the grid environment. As parallel programming libraries such as MPI have been used extensively over the past few years, there were efforts to run MPI style programs on the grid using MPICH-G2 [33], a grid-aware incarnation of a popular MPI implementation. From the programming perspective, Grid application development using MPICH-G2 is little different from MPI programming for clusters or SMP machines. Although existing MPI applications can be ported directly to the grid in principle, such is seldom the case in practice. Only programs with minimal inter-process communication port well.

Alternative higher-level formalisms for grid applications development include various implementations [46, 11] of GridRPC [54]. For certain classes of problems, this approach scales better than MPI-based solutions as they typically do not require as much communication at runtime. There are other classes of formalisms such as virtual distributed shared memory (DSM) [37]. The reader is referred to review by Lee et al. in loc. cit. for a summary of their (un)suitability for Grid programming.

However, with the realization that only certain classes of applications (mainly those with negligible inter-node communication) can be grid enabled, research has been focused on assembling into one solution, various distributed applications which run as services (e.g., web services). Such collections of applications grouped together are often referred to as workflows. Languages used to express workflows have been an area of rigorous research over the past decade. Various types and standards of workflow languages are available to the community such as business process modeling language [1], XML process definition language from the workflow management coalition [4], and Microsoft and IBM's business process execution language for web services (BPEL4WS) [10], which is a combination of Microsoft's XLANG [57] and IBM's WSFL [39]. Although developed for web services, these workflow languages support the basic requirements of sequential and parallel execution of tasks, looping, and conditional control constructs.

There have been many efforts aimed at building workflows based on web services. For example, both Huang's SWFL [31] and Addis et al.'s SCUFL [6] (the workflow component of myGrid [27]) make use of WSFL as a basis to construct their languages, whereas most recently, Wang's Triana Workflow utilized BPEL4WS [43]. It must, however, be remembered that these standards are constantly evolving, and, with the introduction of new web services-oriented languages, it is difficult to foretell the exact standard that will be accepted by the community in future.

There are however a few drawbacks to the services-oriented workflow solutions. For one, these require deployment of the services, that is, installation and publication of applications. As a result, services are less mobile (in the sense that they run only where they have been installed) and the extra overhead can be an obstacle for the development of new applications. Furthermore, services-oriented solutions, such as the GridRPC and DSM approaches, require re-engineering of legacy applications.

There are also security issues that need to be considered while implementing web services because the WSFL approach to workflow composition does not provide the security features of a Grid certificate authentication provided by Globus. Hence, there is a possible cause for concern on abuse and misuse from unauthorized users. Although Amin's GridAnt [9] and Biven's GALE [15] do make an effort to address these issues with the implementation of Grid security features, their present descriptive languages are only able to express simple directed acyclic graphs (DAGs).

The use of grid services also raises similar problems to that of web services. Users would need to first enable their application as a Grid service before they can enact the workflow. Changing standards, with the coming introduction of the open grid service architecture (OGSA) [26], would mean that a workflow built using a solution as Huang's GSiB, which deploys an application as a grid service, would not be a valid composition.

Legacy systems are also a potential problem as such most such applications are not or cannot be readily and easily made available as a web or grid service. Web services though developed to enable enterprises to give access to their legacy applications through the web, do not presently allow for multiple types of applications invocation, for example, MPI, java, PVM, and C/C++ to name a few. Web services are essentially only able to make web service calls.

There are also nonservices-oriented workflow languages such as DAGMan [17], GridANT [9], GALE [15], and APST [14]. However, these languages only support workflows with acyclic dependencies and thus cannot handle iterative loops, and as such are not generic programming languages.

In summary, standards for web services-oriented workflow languages are constantly evolving. They are not semantically suited for data-driven workflows. Additionally, security issues pose concerns for safe grid operations. Furthermore, most legacy applications are not readily available as Grid services. Hence, there is a need to address these issues in a workflow language design. The workflow language should not only provide for suitable semantics and adequate security to drive the workflow, but should also allow for easy inclusion of legacy applications, mobility of applications to the best resource and must be able to easily integrate local applications with remote ones.

23.5 GRID EXECUTION LANGUAGE

There are two different ways of implementing workflows. The first uses a services-oriented approach where each task is implemented as a web or grid service (as mentioned in the previous section). The second approach relies on the use of scripting languages such as bash, perl, and python to pull together disparate tasks and programs into a single application.

A similar approach can be taken for distributing workflows in a grid environment. However, it is difficult to adapt pre-existing scripting languages to a distributed framework. As these languages are not designed for grid computing, the programmer has to explicitly call commands to transfer files and submit jobs on remote schedulers. In addition, the programmer must also impose control flows on programs to ensure that barriers are respected and jobs are scheduled properly. It would be much more efficient to develop a scripting language specifically targeting workflows in a distributed environment.

Such an approach would specify dependencies between jobs implicitly in the syntactic structure of the script, without the need for explicit naming and referencing of dependent jobs. It would also allow for better scheduling, as, at the time of execution, scheduling decisions can be made from a global perspective, that is, by analysis of the whole script. The design of such a grid scripting language should have the following salient features, keeping in mind the Grid-programming aspects delineated earlier [41]:

- A bottom-up design, which is focused on execution in a heterogeneous, distributed environment.
- Enough resource information to allow for the various subtasks to be scheduled in a way that most effectively uses the Grid resources.
- A middleware independent syntax, which allows programs to run on different middleware implementations, provided a suitable interpretor is available.

The last point is meant to provide a measure of independence from middleware platforms. The GEL [41] has been implemented as an interpreted language (cf. bash, perl, and python) keeping the earlier specifications in mind. Most importantly, efforts have been made to keep the language middleware independent by pushing all the middleware dependencies into specific interpretor instances. For example, one interpretor instance uses GridFTP commands to stage files and Globus GRAM requests to execute

Jobs, wheares other instances assume a campus-wide NAS-based filesystem and use SGE [55], OpenPBS [28], or LSF [60] as schedulers to queue jobs for execution.

The first two points are mentioned in more detail in the following sections.

23.5.1   Language Syntax and Semantics

Let us take a look at what it means to execute a program. Semantically, executing a program amounts to executing a collection of binaries in the specified order. Each program conceptually starts with one directory containing its input files and finishes with possibly many directories containing its output files. It must be noted that a sequential program ends with just one directory of output files when compared with a parameter-sweep-style program that ends with one directory for each parameter instance. The case where many output directories are created arises because of a number of parallel composition constructs that are described in detail subsequently.

The basic atomic components of our programs are thus jobs that can be defined informally, as specifying a binary along with other information such as its resource requirements (e.g., processor/OS architecture and memory), which allows the interpretor to correctly stage the required files and execute the binary (be it through an "exec" OS call, SGE/PBS/LSF qsub/bsub, Globus GRAM request, or otherwise). Executing a job consists of staging the input files into the working directory and then running the binary. The files present in the working directory after the binary terminates are deemed to be the output of the job.

Jobs can be more formally defined as a combination of *atomic predicates* (e.g., of the form (exec = bl2seq), (arch = ia64) and (mem ≥ 100M)) using conjunctive (∧) and disjunctive (∨) operators, giving a *predicate*. Predicates are meant to specify resource requirements by imposing constraints on required software/licences/libraries, required data, cpu count, and required scratch space. Disjunction can be interpreted as giving rise to "possible alternatives," wheares conjunction can be interpreted as an "and" formulation.[1]

For example,

```
(exec=ia32/blastall)

∧ (arch=ia32/intel)

∧ (args=-p blastn -d ecoli -i seq.fasta -o seq.out -E 1E-30)
```
$$(23.1)$$

specifies a job whose binary is called `ia32/blastall` and requires an Intel-based 32-bit architecture machine to run. Supposing we also have a binary `sun/blastall`, which requires a `sparc9` architecture and which is functionally

---

[1]See [41] for more details.

equivalent to the previous binary, then the job can be specified as

$$
\left(
\begin{array}{l}
(\text{exec=ia32/blastall}) \wedge (\text{arch} = \text{ia32}) \\
\vee \quad (\text{exec=sun/blastall}) \wedge (\text{arch} = \text{sparc9})
\end{array}
\right)
$$

$$\wedge\, (\text{args} = \text{-i seq1.fasta -j seq2.fasta})$$

which states that to execute this job, you can execute either binary with the same arguments.

For flexibility, we allow parameterization of arguments by way of a function/procedure mechanism. For example, we can name a parameterized job as

$$
\begin{array}{l}
\quad\quad\quad\quad (\text{exec} = \text{ia32/blastall}) \\
B(a,b) := \wedge \quad (\text{arch} = \text{ia32}) \\
\quad\quad\quad \wedge \quad (\text{args} = \text{-blastn -d ecoli -i } a \text{ -E 1E-30 -o } b)
\end{array}
$$

in which case $B(\texttt{seq.fasta}, \texttt{seq.out})$ "instantiates" to Job (23.1).

23.5.1.1 *Sequential Constructs*

Given the earlier definition of a job, programs can then be defined as consisting of combinations of jobs using a collection of sequential and parallel language constructs. The sequential constructs are standard and are a common feature of many programming languages (Fig. 23.2): sequential composition $P \cdot Q$ (execute P, then execute Q); loop iteration while A do P (continually execute P depending on the outcome of executing A); and conditional if A then P else Q (execute A and, depending on its outcome, execute either P or Q). Executing a program $P \cdot Q$ involves executing P, staging the files in all output directories of P into the input directory of Q, and then executing Q. Note that sequential composition involves an implicit merge of directories.

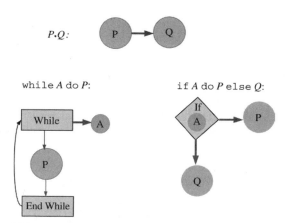

Figure 23.2 The common sequential constructs used are shown here.

23.5.1.2 Parallel Constructs The parallel constructs have been designed with a distributed framework in mind and are described in more detail. There are three main parallel constructs in GEL (Fig. 23.3) and they are discussed subsequently:

1. The parallel composition of programs is the basic mechanism for expressing parameter-sweep-style programs using GEL. The most basic parallel construct is the pair-wise parallel composition operator $- + -$ (cf. the pair-wise sequential composition operator $-.-$). The parallel composition of two programs P and Q is written as $P + Q$. The execution of $P + Q$ consists of the following steps:

   - Staging of files from the input directory to the two input directories for programs P and Q, respectively.
   - Execution of programs P and Q.
   - Staging back and merging of output directories.

   Since P and Q have distinct working directories for P and Q, which are populated from the same input directory, it allows for a transparent implementation on a distributed computer.

   $P + Q$ can be viewed as a mechanism that indicates to the interpretor that P and Q are independent of each other and that their resulting output files do not overlap. Sequential and parallel constructs can, of course, be combined to form complex workflows. For example, a sequential composition of $P + Q$ with another program R, that is, of the form $(P + Q) \cdot R$, involves staging all the output files of $P + Q$ into the input directory of program R. However, there is cause for caution here as the programmer must ensure that programs P and Q do not write to the same files.

2. A very important parallel construct is the *parallel-for* construct. It essentially enables the execution of parameter sweep applications, where a program is run many times with different values for a single parameter and where the number

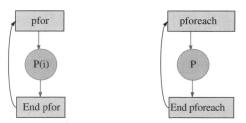

Figure 23.3   The parallel constructs used are illustrated here.

of times the program needs to be executed is known a priori. For example, suppose $A(-)$ is a parameterized job that takes one parameter and needs to be executed for arguments $1, \ldots, 20$. The parallel-for construct is given as

$$\sum_{x=1}^{20} A(x)$$

which is behaviorally equivalent to

$$A(1) + A(2) + \cdots + A(20)$$

As a result, it is fairly straightforward to create distributed parameter sweep applications using GEL.

3. Another useful parallel construct is *parallel-foreach* shown subsequently,

$$\sum_{f \in \{\texttt{gene*.fasta}\}} B(\texttt{q.fasta}, f)$$

which, when executed, finds all files matching glob pattern `gene*.fasta` and instantiates one copy of $B(-, -)$ for each file. For example, if the matching files are `gene1.fasta`, `gene2.fasta`, and `gene3.fasta`, then this is behaviorally equivalent to

$$
\begin{aligned}
& B(\texttt{q.fasta}, \texttt{gene1.fasta}) \\
+\ & B(\texttt{q.fasta}, \texttt{gene2.fasta}) \\
+\ & B(\texttt{q.fasta}, \texttt{gene3.fasta})
\end{aligned}
$$

Of course, $\sum_{x=a}^{b} A(x)$ and $\sum_{f \in \{\{e\}\}} A(f)$ cannot be easily typeset in ASCII and thus more conventional programming syntax such as

```
pfor x = a to b do          pforeach f in e do
   A(x)            and         A(f)
endpfor                     endpforeach
```

is used in our implementations.

The semantics are designed in such a way that it is straightforward to execute programs over a distributed computer, be this a Globus-based Grid, or a heterogeneous collection of clusters within one corporation. An example GEL script is provided in Figure 23.11 for the swarm optimization case study described in Section 23.7.3. The different attributes for the atomic predicates are given in Table 23.1.

23.5.2 GEL Interpretor and Scheduling

Effective utilization of grid resources requires proper job scheduling as well as allocation of resources. One of the primary problems facing a grid application developer

TABLE 23.1 Attributes for Atomic Predicates in Job Definitions

Attribute	Description
exec	File name of executable
dir	Local directory in which executable resides
args	Command line arguments to be passed to executable
ipdir	Local directory containing read-only files
cmdir	Local directory containing read–write files

is that of scheduling the jobs onto the grid in the absence of good metaschedulers. Obviously, an application developer would not want to be tied to any particular middleware. Ideally, an application developer must be able to write an application that can be tested on their own machine and then be ported to the available distributed resource such as a cluster or a grid without having to worry about scheduling mechanisms available on the respective resources. This requires separate interpretor instances for the different cluster-level schedulers as well as for a Globus based scheduler.

For these schedulers to do effective resource allocation, information regarding the workflow must be passed to them. For example, suppose A is a preprocessing step to generate the input files for $B(1), \ldots, B(N)$, for some fixed N, and these jobs are comprised in a pipeline as follows:

$$A \sum_{i=1}^{N} B(i)$$

that is, A is executed first followed by $B(1), \ldots, B(N)$ in parallel. Since $\sum_{i=1}^{N} B(i)$ cannot execute before A completes, if we were to schedule without knowledge of the whole program, A might initially be scheduled on any suitable nearby machine with the least utilization. However, if the entire workflow is known to the scheduler, it might try to run A on a large Beowulf cluster (with at least N CPUs) so that inter-Grid-node file staging before execution of each instance of $B(-)$ could be avoided.

If N is so large (e.g., 10,000 or more) that it is unlikely, there is any one Grid node with as many processors, $\sum_{i=1}^{M} B(i)$ could be run on one node, and $\sum_{i=M+1}^{N} B(i)$ on another, for some M between 1 and N. Alternatively, the program could be transformed into

$$\sum_{i=1}^{N} A \cdot B(i)$$

if A as deterministic. This may give better performance in the case where the instances of $A \cdot B(-)$ were partitioned across many Grid nodes. Of course, such scheduling is only possible if the scheduler has sufficient information. Other than the explicit annotations associated with jobs (e.g., required architecture, memory, disk, libraries, software, and data), there is also implicit information in the language constructs and this information could help the scheduler to make better scheduling decisions.

To preserve all information, the scheduler should take as input the whole program. However, this could introduce its own (unnecessary) complications: the scheduler would have to not only support all the syntactic nuances of the programming language but also be able to deal with apparent cyclic dependencies (e.g., the dependencies present in the while loop). Furthermore, since schedulers must use specific knowledge of the architecture of the distributed computer, different implementations, one for each scheduler type, are necessary, and as such, each scheduler would have to be able to parse, analyze, and interpret programs.

Hence, in the interests of code maintainability, the GEL scheduler and interpretor are separated from one another. Instead, an intermediate description of programs which is essentially that of job instances and their (acyclic) dependencies on other job instances, that is, DAGs, are introduced. These DAGs give more information than simply atomic jobs by themselves; yet at the same time, ease from the scheduler, the burden of the syntactic analyses required for whole programs.

Thus, the monolithic scheduler, which runs programs directly on a distributed computer, is factorized into (1) a (DAG) *generator* which translates from programs to the intermediate DAG form and (2) a (DAG) *executor* which runs DAGs on some target distributed computer. For example, different executor implementations can (1) run jobs on the same computer by calling an exec OS call (useful for development and testing purposes) or (2) interface with the local scheduler on a cluster or use the Globus API (3) or interface with a Grid metascheduler such as Nimrod [5], or APST [14].

23.5.3 Interpretor Anatomy

As mentioned in the previous section, the GEL interpretors are each factored into two components: the (DAG) *builder* and the (DAG) *executor*. The builder encapsulates the language-specific elements of the interpretor, such as the lexical analyzer, parser, and syntax checker. The DAG builder also enables the use of a DAG-based intermediate language between the builder and the executor by translating cyclic dependencies between jobs into DAGs, thereby creating acyclic dependencies.

The executor thus incorporates the job submission aspects of the interpreter. Additionally, it is dependent only on the much simpler DAG-based language without having to bother with cyclic dependcies. Hence, to interface with different middleware formalisms (e.g., SGE), it is only necessary to implement a version of the interpreter that can submit jobs as DAGs to the respective scheduling mechanisms (SGE in this case). Extension of, or changes to, the programming language, in contrast, only require extensions to the builder, as the DAG-based intermediate language remains unchanged.

23.5.3.1 *DAG Builder* DAGs are a commonly used data structure, which are understood by most scheduling mechanisms. This ubiquity of DAGs has been taken advantage of by the GEL interpretor. This is achieved by the builder by translating the

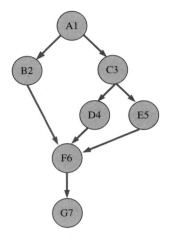

Figure 23.4   An example workflow.

GEL script into a DAG before being passed to the executor. Given a job definition, and for every occurence of a job name in the description syntax, the builder instantiates a copy of the job template. Each instantiation creates a unique job id (the job name with a numerical suffix). After instantiating all jobs, the builder produces a DAG representation of the workflow description and stores it in a data structure.

Figure 23.4 shows an example workflow. The DAG representation of the workflow is shown as follows.

```
A1 (), B2 (A1), C3 (A1), D4 (C3),
E5 (C3), F6 (E5,B2,D4),
G7 (F6)
```

The representation is essentially a comma-separated list of DAG-nodes, where each node consists of an instance name and a list of dependent nodes in parentheses. The dependencies are determined by the builder and passed in the form of a DAG to the executor for execution. There are instances where the *builder* does not instantiate the entire workflow, producing a DAG only as far as it is possible to do so. This occurs when the if-else, while, and pforeach constructs are encountered, as in each of these constructs, the builder does not a priori know the exact number of times the loops are executed (for the while and pforeach constructs) or the particular branch that will be taken (in the case of the if-else construct).

The builder has been designed so that it builds as much of the DAG as possible. It maintains a list of stack machines,[2] which represent the independent execution

---

[2]Each stack machine, in essence, is the stack required to traverse the syntax tree and some extra state variables.

threads of the program. When no more of the DAG can be built for any of the threads, the builder waits for a job to complete, before trying to build more of the DAG.

23.5.3.2 DAG Executor The executor is responsible for executing the workflow by submitting the DAG representation of programs it generates to a scheduler (local, cluster, or grid). Currently, local (fork), cluster (SGE, OpenPBS, and LSF), and grid (Globus) versions of the executor exist. A description of the workflow execution process is given subsequently. The execution process itself is common to all the different executor implementations. The only differences lie in the mechanisms for the copying/staging of files as well as in the scheduling mechanisms that are unique to the different scheduling formalisms.

For each job that the executor submits, a working directory is created on the host on which the job is to be executed. On the basis of information provided in the job definition, the executable and input files on the local machine will be located and then copied (in the case of a local executor) or staged (for cluster and grid versions) to the respective working directories. On completion of the job, the output files needed by a subsequent job are staged directly over to the job's working directory, that is, a third-party transfer, by-passing the local computer (for cluster and grid versions). No user input to the executor regarding the location and sequence of jobs is required.

As such, for jobs running on a remote cluster, the user need only have a valid user account, whereas for jobs on the grid, the user need only has the authority to run on nodes on the Grid (i.e., a valid certificate and entry in the requisite grid-mapfile) and does not have to manually create an executable directory on the remote host. Essentially, the executor makes running a Grid application similar to what one would experience if he/she were to run a workflow on a local machine.

For the grid version of the interpreter, the submission engine developed is a simple round-robin scheduler, which schedules a job to the next host. It also uses a locally stored resource database about the software available on the Grid nodes and will submit a job to a Grid node, only if the required software is installed. More sophisticated executors can be developed, which will understand more resource attributes (e.g., architecture, OS, and memory requirements), use diverse resource discovery tools such as in GRD [42], Ganglia [44], and NWS [59], and perhaps interface with grid meta-schedulers such as Condor-G [17], and Nimrod/G [5].

23.6 GUI-BASED WORKFLOW CONSTRUCTION AND EXECUTION

23.6.1 Background

The GEL described in the previous section makes it easy to execute workflows in a distributed computing environment. However, constructing workflows using GEL is still not intuitive and transparent enough for biologists and bioinformaticians. Suites such as Accelrys and EMBOSS, through consistent user interface elements, have narrowed the usability gap and made individual applications accessible to the nonspecialist bioinformatician.

Additional efforts in narrowing this gap include Jemboss [16], Taverna/Freefluo [47], ICENI [24], and Biopipe [30]. Jemboss addresses usability of bioinformatics applications by providing a GUI to EMBOSS. The user interface replaces the command-line options of the EMBOSS applications with interface elements such as check boxes, drop-down lists, and text boxes; thus simplifying the applications for users unfamiliar with command-line interfaces. Even for command-line enthusiasts, it simplifies learning of new applications, which might only be used occasionally, as the interface is consistent across applications. Jemboss can run the EMBOSS application on the same machine, in "stand-alone" mode, or remotely using a SOAP protocol.

Taverna is a services-oriented workflow engine, which uses web-services for components. The interface requires the user to connect together output and input ports of components to build a workflow. Taverna relies on Soaplab [53] to convert the EMBOSS command-line applications into web services. However, Soaplab appears to have lost the help text annotations of the different input fields, which is characteristic of other EMBOSS interfaces. ICENI is also a service-oriented workflow framework and has a Netbeans-based user interface.

Biopipe [52] is a workflow framework, which also allows for execution of workflows across clusters. However, Biopipe only allows for pipelines, not more general workflows with iterative loops. For instance, workflows containing while loops, in particular, cannot be implemented in Biopipe. In addition, Biopipe currently does not have a user-friendly interface for composing pipelines and workflows.

Wildfire [56] is a GUI-based workflow composition and exection engine introduced in the following section. Wildfire provides a GUI to GEL, thus enabling the easy composition and execution of workflows in a distributed environment. It provides an intuitive interface based on a drawing analogy and, like Jemboss, presents program options using GUI elements. Thus *Wildfire* hides the precise syntax of scripting languages and command-line options from the user. However, unlike Jemboss, which can only run one application at a time, *Wildfire* allows the user to compose multiple applications into a workflow.

In contrast to Taverna and ICENI, it works directly with program executables, rather than web or grid services. This was a design decision based on the fact that bioinformatics abounds in legacy applications, that is, applications that have been in use for a long time. Moreover, the task of converting legacy applications into web and/or grid services is not trivial for a bioinformatician. Additionally, creating web and grid services can tie applications to certain nodes, which thus disallows taking advantage of available compute resources on the grid. This can often lead to performance bottlenecks due to the heavy utilization of node-locked applications in a given workflow. *Wildfire*, keeping in mind the fact that its target audience is the bioinformatics community, incorporates the entire EMBOSS suite of applications. Templates have been provided for all the EMBOSS applications.

23.6.2 WILDFIRE

Wildfire allows the user to visually construct workflows. For execution, *Wildfire* exports the workflow as a GEL script, and then calls a GEL interpretor to execute it.

The GEL interpretor can either run on the same machine as *Wildfire* or on a remote compute server. Figure 23.5 summarizes the interaction between *Wildfire* and GEL.

Wildfire is implemented in Java and has been tested on Windows and Linux platforms. On a Linux platform, the user can run workflows directly on the same machine: ideal for developing and testing small examples on a laptop, while reserving the multi-processor servers and clusters for running the workflow on real data.

The two main activities of *Wildfire*, namely, workflow *construction* and *execution* are discussed subsequently.

23.6.3 Workflow Construction

A user is presented with a graphical workflow canvas, while constructing workflows using *Wildfire*. This obviates the need for the user to work directly with the syntax of scripting languages such as GEL or Perl. There are three main types of workflow components: (1) *atomic components*, which approximately correspond to an EMBOSS application, (2) subworkflows, or (3) loops (both parallel and sequential). Users can select the atomic components from a customizable list, which by default includes all the EMBOSS 2.8.0 applications (as mentioned earlier). Sequential dependencies

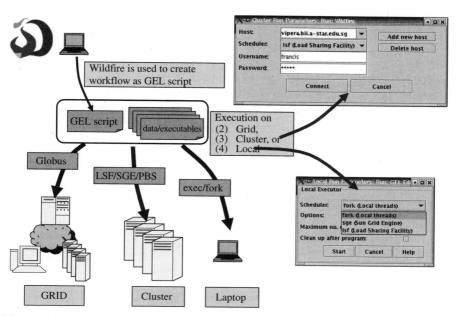

Figure 23.5 Relationship between *Wildfire* and GEL. *Wildfire* is an interactive application, which allows users to draw workflows. The workflow is exported as a GEL script, which is executed using a suitable GEL interpretor. There are GEL interpretors for execution on (1) the Grid, using Globus, (2) a cluster, using LSF, PBS, or SGE, and (3) the same machine, which could be a laptop, desktop, or multiprocessor server.

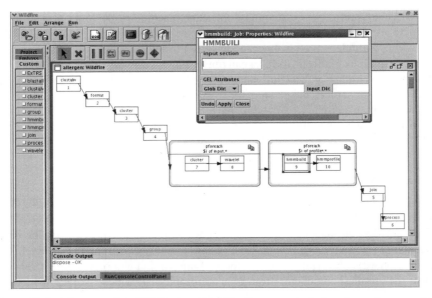

Figure 23.6 Elements of the *Wildfire* interface. The foreground window shows the properties form for the `hmmbuild` program. The main window in the background shows the workflow canvas. Its left panel lists the atomic workflow components; this list is preconfigured with all EMBOSS applications and can be customized.

between components are created by drawing an arrow between them. By default, components not linked by arrows are assumed to be independent (and so can be executed in parallel).

Double clicking on an atomic component in the workflow will bring up properties window resembling that of Jemboss (Fig. 23.6). In addition, the user can add his own command-line programs to the list of atomic components. The *Wildfire* user interface has a facility to help the user create new atomic components.

23.6.4 Workflow Execution

For execution, *Wildfire* exports a programmatic description of the workflow, in GEL, which is passed to a GEL interpretor for execution. When developing small workflows, the user can run the workflow on the same machine.[3] In this way, *Wildfire* can be used as a standalone application without access to the network.

Alternatively, the user can choose to send the workflow to a remote server and run it there. In this case, *Wildfire* uses the SSH and SCP protocols to send the necessary files over and then executes the job/jobs on the remote server (Fig. 23.7). The GEL interpretor can execute the atomic components directly if the server has multiple processors. If the server is a cluster or a grid, then GEL can submit the atomic

---

[3]Currently, standalone mode is not available for Windows.

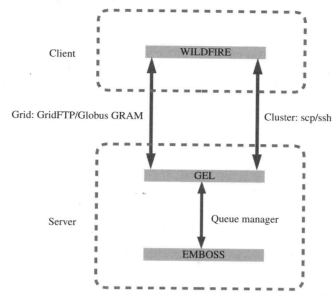

Figure 23.7 Remote execution of workflows. In the case of large workflows or when the applications are not available on the client machine, it is possible to execute the workflow remotely. In this case, *Wildfire* uses SSH and SCP protocols (for clusters) or Globus GRAM and GridFTP (for grids) to the send files to the remote machine/machines and start execution.

components as jobs to the queue manager. In either case, the GEL interpretor will try to use multiple processors where possible. Remote server execution is useful for workflows with large data sets as GEL will make use of multiple processors. It is also useful if the atomic components are not installed on the local machine.

Wildfire can also be used to break up the workflow and run parts of it concurrently on different supercomputers by using the Grid. As GEL uses Globus protocols (Globus GRAM and GridFTP) to transfer files and run the individual components on the different machines, it is useful for very large workflows that require as many compute resources as possible. It is also useful when not all components are available on any one machine or when some machines are more efficient than others for running specific components, because of different hardware or operating system characteristics. A further opportunity for running distributed workflows on the grid exists when idle cycles are available on distributed resources. In such a case, load balancing can be performed to best utilize these available resources.

The execution of the individual atomic components is monitored by *Wildfire* with feedback being provided via annotations on the canvas, which are updated in real time.

The exported GEL script can also be run directly using an interpretor via the command line. This allows a workflow to be run in batch mode independent of *Wildfire* and is useful for very long-running workflows or those that have to be run repeatedly.

23.7   CASE STUDIES

Having described in detail the architectural details of *Wildfire* and its underlying script-ing language, let us now take a look at three different case studies that demonstrate the features of *Wildfire*/GEL as a distributed workflow enactment engine.

The first application is fairly typical of most bioinformatics workflows and deals with the analysis of human tissue-specific transcripts by comparison against known exons. This example shows how *Wildfire* can make use of the parallel capabilities of supercomputers. The second example considers a particle swarm optimization algorithm implemented as a workflow and shows that *Wildfire* can express workflows requiring iteration (while loops). The last example cross validates an allergenicity prediction algorithm. The number of parallel processes in this workflow can only be determined at run time.

23.7.1   Tissue-Specific Gene Expression Analysis

The study of tissue-specific gene expression in humans is very typical of most bio-informatics pipelines or workflows. The idea here is to compare the known exons against a database of 16,385 transcripts obtained from the mammalian gene collec-tion. The workflow is shown in Figure 23.8a. As the human genome contains many exons, the extraction process is time consuming but easily parallelizable. The inherent parallelism in the workflow is shown in Figure 23.8b. The standard organization of the 24 chromosomes into separate files provides a natural partitioning of the exon extrac-tion problem: the exons are extracted from each chromosome in parallel. To further increase the granularity of the problem and thereby exploiting more parallelism, each

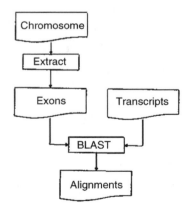

(*a*) Tissue-specific gene expression analysis.

Figure 23.8   Profile of job execution. Time (hh:mm) is shown along horizontal scale. The execution of each job is shown as a line. Total CPU time is 54 m:40 s and wall time is 12 m: 55 s.

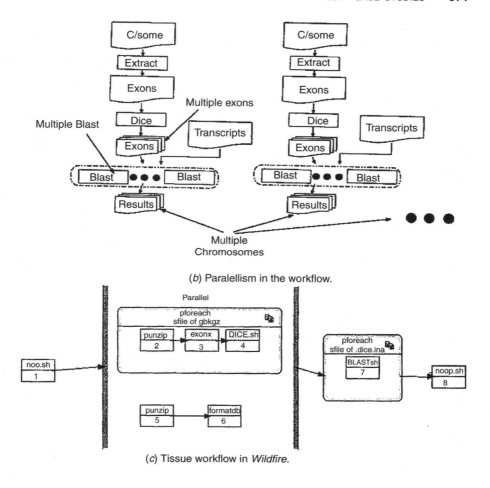

(*b*) Paralellism in the workflow.

(*c*) Tissue workflow in *Wildfire*.

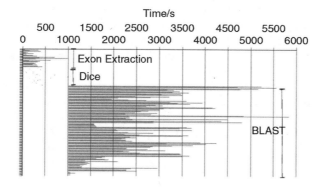

Figure 23.8 *Continued.*

of the 24 files of exons is broken up into five smaller files, resulting in a total of 120 files. These are then BLASTed against the database of transcripts.

The workflow as constructed in *Wildfire* is shown in Figure 23.8*c*. The atomic component `exonx` is a program developed in-house to extract and store exons from a genbank file in fasta format; `dice` is a perl script used to break up a fasta file into smaller pieces. The `noop.sh` components at the beginning and end are required to make sure all the files are in the right place. These will be replaced in future versions by an implicit merge, which will copy all the relevant files into the input directory at the beginning and into the results directory at the end. The remaining components (GNU `gunzip` and NCBI BLAST `formatdb`, and `blastall`) are standard applications that have been incorporated as atomic components using the template builder provided.

The whole workflow takes less than 6000 s to run on a 128 CPU Pentium III cluster, whereas a sequential version of the same workflow required almost nine times longer [41]. The execution profile is shown in Figure 23.8. Further modifications to the workflow should be able to improve this time.

23.7.2 Allergenicity Prediction

Allergens are proteins that induce allergic responses. More specifically, they elicit IgE antibodies and cause the symptoms of allergy, which has been a major health problem in developed countries [49]. With many transgenic proteins introduced into the food chain, the need to predict their potential allergenicity has become a crucial issue. Bioinformatics, more specifically, sequence analysis methods have an important role in the identification of allergenicity [25, 29].

One approach to allergenicity prediction is to determine, automatically, motifs from sequences in an allergenic database and then search for the identified motifs in the query sequences. Li et al. [40] described an approach where protein sequence motifs were identified using wavelet analysis [35]. The particular example consists of 817 sequences in an allergen database. A 10-fold cross-validation test is conducted where 90% of the sequences are used for motif identification with the remaining 10% being used as query sequence for validation. This procedure is carried out a number of times to obtain averaged values for recall and precision. The workflow is shown in Figure 23.9. A brief description of the workflow is discussed as follows.

ClustalW is initially used to generate the pair-wise global alignment distances among the randomly selected protein sequences. The pair-wise distances so obtained are then used to cluster the protein sequences by partitioning around medoids using the statistics tool R [3]. Each cluster of protein sequences is subsequently realigned using *ClustalW*. The wavelet analysis technique developed by Krishnan et al. is then used on each aligned cluster to identify motifs in the protein sequences.

HMM profiles [18, 20] are then generated for each identified motif using `hmmbuild`. We use these profiles to search for the motifs in each query sequence using `hmmprofile`, and thus predict whether it is an allergen. The accuracy of the predictions is computed to assess the effectiveness of this approach.

Figure 23.9*a* shows the workflow (on the left) as well as the inherent parallelisms (on the right). The two main areas of parallelism are in the identification of the motifs using the wavelet analysis technique (one for each cluster) as well as in building the HMM based profile and searching the query sequences (one for each motif identified).

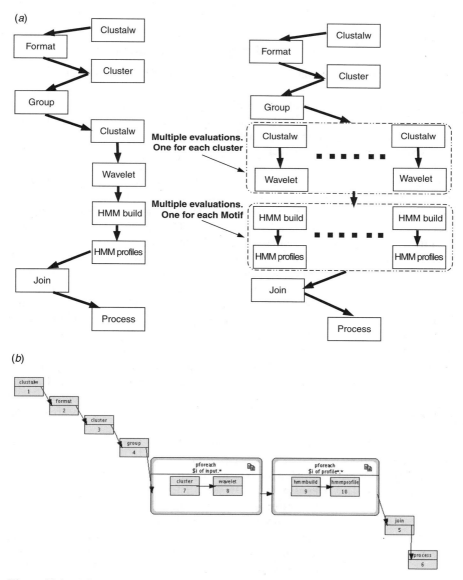

Figure 23.9   Allerginicity workflow. (*a*) Allergen predicition workflow. (*b*) Allergen workflow in Wildlife.

Figure 23.9*b* shows the workflow as comprised in *Wildfire*. The parallel "foreach" construct, *pforeach* has been used to execute in parallel. This is because the number of clusters and the number of motifs are not known a priori. This is a frequent occurence in many bioinformatics workflows and hence this particular example is a good illustration of the *pforeach* construct. This construct allows the pipeline included in the *pforeach* box to be executed as many times as there are files in the directory that match the particular "glob" pattern.

23.7.3 Parameter Estimation Using Swarm Intelligence

The next example demonstrates how to run a swarm intelligence algorithm over the grid.

Real-life optimization problems are often intractable and heuristics are the only choice for finding near optimal solutions. Particle Swarm Optimization [19] is such a heuristic based on simulation of information exchange between leaders and followers observed in, for example, bird flocking.

The algorithm simulates individuals flying through the search space. On each iteration, the individuals are separated into a set of leaders and a set of followers, based on their fitness. The followers use the locations of the leaders to change their flying direction, that is, search velocity. The location of each individual is computed based on its current location and flying direction. The new location is used to rank the fitness of individuals and subsequently the leader and follower sets. This process is repeated again until an optimal solution is found. In the swarm algorithm, each individual of the swarm works independently after obtaining information about the leaders. Hence, it is computationally advantageous to parallelize the algorithm.

The workflow in Figure 23.10 is a simplified implementation of a swarm algorithm by Ray et al. [50]. The algorithm is applied to a parameter estimation problem for a biochemical pathway model consisting of 36 unknowns and eight ODEs [45]. Components `Initialize`, `Evaluate`, and `Collate` are used to initialize and rank the individuals. Component `Test` determines whether the workflow should terminate and `Extract` collects together the results on termination of the simulation. Component `ReEval` is used to evaluate the fitness of an individual; note the outer parallel loop evaluates the fitness of each follower. The remaining components are used to select the leaders and followers.

It is to be noted that there is a cyclic dependency in the workflow as `Classify` depends on both `Collate` and `Reassign` (initially and thereafter on `Reassign` hereditarily), whereas `Reassign` in its turn is dependent hereditarily on `Classify`. The while loop in GEL allows such dependencies and so is crucial for this workflow.

Figure 23.10*b* shows the swarm workflow as comprised in *Wildfire*. Figure 23.11 shows the GEL script generated upon building the workflow in *Wildfire*.

The swarm algorithm script in Figures 23.10*b* and 23.11 shows two new syntax constructs not observed in the previous two examples. These two are the `pfor` and `while` loops. The `pfor` initializes the swarm with some random values. The `while` body contains the stages in the evolution of the swarm and it is the test for ending the algorithm. The `pforeach` in the loop body represents the set of followers updating

(a)

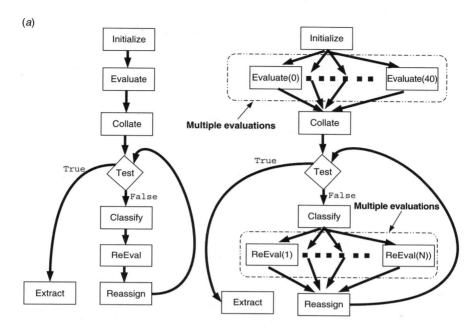

(b)

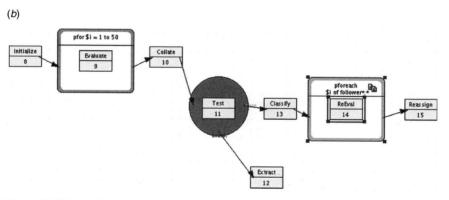

Figure 23.10 (a) Shows the swarm workflow on the left and the same workflow with the parallelisms defined. (b) Shows the swarm workflow as comprised using *Wildfire*.

their *flying* direction. The construct is specifically used because at each evolution, the set of leaders and followers changes and pforeach is able to reflect those changes through the variable number of matches of the pattern it finds at each evolution. The syntax pfor works similar to the pforeach except that it expands in parallel the statement it encloses by stepping from the starting integer to the ending integer in steps of +1.

```
1  Initialize:={exec= "Initialize";
2          dir= "swarm/";
3          cmdir= "model/"}
4  Evaluate(i):={exec= "Evaluate";
5              args= $i;
6              dir= "swarm/"}
7  Collate:={exec= "Collate";
8          dir= "swarm/"}
9  Test:={exec= "Test";
10      dir= "swarm/"}
11 Classify:={exec= "Classify";
12             dir="swarm/";
13             cmdir= "Common/"}
14 ReEval(i):={exec= "ReEval";
15             args= $i;
16             dir= "swarm/"}
17 Reassign:={exec= "Reassign";
18             dir= "swarm/"}
19 Extract:={exec= "Extract";
20          dir= "swarm/";
21          cmdir= "result/"}
22
23 Initialize
24 pfor i = 0 to 49 do
25     Evaluate($i)
26 endpfor
27 Collate
28 while Test do
29     Classify
30     pforeach file of "follower*.*"
31             in "Common" do
32         ReEval($file)
33     endpforeach
34     Reassign
35 endwhile
36 Extract
```

Figure 23.11   Script for swarm algorithm.

TABLE 23.2   Grid Testbed Configuration

Name	Nodes	CPUs	Scheduler
turing	4	8	SGE
church	2	4	PBS
goedel	2	4	LSF

Note: The testbed consists of three Pentium III 800 MHz clusters running Linux and Globus Toolkit 2.2.4.

The `while` loop examines the standard output of `Test` to decide on whether to step into the loop body. The boolean test is false if `Test` writes to standard output and true if nothing is written. As such, this test based on writing to standard output allows us to incorporate conditional constructs for more expressive scripting. In this example, `Test` will test for the convergence of the solution and break out of the loop if the condition of the boolean test is false.

The workflow was run on a test bed consisting of three compute clusters `turing`, `church`, and `goedel`. The grid testbed configuration is given in Table 23.2. The R package was installed only on `church`, and each cluster runs a different local scheduler.

Table 23.3 shows a comparison of the performance of the various interpretors for the swarm optimization workflow. It is intriguing to note that the grid version, running on all 16 processors (across all the clusters) was the fastest, despite the rather naive, round-robin scheduling being used. It was also noticed that the interpretor did not monopolize the resources from the beginning; rather it acquired the resources as and when required, thereby allowing unused CPUs to be utilized by other jobs. As a result, parallel speedup in this case is not directly indicative of the efficiency. Figure 23.12 shows a profile of the execution of each job for a small example run on turing (8 CPU cluster). The consequences of barriers are clearly shown (e.g., jobs 14–18 and 21–25).

TABLE 23.3   Performance of Various Interpretors

Interpretor	CPUs	Time (min)
Local	1	357
Globus Grid	16	89
SGE	8	123
Bash + SGE	8	122

Note: During runtime, the idle CPUs can be used by other users; the interpretors do not monopolize all the CPUs displayed in the table earlier.

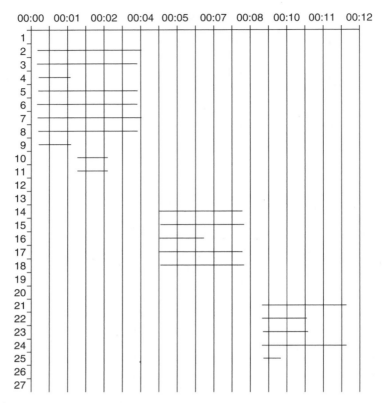

Figure 23.12   Profile of job execution for an example run on the eight processor node turing. Time (hh:mm) is shown along horizontal scale. The execution of each job is shown as a line. Total CPU time is 54 m:40 s and wall time is 12 m:55 s.

23.8 SUMMARY

The rapid strides made in the fields of computational biology, bioinformatics, and distributed and parallel computing provide unique opportunities for furthering the needs of interdisciplinary research. With an explosion in the amount of information collected in bioinformatics, there is a need for new programming and computing paradigms to process this vast storehouse of knowledge. Luckily, the presence of a number of embarrassingly applications make it easy to exploit a high performance computing environment.

Workflows, as a result of occuring naturally in the field of bioinformatics, have been targeted by the distributed computing community as test cases for grid enablement. A number of efforts are underway that use different workflow languages and approaches. There are currently two schools of thought: one that works on a services oriented approach, whereas the other works with legacy applications in a distributed computing framework. There are a number of challenges that are still to be overcome for both these approaches and it may well be that in future these two different approaches merge.

It must however be borne in mind that the different approaches are just enabling technologies and that to find acceptance among the bioinformatics and computational biology communities, the workflow enactment engine has to hide the complexities of the computing side of things from the scientists. A GUI-based front end, which enables easy composition and execution of workflows, is thus extremely important. *Wildfire* has been designed keeping this in mind.

REFERENCES

1. Business Process Modelling Language, www.bpmi.org/bpml.esp.

2. European Datagrid, www.eu-datagrid.org/.

3. R Language Definition, http://www.r-project.org.

4. XML Process Definition Language, 5 2001, xml. coverpages. org/XPDL20010522.pdf.

5. D. Abramson, R. Sosic, J. Giddy, and B. Hall, Nimrod: A Tool for Performing Parameterised Simulations Using Distributed Workstations, in *HPDC*, 1995, pp. 112–121.

6. M. Addis, J. Ferris, M. Greenwood, P. Li, D. Marvin, T Oinn, and A. Wipat, Experiences with e-science Workflow Specification and Enactment in Bioinformatics, in *Proceedings of the UK e-Science All Hands Meeting*, 2003.

7. J. Almond and D. Snelling, LJNICORE: uniform access to supercomputing as an element of electronic commerce, *Future Generation Comp. Sys.*, 15 (5–6), 539–548 (1999).

8. S. F. Altschul, T. L. Madden, A. A. Schaffer, J. Zhang, Z. Zhang, W. Miller, and D. J. Lipman, Gapped BLAST and PSI-BLAST: a new generation of protein database search programs, *Nucleic Acids Res.*, 25, 3389–3402 (1997).

9. K. Amin and G. von Laszewski, GridAnt: A grid workflow system, www.globus.org.

10. T. Andrews, F. Curbera, H. Dholakia, Y. Goland, J. Klein, F. Leymann, K. Liu, D. Roller, D. Smith, S. Thatte, I. Trickovic, and S. Weerawarana, Business Process Execution Language for Web Services (BPEL4WS 1.1), 5 2003, www6.software.ibm.com/software/developer/library/ws-bpel.pdf.

11. H. Cassanova and J. J. Dongarra, "NetSolve: A Network-Enabled Solver; Examples and Users", in *Proc. Seventh Heterogeneous Computing Workshop*, 19–28, 1998.

12. P. Avery and I. Foster, The GriPhyN Project: Towards Petascale Virtual-Data Grids, Technical Report 2000-1, GriPhyN, 2000, www.griphyn.org.

13. K. Baldridge and P. E. Bourne, *The New Biology and The Grid, Gid Computing Making the Global Infrastructure a Reality*, Wiley, 2003.

14. F. D. Berman, R. Wolski, S. Figueira, J. Schopf, and G. Shao, Application-Level Scheduling on Distributed Heterogeneous Networks, in *Proceedings of Supercomputing 1996*, 1996, citeseer.nj.nec.com/124341.html.

15. H. P. Bivens, Grid Workflow.

16. T. Carver and A. Beasby, The design of Jemboss: a graphical user interface to EMBOSS, *Bioinformatics*, 19 (14), 1837–1843 (2003).

17. Condor Team, Condor home page, Feb 2002, http://www.cs.wisc.edu/condor/.

18. R. Durbin, S. Eddy, A. Krogh, and G. Mitchison, *Biological Sequence Analysis*, CUP, 1998.

19. R. C. Eberhart and J. Kennedy, A New Optmizer Using Particle Swarm Theory, in *Sixth International Symposium on Micro Machine and Human Science*, IEEE Service Center, 1995, pp. 39–43.

20. S. Eddy, *HMMER User's Guide*, hmmer.wustl.edu.

21. J. Felsenstein, PHYLIP — Phylogeny Inference Package (version 3.2), *Cladistics*, 5, 164–166 (1989).

22. I. Foster and C. Kesselman, *The Grid: Blueprint for a New Computing Infrastructure*, Morgan-Kaufmann, 1999.

23. I. Foster and C. Kesselman, Globus: a metacomputing infrastructure toolkit, *Int. J. Supercomp. Appl. High Perfor. Comput.*, 11 (2), 115–128 (1997).

24. N. Furmento, W. Lee, A. Mayer, S. Newhouse, and J. Darlington, Iceni: An Open Grid Service Architecture Implemented with jini, in *SuperComputing 2002*, 2002.

25. S. M. Gendel, Sequence analysis for assessing potential allergenicity, *Ann. N.Y. Acad. Sci.*, 964, 87–98 (2002).

26. Globus Alliance, Open Grid Service Architecture, www.globus.org/ogsa/.

27. C. Goble, C. Wroe, and R. Stevens, The myGrid Project: Services, Architecture and Demonstrator, in *Proceedings UK e-Science All Hands Meeting*, 2003.

28. R. Henderson and D. Tweten, Portable Batch System: External Reference Specification, Technical Report, NASA Ames Research Center, 1996.

29. R. E. Hileman, et al., Bioinformatics methods for allergenicity assessment using a comprehensive allergen database, *Int. Arch. Allergy Immunol.*, 128, 380–391 (2002).

30. S. Hoon, K. K. Ratnapu, J. M. Chia, B. Kumarasamy, X. Juguang, M. Clamp, A. Stabenau, S. Potter, L. Clarke, and E. Stupka, Biopipe: a flexible framework for protocol-based bioinformatics analysis, *Genome Res.*, 13, 1904–1915 (2003).

31. Y. Huang, GSiB: PSE Infrastructure for Dynamic Service-Oriented Grid Applications, *Computational Science — ICCS 2003 (Part 4)*, 2003, pp. 430–439.

32. ACCELRYS INC, Accelrys: modeling and simulation tools, http://wwws.accelrys.com/.

33. N. Karoni, B. Toonen, and I. Foster, MPICH-G2: a grid-enabled implementation of the message passing interface, *J. Parallel Distributed Comput.*, 63, 551–563 (2003).

34. A. Krishnan, A survey of life sciences applications on the grid, *New Generation Comput.*, 22, 111–126 (2004).

35. A. Krishnan, K. B. Li, and P. Issac, Rapid detection of conserved regions in protein sequences using wavelets, *In Silico Biol.*, 4, 0013, 2004.

36. A. Krishnan, F. Tang, and S. Ho, GridX: a meta-scheduling architecture for the grid, in press.

37. C. Lee, S. Matsuoka, D. Talia, A. Sussman, M. Mueller, G. Allen, and J. Saltz, A grid programming primer, *Advanced Programming Models Research Group, Global Grid Forum White Paper*, http://www.gridforum.org.

38. W. Leinberger and V. Kumar, Information power grid: the new frontier in parallel computing? *IEEE Concurrency*, 7 (4), 75–84 (1999).

39. F. Leymann, Web services flow language (WSFL 1.0), 5 2001, Available from http://www-3.ibm.com/software/solutions/webservices/pdf/WSFL.pdf.

40. K.-B. Li, P. Issac, and A. Krishnan, Predicting Allergenic Proteins using Wavelet Transform, *Bioinformatics*, 20(16), 2752–2758 (2004). Epub 2004 Apr 29.

41. C.-L. Chua, F. Tang, P. Issac, and A. Krishnan, Grid Execution Language, *Journal of Paralled and Distributed Computing*, 65(7), 857–869 (2005).

42. R. Lim, S. Ho, and A. Krishnan, GRD: A Grid Resource Discovery Framework, in *Proceedings of APAC Conference and Exhibition on Advanced Computing, Grid Applications and eResearch*, 2003.

43. S. Majithia, I. Taylor, M. Shields, and I. Wang, Triana as a Graphical Web Services Composition Toolkit, in *Proceeding of the UK e-Science Programme All Hands Meeting*, 2003.

44. Matthew L. Massie, Brent N. Chun, and David E. Culler, Ganglia, 2003, http://ganglia.sourceforge.net/.

45. G. Carmen, Moles, P. Mendes, and Julio R. Banga, Parameter estimation in biochemical pathways: a comparison of global optimization methods, *Genome Res.*, 13(11), 2467–2474 (2003).

46. H. Nakada, M. Sato, and S. Sekiguchi, Design and implementations of Ninf: towards a global computing infrastructure, *Future Generation Comput. Sys.*, Metacomputing Issue, 15(5), 649–658 (1999).

47. T. Oinn, M. Addis, J. Ferris, D. Marvin, M. Greenwood, T. Carver, Matthew R. Pocock, A. Wipat, and P. Li, Taverna: a tool for the composition and enactment of bioinformatics workflows, *Bioinformatics*, 20(17), 3045–3054 (2004).

48. T. Oinn, M. Addis, J. Ferris, D. Marvin, M. Greenwood, T. Carver, Matthew R. Pocock, A. Wipat, and P. Li, Taverna: a tool for the composition and enactment of bioinformatics workflows, *Bioinformatics Adv. Access*, June, 2004.

49. S. J. Ono, Molecular genetics of allergic diseases, *Annu. Rev. Immunol.*, 18, 347–366 (2000).

50. T. Ray, K. Tai, and K. C. Scow. An Evolutionary Algorithm for Constrained Optimization. In *Proceedings of the Genetic and Evolutionary Computation Conference*, Morgan Kaufmann, 2000, pp. 771–777.

51. P. Rice, I. Longden, and A. Bleasby. EMBOSS: the European molecular biology open software suite, *Trends Genet.*, 16, 276–277 (2000).

52. S. Hoon, K. K. Ratnapu, J. M. Chia, B. Kumarasamy, X. Juguang, M. Clamp, A. Stabenau, S. Potter, L. Clarke, and E. Stupka, Biopipe: a flexible framework for protocolbased bioinformatics analysis. *Genome Res.*, 13 (8), 1904–1915 (2003).

53. M. Senger, P. Rice, and T. Oinn, Soaplab — a Unified Sesame Door to Analysis Tools, in *Proceedings, UK e-Science, All Hands Meeting*, Simon J. Cox, Ed., 2003, pp. 509–513.

54. K. Seymour, H. Nakada, S. Matsuoka, J. Dongarra, C. Lee, and H. Casanova, GridRPC: A Remote Procedure Call API for Grid Computing, *ICL Technical Report ICL-UT-02-06*, 6, 2002.

55. SUN, Sun grid engine: white paper available at 2003, http://wwws.sun.com/software/gridware/sgeee53/wp-sgeee/index.html.

56. C.-L. Chua, F. Tang, H. L. Yoong and A. Krishnan, WILDFIRE: Distributed, Grid-enabled Workflow Construction and Execution for Bioinformatics, *BMC Bioinformatics*, 6, 69, 2004.

57. S. Thatte, XLANG: web services for business process design, 2001, http://www.gotdotnet.com/team/xml$_w$sspecs/xlang — c1default.htm.

58. J. D. Thompson, D. G. Higgins, and T. J. Gibson, CLUSTAL W: improving the sensitivity of progressive multiple sequence alignment through sequence weighting, position-specific gap penalties and weight matrix choice, *Nucleic Acids Res.*, 22 (22), 4673–4680 (1994).

59. R. Wolski, Dynamically forecasting network performance using the network weather service, *Cluster Comput.*, 1 (1), 119–132 (1998).

60. S. Zhou, LSF: Load Sharing in Large-Scale Heterogeneous Distributed System, *Proceedings of Workshop Cluster Computing*, 1992.

CHAPTER 24

Molecular Structure Determination on a Computational and Data Grid

RUSS MILLER and MARK L. GREEN

The focus of this chapter is on the design and implementation of a critical computer program in structural biology on two computational and data grids. The first is the Buffalo-based Advanced Computational Data Center (ACDC) Grid, which uses facilities at SUNY–Buffalo and several research institutions in the greater Buffalo area. The second is Grid2003, an international grid established late in 2003 primarily for physics and astronomy applications. We present an overview of the ACDC Grid and Grid2003, focusing on the implementation of several new tools that we have developed for the integration of computational and data grids, lightweight job monitoring, predictive scheduling, and opportunities for improved Grid utilization through an elegant backfill facility. A new computational framework is developed for the evolutionary determination and an efficient implementation of an algorithm to determine molecular crystal structures using the *Shake-and-Bake* methodology. Finally, the grid-enabled data mining approach that we introduce is able to exploit computational cycles, which would otherwise go unused.

24.1 INTRODUCTION

The grid is a rapidly emerging and expanding technology that allows geographically distributed and independently operated resources [central processing unit (CPU) cycles, data storage, sensors, visualization devices, and a wide variety of Internet-ready instruments] to be linked together in a transparent fashion [1–3]. The power of the grid lies not only in the aggregate computing power, data storage, and network bandwidth that can be readily brought to bear on a particular problem but also on its ease of use.

Parallel Computing for Bioinformatics and Computational Biology, Edited by Albert Y. Zomaya
Copyright © 2006 John Wiley & Sons, Inc.

Grids are now a viable solution to certain computationally and data-intensive computing problems for reasons that include

1. The Internet is reasonably mature and able to serve as fundamental infrastructure for network-based computing.
2. Network bandwidth, which is doubling approximately every 12 months, has increased to the point of being able to provide efficient and reliable services.
3. Motivated by the fact that digital data are doubling approximately every 9 months, storage capacity has now reached commodity levels, where one can purchase a terabyte of disk for roughly the same price as a high-end PC.
4. Many instruments are Internet-aware.
5. Clusters, supercomputers, as well as storage and visualization devices are becoming more mainstream.
6. Major applications, including critical scientific community codes, have been parallelized to increase their performance (faster turnaround) and capabilities (handle larger data sets or provide finer resolution models).
7. Driven by the fact that science is a collaborative activity, often involving groups that are not co-located, collaborative environments (i.e., collaboratories) are moving out of the alpha phase of development and into at least beta testing.

For these and other reasons, grids are starting to move out of the research laboratory and into early-adopter production systems. The focus of grid deployment continues to be on the difficult issue of developing high-quality middleware.

Grids have recently moved from academic settings to corporate thrusts. Numerous grid projects have been initiated [GriPhyN, PPDG, EU DataGrid, NASA's Information Power Grid, TeraGrid, Open Science Grid (OSG), and iVDGL, etc.]. However, the construction of a real general-purpose grid is in its infancy, because a true grid requires coordinated resource-sharing and problem solving in a dynamic, multi-institutional scenario using standard, open, general-purpose protocols and interfaces that deliver a high quality of service.

Many types of computational tasks are naturally suited to grid environments, including data-intensive applications. Grid-based research and development activities have generally focused on applications where data are stored in files. However, in many scientific and commercial domains, database management systems play a central role in data storage, access, organization, and authorization for numerous applications. Part of our research effort is targeted at enabling systems that are more accessible within a grid framework.

As grid computing initiatives move forward, issues of interoperability, security, performance, management, and privacy need to be carefully considered. In fact, security is concerned with various issues relating to authentication to ensure application and data integrity. Grid initiatives are also generating best practice scheduling and resource management documents, protocols, and API specifications to enable interoperability. Several layers of security, data encryption, and certificate authorities already exist in grid-enabling toolkits such as Globus Toolkit 3 [4].

24.2 MOLECULAR STRUCTURE DETERMINATION

SnB [5–7] is a computer program based on the *Shake-and-Bake* [8, 9] method of molecular structure determination from X-ray diffraction data. It is the program of choice for solving such structures in hundreds of laboratories that have acquired it. This computationally intensive procedure is ideally suited to an implementation on a computational and data grid. Such an implementation of *SnB* allows for the processing of a large number of related molecular trial structures [10].

The Shake-and-Bake algorithm for molecular structure determination was listed on the IEEE poster *"Top Algorithms of the 20th Century."* The *SnB* program uses a dual-space direct-methods procedure for determining crystal structures from X-ray diffraction data. This program has been used in a routine fashion to solve difficult atomic resolution structures, containing as many as 1000 unique non-hydrogen atoms, which could not be solved by traditional reciprocal-space routines. Recently, the focus of the Shake-and-Bake research team has been on the application of *SnB* to solve heavy-atom and anomalous-scattering substructures of much larger proteins, provided that 3–4 Å diffraction data can be measured. In fact, direct methods had been applied successfully to substructures containing on the order of a dozen selenium sites, whereas *SnB* has been used to determine as many as 180 selenium sites. Such solutions have led to the determination of complete structures containing hundreds of thousands of atoms.

The Shake-and-Bake procedure consists of generating structure invariants and coordinates for random-atom trial structures. Each such trial structure is subjected to a cyclical automated procedure, which includes computing a Fourier transform to determine phase values from the proposed set of atoms (initially random), determining a figure-of-merit [11] associated with these phases, refining the phases to locally optimize the figure-of-merit, computing a Fourier transform to produce an electron density map, and employing a peak-picking routine to examine the map and find the maxima. These peaks (maxima) are then considered to be atoms, and the cyclical process is repeated for a predetermined (by the user) number of cycles.

The running time of *SnB* varies widely as a function of the size of the structure, the quality of the data, the space group, and the choices of critical input parameters, including the size of the Fourier grid, the number of reflections, the number and type of invariants, and the number of cycles of the procedure used per trial structure, and so on. Therefore, the running time of the procedure can range from seconds or minutes on a PC to weeks or months on a supercomputer. Trial structures are continually and simultaneously processed, with the final figure-of-merit values of all structures stored in a file. The user can review a dynamic histogram during the processing of the trials to determine whether a solution is likely present in the set of completed trial structures.

SnB has recently been augmented with a data repository that stores information for every application of *SnB*, regardless of where the job is run. The information is sent to the repository directly from *SnB* in a transparent fashion. This information is then mined in an automated fashion to optimize 17 key *SnB* parameters in an effort to optimize the procedure for solving previously unknown structures, as discussed later in this chapter.

SnB has also been augmented with a 3D geographically distributed visualization tool so that investigators at geographically distributed locations can collaborate in an interactive fashion on a proposed molecular solution. Further, the tool is being generalized to handle standard formats.

24.3   GRID COMPUTING IN BUFFALO

The *Advanced Computational Data Center (ACDC) Grid* [10, 12–14], which spans organizations throughout Western New York, is a heterogeneous grid initially designed to support *SnB*. ACDC Grid is part of Grid3+, the IBM NE BioGrid, and serves as the base for our proposed WNY-Grid. ACDC Grid incorporates an integrated computational and data grid, lightweight job monitoring, predictive scheduling, and opportunities for improved grid utilization through an elegant backfill facility. The following projects and packages deliver unique and complementary components that allow for the systematic expansion of the ACDC Grid.

- **Globus Toolkit 3** [15] provides APIs and tools using the Java SDK to simplify the development of OGSI-compliant services and clients. It supplies database services and monitoring and discovery system (MDS) index services implemented in Java, GRAM [16] service implemented in C with a Java wrapper, GridFTP [17] services implemented in C, and a full set of Globus Toolkit 2 components based on version 2.4. The Globus Toolkit 3 Java provides C bindings for application development and integration with the existing grid application base. The recently proposed Web Service-Resource Framework (WS-RF) provides the concepts and interfaces developed by the OGSI specification exploiting the Web services architecture [18–21]. These specifications enable defining the conventions for managing state so that applications discover, inspect, and interact with stateful resources in standard and interoperable ways [22, 23].
- **The Python Globus (pyGlobus) Project** [24–26] generated a Python object-oriented interface to the Globus Toolkit versions 2.2.4 and 2.4. This provides high-level scripting language access to the entire Globus Toolkit with similar performance to the underlying Globus Toolkit. Integration with Python offers high-performance scientific computing access to Numerical Python [27], Scientific Python [28], the netCDF library [29], Message Passing Interface (MPI) [30], Bulk Synchronous Parallel Programming (BSPlib) [31, 32], and the SciPy library [33]. The pyGridWare Project [34] provides a migration path for the pyGlobus users, which need a pure Python implementation for developing automated client side tooling to interact with Globus Toolkit 3 implementation of OGSI, whereas Perl provides several different Web services implementations [35] based on SOAP and XML-RPC. The OGSI standard uses SOAP, where the best Perl module for SOAP support is SOAP::Lite [36]. The OGSI::Lite [37] package is a container for grid services, which facilitates writing services in the Perl scripting language. Exporting a Perl class as a grid service can inherit the required standard OGSI classes and communicate using the SOAP::Lite package.

These packages add tremendous flexibility to the ACDC Grid enterprise grid service development effort.

- **Microsoft's .Net technology** for supplying Grid Services [38, 39] to the UK e-Science community is projected to result from a collaboration between Microsoft [40] and National e-Science Centre (NeSC) [41]. The project objectives include developing an implementation of OGSI using .NET technologies and developing a suite of Grid Service demonstrators, which can be deployed under this .NET OGSI implementation. The University of Virginia Grid Computing Group is developing **OGSI.NET** that provides a container framework for the .NET/Windows grid-computing world [42]. This project can bridge the gap between OGSI compliant frameworks that primarily run on Unix-based systems to interoperability with Windows-based platforms within the ACDC Grid.

- **OptimalGrid** is a middleware released by IBM, which aims to simplify the creation and management of large-scale connected, parallel grid applications [43]. OptimalGrid manages problem partitioning, problem piece deployment, runtime management, dynamic level of parallelism, dynamic load balancing, and system fault tolerance and recovery. The SETI@home project [44] and the Folding@home protein-folding project [45] are examples of applications, similar in granularity to applications discussed herein, which can utilize the OptimalGrid infrastructure. These applications work in a simple "scatter/gather" mode and have no requirement for communication between the grid nodes participating in the computation.

The ACDC Grid has been developed with critical grid components that allow for the deployment of a general-purpose regional enterprise grid residing over generally available IP networks. The Shake-and-Bake method of molecular structure determination, as instantiated in SnB, has been used as the prototype application in the development of our general-purpose grid. There are many reasons why SnB was chosen, including the fact that it is an important scientific code, it is widely distributed, both Shake-and-Bake and SnB were developed in Buffalo by members of the Hauptman-Woodward Medical Research Institute and the State University of New York at Buffalo, and that one of the co-developers of Shake-and-Bake and SnB is a member of the leadership team of the ACDC Grid, which means that we have access to the knowledge base associated with SnB as well as all of its internals.

To date, the result of our general-purpose grid effort has been the successful deployment of a campus grid involving a variety of independent organizations throughout SUNY–Buffalo and a Western New York Grid (WNY-Grid), which provides a seamless and transparent mode of operation for grid users in the greater Buffalo region. The WNY-Grid also provides a unique framework for education, outreach, and training of grid technology and its application in the Western New York region. Finally, it should be noted that we are in the process of widening the reach of WNY-Grid to develop a New York State Grid (NYS-Grid). Although, the NYS-Grid is in its infancy, we have already secured commitments for participation by a variety of institutions in Western New York, Southern Tier, Upstate New York, and New York City. Some of these nodes will be brought on-line in early 2005.

24.4 CENTER FOR COMPUTATIONAL RESEARCH

The majority of the work presented in this chapter was performed at the Center for Computational Research, SUNY–Buffalo. The center maintains a wide variety of resources that were used during various phases of the ACDC Grid implementation, including

1. *Compute Systems.* A 3TF peak Dell Pentium4 system with Myrinet; a 6TF peak Dell PentiumIII system with Fast Ethernet; a 3TF IBM Blade Server; a 64 processor SGI Origin 3800; A 64 processor SGI Origin 3700 (Altix); a SUN cluster with Myrinet; an IBM SP; an 18 node Dell P4 visualization cluster; a heterogeneous bioinformatics system; several SGI Onyx systems; networks of workstations.

2. *Storage Systems.* A 40 TB RAID5 HP SAN system with 190 TB of backup tape front-ended by 64 alpha processors, which is directly connected to CCR's high-end compute platforms; several NAS systems, some of which are targeted at CCR's Condor flocks.

3. *Visualization Systems.* An $11' \times 8'$ Tiled Display Wall with 20 projectors; a FakeSpace ImmersaDesk R2; an SGI Reality Center 3300W; several Access Grid Nodes; miscellaneous PC-based visualization systems.

4. *Networking.* SUNY–Buffalo is an Internet2 member and a participant in the Abeline network. CCR is directly connected to Internet2.

24.5 ACDC-GRID OVERVIEW

The development of the heterogeneous ACDC-Grid infrastructure has flourished recently with funding from an NSF/ITR. A variety of applications are available on ACDC-Grid, as are a variety of critical tools that we have developed. An overview of the ACDC-Grid effort follows.

1. *Grid Core Infrastructure.* The core infrastructure for the ACDC Grid includes the installation of standard grid middleware, the deployment of an active web portal for deploying applications, dynamic resource allocation so that clusters and networks of workstations can be scheduled to provide resources on demand, a scalable and dynamic scheduling system, and a dynamic firewall, to name a few.

2. *Grid Monitoring, Scheduling, and Mining.* The ACDC Grid provides an efficient and lightweight grid monitoring system, a sophisticated predictive job scheduler that integrates past performance of users with the knowledge of availability of compute resources and knowledge of the location of the requisite data, a backfill mechanism that allows the ACDC Grid to maximize utilization, while minimizing interference with job scheduling, and a grid-enabled mechanism for data mining.

3. *Data Grid and Storage Services.* The ACDC-Grid Data Grid has been developed from the ground up to transparently integrate with the ACDC Grid Computational Grid and provide the user with a representation of their data that hides critical details such as location, making the Grid appear as a single entity to the user. That is, from the user's point of view, they have access to their data and computational resources upon which to process their data. However, the user does not need to know the location of the data or computational resources. This development included the design, analysis, and implementation of a data grid scenario manager and simulator. The Data Grid can utilize historical information to migrate data to locations that are most efficient for its analysis.

4. *Applications and Collaborations.* The SUNY–Buffalo Grid Team has been working closely with a number of highly visible grids, including the International Virtual Data Grid Laboratory (iVDGL), Grid3+ and its technical workgroups, OSG and its technical workgroups, the Northeast Bio-Grid, MCEER, NEES, NSF funded educational grid projects at SUNY–Buffalo, the NSF/NIH supported Grid-enabled Shake-and-Bake package, transport modeling to support algal bloom tracking for event monitoring and response management, evolutionary aseismic design and retrofit (EADR), and OSTRICH, a general purpose software tool for parameter optimization.

24.5.1 Monitoring

An effective and efficient grid monitoring system was developed during the early stages of the prototype ACDC Grid. This monitoring system was critical to the grid development group and proved useful to early application adopters. The *ACDC-Grid monitoring system* exploits the development of robust database servers. The monitoring system utilizes a MySQL database server, which can maintain millions of records and hundreds of simultaneous connections in a fast and stable manner. In fact, the ACDC-Grid monitoring system currently contains statistics for over 300,000 computational jobs completed on CCR's heterogeneous compute platforms and over 1,600,000 jobs completed on the Grid3 multi-institutional computational resources. The ACDC-Grid monitoring infrastructure has proven to be robust and scalable, but lacks the necessary service-based tooling to be incorporated into a large general-purpose grid infrastructure. Therefore, our current efforts are targeted at a second-generation monitoring service that is more tightly integrated and configured with the unique computational resource it monitors. We believe that this second-generation system will provide an order of magnitude of more scalability, from tens of thousand to hundreds of thousand of servers.

The current ACDC-Grid monitoring system includes the following features:

1. *Running/Queued Jobs.* The ACDC-Grid monitoring system provides summary and statistics of currently running or queued jobs on Grid3. Summary charts are compiled based on total jobs, CPU hours, or runtime for either a user or group [i.e., virtual organization (VO)] over an individual resource, subset of resources,

or the entire grid. Each interactive chart provides the ability to display detailed job information.

2. *Job History.* The ACDC-Grid monitoring system provides detailed historical job information including CPU consumption rates and job production rates for either an individual user or a group over a subset of grid resources. To date, ~1,600,000 jobs have run on Grid3 since October 2003. Summary charts are compiled from usage data based on user jobs or VOs for a given range of dates over a given set of resources. Statistics such as total jobs, average runtime, total CPU time consumed, and so forth are dynamically produced from the available database. Each interactive chart allows for detailed information to be displayed.

3. *ACDC Site Status.* The ACDC-Grid monitoring system generates dynamic ACDC site status logs, reporting successful monitoring events, and specific Grid3 site errors corresponding to monitoring event failures.

24.5.2   Scheduling

The *ACDC-Grid predictive scheduler* uses a database of historical jobs to profile the usage of a given resource on a user, group, or account basis [46–54]. Determining accurate quality of service estimates for grid-enabled applications can be defined in terms of a combination of historical and runtime user parameters, in addition to specific resource information. Such a methodology is incorporated into the ACDC-Grid Portal, which continually refines the predictive scheduler parameters based, partly on the data stored by the monitoring system.

Workload also plays a significant role in determining resource utilization. The native queue schedulers typically use the designated job wall-time for managing resource backfill (i.e., small pockets of unutilized resources that are being held for a scheduled job). However, such systems may also use a weighted combination of node, process, and wall-time to determine a base priority for each job and subsequently modify this priority to impose a fair share resource policy based on historical usage. The backfill system will allow a job with lower priority to overtake a job with higher priority if it does not delay the start of the prioritized job. The *ACDC-Grid predictive scheduler* uses historical information to better profile grid users and more accurately determine execution times. Our prototype predictive scheduling system is based on statistical principles [55] that allow jobs to more effectively run in a backfill mode.

We consider the aforementioned shared- and distributed-memory computational resources at SUNY–Buffalo's CCR. The ACDC-Grid Portal executes many grid-enabled scientific applications on several of the center's heterogeneous resources concurrently. Several applications have inter-dependent execution and data requirements, which require reliable knowledge of job start and completion times.

An explanation of the development of the ACDC-Grid predictive scheduler is best served by considering a snapshot of the queue for a single computational resource. Table 24.1 shows 15 running and queued jobs on this resource (Dell P4 cluster with Myrinet) from six users, which initially completely occupy all processors on all nodes (i.e., all 516 processors on the 258 dual-processor nodes). There are seven running

TABLE 24.1 Sample Computational Resource Queue Snapshot

Job id	User	Nodes	Procs	Wall-Time	Status
1	user2	32	64	360	Running
2	user1	32	64	360	Running
3	user1	32	64	360	Running
4	user1	32	64	360	Running
5	user1	32	64	360	Running
6	user3	64	128	500	Running
7	user5	34	68	720	Running
8	user4	96	192	720	1
9	user5	64	128	360	2
10	user5	64	128	480	3
11	user5	128	256	720	4
12	user6	128	256	720	5
13	user5	128	256	720	6
14	user6	96	192	306	7
15	user5	64	128	480	8

jobs and eight queued jobs, where the queue job priority determines a relative rank for corresponding to the order that the queued jobs will start. Note that the user requests the number of nodes, number of processes, and wall-time queue parameters for each of the running and queued jobs. This information is sufficient to completely define the job execution and the native scheduler priority determination.

The native queue scheduler uses the designated job wall-time for managing resource backfill and estimated job start and end times. Table 24.2 reports the native

TABLE 24.2 Native Queue Job Execution Start and End Time

Job id	Wall-Time	Start Time	End Time
1	360	00:05:41	00:11:41
2	360	00:05:41	00:11:41
3	360	00:05:41	00:11:41
4	360	00:05:41	00:11:41
5	360	00:05:41	00:11:41
6	500	00:05:41	00:14:01
7	720	00:07:36	00:19:36
8	720	00:11:41	00:23:41
9	360	00:11:41	00:17:41
10	480	00:14:01	00:22:01
11	720	00:23:41	01:11:41
12	720	00:22:01	01:10:01
13	720	01:11:41	01:23:41
14	306	01:10:01	01:15:07
15	480	01:23:41	02:07:41

queue scheduler estimates for start and end times for all running and queued jobs. The native scheduler uses a weighted combination of node, process, and wall-time to determine a base priority for each job and subsequently modifies the base priority to impose a fair share resource policy. The fairshare value is based on historical usage and can be divided into user, group, and account associated with the job. This scheduling scheme is also based on advanced wall-time reservations with backfill, where a job with lower priority can overtake a job with higher priority only if it does not delay the start of the prioritized job. The advanced reservation scheme also makes it possible to allocate resource in the future.

The ACDC-Grid predictive scheduler uses a database of historical job executions to provide an improved profile of the usage of a given resource based on a user, group, or account basis. Workload also plays a significant role in determining average system utilization. Users will take advantage of scheduler feedback to determine the type of jobs that have the best turnaround time. The users will submit jobs that give them the best service, resulting in a dynamic workload that adjusts to provide near-optimal utilization. Table 24.3 reports five genetic algorithm (GA) optimized user profile parameters that were used to determine a more efficient job execution.

This methodology is incorporated into the ACDC-Grid Portal, where it continually verifies and evolves the predictive scheduler parameters based on the current computational grid state. The resulting system delivers a self-adapting job start times with a factor of 2–3 times more accurate than the native queue systems.

The ACDC-Grid predictive scheduler backfill algorithm was initially designed to be extensible to a general set of multi-disciplinary applications, although it has only been deployed for the SnB application environment. The prototype results have been impressive. On the basis of predictive analysis, the ACDC-Grid infrastructure determines the length of time idle processors will be available on all computational resources. For example, over a 6 month period, the ACDC-Grid predictive scheduler has allowed 3709 heterogeneous jobs to be completed on an average of 21 processors per job with an average runtime of 7.3 h consuming a total of 410,000 CPU h at the rate of 2250 CPU h/day.

The ACDC-Grid predictive scheduler estimates are used for determining whether a computational grid resource can meet the quality of service requirements defined by the current workload. If a computational grid resource will not meet the quality

TABLE 24.3   ACDC-Grid User Profile Information

User	Efficiency	Node	Wall-Time	Job	Age
user1	0.568	33	382	61	17
user2	0.421	44	447	60	38
user3	0.650	64	426	19	23
user4	0.717	96	424	16	30
user5	0.612	44	255	138	35
user6	0.691	19	423	138	20

of service expectations required, the ACDC-Grid infrastructure will search for a grid resource that can meet the expectations and determine whether it is feasible to migrate the job in question to a more suitable resource. The overall computational grid resource statistics are compiled in the ACDC-Grid database and can be queried by grid users and administrators to better understand the "state of the grid."

24.5.3 Data Grid

The ACDC-Grid enables the transparent migration of data between various storage element resources, while preserving uniform access for the user, where basic file management functions are provided via a platform-independent web interface, as shown in Figure 24.1.

We have identified five use cases for the Data Grid file management infrastructure. The infrastructure architecture description for a general View, Edit, Copy, Upload, and is Download use case is presented in Figure 24.2a–e, respectively.

The View use case copies a designated file from the users, group, or public accessible Data Grid to a temporary Grid Portal scratch space and presents the file contents through the web interface. The temporary copy of the file stored in the Grid Portal scratch space is removed after viewing is complete. The Edit use case copies the

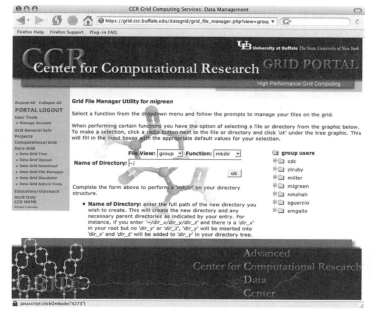

Figure 24.1   ACDC Data Grid File Manager Web user interface.

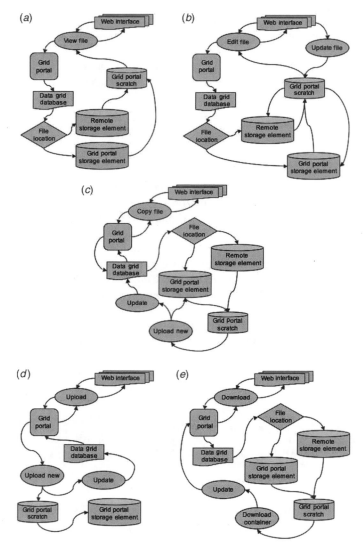

Figure 24.2 (*a* and *b*) ACDC Data Grid View and Edit file use case description. (*c*) ACDC Data Grid Copy file use case description. (*d* and *e*) ACDC Data Grid Upload and Donwload file use case.

file from the users, group, or public accessible Data Grid to a temporary Grid Portal scratch space and presents the file for editing through the web interface. After successfully editing the file, the original file is overwritten by the edited file.

The Copy use case copies a designated file from the users, group, or public accessible Data Grid to a temporary Grid Portal scratch space and uploads the new file into the Grid Portal Storage Element. The new file attributes are updated in the ACDC Data Grid database after a successful upload into the Storage Element.

The Upload use case uploads files via the web interface into a Grid Portal scratch space, applying the directory and file abstractions and copying the files to the Grid Portal storage element. The ACDC Data Grid database is updated with the new directory and file attributes upon successful upload; the Grid Portal scratch files are deleted. The Download use case assembles the requested files by querying the ACDC Data Grid database for individual file and directory locations into the Grid Portal scratch space. A download container is assembled from the abstracted directory and file attributes obtained from the database and compressed for download. The compressed container is then downloaded to the user through the web interface.

The gathering of statistical information and the display of such information through a common web interface are of particular use to developers and administrators. The metadata information and the corresponding data repository for each file are maintained in a global MySQL database table. Algorithms have been implemented to periodically migrate files between repositories to optimize usage of resources based on the users' utilization profile. This leads to localization of data files for the computational resources that require them. Conversely, the Chimera Virtual Data System, which combines a virtual data catalog for representing data derivation procedures and derived data, is used by GriPhyN high-energy physics collaborators [56]. We plan to integrate the Chimera system into the general-purpose ACDC-Grid infrastructure with distributed "Data Grid" services to enable on-demand execution of computation schedules constructed from database queries. In addition, this system will provide a catalog that can be used by application environments to describe a set of application programs and then track all the data files produced by executing those applications.

Storage Resource Managers (SRMs) [57] are middleware components that provide dynamic space allocation and file management on shared storage components of a grid [58]. SRMs support protocol negotiation and reliable replication mechanism. The SRM specification standardizes the interface, thus allowing for a uniform access to heterogeneous storage elements [59–62]. The SRM standard allows independent institutions to implement their own SRMs. SRMs provide a flexible policy decision specification process, which can be made independently by each implementation for all grid-enabled resources. Furthermore, the tight integration of the computational grid predictive scheduler with the data grid network bandwidth availability statistics is essential for scheduling data migrations for computational jobs. The ACDC Grid incorporates the Network Weather Service [63] bandwidth and latency information obtained from the computational and data resources into the predictive scheduler algorithms for job staging and execution requirements. Unfortunately, this information is insufficient for determining network bandwidth availability or forecasting essential network statistics. To address this issue, we have deployed software throughout the existing IP networking infrastructure that can be exploited for the development of network forecasting grid services for the ACDC Grid. This software utilizes the port level network statistics obtained from switches and routers distributed throughout the SUNY–Buffalo network fabric and builds a database for data mining this valuable information. We propose coupling the network information services, predictive scheduler service, and data grid migration forecasting services into a tool that will achieve improved network and computational resource utilization.

24.5.4   Dynamic Integration of Resources

The ACDC-Grid introduced the concept of dynamic resource allocation during the GRID3 intensive application period during Supercomputing 2003 and Supercomputing 2004. The amount of computational resources provided to the GRID3 user base was dynamically rolled into and out of production on a daily basis. As a proof of concept, for a 2-week period, 400 processors of a 600 processor Pentium4 cluster were rolled out of the local CCR pool of resources and into the GRID3 production pool at 8:00 A.M, with the inverse procedure taking place at 8:00 P.M. The production jobs running on dynamically shared resources were managed through the advanced reservation capabilities of the queuing system [64], thus requiring no administrator intervention in managing the job start or completion. These resources, unlike a similar concept used in Condor flocking, were queue managed and reconfigured on the fly with enhanced grid node security, NFS mounted filesystems, grid user accounts and passwords, grid-enabled software infrastructure, and so forth and were ready to accept production jobs without system administrator intervention. We are working to extend this automated ACDC-Grid infrastructure to provide on-demand computational resources from multiple IT domain-managed clusters, which can be configured by the respective administrators using a grid service.

24.6   GRID RESEARCH COLLABORATIONS

The ACDC Grid exploits a grid-enabling template framework, which includes a dynamically created HTML grid console for the detailed monitoring of computational grid jobs. Results from previous studies have been used in the design of the Globus-based ACDC Grid, which serves researchers at the Center for Computational Research and the Hauptman-Woodward Medical Research Institute, located in Buffalo, NY. In particular, the extensive framework of HTML, JavaScript, PHP, MySQL, phpMyAdmin, and the Globus Toolkit provide a production-level ACDC Grid for scientific applications and data integration as required by the applications community. The rapid expansion of the Grid community has facilitated the ACDC-Grid collaboration with many high-quality laboratories and testbeds for developing robust and scalable grid infrastructure. The ACDC Grid has been hardened using grid research collaboration memberships and participation over the past several years.

24.6.1   Grid3

The ACDC-Grid membership in the iVDGL provides access to international heterogeneous computing and storage resources for the purpose of experimentation in grid-enabled data-intensive scientific computing. The ACDC-Grid team participates in the (1) iVDGL iGOC, which is used as the central coordination point for grid technical problem resolution, (2) grid monitoring technical working group, and (3) grid troubleshooting working group. The iVDGL and other US Grid projects have sponsored several Data Grid activities, including the Grid3 collaboration that has deployed an international Data Grid with participation from more than 28 sites across the United States (including the ACDC-Grid site) and Korea. This facility is operated by the US Grid projects iVDGL, Grid Physics Network (GriPhyN) and the Particle Physics Data Grid (PPDG), and the U.S. participants in the Large Hadron Collider (LHC) experiments ATLAS and CMS. The Grid3 collaboration uses the Virtual Data Toolkit (VDT) [65] for providing the Grid cyberinfrastructure for the scientific and computer science applications from a variety of disciplines including physics, astrophysics, biology, and astronomy.

The ACDC-Grid VO provides computational resources, expertise, users, applications, and core grid job monitoring services for the Grid3 collaboration. The Grid3 resources are used by seven different scientific applications, including three high-energy physics simulations and four data analyses in high-energy physics, structural biology (Shake-and-Bake), astrophysics, and astronomy. The ACDC-Grid resources processed over 175,000 computational jobs submitted by all of the scientific applications since October 2003, accounting for over 25% of the total computational jobs processed by the Grid3 resources. The ACDC-Grid resources continue to process computational jobs and provide critical computational job monitoring for the Grid3 collaboration members (ACDC Job Monitoring for Grid3 is at http://acdc.ccr.buffalo.edu).

The iVDGL is a global Data Grid that provides resources for experiments in physics and astronomy [66]. Its computing, storage, and networking resources in the USA, Europe, Asia, and South America provide a unique computational laboratory, which will test and validate Grid technologies at international and global scales. The Grid2003 project [67] was defined and planned by Stakeholder representatives in an effort to align iVDGL project goals with the computational projects associated with the LHC experiments (Fig. 24.3).

The Grid Laboratory Uniform Environment (GLUE) [68] collaboration was created in February 2002 to provide a focused effort to achieve interoperability between the U.S. physics Grid projects and the European projects. Participant U.S. projects include iVDGL, Grid Physics Network (GriPhyN) [69], and Particle Physics Data Grid (PPDG) [70]. Participant European projects include the European Data Grid (EDG) Project [71], Data Transatlantic Grid (DataTAG) [72], and CrossGrid [73]. Since the initial proposal for the GLUE project, the LHC Computing Grid (LCG) project was created at CERN [74] to coordinate the computing and Grid software requirements for the four LHC experiments, with a goal of developing common solutions. One of the main project goals is deploying and supporting global production Grids for the LHC experiments, which resulted in the Grid2003 "production" grid.

24.6.2 Goals of the Grid2003 Project

The iVDGL Steering Committee set the following broad goals for the Grid2003 project.

- Provide the next phase of the iVDGL Laboratory.

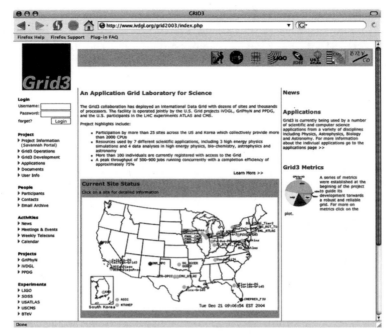

Figure 24.3 Grid2003 project web page site catalog and status.

- Provide the infrastructure and services needed to demonstrate LHC production and analysis applications running at scale in a common grid environment.
- Provide a platform for computer science technology demonstrators.

The goals of this project included meeting a set of performance targets, and using metrics listed in a planning document. The central project milestone can be summarized as delivery of a shared, multi-VO, multi-application grid laboratory, in which performance targets were pursued through deployment and execution of application demonstrations during the period before, during, and after the SC2003 conference in Phoenix (November 16–19). The organization of this project included the creation of teams representing application groups, site administrators, middleware developers, core service providers, and operations. The active period of this project was a 5-month period from July to November 2003. It is interesting to note that subsequent to this period, Grid3 remains largely intact with many applications running.

The Grid2003 Project deployed, integrated, and operated Grid3 with 27 operational processing sites comprising at peak ~2800 CPUs for more than 3 weeks. Progress was made in other areas that are important to the iVDGL mission.

- *Multiple VO Grid.* Six different virtual organizations participated and successfully deployed 10 applications. All applications were able to run on sites that were not owned by the host organization. Further, the applications were all able to run on nondedicated resources.

- *Multi-Disciplinary Grid.* During the project, two new applications, the SnB structural biology application and an application in chemical informatics, were run across Grid3. The fact that these could be installed and run on a Grid infrastructure designed and installed for Particle and Astrophysics Experiments provides the members of iVDGL with confidence that this grid can be adapted to other applications as needed.

- *Use of Shared Resources.* Many of the resources brought into the Grid3 environment were leveraged facilities in use by other VOs.

- *Dynamic Resource Allocation.* In addition to resources that were committed 24×7, the computational research (CCR) configured their local schedulers to bring additional resources into and out of Grid3 on a daily basis, satisfying local requirements and Grid3 users.

- *International connectivity.* One site was located abroad (Kyunpook National University, Korea).

Over the course of several weeks surrounding SC2003, the Grid2003 project met its target goals.

1. *Number of CPUs.* With a target of 400 CPUs, Grid2003 successfully incorporated 2163 processors. More than 60% of available CPU resources are nondedicated facilities. The Grid3 environment effectively shared resources not directly owned by the participating experiments.

2. *Number of Users.* With a target of 10 users, Grid2003 successfully supported 102 users. About 10% of the users are application administrators who do the majority of the job submissions. However, more than 102 users are authorized to use the resources through their respective VOs services.

3. *Number of Applications.* With a target of at least four physics applications, Grid2003 successfully supported 10 applications, including at least one from each of the five GriPhyN–iVDGL–PPDG participating experiments, the SnB program from structural biology, and GADU/Gnare genome analysis. Note that these applications continue to run on Grid3.

4. *Number of Sites Running Concurrent Applications.* With a target of at least 10 concurrent applications, Grid2003 supported 17 concurrent applications. This number is related to the number of computational service sites defined on the catalog page and varies with the application.

5. *Data Transfers Per Day.* With a target of 2–3 TB of data transfer daily, Grid2003 achieved a 4 TB/day transfer rate. This metric was met with the aid of the GridFTP-demo.

6. *Percentage of Resources Used.* With a target of utilizing 90% of the resources, Grid2003 was only able to achieve 40–70% of the resources.

7. *Peak Number of Concurrent Jobs.* With a peak target of 1000 concurrent jobs, Grid2003 was able to support 1100 concurrent jobs. On November 20, 2003, there were sustained periods when over 1100 jobs ran simultaneously.

24.6.3 IBM NE BioGrid

The IBM Northeast Bio-Grid (IBM NE BioGrid) collaboration includes IBM, MIT, Harvard, and the ACDC-Grid. It uses the IBM Grid Toolbox V3 [75] that delivers a set of grid services built with Open Grid Services Architecture (OGSA). OGSA enables the communication across heterogeneous, geographically dispersed environments in addition to the IBM General Purpose File System (GPFS) [76] and provides a parallel scalable global filesystem that is used for the ACDC-Grid computational resources. This 4.3 TB single filesystem uses 34 servers with two hard drives connected by Myrinet and has provided grid-enabled I/O intensive scientific applications bandwidth in excess of 1800 MB/s. The IBM NE BioGrid and the Grid3 collaboration use very different Grid cyberinfrastructure middleware for grid-enabled resource communication and computational job executions.

24.6.4 HP GridLite

The ACDC-Grid collaboration with HP on GridLite provides another Grid cyberinfrastructure which we believe will provide core infrastructure for the SUNY–Buffalo ACDC-Campus-Grid that is currently under construction. GridLite will provide a lightweight infrastructure that can easily be deployed on pocketPCs, laptops, PDAs, cellular phones, and other portable devices on the campus. Many of these devices are also being grid-enabled by our NEESgrid [77] collaborators, SUNY–Buffalo's Structural Engineering and Earthquake Simulation Laboratory (SEESL) [78], which is the flagship laboratory in the Multidisciplinary Center for Earthquake Engineering Research (MCEER) [79], which will be an important node of a nationwide "collaboratory" in the NSFs Network for Earthquake Engineering Simulation (NEES). The NEESgrid software release 3.0 [80] point of presence, tele-presence system, and software integration provide the ACDC-Grid with grid services and testbeds for hardening the core grid-enabling instrument and device cyberinfrastructure. The *MCEER, NEES, CSEE,* and *CCR Collaboration Platform* tightly integrates all of the CCRs common interests and missions. CCR provides the machine room space to house and maintain a high-powered dual processor server capable of (1) serving a custom web site with a Gigabit Ethernet connection to the University backbone, (2) serving a web accessible MySQL database, (3) serving 3D stereo graphics to the SGI 3300W Visualization Display, (4) serving 2D and 3D graphics to the Tiled-Display Wall, (5) serving streaming video to the Access Grid for world-wide presentation, (6) staging and postprocessing platform for CCR's Computational Grid (ACDC-Grid) analysis and results, (7) providing a common platform for exchange of information and visualization, and (8) fostering collaborations with other University departments.

24.6.5 Open Science Grid

The ACDC-Grid is a founding participant of the OSG, a cooperative venture that brings together laboratory and university facilities, grid technology providers, and the application communities, for the purpose of engineering and building a common grid infrastructure, which will ensure the necessary robust, persistent, computational, and data services needed by laboratories, experiments, and application managers. The OSG provides a framework for coordinating activities with the goal of enabling a common grid infrastructure and shared resources for the benefit of scientific applications. The ACDC-Grid team participate in the (1) OSG Security Incident Handling Activity, (2) OSG Storage Services Activity, (3) OSG-0 Activity, and (4) the OSG Blueprint Activity [81]. In accordance with the magnified risk and the circumscribed communities, the Security Incident Handling activity group (SIHag) was established with the goal to reduce risk through the establishment of guidelines, policies, and methods for security incident handling within the OSG and iVDGL communities.

24.7 GRID RESEARCH ADVANCEMENTS

Several distributed monitoring systems have been designed to track the status of large networked systems. Some of these systems are centralized, where the data is collected and analyzed at a single central host, whereas others use a distributed storage and query model. Ganglia [82, 83] uses a hierarchical system, where the attributes are replicated within clusters using multicast and then cluster aggregates are further aggregated along a single tree. Sophia [84, 85] is a distributed monitoring system, currently deployed on Planetlab [86] and is based on a declarative logic-programming model, where the location of query execution is both explicit in the language and can be calculated during the course of evaluation. TAG [87] collects information from a large number of sensors along a single tree. IBM Tivoli Monitoring [88] also provides the foundation for additional automated Best Practices via Proactive Analysis Components (PACs) for managing business critical hardware and software including middleware, applications, and databases. A number of existing grid information systems such as MDS2 [89, 90], global information service (GIS) [91], R-GMA [92, 93], and Hawkeye [94] each provide a core distributed information management system designed to support a range of applications and services such as scheduling, replica selection, service discovery, and system monitoring. All of these systems use a client–server model in which Information Providers collect or generate data and supply this data to Information Services. We currently work with the Globus GIS and the MDS working groups through our Grid3 and OSG collaborations. The ACDC-Grid Monitoring and Information Services–Core Infrastructure (MIS-CI) deployed on our grid-enabled resources has been developed through this collaboration, as shown in Figure 24.4. The MIS-CI is architected to be a lightweight nonintrusive monitoring and information service that can be throttled by the Resource Provider in a dynamic fashion. The MIS-CI is self-monitoring, secure,

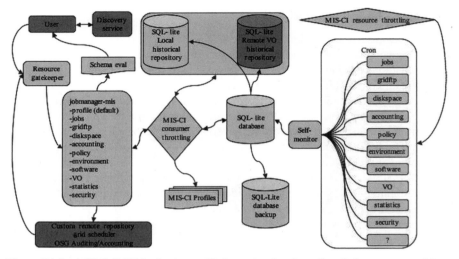

Figure 24.4   ACDC-Grid Monitoring and Information Services–Core Infrastructure architecture description.

and hierarchical in design, making it extremely scalable with tuneable information time scales.

Our monitoring system is being enhanced to

1. Provide a programmatic interface to the ACDC Job Monitoring database for running, queued, or historical jobs, complete with the current site status metrics;
2. Provide integration with MonaLisa [95] and the Grid3 site status catalog for defining difference metrics on job monitoring, resource utilization, and policy metrics;
3. Provide integration with the Globus MDS provider development team for providing XML formatted job information and site status metrics;
4. Provide integration of our predictive scheduling estimates based on resource policy specifications;
5. Provide resource specific CPU availability for Grid3 resources, ACDC-Grid resources, and VOs;
6. Provide currently available free nodes and predictive scheduling capabilities of job execution start times based on running, queued, and submitted job characteristics, including site policy constraints;
7. Provide data grid historical and near real-time estimates of bandwidth and utilization of grid-enabled repositories; and
8. Harden the secure, lightweight, scalable distributed hierarchical imbedded MySQL database ACDC-Grid monitoring daemon infrastructure for heterogeneous computational grid hardware resources and heterogeneous grid infrastructure middleware.

This enhanced and hardened service can then be utilized by several other open source applications and included in the Globus, NMI [96, 97], and VDT software suites for production grid monitoring efforts.

24.8 GRID RESEARCH APPLICATION ABSTRACTIONS AND TOOLS

The grid-enabling application templates (GATs) used for porting scientific and engineering applications to the ACDC-Grid use abstraction as the process of combining multiple smaller operations into a single unit that can be referred to by a stage. Each stage is named and may contain a template for imposing fine-grained application input file generation, automated parallelization, intermediate result file monitoring, exception handling, and overall application performance metrics. Using the ACDC-Grid GAT abstraction allows programmers to solve problems at a high level, while deferring noncritical details. This has proved to be an effective problem solving strategy in porting codes from structural biology, earthquake engineering, and the environmental and hydrodynamic domains to the ACDC-Grid infrastructure. The application developers can drill down into each stage or split stages into logical units for their specific application. For example the Shake-and-Bake application uses seven stages in defining a computational and data grid job: (1) software, (2) template, (3) general information, (4) data preparation, (5) job definition, (6) review, and (7) execution scenario. This GAT defines the grid-enabled software application; required and/or optional data files from the ACDC Data Grid; computational requirements are input or a template defined computational requirement runtime estimate is selected; application specific runtime parameters or default template parameter definitions are used; the grid user accepts the template complete job definition workflow or corrects any part of job definition; the grid user has the ability to input an execution scenario or select a ACDC-Grid determined template defined execution scenario. After these stages have been completed the grid user can view specific grid job completion status, grid job current state, detailed information on all running or queued grid jobs, grid-enabled application specific intermediate and post processing grid job graphics, as well as plots and tables. Figure 24.5 describes a typical ACDC-Grid GATs workflow definition and execution. The current GAT workflow is robust enough to handle quite complicated definitions that integrate intermediate job status and statistics on a dynamic basis. The GAT API is used extensively for integration of the ACDC Computational Grid with the ACDC Data Grid in a seamless fashion.

Leveraging our experience with Grid3 and OSG, it is evident that the current Grid security infrastructure is deficient. Specifically, many Grids use a grid-mapfile for mapping remote users to a single local grid user account. This can lead to several potential security problems. We are currently developing infrastructure to mitigate these problems, as shown in Figure 24.6.

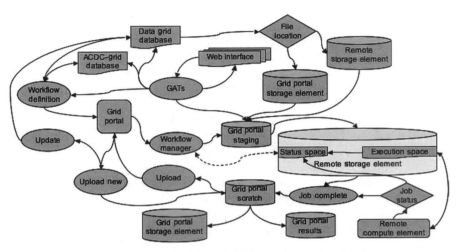

Figure 24.5 ACDC-Grid GAT definition and execution description.

24.8.1 Optimizing SnB on Grids

GAs were developed by Holland [98] and are based on natural selection and population genetics. Traditional optimization methods focus on developing a solution from a single trial, whereas GAs operate with a *population* of candidate solutions.

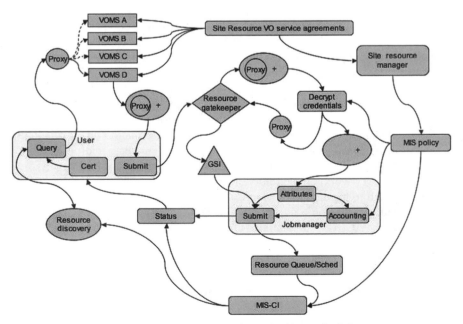

Figure 24.6 ACDC-Grid Proxy+ enhanced grid security infrastructure.

We have constructed a GA to determine an efficient set of *SnB* input parameters in an effort to reduce the time-to-solution for determining a molecular crystal structure from X-ray diffraction data. We use a *population* of candidate *SnB* input parameters. Each member of the population is represented as a string in the population, and a fitness function is used to assign a fitness (quality) value for each member. The members in the population obtain their fitness values by executing the SnB program with the input parameter values represented by their strings. Using "survival-of-the-fittest" selection, strings from the *old* population are used to create a *new* population based on their fitness values. The member strings selected can recombine using crossover and/or mutation operators. A crossover operator creates a new member by exchanging substrings between two candidate members, whereas a mutation operator randomly modifies a piece of an existing candidate. This procedure of combining and randomly perturbing member strings has, in many cases, been shown to produce stronger (i.e., more fit) populations as a function of time (i.e., number of generations).

We use the Sugal [99] (sequential execution) and PGAPack [100, 101] (parallel and sequential execution) GA libraries. The Sugal library provided a sequential GA and has additional capabilities, including a restart function, which proved to be very important when determining fitness values for large molecular structures. The PGAPack library provided a parallel master/slave MPICH/MPI implementation, which proved very efficient on distributed- and shared-memory ACDC-Grid compute platforms. Other key features include C and Fortran interfaces, binary-, integer-, real-, and character-valued native data types, object-oriented design, and multiple choices for GA operators and parameters. In addition, PGAPack is quite extensible. The PGAPack library was extended to include restart functionality and is currently the only library used for the ACDC-Grid production work.

The SnB computer program has approximately 100 input parameters, although not all parameters can be optimized. For the purpose of this study, 17 critical parameters were identified for participation in the optimization procedure. Eight known molecular structures were initially used to evaluate the GA evolutionary molecular structure determination framework performance. These structures are 96016c [102], 96064c [103], crambin [104], gramicidin A [105], isoleucinomycin [106], pr435 [107], triclinic lysozyme [108], and triclinic vancomycin [109].

To efficiently utilize the computational resources of the ACDC-Grid, an accurate estimate must be made in the resource requirements for SnB jobs that are necessary for the GA optimization. This includes runs with varying parameter sets over the complete set of eight known structures from our initial database.

This is accomplished as follows. First, a small number of jobs are run to determine the required running time for each of the necessary jobs. Typically, this consists of running a single trial for each of the job to predict the time required for the required number of trials for the job under consideration.

Approximately 25,000 population members were evaluated for the eight known molecular structures and stored in a MySQL database table, as shown in Figure 24.7.

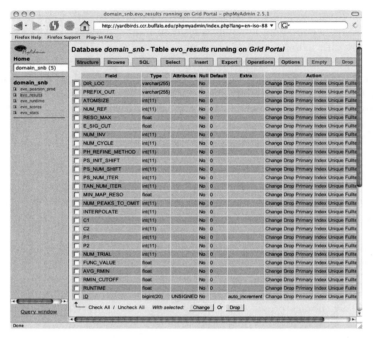

Figure 24.7   MySQL database table for SnB trial results.

From these trial results, the mean $(\overline{X}^j)$ and standard deviations (s^j) are calculated for each input parameter j and used to determine the standard scores (z_i^j) for each trial i,

$$z_i^j = \frac{X_i^j - \overline{X}^j}{s^j},$$

for all i and j, where the trial parameter value for trial i and parameter j is X_i^j. Figure 24.8 shows the standard scores of the parameters under consideration.

The Pearson product–moment correlation coefficients (r_k^j) are calculated for input parameter j and molecular structure k by

$$r_k^j = \frac{\sum z_k^j z_k^{\text{runtime}}}{N - 1},$$

for all j and k, where N denotes the degrees of freedom and z_k^{runtime} represents the standard score of the GA trial runtime (Fig. 24.9).

The input parameters that have the largest absolute magnitude Pearson product–moment correlation coefficient with respect to the observed trial runtimes are selected and used to form a predictive runtime function that is fit using a linear least squares routine

$$X_i^{\text{runtime}} = \sum a_j r_k^j \overline{X}^j,$$

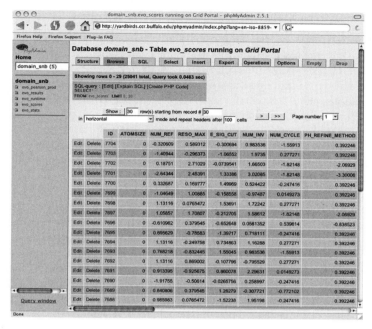

Figure 24.8 Standard scores for Pearson product–moment correlation coefficient calculations.

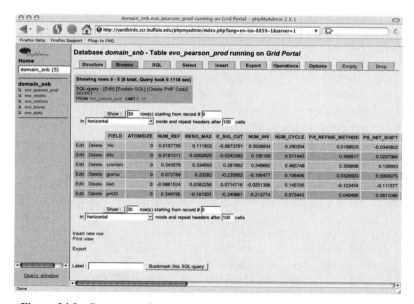

Figure 24.9 Pearson product–moment correlation coefficient database table.

where the observed X_i^{runtime} trial runtime is fit to a selected sub-set of input parameter values j, $\overline{X}^j$ denotes the input parameter value, r_k^j denotes the respective molecular structure k Pearson product–moment correlation coefficient, and a_j denotes the linear least-square fit coefficients for each j input parameter. We use this function within the grid-enabled data-mining infrastructure to estimate the maximum number of SnB GA generations and the maximum size of the population that would run on a given computational resource within the specified time frame.

The ACDC-Grid infrastructure automatically updates the correlation coefficients based on the availability of new trial data appearing in the SnB trial result table. Thus, runtime estimates for any given structure continually evolve throughout the GA optimization process.

For example, if there are 50 processors available for 150 min on ACDC-Grid compute platform "A," we are interested in determining the maximum number of GA generations and the size of the population that can run on "A" and complete within 150 min. On the basis of this information, the data mining algorithms can make intelligent choices of not only which structures to evaluate but also they can completely define the SnB GA job that should be executed. This type of runtime prediction is an essential component of our system for providing a level of quality of service. Further, in our experience, this type of runtime parameter-based prediction is almost always necessary when queue managed computational resources are employed.

24.8.2 Grid-Enabled Data Mining with SnB

The SnB grid-enabled data mining application utilizes the ACDC-Grid infrastructure. A typical SnB job uses the Grid Portal to supply the molecular structures parameter sets to optimize, the data file metadata, the grid-enabled SnB mode of operation (dedicated or back fill), and the SnB termination criteria. The Grid Portal then assembles the required SnB application data and supporting files, execution scripts, database tables, and submits jobs for parameter optimization based on the current database statistics. ACDC-Grid job management automatically determines the appropriate execution times, number of trials, number of processors for each available resource, as well as logging the status of all concurrently executing resource jobs. In addition, it automatically incorporates the SnB trial results into the molecular structure database and initiates post-processing of the updated database for subsequent job submissions.

The Grid Portal then assembles the required SnB application data and supporting files, execution scripts, database tables, and submits jobs for parameter optimization based on the current database statistics. ACDC-Grid job management automatically determines the appropriate execution times, number of trials, number of processors for each available resource, as well as logging and status of all concurrently executing resource jobs. In addition, it automatically incorporates the SnB trial results into the molecular structure database a and initiates post-processing of the updated database for subsequent job submissions. Figure 24.10 shows the logical relationship for the SnB grid-enabled data mining routine described.

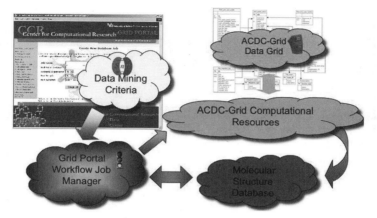

Figure 24.10 ACDC-Grid grid-enabled data mining diagram.

For example, starting September 8, 2003, a backfill data mining SnB job was activated at the Center for Computational Research using the ACDC-Grid computational and data grid resources. The ACDC-Grid historical job-monitoring infrastructure is used to obtain the jobs completed for the period of September 8, 2003 to January 10, 2004, as shown in Figure 24.11.

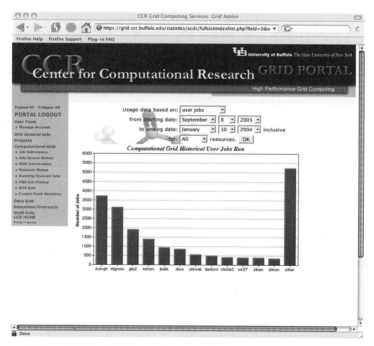

Figure 24.11 ACDC-Grid job monitoring information for all resources and users.

Figure 24.12   ACDC-Grid job monitoring statistics for user mlgreen.

The activated data mining *SnB* job template is being run by user mlgreen. By hovering over the bar in the chart, as shown in Figure 24.12, one can see mlgreen's job statistics. Further, notice that 3118 jobs have been completed on the ACDC-Grid resources over this time period. The ACDC-Grid job monitoring also dynamically reports job statistics for the data mining jobs. The total number of jobs completed by all users on all resource is 19,868, where the data mining jobs represent 15.69% of the total. The average number of processes for a data-mining job was 19.65 and the total number of processors used over this period was 433,552, where the data mining jobs accounted for 16.85% of the total. The data mining jobs consumed 291,987 CPU hours, which was 19.54% of the total CPU hours consumed (1,494,352 CPU hours).

A subsequent mouse click on the bar chart drills down further describing the jobs completed by user mlgreen. Here, we see five computational resources that processed the 3118 data mining jobs. The statistics for the Joplin compute platform are shown in Figure 24.13. Note that all statistics are based only on the jobs completed by the mlgreen user. There were 869 jobs processed by the Joplin compute platform representing 27.87% of the 3118 data mining jobs.

Clicking on the bar chart drills down into a full description of all jobs processed by the Joplin compute platform, as shown in Figure 24.14. The information presented includes job ID, username, group name, queue name, node count, processes per node, queue wait time, wall time used, wall time requested, wall time efficiency, CPU time, physical memory used, virtual memory used, and job completion time/date.

The ACDC-Grid data mining backfill mode of operation only uses computational resources that are currently not scheduled for use by the native queue scheduler. These resources are commonly called "backfill" as users can run jobs on the associated nodes without affecting the queued jobs. Many queues and schedulers give this information

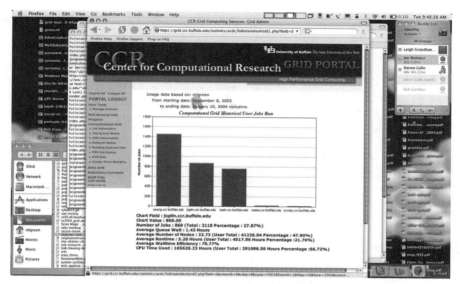

Figure 24.13 ACDC-Grid job monitoring statistics for user mlgreen.

in the X number of nodes available for Y amount of time. The ACDC-Grid infrastructure monitors this information for all of the computational resources and stores this information in a MySQL database table, as shown in Figure 24.15.

Figure 24.15 also shows the number of processors and wall time that are available for each resource. Note a value of -1 for the available wall-time represents an unlimited amount of time (no currently queued job requires the use of these processors).

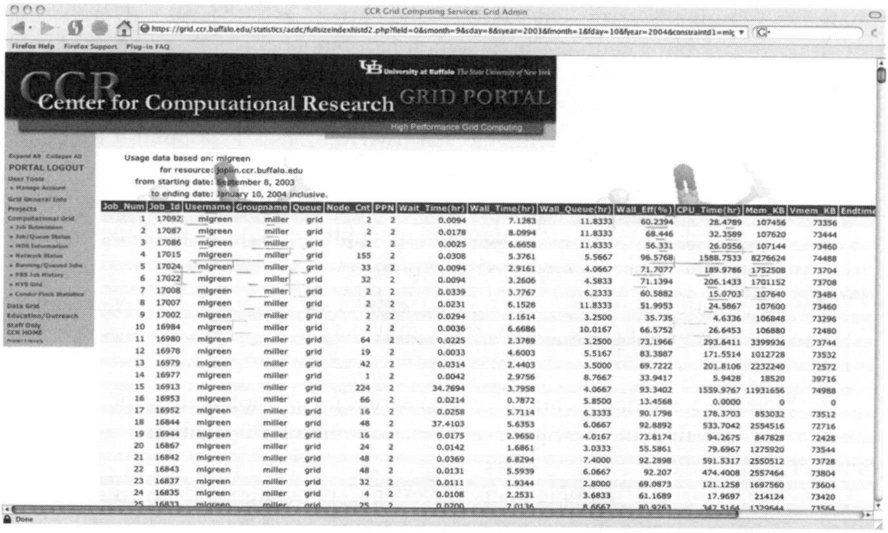

Figure 24.14 ACDC-Grid job monitoring tabular accounting of completed job statistics.

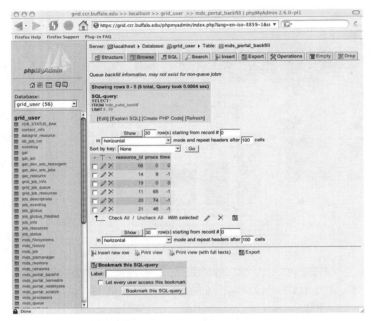

Figure 24.15 ACDC-Grid backfill information for all resources.

The activated data mining template can obtain the number of processors and wall time available for a given compute platform and then check the status of the platform before determining the actual GA *SnB* data mining job parameters (Fig. 24.16).

Using the Pearson product–moment fit function derived earlier, the new data mining job run time is estimated based on the current ACDC-Grid SnB molecular structure database information. The data mining job template is then executed leading to the migration and submission of the designed data-mining job to the respective ACDC-Grid computational resource.

The activated data-mining template has two options of stopping criteria, as follows.

1. Continue submitting SnB data mining application jobs until the optimal parameters have been found based on predetermined criteria.
2. Continue indefinitely (the data mining template is manually deactivated by the user when optimal parameters are found).

This illustrative example summarizes the evolutionary molecular structure determination optimization of the Shake-and-Bake method as instantiated in the SnB computer program.

The ACDC data grid complements the ACDC computational grid in terms of managing and manipulating these data collections. As discussed, the goal of the ACDC data grid is to transparently manage data distributed across heterogeneous

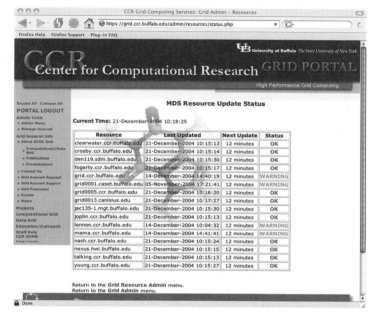

Figure 24.16 ACDC-Grid computational resource status monitor.

resources, providing access via a uniform (web) interface. In addition, we also enable the transparent migration of data between various resources, while preserving uniform access for the user (Fig. 24.17).

The hierarchical display does not list the file attribute data, so a list-based display has also been developed that can be used for sorting data grid files based on available metadata (e.g., filename, file size, modification time, owner, etc.), as shown in Figure 24.18.

Basic file management functions are available via a platform-independent user-friendly Web interface that includes a file transfer capabilities, a simple Web-based file editor, an efficient search utility, and the logical display of files for a given user in three divisions (user/group/public). Collating and displaying statistical information is particularly useful to administrators for optimizing usage of resources. The ACDC data grid infrastructure periodically migrates files between data repositories for optimal usage of resources. The file migration algorithm depends upon a number of factors, including the following:

- User access time.
- Network capacity at time of migration.
- User profile.
- User disk quotas on various resources.

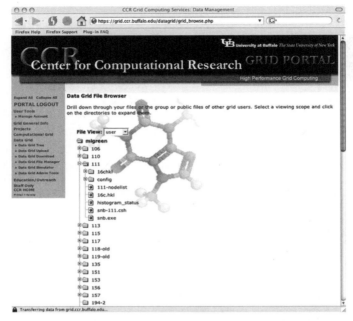

Figure 24.17   ACDC data grid Java tree view of files.

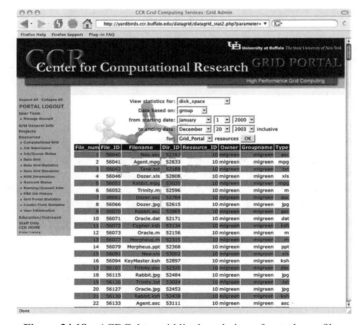

Figure 24.18   ACDC data grid list-based view of sorted user files.

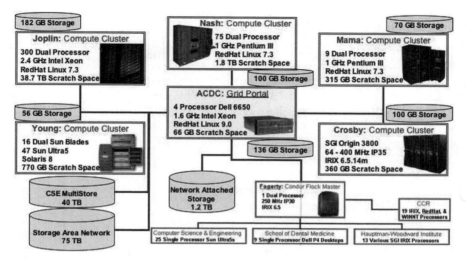

Figure 24.19 ACDC data grid repository location, network bandwidth, and size.

Further, we have the ability to mine log files, which aids in the determination of the following:

• The amount of data to migrate in one cycle.
• The appropriate migration cycle length.
• The file access pattern of a data grid user.
• The access pattern for public or group files.

The user global file-aging attribute is indicative of a user's access across their own files and is an attribute of a user's profile. The local file aging attribute is indicative of overall access of a particular file by users having group or public access. The latter is an attribute of a file and is stored in the file management data grid table. During migration, these attributes are used to determine the files that are to be migrated from the grid portal repository to a remote resource repository. Specifically, file migration is a function of global file aging, local file aging, and resource usage (e.g., the previous use of files on individual compute platforms is a factor in determining file migration). By tracking the file access patterns of all user files and storing this information in the associated database tables, the ACDC data grid infrastructure can automatically determine an effective repository distribution of the data grid files. See Figure 24.19 for a schematic of the physical data ACDC data grid.

Support for multiple access to files in the data grid has been implemented with file locking and synchronization primitives. The ACDC data grid also provides security for authentication and authorization of users, as well as policies and facilities for data access and publication. The ACDC data grid algorithms are continually evolving to minimize network traffic and maximize disk space utilization on a per user basis.

This is accomplished by data mining user usage and disk space requirements in a ubiquitous and an automated fashion.

One advantage of SnB is that it can run in either a loosely coupled or tightly coupled fashion, it uses a database management system, it can take advantage of computational steering, it utilizes a geographically distributed interactive back-end visualization system, and it is amenable to an automated backfill mechanism. Currently, we run SnB on the ACDC-Grid from either a GUI or Web portal.

24.9 CONCLUSIONS

The Grid is a rapidly emerging and expanding technology that allows geographically distributed and independently operated resources (CPU cycles, data storage, sensors, visualization devices, and a wide variety of Internet-ready instruments) to be linked together in a transparent fashion. SnB is a computer program based on the Shake-and-Bake method of molecular structure determination from X-ray diffraction data. The Shake-and-Bake algorithm for molecular structure determination was listed on the IEEE poster *"Top Algorithms of the 20th Century."* In this chapter, we have discussed the development of tools that allow for an efficient grid-based implementation of *SnB* that is extensible to a wide range of scientific programs.

We introduced the ACDC-Grid, which provides an integrated computational and data grid, lightweight job monitoring, predictive scheduling, and opportunities for improved Grid utilization through an elegant backfill facility. The core infrastructure for the ACDC-Grid includes the installation of standard grid middleware, the deployment of an active Web portal for deploying applications, dynamic resource allocation so that clusters and networks of workstations can be scheduled to provide resources on demand, a scalable and dynamic scheduling system, and a dynamic firewall, to name a few.

ACKNOWLEDGMENTS

The authors would like to thank members of the SUNY–Buffalo Grid Team, including Steve Gallo, Naimesh Shah, Jason Rappleye, Cathy Ruby, Jon Bednasz, and Tony Kew, as well as Chuck Weeks, Sam Guercio, Adam Koniak, Martins Innus, Dori Macchioni, Henrique Bucher, and Cynthia Cornelius, for their contributions to the efforts described in this chapter. This research is supported by NSF ITR Grant #0204918 and a post-doctoral fellowship from HP. Computing Resources provided by the Center for Computational Research, SUNY–Buffalo.

REFERENCES

1. Grid Computing Info Centre, http://www.gridcomputing.com/.
2. I. Foster and C. Kesselman, *The Grid: Blueprint for a New Computing Infrastructure*, Morgan Kauffman Publishers, Inc., San Francisco, 1999.

3. F. Berman, G. Fox, and T. Hey, *Grid Computing: Making the Global Infrastructure a Reality*, John Wiley & Sons, 2003.

4. The Globus Alliance, http://www.globus.org.

5. R. Miller, S. M. Gallo, H. G. Khalak, and C. M. Weeks, *SnB*: Crystal structure determination via *Shake-and-Bake, J. Appl. Crystallogr.*, 27, 613–621 (1994)

6. C. M. Weeks and R. Miller, The design and implementation *SnB* v2.0, *J. Appl. Crystallogr.*, 32, 120–124 (1999).

7. J. Rappleye, M. Innus, C. M. Weeks, and R. Miller, *SnB* v2.2: An example of crystallographic multiprocessing, *J. Appl. Crystallogr.*, 35, 374–376 (2002).

8. C. M. Weeks, G. T. DeTitta, H. A. Hauptman, P. Thuman, and R. Miller, Structure solution by minimal function phase refinement and Fourier filtering: II. Implementation and applications, *Acta Cryst.*, A50, 210–220 (1994).

9. G. T. DeTitta, C. M. Weeks, P. Thuman, R. Miller, and H. A. Hauptman, Structure solution by minimal function phase refinement and Fourier filtering: theoretical basis, *Acta Cryst.*, A50, 203–210 (1994).

10. M. L. Green and R. Miller, Grid computing in Buffalo, New York, *Ann. Eur. Acad. Sci.*, 191–218 (2003).

11. H. A. Hauptman, "A minimal principle in the phase problem," in *Crystallographic Computing 5: From Chemistry to Biology*, D. Moras, A. D. Podjarny, and J. C. Thierry, Eds., Oxford: IUCr & Oxford University Press, pp. 324–332.

12. M. L. Green and R. Miller, Molecular Structure Determination on a Computational & Data Grid, Parallel Computing, Volume 30, Issues 9–10, September–October 2004, Pages 1001-1017.

13. M. L. Green and R. Miller, Evolutionary Molecular Structure Determination Using Grid-Enabled Data Mining, Parallel Computing, Volume 30, Issues 9–10, September–October 2004, Pages 1057–1071.

14. M. L. Green and R. Miller, A client–server prototype for application grid-enabling template design, January 2004, http://www.cse.buffalo.edu/pub/WWW/faculty/miller/Papers/PPL04-1.pdf.

15. Globus Toolkit 3, http://www-unix.globus.org/toolkit/.

16. Globus Resource Allocation Manager (GRAM), http://www-unix.globus.org/developer/resource-management.html.

17. GridFTP Data Transfer Protocol, http://www.globus.org/datagrid/gridftp.html.

18. K. Czajkowski, D. Ferguson, I. Foster, J. Frey, S. Graham, T. Maguire, D. Snelling, S. Tuecke, From Open Grid Services Infrastructure to WS-Resource Framework: Refactoring & Evolution, http://www.globus.org/wsrf/OGSI%20to%20WSRF%201.0.pdf.

19. Web Services Resource Lifetime, http://www.globus.org/wsrf/WS-ResourceLifetime.pdf.

20. Web Services Resource Properties, http://www.globus.org/wsrf/WS-ResourceProperties.pdf.

21. Web Services Notification, http://www.globus.org/wsrf/WS-Notification.pdf.

22. Modeling Stateful Resources with Web Services, http://www.globus.org/wsrf/ModelingState.pdf.

23. The Globus Alliance: WS-Resource Framework, http://www.globus.org/wsrf/.

24. pyGlobus Project, http://www-itg.lbl.gov/gtg/projects/pyGlobus/.

25. XML Package for Python, http://pyxml.sourceforge.net/.

26. Python Extensions for the Grid (PEG), http://grail.sdsc.edu/projects/peg/introduction.html.

27. Numerical Python, http://www.pfdubois.com/numpy/.

28. Scientific Python, http://starship.python.net/~hinsen/ScientificPython/.

29. netCDF Library, http://www.unidata.ucar.edu/packages/netcdf/.

30. Message Passing Interface (MPI), http://www-unix.mcs.anl.gov/mpi/.

31. Bulk Synchronous Parallel Programming (BSPlib), http://www.bsp-worldwide.org/.

32. R. H. Bisseling, *Parallel Scientific Computation: A Structured Approach Using BSP and MPI*, Oxford University Press, 2004, 305 pp. (ISBN 0-19-852939-2).

33. SciPy Library, http://www.scipy.org/.

34. pyGridWare Project, http://www-itg.lbl.gov/gtg/projects/pyGridWare/.

35. Integrate Perl into OGSI-based Grid Applications and Services, http://www-106.ibm.com/developerworks/library/gr-perlinf.html.

36. SOAP::Lite, http://www.soaplite.com/.

37. OGSI::Lite, http://www.sve.man.ac.uk/Research/AtoZ/ILCT.

38. MS.NET Grid, http://www.nesc.ac.uk/action/projects/project_action.cfm?title=145.

39. MS.NETGrid Project, http://www.epcc.ed.ac.uk/~ogsanet/.

40. Microsoft, http://www.microsoft.com/.

41. National e-Science Centre, http://www.nesc.ac.uk/.

42. OGSI.NET, http://www.cs.virginia.edu/~humphrey/GCG/ogsi.net.html.

43. Optimalgrid, http://www.alphaworks.ibm.com/tech/optimalgrid.

44. Seti@home, http://setiathome.ssl.berkeley.edu/.

45. Folding@home, http://folding.stanford.edu.

46. MOAB Grid Scheduler (Silver), http://www.supercluster.org/silver/.

47. Sun Grid Engine (SGE), http://gridengine.sunsource.net/.

48. Sphinx Scheduler, http://www.griphyn.org/sphinx/.

49. J. Patton Jones and B. Nitzberg, Scheduling for Parallel Supercomputing: A Historical Perspective of Achievable Utilization, in *Job Scheduling Strategies for Parallel Processing*, Lecture Notes in Computer Science 1659, Springer-Verlag, 1999, pp. 1–16.

50. D. Zotkin and P. J. Keleher, Job-Length Estimation and Performance in Backfilling Schedulers, in *Proceedings of the Eight High Performance Distributed Computing Conference, IEEE*, 1999.

51. S.-H. Chiang and M. Vernon, Production Job Scheduling for Parallel Shared Memory Systems, *in Proceeding of the International Parallel and Distributed Processing Symposium* (IPDPS).

52. W. Smith, V. Taylor, and I. Foster, Using Run-Time Predictions to Estimate Queue Wait Times and Improve Scheduler Performance, in *Job Scheduling Strategies for Parallel in Processing*, D. G. Feitelson and L. Rudolph, Eds., Lecture Notes in Computer Science, Springer Verlag, 1999.

53. R. Gibbons, A Historical Application Profiler for Use by Parallel Schedulers, Lecture Notes on Computer Science, pages 58–75, 1997.

54. W. Smith, V. Taylor, and I. Foster, Using Run-Time Predictions to Estimate Queue Wait Times and Improve Scheduler Performance, in *Job Scheduling Strategies for Parallel*

Processing, D. G. Feitelson and L. Rudolph, Eds., Lecture Notes in Computer Science, Springer-Verlag, 1999.

55. J. K. Talyor, *Statistical Techniques for Data Analysis*, Lewis Publishers, Inc., Chelsea, MI, 1990.

56. I. Foster, J. Vöckler, M. Wilde, and Y. Zhao, Chimera: A Virtual Data System for Representing, Querying, and Automating Data Derivation, in *Proceeding of the 14th International Conference on Scientific and Statistical Database Management* (SSDBM 2002).

57. Storage Resource Manager, http://sdm.lbl.gov/srm-wg.

58. Storage Resource Management: Concepts, Functionality, and Interface Specification, Arie Shoshani, Future of Data Grids Workshop, Berlin, 2004.

59. Storage Element Service, http://www.ivdgl.org/grid2003/news/.

60. SRM Joint Functional Design, Version 1, http://sdm.lbl.gov/srm/documents/joint.docs / SRM.joint.func.design.part1.doc.

61. SRM joint methods specification Version 1, http://sdm.lbl.gov/srm/documents/joint. docs/srm.v1.0.doc.

62. The Storage Resource Manager Interface Specification, Version 2.1, J. Gu, A. Sim, A. Shoshani, Eds., available at http://sdm.lbl.gov/srm/documents/joint.docs/SRM.spec. v2.1.final.doc.

63. The Network Weather Service, http://nws.cs.ucsb.edu/.

64. W. Smith, I. Foster, and V. Taylor, Scheduling with advanced reservations, International Parallel and Distributed Processing Symposium (IPDPS'00), May 2000.

65. The Virtual Data Toolkit, http://www.lsc-group.phys.uwm.edu/vdt/.

66. International Virtual Data Grid Laboratory, http://www.ivdgl.org/.

67. GRID2003, http://www.ivdgl.org/grid2003.

68. The Grid Laboratory Uniform Environment (GLUE), http://www.hicb.org/ glue/glue.htm.

69. Grid Physics Network GriPhyN, http://www.griphyn.org/index.php.

70. Particle Physics Data Grid, http://www.ppdg.net/.

71. European Data Grid, http://eu-datagrid.web.cern.ch/eu-datagrid/.

72. TransAtlantic Grid (DataTAG), http://datatag.web.cern.ch/datatag/.

73. CrossGrid, http://www.eu-crossgrid.org/.

74. CERN, http://public.web.cern.ch/public/.

75. IBM Grid Toolbox, http://www-132.ibm.com/webapp/wcs/stores/servlet/Category Display?storeId=1&catalogId=-840&langId=-1&categoryId=2587007.

76. IBM General Purpose File System (GPFS), http://www-1.ibm.com/servers/eserver/ clusters/software/gpfs.html.

77. NSF Network for Earthquake Engineering Simulation (NEES) Grid, http://www.nees. org/.

78. Structural Engineering Earthquake Simulation Laboratory (SEESL), http://www.civil. buffalo.edu/Facilities/research.html.

79. Multidisciplinary Center for Earthquake Engineering (MCEER), http://mceer.buffalo. edu/.

80. NEESgrid software release 3.0, http://www.neesgrid.org/software/neesgrid3.0/.

81. Open Science Grid Consortium, http://www.opensciencegrid.org/activities/index.html.

82. Ganglia: Distributed Monitoring and Execution System, http://ganglia.sourceforge.net.

83. M. L. Massie, B. N. Chun, and D. E. Culler, The ganglia distributed monitoring system: design, implementation, and experience, *Parallel Comput.*, 30 (7), 2004.

84. M. Wawrzoniak, L. Peterson, and T. Roscoe, Sophia: An Information Plane for Networked Systems, in *Proceedings of the HotNets-II*, Cambridge, MA, USA, 2003.

85. Sophia, http://www.cs.princeton.edu/~mhw/sophia/documents.php.

86. Planetlab, http://www.planet-lab.org.

87. S. R. Madden, M. J. Franklin, J. M. Hellerstein, and W. Hong, TAG: a Tiny AGgregation Service for Ad-Hoc Sensor Networks, in *Proceedings of the Fifth Annual Symposium on Operating Systems Design and Implementation* (OSDI), December 2002.

88. IBM Tivoli Monitoring, http://www.ibm.com/software/tivoli/products/monitor.

89. K. Czajkowski, S. Fitzgerald, I. Foster, and C. Kesselman, Grid Information Services for Distributed Resource Sharing, in *Proceedings of the Tenth IEEE International Symposium on High-Performance Distributed Computing* (HPDC-10), IEEE Press, August 2001.

90. X. Zhang and J. Schopf, Performance Analysis of the Globus Toolkit Monitoring and Discovery Service, MDS2, Proceedings of the International Workshop on Middleware Performance (MP 2004), part of the 23rd International Performance Computing and Communications Workshop (IPCCC), April 2004.

91. Globus Alliance WS information services: Key concepts, http://www-unix.globus.org/toolkit/docs/3.2/infosvcs/ws/key/index.html, 2004.

92. Z. Balaton and G. Gombás, Resource and Job Monitoring in the Grid, in *Proceedings of the Euro-Par 2003 International Conference on Parallel and Distributed Computing*, Klagenfurt, Austria, 2003.

93. R-GMA, http://www.r-gma.org.

94. Hawkeye: A monitoring and management tool for distributed systems, http://www.cs.wisc.edu/condor/hawkeye/.

95. MonaLisa Monitoring, http://gocmon.uits.iupui.edu:8080/index.html.

96. NMI-R4, http://www.nsf-middleware.org/NMIR4/.

97. NMI-R4 New Release, http://www.nsf-middleware.org/Outreach/news_12-16-03.asp.

98. J. Holland, *Adaptation in Natural and Artificial Systems.*, MIT Press, Cambridge, 1992.

99. A. Hunter, SUGAL User Manual v2.0, http://www.dur.ac.uk/andrew1.hunter/Sugal/.

100. D. Levine, PGAPack, 1995. A public-domain parallel genetic algorithm library, Available anonymous ftp from ftp.mcs.anl.gov in the directory pub/pgapack, file pgapack.tar.Z.

101. D. Levine, *Users Guide to the PGAPack Parallel Genetic Algorithm Library*, Technical Report ANL-95/18, Argonne National Laboratory, Mathematics and Computer Science Division, June 23, 1995.

102. D. Ho, Personal communication: C109 H73 N1.

103. D. Ho, Personal communication: C220 H148.

104. M. G. Usha and R. J. Wittebort, Orientational ordering and dynamics of the hydrate and exchangeable hydrogen atoms in crystalline crambin, *J. Mol. Biol.*, 208 (4), 669–678 (1989).

105. D. A. Langs, G. D. Smith, C. Courseille, G. Précigoux, and M. Hospital, Monoclinic uncomplexed double-stranded, antiparallel, left-handed $\beta^{5.6}$-helix ($\uparrow\downarrow \beta^{5.6}$) structure of Gramicidin A: Alternative patterns of helical association and deformation, *Proc. Natl. Acad. Sci. USA*, 88, 5345–5349, June, (1991).

106. V. Pletnev, N. Galitskii, G. D. Smith, C. M. Weeks, and W. L. Duax, Crystal and molecular structure of isoleucinomycin, *cyclo*[-(D-Ile-Lac-Ile-D-Hyi)3-] (C60H102N6O18), *Biopolymers*, 19, 1517–1534 (1980).

107. C. M. Weeks and W. L. Duax, 9α-Chlorocortison, an active cortisol derivative, *Acta Cryst.*, B30, 2516–2519 (1974).

108. J. M. Hodsdon, G. M. Brown, L. C. Sieker, and L. H. Jensen, Refinement of triclinic Lysozyme: I. Fourier and Least-Squares Methods, *Acta Crystallogr.*, B46, 54–62 (1990).

109. P. J. Loll, R. Miller, C. M. Weeks, and P. H. Axelsen, A ligand-mediated dimerization mode for vancomycin, *Chemistry and Biology*, 5, 293–298 (1998).

CHAPTER 25

GIPSY: A Problem-Solving Environment for Bioinformatics Applications

RAJENDRA R. JOSHI, SAMEER INGLE, JANAKI CHINTALAPATI, P. V. JITHESH, UDDHAVESH SONAVANE, SATISH MUMMADI, DATTATRAYA BHAT, and SANTOSH ATANUR

Recently there has been an increase in the number of completely sequenced genomes due to the numerous genome-sequencing projects. The enormous biological sequence data thus generated necessitate the development of efficient tools for mining the information on structural and functional properties of biomolecules. Such a kind of information can prove invaluable for pharmaceutical industries, for in silico drug target identification and new drug discovery. However, the enormity of data and complexity of algorithms make the above tasks computationally demanding, necessitating the use of high-performance computing (HPC). Lately, the cost-effective general-purpose clusters of personal computers (PCs) and workstations have been gaining importance in bioinformatics. However, to use these techniques one must still have significant expertise not only in the bioinformatics domain but also in parallel computing. A problem-solving environment (PSE) relieves the scientist of the burdens associated with the needless and often confidential details of the hardware and software systems by providing a user-friendly environment either through web portals or graphical user interfaces. The PSE thus leaves the scientist free to concentrate on his/her job. This paper describes the design and development of GIPSY, a PSE for bioinformatics applications.

25.1 INTRODUCTION

The last decade has witnessed marvelous achievements in biotechnology and molecular biology. A major achievement deals with the completion of the numerous

Parallel Computing for Bioinformatics and Computational Biology, Edited by Albert Y. Zomaya
Copyright © 2006 John Wiley & Sons, Inc.

genome-sequencing projects including the Human Genome Project. Currently, 242 complete genome sequences are available and another 1001 genome-sequencing projects are in progress [1]. Millions of sequence residues are flooding out of these projects every day, thereby exponentially increasing the size of genome sequence databases such as GenBank and EMBL every year [2, 3]. Bioinformatics plays an important role in interpreting the experimental data generated by sequencing efforts. This includes assembling the sequence fragments and annotating the raw genomic sequences with information on the presence and location of genes and the regulatory regions. A sequence with unknown structure and function can be aligned with the already annotated sequences in a biological database. However, such analysis of sequences alone does not reveal structural and functional properties of gene products that are directly involved in vital cellular processes. We can use, methods like homology modeling to study the structure of an unknown molecule. However, these methods neither provide a high-resolution structure nor provide information on the dynamics and thermodynamics. Therefore, use of techniques such as molecular mechanics, molecular dynamics simulation, and quantum mechanics provides the above information at different levels of precision. Screening the sequence databases for potential drug targets and studying the interaction energies by docking methods help in in silico drug designing. Modeling the metabolic and regulatory pathways as well as the interaction networks will provide a complete picture of the cell. All the above areas dealing with processing and analysis of genomic data demand the usage of HPC [4, 5].

Two major areas that need high-end computation are genome sequence analysis and molecular modeling. Genome sequence analysis involves the searching of sequence databases using the analysis tools for revealing sequence similarities that can throw light into their structural and functional characteristics. Various analysis tools have been developed in the past for genome sequence analysis [6]. The dynamic programming methods like Smith–Waterman [7] gained importance in genome sequence analysis due to their ability to provide an optimal alignment, although heuristic methods like BLAST [8] and FASTA [9] are widely used due to their fast database searching ability. Sequence similarity searches using the above tools become computationally intensive as the query and database sizes increase. The second area of molecular modeling deals with the structure and dynamics of biomolecular systems at the molecular level. This is difficult to discern by conventional methods, viz. x-ray, NMR spectroscopy, and so on. Atomistic computer simulation methods like molecular dynamics (MD) can be used as a complementary method, providing a great deal of information on structure and dynamics of the biomolecule under investigation. MD simulation is a deterministic molecular modeling method where sets of atomic positions are derived in sequence by solving the differential equations embodied in Newton's law of motion. Molecular modeling programs like AMBER (Assisted Model Building with Energy Refinement) [10, 11] and CHARMM (Chemistry at Harvard for Molecular Mechanics) [12] are widely used to carry out MD simulations. However, MD simulations of biomolecules in realistic conditions like the presence of counter ions and water require huge computing power.

Owing to the tremendous demand for computing power, HPC has gained significant importance in sequence analysis and molecular modeling. Bioinformatics applications parallelized using either distributed computing approach or using message-passing interface (MPI)/parallel virtual machine (PVM) libraries are ported on cost-effective general-purpose cluster of workstations and PCs. Parallel computing helps in dividing a complex task into multiple smaller tasks which can be executed on independent processors of a cluster. There is a paradigm shift from conventional supercomputers to clusters due to the better price to performance ratio. Clusters also have the ability to use already existing hardware and software technologies developed for broad applications, flexibility of configuration like number of nodes, memory capacity per node, number of processors per node, and interconnect topology, and the easy adaptability to new trends in technology.

Though parallel computers can help in accelerating the genome sequence database searches and long simulations of biomolecules, it is a complex task for a biologist not trained in advanced computing to execute their codes on parallel computers. The biologist needs to get trained on Unix platforms to execute commands required on a multiprocessor environment and also needs to have expertise in parallel computing. To simplify the task of executing multiple commands on a cluster, a PSE can be used. A PSE provides an easy interface either through a GUI or web-based browser thus shielding the users from the complexities of underlying computer hardware or software, making it easy to run their applications on a sophisticated multiprocessor computing environment. PSEs are very popular and defined as a computational system that provides a complete and convenient set of high-level tools for solving problems from a specific domain. The PSE allows users to define and modify problems, and visualize and analyze results. A user communicates with a PSE in the language of the problem, not in the language of a particular operating system, programming language, or network protocol. PSEs can be used in any field of the computational science to create components involving geometric modeling, scientific visualization, symbolic mathematics, scientific databases, optimization, and so on [13]. The challenge lies in developing frameworks for multidisciplinary applications such as design of airplane engines which requires computational fluid dynamics, structural engineering, and optimizations to get the final solution and such frameworks are referred to as multidisciplinary PSEs (MPPSEs). Some of the frameworks for PSE that were developed earlier for integrating different scientific domain applications are Cactus and Meta-Chaos. Cactus is an open-source framework that enables parallel computation across different architectures [14]. Cactus comes from the design of a central core (or flesh), which connects, to application modules (or thorns) through an extensible interface [15]. Meta-Chaos is another framework that allows interoperability between various data parallel run-time libraries [16]. So far, very few efforts have been made to develop a PSE in biology and some of them include BioSim [17], Biodiversity world [18], Proteus [19], ClusterControl [20], and so on. Proteus is a grid-based PSE for bioinformatics that assist users in formulating bioinformatics problems, running an application on the Grid and for viewing and analyzing results, and so on. It integrates different aspects of bioinformatics resources such as biological data sources (swissprot, PDB, etc.), bioinformatics tools such as BLAST, Ensembl, and so on. Proteus was implemented using Java Application Programming Interface (APIs) as it provides object-oriented abstractions of ontology elements. ClusterControl is a web interface to simplify distributing and monitoring bioinformatics applications on Linux cluster systems. Currently the application modules that are supported in ClusterControl are NCBI-BLAST, WU-BLAST, FASTA, and HMMer.

To the best of our knowledge, there has been no PSE developed for molecular modeling using complex codes like AMBER, CHARMM, and so on. Although some efforts were put in the past to integrate bioinformatics applications, so far there is no PSE available that integrates parallel tools of both sequence analysis and molecular modeling. This work deals with the development and deployment of GIPSY, a PSE for sequence analysis codes such as BLAST, FASTA, Smith–Waterman (S–W), ClustalW and molecular modeling codes such as AMBER and CHARMM. GIPSY was deployed on PARAM Padma, an HPC system, designed and developed in-house. It is envisaged that such an integrated platform would be highly useful to scientific community.

25.2   ARCHITECTURE

25.2.1   Hardware and Software Environment

25.2.1.1   Hardware   PARAM Padma is a cluster of workstations designed and developed in-house. It is developed using the state-of-the-art Power4 RISC processors in Symmetric Multiprocessor (SMP) configurations with AIX operating system. The cluster has 248 processors (fifty-four 4-way SMP pSeries P630 nodes and a 32-way SMP P690) with aggregate memory of 0.5 TB and approximately 1 Tera Flop (1005 Gigaflops) peak computing power. The nodes are connected through a primary high-performance System Area Network, ParamNet-II (designed and developed in-house) and the Gigabit Ethernet Network. The use of such a complex computing environment for solving large problems is a truly challenging task for a domain researcher. This gave the motivation to develop a Web-computing portal for bioinformatics applications which will assist to perform jobs effectively at a faster rate and in user-friendly way. A PSE for BLAST, FASTA, S–W, ClustalW, AMBER, and CHARMM was developed. All the above applications except for BLAST were ported on PARAM Padma using IBM-MPI libraries. BLAST is a threaded version that runs on 32-way SMP machine (P690 Regatta) of PARAM Padma.

25.2.1.2   Software   Java 1.4 programming language was used for building the PSE application server. The other components were built using C (AIX compiler, version 6.0), Perl (5.6.0), shell scripting, and JavaScript. The Web interfaces were designed using tools like Dream weaver (Version 4). The middleware was implemented using JSP 1.0 [Java Server Pages] and servlets 2.0 as a server side presentation layer and controller. The JSP/Servlet container used was Tomcat application server 3.2.0.

25.2.2   Design Goals

Many of the challenging problems in bioinformatics codes require HPC as mentioned in Section 25.1. To execute the job on cluster of workstations from command line, the user needs to be well versed with Unix/Linux commands to create input files. The user also needs to know how to compile and optimize a code on clusters based on underlying operating system using appropriate parallel MPI/PVM libraries. For a biologist, who is a non-specialist in computing, enormous amount of time is consumed in creating the input files, in generating scripts to execute job on cluster of workstations, and to monitor the jobs.

Considering the requirement of HPC for bioinformatics applications and complexities involved in executing a code on clusters, the GIPSY was developed having the following features as design goals.

1. Should provide a framework to use the computing resources remotely.
2. Secure job transactions.
3. Security of user's job input parameters and files.
4. Hide the complexity associated with an HPC system.
5. Dynamic job creation on the fly based on user inputs.
6. Tight coupling with the job managers on the system.
7. Easily portable and should be independent of underlying operating systems.
8. No additional software requirements to be imposed on client/user machine.
9. The output files generated by a particular job of a user should be either downloadable or visualized on the interface itself.
10. To ensure that the PSE architecture can be easily grid enabled to allow resource sharing in environment of multiple computing clusters.

25.2.3 Available Technologies

Some of the Web-based technologies that are available to develop frameworks for a PSE are CGI (common gateway interface), PHP (recursive acronym for "PHP: Hypertext Preprocessor"), ASP (active server page), J2EE (Java 2 Platform, Enterprise Edition), .COM, .NET, and so on. The drawback of technologies like CGI is that it handles Web request by creating an additional process on the server due to which the load on the server increases. J2EE and .NET are component-based technologies that gained significance in enterprise and scientific computing. The component-based technology helps (a) in application maintenance, (b) to add and remove the components, (c) customization and reusability of any of the components, and (d) is more secure. Both J2EE and .NET architecture models use object-oriented (OO) approach for mainstream enterprise computing, use virtual machine, use multi-tiered architecture, and so on. Microsoft .NET is vendor-dependent and runs only on Windows Server operating systems. J2EE is platform-independent and its server applications support operating system portability. The technologies like CORBA (Common Object Request Broker Architecture) can be used as one of the components of middle tier in J2EE. J2EE was chosen for developing GIPSY, as it is platform-independent and can be implemented on AIX operating system of the PARAM Padma. Some of the important features of J2EE are (1) code reusability, (2) faster maintenance due to smaller units of code,

(3) higher scalability of the application, (4) better performance through load-balancing and distribution of components, (5) simplification of the development process, (6) capable of handling complicated logics/flow, (7) built-in security, and so on.

25.2.4 Overview of J2EE

J2EE is a specification or standard and not a language or product. The J2EE architecture is based on Java programming language. The Java 2 Platform, Enterprise Edition, takes advantage of many features of the Java 2 Platform, Standard Edition, such as "Write Once, Run Anywhere" portability, JDBC API for database access, CORBA technology for interaction with existing enterprise resources, and a security model that protects data even in Internet applications. On the basis of this, the Java 2 Enterprise Edition adds full support for Enterprise JavaBeans components, Java Servlets API, JavaServer Pages (JSP), and XML technology. JSP technology enables rapid development of Web-based applications that are platform-independent and easily maintainable, information-rich, dynamic Web pages. JSP performs a dual role of being presentation layer where it can render as plain HTML at the client side and also as servlets at the server side using Java as a scripting language.

The J2EE platform provides a multitier distributed application model. This means that the various parts of an application can run on different devices. The J2EE architecture follows three-tier architecture with a *presentation* or a *client tier*, a *middle tier* (application or Web tier consisting of one or more subtiers), and a *data tier*. The presentation tier takes care of how the data needs to be presented, receives user requests, and controls the user interface. Using the presentation tier, the user communicates with server and receives information regarding the job status. To provide a presentation mode from client side, either a graphical user interface (GUI) or a Web interface can be used. The middle tier is the Web tier that holds application logic and supports client services through Web containers. Middle tier runs on the server and is powered by a Java Application Server. The multitier architecture supported by J2EE was used to build the GIPSY.

25.2.5 GIPSY Implementation

25.2.5.1 Architecture (Model–View–Controller) The GIPSY is based on the J2EE component-based architecture and follows the MVC (*Model–View–Controller*) design pattern. It is configured as three-tier architecture having a client tier to provide the user interface (*View*), one or more middle-tier modules that provide client services and application logic for an application (*Controller*), and a component that handles data management (*Model*) (Fig. 25.1). In the presentation tier (*View*), the Web interfaces were developed for all the applications so that user can easily access the GIPSY. HTML (hyper text markup language) and JavaScripts were used as programming languages and JSP was used for the dynamic content. The *Controller* was implemented using JavaBean components that interact with the services in the middle tier. After the GIPSY gets the users request, the input parameters, and options required to run a particular application, it builds a query string and then submits the jobs to the job manager.

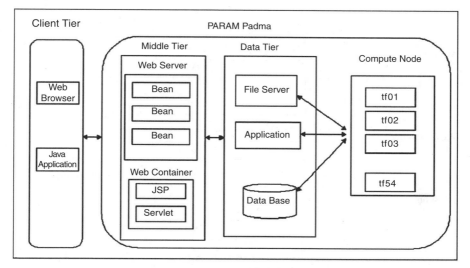

Figure 25.1 Three-tier architecture of GIPSY.

In the data tier (*Model*), two types of data models are supported, viz. RDBMS (relational database management system) and Flat File System. A Flat File System was used as a data model in GIPSY which aptly suits bioinformatics applications. The design pattern of MVC implemented in GIPSY is shown in Figure 25.2.

25.2.5.2   JSP/Servlet Engines   The user request from the client (browser) is forwarded to the Webserver as HTTP protocol and invokes the Java Server Pages (JSP). The JSP in turn initializes the required parameters and stores them in the Java beans. This bean has an in-built application logic so that it creates a query string and a shell script based on user input. When a user submits a particular job, the job manager invokes a shell script, which finally gets executed on the PARAM Padma nodes.

25.2.5.3   Modules in PSE   The main modules used in GIPSY, which acts as building block are

- Authentication module;
- User parameter initialization module (Query Builder);
- Job execution module;
- Job management module;
- Messaging module.

These are the common component modules for all the applications that are integrated within GIPSY. These modules are tightly coupled with each other. The flow of the above modules in GIPSY is shown in Figure 25.3.

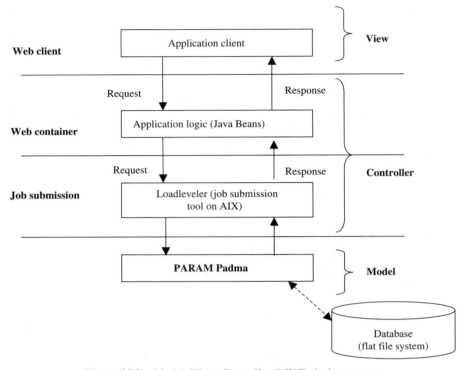

Figure 25.2 Model–View–Controller (MVC) design pattern.

Authentication Module As the user performs on the fly computing, the user authentication is required for system security, for separating one user's session from the other, for job tracking and for retrieving results of a particular user. The authentication service provides authentication using a Flat File System for all PSE applications. This model is based on the simple MVC pattern as described in Section 25.2.5.1.

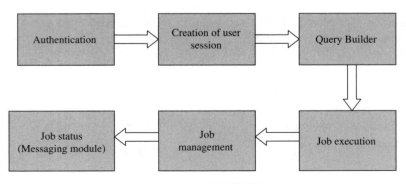

Server environment (PARAM Padma)

Figure 25.3 Flow of modules in GIPSY.

Service is comprised of the GIPSY Login Page (which is used by all the applications for making the portal more secure), the Authentication Client, and the Authentication Server. The client communicates with the server using HTTP protocol and authentication server communicates with the client using an API. The user needs to provide the user name and password for logging in. It is an HTML page that sends request to the Web server. On the server side, JSP/Servlets processes the request and initialize the following bean components:

- User bean component;
- User login verifier component;
- User initialization component.

The *user bean component* encapsulates the user information. A user bean is used for initializing the state of the bean by setting specific properties of the bean, instigating the bean to execute its specific application logic task by calling its "query builder" method, and then getting the values of the bean's properties.

The *user login verifier* component verifies the user by querying the database after taking the user name and password for *user bean component*. Once the user is verified, it transfers the control to the *user initialization component*.

The *user initialization component* is responsible for (a) initializing the input parameter, viz. environmental path, user name and password, session ID, and so on and (b) to create the directory if the user is valid or else forward the request back to the login page. This bean is also responsible for creating the view to display the previous session information if the user is valid. This programming model helps to isolate changes in the Web application by factoring the application logic into fine-grained components that are easily managed and less reliant on other components. This model also allows easier distribution of the processing using serialization to send the bean over IIOP (Inter-ORB Protocol), HTTP, and so on to a remote server to be executed and then sent back with the results. All the above three bean components are illustrated in Figure 25.4.

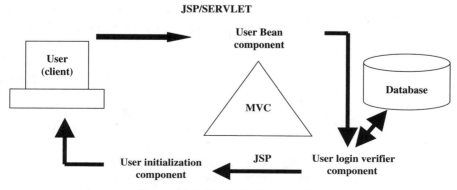

Figure 25.4   Authentication module.

Query Builder Module   The *user parameter initialization module* (Query Builder) is the heart of PSE as it is responsible for the following tasks:

- Creating user input;
- Input confirmation (it helps user in viewing the input, editing, and saving input);
- Creating files required during run time for the program execution;
- Building the query string that will be used to run the shell script;
- Building the shell script dynamically.

The creation of input can be done in two ways:

1. Uploading the input file;
2. Building the input file interactively query with the Web interface.

The user parameter initialization module uses the several bean components, the functions of which are described in detail in Table 25.1.

Job Execution Module   The *execution module* is designed to submit a job to the job manager, which could be a loadleveler or PBS (portable batch system) or a simple fork. In this implementation, IBM loadleveler has been used for job submission. The Execute bean component accepts the query string produced by *Query Builder Bean component* and executes the shell script to submit a particular job through loadleveler.

Job Management Module   The loadleveler manages both serial and parallel jobs over a cluster of servers. On PARAM Padma, under loadleveler, there is a pool of IBM P630/P690 processors for performing batch jobs. Jobs are allocated to machines in

TABLE 25.1   Bean Components Used in Query Builder

Component Name	Function
File Writer Bean	To write the user input in a particular format based on the application; this bean is also responsible for creating files required for the program execution
Input Confirmation Bean	Users can view/edit the input file created dynamically; if the user edits the input file, the changes made will be saved with the help of the JSP
Upload File Bean	Users can upload the input file from client machine to the server; after uploading, the JSP uses Input Confirmation Bean to view/update the uploaded input file
Query Builder Bean	Formulates the Query String and the shell script that will be submitted to job manager on the server

the cluster by a scheduler. A user submits a job by selecting the number of nodes and approximate number of hours the job will take for completion. One can select various job classes and maximum number of nodes through the GIPSY interface, based on which the job gets fired with different priorities. Once the job is submitted, the status of the job is communicated to the user using Job Bean Component.

The results of different application modules can be tracked in two different modes:

1. *Interactive Mode*: If the job submitted by the user is very small, the user can see the job output interactively through dynamically created JSP pages. The output files created during different sessions can be downloaded onto the local hard disk.
2. *E-mail*: If the job submitted by a user is highly compute-intensive and if it takes more than few hours to complete, the result will be mailed to the user using Java mail API.

SESSION HANDLING The GIPSY can be used concurrently by a large number of users to spawn their jobs on the PARAM Padma using the Web-based interface. Session handling is a key factor when multiple users use a PSE concurrently. The interface should ensure that multiple users' job transactions and multiple jobs of a single user are to be separated, as all the communication between the client and the server is via HTTP, which is a stateless protocol. Explicit state maintenance has to be incorporated in the server/client application.

The session object is used to share information of one user across multiple pages while navigating through the Web pages. In other words, a session object is a way of retaining state for a normally stateless HTTP Web site. By default, all JSP pages have access to the implicit session object.

A Web container can use several methods to associate a session with a user, which involve passing an identifier between the client and server as shown in Figure 25.5. The identifier can be maintained on the client as a cookie or the Web component can include the identifier in every URL (uniform resource locator) that is returned to the client. As a job submission involves multiple page submissions, the URLs returned

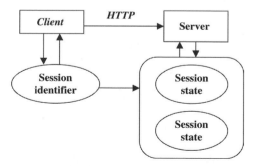

Figure 25.5   Session handling.

in a job transaction contain the session ID. The session ID is basically a random string whose randomness can be guaranteed to ensure that every job transaction gets a different session ID. The session ID is also used to build a directory structure in a particular user space to store input, output, and intermediate files. In GIPSY, each user is mapped on the local server with a specific directory. The user will be able to track the job using the session ID and the user name. This can avoid the conflict between two users or two jobs of the same user and enable persistent state of a user. Each user is allotted one directory and each directory contains maximum of three sessions. As soon as a user starts the fourth session, one of the earlier session results needs to be deleted. This is done automatically and the user has option to select the session to be deleted. This facilitates the optimum utilization of disk space on the system.

Messaging Module   The GIPSY has also a reporting back-mechanism in which users can mention their email address to which the results can be sent. The mail processing system is configured using two different ways:

1. Java Mail API;
2. Simple "mail" command in UNIX.

Java mail API was used in registration and feedback modules of the PSE. When a new user fills the registration form and requests for a user name and password, the above two modules send the confirmation of registration to the user. These are simple java programs and a set of java libraries like mail.jar, activation.jar, and so on that are available along with Java mail API. These are configured along with SMTP server to send and receive mail through given IP address of mail server (SMTP).

25.2.5.4   *Deployment of GIPSY*   The GIPSY has been successfully deployed on the Internet using the Apache server as a proxy Web server and the portal can be viewed at http://bioinfo-portal.cdac.in. PSE sports a generic architecture based on J2EE technologies as described in Section 25.2.5.1. Any new addition of applications involves development of presentation and enterprise logic for the corresponding application. The application can be compiled into a .war (Web Archive) file so that it can be plugged along with existing applications. The JSP/Servlet container architecture defines application format called.war or Web archives.

25.3   CURRENTLY DEPLOYED APPLICATIONS

The current deployment of GIPSY includes applications such as BLAST, FASTA, Smith Waterman, ClustalW for Sequence Analysis and AMBER, CHARMM applications for molecular modeling. This section describes how various applications are modularized and web enabled.

25.3.1 Sequence Analysis

All sequence analysis applications fall into the category of query against database comparison. The GIPSY provides interface for the user to upload a query for sequence similarity search and select any database and program.

25.3.1.1 BLAST

Basic Local Alignment Search Tool (BLAST), developed by Altschul et al. in 1990 [8], is a heuristic method for finding high-scoring segment pairs (HSP) among a pair of biological sequences aligned. It is extremely fast in selecting similar sequences and is more selective in detecting closely related sequences whereas it is less sensitive in detecting homology among distantly related sequences. In the first step of the algorithm, for the query it finds a list of high-scoring words of length "W" and compares the word list to the database to identify exact matches. For each word, the alignment is extended in both directions to find matches that score greater than a particular threshold score "S." For each query and database sequence, there can be more than one HSP region. BLAST being a more selective method can be used in finding similar sequences like ORFs, paralogs, repeat elements, orthologs, and so on. It is being widely used to form cluster of orthologs (COGs) at NCBI (http://www.ncbi.nlm.nih.gov/). The threaded BLAST program available from NCBI was ported on the PARAM Padma and was made available for the BLAST interface in GIPSY. There are five different programs of BLAST available within the interface, viz. blastn (DNA against DNA search), blastp (protein against protein), blastx (nucleotide against protein), tblastn (protein against nucleotide), and tblastx (translated nucleotide against translated nucleotide). The databases that are available for search are Swissprot, yeast, PDB, Print, NR, PIR, SWALL, OWL, Sptrembl, Remtrembl, Synthetic, mitochondria, fungi, bacteriophage, vectors, mammalian, viral, human ESTs, mouse ESTs, other organisms EST sequences, invertebrates, STS, prokaryote, GSS, and so on. When blastp or blastx program is selected, protein databases are listed and if blastn, tblastn, or tblastx is selected nucleotide databases are listed. This was done as part of client side validations. The user can choose options like expect value, maximum score, gap opening, and extension penalties, word size, and scoring matrix from drop down menus to get more sensitive results. If the user does not select an option, then default values are taken. The scoring matrices available are BLOSUM 45, BLOSUM 62, BLOSUM 80, BLOSUM 50, PAM 250, PAM 120, MD20, and MD10. In the client side validations, the scoring matrices, word size, gap opening, and extension penalties change according to the program selected. The user needs to provide their email address, otherwise an error command pops up. The query sequence can either be pasted in the given text box or can be uploaded from the local hard disk. A query file of maximum of 15 MB (megabytes) can be uploaded. For viewing the results, user can choose an option of whether to get the results through email or in an interactive way. The snapshot of BLAST job submission interface is given in Figure 25.6. In the figure, links for "Help" and 'logout' are also seen. A help page is available for all the applications. The left-hand side menu bar shows that any of the four sequence analysis modules can be selected.

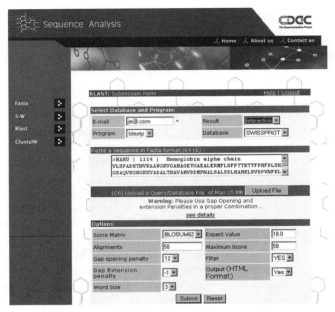

Figure 25.6   BLAST interface of GIPSY.

25.3.1.2 FASTA Fast Alignment Search Tool (FASTA) is an algorithm capable of providing the best local optimal alignments of genomic sequences using the combined heuristic and dynamic programming methods. The FASTA algorithm initially finds the regions shared by a pair of sequences having high density of identities, subsequently rescanning the top 10 best scoring regions using scoring matrices like PAM. A joining penalty can be given to connect the high-scoring regions, whereas an optimal alignment is obtained in the final step by using a dynamic programming method. Though the FASTA algorithm is comparatively slower than BLAST, the sensitivity in finding high-ranking scores among distantly related sequences is higher. FASTA, which has immense applications in studying protein functions, becomes more compute-intensive especially for longer query sequences (more than 1 MB) when searched against large databases like human genome sequence database, nonredundant (nr) database and the like. Parallel FASTA programs were obtained from the Virginia University and were ported and optimized on PARAM Padma. The FASTA interface in GIPSY has programs, namely FASTA (protein against protein or nucleotide against nucleotide database search), FASTX (nucleotide against protein), TFASTX (translated nucleotide against translated nucleotide database), and TFASTY (protein against nucleotide) (Fig. 25.7). The sequence databases to search and the scoring matrices to choose are the same as that of the BLAST interface. The options that are available for users are K-tuple value, histogram (whether to display or not), Expect value, and maximum score. Default values are used if the users do not select any options. Similar to BLAST PSE, client-side validations are done in FASTA PSE also.

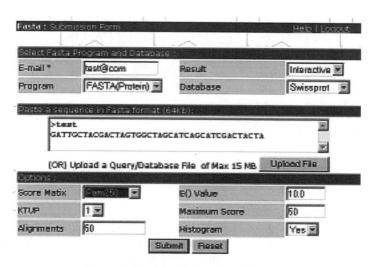

Figure 25.7 FASTA interface of GIPSY.

25.3.1.3 Smith–Waterman The Smith–Waterman (S–W) algorithm is a dynamic programming method that yields local optimal alignment between a pair of sequences. The SSEARCH program available with FASTA package implements the S–W algorithm and has been reported to be more sensitive as compared with heuristic methods mentioned above [21]. The S–W algorithm is extremely useful when all possible alignments have to be found within the pair of sequences to be compared, for example, detecting single nucleotide polymorphs (Snips) from expression sequence tag (EST) databases where a single base variation can occur in any possible sub-segment. The S–W algorithm can report significant hits that can be missed using heuristic methods like BLAST or FASTA. However, the S–W algorithm is computationally demanding and is extremely slow to perform on a single-processor machine, as a scoring matrix of $M \times N$ size (M and N are lengths of two sequences) has to be built by assigning value to each cell of the matrix dynamically, penalizing gap openings and extensions. Performing database against database searches using the S–W algorithm becomes impractical, as it has to calculate the matrix for every pair of sequences in the database. Parallel SSEARCH, an implementation of the S–W algorithm, was developed to reduce the computational complexity. The parallel code available from the ftp site of University of Virginia was ported and optimized on PARAM Padma and is made available in GIPSY. The interface of S–W is similar to that of FASTA, having same options and databases, except that the options to choose gap opening and extension penalties are available in the S–W interface.

25.3.1.4 ClustalW ClustalW is an algorithm for multiple sequence alignment of DNA or protein sequences [22]. It produces biologically meaningful multiple sequence alignments of divergent sequences. The algorithm consists mainly of the following three steps: (i) pairwise alignment of all the sequences, (ii) building up of guide tree using alignment scores, and (iii) progressive alignment of sequences. It calculates the best match for the selected sequences, and lines them up so that the identities, similarities, and differences can be seen within the aligned sequences. Multiple sequence alignments have wide applications such as to find diagnostic patterns for characterizing protein families, to detect or demonstrate homology between new sequences and existing families of sequences, to help predict the secondary and tertiary structures of new sequences, and so on. The interface for executing ClustalW is very simple and the user needs to provide email address and a multiple sequence file in FASTA format. The sequences can be either pasted in a given text box or can be uploaded from the local hard disk.

25.3.2 Molecular Modeling

In molecular modeling, molecular mechanics and dynamics methods are widely used for studying biomolecular structures. The classical molecular modeling techniques are based on assumptions of (a) atoms as point mass, (b) atoms perform simple harmonic motion, and (c) these point-like mass atoms obey Newton's laws of motion. The energy equation is known as force field consisting of various bonded and nonbonded terms. The molecular mechanics has energy evaluator and energy minimizer. In molecular dynamics simulation, successive configurations of the system are generated by integrating Newtonian equations of motion;

$$\frac{d^2 x_i}{dt^2} = \frac{F_{x_i}}{m_i}, \qquad i = 1, 2, \ldots, N \tag{25.1}$$

Equation (25.1) describes the motion of a particle of mass m_i along one coordinate (x_i) with Fx_i being the force on the particle in that direction. As the particles interact pairwise, computational time for the force interactions is proportional to $N(N-1)/2$, where N is the number of particles in the system. This becomes highly compute-intensive as the number of atoms increases, which is the case when macromolecules are simulated in "real" conditions like the presence of ions and water. While using present methods, a small time step such as a femtosecond is necessary to accurately model the vibrational motions in molecules. To study the true evolution of particle by integration of Newton's laws of motions, it is necessary to investigate this development for a sufficient length of time. So the length of the run in the nanosecond scale with femtosecond time steps makes the calculation huge. Programs like AMBER and CHARMM are widely used for molecular simulations. Keeping in mind the highly compute-intensive nature of the calculations, the above programs have been parallelized. This, therefore, makes it more complicated for a scientist to run their applications on a parallel computer.

Both the AMBER and CHARMM web interface provide secure user authentication and retrieval of previous sessions. A user working on a molecule can log off and return to the same work by retrieving previous sessions. At a time, a total of three sessions belonging to three different molecules can be saved. AMBER and CHARMM interfaces allow the user to view the job input files generated and also to download them. The output in PDB format can be downloaded and viewed from visualization tool like Rasmol [23].

25.3.2.1 *AMBER*

AMBER is the collective name for a suite of programs that allow users to carry out molecular dynamics simulations, particularly on biomolecules. AMBER is a highly modular package with programs for building molecules, energy calculations, and analysis of the simulation. The flow of main modules in AMBER 5 package is shown in Figure 25.8. LEaP consists of three modules, viz. Link, Edit, and Parm, and is used for building topology and generating parameters, and coordinates for the molecules. The Edit module additionally can do solvation and used for setting periodic boundary condition (PBC). The Prep module is useful for building nonstandard nucleotide/amino acid or organic molecule, while Protonate is used only for protein molecules. LEaP along with Prep and Protonate form preprocessing unit of AMBER simulation package. Among the energy programs, Sander (simulated annealing using NMR-derived energy restraints) is the basic energy minimizer and molecular dynamics program in AMBER. Gibbs is a free energy calculator whereas ptraj, carnal, mdanal, and anal are used for analysis.

Performing molecular dynamics simulations using AMBER is a highly complex task, as it requires good computational background mainly in Unix and Fortran programming. At the start of each module, the user has to prepare input with proper options and should follow Fortran file format. Understanding the fundamentals of each module and following the stringent file formats is a laborious task. These intricacies are the main hurdles, which restrict biologists from using molecular modeling techniques. Also executing parallel AMBER to enhance the speed of MD simulations requires knowledge of parallel computing. Thus, efforts have been made to develop a user-friendly environment that automatically handles all these intricacies in background and the user can directly setup simulation experiment with minimal understanding of the program.

The module for parallel AMBER 5 in GIPSY has been developed in the modular fashion to provide interfaces for building the molecule, for preprocessing, and for simulation of DNA/RNA and protein molecules. There is a login page to check

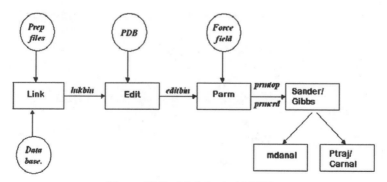

Figure 25.8 Modules in AMBER.

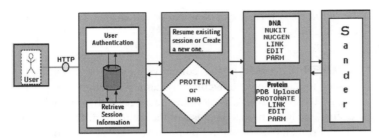

Figure 25.9   Information flow in GIPSY for AMBER.

for user authentication and once the user logins, a new session can be either created or old session can be resumed before actually starting with the preprocessing modules of AMBER. Figure 25.9 describes the information flow in GIPSY for AMBER. There are interfaces to execute LEAP (Link Edit and Parm) tools, which are the preprocessing modules for both DNA and protein. LEAP is followed by Sander, which is the core program for molecular dynamics simulations, and is also used for replica exchange, thermodynamic integration, and potential of mean force (PMF) calculations.

Simulation of DNA/RNA Molecules

(A) NUKIT: If a good starting structure is not available for DNA/RNA from X-ray crystallography or NMR studies, then programs like Nukit and Nucgen can be used to build the model nucleic acid structures. Nukit is a utility program that helps to create input files for Nucgen and for the Link module of AMBER. Figure 25.10 shows the snapshot of the Nukit interface in the PSE. The user needs to provide the sequence information of DNA from 5′ to 3′ end for both strands and can select any one of the conformations like ABDNA, ARNA, APRNA, LBDNA, SBDNA, and LDNA to build the DNA molecule. Once the input sequence is provided, the output is generated using Nucgen and Nukit.

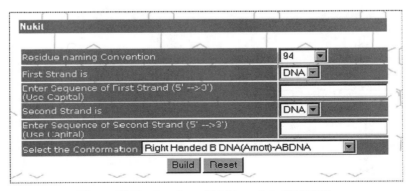

Figure 25.10   Interface of Nukit module (AMBER).

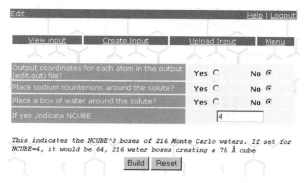

This indicates the NCUBE^3 boxes of 216 Monte Carlo waters. If set for
NCUBE=4, it would be 64, 216 water boxes creating a 75 Å cube

Figure 25.11   Interface of Edit module (AMBER).

(B) LINK: The purpose of this module is to create a molecular topology file for the input sequence provided by the user. The program reads the topology of individual residues from one of the standard databases and links them together to create the topology of the final system. It always connects the first main type atom of the current residue to the last main type atom of the previous residue. It can also crosslink specified atoms in a molecule or different molecules to form a covalent bond. The user can either upload the input files for the Link module or can create input using Nukit and Nucgen modules as mentioned in earlier section. The output generated by Link module can be either viewed/downloaded and is used as input for Edit module.

(C) EDIT: The environment for Edit module consists of three different interfaces. The first interface as shown in Figure 25.11 provides options to place water box, counterions around the solute, and to add coordinates for the missing atoms. The second interface is to build input file for Edit, which can be modified and saved before submitting for execution in the third interface. The Edit output is saved and is provided as input to the Parm module. The user can download the intermediate files including edit.pdb and view using visualizing tools like Rasmol.

(D) PARM: This module is used to allocate the force field parameters for all the constants in the potential energy function to the topology file created by Edit. The constants such as equilibrium bond lengths, bond angles, dihedral angles, and their force constants are read from a parameter file. Parameters are allocated based on AMBER atom types. Parm creates both a molecular topology file and a coordinate file that can be read by the Sander module. As shown in Figure 25.12, GIPSY interface provides output options (formatted/binary) and name of nonbonded parameters (MOD4/STUB/STDA). The user can even upload the Parm input file created manually.

(E) SANDER: Sander is the core module of AMBER suite, which carries out the energy minimization, molecular dynamics, and NMR restraints. GIPSY provides an easy to use interface to set various options to run parallel Sander on the PARAM Padma.

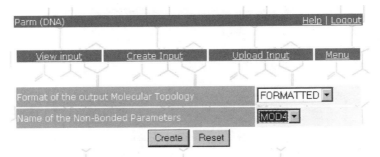

Figure 25.12   Interface of Parm module (AMBER).

Three interfaces were developed for Sander module, due to its high complexity and the large number of parameters that are required as input. The snapshots of three interfaces of Sander are shown in Figure 25.13. It also provides an option to start a new MD run or restart from a previous run which is one of the important features of AMBER PSE, which helps users in working on previous MD runs. The interfaces for taking inputs of parameters of Sander has been categorized as (1) nature of simulation, restart, and NMR-restrained options, (2) nature and format of input/output, (3) setting for potential functions, (4) freezing/restraining atoms, (5) energy minimization, (6) molecular dynamics options along with setting temperature/pressure conditions,

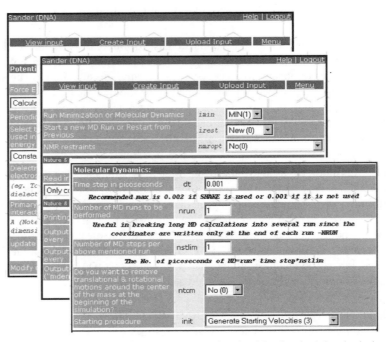

Figure 25.13   A cascade of multiple screens involved for Sander job submission.

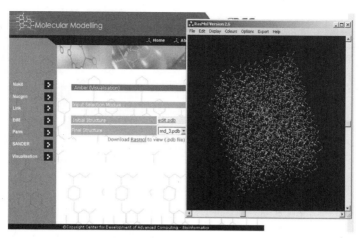

Figure 25.14 Output generated by Sander and viewed in Rasmol.

and (7) SHAKE options for hydrogen atoms. All these parameters/variables can be selected by drop down menu facility or the values can be set. The user can also download or view the output file generated by Sander.

The other important feature of AMBER module in GIPSY is that during the intermediate stages from Link to Sander, it provides an option for the end user to download the intermediate input and output files. After the Sander run is completed, the output file, trajectory, velocity, and energy files can be downloaded onto the local hard disk. The restart file can be used as starting coordinates for next simulation run. The PDB output generated by Sander and other modules can be viewed in Rasmol (Fig. 25.14).

Simulation of Protein Molecule A protein simulation using AMBER involves Protonate, Link, Edit, Parm, Sander modules. Except for Protonate, all the other modules were described in Section "simulation of DNA/RNA molecules". The GIPSY provides an interface to upload a protein in PDB format (Fig. 25.15) and the Protonate module adds hydrogen atoms to the structure. Link input will be created for uploaded PDB using a parser written in Perl. This parser extracts sequence and disulfide bonds information from uploaded PDB file. The outputs generated by LEAP will be provided as input to SANDER for simulation jobs through the GIPSY interfaces.

25.3.2.2 *CHARMM* CHARMM (Chemistry at Harvard Macromolecular Mechanics) is a highly flexible molecular dynamics program using empirical energy functions to model macromolecular systems. The algorithm implemented in CHARMM is similar to the one discussed in Section 25.3.2.1. It performs standard molecular dynamics using state-of-the-art algorithms for time stepping, long-range force calculation, and periodic images. CHARMM has been modified to allow computationally intensive simulations to be run on multi-processor machines using a

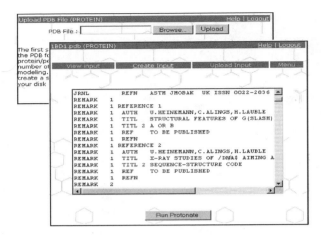

Figure 25.15 Interface of PDB file upload and view of PDB file uploaded (AMBER).

replicated data model [24]. All computationally intensive steps have been fully parallelized.

The GIPSY provides an interface to run CHARMM jobs on the PARAM Padma. Unlike AMBER, which is a collection of various programs for modules like preprocessing, simulation, and postprocessing, CHARMM has a single executable for all the above operations. Hence, efforts have been put in modularizing CHARMM interfaces for preprocessing, production simulation run, and postprocessing. The program has been broken up into following modules:

(1) Creating initial structure;
(2) Solvation;
(3) Minimization;
(4) Equilibration;
(5) Production.

The information flow of CHARMM PSE module in GIPSY is shown in Figure 25.16. Currently, the CHARMM module in GIPSY is available for simulation of protein molecules only.

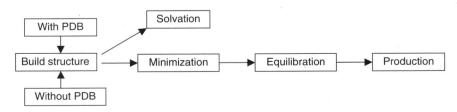

Figure 25.16 Information flow in GIPSY for CHARMM.

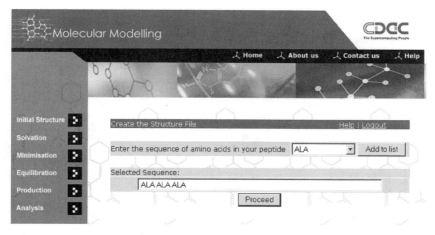

Figure 25.17   Structure building interface (CHARMM).

Initial Structure Building   This interface provides facility to either build protein molecule by providing sequence information as shown in Figure 25.17 or by uploading PDB format coordinate file. The input file is created dynamically in the CHARMM format to generate parameter, topology, and coordinates information.

Minimization   For minimization using CHARMM, the user can select methods like steepest descent, conjugate gradient, Newton–Raphson, and so on provided on the interface (Fig. 25.18). The standard set of parameter values for treatment of non-bonded interactions has options of atom-based cutoff, group-based cutoff, extended electrostatics, or no cutoff periodic system.

Equilibration   User-friendly interfaces have been created for heating and equili-bration module. The user needs to select or provide appropriate values to simulate thermodynamical conditions. The interface has parameters for controlling tempera-ture and pressure, periodic boundary conditions, hydrogen atoms, and various other nonbonded interaction parameters along with MD options. Figure 25.19 shows snap-shot of simulation control parameters for the heating module. An output file will be generated based on the parameters selected, which in turn will be used as an input for execution of parallel CHARMM.

Production   The equilibrated structure can be carried further for production runs. As shown in Figure 25.20, various parameters can be selected for production mode. An input file will be created based on parameters selected and this is used for production runs. The resulting molecule in PDB format can be downloaded or viewed through Rasmol molecule visualizer.

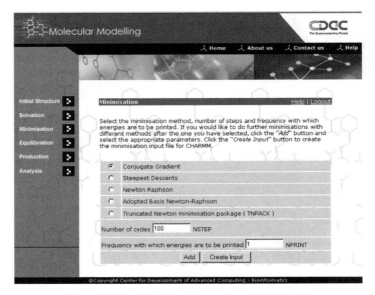

Figure 25.18   Minimization module (CHARMM).

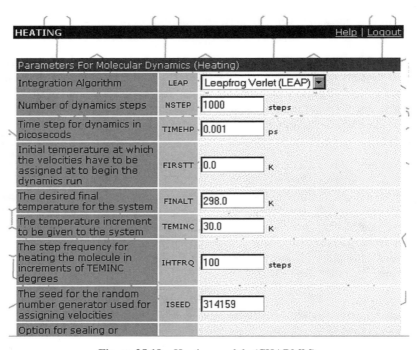

Figure 25.19   Heating module (CHARMM).

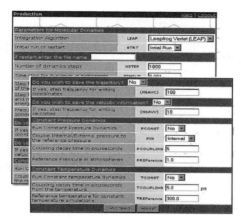

Figure 25.20   Production module (CHARMM).

25.4 CONCLUSION

A PSE is an environment that provides all the computational facilities needed to solve a target class of problems. The advantage here is that PSEs use the language of the target class of problems, so users can run them without specialized knowledge of the underlying computer hardware or software. GIPSY deals with the area of bioinformatics and ensures that the biologists can perform complex calculations on their data sets using large clusters of computers. In general, bioinformatics problems fit into two categories: floating point or integer. This implementation of GIPSY has popular codes in the genome sequence area like FASTA, BLAST, Smith–Waterman, ClustalW, and complex molecular modeling codes like AMBER and CHARMM. To the best of our knowledge, this is the first implementation of a web-based computing system for AMBER and CHARMM. Similarly this is probably the first implementation, which integrates the popular sequence analysis and molecular modeling codes in the same portal or environment.

However, as can be seen this implementation has all the bioinformatics applications codes which are plugged in as standalone applications. Currently, carrying out full genome analysis and comparative genomics involves many distinct but interrelated steps, each requiring a different algorithm or application. The obvious solution to such problems would be to build workflows comprised discrete components linked by logical constructs. Such a kind of integrated workflow environment would be a boon for researchers in life sciences, who usually spend enormous amount of time in executing individual applications, converting file formats, and manually building the entire pipeline for analysis. Building a completely automated workflow in the GIPSY, which can take initial inputs in the form of genome sequence and finally allow the user to carry out molecular modeling is one of our future plans. Presently, work is in progress to grid enable the GIPSY, which would allow scientists to solve larger or new problems by pooling resources together. The main motivation behind this work is to build an integrated HPC environment so that a domain expert can be relieved of the burdens associated with learning the intricacies of the parallel processing and grid technology. We envisage that such an environment would be extremely beneficial in the genome-based drug discovery process, where the concept of gene to drug can be successfully demonstrated.

ACKNOWLEDGMENTS

The authors acknowledge the help received from the C-DAC's Tera Scale Computing Facility (CTSF), Web and Network operations team of SANG group, and Corporate communications team in the deployment of GIPSY.

REFERENCES

1. A. Bernal, U. Ear, and N. Kyrpides, Genomes OnLine Database (GOLD): a monitor of genome projects world-wide, *Nucl. Acids Res.*, 29 (1), 126–127 (2001).
2. D. A. Benson, et al., GenBank: update, *Nucl. Acids Res.*, 32, Database issue D23–D26 (2004).
3. T. Kulikova, et al., The EMBL Nucleotide Sequence Database, *Nucl. Acids Res.*, 32, Database issue D27–D30 (2004).
4. T. Head-Gordon and J. C. Wooley, Computational challenges in structural and functional genomics, *IBM Sys. J.*, 40, 265–296 (2001).
5. D. L. Brutlag, Genomics and computational molecular biology, *Curr. Opin. Microbiol.*, 1, 340–345 (1998).
6. J. C. Wooley, Trends in computational biology: a summary based on a RECOMB, Plenary Lecture, *J. Comput. Biol.*, 6, 459–474 (1999).
7. T. F. Smith and M. S. Waterman, Identification of common molecular subsequences, *J. Mol. Biol.*, 147, 195–197 (1981).
8. Altschul, et al., Gapped BLAST and PSI-BLAST: a new generation of protein database search programs, *Nucl. Acids Res.*, 25, 3389–3402 (1997).
9. W. R. Pearson and D. J. Lipman, Improved tools for biological sequence comparison, *Proc. Natl. Acad. Sci. USA*, 85, 2444–2448 (1988).
10. D. A. Pearlman, et al., AMBER, a package of computer programs for applying molecular mechanics, normal mode analysis, molecular dynamics and free energy calculations to simulate the structural and energetic properties of molecules, *Comput. Phys. Commun.*, 91, 1–41 (1995).
11. D. A. Case, et al., AMBER 5, University of California, San Francisco, 1997.
12. B. R. Brooks, et al., Charmm: a program for macromolecular energy, minimization, and dynamics calculations, *J. Comp. Chem.*, 4, 187–217 (1983).
13. E. Houstis, E. Gallapoulos, R. Bramley, and J. Rice, Problem-solving environments for computational science, *IEEE Comput. Sci. Eng.*, 4, 18–21 (1997).
14. A. Gabrielle, Solving Einstein's equations on supercomputers, *Computer*, 32, 52–58 (1999).

15. D. Laforenza, Grid programming: some indications where we are headed, *Parallel Comput.*, 28, 1733–1752 (2002).

16. G. Edjlali, S. Alan, and S. Joel, Interoperability of Data Parallel Runtime Libraries with Meta-Chaos, in *Proceedings of the Eleventh International Parallel Processing Symposium*, IEEE Computer Society Press, 1997.

17. C. Yang, et al., BioSim — a biomedical character-based problem solving environment, *Future Gen. Comput. Syst.*, 21, 1145–1156 (2005).

18. W. Richard, et al., Building a Biodiversity Problem-Solving Environment, in *Proceedings of the UK e-Science*, All Hands Meeting, 2004.

19. M. Cannataro, et al., Proteus, a Grid based problem solving environment for bioinformatics: architecture and experiments, *IEEE Comput. Intelligence Bull.*, 3, 7–18 (2004).

20. G. Stocker, D. Rieder, and Z. Trajanoski, ClusterControl: a web interface for distributing and monitoring bioinformatics applications on a Linux cluster, *Bioinformatics*, 20 (5), 805–807 (2004).

21. W. Pearson, Comparison of methods for searching protein-sequence databases, *Protein Sci.*, 4, 1145–1160 (1995).

22. J. D. Thompson, D. G. Higgins, and T. J. Gibson, CLUSTAL W: improving the sensitivity of progressive multiple sequence alignment through sequence weighting, positions-specific gap penalties and weight matrix choice, *Nucl. Acids Res.*, 22, 4673–4680 (1994).

23. http://www.openrasmol.org/doc/rasmol.html.

24. B. R. Brooks and M. Hodoscek, Parallelization of CHARMM for MIMD machines, *Chemical Design Automation News*, July 1992, pp. 16.

CHAPTER 26

TaskSpaces: A Software Framework for Parallel Bioinformatics on Computational Grids

HANS DE STERCK, ROB MARKEL, and ROB KNIGHT

Owing to ever-increasing data sizes and the high computational complexity of many algorithms, there is a natural drive towards applying parallel and distributed computing to bioinformatics problems. Grid computing techniques can provide flexible, portable, and scalable software solutions for parallel bioinformatics. Here, we describe the TaskSpaces software framework for grid computing. TaskSpaces is characterized by two major design choices: decentralization, provided by an underlying tuple space concept, and platform independence, provided by implementation in Java. We discuss advantages and disadvantages of this approach and demonstrate seamless performance on an ad hoc grid comprised of a wide variety of hardware for a real-life parallel bioinformatics problem. Specifically, we performed virtual experiments in RNA folding on computational grids comprised of fast supercomputers, to estimate the smallest pool of random RNA molecules, which would contain enough catalytic motifs for initiating a primitive metabolism. These experiments may establish one of the missing links in the chain of events that led to the origin of life.

26.1 INTRODUCTION

In recent years, parallel and distributed computing techniques have steadily been gaining popularity for tackling difficult bioinformatics problems. Two important reasons for the use of parallel techniques can be identified easily. First, bioinformatics problems involve increasingly large data sets. For example, the 2003 release of GenBank contained 36.6 billion basepairs and 118,689 different species, and in routine

Parallel Computing for Bioinformatics and Computational Biology, Edited by Albert Y. Zomaya
Copyright © 2006 John Wiley & Sons, Inc.

proteomics experiments, examination of a single sample may easily produce millions of peptide spectra to be processed. Secondly, the algorithms used in many bioinformatics applications can be computationally prohibitive. For example, the computational complexity of algorithms for phylogenetics typically scales cubically to exponentially in the number of species, and in proteomics data processing applications, the algorithms used to identify proteins and genes from peptide spectra involve searches with high complexity. Therefore, for many bioinformatics problems, it is clear that computations limited to a single CPU cannot deliver the required computing power and that parallel and distributed computing approaches are necessary. A large class of bioinformatics problems can be parallelized easily, with minimal or no interprocess communication. These types of problems are called loosely coupled, and they are especially suitable for distributed processing. More tightly coupled problems require intensive interprocess communication. Efficient parallel and distributed computing is typically more challenging for these types of problems. In the present chapter, we discuss both types of problems.

Consider, for example, the case of a university researcher who is confronted with a complex bioinformatics problem. The researcher typically has access to a wide range of computational resources on different scales. These resources include desktop machines that may be available in the researcher's own lab (of the order of 10 CPUs or so), PC clusters that may be available at the department level (order of 100 CPUs), parallel computers that may be available in the university's computer center (order of 100–1000 CPUs), and large parallel supercomputers (up to several thousand CPUs) that can be accessed at national supercomputer centers such as the US National Center for Supercomputing Applications (NCSA) and the San Diego Supercomputer Center (SDSC). In this chapter, we propose an approach to parallel bioinformatics that ideally allows the researcher to develop the bioinformatics software locally on a single PC. Then, depending on the size of the problem at hand, the task can be distributed seamlessly over any or all of the wide variety of machines available.

This "universal computing dream" is hard to realize for several reasons. The hardware, operating systems (and versions of operating systems), supporting software, and queuing systems may all vary among available machines. The researcher will wonder how to install and maintain code on all these machines, how to distribute tasks and data, how the results will be collected and centralized, and so on. Scripts that automate some of these tasks will be brittle when software is upgraded or when machines are added or removed. In the light of these obstacles, the "universal computing dream" seems little more than an ever-receding mirage.

However, in this chapter, we describe TaskSpaces, a system we developed, which demonstrates that many components of the "universal computing dream" can be realized on today's infrastructure using grid computing. The grid computing concept can be easily understood by considering the analogy with a power grid. A power grid user accesses the grid to obtain electrical power, which is an interchangeable commodity. Indeed, the user's machines do not care where or how the power they use is produced (the user may have ethical concerns that affect the desirability of particular power sources, but, to the hardware, all electricity is equivalent).

Two crucial properties make the power grid work

1. The grid can be accessed through a standard interface. In the case of a power grid, the standard interface is simply the electrical plug, which gives access to the power grid that operates at standard voltages and frequencies.
2. The grid is scalable. This scalability works both from the user's side (the user can access more power as needed) and from the power producer's side (the grid operator can switch in additional power generators as demand rises).

Ideally, grid computing would work in exactly the same way: A user accesses the geographically distributed grid to obtain CPU cycles, which are considered as an interchangeable commodity (the user does not care where the computing cycles are produced) (Fig. 26.1). Unfortunately, accessibility through a standard interface (the first of the two essential properties of a grid) can be difficult to achieve with computers. In TaskSpaces, the standard interface is provided by the Java virtual machine, which is almost universally available. Java behaves almost exactly in the same way on all those machines, and Java's "executable bytecode" is, in theory, fully interchangeable between machines. In TaskSpaces, the second essential grid property, scalability, is realized through the concepts of "bag-of-tasks" computing and tuple spaces. Consequently, each user can submit many tasks concurrently and the grid operator can switch in additional compute farms when demand is high.

The analogy between computational and power grids is not perfect: Computing cycles and data are more complex than electrical power units. We can identify the following additional requirements for computing grids, some essential and others pragmatic.

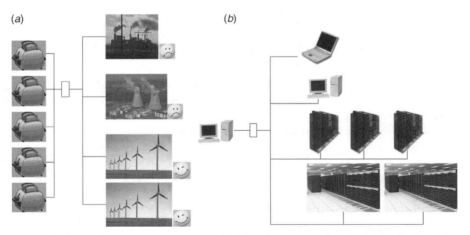

(a)   (b)

Figure 26.1 Analogy between a power grid (*a*) and a computational grid (*b*). Both exhibit scalability from the user's and the producer's sides and need to be accessible through a standard interface.

3. Information is not interchangeable and must often be kept confidential (unlike electrical power). The grid must allow secure resource sharing.
4. Information is not easily replaceable (unlike electrical power). The grid must provide fault-tolerance mechanisms such as transactions.
5. Parallel computers use many different queuing systems. The grid must provide resource allocation and scheduling.
6. Large problems may require deployment on heterogeneous hardware and software. The grid must provide a mechanism for distributing the application code transparently to the machines on which calculations are ultimately performed.
7. Many problems require interprocess communication. The grid must allow efficient communication between processes.
8. Computing resources are expensive. The grid must allow users to be billed according to cycle usage.
9. Some problems require specific turnaround time, data transfer bandwidth, fault-tolerance, and so on. The grid may need to provide quality-of-service guarantees.
10. Problems must be connected with computing resources. Either the grid must allow the user to discover resources or the grid must be able to discover tasks as they are presented (TaskSpaces uses the latter approach, resembling a real power grid).

Many efforts to realize the concepts of grid computing are now underway. Some projects, such as Globus, try to define standards for what eventually may become a worldwide, unified, computational grid ("The Grid"), very much along the lines of "The Internet" and "The World Wide Web." However, many of the difficulties summarized earlier are still far from being resolved in a general, satisfactory way, and it is not clear that generally usable standards for grid computing will become available and accepted soon. Therefore, we have developed TaskSpaces, a software framework for a smaller-scale computational grid. TaskSpaces is based on the design criteria of decentralization, provided by an underlying tuple space concept, and platform independence, provided by implementation in Java. Our goal was to produce a lightweight grid environment that is easy to install and operate and to demonstrate that it can be used efficiently for real-world parallel bioinformatics problems. In this effort, we have attempted to deal with some, but not all, of the challenges listed earlier. Besides providing an environment for solving real bioinformatics problems on small, "privately operated" grids, we hope that our experiences may reveal some methods of overcoming the challenges mentioned earlier and that these methods may become more generally useful in guiding standards adopted for larger grids. At present, many different approaches are being tested on small-scale, privately operated grids, both in research and commercial settings. The successful approaches will survive, and, driven by demand and cost savings through efficiency gains, these privately run grids may eventually become connected to form a World Wide Grid, very much like national power grids are presently connected to neighboring grids throughout most of the world.

The rest of this chapter is organized as follows. The next section describes TaskSpaces, our prototype software framework for grid computing, which is based on tuple space concepts and implemented in Java. Section 26.3 describes a loosely coupled parallel bioinformatics application that we investigated on a computational grid, namely, the problem of finding correctly folded RNA motifs in sequence space. Section 26.4 describes our experience with operating the software framework on a computational grid comprised of local workstations and parallel clusters at supercomputer centers. Brief results for the RNA motif problem are presented in Section 26.5. The chapter concludes with a section on future work and a summary.

26.2 THE TASKSPACES FRAMEWORK

TaskSpaces is a prototype lightweight grid computing framework for scientific computing characterized by two major design choices: decentralization, provided by an underlying tuple space concept, and object-orientation and platform-independence, provided by implementation in Java. The TaskSpaces framework has been described in detail in Ref. [1]; in this section, we summarize its main properties.

Tuple spaces were pioneered in the late 1970s and were first realized in the Linda system and language [2]. In a tuple space distributed computing environment, processes communicate solely by adding tuples to and taking them from a tuple space, a form of independent associative memory. A tuple is a sequence of fields, each of which has a type and contains a value. Figure 26.2 shows conceptually how distributed computation works in a tuple space environment. An application program places subtasks resulting from the partitioning of a large computational problem into a tuple space (which in the bag-of-tasks paradigm is called a "task bag" [3]), in which each subtask is represented as a tuple. "Worker processes" take the task objects from the task bag, execute the tasks, and place the result in a "result bag" as another tuple. The tuple space

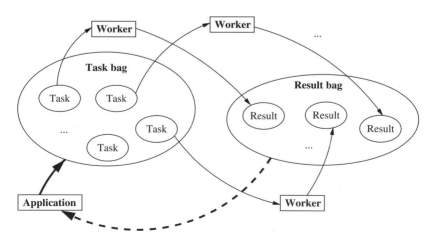

Figure 26.2 The tuple space paradigm for distributed computing.

concept allows tasks to be decoupled both in space and time. The distributed computing process is decoupled in space, as the application, task and results bags, and the various worker processes may reside on a heterogeneous collection of machines that are connected by a network but that are otherwise widely geographically distributed. This decoupling allows flexible topology for the computation, permitting automatic configuration based on the availability of worker processes. The distributed computing process is also decoupled in time: as spaces are persistent, tuples are persistent while resident in the space, and processes can access tuples long after the depositing process has completed execution.

Figure 26.3 shows a conceptual deployment diagram of the TaskSpaces framework. TaskSpaces uses an event-driven model. On startup, worker processes register with a task bag. The application process sends subtask objects to the task bag, and the task bag sends those task objects to available workers. The task bag acts as a "superqueue," and thus alleviates the problem of scheduling when multiple supercomputers with different unsynchronized queuing systems are used. Scalability is inherent because users may put several applications in the task bag at the same time and the grid operator can add "worker farms" when needed. After a task is processed, the worker puts a result object in the result bag, from which the result objects are collected for final assembly by the application. TaskSpaces is implemented in Java, providing a standard, platform-independent interface to the grid system and exploiting Java's built-in networking and security features.

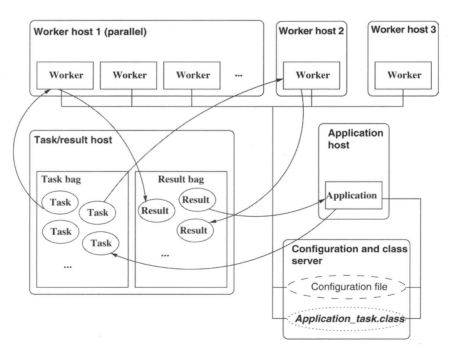

Figure 26.3   TaskSpaces framework deployment diagram.

The TaskSpaces code consists of several classes. All classes, except for the Runner class, are served to participant machines via HTTP servers. Configurable properties files which contain system information and parameters, described further subsequently, are also served by HTTP servers.

The Runner class is the driver of the system; it is a 2 kB Java bytecode executable which contains a main() method and it is executed from the command line (or from a queue script). This is the only file which must be installed on a machine to enable the machine to participate in the grid system in any of the possible functions such as running an application, running a bag, or running a compute node. The Runner accepts as a command line argument the URL identifier of a Java properties file, which contains any number of resource URLs. These resource URLs contain compiled Java classes or JAR format archive files, with methods that can be used during operation. The built-in security features of Java, such as digitally signed JAR files and tools for creating a configurable sand box for the JVM interpreter which can restrict access to local and remote resources for the downloaded code, can be incorporated at this level. The final argument passed to a Runner process is the name of the class to run. This is typically Node (for a compute node), Space (for a tuple space bag), or the name of a TaskSpaces application. The Runner downloads the appropriate class from the input argument set of URL resources, casts it to an instance of the Java class Runnable, and begins execution by calling its run() method. Any additional classes required for execution are automatically downloaded, provided they are present in the set of URL resources.

The Node class represents a compute node which participates in the system. The properties file, also identified by command line argument, contains a property named "spaces," which identifies the IP address and port number of any existing Space servers. The Node registers with these Space server objects on startup. Other properties define the maximum run time for the Node, after which it automatically terminates, a default port number on which to begin to run the Node, and the maximum number of Task objects to process before termination. Upon startup, the Node creates an instance of the Server class and an instance of the Worker class. The Server registers with the remote TaskSpace object that is identified in the properties file and then waits for incoming requests. Incoming requests may be of three possible object types, task, agent, and message. Task objects are applications or application components to be executed. These objects are passed to a TaskStore object, which was created by the Node on startup, and is monitored by the Worker thread. The Worker executes the Task, which may, for applications with interprocessor communication, contain code to monitor the local MessageStore object, also initiated in a separate Thread by the Node at startup. When received, Message objects are placed by the Server into the MessageStore. The MessageStore is monitored by the Task, and the Message objects are pulled into the Task and the data is extracted and used by the Task during execution. Agents are executed immediately by the Server upon arrival and may be used for a variety of system functions, including shutting down the Node or extracting data held in a Node data structure, which is available to the application for storing data or system or state information.

The Space class contains several data structures (mainly synchronized ArrayLists) and methods for accepting and storing the addresses of registering Nodes and Task Objects. IP addresses and port numbers of registered Nodes are stored in two structures, one of which is permanent and other from which address and port identifiers are deleted as individual Tasks are sent to the registered Nodes in FIFO order. The permanent addresses can be used by Agents to identify all Nodes which may be participating in the system. This information can be used by Agents to shut down running Nodes or perform other application-dependent functions. Space objects are created in the same manner as starting a Node. The system property file mentioned earlier specifies the IP address and port number of Spaces in the system that act as task or result bags. On startup, a Space creates a server on a port specified in the properties file. It is expected that the Spaces will typically be started once and then left running as long as worker nodes may be active, similar to HTTP servers. Spaces are multi-threaded and create a new thread for each incoming request. Each new thread is an instance of the SpaceConnection class, within which the nature of the request is identified and internal processing is performed. When a Task object arrives, it is sent to a worker node if any Nodes are currently registered as available Nodes. If not, the Task is temporarily stored until worker Nodes register with the TaskSpace to indicate their availability. Spaces can also transmit messages to Nodes running applications and can be used as an intermediary messaging store or as the medium for Nodes to exchange addressing information in case applications require direct Task to Task communication [1].

An additional optimization can be made for applications for which the subtasks do not have a large input data set and have a limited number of input parameters that vary in a systematic way. In this case, it is beneficial to generate the (potentially many) Task objects within the TaskSpace, rather than have the Application process to generate all the separate Task objects, and then send them to the TaskSpace one by one. The Application process can define an object of class TaskAgent. The TaskAgent is sent to the TaskSpace, and there a method is called on the TaskAgent to create a new application task. The Space advances the data by calling the next() method of the TaskAgent, which calls the internally held application Task object to advance its state (whatever this may mean in the context of the application) to create a new application Task. The new Task is returned to the Space and the Space sends this Task to an available Node.

Application processes can choose to have Nodes, which send result data to a result Space, or directly back to the application. In the first case, the Application registers with the result Space to receive any arriving results, which are sub-classes of the Result class. The application can then store the data locally on the file system, send it to a database, or process the data and display output on a connected display device.

The final class of the TaskSpaces system is the Communicator. The Communicator contains methods and a protocol definition for all of the other components to communicate with each other. All the components sub-class Communicator to enable remote communication with the other components of the system. The Communicator class centralizes communication in a single object for simplified error tracking and

TABLE 26.1 High-Throughput Grid Experiment for a Tightly Coupled Numerical Linear Algebra Scientific Computing Problem with 500^2 Grid Points per Worker

Blue Horizon, SDSC, San Diego, CA (4 workers/processor)	64	128	240
P4 Linux, CU Boulder, CO (2 workers/processor)	4	4	4
Itanium Linux, CU Boulder, CO (2 workers/processor)	4	4	4
forseti1, NCSA, Urbana, IL (1 worker/processor)	16	16	16
hermod, NCSA, Urbana, IL (1 worker/processor)	16	16	16
Total number of workers	104	168	280
Total execution time (s)	105	103	101

Note: The number of worker processes and the total execution times are shown. The problem size is constant per worker process, so the nearly constant total execution times indicate almost perfect scalability.

modification, which are complex problems in such widely distributed systems. The communication is performed using integer identifiers and serialized Java objects over sockets.

Application code need not be installed and maintained on workers, because it is downloaded from a central server when task objects arrive at each worker. Installing and executing a Java bytecode executable of size <2 kB allow any worker host to participate in the grid. Thus, installation and maintenance of TaskSpaces are extremely lightweight and easy. In fact, the complete TaskSpaces codebase is extremely small and compact, due to the simplicity of the design and the availability of Java's built-in networking and object manipulation capabilities.

TaskSpaces can be used in taskfarming mode for problems that do not require interprocess communication, such as independent folding of many RNA sequences (discussed subsequently). It can also be used for other applications that do require interprocess communication, handling such communication in a scalable way by transmitting serialized Java objects over sockets. Table 26.1 demonstrates that TaskSpaces scales well on large grids comprised of supercomputers at NCSA, SDSC, and other supercomputer centers, connected over the Internet, for a parallel computing problem in numerical linear algebra [1]. This problem requires neighbor–neighbor interprocess communication, and it is thus surprising that the scalability for this problem in the heterogeneous grid environment is so good.

Looking back at the prerequisites we set out in the previous section for the "universal computing dream" we pursue, it is instructive to consider how our prototype grid implementation performs with respect to our aspirations. Some of the functionality is only present in a rudimentary way in our prototype implementation, but more sophisticated versions based on the general concepts presented can be easily imagined.

1. Standard interface: YES.
   Through implementation in Java. In the strict sense, this limits the applications

to code written in Java, but, with limited sacrifices in generality, application code in other languages can be used as well (discussed subsequently).

2. Scalable: YES.
   Through the tuple space concept. Scalability from the producer side is currently performed "by hand," but automated strategies can be easily imagined. In addition, bags can, in principle, be replicated when access loads become high and bottlenecks arise and automatic strategies to this end can be considered as well.

3. Secure resource sharing: not implemented yet in TaskSpaces.
   However, definitely feasible using Java's built-in mechanisms of digital signatures and public–private key cryptography.

4. Fault-tolerance: not implemented yet in TaskSpaces.
   However, for instance, automatic duplication of bags for backup reasons could easily be achieved via simple cloning of Java objects.

5. Resource allocation and scheduling: YES.
   The task bag acts as a "superqueue."

6. Automatic distribution of application code to worker machines: YES.
   By downloading Java objects from the task bags. The objects contain both the data and references to the application code, which is downloaded automatically from the class server upon first use by a worker.

7. Scalable interprocess communication: YES.
   Through direct exchange of serialized Java objects over sockets between workers [1]. Efficient collective communications would require additional features such as multi-level communication schemes (discussed subsequently).

8. User charging algorithms: not implemented yet in TaskSpaces.
   Simple charging strategies are straightforward to implement.

9. Quality-of-service: not implemented yet in TaskSpaces.
   This may require thorough study of the particular grid environments considered and instrumentation of objects and worker machines with performance measures and priority mechanisms.

10. Resource discovery: YES.
    Computing resources discover tasks by making themselves available to the task bags, rather than the other way around. Compute farms are presently assigned to task bags by hand, but automatic, multi-level assignment strategies are feasible.

The overview mentioned earlier shows that the TaskSpaces design, despite its simplicity, is quite effective in realizing many of the conceptual aspirations of the "universal computing dream." In the following sections, we illustrate how the framework, with minimal effort, can be used for a practical, real-life parallel bioinformatics application on ad hoc computational grids comprised of a variety of widely available hardware types.

26.3   APPLICATION: FINDING CORRECTLY FOLDED RNA MOTIFS IN SEQUENCE SPACE

We have applied the TaskSpaces framework to the following problem, which is relevant both to natural evolution and to a process of artificial evolution called SELEX, which has been widely used to select new molecular functions from random pools of RNA. Given a pool of random RNA molecules of a specified length (typically 50–200 bases), what is the probability that the random pool contains molecules that have the right sequence and are folded into the right structure needed for a particular chemical function? This question is critical for the RNA world hypothesis: if molecules that can catalyze a particular reaction are especially common, the idea that the little amounts of RNA that would be produced by prebiotic synthesis could produce an RNA metabolism becomes more plausible (Fig. 26.4) [4]. Chemically active RNA molecules are also routinely synthesized, in SELEX laboratory experiments, from intially random pools of RNA molecules [5]. Specifically, we have focused on determining the abundance of isoleucine and hammerhead RNA motifs in random molecules [5]. The isoleucine motif is the shortest RNA motif capable of binding specifically to the amino acid isoleucine, whereas the hammerhead motif cuts RNA at specific locations and has been found both in cells and through SELEX. It has been determined experimentally that chemical function of a certain type appears when the random RNA molecule contains a prescribed motif, which

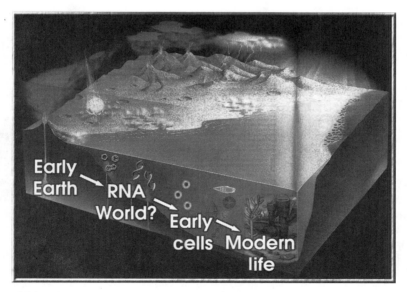

Figure 26.4   The RNA world hypothesis: If a small number of random RNA molecules, say a pool of 10^6 to 10^9 sequences, has a reasonable probability of containing molecules with various chemical functions, then primitive metabolisms would be expected to have arisen many times on the early Earth. Figure adapted from Horgan, J. (1991), Sci. Am. 264: 116–125.

is comprised of several modules with partially specified sequence, and has a pre-scribed folding structure (Fig. 26.5). The probability that a random molecule matches both the prescribed sequence and the structure, $P(\text{seq}, \text{struct})$, is calculated in two steps as $P(\text{seq}, \text{struct}) = P(\text{seq})\, P(\text{struct}|\text{seq})$. The sequence probability $P(\text{seq})$ can be approximated accurately by combinatorial formulas [4, 5]. The conditional proba-bility of obtaining the right folding structure, given a partially random molecule that contains the right sequence, cannot be approximated analytically. Instead, we approx-imate this probability by computational folding of large samples of RNA molecules (a sample size of 10,000 is typically used): the probability is approximated by the number of partially random molecules that fold into the correct structure divided by the total number of molecules in the sample. One important question of interest is the variation of the probability $P(\text{seq}, \text{struct})$ as the composition of the random pool changes, because the composition of RNA pools may have varied widely on the primitive earth and because modern genomes vary widely in composition, possibly affecting the evolution of specific functions. We set out to investigate whether specific kinds of chemical function arise more often in pools with overall composition biases in particular directions. This required the computational folding of many samples in

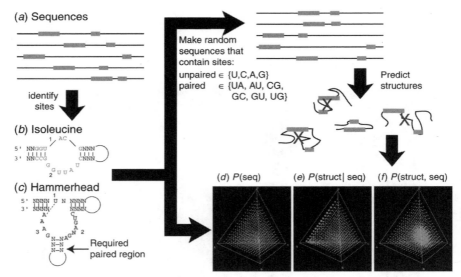

Figure 26.5 Procedure for determining the effects of folding and sequence composition on motif abundance. (*a*) The motifs are identified by comparing sequences with the same function. The isoleucine aptamer (*b*) and the hammerhead ribozyme (*c*) both consist of modules that must have an exact sequence and flanking helices that must base pair but need meet no other constraints. These diagrams show the exact sequence and structure requirements that were used in the calculations: base pairs are indicated by connecting lines. We calculate $P(\text{sequence})$ (*d*) from the sequence requirements and $P(\text{structure}|\text{sequence})$ (*e*) by constructing large samples of random sequences that contain the motif and computationally predicting their structures. The overall probability of finding a correctly folded sequence (*f*) is obtained by multiplying the probabilities from (*d*) and (*e*).

{A, C, G, U} composition space. We used 5% intervals in composition space, leading to 969 different compositions to be tested. Varying the length of the random molecules (we have considered lengths of 50, 100, and 150 nucleotides), further increased the number of foldings required. For the results to be discussed briefly subsequently (see [5] for a more detailed discussion), we performed about hundred million computational foldings. This constitutes a computational problem of moderately large size, which would require weeks to months on a single fast workstation. We decided to use a grid computing approach, mainly for flexibility, portability, and scalability reasons.

We used the Vienna RNA folding package [6], which is written in C, for folding individual sequences. The RNAfold executable is called by the Java application on each worker node as needed. Non-Java executables must be compiled in advance for each worker architecture and can be downloaded from the code server by the workers upon first use. Thus, although reliance on code written in other languages increases the effort required for cross-platform operation, it is still feasible.

26.4 CASE STUDY: OPERATING THE FRAMEWORK ON A COMPUTATIONAL GRID

We simulated the RNA function probability problem on a grid comprised of the NCSA IA32 Linux Platinum Supercluster and various P4 Linux workstations at CU Boulder, Colorado. The Platinum machine features 968 P3 compute processors (1 GHz). For code development and execution of some smaller subproblems, only the local workstations were used, whereas for larger problems, the local workstations were combined with up to 200 Platinum processors concurrently. The total computing time used for this project so far, including extensive initial runs for exploring the problem and determining the right approach and questions to be answered, amounts to approximately 10,000 Platinum processor hours.

The framework was easy to install on candidate worker machines. Even though Java is normally not thought of very much as a language for supercomputing, it is actually available on all machines we obtained access to, even the largest parallel supercomputers. In fact, Java is catching up fast in execution speed with other languages and the advantages in ease of use and portability may actually give it a good future in scientific computing. Locating the Java executable (which is typically not included in the standard path), copying the Java worker bytecode to the worker machine and starting the workers, was typically very fast: for most machines, it did not take more than 15 min to make them participate in the grid. On parallel computes, the standard queuing systems were used. Varying queue delays on concurrently participating machines did not cause a problem, because the task bag (typically located on a workstation in Boulder) acts as a superqueue and the RNA folding tasks are loosely coupled and do not require any interprocess communication and synchronization. The Internet was used as network connection between the grid machines, and network performance was adequate at all times.

A major obstacle in constructing ad hoc grids like this is security, which will become increasingly important as research networks and institutions are increasingly targeted by malicious intruders. Under pressure from malicious attacks, potential worker machines will often be protected by firewalls. Participation in a grid then requires additional firewall configuration, as our framework requires at present worker nodes with externally accessible IP addresses. Security is another reason why we expect, as argued before, that grids will develop as "islands" for the foreseeable future, further delaying the concept of a "World Wide Grid." Another inconvenience in operating a grid is the variety of queuing systems operating on parallel computers and clusters. If machines were available where TaskSpaces workers would be the only, continuously running processes, then much of the queuing considerations could be dealt with in more efficient ways that decrease turnaround times, for instance, by extending the use and functionality of task bags as superqueues.

We can summarize our experiences with operating the grid framework for a real problem on a real moderately sized grid, by saying that the framework mostly delivered the promised flexibility, portability, and scalability.

26.5   RESULTS FOR THE RNA MOTIF PROBLEM

We estimated the abundance of two motifs, the hammerhead ribozyme and the isoleucine aptamer, in random-sequence pools of many compositions and several lengths. These two well-studied motifs provide test cases for our code on the TaskSpaces framework, with which we plan to analyze dozens to hundreds of motifs. Knowing where particular kinds of RNA sequences are most likely to be found in the space of possible compositions and where these sequences are most likely to fold into the correct structure if they are found will provide striking new insight into the conditions under which particular RNA activities can evolve.

To test the effects of nucleotide composition on the probability of meeting the sequence requirements and the probability of correct folding, we generated 10,000 random sequences at each of the 969 possible 5% intervals of sequence composition. The sequences were of total length 50, 100, and 150 nucleotides, meeting the sequence requirements for each of the hammerhead and isoleucine motifs. We repeated the analysis for sequence length 50 allowing G-U base pairs (a weaker type of pairing than the more familiar "Watson–Crick" G-C and A-U base pairs, which are found at a small but not negligible frequency in biological RNA structures). Thus, we folded a total of 77,520,000 sequences for this experiment.

We found that the composition of the randomized sequences had a striking effect on both the probability of finding each motif and the probability of correct folding. Figure 26.6 shows the probability of meeting the sequence requirements, the probability of correct folding given that the sequence requirements were met, and the overall probability of finding the motif, for each of the 969 internal 5% interval compositions that include atleast some of each of the four nucleotides U, C, A, and G. The patterns in the different diagrams are strikingly different, indicating that folding and sequence abundance can actually have antagonistic effects on the overall probability of finding a correctly folded motif.

The probability of correct folding ranged over many orders of magnitude. Figure 26.6 shows, for all 5% intervals of nucleotide composition in the space of possible compositions, the probability of meeting the sequence requirements in a completely random sequence for the hammerhead and isoleucine motifs (left and right, respectively; Fig. 26.6a and b), the probability of correct folding in partially random sequences that already meet the sequence requirements (Fig. 26.6c and d), and the combined probability of finding the correctly folded motif. In sequences of total length 100, the probability of finding the isoleucine motif ranged from 1.44×10^{-21} to 5.71×10^{-10} with a mean of 3.62×10^{-11}, reaching a value of 1.71×10^{-10} at unbiased nucleotide frequency and a maximum at the coordinates 15%A, 25%C, 35%G, and 25%U. The probability of finding the hammerhead motif ranged from 0 to 4.58×10^{-10} with a mean of 7.37×10^{-12}, reaching a value of 3.38×10^{-11} at unbiased nucleotide frequency and a maximum at the coordinates 35%A, 10%C, 25%G, and 30%U.

Sequence length also had a substantial effect on the probability of correct folding. As expected [4, 7, 8], longer sequences had a large combinatorial advantage over short sequences in meeting the sequence requirements (maximum probabilities of 1.74×10^{-8}, 1.42×10^{-6}, and 7.87×10^{-6} for 50, 100, and 150 nucleotides for the hammerhead motif and 3.46×10^{-9}, 3.20×10^{-8}, and 8.94×10^{-8} for isoleucine: the probability for the isoleucine aptamer changes more slowly because it has two modules instead of three for the hammerhead). However, this combinatorial advantage was offset somewhat by substantially worse folding at greater sequence lengths (maximum probabilities of 5.64×10^{-2}, 2.49×10^{-2}, and 1.08×10^{-2} for 50, 100, and 150 nucleotides for the hammerhead motif and 3.17×10^{-1}, 1.78×10^{-1}, and 1.29×10^{-1} for isoleucine). The maximum overall probabilities for the two sites were 4.27×10^{-12}, 4.57×10^{-10}, and 8.61×10^{-10} for 50, 100, and 150 nucleotides for the hammerhead motif and 1.88×10^{-10}, 5.71×10^{-10}, and 1.06×10^{-9} for isoleucine (note that these are not the products of the best probabilities for finding the sequence requirements and for folding, because the optima occurred at different compositions). These findings are difficult to reconcile with experiments that show that motifs are much more difficult to find in longer random regions [9, 10]. One possibility is that the computational folding systematically overestimates the probability of a correct fold in longer sequences; another is that other effects of sequence length, notably amplification efficiency, outweigh the effects of function at the RNA level. We plan to test these effects directly by synthesizing sequences that are computationally predicted to fold into one motif or the other. We will then use chemical and enzymatic probing to test the structural predictions around each motif and assay the relevant catalytic and binding parameters to determine whether the molecules perform the predicted function.

To test whether the compositional grid was sufficiently fine to locate the region of maximum probability, we performed a more detailed analysis of the transect between the two best-folding points for the isoleucine aptamer using a larger sample size of 100,000 sequences per point to reduce the effects of sampling error. Figure 26.7 shows the folding probabilities at 10 intervals between the two best points at sequence length 50: 10%A, 30%C, 35%G, 25%U and 10%A, 30%C, 40%G, 20%U. Interestingly, the

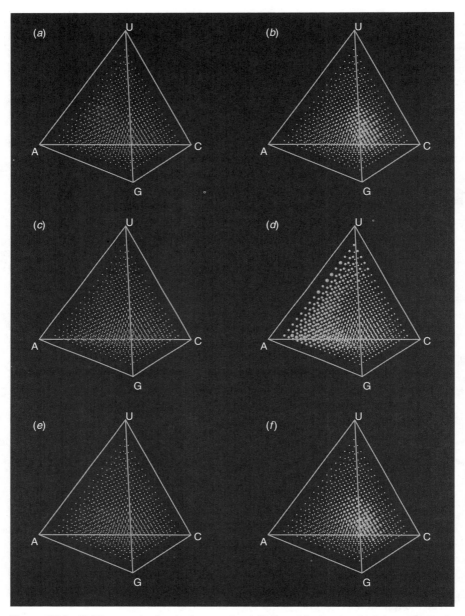

Figure 26.6 Folding results for the hammerhead (left) and isoleucine (right) motifs. Probability of finding the required sequence elements (*a* and *b*), probability of folding correctly given that the required sequence elements were present (*c* and *d*), and overall probability of having the required sequence elements and folding correctly (*e* and *f*). Volume of each sphere is proportional to the probability at each of the 969 internal 5% intervals in the space of possible compositions. Radii are scaled such that the maximum radius in each diagram is set to 0.01 composition unit. These results are for sequence length 100.

region of maximum probability was insensitive to the length of the sequence, although (as seen earlier) the length of the sequence changed the probability at each point by orders of magnitude.

These results demonstrate striking relationships between nucleotide composition and the probability of finding specific sequences and suggest that we may be able to predict which kinds of random-sequence pools (for SELEX or in organisms) might be most able to evolve particular functions. The probability of finding the specific functions we searched for (10^{-8} to 10^{-12}) are rather lower than we had predicted from previous work, demonstrating that the effects of folding are important and cannot be ignored. These figures are consistent with the observation that new RNA activities are routinely isolated in the laboratory from random-sequence pools of 10^{12} to 10^{15} molecules, although they do not provide support for the idea that an RNA metabolism could have arisen from only a few hundred thousand random RNA molecules as might have been present on the prebiotic Earth. Owing to the chemical problems in synthesizing large amounts of RNA without enzymes, it has often been suggested that a simpler self-reproducing RNA system preceded the RNA World. However,

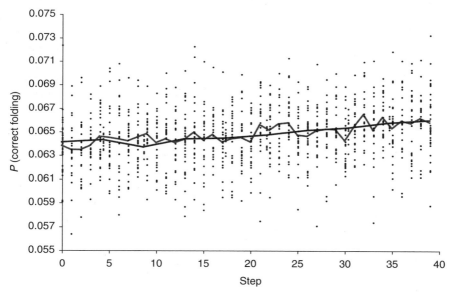

Figure 26.7 Fine-grained analysis of regions between the two most probable points for isoleucine aptamer folding, which were ACGU = [10, 30, 35, 25] and ACGU = [10, 30, 40, 20] with a total sequence length of 50 nucleotides. We made 10 independent samples (dots), each of 100,000 sequences, at each of 10 equal intervals between the two most probable points (smoother line shows the mean) and made 25 independent samples (dots), each of 10,000 sequences, at each of 40 equal intervals between these same two points (more wiggly line shows the mean). Both series are shown at the same scale in terms of absolute composition. The lines for the means are smooth in both cases, although (as expected) the scatter is lower for the points at the larger sample size.

once RNA was first synthesized (perhaps for an entirely different reason), our results show that catalytic activity would soon be likely to emerge: 10^{15} 100-nucleotide RNA molecules is about 50 µg of RNA, less than the amount of RNA found in a single gram of modern tissue.

26.6 FUTURE WORK

As demonstrated earlier, our prototype grid framework delivers promising flexibility, portability, and scalability for real-life applications on ad hoc grids. However, there are many interesting ways in which the framework can be extended.

First of all, we are planning to build full Python language functionality into the framework to allow researchers familiar with that language to scale their single-CPU tasks easily to the grid. Python is becoming increasingly popular as a language for bioinformatics, mirroring its success for other scientific computing tasks. Secondly, as indicated in the enumeration in Section 26.2, the framework implementation needs to be extended with regards to scalability, fault-tolerance, security, charging algorithms, and quality-of-service. For example, fault-tolerance may be enhanced by cloning of objects and bags and transaction-type communication. Thirdly, we plan to add more extensive functionality, in terms of support for complex parallel workflows (Fig. 26.8), connection with databases for data furnishing and result collection, and multilevel tree-based collective communication for tightly coupled parallel applications.

On the parallel bioinformatics application side, additional loosely coupled parallel bioinformatics applications will be studied, including variants of the previously

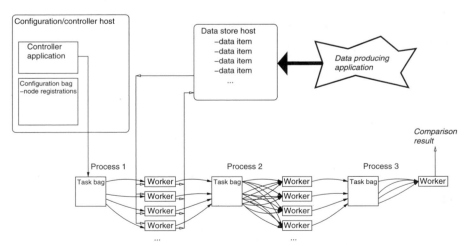

Figure 26.8 Proposed agent-mediated workflow diagram. In the first phase, a configuration agent sets up a workflow topology for a workflow, consisting of two parallel processes and a serial process in this example. In the second phase, the data are carried through the workflow by execution agents. For fault-tolerance purposes, the workflow could be made self-migrating.

considered RNA folding statistics problem (for instance, investigation of the effect of the length of the molecules on correct folding) and an examination of whether certain compositional features of ribosomal RNA are universal across organisms or across RNA molecules. We are also considering more challenging applications, including proteomics workflows and tightly coupled problems such as building large phylogenies.

26.7 SUMMARY AND CONCLUSION

We have described a software framework for scientific computing on computational grids that is based on tuple space principles and implemented in Java and we have demonstrated that seamless simulation on an ad hoc grid comprised of a wide variety of hardware is feasible for real-life parallel bioinformatics problems. The language and general approach we used is most appropriate in cases in which flexibility and ease of configuration outweigh concerns about extracting maximal performance on a given architecture for a given, fixed, application with fixed, large problem size that must be executed repeatedly. In this latter situation, it is often a good investment to develop specific optimized software solutions of "high-performance computing" type. In many situations, however, research is dynamic and research goals and directions change continuously. In such a rapid-prototyping environment with wide variations in problem sizes, with complex changing workflows, and with fast variations in application code, a platform-independent "high-throughput computing" grid solution of the type proposed in this chapter may be most appropriate, because of the gains in flexibility, portability, and cross-platform scalability.

ACKNOWLEDGMENTS

This work was partially supported by the National Computational Science Alliance under grant MCB020011 and utilized the NCSA IA32 Linux Supercluster Platinum.

REFERENCES

1. H. D. Sterck, R. Markel, T. Pohl, and U. Rüde, A Lightweight Java TaskSpaces Framework for Scientific Computing on Computational Grids, in *Proceedings of the ACM Symposium on Applied Computing, Track on Parallel and Distributed Systems and Networking*, 2003, pp. 1024–1030.

2. D. Gelertner, Generative communication in Linda. *ACM Trans. Programm. Lang. Sys.*, 7 (1), 80–112 (1985).

3. G. R. Andrews, *Foundations of Multithreaded, Parallel, and Distributed Programming*, Addison Wesley, Boston, 2000.

4. R. Knight and M. Yarus, Finding specific RNA motifs: function in a zeptomole world? *RNA*, 9 (2), 218–230 (2003).

5. R. Knight, H. De Sterck, R. S. Markel, S. Smit, A. Oshmyansky, and M. Yarus, Finding correctly folded active RNA motifs in sequence space using computational grids, *NAR*, submitted for publication.

6. I. Hofacker, W. Fontana, P. Stadler, L. Bonhoeffer, M. Tacker, and P. Schuster, Fast folding and comparison of RNA secondary structures, *Monatshefte Fur Chemie*, 125 (2), 167–188 (1994).

7. P. C. Sabeti, P. J. Unrau, and D. P. Bartel, Accessing rare activities from random RNA sequences: the importance of the length of molecules in the starting pool, *Chem Biol.*, 4 (10), 767–774 (1997).

8. M. Yarus and R. Knight, *Translation Mechanisms*, Landes Bioscience, 2003.

9. F. Huang, C. W. Bugg, and M. Yarus, RNA-catalyzed CoA, NAD, and FAD synthesis from phosphopantetheine, NMN, and FMN, *Biochemistry*, 39 (50), 15548–15555 (2000).

10. C. Lozupone, S. Changayil, I. Majerfeld, and M. Yarus, Selection of the simplest RNA that binds isoleucine, *RNA*, 9 (11), 1315–1322 (2003).

■■■■■ **CHAPTER 27**

The Organic Grid: Self-organizing Computational Biology on Desktop Grids

ARJAV J. CHAKRAVARTI, GERALD BAUMGARTNER, and MARIO LAURIA

Machines take me by surprise with great frequency.

—A. Turing

I think there's a world market for about five computers.

—T. J. Watson

Desktop grids have been used to perform some of the largest computations in the world and have the potential to grow by several more orders of magnitude. However, current approaches to utilizing desktop resources require either centralized servers or extensive knowledge of the underlying system, limiting their scalability.

We propose a new design for desktop grids that relies on a self-organizing, fully decentralized approach to the organization of the computation. Our approach, called the Organic Grid, is a radical departure from current approaches and is modeled after the way complex biological systems organize themselves. Similarly to current desktop grids, a large computational task is broken down into sufficiently small subtasks. Each subtask is encapsulated into a mobile agent, which is then released on the grid and discovers computational resources using autonomous behavior. In the process of "colonization" of available resources, the judicious design of the agent behavior produces the emergence of crucial properties of the computation that can be tailored to specific classes of applications.

We demonstrate this concept with a reduced-scale proof-of-concept implementation that executes a data-intensive independent-task application on a set of heterogeneous, geographically distributed machines. We present a detailed exploration of the design space of our system and a performance evaluation of our implementation using metrics appropriate for assessing self-organizing desktop grids.

Parallel Computing for Bioinformatics and Computational Biology, Edited by Albert Y. Zomaya
Copyright © 2006 John Wiley & Sons, Inc.

27.1 INTRODUCTION

Many scientific fields, such as genomics, phylogenetics, astrophysics, geophysics, computational neuroscience, bioinformatics, require massive computational power and resources, which might exceed those available on a single supercomputer. There are two drastically different approaches for harnessing the combined resources of a distributed collection of machines: large-scale desktop-based master–worker schemes and more traditional computational grid schemes.

Some of the largest computations in the world have been carried out on collections of personal computers (PCs) and workstations over the Internet. Tera-flop levels of computational power have been achieved by systems comprised heterogeneous computing resources that ranged from hundreds of thousands to the millions in number. This extreme form of distributed computing is often called *Internet computing*, and has allowed scientists to run applications at unprecedented scales at a comparably modest cost. The desktop-based platforms on which Internet-scale computations are carried out are often referred to as *desktop grids*. In analogy to computational grids [1, 2], these collections of distributed machines are connected together by a layer of middleware software that provides the illusion of a single system [3–5]. Although impressive, these efforts only use a tiny fraction of the desktops connected to the Internet. Improvements of several orders of magnitudes could be achieved if novel systems of organization of the computation were to be introduced that overcome the limits of present systems.

A number of large-scale systems are based on variants of the master–workers model [3–13]. Some of these systems have resulted in commercial enterprises, which shows the level of technical maturity reached by the technology. However, the obtainable computing power is constrained by the performance of the master (especially for data-intensive applications) and by the difficulty of deploying the supporting software on a large number of workers. As networks cannot be assumed to be reliable, large desktop grids are designed for independent task applications (ITAs) with relatively long-running individual tasks.

By contrast, research on traditional grid scheduling has focused on algorithms to determine an optimal computation schedule based on the assumption that sufficient and up-to-date knowledge of the system state is available to a single entity (the metascheduler) [14–17]. Although this approach results in a very efficient utilization of the resources, it does not scale to large numbers of machines. Maintaining a global view of the system becomes prohibitively expensive and unreliable networks might even make it impossible.

Table 27.1 summarizes different design strategies of the existing approaches to harnessing machine resources. Traditional grid approaches limit the size of the system and assume a fairly reliable network in exchange for being able to run arbitrary tasks, such as message-passing interface (MPI) tasks. Desktop grid approaches restrict the type of the application to independent (or nearly independent) tasks of fairly large task granularity in exchange for being able to run on very large numbers of machines with potentially unreliable network connections. The best of both worlds, arbitrary tasks

TABLE 27.1   Classification of Approaches to Large-Scale Computation

	Large Desktop Grids (e.g., BOINC)	Small Desktop Grids (Condor)	Traditional Grids (e.g., Globus)	Organic Grid
Network	Large, unreliable	Small, reliable	Small, reliable	Large, unreliable
Task granularity	Large	Medium to large	Medium to large	Medium to large
Task model	Independent task	Any	Any	Any
Task scheduling	Centralized	Centralized	Centralized	Decentralized

and large numbers of machines, is not possible because the central task scheduler would become a bottleneck.

We present a new approach to grid computing, called the Organic Grid, that does not have the restrictions of either of the existing approaches. By using a decentralized, adaptive scheduling scheme, we attempt to allow arbitrary tasks to be run on large numbers of machines or in conditions with unreliable networks. Our approach can be used to broaden the class of applications that can be run on a large desktop grid, or to extend a traditional grid computing approach to machines with unreliable connections. The trade-off of our approach is that the distributed scheduling scheme may not result in as good resource usage as with a centralized scheduler.

The Organic Grid project is an effort to redesign, from scratch, the infrastructure for distributed computation on desktop grids. Our middleware represents a radical departure from current grid or peer-to-peer concepts, and does not rely on existing grid technology. In designing our Organic Grid infrastructure, we have tried to address the following questions:

- What is the best model of use of a system based on the harvesting of idle cycles of hundreds of thousands to millions of PCs?
- How should the system be designed to make it consistent with the grid computing ideals of computation as a ubiquitous and easily accessible utility?

Nature provides numerous examples of the emergence of complex patterns derived from the interactions of millions of organisms that organize themselves in an autonomous, adaptive way relatively simple behavior. To apply this approach to the task of organizing computation over complex systems such as desktop grids, one would have to devise a way of breaking a large computation into small autonomous chunks, and then endowing each chunk with the appropriate behavior.

Our approach is to encapsulate computation and behavior into mobile agents. A similar concept was first explored by Montresor et al. [18] in a project showing how an ant algorithm could be used to solve the problem of dispersing tasks uniformly over a network. In our approach, the behavior is designed to produce desirable patterns of execution according to current grid engineering principles. Kreaseck et al. [19] studied the pattern of computation resulting from the synthetic behavior of our agents reflecting some general concepts about autonomous grid scheduling protocols. Our approach extends previous results by showing (i) how the basic concepts can be extended to accommodate highly dynamic systems and (ii) a practical implementation of these concepts.

One result of the encapsulation of behavior and computation into agents is that they can be easily customized for different classes of applications. Another useful result is that the underlying support infrastructure for our system is extremely simple. Therefore, our approach naturally lends itself to a true peer-to-peer implementation, where each node can be both provider and user of the computing utility infrastructure. Our scheme can be easily adapted to the case where the source of computation (the node initiating a computing job) is different from the source of the data.

The purpose of this work is the initial exploration of a novel concept, and as such it is not intended to give a quantitative assessment of all aspects and implications of our new approach. In particular, detailed evaluations of scalability, degree of tolerance to faults, adaptivity to rapidly changing systems, or security issues have been left for future studies.

27.2   BACKGROUND AND RELATED WORK

This section contains a brief introduction to the critical concepts and technologies used in our work, as well as the related work in these areas. These include: grid computing, peer-to-peer and Internet computing, scheduling, self-organizing systems and the concept of emergence, strongly mobile agents, and autonomic scheduling.

27.2.1   Grid Computing

Grid computing is a term often used to indicate some form of distributed computation on geographically distributed resources. We use the term not as referring to a particular technology, which is consistent with the following definition of grid computing given by Foster and Kesselman:

> coordinated resource sharing and problem solving in dynamic, multi-institutional virtual organizations

where virtual organizations (VOs) are defined as "dynamic collections of individuals, institutions, and resources" [1]. Examples of VOs are members of an industrial consortium bidding on a new aircraft; participants of a large, international, multi-year high-energy physics collaboration; peer-to-peer computing (as implemented, e.g., in the Napster, Gnutella, and Freenet file-sharing systems); and Internet computing (as implemented, e.g., by the SETI@home, Parabon, and Entropia systems) [1].

As these examples show, VOs encompass entities with very different characteristics. Nevertheless, to achieve the grid computing the following set of common requirements can be identified [1]:

- Mechanisms for sharing varied resources, ranging from programs, files, and data to computers, sensors, and networks.

- Mechanisms for highly flexible sharing relationships, ranging from client–server to peer-to-peer.
- Mechanisms for sophisticated and precise levels of control over how shared resources are used, including fine-grained and multi-stakeholder access control, delegation, and application of local and global policies.
- Mechanisms for diverse usage models, ranging from single user to multi-user and from performance-sensitive to cost-sensitive, and hence embracing issues of quality of service, scheduling, co-allocation, and accounting.

Currently, the Globus toolkit [20] (both in its initial version and in its recent redesign following the web services architecture known as open grid services architecture (OGSA) [2]) represents the *de facto* standard model for grid applications development and deployment. The Globus toolkit is a collection of tools for grid application development, each targeted to a particular area of grid computing (application scheduling, security management, resource monitoring, etc.). An unintended consequence of its popularity is the common misconception that grid technology and Globus (or OGSA) are one and the same thing. In reality, the grid concept as defined above is much more general, and a lot of research opportunities exist on the study of novel forms of grid computing.

Peer-to-peer and Internet computing are examples of the more general "beyond client–server" sharing modalities and computational structures that we referred to in our characterization of VOs. As such, they have much in common with grid technologies. In practice, however, so far there has been very little work done at the intersections of these domains.

The Organic Grid is a novel type of grid that is based on a peer-to-peer model of interaction, where the code (in addition to the data) is exchanged between peers. It therefore requires some type of mobility of the code. We use mobile agents as the underlying technology for building our grid infrastructure. In peer-to-peer systems like Napster or Kazaa, the peers exchange files. We demonstrate that by connecting agent platforms into a peer-to-peer network and by exchanging computation in the form of agents, it is possible to build a novel grid computing infrastructure.

At a very high level of abstraction, the Organic Grid is similar to Globus in that a user can submit an application to the system and the application will be executed somewhere on the grid. The innovative approach employed by the Organic Grid is that the user's application is encapsulated in a mobile agent together with scheduling code; the mobile agent then carries the application to a machine that has declared it has available computing resources. Instead of relying on a centralized scheduler as in existing grid approaches, agents make simple decentralized scheduling decisions on their own.

A grid architecture like ours with decentralized scheduling could have been built without employing mobile agents, using, for example, a service architecture (after all, mobile agents are implemented on top of remote method invocation, which is implemented on top of client-server communication). However, mobile agents provide a particularly convenient abstraction that makes building such a system, and experimenting with different scheduling strategies, much easier and more flexible.

In addition, the use of strong mobility will enable future implementations of the Organic Grid to transparently checkpoint and migrate user applications.

27.2.2   Peer-to-Peer and Internet Computing

The goal of utilizing the central processing unit (CPU) cycles of idle machines was first realized by the Worm project [21] at Xerox PARC. Further progress was made by academic projects such as Condor [8]. The growth of the Internet made large-scale efforts like GIMPS [7], SETI@home [3] and folding@home [4] feasible. Recently, commercial solutions such as Entropia [5] and United Devices [22] have also been developed.

Peer-to-peer computing adopts a highly decentralized approach to resource sharing in which every node in the system can assume the role of client or server [23, 24]. Current peer-to-peer systems often rely on highly available central servers and are mainly used for high-profile, large-scale computational projects such as SETI@home, or for popular data-centric applications like file sharing [25].

The idea of combining Internet and peer-to-peer computing is attractive because of the potential for almost unlimited computational power, low cost, ease and universality of access — the dream of a true computational grid. Among the technical challenges posed by such an architecture, scheduling is one of the most formidable — how to organize computation on a highly dynamic system at a planetary scale while relying on a negligible amount of knowledge about its state.

27.2.3   Scheduling

Decentralized scheduling is a field that has recently attracted considerable attention. Two-level scheduling schemes have been considered [26, 27], but these are not scalable enough for the Internet. In the scheduling heuristic described by Leangsuksun et al. [28], each machine attempts to map tasks onto itself and its K nearest-neighbors. This appears to require that each machine have an estimate of the execution time of subtasks on each of its neighbors, as well as of the bandwidth of the links to these other machines. It is not clear that this information will be available in large-scale and dynamic environments.

G-Commerce was a study of dynamic resource allocation on a grid in terms of computational market economies in which applications must buy resources at a market price influenced by demand [29]. Although conceptually decentralized, if implemented this scheme would require the equivalent of centralized commodity markets (or banks, auction houses, etc.) where offer and demand meet, and commodity prices can be determined.

Recently, a new autonomous and decentralized approach to scheduling has been proposed to address specifically the needs of large grid and peer-to-peer platforms. In this bandwidth-centric protocol, the computation is organized around a tree-structured overlay network with the origin of the tasks at the root [19]. Each node in the system sends tasks to and receives results from its K nearest-neighbors, according to bandwidth constraints. One shortcoming of this scheme is that the structure of the tree, and consequently the performance of the system, depends completely on the initial structure of the overlay network. This lack of dynamism is bound to affect the performance of the scheme and might also limit the number of machines that can participate in a computation.

27.2.4 Self-Organization of Complex Systems

The organization of many complex biological and social systems has been explained in terms of the aggregations of a large number of autonomous entities that behave according to simple rules. According to this theory, complicated patterns can emerge from the interplay of many agents despite the simplicity of the rules [30, 31]. The existence of this mechanism, often referred to as *emergence*, has been proposed to explain patterns such as shell motifs, animal coats, neural structures, and social behavior. In particular, certain complex behaviors of social insects such as ants and bees have been studied in detail, and their applications to the solution of specific computer science problems has been proposed [18, 32]. In a departure from the methodological approach followed in previous projects, we did not try to accurately reproduce a naturally occurring behavior. Rather, we started with a problem and then designed a completely artificial behavior that would result in a satisfactory solution to it. Our work was inspired by a particular version of the emergence principle called Local Activation, Long-range Inhibition (LALI), which was recently shown to be responsible for the formation of a complex pattern using a clever experiment on ants [33].

27.2.5 Strongly Mobile Agents

To make progress with frequent reclamations of desktop machines, current systems rely on different forms of checkpointing: automatic, for example, SETI@home, or voluntary, for example, Legion. The storage and computational overheads of checkpointing put constraints on the design of a system. To avoid this drawback, desktop grids need to support the asynchronous and transparent migration of processes across machine boundaries.

Mobile agents [34] have relocation autonomy. These agents offer a flexible means of distributing data and code around a network, of dynamically moving between hosts as resource availability varies, and of carrying multiple threads of execution to simultaneously perform computation, decentralized scheduling, and communication with other agents. There have been some previous attempts to use mobile agents for grid computing or distributed computing [35–38].

Most of the mobile agent systems that have been developed until now are Java-based. However, the execution model of the Java Virtual Machine does not permit an agent to access its execution state, which is why Java-based mobility libraries can only provide *weak mobility* [39]. Weak mobile agent systems such as IBM's Aglets framework [40] do not migrate the execution state of methods. The go() method, used to move an agent from one virtual machine to another, simply does not return. When an agent moves to a new location, the threads currently executing in it are killed without saving their state. The lifeless agent is then shipped to its destination and restarted there. Weak mobility forces programmers to use a difficult programming style, that is, the use of callback methods, to account for the absence of migration transparency.

By contrast, agent systems with *strong mobility* provide the abstraction that the execution of the agent is uninterrupted, even as its location changes. Applications where agents migrate from host to host while communicating with one another are severely restricted by the absence of strong mobility. Strong mobility also allows programmers to use a far more natural programming style.

The ability of a system to support the migration of an agent at any time by an external thread is termed *forced mobility*. This is essential in desktop grid systems, because owners need to be able to reclaim their resources. Forced mobility is difficult to implement without strong mobility.

We provide strong and forced mobility for the full Java programming language by using a preprocessor that translates an extension of Java with strong mobility into weakly mobile Java code that explicitly maintains the execution state for all threads as a mobile data structure [41, 42]. For the weakly mobile code, target, we currently use IBM's Aglets framework [40]. The generated weakly mobile code maintains a movable execution state for each thread at all times.

27.2.6   Organic Grid Architecture

27.2.6.1   Overview   One of the works that inspired our project was the bandwidth-centric protocol proposed by Kreaseck et al. [19], in which a grid computation is organized around a tree-structured overlay network with the origin of the tasks at the root. A tree overlay network represents a natural and intuitive way of distributing tasks and collecting results. The drawback of the original scheme is that the performance and the degree of utilization of the system depend entirely on the initial assignment of the overlay network.

In contrast, we have developed our systems to be adaptive without any knowledge about machine configurations, connection bandwidths, network topology, and assuming only a minimal amount of initial information. While our scheme is also based on a tree structure, our overlay network keeps changing to adapt to system conditions. Our tree adaptation mechanism is driven by the perceived performance of a node's children, measured passively as part of the ongoing computation [43]. From the point of view of network topology, our system starts with a small amount of knowledge in the form of a "friends list," and then keeps building its own overlay network on the fly. Information from each node's "friends list" is shared with other nodes, so the initial configuration of the lists is not critical. The only assumption we rely upon is that a "friends list" is available initially on each node to prime the system; solutions for the construction of such lists have been developed in the context of peer-to-peer file sharing [25, 44] and will not be addressed in this paper.

To make the tree adaptive, we rely on a particular version of the emergence principle called LALI. The LALI rule is based on two types of interactions: a positive, reinforcing one that works over a short range, and a negative, destructive one that works over longer distances. We retain the LALI principle but with the following modification: we use a definition of distance which is based on a performance-based metric. In our experiment, distance is based on the perceived throughput, which is a function of communication bandwidth and computational throughput. Nodes are initially recruited using the "friends list" in a way that is completely oblivious of distance, therefore propagating computation on distant nodes with same probability as close ones. During the course of the computation agents behavior encourages the propagation of computation among well-connected nodes while discouraging the inclusion of distant (i.e. less responsive) agents.

In the natural phenomena, the emergence principle is often invoked to explain the formation of patterns. In the Organic Grid it is possible to define the physical pattern of a computation as the physical allocation of the agents to computing resources such as communication links, computing nodes, data repositories. Two examples of computation patterns on a grid are illustrated in Figure 27.1, where nodes are represented as dots (double circle is the starting node) and links as lines of thickness proportional to the bandwidth. Figure 27.1a represents a pattern that could be obtained by recruiting nodes at random. A more desirable pattern would be one where the availability of resources is taken into account in deciding where to run agents. For example, in a data-intensive, ITA such as BLAST [45], a factor of merit should be not only the processing power of a node but also the available bandwidth of the intervening link. Assuming for simplicity that nodes are homogeneous, a desirable pattern of computation is one where nodes connected to high bandwidth links are eventually more likely to be retained in the computation, as in Figure 27.1b.

The main challenge of programming the Organic Grid is designing an agent behavior that produces a desirable physical pattern of computation. The agent design we adopted for running BLAST promotes the formation of a physical pattern that approximates the one shown in Figure 27.1b. It is important to note that the criteria defining what is a desirable pattern are specific for each class of application, and therefore the agent design must be taylored to the requirement of each class.

The methodology we followed to design the agent behavior is as follows. We selected a tree-structured overlay network as the fundamental logical pattern around which to organize the computation. We then empirically determined the simplest agent

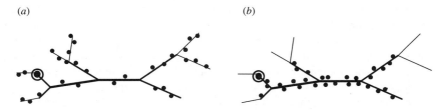

(a) (b)

Figure 27.1 Example of physical pattern of computation on a network; nodes are represented as dots (double circle is starting node) and links as lines of thickness proportional to the bandwidth. (a) A configuration obtained by recruiting nodes at random and (b) a desirable pattern showing clustering of the computation around available resources by selective recruitment and dropping of nodes.

behavior that would (i) generate the tree overlay and (ii) organize basic tasks such as agent-to-agent communication and task distribution according to such tree pattern. We then augmented the basic behavior in such a way that introduced other desirable properties. With the total computation time as the performance metric, every addition to the basic scheme was separately evaluated and its contribution to total performance, assessed quantitatively.

One such property is the continuous monitoring of the performance of the child nodes. We assumed that no knowledge is initially available on the system, instead passive feedback from child nodes is used to measure their effective performance, for example, the product of computational speed and communication bandwidth.

Another property is continuous, on-the-fly adaptation using the restructuring algorithm presented in Section 27.2.6.4. Basically, the overlay tree is incrementally restructured while the computation is in progress by pushing fast nodes up toward the root of the tree. Other functions that were found to be critical for performance were the automatic determination of parameters such as prefetching and task size, the detection of cycles, the detection of dead nodes, and the end of the computation.

In this paper, we focus on the solution to one particular problem: the scheduling of the independent, identical subtasks of an ITA whose data initially reside at one location. The size of individual subtasks and of their results is large, and so transfer times cannot be neglected. The application that we have used for our experiments is NCBI's nucleotide–nucleotide sequence comparison tool BLAST [45].

Our choice of using an ITA for our proof-of-concept implementation follows a common practice in grid scheduling research. However, our scheme is enough to accommodate other classes of applications. In a recent article, we have demonstrated using a fault-tolerant implementation of Cannon's matrix multiplication algorithm that our scheduling scheme can be adapted to applications with communicating tasks [46, 47].

27.2.6.2   *Basic Agent Design*   A large computational task is encapsulated in a strongly mobile agent. This task should be divisible into a number of independent subtasks. A user starts the computation agent on his/her machine. One thread of the agent begins executing subtasks sequentially. The agent is also prepared to receive requests for work from other machines. If the machine has any uncomputed subtask, and receives a request for work from another machine, it sends a clone of itself to the requesting machine. The requester is now this machine's *child*.

The clone asks its parent for a certain number of subtasks to work on, s. A thread begins to compute the subtasks. Other threads are created — when required — to communicate with the parent or other machines. When work requests are received, the agent dispatches its own clone to the requester. The computation spreads in this manner. The topology of the resulting overlay network is a tree with the originating machine at the root node.

An agent requests its parent for more work when it has executed its own subtasks. Even if the parent does not have the requested number of subtasks, it will respond and send its child what it can. The parent keeps a record of the number of subtasks that remain to be sent, and sends a request to its own parent. Every time a node of

```
receive request for s subtasks from node c

// c may be the node itself

if subtask_list.size>=s

  c.send_subtasks(s)

else

  c.send_subtasks(subtask_list.size)

  outstanding_subtask_queue.

    add(c,s--subtask_list.size)

  parent.

    send_request(outstanding_subtask_queue.

        total_subtasks)
```

Figure 27.2 Behavior of node on receiving request.

the tree obtains *r* results, either computed by itself or obtained from a child, it sends them to its parent. This message includes a request for all pending subtasks. This can be seen in Figures 27.2 and 27.3.

27.2.6.3 *Maintenance of Child-Lists* Each node has up to *c* active children, and up to *p* potential children. Ideally, $c + p$ is chosen so as to strike a balance between a tree that is too deep (long delays in data propagation) and one that is too wide (inefficient distribution of data).

```
receive t subtasks from parent

subtask_list.add(t)

if outstanding_subtask_queue.

    total_subtasks>=t

  <send t subtasks to nodes in

  outstanding_subtask_queue>

else

  <send outstanding_subtask_queue.

  total_subtasks subtasks to nodes in

  outstanding_subtask_queue>

// may include subtasks for node itself
```

Figure 27.3 Behavior of node on receiving subtasks.

```
receive feedback from node c
if child_list.contains(c)
    child_list.update_rank(c)
else
    child_list.add(c)
    if child_list.size>MAX_CHILD_LIST_SIZE
        sc:=child_list.slowest
        child_list.remove(sc)
        old_child_list.add(sc)
        inverted_child_list:=inv(child_list)
        sc.send_ancestor_list(inverted_child_list)
```

Figure 27.4   Behavior of parent node on receiving feedback.

The active children are ranked by their performance. The performance metric is application-dependent. For an ITA, a child is evaluated by the rate at which it sends in results. When a child sends r results, the node measures the time interval since the last time it sent r results. The final result-rate of this child is calculated as an average of the last R such time intervals. This ranking is a reflection of the performance of not just a child, but of the entire subtree with the child node at its root.

Potential children are the ones which the current node has not yet been able to evaluate. A potential child is added to the active child-list once it has sent enough results to the current node. If the node now has more than c children, the slowest child, sc, is removed from the child-list. As described below, sc is then given a list of other nodes, which it can contact to try and get back into the tree. The current node keeps a record of the last o former children, and sc is now placed in this list. Nodes are purged from this list once a sufficient, user-defined time period elapses. During that interval of time, messages from sc will be ignored. This avoids thrashing and excessive dynamism in the tree. The pseudo-code for the maintenance of child-lists has been presented in Figure 27.4.

27.2.6.4   *Restructuring of the Overlay Network*   The topology of the overlay network is a tree, and it is desirable for the best-performing nodes to be close to the root. In the case of an ITA, both computational speed and link bandwidth contribute to a node's effective performance. Having well-connected nodes close to the top enhances the extraction of subtasks from the root and minimizes the communication delay between the root and the best nodes. Therefore the overlay network is constantly being restructured so that the nodes with the highest throughput migrate toward the root, pushing those with low throughput toward the leaves.

A node periodically informs its parent about its best-performing child. The parent then checks whether its grandchild is present in its list of former children. If not, it

```
receive node b from node c

if old_child_list.not_contains(b)

  potential_child_list.add(b)

  c.send_accept_child(b)

else

  c.send_reject_child(b)
```

Figure 27.5 Behavior of parent node on receiving propagated child.

adds the grandchild to its list of potential children and tells this node that it is willing to consider the grandchild. The node then instructs its child to contact its grandparent directly. If the contact ends in a promotion, the entire subtree with the child node at its root will move one level higher in the tree. This constant restructuring results in fast nodes percolating toward the root of the tree and has been detailed in Figures 27.5 and 27.6. The checking of a promising child against a list of former children prevents the occurrence of trashing due to consecutive promotions and demotions of the same node.

When a node updates its child-list and decides to remove its slowest child, *sc*, it does not simply discard the child. It prepares a list of its children in descending order of performance, that is, slowest node first. The list is sent to *sc*, which attempts to contact those nodes in turn. As the first nodes that are contacted are the slower ones, the tree is sought to be kept balanced. The actions of a node on receipt of a new list of ancestors are shown in Figure 27.7.

```
receive accept_child(b) from parent

// a request was earlier made to parent

// about node b

b.send_ancestor_list(ancestor_list)

// b will now contact parent directly
```

Figure 27.6 Behavior of child node on receiving positive response.

```
receive message from parent

ancestor_list := message.ancestor_list

if parent != ancestor_list.last

  parent:=ancestor_list.last
```

Figure 27.7 Behavior of node on receiving new ancestor-list.

27.2.6.5 Size of Result Burst   Each agent of an ITA ranks its children on the basis of the time taken to send some results to this node. The time required to obtain just one result-burst, or a result-burst of size 1, might not be a good measure of the performance of a child. Nodes might make poor decisions about which children to keep and discard. The child propagation algorithm benefits from using the average of R result-burst intervals and from setting r, the result-burst size, to be greater than 1. A better measure for the performance of a child is the time taken by a node to obtain $r * (R + 1)$ results. However, r and R should not be set to very large values because the overlay network would take too much time to take form and to get updated.

27.2.6.6 Fault Tolerance   If the parent of a node were to become inaccessible due to machine or link failures, the node and its own descendants would be disconnected from the tree. The application might require that a node remain in the tree at all times. In this scenario, the node must be able to contact its parent's ancestors. Every node keeps a (constant size) list of a of its ancestors. This list is updated every time its parent sends it a message. The updates to the ancestor-list take into account the possibility of the topology of the overlay network changing frequently.

A child sends a message to its parent — the ath node in its ancestor-list. If it is unable to contact the parent, it sends a message to the $(a - 1)$th node in that list. This goes on until an ancestor responds to this node's request. The ancestor becomes the parent of the current node and normal operation resumes.

If a node's ancestor-list goes down to size 0, it attempts to obtain the address of some other agent by checking its data distribution and communication overlays. If these are the same as the scheduling tree, the node has no means of obtaining any more work to do. The mobile agent informs the agent environment that no useful work is being done by this machine, before self-destructing. The environment begins to send out requests for work to a list of friends. The pseudo-code for the fault tolerance algorithm is shown in Figure 27.8.

To recover from the loss of tasks by failing nodes, every node keeps track of unfinished subtasks that were sent to children. If a child requests additional work and no new task can be obtained from the parent, unfinished tasks are handed out again.

```
while true

  send message to parent

  if <unable to contact parent>

    ancestor_list.remove(parent)

    if ancestor_list.size = 0

      <find-new-parent or self-destruct>

    parent := ancestor_list.last
```

Figure 27.8   Fault tolerance — contacting ancestors.

27.2.6.7 Cycles in the Overlay Network Even though the scheduling overlay network should be a tree, failures could cause the formation of a cycle of nodes. The system recovers from this situation by having each node examines its ancestor-list on receiving it from its parent. If a node finds itself in that list, it knows that a cycle has occurred. The node attempts to break the cycle by obtaining the address of some other agent on its data distribution or communication overlays. However, if these are identical to the scheduling overlay, the node will be starved of work. If the agent is starved of work for more than a specified time, it self-destructs.

27.2.6.8 Termination The root of the tree is informed when the computational task has been completed. It sends a termination message to each of its actual, potential, and former children. The computation agent on the root then self-destructs. The children of the root do the same. Termination messages spread down to the leaves and the computation terminates. There are two scenarios in which termination could be incomplete:

1. A termination message might not reach a node. The situation is the same as that described in Section 27.2.6.6.
2. Consider that computation agents are executing on nodes $n1$ and $n2$. $n1$ receives a termination message, but $n2$ does not because of a failure. The agent on $n1$ destroys itself. $n1$ now sends request messages to its friends. If one of these is $n2$, a clone of $n2$'s agent is sent to $n1$.

An unchecked spread of computation will not occur because agents send out clones only if they do not have any uncomputed subtasks. $n1$ and $n2$ will eventually run out of subtasks and destroy themselves as explained in Section 27.2.6.6.

27.2.6.9 Self-Adjustment of Task List Size A node always requests a certain number of subtasks and obtains their results before requesting more subtasks to work on. The size of a subtask is simply an estimation of the smallest unit of work that every machine on the peer-to-peer network should be able to compute in a time that the user considers reasonable; scheduling should not be inordinately slow on account of subtasks that take a long time to compute. However, in an ITA-type application, the utilization of a high-performance machine may be poor because it is only requesting a fixed number of subtasks at a time.

A node may request more subtasks to increase the utilization of its resources and to improve the system computation-to-data ratio. A node requests a certain number of subtasks, t, that it will compute itself. Once it has finished computing the t subtasks, it compares the average time to compute a subtask on this run with that of the previous run. Depending on whether it performed better, worse, or about the same, the node requests $i(t)$, $d(t)$, or t subtasks for its next run, where $i(t) > t$ and $d(t) < t$.

27.2.6.10 Prefetching A potential cause of slowdown in the basic scheduling scheme described earlier is the delay at each node due to its waiting for new subtasks.

This is because it needs to wait while its requests propagate up the tree to the root and subtasks propagate down the tree to the node.

It might be beneficial to use prefetching to reduce the time that a node waits for subtasks. A node determines that it should request t subtasks from its parent. It also makes an optimistic prediction of how many subtasks it might require in future by using the i function that is used for self-adjustment. $i(t)$ subtasks are then requested from the parent. When a node finishes computing one set of subtasks, more subtasks are readily available for it to work on, even as a request is submitted to the parent. This interleaving of computation and communication reduces the time for which a node is idle.

Although prefetching will reduce the delay in obtaining new subtasks to work on, it increases the amount of data that need to be transferred at a time from the root to the current node, thus increasing the synchronization delay and data transfer time. This is why excessively aggressive prefetching will result in a performance degradation.

27.3 MEASUREMENTS

We have conducted experiments to evaluate the performance of each aspect of our scheduling scheme. The experiments were performed on a cluster of 18 heterogeneous machines at different locations around Ohio. The machines ran the `Aglets` weak mobility agent environment on top of either Linux or Solaris.

The application we used to test our system was the gene sequence similarity search tool, NCBI's nucleotide–nucleotide BLAST [45] — a representative ITA. The mobile agents started up a BLAST executable to perform the actual computation. The task was to match a 256 kB sequence against 320 data chunks, each of size 512 kB. Each subtask was to match the sequence against one chunk. Chunks flow down the overlay tree whereas results flow up to the root. An agent cannot migrate during the execution of the BLAST code; as our experiments do not require strong mobility, this limitation is irrelevant to our measurements.

All 18 machines would have offered good performance as they all had fast connections to the Internet, high processor speeds, and large memories. To obtain more heterogeneity in their performance, we introduced delays in the application code so that we could simulate the effect of slower machines and slower network connections. We divided the machines into fast, medium, and slow categories by introducing delays in the application code.

As shown in Figure 27.9, the nodes were initially organized randomly. The dotted arrows indicate the directions in which request messages for work were sent to friends. The only thing a machine knew about a friend was its URL. We ran the computation with the parameters described in Table 27.2. Linear self-adjustment means that the increasing and decreasing functions of the number of subtasks requested at each node are linear. The time required for the code and the first subtask to arrive at the different nodes can be seen in Figure 27.10. This is the same for all experiments.

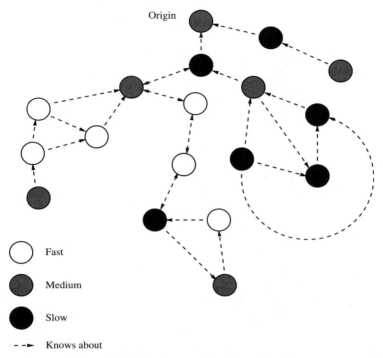

Figure 27.9 Random configuration of machines.

27.3.1 Comparison with Knowledge-Based Scheme

The purpose of this chapter is to evaluate the quality of the configuration which is autonomously determined by our scheme for different initial conditions.

Two experiments were conducted using the parameters described in Table 27.2. In the first, we manually created a good initial configuration assuming *a priori* knowledge of system parameters. We then ran the application and verified that the final configuration did not substantially depart from the initial one. We consider a good

TABLE 27.2 Original Parameters

Parameter Name	Parameter Value
Maximum children	5
Maximum potential children	5
Result-burst size	3
Self-adjustment	Linear
Number of subtasks initially requested	1
Child-propagation	On

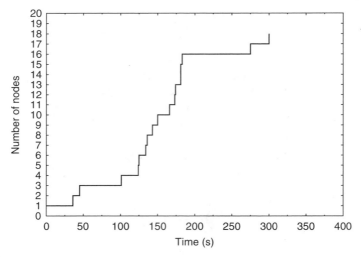

Figure 27.10   Code ramp-up.

configuration to be one in which fast nodes are nearer the root. Figures 27.11 and 27.12 represent the start and end of this experiment. The final tree configuration shows that fast nodes are kept near the root and that the system is constantly re-evaluating every node for possible relocation (as shown by the three rightmost children which are under evaluation by the root).

We began the second experiment with the completely random configuration shown in Figure 27.9. The resulting configuration shown in Figure 27.13 is substantially similar to the good configurations of the previous experiment; if the execution time had been longer, the migration toward the root of the two fast nodes at depths 2 and

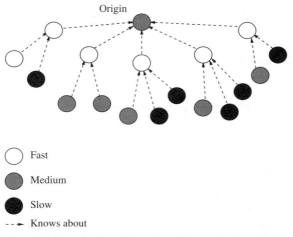

Figure 27.11   Good configuration with a priori knowledge.

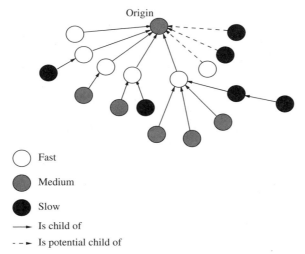

Figure 27.12   Final node organization, result-burst size = 3, good initial configuration.

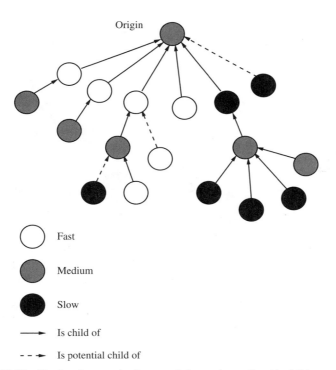

Figure 27.13   Final node organization, result-burst size = 3, with child propagation.

TABLE 27.3   Effect of Prior Knowledge

Configuration	Running Time (s)
Original	2294
Good	1781

3 would have been complete. Table 27.3 shows the difference in running time in the two experiments.

27.3.2 Effect of Child Propagation

We performed our computation with the child-propagation aspect of the scheduling scheme disabled. Comparisons of the running times and topologies are in Table 27.4

TABLE 27.4   Effect of Child Propagation

Scheme	Running Time (s)
With	2294
Without	3035

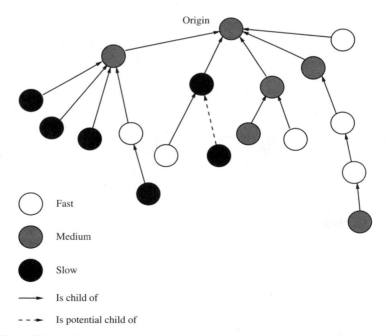

Figure 27.14 Final node organization, result-burst size = 3, no child propagation.

TABLE 27.5   **Effect of Result-Burst Size**

Result-Burst Size	Running Time (s)
1	3050
3	2294
5	2320
8	3020

and Figures 27.13 and 27.14. The child-propagation mechanism results in a 32% improvement in the running time. The reason for this improvement is the difference in the topologies. With child-propagation turned on, the best-performing nodes are closer to the root. Subtasks and results travel to and from these nodes at a faster rate, thus improving system throughput and preventing the root from becoming a bottleneck. This mechanism is the most effective aspect of our scheduling scheme.

27.3.3 Result-Burst Size

The experimental setup in Table 27.2 was again used. We then ran the experiment with different result-burst sizes. The running times have been tabulated in Table 27.5. The child evaluations that are made by nodes from one result are poor. The nodes' child-lists change frequently and are far from ideal, as in Figure 27.15.

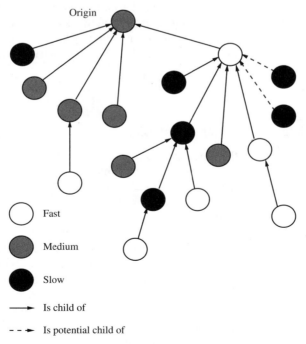

Figure 27.15   Node organization, result-burst size = 1.

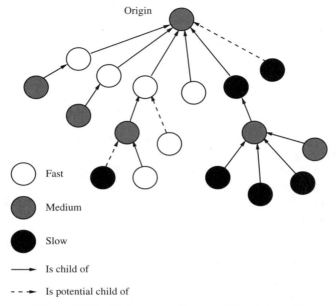

Figure 27.16   Node organization, result-burst size = 3.

There is a qualitative improvement in the child-lists as the result-burst size increases. The structure of the resulting overlay networks for result-burst sizes 3 and 5 are in Figures 27.16 and 27.17. However, with very large result-bursts, it takes longer for the tree overlay to form and adapt, thus slowing down the experiment. This can be seen in Figure 27.18.

27.3.4   Prefetching and Initial Task Size

The data ramp-up time is the time required for subtasks to reach every single node. Prefetching has a positive effect on this. The minimum number of subtasks that each node requests also affects the data ramp-up. The greater this number, the greater the amount of data that need to be sent to each node, and the slower the data ramp-up. This can be seen in Table 27.6 and Figures 27.19–27.23.

Prefetching does improves the ramp-up, but its effect on the overall running time of an experiment is of paramount importance. This is also closely related to the minimum number of subtasks requested by each node. Prefetching improves system throughput when the minimum number of subtasks requested is 1. As the minimum number of subtasks requested by a node increases, more data need to be transferred at a time from the root to this node, and the effect of prefetching becomes negligible. As this number increases further, prefetching actually causes a degradation in throughput. Table 27.6 and Figure 27.24 summarize these results.

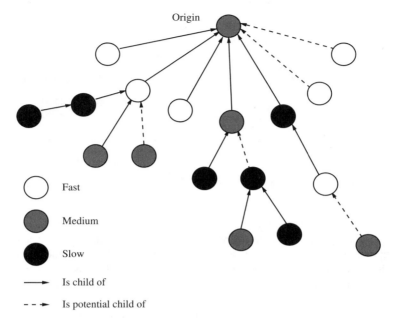

Figure 27.17   Node organization, result-burst size = 5.

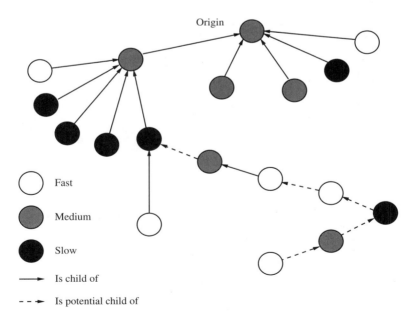

Figure 27.18   Node organization, result-burst size = 8.

TABLE 27.6   Effect of Prefetching and Minimum Number of Subtasks

No. of Subtasks	Ramp-up Time (s)		Running Time (s)	
	Prefetching	No Prefetching	Prefetching	No Prefetching
1	406	590	2308	2520
2	825	979	2302	2190
5	939	1575	2584	2197

27.3.5 Self-Adjustment

We ran an experiment using the configuration in Table 27.2 and then did the same using constant and exponential self-adjustment functions instead of the linear one. The data ramp-ups have been compared in Table 27.7 and Figure 27.25. The ramp-up with exponential self-adjustment is appreciably faster than that with linear or constant self-adjustment. The aggressive approach performs better because nodes prefetch a larger amount of subtasks, and subtasks quickly reach the nodes farthest from the root.

We also compared the running times of the three runs which are given in Table 27.7. Interestingly, the run with the exponential self-adjustment performed poorly for other runs. This is due to nodes prefetching extremely large numbers of subtasks. Nodes now

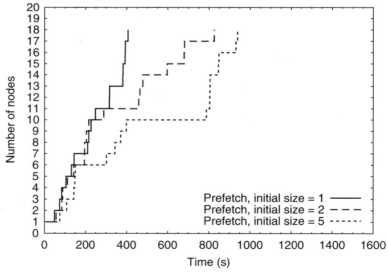

Figure 27.19   Effect of minimum number of subtasks on data ramp-up with prefetching.

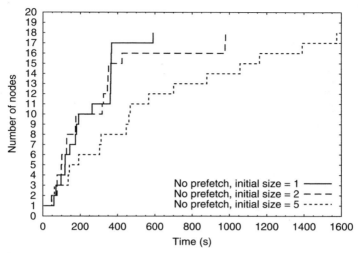

Figure 27.20 Effect of minimum number of subtasks on data ramp-up without prefetching.

spend more time waiting for their requests to be satisfied, resulting in a degradation in the throughput at that node.

The linear case was expected to perform better than the constant one, but the observed difference was insignificant. We expect this difference to be more pronounced with longer experimental runs and a larger number of subtasks.

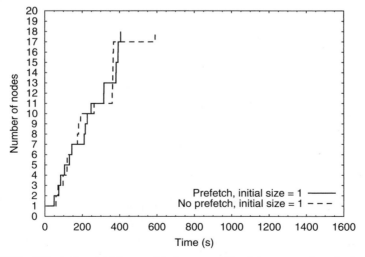

Figure 27.21 Effect of prefetching on data ramp-up with minimum number of subtasks = 1.

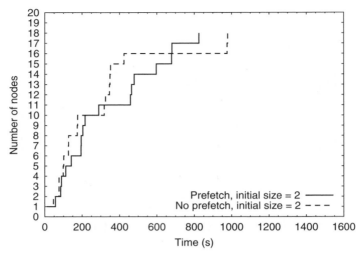

Figure 27.22 Effect of prefetching on data ramp-up with minimum number of subtasks = 2.

27.3.6 Number of Children

We conducted experiments with different child-list sizes and found that the data ramp-up time with the maximum number of children set to 5 was less than that with the maximum number of children set to 10 or 20. These results are given in Table 27.8. The root is able to take on more children in the latter cases and the spread of subtasks to nodes that were originally far from the root takes less time.

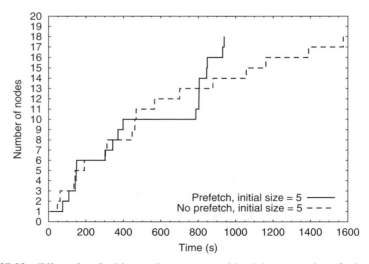

Figure 27.23 Effect of prefetching on data ramp-up with minimum number of subtasks = 5.

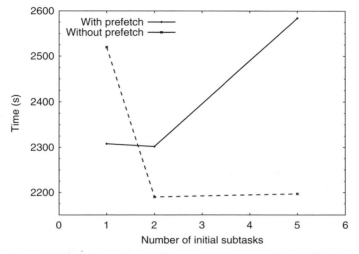

Figure 27.24 Effect of prefetching and minimum number of subtasks.

TABLE 27.7   Effect of Self-Adjustment Function

Self-Adjustment Function	Ramp-Up Time (s)	Running Time (s)
Linear	1068	2302
Constant	1142	2308
Exponential	681	2584

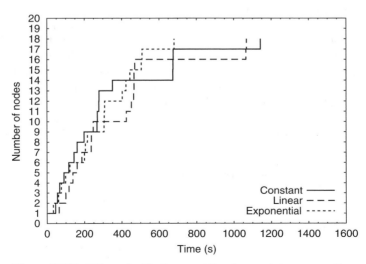

Figure 27.25 Effect of self-adjustment function on data ramp-up time.

TABLE 27.8   Effect of Number of Children on Data Ramp-up

Maximum Number of Children	Time (s)
5	1068
10	760
20	778

Instead of exhibiting better performance, the runs where large numbers of children were allowed had approximately the same total running time as the run with the maximum number of children set to 5. This is because children have to wait for a longer time for their requests to be satisfied.

To obtain a better idea of the effect of several children waiting for their requests to be satisfied, we ran two experiments: one with the good initial configuration of Figure 27.11 and the other using a star topology — every non-root node was adjacent to the root at the beginning of the experiment itself. The maximum sizes of the child-lists were set to 5 and 20, respectively. As the overlay networks were already organized such that there would be little change in their topology as the computation progressed, there was minimal impact of these changes on the overall running time. The effect of the size of the child-list was then clearly observed as in Table 27.9. Similar results were observed even when the child-propagation mechanisms were turned off.

27.4   CONCLUSIONS

We have designed an autonomic scheduling algorithm in which multi-threaded agents with strong mobility form a tree-structured overlay network. The structure of this tree is varied dynamically such that the nodes that currently exhibit good performance are brought closer to the root, thus improving the performance of the system.

We have described experiments with scheduling a representative computational biology application whose data initially resides at one location and whose subtasks have considerable data transfer times. The experiments were conducted on a set of machines distributed across Ohio. Although this paper concentrated on a scheduling scheme for ITAs, we are experimenting with adapting the algorithm for a wide class of

TABLE 27.9   Effect of Number of Children on Running Time

Maximum Number of Children	Time (s)
5	1781
20	2041

applications. Recent results show that our approach can be adapted to communicating applications, such as Cannon's algorithm for parallel matrix multiplication [46, 47].

It is our intention to present a desktop grid application developer with a simple application programming interface that will allow him/her to customize the scheduling scheme to the characteristics of an application. A prototype of this has already been implemented.

An important problem that we will address in future is the initial assignment of the friend-list. There has been some research on the problem of assigning friend-lists [25, 44], and we will consider how best to apply this to our own work.

The experimental platform was a set of 18 heterogeneous machines. In future, we plan to harness the computing power of idle machines across the Internet by running a mobile agent platform inside a screen saver to create a desktop grid of a scale of the tens or hundreds of thousands. Researchers will then be free to deploy scientific applications on this system.

27.5 FUTURE DIRECTIONS

Despite the obvious success of current master–workers Internet computing systems such as SETI@home and folding@home, the range of applications that can be successfully employed with this approach is still limited. In this section, we describe some applicative scenarios that showcase the Organic Grid advantage over current approaches, and how it could substantially expand the use of large-scale Internet computing.

Ab initio prediction of protein folding involves the simulation of molecule folding using interatomic forces. This type of simulation requires the analysis of a very large number of atomic conformations over an energy landscape. The exploration of the conformational space can in principle be parceled to different nodes, but some kind of periodic data exchange is needed to ensure that only the simulation of the most promising conformations are carried forward.

An example of this approach is the "synchronize and exchange" algorithm called replica exchange molecular dynamics used in the Folding@home project [48]. This requires light communication that can go through the root but could be made more scalable with horizontal communication. Furthermore, so far only simple proteins have been studied with the folding@home system. Complex molecular systems (i.e., protein–solvent interaction) could be studied by adopting more sophisticated molecular dynamic simulation algorithms, which typically need more internode communication. One of these algorithms is GROMACS, which assumes a ring node topology and has been parallelized using PVM and MPI [49, 50].

Another promising applicative scenario for the Organic Grid is phylogenetic analysis. To make evolutionary and functional inferences, biologists use evolutionary trees to find correlated features in DNA and phenotypes and derive evolutionary or functional inferences. Evolutionary tree search is computationally intensive as the number of candidate trees is combinatorially explosive as more organisms are considered.

Commonly used heuristics include the consideration of many candidate trees with randomization of the order in which organisms are added as trees are built.

Most advances in parallel computing for evolutionary trees follow a coarse-grained approach in which candidate trees are evaluated independently in a one-replica-per-processor strategy. This strategy reduces overall search time but only allows the investigator to evaluate a number of trees concurrently rather than evaluating a single tree faster. An Organic Grid implementation could allow the parallelization of a candidate tree analysis by enabling horizontal communication between same level nodes in a tree overlay. Faster methods to evalutate single trees are crucial because with the advent of rapid whole genome-sequencing technologies researchers are beginning to consider entire genomes for tens to hundreds of organisms.

The Organic Grid support for arbitrary communication topologies could open the door to the use of algorithms previously unfit for implementation on a desktop grid. As demonstrated in our matrix multiplication experiment [46, 47], the agent behavior can be personalized to build an application-specific communication overlay in addition to the service tree overlay, with only a minimal amount of modifications required to the application itself.

ACKNOWLEDGMENTS

This work was partially funded with Ohio Supercomputer Center grants PAS0036-1 and PAS0121-1.

REFERENCES

1. I. Foster, C. Kesselman, and S. Tuecke, The anatomy of the grid: enabling scalable virtual organizations, *Int. J. High Perform. Comput. Appl.*, 15 (3), 2001.
2. I. Foster, C. Kesselman, J. Nick, and S. Tuecke, The physiology of the grid: an open grid services architecture for distributed systems integration, 2002. http://www.globus.org/research/papers.html.
3. The SETI@home project. http://setiathome.ssl.berkeley.edu.
4. The folding@home project. http://folding.stanford.edu.
5. A. A. Chien, B. Calder, S. Elbert, and K. Bhatia, Entropia: architecture and performance of an enterprise desktop grid system, *J. Parall. Distr. Comput.*, 63 (5), 597–610 (2003).
6. Berkeley Open Infrastructure for Network Computing (BOINC). http://boinc.berkeley.edu/.
7. G. Woltman, Web site for the Marsenne Prime project at http://www.mersenne.org/prime.htm.
8. M. Litzkow, M. Livny, and M. Mutka, Condor — a Hunter of Idle Workstations, in *Proceedings of the Eigth International Conference of Distributed Computing Systems*, June 1988.

9. M. Maheswaran, S. Ali, H. J. Siegel, D. A. Hensgen, and R. F. Freund, Dynamic Matching and Scheduling of a Class of Independent Tasks onto Heterogeneous Computing Systems, in *Proceedings of the Eighth Heterogeneous Computing Workshop*, April 1999, pp. 30–44.

10. E. Heymann, M. A. Senar, E. Luque, and M. Livny, Adaptive Scheduling for Master–Worker Applications on the Computational Grid, in *Proceedings of the First International Workshop on Grid Computing*, 2000.

11. T. Kindberg, A. Sahiner, and Y. Paker, Adaptive Parallelism Under Equus, in *Proceedings of the Second International Workshop on Configurable Distributed Systems*, March 1994, pp. 172–184.

12. D. Buaklee, G. Tracy, M. K. Vernon, and S. Wright, Near-Optimal Adaptive Control of a Large Grid Application, in *Proceedings of the International Conference on Supercomputing*, June 2002.

13. N. T. Karonis, B. Toonen, and I. Foster, MPICH-G2: a grid-enabled implementation of the message passing interface, *J. Parall. Distr. Compu.*, 63 (5), 551–563 (2003).

14. A. S. Grimshaw and W. A. Wulf, The legion vision of a worldwide virtual computer, *Commun. ACM*, 40 (1), 39–45 (1997).

15. F. Berman, R. Wolski, H. Casanova, W. Cirne, H. Dail, M. Faerman, S. Figueira, J. Hayes, G. Obertelli, J. Schopf, G. Shao, S. Smallen, N. Spring, A. Su, and D. Zagorodnov, Adaptive computing on the grid using AppLeS, *IEEE Trans. Parall. Distr. Syst.*, 14 (4), 369–382 (2003).

16. D. Abramson, J. Giddy, and L. Kotler, High-Performance Parametric Modeling with Nimrod/G: Killer Application for the Global Grid? in *Proceedings of International Parallel and Distributed Processing Symposium*, May 2000, pp. 520–528.

17. I. Taylor, M. Shields, and I. Wang, *Grid Resource Management*, Chapter 1 — Resource Management of Triana P2P Services, Kluwer Academic Publishers, 2003.

18. A. Montresor, H. Meling, and O. Babaoglu, Messor: Load-Balancing Through a Swarm of Autonomous Agents, in *Proceedings of the First Workshop on Agent and Peer-to-Peer Systems*, July 2002.

19. B. Kreaseck, L. Carter, H. Casanova, and J. Ferrante, Autonomous Protocols for Bandwidth-Centric Scheduling of Independent-Task Applications, in *Proceedings of the International Parallel and Distributed Processing Symposium*, April 2003, pp. 23–25.

20. The Globus Project. http://www.globus.org.

21. J. F. Shoch and J. A. Hupp, The "worm" programs — early experience with a distributed computation, *Commun. ACM*, 25 (3), 172–180 (1982).

22. United Devices. http://www.ud.com.

23. A. Oram, *Peer-to-Peer: Harnessing the Power of Disruptive Technologies*, O'Reilly, 2001.

24. C. Shirky, What is P2P … and what isn't? *O'Reilly Network*, November 2000.

25. The Gnutella download. http://www.gnutelliums.com.

26. H. James, K. Hawick, and P. Coddington, Scheduling Independent Tasks on Metacomputing Systems, in *Proceedings of the Parallel and Distributed Computing Systems*, August 1999.

27. J. Santoso, G. D. van Albada, B. A. A. Nazief, and P. M. A. Sloot, Hierarchical Job Scheduling for Clusters Of Workstations, in *Proceedings of the Sixth Annual Conference of the Advanced School for Computing and Imaging*, June 2000, pp. 99–105.

28. C. Leangsuksun, J. Potter, and S. Scott, Dynamic Task Mapping Algorithms for a Distributed Heterogeneous Computing Environment, in *Proceedings of the Heterogeneous Computing Workshop*, April 1995, pp. 30–34.

29. R. Wolski, J. Plank, J. Brevik, and T. Bryan. Analyzing market-based resource allocation strategies for the computational grid, *Int. J. High Perform. Comput. Appl.*, 15 (3), 258–281, (2001).

30. A. Turing, The chemical basis of morphogenesis, *Philos. Trans. R. Soc. London B*, 237, 37–72 (1952).

31. A. Gierer and H. Meinhardt, A theory of biological pattern formation, *Kybernetik*, 12, 30–39 (1972).

32. E. Bonabeau, M. Dorigo, and G. Theraulaz, *Swarm Intelligence: From Natural to Artificial Systems*, Oxford University Press, Santa Fe Institute Studies in the Sciences of Complexity, 1999.

33. G. Theraulaz, E. Bonabeau, S. C. Nicolis, R. V. Solé, V. Fourcassié, S. Blanco, R. Fournier, J.-L. Joly, P. Fernández, A. Grimal, P. Dalle, and J.-L. Deneubourg, Spatial patterns in ant colonies, *Proc. Nat. Acad. Sci*, 99 (15), 9645–9649 (2002).

34. D. B. Lange and M. Oshima, Seven good reasons for mobile agents, *Commun. ACM*, 42, 88–89 (1999).

35. J. Bradshaw, N. Suri, A. J. Cañas, R. Davis, K. M. Ford, R. R. Hoffman, R. Jeffers, and T. Reichherzer, Terraforming Cyberspace, in *Computer*, Vol. 34 (7), IEEE, 2001.

36. O. F. Rana and D. W. Walker, The Agent Grid: Agent-Based Resource Integration in PSEs, in *Proceeding, of the 16th IMACS World Congress on Scientific Computation, Applied Mathematics and Simulation*, Lausanne, Switzerland, August 2000.

37. B. J. Overeinder, N. J. E. Wijngaards, M. van Steen, and F. M. T. Brazier, Multi-Agent Support for Internet-Scale Grid Management, in O. Rana and M. Schroeder, Eds., *Proceeding Symposium on AI and Grid Computing (AISB'02)*, April 2002, pp. 18–22.

38. R. Ghanea-Hercock, J. C. Collis, and D. T. Ndumu. Co-operating Mobile Agents for Distributed Parallel Processing, in *Proceedings of the Third International Conference on Autonomous Agents (AA '99)*, ACM Press, Mineapolis, MN, May 1999.

39. G. Cugola, C. Ghezzi, G. Pietro Picco, and G. Vigna, Analyzing Mobile Code Languages, in Selected Presentations and Invited Papers Second International Workshop on Mobile Object Systems – Towards the Programmable Internet (July 8–9, 1996). J. Vitek and C.F. Tschndin, eds., Lecture Notes in Computer Science, Vol. 1222, Springer-Verlag, London, 93–110.

40. D. B. Lange and M. Oshima, *Programming and Deploying Mobile Agents with Java Aglets*, Addison-Wesley, 1998.

41. A. J. Chakravarti, X. Wang, J. O. Hallstrom, and G. Baumgartner, Implementation of Strong Mobility for Multi-Threaded Agents in Java, in *Proceedings of the International Conference on Parallel Processing*, IEEE Computer Society, October 2003.

42. A. J. Chakravarti, X. Wang, J. O. Hallstrom, and G. Baumgartner, Implementation of strong mobility for multi-threaded agents in Java, Technical Report OSU-CISRC-2/03-TR06, Department of Computer and Information Science, The Ohio State University, February 2003.

43. A. J. Chakravarti, G. Baumgartner, and M. Lauria, The Organic Grid: self-organizing computation on a peer-to-peer network, Technical Report OSU-CISRC-10/03-TR55,

Department of Computer and Information Science, The Ohio State University, October 2003.

44. S. Ratnasamy, P. Francis, M. Handley, R. Karp, and S. Shenker, A Scalable Content Addressable Network, in *Proceedings of ACM SIGCOMM'01*, 2001.

45. Basic Local Alignment Search Tool (BLAST). http://www.ncbi.nlm.nih.gov/BLAST/.

46. A. J. Chakravarti, G. Baumgartner, and M. Lauria, Application-specific scheduling for the Organic Grid, Technical Report OSU-CISRC-4/04-TR23, Department of Computer and Information Science, The Ohio State University, April 2004.

47. A. J. Chakravarti, G. Baumgartner, and M. Lauria, Application-Specific Scheduling for the Organic Grid, in *Proceedings of the Fifth IEEE/ACM International Workshop on Grid Computing (GRID 2004)*, Pittsburgh, November 2004.

48. Y. M. Rhee and V. S. Pande, Multiplexed-replica exchange molecular dynamics method for protein folding simulation, *Biophys. J.*, 84 (2), 775–786 (2003).

49. B. Hess, E. Lindahl, and D. van der Spoel, Gromacs 3.0: A package for molecular simulation and trajectory analysis, *J. Mol. Mod.*, 7 (8), 306–317 (2001).

50. GROMACS Web site. http://www.gromacs.org/.

CHAPTER 28

FPGA Computing in Modern Bioinformatics

H. SIMMLER

Modern bioinformatics is one research area that has a strong demand for high performance computing systems. The solutions for this area are predominated by cluster or grid implementations where the applications are distributed and processed in parallel. Unfortunatly, not all bioinformatics applications can be accelerated by a cluster or a grid. Therefore, a new computing approach is introduced that make use of field programmable gate arrays. This new approach uses field programmable gate array (FPGA) processors that are integrated into existing computing nodes. The FPGA processors provide a computing structure that enables to execute the algorithms in a parallel architecture. The transformation from the sequential algorithm to the parallel architecture is described by the energy calculation part of a protein structure prediction task.

The increased research activities in modern biology and computer science have led us to a huge amount of data that is stored in public databases like the NCBI or EMBL GenBank. There are three main reasons for the dramatic increase in database size in the last few years. One reason is the increasing amount of research institutes that work in various fields of biology and generate this data. The second reason are modern high throughput experiments and workflows. Modern biological experiments like microarrays generate a huge amount of data and information about gene expression because thousands of experiments are performed at the same time. Finally, the third reason for the increased amount of data comes from the combination of information and data from several independent databases. Particular research questions are solved in this way, whereas the generated information is stored in new databases. In addition to the increasing amount of data, new applications and algorithms used in the area of bioinformatics were invented to increase the quality of the results.

Driven by the huge database sizes and challenging computational algorithms new forms of parallel and distributed computing were developed to tackle the huge

Parallel Computing for Bioinformatics and Computational Biology, Edited by Albert Y. Zomaya
Copyright © 2006 John Wiley & Sons, Inc.

computing demand in modern bioinformatics. The predominant approaches are cluster or grid solutions. The basic idea is to use standard off-the-shelf computing nodes and connect them through a high speed network. The application that runs on the cluster or grid are parallelized either on process or on thread level and distributed over the available computing nodes.

This approach of parallel and distributed computing is well suited for lots of applications where the processed data can be separated for the execution and distributed through the network to the cluster or grid. Other applications were the data or the execution cannot be separated to several nodes will not benefit from a cluster or grid solution. Therefore, new computing approaches have to be developed to enable a fast and parallel execution for these specific applications and also for other applications that are well suited for a cluster.

Subsequently, a new computing approach will be described that makes use of field programmable gate array (FPGA) devices. In the first part of this chapter it is shown that applications which are divided for a distributed execution usually have at least one algorithm part that will not benefit from a parallelization on a cluster or grid. This will be shown by an image processing example. The new computing approach using FPGA devices will be described by a solution for the image processing example. In addition, details of the FPGA devices and processors are shown. This new approach is universal and it can be applied for many types of applications. Furthermore, the new computing approach can be used in conjunction with existing computing nodes of clusters or grids because the new FPGA processors are integrated into host systems and run as a coprocessor. Rather than brief summaries of possible bioinformatics implementations, the second part of this chapter will provide an in-depth description of one application. The chosen application performs a protein structure prediction and it is described how this sequential algorithm will be transformed to a parallel architecture that is executed on an FPGA processor.

28.1 PARALLEL PROCESSING MODELS

Today, there are innumerable ways to connect single processor systems. In general parallel processing systems consist of several single processors mounted on a single mainboard or they are built as a network where each processor is connected through a physical network like Ethernet. Both the basic methods have in common that they can be scaled to huge systems with hundreds or thousands of computing nodes which are connected [1, 2].

The most common approach for the classification of various architectures is to use executed instructions and processed data words [2]. Based on these two classifiers four parallel processing models can be generated: SISD, SIMD, MISD, and MIMD. In the following, three of these four parallel processing models are described. The Multiple Instruction–Single Data (MISD) model is more or less a theoretical model which is not used in real applications.

The first and simplest processing model is the Single Instruction–Single Data (SISD) case. SISD models process an algorithm or an application as a sequential instruction stream where each instruction processes only a single data word. Traditionally, the von Neumann computing architecture is based on a SISD processing model.

The Single Instruction–Multiple Data (SIMD) processing model also executes the instruction stream in a sequential mode. In comparison to the SISD model, the SIMD model performs the instructions on multiple data words in parallel. Typical processors that are based on the SIMD model are vector processors or super-scalar processors [2]. The SIMD model is also used in a more general view for large multiprocessor systems with many simple processors.

The Multiple Instruction–Multiple Data (MIMD) processing model executes several instruction streams that can use multiple data words. Typical MIMD processing models can be found in clusters or grids where the single processors run as independent nodes. These nodes are connected and synchronized to perform the complete application.

Typically, one of the four described parallel processing models will be chosen for the execution of an algorithm or a program. The selection of the best suited model is mainly affected by the computing task itself but also takes the executed algorithms and the processed data into account. Both selection criteria have to be analyzed properly to choose the right model for an efficient execution.

The analysis of the computing task shows whether parallel processing of the complete task is possible or not. This analysis step uses a high-level abstraction of the computing task to see if blocks of data sets can be processed independently on several single processors. A well suited example for such a parallelized computing task is the processing of a large set of independent images. Let us assume a cluster (MIMD) with single processing nodes is available, the complete image processing task can be spread onto the single nodes where each node processes a single image. This distribution of the complete computing task will lead to a reduced overall computing time because each node is running in parallel executing different data. If only one image has to be processed, this parallelized solution is not appropriate because only one single computing node would be needed. Therefore, a single processor solution (SISD) would be selected for this task.

The second criterion for the selection of the suitable parallel processing model is the executed algorithm itself. Each used algorithm is analyzed at a low abstraction level to identify which instructions can be distributed onto parallel working processors and which data separation can be applied to parallelize the execution of the algorithm using a parallel processing model. Looking at the previous image processing example, a parallel execution of independent filter operations can be executed by different processors. Furthermore, each image can be split into several subimages which can be distributed onto independent processing nodes for their execution. The selection of the appropriate parallel processing model depends, in the case of independent filters, on the amount of filter operations. In case of split images the communication overhead needed for different subimage sizes will define the best suitable parallel processing model for the algorithm execution.

The communication overhead factor is very important for the selection of an appropriate parallel processing model as well as for the implementation of the computing task on the selected model. The communication overhead is specified by the granularity [3]. This granularity is defined as the ratio of computing time to communication time. A computing task or algorithm that requires data exchange after a small amount of processed instructions has a fine-grained granularity, whereas tasks or algorithms that exchange data only very rarely between large instruction blocks have a coarse-grain granularity.

Algorithms which have a coarse-grain granularity are generally suited for SISD or MIMD processing models which are connected by a network or by shared memory. The individual performance of the chosen parallel processing model depends on the connection speed, the data exchange amount, and data exchange rate. Fine-grain granularity algorithms, on the other hand, are suited mainly for SIMD and MIMD processing models where the individual processors are connected by shared memory or other low latency links. High latency network based systems are not suited because the execution time is shifted from processing time to communication time.

Looking back to the image processing example, the possibilities and the limitations are described in more detail in the subsequent section.

28.2 IMAGE PROCESSING TASK

Image processing tasks are needed and used in many research areas and also in many industrial applications. Examples can be found in quality control applications in industry [4] as well as pattern matching applications, for example, for robot control [4] or high energy physics [5, 6]. Image processing is also an important issue especially in the research field of bioinformatics where many biological experiments like Microarray scans are analyzed using specific image processing applications.

Image processing is the umbrella term for all kinds of algorithms that process image data. Subgroups of image processing tasks are image generation, image compression, image filtering, pattern matching, pattern extraction, motion detection, transformation, and many others. Image filtering is chosen from the incomplete list of image processing tasks to describe the mapping of an algorithm and programming details that have to be taken into account when a computing task is mapped onto a parallel processing model.

28.2.1 Image Filtering

Filtering image data is usually done by a two-dimensional finite impulse response (FIR) filter [4] as shown in Figure 28.1. The filter operation itself is performed for each single pixel in the image. As shown in the figure, the filter uses the surrounding pixels to perform the filter operation.

Assuming that the filter performs a median operation, the sum of the processed pixel and all surrounding pixels are computed and finally divided through the amount

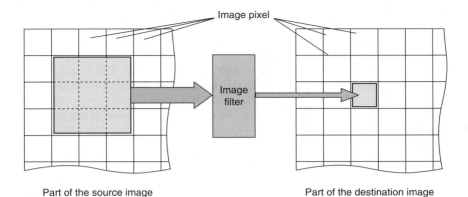

Figure 28.1 FIR image filter operation. Left part contains the source image and the right part the destination image.

of used pixels. This operation is performed for all image pixels.[1] The complete code is shown in the following code example. The used median filter has a size of 3×3 pixel and the image border is not taken into account.

Based on this example for a 3×3 median image filter almost any filter operation and filter size can be generated using the same basic principle. Each individual pixel position of the filter can be supplemented with a coefficient to perform operations like edge detection or image smoothing. The filter size can also be increased simply by adding summation operations to the innermost instruction block.

```
Median filter on an image: img[x,y]
loop y = 2 to img.height-1  // Loop over all image lines
  loop x = 2 to img.width-1   // Loop over all image columns
    sum   = img[x-1,y-1]
    sum += img[x,y-1]
    sum += img[x+1,y-1]
    sum += img[x-1,y]
    sum += img[x,y]
    sum += img[x+1,y]
    sum += img[x-1,y+1]
    sum += img[x,y+1]
    sum += img[x+1,y+1]
    img_dest[x,y] = sum/9; //Compute and store filtered pixel
  end loop x
end loop y
```

---

[1]The pixels at the image borders are either ignored or a copy of the last row or column is used for the calculation.

28.2.2   Parallel Processing Model for the Image Filter

The following case study describes the mapping of the image filter algorithm. This case study shows the concrete procedure starting from a sequential computing task or algorithm until a parallel working architecture is generated. The purpose of this parallel architecture is to reduce the execution time for the complete image filter application.

This case study is performed with the following assumptions in mind: The image size will be 256×256 pixel and the application will only process one image at one time. A 16-node cluster connected by a network is assumed for the parallel processing.

A first look at these basic conditions of the computing task makes it clear that a filter operation which processes the complete image would request only a single processor (SISD). Therefore, the first approach for a parallel working image filter is to split the complete image into several subimages and distribute these subimages onto the nodes of the cluster. Each cluster node processes the received subimage and returns the computed result subimage back to the controller. After all subimages are processed, the filtered image is rebuilt using the processed subimages and the result is returned and stored. The execution of the filter operation on the subimage has a coarse-grain granularity because the filter process can be performed without communication. This is the reason why this parallel approach scales almost linear with the amount of nodes that are available in the cluster. For the 16-node cluster an optimum subimage size will be 64×64 pixel, so that each cluster node can be used to compute the complete image. The resulting speedup of the image filter application will be 16-fold[2] compared to a single processor.

The speedup of the execution time can be increased by extending the cluster with additional nodes and adjusting the subimage size accordingly. The speedup will scale almost linear until the cluster nodes process only one pixel of the image.

28.2.2.1   *Is a parallel execution of the innermost loop possible?*   Let me first make a remark on this question, because it is purely theoretical: Splitting the image filter task to subimages with a 1×1 pixel size is useless because the ratio between communication time and computation time would be very high. In contrast to the coarse-grain granularity character of the subimage separation, the innermost part of the filter loop has a fine-grain granularity, if it is distributed across a network. Because of this granularity the summation results have to be exchanged between the computing nodes and this will lead to a high network traffic on a cluster. This is counterproductive for a high speedup and the final result would be an increase in the execution time rather than a reduction.

Shown for an example, a separation of the innermost loop is useless but on the other hand, there are many real applications which are very similar to the innermost loop of the filter instruction. A cluster is not suited because of the increasing communication time. The usage of a multi processor computer system that comes with a shared memory has the advantage of a direct data exchange through the shared memory but

---

[2]The communication time for the data transfer of the images is not taken into account.

is limited to the amount of connected processors and other computing architectures like vector processors also have to face the same data exchange problem.

The image filter application is a typical application which benefits from the execution on a parallel processing model like a cluster. But the example shows also that there are algorithm parts that cannot be executed in parallel, because of the algorithm granularity.

An accelerator of the fine-grain granularity algorithm parts could boost the performance of the complete cluster even more, or it can result in a smaller cluster size, because each node can execute a larger subimage in the same time. Assuming each cluster node has an accelerator that reduces the execution time of the innermost loop by a factor of 10, the total speedup of the 16-node cluster will be 160 instead of only 16. Moreover, such an accelerator could also reduce the cluster size to only two nodes. Such an accelerated two-node cluster would have around 25% more performance than the 16-node cluster without accelerators.

As shown in the image processing example, such an accelerator would be very useful for the parallel processing of several kinds of algorithms that have to compute algorithm parts which have a fine-grain granularity. The next section will describe a hardware accelerator which is excellently suited for the execution of fine-grain algorithm parts like the image filter.

28.3 FPGA HARDWARE ACCELERATORS

As we have seen in the previous image processing task section there are algorithms which are not suited for an acceleration on a cluster or other parallel computing architectures, because of their fine-grain granularity.

The innermost loop of the image processing task has shown that up to nine additions and one division have to be processed in the innermost loop. If additional coefficients are used for the filter operation, then another nine multiplications have to be computed. If the innermost loop of the image filter is executed an optimal solution for the computation would be a parallel architecture where each operation is performed by an individual processor. All these processors must be connected according to the image filtering algorithm to perform the complete innermost loop operation.

A general-purpose processor is inappropriate for the implementation of such a parallel architecture, because there are only limited parallel execution units available. Therefore, the optimum solution would be an application specific hardware architecture that fulfils the needed requirements and executes each operation in an independent processor.

One possible technology that can be used for the implementation of such a parallel working architecture is an application specific integrated circuit (ASIC) [7]. Such an ASIC allows the implementation of individual and independent processors on one chip. These processors are connected to execute the specific algorithm. The ASIC technology is powerful and allows to implement only the needed operations in the form of specific processors, so that there is no dissipated space on the integrated circuit. All operations are implemented directly on the hardware circuit itself and perform the operations without any instruction decoding steps. The two most important disadvantages of the ASIC technology are the long design process time and the total costs of the fabrication setup. Furthermore, the parallel architecture is implemented as an inflexible structure of transistors and connections which are highly optimized for the selected ASIC manufacturing process. This structure optimization together with the inflexible structure on the ASIC leads to a long design process for such a chip. This is the reason why the ASIC technology is usually restricted to applications that are needed at high volumes. Good examples are specific image processing chips like digital cameras or network chips.

An alternative technology that provides the possibility to implement application specific parallel architectures are FPGAs [8–10]. The FPGA technology provides a flexible and programmable network of processing units that can be programmed and connected to implement a parallel working architecture. This relatively new technology eliminates the long design process times and the inflexibility of ASICs and can be used as an alternative for applications that are needed at low or medium volumes.

28.3.1 FPGA Devices

FPGAs devices are the basis for the execution of parallel applications. The FPGAs are programmable logic devices which have a matrix of processors connected by an interconnection network. This matrix of processors and the interconnects are surrounded by I/O cells used for all kinds of data transfers. Figure 28.2 shows the schematic layout of the internal FPGA architecture.

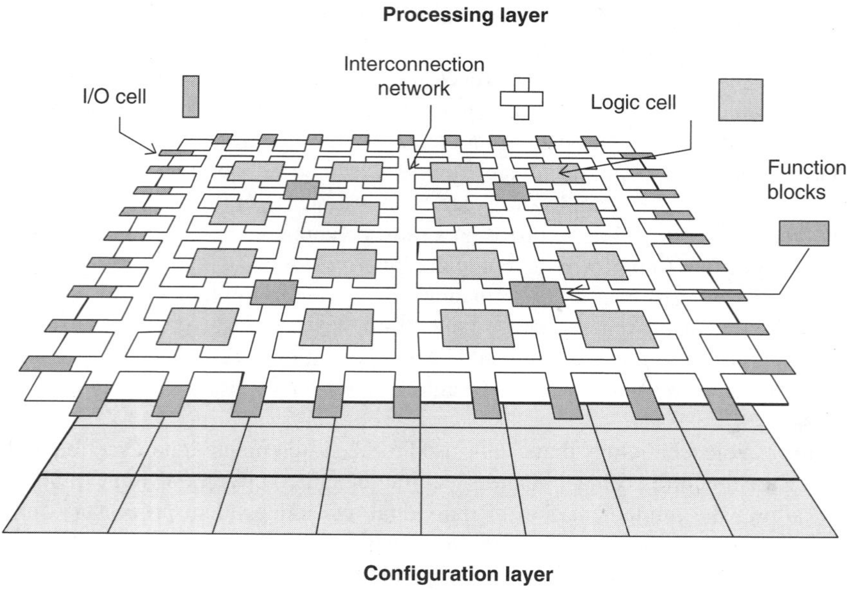

Figure 28.2 FPGA architecture.

In general an FPGA architecture consist of four main components:

(1) Logic cells;
(2) Interconnection network;
(3) I/O cells;
(4) Hardcoded function blocks.

Logic Cells Logic cells are small processing units which are able to process a limited number of input bits. The logic cells also contain register elements for bit storage. The typical bit size range of these logic elements vary from 1 to 8 bits depending on the manufacturer. Modern FPGAs typically contain up to 100,000 logic cells arranged in a matrix. Each cell in this matrix can be programmed to perform an individual operation.

Interconnection Network The interconnection network surrounds all matrix cells and provides the connections between the individually programmed logic cells. The interconnection network is also free programmable.

I/O Cells I/O cells are arranged at the border of the matrix. They provide a connection between the internal logic cells or the network and any external device like a communication bus or a memory device.

Hardcoded Function Blocks Modern FPGAs have included specific hardcoded function blocks that can be connected to the matrix of logic cells. These blocks perform specific operations like multiplications or provide small memory blocks with flexible bit width and address space. Some FPGA device families have complete CPU cores [9, 10] embedded into the logic cell matrix. These hardcoded blocks are also connected to the internal network, so that the function blocks can be integrated for the individual parallel architectures.

This matrix architecture and the free programmable logic cells, I/O cells, and the interconnection network are the reason for the flexible usage of the devices. Other features of FPGA devices are:

1. Flexible and free programmable resources.
2. Direct execution of operations in hardware.
3. Reconfigure flexibility.

Flexible and Free Programmable Resources This means the available logic cells can be individually programmed and combined through the interconnection network to implement even sophisticated operations like divisions or a 128 bit multiplication.

Direct Execution of Operations in Hardware The parallel architecture is mapped directly to the available cells in the FPGA in a way that only the necessary amount of resources will be used for the execution. In addition, the amount of available and connectable logic cells makes it possible to execute several operations in different logic cells in parallel. This is the main reason why the highly flexible and programmable structure of an FPGA is perfectly suited for the mapping and the execution of fine-grain granularity processes.

Reconfigure Flexibility Reconfigurability is used in two different ways. The reconfigurability in conjunction with the application means that modifications (e.g., extending the data path) of an application can easily be done by adapting the operations using more logic cells and by programming the supplementary interconnects in the FPGA. The application is flexible and can be adapted fast and easily to new requirements. Nevertheless, the application is executed in hardware.

Second, the FPGA device can be reconfigured simply by downloading a new configuration into the configuration layer shown in Figure 28.2. This makes the FPGA a general processing device that can execute different kinds of parallel working applications. Typically, a reconfiguration of a FPGA device takes less than a second.

All this shows that FPGA devices are well suited for the implementation of parallel architectures used in fine-grain but also in course-grain applications. Their specific internal architecture, the flexibility, and the reconfigurability enable an utilization within a broad range of applications.

28.3.2 FPGA Processor Boards

In principle, the FPGA device acts as a highly flexible coprocessor which has to be integrated into a host system. The FPGA device is utilized for the parallel execution of algorithms or applications by a connection between the FPGA and the processor and the memory of the host system. Data words are transferred from the memory to the FPGA and processed data words are written back to the memory for further processing or data I/O.

This data transfer requires a low latency and a high bandwidth to ensure that the communication does not affect the processing time. On the other hand, specific or proprietary processor or system interfaces should be avoided to make the FPGA available for various systems. To meet this divergency demands most FPGAs are connected to the processor by the PCI-Bus [11].[3]

In general the FPGA devices are mounted on a PCI board that can be plugged into modern PCI based computer systems. The modern PCI bus provides data transfer rates with up to 528 MB/s (64 bit/66 MHz PCI-Bus), which is sufficient for most applications. A generalized FPGA processor board structure is shown in Figure 28.3.

Besides the PCI bridge and the FPGA device, a clock generator creates the base clock frequency for the board. The glue logic controller can be seen as an operating system for the FPGA board, because it provides access to set up the clock generator or to configure the FPGA device. Another important component on an FPGA board is local memory (RAM) that stores data values. The type of this local RAM differs in

---

[3]PCI-Bus: peripheral component interconnect bus.

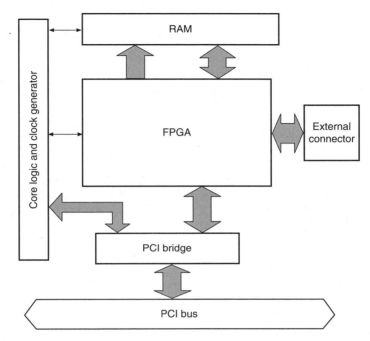

Figure 28.3 A generalized FPGA processor board structure.

each FPGA board. Static synchronous RAM is used as well as synchronous dynamic RAM for larger memory requirements.

Other specific devices can be attached to the FPGA by an external connector. Typically, specialized interfaces to CCD cameras [12] or network interface devices [13] are available.

As shown in the schematic block diagram in Figure 28.3 all additional devices on the FPGA board are connected directly to the FPGA device. This ensures that each device can be accessed in parallel and with the maximum bandwidth which is particularly important for the memory connection and the PCI bridge connection, because in many cases the data values are processed with every clock cycle and therefore a maximum bandwidth usage is mandatory to ensure a maximum overall performance.

Today, several FPGA boards which follow the described schematic block layout are commercially available. Nevertheless, the appropriate board for a specific application or a range of applications must be chosen. Beside the described PCI board there are also FPGA boards that have an alternative system integration interface like Compact-PCI [14], Universal Serial Bus (USB) [15], or an application specific interface for example, in high-energy physics [6].

The future trend in the area of FPGA technology will integrate traditional processor cores into FPGAs [9, 10] and vice versa. Programmable FPGA space will be directly attached to processors so that the data can be exchanged instantly.

28.3.3 FPGA Processor Integration

The FPGA boards are used to execute the time-consuming part of an application. These parts are implemented as parallel architectures which are running on the FPGA. All the other application parts (e.g., parameter settings or file handling) which are not time consuming are still executed on the processor of the host system. The control of the FPGA board and the exchange of data words between the host system memory and the FPGA board is performed using a board specific application programmer interface (API) [16]. This API provides all necessary methods and functions to transfer the data words from the host system memory to either the FPGA or to the available local memory on the FPGA board. The API also provides functions which are used to read status and result registers or to write to control registers on the board or within the FPGA architecture. The content and the structure of the exchanges data is defined by the application and the implemented parallel architecture that is running on the FPGA device.

28.4 IMAGE PROCESSING EXAMPLE

This section shows an example of how an existing algorithm is mapped onto a parallel working architecture that can be executed on an FPGA processor. The FIR image filter from Section 28.2.1 is used to describe the generation of a parallel system that performs this operation on an FPGA hardware.

The filter operation shown in Figure 28.1 computes the new pixel value by using the surrounding pixel data. The result of the described mapping process is an optimal parallel architecture that is able to process a single result pixel with every clock cycle. In the following part of this section it is shown how a sequential workflow can be transformed into an optimal parallel workflow that fulfils the wanted processing time of only one clock cycle per pixel. Two independent optimizations are presented in detail and it is shown that these optimizations can be exemplarily realized in a parallel working architecture.

Starting from the described 3×3 image filter each filter operation requires nine pixel input data to process the output pixel value. Each pixel data value must be read from the local memory on the FPGA board, a coefficient multiplication must be performed for each read pixel and the result must be summarized and divided by another coefficient. Due to the available logic cells and the interconnection network in the FPGA matrix all the mentioned mathematical operations can be performed in parallel. Assuming that the first approach performs all mathematical operations in parallel, the architecture would still need nine clock cycles for each image pixel, because each pixel data value must be read from the memory.

The first optimization is used to reduce the amount of reads that are necessary to process two contiguous pixel data. As shown on the left side of Figure 28.4 the image filter mask is shifted to the right to process the next following pixel result. It can easily be seen that six of nine pixel data are already read for the previous filter operation. A parallel working architecture that is able to store these pixel data and

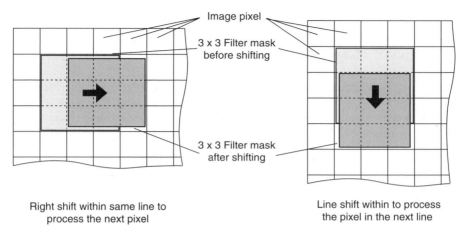

Image pixel

3 x 3 Filter mask
before shifting

3 x 3 Filter mask
after shifting

Right shift within same line to
process the next pixel

Line shift within to process
the pixel in the next line

Figure 28.4   Examples showing the shift of the filter mask.

make it available for the next filter operation can save up to six memory accesses. This means that together with the parallel executed operations each filter operation can be performed within only three clock cycles instead of nine clock cycles.

The second optimization reduces the read access to the local memory for two pixel data which are in the next contiguous image line. The image filtering is usually done line by line. After computing the last pixel of a line, the process starts with the first pixel of the next line. As shown in Figure 28.4 on the right side, the filter mask is shifted to the same pixel column in the next line. Like before, six of the nine needed pixel data are already read. Therefore, only three pixel data must be read to process the result. Although it is the same kind of optimization, the extension of the parallel architecture is different. This architecture extention must be able to store and delay the data values of the complete line until the data is needed for the next line. If this data delay is integrated in the architecture, the needed clock cycles for the execution are also reduced from nine to only three clock cycles.

Both extensions reduce the amount of needed clock cycles by a factor of three. Unfortunately, in both cases there are still three clock cycles necessary to process each pixel data word. Because both optimizations can be combined in one parallel architecture the total amount of needed clock cycles can be reduced to only one.

28.4.1   Parallel Image Filtering Architecture

Here the parallel architecture with the two described optimizations is shown in Figure 28.5. This architecture is separated into a part that is responsible for storing the pixel data and another part that computes the 3×3 image filter.

The pixel data storage architecture is shown in the upper part of the block diagram. nine registers are arranged in a 3×3 matrix to store all needed pixel data for the filter mask. Because of the separated registers each pixel value is available for a parallel computation. Each column register of the matrix is connected to the next column

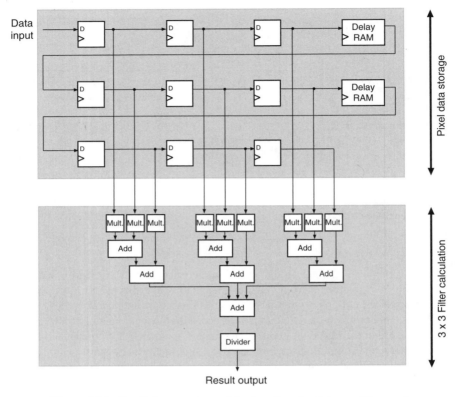

Figure 28.5   Parallel processing architecture for a 3×3 image filter mask.

register at the same row of matrix. This connection scheme ensures that the pixel data are shifted at each clock cycle, so that they are available at the appropriate position for the filter calculation. The described register matrix implements the first part of the optimized parallel architecture. The integration of the second optimization requires to store the pixel data of the complete lines to make them available when the next line will be processed. This can be done by extending the symmetrical 3×3 matrix to a matrix that has the size $3 \times ImageWidth$. Such an asymmetrical matrix would require large amount of registers within the hardware which will only be used for storing the data. Therefore, the storage of pixel data from a complete line is done by a delay memory. This delay memory is a RAM that stores the pixel data and outputs the input data after a selectable amount of clock cycles. Such a solution requires fewer resources in contrast to the registers, because specific hardcoded RAM blocks could be used for the storage. The output data of the delay memory is applied to the register matrix to make the data available for processing the next line.

The filter operation itself is performed by the 3×3 filter calculation that is shown in the lower part of the block diagram. Due to the 3×3 register matrix, all necessary pixel data values are available for the calculation. In the first computation layer all coefficient multiplications are performed in parallel. The modified pixel data are summarized in the second computation layer. This second layer is directly connected to the multipliers and adds the nine input values to one output result value. The third computation layer performs the division of the summarized value and outputs the computed filter value at the output of the calculation block. All shown mathematical operations are implemented as logic and therefore the filter result data word can be processed within one clock cycle.

Altogether, this parallel architecture of a 3 × 3 image filter mask is able to process a filter operation within only one clock cycle and it needs only one new pixel data value at each clock cycle. This parallel architecture works faster than the described sequential workflow that is shown in the code fragment 1.2.1. This sequential workflow requires all nine image values to be read before they can be processed in a sequential order. In addition, the execution is done directly in hardware, where in contrast to the software execution no operation decoding is necessary.

28.4.2   Extended Parallel Image Filtering Architecture

As shown in the previous section, the computation of an image filter can be computed within a single clock cycle using an appropriated parallel architecture. Assuming that the data input can provide more than one new pixel data word, the 3 × 3 filter calculation can be duplicated to process the amount of input data within one clock cycle. An example architecture for four pixel data words is shown in Figure 28.6.

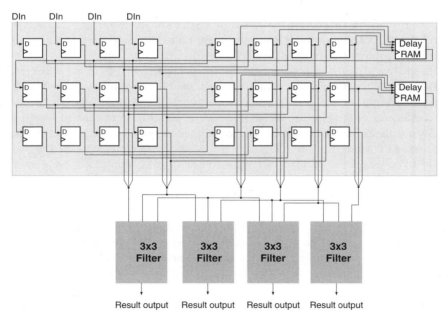

Figure 28.6 Extended parallel processing architecture with four 3 × 3 image filter calculations.

As shown in the block diagram up to four 3×3 filter calculations can be performed in parallel if the data input can provide four consecutive data words. Besides four implementations of the 3×3 filter calculation blocks, the register matrix and the delay memory must be extended and reconnected to provide the appropriate pixel data for each filter calculation block.

This extended parallel architecture has a four times faster execution time compared to the solution with only one filter block. Mainly because each filter block uses its own mathematical operations which run completely parallel to the others. Compared to the first initial approach where the pixel data were processed sequentially the speedup is 36.

28.4.3   Image Filter Example Conclusions

Starting from the question if the innermost loop of the FIR 3×3 image filter task can be executed in parallel this section has shown a possible solution in form of a parallel architecture. The basic principles of a parallel execution and the optimization steps have been shown in detail.

In principle, the innermost loop of the FIR image filter is an algorithm that has a fine-grain granularity and therefore it is not suited to be accelerated by using clusters. It is shown that especially these fine-grain granularity algorithms are very well suited for an execution by a parallel working architecture, because the operations are connected directly using dedicated buses and connections.

The described architecture for the 3×3 FIR filter can be implemented on an FPGA processor board where a connection to the local memory is given. The parallel architecture is implemented within the FPGA processor and the available local memory can be used for temporary storage of the image data. The integration of the parallel architecture into the software is done by the API.

In summary it can be ascertained that the direct implementation of the architecture and the flexibility of the FPGA processors make the FPGA coprocessor an ideal platform for this type of fine-grain granularity algorithms. Furthermore, the modification of coefficients or the increase of the filter size or the data words can be integrated easily into the existing architecture and the modified algorithm can be executed within the same FPGA processor.

28.5   CASE STUDY: PROTEIN STRUCTURE PREDICTION

The described FPGA processor is able to execute several kinds of applications. It can be seen as a general-purpose computing processor. The general usability will be presented in this section using a concrete application from the field of bioinformatics. The complete application for protein structure prediction, a view of the parallelized architecture, and the integration into an existing software environment is described in this section. This protein structure prediction approach is shown in specific detail rather than showing numerous application examples that are suitable for an execution on an FPGA processor.

Protein structure prediction is one of the basic research fields in modern bio-informatics. Today, biologists are interested in the structure of a protein, because this structure will lead them to the protein function in a specific environment. The structure can be determined by several methods starting from experimental analysis and ending in a pure virtual simulation of possible protein structures.

Experiments are performed using methods like X-ray crystallography or nuclear magnetic resonance (NMR). Both methods are used to determine the three-dimensional molecular structure of proteins. For X-ray crystallography the protein molecules must be crystallized, whereas the crystal must have a high quality to achieve accurate results. Many important molecules cannot be determined, because the attempt to produce suitable crystals failed [17]. NMR is the other experiment that is used to determine the three-dimensional molecular structure of a protein. This method uses chemical shifts of atomic nuclei with nonzero spins to detect the distances between nearby atoms. For the detection a strong magnetic field is required.

NMR is used for small and medium proteins which must be soluble at high concentrations and stable for days without aggregation under the experimental conditions. The result of an NMR study is not as detailed and accurate as the result obtained using X-ray crystallography [18]. On the other hand, X-ray crystallography requires the generation of a pure crystal which is not always possible. Looking at the protein data bank (PDB) [17] over 80 percent of the stored three-dimensional structures are determined with X-ray crystallography and only about 16 percent are determined using NMR.

Besides the two briefly described experimental methods to determine the three-dimensional structure of a protein, there are several other approaches to determine the structures using a virtual simulation. These simulation approaches make use of more or less simple models which base on a classical force field [19]. These molecular models are of great scientific interest for two reasons: First, until now there has been no universal model defined that computes reasonable results for different kinds of proteins. Second, the simulation of protein structures is the only possible approach to deal with proteins that cannot be determined by X-ray crystallography or NMR.

Homology modeling is the most commonly used for "in silico" simulation. This approach is separated into a workflow with several steps [20]. The first step makes use of a protein domain databases. These databases contain protein sequences of all proteins where the three-dimensional structure is already known and where these proteins are classified into so called protein domains. The aim of the database searches is to find suitable protein domain classes for the unknown protein sequence. In case of a high homology between the given protein sequence and a protein domain, this secondary structure of the protein domain is used as the base structure. After determining an appropriate base structure, the loops of the protein are modeled in the second step. These loops are mostly at the protein surface and therefore important to determine the protein function. The final result of the complete workflow will be a predicted protein structure that can be used to study the functions of the protein.

This homology modeling approach is very useful unless there is no protein domain found that has a high homology. In this case the protein structure must be modeled from scratch without a probable starting structure. Protein structure prediction that does not use protein domains are called "ab initio" protein structure prediction.

Within the following sections a possible solution of an "ab initio" protein structure prediction approach will be described and discussed. Then the possibilities of a parallel execution of the task is shown. Finally, the implementation aspects are discussed and the layout of a parallel architecture is presented.

28.5.1 "Ab Initio" Protein Structure Prediction

In general "ab initio" protein structure prediction is a problem which is still unsolved today [21] although interesting progress in this field has been reported [22–24]. The "ab initio" structure prediction problem can be formulated as an optimization problem, because it leads to the task of finding the free enthalpy minimum in the conformational space of the protein.

Thus protein structure prediction can be divided into two subproblems:

1. Search method/structure generator for different structures.
2. Evaluation of the protein structure energy.

The protein structures are generated in the first step by the structure generator using different strategies. The first step models the protein and describes it as the combination of the amino acid atoms. Each atom is defined by its three-dimensional coordinates and an atom type number. This representation must be recomputed every time a modification in the protein structure is performed.

Once a protein structure is generated or modified it must be evaluated within the second step. Important for this evaluation of the protein is its free enthalpy. Because the free enthalpy is related to the energy, this energy value is computed using the atom type classifications and van der Waals radii as devised by Nussinov et al. [25]. The computed energy is returned back to the first step and compared to the already evaluated protein structures.

This two-step workflow is computed within a loop to check all the generated protein structures and to find the protein structure with the lowest energy. The number of possible protein structure conformations is enormous and no efficient algorithm is known which can guarantee to find the global optimum of this energy landscape. This is the reason why it is necessary to compute a vast number of protein structures in order to find the global energy minimum of a protein. Hence, the faster the computation of protein energies can be performed the bigger the size of proteins which can be computed in a feasible time. This is especially the case for the energy calculation, because this step requires more than 90% of the complete execution time.

The focus of the subsequent section is on the efficient and powerful implementation of this energy calculation as it is computed by a FPGA processor. First, the requirements for the energy computation are presented and the used calculation models are discussed. Second, a possible execution architecture for this energy calculation is shown and finally the parallel architecture will be described and outlined in detail before the results of the implementation are presented.

28.5.2 Protein and Energy Model

The energy calculation for a given protein structure, makes use of two basic models. One model is used for the description of the protein structure, whereas the other one defines the calculation that is used for the energy computation.

The protein model uses a unified atom approach. Proteins are chains of amino acids. These amino acids are further separated into backbone atoms and side-chain atoms. The model for the protein structure representation uses all nonhydrogen atoms of the amino acids and describes these atoms by their three-dimensional coordinates and an atom type number. Both atom attributes are needed for the later described energy computation. The coordinates are defined in Angstrom (Å) and are given as an absolute value from a virtual three-dimensional space centre.

The used energy model is very simple for a practical realization on FPGA processors. On the other hand, it is also realistic in the sense, that it is used for protein structure computation [25] purposes even without special hardware support. Like many other energy models we also use a simple algebraic form: A pair potential model.

This means that in our model the total energy is the result of the interaction energies from all possible atom pairs. This interaction energy is computed using the distance between atom pairs and an energy function. The total energy has the form:

$$E_{\text{total}} = \sum_{i<j} E_{ij}(r_{ij}) \tag{28.1}$$

E_{ij} is the interaction energy between atoms i and j. The distance between the sites i and j is denoted as r_{ij}. This approach for the pair interaction energy uses a very simple form of interaction potentials which are called the contact potentials [26]. The interaction energy that is used in the energy model has the form:

$$E_{ij}(r_{ij}) = \begin{cases} E_{\text{penalty}} & \text{if } r_{ij} < r_{t(i)t(j)}^{\text{collision}} \\ \epsilon_{t(i)t(j)} s(i,j) & \text{if } r_{t(i)t(j)}^{\text{collision}} < r < r_{t(i)t(j)}^{\text{cutoff}} \\ 0 & \text{if } r_{ij} > r_{t(i)t(j)}^{\text{cutoff}} \end{cases} \tag{28.2}$$

The pair potential depend on the two atom types that are evaluated. This is the reason why the used radius in the interaction energy formula depend on the atom types. The atom type is denoted by the function $t()$. The term $s(i,j)$ denotes the amino acid sequence separation of the two atoms under consideration. All atom distances smaller than the collision distance ($r_{t(i)t(j)}^{\text{collision}}$) are treated with an energy penalty (E_{penalty}) to indicate that the given protein conformation is invalid. Atom distances which are greater than the cutoff distance ($r_{t(i)t(j)}^{\text{cutoff}}$) are set to zero, because the distance between these atom pairs is to large to contribute an energy term to the complete energy. All distances between the collision and the cutoff value are counted using the atom pair specific energy value. The interaction energy according to this model is shown in Figure 28.7. The cutoff and collision values are denoted as Minimum and Maximum distances. The used energy model also takes the atom neighboring relation

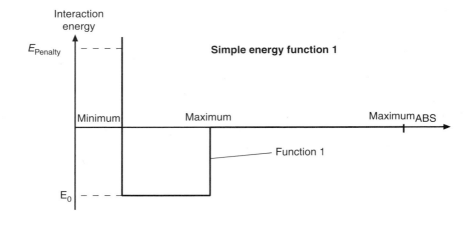

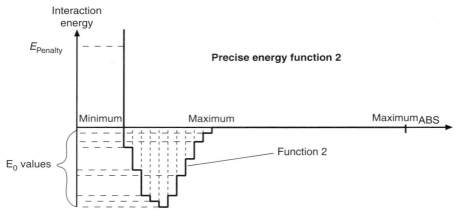

Figure 28.7   Used energy function for the contact pair potentials. The upper diagram shows the applied simple energy function 1 and the lower diagram shows the more precise energy function 2.

into account and checks if the evaluated atoms are from the same amino acid, from a neighboring amino acid or from a non-neighboring amino acid. Atom pair interactions from atoms that are located within the same amino acid do not contribute an energy term to the total energy. These energy values are set to zero. Atom pairs from neighboring amino acids are evaluated using a different interaction value table as it is used for atom pairs which are from non-neighbor amino acids.

28.5.3   Energy Calculation Algorithm

The total energy of a protein in this model is the sum of the contact energies between all atom pairs. Therefore, the algorithm for calculating the total energy must loop over all atom pairs and calculate the individual distance between the two selected atoms.

The atom pair energy term is then determined using this atom distance and the atom type numbers, before the energy term is added to the total energy.

Atom distances are computed using the difference vector and building the vector sum of this distance vector. This calculation step is called the vector sum in the following text. The atom positions are defined through its position vector in the three-dimensional space. The vector sum is calculated using the following formula:

$$|\vec{ab}| = \sqrt{(a_x - b_x)^2 + (a_y - b_y)^2 + (a_z - b_z)^2} \qquad (28.3)$$

After the atom distances are computed for an atom pair the interaction energy of this atom pair is estimated. Besides the computed distance this second step also uses the atom type information of both atoms to get the corresponding limiting values for the determination of the atom pair energy term. Figure 28.7 shows the energy functions with the applied limiting values. For the energy term determination only four dedicated limiting values are necessary. These values are Minimum, Maximum, Maximum$_{ABS}$, and the energy E_0. The E_0 value is equal to the ϵ_{ij} in Equation 28.2. The Minimum boundary defines the lowest possible distance between the two atoms. If the distance falls below this minimum value, the atoms will collide. This case indicates that the protein conformation is not valid and the algorithm will stop its execution instantly. If the atom pair distance is between the Minimum and the Maximum boundaries, the interaction energy is taken into account for the total energy. Therefore, the energy E_0 is added to the current total energy value for the protein structure. All distances above the Maximum boundary do not contribute an energy term to the total energy. The total energy value is left unchanged in this case. The additionally introduced value Maximum$_{ABS}$ is used as an optimization step, because if the distance of a calculated atom pair is far above the Maximum boundary it can be assumed that no other atom pairs of the same two involved amino acids will contribute an energy term to the total energy. Therefore, the calculation for this amino acid pair is skipped and the algorithm continues with the next amino acid pair.

The complete algorithm with the two steps is defined in the following algorithm.

```
Energy Calculation Algorithm
E sum = 0
for each atom A(1,..., N - 1){
  for each atom B(A+1,..., N){
    // Calculate the vector sum for the atom pair
    distance = (atomAx - atomBx)²
    distance += (atomAy - atomBy)²
    distance += (atomAz - atomBz)²
    distance = √dist;

    Read the energy function values for the atom pair

    // atom pair value below the minimum
    if(distance < minimum)
```

```
        Skip the calculation instantly

    // Determine the energy term of the atom pair
    E_sum += E_0 (atomA, atomB)
  }
}
```

28.5.4   Parallelized Algorithm Solutions

With the detailed algorithm description of the energy calculation and the overall work-flow steps of the protein structure calculation in mind a parallel working architecture has to be defined. The main goal of this parallel architecture is to reduce the execution time to a minimum to be able to process a maximum number of possible protein conformations within a feasible time.

Looking at the overall workflow with the alternate processed protein structure generator step and the following energy calculation step, the only possible parallel execution would be to split the complete workflow into several parallel running threads. Each thread will be started with a different initial structure. The individual threads run independently without any interaction. This kind of parallelization has a particular low coarse-grain granularity and is therefore, extremely well suited for an execution on independently running processors or computing nodes in a cluster or a grid.

Now that we have determined a possible parallel execution of the complete task, we should also look at the inner workflow with the protein structure generator and the energy calculation unit. An analysis of the execution times has shown that over 90% of the time is needed for the energy calculation whereas the remaining time is needed for the protein structure generation. This fact motivates a more precise analysis of the used energy calculation algorithm that is shown in Section 28.5.3.

The algorithm computes the vector sum using the two, three-dimensional coordinates of the atoms. This vector sum calculation requires three subtractions, three multiplications, and the summation of the individual distances. A square root operation at the end will finally generate the distance value for the two atoms. This complete vector sum operation has a fine-grain granularity, because the results of each operation are used as the input value in the next subsequent operation. This behavior will lead to a high communication time if the operations are performed on independent processors.

Subsequent to this vector sum calculation the result is compared to the limit values. These values have to be read according to the two used atom types and they are used for the energy determination. The fact that the read energy values are directly compared to the computed distance shows that also the second part of the complete energy calculation algorithm has a fine-grain granularity. Due to the fact that both parts of the energy calculation have a fine-grain granularity this innermost energy calculation is not suited for a distribution on a cluster.

Looking at the two nested loops that are performed for the calculation of the total energy it can be seen that in principle it is possible to split the execution and process it on different computing nodes. This is possible, because the relation between each executed loop is only the summation of the energy terms. Each loop run can be executed in parallel, whereas the energy sums must be accumulated at the end to the total protein energy. Although the execution of the individual loop runs can be distributed, almost the complete set of protein atom coordinates must be distributed to each computing node. This fact moves the distributed and parallel loop execution concept from a coarse-grain to a more fine-grain granularity implementation which is acceptable only if the amount of atoms that are computed on one node exceeds a minimum amount. The distributed loop execution is also not optimal if the individual computing nodes do not instantly react on a detected atom collision and abort the calculation. Assuming the loop runs are distributed to a parallel working computing node and each of them is programmed to receive a request, to execute this request completely, and to return the calculated energy value. The occurrence of an atom collision on one computing node would terminate the execution on this node, but all other nodes would continue when the abort signal is not distributed. The time spent on the other computing nodes would be wasted, because the complete protein structure is invalid and no energy is defined.

Taking all the discussed issues for a parallel working architecture into account, a suitable solution would separate the search in the huge search space into several search threads and distribute them onto a cluster or a grid. No communication is needed between the threads and therefore it is perfectly suited for this parallel architecture.

A further acceleration of the individual threads can be achieved by an acceleration of the energy calculation, because this part requires over 90% of the complete execution time. As we have seen in the previous discussion a separation of the energy calculation loop onto several computing nodes in a cluster only makes sense when the protein is split into portions which have a certain atom amount. In addition, a fast signaling mechanism must be implemented to avoid the execution of unnecessary calculations.

An alternative to the limited possibilities of using several computing nodes is to use FPGA processors instead. These FPGA processors will be integrated into the existing computing nodes that perform the search threads. FPGA processors are perfectly suited for the execution of the fine-grain granularity algorithm parts like the one that computes the energy contribution of a given atom pair.

The following sections will describe the implementation aspects and the realization of the parallel architecture that is generated for an execution on an FPGA processor.

28.5.5 FPGA Processor Implementation Aspects

Before the parallel architecture is planned, some aspects regarding the necessary operations, the data representations, and the requirements to the used FPGA processor must be evaluated. The considerations and evaluation that were made for the parallel architecture and the general usage of the energy calculation are discussed in the following.

One of the first analyses that are made examine the necessary data representations needed for the task. The input for the energy calculation is mainly the three-dimensional atom coordinates of each atom. The coordinates are given in Å and measure the absolute distance of the atom to a three-dimensional origin. The origin is located at one corner of the three-dimensional space which leads to the fact that all coordinate values are positive and no negative values are needed for the protein structure representation. The precision of the given coordinates is limited to three positions after the decimal point. This precision is sufficient for the calculation and enables that the coordinates can be processed as a fix-point representation. The three-dimensional space is limited to a cube with 65.535 Å dimension on each axis. This space limitation is introduced, because the protein structures with the lowest energy usually form a compact structure rather than a stretched structure across the three-dimensional space. The used atom coordinate values are defined as:

$$\text{Atom coordinates}_{x,y,z} = [0, 65.535]\text{Å} \qquad (28.4)$$

This atom coordinate representation is sufficient for the calculation and has the advantage that all coordinate values can be stored and processed as 16-bit data words. Another important point is that the fix-point representation of the coordinates enables a less resource intensive implementation of the necessary mathematical operations.

The second analysis examines these mathematical operations and the dependency of the individual operations. Looking at the vector sum calculation the needed operations are defined by the formula and the 16-bit input data words. No optimization can be applied for this step. The result of the vector sum calculation is afterwards compared against the minimum and maximum values to determine if the atom pair contributes an energy term to the total energy or not. Knowing that the implementation of a square root operation in hardware requires lots of resources and limits the throughput of the complete computation, an optimized algorithm would eliminate the square root operation if possible.

This square root operation can be eliminated, because the computed distance value is solely used for the comparison of the minimum and maximum values. Therefore the square root operation can be eliminated if in return the comparison values are adjusted accordingly. This optimization of the complete algorithm will save resources in the FPGA architecture and even more important it makes the complete parallel architecture more efficient and faster.

Another more general aspect of the complete implementation is its flexible usage. The biologist should be able to set and change the used energy values which are used for the comparison. This modification of the energy values has to be taken into account when the parallel architecture is designed. The required flexibility of the parallel architecture must be combined with the requirement of an efficient and fast execution. Therefore energy values are stored within a so called lookup table to fulfil these flexibility and performance aspects. This lookup table is a memory block which stores the energy values that are assigned to specific atom distances. The lookup table is loaded with user values to provide the flexibility in the energy value, and on the other hand, an access to the stored energy values can be performed with every clock cycle when a protein structure is processed by the architecture.

The usage of the lookup table has a second advantage which is needed should the used energy function (Function 1 in Fig. 28.7) not be precise enough. In this case the lookup table can be extended and multiple E_0 energy terms can be stored according to the defined distance values to achieve a more realistic energy value of the protein. An example for a more precise function is named as Function 2 and can be seen in the lower part of Figure 28.7.

One requirement that has to be emphasized is the data exchange rate between the host memory and the FPGA processor. The atom coordinates of a protein must be transferred from the host memory to the FPGA processor and the computed total energy together with some control signals are returned from the FPGA processor. The time needed for this data exchange must be added to the total execution time, because the computation can only start after all atom coordinates have been transferred to the FPGA Processor.

Modern PCI systems provide a maximum data exchange rate of up to 528 MB/s. The maximum protein size is assumed to have 8192 amino acids with up to 32 atoms each. This requires a memory space of 2 MB to store the total of 262,144 atoms. The resulting transfer time for the complete atom space is less than 4.1 ms, whereas coordination data of smaller proteins have fewer data to transfer.

The previously mentioned aspects and requirements must be taken into account for the implementation as well as for the board selection. The last mentioned requirement restrict the FPGA processor selection to a PCI board with a high data exchange rate.

A second aspect regarding the FPGA processor selection is the amount and the access to local memory banks on the FPGA processor. One memory bank has to be used for the storage of the complete atom coordinates, because these data values are accessed on average more than once during one complete energy calculation. Each atom data word consists of three coordinates for the three dimensions and an atom type number. All these words are defined as 16-bit data words so that an atom data word has 64 bits. The optimum architecture requires that all atom data can be read within one clock cycle. This requires a memory interface for the atom data with a 64-bit data bus interface. The efficient processing of one atom pair in each clock cycle leads to the fact that also the lookup table must be accessible with each clock cycle. The stored complete energy information for one atom pair is also stored within a 64-bit data word which has to be read out in one clock cycle. Therefore a second independent memory interface with a 64-bit data bus must be provided by the FPGA processor.

Besides these necessary requirements for an optimum parallel architecture the amount of available resources in the FPGA device must also be given to map the architecture onto the FPGA. This is usually a less important requirement, because the FPGA processor boards are available with a broad range of different FPGA devices that have a different amount of available resources.

28.5.6 Energy Calculation Architecture

After all implementation aspects are discussed and simulated, the layout of the actual parallel architecture for the FPGA device and the complete data workflow in the system can be designed and optimized. For the energy calculation used in the "ab-initio" protein structure prediction the following overall system architecture is defined.

The complete architecture, shown in Figure 28.8, shows the FPGA processor and the host computer where the PCI card is plugged in. Here we focus on the FPGA outline with its architecture. The module *Host-Interface* manages the atom and the lookup table data when it is transferred from the host memory into the local memory banks of the FPGA processor. This module also provides a set of register where the host processor can read result and status information and write control commands to the parallel architecture. The two *RAM* modules are needed to handle the data transfer which load the data during the initialization process and performs the data readout when the energy calculation is executed. The two *RAM* modules work independently and are able to transfer a 64-bit data words with each single clock cycle. The complete workflow is controlled by the *Design Workflow Control* module. This module generates all internal signals which are necessary to synchronize the independent modules and to exchange data words.

Apart from these necessary access and control structures the real energy calculation is performed by the *Distance Calculation*, the *Energy Determination*, and the *Energy Summation* module. These three modules are arranged within a pipeline and run in parallel. The calculated distance values are generated and directly passed forward to the energy determination and the determined energy value is then further passed to the energy summation. This pipeline structure enables that the distance of the next atom

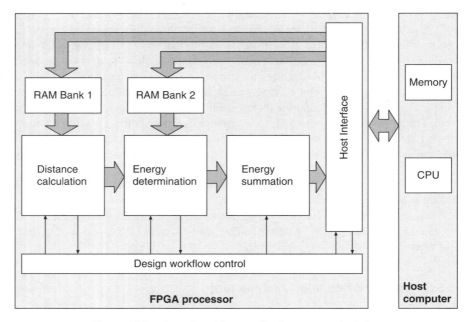

Figure 28.8 Overall architecture for the energy calculation.

pair can be calculated while the energy value of the current atom pair is determined in the second stage. Altogether, the pipeline structure allows that a new atom pair can be processed with each single clock cycle. The bit width of the data path along the pipeline flow differs because only necessary data values are passed from one stage to the next stage. The individual energy contributions are passed as an 18-bit data word into the last stage, where the terms are summarized to the total 32-bit energy value.

The same pipeline principle is also used within the energy calculation modules. The principles of the pipelining model is described using the distance calculation and the advantages in conjunction with the FPGA execution are shown. Basically, pipelining is another way, to execute operations in a parallel manner. It is a very efficient way especially to execute mathematical operations like the vector sum computation. This vector sum computation can be seen as a combination of multiplications, additions, and subtractions as shown in Eq. (28.3). As illustrated in Figure 28.9 the individual arithmetic operations are all running in parallel using dedicated modules. These modules are connected by registers which store the interim results for only one clock cycle. These individual interim results are shifted through the whole pipeline until the last stage calculates the vector sum result. The advantage of such a pipeline structure is the parallel execution of the single operations and the higher frequency that can be applied to the complete parallel architecture.

The time needed to process one arithmetic operation is defined by the logic levels that are needed for the operation. This time is called the propagation delay time and defines the maximum frequency for the operation. Computing two consecutive operations without a register stage in between increases the total propagation delay

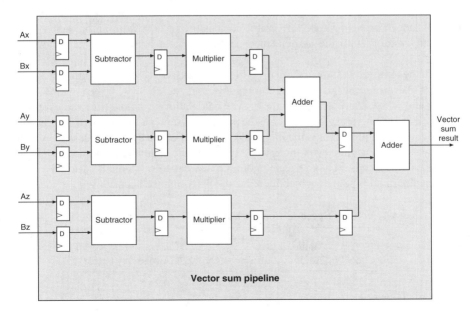

Figure 28.9 Parallel architecture of the vector sum calculation pipeline.

time to the sum of both single propagation times and reduces the maximum frequency accordingly. Thus, one operation is split into two parts separated by one register and the maximum frequency will raise because the propagation delay time is reduced. Another advantage of the pipeline structure is the point that a new data word can be processed with every single clock cycle which leads to extremely high throughputs. Only the fact that the result is only available after a certain amount of clock cycles must be taken into account in the design process of the parallel architectures.

Both the high frequency and the possibility to process operations at each clock cycle result in an excellent overall performance especially for arithmetic computations like the vector sum shown earlier.

28.5.7   Results

The overall performance of the parallel working architecture has been compared between a software-executed energy calculation and the FPGA processor-accelerated implementation. The software implementation has been executed on a Pentium III system with 450 MHz and the FPGA-supported application has been run on the same system but makes use of the described FPGA architecture. The FPGA design itself was clocked with 60 MHz.

For the estimation of the speedup, we switched off the collision detection to prevent aborts of calculations and we set the Maximum$_{ABS}$ value to the maximum to prevent an amino acid calculation from being aborted. The intention for this settings were to achieve results that depend only on the amount of protein atoms rather than on the somewhat arbitrary cutoff distances.

Three proteins were taken from the PDB database and supplemented with a hypothetical (not-existent) protein "Polyvalin" consisting of 100 Valin amino acids. The executed proteins with the associated execution times are shown in the following Table 28.1.

Both the Pentium system and the used FPGA processor were built around the same time and therefore, the systems are comparable.

The shown speedup factors for the energy calculation task are still valid even for modern state-of-the-art systems, where the processors run $\approx$ 8 times faster. The reason for the equal speedup factor is the increased frequency of the FPGA processors which is today twice as fast and even more important than the available resource amount in the FPGAs. Modern FPGAs provide enough resources to implement up to 25 of the described parallel pipelines which increase the performance accordingly.

TABLE 28.1   Speedup Comparison Table

Proteins (PDB Codes)	Amino Acids	Execution Time		Speed-up Factor
		Software (ms)	FPGA (ms)	
1knb	186	1560	40.2	39
Polyvalin	100	360	10.4	35
1crn	46	75	2.16	35
1vii	35	60	1.60	38

28.6   CONCLUSION

Modern bioinformatics have to face two major problems. First, the huge and increasing data amount that have to be analyzed and second, the usage of more complex and sophisticated algorithms for the computation. Both facts automatically lead to longer computing times. The general approach to keep the computing time feasible or to reduce the computing times is to use the general approach of parallelization.

The parallelization of applications is usually performed on the process or on the thread level using multi processor systems, clusters, or grids. Especially, the clusters, and grids are very popular, because these systems can be build up easily using of-the-shelf components like computing systems and a high speed network to connect them. They are also easy to handle, because the complex task of distributing an application to a cluster and programming the cluster is supported by several programming environments which take over the complete communication and synchronization between the nodes. But on the other hand clusters also have specific characteristics which limits their usage for the parallel execution of applications. One important limitation are the costs of an cluster. Even if an application can be ideally distributed to a cluster, because of a linear decrease in computing time, the size of the cluster will be limited by the costs of the hardware components and sometimes also by the cost of the software licenses. The second limitation are the applications itself. Every distributed application that has a high communication rate has a optimum cluster size. A further distribution to more nodes will increase the total execution time because of the additional need in communication time.

In summary, it can be ascertained that there are some applications which are limited in their parallelization and even more important that there are applications that cannot be accelerated by using clusters or grids. This is especially the case if the parallelization has to be done on instruction level rather than on thread or process level. New computing approaches have to be developed to enable the fast and parallel execution also on the instruction level.

One solution for a new computing approach that can execute applications on a parallelized instruction level are shown in this chapter. FPGA devices are used to execute the parallel architectures. The advantages of this computing devices is their massively parallel structure and their flexibility. Within one FPGA up to several thousand operations are executed in parallel like it is known from ASICs. The flexibility of the FPGAs allows to reprogram them in less than a second to perform a completely different parallel architecture. These two features of the FPGA devices makes them ideally suited for the execution of an application that is parallelized on instruction level. The advantage of the parallelized execution is shown by the implementation of the energy calculation part used in a protein structure prediction application. The used algorithm for this task is not well suited for a cluster or grid execution. Therefore, the algorithm is transformed into a parallel working architecture which achieves at least a 35-fold speedup compared to one cluster node.

This new computing approach can be integrated in standard computing systems as coprocessor cards. Therefore, it can be used also in conjunction with existing clusters to boost the computing performance. As it is shown in the chapter the utilization of these FPGA processors can improve the performance of an existing cluster or it can reduce the cluster size without reducing the overall performance.

It is believed that, the reader will leave this chapter with an appreciation of the possibilities that the described new computing approach using FPGA processor may offer. This new FPGA processors are general computing devices and they can be used in almost all scientific and industrial solutions. The chapter shows the transformation from a sequential algorithm into a parallel working architecture for two concrete examples. These examples might give the reader an idea for their specific application to think of a parallelization on the instruction level.

ACKNOWLEDGMENTS

The author wishes to thank Dr. Eckart Bindewald and Prof. Dr. Silvio Tosatto for the work that was done to implement the protein structure prediction application.

REFERENCES

1. J. L. Hennessy and D. A. Patterson, *Computer Architecture: A Quantitative Approach*, Morgan Kaufmann Publisher Inc., CA, USA, 1996.

2. A. S. Tanenbaum, *Structured Computer Organization,* 3rd Ed., Prentice-Hall International Inc., USA, 1990.

3. A. Y. Żomaya, Ed., *Parallel and Distributed Computing Handbook*, McGraw-Hill, New York, 1996.

4. B. Jähne, H. Hauecker, and P. Geiler, *Handbook of Computer Vision and Applications*, Academic Press, San Diego, CA, USA, 1999.

5. A. Kugel, et al., 50 kHz Pattern Recognition on a Large FPGA Processor Enable++, *IEEE Symposium on FPGAs for Custom Computing Machines*, pp. 262–263, 1998.

6. H. Högl, et al., Enable++: A Second Generation FPGA Processor, *IEEE Symposium on FPGAs for Custom Computing Machines*, pp. 45–53, 1995.

7. N. G. Einspruch and J. L. Hilbert, Eds., *Application Specific Integrated Circuit (ASIC) Technology*, Academic Press, San Diego, CA, USA, 1991.

8. S. D. Brown, R. J. Francis, J. Rose, and Z. G. Vranesic, *Field-Programmable Gate Arrays*, Kluwert Academic Press, Norwell, MA, USA, 1992.

9. Xilinx Inc., *Xilinx Virtex II Pro and Virtex II Pro X Platform FPGAs: Complete Data Sheet*, Xilinx Inc., San Jose, CA, USA, 2004.

10. Altera Corporation, *Altera — Excalibur Device Overview*, Altera Corporation, San Jose, CA, USA, 2002.

11. T. Shanley and D. Anderson, *PCI System Architecture*, Addison Wesley Longman Ltd., Essex, England, 1999.

12. S. A. Cuenca, F. Ibarra, and R. Alvarez, *Reconfigurable Frame-Grabber For Real-Timer Automated Visual Inspection Systems*, Field-Programmable Logic and Applications FPL 2001, LNCS 2147, pp. 223–231, 2001.

13. B. Gorini, M. Joos, J. Petersen, A. Kugel, R. Männer, M. Müller, M. Yu, B. Green, and G. Kieft, A RobIn prototype for a PCI-Bus based atlas readout-system, in Proceeding of the Ninth *Workshop on Electronics for LHC Experiments 2003*, Amsterdam, Netherland, 2003.

14. J. Hesser, C. Hinkelbein, K. Kornmesser, T. Kuberka, A. Kugel, R. Männer, H. Singpiel, and B. Vettermann, ATLANTIS — A Hybrid Approach Combining the Power of FPGA and RISC Processors based on CompactPCI, *Proceedings of the IEEE Symposium on FPGAs for Custom Computing Machines*, 1999.

15. A. Kugel, *The usbFPGA Co-Processor*, http://www-li5.ti.uni-mannheim.de/fpga/usbfpga.

16. C. Hinkelbein and R. Männer, Reconfigurable Hardware Control Software using Anonymous Libraries, Proceedings of the First International Conference on Field-Programmable Technology, Hong Kong, pp. 426–428, 2002.

17. H. M. Berman, J. Westbrook, Z. Feng, G. Gilliland, T. N. Bhat, H. Weissig, I. N. Shindyalov, and P. E. Bourne *The Protein Data Bank*, Nucleic Acids Research, 28 pp. 235–242, 2000.

18. T. E. Creighton, *Protein Structures and Molecular Properties*, W.H. Freeman and Co., New York, USA, 1993.

19. R. Buckert and N. L. Allinger, *Molecular Mechanics*, American Chemical Society, Washington D.C., USA, 1982.

20. A. Fiser, R. Sanchez, F. Melo, and A. Sali, Comparative protein structure modeling, *Comput. Biochem. Biophys.* 275–312 (2001).

21. D. Jones, Progress in protein structure prediction, *Curr. Opin. Struct. Biol.* 7, 377–387 (1997).

22. C. A. Orengo, J. E. Bray, T. Hubbard, L. Loconte, and I. Silitoe, Analysis and assessment of ab initio three-dimensional prediction, secondary structure, and contacts prediction, *Proteins* Suppl. 3, 149–170 (1999).

23. A. Finkelstein, Protein structure: what is possible to predict now? *Curr. Opin. Struct. Biol.*, 7, 60–71 (1997).

24. D. J. Osguthorpe, Ab initio protein folding, *Curr. Opin. Struct. Biol.* 10, 146–152 (2000).

25. A.-J. Li and R. Nussinov, A set of van der Waals and coulombic radii of protein atoms for molecular and solvent-accessible surface calculation, packing evaluation, and docking, *Proteins* 32, 111–127, (1998).

26. V. N. Maiorov and G. M. Crippen, Contact potential that recognizes the correct folding of globular proteins, *J. Mol. Biol.* 227 876–888 (1992).

ADDITIONAL INFORMATION

A. S. Tanenbaum, *Computer Networks,* 2nd Ed., Prentice-Hall International Inc., Englewood Cliffs, NY, USA, 1988.

A. R. Leach, *Molecular Modelling*, Addison Wesley Longman Ltd., Essex, England, 1996.

G. E. Schulz and R. H. Schirmer, *Principles of Protein Structure*, Springer-Verlag New York Inc., New York, NY, USA, 1996.

S. Mullender, *Distributed Systems*, 2nd Ed., ACM Press New York, New York, NY, USA, 1993.

R. W. Hockney, *Parallel Computers 2*, IOP Publishing Ltd., Bristol, England, 1988.

D. A. Buell, J. M. Arnold, and W. J. Kleinfelder, *Splash 2 — FPGAs in a Custom Computing Machine*, IEEE Computer Society Press, Los Alamitos, CA, USA, 1996.

K. M. Merz and S. M. Le Grand, *The Protein Folding Problem and Tertiary Structure Prediction*, Birkhäuser, 1994.

B. Rost and C. Sander, Bridging the protein sequence-structure gap by structure predictions, *Ann. Rev. Biophys. Biomol. Struct.*, 25, 113–136 (1996).

G. M. Crippen and Y. Z. Ohkubo, Statistical mechaics of protein folding by exhaustive enumeration, *Proteins* 32, 425–437 (1998).

G. M. Crippen and M. E. Snow, A 1.8 A resolution potential function for protein folding, *Biopolymers* 29, 1479–1489 (1990).

M. Sippl, Calculation of the knowledge-based prediction of local structures in globular proteins, *J. Mol. Biol.*, 213 859–883 (1990).

Virtual Microscopy: Distributed Image Storage, Retrieval, Analysis, and Visualization

T. PAN, S. JEWEL, U. CATALYUREK, P. WENZEL, G. LEONE, S. HASTINGS, S. OSTER, S. LANGELLA, T. KURC, J. SALTZ, and D. COWDEN

Technological advances in microscopy, digital image acquisition, and automation have allowed digital, virtual slides to be used in pathology and microbiology. Virtual microscopy has the benefits of parallel distribution, on-demand reviews, rapid diagnosis, and long-term warehousing of slides. Sensor technologies combined with high power magnification generate uncompressed images, which can reach 50 GB per image in size. In a clinical or research environment, the number of slides scanned can compound the challenges in storing and managing these images. A distributed storage system coupled with a distributed execution framework is currently the best way to overcome these challenges to perform large-scale analysis and visualization. We demonstrate an implementation that integrates several middleware components in a distributed environment to enable and optimize the storage and analysis of the digital information. These systems support and enable virtual slide reviews, pathology image analysis, and 3D reconstruction and visualization of microscopy data sets in both clinical and research settings.

29.1 INTRODUCTION

In the past few years, there has been an explosion of technology in the area of virtual microscopy. Virtual microscopy is the digitization of whole slides and the subsequent visualization and interaction with the electronic image purely in silica. Although, the technology has matured to the point where commercial products have now become

Parallel Computing for Bioinformatics and Computational Biology, Edited by Albert Y. Zomaya
Copyright © 2006 John Wiley & Sons, Inc.

available, virtual microscopy remains an area of active research from systems to acquisition technology to image analysis applications.

A complete virtual microscopy system must integrate both hardware and software into an end-to-end solution. The system must satisfy several criteria from the user perspective: (1) fast scanning speed, (2) acceptable image quality, (3) easy data management, (4) interactive image review, and (5) integration with image processing and analysis.

Telepathology, the technologies that make it possible to examine specimens at a distance, has been an active research in last decade [1–5]. Virtual microscopy is a completely digital telepathology application [6] which has become popular in the past few years. The first virtual microscope implementation has been presented by Ferreira et al. [7, 8]. They designed and implemented a realistic digital emulation of a high power light microscope, through a client–server architecture. Catalyurek et al. [6] extended this design to utilize distributed architecture to serve microscopy images to multiple clients, which prefetches and caches portions of the image to ensure interactive navigation of the images.

Similarly, scanning hardware have been in existence long before the current commercial trend. Romer et al. at OSU's Pathology Department constructed their own scanner from a standard Olympus microscope. It is coupled with a robotic stage and a color video camera. The scanner allows whole slides to be captured as a grid of microscopy views, which are then stitched into a single collage using commercial software [9]. Commercial products offer a level of quality and reliability assurance, however, that is well suited for production use in clinical settings.

In the commercial arena, several companies have established themselves with viable products or and promising next generation technologies. Aperio [10] provides scanners for whole slide digitization as well as the data management system and the review software. Aperio utilizes a traditional robotic stage along with a line camera for image capture. Interscope [11] and Trestle [12] have similar products that utilize area cameras. D'metrix [13] has developed scanner technology that utilizes a miniature objective lens array to parallelize acquisition.

Each of these scanner manufacturers also provide their own data management and slide review software that interact closely with their own hardware platforms. Some companies, such as Bacus [14], are offering review and management software alone. The lack of a common standard, however, limits interoperability between the different vendors at the moment.

This chapter discusses the infrastructure required to support slide digitization and data management in both clinical and research environments. Several applications, for both production and research, are provided to demonstrate the capability of virtual microscopy. Finally, some challenges facing virtual microscopy are outlined.

29.2   ARCHITECTURE

In the heterogeneous environment of an academic research hospital, a virtual microscopy system needs to support different types of usages, specifically production and research. In this section, technical requirements for the different types of usages are highlighted. Different aspects of the system architecture, including acquisition, storage and data management, and review and analysis, are described.

29.2.1 Slide Scanner

Central to a virtual microscopy system is the slide scanner. Within the Ohio State University healthcare organization, two Aperio scanners as well as a custom-built scanner forms the acquisition core. The custom scanner and one of the Aperio scanners are located in the Pathology Department of the OSU Medical Center. The remaining Aperio scanner is located at the Columbus Children's Hospital, where it is used primarily as clinical support for pediatric oncology.

Although custom hardware systems are good research and proof-of-concept systems, they are typically more expensive to construct, operate, and support. In contrast, the Aperio system is a commercial off-the-shelf technology with vendor and user group support. Similar to the OSU custom scanner, the Aperio scanner also utilizes robotic stage and digital camera. However, design decisions reflect the goal of high throughput and high quality microscopy image digitization. Using a line camera for image acquisition improves acquisition speed and quality as the stage does not need to stop during the acquisition process, unlike tile-based systems [15].

The incorporation of a slide autoloader in the Aperio system further improves throughput. The automated tissue location and auto-focus features enable automated scanning, which when coupled with the autoloader, allow slides to be processed in batch mode during off-peak hours. Designing and building an autoloader for a custom-built scanner, although feasible, do not represent a cost-effective solution. The economics of scale played an important role in the decision to acquire a commercial scanner. For the remainder of this section, discussions assume the Aperio scanner to be the image acquisition device.

The Aperio scanner scans whole slides that are up to $75 \times 50 \, \text{mm}^2$ in size, but typically $75 \times 25 \, \text{mm}^2$ slides are used for microscopy and pathology. At $200\times$ magnification, the scanner has a resolution of $0.47 \, \mu\text{m}$ in the x and y directions. As the specimen being scanned may cover up to $50 \times 25 \, \text{mm}^2$ of the slide area, the resulting image may contain up to $108,000 \times 54,000$ or 5.9 billion pixels. Each uncompressed color image, with 24 bit RGB pixels, can reach up to 16.3 GB in size. Using $400\times$ magnification implies roughly double the scan time and a quadruple increase in data size. The impact of the large data size will be discussed further in the remainder of this section. The uncompressed images are stored in stripes that have the same width as the line camera acquisition and full height of the slide.

29.2.2 Image Management System

Postacquisition data management is a task that is common to many disciplines. For radiology, this task has largely become a commercial solution through the widespread use of Picture Archive and Communications System (PACS) and common protocol for encoding and communication via the Digital Imaging and Communications in

Medicine (DICOM) standard [16]. Virtual microscopy, as an emerging technology, does not yet have the luxury of industry standards. However, basic components need to exist to create a generally usable system for virtual microscopy. These components include image storage subsystem, image server for on-demand retrieval, computation subsystem, review client, annotation database, and image storage and communication standard.

At the bare minimum, the image storage system provides basic capability for archival, whether long-term, short-term, or a mixture of durations. It can employ a distributed storage mechanism to take advantage of larger aggregated storage and bandwidth. The image server provides an interface to the image store, from which images are retrieved on the basis of client queries. It acts as both a database engine and execution manager for computation subsystem. Computation subsystem is used to execute compute-intensive tasks varying from simple image decoding to more complex image analysis. It can also employ distributed execution mechanism. The review client is responsible for presenting the image to the user in a user-friendly manner and provides basic image analysis and annotation capabilities. The annotation database allows the reviewer's annotations to be captured and stored by a structured process. Finally, the image store and communications standard provide the glue through which all of the components are integrated and the abstraction layer above which components from different vendors inter-operate.

29.2.2.1 *Production Infrastructure*

In a production environment, a virtual microscopy system has to function reliably in managing and delivering the images to the end users. The primary applications in a clinical setting are slide archival, telepathology, and education. These applications require common functionalities, which includes: (1) query for image based on metadata, (2) retrieve and view image, and (3) annotate image.

The requirement of mass storage is common to all three applications. Telepathology in most cases requires efficient use of available bandwidth, which implies image compression, progressive retrieval, prefetching, and caching. In addition, client support for virtual conferencing is sometimes necessary for teleconferencing. Educational use of the system requires server support for high volume slide browsing.

Aperio provides various components for addressing these functional needs. Fundamental to meeting these requirements is the design of an efficient image compression scheme. Aperio designed a proprietary file format that supports multiple levels of details, random retrieval of image blocks, and JPEG2000 compression of these blocks. Compression ratio for these images ranges from 15 : 1 to 70 : 1, depending on information content. These file format features allow efficient retrieval of only the data that is required for the current region of interest at the current magnification of interest.

Aperio's image server represents the mass storage subsystem as well as the image database and computation subsystem. Two different types of clients communicate with the server. ImageScope is a thick client, which retrieves compressed images and performs client side prefetching and caching to improve performance. The image data is decompressed on the client as needed. The web client is a simple Macromedia Flash web application that requests a region of interest at a particular magnification.

The image server, upon receiving the HTTP request, retrieves the designated portion of the image and re-encoded it into a JPEG image to send back to the web client. In this case, the server performs most of the computationally intensive tasks, as well as acting as a web server. Although the web client is designed for quick review of the microscopy images, the ImageScope client allows virtual slide conferencing as well as annotation of the images.

Today's commercial image server and the viewing clients, along with the scanner, form a complete, end-to-end system, which is adequate and well suited for a small to medium size organization, where the scientific or clinical applications are well defined and limited to telepathology, slide archival, and education. However, as the size of the organization, the number of organizations involved, and the number of slides scanned increase, their end-to-end solutions become less scalable. Distributed computing and storage technologies become necessary complements.

29.2.3 Research Infrastructure

In contrast to production usage, research infrastructure affords more flexibility and potentially more diverse requirements. In this case, the goal is to provide advanced capabilities in managing and processing large virtual microscopy images.

The lack of a standard for image encoding and communication implies that each vendor as well as research group must develop their own set of "standards." The case is similar for the research infrastructure at the Ohio State University. However, care was taken to develop components that are generic and reusable. The research infrastructure encompasses all six components as described in Section 29.2.2 with a research emphasis on distributed storage and computation subsystems.

29.2.3.1 Storage Subsystem   On the storage subsystem, one solution that has been investigated by both the Department of Biomedical Informatics and Columbus Children's Hospital involves using a hierarchical mass storage system. The Ohio Supercomputing Center recently installed an IBM StorageTank mass storage system. This system provides 450 TB of online storage. The system consists of a core with 50 TB of high speed fiber channel (FC) disks, a 400 TB pool of inexpensive IDE disks attached through FC switches to a cluster of machines, namely, active disk managers, and a tape backup system (currently 128 TB) connected through same FC switches. The storage space is shared among multiple projects across the state of Ohio. Existing plan for large-scale clinical virtual microscopy calls for interfacing the Aperio image server with StorageTank. As for the research use, we have been using our Mobius [17, 18] and STORM [19, 20] middlewares to implement storage subsystem.

The large image size created challenges for image analysis as an application in several ways. The first, and the most fundamental, is the representation of the images. Aperio created a proprietary file format that utilizes lossy compression to reach reasonable file sizes in the sub-GB range for 200× magnification scanning. However, the nature of proprietary file format exclude easy access to the data content from analysis algorithms without using commercial software, which are not extensible except via vendor licensing. As a consequence, the research system at Department of Biomedical Informatics currently interacts with the raw stripe data, which are specifically saved for this purpose. Once the raw data is obtained, standard image compression schemes may be used to reduce storage system load and to improve access time.

Another motivation for working with uncompressed images as opposed to the compressed is that lossy compression invariably reduces image quality. Although it is unclear how much a compression algorithm such as JPEG2000 affects image data content, uncompressed images always provide the maximum quality for the analysis algorithms.

29.2.3.2   *Computation Subsystem*   The large amount of data, particularly in the uncompressed form, not only require large amount of storage capacity but also analysis of these images are most efficiently handled by parallel and distributed algorithms. This implies the use of clusters of machines for storage and computation. At the Ohio State University, we have various small size storage and computation clusters and we also have direct access to Ohio Super Computer's large computation clusters. Our computational infrastructure is built on top of DataCutter, STORM, and Mobius middlewares that our group have been developing.

DataCutter [21–24] is a component-based middleware framework [25–32] designed to provide support for user-defined processing of large multi-dimensional data sets across a wide-area network. In DataCutter, application processing structure is implemented as a set of components, referred to as *filters*, which exchange data through a *stream* abstraction. The interface for a *filter* consists of three functions: (1) an initialization function (*init*), in which any required resources such as memory for data structures are allocated and initialized; (2) a processing function (*process*), in which user-defined operations are applied on data elements; and (3) a finalization function (*finalize*), in which the resources allocated in *init* are released. Filters are connected via *logical streams*. A *stream* denotes a uni-directional data flow from one filter (i.e., the producer) to another (i.e., the consumer). A filter is required to read data from its input streams and write data to its output streams only. The DataCutter runtime system supports execution of filters on heterogeneous collections of storage and compute clusters in a distributed environment. Processing, network, and data copying overheads are minimized by the ability to place filters on different platforms. DataCutter is capable of implementing support for instantiation and execution of the various services, which can be implemented as DataCutter filters or filter groups, in the proposed framework. The filtering service as DataCutter performs most steps necessary to instantiate filters on the desired hosts, to connect all logical endpoints and to call the filter's interface functions for processing work. Data exchange between two filters on the same host is carried out by memory copy operations, whereas TCP sockets are employed for communication between filters on different hosts.

STORM is a services-based middleware [19, 20], implemented using DataCutter, which is designed to provide basic database support for: (1) *Selection of the data of interest.* The data of interest is selected based on either the values of particular attributes or ranges of attribute values (i.e., range queries). The selection operation can also involve joins between multiple data sets and user-defined filtering operations; and (2) *Transfer of data from storage nodes to compute nodes for processing.* After the data of interest has been selected, it can be transferred from storage systems to processor memories for processing by a data analysis program. If the data analysis program runs on a cluster, STORM supports partitioning of data elements in an application-specific way among the destination processors. To provide these capabilities, STORM is designed as a set of coupled services. The *query service* provides an entry point for clients to submit queries to the database middleware. It is responsible for parsing the client query to determine which services should be instantiated to answer the query. The *metadata service* maintains information about data sets and indexes and user-defined filters associated with the data sets. The *data source* service provides a view of a data set in the form of virtual tables to other services. Efficient execution of select operations is supported by two services: *indexing service* and *filtering service.* The *indexing service* encapsulates indexes for a data set. The *filtering service* is responsible for efficient execution of user-defined filters. The purpose of the *partition generation service* is to make it possible for an application developer to export the data distribution scheme employed in a parallel client program. The *data mover* is responsible for transferring the selected data elements to the client based on the partitioning information returned from the *partition generation service.*

Mobius is a metadata management middleware [17, 18]. It is developed using Java, therefore, allowing rapid deployment on different platforms. Mobius provides two key services that are well suited for a distributed image management system. The first service is the schema management system, Global Model Exchange (GME). GME acts as the global authority for the different database schema, which allows users from different organizations to share and reuse portions of common schema (Fig. 29.1). GME also allows versioning of schemas. This promotes common best practices in syntactic structure of data as well as facilitates data sharing between collaborators. The second service of importance is the Mako XML database service. Mako creates databases based on user-defined schemas and allows storage and retrieval of XML documents that conform to these schema. Because of this constraint, the database is guaranteed to contain well-formed data. Mako supports indexing at different element levels within the XML document, as well as referencing and including remote XML documents. This indexing and virtual inclusion capability allow efficient query and retrieval of regions of interest in an image, which may be partitioned and distributed across multiple nodes. Mako supports XPath and XQuery, which are XML protocols for query and retrieval of data within the database. Once the user obtains the schema, he or she can query and retrieve portions of the XML documents within the database.

29.2.3.3 *Distributed PACS* Picture Archive and Communication Systems (PACS) have become a common component of radiology information systems during the last two decades. As virtual microscopy gain acceptance in pathology departments and research organizations, microscopy PACS will similarly become a standard component. When compared with single server configuration, distributed architecture offers several benefits:

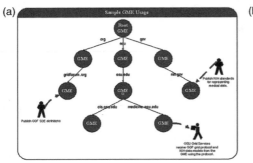 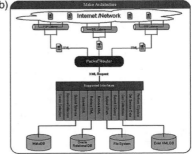

Figure 29.1 (*a*) GME using a hierarchy of authorities to manage metadata schemas. (*b*) The flexibility of Mako database service architecture.

- Distributed storage of data sets allows parallel access to improve single user performance.
- Distributed storage of images allows multiplexed access to improve multi-user performance.
- Distributed location of images allows parallel image processing.

BMI developed a distributed PACS system [33], GridPACS, based on the Mobius metadata management middleware [17, 18]. GridPACS is an application built on top of the Mobius middleware to leverage its features. It consists of a generic image data set schema for use with Mako to setup databases, several image ingestors for ingesting images into the databases, and a front-end user interface for querying and reviewing data sets. GridPACS was designed to handle both radiology and microscopy images, mainly through different ways of using the same data schema (Fig. 29.2). To support the widest possible types of images, the schema separates the metadata from the actual image data. Image metadata subschema allows arbitrary name-value pairs, therefore providing a great deal of flexibility. The image data subschema organizes data hierarchically, from image stack, to image grid, to image, and finally to tiles. Image stack represents a sequence of images, either temporal or spatial along z-axis. The use of tiles allows efficient storage of very large images by partitioning it into smaller, more manageable chunks. Each tile has been labeled with the data set source, as well as the x, y, and z extents of the bounding box. This allows efficient query and retrieval of tiles directly given the data set id and a region of interest.

The XML schema allows Mako to rapidly create databases that are customized for a particular application, in this case, for image management. Matching ingestors are developed to transform source images into XML documents with the accepted syntax and store them in the database. Two types of XML documents are submitted for each image data set. The first is for the tiles. The Aperio ingestor imports the uncompressed stripes, partition them into tiles, and generates an XML document for each of the tile, attaching position and data set information. The tile XMLs are submitted to Mako, and document references are returned and added to the data set XML document, which is submitted to Mako after all tiles have been ingested. The actual image tiles

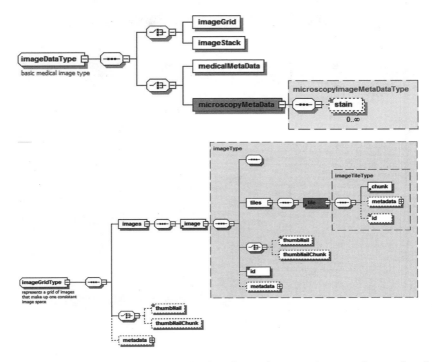

Figure 29.2   Hierarchical schema organization allows microscopy images to be stored as tiles.

are stored as binary attachments to the tile XML documents and can be compressed using a preselected compression scheme. In this case, the image have been stored uncompressed, partly to illustrate large-scale computing capabilities.

The GridPACS user interface, as shown in Figure 29.3, is a tool for navigating through the available data sets. The user specifies the databases to connect to and the available data sets are listed along with thumbnails of the images. The front-end client allows queries of basic information, such as patient id. Once the query results are retrieved, additional metadata can be viewed in the application. Depending on whether the data sets are radiological or microscopic, the user interface changes to reflect the different organization of the images. For radiology, retrieved images are displayed at full resolution. For microscopy, however, full magnification becomes impractical due to the amount of data to be transfered. Instead, an $1\times$ magnification subsampled image is displayed. The subsampled image allows specification of regions of interest for further image analysis, as described later in this section.

For interactive review of the images, as well as annotation in the research environment, a simple viewer that works with the native data structure as well as the GridPACS system is needed. Previous work by Catalyurek used a pyramidal data presentation and integrates prefetching and caching [34]. It allows storage of data across multiple nodes in a cluster, managed using DataCutter or Active Data Repository (ADR) [35, 36]. The integration of this virtual microscopy viewer (Fig. 29.4) with

Figure 29.3 GridPACS front end GUI, showing an H&E stained virtual slide.

the GridPACS application would allow interactive reviews of the microscopy slides from within the image management tool and provide single point of entry for image review, annotation, and analysis.

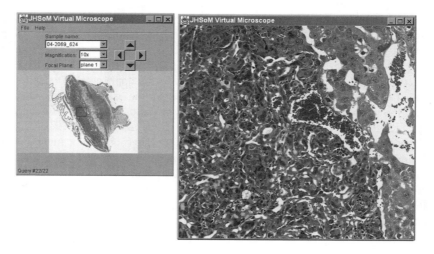

Figure 29.4 The virtual microscope client.

29.2.3.4 Distributed Image Analysis The digitization of histology and microscopy images provide a natural research opportunity for advanced images analysis, including feature detection and automated quantification. The large data size of the images implies that parallel and distributed computation is necessary for timely execution of analysis algorithms. In a cluster-based research infrastructure, the storage nodes typically also carry computational resources, which forms a convenient topology for distributed computation and reduces data movement overhead.

The distributed image processing depends on the DataCutter middleware. Although the DataCutter provides the distributed process execution engine, algorithms need to be developed for image analysis. Several toolkits, such as the Visualization Toolkit (VTK) [37] and Insight Segmentation and Registration Toolkit (ITK) [38], are available publicly, which provide well documented, tested, and community accepted algorithms. Image Processing for the Grid toolkit (IP4G) provides the integration layer for deploying these algorithm implementations, along with custom algorithms, in analysis pipelines [39].

IP4G includes a set of classes that encapsulate the image chunks for movement between DataCutter filters. The classes are extended with ITK, VTK, or custom algorithm functionalities to operate on the image chunks. When multiple copies of these filters are executed in the DataCutter framework, the algorithms used are in essence parallelized at the data level.

The GridPACS user interface tool has been extended, for microscopy images, to allow the user to invoke distributed image processing using the IP4G and DataCutter middleware (Fig. 29.5). The user first specifies a region of interest and then either retrieve a previous analysis pipeline or construct a new pipeline. The user can select the filters being used in the pipeline, specify the parameters and input, and submit the generated XML configuration file to the listening DataCutter server, which then executes the pipeline. Filters are designed to retrieve tiles directly from the GridPACS database, thus avoiding retrieval and forwarding of data by the GridPACS client. The analysis can be performed on-demand or in batch, where the results are stored in Mobius result databases.

29.3 IMAGE ANALYSIS

As previously described, digital microscopy creates a need for image analysis due in part to the large scale of the images and provides an opportunity to introduce more systematic reproducibility and objectivity to the microscopy image assessment process. The infrastructure described in Section 29.2.3.4 enables feature quantification and classification and provides a framework for rapid algorithm development and comparison. The spectrum of applications of image analysis for microscopy range from pathology decision support, to clinical studies, to basic scientific research. This section describes use cases, that illustrate the importance of image analysis for large-scale virtual microscopy.

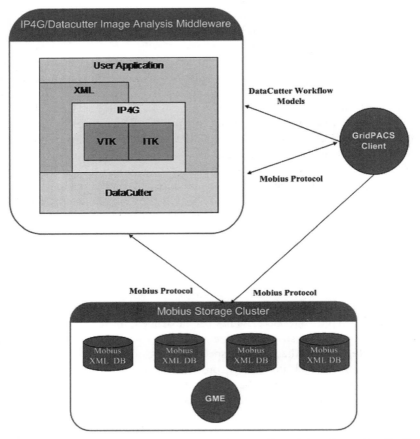

Figure 29.5 GridPACS system architecture utilizes IP4G and DataCutter for distributed processing, Mobius cluster for image storage, and GridPACS client for user navigation and analysis invocation.

In this section, we examine three application use cases, which leverage the virtual microscopy infrastructure. These include mouse placenta reconstruction and analysis and confocal mouse brain imaging analysis.

29.3.1 Mouse Placenta

Mouse placenta offers a convenient and controlled model for studying developmental biology as well as cancer genetics. Rb gene, which is a known oncogene, has been previously demonstrated by Gustavo Leone, Ph.D., at OSU to regulate mouse placenta development. Rb-knockout placenta shows morphological differences from wild type [41, 42]. The differences have been qualitatively described and manually measured in histological sections of the placenta. Three tissue layers show involvement in the morphologic changes: labyrinth layer, spongiotropoblast layer, and giant cell layer.

In Rb-knockout placenta, labyrinth layer shows higher level of spongiotropoblast invasion, which reduces blood space and, therefore, gas exchange capacity.

Virtual microscopy presents two opportunities in the assessment of these morphological changes. First, digitization of slides allow objective, computer aided analysis to be performed. Secondly, sequential sections can be used to reconstruct a placenta model, which would aid in visualization and quantification of the morphological changes, as well as providing an atlas for comparison of placentae. The project consist of two initial tasks. The first task is to perform a 3D reconstruction of placental sections for visualization and quantification, which is described in further detail subsequently. The second task is to classify and segment the tissue layers, which allows for measurement of cell layer changes.

The placenta is fixed in paraffin and cut into 3 μm sections. The slides are stained with H&E stains for structural presentation. A single mouse placenta yields approximately 1200 sections. The first two placentae were digitized by scanning every fifth section. The latest placenta was scanned in its entirety at 200× magnification on the Aperio scanner using the autoloader. The total data size for a single, complete placenta is approximately 800 GB. The data were processed with VTK and ITK algorithms using the infrastructure described in Section 29.2.3.4.

29.3.1.1 3D Reconstruction
Reconstructing serial section into a single volume is essentially a registration process to register the successive images [43]. Owing to the large data size, direct image based registration, such as mutual information registration, is not practical, since both the source and target images need to reside in memory. For microscopy data sets, a single image can exceed the memory capacity of the workstation. Multiresolution approaches can potentially bypass this limitation. Alternatively, mutual information registration may be modifiable to utilize a distributed environment.

Currently, the approach taken for image registration is feature based. Instead of aligning images, features of the images are matched and aligned. This simplifies the movement of data as well as allowing the registration to be parallelized at the individual image level.

The first step in the registration process is detecting primary edges in the images. The points along these edges form the feature sets. The features of successive images are aligned to each other, and a transformation matrix is obtained for each successive image. The registration algorithm selected for this task is iterative closest points (ICP) registration [44]. ICP chooses from the target feature set a subset of points that are closest to each of the source feature set. The corresponding points are aligned with a least-squares minimum distance algorithm. The transformation is then applied to the source feature set and a new set of corresponding points are selected from the target features. The process iterates until either there is convergence or the maximum number of iterations have reached.

The final transformation matrix for each image is concatenated with the preceding images in a recursive process, so that each transformation matrix becomes relative to the first image and the global coordinate system. Each image is then transformed into the global coordinate system and stacked together to form a volume (Fig. 29.6).

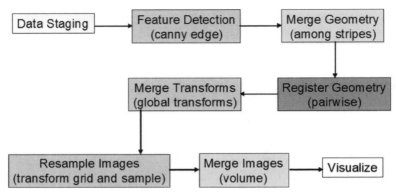

Figure 29.6 Virtual placenta 3D reconstruction process pipeline shows the different stages of computation. Feature Detection and Image Resample are operations that can be performed locally, whereas green steps merge geometry and merge images are aggregation operations. Register Geometry is pairwise operation that requires some local communications between nodes. The Merge Transform step is a sequential operation as the matrices are concatenated for all images.

Preliminary results suggest that 3D registration is feasible for serial sections of placenta (Fig. 29.7). Challenges remain, including the irregularity in the slide spacing due to lost sections, and large orientation changes of successive tissue sections. Visualization of these volumes with high frequency textures also presents interesting challenges. Texture segmentation and tissue layer representation will help in simplifying the visual presentation of information.

Figure 29.7 Image on left shows the first placenta section along with the outline of six consecutive sections before registration. The image on the right shows the outlines of the sections relative to the first section after registration process. Specimens courtesy of Pamela Wenzel and Gustavo Leone at OSU.

29.3.2 Multi-photon Confocal Neuroimaging

The Bioinformatics Research Network (BIRN) is a collaborative effort, which focuses on research and understanding of brain structure and function. Mouse BIRN studies mouse brain in order to provide insight into neuroscience, human and otherwise. One of the goals of Mouse BIRN is to create an integrated anatomical atlas, which provides spatial correlation for data sets ranging from CT, MR, bright-field microscopy, confocal microscopy, as well as molecular data such as genomic and protenomic data. The atlas also serves as a visual-based query system. Maryann Martone, Ph.D., at University of California at San Diego has been using two-photon confocal microscopy to study fluorescence labeled mouse brain sections. This project provides an opportunity to use distributed computing capability for the large amount of data generated by Martone's group. In addition, it provides an opportunity to exercise the system against microscopy modalities other than bright-field light microscopy.

The confocal microscope captures the 3D tissue volume as a sequence of 2D image tiles that are individually small at 512×480 pixels each (Fig. 29.8). The images in the same z focal plane are stitched together using Martone's own software. As larger volumes of the tissue is captured, the total amount of data began to exceed the memory capacity of single workstations.

To solve this problem, OSU began developing a distributed version of the image stitching algorithm using the DataCutter and IP4G framework. At the same time, Martone's group modified their stitching code to operate in out-of-core mode on a single workstation, where tiles are loaded into memory as needed. The two solutions are equivalent, except that the distributed version used additional machines to reduce processing time. The OSU version of application next converted the stitched images into image stripes that are compatible with Aperio's ImageScope viewing software. This allows interactive review of the stitched images.

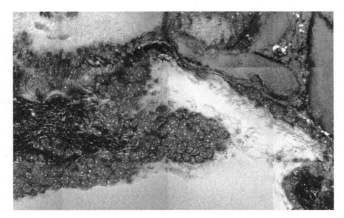

Figure 29.8   Confocal microscopy image of the mouse brain, after stitching. Data courtesy of Maryann Martone, Diana Price, Natalie MacLean, and Sunny Chow at UCSD NCMIR.

The distributed processing architecture is also used to analyze the confocal images by executing Martone's application for protein quantification. The use case illustrates one of the strengths of the architecture, where third party applications can be treated as black-boxes and executed on large images in a distributed fashion.

29.4   CLINICAL USE

Virtual microscopy provides two key clinical benefits: slide archival and telepathology, as mentioned in Section 29.2.2.1. In this section, we describe a use case are described to illustrate the benefits of virtual microscopy in the clinical setting.

29.4.1   Cancer and Leukemia Group B

The virtual microscope concept has been extended to the evaluation and quality control of pathology specimens submitted for clinical trial correlative science use. Web-enabled virtual microscopy system can be accessed from anywhere at anytime via the Internet to review the histopathology in tissue sections. Virtual microscopy offers several advantages to the reviewing pathologist and improves the efficiency of the review process.

29.4.1.1   Function of the Pathology Coordinating Office (PCO)   The Cancer and Leukemia Group B (CALGB) funded by the National Cancer Institute is a clinical cooperative group with 35 main member institutions and approximately 200 affiliated hospitals. When solid tumor specimens are submitted to the CALGB as part of the clinical trial's scientific study of the treatment or disease, these specimens are sent to the CALGB PCO at The Ohio State University. The paraffin-embedded tissue specimens are sent to the PCO by the submitting institution as cut sections either $(4-5\,\mu m)$ placed on microscope slides or on the paraffin block containing the tissue. The PCO reviews the submitted material against the pathology report to ensure that the proper specimen was sent according to the clinical trial protocol requirements. The pathology report is cross-checked with the tissue blocks or sections derived from blocks to determine whether the requested tissue was appropriately submitted. The PCO selects the first, middle, and last sections in a series of tissue sections and stains them with Harris H&E for morphologic review by a pathologist. The histopathology review by the CALGB cadre pathologist controls for the accuracy of the submitted tissue and also the presence of tumor or normal tissue types throughout the series of tissue sections. The CALGB pathologist cadres have documented on a number of occasions the absence of tumor or normal tissues in series of tissue sections and more importantly have uncovered frank prevented in the tissue type submitted classification errors. The CALGB Correlative Science Committee, which reviews the PCO procedures, believes it is of utmost importance to perform this quality control review to ensure that the correct target tissue is being studied for correlative science. Moreover, it may not be possible to provide this review at a subsequent point in the scientific analysis via another pathologist, especially if the tissue and/or morphology are destroyed when used in molecular tests such as CGH, LOH, PCR, and so on. Thus, this review not only ensures accuracy in correlative science but also lowers research costs by minimizing testing on inappropriate tissue.

29.4.1.2 *Traditional Quality Control Process* The number of CALGB cadre pathology reviewers involved in the quality control process has been typically between 10 and 20 pathologists, who are located throughout the United States. The CALGB clinical trials involve several solid organ systems where cancer arises including breast, gastrointestinal, genitourinary, lymphoma, melanoma, and respiratory. Most of the CALGB clinical trials enrollments that range from several hundred patients to thousands of patients. As mentioned before, the top, middle, and bottom sections of a slide schema, which are often between 20 and 40 slides, are H&E stained and reviewed for quality control. These slide sets are then batch shipped to a designated cadre pathologist for review. Subsequently, these slides must be returned to the PCO for future use, documentation, and long-term storage. The quality control process for one large clinical trial could require the movement of 12,000 slides through mail services. The PCO packages these slides in batches of 100 per slide box and ships not more than three boxes at one time to reduce the risk of losing original material should they be lost or broken in shipment or in the care of a pathologist. Shipping costs for a single project of this size would approach $1200 to $1500. If original material was lost, the cost would be significantly higher and would potentially harm the ability to include cases in correlative science study. If treatment subject's tissue material is lost before correlative science studies are performed, the scientific power of the results could be negatively affected, jeopardizing the value of the research. Personnel expenses are also a large component of the expense associated with the cost of packaging and shipping slides.

The traditional histopathology review by CALGB cadre pathologists uses the standalone microscope. The pathologist records the results on a checklist with room for along with their comments, which after completion is faxed to the PCO. The review determines which patient cases meet the study requirements and verifies that the appropriate tissue type, that is, tumor or normal, is represented throughout the slide set. Slides are returned to the PCO before the next slide set is sent to the pathologist for review.

Some situations of the review process are complicated by agreements with the submitting institutions. Approximately 5% of institutions that submit paraffin blocks to the PCO request that the blocks be returned in a timely manner, that is, approximately within 1 month. This may cause small subsets of H&Es from individual cases to be sent to pathologists so that the quality control process can be completed in an attempt to minimize errors and confusion downstream in the process of supplying tissue sections for research. In addition, insufficient amounts of tissue or incorrect tissue blocks may be sent to the PCO. In these cases, the PCO must request the resubmission of new, more representative tissue. This process is very time consuming and the quicker that the PCO can discover and communicate errors in submitted tissue blocks, the more likely the submitting institution will comply.

Another more recent development that significantly affects the management of the submitted tissue blocks to the PCO involves the manufacturing of tissue microarray (TMA) blocks for each clinical trial [45, 46]. One TMA block can include representative tissue cores of up to 300 patients or approximately 900 tissues. TMA tissue sections can then be used to provide quick analysis for research questions in a very cost effective way [47–49]. The CALGB Correlative Science Committee has recommended that TMA blocks be made for every clinical trial where tissue is submitted. As TMA blocks contain the greatest length in tissue cores, they need to be removed from the blocks prior to sectioning of the blocks. Prior to the removal of representative tissue cores, a pathologist must select their location in the tissue. Therefore, it is most efficient that the process to mark the areas in blocks that are to be returned in a timely fashion as well as blocks that are stored long-term should be included in the quality control procedure.

29.4.1.3 *Virtual Microscopy Use for the CALGB*   To provide quality control, timely return of submitted tissue blocks and marking slides for TMA coring, the CALGB PCO has chosen to use digital imaging and virtual slide microscopy to improve this process. The appealing factors of virtual microscopy are that it reduces the personnel costs in handling and shipping thousands of microscope slides, reduces the risk of losing original material when shipping the slides to distant locations, provides a more timely return of the tissues to submitting institutions, and provides an annotation feature to mark pertinent tissue areas for TMA production. The PCO laboratory supplies the Virtual Slide Facility with the H&E slides, which are then scanned using the Aperio ScanScope. The digitized images are saved to the virtual slide server.

This slide server has 1 TB of storage with a much larger storage bank (50 TB) located at the Ohio Supercomputer Center. Cadre pathologists are notified when the slides are available for review and they then access the images using the Internet following a standard procedure. The pathologist records his or her remarks about each VM slide using an Excel spreadsheet. They can also annotate each slide using the Aperio ScanScope software. The annotation is similar to drawing tools in Microsoft Word and Excel software where different shapes can be used and expanded to circumscribe an area of interest. Squares are used to mark areas of tumor and circles mark areas of tissue that are representative of normal tissue. Slides are only identified with the PCO sample number and the CALGB protocol to protect patient confidentiality. The PCO can then use the Excel spreadsheets to base further decisions on use and/or clarifications with submitting institutions. Moreover, the TMA technician can use the annotated images to compare to the original tissue blocks and core the blocks appropriately. The fact that all of this information is in an electronic format provides even more opportunity to improve the use of these materials. One such improvement is the use of the digitized image to match annotated core locations with the tissue block to automatically align the coring needles to the location in the block.

29.5 EDUCATION

The benefits arising out of virtual microscope are clearly tangible in the arena of medical education. One of the limitation of educating a group of students was that it had to be done at a one-by-one basis. This was because the tools of the time, the microscope, had a limited number of viewers. There is generally a limit on the number of users that can review a case under a multi-headed scope and this is approximately 10 users. Additionally, the review of a case was dependent on the person presenting the case. As the presenter (or mentor) moved through the various regions of interest on the slide, all of his or her mentees could only evaluate the region of the slide that was currently being illuminated. Thus, all students being mentored were unable to review the slide independent of the mentor, and as such, the students had to learn from what was presented. The virtual microscopy removes these barriers. Classes with sizes larger than 10 are now feasible without increasing the cost drastically. In a teaching environment that employs virtual microscopy, each student can access the same virtual slide either dependently, also called *virtual conferencing*, or independently. Paradoxically, the virtual microscopy system is challenged not by the masses, the dependently coupled situation of virtual conferencing technologies, but by the few, multiple single users accessing independent areas of the virtual slide. This is because the service has to be equipped with large aggregate memory cache to enable multiple independent users to access multiple slides at the same time.

Virtual microscopy also permits improvement in teaching methodologies in the classroom. Annotation softwares can be used to reveal the region of interest with which the instructor wants the students to review. Both at general areas and then at specific and diagnostic areas can easily be captured and coordinated for teaching and review. Therefore, architectural patterns as well as detailed diagnostic features can be discussed. All the while, the student is honing his investigatory skills as the process of focusing in and out ($4\times$, $10\times$, $20\times$, or $40\times$) to understand that the virtual slide is in under his control. This secondary skill set quickly becomes second hand to the students as does the use specific buttons, like a mouse click or a simple roll. The slides may be zoomed in or out more rapidly than while using a microscope and the student may "pan" the image to move it in different directions. The annotation layers can be used not only for teaching but also for testing. Given nothing else that a virtual slide, the students can be tested on that image. They can be asked, for example, to identify areas of necrosis and mitosis and make a diagnosis. When they have rendered their findings, the annotation layer can be sent to the teacher. In addition, the results either graded manually by the professor or automatically by the virtual microscopy system. As the annotation layer records the text-based responses in an x- and y-axes, if the virtual slide that is being tested had been previously marked up by the experts, any matching textual response that fell within borders of the expert markup would be graded as a correct response, whereas those falling outside that area or unmatching the expert text would be graded as incorrect. Comparison of textual responses has to be controlled at the testing level or can be generated in drop-down multiple choice or k-type questions. The idea of automatic grading has a great appeal to faculty, but even more beneficial is that the process of gathering these gold standard data from the experts can be enabling for knowledge discover with regards to future image analysis.

29.6   FUTURE DIRECTIONS

As the virtual microscopy matures and develops into accepted practices in clinical pathology departments as well as scientific communities, data management support will need to accommodate technological advances and standards emergence.

29.6.1   Mass Storage for Large-Scale Clinical Infrastructure

Assuming virtual microscopy follows the same trend as radiological imaging modalities, increasing number of hospitals will begin to recognize the benefits of slide archival, telepathology, and electronic record management. The cost of adopting virtual microscopy in a clinical setting is partly attributed to the mass storage requirements for long-term archival. As illustrated by the CALGB use case, single clinical trials may accrue 6000 slides for quality control alone. A clinical pathology department of a large hospital may reach 500,000 cases a year, yielding in excess of 25 PB (uncompressed) required storage per year.

The need to integrate mass storage system, either through clusters or through dedicated storage networks, presents challenges to the current commercial offerings. In the current production system, all images are stored on the image server, which has 1 TB of storage. The server storage is backed up manually to a different server, and is, at the moment, a complete mirror of the image server content. As data accumulates at a faster rate, it will become necessary to establish more formal data management policies. The active cases will need to be readily accessible on the image server. Recently, active cases and clinical trials cases need to be easily retrievable, yet does not require immediate accessibility. Older cases can be archived and are used to audit and kept as long-term patient record. This suggests a storage architecture with three or more tiers of availability, short-term, near-term, and long-term storage.

Data movement among the different tiers also present interesting challenges. Establishing the policy for archival depends on the workflow, end-user requirements, as well as health regulations such as the duration for maintaining patient records. User interface needs to be designed, so end users may navigate the catalog and selectively archive or retrieve cases. Network connections between the different storage systems also need to satisfy performance requirements, as the data being moved are large in size, and the utility of the storage subsystem depend on how efficient data can be moved between components.

An interesting challenge is how to integrate a large-scale storage solution to the commercial virtual microscopy system. Loose integration allows an organization to easily accommodate different vendors, whereas a tight integration provides additional functionalities as well as streamlined operation to the end users.

29.6.2 Microscopy Modalities

Microscopy is a rich discipline. Microscopy modalities differ from each other by acquisition methodology, tissue preparation, or a combination of both. The system at OSU deals primarily with bright-field light microscopy. There are numerous other methods for capturing images, such as dark-field, phase-contrast, and fluorescence microscopies. Additionally, transmission electron microscopy generates images that have similar characteristics in size but at far greater resolution. Confocal microscopy, as mentioned in Section 29.3.2 forms another mode of image acquisition, albeit volumetric instead of planar.

On the tissue preparation slide, tissue may be stained with different types of chemicals to illustrate different features. Basic stains, such as H&E, are non-specific and delineate the structure and morphology of the tissue via acid–base interaction. Histochemical stains bind to macromolecules to illustrate specific structures such as cytoskeleton. Immunohistochemical stains, in contrast, targets specific molecules using antigen–antibody interaction to provide structure and/or functional information [50].

An emerging technology is multi-spectral microscopy, where a diffraction grating is used to capture images at individual wavelengths. The technology in many respect has similarity to satellite imaging, where multiple channels of data are captured at each pixel location. Multispectral imaging has been shown to have improved differentiation power of different cellular structures as well as cell types [51, 52].

The image management infrastructure should be able to accommodate data sets that differ as results of difference in scanner types, acquisition channels, image formats, tissue preparations, and consequently the information content. The system needs to be able to support query, retrieval, browse and image processing of these diverse set of images in a generic way.

29.6.3 Multiple Focal Plane 3D Reconstruction

One of the significant difference between traditional microscopy and virtual microscopy today is the lack of z-depth in the digital image. On a conventional microscope, a user can adjust the focal depth to examine the structure at different z positions, therefore, mentally recreating the structure in 3D. This capability is not present in the existing virtual microscopy system, as the images themselves are not usually 3D. Although confocal microscopy acquires volumetric data natively, bright-field microscopes such as Aperio's scanner do not support 3D acquisition.

Recent development in 3D reconstruction of microscopy images using numerical methods has shown success. The basic process involves acquiring images at multiple focal depths and then estimating the 3D position of structures based on how they change in sharpness across successive z slices [53, 54], where the structure sharpest in z represents the location of that structure in z.

To support such use case, the client need to support volumetric data sets and z-depth browsing. Additionally, the scanner control software has not been designed to acquire at multiple focal depths, which necessitates manual focus and scanning at each of the focal depths to be captured. The image server also would need to be able to store and retrieve multi-dimensional data sets. Once these technical issues are solved, reconstruction can allow users to interact with the images in a more natural and informative way.

29.6.4   Multi-modal Data Integration

Digitalization of microscopy slides exposes opportunities to integrate data from different modalities of data acquisition. Successive sections from a single tissue block may be treated with basic stains and immunohistochemical stains to show cellular structure and functions. The images can then be registered to show correlation between structure and function. Additionally, the same slide may be digitized using bright-field as well as field microscopes. Extending beyond microscopy acquisition, micro-CT, micro-MR, and ultrasound of the same tissue can show data of different scales and characteristics. Beyond imaging, molecular data such as DNA sequence and protein expression may be integrated with the image data, using the image as an atlas for navigation.

Integration of these various data types is a significant technical effort, which can provide new ways of exploring data and understanding cellular and molecular biology, pathology, and oncology.

29.6.5   Common Standard

One of the biggest challenges in virtual microscopy as an emerging technology is the lack of communications standards. Unlike radiology, there has not been a universal standard like DICOM that defines image file formats and communications protocol between storage servers. This is partly due to the fact that virtual microscopy, particularly for pathology, is only recently becoming a technology that is mature enough for clinical use.

There have been some attempts to extend DICOM to support image storage. However, they have been hindered by the inability of DICOM to support extremely large images. DICOM has been designed to store and transmit CT, MR, and X-ray images, which typically are two orders of magnitude smaller in each dimension than microscopy images. Microscopy images require different data set organization strategies such as tiling, multi-resolution representation, and efficient compression techniques. The DICOM visible light extension is intended to include microscopy as a standard modality [55]. However, the image sizes of whole, digitized slides remain a unmet challenge for DICOM.

To properly support virtual microscopy, a data storage and communications standard must have the following characteristics:

- Allow image to be specified as tiles, which are stored in separate files,
- Support multi-image volumes for serial section studies,
- Organize data set in a similar way as DICOM: patient, study, exam, and series,

- Provide storage for imaging acquisition metadata, such as type of microscope and magnification,
- Store sample preparation protocol: section thickness, tissue source, and stains used,
- Provide access security, user authentication, and authorization,
- Protect patient privacy where necessary via deidentification and anonymization tools.

Presently, each vendor and research organization continue to define their own storage format independently, whereas other requirements such as security and acquisition metadata are ignored. As the virtual microscopy community grows, these requirements will be developed into standards, thus facilitating collaboration, data sharing, and systems interaction and integration.

29.7 SUMMARY

Virtual microscopy is an emerging technology that is gaining popularity among clinical and research communities. The ability to digitize whole slides and to review these slides in silica allows large volume slide archival, telepathology, and electronic education. Commercial offering has reached a level of maturity where production usage for whole organization is now technically and financially feasible. For systems and image research, however, the large amount of data remain a challenge that are better solved with distributed infrastructure for storage and analysis. A clinical use case, CALGB quality control, was described, which illustrate the value of virtual microscopy in production setting. For research applications, virtual placenta 3D reconstruction, and confocal image processing illustrate the need for distributed analysis infrastructure.

Although the commercial and research infrastructures are continually improved, there remain significant challenges. The integration of mass storage into clinical infrastructure provides a growth path for large-scale clinical use. Support for additional microscopy modalities and image types will facilitate multi-modal data integration and subsequent analysis. Volumetric image acquisition and reconstruction will not only allow users to interact with the virtual slides more naturally but also enable more informative image analysis. One of the biggest challenges facing virtual microscopy, however, is the establishment of a common communications and image storage standard, which will further accelerate the acceptance of virtual microscopy as a productive technology.

ACKNOWLEDGMENTS

The authors would like to thank Gustavo Leone, Ph.D., and Pam Wenzel for supplying mouse placenta serial sections and assistance in learning about placenta anatomy and pathological changes; Maryann Martone, Ph.D., and associates for providing confocal microscopy of mouse brain tissue sections.

REFERENCES

1. D. Comaniciu, W. Chen, P. Meer, and D. J. Foran, Multiuser Workspaces for Remote Microscopy in Telepathology, in *IEEE Proceedings on Computer-Based Medical Systems*, vol. 2, 1999, pp. 150–155.

2. S. Olsson and C. Busch, A national telepathology trial in Sweden: Feasibility and assessment, *Arch. Anat. Cytol. Pathol.*, 43, 234–241 (1995).

3. J. Z. Wang, J. Nguyen, K.-K. Lo, C. Law, and D. Regula, Multiresolution Browsing of Pathology Images Using Wavelets, in *Proceedings of the 1999 AMIA Annual Fall Symposium*, American Medical Informatics Association, Hanley and Belfus, Inc., November 1999, pp. 340–344.

4. M. Weinstein and J. I. Epstein, Telepathology diagnosis of prostate needle biopsies, *Hum. Pathol.*, 28 (1), 22–29 (1997).

5. R. S. Weinstein, A. K. Bhattacharyya, A. R. Graham, and J. R. Davis, Telepathology: A ten-year progress report, *Hum. Pathol.*, 28 (1), 1–7 (1997).

6. U. Catalyurek, M. Gray, T. Kurc, J. Saltz, E. Stahlberg, and R. Ferreira, A Component-Based Implementation of Multiple Sequence Alignment, in *18th ACM Symposium on Applied Computing (SAC2003) Bioinformatics Track*, Melbourne, FL, March 2003.

7. R. Ferreira, B. Moon, J. Humphries, A. Sussman, J. Saltz, R. Miller, and A. Demarzo, The Virtual Microscope, in *Proceedings of the 1997 AMIA Annual Fall Symposium*, American Medical Informatics Association, Hanley and Belfus, Inc., October 1997, pp. 449–453.

8. A. Afework, M. D. Beynon, F. Bustamante, A. Demarzo, R. Ferreira, R. Miller, M. Silberman, J. Saltz, A. Sussman, and H. Tsang, Digital Dynamic Telepathology — the Virtual Microscope, in *Proceedings of the 1998 AMIA Annual Fall Symposium*, American Medical Informatics Association, November 1998.

9. D. J. Romer, K. H. Yearsley, and L. W. Ayers, Using a modified standard microscope to general virtual slides, *The Anat. Rec. (Part B: New Anat.)*, 272B, 91–97 (2003).

10. Aperio Technologies, Inc., http://www.aperio.com.

11. Interscope Technologies, http://www.interscopetech.com, 2001.

12. Trestle Corporation, http://www.trestlecorp.com.

13. D'metrix, http://www.dmetrix.net.

14. Bacus Laboratories, Inc., http://www.bacuslabs.com.

15. Aperio Technology brief, http://www.aperio.com/products-technology.asp.

16. Digital imaging and communications in medicine, http://medical.nema.org.

17. The mobius project, http://www.projectmobius.org.

18. S. Hastings, S. Langella, S. Oster, and J. Saltz, Distributed data Management and Integration Framework: The Mobius Project, in *Proceedings of the Global Grid Forum 11 (GGF11) Semantic Grid Applications Workshop*, 2004, pp. 20–38.

19. S. Narayanan, T. Kurc, U. Catalyurek, and J. Saltz, Database support for data-driven scientific applications in the grid, *Parallel Process. Lett.*, 13 (2), 245–271 (2003).

20. S. Narayanan, U. Catalyurek, T. Kurc, X. Zhang, and J. Saltz, Applying Database Support for Large Scale Data Driven Science in Distributed Environments, in *Proceedings of the Fourth International Workshop on Grid Computing (Grid 2003)*, Phoenix, Arizona, November 2003, pp. 141–148.

21. M. D. Beynon, R. Ferreira, T. Kurc, A. Sussman, and J. Saltz, DataCutter: Middleware for Filtering Very Large Scientific Datasets on Archival Storage Systems, in *Proceedings of the Eighth Goddard Conference on Mass Storage Systems and Technologies/17th IEEE Symposium on Mass Storage Systems*, National Aeronautics and Space Administration, March 2000, NASA/CP 2000-209888, pp. 119–133.

22. M. D. Beynon, T. Kurc, A. Sussman, and J. Saltz, Optimizing Execution of Component-Based Applications Using Group Instances, in *Proceedings of CCGrid2001: IEEE International Symposium on Cluster Computing and the Grid*, IEEE Computer Society Press, May 2001, pp. 56–63.

23. M. Beynon, T. Kurc, A. Sussman, and J. Saltz. Design of a Framework for Data-intensive Wide-Area Applications, in *Proceedings of the Nineth Heterogeneous Computing Workshop (HCW2000)*, IEEE Computer Society Press, May 2000, pp. 116–130.

24. M. D. Beynon, T. Kurc, U. Catalyurek, C. Chang, A. Sussman, and J. Saltz, Distributed processing of very large datasets with DataCutter, *Parallel Comput.*, 27 (11), 1457–1478 (2001).

25. R. Oldfield and D. Kotz, Armada: A Parallel File System for Computational, in *Proceedings of CCGrid2001: IEEE International Symposium on Cluster Computing and the Grid*, Brisbane, Australia, May 2001, IEEE Computer Society Press.

26. B. Plale and K. Schwan, dQUOB: Managing Large Data Flows Using Dynamic Embedded Queries, in *IEEE International High Performance Distributed Computing (HPDC)*, August 2000.

27. C. Isert and K. Schwan, ACDS: Adapting Computational Data Streams for High Performance, in *Proceedings of the 14th International Parallel and Distributed Processing Symposium (IPDPS 2000)*, Cancun, Mexico, May 2000, IEEE Computer Society Press, pp. 641–646.

28. The ABACUS project, *http://www.cs.cmu.edu/~amiri/abacus.html*.

29. K. Amiri, D. Petrou, G. R. Ganger, and G. A. Gibson, Dynamic Function Placement for Data-Intensive Cluster Computing, in *The USENIX Annual Technical Conference*, San Diego, CA, June 2000.

30. M. Aeschlimann, P. Dinda, J. Lopez, B. Lowekamp, L. Kallivokas, and D. O'Hallaron, Preliminary Report on the Design of a Framework for Distributed Visualization, in *Proceedings of the International Conference on Parallel and Distributed Processing Techniques and Applications (PDPTA'99)*, Las Vegas, NV, June 1999, pp. 1833–1839.

31. Common Component Architecture Forum, http://www.cca-forum.org.

32. R. H. Arpaci-Dusseau, E. Anderson, N. Treuhaft, D. E. Culler, J. M. Hellerstein, D. A. Patterson, and K. Yelick, Cluster i/o with River: Making the Fast Case Common, in *IOPADS '99: Input/Output for Parallel and Distributed Systems*, Atlanta, GA, May 1999.

33. S. Hastings, S. Oster, S. Langella, T. Kurc, T. C. Pan, U. Catalyurek, and J. Saltz, A Grid Based Image Archival and Analysis System, BMI technical report: Osubmi_tr_2004_n04, The Ohio State University, Department of Biomedical Informatics, 2004.

34. U. Catalyurek, M. D. Beynon, C. Chang, T. Kurc, A. Sussman, and J. Saltz. The virtual microscope, *IEEE Trans. Inform. Technol. BioMed.*, 7 (4), 230–248 (2003).

35. C. Chang, R. Ferreira, A. Sussman, and J. Saltz, Infrastructure for Building Parallel Database Systems for Multidimensional Data, in *Proceedings of the Second Merged IPPS/SPDP Symposiums*, IEEE Computer Society Press, April 1999.

36. R. Ferreira, T. Kurc, M. Beynon, C. Chang, A. Sussman, and J. Saltz, Object-relational queries into multi-dimensional databases with the Active Data Repository, *Parallel Process. Lett.*, 9 (2), 173–195 (1999).

37. W. Schroeder, K. Martin, and B. Lorensen, *The Visualization Toolkit: An Object-Oriented Approach to 3D Graphics*, 2nd ed., Prentice Hall, 1997.

38. National Library of Medicine, Insight Segmentation and Registration Toolkit (ITK), http://www.itk.org/.

39. S. Hastings, T. Kurc, S. Langella, U. Catalyurek, T. Pan, and J. Saltz, Image Processing for the Grid: A Toolkit for Building Grid-Enabled Image Processing Applications, in *CCGrid: IEEE International Symposium on Cluster Computing and the Grid*, IEEE Press, May 2003.

40. K. R. Mosaliganti, T. Pan, D. Cowden, R. Machiraju, and J. Saltz, Generalized Clustering Methods for Multivariate Data, BMI technical report: Osubmi_tr_2004_n08, The Ohio State University, Department of Biomedical Informatics, 2004.

41. L. Wu, A. de Bruin, H. I. Saavedra, M. Starovic, A. Trimboli, Y. Yang, J. Opavska, P. Wilson, J. C. Thompson, M. C. Ostrowski, T. J. Rosol, L. A. Woollett, M. Weinstein, J. C. Cross, M. L. Robinson, and G. Leone, Extra-embryonic function of rb is essential for embryonic development and viability, *Nature*, 421, 942–947 (2003).

42. J. Rinkenberger and Z. Werb, The labyrinthine placenta, *Nat. Genet.*, 25, 248–250 (2000).

43. T. C. Pan, Three Dimensional Reconstruction of Microscopy Images, BMI Technical Report: Osubmi_tr_2004_n09, The Ohio State University, Department of Biomedical Informatics, 2004.

44. Z. Zhang, Iterative point matching for registration of free form curves and surfaces, *Int. J. Comp. Vis.*, 13, 119–152 (1994).

45. O. P. Kallioniemi, U. Wagner, J. Kononen, and G. Sauter, Tissue microarray technology for high-throughput molecular profiling of cancer, *Hum. Mol. Genet.*, 10 (7), 657–662 (2001).

46. A. Nocito, J. Kononen, O. P. Kallioniemi, and G. Sauter, Tissue microarrays (tmas) for high-throughput molecular pathology research, *Int. J. Cancer*, 94 (1), 1–5 (2001).

47. J. Torhorst, C. Bucher, J. Kononen, P. Haas, M. Zuber, O. R. Kochli, F. Mross, H. Dieterich, H. Moch, M. Mihatsch, O. P. Kallioniemi, and G. Sauter, Tissue microarrays for rapid linking of molecular changes to clinical endpoints, *Am. J. Pathol.*, 159 (6), 2249–2256 (2001).

48. I. S. Shergill, N. K. Shergill, M. Arya, and H. R. Patel, Tissue microarrays: A current medical research tool, *Curr. Med. Res. Opin.*, 20 (5), 707–712 (2004).

49. A. M. Velasco, K. A. Gillis, Y. Li, E. L. Brown, T. M. Sadler, M. Achilleos, L. M. Greenberger, P. Frost, W. Bai, and Y. Zhang, Identification and validation of novel androgen-regulated genes in prostate, *Endocrinology*, 145 (8), 3913–3924 (2004).

50. Pathology, http://members.cox.net/stokman1c/PrimerPathology.html#ViewingMethodologies.

51. R. Zhou, E. H. Hammond, and D. L. Parker, A multiple wavelength algorithm in color image analysis and its application in stain decomposition in microscopy images, *Med. Phys.*, 23 (12), 1977–1986 (1996).

52. R. M. Levenson and C. C. Hoyt, Spectral Imaging and Microscopy, *American Laboratory*, November 2000, pp. 26–33.

53. A. J. Lipton, E. J. Breen, and C. Glasby, 3D Deconvolution of Microscopy Images, Technical Report, CSIRO Technical Report, 1995.

54. J. Philip and K. Carlsson, 3D Image Deconvolution in Light Microscopy: Theory and Practice, Report TRITA-MAT-04-ma03, Royal Institute of Technology, Stockholm, Sweden.

55. Dicom visible light supplement, ftp://medical.nema.org/medical/dicom/final/sup15_ft.pdf.

ACDC-grid, 588–596
  collaborations, 596–601
  data grid, 593–595
  dynamic integration, 596
  generally, 588–589
  molecular structure determination on grid, 603–616
  monitoring, 589–590
  scheduling, 590–593
Agent design, desktop organic grids (self-organizing), organic grid architecture, 680–681
Alelle, computational biology, 4
Algorithm construction, evolutionary computation, computational biology applications, 22–23
Algorithms. *See* specific algorithms
Allergenicity prediction, bioinformatics distributed workflows, 572–574
α-helix, replica exchange molecular dynamics (REMD) method, 405–408
AMBER, GIPSY applications, 638–643
Amdahl's law, parallel performance, phylogenetic parameter estimation, 348–349
Anaplerotic reactions, kinetic rate expressions, differential evolutionary algorithms in *Escherichia coli,* 64
Anisotropic diffusion (human brain diffusion and deformation simulation), 122–132
  background, 122–125
  parallel implementation, 130–132
  process simulation, 125–130
Antibody surveillance adaptation, HIV-1 molecular evolution (parallel Monte Carlo simulation), 50–52, 51–52
Approximate string matching, Cray MTA system bioinformatics, 517–519

Arbitrary branch, phylogenetic trees, 331
Artificial neural net (ANN), protein structure prediction, 466–469
Asia, bioinformatics grid activities, 498
Association rule(s) (DNA microarrays), 306–308
  data and, 308
  initial problem, 306
  multi-objective optimization plan, 307
Association rule operators, multi-objective algorithm, DNA microarrays, 309–312
Atomistic lattice simulation, protein structure prediction, 463
Australia, bioinformatics grid activities, 499

Batch query optimizations, high-performance BLASTs, 219–220
β-hairpin, replica exchange molecular dynamics (REMD) method, 408–410
Bioinformatics. *See also* specific bioinformatics resources and applications
  computational biology, 13–20
  defined, 13
  genetic linkage analysis, 19–20
  parallelization of, 15–20
    applications, 17–20
    generally, 15–16
    parallel programming models, 16–17
Bioinformatics distributed workflows, 551–582. *See also* Cluster and grid infrastructure
  applications, 554–555
  case studies, 570–578
    allergenicity prediction, 572–574
    swarm intelligence, 574–578
    tissue-specific gene expression analysis, 570–572
  challenges of, 553–554

Parallel Computing for Bioinformatics and Computational Biology, Edited by Albert Y. Zomaya
Copyright © 2006 John Wiley & Sons, Inc.

Bioinformatics distributed workflows (*Continued*)
execution language, 557–565
GEL interpretor and scheduling, 561–563
generally, 557–558
interpreter anatomy, 563–565
syntax and semantics, 558–561
GUI-based workflow, 565–569
construction, 567–568
execution, 568–569
generally, 565–566
Wildfire, 566–567
overview, 551–553, 578–579
programming, 555–557
Bioinformatics grid activities, 489–508
applications, 491
Asia and Japan, 498
Australia, 499
Europe, 492–494
future directions, 500–501
grid computing, 490, 491–492
international collaborations, 499–500
overview, 489–490
United Kingdom, 494–497
United States, 497
Bioinformatics parallel algorithms, 509–529
computational challenge, 509–510
computer architecture, 511–517
Cray MTA system, 517–527
approximate string matching, 517–519
exact string matching, 526–527
molecular dynamics, 519–522
Cray MTA system bioinformatics, DNA sequencing with very long reads, 522–525
overview, 509, 527–528
representative algorithms, 510–511
Biological sequence alignment, global and local, computational molecular biology, 152–157. *See also* Sequence analysis
Biological sequence comparison, heuristic approaches, 158–160. *See also* Sequence analysis
Biosynthetic reactions, kinetic rate expressions, differential evolutionary algorithms in *Escherichia coli,* 64
BLAST. *See also* High-performance BLASTs
biological sequence comparison, heuristic approaches, 159–160
distributed sequence comparison, 163
high-performance BLASTs, 211–232

local sequence alignment, 245–249
generally, 245–246
green destiny, 249
mpiBLAST, 247–249
TurboBLAST, 246–247
sequence analysis, GIPSY, 635–636
Brain. *See* Human brain diffusion and deformation simulation
Branch and bound (B&B) algorithm:
exact maximum parsimony (MP), phylogeny reconstruction (high-performance), 378–381
mixed integer programming models, LS algorithm and self-threading case, 442
Brownian motion, compute-intensive simulations (cellular models), spatial modeling, 106–108
Buffalo, New York, grid computing in, 586–587
Building block experiment (protein structure prediction):
performance evaluation, 478
results, 482–483
Build list, BLAST algorithm, 213

CALGB PCO, virtual microscopy clinical use, 754
Cancer, virtual microscopy clinical use, 752–754
Cell colonies (compute-intensive simulations), 109–115
applications, 114–115
generally, 109–110
inter-cell forces, 110–111
model extension, 111–113
parallelization and visualization, 113–114
Cell data structure, HIV-1 molecular evolution (parallel Monte Carlo simulation) model, 32
Cell superinfection and recombination, HIV-1 molecular evolution (parallel Monte Carlo simulation), 31
Cellular models. *See* Compute-intensive simulations (cellular models)
Center for Computational Research, grid computing, 588
Chemistry at HARvard Molecular Mechanics (CHARMm) model. *See also* Protein structure prediction
GIPSY applications, 638, 643–647
protein structure prediction, 460, 463–466, 470

Child-list maintenance, desktop organic grids (self-organizing), organic grid architecture, 681–682

Child-list sizes, desktop organic grids (self-organizing) measurements, 696–698

Child propagation effect, desktop organic grids (self-organizing) measurements, 690–691

Chromosome, computational biology, 4

Classification, gene expression relationship analysis, 274–280

ClustalW, 194–201
  distance matrix calculation, 194–196
  guide tree construction, 196–200
  local sequence alignment, 252–257
    ClustalW-MPI, 253–254
    generally, 252–253
    parallel ClustalW, HT ClustalW, and MULTICLUSTAL, 254–257
  progressive alignment process, 200–201
  sequence analysis, GIPSY, 637–638

ClustalW-MPI, local sequence alignment, 253–254

Cluster and grid infrastructure, 531–550. *See also* Bioinformatics distributed workflows
  GAMESS, 532–536
  GAMESS with Nimrod, 538–542
  overview, 531–532, 546–547
  portal technology, 537–538
  workflow environments, 542–546

Clusters of workstations (COWS), phylogenetic parameter estimation on, 347–368. *See also* Phylogenetic parameter estimation

Coarse-grain parallelism:
  local sequence alignment basics, 235–236
  Smith–Waterman algorithm, local sequence alignment, 243–244

Codetermination analysis, multivariate gene expression analysis, 267–274
  algorithm, 267–269
  parallel implementation, 270–274
  prediction system design, 269–270

Communication register (C-register), hybrid parallel computer, 171

Competitive template generation (protein structure prediction):
  performance evaluation, 478
  results, 479–480

Computational biology, 3–28
  alelle, 4
  bioinformatics, 13–20

chromosome, 4
defined, 13
evolutionary computation applied to, 20–23
  algorithm construction, 22–23
  approaches, 21–22
  generally, 20–21
  genetic algorithms, 23
expected frequency of offspring, 6–7
factors driving, 13–14
genetic linkage, 5–6
key areas of, 14–15
meiosis, 5
multipoint linkage analysis, 7–11
  generally, 7–9
  joint distribution of genotype, 10–11
  joint genotype probabilities, 9–10
overview, 3–4, 23–25
parallelization of bioinformatics, 15–20
  applications, 17–19
  generally, 15–16
  parallel programming models, 16–17
pedigree probabilities, 11–12
  methods, 12
  probability types, 11–12
recombination, 4–5

Computational molecular biology, 149–166
  biological sequence alignment, global and local, 152–157
  biological sequence comparison, heuristic approaches, 158–160
  molecular biology concepts, 150–151
  overview, 149–150, 164
  parallel and distributed sequence comparison, 161–163

Compute-intensive simulations (cellular models), 79–119
  cell colonies, 109–115
    applications, 114–115
    generally, 109–110
    inter-cell forces, 110–111
    model extension, 111–113
    parallelization and visualization, 113–114
  genetic regulation, 92–96
  overview, 79–81
  parallel computing, 96–100
    across methods, 98–100
    across simulations, 96–98
    performance, 100
  parallel simulations, 100–103
  spatial modeling, 104–109
    Brownian motion, 106–108
    issues in, 108–109

Compute-intensive simulations (cellular models) (*Continued*)
  Turing models, 104–105
  stochastic chemical kinetics, 81–92
    algorithm, 81–87
    continuous models, 87–88
    generally, 81–82
    multi-scaled methods, 90–92
    Poisson Runge–Kutta methods, 88–90
Continuous models, compute-intensive simulations (cellular models), 87–88
Control characteristics, differential evolutionary algorithms in *Escherichia coli,* 73–75
Cooperative multi-objective algorithm (PMGA), DNA microarrays, 313–315
Coreceptor usage phenotype, V3 functional component, HIV-1 molecular evolution (parallel Monte Carlo simulation) model fitness, 34–36
Cray MTA system, 512–527
  approximate string matching, 517–519
  DNA sequencing with very long reads, 522–525
  exact string matching, 526–527
  generally, 517–519
  molecular dynamics, 519–522
Criteria-based methods, phylogeny reconstruction (high-performance), 372–373
Critical assessment of protein structure prediction (CASP), replica exchange molecular dynamics (REMD) method, 420–422
Crossover operator analysis, DNA fragment assembly (distributed genetic algorithm), 295–296

DAG builder, bioinformatics distributed workflows, execution language, 563–565
DAG executor, bioinformatics distributed workflows, execution language, 565
Database comparisons, BLAST use, 214
Database searching:
  high-performance BLASTs for, 211–232
    (*See also* High-performance BLASTs)
  parallelization of bioinformatics applications, 16–18
Database size, BLAST performance, 215, 222–223
Data collection, BLAST use, 214

Data-driven applications, bioinformatics distributed workflows, 555
Data grid, ACDC-grid, 593–595
Data preprocessing, DNA microarrays, 304–305
Data presentation, DNA microarrays, association rules, 308
Data processing, DNA microarrays, 305–306
Data sets, phylogenetic parameter estimation, 355
Deformation simulation (image-guided neurosurgery, human brain diffusion and deformation simulation), 132–142
  background, 132–133
  biomechanical models, 135–142
    elastic deformation integrated with optical flow, 136–138
    elastic deformation of volumetric solid, 135–136
    linear elastic model, 138–140
    physics-based models, 133–135
Desktop organic grids (self-organizing), 671–703
  future directions, 699–700
  grid computing, 674–676
  measurements, 686–698
    child-list sizes, 696–698
    child propagation effect, 690–691
    generally, 686
    knowledge-based schemes compared, 687–690
    prefetching and initial task size, 692–694
    result-burst size, 691–692
    self-adjustment, 694–696
  organic grid architecture, 678–686
    agent design, 680–681
    child-list maintenance, 681–682
    fault tolerance, 684
    generally, 678–680
    overlay network cycles, 685
    overlay network restructuring, 682–683
    prefetching, 685–686
    result burst size, 684
    task list size self-adjustment, 685
    termination, 685
  overview, 671–674, 698–699
  peer-to-peer and Internet computing, 676
  scheduling, 676–677
  self-organization, 677
  strongly mobile agents, 677–678
DICOM, virtual microscopy, 758–759

Differential evolutionary algorithms (in *Escherichia coli*), 59–78
  control characteristics, 73–75
  kinetic parameters estimation, 69–70
  mathematical model, 61–67
    kinetic rate expressions, 63–66
      biosynthetic and anaplerotic reactions, 64
      glucose transport system, 64
      glycolysis, 64
      pentose phosphate pathway, 65–66
    maximum reaction rate estimation, 62–63
    metabolite flux balancing, 61
    steady-state concentration (estimation of non-measured), 66–67
    structure of model, 61–62
  model parameters estimation, 67–69
  overview, 59–61, 75
  simulation and results, 70–72
  stability analysis, 73
Direct execution, FPGA devices, 713–714
Disk-covering methods, maximum parsimony (MP) heuristics, 381–390
  DCM3, 382–385
  experimental design, 385–387
  generally, 381–382
  results, 387–390
Distance matrix calculation:
  CLUSTRAL W, 194–196
  implementation, 202–204
  results, 207
Distance methods, phylogeny reconstruction (high-performance), 371–372
Distributed databases, high-performance BLASTs, 218–219
Distributed genetic algorithm, 285–302. *See also* DNA fragment assembly (distributed genetic algorithm)
Distributed RAxML-III, HPC solutions in, 339–341
Distributed sequence comparison, computational molecular biology, 161–163
Divide-and-conquer technique, protein threading problem (PTP), 444–448
DNA fragment assembly (distributed genetic algorithm), 285–302
  overview, 285–286, 301
  parallel GA, 292–294
    generally, 292–293
    MALLBA project, 293–294
  problem statement, 286–289

generally, 286–287
  sequencing process, 287–289
  results, 294–300
    algorithm analysis, 294–297
    problem analysis, 297–300
  sequential GA, 289–292
DNA microarrays, 303–324
  association rules, 306–308
    data and, 308
    initial problem, 306
    multi-objective optimization plan, 307
  cooperative multi-objective algorithm (PMGA), 313–315
  data preprocessing, 304–305
  data processing, 305–306
  experiments, 315–321
    design of, 318
    indicators for, 316–317
    parallel vs nonparallel, 320–321
    parameter selection, 318–320
  multi-objective algorithm, 308–313
    association rule operators, 309–312
    generally, 308–309
    multi-objective operators, 312–313
    multi-objective optimization, 312
  overview, 303–304
  technology, 304
DNA sequencing with very long reads, Cray MTA system bioinformatics, 522–525
Dynamic programming communication pattern, 172–179
  special-purpose computing:
    linear systolic array, 176–177
    mapping, 177–179
    Smith–Waterman algorithm, 173–174
    Viterbi algorithm, 174–176

Education, virtual microscopy, 755–756
Elastic deformation:
  integrated with optical flow, human brain diffusion and deformation simulation, 136–138
  of volumetric solid, human brain diffusion and deformation simulation, deformation simulation (image-guided neurosurgery), biomechanical models, 135–136
Electron microscopy, parallelization of bioinformatics applications, 17–18. *See also* Virtual microscopy

Elston–Stewart algorithm:
  parallelization of bioinformatics,
    computational biology, 19
  pedigree probabilities, computational
    biology, 12
Energy fitness approximation, protein
  structure prediction, 466–469. *See also*
  Fitness
Energy minimizations models, protein
  structure prediction, 463
Entropy, DNA microarray experiments,
  indicators for, 317
Escherichia coli. See Differential
  evolutionary algorithms (in *Escherichia
  coli*)
Estimation of steady-state concentration
  (non-measured), differential
  evolutionary algorithms in *Escherichia
  coli,* 66–67
Europe, bioinformatics grid activities,
  492–494
Evolutionary algorithms (EAs), 471–479.
  See also Differential evolutionary
  algorithms (in *Escherichia coli*)
  fast messy GA, 471–474
  multiobjective fmGA (FMfmGA), 475
  parallel fast messy GA, 474–475
  Ramachandran experiment, 475–477
Evolutionary computation (applications),
  20–23
  algorithm construction, 22–23
  approaches, 21–22
  generally, 20–21
  genetic algorithms, 23
Evolutionary trees. *See* Phylogenetic tree(s)
Exact maximum parsimony (MP),
  phylogeny reconstruction
  (high-performance), 378–381. *See also*
  Maximum parsimony (MP)
Exact string matching, Cray MTA system
  bioinformatics, 526–527
Expected frequency of offspring,
  computational biology, 6–7
Extend, BLAST algorithm, 213–214

Farming model:
  performance evaluation, 479
  protein structure prediction, 469–471
  results, 480–482
FASTA:
  biological sequence comparison, heuristic
    approaches, 158–159
  local sequence alignment, 244–245

sequence analysis, GIPSY, 636–637
Fast messy GA:
  parallel, evolutionary algorithms (EAs),
    protein structure prediction, 474–475
  protein structure prediction, evolutionary
    algorithms (EAs), 471–474
Fault tolerance, desktop organic grids
  (self-organizing), organic grid
  architecture, 684
Field programmable gate array (FPGA),
  705–736
  case study (protein structure prediction),
    720–732
    "ab initio," 722
    energy calculation algorithm, 724–726
    energy calculation architecture,
      729–732
    generally, 720–722
    parallelized algorithm solutions,
      726–727
    processor implementation, 727–729
    protein and energy model, 723–724
    results, 732
  example, 716–720
    conclusions, 720
    extended parallel image filtering
      architecture, 719–720
    generally, 716–717
    parallel image filtering architecture,
      717–719
  hardware accelerators, 711–716
    devices, 712–714
    generally, 711–712
    processor boards, 714–715
    processor integration, 716
  image processing, 708–711
    filtering, 708–709
    filter parallel processing model,
      710–711
  overview, 705–706, 733–734
  parallel processing models, 706–708
  special-purpose parallel computers, 238
Filtering, image processing, field
  programmable gate array (FPGA),
  708–709
Fine-grain parallelism:
  local sequence alignment basics, 235–236
  Smith–Waterman algorithm, local
    sequence alignment, 242–243
Fitness:
  HIV-1 molecular evolution (parallel
    Monte Carlo simulation), results
    (preliminary), 47, 50–51

HIV-1 molecular evolution (parallel Monte Carlo simulation) model, 34–38
V3 functional component, 34–37
V3 neutralization component, 37–38
Fitness approximation, protein structure prediction, 466–469
Fitness function, sequential GA, DNA fragment assembly, 290–291
Fixed tree scoring, maximum parsimony (MP), phylogeny reconstruction (high-performance), 374–375
Flexible and free programmable resources, FPGA devices, 713
Forced mobile agents, desktop organic grids (self-organizing), 678
Force fields, solvation models and, replica exchange molecular dynamics (REMD) method, 410–420
FPGA technology:
local sequence alignment, 257–262
generally, 257–258
implementation, 258–262
special-purpose computing, 168–169
Function analysis, DNA fragment assembly (distributed genetic algorithm), 295
Function prediction, computational biology, 15

GAMESS:
execution of, 532–536
with Nimrod, 538–542
GEL interpretor and scheduling, bioinformatics distributed workflows, 561–563
Gene expression relationship analysis, 265–283
classification, 274–280
future directions, 280–282
multivariate gene expression, codetermination analysis, 267–274
algorithm, 267–269
generally, 267
parallel implementation, 270–274
prediction system design, 269–270
overview, 265
significance of, 265–266
Genehunter algorithm, pedigree probabilities, computational biology, 20
General-purpose parallel computers, local sequence alignment basics, 237–238
Genetic algorithms (GAs):
evolutionary computation, computational biology applications, 23

maximum likelihood (ML) algorithms, 333
Genetic linkage analysis:
bioinformatics, computational biology, 19–20
computational biology, 5–6
Genetic regulation, compute-intensive simulations (cellular models), 92–96
Genome databases, availability of, 151
Genome-sequencing project, goal of, 151
Genotype, joint distribution of, multipoint linkage analysis, computational biology, 10–11
GIPSY, 623–649
applications, 634–647
molecular modeling, 638–647
sequence analysis, 635–638
deployment, 634
design goals, 626–627
hardware, 626
implementation, 628–634
J2EE overview, 628
overview, 623–626, 647–648
software, 626
technologies, 627–628
Global algorithms, maximum likelihood (ML), phylogenetic trees, 332–333
Global biological sequence alignment, computational molecular biology, 152–157
Glucose transport system, differential evolutionary algorithms in *Escherichia coli,* kinetic rate expressions, 64
Glycolysis, differential evolutionary algorithms in *Escherichia coli,* 64. *See also* Differential evolutionary algorithms (in *Escherichia coli*)
Green destiny, BLAST local sequence alignment, 249
Grid3, research collaborations, 596–597
Grid computing, desktop organic grids (self-organizing), 674–676. *See also* Bioinformatics grid activities; Desktop organic grids (self-organizing); Molecular structure determination on grid; specific grid computing types
Grid infrastructure. *See* Cluster and grid infrastructure
Grid2003 project, research collaborations, 597–600
GT stage optimization, local sequence alignment, parallel ClustalW, HT ClustalW, and MULTICLUSTAL, 255–256

GUI-based workflow, 565–569
  construction, 567–568
  execution, 568–569
  generally, 565–566
  Wildfire, 566–567
Guide tree construction:
  CLUSTRAL W, 196–200
  results, 207

Hardcoded function blocks, FPGA devices,
    713
Hardware accelerators (field programmable
    gate array), 711–716
  devices, 712–714
  generally, 711–712
  processor boards, 714–715
  processor integration, 716
Health applications. *See* Bioinformatics grid
    activities
Heuristic approaches, biological sequence
    comparison, 158–160
Hidden Markov algorithm:
  parallelization of bioinformatics,
      computational biology, 19
  pedigree probabilities, computational
      biology, 12
  Viterbi algorithm, special-purpose
      computing, dynamic programming
      communication pattern, 174–176
Hidden Markov models:
  local sequence alignment, 249–252
    generally, 249–250
    parallel implementation, 251–252
  local sequence alignment, sequence
      scoring with, 251
Hierarchical parallelism, bioinformatics
    distributed workflows, 554
High-performance alignment methods for
    protein threading. *See* Protein threading
    problem (PTP)
High-performance BLASTs, 211–232. *See
    also* BLAST
  algorithm, 212–214
  batch query optimizations, 219–220
  distributed databases, 218–219
  future directions, 228
  multithreading, 216–217
  overview, 211–212, 230

performance comparisons, 221–226
    batch size, 222–223
    database size, 221–222
    experimental environment, 221
    observations, 225–226
    parallel performance, 224–225
    query length, 223–224
  performance factors, 215
  related work, 229–230
  replicated databases, 217–218
  UMD-BLAST, 225–228
  usage, 214
  vector instructions, 215–216
High performance computing (HPC)
    solutions (RAxML-III), 337–341
  distributed, 339–341
  parallel, 337–339
High-performance phylogeny
    reconstruction. *See* Phylogeny
    reconstruction (high-performance)
Hill-climbing, maximum likelihood (ML)
    algorithms, 333
HIV-1 molecular evolution (parallel Monte
    Carlo simulation), 29–57
  future directions, 52–55
    computing limitations, 55
    model expansion, 54
    parameter values refining, 53–54
  model, 32–39
    cell data structure, 32
    expansion of, 54
    fitness, 34–38
      V3 functional component, 34–37
      V3 neutralization component, 37–38
    genetic variation, 33–34
    parameter values, 38–39
    simulation flow, 33
  overview, 29–30
  parallelization with message-passing
      interface (MPI), 39–43
    initialization and termination, 39–40
    replicate simulation results
        consolidation, 41–43
  parallel random number generation, 43–46
  problem statement, 30–31
    cell superinfection and recombination,
        31
    HIV replication cycle, 31
    V3 loop, 30–31
  results (preliminary), 46–52
    adaptation to CCR5, 47–49
    antibody surveillance adaptation, 50–52
    model parameters, 46–47
    parallel computing environment, 46

recombination effects, 49–50
superinfection effects, 49
HP GridLite, research collaborations, 600
HT ClustalW, local sequence alignment, 254–257
Human brain diffusion and deformation simulation, 121–146
anisotropic diffusion (white matter tractography), 122–132
background, 122–125
parallel implementation, 130–132
process simulation, 125–130
deformation simulation (image-guided neurosurgery), 132–142
background, 132–133
biomechanical models, 135–142
elastic deformation integrated with optical flow, 136–138
elastic deformation of volumetric solid, 135–136
linear elastic model, 138–140
volumetric, with a priori knowledge, 140–142
physics-based models, 133–135
overview, 121–122
Human immunodeficiency virus type 1 (HIV-1) molecular evolution. *See* HIV-1 molecular evolution (parallel Monte Carlo simulation)
Hybrid parallel computer, special-purpose computing, 169–172

IBM NE BioGrid, research collaborations, 600
Image management system, virtual microscopy architecture, 739–741
Image processing, field programmable gate array (FPGA), 708–711
filtering, 708–709
filter parallel processing model, 710–711
Initialization, message-passing interface (MPI) parallelization, 39–40
Initial task size, measurements, desktop organic grids (self-organizing), 692–694
Instructional systolic array (ISA):
hybrid parallel computer, 171
special-purpose computing, 169
Interactive visualization tools, special-purpose computing, future directions, 186
Inter-cell forces, compute-intensive simulations (cellular models), 110–111

Interconnection network, FPGA devices, 713
Internet computing, desktop organic grids (self-organizing), 676
Inter-process communication, local sequence alignment basics, parallel programming models, 236–237
I/O cells, FPGA devices, 713
Irregular computational pattern, parallelization of bioinformatics applications, 19
Island model, DNA microarrays, cooperative multi-objective algorithm (PMGA), 313–315

Japan, bioinformatics grid activities, 498
Joint distribution of genotype, multipoint linkage analysis, computational biology, 10–11
Joint genotype probabilities, multipoint linkage analysis, computational biology, 9–10

Kinetic rate expressions (differential evolutionary algorithms in *Escherichia coli*), 63–66
biosynthetic and anaplerotic reactions, 64
glucose transport system, 64
glycolysis, 64
pentose phosphate pathway, 65–66
Knowledge-based schemes, desktop organic grids (self-organizing) compared, 687–690

Large-scale phylogenies, phylogeny reconstruction (high-performance), 373–374
Lathrop–Smith algorithm. *See* Branch and bound (B&B) algorithm
Least-square branch lengths, PEst, phylogenetic parameter estimation, 359
Leukemia Group B, virtual microscopy clinical use, 752–754
Likelihood vector, phylogenetic trees, 331
Linear elastic model, human brain diffusion and deformation simulation, deformation simulation (image-guided neurosurgery), biomechanical models, 138–140
Linear systolic array, special-purpose computing, dynamic programming communication pattern, 176–177

Linkage analysis:
  multipoint, computational biology, joint
    genotype probabilities, 9–10
  parallelization of bioinformatics
    applications, 18
Local sequence alignment, 233–264
  basics, 235–240
    local sequence alignment software,
      238–240
    parallelization, 238–240
    parallel computer architecture, 237–238
    general-purpose parallel computers,
      237–238
    special-purpose parallel computers,
      238
    parallel programming models, 235–237
    coarse and fine-grain parallelism,
      235–236
    inter-process communication,
      236–237
  BLAST, 245–249
    generally, 245–246
    green destiny, 249
    mpiBLAST, 247–249
    TurboBLAST, 246–247
  ClustalW, 252–257
    ClustalW-MPI, 253–254
    generally, 252–253
    parallel ClustalW, HT ClustalW, and
      MULTICLUSTAL, 254–257
  computational molecular biology,
    152–157
  FASTA, 244–245
  hardware (FPGA), 257–262
    generally, 257–258
    implementation, 258–262
  hidden Markov models:
    parallel implementation, 251–252
    sequence scoring with, 251
  hidden Markov models (HMMER),
    249–252
    generally, 249–250
  overview, 233–234
  Smith–Waterman algorithm, 240–244
  software for, 238–240
  types of, 234–235
    generally, 234–235
    multiple sequence alignment, 235
    pairwise alignment, 235
Logic cells, FPGA devices, 713

MALLBA project, DNA fragment assembly,
  parallel GA, 293–294

Mapping, special-purpose computing,
  dynamic programming communication
  pattern, 177–179
Markov algorithm (hidden). *See* Hidden
  Markov algorithm
Maximum likelihood (ML). *See also*
  Phylogenetic tree(s)
  algorithms classification, phylogenetic
    trees, 332–334
  HPC solutions in RAxML-III, 337–341
    distributed, 339–341
    parallel, 337–339
  phylogenetic trees, 329, 330–332
  RAxML-III heuristics, 334–337
Maximum parsimony (MP). *See also* Exact
  maximum parsimony (MP); Phylogeny
  reconstruction (high-performance)
  exact, phylogeny reconstruction
    (high-performance), 378–381
  phylogenetic trees, 329
  phylogeny reconstruction
    (high-performance), 369–394,
    374–377 (*See also* Phylogeny
    reconstruction (high-performance))
  exact search, 376–377
  fixed tree scoring, 374–375
  heuristics, 377
  informative sites, 375–376
Maximum reaction rate estimation,
  differential evolutionary algorithms in
  Escherichia coli, 62–63
Measurements, (desktop organic grids,
  self-organizing), 686–698
  child-list sizes, 696–698
  child propagation effect, 690–691
  generally, 686
  knowledge-based schemes compared,
    687–690
  prefetching and initial task size, 692–694
  result-burst size, 691–692
  self-adjustment, 694–696
Meiosis, computational biology, 5
Message-passing interface (MPI), HIV-1
  molecular evolution (parallel Monte
  Carlo simulation), 30, 41–43
Message-passing interface (MPI)
  parallelization, HIV-1 molecular
  evolution (parallel Monte Carlo
  simulation), 39–43
Metabolite flux balancing, differential
  evolutionary algorithms in *Escherichia
  coli*, 61

Michaelis–Menten reaction,
   compute-intensive simulations (cellular
   models), 91
Microparallelism, general-purpose parallel
   computers, 237–238
Microscopy. *See* Electron microscopy;
   Virtual microscopy
Migration policy analysis, DNA fragment
   assembly (distributed genetic
   algorithm), 297
MIMD architecture, special-purpose
   computing, 167–168, 169–170
Mixed integer programming models,
   434–444
   comparisons of, 443–444
   generally, 434–435
   LS algorithm and self-threading
      case, 442
   MXYZ model, 439–441
   MXZ model, 439
   MYZ model, 441–442
   network flow formulation, 435–438
   nonlinear model using vertices, 438–439
   RAPTOR model, 442
Mobile agents, desktop organic grids
   (self-organizing), 677–678
Molecular biology, concepts in, 150–151.
   See also Computational molecular
   biology
Molecular dynamics, Cray MTA system
   bioinformatics, 519–522
Molecular evolution modeling, phylogenetic
   parameter estimation, phylogenetic tree
   reconstruction, 349–351
Molecular modeling, GIPSY applications,
   638–647
Molecular structure determination on grid,
   583–621
   ACDC-grid, 588–596
      data grid, 593–595
      dynamic integration, 596
      generally, 588–589
      monitoring, 589–590
      scheduling, 590–593
   Buffalo, New York, 586–587
   Center for Computational Research, 588
   overview, 583–584
   process of, 585–586
   research advancements, 601–603
   research application abstractions and
      tools, 603–616
      data mining with SnB, 608–616
      generally, 603–604
      optimizing SnB on grids, 604–608

research collaborations, 596–601
   Grid3, 596–597
   Grid2003 project, 597–600
   HP GridLite, 600
   IBM NE BioGrid, 600
   open science grid, 601
Monte Carlo simulation (parallel). *See*
   HIV-1 molecular evolution (parallel
   Monte Carlo simulation)
Mouse placenta model, virtual microscopy,
   748–750
MPI. *See* Message-passing interface (MPI)
mpiBLAST, local sequence alignment,
   247–249
MULTICLUSTAL, local sequence
   alignment, 254–257
Multi-objective algorithm (DNA
   microarrays), 308–313
   association rule operators, 309–312
   generally, 308–309
Multiobjective experiment, protein structure
   prediction, performance evaluation, 478
Multiobjective fmGA (FMfmGA), protein
   structure prediction, evolutionary
   algorithms (EAs), 475
Multi-objective operators, DNA microarrays,
   multi-objective algorithm, 312–313
Multi-objective optimization:
   association rules, DNA microarrays, 307
   DNA microarrays, multi-objective
      algorithm, 312
Multi-photon confocal neuroimaging, virtual
   microscopy, 751–752
Multiple Instruction-Multiple Data (MIMD):
   field programmable gate array (FPGA),
      707–708
   general-purpose parallel computers,
      237–238
Multiple sequence alignment in parallel,
   193–210
   CLUSTAL W, 194–201
      distance matrix calculation, 194–196
      guide tree construction, 196–200
      progressive alignment process, 200–201
   implementation, 201–206
      distance matrix calculation, 202–204
      generally, 201–202
      progressive alignment process, 204–206
   overview, 193–194, 209
   results, 207–209
      distance matrix, 207
      guide tree construction, 207
      overall, 208–209
      progressive alignment process, 207–208

Multipoint linkage analysis (computational biology), 7–11
  generally, 7–9
  joint distribution of genotype, 10–11
  joint genotype probabilities, 9–10
Multi-scaled methods, compute-intensive simulations (cellular models), stochastic chemical kinetics, 90–92
Multi-threaded computation, FPGA technology, local sequence alignment, 258–259
Multithreading, high-performance BLASTs, 216–217
Multivariate gene expression analysis (codetermination analysis), 267–274
  algorithm, 267–269
  parallel implementation, 270–274
  prediction system design, 269–270
Mutation operator, sequential GA, DNA fragment assembly, 292
MXYZ model, mixed integer programming models, 439–441
MXZ model, mixed integer programming models, 439
MYZ model:
  divide-and-conquer technique, 445
  mixed integer programming models, 441–442

Nearest-neighbor interchange (NNI), maximum parsimony (MP) heuristics, phylogeny reconstruction (high-performance), 377
Neighbor-joining tree, PEst, phylogenetic parameter estimation, 359
Network flow formulation, mixed integer programming models, 435–438
Nimrod, GAMESS with, 538–542
Nonatomistic lattice simulation, protein structure prediction, 463
Nonlinear model, vertices, mixed integer programming models, 438–439
Non-measured steady-state concentrations, estimation of, differential evolutionary algorithms in *Escherichia coli,* 66–67

Offspring, expected frequency of, computational biology, 6–7
Open grid services architecture (OGSA), desktop organic grids (self-organizing), 675
Open science grid, research collaborations, 601

Operator rate analysis, DNA fragment assembly (distributed genetic algorithm), 296
Optical flow, elastic deformation integrated with, human brain diffusion and deformation simulation, 136–138
Organic grid architecture (desktop organic grids, self-organizing), 678–686
  agent design, 680–681
  child-list maintenance, 681–682
  fault tolerance, 684
  generally, 678–680
  overlay network cycles, 685
  overlay network restructuring, 682–683
  prefetching, 685–686
  result burst size, 684
  task list size self-adjustment, 685
  termination, 685
Overlay network cycles, organic grid architecture, desktop organic grids (self-organizing), 685
Overlay network restructuring, desktop organic grids (self-organizing), organic grid architecture, 682–683

Pairwise alignment, local sequence alignment, 235
Parallel ClustalW, local sequence alignment, 254–257. *See also* ClustalW
Parallel computer, hybrid, special-purpose computing, 169–172
Parallel computer architecture:
  bioinformatics parallel algorithms, 511–517
  local sequence alignment basics, 237–238
Parallel computing. *See also* Human brain diffusion and deformation simulation
  compute-intensive simulations (cellular models), 96–100
    across methods, 98–100
    across simulations, 96–98
    performance, 100
  phylogeny reconstruction (high-performance), branch and bound (B&B) algorithm, 380–381
Parallel fast messy GA, evolutionary algorithms (EAs), protein structure prediction, 474–475
Parallel hardware, phylogenetic parameter estimation, 354–355
Parallel image filtering architecture, field programmable gate array (FPGA), 717–720

Parallel implementation:
  hidden Markov models, local sequence
    alignment, 251–252
  multivariate gene expression analysis,
    codetermination analysis, 270–274
Parallelization:
  bioinformatics, 15–20
    applications, 16–20
    generally, 15–16
  message-passing interface (MPI), HIV-1
    molecular evolution (parallel Monte
    Carlo simulation), 39–43
    initialization and termination, 39–40
    replicate simulation results
      consolidation, 41–43
  protein threading problem (PTP), 448–453
    algorithm, 449
    computational experiments, 449–453
    generally, 448–449
  visualization and, compute-intensive
    simulations (cellular models), cell
    colonies, 113–114
Parallel Monte Carlo simulation. *See* HIV-1
  molecular evolution (parallel Monte
  Carlo simulation)
Parallel processing models, field
  programmable gate array (FPGA),
  706–708
Parallel programming models, local
  sequence alignment, 235–237
Parallel random number generation, HIV-1
  molecular evolution (parallel Monte
  Carlo simulation), 43–46
Parallel RAxML-III, HPC solutions in,
  337–339
Parallel replica exchange molecular
  dynamics (REMD) method. *See*
  Replica exchange molecular dynamics
  (REMD) method
Parallel sequence comparison, computational
  molecular biology, 161–163
Parallel simulations, compute-intensive
  simulations (cellular models), 100–103
Parameter selection, DNA microarray
  experiments, 318–320
Parameter values, HIV-1 molecular
  evolution, 38–39
Parsimony-Informative sites, phylogeny
  reconstruction (high-performance),
  375–376
Pedigree probabilities, computational
  biology, 11–12
  methods, 12
  probability types, 11–12

Peer-to-peer computing, desktop organic
  grids (self-organizing), 676
Pentose phosphate pathway, kinetic rate
  expressions, differential evolutionary
  algorithms in *Escherichia coli,* 65–66.
  See also Differential evolutionary
  algorithms (in *Escherichia coli*)
Perfect phylogeny problem, phylogenetic
  trees, 329
Performance evaluation:
  parallel computing, compute-intensive
    simulations (cellular models), 100
  special-purpose computing, 179–185
PEst, phylogenetic parameter estimation,
  356–365
  coverage extension, 359–365
  heterogeneous COW, 357–359
  ML distance estimation, 356
  neighbor-joining and least-square branch
    lengths, 359
Pharmacology, bioinformatics grid activities,
  497, 499–500
Phylogenetic parameter estimation,
  347–368. *See also* Phylogenetic tree(s)
  data sets, 355
  overview, 347–348, 365–366
  parallel hardware, 354–355
  parallel performance, 348–349
  parallel platforms, 348
  PEst, 356–365
    coverage extension, 359–365
    heterogeneous COW, 357–359
    ML distance estimation, 356
    neighbor-joining and least-square
      branch lengths, 359
  phylogenetic tree reconstruction, 349–354
    molecular evolution modeling, 349–351
    quartet puzzling algorithm, 351–354
  scheduling algorithms, 355–356
Phylogenetic tree(s), 327–346. *See also*
  Phylogenetic parameter estimation
  future directions, 341–344
    algorithmic, 341–343
    technical, 343–344
  high performance computing (HPC)
    solutions in RAxML-III, 337–341
    distributed, 339–341
    parallel, 337–339
  maximum likelihood (ML), 329, 330–332
  maximum likelihood (ML) algorithms,
    332–334
  overview, 327–330
  RAxML-III heuristics, 334–337

Phylogenetic tree reconstruction,
  phylogenetic parameter estimation,
  349–354
  molecular evolution modeling, 349–351
  quartet puzzling algorithm, 351–354
Phylogeny reconstruction
  (high-performance), 369–394
  exact maximum parsimony (MP),
    378–381
  large-scale phylogenies, 373–374
  maximum parsimony (MP), 374–377
    exact search, 376–377
    fixed tree scoring, 374–375
    heuristics, 377
    informative sites, 375–376
  maximum parsimony (MP) heuristics
    (disk-covering methods), 381–390
    DCM3, 382–385
    experimental design, 385–387
    generally, 381–382
    results, 387–390
  overview, 369, 390–391
  phylogenetic data, 370–371
  phylogenetic methods, 371–373
    criteria-based methods, 372–373
    distance methods, 371–372
Physics-based models, human brain
  diffusion and deformation simulation,
  deformation simulation (image-guided
  neurosurgery), 133–135
Poisson Runge–Kutta methods,
  compute-intensive simulations (cellular
  models), stochastic chemical kinetics,
  88–90
Population representation, sequential GA,
  DNA fragment assembly, 290
Population size analysis, DNA fragment
  assembly (distributed genetic
  algorithm), 296, 297
Portal technology, cluster and grid
  infrastructure, 537–538
Prediction system design, multivariate gene
  expression analysis, codetermination,
  269–270
Prefetching:
  desktop organic grids (self-organizing),
    organic grid architecture, 685–686
  measurements, desktop organic grids
    (self-organizing), 692–694
Probability types, pedigree probabilities,
  computational biology, 11–12
Processor boards, FPGA hardware
  accelerators, 714–715

Processor integration, FPGA hardware
  accelerators, 716
Production infrastructure, virtual microscopy
  architecture, image management
  system, 740–741
Progressive algorithms, maximum
  likelihood (ML), phylogenetic trees,
  332–333
Progressive alignment process:
  CLUSTRAL W, 200–201
  implementation, 204–206
  results, 207–208
Protein folding, 397–425. *See also* Protein
  threading problem (PTP); Replica
  exchange molecular dynamics (REMD)
  method
Proteins:
  computational molecular biology,
    149–150
  makeup of, 151
Protein structure prediction, 459–486
  discernment methods, 461–471
    atomistic and nonatomistic lattice
      simulation, 463
    Chemistry at HARvard Molecular
      Mechanics (CHARMm) model,
      463–466
    energy fitness approximation, 466–469
    farming model, 469–471
    generally, 461–462
  evolutionary algorithms (EAs), 471–479
    fast messy GA, 471–474
    multiobjective fmGA (FMfmGA),
      475
    parallel fast messy GA, 474–475
    performance evaluations, 477–479
    Ramachandran experiment, 475–477
  field programmable gate array (FPGA)
    case study, 720–732
    "ab initio," 722
    energy calculation algorithm, 724–726
    energy calculation architecture,
      729–732
    generally, 720–722
    parallelized algorithm solutions,
      726–727
    processor implementation, 727–729
    protein and energy model, 723–724
    results, 732
  future directions, 483
  overview, 459–460
  parallelization of bioinformatics
    applications, 18
  problem statement, 460–461

results, 479–483
  building block experiment, 482–483
  competitive template generation,
    479–480
  farming model experiment, 480–482
Protein structure refinement, replica
  exchange molecular dynamics (REMD)
  method, 420–422
Protein threading problem (PTP), 427–457
  defined, 431–434
  divide-and-conquer technique, 444–448
  future directions, 453–454
  mixed integer programming models,
    434–444
    comparisons of, 443–444
    generally, 434–435
    LS algorithm and self-threading
      case, 442
    MXYZ model, 439–441
    MXZ model, 439
    MYZ model, 441–442
    network flow formulation, 435–438
    nonlinear model using vertices,
      438–439
    RAPTOR model, 442
  overview, 427–431, 454–455
  parallelization, 448–453
    algorithm, 449
    computational experiments, 449–453
    generally, 448–449
PW stage optimization, local sequence
  alignment, parallel ClustalW, HT
  ClustalW, and MULTICLUSTAL, 255

Quality control, virtual microscopy clinical
  use, 753–754
Quartet puzzling algorithm, phylogenetic
  parameter estimation, 351–354
Query batch size, BLAST performance, 215
Query length, BLAST performance,
  223–224
Query sequence, protein threading problem
  (PTP), 431

Ramachandran experiment, protein structure
  prediction, evolutionary algorithms
  (EAs), 475–477
Ramachandran maps, protein structure
  prediction, performance evaluation, 478
RAPTOR model, mixed integer
  programming models, 442

RAxML-III:
  high performance computing (HPC)
    solutions, 337–341
  phylogenetic trees, 334–337
Reaction rate estimation, maximum,
  differential evolutionary algorithms in
  Escherichia coli, 62–63
Recombination:
  computational biology, 4–5
  effects of, HIV-1 molecular evolution
    (parallel Monte Carlo simulation),
    49–50, 54
Recombination operator, sequential GA,
  DNA fragment assembly, 291
Reconfigurability, FPGA devices, 713–714
Regular computational pattern (database
  searching), parallelization of
  bioinformatics applications, 16–18
Replica exchange molecular dynamics
  (REMD) method, 397–425
  described, 399–403
  overview, 397–399, 422–423
  protein folding, 403–420
    α-helix, 405–408
    β-hairpin, 408–410
    examples, 403–404
    solvation models and force fields
      assessment, 410–420
    temperature sequences, 404–405
  protein structure refinement with, 420–422
Replicated databases, high-performance
  BLASTs, 217–218
Replicate simulation results, consolidation
  of, message-passing interface (MPI),
  HIV-1 molecular evolution (parallel
  Monte Carlo simulation), 41–43
Result-burst size, desktop organic grids
  (self-organizing), 684, 691–692
Row broadcast, instructional systolic array
  (ISA), 169
Row ringshift, instructional systolic array
  (ISA), 169–170
Runtime reconfiguration, FPGA technology,
  local sequence alignment, 261–262

Scheduling:
  ACDC-grid, 590–593
  algorithms for, phylogenetic parameter
    estimation, 355–356
  desktop organic grids (self-organizing),
    676–677
  GEL interpretor and, bioinformatics
    distributed workflows, 561–563

Score, BLAST algorithm, 214
Score function, protein threading problem
  (PTP), 433–434
Scoring matrices:
  BLAST algorithm, 212
  global biological sequence alignment,
    156–157
Search sequence length, BLAST
  performance, 215, 223–224
Seeds and seeding:
  BLAST, biological sequence comparison,
    159–160
  BLAST algorithm, 213
Selection operator, sequential GA, DNA
  fragment assembly, 292
Self-adjustment, desktop organic grids
  (self-organizing) measurements,
    694–696
Self comparisons, BLAST use, 214
Self-organization, desktop organic grids
  (self-organizing). *See* Desktop organic
  grids (self-organizing)
Semi-global threading, protein threading
  problem (PTP), 454
Semi-regular computational pattern,
  parallelization of bioinformatics
  applications, 18–19
Sequence analysis. *See also* Computational
  molecular biology; Multiple sequence
  alignment in parallel; Special-purpose
  computing
  computational biology, 14
  computational molecular biology,
    149–166
  GIPSY, 635–638
  multiple sequence alignment in parallel,
    193–210
  special-purpose computing for, 167–192
Sequence database searching,
  high-performance BLASTs for,
    211–232. *See also* High-performance
  BLASTs
Sequence evolution, HIV-1 molecular
  evolution (parallel Monte Carlo
  simulation), 47–49, 51
Sequence scoring, hidden Markov models,
  local sequence alignment, 251
Sib pair analysis, computational biology,
  multipoint linkage analysis, 8–9
F-classifiers and feature selection, gene
  expression relationship analysis
  classification, 275–280
SIMD architecture, special-purpose
  computing, 167–170

Similarity array calculation, global
  biological sequence alignment,
    153–154
Single Instruction–Multiple Data (SIMD):
  bioinformatics distributed workflows, 554
  field programmable gate array (FPGA),
    707–708
  general-purpose parallel computers,
    237–238
Single Instruction–Single Data (SISD), field
  programmable gate array (FPGA),
    707–708
Site independence, V3 functional
  component, HIV-1 molecular evolution
  (parallel Monte Carlo simulation)
  model fitness, 36–38
Slide scanner, virtual microscopy
  architecture, 739
Smith–Waterman algorithm:
  local sequence alignment, 240–244
  sequence analysis, GIPSY, 637
  special-purpose computing, dynamic
    programming communication
    pattern, 173–174
Solvation models, force fields and, replica
  exchange molecular dynamics (REMD)
  method, 410–420
Spatial modeling, 104–109
  Brownian motion, 106–108
  issues in, 108–109
  Turing models, 104–105
Special case reconstruction, pedigree
  probabilities, computational biology, 12
Special-purpose computing, 167–192
  dynamic programming communication
    pattern, 172–179
    linear systolic array, 176–177
    mapping, 177–179
    Smith–Waterman algorithm, 173–174
    Viterbi algorithm, 174–176
  future directions, 185–188
    dihedral angles, 186–187
    fast algorithms and short patterns, 185
    interactive visualization tools, 186
    ISA architecture with nonidentical
      processors, 187–188
    optimal context, 186
    protein structure predictions, 187
  hybrid parallel computer, 169–172
  overview, 167–169
  parallel computers, local sequence
    alignment basics, 238
  performance evaluation, 179–185
  tutorial, 188–190

Stability analysis, differential evolutionary algorithms in *Escherichia coli,* 73

Steady-state concentration, estimation of non-measured, differential evolutionary algorithms in *Escherichia coli,* 66–67

Stochastic chemical kinetics (compute-intensive simulations, cellular models), 81–92
  continuous models, 87–88
  generally, 81–82
  multi-scaled methods, 90–92
  Poisson Runge–Kutta methods, 88–90

Stochastic optimization, maximum likelihood (ML) algorithms, 333

Strongly mobile agents, desktop organic grids (self-organizing), 677–678

Structural biology (electron microscopy), parallelization of bioinformatics applications, 18

Structure analysis, computational biology, 14

Structure template, protein threading problem (PTP), 431–432

Subtree pruning and regrafting (SPR), maximum parsimony (MP) heuristics, phylogeny reconstruction (high-performance), 377

Superinfection effects, HIV-1 molecular evolution (parallel Monte Carlo simulation), 49, 54

Swarm intelligence, bioinformatics distributed workflows, 574–578

Systola 1024 architecture, hybrid parallel computer, 172

Systolic sequence comparison, FPGA technology, local sequence alignment, 259–260

Task list size self-adjustment, desktop organic grids (self-organizing), 685

TaskSpaces, 651–670
  application example, 661–663
  case study, 663–664
  framework, 655–660
  future directions, 668–669
  overview, 651–655, 669
  RNA motif problem, 664–668

Temperature sequences, replica exchange molecular dynamics (REMD) method, 404–405

Termination:
  desktop organic grids (self-organizing), organic grid architecture, 685

message-passing interface (MPI) parallelization, HIV-1 molecular evolution, 39–40

Threading, protein threading problem (PTP), 432–433. *See also* Protein threading problem (PTP)

Three-dimensional structure databases, parallelization of bioinformatics applications, 18

Tissue-specific gene expression analysis, bioinformatics distributed workflows, 570–572

Tree-bisection reconnection, maximum parsimony (MP) heuristics, phylogeny reconstruction (high-performance), 377

TurboBLAST, local sequence alignment, 246–247

Turing models, compute-intensive simulations (cellular models), spatial modeling, 104–105

UMD-BLAST, 225–228

United Kingdom, bioinformatics grid activities, 494–497

United States, bioinformatics grid activities, 497

Vector instructions, high-performance BLASTs, 215–216

Vertices, mixed integer programming models, 438–442

Very large scale integration (VLSI) technology, special-purpose parallel computers, 238

Virtual microscopy, 737–763. *See also* Electron microscopy
  architecture, 738–747
    generally, 738–739
    image management system, 739–741
    research infrastructure, 741–747
      computation subsystem, 742–743
      distributed image analysis, 747
      distributed PACs, 743–746
      storage subsystem, 741–742
    slide scanner, 739
  clinical use, 752–754
  education, 755–756
  future directions, 756–759
    common standard, 758–759
    large-scale clinical infrastructure storage, 756
    microscopy modalities, 757
    multi-modal data integration, 758

Virtual microscopy (*Continued*)
multiple focal plane 3D reconstruction, 757–758
image analysis, 747–752
generally, 747–748
mouse placenta model, 748–750
multi-photon confocal neuroimaging, 751–752
overview, 737–738, 759
Virtual root, phylogenetic trees, 331
Visualization, parallelization and, compute-intensive simulations (cellular models), 113–114
Viterbi algorithm, special-purpose computing, dynamic programming communication pattern, 174–176
Volumetric biomechanical model, with a priori knowledge, human brain diffusion and deformation simulation, deformation simulation (image-guided neurosurgery), 140–142
V3 functional component, HIV-1 molecular evolution (parallel Monte Carlo simulation) model fitness, 34–37

V3 loop, HIV-1 molecular evolution (parallel Monte Carlo simulation), 30–31
V3 neutralization component, HIV-1 molecular evolution (parallel Monte Carlo simulation) model fitness, 37–38

White matter tractograhy (human brain diffusion and deformation simulation), 122–132
background, 122–125
parallel implementation, 130–132
process simulation, 125–130
Wildfire, GUI-based workflow, 566–569
Workflow, bioinformatics distributed workflows, 555
Workflow environments, cluster and grid infrastructure, 542–546

X-arcs, mixed integer programming models, 439–441

Z-arcs, mixed integer programming models, 439–442